ANGLO-SAXON
BIBLIOGRAPHY

AN
ANGLO-SAXON
AND CELTIC
BIBLIOGRAPHY
(450–1087)

By WILFRID BONSER

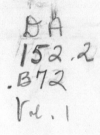
UNIVERSITY OF CALIFORNIA PRESS

BERKELEY AND LOS ANGELES

1957

PRINTED IN GREAT BRITAIN
BY A. T. BROOME AND SON, ST. CLEMENT'S, OXFORD
AND BOUND BY THE KEMP HALL BINDERY, OXFORD

CONTENTS

INDICES ARE CONTAINED IN VOL. II.

ERRATA

P. 225 **4671** For Lerins read Lérins.

231 **4813** For Stieve read Slieve

246 **5161** For Sitgungsb. read Sitzungsb.

250 **5253** For *scries* read *series*

257 **5400** Delete this entry [= **5159**]

280 **5877** For *Same jnl.* read J. Brit. Archaeol. Assoc.

310 **6501** For Camb. read Cant.

320 **6751** For A.-S., c. read A.-S.C.

332 **7019** 4th edition, 1902 repeats entry **7018**

368 **7727** For Aarberg read Aaberg

385 **8081** Delete this entry [= **8501**]

INTRODUCTION

This bibliography was begun in Birmingham, when I was the Librarian of its University, and has been finished in London since I retired in 1952. It includes material published to the end of 1953.

Its justification—apart from personal interest—is that, though text-books and monographs on a specific subject can be found in the subject-catalogues of most large libraries, no complete index to articles in periodicals in an 'Arts' subject is usually available. The books were added later for completeness.

As I proceeded, the problem as to what should be included became more and more insistent; later this developed into the problem of where I should stop.

No one but a Stenton or a Hamilton Thompson, with an encyclo-paedic knowledge of the period and its many problems would be completely competent to produce a systematic bibliography of it. But it is equally obvious that such a scholar would not have the time to spend upon it, and it therefore seemed to me to be the function of a librarian, provided he has the requisite subject-background.

In these circumstances, I wrote to Sir Frank Stenton, stating the difficulties I was encountering, and asking for his advice as to the scope of the work.

1 (*a*) *Material included, subjects.*

I have endeavoured in these two volumes to follow the extremely valuable advice which Sir Frank Stenton gave me, making the work comprehensive in the extreme. It therefore covers all aspects of the period, as pertaining to the whole of the British Isles, from the coming of the Saxons, c. 450 A.D. till 1087. This latter date is chosen as the later limit so that the all-important Domesday material may be included, and also so as to terminate at the same date as Sir Frank Stenton's volume 'Anglo-Saxon England'. I have also included some topics which at first seemed to be slightly extraneous, such as Celtic missionary and cultural work on the continent, since they were not only indicated as necessary by Sir Frank Stenton but also because they are included as relevant by Kenney in his Irish bibliography.

1 (*b*) *Material included, its sources.*

I have prefaced this bibliography with a list of all the periodicals which I have abstracted for articles, to the year 1953. These periodicals are of five types : (1) 'trade' journals (such as the English Historical

Review) which contain research material; (2) journals published by learned societies in the British Isles, both general and local; (3) older material of the local 'Notes and Queries' variety; (4) American journals containing research material; and (5) continental journals (French, German, Italian, Dutch, Belgian, Scandinavian and Finnish). I have also included articles in Collected Works and in Festschriften. Those periodicals (and Festschriften) which I have listed I have exhaustively examined, and I can vouch for the accuracy of the work I have done thereon. Articles from other periodicals have also been included, but these have not been seen in all cases.

I long delayed including text-books and monographs in this work, but eventually was persuaded to do so for its greater completeness. But here I cannot guarantee that I have found all the relevant material. I know of no exhaustive method of collecting such material as there is in the case of articles, but I have searched the shelves of many libraries both in London and in the provinces, and have also included material from other bibliographies. The few thousand books thus found I think sufficient to make their inclusion a useful one.

Records of 'finds' of coins, weapons or cross-fragments, and similar source-material (even if consisting of single paragraphs) have been included in case this information does not appear elsewhere.

In no case has an evaluation of a book or article been attempted (unless 'nothing new' is such). But a few quotations from Gross, after a reference to his bibliography, have been added. Evaluation I hold to be the function and responsibility of the user of such a bibliography as this, and not of its compiler. It is also considered to be for the user to discern what is obsolete, what is accurate, what is now redundant, or what is prejudiced.

(2) (a) Material excluded, subjects.

For fear of making the size of this work too unwieldy, I have reluctantly excluded all material dealing with literature and linguistics as such, since this is a bibliography on Anglo-Saxon and Celtic *history* in the widest sense of the term. But I have included articles on the manuscript or on the magic of 'Beowulf' as adjuncts to the sections on manuscripts and magic, and I have also included those on specific law terms as adjuncts to the section on law.

(2) (b) Material excluded, its sources.

Reviews, except in very exceptional cases, have not found a place here.

In a few cases, 'chatty' articles or a series of indifferent photographs connected by a couple of paragraphs have been omitted.

Matter contained in existing bibliographies such as those of Chevalier (Repertoire des sources historiques du moyen âge, 2 and 3) and Potthast (Bibliotheca historica medii aevi, 9) have not been systematically incorporated. These works must, therefore, also be consulted. This, again, is partly to avoid the resultant unwieldyness of this work, and partly because no purpose would be served by such repetition. Much of the material in these may, however, appear here : for example, all the articles contained in the periodicals which I have systematically abstracted. I have not checked to see.

The source-material contained in the bibliographies of Kenney (Sources for the early history of Ireland, 1, ecclesiastical : 1929, 7) and of Gross (The Sources and literature of English history, 2nd edition, 1915, 5)—of which latter, I believe, a third edition is urgently called for —has been omitted. In other words, older editions of such writers as Bede, Alfred, St. Aldhelm, or St. Patrick have not been included here. But editions of these authors which have been published since ' Gross ' (i.e. after the first decade of this century) do appear here. Works *on* these Anglo-Saxon or Celtic authors and on their writings, although they appear in ' Kenney ' and in ' Gross ', have been included, and references to the numbers of ' Kenney ' and ' Gross ' have been inserted in each case.

For the older editions, the printed Catalogue of the British Museum (as well as ' Potthast ', ' Kenney ' and ' Gross ') may profitably be consulted.

3. *Classification and subject-index.*

The compilation of this work has proved an interesting experiment in classification. Naturally so complicated a period as the Anglo-Saxon could not be subjected to a classification such as ' Dewey ' or that of the Library of Congress. But one had to be created for the purpose.

The material for the history of the Anglo-Saxon period often consists of unwritten evidence rather than of recorded facts. The classification has therefore had to be entirely different from what it would have been for later periods for which contemporary written documents exist to a far greater extent. The unwritten evidence in many cases is highly controversial, and my explanatory notes are intended to show the opinions of the various writers of the articles as well as the evidence produced.

Any classification (especially if not standardized and ' accepted ') must, in the opinion of the various users, be arbitrary. I have endeavoured to classify in such a way as to collect the mass of material available under headings most useful for research purposes rather than placing it in what at first might appear to be the easiest place. But my way of classifying may prove most annoying to some of my users, and I crave the indulgence of these hoping that they will rejoice at finding some material of which they were unaware rather than complaining of omissions in places where they would expect their material to be.

In a work of this magnitude it has been found impossible to enter

the same book or article in more than one place, though in most cases
it could, and should, be placed in several. I have therefore endeavoured
to cover this deficiency by the provision of a large subject-index, and it is
essential (to counteract constant irritation) that this should be consulted
—but only as a guide—in all cases of doubt. The index is therefore
designed to cover disputable points of classification as well as for finding
individual themes.

The user is also reminded that in most cases he must consult the
more general sections as well as particular ones in which he is interested
—also probably other sections which the table of contents may suggest.
For instance, references to jewellery will be found not only in the sub-
division so named, but also under the general section of Art. The user
will also find much of this material in the various sub-sections of
Archaeology which are entitled cemeteries and ' finds ' in them, since
articles on the jewellery alone have been separated from the rest of
those dealing with the ' finds ', and placed under Art. A worker on
manuscripts and scriptoria may find his material under the main division
of General Culture with its various sub-divisions on manuscripts, or
under Art with its various sub-divisions on illuminations, or he may
even find it under Religion, with its various sub-divisions on missals
and other service-books. Yet again, material relating to king Arthur
will be found in at least three different places—under Political History
('Arthuriana ') for the purely historical side, under Geography for
Arthurian sites, and also under Folklore. The material on special
subjects must fall in different places according to the initial choice of the
main divisions of the bibliography.

It is obvious that I, as compiler, am personally better acquainted
with some of the subject-matter of this mass of material than with
others, and again I claim indulgence in cases where my knowledge is
more limited.

Some sections of the work are fuller and more detailed than others.
For instance, I have endeavoured to insert *all* the Domesday material,
including the sources whether published before ' Gross ' or later, so
as to give a comprehensive view. I have done the same with Law and
Medicine. In some cases also the editorial notes are fuller than in
others, e.g. in Medicine with which I am best acquainted.

I have elaborated the subject-index in certain cases where I think
extra information may be useful. For instance, an entry has been made
for every shire so as to show the part it has played in the period, with
references to each of its towns and villages which have featured in some
way or other.

I have also added, under the heading Manuscripts, references to
those, in this country and abroad, which contain material relating to the
period as far as it has appeared in print and is cited here. For further
information on Anglo-Saxon manuscripts, Potthast's work must, of
course, be consulted.

4. *Problems of dating.*

One difficulty that I have especially encountered in the course of compilation is that affecting dating, more particularly in the case of Celtic material. I have often read through an article in the hope that the building or inscription which forms its subject is dated by the author. But in many cases there is no mention of any date ; often it becomes obvious that the date is not known, thus accounting for its omission. If I have attached a date in my editorial notes, it is usually that attributed to the object by the writer. If a controversy has arisen as to dating, I have included both sides, even if the latest research has proved the object not to be Anglo-Saxon at all, e.g. in the case of the Roos-Carr figures or of the bones in the crypt of Hythe church. If, however, I have had reason to believe that an object should be dated to the Anglo-Saxon period, I have included the description of it on the assumption that it is better to include erroneously rather than to deprive the research-worker (who may know more than I do of the topic in question) of information that he might otherwise lose. If a building was erected—or may have been erected—or a road or dyke constructed, in a previous period but was obviously in active use in Anglo-Saxon times, its description may have been included here : the Scottish brochs are an example of this. In some cases I have included the description of a pre-historic or Roman tumulus or grave because of its appropriation as a burying-place by an Anglo-Saxon.

5. *Gaps.*

Sir Frank Stenton in the course of his 'Anglo-Saxon England' (1943), has noted various gaps in the literature of this period. In compiling this bibliography, I also, naturally, have found many such lacunae. Some are owing to the fact that the subjects have not yet been ' written up ', even in article form : others indicate that the necessary source material has either been destroyed or for some reason or other does not exist. An obvious example of the latter is the lack of information on Anglo-Saxon crosses in East Anglia : perhaps the East Anglians were not sculptors by nature, or perhaps the crosses themselves were destroyed during the incursions of the Norsemen. It is also obvious that many topics could well be dealt with more fully than has been done already. The noting of these bare patches through this bibliography may encourage writers to fill them where the information is still available.

6. *Acknowledgements.*

In the compilation of this bibliography I have naturally made use of the resources of many libraries.

In addition to that of the University of Birmingham, I have worked in the following :

Birmingham : Barber Institute of Fine Art, Birmingham Archaeological Society, City Reference Library.

Bristol : University Library.

Leeds : University Library, Yorkshire Archaeological Society.

Leicester : University College.

Manchester : University Library.

London : University Library, University College, Institute of
Archaeology, Institute of Historical Research, Warburg Institute,
Society of Antiquaries, Royal Anthropological Institute, Royal Institute
of British Architects, Folk-lore Society, Victoria and Albert Museum,
S. Kensington : and finally the British Museum, where (as in other
places) I have most generously been accorded special privileges.

I wish to thank the Librarians of these libraries (and their staffs) for
the facilities so liberally afforded me, and especially Mr. Ronald Pick,
of the British–Museum, whose intimate knowledge of the museum
labyrinth, with its galleries, ' quadrants ' and ' tangents ', has been
unstintingly placed at my disposal.

Incomplete references have very occasionally been copied from other
bibliographies and have been added (with some misgivings) for what
they are worth, in case others may be more successful than I in tracing
the works to which they refer. Apart from this, I might add that there
are no details in this work the responsibility for which I can pass on to
another person. I must bear the blame for all its faults and deficiencies.

Finally, I would like to thank Sir Basil Blackwell for the personal
interest he has taken in my work—for his active co-operation and for
his professional advice which I have gratefully accepted.

CLASSIFICATION

I. GENERAL TOPICS AND HISTORICAL SOURCE MATERIAL

IX. ARCHAEOLOGY

PERIODICALS AND COLLECTIVE WORKS ABSTRACTED

(a) PERIODICALS

Journals in progress appear here as : x (date)—y (date)—usually 1953. Journals which have ceased publication appear as : x—y (date to date).

1 Aberystwyth Studies. 1 [1910–11]–14 (1912–36)
2 Abhandlungen der (k.) preussischen Akademie der Wissenschaften. Phil.-hist. Classe. [1] 1908–52 ix (1953)
3 Acta Archaeologica (Copenhagen). 1 (1930)–23 (1952)
4 Acta Philologica Scandinavica (Copenhagen). 1 (1926)–21 (1952)
  Acta Regiae Societatis Humaniorum Litterarum Lundensis. *See* **280**
5 Acta Universitatis Lundensis (Lunds Universitets Årsskrift). N.F. 1 (1905)–47 (1951)
6 Akademie der Wissenschaften und der Literatur, Mainz. Abhandlungen der Geistes-und-Sozialwissenchaftliche Klasse. [1] 1950–[3] 1952
7 Amateur Historian. 1 i–x (1952–54)
8 American Historical Review. 1 (1893)–58 (1953)
9 Analecta Bollandiana. 1 (1882)–71 (1953)
10 Anglesey Antiquarian Society and Field Club. Transactions. 1913–53
11 Anglia. 1 (1878)–70 (1951)
12 Anglia Beiblatt. 1–55 (1890–1944)
13 Anglistische Forschungen. 1–88 (1901–48)
14 Annales de Bretagne. 1 (1886)–59 (1952)
15 Annals of Archaeology (University of Liverpool). 1–27 (1908–40)
16 Annual Report of the Rutland Archaeological and Natural History Society. 1 [1902–03]–51 (1953)
17 Annual Report of the Yorkshire Philosophical Society. 1825–1952 (1953). *Also* Proceedings. 1 (1848–49), 1849, *and* Communications, 1870
18 Annual Reports and Proceedings of the Belfast Naturalists' Field Club, N.S. 1–10 (1873–1946) : 3rd S. 1 i–iv (1947–51)
19 Antiquarian Communications. 1–2 (1859–64). *Contd. as* : Cambridge Antiquarian Communications. 3–6 (1864–88). *Contd. as* : Proceedings of the Cambridge Antiquarian Society. 7 (1888)–46 (1952). 1953
20 Antiquarian Magazine and Bibliographer. 1–7 (1882–85). *Contd. as* : Walford's Antiquarian. 8–12 (1885–87)
21 Antiquaries Journal. 1 (1921)–33 (1953)
22 Antiquary. 1–51 (1880–1915)
23 Antiquities of Sunderland. 1 (1900)–20 (1932/43). 1902–51
24 Antiquity. 1 (1927)–27 (1953)
25 Apollo. 1 (1925)–54 (1951)
26 Archaeologia. 1 (1770)–95 (1953)
27 Archaeologia Æliana. 1st S. 1 (1822)–4 : 2nd S. 1–25 : 3rd S. 1–21 : 4th S. 1–31 (1953)
28 Archaeologia Cambrensis. 1–4 (1846–49) : N.S. 1–5 (1850–54) : 3rd S. 1–15 (1855–69) : 4th S. 1–14 (1870–83) : 5th S. 1–17 (1884–1900) : 6th S. 1 (1901)–102 i (1952)
29 Archaeologia Cantiana. 1 (1858)–65 (1952). 1953

30 Archaeologia Oxoniensis. 1–6 (1892–95)
31 Archaeologia Scotica (Trans. R. Soc. Antiquaries of Scotland). 1–5 (1792–1890)
32 Archaeological and historical Collections relating to the counties of Ayr and Wigton (Ayrshire and Galloway). 1–15 (1878–99)
33 Archaeological Journal. 1 (1844)–109 (1953)
33a Archaeological News Letter. 1 (1948)–5 iv (Aug. 1954)
34 Archaeological Review. 1–4 (1888–90)
35 Archaeology. (Archaeological Institute of America). 1 (1948)–6 (1953)
36 Archiv der Gesellschaft für ältere deutsche Geschichtskunde. 1–12 (1820–74). *Contd. as* : Neues Archiv der Gesellschaft, *etc.* 1–50 (1876–1935)
37 Archiv für celtische Lexikographie. 1–3 (1898–1907)
38 Archiv für das Studium der neueren Sprachen und Literaturen. Bd. 1 (1846)–188 (1951).
39 Archiv für Urkundenforschung. 1–18 i (1908–44).
40 Archivium Hibernicum, or Irish Historical Records. (Catholic Record Society of Ireland). 1 (1912)–17 (1953)
41 Arkiv for nordisk filologi. 1 (1883)–68 (1953)
Art Bulletin. *See* 58
42 Art Studies, Medieval, Renaissance and Modern. (Harvard and Princeton Universities). 1–8 ii (1932–31)
Associated Archaeological Societies' Reports and Papers. *See* 256
Bedfordshire Historical Record Society. Publications. *See* 247
43 Bedfordshire Notes and Queries. 1–3 (1886–93)
44 Beiträge zur Geschichte der deutschen Sprache und Literatur. *See* 220
45 Berks., Bucks. and Oxon. Archaeological Journal. 1–34 i (1895–1930). *Contd. as* : Berkshire Archaeological Journal. 34 ii (1931)–52 (1950–1)
46 Berkshire Notes and Queries. 1 ii–iii (1890–91)
47 Bibliographica. 1–3 (1895–97)
48 Biometrika. 1 (1901)–40 (1953)
49 Birmingham Historical Society. Transactions. 1–4 (1880–84). 1881–84
50 Bonner Beiträge zur Anglistik. 1–25 (1898–1908)
51 Bradford Antiquary. 1 (1881)–10 i (pt. 36) (1952). 1888–52
52 Breifny Antiquarian Society's Journal. 1 ii–3 ii (1921–30)
53 Brighton and Hove Archaeologist. 1–3 (1914–26)
54 British Museum Quarterly. 1 (1926)–18 ii (1953)
55 British Numismatic Journal. 1 (1905)–27 i (1952). 1953
56 Bulletin d'ancienne Littérature et d'Archéologie Chrétienne. 1–4 (1911–14)
Bulletin de la Société royale des lettres de Lund. *See* 163
57 Bulletin of the Board of Celtic Studies. 1 (1921)–15 iii (Nov. 1953)
58 Bulletin of the College of Art Association (of America). 1 (1913–18). *Contd. as* : Art Bulletin. 2 (1919)–35 (1953)
59 Bulletin of the Institute of Historical Research. 1 (1923)–26 (1953)
60 Bulletin of the John Rylands Library. 1 (1903)–36 (1954)
61 Burlington Magazine. 1 (1903)–95 (1953)
62 Caernarvonshire Historical Society. Transactions. 1 (1939)–13 (1952)
Cambridge Antiquarian Communications. *See* 19
63 Cambridge Antiquarian Society. 8° Publications. 1 (1851)–55 (1942)
64 Cambridge Antiquarian Society 4° Publications. 1–2 (1840–49) : N.S. 1 (1908)–6 (1951)
65 Cambridge Historical Journal. 1 (1923)–11 i (1953)
66 Cardiff Naturalists' Society. Report and Transactions. 1 (1867)–79 (1945/48). 1951
67 Catholic Historical Review. 1 (1915)–38 (1953)
68 Celtic Review. 1–10 (1904–16)

147 Journal of the Flintshire Historical Society (Flintshire Historical Society Publications). 1 (1911)–13 (1953)
148 Journal of the Galway Archaeological and Historical Society. 1 (1906)–25 ii. (1952)
149 Journal of the Historical Society of the Church in Wales. 1 (1947)–3 (1953)
150 Journal of the History of Medicine and Allied Sciences. 1 (1946)–8 (1953)
151 Journal of the Invernian Society. 1–7 (1908–15)
152 Journal of the Limerick Field Club. 1–3 (1897–1908). *Contd. as* : **154**
153 Journal of the Manx Museum. 1 (1924)–5 (no. 72/73, 1945/46)
154 Journal of the North Munster Archaeological Society. 1–3 (1909–15). *Contd. as*: North Munster Antiquarian Journal. 4 (1936)–5 iv (1948)
155 Journal of the Northampton(shire) Natural History Society and Field Club. 1 (1880)–32, no. 235 (1952)
156 Journal of the (Royal) Anthropological Institute. 1 (1872)–82 (1952)
     Journal of the (Royal) Historical and Archaeological Association of Ireland. *See* **329**
157 Journal of the Royal Institute of British Architects. 3rd S. 1 (1893–94)–60 (1953)
158 Journal of the Royal Institution of Cornwall. 1 (1864)–25 : N.S. 1–2 i (1953)
     Journal of the Royal Society of Antiquaries of Ireland. *See* **329**
159 Journal of the Warburg (and Courtauld) Institutes. 1 (1937)–16 ii (1953)
160 Journal of the Waterford and South-East Ireland Archaeological Society. 1–19 i (1894–1920)
161 Journal of Theological Studies. 1(1900)–50 : N.S. 1–4 (1953)
162 Kerry Archaeological Magazine. 1–5 ii (no. 22) (1908–20)
163 Kungl. Humanistiska Vetenskapssamfundet i Lund : Årsberättelse. 1918–52/53
164 Kungl. Vitterhets Historie och Antiquitets Akademiens Handlingar. 21 (N.F. 1) (1861)–86 (1953)
165 Laudate (Benedictines of Pershore, Worcs.–Nashdom, Bucks.). 1 (1923)–31 (1953)
166 Law Quarterly Review. 1 (1885)–69 (1953)
167 Leeds Studies in English. 1 (1932)–8 (1952)
168 Leicestershire and Rutland Notes and Queries and Antiquarian Gleaner. 1–3 (1889–95). 1891–95
     Lincolnshire Architectural and Archaeological Society. Reports and Papers. *See* **256**
169 Lincolnshire Historian. 1 (1947)–11 (1953)
170 Lincolnshire Notes and Queries. 1 (1888)–24 (1889–1936)
171 Lioar Manninagh, Yn. 1–4 (1889–1910)
172 Man. 1 (1901)–53 (1953)
173 Mannin. Nos. 1–9 (1913–17)
174 Manx Note Book. 1–3 (1885–87)
175 Mediaeval and Renaissance Studies (Warburg Institute). 1 (1941)–2 (1950)
176 Mediaeval Studies (Institute of Mediaeval Studies). 1 (1939)–14 (1952)
177 Medievalia et Humanistica. 1 (1943)–8 (1954)
178 Medium Aevum. 1 (1923)–22 (1953)
179 Mémoires de la Société archéologique et historique des Côtes-du-Nord. 1–4 : 2e S., 1–6 (1852–74)
180 Mémoires de la Société d'Histoire et d'Archéologie de Bretagne. 1 (1920)–33 (1953)
181 Mémoires de la Société néo-philologique de Helsingfors. 1 (1893)–16 (1951)
182 Mémoires de la Sociéte royale des Antiquaires du Nord. [1] 1836/39–1934
     Memoirs . . . communicated to the . . . Archaeological Institute. *See* **223**
183 Midland Antiquary. 1–4 (1882–87)

184   Midland Counties Historical Collector. 1–2 (1855–56)
185   Mitteilungen des oberhessischen Geschichtsverein in Giessen. N.S. 1–35 (1889–1938)
186   Modern Language Notes. 1 (1886)–68 (1953)
186a Modern Language Quarterly (Univ. of Washington). 1 (1940)–13 (1952)
187   Modern Language Review. 1 (1905)–48 (1953)
188   Modern Philology. 1 (1903)–49 (1952)
      Montgomeryshire Collections. *See* **78**
189   Moyen Âge. 1 (1888)–59 ii (1953)
190   National Library of Wales Journal. 1 (1939)–7 (1952)
191   Neath Antiquarian Society. Transactions. 2nd S. 1–7 (1930–39)
192   Neophilologus. 1 (1916)–37 (1953)
      Neues Archiv. *See* **36**
193   Nomina Germanica: Arkiv for Germanisk namenforskning. 1 (1937)–9 (1950)
194   Norfolk Antiquarian Miscellany. 1–3 (1873–87)
195   Norfolk Archaeology (Norfolk and Norwich Archaeological Society). 1 (1847)–30 (1952)
196   Norsk Tidsskrift for Sprogvidenskap. 1 (1928)–16 (1952)
      North Munster Antiquarian Journal. *See* **154**
197   North Staffordshire Field Club. (Annual Report and) Transactions. [1] 1866–86 (1951–52). 1952
198   Northamptonshire Notes and Queries. 1–6 (1886–96): N.S. 1–6 (1905–31)
199   Northern Counties Magazine. 1–2 (1900–01)
200   Northern Notes and Queries. 1–4 (1886–90). *Contd. as*: Scottish Antiquary. 5–17 (1881–1903). *Contd. as*: **275**
201   Notes and Gleanings [Devon and Cornwall]. 1–5, no. 60. (1888–92)
202   Notes and Queries. 1 (1849)–198 (1953)
203   Notes and Queries for Somerset and Dorset. 1 (1890)–26 (1952)
204   Notes of the Bedfordshire Architectural and Archaeological Society. 1 (1853–67)
205   Notts. and Derbyshire Notes and Queries. 1–6 (1893–98)
206   Nouvelle revue historique de droit français et étranger. 1–45 (1877–1921)
207   Numismatic Chronicle and Journal of the Numismatic Society. 1 (1838/9)–6th S. 12 (1952)
208   Numismatic Journal. 1–2 (1836–38). *Contd. as*: **207**
208a Occasional papers printed for the Department of Anglo-Saxon, Cambridge. 1(1952)–3 (1953)
209   Old-lore Miscellany of Orkney, Shetland, Caithness and Sutherland (Viking Society). 1 (1907)–10 (1946)
210   Orkney Miscellany, being Orkney Record and Antiquarian Society Papers. 1 (1953)
211   Ortnamnssälskapets i Uppsala årsskrift. 1 (1936)–1952
212   Otia Merseiana: the publication of the Arts Faculty of University College, Liverpool. 1–4 (1899–1904)
213   Oxfordshire Archaeological Society. Reports. 1 (1853)–87 (1949). 1951
214   Oxoniensia. 1 (1936)–16 (1951). 1953
      P.B.B. *See* **220**
      P.M.L.A. *See* **333**
215   Palaestra. 1–217 (1898–1939)
216   Palatine Note-Book, for . . . the counties of Lancaster, Cheshire, etc. 1–5 i (1881–85)
217   Papers and Proceedings of the Hampshire Field Club (and Archaeological Society). 1 (1885/89)–18 ii (1953)
      Papers read at the Royal Institute of British Architect. *See* **336**

218 Papers, Reports, etc., read before (Transactions of) the Halifax Antiquarian Society. 1901–52
219 Past, The (The organ of the Ui Ceinnsealaigh Historical Society, Wexford). 1–2 (1920–21)
220 Paul und Braunes Beiträge zur Geschichte der deutschen Sprache und Literatur. [P.B.B.]. 1 (1874)–74 (1952)
221 Philological Quarterly (Iowa City). 1 (1922)–32 (1953)
222 Proceedings and Transactions of the Croydon Microscopical and Natural History Club (Natural History and Scientific Society). 1 (1871)–12 i (1948/51). 1951
    Proceedings and Transactions of the Kilkenny Archaeological Society. *See* 329
223 Proceedings at the annual meeting of the Archaeological Institute of Great Britain and Ireland. [1] 1845. (1846). *Contd. as* : Memoirs ... communicated to the annual meeting, etc. [2–8], 1846–52 (1848–58). *Contd. as* : Report of the Transactions, *etc.* [9] 1853. (1856)
224 Proceedings of the Bath Natural History and Antiquarian Field Club. 1–11 iii (1867–1909)
225 Proceedings of the Belfast Natural History and Philosophical Society. 1894/95–1934/35 : 2nd S. 1 (1935)–3 (1949/50). 1951
226 Proceedings of the British Academy. [1] 1903 (1904)–37 (1951)
227 Proceedings of the Bury and West Suffolk Archaeological Institute. 1 (1849–53). *Contd. as* : Proceedings of the Suffolk Institute of Archaeology. 2 (1854)–26 i (1952). 1953
    Proceedings of the Cambridge Antiquarian Society. *See* 19
228 Proceedings of the Clapton Architectural Club. 1–14 (1890–1903)
229 Proceedings of the Clifton Antiquarian Club. 1–7 (1884–1912)
230 Proceedings of the Cotteswold Naturalists' (Field) Club. 1 (1853)–31 i (1951). 1953
231 Proceedings of the Coventry and district Natural History and Scientific Society. 1 (1930)–2 vii (1953)
232 Proceedings of the Dorset Natural History and Antiquarian Field Club (Archaeological Society). 1 (1877)–74 (1952). 1953
233 Proceedings of the evening meetings of the London and Middlesex Archaeological Society. 1871–74 (1872–77)
234 Proceedings of the Leeds Philosophical and Literary Society. Literary and Historical Section. 1 (1925)–6 ix (1952)
235 Proceedings of the Manchester Numismatic Society. 1–2 i (1864–71)
236 Proceedings of the Orkney Antiquarian Society. 1–15 (1922–39)
237 Proceedings of the Oxford Architectural and Historical Society. N.S. 1–6 (1860–1900)
238 Proceedings of the Philological Society. 1–6 (1842–53). *Contd. as* : Transactions of the Philological Society. 1854–1953
239 Proceedings of the Royal Irish Academy. 1 (1836)–56 iv (1954)
240 Proceedings of the Society of Medicine, History of Medicine Section. [1] (in Proceedings, 6) (1913) –45 (1952)
241 Proceedings of the Scottish Anthropological (and Folklore) Society. 1 (1934)–5 i (1954)
242 Proceedings of the Society of Antiquaries of London. 1–4 (1843–59) : 2nd S. 1–32 (1859–1920). *Contd. as* : 21
243 Proceedings of the Society of Antiquaries of Newcastle-upon-Tyne. 1 (1855)–5th S. 1 (1953)
244 Proceedings of the Society of Antiquaries of Scotland. 1 (1851)–85 (1950/1). 1953
245 Proceedings of the Somerset Archaeological and Natural History Society. 1 (1849)–97 (1952). 1953

280 Skrifter utgivna av Kungl. humanistiska Videnskapssamfundet i Lund (Acta Reg. Societatis humaniorum litterarum Lundensis). 1 (1920)–50 (1952)
281 Skrifter utgivna av Kungl. humanistiska Videnskapssamfundet i Upsala. 1 (1890)–38 (1948)
282 Skrifter utgivna af Videnskabsselskabet i Christiania. 1894–1924. *Contd. as*: Skrifter utgitt av der Norske Videnskaps-Akademi i Oslo. 2. Historisk-filosofisk Klasse. 1925–1951
283 Somerset Archaeological and Natural History Society. Proceedings of the Bath and district branch, [1]–8 (1904/08–1934/38) 1904–47
284 South–Eastern Naturalist (and Antiquary), being the Transactions of the South Eastern Union of Scientific Societies. 1 (1896)–57 (1952)
285 South Wales and Monmouth Record Society, Publications. 1 (1932)–2 (1950)
286 Speculum. 1 (1926)– 28 (1953)
287 Studi Gregoriani (abbazia di San Paolo di Roma). 1(1947)–4 (1952)
288 Studia Neophilologica (Uppsala). 1 (1928)–25 (1953)
289 Studien zur englischen Philologie, hrsg. von L. Morsbach. 1–68 (1897–1925)
290 Studier i modern Språkvetenskap. 1 (1898)–16 (1946)
291 Studies : an Irish quarterly review, etc. 1 (1912)–42 (1953)
292 Studies and Notes in Philology and Literature . . . Harvard University. 1–11 (1892–1907). *Contd. as*: Harvard Studies and Notes in Philology and Liturature. 12–20 (1930–38)
293 Studies in Philology (University of N. Carolina). 1 (1906)–50 (1953)
294 Surrey Archaeological Collections. 1 (1854)–52 (1952)
295 Surtees Society, Publications. [Since publication of ' Gross ']. 120 (1911)–160, 162 [1952]
296 Sussex Archaeological Collections. 1 (1884)–91 (1953)
297 Sussex County Magazine. 1 (1927)–27 (1953)
298 Sussex Notes and Queries. 1 (1926)–13 xvi (Nov. 1953)
299 Traditio. 1 (1943)–8 (1952)
300 Transactions and Journal of the Proceedings of the Dumfriesshire and Galloway Natural History and Antiquarian Society. [1] 1862/63–30 (1952)
301 Transactions of the Aberafan and District (and Margam) Historical Society. 1–6 (1928–34)
302 Transactions of the Aberdeen Ecclesiological Society. 1–4 (1886–1905). *Contd. as*: **342**
303 Transactions of the Architectural and Archaeological Society of Durham and Northumberland. 1, for 1862–68 (1870)– 10 iv (1953)
304 Transactions of the Birmingham Archaeological Society (formerly Birmingham and Midland Institute, Archaeological Section). 1 (1870)–69 (1951). 1953
305 Transactions of the Bristol and Gloucestershire Archaeological Society. 1 (1876)–72 (1953). 1954
306 Transactions of the British Archaeological Association at the 1st (2nd, 3rd, 5th) Congress. [1. Canterbury (1844) 1845 : 2. Winchester (1845) 1846 : 3. Gloucester (1846) 1847 : 5. Worcester (1848) 1851]
307 Transactions of the Buchan (Field) Club. 1–16 i (1887–1940)
308 Transactions of the Burton-on-Trent Natural History and Archaeological Society. 1–8 (1889–1926)
309 Transactions of the Cambridgeshire and Huntingdonshire Archaeological Society. 1, for 1900–03 (1904)–7 (1952)
310 Transactions of the Cardiganshire Antiquarian Society and Archaeological record. 1–13 (1909–1938)
311 Transactions of the Connecticut Academy of Arts and Sciences. 1–36 (1866–1945)
312 Transactions of the Cumberland and Westmorland Antiquarian and Archaeological Society. 1 (1866)– N.S. 52 (1953)

313   Transactions of the Dartford District Antiquarian Society. 1–7 (1931–38)
314   Transactions of the East Lothian Antiquarian and Field Naturalists' Society.
      1 (1924/25)–2 (1931/33). 1925–34
315   Transactions of the East Riding Antiquarian Society. 1 (1893)–29 (1949)
316   Transactions of the Essex Archaeological Society. 1 (1852)–N.S. 24 (1951)
317   Transactions of the Ethnological Society of London. N.S. 1–7 (1861–69)
318   Transactions of the Exeter Diocesan Architectural and Archaeological Society.
      1–16 i [1st S. 1–6 (1843–61) : 2nd S. 1–5 (1867–92) : 3rd S. 1–5 i (1892–1933)]
319   Transactions of the Gaelic Society of Inverness. 1–37 (1871–1946)
320   Transaction of the Glasgow Archaeological Society. 1 (1868)—N.S. 12 (1953)
321   Transactions of the Glasgow Ecclesiological Society. 1–3 (1895–1901).
      Contd. in : **342**
322   Transactions of the Greenwich (and Lewisham) Antiquarian Society. 1 (1905)–
      4 v (1950/51). 1952
323   Transactions of the Hampstead Antiquarian and Historical Society. [1–6]
      (1898–1904/05). 1899–1907
324   Transactions of the Hawick Archaeological Society. 1863–1952
      Transactions of the Historic Society of Lancashire and Cheshire. *See* **121**
325   Transactions of the Honorable Society of Cymmrodorion. [1] 1892/94–1949/51.
      1953
326   Transactions of the Hull Scientific and Field Naturalists' Club. 1–4 (1898–1919)
327   Transactions of the Hunter Archaeological Society (Sheffield). 1 (1914)–7 iii
      (1953/4). 1954
328   Transactions of the Isle of Man Natural History and Antiquarian Society. 1
      for 1879/84. (1888)
329   Transactions of the Kilkenny Archaeological Society. 1–2, for 1849–53
      (1850–55) : *Contd. as* : Proceedings and Transactions of the Kilkenny ... Arch-
      eological Society. 3 for 1854–55–[9] N.S. 6 for 1867 (1856–71) : *Contd. as* :
      Journal of the Royal Historical and Archaeological Association of Ireland.
      [10–19] 3rd S. 1, 4th S. 1–9 (1868–89) : *Contd. as* : Journal of the Royal
      Society of Antiquaries of Ireland. [20] 5th S. 1, for 1890–91 (1892)–83 (1953)
330   Transactions of the Lancashire and Cheshire Antiquarian Society. 1, for 1883
      (1884)–62 (1950/1). 1953
331   Transactions of the Leicestershire (Architectural and) Archaeological Society.
      1 (1866)–29 (1953)
332   Transactions of the London and Middlesex Archaeological Society. 1–6 (1860–
      90) : N.S. 1 (1891)–11 ii (1953)
333   Transactions of the Modern Language Association of America. 1–3, for
      1884–87 (1886–88) : *Contd. as* : Publications of the Modern Language Associ-
      ation of America, 4 (1889)–67 (1952)
334   Transactions of the Newbury District Field Club. 1 (1870)–10 i (1953)
      Transactions of the Philological Society. *See* **238**
335   Transactions of the Royal Historical Society. 1, for 1869 (1872)–5th S. 3 (1953)
336   Transactions of the (Royal) Institute of British Architects. [1] 1835–1842 :
      Contd. as : Papers read at the Institute . . . 1849–78 : *Contd. as* : Transactions.
      1878–92 : *Contd. as* : **157**
337   Transactions of the Royal Irish Academy. 1–33 (1787–1907)
338   Transactions of the Royal Society of Literature of the United Kingdom. 1–2nd
      S. 37 (1827–1919)
339   Transactions of the St. Albans and Hertfordshire Architectural and Archaeo-
      logical Society. [1] 1884–94 : N.S. 1–2 (1895–1914) : 3rd S. 1–6 (1953)
340   Transactions of the St. Paul's Ecclesiological Society. 1–10 (1881–1938)
341   Transactions of the Salisbury Field Club. 1 (1891–94)
342   Transactions of the Scottish Ecclesiological Society. 1 (1903)–14 iii (1951)
343   Transactions of the Shropshire Archaeological Society. 1 (1878)–54 i (1951/52)

344 Transactions of the Southend-on-Sea and District Antiquarian and Historical Society. 1 (1921)–4 ii (1951)
345 Transactions of the Stirling Natural History and Archaeological Society. 1–61 (1878–1939)
346 Transactions of the Thoroton Society of Nottinghamshire. 1 (1897)–56 (1952). 1953
347 Transactions of the Woolhope Naturalists' Field Club (Hereford). 1 (1852)–34 i (1952). 1953
348 Transactions of the Worcestershire Archaeological Society. N.S. 1 (1923)–29 (1952). 1953
349 Transactions of the Yorkshire Dialect Society. 1 (1898)–9 (1951)
350 Transactions of the Yorkshire Numismatic Society. 1–3 (1909–29) : 2nd S. 1 i (1951)
351 Ulster Journal of Archaeology. 1st S. 1–9 (1853–62) : 2nd S. 1–17 (1894–1911) : 3rd S. 1 (1938)–15 (1952). 1953
352 University of California, Publications in English. 1 (1929)–20 (1951)
353 University of Colorado Studies. 1–25 (1902–38) : *Contd. as* : University of Colorado, Series B. Studies in the Humanities. 1 (1939)–2 iv (1945)
354 Uppsala Universitets Årsskrift. Filosofi, etc. 1861–1951
355 Vetusta Monumenta (Society of Antiquaries). 1–7 (1747–1906)
356 Viking : tidsskrift for norrøn arkeologi. 1 (1937)–16 (1953).
     Walford's Antiquarian. *See* 20
357 Wessex (University College, Southampton). 1–4 (1928–38)
358 Wiltshire Archaeological and Natural History Magazine. 1 (1854)–55 (pt. 200) (1954)
359 Wiltshire Notes and Queries. 1–8 (1893–1916)
360 Woolwich and District Antiquarian Society. Annual Report (and Transactions). 1 (1895)–29 (1949). 1896–1950
361 Word-lore. 1–3 (1926–28)
362 Worthing Archaeological Society. Annual Report. 1 (1923)—31 (1953)
363 Year-book of the Viking Club (Society). 1–24 (1909–32)
364 Yorkshire Archaeological Journal. 1 (1869)–38 ii (1953)
365 Yorkshire Celtic Studies. 1 (1937/38)–5 (1949/52)
366 Yorkshire Notes and Queries. 1–2 (1888–90)
367 Yorkshire Notes and Queries. 1–5 (1904–09)
368 Yorkshire Society for Celtic Studies, Report for 1932/33–1937/38
369 Zeitschrift des Vereins für hessische Geschichte und Landeskunde. 1–61 (1837–1936)
370 Zeitschrift für celtische Philologie. 1 (1897)–24 (1954)
371 Zeitschrift für christliche Archäologie und Kunst. 1–2 (1856–60)
372 Zeitschrift für deutsche Philologie [Z.f.d.P.]. 1 (1869)–71 (1953)
373 Zeitschrift für deutsches Alterthum [Z.f.d.A.]. 1 (1841)–84 (1953)
374 Zeitschrift für Kirchengeschichte. 1 (1876)–64 (1953)
375 Zeitschrift für Rechsgeschichte 1 (1861)–81 (1951). (Zeitschrift der Savigny-stiftung für Rechtsgeschichte, Germanistische Abteilung. 1 (1880)–68 (1951) : Kanonistische Abteilung. 1 (1911)–37 (1951))
376 Zentralblatt für Bibliothekswesen. 1 (1884)–67 (1953)

(*b*) COLLECTIVE WORKS (' Festschriften,' etc.)

377 Abhandlungen . . . zum 70. Geburtstag Heinrich Finke. 1925
378 Aspects of archaeology in Britain and beyond : essays presented to O. G. S. Crawford. Ed. W. F. Grimes. 1951
379 Bede, 12th centenary essays, ed. A. H. Thompson. 1935
     Bémont (Charles). *See* 403

380 Birmingham and its regional setting. British Association, 1950
381 Cambridge Economic History. 1–2 (1941–52)
382 Cambridge Medieval History. 1–3, 5 (1911–26)
     Chadwick (H. M.). *See* 385
     Crawford (O. G. S.). *See* 378
383 Custom is king : essays presented to R. R. Marett on his 70th birthday. Ed.
     E. H. D. Buxton. 1936
     Darby (H. C.). *See* 399
384 Domesday Studies, ed. P. E. Dove. 2 vol. 1888–91
     Dopsch (A.). *See* 422
385 Early cultures of north-west Europe. H. M. Chadwick Memorial Studies.
     Ed. Sir C. Fox and B. Dickins. 1950
386 English miscellany presented to F. J. Furnivall. 1901
387 Essays and studies presented to Eoin MacNeill. 1940
388 Essays and studies presented to Tadhg ua Donnchadha (Torna) 1944 : ed. S.
     Pender. 1947
389 Essays in Anglo-Saxon law. Boston, 1876
390 Essays in history presented to Reginald Lane Poole : ed. H. W. C. Davis. 1927
391 Essays in medieval history presented to T. F. Tout. Ed. A. G. Little and F. M.
     Powicke. 1925
392 Festgabe Alois Knöpfler zur Vollendung des 60. Lebensjahres. 1907. (Veröff-
     entlichungen a.d. Kirchenhistorischen Seminar, München, III. Reiche, Nr. 1)
393 Festgabe Alois Knöpfler zur Vollendung des 70. Lebensjahres. 1917
394 Festgabe für L. Schmitz-Kallenberg. 1927
395 Festschrift für Lorenz Morsbach. (Studien zur englischen Philologie, 50).
     1913
396 Festschrift zu Ehren Oswald Redlichs. (Veröffentlichungen des Museums
     Ferdinandeum in Innsbruck, 8). 1928
     Finke (H.). *See* 377
     Fitting (H.). *See* 404
     Furnivall (F. J.). *See* 386
397 Grammatical miscellany offered to Otto Jespersen on his 70th birthday. 1930
398 Historical essays in honour of James Tait : ed. J. G. Edwards. 1933
399 Historical geography of England before A.D. 1800. 14 studies ed. H. C. Darby.
     1936
     Jespersen (O.). *See* 397
     Klaeber (F.). *See* 417
     Knoepfler (A.). *See* 392 and 393
     Liebermann (F.). *See* 419
     Loomis (G. S.). *See* 401
     Lot (F.). *See* 402
     Luick (K.). *See* 409
     MacNeill (Eoin). *See* 387
     Malone (Kemp). *See* 410
     Marett (R. R.). *See* 383
400 Medieval studies in memory of A. Kingsley Porter, ed. W. R. W. Koehler :
     2 § vii. Medieval art in Scandinavia and the British Isles. 1939
401 Medieval studies in honour of Gertrude Schoepperle Loomis. 1927
402 Mélanges d'histoire du moyen âge offerts à F. Lot. 1925
403 Mélanges d'histoire offerts à Charles Bémont. 1913
404 Mélanges Hermann Fitting. LXXVe anniversaire. 2. 1908.
     Meyer (A. de). *See* 407
405 Miscellanea Ceriani (Biblioteca Ambrosiana, Milano). 1910
406 Miscellanea hagiographica hibernica, ed. C. Plummer. (Studia hagiographica,
     13. Société des Bollandistes). 1925

GUIDE FOR USERS

Editorial notes are placed between [ ]. They are (1) to indicate the scope of the book or article—often by quoting the sub-headings in its text, if these are set out : (2) to clarify ambiguous points, and (3) to explain my classification of an entry (e.g. 'An ancient deed,' with no more in its title to explain its nature or its date).

Topographical sub-divisions in the classification though appearing for brevity and convenience as the names of the various kingdoms of the Heptarchy, indicate in almost all cases definite geographical areas and not necessarily material dealing with the actual kingdoms whose confines varied from century to century. Thus ' Northumbria ' signifies here the district north of the line from the Mersey to the Humber, often extending (as in the case of sculpture) as far north as the Firth of Forth —the frontier of Bernicia : ' East Anglia ' signifies here the three counties of Norfolk, Suffolk and Cambridge, and often Essex also when it is not treated as a separate kingdom : ' Mercia ' signifies here the rest of the English counties north of the Thames and south of ' Northumbria ' : ' Wessex ' signifies here the counties south of the Thames, except for Kent and Sussex, which counties usually contain sufficient material to be treated as separate divisions, as well as being separate kingdoms of the Heptarchy.

Abbreviations. The letters ' A.–S. ' have been used in my editorial notes to indicate the period from c. 450 to 1087. This symbol therefore covers all material, Anglian, Saxon, Jutish, Celtic, Viking, etc. Abbreviations used in the case of periodicals cited are such as are usually used (e.g. E.H.R. for the English Historical Review), or else they are obvious. The *latest edition* of a work is usually the only one which appears—unless more details (as to pagination, etc.) are available for an older edition, in which case this also is given.

Anonymous works usually appear under their titles rather than under their editors, but the names of the latter are given in the author index.

THE USER SHOULD CONSULT THE TABLE OF CONTENTS AND THE INDEX—AS A POSSIBLE AID—IN ALL CASES OF DIFFICULTY.

I. GENERAL TOPICS AND HISTORICAL SOURCE MATERAL

1. BIBLIOGRAPHIES

(n.b. **4a, 5** and **7** have been abstracted and included here, except for sources)

1 Baxter (James Houston), **Johnson** (Charles) and **Willard** (James Field). An index of British and Irish Latin writers, A.D. 400–1520. [Pp. 7–26, 4th–11th c.]. Archivum Lat. Med. Aevi (Bull. Du Cange), 7, pp. 7–219. 1932.

2 Chevalier (Ulysse). Repertoire des sources historiques du moyen âge. Bio-bibliographie. Nouvelle édition. coll. 4832. 2 vol. 4° Paris, 1905 [1903]–07. [Gross, 19.]

3 —— Repertoire des sources historiques du moyen âge. Topo-bibliographie. 2 vol. 4° Montbéliard, 1894–1903. [Gross, 20. Under Angleterre, etc.]

4 Esposito (Mario). A bibliography of the Latin writers of mediaeval Ireland. [To supplement works of Potthast, Chevalier, and Manitius.] Studies, 2 pp. 495–521. 1913.

4a Gomme (*Sir* George Laurence *and* Bernard), *ed*. Index of archaeological papers, 1665–1890. pp. xi, 910. 8° London, 1907. [Continued annually as :] Index of archaeological papers published in 1891(–1909). 1892–1910. [Items included in this bibliography.]

5 Gross (Charles). The sources and literature of English history, from the earliest times to about 1485. 2nd edition, revised and enlarged [to 1910]. pp. xxiii, 820. 8° London, 1915. [Especially : Part 3, the A.-S. period, pp. 233–324. Items included in this bibliography, excepting source material.]

6 Heusinkveld (Arthur Helenus) and **Bashe** (Edwin J.). A bibliographical guide to Old English. A selective bibliography of the language, literature and history of the Anglo-Saxons. pp. 153. Univ. Iowa Studies, Humanistic Studies, 4 : no. 5 (202). 1931.

7 Kenney (James Francis). Sources for the early history of Ireland. Vol. 1 : ecclesiastical. pp. xvi, 807, + 2 maps.

8° New York, 1929. [Items included in this bibliography, excepting source material.]

8 Paetow (Louis John). A guide to the study of mediaeval history. Revised edition. pp. xix, 643. 8° London, 1931.

9 Potthast (August). Bibliotheca historica medii aevi. Wegweiser, *etc*. 2. Auflage. 2 vol. 8° Berlin, 1896. [Gross, 25.]

10 Williams (Harry Franklin), *compiler*. An index to mediaeval studies published in Festschriften, 1865–1946. pp. x, 165. 4° Berkeley, 1951.

2. GENERAL

11 Abegg (Daniel). Zur Entwicklung der historischen Dichtung bei den Angelsachsen. *Quellen und Forschungen*, 73. pp. xii, 126. 8° Strassburg, 1894.

12 Anderson *afterwards* **Cox** (Mary Desirée), *Mrs. Trenchard Cox*. Looking for history in British churches. pp. xv, 328, + map + 24 plates. 8° London, 1951. [Much A.-S. background : saints, crosses, etc.]

13 Baxter (James Houston), **Johnson** (Charles) and **Abrahams** (Phyllis), *eds*. Mediaeval Latin word-list from British and Irish sources. *British Academy*. pp. xiii, 466. 4° Oxford, 1934. [5th–16th c.]

14 Blair (Peter Hunter). The foundations of England. The heritage of early Britain, pp. 128–52. 1952.

15 Buckley (W. E.), *etc*. 'Anglo-Saxon.' [Use of the term.] N. and Q., 6th S., 3, pp. 390–1. 1881.

16 Chadwick (Nora Kershaw). The Celtic West. The heritage of early Britain. pp. 104–27. 1952.

17 Collen (George William). Britannia Saxonica. A map ... accompanied by a table showing the contemporary sovereigns. The genealogies of the ... kings, *etc*. pp. 55, + map. 4° London, 1833.

18 Crawford (Samuel John). Anglo-Saxon influence on western Christendom, 600–800. pp. 109. 8° London, 1933.

19 Davis (Henry William Carless), *ed.* Mediaeval England: a new edition of Barnard's Companion to English history. pp. xxi, 632. 8° Oxford, 1924. [A.-S. *passim*: e.g. pp. 110–17, the art of war, from the A.-S. conquest to Hastings: pp. 150–51, civil costume: pp. 170–72, military costume: pp. 245–49, shipping: pp. 281–89, town life: pp. 319–22, country life: pp. 345–58, monasticism: pp. 483–92, art: pp. 532–52, coinage.]

20 Dictionary of National Biography. 21 vol. 8° London, 1908–09. [Still contains the best, or only, lives available in many cases.]

20a Jackson (Kenneth). Language and history in early Britain. A chronological survey of the Brittonic languages, first to twelfth century A.D. pp. xxvi, 752. 8° Edinburgh, 1953. [Pp. 149–193, the early Christian inscriptions: pp. 194–261, Britons and Saxons in the 5th–8th c.: pp. 701–05, the name Bernicia.]

21 Malone (Kemp). On *Anglo-Saxon* as a technical term. Anglia, 55 (N.F. 43), pp. 4–7. 1931.

22 Robertson (Eben William). Historical essays in connexion with the land, the Church, *etc.* 8° Edinburgh, 1872. [Gross, 1499. Pp. 92–102, the hide; pp. 112–33, the shire; pp. 177–89, the king's kin; pp. 189–203, Dunstan; pp. 203–15, Edgar's coronation.]

23 Skeat (Walter William), **Lynn** (William Thynne), and **Krebs** (H.). Whitsunday (in the Anglo-Saxon Chronicle). [Names for Whitsun in German, A-S., or Welsh.] N. and Q., 10th S., 2, pp. 121–22, 166, 313–14. 1904.

24 Smith (*Sir* William) and **Cheetham** (Samuel). A dictionary of Christian antiquities. 2 vol. 8° London, 1875–80. [Passim.]

25 Smith (*Sir* William) and **Wace** (Henry). A dictionary of Christian biography, *etc.* 4 vol. 8° London, 1877–87. [Passim.]

26 Stenton (*Sir* Frank Merry). Early English history, 1895–1920. [Review of work done in the quarter century.] Trans. R. Hist. Soc., 4th S. 28, pp. 7–19. 1946.

27 Stenton (Sir Frank Merry). The foundations of English history. [? restatement of A.-S. history necessary owing to growth of material.] *Same jnl.*, 4th S., 9, pp. 159–73. 1926.

28 Strunk (W.), *jr.* Anglo-Saxon as a name of the language. J. Engl. and German. Philol., 7, pp. 92–93. 1908.

29 Toller (Thomas Northcote). Additions (further additions) to the supplement of the Bosworth-Toller 'Anglo-Saxon dictionary'. Mod. Lang. Rev., 17, pp. 164–65; 19, pp. 200–04. 1922–24.

30 Weigall (Arthur Edward Pearse Brome). Wanderings in Anglo-Saxon Britain. pp. 286. 8° London, [1927].

31 Whitelock (Dorothy). Anglo-Saxon poetry and the historian. Trans. Roy. Hist. Soc., 4th S. 31, pp. 75–94. 1949.

32 Wright (Cyril Ernest). The cultivation of saga in Anglo-Saxon England. pp. xi, 310. 8° Edinburgh, 1939.

33 Wright (Thomas) and **Wuelcker** (Richard Paul). Anglo-Saxon and Old English vocabularies. 2nd edition. 2 vol. 8° London, 1902.

3. ANGLO-SAXON SCHOLARS AND STUDY

34 Adams (Eleanor Nathalie). Old English scholarship in England from 1566–1800. *Yale Studies in English*, 55. pp. 209. 8° New Haven, 1917.

35 Ashdown (Margaret). Elizabeth Elstob, the learned Saxonist. [Biography of first woman student of A.-S.] Mod. Lang. Rev., 20, pp. 125–46. 1925.

36 Dickins (Bruce). John Mitchell Kemble and Old English scholarship. (With a bibliography of his writings.) Proc. Brit. Acad., 25, pp. 51–84. 1939.

37 Douglas (David Charles). English scholars. pp. 381. 8° London, 1943. [Pp. 60–147: The Saxon past, George Hickes, Humphrey Wanley.]

38 Liebermann (Felix). Zu Matthaeus Parkers altenglischen Studien. Arch. Stud. neueren Spr., Bd. 92, pp. 415–16. 1894.

39 Metcalfe (Frederick). The Englishman and the Scandinavian; or a comparison of Anglo-Saxon and Old Norse Literature. pp. xxvi, 514. 8° London, 1880. [Study of A.S. revived by Parker, Spelman, Cotton, etc.; Bede; letters of Aldhelm, Boniface and Alcuin; laws; charters; runes; etc.]

40 Tout (Thomas Frederick). Felix Liebermann (1851–1925). History, N.S., 10, pp. 311–19. 1926.

41 Wright (Cyril Ernest). The dispersal of the monastic libraries and the beginnings of Anglo-Saxon studies. Matthew Parker and his circle. Trans. Camb. Bibliogr. Soc., 3, pp. 208–37. 1951.

4. SOURCE MATERIAL FOR THE HISTORY OF THE PERIOD

§a. General and Miscellaneous

42 Arbois de Jubainville (Marie Henry d'). Compte des manuscrits irlandais des bibliothèques d'Angleterre et d'Irlande. Bibl. École Chartes, 42. 1881.

43 Arnold (A. A.). Preliminary account of ' notes on the Textus Roffensis, by Dr. F. Liebermann'. Arch. Cant., 23, pp. 94–100, + 1 plate. 1898.

44 Barker (Eric E.). The Cottonian fragments of Æthelweard's Chronicle. Bull. Inst. Hist. Res., 24, pp. 46–56. 1951.

45 Birch (Walter de Gray). On the life and writings of William of Malmesbury. Trans. Roy. Soc. Lit., 2nd S. 10, pp. 318–82. 1874.

46 —— On two Anglo-Saxon manuscripts in the British Museum. [*i.e.* Cotton Titus D xxvi and xxvii. Prognostics, etc. 10th c.] *Same jnl.*, series 2, 11, pp. 463–512. 1875.

47 Blair (Peter Hunter). Symeon's History of the kings. [His sources of information: Bede, etc.] Archaeol. Æl., 4th S., 16, pp. 87–100. 1939.

48 Brauer (H.). Capitula Caroli angelsächsisch und althochdeutsch. [Query origin of Rz commentary on Capitula in Canterbury at end of 7th c.] Z.f.d.P., 53, pp. 183–84. 1928.

49 Chambers (Raymond Wilson). The lost literature of medieval England. [Bede, etc.] Library, 4th S., 5, pp. 293–321. 1925.

50 Cook (Albert Stanburrough). The possible begetter of the Old English Beowulf and Widsith. [Aldfrith, king of Northumbria.] Trans. Conn. Acad. Arts and Sci., 25, pp. 281–346. 1922.

51 Douglas (David Charles) and **Greenaway** (George William), *ed.* English historical documents [vol. 2], 1042–1189. pp. xxiv, 1014. 8° London, 1953. [Pp. 107–65, A.-S.C. (1042–87): pp. 204–14, Florence of Worcester: pp. 215–16, William of Jumièges: pp. 217–31, William of Poitiers: pp. 232–78, the Bayeux tapestry (pp. 239–78, plates), etc.]

52 Floyer (John K.). The early monastic writers of Worcester. [Milred, Werefrith, Dunstan, Oswald, Abbo, Wulstan, etc.] Assoc. Archit. Socs'. Rpts., 25, pp. 146–64. 1899.

53 Foerster (Max). Die altenglischen Texte der Pariser Nationalbibliothek. Engl. Studien, 62, pp. 113–131. 1927.

54 Gairdner (James). Early chroniclers of Europe: England. pp. viii, 328. 8° London, [1879]. [Gross, 42.]

55 Gomme (*Sir* George Laurence). The Historical Manuscripts Commission. —Notes on documents relating to pre-Norman history. Reliquary, 20, pp. 91–152–56. 1879–80.

56 Gross (Max). Geffrei Gaimar, die Komposition seiner Reimchronik und sein Verhältnis zu den Quellen [to A.D. 975]. pp. 136. 8° Erlangen, 1902. [Gross, 1778, note.]

57 Haigh (David Henry). The Anglo-Saxon sagas; an examination of their value as aids to history. pp. xi, 178. 8° London, 1861.

58 Hamel (Anton Gerard van), *the younger.* De oudste keltishe en angelsaksische Geschiedbronnen. *Acad. proefschrift.* pp. xii, 196. 8° Middleburg, 1911.

59 Hardy (*Sir* Thomas Duffus). Descriptive catalogue of materials relating to the history of Great Britain and Ireland [to 1327]. *Rolls Series.* 3 vol. (in 4). 8° London, 1862–71. [Gross, 45.]

60 Harmer (Florence Elizabeth), *ed.* Select English historical documents of the ninth and tenth centuries. pp. 142. 8° Cambridge, 1914.

61 Henel (Heinrich). Byrhtferth's *Preface* : the epilogue of his Manual ? Speculum, 18, pp. 288–302. 1893.

62 Herben (Stephen J.). The Vercelli Book : a new hypothesis. [How did it get to Vercelli?] Speculum, 10, pp. 91–94. 1935.

63 Jeudwine (John Wynne). The manufacture of historical material. An elementary study in the sources of story. pp. xxvii, 268. 8° London, 1916. [Including A.-S. and Celtic source material.]

64 Ker (Neil Ripley). Two notes on MS. Ashmole 328 (Byrhtferth's Manual). [A. Dislocation of the contents of pp. 26–40[1] : B. The loss of a leaf after p. 168.] Medium Ævum, 4, pp. 16–19. 1935.

65 Liebermann (Felix). Heinrich von Huntingdon. [Gross, 1801, note. ' Details presented in the Historia Anglorum which are not found elsewhere are figments of the imagination.'] Forsch. z. deut. Gesch., 18, pp. 265–95. 1878.

66 —— Notes on the Textus Roffensis. Arch. Cant., 23, pp. 101–12. 1898.

67 —— Ueber ostenglische Geschichtsquellen des 12–14. Jh., bes. den falschen Ingulf. Neues Archiv, 18, pp. 225–67. 1892.

68 Marx (Jean). Guillaume de Poitiers et Guillaume de Jumièges. [Disputes Körting's theory of a common source for their lives of William I.] Mélanges d'histoire du moyen âge offerts à F Lot, pp. 543–48. 1925.

69 Paasche (Fredrik). Æthelstan-Adalstein. [Old Norse sources as regards king Æthelstan.] Studia Neophil., 14, pp. 366–68. 1942.

70 Riley (Henry Thomas). The Chronicle of Fabius Ethelwerd. [Gross, 1366, note.] Gent. Mag., 203, pp. 120–31. 1857.

71 Robinson (Joseph Armitage). Byrhtferth and the Life of St. Oswald [of York]. [Question of authorship.] J. Theol. Stud., 31, pp. 35–42. 1930.

72 Sisam (Kenneth). An Old English translation of a letter from Wynfrith to Eadburga. [Latin text, and discussion.] Mod. Lang. Rev., 18. pp. 253–72. 1923.

73 Theopold (Ludwig). Kritische Untersuchungen über die Quellen zur angelsächsischen Geschichte des achten Jahrhunderts, mit besonderer Rücksicht auf die Zeit Koenig Offas. *Diss.* pp. 128. 8° Lemgo, 1872. [Gross, 1349 : Lit. Says A.-S.C. dates from 754 to 828 are 2 years too early, and from 829–839 are 3 years too early.]

73a Whitelock (Dorothy), *ed.* English historical documents [vol. 1], c. 500–1042. 8° London [announced].

74 Wilson (R. M.). Lost literature in Old and Middle English. Leeds Studies in English, 2, pp. 14–37 ; 5, pp. 1–49. 1933, 36.

75 Winters (William). Historical notes on some of the ancient manuscripts formerly belonging to the monastic library of Waltham Holy Cross. [Includes transcript of charter from MS. Cotton, Tib. C. IX, f. 40, etc.] Trans. R.H.S., 6, pp. 204–66. 1877.

§ b. The Anglo-Saxon Chronicle

MS. A. (Parker Chronicle). From Winchester and Christ Church, Canterbury. MS. C.C.C.C. 173.

MS. B. From Abingdon. MS. Cotton Tib. A. VI.

MS. C. From Abingdon. MS. Cotton Tib. B. I.

MS. D. From Worcester or Evesham. MS. Cotton Tib. B. IV.

MS. E. From Peterborough. MS. Bodl. Laud, 636.

MS. F. From St. Augustine's, Canterbury. MS. Cotton Domitian A. VIII.

MS. G. (Fragments). MS. Cotton Otho B. XI.

76 Anglo-Saxon Chronicle. An Anglo-Saxon Chronicle, from British Museum, Cotton MS. Tiberius B. IV. Edited by E. Classen and F. E. Harmer. *Modern Language Texts : English Series.* pp. xvi, 150. 8° Manchester, 1926. [MS. D. A.-S. text and glossary.]

77 Anglo-Saxon Chronicle. Newly translated by E. E. C. Gomme. pp. xvi, 115. 8° London, 1909. [Parker.]

78 —— The Anglo-Saxon Chronicle, translated with an introduction by George Norman Garmonsway. *Everyman's Library*, 624. pp. xlviii, 295. 8° London, 1953. [Parker Chronicle (A) and Laud Chronicle (E) translations, parallel.]

79 —— The C-text of the Old English Chronicles, edited by Harry August Rositzke. *Beiträge zur englischen Philologie*, 34. pp. 100. 8° Bochum-Langendreer, 1940.

80 —— Parker's Chronicle (832–900). Edited by A. H. Smith. *Methuen's Old English library*. B-Prose selections, 1. pp. viii, 72. 8° London, 1935. [Introduction, text, and notes.]

81 —— The Parker Chronicle and laws (Corpus Christi College, Cambridge, MS. 173), a facsimile. Edited by Robin Flower and Hugh Smith. *Early English Text Society*, O.S. 208. pp. vi, + 112 plates. fol. London, 1941.

82 —— The Peterborough Chronicle. Translated with an introduction by Harry August Rositzke. *Records of civilization, sources and studies*, 44. pp. 193. 8° New York, 1951.

83 Ashdown (Margaret). English and Norse documents relating to the reign of Ethelred the Unready. pp. xiii, 311. 8° Cambridge, 1930. [Texts and translations, and appendices. Continuation of A.-S.C., MS. C. (Abingdon Chronicle).]

84 Atkins (*Sir* Ivor). The origin of the later part of the Saxon Chronicle known as D. E.H.R. 55, pp. 8–26. 1940.

84a Dahl (Sejr Torsten Frantz Granzow). Den oldengelske krønike i udvalg, oversat med indledning og noter. 8° København, 1936. [Extracts mainly concerned with Anglo-Scandinavian affairs.]

85 Dickins (Bruce). The genealogical preface to the Anglo-Saxon Chronicle. Four texts edited to supplement Earle-Plummer. Occas. Papers. Dept. A.-S., Camb., 2. pp. 8. 1952.

86 English (Henry Scale). Ancient history, English and French, exemplified in a dissection of the Saxon Chronicle. 8° London, 1830.

87 Fernquist (Carl-Henric). Study on the O.E. version of the Anglo-Saxon Chronicle in Cott. Domitian A. VIII. Studier mod. Språkvetenskap, 13, pp. 39–103. 1937.

88 Field (John Edward). Some notes on the Abingdon Chronicle. Berks, Bucks and Oxon Archaeol. J., 10, pp. 108–14. 1905.

89 Flohrschuetz (Armin). Die Sprache der Handschrift D der angelsächsischen Annalen im MS. Cotton Tib. B. IV. *Diss., Jena*. pp. 45. 8° Hildburghausen. (1909).

90 Grubitz (Ernest). Kritische Untersuchungen über die angelsächsischen Annalen bis zum Jahre 893. *Diss*. pp. 34. 8° Göttingen, 1868. [Gross, 1349 : Lit.]

90a Hoffman-Hirtz (Marie). Une chronique anglo-saxonne, traduite d'après le manuscrit 173 de Corpus Christi College, Cambridge. pp. 173. 8° Strasbourg, 1933. [Text A.]

91 Horst (Karl). Beiträge zur Kenntniss der altenglischer Annalen. Engl. Studien, 24, pp. 1–16 ; 25, pp. 195–218. 1898.

92 —— Die Reste der Handschrift G der altenglischen Annalen. [MS. Cotton Otho B. XI, ff. 39–48. A.-S. text of unburnt fragments.] *Same jnl.*, 22, pp. 447–50. 1896.

93 —— Zur Kritik der altenglischen Annalen. pp. 39. 8° Darmstadt, 1896. [Gross, 1349 : Lit.]

94 Howorth (*Sir* Henry Hoyle). The Anglo-Saxon Chronicle. Athenaeum, Sept. 8, 1877, pp. 308–10 ; Sept. 20, 1879, pp. 367–69 ; Oct. 9, 1880, pp. 465–67 ; Aug. 12, 1882, pp. 207–08. 1877–82.

95 —— The Anglo-Saxon Chronicle, its origin and history. Part 1 : The so-called 'Peterborough Chronicle' or MS. E. (Part 2 : The second Christ Church Canterbury Chronicle or MS. F. Part 3 : The lost MS. EE. and its relations to MS. D, the Waverley annals, the history of Henry of Huntingdon and the poem of Gaimar). Archaeol. J., 65, pp. 141–204 : 66, pp. 105–44 : 69, pp. 312–70. 1908, 09, 12.

96 Howorth (*Sir* Henry Hoyle). Notes on the Anglo-Saxon Chronicle. 1. The value of Codex A. [*See also* note by F. Liebermann *in* Archiv Stud. neueren Spr., Bd. 106, p. 345, 1901.] E.H.R., 15, pp. 748–54. 1900.

97 Jost (Karl Theodor). Wulfstan und die angelsächsische Chronik. [? Wulfstan author of two Eadgar poems in A.-S.C.] Anglia, 47 (N.F. 35), pp. 105–23. 1923.

98 Keller (Wolfgang). Die litterarischen Bestrebungen von Worcester in angelsächsischer Zeit. pp. 104. Strasburg, 1900. [Gross, 1349, Lit. Deals mainly with the Worcester version of the Chronicle.]

99 Kube (Emil). Die Wortstellung in der Sachsenchronik (Parker Manuscript). pp. 55. 8° Jena, 1886.

100 Kupferschmidt (Max.). Ueber das Handschriftenverhältniss der Winchester-Annalen. Engl. Studien, 13, pp. 165–87. 1889.

101 Magoun (Francis Peabody), *jr.* Annales Domitiani Latini : an edition. [The Latin text in B.M., MS. Cotton Domitian A. VIII, with foreword and indices.] Mediaeval Stud., 9, pp. 235–95. 1947.

101a —— The Domitian bilingual of the *Old-English Annals* : the Latin preface. [MS. Cotton Domitian A. VIII, fol. 29r–69v. (Text F).] Speculum, 20, pp. 65–72. 1945.

101b —— The Domitian bilingual of the Old-English annals : notes on the F-text. Mod. Lang. Quart., 6, pp. 371–80. 1945.

102 Robertson (William Allan). Tempus und Modus in der altenglischen Chronik. Hss. A und E. (C.C.C.C. 173 ; Laud, 636). *Diss., Marburg.* pp. 80. 8° Marburg, 1906.

103 Robinson (Joseph Armitage). The Anglo-Saxon Chronicle. Downside Rev., 53, pp. 229–45, 383–93. 1935.

104 Sweet (Henry). Some of the sources of the Anglo-Saxon Chronicle. [Points out poetical character of some passages, e.g. for 473 and 584, in the Winchester Chronicle.] Engl. Studien, 2, pp. 310–12. 1879.

104a Viglione (Francesco). Studio critico-fililogica sul' Anglo-Saxon Chronicle, con saggi di traduzioni. pp. viii, 168. 8° Pavia, 1922. [Translation of extracts, mainly from A. and E.]

§ *c* **Asser**

105 Adamson (John William). Who was 'Asser'? [Thesis : i, that 'Asser's' Life of Alfred, from a minute study of its text and its chronology was written in the 12th c., and ii, that it may have been written by Giraldus Cambrensis for political and personal ends.] 'The illiterate Anglo-Saxon' and other essays … by J. W. Adamson, pp. 21–37. 1946.

106 Asser (Joannes), *bp. of Sherburn.* Asser's Life of King Alfred. Translated from the text of Stevenson's edition by Albert Stanburrough Cook. pp. xii, 83. 8° Boston. 1906.

107 Asser (Joannes), *bp. of Sherburn.* Life of King Alfred, translated with introduction and notes by L. C. Jane. *King's Classics.* pp. lix, 163. 8° London, 1926.

108 Asser (Joannes), *bp. of Sherburn.* Asser's Life of King Alfred. *Medieval Library*, 22. 8° London, 1926. [A reissue.]

109 Howorth (*Sir* Henry Hoyle). Asser's life of Alfred. [Regards Annales as written early in 11th c.] Athenaeum, Jan. 15, p. 88 ; Mch. 25, p. 25 ; May 27, p. 427 ; Sept. 2, p. 307, 1876 ; Aug. 4, 1877, p. 145. Answered by William Clifford, June 24, 1876, p. 859. 1876–77.

110 ?Leach (Arthur Francis). The real Alfred : from a Correspondent. [?that 'Asser's' Life was compounded by a Welshman, perhaps with some political purpose, from A.-S.C., Florence of Worcester, a life of St. Neot, and some imaginary stories.] Times, for Mch. 17, 1898. 1898.

111 Shirley (Walter Waddington). Asser's Life of Alfred. [Discusses genuineness.] Proc. Oxford Archit. and Hist. Soc., N.S. 1, pp. 313–21. 1864.

112 Wheeler (G. M.). Textual emendations to Asser's Life of Alfred. E.H.R., 47, pp. 86–87. 1932.

113 Wright (Thomas). On the true character of the biographer Asser. *In his* Essays on archaeological subjects, 1, pp. 172–85. 1861.

114 —— Some historical doubts relating to the biographer Asser. Archaeologia, 29, pp. 192–201. 1842.

§ d. Domesday Book
(The document)

115 [Anon.] The early custody of Domesday Book. Walford's Antiquarian, 11, pp. 269–71. 1887.

116 Baker (H. Kendra) and **Armstrong** (T. Percy). Domesday. [Name and definition of the work.] N. and Q., 159, pp. 228–29. 1930.

117 Baring (*Hon.* Francis Henry). Domesday Book and the Burton Cartulary. E.H.R., 11, pp. 98–102. 1896.

118 Birch (Walter de Gray). The Domesday Book. J. Brit. Archaeol. Assn., 41, pp. 241–61. 1885.

119 Birch (Walter de Gray). The materials for the re-editing of the Domesday Book, and suggestions for the formation of a Domesday Book Society. Domesday Studies, 2, pp. 485–515. 1891.

120 British Museum. Domesday commemoration, 1886. Notes on the manuscripts and printed books exhibited at the British Museum. *Same series*, 2, pp. 651–62. 1891.

121 Burtt (Joseph). On a reproduction of a portion of the Domesday Book by the photo-zincographic process. Archaeol. J., 18, pp. 128–33. 1861.

122 Clarke (Hyde). Note on the order of Domesday Book. Domesday Studies, 2, pp. 387–97. 1891.

123 Finn (Reginald Arthur Welldon). The evolution of successive versions of Domesday Book. E.H.R., 66, pp. 561–64, + 2 plates. 1951.

124 Hall (Hubert). The official custody of Domesday Book. Domesday Studies, 2, pp. 517–37. 1891.

125 Le Schonix (Roach). On the Domesday Book. [' Condition, custody, and past bibliography.'] Reliquary, N. [2nd] S., 1, pp. 43–47, + 1 plate. 1887.

126 Public Record Office. Domesday commemoration, 1886. Notes on the manuscripts, etc., exhibited at H.M. Public Record Office. Domesday Studies, 2, pp. 623–47. 1891.

127 Stephenson (Carl). Notes on the composition and interpretation of Domesday Book. Speculum, 22, pp. 1–15. 1947.

§ e. Geoffrey of Monmouth. (*See also* Section 20)

128 Geoffrey, *of Monmouth.* Historia regum Britanniae. A variant version edited from manuscripts by Jacob Hammer. *Mediaeval Academy of America*, 57. pp. viii, 292. 8° Cambridge, Mass., 1951.

129 —— The Historia regum Britanniae. With contributions to its place in early British history by Acton Griscom, *etc.* pp. xiii, 672, + 16 plates. 8° New York, London, 1929.

130 —— Histories of the kings of Britain. Translated by Sebastian Evans. [With an introduction by Lucy Allen Paton, and indices to personal names, place-names and folk-lore, by Wilfrid Bonser.] *Everyman's Library.* pp. xxvi, 262. 8° London, [c. 1920].

131 Hamel (Anton Gerard van). The Old-Norse version of the Historia regum Britanniae and the text of Geoffrey of Monmouth. [Pp. 237–47, The history of Anglo-Saxon kings.] Études celtiques, 1, pp. 197–247. 1936.

132 Jones (W. Lewis). Geoffrey of Monmouth. Trans. Hon. Soc. Cymm., 1898–99, pp. 52–95. 1900.

133 Parry (John Jay). The Welsh texts of Geoffrey of Monmouth's Historia. Speculum, 5, pp. 424–31. 1930.

134 Piggott (Stuart). The sources of Geoffrey of Monmouth. Antiquity, 15, pp. 269–86, 305–19. 1941.

135 Tatlock (John Strong Perry). The legendary history of Britain. Geoffrey of Monmouth's Historia regum Britanniae and its early vernacular versions. pp. xi, 545. 8° Berkeley, 1950. [Sources, geography, names, Arthur, imperialism, motives in writing, etc.]

§ƒ. Gildas

136 Anscombe (Alfred). The date of the De excidio. Academy, 48, pp. 411–13. 1895.

137 La Borderie (Louis Arthur Le Moyne de). La date de la naissance de Gildas. Rev. celt., 6, pp. 1–13. 1883.

138 Lot (Ferdinand). De la valeur historique du De excidio et conquestu Britanniae de Gildas. Medieval studies in memory of G. S. Loomis, pp. 229–64. 1927.

139 Lot (Ferdinand). Nennius et Gildas. [Gross, 1375 note.] Moyen Âge, 1 s. 7, pp. 1–5, 26–31 ; 8, pp. 177–84 ; 9 (2s. 1), pp. 1–13, 25–32. 1894–96.

140 Lynn (William Thynne). Gildas and the battle of Mons Badonicus. N. and Q., 6th S. 12, pp. 461–62 : 7th S. 4, pp. 372–73 ; 8th S. 8, pp. 406, 452. 1885, 1887, 1895.

141 Meyer (Wilhelm). Gildae Oratio rhythmica. Nachrichten k. Gesellschaft Wiss. Göttingen, Phil. hist. Kl., 1912, pp. 48–108. 1912.

142 Nicholson (Edward Williams Byron). Gildas vindicatus. Academy, 48, pp. 364–65. 1895.

143 Stevens (Courtenay Edward)· Gildas sapiens. E.H.R., 56, pp. 353–73· 1941.

144 Stevenson (William Henry). The date of Gildas's De excidio Britanniae. Academy, 48, pp. 340–42. 1895.

145 Tregelles (S. Prideaux), etc· Gildas. [Authenticity.] N. and Q., 4th S. 1, pp. 271–772, 511–12. 1868.

146 Wade-Evans (Arthur Wade)· Further remarks on the ' De excidio '. Arch. Camb., 98, pp. 113–28. 1944.

147 —— Gildas and modern professors. Y Cymmrodor, 31, pp. 60–80. 1921.

148 —— Notes on the Excidium Britanniae : a contribution towards a re-statement of early Saxo-Welsh history. Celtic Rev., 1, pp. 289–95. 1905.

149 —— 'The ruin of Britannia' : a contribution towards a re-statement of Saxo-Welsh history. Celtic Rev., 2, pp. 46–58, 126–35. 1905.

150 —— The Saxones in the Excidium Britanniae. Arch. Camb., 6th S, 11, pp. 170–83. 1911.

151 —— The *Saxones* in the *Excidium Brittaniae*. Celtic Rev., 10, pp. 215–27, 322–33. 1915–16.

152 —— Some insular sources of the ' Excidium Britanniae '. Y Cymmrodor, 27, pp. 37–69. 1917.

153 Wheeler (G. H.). Gildas de excidio Britanniae, chapter 26. [Mons Badonicus, date.] E.H.R., 41, pp. 497–503. 1926.

§g. Nennius

154 Duchesne (Louis). *L'Historia Britonum*. Rev. celt., 17, pp. 1–5. 1896.

155 —— Nennius retractatus. pp. 24. 12° Chartres, [1894]. [A criticism of Zimmer, **178**.]

156 —— Nennius retractatus. [i. L'Historia Britonum du manuscrit de Chartres (with Latin text) : ii. Spécialités du nouveau texte : iii. La primitive Historia Britonum : iv. Les sources irlandaises : v. Nennius.] Rev. celt., 15, pp. 174–97. 1894.

157 Foerster (Max). War Nennius ein Ire ? Abhandlungen a.d. Gebiete der mittleren . . . Geschichte. Festgabe H. Finke, pp. 36–42. 1925.

158 Howorth (*Sir* Henry Hoyle). 'Nennius' and the Historia Britonum. Arch. Camb., 6th S. 17, pp. 87–122, 321–45 : 18, pp. 199–262. 1917–18.

159 Leabhar Bretnach. Lebor Bretnach ; the Irish version of the Historia Britonum ascribed to Nennius. Edited from all the MSS. by A. G. van Hamel. *Irish Manuscripts Commission.* pp. xxxix, 98. 8° Dublin, 1932. [Introduction : text in Irish and Latin.]

160 Liebermann (Felix). Nennius the author of the *Historia Brittonum*. Essays . . . presented to F. T. Tout, pp. 25–44. 1925.

161 Lot (Ferdinand). Nennius et l'Historia Brittonum; étude critique, suivie d'une édition des diverses versions de ce texte. *Bibliothèque de l'École des Hautes Études*, 263. pp. 282, + 8 plates. 8° Paris, 1934.

162 Loth (Joseph). A propos de *Nennius vindicatus*. [On two passages : ' Ida junxit Din Guayrdi guurth Bryneich ' and ' Tunc Talhaern Tataguen in poemate claruit et *Neiren* et Taliessin.'] Rev. celt., 16, pp. 267–68. 1895.

163 —— Remarques à *l'Historia Britonum* dite de Nennius. [i. Le sens d' ' Exberta ' dans la manuscrit de Chartres : ii. Le latin et le celtique de Nennius.] Rev. celtique, 49, pp. 150–65 : 51, pp. 1–31. 1932, 34.

164 —— Sur une faute d'un copiste de *l'Historia* de Nennius. [On two passages : *see* **162**.] Rev. celt., 10, pp. 357–58. 1889.

165 Nennius, *abbot of Bangor.* Lebor Bretnach. The Irish version of the Historia Britonum ascribed to Nennius. Edited from all the manuscripts by A. G. van Hamel. *Irish Manuscripts Commission.* pp. xxxix, 98. 8° Dublin, [1932].

166 —— Nennius' History of the Britons. Together with the Annals of the Britons and Court pedigree of Hywel the Good, also the Story of the loss of Britain. [An English translation with introduction and notes] by A. W. Wade-Evans. *Publications of the Church Historical Society*, N.S. 34. pp. 156, + map. 8° London, 1938.

167 Newell (William Wells). Doubts concerning the British history attributed to Nennius. P.M. L.A., 20, pp. 622–72. 1905.

168 Reynolds (Llywarch). Nennius and Geoffrey of Monmouth. [Criticism of La Borderie's work.] Y Cymmrodor, 7, pp. 155–65. 1886.

169 Ross (Alan Strode Campbell). Hengist's watchword. [Used in his treacherous attack on Vortigern's men.

Philological details throw light on date of composition of ' Nennius '.] Engl. and Germ. Stud., 2, pp. 81–101. 1949.

170 Thurneysen (Rudolf). Zu Nemnius (Nennius). (Nochmals Nemnius). Zeit. f. celt. Philol., 20, pp. 97–137, 185–91. 1935.

171 Traube (Ludwig). Zu Nennius. Neues Archiv, 24, pp. 721–24. 1899.

172 Wade-Evans (Arthur Wade). The Chartres Historia Brittonum. [Text and notes.] Arch. Camb., 92, pp. 64–85. 1937.

173 Williams (*Sir* Ifor). Mommsen and the Vatican Nennius. [Vatican text derives from a recension of the Historia made by an A.-S. in 10th c.] Bull. Bd. Celtic Stud., 11, pp. 43–48. 1941.

174 —— The Nennian preface : a possible emendation. *Same jnl.*, 9, pp. 342–44. 1939.

175 —— Notes on Nennius. *Same jnl.*, 7, pp. 380–89, + 2 plates. 1935.

176 Zimmer (Heinrich). Ein weiterer irisches Zeugnis für Nennius als Autos der Historia Brittonum. Neues Archiv, 19, pp. 436–43. 1894.

177 —— Ein weiteres Zeugnis für die nordwelsche Herkunft der Samuel-Beulan-Recension der Historia Brittonum. *Same jnl.*, 19, pp. 667–69. 1894.

178 —— Nennius vindicatus. Über Entstehung, Geschichte und Quellen der Historia Brittonum. pp. viii, 342. 8° Berlin, 1893.

§ *h.* Irish

179 [Anon.] The Leabhar na-Huidhri. [Book of the Dun Cow, 11th c. In R.I.A.] Irish Eccles. Rec., 7, pp. 224–35. 1871.

180 Coleman (James). The early Irish manuscripts of Munster. J. Cork Hist. Soc., 2nd S. 14, pp. 83–92. 1908.

181 Flower (Robin Ernest William). The annals in Cotton MS. Titus A. XXV.—The origin and history of the Cottonian Annals. Rev. celt., 44, pp. 339–44. 1927.

182 Freeman (A. Martin), *ed.* The annals in Cotton MS. Titus A. XXV. [Latin text to 1087, and notes : marginalia : preface and indices.] Rev. celt., 41, pp. 301–30 : 43, pp. 358–84 : 44, pp. 336–61. 1924, 1926–27.

183 Gougaud (Louis). Le témoignage des manuscrits sur l'oeuvre littéraire du moine Lathren. [Or Loding, or Laidgen, who composed Lorica. Died 660 or 661.] Rev. celt., 30, pp. 37–46. 1909.

184 Graves (Charles), *bp. of Limerick.* On the date of the MS. called the Book of Armagh. Proc. R.I.A., 3 (1846–47), pp. 316–24, 356–59. 1847.

185 Grosjean (Paul). Analyse du Livre d'Armagh. Anal. Boll., 62, pp. 33–41. 1944.

186 Hamel (Anton Gerard van). The foreign notes in the Three Fragments of Irish annals. [i.e. notes on A.-S. history in : 'Annals of Ireland. Three Fragments copied from ancient sources by Dubhaltach mac Firbisigh. Ed. O'Donovan, 1860.' (573–628 & 713–35: 662–704 : 851–913).] Rev. celt., 36, pp. 1–22. 1915.

187 —— On Lebor Gabála [or the Book of Invasions]. [Growth, before 800, 800–1000, 1000–1200, 1200–1600.] Zeit. celt. Phil., 10, pp. 97–197. 1915.

188 Healy (John), *abp. of Tuam.* The Book of Deer. Irish Eccles. Rec., 3rd S. 13, pp. 865–73. 1892.

189 —— The Four Masters. *Same jnl.,* 3rd S. 15, pp. 385–403. 1894.

190 Inisfallen, *Annals of.* Extracts from the Annals of Innisfallen. [These pp. cover A.-S. period.] Kerry Archaeol. Mag., 1, pp. 480–88 : 2, pp. 32–40, 93–97, 173–78. 1912–13.

191 —— Reproduced in facsimile from the original manuscript (Rawlinson B 503) in the Bodleian Library, with a descriptive introduction by R. I. Best and E. MacNeill. *Royal Irish Academy.* pp. viii, 29. fol. Dublin, 1933.

192 Joyce (Patrick Weston). The truthfulness of ancient Irish historical records. [Tests of accuracy : physical phenomena : testimony of foreign writers : consistency of the records among themselves.] Archaeol. J., 57, pp. 259–69. 1900.

193 Leabhar Gabhála. The Book of the Conquests of Ireland. The recension of Micheál Ó Cléirigh. Part 1, edited by R. A. S. Macalister and John MacNeill. pp. 285. 8° Dublin, 1916. [Irish and English.]

194 Macalister (Robert Alexander Stewart). The sources of the preface to the 'Tigernach' Annals. [i.e. to the pre-Patrick period=a scrap-book of cuttings from Isidore, Bede, Orosius and Eusebius. How the 'Irish Annals' were compiled, copied, dated, etc.] Irish Hist. Stud., 4, pp. 38–57. 1944.

195 MacCarthy (Bartholomew). Hibernia Christiana. [Early and mediaeval Latin Literature of the Irish Church.] Irish Eccles. Rec., 3rd S., 16, pp. 442–52. 1895.

196 MacDonnell (Charles P.). On a MS. in the Library of Cambray. [MS. 619 : Canones Hibernici, 8th c.] Proc. R.I.A., 5, pp. 222–24. 1853.

197 MacNeill (Eoin). The authorship and structure of the 'Annals of Tigernach'. Ériu, 7, pp. 30–113. 1913.

198 —— The Book of Rights. [c. temp. Brian Boru. Account of rights of Irish kings and of revenues payable to them.] New Ireland Rev., 26, pp. 348–54. 1906.

199 —— The Irish synthetic historians. *Same jnl.,* 26, pp. 193–206. 1906.

200 MacSuibhne (Padraic). A great historical work : the Annals of the Four Masters. J. Ivernian Soc., 7, pp. 66–93. 1915.

201 Malone (Sylvester). The Book of Armagh and its Irish puzzles. Irish Eccles. Rec., 3rd S. 7, pp. 325–39. 1886.

202 Meyer (Kuno), *ed.* Rawlinson B. 502. A collection of pieces in prose and verse in the Irish language, compiled during the eleventh or twelfth centuries. Now published in facsimile from the original manuscript in the Bodleian Library. pp. xiv, 168, 42. fol. Oxford, 1909.

203 Nuallain (Tomas Ua). Sources of Irish history. Irish Eccles. Rec., 4th S. 21, pp. 379–92 : 23, pp. 32–42, 289–99. 1907–08.

204 O'Curry (Eugene). Lectures on the manuscript materials of ancient Irish history. pp. xxviii, 722. 8° Dublin, 1861 ; reprinted, 1873. [Gross, 50, who gives list of older material.]

205 O'Farrelly (J. J.). The Annals of Innisfallen. [MSS., printed edition, authority, chronology, 'Dublin copy'.] J. Ivernian Soc., 1, pp. 110–18, + 1 plate. 1908.

206 Reeves (William), *bp. of Down.* On Augiestin, an Irish writer of the seventh century. Proc. R.I.A., 7 (1861), pp. 514–22. 1862.

207 Stokes (Whitley). The Annals of Ulster. [Corrections to text, translation and notes of vol. 2 of Hennessy's edition (1057–1131).] Rev. celt., 18, pp. 74–86. 1897.

208 —— Old-Norse names in the Irish Annals. Academy, 38, pp. 248–49. 1890.

209 —— On the Calendar of Oengus. [10th c. MSS., the author, contents, etc.]. Rev. celt., 5, pp. 339–80. 1882.

210 Thurneysen (Rudolf). Saltair na Rann. Rev. celt., 6, pp. 96–109. 1883.

211 —— Zum Lebor Gabála. Zeit. celt. Phil., 10, pp. 384–95. 1915.

212 Tigernach, *Annals of.* The Annals of Tigernach. Edited with translation, by Whitley Stokes. [Irish text and English translation, Third fragment, A.D. 489–766 (MS. Rawlinson B. 488, folio 7a 1–14 b2). Fourth fragment, A.D. 973–1088 (*ditto*, folio 15a–19a).] Rev. celtique, 17, pp. 119–263, 337–420. 1896.

213 Todd (James Henthorn). Account of an ancient Irish MS. preserved in the Bodleian Library, Oxford. [MS. Laud 610. 'Psalter of Mac Richard Butler'. Contains sundry documents relating to the pre-1087 period in Ireland.] Proc. R.I.A., 2, pp. 336–45. 1843.

214 —— On the Irish MSS. in the Bodleian library. [Short description of sundry MSS. seen by him on a visit.] Proc. R.I.A., 5, pp. 162–76. 1853.

215 Vries (Jan de). Om Betydningen av Three fragments of Irish Annals for Vikingertidens Historie. Historisk Tidsskrift : Norsk Hist. Forening, Raekke 5, 5, pp. 509–32. 1924.

216 Wainwright (Frederick Threlfall). Duald's ' Three fragments '. [Brussels, Bibl. Royale, MS. 5301–20. Irish annals, 571–910.] Scriptorium, 2, pp. 56–58. 1948.

217 Walsh (Paul). The annals attributed to Tigernach. Irish Hist. Stud., 2, pp. 154–59. 1940.

218 —— The Four Masters and their work. pp. 44. 8° Dublin, 1944.

219 —— The Book of the Dun Cow. Irish Eccles. Rec., 5th S. 34, pp. 447–64. 1929.

§ *i.* Scottish

220 Anderson (Alan Orr). Early sources of Scottish history, A.D. 500–1286. 2 vol. 8° Edinburgh, 1922. [With bibliography.]

221 —— Scottish annals from the English chronicles, A.D. 500–1286. pp. xiii, 403. 8° London, 1908. [Translations.]

222 Dickinson (William Croft), **Donaldson** (Gordon) and **Miller** (Isobel A.) A source book of Scottish history. Vol. 1, from the earliest times to 1424. pp. 218. 8° London. 1952.

223 Holyrood, *Chronicle of.* A Scottish chronicle known as the Chronicle of Holyrood. Edited by Marjorie Ogilvie Anderson, with some additional notes by Alan Orr Anderson. *Scottish History Society,* 3rd S., 30. pp. ix, 221. 8° Edinburgh, 1938. [Pp. 75–110, text to 1087.]

224 Johnston (Alfred Wintle). Orkneyinga Saga. [Edited in present form after 1098.] Scot. H.R., 13, pp. 393–400. 1916.

225 Maxwell (*Sir* Herbert Eustace), *7th bart.* The early chronicles relating to Scotland. *Rhind Lectures,* 1912. pp. xiii, 261. 8° Glasgow, 1912.

226 Melrose, *Chronicle of.* The Chronicle of Melrose from the Cottonian manuscript, Faustina B. IX in the

British Museum. A complete and full-size facsimile in collotype, with an introduction by Alan Orr Anderson and Marjorie Ogilvie Anderson, with an index by William Croft Dickinson. pp. lxxxii, 264. 4° London, 1936. [Pp. 1–29, A.-S. period. Pp. 1–148, facsimile.]

227 Orkneyinga Saga. Translated from the Icelandic by Jom A. Hjaltalin and Gilbert Goudie. Edited, with notes and introduction by Joseph Anderson. pp. cxxxiv, 227, + 3 maps. 8° Edinburgh, 1873. [Introduction contains : earliest historical notices of the Orkneys : early Christianity, arrival of Northmen, Norse earldom 872–1231, ancient churches, Maeshow, Mousa and Pictish towers, remains of Northmen, etc.]

228 Orkneyinga Saga. A new translation with introduction and notes by Alexander Burt Taylor. pp. xvii, 435, + 8 plates, and 3 maps. 8° Edinburgh, 1938.

§ j. Welsh and Cornish

229 Aneurin Gwawdrydd. The Gododin. An English translation, with . . . notes, a life of Aneurin, and . . . dissertations . . . by Thomas Stephens. Edited by Thomas Powel. *Hon. Soc. Cymmrodorion.* pp. xi, 440. 8° London, 1888. [Introduction on social history, battle of Cattraeth, etc.].

230 Anwyl (*Sir* Edward). The Book of Aneirin. [As a source for Northumbrian and Scottish history of 6th–7th centuries.] Trans. Hon. Soc. Cymm., 1909–10, pp. 95–136, and 2 plates. 1911.

231 —— Corrigenda to Skene's text of the Book of Taliessin, made from the original, now in the National Library of Wales, Aberystwyth. Rev. celt., 32, pp. 232–42. 1911.

232 —— The four branches of the Mabinogi. [i. Introductory : ii. Structure.] Zeit. celt. Phil., 1, pp. 277–93 ; 2, pp. 124–33 ; 3, pp. 123–34. 1897–1901.

233 Black (W. H.) On the 'Llyfr Teilo', or the Liber Landavensis, the Book of Llandaff. J. Brit. Archaeol. Assoc., 10, pp. 237–48. 1855.

234 Brut y Tywysogyon. Brut y Tywysogyon, Peniarth MS. 20. (The Chronicle of the princes, in the National Library of Wales). Edited by Thomas Jones. pp. xxiv, 255. 8° Cardiff, 1941.

235 —— Or the Chronicle of the princes. Peniarth MS. 20 version. Translated with introduction and notes by Thomas Jones. *Board of Celtic Studies, University of Wales, Hist. & Law Series*, 11. pp. lxxvii, 272. 8° Cardiff, 1952.

236 Evans (John Gwenogvryn) and **Rhys** (*Sir* John). The text of the Book of Llan Dâv, reproduced from the Gwysaney manuscript. pp. l, 422. 8° Oxford, 1893. [Kenney, 1, p. 173.]

237 Gresham (Colin A.). The Book of Aneirin. [Pp. 242–57, battle of Catraeth ?=Catterick : ? end of 6th c.] Antiquity, 16, pp. 237–57. 1942.

238 Griscom (Acton). The 'Book of Basingwerk' of MS. Cotton Cleopatra B.V. [Best MS. of Tysilio's Chronicle.] Y Cymmrodor, 35, pp. 49–116, + 2 plates : 36, pp. 1–33, + 2 plates. 1925–26.

239 Gruffydd (W. J.). The Mabinogion. [i. The cycles and their homes : ii, The mabinogi : iii. The sources and origins.] Trans. Hon. Soc. Cymm., 1912–13, pp. 14–80. 1914.

240 Jackson (Kenneth). The 'Gododdin' of Aneirin. [6th c.] Antiquity, 13, pp. 25–34. 1939.

241 Lloyd (*Sir* John Edward). The Welsh Chronicles. Proc. Brit. Acad., 14, pp. 369–91. 1928.

242 Loth (Joseph). Remarques aux Four ancient Books of Wales. [i. Le Livre d'Aneurin : ii. Le Livre de Taliesin.] Rev. celt., 21, pp. 328–37. 1900.

243 Parry (Henry). Brut y Saeson : translation [from 683 to 977 A.D.]. Arch. Camb., 3rd S. 9, pp. 59–67. 1863.

244 Phillimore (Egerton). The publication of Welsh historical records. [i.e. of Annales Cambriae and Brut y Tywysogion. From departure of Romans to death of Llewelyn ap Gruffud.] Y Cymmrodor, 11, pp. 133–75. 1892.

245 Poste (Beale). The chronicle of Tysilio, the primary chronicle of the Cambrians. (Further remarks, *etc.*)

['Written c. 1000.' *See also* **251–52.**] J. Brit. Archaeol. Assoc., 10, pp. 231–36; 11, pp. 56–63. 1855.

246 —— Data on Tysilio's Chronicle, relating to the time of its publication, the festival of the Round Table, *etc.* (Data on Vortigern). *Same jnl.*, 11, pp. 248–53. 1855.

247 Skene (William Forbes). The Book of Aneurin. Arch. Camb., 3rd S. 11, pp. 383–93. 1865.

248 Stephens (Thomas). The Book of Aberpergwm, improperly called the Chronicle of Caradoc. [16th c. source. Points out unwarranted additions to original sources.] Arch. Camb., 3rd S., 4, pp. 77–96. 1858.

249 —— The literature of the Kymry. 8° Llandovery, 1849. 2nd edition. 8° London, 1876. [Gross 51. Pp. 295–317, the chroniclers.]

250 Wade-Evans (Arthur Wade). The Brychan documents. [Introduction: text: notes.] Y Cymmrodor, 19, pp. 18–50. 1906.

251 Wakeman (Thomas). Note on the territories of Vortigern and the Chronicle of Tysilio. [On two papers by Beale Poste, *q.v.*, **245–46.**] J. Brit. Archaeol. Assoc., 10, pp. pp. 367–72. 1855.

252 —— On the Chronicle of Tysilio and the territories of Vortigern. *Same jnl.*, 11, pp. 134–42, + plan. 1855.

5. CHARTERS, GRANTS, ETC.

§ *a*. General

253 Aronius (Julius). Diplomatische Studien über die älteren angelsächsischen Urkunden. *Diss.* pp. 90. 8° Königsberg, [1884]. [Gross, 1410.]

254 Ballard (Adolphus), *ed.* British borough charters, 1042–1216. pp. cxlvii, 266. 8° Cambridge, 1913.

255 Birch (Walter de Gray). Cartularium Saxonicum: a collection of charters relating to Anglo-Saxon history. (Index Saxonicus: an index to all the names of persons in Cartularium Saxonicum). 4 vol. 8° London, 1885 [1883]–99. [Gross, 1411. 1354 documents, many not in Kemble.]

256 British Museum. Facsimiles of ancient charters in the British Museum. 144 plates. 4 vol. fol. London, 1873–78. [Gross, 257. Vol. 1, 17 facsimiles with transcriptions, A.-S. period, (679–838), ed. E. A. Bond.]

257 Brunner (Heinrich). Zur Rechtsgeschichte der römischen und germanischen Urkunde, . . . Bd. 1. pp. xvi, 316. *No more published.* 8° Berlin, 1880. [Gross, 1412. Pp. 149–208, das angelsächsische Landbuch. Examines the structure of the charters. Deals mainly with bookland.]

258 Bryan (William Frank). Studies in the dialects of the Kentish charters of the Old English period. *Diss.* 8° Chicago, 1915.

259 Davis (Henry William Carless), *ed.* Regesta regum Anglo-Normannorum, 1066–1154. Vol. 1, Regesta Willelmi Conquestoris et Willelmi Rufi. pp. xliii, 159. fol. Oxford, 1913. [Pp. 1–76, 50 charters in full and abstracts of 250 more, temp. William I.]

260 Earle (John), *ed.* A handbook to the land charters and other Saxonic documents. pp. cxiii, 519. 8° Oxford, 1888. [Gross, 1416. c. 250 documents, some not in Kemble or Birch.]

261 Farrer (William). Early Yorkshire charters. 4 vol. 8° Edinburgh, 1914–42. [Vol. 1, pp. 1–28, pre-Norman documents (and a few others). Latin and A.-S. with notes. Consolidated index to vol. 1–3, *Yorks. Archaeol. Soc., Records, extra s.*, 4, 1942.]

262 Galbraith (Vivian Hunter). Monastic foundation charters of the eleventh and twelfth centuries. Camb. Hist. J., 4, pp. 205–22, 296–9 (appendices of documents). 1934.

263 Gelling (Margaret). Pre-Conquest local history: evidence from Anglo-Saxon charters. Amateur Historian, 1, pp. 241–45. 1953.

264 Grundy (George Beardoe). On the meaning of certain terms in the Anglo-Saxon charters. Essays and studies (English Assoc.), 8, pp. 37–69. 1922.

265 Hampson (R. T.). Medii aevi kalendarium, or dates, charters and customs of the Middle Ages ; with kalendars from the tenth to the fifteenth centuries, *etc.* 2 vol. 8° London, [1841]. [Pp. 9–34, dates of A.-S. charters, etc.]

266 Harmer (Florence Elizabeth). Anglo-Saxon charters and the historian. Bull. John Rylands Library, 22, pp. 339–67, + 1 plate. 1938.

267 Kemble (John Mitchell). Codex diplomaticus aevi Saxonici. *English Historical Society.* 6 vol. 8° London, 1839–48. [Gross, 1419. 1369 documents, from 604 to c. 1061, some inaccurately printed. Texts. A.-S. and Latin.]

268 —— Notices of heathen interment in the Codex Diplomaticus. [Heathen burial places noted as defining boundaries of estates.] Archaeol. J., 14, pp. 119–39. 1857.

269 Leach (Arthur Francis). Educational charters and documents (598–1909). pp. 634. 8° Cambridge, 1911. [Pp. 1–71, A.-S. period.]

270 Napier (Arthur Sampson) and **Stevenson** (William Henry), *ed.* The Crawford collection of early charters and documents, now in the Bodleian Library, *Anecdota Oxoniensia, Medieval and modern series,* 7. pp. xi, 167. 8° Oxford. 1895. [Gross, 1420. 19 documents, A.D. 739–1150, eight of them never published before, with elaborate notes.]

271 Parsons (Mary Prescott). Beiträge zur angelsächsischen Urkundenwesen bis zu Ausgang des 9. Jahrhunderts. *Diss., Vienna,* 1937. *Unpublished.*

272 —— Some scribal memoranda for Anglo-Saxon charters of the 8th and 9th centuries. Mitt. Inst. österreich. Geschichtforschung, Erg.–Bd. 14, pp. 13–32, + 3 plates. 1939.

273 Pierquin (Hubert). Recueil général des chartes anglo-saxonnes. Les Saxons en Angleterre, 604–1061. pp. 871. 8° Paris, 1912.

274 Poole (Reginald Lane). Seals and documents. [§ iv, in A.-S. England. Reprinted, with corrections, in his Studies in chronology and history, 1934.] Proc. Brit. Acad., 9, pp. 319–39, + 1 plate. 1919.

275 Public Record Office. Calendar of royal charters which occur in letters of inspeximus, exemplification, or confirmation, and in cartularies in the Public Record Office. Part 1, from Æthelbert of Kent to William II. [Gross, 1413. Contains an abstract of their contents.] Rept. Deputy Keeper Pub. Records, 29, pp. 7–48. 1868.

276 Robertson (Agnes Jane), *ed.* Anglo-Saxon charters, edited with translation and notes. pp. xxviii, 555. [120 documents.] 8° Cambridge, 1939.

277 Robinson (Joseph Armitage) and **Rose-Troup** (Frances). Le Thurleston. [A.-S. *Thyrel,* perforated. Use of term as a boundary in A.-S. charters, e.g. Birch 451, 670, 973.] N. and Q. Som. and Dorset, 19, pp. 223–24, 261–62. 1929.

278 Smith (Edward). Cartularium Saxonicum. [Further identifications to those in Birch.] N. and Q., 10th S. 7, pp. 185, 287, 466 : 12, p. 186. 1907, 1909.

279 Taxweiler (Richard Karl Wilhelm). Angelsächsische Urkundenbücher von kentischem Lokalcharakter. *Diss., Berlin.* pp. 59. 8° Berlin, 1906.

280 Thorpe (Benjamin). Diplomatarium Anglicum aevi Saxonici. A collection of English charters, from . . . A.D. 605 to William the Conqueror, with a translation of the Anglo-Saxon. 8° London, 1865. [Gross, 1422. c. 325 documents, of which some 20 not printed by Kemble. i. Miscellaneous charters : ii. Wills ; iii. Guilds : iv. Manumissions and acquittances.]

281 Treiter (M.) Die Urkundendatierung in angelsächsischen Zeit. Archiv f. Urkundenforschung, 7, pp. 53–160. 1921.

282 Weightman (Jane). Vowel-levelling in early Kentish and the use of the symbol ę in OE. charters. Engl. Studien, 35, pp. 337–49. 1905.

283 Wright (Cyril Ernest). Sir Edward Dering : a seventeenth-century antiquary and his ' Saxon ' charters. Chadwick Mem. Stud., pp. 369–93. 1950.

§ b. Individual

284 [Anon.] Ancient charters relating to Woodchester [Glos.]. [Latin and English translation by J. Earle: i. Charter of Æthelbald of Mercia: ii. Charter of Æthelred of Mercia. Both reprinted from Kemble.] Trans. Bristol and Glos. Arch. Soc., 5, pp. 148–53. 1881.

285 [Anon.] Observations on a charter in Mr. [Thomas] Astle's library, which is indorsed, in a hand co-eval with it; 'Haec est carta regis Eadgari, de institutione abbatiae Eliensis, et duplicatus'. [=2nd foundation, 970.] Archaeologia, 10, pp. 226–31. 1792.

286 Alexander (John James). Bishop Conon and St. Buryan. [?Date of endowment by Athelstan of a college of secular canons on site of hermitage of St. Beriana. (Birch, 785 : Kemble, 1143.)] Devon and Cornwall N. and Q., 15, p. 78. 1928.

287 Andrews (Robert T.) The charter of Oxhey, A.D. 790 : 'the manor of Rodenhanger, [Herts.]. Antiquary, 48, pp. 329–36, 414–17, 465–68. 1912.

288 Angus (William). Two early East Lothian charters. [i. By Duncan II to monks of St. Cuthbert of Durham, 1094 : 'The only surviving example of a Scottish charter executed in the A.-S. style.' Latin text, and translation.] Trans. E. Lothian Antiq. Soc., 1, pp. 5–11, + 1 plate. 1925.

289 Anscombe (Alfred) and **Stevenson** (William Henry). The charter [of Wulfrun, sister of Æthelred II] relating to St. Peter's, Wolverhampton. N. and Q., 9th S. 3, pp. 70–71, 149–51. 1899.

290 Anscombe (Alfred). Landavensium ordo chartarum. Celtic Rev., 6, pp. 123–29, 272–77, 289–95 : 7, pp. 63–67. 1909–11.

291 Astle (Thomas). Observations on a charter of king Eadgar. [Showing it to be a forgery.] Archaeologia, 10, pp. 232–40. 1792.

292 Balfour-Melville (E. W. M.) A Northamptonshire estate of Malcolm Canmore. [3 hides in Corby hundred in Northants geld roll. ? granted to Malcolm when an exile from Macbeth by his kinsman, Siward, who held the earldom of Northampton.] Scott. Hist. Rev., 27, pp. 101–02. 1948.

293 Barker (Eric E.). Sussex Anglo-Saxon charters. [Text, translation and notes.] Sussex Archaeol. Coll., 86, pp. 42–101 : 87, pp. 112–63 : 88, pp. 51–113. 1947–49.

294 Barrett (W. Bowles). Wyke Regis, Dorset, Ethelred [II]'s charter, cir. 988. [Latin text, with boundaries in A.-S., and notes.] N. and Q. Som. and Dorset, 9, pp. 345–46. 1905.

295 Bennet (E. K.). Cheveley church, [Cambs.]. [Pp. 238–40, Latin text of deed of exchange of manor of Dictune (Woodditton) for that of Cheaflea between Canute and Ely monastery : also Domesday entry.] Proc. Bury and W. Suffolk Archaeol. Inst., 1, pp. 237–49, + 1 plate. 1882.

296 Bibliographer, *pseud.* and **B.** (B. H.). List of Anglo-Saxon charters, A.D. 680–824; (ditto : 848–947 : 947–[1181]) [relating to Gloucestershire]. [Collected from Birch.] Glos. N. and Q., 3, pp. 331–33, 604–05 : 5, p. 40. 1887, 94.

297 Birch (Walter de Gray). The Anglo-Saxon charter of Oslac. *Privately printed,* 1892. [In Library of Chichester Cathedral. Confirmation by Offa, c. 787–94, on verso. B.C.S. 1334 (2373).]

298 —— The Anglo-Saxon charters of Worcester Cathedral. J. Brit. Archaeol. Assoc., 38, pp. 24–54. 1882.

299 —— Notes on an unpublished charter of Edgar in the possession of the dean and chapter of Wells. [958. A grant to Ealhstan of land at Stantun, in the territory of the Magosaetae. Latin text given.] Proc. Soc. Antiq., 2nd S. 8, pp. 225–30. 1880.

300 —— Notes on some Anglo-Saxon charters of the seventh and eighth centuries relating to Sussex. J. Brit. Archaeol. Assoc., 42, pp. 400–09. 1886.

301 —— Notes on the Isis in the Saxon charters, of the significance of [the name of] Berkshire. *Same jnl.,* 49, pp. 251–56. 1893.

302 Birch (Walter de Gray). On an unpublished charter of Uhtred of the Huuiccas, in the possession of the dean and chapter of Worcester. [770. Grant of land to Æthelmund, his minister. With particulars of four other charters of Uhtred.] Trans. Roy. Soc. Lit., 2nd S. 11, pp. 338–54, + one facsimile. 1878.

303 —— Original Anglo-Saxon charter in possession of the dean and chapter of Ely. [Latin text, 974. Kemble, vi, 103–5.] J. Brit. Archaeol. Assoc., 38, pp. 382–3. 1882.

304 Blaauw (William Henry). Buncton. The grant of part of a wood in Cealtborgsteal by Ealdwulf, heretoga of the South Saxons, dated from the hill of Biohchandoune, A.D. 791. [Notes on various A.-S. grants in Sussex. *See also* : Thorpe (B.) in 21, p. 22. 1869.] Sussex Archaeol. Collns., 8, pp. 177–88. 1856.

305 Brackenbury (Henry). [Exhibition of] two ancient charters to Battle Abbey. [Text (Latin) of charter of William I.] Proc. Soc. Antiq., 2nd S. 3, pp. 408, 410. 1867.

306 Brentnall (Harold Cresswell). The botany of the Anglo-Saxon charters. [Comments on **346.**] Wilts. Archaeol. Mag., 52, pp. 127–29. 1947.

307 —— Heathen burials. [Occurence as landmarks in A.-.S. charters. Wiltshire cases collected from Birch, etc.] *Same jnl.*, 53, pp. 373–74. 1950.

308 Bridgeman (Charles George Orlando). Staffordshire preconquest charters. [Includes texts in English, of 28 charters, with notes.] Collectns. for a history of Staffs., 1916, pp. 69–137. 1918.

309 Bruce (John). Saxon charter, belonging to Sir Edward Dering, Bart. [Conveyance of lands at Swithraedingdaenne, now Surrenden, Kent. c. 1020. A.-S. text.] Proc. Soc. Antiq., 4, p. 76. 1857.

310 Buddicom (R. A.). A.D. 901. Grant by Aeldered and Aedelflaed of the Mercians to Wenlock Abbey, of land at Easthope and Patton, co. Salop in exchange for land at Stanton, (Long Stanton, co. Salop). [Cart. Cott. viii,

27.] Transcribed and translated. Trans. Shrop. Arch. Soc., 50, pp. 185–87. 1940.

311 Burrows (Montagu). The antiquity of the Cinque Ports charters. [Date of confederation— ? from reign of Edward the Confessor.] Archaeol. Rev., 4, pp. 438–44. 1890.

312 Canham (A. S.). Notes on the history, charters, and ancient crosses of Crowland. Fenland N. and Q., 2, pp. 236–52. 1893.

313 Canterbury, *Cathedral library*. A summary of the Anglo-Saxon letter to King Edward. (A free translation of a letter to king Edward the Elder, from the Anglo-Saxon. Date circa 901–924. MS. in Canterbury Cathedral Library, Charta antiqua, c. 1282). [Re 5 hides of land at Fonthill, Wilts.] Canterbury Cath. Chronicle, no. 25, pp. 9–15, + 1 plate. 1936.

314 Carrie (John). The thane of Fife. [Grant by Malcolm Canmore of a place of refuge to Macduff's descendants.] Scottish N. and Q., 3, p. 56. 1889.

315 Civil (G.). Saxon Gosport and a royal charter of Alverstoke. [Grant of 11 hides *at Stocé* to Ælfric his thegn by Eadred, 948. Kemble MCLXIII.] Papers and Proc. Hants. F.C., 18, pp. 36–46. 1953.

316 Collingwood (William Gershom). Gospatric's Cumberland Charter. Saga-Book V. C., 3, pp. 300–02. 1904.

317 Cook (Albert Stanburrough). A putative charter to Aldhelm. [?Grant by Leutherius, bp. of Winchester, to Malmesbury, 675. (Gesta Pontificum, pp. 347–49).] Studies in English philology in honor of F. Klaeber, pp. 254–57. 1929.

318 Corner (George Richard). On the Anglo-Saxon charters of Friðwald, Ælfred, and Edward the Confessor, to Chertsey abbey. [With text, A.-S. and Latin, of first two.] Surrey archaeol. Collns., 1, pp. 77–96. 1858.

319 Coventry, *Minster*. The Anglo-Saxon charters of king Edward the Confessor to Coventry minster. With an autotype facsimile, and a translation by Walter de Gray Birch. pp. 4. 4° London, 1889.

320 Cowper (Henry Swainson). A wealden charter of A.D. 814. (Harleian charter 83 A.I.). [Text in Latin and transl.; identification of 13 place names in it.] Arch. Cant., 31, pp. 203–06. 1915.

321 Crediton. The early charters of Crediton. [Transcripts, in English, of Crawford charters 1–4, 7, 10 and 13, now in the Bodleian Library. For comments and corrections, see 7, pp. 267–72.] Devon and Cornwall N. and Q., 7, pp. 184–200. 1913.

322 Crofts (C. B.). St. Buryan. An attempt to restore and identify the charter place names. *Same jnl.*, 24 pp. 6–9. 1950.

323 Davidson (James Bridge). On some Anglo-Saxon charters at Exeter. [15 documents, A.D. 938–1069, five never before printed: four only in Kemble.] J. Brit. Archaeol. Assoc., 39, pp. 259–303. 1883.

324 —— On the charters of king Ine. [Appendix 1, 'abbots of Glastonbury': Appendix 2, 'table of charters of king Ine': Appendix 3, 'list of reputed charters to Glastonbury to 740': Appendix 4, 'William of Malmesbury, A.D. 709'.] Proc. Somerset Arch. Soc., 30 (1884), pp. 1–31, and map of Saxon boundaries of Shepton, Croscombe, and Pilton. 1885.

325 Davis (Henry William Carless). The liberties of Bury St. Edmunds. [§ 2, The grants of Edward the Confessor.] E.H.R., 24, pp. 417–31. 1909.

326 Dickinson (Francis Henry). West Monkton charter. [Grant, in MS. at Longleat, by Centwine, of West Monkton to abbot Hamegils of Glastonbury, 682. Includes transcript, in Latin.] Proc. Somerset Arch. Soc., 28 (1882), pp. 89–98. 1883.

327 Douglas (David Charles). A charter of enfeoffment under William the Conqueror. [To Bury. With transcript.] E.H.R., 42, pp. 245–47. 1927.

328 —— Fragments of an Anglo-Saxon survey from Bury St. Edmunds. [With A.-S. and Latin text from C.C.C. Oxford, MS. CXCVII, fol. 106 b. Economic conditions of abbey estates temp. Leofstan, 1045–65.] E.H.R., 43, pp. 376–83. 1928.

329 Dowdeswell (E. R.). Anglo-Saxon charter: Dowdeswell, [Glos.] [Reversionary grant by Headda, abbot, to Worcester monastery, of land at Dogodes well . . . 781 × 798.] Glos. N. and Q., 3, p. 400. 1887.

330 Duignan (William Henry) and **Carter** (William Fowler). King Ethelred's [II] charter confirming the foundation of Burton Abbey, and the will of Wulfric Spott, the founder. [1002–4; texts, translated.] Midland Antiquary, 4, pp. 97–115. 1886.

331 Ekwall (Eilert). On some Old English charters. Neusprachliche Studien. Festgabe K. Luick, pp. 152–57. 1925.

332 Eyton (Robert William). The Staffordshire chartulary of ancient deeds. Annotated by R.W.E. [Series 1, no. 1, is the only one before 1087. Robert de Stafford's grant of Wrottesley to the abbey of Evesham, 1072, MS. Harl. 408. Text, in English, and notes.] Collns. for a history of Staffs (Wm. Salt Arch. Soc.), 2i, pp. 178–82. 1881.

333 Field (John Edward). The Saxon charters of Brightwell, Sotwell and Mackney, Berks. [No texts.] Berks, Bucks and Oxon Archaeol. J., 11, pp. 108-12; 12, pp. 7–12, 49–52, 82–86. 1906.

334 Finberg (Herbert Patrick Reginald). The early charters of Devon and Cornwall. *Univ. Coll. Leicester, Dept. English Local Hist., Occ. Papers*, 2. pp. 31. 4° Leicester, 1953. [List of 99 A.-S. charters.]

335 Forsberg (Rune). Topographical notes on some Anglo-Saxon charters. Namn och Bygd, Lund, 30, pp. 150–58. 1942.

336 Fowler (George Herbert). Some Saxon charters. [Translations of 16 A.-S. Bedfordshire charters, with notes.] Pubs. Beds. Hist. Rec. Soc., 5, pp. 39–57. 1920.

337 Galbraith (Vivian Hunter). An episcopal land-grant of 1085. [Holme Lacy and Onibury, Salop: between Robert, bp. of Hereford and Roger de Lacy.] E.H.R., 44, pp. 353–72, + 1 plate. 1929.

C

338   Galbraith (Vivian Hunter). Royal charters to Winchester. [With texts of 49 charters, 1032–1178.] E.H.R., 35, pp. 382–400. 1920.

339 Gelling (Margaret). The boundaries of the Westminster charters. [Of Edgar and Ethelred. With A.-S. texts and translations.] Trans. London and Middlesex Arch. Soc., N. S. 11, pp. 101–04. 1953.

340 Goodchild (W.). Tisbury in the Anglo-Saxon charters. Wilts. Archaeol. Mag., 44, pp. 322–31. 1929.

341 Greaves (C. S.) and **Lee-Warner** (J.). Charter of Cuthwulf, bishop of Hereford, A.D. 840. [Transcript of original Latin, and notes.] Archaeol. J., 30, pp. 174–80, + 2 plates. 1873.

342 Greswell (William Henry Parr). King Ina's grant of Brent to Glastonbury. [663. Birch, 121.] N. and Q. Som. and Dorset, 7, p. 255. 1901.

343 Grinsell (Leslie Valentine). An analysis and list of Berkshire barrows. [Pp. 186–88, ' Saxon land charters ', i.e. ' barrows used as boundary-marks in Saxon times '.] Berks. Archaeol. J., 39, pp. 171–91, *etc.* 1935.

344 —— Berkshire barrows : part 3, Evidence from the Saxon charters. *Same jnl.*, 42, pp. 102–16. 1938.

345 —— Hampshire barrows. [Pp. 30–36, 197, references in the Saxon land charters.] Papers and Proc. Hants. F.C., 14, pp. 9–40, 195–229, 346–65, + 15 plates, + 5 maps. 1938–40.

346 Grose (J. Donald). Botanical references in the Saxon charters of Wiltshire. [Notes by H. C. Brentnall, **306**.] Wilts. Archaeol. Mag., 51, pp. 555–83. 1947.

347 Grundy (George Beardoe). Berkshire charters. [pp. 96–102, 137–44, Abingdon.] Berks, Bucks and Oxon Archaeol. J., 27, pp. 96–102, 137–71, 193–247; 28, pp. 64–80; 29, pp. 87–128, 196–220; 30, pp. 48–63, 102–20; 31, pp. 31–62, 111–45; 32, pp. 16–30, 62–68 (index). 1922–28.

348 —— Dorset charters (Saxon charters of Dorset.) [61, pp. 72–78, list of charters and their topographical identifications.] Proc. Dorset Archaeol. Soc., 55 (for 1933), pp. 239–68 : 56, pp. 110–30 : 57, pp. 114–39 : 58, pp. 103–36 : 59, pp. 95–118 : 60, pp. 75–89 ; 61, pp. 60–78. 1934–40.

349 —— Saxon charters and field names of Gloucestershire. *Bristol and Glos. Archaeol. Soc.* pp. 306. 8° Gloucester, 1935–36.

350 —— The Saxon charters and field names of Somerset. Proc. Somerset Arch. Soc., Supplements to 73–80 (1927–34). 1935.

351 —— The Saxon charters of Somerset : West Monkton. Revised notes of its charter. [*See* his Somerset charters, pp. 51–54.] *Same jnl.*, 84 (1938), pp. 104–06. 1939.

352 —— Saxon charters of Worcestershire. Trans. B'ham. Arch. Soc., 52 (for 1927), pp. 1–183 : 53 (for 1928), pp. 18–131, + 1 map. 1929–31.

353 —— The Saxon land charters of Hampshire, with notes on place and field names. Archaeol. J., 78, pp. 55–173 : 81, pp. 31–126 : 83, pp. 91–253 : 84 (1927), pp. 160–340 : 85 (1928), pp. 188–96 (index). 1921–29.

354 —— The Saxon land charters of Wiltshire. *Same jnl.*, 76, pp. 143–301 : 77, pp. 8–126. 1919–20.

355 —— Saxon Oxfordshire. Charters and ancient highways. *Oxfordshire Record Society*, 15. pp. x, 120. 8° Oxford, 1933.

356 Hales (John W.). Notes on two Anglo-Saxon charters relating to Hampstead in the times of kings Eadgar and Æthelred. [Extracts in A.-S. and translation and notes : map of ' Hampstead in Saxon times '.] Trans. London and Middx. Archaeol. Soc., 6, pp. 560–70, + map. 1890.

357 Hamper (William). Disquisition on a passage in king Athelstan's grant to the abbey of Wilton [in 937]. [MS. Harl. 436. ' From Noddre bank upwards over Eastcombe, as the Stone Ridge shoots to the heathen burial-place '.] Archaeologia, 22, pp. 399–402. 1829.

358 Haskins (Charles Homer). A charter of Canute for Fécamp. [Extract (quoted) from cartulary of 12th c., now lost, shows grant planned by Ethelred and actually made by Canute.] E.H.R., 33, pp. 342–44. 1918.

359 Haskins (George Lee). A forged charter of William the Conqueror. [MS., B.M. Add. Charter 11205: a confirmation to Coventry abbey.] Speculum, 18, pp. 496–97. 1943.

360 Hemingus. Chartularium ecclesiae Wigornensis, e codibus MS. penes R. Graves . . . descripsit ediditque T. Hearnius, qui et eam partem libri de Domesday quae ad Ecclesiam pertinet Wigornensem . . subnexuit. 2 vol. 8° Oxonii, 1723. [Gross, 1417. Royal grants of 9th–10th c., reprinted by Kemble. Heming was sub-prior while Wulfstan was bp., and at whose command he compiled his chartulary.]

361 Hoare (*Sir* Richard Colt), *bart.*, *ed.* Registrum Wiltunense, Saxonicum et Latinum, A.D. 892–1045. fol. London, 1827. [Gross, 1418. In B.M. 34 documents, all printed in Kemble.]

362 Hughes (J. C.). An unrecognised charter of Alverstoke. [Charter of Eadred, 948, granting xi hides to his thegn Ælfric *aet Stoc*. Assigned by Birch to Bishopstoke, and by Kemble to Stoke. Boundaries (given in A.-S.) indicate Alverstoke.] Papers and Proc. Hants. F.C., 8, pp. 239–41. 1918.

363 Jeffcock (John Thomas). A record of the . . . 900th anniversary of the granting of the charter of the pious lady Wulfrun in 994 A.D., to the collegiate church of Wolverhampton. pp. 86 + 16, + 5 plates. 8° Wolverhampton, 1894. [With (Latin) text of her charter.]

364 Jessop (Ronald Frederick). Notes on a Saxon charter of Higham. [MS. Cotton, Aug. II. 99. Grant of 5 ploughlands by Offa to abp. Jaenberht in 774.] Arch. Cant., 55 (1942), pp. 12–15, + map. 1943.

365 Jones (William Henry). On an Anglo-Saxon charter relating to the parish of Stockton, in Wilts. [Kemble, 1078: date 901. Including text in A.-S. and translation.] Wilts. Archaeol. Mag., 12, pp. 216–220, + map. 1870.

366 Jones (William Henry). On some ancient charters relating to North Newenton. [Alfred, 892 and Athelstan, 933 (Kemble, nos. 320 and 1109. Texts in A.-S. and English, with notes. *Same jnl.*, 19, pp. 302–06. 1881.

367 Judge (Cyril Bathurst). Anglo-Saxonica in Hereford cathedral library. [MSS. of Caedmon's hymn, the vision of a certain prior of England, a lawsuit brought against his mother by Eadwine (Kemble 755) A.-S. text and translation, and a deed of purchase of land by Leofwine (Kemble 802) A.-S. text and translation.] Harvard Stud. and Notes in Phil. and Lit., 16, pp. 89–96, + 1 plate. 1934.

368 Keays-Young (Julia). The Éadmund-Ælfric charter, 944 A.D. [Grant of land near Daventry to bp. Ælfric of Hereford. Map on p. 274. Text, translation and notes.] Rev. Engl. Stud., 6, pp. 271–83. 1930.

369 Kemble (John Mitchell). Anglo-Saxon document relating to lands at Send and Sunbury, in Middlesex, in the time of Eadgar [962]: of the writ of Cnut, on the accession of archbishop Æthelnoth to the see of Canterbury, A.D. 1020. [Including texts in A.-S. and English. Former document is a title-deed of Westminster.] Archaeol. J., 14, pp. 58–62. 1857.

370 Larking (Lambert Blackwell). On the Surrenden charters. [With plate of grant by Godwin to Leofwine the Red of swine-pastures at Swidraedingden (i.e. ?Surrenden), c. 1016–20.] Arch. Cant., 1, pp. 50–65. 1858.

371 Lawrie (*Sir* Archibald Campbell), *ed.* Early Scottish charters, prior to A.D. 1153. pp. xxix, 515. 8° Glasgow, 1905. [First 10 only pre 1087. Texts and notes.]

372 Leigh (*Hon.* James Wentworth), *dean of Hereford.* Some archives and seals of Hereford cathedral. [Plates of charter of Cuthwulf, bp. of Hereford, 840, to Bromyard monastery, and of portion of instrument recording a suit in county court under Canute (=Kemble, 757), etc.] Trans. Woolhope N.F. Club, 1900–2, pp. 107–21, + 9 plates. 1903.

373 Liebermann (Felix). Drei north-umbrische Urkunden um 1100. [ii. Rights of archbishop Thomas I of York (1070–1100) in the city of York. A.-S. text and German translation, with notes.] Archiv Stud. neueren Spr., Bd. 111, pp 275–84, + 1 plate. 1903.

374 —— An English document of about 1080 : privileges of archbishop Thomas I of York (1070–1100), in the city of York. [Translation by M. H. Peacock, of 373. Text of document, A.-S., French and English translation.] Yorks. Archaeol. J., 18, pp. 412–16. 1905.

375 Madden (*Sir* Frederick). Re-marks on the Anglo-Saxon charters [of Eadgar and Offa] granted to the abbey of St. Denis, in France, and on the seals attached to them. [Including the texts, in Latin. 790 and 960 A.D.] Archaeol.J., 13, pp. 355–71, + 1 plate : 14, p. 57. 1856.

376 Maitland (George). Lindfield church from Saxon times. [Charter of Aldwulf, 765 : confirmed by Offa.] Sussex N. and Q., 12, pp. 143–49. 1949.

377 Morgan (Thomas). Grant from Offa, king of the Mercians, to Æthel-mund, of land in Westbury, in the pro-vince of the Wiccas, A.D., 791–796. [Latin text and translation. Postscript to **1875**, *q.v.*]. J. Brit. Archaeol. Assoc., 32, pp. 190–92, + 2 plates, 1876.

378 O'Donovan (John). The Irish charters in the Book of Kells. [Kenney, 1, p. 753. Charters 2 and 4 (11th c.). Text, transl., and commentary. On blank ff. 6, 7, 27 of the Book of Kells for safe keeping, as records concerning the property of the Church. 12th c. hand.] Miscellany Irish Archaeol. Soc., pp. 127–58. 1841.

379 Pafford (John Henry Pyle). Bradford-on-Avon. The Saxon bound-aries in Ethelred's charter of 1001 A.D. [A.-S. text of charter, and translation and notes.] Wilts. Archaeol. Mag., 54, pp. 210–18, + 1 plate. 1951.

380 Peake (Harold John Edward). Brihtric's charter. [Corrections to p. 82 of J. E. Field's paper ' Some notes on the Domesday Survey of Berkshire ', *q.v.* **2831** : 'Lulla, to whom in 801

Brihtric, king of Wessex, gave a manor in Aston ', etc.] Berks, Bucks and Oxon Archaeol. J., 10, pp. 122–23. 1905.

381 Peckham (W. D.). Ceadwalla's charter and the hundred of Manwood. [Question of parish boundaries in 1524.] Sussex N. and Q., 1, pp. 233–34. 1927.

382 —— The text of Ceadwalla's charter. [Of land for his monastery at Selsey, to Wilfrid. With translation.] *Same jnl.*, 2, pp. 45–47. 1928.

383 Pegge (Samuel). A copy of a deed in Latin and Saxon, of Odo, bishop of Baieux . . . ; with some observ-ations thereon. [Trendley, Wickham-breux, Kent.] Archaeologia, 1, pp. 361–72, + 1 plate. 1770.

384 Perceval (Charles Spencer). Re-marks on an unpublished portion of a charter of king Ethelred, A.D. 1012 [from] the Textus Roffensis [c. 79]. [The land-boundaries of Stanton, Hunts. A.-S. text and translation.] Proc. Soc. Antiq., 2nd S. 3, pp. 47–50. 1865.

385 Phillipps (*Sir* Thomas), *bart.*, *ed.* Cartularium Saxonicum Malmesburiense. pp. 25. fol. Typis Medio-Montanis, [1831]. [Gross, 1414. 29 Latin charters (in Kemble) mostly before 1066.]

386 —— Three unedited Saxon char-ters, from the cartulary of Cirencester abbey. [Texts in A.-S. only.] Arch-aeologia, 26, pp. 255–56. 1836.

387 Pope (William). The Copplestone charter. [Birch, 1303. Grant by Edgar in 974 of ' three hides of land at Nymed ' to his thegn Ælfhere.] Devon and Corn-wall N. and Q., 17, pp. 322–24, + 1 plate (of Copplestone cross). 1933.

388 Radcliffe (P. Delme). ' Deed of gift of North Nywantune [Newenton] to the monastery of Wilton, in the county of Wilts, by king Athelstan, A.D. 933.' Extracted from Dugdale's Mon-asticon Anglicanum, and translated by F. A. Radcliffe. [Latin text with trans-lation, and notes]. Wilts. Archaeol. Mag., 19, pp. 228–31. 1881.

389 Ragg (Frederick William). A charter of Gospatrick. [Text in A.-S., and translation.] Ancestor, 7, pp. 244–47. 1903.

390 Rag (Frederick William). Five Strathclyde and Galloway charters— four concerning Cardew, and one the Westmorland Newbigging. [i. Gospatric's charter (pp. 198–218, and first plate).] Trans. Cumb. and Westm. Antiq. Soc., N.S. 17, pp. 198–233, + 3 plates. 1917.

391 —— Five Strathclyde or Galloway charters . . . [pp. 231–49 and plate 1, Gospatric's charter: including text as it stands, text amended, and translation.] Trans. Dumfries. Antiq. Soc., 3rd S. 5, pp. 231–64, + 3 plates. 1918.

392 —— Gospatrick's charter. [Text in A.-S. and in translation, and notes.] Trans. Cumb. and Westm. Antiq. Soc., 5, pp. 71–84. 1905.

393 Reichel (Oswald Joseph). Church right and church charters in Devonshire. [On a charter of Aethelred of Mercia to Dunne and her daughter Bucge (Cart. Sax., i, 225).] Devon N. and Q., 1, pp. 39–41. 1900.

394 Riley (Henry Thomas). The history and charters of Ingulfus considered. [Spuriousness of charters of Wichtlaf (833), of Burghred (868), Thorold (1051), etc.] Archaeol. J., 19, pp. 32–49, 114–33. 1862.

395 Robinson (Joseph Armitage). Chats on charters. [Discrepancies of Athelstan dates in two Worcester charters, (B.C.S., 665, 666; K.C.D., 347, 348) from MS. Cotton Tib. A. XIII.] Downside Rev., 56, pp. 180–90. 1938.

396 —— Westwood manor and Farleigh Hungerford. [Charter of Ethelred II in 987 to his huntsman Leofwine (Kemble, 658).] N. and Q. Som. and Dorset, 18, pp. 105–10. 1925.

397 Robson (John). On the early charters of St. Werburgh's in Chester. [Of Edgar, 958, etc.] Trans. Hist. Soc. Lancs. and Ches., 11, pp. 187–98. 1859.

398 Rose-Troup (Frances). The Anglo-Saxon charter of Brentford (Brampford), Devon. [Includes Latin text (with facsimile): appendix B gives ' estates in Devon held by Glastonbury abbey '.] Rept. and Trans. Devon. Assoc., 70, pp. 253–75, and 1 plate. 1938.

399 Rose-Troup (Frances). The Anglo-Saxon charter of Ottery St. Mary. [Text and facsimile. Notes: the battle of Wicganbeorg, 851: enclosures for land marks: etc.] *Same jnl.*, 71, pp. 201–20, + 1 plate. 1939.

400 —— Anglo-Saxon charters of Devon. [Remarks on boundaries in Birch 723 (Stoke Canon), 721 (Topsham), 952 (Ippleden, Daignton and Abbot's Kerswell), 1103 (Clyst Wicon), 1303 (Nymet), 725 (Newton St. Petrock), 1323 (Peadington),Kemble 744 (Meavy).] Devon and Cornwall N. and Q., 17, pp. 55–58, 124–26. 1932.

401 —— Crediton charters of the tenth century. Rept. and Trans. Devon. Assoc., 74, pp. 237–61. 1942.

402 —— The new Edgar charter and the South Hams. [962. Text in Latin, A.-S., and translation. Plates show facsimile of Hiwisce charter, map of Dartmoor (16th c.), Om Homme charter, Derentune charter: map is of the South Hams.] *Same jnl.*, 61, pp. 249–80, + 4 plates, + map. 1929.

403 —— St. Buryan charter. [Confirmation in Bishop Grandisson's Register fol. 25b of a grant by Athelstan in 943. 9 serious errors which make it spurious.] Devon and Cornwall N. and Q., 18, pp. 294–99. 1935.

404 Round (John Horace). Some early Sussex charters. [Preserved in France, temp. Edward the Confessor to 1207. Endowments of Norman monasteries with possessions in Sussex.] Sussex Archaeol. Collns., 42, pp. 75–86. 1899.

405 —— and **Stevenson** (William Henry). An Old-English charter of William the Conqueror, 1068 (?) [in favour of St. Martin's-le-Grand, London]. [?did A.-S. kings possess a chancery. Criticism of W. H. Stevenson's article, **412**, together with his reply.] E.H.R., 12, pp. 105–07. 1897.

406 Rowe (Joseph Hambley). Identification of Caellwic, [Cornwall]. [? where. Assigned by king Egbert to bp. of Sherborne between 810 and 840.] N. and Q., 12th S., 6, p. 332. 1920.

407 Rundell (T. W.). The early charters of Crediton. [Comments on **321**, with corrections from Napier and Stevenson's work, **270**.] Devon and Cornwall N. and Q., 7, pp. 267–72. 1913.

408 Shoosmith (Edward). The vanishing South Saxon. [Charter of Offa, 772. Grant of 8 carucates of land in Bixlea to bp. Oswald, with boundaries.] Sussex County Mag., 4, pp. 478–80. 1930.

409 Stevenson (William Henry) and **Duignan** (William Henry). Anglo-Saxon charters relating to Shropshire. Trans. Shrop. Arch. Soc., 34, pp. 1–22. 1911.

410 Stevenson (William Henry). The charter of Wulfrun to the monastery at Hamtun (Wolverhampton). [The text translated and revised by W. H. Stevenson, and edited] by W. H. Duignan. pp. 19. 8° Wolverhampton, [1888].

411 —— The Old English charters to St. Denis. [?later French fabrications, and not copies of lost English originals.] E.H.R., 6, pp. 736–42. 1891.

412 —— An Old English charter of William the Conqueror in favour of St. Martin's-le-Grand, London, A.D. 1068. [Text in Latin and in A.-S.: did A.-S. kings possess a chancery? *see also* **405**.] E.H.R., 11, pp. 731–44. 1896.

413 —— Yorkshire surveys and other eleventh-century documents in the York Gospels. E.H.R., 27, pp. 1–25. 1912.

414 Tait (James). An alleged charter of William the Conqueror. [B.M. Add. Charter 11205, purporting to confirm to Coventry abbey the gifts of earl Leofric its founder.] Essays . . . presented to R. L. Poole, pp. 151–67. 1927.

415 Tapp (William Henry) and **Draper** (F. W. M.). The Saxon charter of Sunbury-on-Thames. [962 (Edgar). A.-S. and translation. The boundaries. Map.] Trans. London and Middsx. Archaeol. Soc., N.S. 10, pp. 302–06. 1951.

416 Tapp (William Henry). The Sunbury charter. (King Eadgar's charter, granting land at Sunbury [Middlesex], to his kinsman Ælfheh, c. A.D. 962, with

reference in the legend to an earlier charter in the possession of Æthelstan's family (possibly before A.D. 900). pp. 29. 4° Sunbury-on-Thames, [1951]. [3 facsimiles and map in text.]

417 Wade-Evans (Arthur Wade). The Llancarfan charters. [6th c.–] Arch. Camb., 87, pp. 151–65. 1932.

418 Ward (Gordon). Dudda's land in Canterbury. [Charter of Æthelwulf, 837. (Birch, 426).] Arch. Cant., 64 (1951), pp. 13–19. 1952.

419 —— The Hæselerc charter of 1018. [B. M. Stowe, 38 (plate). ' I, Cnut, . . . grant to . . . abp. Ælfstan . . . a certain little woodland pasture in . . . Andredeswealde, which is commonly called Hæselersc.' = Haslesse of Domesday and now Hazelhurst in Ticehurst parish.] Sussex Archaeol. Collns., 77, pp. 119–29. 1936.

420 —— King Nothelm's charter. [To Selsey, c. 682–85.] Sussex County Mag., 20, pp. 21–24. 1946.

421 —— King Wihtred's charter of A.D. 699. Arch. Cant., 60 (1947), pp. 1–14, + 2 plates. 1948.

422 —— Sand tunes boc. [Grant by Æthelberht 1 of Kent to Sandtun (Sampton in West Hythe), endorsed in a charter of 732 : grant repeated by Ecgberht in 833. MSS. B.M. Cotton Augustus II. 91 and 102 (Birch, 148 and 411). Geographical identifications, etc. Sketch map on p. 41.] Arch. Cant., 43, pp. 39–47. 1931.

423 —— The Saxon charters of Burmarsh [Romney marsh]. [Including texts and translations. With map.] Arch. Cant., 45, pp. 133–41. 1933.

424 —— The Westernhanger charter of 1035. [Identification of places mentioned.] Arch. Cant., 47, pp. 144–52, + plate (facsimile), + map. 1935.

425 —— The Wilmington [Kent] charter of A.D. 700. [Birch, 97 and 98. Identification of places mentioned : with map.] Arch. Cant., 48, pp. 11–28, + 3 plates (facsimiles). 1936.

426 Watson (Christopher Knight). Remarks on exhibition by the dean and chapter of Canterbury of a volume of

Saxon charters entitled ' Diplanata vet-ustissima chartarum ecclesiae Christi Cantuariensis.' [Gives text, hitherto unprinted, of Privilege of Æthelbald of Mercia, 742 ; the boundaries in Privilege of Egbert, 830 (Kemble, 224) ; the boundaries of Privilege of Alfred, 898 (Kemble 324).] Proc. Soc. Antiq., 2nd S. 6, pp. 165–67. 1874.

427 Wethered (F. T.). Hurley. [Pp. 58–61 : ' The dedication and endowment of St. Mary's church and foundation of the Benedictine monastery of Hurley, Berks., in the reign of William the Conqueror . . . a translation of the original charter in the custody of the dean and chapter of Westminster.'] Q.J. Berks Archaeol. Soc., 2, pp. 27–34, 53–61, *etc.* Notes on pp. 145–46 (1892). 1891.

428 Whitley (T. W.). The charters and manuscripts of Coventry : their story and purport (with translations). The royal and noble charters of the eleventh century founding the Coventry minster. [Gross, 2681.] Proc. Warw. Archaeol. F.C., 41, pp. 53–94 : 42, pp. 35–71. 1896–97.

429 Wilson (James). An English letter of Gospatric. [Charter, including text and translation.] Scot. Hist. Rev., 1, pp. 62–69 : *See also* pp. 105–06, 240–41, 353–54 : 2, pp. 340–41. 1904–05.

430 Wrottesley (*Hon.* George). The Burton chartulary (Derbyshire portion). [Pp. 97–100, A.-S. and Domesday.] J. Derbs. Archaeol. Soc., 7, pp. 97–153. 1885.

431 Wyatt (Alfred John). Notes on Anglo-Saxon charters, etc. [i. Bishop Denewulf : ii. King Alfred's will : iii. The stolen belt.] Mod. Lang. Rev., 13, pp. 83–84. 1918.

6. CHRONOLOGICAL PROBLEMS

432 Angus (W. S.). The chronology of the reign of Edward the Elder. E.H.R., 53, pp. 194–210. 1938.

433 —— The eighth scribe's dates in the Parker manuscript of the Anglo-Saxon Chronicle. Medium Ævum, 10, pp. 130–49, + 2 plates. 1941.

434 Anscombe (Alfred). The Anglo-Saxon computation of historic time in the ninth century. Brit. Num. J., 4, pp. 241–310, + 1 plate : 5, pp. 381–407. 1908–09.

435 —— The obit of St. Columba and the chronology of the early kings of Alban. E.H.R., 7, pp. 510–31. 1892.

436 —— St. Gildas of Ruys and the Irish regal chronology of the sixth century. pp. 66. 8° Tottenham, 1893. [Gross, 1370 : Lit.]

437 B. (A. E.). Venerable Bede's mental almanach. ['Quae sit feria in calendis.'] N. and Q., 1st S. 4, pp. 201–03. 1851.

438 Beaven (Murray Lowthian Randolph). The beginning of the year in the Alfredian chronicle (866–87). E.H.R. 33, pp. 328–42. 1918.

439 —— The regnal dates of Alfred, Edward the Elder, and Athelstan. E.H.R., 32, pp. 517–31. 1917.

440 Dickins (Bruce). The day of Byrhtnoth's death and other obits from a twelfth-century Ely calendar. [Aug. 10, 991.] Leeds studies in English, 6, pp. 14–24. 1937.

441 Hodgkin (Robert Howard). The beginning of the year in the English Chronicle. E.H.R., 39, pp. 497–510. 1924.

442 Lenmacher (Gustav). The ancient Celtic year. J. Celtic Stud., 1, pp. 144–47. 1950.

443 Loth (Joseph). L'année celtique d'après les textes irlandais, gallois, bretons et le calendrier de Coligny. Des nombres et du systême de numération chez les Celtes. Rev. celtique, 25, pp. 113–62. 1904.

444 MacCarthy (Bartholomew), *ed.* The Codex Palatino-Vaticanus no. 830. Texts, translations and indices. *Royal Irish Academy* : *Todd Lecture Series*, 3. pp. 450. 8° Dublin, 1892. [Pp. 335–95, Irish chronology.]

445 MacNeill (John). An Irish historical tract dated A.D. 721. [On synchronisms.] Proc. R.I.A., 28 c, pp. 123–48. 1910.

446 MacNeill (John). On the reconstruction and date of the Laud synchronisms. Zeit. celt. Phil., 10, pp. 81–96. 1915.

447 Nichols (Robert Cradock). On a Latin note to the Bodleian ms. of the Anglo-Saxon Chronicle [E] concerning the origin of the Æra Dionysiana. Archaeologia, 47, pp. 481–82. 1883.

448 Oppert (Gustav). On the origin of the Aera Dionysiana, or Aera vulgaris, or Aera Christiana. [Pp. 347–52, evidence from A.-S.C. and from Bede.] *Same jnl.*, 44, pp. 335–52. 1873.

449 Poole (Reginald Lane). The beginnings of the year in the Anglo-Saxon Chronicles. E.H.R., 16, pp. 719–21. 1901.

450 —— The beginning of the year in the Middle Ages. [Contains A.-S. material.] Proc. Brit. Acad., 10, pp. 113–37. 1921.

451 —— The chronology of Bede's Historia ecclesiastica and the councils of 679–680. [Reprinted in his Studies in chronology and history, pp. 38–53. 1934.] J. Theol. Stud., 20, pp. 24–40. 1919.

452 —— Studies in chronology and history. Collected and edited by Austin Lane Poole. pp. 328. 8° Oxford. 1934.

453 Powicke (*Sir* Frederick Maurice), *ed.* Handbook of British chronology. *Royal Historical Society*: *Guides and handbooks*, 2. pp. xii, 424. 8° London, 1939. [Pp. 6–33, A.-S. period, and *passim*. Rulers, bishops, Church councils, etc.].

454 Stevenson (William Henry). The date of king Alfred's death. [His conclusion is 26.x.899.] E.H.R., 13, pp. 71–77. 1898.

455 Thurneysen (Rudolf). Synchronismen der irischen Könige. Zeit. celt. Philol., 19, pp. 81–99. 1933.

456 Tille (Alexander). Yule and Christmas : their place in the Germanic year. ['i. The Germanic year : ii. The beginning of the Anglo-German year : iii. Solstices and equinoxes : iv. The Calends of January : v. Beda, de mensibus Anglorum'.] Trans. Glasgow Archaeol. Soc., N.S. 3, pp. 426–97. 1899.

457 Wade (John R.). Celtic chronology. J. Roy. Soc. Antiq. Ireland, 67 (7th S. 7), p. 310. 1937.

458 Wade-Evans (Arthur Wade). The chronology of Arthur. Y Cymmrodor, 22, pp. 125–49. 1910.

459 Wainwright (Frederick Threlfall). The chronology of the 'Mercian Register'. [Annals temp. Edward the Elder incorporated into A.-S. C., MSS. B, C, and D.] E.H.R., 60, pp. 385–92. 1945.

460 Walsh (Paul). Dating of the Annals of Inisfallen. Catholic Bulletin, 29, pp. 677–82. 1939.

461 —— The dating of the Irish Annals. Irish Hist. Stud., 2, pp. 355–75. 1941.

462 Wildhagen (Karl). Das Kalendarium der Handschrift Vitellius E. XVIII. [First half of 11th c. Written at Winchester.] Texte u. Forschungen : Festgabe für F. Liebermann, pp. 68–118. 1921.

7. GENEALOGY

§ *a*. Anglo-Saxon, General

463 Anscombe (Alfred). The pedigree of earl Godwin. Trans. R.H.S., 3rd S., 7, pp. 129–49. 1913.

464 Bell (Alexander). The West Saxon genealogy in Gaimar. Philol. Quart., 2, pp. 173–86. 1923.

465 Bjoerkman (Erik). Bedwig in den westsächsischen Genealogien. Anglia, Beibl., 30, pp. 23–25. 1919.

466 Boeddeker (K.). Ein Stammbaum der englischen Könige zurückgeführt bis auf Adam. Nach einem Manuscripte der Harleianischen Bibliothek [53] des Britischen Museums. Archiv Stud. neueren Spr., Bd. 53, pp. 205–18. 1874.

467 Brandl (Alois). Die Urstammtafel der Westsachsen und das Beowulf-Epos. *Same jnl.*, Bd. 137, pp. 6–24. 1918.

468 Bridgeman (Charles George Orlando). The royal descent of the Mercian earls. Collectns. for a history of Staffs., 1919, pp. 128–31. 1920.

469 Buckley (W. E.). Cerdic. [His descent from Woden.] N. and Q., 7th S. 5, pp. 34–35. 1888.

470 Chambers (Raymond Wilson). Beowulf, an introduction, *etc.*, pp. xii, 417, + 8 plates. 8° Cambridge, 1921. [Pp. 195–201, the Old English genealogies.]

471 —— The mythical ancestor of the kings of East Anglia. [' Casere ' succeeds Woden in earliest genealogy, in 9th c. MS. Cotton Vesp. B.VI.] Mod. Lang. Rev., 4, pp. 508–09. 1909.

472 Ellis (Alfred Shelley). The lady Godiva and the countess Lucy. [With tree.] N. and Q., 12th S. 2, pp. 387–88. 1916.

473 Hackenberg (Erna). Die Stammtafeln der angelsächsischen Königreiche. *Diss., Berlin.* pp. ix, 117. 8° Berlin, 1918.

474 Haigh (Daniel Henry). On the Jute, Angle, and Saxon royal pedigrees. Arch. Cant., 8, pp. 18–49, + 1 tree. 1872.

475 Hodgkin (Thomas). Origins of barbarian history. [Pp. 3–6, the genealogies of the Anglo-Saxons.] Hermathena, 12, pp. 1–16. 1902.

476 Kemble (John Mitchell). Ueber die Stammtafel der Westsachsen. pp. 35. 8° München, 1836. [Gross, 1368 : Lit.]

477 Magoun (Francis Peabody), *jr.* King Aethelwulf's biblical ancestors. [In A.-S. C. under 855. A collateral relative of Our Lord !] Mod. Lang. Rev., 46, pp. 249–50. 1951.

478 Napier (Arthur Sampson). Two Old English fragments. [1] Genealogy of the West Saxon kings. Mod. Lang. Notes, 12, coll. 105–13. 1897.

479 Schroeder (Edward). Die nordhumbrische Königsgenealogie. Mit Exkursen zur festländischen Namenkunde. Nachr. Gesell. Wiss. zu Göttingen, Phil. Hist. Kl., N.F., 2, pp. 127–38. 1939.

480 Searle (William George). Anglo-Saxon bishops, kings and nobles, the succession of the bishops and the pedigrees of the kings and nobles. pp. xii, 469. 8° Cambridge, 1899. [Gross, 1500.]

481 Statham (S. P. H.). The parentage of William de Percy. Yorks. Archaeol. J., 28, pp. 101–04. 1926.

482 Welby (*Sir* Alfred Cholmeley Earle). Pedigree of earl Godwin. N. and Q. for Som. and Dorset, 21, pp. 46–47. 1933.

483 Wheeler (G. H.). The genealogy of the early West Saxon kings. E.H.R., 36, pp. 161–171. 1921.

484 Woolrych (E. B.). Anglo-Saxon descent of Danish kings of England. N. and Q., 174, pp. 318–19, 354–55. 1938.

§ *b*. Gundrada de Warenne

(Important owing to papal prohibition on marriage of William I and Matilda. The Council of Rheims, in 1049, prohibited the marriage, thus affecting all their children, e.g. Gundrada and Robert of Normandy, born before that date.)

485 Blaauw (William Henry). Remarks on Matilda, queen of William the Conqueror, and her daughter Gundrada. [Answer to **499**.] Proc. Soc. Antiq., 1, pp. 159–60. 1846. *Same title*. Archaeologia, 32, pp. 108–25. 1847.

486 Duckett (*Sir* George Floyd), *bart.* Observations on the parentage of Gundreda, the daughter of William, duke of Normandy, and wife of William de Warenne. Trans. Cumb. and Westm. Antiq. Soc., 3, pp. 321–36. 1878. *Same title*. Sussex Archaeol. Collns., 28, pp. 114–26. 1878. *Same title*. Yorks. Archaeol. J., 9, pp. 421–37. 1886.

487 —— Supplementary observations on the parentage of the countess Gundreda, *etc.* Sussex Archaeol. Collns., 34, pp. 1–20. 1886.

488 —— Gundreda, a parting word about her. [Practically same article as **489**.] *Same jnl.*, 38, pp. 166–76. 1892.

489 —— Gundreda, . . . a parting word about her. (——. Final and conclusive evidence). Yorks. Archaeol. J., 12, pp. 123–32 : 15, pp. 428–33. 1893, 1900.

490 Freeman (Edward Augustus) The parentage of Gundreda, *etc.* [Till 1846 believed to be daughter of William I and Matilda. Parentage still a query.] E.H.R., 3, pp. 680–701. 1888.

491 Fry (H. A.), *etc.* Queen Matilda's daughter Gundred. N. and Q., 168, pp. 283–84, 320, 426. 1935.

492 Hall (A.). Gundrada de Warren. N. and Q., 7th S. 7, pp. 64–65, 311. 1889.

493 Hall (Hamilton). Gundrada de Warenne. Archaeol, J., 56, pp. 159–74. 1899.

494 —— Gundrada de Warenne : a legend. [*Ante* Duckett.] Yorks. Archaeol. J., 16, pp. 305–18. 1902.

495 Munford (George), *etc.* William de Warenne, first earl of Surrey, and Gundrada, daughter of William the Conqueror. N. and Q., 2nd S. 5, pp. 269–70, 364–65, 447. 1858.

496 Shoosmith (Edward). Brihtric and Matilda. [Gundreda her daughter by Brihtric who held the Honour of Gloucester and was 6th generation from Ethelred, brother to king Alfred.] Sussex County Mag., 5, p. 438. 1931.

497 Snowden (C. E.). The de Warennes of Lewes. [William de Warenne and Gundrada.] *Same jnl.*, 6, pp. 116–21. 1932.

498 —— Gundrada, wife of William de Warenne. Sussex N. and Q., 6, pp. 249–52. 1937.

499 Stapleton (Thomas). Observations in disproof of the pretended marriage of William de Warren, earl of Surrey, with a daughter begotten of Matildis, daughter of Baldwin, comte of Flanders, by William the Conqueror, and illustrative of the origin and early history of the family in Normandy. Archaeol. J., 3, pp. 1–26. 1846.

500 Waters (Edmond Chester). Gundrada de Warenne. Archaeol. J., 41, pp. 300–123 : 43, pp. 306–10. 1884–86.

501 —— The parentage of Gundred, wife of William de Warrenne, created earl of Surrey by William II. [Answered by E. A. Freeman *in* 15, pp. 97–98, and reply by E. C. Waters *in* 15, pp. 457–58.] Academy, 14, pp. 597–98. 1878–79.

§ *c*. **Celtic**

502 Anscombe (Alfred). Indexes to Old-Welsh genealogies. [i. Pedigrees in the Harley Ms. no. 3859 : ii. The Concenn pedigree : iii. The Fernmail pedigree : iv. De Situ Brecheniavc : v. Progenies Keredic regis de Keredigan : vi. Pedigrees from the Mostyn 'Historia regum Britanniae' : vii. Bonhed Gwyr y Gogled : viii. The Rhydderch and Hafod pedigrees : [1]x : The pedigrees in the Book of Llewelyn the Priest.] Arch. celt. Lexik., 1, pp. 187–212, 513–49 : 2, pp. 147–96 : 3, pp. 57–103. 1898–1906.

503 —— Some Old-Welsh pedigrees. Y Cymmrodor, 24, pp. 74–85. 1913.

504 Barbier (Paul). The old Welsh genealogies. [Original ms. written for Owain (d. 987), son of Howel Dda.] Yorks. Soc. Celtic Stud., Rpt. for 1936–37, pp. 12–15.   1937.

505 Diefenbach (Lorenz). Celtica II. Versuch einer genealogischen Geschichte der Kelten. 2 vol. 8° Stuttgart, 1840.

506 Dobbs (Margaret E.) [Maíghréad ní C. Dobs]. The genealogies of the southern Ui Neill. Zeit. celt. Philol., 20, pp. 1–29. 1935.

507 —— Miscellany from H.2.7. (T.C.D.). [Irish genealogies prior to 800.] *Same jnl.*, 21, pp. 307–18. 1940.

508 —— The origin of the surname 'Mulholland'. [Ui Mail Challainn, official guardians of St. Patrick's bell.] Ulster J. Archaeol., 3rd S. 1, pp. 115–17. 1938.

509 —— References to Erc daughter of Loarn in Irish MSS. [?' ancestress of many families'. 5th–6th c.] Scot. Gaelic Stud., 6, pp. 50–57. 1947.

510 Jones (Gwilym Peredur). Brychan. ['No reliable genealogical evidence in favour of a 5th c. Brychan, but indications of a 10th c. Brychan, of Hiberno-Scandinavian origin.'] Arch. Camb., 81 (7th S. 6), pp. 363–76. 1926.

511 Loth (Joseph). Une généalogie des rois de Stratclut, remontant de la fin du IXe. au Ve. siècle. Rev. celt., 47, pp. 176–83. 1930.

512 MacNeill (John). Notes on the Laud genealogies. Zeit. celt. Phil., 8, pp. 411–19. 1912.

513 Meyer (Kuno). The Laud genealogies and tribal histories : from Laud 610, fo. 75 a1. [Text, partly Latin, partly Irish.] *Same jnl.*, 8, pp. 291–338. 1912.

514 Nicholson (Edward Williams Byron). The dynasty of Cunedag and the 'Harleian genealogies'. Y Cymmrodor, 21, pp. 63–104, + tree. 1908.

515 Pender (Séamus). Uí Bruice, Ríg na nDéssi. Essays presented to E. MacNeill, pp. 475–79. 1940.

516 —— The Uí Liatháin genealogies from the Book of Ballymote. [The Eóghanachta, who ruled Munster from 5th c.] J. Cork Hist. Soc., 2nd S. 43, pp. 32–38, + tree. 1938.

517 Phillimore (Egerton). The Annales Cambriae and Old-Welsh genealogies from Harleian MS. 3859. [With complete text.] Y Cymmrodor, 9, pp. 141–83. 1888.

518 Vaughan (Henry F. J.). Chief of the noble tribes of Gwynedd. [Genealogy of early princes of Gwynedd.] Arch. Camb., 5th S. 8, pp. 241–61. 1891.

519 —— Welsh pedigrees. Y Cymmrodor, 10, pp. 72–156. 1889.

520 Waller (Evangelia H.) A Welsh branch of the Arthur family-tree. ['Gwalchmei [Gawain] the son of Gwyar': who was Gwyar?] Speculum, 1, pp. 344–46. 1926.

521 Walsh (Paul), *ed.* Genealogiae regum et sanctorum Hiberniae by the Four Masters. Edited from the manuscripts of Michel O Cleirigh, with appendices and index. *Catholic Record Society of Ireland.* pp. viii, 164. 8° Dublin, 1918. [Irish text.]

8. MENSURATION

522 Anscombe (Alfred). Dr. MacCarthy's lunar computations. [On the introduction to his Annals of Ulster, respecting Pascal lunar cycle employed by St. Patrick and St. Columba.] Zeit. celt. Phil., 4, pp. 332–38. 1903.

523 Belaiew (Nikolai Timothyeevich). A note on the use of Russian and Norse measurements by early Norman builders. [' Norse measurements were brought by the Normans to Russia in the ninth century, to Normandy . . . in the next century, and to England with the Conqueror.'] Archaeol. J., 77, pp. 190–91. 1920.

524 Bryce (Thomas H.). Note on a balance and weights of the Viking period found in the island of Gigha. [Pp. 442–43, note on the metallurgy of the balance and weights, by Cecil H. Desch.] Proc. Soc. Antiq. Scot., 47 (4th S. 11, 1912–13), pp. 436–43. 1913.

525 Cole (T. W.). Church sundials in mediaeval England. (Summarized by A. J. Hatley). [Era i, the Anglian and Saxon dials (7th c. to Conquest).] J. Brit. Archaeol. Assoc., 3rd S. 10 (1945–47), pp. 77–80, + 3 plates. 1948.

526 Davis (Joseph Barnard). Some account of runic calendars and ' Staffordshire clog' almanacs. Archaeologia, 41, pp. 453–78, + 1 plate. 1867.

527 Findlay (*Sir* John Ritchie), *bart.* The construction and use of wheel dials. [E.g. that on the Bewcastle cross : fig. 1.] Antiq. J., 7, pp. 134–38. 1927.

528 Fowler (James). On mediaeval representations of the months and seasons. [Calendar in MS. Cotton, Tib. B.V., 10th c., etc.] Archaeologia, 44, pp. 137–224, + 3 plates. 1873.

529 Green (Arthur Robert). The Anglo-Saxon sundial at Birton, [Worcs.]. Trans. Worcs. Archaeol. Soc., 9 (1932), pp. 25–26. 1933.

530 —— Anglo-Saxon sundials. [22 figures in text.] Antiq. J., 8, pp. 489–516. 1928.

531 Gresham (Colin A.). A further note [to **539**] on ancient Welsh measurements of land. Arch. Camb., 101, pp. 118–22. 1951.

532 Grundy (George Beardoe). The old English mile and the Gallic league. [Saxon measures, etc.] Geog. J., 91, pp. 251–59. 1938.

533 Haigh (Daniel Henry). Yorkshire dials [of A.S. period.] Yorks. Archaeol. J., pp. 134–222, + 3 plates. 1879.

534 Houghton (John F.). Money scales. [Pp. 218–19, on A.-S. scales and weights.] Proc. Soc. Antiq. Newcastle, 4th S. 9, pp. 218–21. 1941.

535 Hughes (Henry Harold). An ancient sun-dial at Clynnog, [Carnarvonshire]. [2 figures in text.] Arch. Camb., 86, pp. 181–83. 1931.

536 Loth (Joseph). L'année celtique d'après les textes irlandais, gallois, bretons, et le calendrier de Coligny. Rev. celt., 25, pp. 113–62. 1904.

537 MacRitchie (David). The Celtic numerals of Strathclyde. Proc. Soc. Antiq. Scot., 49 (5th S. 1, 1914–15), pp. 276–85. 1915.

538 N. (J. G.). Saxon sundial at Bishopston, . . . Sussex [References.] N. and Q., 4th S., 4, p. 276. 1863.

539 Palmer (Alfred Neobard). Notes on ancient Welsh measures of land. [Howel Dda, etc.] Arch. Camb., 5th S. 13, pp. 1–19. 1896.

540 Pegge (Samuel). The commencement of day amongst the Saxons and Britons ascertained. Archaeologia, 6, pp. 150–53. 1782.

541 Pell (O. C.). The long hundred. [Comment on **545.**] Archaeol. Rev., 4, pp. 460–63. 1890.

542 Pierce (T. Jones). A note on ancient Welsh measurements of land. Arch. Camb., 97, pp. 195–204. 1943.

543 Prior (W. H.). Notes on the weights and measures of medieval England. *Bulletin du Cange.* pp. 50. [A little A.-S. With glossary.] 8° Paris, 1924.

544 Skeat (Walter William). The Anglo-Saxon names of the months. N. and Q., 7th S., 7, p. 301. 1889.

545 Stevenson (William Henry). The long hundred and its use in England. [The hundred of 120 was the original hundred of the Teutonic tribes, and O.E. measurements were on this basis.] Archaeol. Rev., 4, pp. 313–27. 1889.

546 Tupper (Frederick), *jr.* Anglo-Saxon *dæg-mæl*. [i. The A.-S. day: canonical hours: ii. The rubrics to the A.-S. Gospels.] P.M.L.A., 10, pp. 111–241. 1895.

547 Way (Albert). Ancient sun-dials : especially Irish examples, *etc.* [A.-S., e.g. at Bishopstone, Kirkdale, Edstone, Corhampton, etc.] Archaeol. J., 25, pp. 207–23, + 2 plates. 1868.

548 Wrottesley (*Hon.* George). Mediæval mensuration of land. [Extracted from Evesham chartulary, MS. Harl. 3763.] Collections for a history of Staffs., 5.i, pp. 103–04. 1884.

9. PERSONAL NAMES

§ *a.* Anglo-Saxon

549 Anderson *afterwards* **Anderson-Arngart** (Olof Sigfrid). The Calendar of St. Willibrord. A little used source of Old English personal names. Studia Neophil., 16, pp. 128–34. 1944.

550 Anscombe (Alfred). The name of Cerdic. Y Cymmrodor, 29, pp. 151–202. 1919.

551 —— The name of Penda. N. and Q., 12th S., 6, p. 246. 1920.

552 B. (A.). Midland surnames in the so-called Roll of Battle Abbey. Midland Antiquary, 4, pp. 129–31. 1887.

553 Bardsley (Charles Wareing). A dictionary of English and Welsh surnames. pp. xvi, 837. 8° London, 1901.

554 —— English surnames. 7th edition. pp. xxv, 612. 8° London, 1901.

555 Baring-Gould (Sabin). Family names and their story. pp. 432. 8° London, 1910. [Pp. 154–83, place-names : pp. 184–90, A.-S. names, Domesday, etc.]

556 Bjoerkman (Erik). Aeltere englische Personennamen mit -*god*, -*got* im zweiten Gliede. Engl. Studien, 51, pp. 161–79. 1917.

557 —— Ae. *Cnytel.* Arch. Stud. neueren Spr., Bd. 125, pp. 162–63. 1910.

558 —— *Hæþcyn* und Hákon. [Hákon the Scandinavian equivalent of A.-S. *Hæþcyn.* Argument that *Hæþcyn* is derived from *Hapu.*] Engl. Studien, 54, pp. 24–34. 1920.

559 —— Nordische Personennamen in England in alt-und frühmittelenglische Zeit. Ein Beitrag zur englische Namenkunde. *Studien zur englischen Philologie*, 37. pp. xiii, 217. 8° Halle, 1910.

560 Bjoerkman (Erik) *Sculf, Scolfus* im Liber Vitae Dunelmensis. [Searle : Onomasticon Saxonicum, p. xxix, queries Celtic names, or corrupt forms. ?= *Seulf, Seolfus.*] Arch. Stud. neueren Spr., Bd. 123, p. 154. 1909.

561 —— Tiernamen als Taufnamen im Altenglischen. Anglia, Beibl., 29, pp. 239–41. 1918.

562 —— Two derivations. English-Latin : Scaldingi-Old English wicing. Saga-Book V.C., 7, pp. 132–40. 1912.

563 —— Zur englischen Namenkunde. *Studien zur englischen Philologie,* 47. pp. x, 94. 8° Halle, 1912.

564 Boehler (Maria). Die altenglischen Frauennamen. *Germanische Studien,* 98. pp. 261. 8° Berlin, 1930.

565 Brunner (Karl). Einige Dialekttaufnahmen aus Lancashire. Neusprachliche Studien. Festgabe K. Luick, pp. 47–59. 1925.

566 Buckley (W. E.), **Picton** (*Sir* John Allanson), **Krebs** (H.) and **Taylor** (Isaac). Anglo-Saxon names. [Especially with prefix Os—.] N. and Q., 7th S., 1, pp. 329–31. 1886.

567 Cole (Edward Maule). Ancient Danish mensnames in Yorkshire. [Yorks Dano-English name-roll from c. 1023 (Knut), by George Stephens, with Domesday equivalents.] Trans. Yorks. Dialect Soc., 1, pt. 7, pp. 43–49. 1906.

568 Cook (Albert Stanburrough). The name Cædmon. P.M.L.A., 6, pp.. 9–28. 1891.

569 Coote (Henry Charles). On the existence of Anglo-Saxon baptismal names. Proc. evening meetings London and Middlesex Archaeol. Soc., 1874, pp. 162–84. 1877.

570 Ekwall (Eilert). Early London personal names. *Skrifter utgivna [av Kungl. Humanistiska Vetenskapssamfundet i Lund,* 43. pp. xix, 208. 8° Lund, 1947.

571 Elwes (G. R.). Dorset surnames. [Pp. 195–96 : table of Saxon surnames in Dorset.] Proc. Dorset Antiq. F.C., 19, pp. 184–201. 1898.

572 Ewen (Cecil Henry L'Estrage). A history of surnames of the British Isles. pp. xx, 508. 8° London, 1931. [Pp. 12–14, Picts ; pp. 36–37, Ogams : pp. 48–62, A.-S. : pp. 62–65, Domesday ; pp. 65–68, Northmen.]

573 Federer (Charles Antoine). The genesis of English surnames. Bradford Antiquary, 3, pp. 81–98. 1900.

574 Feilitzen (Olof von). Old Welsh *Enniaun* and the Old English personal name element *wen.* Mod. Lang. Notes, 62, pp. 155–65. 1947.

575 —— The pre-Conquest personal names of Domesday Book. *Nomina Germanica,* 3. pp. xxxi, 430. 8° Uppsala, 1937.

576 Foerster (Max). The etymology of Sidwell. (Notes on St. Sidwell contributions [4373–75, 4378–79, 590]). [Sidefulle (=full of purity), Latinised as Sativola.] Devon and Cornwall N. and Q., 17, pp. 243–45, 326–28. 1933.

577 —— The name of St. Sidwell. *Same jnl.,* 19, pp. 291–92. 1937.

578 Folkard (Arthur). The antiquity of surnames. [' Chiefly as it affects the antiquity of the practice among our Anglo-Saxon forefathers.'] Antiquary, 13, pp. 61–65, 101–04. 1886.

579 Forssner (Thorvald). Continental-Germanic personal names in England in Old and Middle English times. *Diss., Upsala.* pp. lxiii, 289. 8° Uppsala, 1916.

580 G. (M. P.). The pronunciation of Anglo-Saxon names. N. and Q., 186, pp. 226–28. 1944.

581 Gentry (Thomas G.). Family names from the Irish, Anglo-Saxon, Anglo-Norman and Scotch considered in relation to their etymology. pp. 225. 8° Philadelphia, 1892.

582 Gordon (Eric Valentine). *Wealhpeow* and related names. [Beowulf. ?= British servant. ?Scandinavian origin for names in *-peow.*] Medium Ævum, 4, pp. 169–75. 1935.

583 Hellwig (H.). Untersuchungen über die Namen des northumbrischen Liber Vitae. I. *Diss., Berlin.* 8° Berlin, 1888.

584 Hutson (Arthur E.). British personal names in the Historia regum Britanniæ. [Pp. 55–88, iv. Post-Roman Britain : v. Arthurian Britain : vi. Decline of Britain.] Univ. Cal., Pubns. in English, 5, pp. 1–160. 1940.

585 Jerram (Charles Stanger), *etc.* Oscar. [*Os-* in A.-S. personal names.] N. and Q., 5th S. 3, pp. 10–11. 1875.

586 Just (John). A dissertation on the Anglo-Saxon patronymics. Mems. Manch. Lit. and Phil. Soc., 2nd S. 7, pp. 440-63. 1846.

587 Kemble (John Mitchell). The names, surnames, and nicknames of the Anglosaxons. [Difficulty of identifying individuals with the same name, *etc.*] Proc. Archaeol. Inst., [1] (1845), pp. 81–102. 1846.

588 —— On a peculiar use of the Anglo-Saxon patronymical termination *-ing*. Proc. Philol. Soc., 4, pp. 1–10. 1848.

589 Koepke (Johannes). Altnordische Personennamen bei den Angelsachsen. I. *Diss. Berlin.* pp. vii, 48. 8° Berlin, 1909.

590 Lega-Weekes (Ethel). St. Sidwell and her fee. [Latin and English forms of her name.] Devon and Cornwall N. and Q., 17, pp. 253–56. 1933.

591 McClure (Edmund). Some notes on personal names, chiefly those of the British Isles. N. and Q., 6th S. 7, pp. 241–42, 381–83. 1883.

592 Mueller (Rudolph). Untersuchungen über die Namen des nordhumbrischen Liber Vitae. *Palaestra*, 9. pp. xvi, 186. 8° Berlin, 1901.

593 Murray (Margaret Alice). The divine king in Northumbria. [Names beginning with Os—.] Folk-lore, 53, pp. 214–15. 1942.

594 Reaney (Percy Hide). Onomasticon Essexiense. A proposal for the systematic collection of the personal-names and surnames of Essex. [Especially, pp. 202–03, survival of O.E. names.] Essex Rev., 61, pp. 133–42, 202–15. 1952.

595 —— Three unrecorded O.E. personal names of a late type. [Additional to Feilitzen, **575.**] Mod. Lang. Rev., 47, p. 374. 1952.

596 Redin (Mats). Studies in uncompounded personal names in Old English. *Diss., Upsala.* Uppsala Univ. Årsskr., Filos., 1919, No. 2. Pp. xlv, 195. 1919.

597 Searle (William George). Onomasticon Anglo-Saxonicum ; a list of Anglo-Saxon proper names from the time of Bede to that of king John. pp. lvii, 601. 8° Cambridge, 1897. [Gross, 341.]

598 Skeat (Walter William). Anglo-Saxon names as surnames. N. and Q., 10th S., 5, p. 442. 1906.

599 —— The corrupt spelling of Old English names. Proc. Camb. Antiq. Soc., 13, pp. 15–29. 1909.

600 —— On the survival of Anglo-Saxon names as modern surnames. Trans. Philolog. Soc., 1907–1910, pp. 57–85. 1910.

601 Smith (Albert Hugh). Early Northern nick-names and surnames. [A little A.-S. material.] Saga-Book V. C., 11 (1928–33), pp. 30–60. 1934.

602 Spiegelhalter (Cecil). Surnames of Devon. ii. The Saxon element. Rept. and Trans. Devon. Assoc., 69, pp. 470-77. 1937.

603 Stefansson (Jón). The oldest known list of Scandinavian names. [Facsimile and transcript from 10th c. codex in York Minster, with comments.] Saga-Book V. C., 4, pp. 294–311. 1906.

604 Stephens (George). Yorkshire Dano-English name-roll from about the time of king Knut, A.D. 1023. Trans. Yorks. Dialect Soc., 1, pp. 43–49. 1906.

605 Strachan (Lionel Richard Mortimer). —*Flæd* in feminine Anglo-Saxon names. N. and Q., 168, p. 247. 1935.

606 Stroem (Hilmer). Old English personal names in Bede's History. *Lund Studies in English*, 8. pp. xliii, 180. 8° Lund, 1939.

607 Taylor (Isaac) and **Skeat** (Walter William). Anglo-Saxon personal names. N. and Q., 7th S. 11, pp. 352–53, 376–77. 1891.

608 Taylor (Winifred M.). An historical investigation into the survival of Anglo-Saxon personal names into the English surname period. *M.A. thesis, London.* 1914. [Apply Univ. Library.]

609 Tengvik (Gösta). Old-English bynames. *Dissertation. Nomina Germanica*, 4. pp. xxii, 407. 8° Uppsala, 1938.

610 Whitelock (Dorothy). Scandinavian personal names in the Liber Vitae of Thorney Abbey. Saga-Book V. C., 12 (1937–38), pp. 127–53. 1940.

611 Woolf (Henry Bosley). The name of Beowulf. [?Ælfhere his real name, as 'Beowulf' does not alliterate with other names in his family.] Engl. Studien, 72, pp. 7–9. 1937.

612 —— The naming of women in Old English times. Mod. Philol., 36, pp. 113–20. 1938.

613 —— The personal names in *The Battle of Malden*. [27 fall into groups of kinsmen. 5th c. alliteration still followed in 10th c.] Mod. Lang. Notes, 53, pp. 109–12. 1938.

614 Wrenn (Charles Leslie). Late Old English rune-names. [Postscript, by C. E. Wright, in 5, pp. 149–51.] Medium Ævum, 1, pp. 24–34. 1932, 1936.

615 Zachrisson (Robert Eugen). Notes on early English names in *-god, -got*. Engl. Studien, 50, pp. 341–58 ; 52, pp. 194–203. 1917–18.

616 —— Notes on early English personal names. [Pp. 274–80, Scandinavian or Anglo-Saxon names ? pp. 294–97, nick names and descriptive epithets.] Studier mod. Språkvetenskap, 6, pp. 269–98. 1917.

617 —— Notes on early Germanic personal names. Stud. Neophilol., 1, pp. 74–77. 1928.

618 —— Scandinavian or Anglo-Saxon names ? Mod. Lang. Rev., 14, pp. 391–97. 1919.

619 —— Some notes on early English nicknames. Anglia, Beibl., 28, pp. 369–75. 1917.

620 Zimmer (Heinrich). Zur Orthographie des Namens Beda. Neues Archiv, 16, pp. 599–601. 1891.

§ *b*. Celtic

621 Anscombe (Alfred). The name of Sir Lancelot du Lake. Celtic Rev., 8, pp. 365–66. 1913.

622 Foerster (Max). The Breton name of St. Budoc. Devon and Cornwall N. and Q., 19, pp. 370–71. 1937.

623 Jones (Gwilym Peredur). The Scandinavian element in Welsh. 1. Personal names. Zeit. celt. Philol., 16, pp. 162–66. 1927.

624 Kneen (John Joseph). The personal names of the Isle of Man. pp. lx, 295. 8° Oxford, 1937. [Pp. 258–66, the personal names of the Ogam, early Christian and runic monuments.]

625 Lloyd (*Sir* John Edward). The personal name-system in Old Welsh. Y Cymmrodor, 9, pp. 39–55. 1888.

626 Loomis (Roger Sherman). Some names in Arthurian romance. [Winlogee, Mardoc, Carrado, Lionel, Niniane, Uentres.] P.M.L.A., 45, pp. 416–43. 1930.

627 Loth (Joseph). Les formes celtiques du nom des Calédoniens : Calēdō, Calēdon-es, Calēdòno-s ; Gallois Celyðon-Lossio Veda Nepos Vepogeni Caledo ; le sens de Nepos. Rev. celt., 47, pp. 1–9. 1930.

628 MacBain (Alexander). Early Highland personal names. [Mostly later.] Trans. Gaelic Soc. Inverness, 22, pp. 152–68. 1900.

629 —— The old Gaelic system of personal names. *Same jnl.*, 20, pp. 279–315. 1897.

630 McClure (Edmund). Early Welsh (in relation to other Aryan) personal names. Arch. Camb., 5th S. 7, pp. 257–73. 1890.

631 —— On Irish personal names. [Irish surnames from genitive of names of 10th–11th c. ancestors. Localities, physical peculiarities, occupations, etc.] Proc. R.I.A., 2nd S. 1 (Antiq.), pp. 307–14. 1879.

632 MacNeil (John). Early Irish population-groups ; their nomenclature, classification, and chronology. [i. Plural names : ii. Collective names : iii. Sept names : iv. The Tuath : v. The Tricha cét = Thirty Hundreds.] Proc. R.I.A., 29 c, pp. 59–114. 1911.

633 Meyer (Kuno). Ags. Berecht-wine in Alt-Irland. Arch. Stud. neueren Spr., Bd. 130, pp. 155–56. 1913.

634 —— Brian Borumha. [i. The name Brian : 2. Borumha.] Ériu, 4, pp. 68–73. 1908.

635 Moore (Arthur William). Manx names, or the surnames and place-names of the Isle of Man. Cheap edition, revised. pp. xvi, 261. 8° London, 1906.

636 —— Manx surnames. [i. Intro-ductory : ii. Surnames of Celtic origin derived from personal names : iii. Celtic surnames from trades or occupations, from descriptive nicknames, from de-signations of residence or birthplace : iv. (in vol. 3) Names of Scandinavian origin : v. Exotic surnames.] Manx Note Bk., 1, pp. 44–50, 83–89, 130–35 : 2, pp. 20–30, 58–65, 114–20, 149–58 : 3, pp. 53–60, 112–19, 151–56. 1885–87.

637 —— The surnames and place-names of the Isle of Man. pp. xiv, 365. 8° London, 1890.

638 Mossé (F.). Sur le nom d'homme *Ketill* en Scandinave. [And its Irish derivation : first Ketill (the White) was Caitill Finn, who died in Ireland, 857 or 856.] Rev. celt., 50, pp. 248–53. 1933.

639 Ó Briain (Micheál). Studien zu irischen Völkernamen. [i. Die Stam-mesnamen auf -*rige*.] Zeit. celt. Philol., 15, pp. 222–37. 1925.

640 Stokes (Whitley). On the Gaelic names in the Landnamabok and runic inscriptions. [In Man, etc.] Rev. celt., 3, pp. 186–91. 1877.

641 —— On the linguistic value of the Irish annals. [III. i. Cymric names of persons and places which occur in the Irish annals : IV. Pictish names : V. i. Old Norse names : VI. i. Anglo-Saxon names, i.e. Irish form followed by A.-S. identification.] Trans. Philol. Soc., 1888–90, pp. 365–433. 1891.

642 Wade-Evans (Arthur Wade). Notes on names in the Mabinogi. Arch. Camb., 89, pp. 176–79. 1934.

643 Watson (William John). Personal names : the influence of the saints. Trans. Gaelic Soc. Inverness, 32 (1924–25), pp. 220–47. 1929.

644 Williams (*Sir* Ifor). The personal names in the early inscriptions [in Anglesey]. Roy. Commission on hist. mon., Anglesey, pp. cxiv–vii. 1937.

645 Woulfe (Patrick). Irish names and surnames. With explanatory and his-torical notes. pp. xlvi, 696. 8° Dublin, 1923.

II. POLITICAL HISTORY

10. GENERAL (ANGLO-SAXON)

646 Allen (Grant). Anglo-Saxon Britain. *Early Britain Series.* pp. viii, 237, + map. 8° London, [19 . . .].

647 Bryant (Arthur). The story of England : makers of the realm. pp. 399. 8° London, 1953. [Pp. 53–176, A.-S., period (pp. 92–113, Alfred).]

648 Cam (Helen Maud). England before Elizabeth. pp. 184. 8° London, 1950. [Pp. 1–78, A.-S. period.]

649 Chadwick (Nora Kershaw). The Celtic background of Anglo-Saxon England. Yorks. Soc. Celtic Stud., 3, pp. 13–32. 1946.

650 Chambers (Raymond Wilson). England before the Norman Conquest. *University of London intermediate source-books of history,* 7. pp. xxvi, 334. 8° London, 1928. [Translated passages. From contemporary documents.]

651 Church (Alfred John). Early Britain. *Story of the Nations.* pp. xx, 382, + map. 8° London, 1889. [Pp. 92–375, A.-S. period.]

652 Collingwood (Robin George) and **Myres** (John Nowell Linton). Roman Britain and the English settlements. *Oxford History of England,* 1. 2nd edition. pp. xxv, 515. 8° Oxford, 1937.

653 Corbett (William John). England (to c. 800) and English institutions. Camb. Med. Hist., 2, pp. 543–74. 1913.

654 —— England from A.D. 954 to the death of Edward the Confessor. Camb. Med. Hist., 3, pp. 371–408. 1922.

655 —— The foundation of the kingdom of England. [786–954.] Camb. Med. Hist., 3, pp. 340–70. 1922.

656 Creighton (Mandell), *bp. of London.* The story of some English shires. pp. 384. 8° London, 1897. [A.-S. period : pp. 17–22, Northumberland : pp. 50–60, Durham : pp. 84–97, Yorks, etc.]

657 Freeman (Edward Augustus). The mythical and romantic elements in early English history. [Reprinted in his Historical Essays, first series, pp. 1–39.] Fortnightly Rev., 4, pp. 641–68. 1866.

658 —— Old-English history. pp. xxxiv, 371. 8° London, 1881. [To 1066.]

659 Giles (John Allen). The invasions of England from the earliest times, a lecture. 4° London, 1861.

660 Green (John Richard). The making of England. 4th edition. 2 vol. 8° London, 1897. [Gross, 1510. 449–829.]

661 —— The conquest of England. 2 vol. 8° London, 1899. [Gross, 1526. Egbert to 1071.]

662 Hearnshaw (Fossy John Cobb). England in the making (before 1066). pp. 96. 8° London, [1913].

663 Hodgkin (Robert Howard). A history of the Anglo-Saxons. 3rd edition. pp. xxxi, xii, 796, + 89 plates, + 9 maps. 2 vol. 8° Oxford, 1952. [To the death of Alfred. In editions 1 and 2 the frontispieces were in colour. Appendix (pp. 696–734, with 6 plates) added to 3rd ed. : The Sutton Hoo ship-burial, by R. S. L. Bruce-Mitford.]

664 Hodgkin (Thomas). The history of England from the earliest times to the Norman Conquest. *Political history of England,* 1. pp. xxi, 528, + 2 maps. 8° London, 1906. [Gross, 1491 a.]

664a Huebener (Gustav). England und die Gesittungsgrundlage der europäischen Frühgeschichte. pp. v, 325. 8° Frankfurt a. M., 1930.

665 Jerrold (Douglas). An introduction to the history of England, from the earliest times to 1204. pp. 614, + maps. 8° London, 1949. [Pp. 194–352, A.-S.]

666 Kemble (John Mitchell). The Saxons in England. New edition, by W. de Gray Birch. 2 vol. 8° London, 1876. [Gross, 1492.]

D

667 Langhorne (Daniel). Chronicon regum Anglorum, insignia omnia eorum gesta . . . ab Hengisto, rege primo, usque ad Heptarchiæ finem, *etc.* pp. xv, 344, + 18 tables. 8° Londini, 1679.

668 Lappenberg (Johann Martin). A history of England under the Anglo-Saxons kings, translated . . . by Benjamin Thorpe. 2 vol. 8° London, 1845.

669 Liebermann (Felix). Vorstufen zur staatlichen Einheit Britanniens bis 1066. Engl. Studien, 60, pp. 94–118. 1925.

670 Lot (Ferdinand), *etc.* Les destinées de l'empire en occident de 395 à 888. *Glotz* (G.): *Histoire du Moyen Âge*, 1. pp. xxv, 832. 8° Paris, 1928. [Pp. 678–739, Les îles britanniques du Ve au Xe siècle : i. Les Bretons : ii. Les Anglo-Saxons : iii. L'Irlande : iv. L'Écosse.]

671 Lukman (N.). British and Danish traditions : some contacts and relations. [Agreements in narratives of Saxo and Geoffrey of Monmouth. iv. Gormund and Godrum : vi Ambrosius and Amleth : vii. Arthur and Frode.] Classica et mediaevalia, 6, pp. 72–109. 1944.

671a Miller (Thomas). History of the Anglo-Saxons. 3rd edition. *Bohn's illustrated library*. 8° London, 1849.

672 Milton (John). The history of Britain, that part especially now call'd England ; continu'd to the Norman Conquest. *Works, Columbia University Press*, 10, pp. 1–325. 8° New York, 1932.

673 Oman (*Sir* Charles William Chadwick). England before the Norman Conquest. *Methuen's History of England*, 1. 8th edition, revised. pp. xiv, 679, + 3 maps. 8° London, 1938. [Gross, 1495.]

674 Owen (Thomas Morgan). A history of England and Wales, from the Roman to the Norman conquest. 2nd edition, enlarged. pp. x, 228. 8° London, 1882. [Gross, 1496.]

675 Palgrave (*Sir* Francis). A history of Normandy and of England. 4 vol. 8° London, 1851–64. [Gross, 2823. To 1101. Also forms vol. 1–4 of his Collected works. 8° Cambridge, 1919–21.]

676 —— History of the Anglo-Saxons. New edition. pp. xliii, 332, +

plates, + maps. 8° London, 1867. —A re-issue. pp. xlviii, 332. 8° London, [1887]. [Gross, 1497, note.]

677 Pearson (Charles Henry). The early and middle ages of England. pp. xvi, 472. 8° London, 1861. History of England during the early and middle ages, 1. [=2nd edition.] 8° London, 1867.

678 Pierquin (Hubert). Histoire politique de la monarchie anglo-saxonne, 449–1066. pp. 307. 8° Paris, 1912.

679 Previté-Orton (Charles William). The shorter Cambridge medieval history. 2 vol. 8° Cambridge, 1952. [Vol. 1, pp. 379–417 : England in the 9th c. : the successors of Alfred : England and Danish kings : government and institutions on the eve of the Conquest : the Celtic kingdoms.]

680 Ramsay (*Sir* James Henry), *bart.* The foundations of England, or twelve centuries of British history, B.C. 55–A.D. 1154. 2 vol. 8° London, 1898. [Gross, 636. Maps and illustrations.]

681 Saint John (James Augustus). History of the four conquests of England. [B.C. 55–A.D. 1087.] 2 vol. 8° London, 1862 [1861.] [Gross, 637.]

682 Sayles (George Osborne). Medival foundations of England, pp. xi, 480. 8° London, 1948. [Pp. 1–278, A.-S.]

683 Shore (Thomas William). Ancient Kentish colonies in Anglo-Saxon England. [i. Settlements in the Thames valley : ii. Settlements in the southern and western counties : iii. Settlements in the northern and midland counties.] Antiquary, 35, pp. 133–37, 233–36, 339–42. 1899.

684 Stenton (*Sir* Frank Merry). Anglo-Saxon England. *Oxford History of England*, 2. 2nd edition (with a few corrections.) pp. vii, 747, + map. 8° Oxford, 1947. [Pp. 679–713, bibliography.]

685 Stone (Gilbert). England from the earliest times to the Great Charter. pp. xx, 618, + 51 plates. 8° London, 1916. [Pp. 74–367, + plates 14–35, A.-S. period.]

686 Trevelyan (George Macaulay). History of England. Third edition (re-issue, with minor corrections). pp. xxii, 756. 8° London, 1952. [Pp. 28–117, A.-S.]

686a Trevelyan (George Macaulay). The mingling of the races. Being Book one of the History of England. pp. 192, + map. 8° London, 1934.

687 Turner (Sharon). The history of the Anglo-Saxons from their first appearance above the Elbe to the Norman Conquest. Seventh edition. 3 vol. 8° London, 1852. [Gross, 1502.]

688 Wall (James Charles). The tombs of the kings of England. pp. viii, 485. 8° London, 1891. [pp. 45–212, A.-S. period.]

689 Williamson (James Alexander). The evolution of England. pp. xii, 481. 8° Oxford, 1931. [Pp. 26–80, A.-S.]

690 Wingfield-Stratford (Esmé). The history of British civilization. pp. xix, 1332. 8° London, 1930. [Pp. 36–82, A.-S. : pp. 83–108, Celtic : pp. 109–16, Viking.]

691 Winkelmann (Eduard). Geschichte der Angelsachsen bis zum Tode Königs Ælfreds. *Oncken (W.)* : *Allgemeine Geschichte*, II. 3. pp. 185. 8° Berlin, 1883. [Gross, 1503.]

892 Wright (Thomas). Biographia Britannica literaria. Anglo-Saxon period. 8° London, 1842. —Anglo-Norman period. 8° London, 1846. [Gross, 334.]

11. GENERAL (NORSEMEN, VIKINGS)

(*See also* 84 § *b*, 134, 139 § *b*, 140 § *b*, 171 § *b*, 198 for other Viking material.)

693 Abeel (Neilson). Vikings in Ireland. Am. Scand. Rev., 23, pp. 140–47. 1935.

694 Anderson (Sven Axel). Viking enterprise. pp. 164. 8° New York, 1936. [Pp. 99–122, operations in the insular regions of north western Europe.]

695 Berry (R. G.). The Scandinavians in Ireland. [Synopsis of lecture.] Ann. Rep. and Proc. Belfast Nat. F.C., N.S. 6, pp. 67–69. 1908.

696 Birch (Walter de Gray). The early notices of the Danes in England to the battle of Brunanburgh, A.D. 937, and the rebuilding of the city of London by king Alfred, A.D. 886. J.Brit. Archaeol. Assoc., 44, pp. 326–42. 1888.

697 Boult (Joseph). The Danish intrusion into south Britain. Proc. Lit. and Phil. Soc., Liverpool, 28, pp. 189–220. 1874.

698 Bremner (Robert Locke). The Norsemen in Alban. pp. xvii, 286, + 4 maps. 8° Glasgow, 1923. [200–1263.]

699 Broegger (Anton Wilhelm). Ancient emigrants. A history of the Norse settlements in Scotland. Translated by D. N. Crane. *Rhind Lectures*, 1928. pp. xi, 208, + 30 plates and maps. 8° Oxford, 1929.

700 —— Den norke bosetningen pa Shetland-Orknøyene : studier og resultater. [Pp. 271–84, English summary : the Norwegian colonisation of Shetland and the Orkney islands. Pp. 1–33, introduction : pp. 34–140, pre-Celts and Celts (archaeology, brochs., etc.) : pp. 141–247, the Norse colonisation (A.D. 800–), including Caithness, Sutherland and the Sudreys : pp. 248–70, origin and character of the early settlement. 151 figures in text.] Skr. Norske Vid.-Akad., Hist.-filos. Kl., 1930, no. 3. pp. 290. 1931.

701 Bugge (Alexander). Contributions to the history of the Norsemen in Ireland. [Gross, 1523a, note. i. The royal race of Dublin : ii. Norse elements in Gaelic tradition of modern times : iii. Norse settlements round the British channel.] Skr. Vid.-Selsk., Christiania, Hist.-filos. Kl., 1900, no. 4–6. pp. 17, 32, 11. 1900.

702 —— Vikingerne. Billeder fra vore forfædres liv. 2 series. 8° København, 1904–06. [Gross, 1523a. i, pp. 114–69, Northmen in Ireland ; ii, pp. 237–342, Northmen in England.]

703 —— Vesterlandenes indflydelse paa Nordboernes og særlig Nordmændenes ydre kultur, levesæt og samfundsforhold i vikingetiden. Skr. Vid.-Selsk., Christiania, Hist.-filos. Kl., 1904, no. 1. pp. 425, + 3 plates. 1905.

704 Bugge (Sophus). Norsk Saga-skrivning og Sagafortælling i Irland. *Utgivet af den Norske Historiske Forening.* pp. 286. 8° Kristiania, 1908. [Clontarf, etc.]

705 Busch (Fritz Otto). Germanische Seefahrt. pp. 322, + 26 maps. 8° Berlin, 1935. [Including Viking invasions.]

706 Capper (Douglas Parodé). The Vikings of Britain. pp. 219, + 13 plates. 8° London, 1937.

707 Charles (Bertie George). Old Norse relations with Wales. pp. xix, 172. 8° Cardiff, 1934.

708 Christiansen (Reidar Thoralf). The Vikings and the Viking wars in Irish and Gaelic tradition. [Largely literary : ballads, etc.] Skr. Norske Vid.-Akad., Hist. Filos. Kl., 1930, pp. 1–429. 1931.

709 Craigie (*Sir* William Alexander). The Norse-Irish question. [Influence of Northmen on Irish, and vice-versa, during Viking period.] Arkiv nord. Filol., 19, pp. 173–80. 1903.

710 Collingwood (William Gershom). Scandinavian Britain. . . . With chapters introductory to the subject by . . . F. York Powell. pp. 272, + map. 8° London, 1908. [Gross, 1523b.]

711 Cunnington (S.). The Danish element in English life and thought. History, 3, pp. 197–202. 1914.

712 Dasent (*Sir* George Webb). England and Norway in the eleventh century. [Reprinted from North British Rev., Dec. 1865.] Dasent : Jest and earnest, vol. 1, pp. 198–309. 1873.

713 Du Chaillu (Paul Belloni). The Viking age : the early history, manners, and customs of the ancestors of the English-speaking nations, illustrated from the antiquities, *etc.* 2 vol. 8° London, 1889.

714 Gray (Harold St. George). Notes on ' Danes' skins '. [e.g. on church doors.] Saga-Book, V.C., 5, pp. 218–29, + 1 plate. 1908.

715 Haliday (Charles). The Scandinavian kingdom of Dublin, edited by J. P. Prendergast. 2nd edition. pp.

cxxiii, 300. 8° Dublin, 1884. [Gross, 960.]

716 Hamilton (John R. C.). Life in a Viking settlement. [10 figures in text. Evidence from Jarlshof, Shetland.] Archaeology, 4, pp. 218–22. 1951.

717 Healy (John), *abp. of Tuam.* The Vikings in Ireland and the triumph of Brian Boru. *Lectures on Irish Church history*, 4. pp. 35. 8° Dublin, 1899.

718 Henderson (George). The Norse influence on Celtic Scotland. pp. xiii, 371, + 9 plates. 8° Glasgow, 1910. [Gross, 1526 b. Historic background, art, personal names, belief, linguistic influence, etc.]

719 Hull (Eleanor). The Northmen in England. pp. 256. 8° London, 1913.

720 Jones (Gwilym Peredur.) The Scandinavian settlement in Ystrad Tywi. Y Cymmrodor, 35, pp. 117–56. 1925.

721 Keary (Charles Francis). The Vikings in Western Christendom, 789–888 . . . with map and tables. pp. xv, 511. 8° London, 1891 (1890). [Gross, 1528. Ch. 12 deals with England.]

722 Kendrick (*Sir* Thomas Downing). A history of the Vikings. pp. xi, 412, + 12 plates. 8° London, 1930. [Pp. 227–327, England, Ireland, Scotland and Man, Wales.]

723 Keyser (Jacob Rudolph). The private life of the old Northmen, translated . . . by M. R. Barnard. 8° London, 1868.

724 Klindt-Jensen (Ole). The Vikings in England. [Translated . . . by J. R. B. Gosney.) pp. 37. 8° Copenhagen, 1948. [18 figures (on Viking art) in text.]

725 Leeds (Edward Thurlow). Denmark and early England. [Evidence from brooches and from the 20 gold bracteates found in Kent and elsewhere.] Antiq. J., 26, pp. 22–37, + 3 plates. 1946.

726 Lowry (David E.). Jomsburg Vikings and the Thingmannalid. Proc. Belfast N.H. and Phil. Soc., 1930–31, pp. 1–8. 1932.

727 MacFirbisigh (Duald). On the Formorians and the Norsemen. The original Irish text, edited with translation and notes by Alexander Bugge. *Norske Historiske Kildeskriftfond.* pp. viii, 37. 8° Christiania, 1905. [Gross, 1523a, note.]

728 MacNeill (Eoin). Chapter of Hebridean history: Norse history. [*See also in* Section 31.] Scottish Review, 39, pp. 254–76. 1916.

729 Marstrander (Carl Johan Sverstrup). Killaloekorset og de norske Kolonier i Irland. Norsk Tidsskr. f. Sprogvid., 4, pp. 378–400. 1930.

730 Mawer (*Sir* Allen). The Viking age. History, 1, pp. 94–107. 1912.

731 —— The Vikings. *Cambridge manuals of science and literature.* pp. 150, + 3 plates. 8° Cambridge, 1913.

732 —— The Vikings. Camb. Med. Hist., 3, pp. 309–39. 1922.

733 —— The Vikings. (Historical revisions, -xxx). [Necessity ' for studying these movements as a whole, and not merely as events affecting the history of this or that country.'] History, N.S., 9, pp. 116–20. 1924.

734 Mayo (Dermot Robert Wyndham Bourke), *7th earl.* Some notes on the Vikings, their ships, and how they harassed Ireland. J. co. Kildare Archaeol. Soc., 4, pp. 280–84. 1904.

735 Megaw (Basil R. S. and Eleanor M.). The Norse heritage in the Isle of Man. [Viking burials and carved stone monuments: land divisions and the Keeills, *etc.*] Chadwick mem. Stud., pp. 141–70. 1950.

736 Megaw (Eleanor M.) and **Cowin** (W. S.). Odin's bird: notes on the raven past and present. [Viking raven-banners.] J. Manx Mus., 5, pp. 104–6, + plate 207. 1943.

737 Munch (Peder Andreas). Det norske folks historie. 6 pts. (in 8 vol.) 8° Christiania, 1852–63. [Gross, 1531. Vol. 1–3, Danes in England and Ireland.]

738 Olrik (Axel). Viking civilization. Revised by Hans Ellekilde. Translated by Jacob Wittmer Hartmann. pp. 246, and plates. 8° London, 1930.

739 Ormonde (L.). The Danish invasion [of Ireland]. J. Ivernian Soc., 3, pp. 82–88. 1911.

740 Partridge (Charles). Skin of a Viking from Hadstock church, Essex. East Anglian (N. and Q.), N.S. 11, pp. 32, 96. 1905.

741 Piggot (John), *jun.* Saxon [=Danish] cuticle on a church door. [Worcester cathedral, Hadstock and Copford, Essex.] N. and Q., 4th S. 4, pp. 101–02. 1869.

742 Shetelig (Haakon). Vikingetidens utvandring og bosetning i Vest-Europa. Nordisk Kultur, 1, pp. 105–20. 1936.

743 Smith (Charles Marshall). Northmen of adventure. A survey of the exploits of dominant Northmen from the earliest times to the Norman Conquest. pp. xi, 389, + 3 maps. 8° London, 1932. [Pp. 63–86, the Viking age: pp. 87–138, a Viking who's who: pp. 226–41, Canute the Great: pp. 287–93, Harald Hardrada in England: pp. 294–308, the jarls of Orkney.]

744 Sparvel-Bayly (John Anthony). The Daneland. East Anglian (N. and Q.), N.S. 4, pp. 241–45. 1892.

745 Steenstrup (Johannes Christoffer Hagemann Reinhardt). Normannerne. 4 Bde. 8° Kjøbenhavn, 1876–82.—Études préliminaires à l'histoire des Normands et de leurs invasions. [A translation of part of Normannerne]. Avec une introduction de E. de Beaurepaire. pp. 240. *In* Bull. Soc. Antiq. de Normandie, 1880. 8° Caen, 1880. [Gross, 1535. i. Introduction to Norman times: ii. Expeditions of Vikings in 9th c.: iii. Their kingdoms in the British Isles, 10th–11th c.: iv. 'Danelag': Danish institutions in England and their influence; a study in co-operative legal history.]

746 Stenton (*Sir* Frank Merry). The Danes in England. Proc. Brit. Acad., 13, pp. 203–46. 1927.

747 —— The Danes in England. (Historical revisions, -xvi). [Extent of Danish settlement.] History, N.S., 5, pp. 173–77. 1920.

748 Stenton (*Sir* Frank Merry) The Scandinavian colonies in England and Normandy. [Colonies in eastern England founded between 876 and 879.] Trans. R.H.S., 4th S. 27, pp. 1–12. 1945.

749 Todd (James Henthorn), *ed.* The war of the Gaedhil with the Gaill, or the invasions of Ireland by the Danes and other Norsemen. The original Irish text, edited with translation and introduction. *Rolls Series.* pp. ccvii, 349, + 2 plates. 8° London, 1867.

750 Turville-Petre (Edward Oswald Gabriel). The heroic age of Scandinavia. *Hutchinson's University Library.* pp. 196. 8° London, 1951. [Pp. 59–77, the Viking wars of the 9th c. (England and Ireland).]

751 Walsh (Annie). Scandinavian relations with Ireland during the Viking period. pp. 82. 8° Dublin, 1922.

752 Wheaton (Henry). History of the Northmen, or Danes and Normans, from the earliest times to the conquest of England by William of Normandy. 8° London, 1831. —. Histoire des peuples du nord, *etc.* Édition revue et augmentée, . . . traduit par E. Guillot. 8° Paris, 1844.

753 Worsaae (Jens Jacob Asmussen). Den danske Erobring af England og Normandiet. 8° Kjøbenhavn, 1863. [Gross, 1540.]

754 —— Minder om de Danske og Nord Maendene i England, Skotland og Irland. 8° Kjøbenhavn, 1851. An account of the Danes and Norwegians in England, Scotland and Ireland. pp. xii, 359. 8° London, 1852. [Gross, 1539. Influence of the Danes upon English institutions.]

755 Young (Jean I.). A note on the Norse occupation of Ireland. History, N.S. 35, pp. 11–33. 1950.

12. GENERAL HISTORY (CELTIC)

756 Anderson (Alan Orr). The prophecy of Berchan. [Pretended date of composition, 461 A.D. Prophecy re Irish kings' reigns. Introduction, Irish text, and notes.] Zeit. celt. Philol., 18, pp. 1–56. 1930.

757 Anderson (Marjorie Ogilvie). The lists of the kings. [i. Kings of the Scots : ii. Kings of the Picts.] Scot. Hist. Rev., 28, pp. 108–118 : 29, pp. 13–22. 1949–50.

758 Bremer (Walther Erich Emanuel Friedrich). [Die Stellung Irlands in der Vor- und Frühgeschichte Europas.] Ireland's place in prehistoric and early historic Europe. A translation [by R. A. S. Macalister] of an essay, *etc. Royal Irish Academy.* pp. 38. 8° Dublin, 1928. [*Appeared in* Festschrift des roem.-germ. Zentral-Museums 3u Mainz, pp. 171–85. 1927.]

759 Bryant (Sophie). Celtic Ireland. pp. xviii, 219. 8° London, 1889.

760 Cahill (E.). Irish in the Danish and pre-Norman period. Irish Eccles. Rec., 5th S. 47, pp. 337–54. 1936.

761 Chadwick (Hector Munro). Early Scotland : the Picts, the Scots and the Welsh of southern Scotland. pp. xxvi, 171, + 12 plates, + map. 8° Cambridge, 1949.

762 D'Alton (John). Essay on the ancient history, religion, learning, arts, and government of Ireland. [Pp. 171–251, period second, from the arrival of Saint Patrick in 431 to the Danish invasion, A.D. 795 : pp. 252–96, period third, from the Danish invasion to the battle of Clontarf in A.D. 1014 : pp. 297–365, from the battle of Clontarf to the English invasion.] Trans. R.I.A., 16 (Antiq.), pp. 3–380. 1830.

763 Dinan (W.). The early inhabitants of Ireland. J. Ivernian Soc., 3, pp. 214–21 : 4, pp. 10–18, 93–108, 164–80, + 4 plates. 1911–12.

764 Graham (Angus). Archaeological gleanings from dark-age records. (Scottish forts, houses, monasteries, churches, towns, etc.] Proc. Soc. Antiq. Scot., 85 (1950–51), pp. 64–91. 1953.

765 Green (Alice Stopford). History of the Irish state to 1014. pp. 449. 8° London, 1925.

766 —— The Old Irish world. pp. 212. 8° London, 1912.

767 Gunn (Æneas). Ancient north Scotland. Highland Monthly, 2, pp. 538–46. 1890.

768 Hubert (Henri). The greatness and decline of the Celts. *History of civilization.* pp. xvi, 314. 8° London, 1934. [Pp. 165–84, Saxons, Scots and Norsemen : pp. 185–276, civilization of the Celts. 3 maps.]

769 Hull (Eleanor). Early Christian Ireland. pp. xxviii, 283. 8° London, 1905. [429–794. i. Ireland under her native rulers : ii. The island of saints : iii. Irish art and architecture (round towers, books and illumination, learning and learned men, Irish libraries abroad).]

770 —— A history of Ireland and her people to the close of the Tudor period. pp. 525. 8° London, 1926.

771 Hyde (Douglas). A literary history of Ireland. pp. xviii, 654. 8° London, 1899. [Gross, 46. Ch. 13, St. Patrick : ch. 41, Irish annals : ch. 42, Brehon laws.]

772 Innes (Cosmo). Scotland in the Middle Ages. pp. xliv, 368, + 3 maps. 8° Edinburgh, 1860. [Pp. 48–119, + map 1, A.-S. period.]

773 Innes (Thomas). The civil and ecclesiastical history of Scotland. A.D. 80–818. [Edited by George Grub.] *Spalding Club*, 25. pp. lxiv, 340. 4° Aberdeen, 1853.

774 —— A critical essay on the ancient inhabitants of the northern parts of Britain or Scotland, containing an account of . . . the Picts, and particularly of the Scots. *Historians of Scotland, vol.* 8. pp. xxx, 440. 8° Edinburgh, 1879.

775 Jeudwine (John Wynne). The first twelve centuries of British story. . . . Social and political conditions, *etc.* with 24 maps. pp. lix, 436. 8° London, 1912. [Kenney, 1, p. 107. Uses Irish sources.]

776 Keating (Geoffrey). The history of Ireland from the earliest times to the Anglo-Norman invasion. Edited by David Comyn and P. S. Dinneen. *Irish Texts Society*, 4, 8, 9, 15. 4 vol. 8° Dublin, 1902–14.

777 Keith (Duncan). A history of Scotland, civil and ecclesiastical, from the earliest times to the death of David I : 1153. 2 vol. 8° Edinburgh, 1886.

778 Kerslake (Thomas). The Celtic substratum of England. [i. Celtic sanctuaries overshadowed : ii. ing = ynys = inch, etc.] N. and Q., 6th S. 7, pp. 281–84, 301–03. 1883.

779 Lach-Szyrma (Wladyslaw Somerville). Wales and west Wales. [The relation of Wales and Cornwall in the 5th, 6th, and 7th centuries.] J. Brit. Archaeol. Assoc., 44, pp. 279–83, *see also* p. 97. 1888.

780 Lloyd (*Sir* John Edward). A history of Wales from the earliest times to the Edwardian conquest. 3rd edition. pp. lv, vii, 815. 2 vol. 8° London, 1939. [Gross, 1113a.]

781 Macalister (Robert Alexander Stewart). Ancient Ireland : a study in the lessons of archaeology and history. pp. xii, 307, + 24 plates, and map. 8° London, 1935.

782 —— The legendary kings of Ireland. J. Roy. Soc. Antiq. Ireland, 38 (5th S. 18), pp. 1–16, 181. 1908.

783 Macandrew (*Sir* Henry Cockburn). Ireland before the Conquest. [432–795, 795–1014, 1014–1172.] Highland Monthly, 3, pp. 679–92, 705–25 : 4, pp. 49–65. 1892.

784 MacKenzie (Donald A.). Scotland : the ancient kingdom. pp. 384. 8° London, 1930.

785 MacNeill (Eoin). Celtic Ireland. pp. xvi, 182, + 3 maps. 8° Dublin, 1921.

786 —— Phases of Irish history. pp. 364. 8° Dublin, 1920. [Introduction of Christianity : Irish kingdom in Scotland : Ireland's golden age : struggle with the Norsemen : etc.]

787 Merriman (P. J.). The Irish chief in Irish history.]. Ivernian Soc., 6, pp. 164–75, 216–30. 1914.

788 Morgan (Thomas). Sketch of early Scottish history. J. Brit. Archaeol. Assoc., 45, pp. 348–61 : 46, pp. 29–42. 1889–90.

789 Nugent (William). Church and state in early Christian Ireland. *M.A. Thesis, Univ. Coll., Dublin.* 1949.

790 O'Ceallaigh (Seán). Ireland : elements of her early story, from the coming of Ceasair to the Anglo-Norman invasion. pp. xxxi, 416. 8° Dublin, 1921.

791 O'Rahilly (Cecile). Ireland and Wales : their historical and literary associations. pp. viii, 154. 8° London, 1924. [Pp. 46–80, A.-S. period.]

792 O'Rahilly (Thomas Francis). Early Irish history and mythology. pp. x, 568. 8° Dublin, 1946. [Pp. 235–59 : 'some questions of dating in early Irish annals.']

793 —— Notes on [his] Early Irish history and mythology [**792.**] [i. The five provinces : ii. Additions and corrections.] Celtica, 1, pp. 387–402. 1950.

794 Rhys (*Sir* John). Celtic Britain. 3rd edition, revised. pp. xv, 339. 8° London, 1904.

795 —— Studies in early Irish history. *British Academy*. pp. 60. 8° London, [1893].

796 —— and **Brynmore-Jones** (*Sir* David). The Welsh people. pp. xxvi, 678, + 2 maps. 8° London, 1900. [Picts : history, laws, land tenure, etc.]

797 Robertson (Eben William). Scotland under her early kings. 2 vol. 8° Edinburgh, 1862. [11th–13th c.]

798 Roessler (Charles). Les influences celtiques avant et après Colomban. pp. 102, + 8 plates. 8° Paris, 1901.

799 Ryan (John). Ireland from the earliest times to A.D. 800. pp. viii, 190, + map. 8° Dublin, [1928].

800 Shearman (John Francis). A catalogue of the kings of Ireland, from the Christian era. J. Roy. Hist. & Arch. Assoc. Ireland, [14], 4th S. 4, (1876–78), pp. 476–81. 1879.

801 Skene (William Forbes). Celtic Scotland. 3 vol. 8° Edinburgh, 1876–90.

802 Stokes (Whitley), *ed.* The Boroma. [A mediaeval historical romance. The Boroma = an eric fine imposed in 2nd c. on Leinster, which lasted for 500 years, when remitted by St. Molling. Irish text, with English translation.] Rev. celt., 13, pp. 32–124. 1892.

803 Vaughan (Arthur Owen). ' The matter of Wales '. pp. viii, 192. 4° Cardiff, 1913. [Pp. 27–81, ' Saxon Wales ' : pp. 126–43, Howel Dda.]

804 Wakeman (William Frederick). Archaeologia Hiberniae : a handbook of Irish antiquities, pagan and Christian. 3rd edition. Edited by J. Cooke. pp. 430. 8° London, 1903. [Gross, 415.]

805 Watson (William John). Early Irish influences in Scotland. Trans. Gaelic Soc. Inverness, 35 (1929–30), pp. 178–202. 1939.

806 Williams (Albert Hughes). An introduction to the history of Wales. Vol. 1 : prehistoric times to A.D. 1063. pp. x, 192, + 3 plates. 8° Cardiff, 1941.

13. THE PICTS

(All aspects, historical, racial, etc. The oldest of the five races mentioned by Bede in E.H. i. 1. Absorbed by Scots of Dalriada from mid 9th c.)

807 Anderson (Alan Orr). Ninian and the southern Picts. [Also sundry remarks on the Picts, especially of Fortriu, and philology.] Scot. Hist. Rev., 27, pp. 25–47. 1948.

808 Anderson (Marjorie Ogilvie). The Scottish materials in the Paris manuscript Bib. Nat., Latin 4126. [Pictish history.] Scot. Hist. Rev., 28, pp. 31–42. 1949.

809 Clarke (Hyde). The Picts and preceltic Britain. [Descent of queen Victoria from kings of the Picts, etc. !] Trans. R.H.S., N.S. 3, pp. 243–80. 1886.

810 Dobbs (Margaret E.). The Ui Dercco Céin. [Picts of Dal nAraide.] Ulster J. Archaeol., 3rd S. 2, pp. 112–19. 1939.

811 Elton (Charles). The Picts of Galloway. Archaeol. Rev., 1, pp. 48–54. 1888.

812 Ferguson (James). The Pictish race and kingdom. Celtic Rev., 7, pp. 18–36, 122–38. 1911.

813 Fraser (John). The alleged matriarchy of the Picts. Med. Stud. in memory of G. S. Loomis, pp. 407–12. 1927.

814 —— The question of the Picts. [Kenney, 1, p. 775.] Scot. Gaelic Stud., 2, pp. 172–201. 1927.

815 Garnett (Richard). On the probable relations of the Picts and Gael with the other tribes of Great Britain. Proc. Philol. Soc., 1, pp. 199–26. 1843.

816 Gray (John). The origin of the Picts and Scots. Trans. Buchan F.C., 5, pp. 163–68. 1900.

817 Hall (A.). The extinction of Pictish. N. and Q., 6th S. 6, pp. 241–42, 316–17, 406 : 7, p. 34. 1882–83.

818 Jamieson (—), *Rev. Dr.* Remarks on [Alexander] Murray's observations on the history of language of the Pehts. [*q.v.*, **831**.] Archaeol. Scot., 2, pp. 253–85. 1822.

819 Langhorne (Daniel). An introduction to the history of England . . . to the coming of the English Saxons. Together with a Catalogue of the British and Pictish kings. pp. 200. 8° London, 1676.

820 Loth (Joseph). Les Pictes d'après des travaux récents. [Kenney, p. 775.] Ann. de Bretagne, 6, pp. 111–16. 1890.

821 Macandrew (—), *Provost*. The Picts. Trans. Gaelic Soc. Inverness, 13, pp. 230–40. 1888.

822 MacCulloch (J. A.). The Picts of history and tradition. Proc. Scot. Anthrop. Soc., 1, ii, pp. 11–24. 1935.

823 MacDonald (Alasdair). Some knotty points in British ethnology. [Pp. 100–11, Picts.] Celtic Rev., 9, pp. 1–15, 97–111. 1913.

824 Maclean (Hector). The Picts. Trans. Gaelic Soc. Inverness, 16, pp. 228–52. 1891.

825 MacNeill (Eoin). The language of the Picts. [Including history, personal names, etc.] Yorks. Celtic Stud., 2, pp. 3–45. 1939.

826 Macnish (Neil). The Picts. Trans. Canadian Institute, 5, pp. 295–304. 1897.

826a Macpherson (John). Critical dissertations on the . . . Caledonians, . . . the Picts, and the British and Irish Scots. 8° Dublin (and 4° London), 1768.

827 MacRitchie (David). British dwarfs. [Picts.] Archaeol. Rev., 4, pp. 184–207. 1889.

828 MacRitchie (David). Fians, fairies and Picts. pp. 77, + 22 plates. 8° London, 1893.

829 —— Memories of the Picts. Scottish Antiquary, 14, pp. 121–39. 1900.

830 Marshall (Edward H.). The Picts a Scandinavian people ? N. and Q., 6th S. 3, p. 515 : 4, p. 115. 1881.

830a Miscellanea Pictica : containing the history of the Picts by Henry Maule [or ? by Sir James Balfour], Sir Robert Sibbald's account of the Picts, . . . and a description of Pictish antiquities remaining in Scotland and the northern islands. pp. 116. 12° Edinburgh, 1818.

831 Murray (Alexander). Observations on the history and language and the Pehts. [*See also* **818**.] Archaeol. Scot., 2, pp. 134–53. 1822.

832 Nicholson (Edward Williams Byron). Keltic researches. pp. xix, 212. 8° London, 1904. [The Picts, Pictish geographical names, place names in the Pictish Chronicle, the Pictish kingdom, Pictish inscriptions, legend of the ' Scottish conquest ', names of Pictish kings in Ireland, etc.]

833 Phillipps (*Sir* Thomas), *bart.* Catalogue of Pictish [and Scottish] kings. [From a 13th c. Phillipps ms.] Trans. Roy. Soc. Lit., 2, pp. 471–75. 1834.

834 Ross (J. Lockhart). The Picts. Wilts. Archaeol. Mag., 6, pp. 224–44, and 1 plate. 1860.

835 Scott (Archibald Black). The Pictish nation : its people and its Church. pp. 585. 4° Edinburgh, 1918.

836 Skene (William Forbes). The race and language of the Picts. Arch. Camb., 3rd S. 11, pp. 138–57, 286–307, 25–43, + table. 1865.

837 Smith (Roland M.). Sir Walter Scott and the Pictish question. Mod. Lang. Notes, 66, pp. 175–80. 1951.

838 Spence (John). Shetland folklore. pp. 256. 8° Lerwick, 1899. [Pp. 1–58, the Picts and their brochs.]

839 Taylor (Isaac), *etc.* Picts and Scots. N. and Q., 9th S. 5, pp. 261–62, 418–21 : 6, pp. 90–91, 196–97. 1900.

840 Walker (John). On the ancient Camelon, and the Picts. Archaeologia, 1, pp. 252–59. 1770.

841 Watson (William John). The Picts, their original position in Scotland. Trans. Gaelic Soc. Inverness, 30 (1919–22), pp. 240–61. 1924.

842 Zimmer (Heinrich). Das Mutterrecht der Pikten und seine Bedeutung für die arische Alterthumswissenschaft. [Disputed by Gougaud and Fraser.] Zeit. Rechtsgesch., 28 (Romanist. Abt.), pp. 209–40. 1894.

BY PERIOD :

14. INVASION AND SETTLE-MENT (c. 450–c. 600)

§ *a*. **The Anglo-Saxon Urheimat**

843 Barnes (William). Early England and the Saxon-English; with some notes on the father-stock of the Saxon-English, the Frisians. pp. 178. 8° London, 1869.

844 Boeles (Pieter Catharinus Johannes Albertus). Friesland for de elfde eeuw. Tweede druk. pp. xix, 598, + 55 plates, + 2 maps. 8° 's Gravenhage, 1951. [Pp. 207–49, De tijd der immigratie en expansie. De Angelsaksische invasie in Engelund, etc. With English summary.]

845 Erdmann (Axel). Über die Heimat und den Namen der Angeln. *Skrifter Hum. Vetenskapsamfundet, II.* 1. 1. pp. 118. 8° Upsala, 1890. [Gross, 1506. Invading Angles came from Sleswick.]

845a Foerste (W.), *etc.* [5 others] Die angelsächsische Wanderung der Völkerwanderungszeit, eine völkisch-kulturelle Bindung zwischen Deutschland und England. 8° Hamburg, 1936. [Maschinenschrift.]

846 Jankuhn (H.). The continental home of the English. [7 maps and plans in text. Dense population from Angeln migrated to England in 5th and 6th c.] Antiquity, 26, pp. 14–24, + 2 plates. 1952.

847 —— Siedlungs-und Kulturgeschichte der Angeln vor ihrer Auswanderung nach England. Jahrbuch des Angler Heimatvereins, 14, pp. 54–132. 1950.

848 Jankuhn (H.). Zur Frage nach der Urheimat der Angeln. Zeit. Ges. Schlesw.-Holst. Gesch., 70–1, pp. 20–. 1943.

848a Jordan (R.). Die Heimat der Angelsachsen. Verh. Baseler Philolog.-Vers., 1907, pp. 138–40. 1907.

849 Krom (Nicolaus Johannes). De populis Germanis antiquo tempore, patriam nostram incolentibus Anglosaxonumque migrationibus. *Dissertation.* pp. 172. 8° Lugduni Batavorum, 1908. [Gross, 1506 note. Holds that invading Angles came from the Netherlands.]

850 Langenfelt (Gösta). Notes on the Anglo-Saxon pioneers. [i. Earliest homesteads on the Continent : ii. Native traditions : iii. The A.-S. runes : iv. Colonists in Britain, literary and artistic work : v. Communications with the North: vi. The Widsith folk-names : vii. Beowulf problems.] Engl. Studien, 66, pp. 161–244. 1931.

851 Laur (W.). Angelns alteste Ortsnamen. Jahrbuch des Angler Heimatvereins, 14, pp. 133–40. 1950.

851a Moeller (H.). Besprechung von Erdmann. Über die Heimat und den Namen der Angeln. Anz. deut. Altertum, 22, pp. 129–64. 1896.

851b Ohlhaver (H.). Die angelsächsische Landnahme der Völkerwanderungszeit-eine völkischkulturelle Bindung zwischen Deutschland und England. Die Kunde, 4, pp. 185–207. 1936.

852 Pike (Luke Owen). The English and their origin. pp. xxiv, 267. 8° London, 1866. [Historical and philological evidence : evidence of physical and psychical characteristics.]

853 Plettke (Alfred). Ursprung und Ausbreitung der Angelsachsen. Mannus, 7, pp. 347–55. 1915.

854 —— Ursprung und Ausbreitung der Angeln und Sachsen. Beiträge zur Siedlungsarchäologie der Ingväonen. *Urnenfriedhöfe in Niedersachsen, III.* 1. pp. vii, 110, + 55 plates. 4° Hildesheim, 1921.

854a Riemann (Erhard). Germanen erobern Britannien. Die Ergebnisse der Vorgeschichte und der Sprachwissenschaft über die Einwanderung der Sachsen, Angeln und Jüten nach England. *Schriften der Albertus-Universität. Geisteswiss. Reihe*, 27. pp. 143, + 9 plates. 8° Königsberg, 1939.

855 Schaumann (Adolf Friedrich Heinrich). Zur Geschichte der Eroberung Englands durch germanische Stämme. *Göttinger Studien, redigert von A. B. Krische.* pp. 49. 8° Göttingen, 1845. [Gross, 1517. 'Contends that Saxons from the Litus Saxonicum in Gaul took a prominent part in the conquest of Britain.']

855a Schmidt (Ludwig). Die frühgermanische Bevölkerung der jütischen Halbinsel. (Zur Sachsenfrage). Zeit. d. Gesellschaft f. Schleswig-Holsteinische Geschichte, 63, pp. 347–56 (356–57). 1935.

856 Schuette (Gudmund). Die Wohnsitze der Angeln und Kindern. Acta phil. Scand., 14, pp. 21–30. 1914.

857 Seelmann (W.). Die ags. Erce. Zur Herkunft der sächsischen Eroberer Englands. Jahrb. d. Ver. f. niederd. Sprachforschung, 49, pp. 55–57. 1923.

858 Wade-Evans (Arthur Wade). The Frisian origin of the English. N. and Q., 196, pp. 332–33. 1951.

859 Wadstein (Elis). On the origin of the English. Skrifter K. Hum. Vet.-Samf. Uppsala, 24, no. 14. pp. 41. 1927.

860 Weiland (Ludwig). Die Angeln : ein Capitel aus der deutschen Altertumskunde. pp. 40. 8° Tübingen, 1889. [Gross, 1519. *In* Festgabe für Georg Hamssen. 'Maintains that the Angles came from Sleswick, and that the Germans who settled in Kent were not Jutes but that they came from the region of the lower Weser.']

§ *b*. **Anglo-Saxon, General**

861 [Anon.] Saxon invasion of the Severn valley. [By West Saxons, 577.] Glos. N. and Q., 3, pp. 265–67. 1887.

862 Alexander (John James). The Saxon conquest and settlement. [i. The preparation of evidence : ii. The history in outline : iii. Corroborations from place-names : iv. Conclusions : v. Appendices—(a) Chronology, 350–650 : (b)

Wilts., Glos., and Hants. : (c) Early references to the name Cornwall: (d) The Crediton charter of 739 : (e) Celtic invasions.] Rept. and Trans. Devon. Assoc., 64, pp. 75–112. 1932.

863 —— The Saxon conquest of Devon. [i. 440–540 : ii. 540–640 : iii. 640–740 : iv. 740–840 : v. 840–940.] History, 3, pp. 157–68. 1914.

864 Anscombe (Alfred). The date of the first settlement of the Saxons in Britain. [*See also* criticism by E. W. B. Nicholson, **952**.] Zeit. celt. Phil., 3, pp. 492–514 ; 6, pp. 339–98. 1901, 1908.

865 —— The *exordium* of the 'Annales Cambriae '. [Chronological queries, especially as to the coming of the Saxons.] Ériu, 3, pp. 117–34. 1907.

866 —— The historical side of the Old English poem of ' Widsith '. [With R. W. Chambers' reply.] Trans R.H.S., 3rd S. 9, pp. 123–65. 1915.

867 —— Mr. E. W. B. Nicholson and the ' Exordium ' of the 'Annales Cambriae '. Zeit. celt. Phil., 7, pp. 419–38. 1910.

868 Aurner (Nellie Slayton). Hengest, a study in early English hero legend. Univ. Iowa Studies, Humanistic Studies, 2 : no. 1, 1921.

869 Babcock (William Henry). The two lost centuries [5th and 6th] of Britain. pp. 239. 8° Philadelphia, 1890. [Gross, 1505.]

870 Baddeley (Welbore St. Clair). The battle of Dyrham, A.D. 577. [With plan.] Trans. Bristol and Glos. Arch. Soc., 51, pp. 95–101. 1929.

871 Bannard (Henry E.). A new theory of Cuthwulf's campaign in 571. Nineteenth century, 133, pp. 274–76. 1943.

872 Barns (Thomas). The making of Mercia. [i. Sources : ii. Making of Mercia : iii. Genealogy of Penda : iv. Borders of Mercia : v. Battle of Maserfield : vi. Last expedition of Penda : vii. Earlier traditions of Mercia.] North Staffs., F.C., Trans., 46, pp. 49–78. 1912.

873 Beck (F. G. M.). Teutonic conquest of Britain. Camb. Med. Hist., 1 pp. 382–91. 1911.

874 Beddoe (John). On the northern settlements of the West-Saxons. [P. 18, table showing ' colour of hair and eyes on the eastern slope of the Cotswolds.'] J.R.A.I., 25, pp. 16–20. 1896.

875 Bening (H.). Welches Volk hat mit den Sachsen Britannien erobert und diesem den Namen England gegeben ? Zeit. Hist. Ver. f. Niedersachsen, [53], pp. 1–19. 1888.

876 Betts (Reginald Robert). The beginnings of Wessex. Wessex, 3, pp. 19–21. 1936.

877 —— The origins of Wessex. Wessex, 4, pp. 179–81. 1938.

878 Blair (Peter Hunter). The origins of Northumbria. [i. The Gildas tradition: ii. The veracity of Gildas.] Arch. Æl., 4th S. 25, pp. 1–51. 1947.

879 Blasche (Herbert). Angelsachsen und Kelten im Urteil der Historia Ecclesiastica gentis Anglorum des Beda. pp. 55. 8° Göttingen, 1940. [Evidence of Bede for struggle between Anglo-Saxons and Celts.]

880 Boult (Joseph). The Angles, Jutes, and Saxons. Trans. Hist. Soc. Lancs. and Ches., N.S. 13 [=25], pp. 25–54. 1873.

881 Browne (George Forrest), *bp. of Bristol*. Some results of the battles of Deorham and Wanborough. [577, 591.] Proc. Clifton Antiq. Club., 4 (1897–99), pp. 264–76, + map. 1900.

882 Bryant (Arthur). The coming of the English. History to-day, 3, pp. 381–89. 1953.

883 Chadwick (Hector Munro). The origin of the English nation. pp. vii, 331, + 4 maps. 8° Cambridge, 1907. [Gross, 1505a. ' Excludes the Saxons from a share in the conquest of Britain.']

884 Clarke (F.). The West-Saxon occupation of Hampshire. Papers and Proc. Hants. F-C., 6, pp. 318–25, + map. 1910.

885 Coote (Henry Charles). Vortigern, not Hengist, the invader of Kent. Archaeologia, 44, pp. 363–72. 1873.

885a Copley (Gordon J.). The conquest of Wessex in the sixth century. pp. 240, + 12 plates. [10 maps in text.] 8° London, 1954.

886 Corbett (E. C.). The Anglo-Saxon conquest of Worcestershire. Trans. Worcs. Archaeol. Soc., N.S. 22, pp. 1–15. 1946.

887 Cowper (Henry Swainson). The influence of the Roman occupation upon the distribution of population in Cumberland and Westmorland. [Pp. 21–28, the Teutonic settlements.] Trans. Cumb. and Westm. Antiq. Soc., 16, pp. 16–40. 1900.

888 Crawford (Osbert Guy Stanhope). Cerdic and the Cloven Way. [With 6 maps.] Antiquity, 5, pp. 441–58, and 6 plates. 1931.

889 —— Cerdic's landing-place. [Cerdic's ora on coast between Calshot and the mouth of the Beaulieu river, correcting his former location at Totton.] Antiquity, 26, pp. 193–200, + plate, + map. 1952.

890 Dauncey (Kenneth Douglas Masson). The strategy of Anglo-Saxon invasion. Antiquity, 16, pp. 51–63. 1942.

891 Davidson (James Bridge). The Saxon conquest of Devonshire. Rept. and Trans. Devon. Assoc., 9, pp. 198–221. 1877.

892 Dawkins (*Sir* William Boyd). The retreat of the Welsh from Wiltshire. [Pp. 101–11 : ix. The conquest of Wiltshire by the West Saxons : x. The nature of the conquest : xi. The making of Wiltshire : xii. The place of Bockerly dyke and Wansdyke in the history of Wiltshire.] Arch. Camb., 6th S. 14, pp. 87–112. 1914.

893 Deanesly (Margaret). The court of king Æthelberht of Kent. Camb. Hist. J., 7, pp. 101–14, + 1 plate. 1942.

894 Elton (Charles Isaac). Origins of English history. 2nd edition, revised. pp. xxiii, 450. 8° London, 1890. [Gross, 1247. Ch. 12, A.-S. to c. 597.]

895 Evans (John H.). The tomb of Horsa. [? location. ? killed at battle of Aylesford.] Arch. Cant., 65 (1952), pp. 101–13. 1953.

896 Fletcher (Eric George Molyneux). Did Hengist settle in Kent ? Antiquity, 17, pp. 91–93. 1943.

897 Friedel (Victor H.). L'arrivée des Saxons en Angleterre d'après le texte de Chartres et l'Historia Britonum. Beiträge zur . . . Philologie. Festgabe für W. Foerster, pp. 280–96. 1902.

898 Gaupp (Ernst Theodor). Die germanischen Ansiedlungen, *etc.* 8° Breslau, 1844. [Gross, 1509. Pp. 538–50, A.-S.]

899 George (T. J.). The invasions of the Saxons and Angles, and the part Northamptonshire played in them. [Plate shows 3 brooches.] J. Northants. Nat. Hist. Soc., 20, pp. 35–44, + 1 plate. 1919.

900 Godsal (Philip Thomas). Ceawlin, the second Bretwalda and the conquest of the Midlands. Trans. B'ham. Arch. Soc., 40, pp. 53–68. 1914.

901 —— The conquest of Britain by the Angles ; in the light of military science. [Map shows ' The conquest of the Dee valley.'] J. Archit., and Hist. Soc. of Chester, N.S. 16, pp. 70–96, + map. 1909.

902 —— The conquests of Ceawlin, the second Bretwalda. pp. xi, 254, + plans. 8° London, 1924.

903 —— A military study of the conquest of Britain by the English. An abbreviated report of a lecture delivered before the Berks Archaeological Society. Berks, Bucks and Oxon Archaeol. J., 13, pp. 110–18. 1908.

904 —— The storming of London and the Thames valley campaign. A military study of the conquest of Britain by the Angles. pp. xxxv, 288, + 6 maps. 8° London, 1908.

905 Gray (Arthur). The first English settlement of Cambridgeshire. [Abstract only.] Proc. Camb. Antiq. Soc., 23, p. 11. 1922.

906 Greswell (William Henry Parr). The Saxon conquest of Somerset. [In reply to C. W. Whistler and Albany Major, *q.v.* **998**, with their rejoinder, pp. 119–20.] Antiquary, 48, pp. 39–40. 1912.

907 Grundy (George Beardoe). The Saxon settlement in Worcestershire. Trans. B'ham. Arch. Soc., 53 (for 1928), pp. 1–17, + map. 1931.

907a Guest (Edwin). Fethanleag-Uriconium. [A.-S. 584, ? Destruction of Uriconium by Ceawlin in his Fethanleag campaign. ? = Fotherley, Staffs.] Arch. Camb., 3rd, S. 9, pp. 334–35. 1863.

908 Guest (Edwin). On the early English settlements in South Britain. [Map of S.E. England in 520.] Mems. Archaeol. Inst., [5] (1849), pp. 28–72, + folding map. 1851.

909 —— On the English conquest of the Severn valley. [*See also* **1028–29**, **1038**.] Archaeol. J., 19. pp. 193–218, and folding map. 1862. *Same title.* Arch. Camb., 3rd S. 9, pp. 134–56, + map. 1863.

910 —— Origines Celticae (a fragment) and other contributions to the history of Britain. 2 vol. 8° London, 1883. [Gross, 1263. Vol. 2 contains reprints of **908, 5937, 909, 7796, 907a**.]

911 Gummere (Francis Barton). Founders of England, with supplementary notes by Francis Peabody Magoun, jr. pp. xii, 506. 8° New York, 1930. [Revised ed. of Germanic origins.]

912 Haigh (Daniel Henry). The conquest of Britain by the Saxons : a harmony of the ' Historia Britonum ', the writings of Gildas, the ' Brut ', and the Saxon Chronicle with reference to the events of the fifth and sixth centuries. pp. xvi, 367, + 6 plates. 8° London, 1861. [Gross, 1511. Uses early and late evidence as if of equal value !]

913 Hald (Kristian). Angles and Vandals. Classica et mediaevalia, 4, pp. 62–78. 1941.

914 Hallett (T. G. P.). The battle of Deorham, and its relations to Bath. Trans. Bristol and Glos. Arch. Soc., 8, pp. 62–73, + 2 maps. 1884.

915 Hamel (Anton Gerard van). Hengest and his namesake. [Are Hengist of the Saxon conquest and Hengest thane of Hnæf the Dane at Finnsburuh the same person ?] Studies in English philology in honor of F. Klaeber, pp. 159–71. 1929.

916 Hill (Geoffrey). Cerdic's landing place. pp. 24. 8° Salisbury, 1911.

917 Howorth (*Sir* Henry Hoyle). The beginnings of Wessex. [*See also* **982.**] E.H.R., 13, pp. 667–71. 1898.

918 —— The ethnology of Germany. Part 3. The migration of the Saxons. J.R.A.I., 7, pp. 293–320. 1878.

919 Hughes (Michael W.). Grims ditch and Cuthwulf's expedition to the Chilterns in A.D. 571. [With plate from Corpus MS. of A-.S. C. recording battle of Bedcan ford.] Antiquity, 5, pp. 291–314. 1931.

920 International Congress of Pre-historic and Protohistoric Sciences. [Synopsis of papers in] Section 5 . . . Anglo-Saxons. Man, 32, pp. 217–18. 1932.

921 Johnstone (P. K.). Cerdic and his ancestors. [With notes on A.-S. personal names in C.] Antiquity, 20, pp. 31–37. 1946.

922 —— Vortigern and Aetius—a re-appraisal. Antiquity, 20, pp. 16–20. 1946.

923 Kermack (W. R.). Early English settlement, southwest Scotland. [With place-name evidence.] Antiquity, 15, pp. 83–86. 1941.

924 Kerslake (Thomas). The first West-Saxon penetration into Somerset-shire [658 A.D.]. Proc. Somerset Arch. Soc., 22 (1876), pp. 61–70. 1877.

925 King (Richard John). The birth-place of Wynfrith, or St. Boniface, as bearing on the Saxon conquest of Devon-shire. Proc. Somerset Arch. Soc., 20 (1874), pp. 58–73. 1875.

926 Leeds (Edward Thurlow). The early Saxon penetration of the upper Thames area. Antiq. J., pp. 229–51, and 5 plates, + map. 1933.

927 —— Early settlement in the upper Thames basin. [Pp. 534–5, Saxon period, with map.] Geography, 14, pp. 527–35. 1928.

927a —— The Saxon penetration of the upper Thames region. Proc. First Internat. Congress Prehist. and Proto-hist. Sciences, pp. 298–99. 1934.

928 —— The West Saxon invasion and the Icknield Way. [With sketch map to show Saxon burials to A.D. 650.] History, N.S., 10, pp. 97–109. 1925.

929 Lennard (Reginald). The char-acter of the Anglo-Saxon conquests : a disputed point. History, N.S. 18, pp. 204–15. 1933.

930 Lloyd (*Sir* John Edward). North-umbria under Celtic rule. [400–600.] Yorks. Soc. Celtic Stud., Rpt. for 1932–33, pp. 12–14. 1933.

931 Lot (Ferdinand). Bretons et Anglais aux Ve et VI. siècles. Proc. Brit. Acad., 16, pp. 327–44. 1930.

932 —— Hengist, Hors, Vortigern: la conquête de la Grande-Bretagne par les Saxons. Mélanges d'histoire offert à C. Bémont, pp. 1–19. 1913.

933 —— Les invasions germaniques. *Bibliothèque historique.* pp. 340. 8° Paris, 1945. [Pp. 294–320, (chap. 9), 'les Anglo-Saxons en Grande-Bretagne.']

934 —— Les migrations saxonnes en Gaule et en Grande-Bretagne du IIIe au Ve siècle. Rev. hist., 119, pp. 1–40. 1915.

955 Luedeke (H.). The London basin in the Saxon invasion. [Map on p. 106.] Malone (K.) : Philologica, pp. 105–09. 1949.

936 Major (Albany Featherstone-haugh). Early wars of Wessex : being studies from England's school of arms in the west. Edited by Charles W. Whistler. pp. 254. 8° Cambridge, 1913.

937 —— The Saxon settlement of north-east Surrey. Proc. Croydon N.H. Soc., 9, pp. 53–79, + map. 1921.

938 —— Surrey, London and the Saxon conquest. *Same jnl.*, 9, pp. 1–27, + map. 1920.

939 Malden (Henry Elliot). The West-Saxon conquest of Surrey. E.H.R., 3, pp. 422–30. 1888.

940 Malone (Kemp). Hildeburg and Hengist. E.L.H., 10, pp. 257–84. 1943.

941 —— The meaning of Bede's *Iutae.* Anglia, Beiblatt, 51, pp. 262–64. 1940.

942 Martin (John May). The Angli-can [*sic*] invasion of Devon, with some notes on the place-name '-worthy'. [Map shows 'Anglian [*sic*] invasion of Devon, A.D. 743.'] Rept. and Trans. Devon. Assoc., 46, pp. 386–410, + map. 1914.

943 Meyer (Willi). Beiträge zur Geschichte der Eroberung Englands durch die Angelsachsen. *Diss. Halle.* pp. 87. 8° Halle, 1912.

944 Mutton (Alice F. A.). The process and pattern of the Saxon settlement of West Sussex. [5 pp. of maps.] Sussex Archaeol. Collns., 78, pp. 184–94. 1937.

945 Myres (John Nowell Linton). The Adventus Saxonum. Aspects of archaeology : Essays pres. to O.G.S. Crawford, pp. 221–41. 1951.

946 —— The coming of the Saxons. [Re-examines literary and archaeological evidence relating to the Adventus Saxonum.] New English Rev., 13, pp. 271–82. 1946.

947 —— The Teutonic settlement of northern England. (Historical revisions. -lxxx). History, N.S., 20, pp. 250–62. 1935.

948 Napper (H. F.). On the landing of Ella and his sons. Sussex Archaeol. Collns., 38, pp. 211–13. 1892.

949 Neville (Ralph). Wimbledon, the camp and the battle. [A.-S. C., 568.] Surrey Archaeol. Collns., 10, pp. 273–79. 1891.

950 Nichols (John Gough). On the site of Cerdicesora. Sussex Archaeol. Collns., 12, pp. 263–64. 1860.

951 Nicholson (Edward Williams Byron). The 'Annales Cambriae' and their so-called ' Exordium '. [Pp. 121–22, states the quadripartite nature of this controversy between himself, A. Anscombe and A. W. Wade-Evans, *q.v.*] Zeit. celt. Phil., 8, pp. 121–50. 1912.

952 —— Remarks on ' The date of the first settlement of the Saxons in Britain ' [by Alfred Anscombe, **864**]. *Same jnl.*, pp. 439–53. 1908.

953 —— The ruin of history. (A reply to ' The ruin of Britannia ') [by A. W. Wade-Evans, *q.v.* **149**]. Celtic Rev., 2, pp. 369–80. 1905.

954 —— The Vandals in Wessex and the battle of Deorham. (Gormund and Isembard. A postscript). Y Cymmrodor, 19, pp. 5–17 : 22, pp. 150–59. 1906, 1910.

955 Norman (George Warde). Remarks on the Saxon invasion. Arch. Cant., 13, pp. 97–110. 1880.

956 O'Neil (B. H. St. J.). The Silchester region in the 5th and 6th centuries A.D. Antiquity, 18, pp. 113–22, + folding map. 1944.

957 Petrie (*Sir* William Matthew Flinders). British and Saxon fusion. Man, 37, pp. 97–98. 1937.

958 —— Neglected British history. [?date of Hengist and Arthur, etc.] Proc. Brit. Acad., [8], pp. 251–78. 1917.

959 Picton (*Sir* James Allanson). Traces of the settlement of the Saxons in England, particularly in reference to Lancashire. Proc. Lit. and Phil. Soc. L'pool, 6, pp. 89–103. 1850.

960 Poste (Beale). Britannia antiqua. 8° London, 1857. [Gross, 1516. ch. 1–2, Asser, Gildas, Nennius ; ch. 3–4, British history in 6th c.]

961 —— Territories of the ancient British king Vortigern on the Wye, and in the south of Wales. (Further remarks, *etc.*). J. Brit. Archaeol. Assoc., 10, pp. 226–31, + map : 11, pp. 56–63. 1855.

962 Raglan (Fitzroy Raglan Somerset), *4th baron.* The hero : a study in tradition, myth, and drama. pp. xi, 311. 8° London, 1936. [Pp. 73–81, king Arthur : pp. 82–91, Hengist and Horsa.]

963 Reed (Trelawney Dayrell). The battle for Britain in the fifth century. An essay in Dark Age history. pp. viii, 208. 8° London, 1944.

964 —— The rise of Wessex ; a further essay in Dark Age history. pp. ix, 354. 8° London, 1947. [6 maps in text.]

965 —— ' The strategy of Anglo-Saxon invasion '. [Criticism of K. D. M. Dauncey's paper, *q.v.*, **890**.] Antiquity, 16, pp. 177–80. 1942.

966 Robson (John). On the Allelujah victory [429], and the state of England in the fifth century. Archaeol. J., 14, pp. 320–30. 1857.

967 Rolleston (George). On the character and influence of the Anglo-Saxon conquest of England as illustrated by archaeological research. Proc. Roy. Institution, 6, pp. 116–19. 1870.

968 Romer (H. G.). The battle of Mercredsburn. [486. Ælle v. Welsh. ? in Cuckmere valley. *See also* 6, p. 67.] Sussex County Mag., 5, pp. 656–61. 1931.

969 Round (John Horace). On the settlement of the South Saxons and East Saxons, based on a study of the place-names in Sussex and Essex. [Abstract of a paper.] Proc. Soc. Antiq., 2nd S. 16, pp. 84–85. 1896.

970 —— The settlement of the South —and East Saxons. The commune of London and other studies, by J. H. Round, pp. 1–27. [= study, no. 1.] 1899.

971 Russell (—), *Miss*. The acquisition of Lothian by Northumbria : probably a suppressed chapter of Bede. [Theory ' that Edwin's acceptance of Christianity must have been the price he paid for Lothian '—based on dedications to St. Helena.] J. Brit. Archaeol. Assoc., 47, pp. 197–204. 1891.

972 Sargant (W. L.). The pattern of the Anglo-Saxon settlement of Rutland. [Map of ' the villages of Rutland ', on p. 64.] Geography, 31, pp. 62–65. 1946.

973 Savage (Henry Edwin), *dean of Lichfield*. Northumbria after the departure of the Roman forces. Pubs. Thoresby Soc., 22 (1912–14), pp. 1–40. 1915.

974 Schreiner (Katharina). Die Sage von Hengist und Horsa. *Germanische Studien*, 12. pp. xii, 166. 8° Berlin, 1921.

975 Schroeder (Edward). *Hengist* und *Horsa*. [Contends that legend of Hengist is not Germanic, but is probably of Celtic origin.] Z. f. d. A., 77, pp. 69–72. 1940.

976 Schuette (Gudmund). Our forefathers ; the Gothonic nations. A manual of the ethnography of the Gothic, German, Dutch, Anglo-Saxon, Frisian and Scandinavian peoples. 2 vol. 8° Cambridge, 1929–33. [Vol. 2, pp. 221–76, A.-S. conquest : linguistic, archaeological evidence.]

977 Schuette (Gudmund). Vidsid og Slægtsagnene om Hengest og Angantyr. [i. Remsedigtningens almindelige Væsen og Udvikling : ii. Hengests Forfædre : iii. Hengests Nationalitet : etc.] Arkiv nord. Filol., 36 (N.F. 32), pp. 1–32. 1920.

978 Sedgefield (Walter John). The Finn ' episode ' in ' Beowulf '. [?Eotens and Jutes.] Mod. Lang. Rev., 28, pp. 480–82. 1933.

979 Shore (Thomas William). The Anglo-Saxon settlement round London and glimpses of Anglo-Saxon life in and near it. Trans. Lond. and Middsx. Archaeol. Soc., N.S. 1, pp. 283–318. 1905.

980 —— Origin of the Anglo-Saxon race ; a study of the settlement of England and the tribal origin of the Old English people. pp. vii, 416. 8° London, 1906.

981 —— Surviving traces of the West Saxon conquest of Hampshire. Hants. N. and Q., 8, pp. 1–4. 1896.

982 Stevenson (William Henry). The beginnings of Wessex. [*See also* **917**.] E.H.R., 14, pp. 32–46. 1899.

983 —— Dr. Guest and the English conquest of south Britain. E.H.R., 17, pp. 625–42. 1902.

984 Thurneysen (Rudolf). Wann sind die Germanen nach England gekommen ? [Pre-dates Bede's 449 to about 440.] Engl. Studien, 22. pp. 163–79. 1896.

985 Trevelyan (George Macaulay). The coming of the Anglo-Saxons. Trevelyan (G. M.). An autobiography and other essays, pp. 129–48. 1949.

986 Varin [?Pierre Joseph]. Études relatives à l'état politique et religieux des îles britanniques au moment de l'invasion saxonne [A.D. 411–731]. [Gross, 1518.] Mém. Acad. Inscr., Paris, [série 1] 5, pp. 1–270. 1857.

987 Wade-Evans (Arthur Wade). Ælle, the first Bretwalda. [Became Bretwalda owing to his victory (with Cissa) over the Jutes at Andredescester in 491. Argues also that Jutes again invaded in 514, and after 150 years were finally defeated (see De excidio, 23): this 'famous victory' over them was Mons Badonicus.] N. and Q., 193, pp. 542–44. 1948.

988 —— Arthur and Octa. ['Hengist' and 'Horsa' nicknames of Octa and Ebissa, Frisians in the Roman service. Arthur, a Roman provincial (Britannus) was also in same service, but employed against the Picts and Scots, not against the Saxons, as usually supposed.] N. and Q., 193, pp. 508–09. 1948.

989 —— Dr. Haverfield and the Saxon advent in Britain. [*See* Cambridge Medieval History, 1, pp. 380–81. i. Date of Saxon advent: ii. Occasion of Saxon settlement: iii. Course of Saxon invasion: iv. Region of the uplands.] Celtic Rev., 8, pp. 251–55. 1913.

990 —— The Jutish invasion of 514. Arch. Camb., 97, pp. 161–68. 1943.

991 —— —— Vortigern. [End of 4th c. Evidence of pillar of Eliseg.] N. and Q., 195, pp. 200–03. 1950.

992 —— Vortimer, son of Vortigern. Arch. Camb., 96, pp. 193–95. 1941.

993 —— The year of the reception of the Saxones. Y Cymmrodor, 27, pp. 26–36. 1917.

994 Wainwright (Frederick Threlfall). The Anglian settlement of Lancashire. Trans. Hist. Soc. Lancs. and Ches., 93 (1941), pp. 1–44, + folding map. 1942.

995 Ward (Gordon). The first Danes come to England. 15th centenary of Hengist's landing, 449–1949. pp. 15. 8° London, [1949]. [Reprinted from Denmark, a monthly review of Anglo-Danish relations.]

996 —— Hengest. Arch. Cant., 61 (1948), pp. 77–97. 1949.

997 —— Hengist, an historical study of his Danish origins and of his campaigns in Frisia and south-east England. pp. 58. 8° London, 1949. [7 maps in text.]

998 Whistler (Charles Watts) and **Major** (Albany Featherstonehaugh). The Saxon conquest of Somerset. [With map. *See also* **906**.] Antiquary, 47, pp. 376–83, 425–29, 460–63. 1911.

E

999 Williamson (F.). Anglo-Saxon tribal offshoots. ['Offshoots from Old English tribes settled in the territory of other tribes.'] N. and Q., 184, pp. 363–65. 1943.

1000 Willis (F. M.). Notes on the Jutes. Antiquary, 30, pp. 152–56. 1894.

1001 Wilson (Arthur Ernest). The end of Roman Sussex and the early Saxon settlements. Sussex Archaeol. Collns., 82, pp. 35–58. 1942.

1002 —— Sussex, Kent, and the continent in early Saxon times. *Same jnl.*, 83, pp. 55–72. 1943.

1003 Winbolt (Samuel Edward). The Eashing burials: an attempt to explain them. [Roman-British (or Welsh) killed by Saxons. 'Possible settings in history.'] Surrey Archaeol. Collns., 44, pp. 149–52. 1936.

1004 Windle (*Sir* Bertram Coghill Allan). Life in early Britain. Being an account of the early inhabitants of this island and the memorials which they have left behind them. pp. xiii, 244. 8° London, 1897. [Pp. 171–86, the Saxon occupation; pp. 187–206, tribal and village communities.]

1005 Wright (Thomas). The Celt, the Roman and the Saxon: a history . . . down to the conversion of the Anglo-Saxons to Christianity. 3rd edition . . . with additions. pp. xiv, 562. 8° London, 1875. [Pp. 453–529, A.-S. period.]

1006 Young (George Malcolm). The origin of the West-Saxon kingdom. A lecture. pp. 36. 8° Oxford. 1934.

1007 Zachrisson (Robert Eugen). Romans, Kelts and Saxons in ancient Britain. An investigation into the two dark centuries (400–600) of English history. [Historical, archaeological and linguistic evidence: place-names containing O.E. *Wealh, Weall, Weala.*] Skrifter K. Hum. Vet.-Samf., Uppsala, 24, no. 12, pp. 95. 1927.

§ *c.* **Celtic** (c. 450–c. 600)

1008 Anscombe (Alfred). The identification of 'Libine abas Iae' in the Historia Brittonum. [? 'Libine' = Slebhine, abbot of Iona from 752.] Zeit. Celt. Phil., 1, pp. 274–76. 1897.

1009 Baring-Gould (Sabin). Irish conquests and colonies in Domnonia and Wales. [To end of 6th c.] Rept. and Trans. Devon. Assoc., 31, pp. 430–55. 1899.

1010 Barnes (Henry). On the battle of Ardderyd. With plan and description of the earthworks at Arthuret by T. H. Hodgson and Mrs. Hodgson. [c. 573 (Annales Cambriae). Between Peredwr, leader of the N. Welsh and Gwenddolau, a king in Scotland?] Trans. Cumb. and Westm. Antiq. Soc., N.S. 8, pp. 236–46, + plan, + plate. 1908.

1011 Chadwick (Norah Kershaw). The lost literature of Celtic Scotland : Law of Pritdin [Pictish king] and Arthur of Britain. [Relating to events of 5th and 6th c.] Scot. Gaelic Stud., 7, pp. 115–83. 1953.

1012 Chevalier (Jacques). Essai sur la formation de la nationalité . . . au pays de Galles à la fin du 6e siècle. *Annales de l'Université de Lyon, n.s. II. Droit, lettres*, 34. pp. xxxviii, 439. 8° Paris, 1923.

1013 Dobbs (Margaret E.). Aedan Mac Gabrain. [Died 605, A.U.] Scot. Gaelic Stud., 7, pp. 89–93. 1951.

1014 —— Dún Eogain Bél. [Dún located on Lough Mask. Eogan Bél, king of Connaught, died 542 or 546.] J. Galway Archaeol. Soc., 23, pp. 75–76. 1948.

1015 Elston (Charles Sidney). The earliest relations between Celts and Germans. *Birkbeck College monographs, Germanic section*, 1. pp. ix, 198. 8° London, 1934.

1016 Ferguson (James). The British race and kingdom in Scotland. [Arthur and early struggles with Saxons.] Celtic Rev., 8, pp. 170–89, 193–217. 1912–13.

1017 Gourlay (W. R.). The battle of Arthuret, c. 573 A.D. Trans. Dumfries. Antiq. Soc., 3rd S. 16 (1929–30), pp. 104–12. 1931.

1018 Hubert (Henri). Les Celtes depuis l'époque de la Tène, et la civilisation celtique. *L'évolution de l'humanité.* pp. xxiv, 368. 8° Paris, 1932. [Pp. 198–216, Saxons, Scots et Scandinaves.]

1018a Hull (Vernam Edward). The Book of Uí Maine version of the expulsion of the Déssi. Zeit. celt. Philol., 24, pp. 266–71. 1954.

1019 Kermode (Philip Moore Callow). Inquiry as to the conditions of the Isle of Man and its inhabitants in the fifth century. I.O.M., N.H. and Antiq. Soc., Proc., N.S. 1, pp. 471–76. 1913.

1020 Lehmacher (Gustav). Eine Brüsseler Handschrift [6131] der Eachtra Conaill Gulban. [5th c. episode. Irish text and German translation. For identification of the place-names, *see* **6807**.] Zeit. celt. Philol., 14, pp. 212–69. 1923.

1021 Morris (Henry). The battle of Ocha and the burial place of Niall of the Nine Hostages. [Probably in 482]. J. Roy. Soc. Antiq. Ireland, 56 (6th S. 16), pp. 29–42. 1926.

1022 —— Where king Laeghaire was killed. [' Between Erin and Alban.' 457, –8, –9, or 461.] *Same jnl.*, 68 (7th S., 8), pp. 123–29. 1938.

1023 Nicholson (Edward Williams Byron). The battle of Raith and its song-cycle : attributed to Haneirin. (A postscript to ' The battle of Raith '—and, the origins of Bernicia and Lindsey). [596.] Celtic Rev., 6, pp. 214–36 : 7, pp. 81–88. 1910–11.

1024 Omurethi. The battle of Dunbolg, near Baltinglass, fought in 594, and what led up to it. J. Kildare Archaeol. Soc., 5, pp. 285–92, + map. 1907.

1025 Pender (Séamus). Two unpublished versions of the expulsion of the Déssi [from around Tara to south Ireland and Wales.] [Mid 5th c. Earliest version mid 8th c. Irish texts.] Essays presented to . . . Torna, pp. 209–17. 1947.

1026 Plummer (Charles). The conversion of Loegaire, and his death. [In Leabhar na hUidhre, pp. 117–18 of the facsimile. With text in Irish and English, and notes.] Rev. celt., 6, pp. 162–63. 1884.

1027 Ryan (John). The convention of Druim Ceat (A.U. 575). [Between Columcille and king Aed, son of Ainmire.] J. Roy. Soc. Antiq. Ireland, 76, pp. 35–55. 1946.

1028 Skene (William Forbes). [Llywarch Hen and Uriconium]. [*See also* **909, 1029, 1038.**] Arch. Camb., 3rd S. 10, pp. 152–56. 1864.

1029 Stephens (Thomas). Llywarch Hen and Uriconium. [*See also* **909, 1028, 1038.**] Arch. Camb., 3rd S. 10, pp. 62–74. 1864.

1030 —— The Poems of Taliesin. [And the historical matter therein. i. Corroy, son of Dairy and Cuichelm: ii. Anrec Urien: iii. Aeddon of Mona: iv. Cunedda: v. Cynan Garwyn: vi. Gwallawg ab Lleenawg: vii. To Gwallawg.] Arch. Camb., N.S. 2, pp. 149–55, 204–19, 261–74: 3, pp. 47–64, 105–14, 241–58: 4, pp. 43–62. 1851–53.

1031 Stokes (Whitley), *ed.* The death of Muirchertach mac Erca. [Irish text and English translation. Annals of Ulster, A.D. 533: 'The drowning of Muirchertach Mac Erca . . . in a vat full of wine, in the fort of Cletech, over the Boyne.'] Rev. celt., 23, pp. 395–437. 1902.

1032 Wade-Evans (Arthur Wade). Gododdin, Lleuddiniawn, Brynaich. [Territories of Celts and Northumbrians, 2nd to 6th c.] Arch. Camb., 98, pp. 143–45. 1944.

1033 Walshe (Patrick T.). The antiquities of the Dunlavin-Donard district (Counties of Wicklow and Kildare.) [Ancient battle-sites: pp. 118–19, The battle of Dunbolg, co. Wicklow, 594 A.D.] J. Roy. Soc. Antiq. Ireland, 61 (7th S. 1), pp. 113–41, + 4 plates. 1931.

1034 Watson (James). Notes on the early history of Scotland. pp. 88, 84, 64. 8° Peebles, 1883. [i. An examination of the ancient history of Ireland and Iceland in so far as it concerns the origin of the Scots: ii. Interpolations in Bede's Ecclesiastical history and other ancient annals affecting the early history of Scotland and Ireland: iii. Ireland not the Hibernia of the ancients.]

1035 Wilkins (C.). Gwladys, sister of Tydvil. [5th c.] Arch. Camb., 6th S. 1, pp. 151–53. 1901.

1036 Wilson (Daniel). Prehistoric annals of Scotland. 2nd edition. 2 vol. 8° London, 1863. [Vol. 2, pt. 4, Christian period: especially (iii, iv, v.) sculptured standing stones, Scoto- Scandinavian relics, A.-S. relics.]

1037 Windisch (Ernst). Das keltische Britannien bis zu Kaiser Arthur. Abhandl. k. sächs. Gesell. Wiss., phil.-hist. Kl., 29. vi. pp. 301. 1912.

1038 Wright (Thomas). On Llywarch Hen and the destruction of Uriconium. [Criticism of passages in Dr. Guests' paper, **909**, rejoinders by Dr. Guest, 9, pp. 334–35: 10, pp. 156–64, 260–62.] Arch. Camb., 3rd S. 9, pp. 249–54: 10, pp. 164–76. 1863–64.

§ *d* Arthuriana

(*See also* 87 § *a and* 119 § *c, and see* 4 § *f* for date of Mons Badonicus.)

1039 Anderson (Alan Orr). The dating passage in Gildas's Excidium. [i.e. from the siege of Mons Badonicus.] Scot. H.R., 25, pp. 384–85. 1928.

1040 —— Gildas and Arthur. [Date of Badon, etc.] Celtic Rev. 8, pp. 149–65. 1912.

1041 —— Varia. 1. The dating passage in Gildas's Excidium. 2. Gildas and Arthur. Zeit. celt. Philol., 17, pp. 403–06. 1928.

1042 Anscombe (Alfred). King Arthur and Pope Simplicius. [Passage in Geoffrey, ix 1.] N. and Q., 155, pp. 292–94. 1928.

1043 —— King Arthur in Gildas. Academy, 48, pp. 318–19. 1895.

1044 —— King Arthur [Ursus] in Gildas. N. and Q., 155, p. 115. 1928.

1045 Bennett (James Arthur). Camelot. ['Chat' about Cadbury, etc.]. Proc. Somerset Arch. Soc., 36 (1890), pp. 1–19. 1891.

1046 Bilderbeck (Alured Alcock Stokes). Lancashire and king Arthur. pp. 32. 8° Stockport, 1903.

1047 Blenner-Hassett (Roland). Geoffrey of Monmouth's Mons Agned and Castellum Puellarum. Speculum, 17, pp. 250–54. 1942.

1048 Blount (Alma). An index of abbreviations in Miss Alma Blount's unpublished Onomasticon Arthurianum. [Contains a useful Arthurian bibliography, though mostly literary.] Speculum, 1, pp. 190–216. 1926.

1049 Boeddeker (K.). Die Geschichte des König Arthur, nach eines Chronik des Britischen Museums. [Harl. 24. With M.E. text.] Archiv Stud. neueren Spr., Bd. 52, pp. 1–32. 1874.

1050 Boger (*Mrs*. Charlotte G.). The legend of king Arthur in Somerset. Antiq. Mag., 5, pp. 225–28 : 6, pp. 12–19, 267–69. 1884.

1051 Brodeur (Arthur G.). Arthur, dux bellorum. Univ. Cal., Pubns. in English, 3, pp. 233–83. 1939.

1052 Brown (Arthur Charles Lewis). Arthur's loss of queen and kingdom. Speculum, 15, pp. 3–11. 1940.

1053 Bruce (James Douglas). The evolution of Arthurian romance from the beginnings down to the year 1300. 2nd edition. *Hesperia, Ergänzungsreihe*, 8–9. 2 vol. 8° Göttingen, 1928. [Vol. 1, pp. 3–36, early traditions concerning Arthur in the chronicles and elsewhere : vol. 2, pp. 45–50, date of the battle of Badon hill.]

1054 Chambers (*Sir* Edmund Kerchever). Arthur of Britain. pp. vii, 299. 8° London, 1927. [i. Early tradition : ii. Geoffrey of Monmouth : iii. Sources of Geoffrey : iv. Acceptance of Arthur : v. Arthur and the round table : vi. Historicity of Arthur : vii. Arthur and mythology : Records (in Latin) : Bibliography.]

1055 Clarke (John Randall). King Arthur : his relation to history and fiction. A lecture. pp. 36. 8° Gloucester, [1880 ?].

1056 Colfi (B.). Di una recente interpretazione data alla sculture dell' archivolto nella porta settentrionale del duomo di Modena. Atti e mem. Deput. storia patria provincie modenesi, ser. 4, 9. 1899.

1057 Cooksey (Charles Frederick). Who was king Arthur ? pp. 54. 8°. Southampton, 1910.

1058 Cornish (J. B.). King Arthur's castle. [But not Tintagel.] J. Roy. Inst. Cornwall, 21, pp. 280–84. 1924.

1059 Crawford (Osbert Guy Stanhope). Arthur and his battles. Antiquity, 9, pp. 277–91, + map and 2 plates. 1935.

1060 —— King Arthur's last battle [Mons Badonicus]. [?Date.] Antiquity, 5, pp. 236–39. 1931.

1061 De Montmorency (James Edward Geoffrey). Who was king Arthur? [Roman origin.] Contemp. Rev., 92, pp. 651–58. 1907.

1062 Dempe (A.). Beda und die Entstehung der Artursaga. Zeit. deut. Geistesgesch., 1, pp. 304–10. 1936.

1063 Dickinson (L. J.). The story of king Arthur in Cornwall : to which is appended an account of the historical king Arthur, compiled from ancient and modern writers. 4th edition. pp. 31. 8° Tintagel, 1933.

1064 Dickinson (William Howship). King Arthur in Cornwall. pp. xii, 86. 8° London, 1900. [Traditions and history bearing upon the life of Arthur : Arthur's last battle : the doubts which surround his place of burial : topographical associations.]

1065 Eyre-Todd (George). The real king Arthur. History *versus* romance. Scotia (St. Andrew Soc.), 2, pp. 12–20, 89–92. 1908.

1066 Faral (Edmond). L'abbaye de Glastonbury et la légende du roi Arthur. Rev. hist., 160, pp. 1–49. 1929.

1067 Fletcher (Robert Huntington). The Arthurian material in the Chronicles, especially those of Great Britain and France. Harvard Stud. and Notes in Philol. and Lit., 10, pp. x, 313. 1906.

1068 Foerster (W.). Ein neues Artusdocument. [Modena.] Zeit. roman. Philol., 22, pp. 243–48, 526–29. 1898.

1069 Gardner (John Edmund Garratt). The Arthurian legend in Italian literature. pp. xiv, 349, + 16 plates. 8° London, 1930. [Pp. 4–6, + plates 2 and 3, Arthurian sculpture at Modena, c. 1100.]

1070 Godsal (Philip Thomas). Mons Badonicus : the battle of Bath. pp. 6. 8° Bath, 1914.

1071 Gourlay (W. R.). Notes of an informal talk given at Merlin's grave. [Argument for Strathclyde as scene of Arthur's battles, and myth of last days of Merlin after battle of Arterid in 573.] Trans. Dumfries. Antiq. Soc., 3rd S. 18 (1931–33), pp. 391–96. 1934.

1072 Hamel (Anton Gerard van). Koning Arthur's vader. Neophilol., 12, pp. 84–41. 1927.

1073 Hardwick (Charles). Ancient Lancashire battle-fields. 1. King Arthur's presumed victories. Papers Manchester Lit. Club, 2, pp. 151–53. 1876.

1074 Hopkins (Annette Brown). Ritson's Life of king Arthur. P.M.L.A., 43, pp. 251–87. 1928.

1075 Howard (F. T.). The geographical background to Welsh Arthurian stories. [i. Identification of Arthur : ii. Early references to Arthur : iii. Identification of Arthur with Alfred the Great : iv. Battle of Guinnion : v. Battle of Trat Treucoit : vi. Meaning of the name and title of Arthur : vii. Avallon : viii. Gelliwic : ix. Cavall the dog and the Twrch Trwyth : x. Hunt of the boar Trwyth : xi. Cahal : xii. Llyn Uiwan : xiii. Ancient style of story-telling in Wales.] Cardiff Nat. Soc., Rpt. and Trans., 51 (1918), pp. 20–47. 1920.

1076 Jackson (Kenneth). Once again Arthur's battles. [A review of what has been written, and ' to define the problems for future research '.] Mod. Phil., 43, pp. 44–57. 1945.

1077 Jenner (Henry). The Arthurian sculptures on the Porta della Pescheria of Modena cathedral. [Evidence of Arthurian names in Italy in late 11th c.] J. Roy. Inst. Cornwall, 22, pp. 77–92, + 1 plate. 1926.

1078 Johnstone (P. K.). Caw of Pictland. [Father of St. Gildas and father-in-law of ' Sir Modred '.] Antiquity, 12, pp. 340–41. 1938.

1079 —— The date of Camlann. [Annales Cambriae, 537.] Antiquity, 24, p. 44. 1950.

1080 Johnstone (P. K.) Domangart and Arthur. [King of Dalriada, c. 506–11.] Antiquity, 22, pp. 45–46. 1948.

1081 —— Mons Badonicus and Cerdic of Wessex. Antiquity, 13, pp. 92–96. 1939.

1082 Jones (William Lewis). King Arthur in history and legend. *Cambridge manuals of science and literature.* pp. viii, 145. 8° London 1911.

1083 Kerr (John Edward), *jr.* The character of Marc in myth and legend. Mod. Lang. Notes, 9, col. 30–40. 1894.

1084 Lloyd (*Sir* John Edward). The death of Arthur. Bull. Board Celt. Stud., 11, pp. 158–60. 1944.

1085 Loomis (Roger Sherman). The story of the Modena archivolt and its mythological roots. Romanic Rev., 15, pp. 266–84. 1924.

1086 —— The Arthurian legend before 1139. [Links between romance and history.] Romanic Rev., 32, pp. 3–38. 1941.

1087 —— The Modena sculpture and Arthurian romance. Studi medievali, N.S. 9, pp. 1–17, + 4 plates. 1936.

1088 Loth (Joseph). L'historicité d'Arthur d'après un travail récent. Rev. celt., 42, pp. 306–19. 1925.

1089 —— L'origine de la légende d'Arthur fils d'Uther Pendragon. Rev. celt., 49, pp. 132–49. 1932.

1090 —— Le roi Loth des romans de la Table Ronde. Rev. celt., 16, pp. 84–88. 1895.

1091 Malone (Kemp). Artorius. [Was L. Artorius Castor the historical prototype of Arthur ? 2nd century A.D. Praefectus at York and dux against rebellion in Armorica.] Mod. Philol., 22, pp. 367–74. 1925.

1092 —— The historicity of Arthur. J. Engl. and Germ. Phil., 23, pp. 463–91. 1924.

1093 Newell (William Wells). Arthurian notes. [ii. Gawain : ?king of Galloway.] Mod. Lang. Notes, 17, col. 277–78. 1902.

1094 Nicholson (Edward Williams Byron). Mons Badonicus and Geoffrey of Monmouth. Academy, 49, pp. 305–07. 1896.

1095 —— King Arthur in Gildas. Academy, 48, pp. 297–98. 1895.

1096 Nitze (William Albert). Bédier's epic theory and the Arthuriana of Nennius. Mod. Philol., 39, pp. 1–14. 1941.

1097 Robinson (Joseph Armitage). King Arthur and Cadbury castle. N. and Q. for Som. and Dorset, 17, pp. 85–86. 1921.

1098 —— Two Glastonbury legends : king Arthur and St. Joseph of Arimathea. pp. xi, 68, + 6 plates. 8° Cambridge, 1926. [Pp. 1–27, King Arthur : i. The early Glastonbury tradition : ii. The appropriation of the story.]

1099 Scott-Gatty (A. S.). King Arthur. [His genealogy. Identity of Uther and Ambrosius, and of Constantine the Blessed and Constantine the Usurper. *See also* 19, pp. 18–22, king Arthur, a criticism, by W.H.B.B. : *also* A rejoinder, pp. 170–73.] Genealogist, N.S. 18, pp. 209–16 : 19, pp. 73–82. 1902–03.

1100 Shore (Thomas William). King Arthur and the round table at Winchester. [The historical Arthur and his associations with Glastonbury, Silchester and Winchester.] Papers and Proc. Hants. F.C., 4 (1898–1903), pp. 187–204, + 1 plate. 1905.

1101 Thurneysen (Rudolf). Zum Geburtsjahr des Gildas. Zeit. celt. Philol., 14, pp. 13–15. 1923.

1102 White (Jon Manchip). Tristan and Isolt. [?historical basis.] History to-day, 3, pp. 233–39. 1953.

15. RISE OF THE TRIBAL KINGDOMS (c. 600–c. 800)

§ *a*. General (Anglo-Saxon)

1103 Alexander (John James). Ethelbald of Mercia [716–57]. Devon and Cornwall N. and Q., 19, 358–61 ; 20, pp. 43–44. 1937–38.

1104 Bates (Cadwallader John). Winwedfield : the overthrow of English paganism. [655.] Archaeol. Æl., N.S. 19, pp. 182–91. 1898.

1105 Bell (Alexander). Cynewulf and Cyneheard in Gaimar. Mod. Lang. Rev., 10, pp. 42–46. 1915.

1106 —— The fictitious battle of Portsmouth in Gaimar. [Expanded from A.-S.C. under 779.] Mod. Lang. Rev., 15, pp. 422–25. 1920.

1107 Boger (*Mrs*. Charlotte G.). King Ina in Somerset. ['Ina and Aldhelm, A.D. 688–728.'] Walford's Antiquarian, 8, pp. 256–60 : 9, pp. 21–26. 1885–86.

1108 Bond (George). Links between *Beowulf* and Mercian history. [i. Connections between names : ii. Similarity between situations involving Mercian kings and those in the poem : iii. Political implications in the poem fitting Mercian circumstances.] Stud. in philol., 40, pp. 481–93. 1943.

1109 Brandl (Alois). The Beowulf epic and the crisis in the Mercian dynasty about the year A.D. 700. [German version *in* Forschungen und Fortschritte, 12, pp. 165–68, 1936.] Research and progress, 2, pp. 195–203. 1936.

1110 —— Zu den angeblichen Schreiben des altmercischen König Æþelweald [ruled 716–57] an Aldhelm (+ 709). [Disagrees with Ehwald for including these works in his Aldhelm-Ausgabe, **3912**, as genuine works of Æþelweald.] Archiv Stud. neueren Spr., Bd. 171, p. 70. 1937.

1111 Cockayne (Oswald), *etc*. Death of king Oswald. [Winwic, Lancs. Relics. (Nothing new).] N. and Q., 4th S. 11, pp. 397–98 : 12, pp. 56, 117–18. 1873.

1112 Cooper (A. N.). Alfred, king of Northumbria. [Aldfrith.] Trans. East Riding Antiq. Soc., 3, pp. 17–20. 1895.

1113 Dawkins (*Sir* William Boyd). On the date of the conquest of south Lancashire by the English. [After battle of Chester, 607.] Arch. Camb., 4th S. 4, pp. 236–39. 1873.

1114 Dickins (Bruce). Queen Cynethryth of Mercia. Proc. Leeds Phil. and Lit. Soc., 4, p. 54. 1936.

1115 Foster (J. T.). Aldfrid, king of Northumbria. [Query re tablet, dated 705, in Little Driffield church. Answer, by W. C. Wade, *q.v.* **1142.**] Antiquary, 3, p. 191. 1881.

1116 Freeman (Edward Augustus). King Ine. Proc. Somerset Arch. Soc., 18 (1872), pp. 1–59 : 20 (1874), pp. 1–57. 1874–75.

1117 Hammer (Jacob). An unrecorded epitaphium Ceadwallae, [regis Saxonum]. Speculum, 6, pp. 607–08. 1931.

1118 Hardwick (Charles). Ancient Lancashire battle-fields. 2. The defeat of St. Oswald at Maserfelt. [Near Winwick.] Papers Manchester Lit. Club, 2, pp. 153–55. 1876.

1119 —— [Ancient Lancashire battle-fields, 3.] Battles near Whalley and Clitheroe. [A.-S. C., 796 (Hwelleage, = Whalley).] *Same jnl.*, 3, pp. 53–64, + plan. 1877.

1120 Harrison (P. Walton). King Ethelbert's [of E. Anglia] fatal courtship. Antiquary, 46, pp. 334–37. 1910.

121 Heinsch (Joseph). Die Reiche der Angelsachsen zur Zeit Karls des Grossen. pp. 105. 8° Breslau, 1875. [Gross, 1512. ' Deals mainly with Mercia and Northumbria in the 8th c.']

1122 Holderness (Thomas). The funeral of king Alfred [i.e. Aldfrith of Northumbria], at Driffield. Anno 705. pp. 20. 8° Driffield, 1878.

1123 Kern (J. H.). Zur angelsächsischen Chronik. [Cynewulf-Cyneheard episode.] P.B.B., 16, pp. 553–54. 1892.

1124 Kerslake (Thomas). Bindon hill, or the Swines-back. [Re battle there ? in 614, between Britons and A.-S. under Cynegils and Cwichelm.] Proc. Dorset Antiq. F.C., 4, pp. 53–55. [1882.]

1125 —— Vestiges of the supremacy of Mercia in the south of England, during the eighth century. Trans. Bristol and Glos. Arch. Soc., 3, pp. 106–67. 1878.

1126 Leadman (Alexander D. H.). The battles of Heathfield and Winwæd. [633, 655.] Yorks. Archaeol. J., 11, pp. 139–43. 1891.

1127 Levison (Wilhelm). England and the Continent in the eighth century. *Ford Lectures*, 1943. pp. xii, 347. 8° Oxford, 1946.

1128 MacKenzie (Henry), *bp. of Nottingham*. Essay on the life and institutions of Offa, king of Mercia, A.D. 755–794. pp. 36. 8° London. 1840.

1129 Mackinlay (James Murray). Celtic relations of St. Oswald of Northumbria. Celt. Rev., 5, pp. 304–09. 1909.

1130 Magoun (Francis Peabody), *jr.* Cynewulf, Cyneheard, and Osric. Anglia, 57 (N.F. 45), pp. 361–76. 1933.

1131 Marshall (Edward). King Oswy. [Dedication of daughter, etc., after victory of 655 over Penda.] N. and Q., 5th S. 11, p. 354. 1879.

1132 Mathews (—), *canon of Lincoln*. The battle of Hatfield [633] and royal hunting lodge. Assoc. Archit. Socs'. Repts., 31, pp. 369–74. 1912.

1133 Mills (Joseph Travis). The great days of Northumbria ; three lectures. pp. vii, 214, + map. 8° London, 1911.

1133a Moorman (Charles). The A.-S. Chronicle for 755. [Sigeberht, Cynewulf and Cyneheard. *See also* pp. 225, 316 (Cumbra).] N. and Q., 199, pp. 94–98. 1954.

1134 Murray (*Sir* James Augustus Henry). Kinborough as a female Christian name. [Kyneburh, dau. of Penda : married (653) to Alchfrid of Northumbria.] N. and Q., 9th S. 9, pp. 30, 156. 1902.

1135 Radford (W. Locke). The tithing and rectory of Hilcombe [Somerset]. [i. ? the ' sea ' (in A.-S. C.) to which Kenwalch drove the Britons after battle of the Pens (Paonna), 688. ii. Saxon church at Hilcombe.] N. and Q., 191, pp. 134–37. 1946. *Same title*, N. and Q. Som. and Dorset, 25, pp. 31–35. 1947.

1136 Roberts (Askew). Where did king Oswald die ? [Citing Howel W. Lloyd who advocated Oswestry and Oswald Cockayne who advocated Winwick.] Trans. Shrop. Arch. Soc., 2, pp. 97–140. 1879.

1137 Rose-Troup (Frances) and **Alexander** (John James). Cynewulf and Cyneheard. [Cyneheard buried at Axminster, etc.] Devon and Cornwall N. and Q., 17, pp. 216–18, 274–78. 1933.

1138 Savage (Henry Edwin), *dean of Lichfield*. Northumbria in the eighth century. [General history : monasteries : court : popular manners and customs.] Archaeol. Æl., 21, pp. 259–80. 1899.

1139 Shore (Thomas William). An early Anglo-Saxon migration from east Sussex to the vale of Taunton. [Temp. Ine.] Antiquary, 41, pp. 251–54. 1905.

1140 Stenton (*Sir* Frank Merry). The supremacy of the Mercian kings. E.H.R., 33, pp. 433–52. 1918.

1141 Taylor (Charles Samuel). Gloucestershire in the eighth century. Trans. Bristol and Glos. Arch. Soc., 16, pp. 208–30. 1892.

1142 Wade (W. C.). Alfred [i.e. Aldfrith], king of Northumbria. [Answer to a query by J. T. Foster, *q.v.* **1115.**] Antiquary, 4, p. 228. 1881.

1143 Wainwright (Frederick Threlfall). Nechtanesmere. [Sources for history of the battle. Draining of Dunnichar loch (=Nechtanesmere) in c. 1760–1818 for peat : restored by floods in winter of 1946–47.] Antiquity, 22, pp. 82–97. 1948.

1144 Walker (John William). The battle of Winwaed, A.D. 655. [Also synopsis of events preceding it.] Yorks. Archaeol. J., 36, pp. 394–408, + map. 1947.

1145 Ward (Gordon). King Oswin— a forgotten ruler of Kent. [673–74]. Arch. Cant., 50, pp. 60–65. 1939.

1146 —— The life and records of Eadberht, son of king Wihtred. [c. 690– 768.] Arch. Cant., 51, pp. 9–26. 1940.

1147 —— The usurpation of king Sweabheard [of Kent, 675–76]. Arch. Cant., 50, pp. 66–71. 1939.

1148 Williams (*Sir* Ifor). A reference to the Nennian Bellum Cocboy. [' Bede gives Maserfelth as the English name of the place where Oswald of Northumbria fell . . . the Bellum Cocboy of Nennius and the Annales Cambriae.'] Bull. Bd. Celtic Stud., 3, pp. 59–62. 1927.

1149 Wrenn (Charles Leslie). A saga of the Anglo-Saxons. [Cynewulf and Cyneheard episode, 755.] History, N.S., 25, pp. 208–15. 1940.

§ *b*. Sutton Hoo

(**Historical Aspects.** *See also* in index).

1150 Chadwick (Hector Munro). The Sutton Hoo ship-burial. 8. Who was He ? Antiquity, 14, pp. 76–87. 1940.

1151 Crawford (Osbert Guy Stanhope). Sutton Hoo ? a summary. [A king's burial. ? pagan or Christian— ? Anna or Aethelhere. The Swedish connection : 7th c. boat-burial only in E. Anglia and Uppland-chequered inlays of millefiori enamel not continental, but ? presence of ancient Swedish sword and helmets.] Antiquity, 26, pp. 4–8. 1952.

1152 Lantier (Raymond). La tombe royale de Sutton Hoo. [7 figures in text.] Revue archéol., 6e série, 17, pp. 46–57. 1941.

1153 Lindqvist (Sune). Sutton Hoo and Beowulf. Translated by R. L. S. Bruce-Mitford [from next entry]. [Legal title to the find decided by help of passages from Beowulf. Not necessarily a cenotaph as assumed by Bruce-Mitford. Probably of Christian Æthelwald rather than of (?pagan) Æthelhere.] Antiquity, 22, pp. 131–40. 1948.

1153a —— Sutton Hoo och Beowulf. [?Swedish shield and helmet (500–600) mural decorations of a hall before burial, and practice of boat-burial contemporary with them. ?8th c., author of Beowulf cognizant of Sutton Hoo burial from his accurate description of Scyld's pagan boat-burial. ?Beowulf written for an Anglian family, e.g. Uffingas of E. Anglia, originating from Uppland.] Fornvännen, 43, pp. 94–110. 1948.

1154 Nerman (Birger). Sutton Hoo —en svensk kunga-eller hövdinggrav? [26 figures in text. Short account of excavation and finds. Arrangement of grave-goods implies the presence of a body. ?Swedish king or chieftain from weapons, and not Æthelhere of E. Anglia. Coins show 650–670 as date. ?Ivar Vidfamne who conquered part of England (but? Northumbria, not E. Anglia). Pp. 82–93, English summary.] Fornvännen, 43, pp. 65–93. 1948.

1155 Walker (John William). The battle of Winwaed and the Sutton Hoo ship burial. [Argument that Sutton Hoo was a cenotaph to Æthelhere, king of East Anglia, who was slain at Winwaed (?body carried away by the stream), 655.] Yorks. Archaeol. J., 37. pp. 99–104. 1948.

1156 Ward (Gordon). The silver spoons from Sutton Hoo. [6th c., inscribed Saul and Paul in Greek letters. The presence of these—and other arguments—points to Redwald (died c. 625). Standard copied by Edwin who had been at Redwald's court.] Antiquity, 26, pp. 9–13. 1952.

§ *c.* **Celtic** (c. 600–c. 800)

1157 Bartrum (P. C.). Noë, king of Powys. Y Cymmrodor, 43, pp. 53–61. 1932.

1158 Clowston (Joseph Storer). A fresh view of the settlement of Orkney. Proc. Orkney Antiq. Soc., 9 (1930–31), pp. 35–40. 1931.

1159 Dillon (Myles). The wooing of Becfhola and the stories of Cano, son of Gartnán. [Two sagas of the cycle of Diarmait, son of Áed Slaine, and Guaire Aidne, of 7th c.] Mod. Philol., 43, pp. 11–17. 1945.

1160 Dobbs (Margaret E.). The battle of Corann. [Co. Sligo. 701 F.M., or 702 A.U. Between Loingsech, highking and Cellach, king of Connaught.] J. Galway Archaeol. Soc., 23, pp. 154–58. 1949.

1161 Knox (Hubert Thomas). King Guaire [of Aidhne] and bishop Cellach. [Confusion of identities : Guaire did not murder the bishop.] *Same jnl.*, 2, pp. 34–38. 1902.

1162 O'Brien (M. A.). A wrong entry in A.U. and F.M. [A.U. 603, F.M. 600 : Cuu cen mathair mortui sunt : ?read Conchenn (dog-head) a mathair.] Études celt., 3, pp. 365–66. 1938.

1163 Smith (Archibald). Argyllshire invaded, but not subdued, by Ungus, king of the Picts, in the years 736 and 741. Proc. Soc. Antiq. Scot., 7, pp. 412–22. 1870.

1164 Stokes (Whitley), *ed.* The Battle of Allen. [Irish text and English translation. 718, battle at hill of Almain [=Allen], 5 miles north of Kildare, in which Fergal, overking of Ireland, was defeated by Dunchad, king of Leinster.] Rev. celt., 24, pp. 41–70. 1903.

1165 Stokes (Whitley). The battle of Carn Conaill. [645, won by Diarmait, son of Aed Sláne, over Guare, king of Aidne in Connaught. Irish text and English translation from the Book of the Dun Cow.] Zeit. celt. Phil., 3, pp. 203–19. 1901.

16. NINTH CENTURY
§ *a.* General

1166 Amyot (Thomas). An inquiry concerning the kings of the East Angles, from the murder of Ethelbert in 792, to the accession of Edmund the Martyr in 855. Archaeologia, 19, pp. 302–07. 1821.

1167 Bell (Alexander). Buern Bucecarle in ' Gaimar '. [Cf. A.-S. C. under 867 : battle of York. Osbriht, king of Northumbria deposed owing to wrong to wife of his subject, Buern Bucecarle. Story treated by Gaimar.] Mod. Lang. Rev., 27, pp. 168–74. 1932.

1168 Blair (Peter Hunter). Olaf the White and the Three fragments of Irish annals. [Amhlaeibh, ' son of the king of Lochlann '. First arrived in Ireland, 853.] Viking, 3, pp. 1–35. 1939.

1168a Burne (Alfred H.). The battle of Ashdown. [' Fought under the lee of Lowbury hill.'] Trans. Newbury F.C., 10, pp. 71–85. 1953.

1169 Clarke (W. Nelson). The battle of Ashdown, A.D. 871. Archaeol. J., 9, pp. 320–28. 1852.

1170 Ditchfield (Peter Hampson) and **Gardiner** (E. R.). The battle of Æscendune. Q. J. Berks. Archaeol. Soc., 1, pp. 145–48. 1890.

1171 Fletcher (James Michael John). The tomb of king Ethelred [I] in Wimborne minster. [Sketch of reign, etc.] Proc. Dorset Antiq. F.C., 40 (1918–19), pp. 24–34. 1920.

1172 Haigh (Daniel Henry). On runic inscriptions discovered at Thornhill, [Yorks.]. [Concerning king Osberht: see A.-S. C. under 867.] Yorks. Archaeol. J., 4, pp. 418–55, + 4 plates. 1877.

1173 Loomis (Grant). Growth of the Saint Edmund legend. Harvard Stud. and Notes in Phil. and Lit., 14, pp. 83–113. 1932.

1174 —— Saint Edmund and the Lodbrok (Lothbroc) legend. [What are stories told concerning the coming of the Danes ? Where did they originate ? Who was Ragnar Lodbrok ? Who were his sons ? What did actually take place in E. Anglia ?] Harvard Stud. and Notes in Phil. and Lit., 15, pp. 1–23, 1933.

1175 Marstrander (Carl Johan Sverstrup). Det norske landnåm på Man. (The Norwegian conquest of the Isle of Man). With summary in English [pp. 333–55.] Norsk Tidskr. Sprogvid., 6, pp. 40–386, + 2 maps. 1932.

1176 Mawer (Sir Allen). Ragnar Lothbrók and his sons. Saga-Book V.C., 6, pp. 68–89. 1909.

1177 —— The Scandinavian kingdom of Northumbria. Same jnl., 7, pp. 38–64. 1911.

1179 Parker (James). The battle of Ashdown, A.D. 871. Proc. Oxford Archit. and Hist. Soc., N.S. 2, pp. 315–22. 1871.

1180 —— Cuckhamsley hill, Æcesdun and the battle of Ashdown. Trans. Newbury F.C., 3 (1875–86), pp. 65–72. 1886.

1181 Pauli (Reinhold). Karl der Grosse in northumbrischen Annalen. [Gross, 1376 note.] Forschungen zur deutschen Geschichte, 12, pp. 137–66. 1872.

1182 Plenderleath (William Charles). The white horses of the west of England. pp. 41. 8° Bristol, 1885. [Uffington horse.]

1183 Rhys (Sir John). Note on Guriat. [? 9th c. name of Welsh prince connected with Isle of Man.] Zeit. celt. Phil., 1, pp. 52–53. 1897.

1184 Schuette (Gudmund). Offa I reduced ad absurdum. [A criticism of 671.] Acta philol. Scand., 19, pp. 179–96. 1947.

1185 Simcox (William Henry). The house of Ethelwulf. E.H.R., 2, pp. 520–25. 1887.

1186 Smith (Albert Hugh). The sons of Ragnar Lothbrok. Saga-Book V.C., 11 (1928–36), pp. 173–91. 1935.

1187 Sproemberg (H.). Judith, Koenigin von England, Graefin von Flandern. Revue belge de Philol, 15, pp. 397–428, 915–50. 1936.

1188 Taylor (Charles Samuel). The Danes in Gloucestershire. [Political; mostly 9th c.] Trans. Bristol and Glos. Arch. Soc., 17, pp. 68–95. 1893.

1189 Thorkelin (Grímr Jónsson). Fragments of English and Irish history in the ninth and tenth centuries. *Bibliotheca Topographica Britannica* [ed. J. Nichols], vol. 6. 2 pt. 4° London, 1788.

1190 Thorogood (A. Jean). The Anglo-Saxon Chronicle in the reign of Ecgberht. E.H.R., 48, pp. 353–63. 1933.

1191 Vigfusson (Gudbrand). Picts and Caledones in the ninth century. E.H.R., 1, pp. 509–13. 1886.

1192 Wilson (J.). The battle of Aescesdun. Trans. Newbury F.C., 1 (1870–71), pp. 158–77. 1871.

1192a Wise (Francis). A letter (Further observations) . . . concerning . . . the White horse . . . made in memory of a great victory obtained over the Danes, A.D. 871. 4° Oxford, 1738.

§ *b*. **Reign of Alfred** (871–99)

1193 [Anon.] The Alfred literature and commemoration. Church Q. Rev., 53, pp. 139–60. 1901.

1194 Abbott (Jacob). The history of Alfred the Great. pp. 184. 8° London, 1853. [Popular.]

1195 Abbott (Wilbur Cortez). Hasting. [Hæsten, Viking chief v. Alfred, c. 840–c. 910.] E.H.R., 13, pp. 439–63. 1898.

1196 Alfred, *king.* Whole works of king Alfred the Great, with preliminary essays illustrative of the history, arts, and manners of the ninth century. *Alfred Committee.* 3 vol. 8° Oxford, 1852–53. — Reprinted. 8° London, 1858. [Gross, 1537. i, pp. 255–325, T. Forester, The age of Alfred : i, pp. 337–78, C. Hook, The Danes : i, pp. 493–542, T. Forester, Traces of Danes in England.]

1197 Bayley (Arthur R.). Alfritha, daughter of Alfred the Great. N. and Q., 173, pp. 49–50. 1937.

1198 Besant (*Sir* Walter). Alfred. (Lecture on king Alfred, at the Guildhall, Winchester). 3rd edition. pp. 60. 8° London, 1899.

1199 —— The story of king Alfred. pp. 207, + map. 8° London, 1901.

1200 Bicknell (Alexander). The life of Alfred the Great. pp. xv, 404. 8° London, 1777.

1201 Boger (*Mrs*. Charlotte G.). King Alfred : [?his eldest brother] Athelstan or [i.e. ?=] St. Neot : Osburga and Judith. N. and Q., 9th S. 1, pp. 801–02. 1898.

1202 —— King Alfred in Somerset and the legend of St. Neot. Antiq. Mag., 7, pp. 14–21, 58–63, 118–21. 1885.

1203 Bosworth (George Frederick). Alfred the Great. His life and times . . . with maps and illustrations, and an introduction by F. S. Marvin. pp. xvi, 200. 8° London, 1901. [Gross, 1532a. ' Popular '.]

1204 Bowker (Alfred), *ed.* Alfred the Great : containing chapters on his life and times by Frederic Harrison, Charles Oman, Sir Clements Markham, John Earle, Sir Frederick Pollock, and W. J. Loftie. 8° London, 1899. [Gross, 1520.]

1205 —— The king Alfred millenary. A record of the proceedings of the national commemoration. [At Winchester, Sept. 18–20, 1901.] pp. xvii, 212, + plates. 8° London, 1902. [Gross, 1532a, note.]

1206 Browne (George Forrest), *bp. of Bristol.* King Alfred's books. pp. xxxii, 390. 8° London, 1920.

1207 Bryant (Arthur). King Alfred and the Danes. History to-day, 3, pp. 451–60. 1953.

1208 Burrows (Montagu). King Alfred the Great. pp. 29. 8° London, 1898.

1209 Cashmore (Herbert Maurice). ' King Alfred and Ilmington.' [5 scholars he collected round him.] N. and Q., 158, p. 359. 1930.

1210 Chope (Richard Pearse). King Alfred and Devonshire. Devon N. and Q., 2, pp. 114–17, 178–81. 1902–03.

1211 Clifford (William Joseph Hugh), *bp. of Clifton.* President's address, 1877 [on the isle of Athelney, temp. Alfred]. Proc. Somerset Arch. Soc., 23 (1877), pp. 9–27, + folding map. 1878.

1212 Conybeare (John William Edward). Alfred in the chroniclers. 2nd edition. pp. 284, + map. 8° London, 1914. [Gross, 1532a. Introduction, extracts.]

1213 Draper (Warwick Herbert). Alfred the Great : a sketch and seven studies. 2nd edition, revised. pp. xv, 144. 8° London, 1901. [Gross, 1532a, note. ' Unscholarly '.]

1214 —— The burial-place of king Alfred. [With plan of Hyde abbey in 1798.] Antiquary, 35, pp. 299–305. 1899.

1215 Earle (John). The peace of Wedmore, and how it touches the history of the English language. A . . lecture, *etc.* 8° Oxford, 1878.

1216 Engstroem (Charles Robert Lloyd). The millenary of Alfred the Great, warrior and saint, scholar and king. A sermon. pp. 36. 8° London, 1901.

1217 French (John). Alfred the Great and the river Lea. [896. ' The king caused the waters of the Lea to be diverted into three channels that they (the Danes) might not be able to bring out their ships.' At Waltham.] Essex Rev., 20, pp. 121–29. 1911.

1218 Giles (John Allen). The life and times of Alfred the Great. 2nd edition. 8° London, 1854. [Gross, 1525.]

1219 Green (Emanuel). Had king Alfred a palace at Wedmore ? with some notes on the manors of Mudsley and Wedmore. Proc. Bath F. C., 4, pp. 313–44. 1881.

1220 Green (Everard). Alfred the Great. [General sketch.] Downside Rev., 19, pp. 214–20. 1900.

1221 Greswell (William Henry Parr). The sequel to the battle of Edington, A.D. 878. ['Alfred pursued the fugitives to their *geweorc.*'—Asser.? its site.] Proc. Somerset Arch. Soc., 53 (1907), pp. 174–78. 1908.

1222 —— The story of the battle of Edington. pp. iv, 80, + 4 plates, + 4 maps. 8° Taunton, 1910. [Reviewed *in* Antiquary, 46, p. 437, 1910. His criticism of the review on p. 480.]

1223 Hales (John W.). The fame of king Alfred. [Millenary celebration.] Trans. Hampstead Antiq. Soc., 1901, pp. 50–72. 1902.

1224 Haller (Albrecht von), *baron.* Alfred, König der Angel-Sachsen. pp. 212. 8° Carlsruhe, 1779. Life of Alfred the Great, with his maxims, and those of his councillors. [Trans.] with notes and commentaries by Francis Steinitz. pp. xxviii, 344.   8° London, 1849. Alfred, roi des Anglo-Saxons . . . traduit de l'allemand (par C. P.). pp. 232. 8° Lausanne, 1775.

1225 Harrison (Frederic). The writings of king Alfred. An address delivered at Harvard College, Mass. pp. 31. 8° New York, 1901.

1226 Hayward (Frank Herbert). Alfred the Great. *Great lives series*, 62. pp. 141. 8° London, 1936.

1227 Hearnshaw (Fossy John Cobb). Outlines of the life and work of king Alfred the Great. 8° Southampton, 1901.

1228 Hodgkin (John), **Skeat** (Walter William), etc.   Alfred and the cakes. [Sources for story : interpolation in Asser from Latin Life of St. Neot (MS. Cotton Vesp. D. XIV).] N. and Q., 11th S., 1, pp. 211–12, 250–51. 1910.

1229 Horne (Ethelbert), *etc.*   The Ecbright stone.   [? where Alfred gathered his forces before battle of Eddington.] N. and Q. for Som. and Dorset, 23, pp. 220–21, 246–47. 1941.

1230 Howard (Eliot). King Alfred and the Lea. [A.-S. C., 895.] Trans. Essex Archaeol. Soc., N.S. 10, pp. 82–83. 1909.

1231 —— The position of the Danish camp on the Lea. [895 or 896. On Widburg hill, between valleys of the Lea and the Ash.] Essex Rev., 20, pp. 184–186. 1911.

1232 Howard (Henry). Enquiries concerning the tomb of king Alfred, at Hyde abbey, near Winchester. Archaeologia, 13, pp. 309–12, + plan. 1798.

1233 Hughes (Thomas). Alfred the Great. Reprinted. pp. vi, 334, + 3 plates. 8° London, 1901. [Gross, 1532a, note.]

1234 J. (H. T.). The white horse of Westbury. [To commemorate Ethandune, 878?] Wilts. N. and Q., 1, pp. 193–94, + 1 plate. 1894.

1235 Jeffrey (F. B.). A perfect prince [Alfred the Great] ; the story of England a thousand years ago. pp. 144.   8° London, 1901.   [Gross, 1532a, note. ' Popular '.]

1236 Krapp (George Philip). Anglo-Saxon Chronicle, 897. [Question of tides in fight off Isle of Wight.] Mod. Lang. Notes, 19, 232–34. 1904.

1237 Laver (Henry). Mersea [Essex]. [Doings of the Danes there in 894 and 895, and ? remains of their fortress.] Proc. Soc. Antiq., 2nd S. 16, pp. 423–25. 1897.

1238 Lees (Beatrice Adelaide). Alfred the Great . . . 888–99. *Heroes of the Nations.* pp. xv, 493, + 42 plates, + table. 8° New York, 1919.

1239 MacFadyen (Dugald). Alfred the West Saxon king of the English. pp. 388. 8° London, 1901. [Gross, 1532a, note.]

1240 MacKilliam (Annie E.). The story of Alfred the Great. *Heroes of all time.* pp. 191. 8° London, 1914.

1241 McKnight (George Harley). Alfred the Great in popular tradition. Studies . . . in celebration of J. M. Hart, pp. 351–65. 1910.

1242 Magoun (Francis Peabody), *jr.* King Alfred's naval and beach battle with the Danes in 896. Mod. Lang. Rev., 37, pp. 409–14. 1942.

1243 Matcham (George). The battle of Ethandun. (A reply to the strictures of G. P. Scrope [*q.v.*, **1258**].) Wilts. Archaeol. Mag., 4, pp. 175–88 : 5, pp. 255–64. 1858–59.

1244 May (George Lacey). Alfred the Great. *Little books on religion,* 146. pp. 23. 8° London, [1938].

1245 Mead (E. D.). The king Alfred millennial. [Gross, 1532a, note.] Proc. Am. Antiq. Soc., 15, pp. 70–97. 1902.

1246 Mellor (John). The curious particulars relating to king Alfred's death and burial, never before made public. pp. 23. 8° Canterbury, (1871). [Bones ' rescued ' by him from ruins of Hyde abbey, Winchester in 1866.]

1247 Miles (Louis Wardlaw). King Alfred in literature. *Diss., Johns Hopkins.* pp. 130. 8° Baltimore, 1902.

1248 Owen (Thomas Morgan). The battle of Buttington, 894 ; with a brief sketch of the affairs of Powys and Mercia. Collns. hist. and archaeol., rel. to Montgom., 7, pp. 249–66. 1874.

1249 Pauli (Reinhold). König Ælfred und seine Stellung in der Geschichte Englands. pp. x, 331. 8° Berlin, 1851. The life of king Alfred, translated, *etc. Bohn's Antiquarian Library,* pp. lx, 582. 8° London, 1853. [Gross, 1532.]

1250 Plummer (Charles). The life and times of Alfred the Great. *Ford Lectures,* 1901. pp. xii, 232, + map. 8° Oxford, 1902. [Gross, 1532a.]

1251 Pollard (C. J. K.). The campaign of Ethandune, A.D. 877–878. J. Roy. Artillery, 64, pp. 532–38. 1938.

1252 Potter (Simeon). Alfred of Wessex. Wessex, 2, pp. 57–64. 1933.

1253 Powell (Frederick York). The Alfred millenary of 1901. [Gross, 1532a, note.] North Am. Rev., 173, pp. 518–32. 1901.

1254 Reichel (Oswald Joseph). King Alfred and Devonshire. Devon N. and Q., 2, pp. 147–48. 1903.

1255 Rimington (Joseph Cameron). A man of his people . . . A nutshell history of king Alfred. *New Twentieth Century Publications.* pp. 63, + plates. 8° [London, 1939].

1256 Rogers (Inkerman). The invasion of north Devon by Hubba the Dane in the year A.D. 878. Rep. and Trans. Devon. Ass., 80, pp. 119–26, + 4 plates. 1948.

1257 Scott (Mary Monica Constable Maxwell) *Hon. Mrs. Joseph Constable-Maxwell-Scott.* Alfred the Great. *Catholic Truth Society.* pp. 31. 8° London, [1902].

1258 Scrope (G. Poulett). The battle of Ethandun. [*See also* **1243.**] Wilts. Archaeol. Mag., 4, pp.298–308. 1858.

1259 Simcox (William Henry). Alfred's year of battles. E.H.R., 1, pp. 218–34. 1886.

1260 Skrine (H. D.). Ethandune. Proc. Bath F.C., 3, pp. 34–43. 1874.

1261 Smith (Goldwin). Lectures and essays. pp. viii, 336. 8° Toronto, 1881. [Gross, 1533. Pp. 267–85, Alfredus rex fundator.]

1262 Spaul (J. R.). A note on the Anglo-Saxon Chronicle, ann. 897. [Locates sea-fight with Danes in Southampton Water.] N. and Q., 12th S. 10, pp. 187–188. 1922. *Also in* Durham Univ. J., 22, p. 406. 1922.

1263 Spelman (Sir John). The life of Ælfred the Great . . . from the original manuscript in the Bodleian Library : with . . . additions . . . by T. Hearne. pp. 238. 8° Oxford, 1709. [Gross, 1534. Latin translation (Ælfredi Magni vita) by Christopher Wase. pp. 220. fol. Oxonii, 1678.]

1264 Stenton (*Sir* Frank Merry). Æthelwerd's account of the last eight years of king Alfred's reign. E.H.R., 24, pp. 79–84. 1909.

1265 —— The Danes at Thorney Island in 893. E.H.R., 27, pp. 512–13. 1912.

1266 Stevenson (William Henry). Ælthelred-Mucil, Gainorum comes. [Father-in-law to king Alfred (Simeon of Durham). List of 6 occurences of name Mucel. *See also* pp. 157–58.] Academy, 45, pp. 536–37. 1894.

1267 —— The date of king Alfred's death. [Oct., 26, 899. *See also* **439.**] E.H.R., 13, pp. 71–77. 1898.

1268 —— King Alfred's parliament at Shifford [Oxon.]. [More probably at Seaford, Sussex.] N. and Q., 9th S. 4, pp. 344–45. 1899.

1269 Stolberg (Friedrich Leopold zu), *Count.* Leben Alfred des Grosses, Königes in England. . . . 2. Auflage. 12° Münster, 1836.

1270 Stubbs (Charles William), *bp. of Truro.* Alfred the Great, king and patron saint of England. A sermon, *etc.* 8° Winchester, 1901.

1271 Taylor (Charles Samuel). King Alfred and his family in Mercia. Trans. Trans. Bristol and Glos. Arch. Soc., 24, pp. 330–53. 1901.

1272 Thurnam (John). On the barrow at Lanhill near Chippenham, with remarks on the site of, and on the events connected with, the battles of Cynuit and Ethandun, A.D. 878. Wilts. Archaeol. Mag., 3, pp. 67–86, + map. 1857.

1273 Wainwright (Frederick Threlfall). North-west Mercia, A.D. 871–924. Trans. Hist. Soc. Lancs. and Ches., 94 (1942), pp. 3–55. 1943.

1274 Wall (James Charles). Alfred the Great. His abbeys of Hyde, Athelney and Shaftesbury. pp. xiv, 162. 8° London, 1900. [Gross, 1532a, note.]

1275 Whistler (Charles Watts). Ethandune, A.D. 878–King Alfred's campaign from Athelney. Saga-Book V. C., 2, pp. 153–97, + map. 1899.

1276 Williams (W.). King Alfred's remains. [A discovery by John Mellor at Hyde abbey, 1868.] N. and Q., 4th S. 1, pp. 555–56. 1868.

1276a Williams-Freeman (J. P.). A topography of Alfred's wars in Wessex. Papers and Proc. Hants. F.C., 18, pp. 103–18. 1953.

17. TENTH CENTURY

1277 [Anon.] Millenary of Ethelfleda. [Very brief life of her.] Shrop. N. and Q., 3rd S. 2, pp. 31–32. 1912.

1278 Alexander (John James). Athelstan. [Read to Exeter Hist. Assoc.] Devon and Cornwall N. and Q., 13, pp. 203–06. 1925.

1278a —— Athelstan in the west of England. Devonian Y.B., 21, pp. 59–62. 1930.

1279 —— The Athelstan myth. Rept. and Trans. Devon. Assoc., 48, pp. 174–79. 1916.

1280 Angus (W. S.). The annals for the tenth century in Symeon of Durham's Historia regum. Durham Univ. J., 32 (N.S. 1), pp. 213–29. 1940.

1281 Ashdown (Margaret). The attitude of the Anglo-Saxons to their Scandinavian invaders. Saga-Book V.C., 10, pp. 75–99. 1928.

1282 Baring-Gould (Sabin). The battle of Brunanburh. Yorks. Archaeol. J., 22, pp. 16–29. 1913.

1283 —— Eric Bloodaxe in York. *Same jnl.*, 22, pp. 241–52. 1913.

1284 The Battle of Brunanburh. Edited by Alistair Campbell. pp. xvi, 168. 8° London, 1938. [Mainly textual criticism of the poem, but including historical references to the battle and its site.]

1285 The Battle of Maldon. The battle and song of Maldon. [Translated] by Henry J. Rowles. pp. 15. 8° Colchester, [c. 1930]. [Text, with an introduction : site.]

1286 —— (Edited) by Eric V. Gordon. *Methuen's Old English library. A–Poetic texts,* 6. pp. 86, + map. 8° London, 1937.

1287 —— and short poems of the Saxon Chronicle. Edited . . . by W. J. Sedgefield. pp. xxiii, 96. 8° Boston, 1904.

1288 Beaven (Murray Lowthian Randolph). King Edmund I and the Danes of York. E.H.R., 33, pp. 1–9. 1918.

1289 Bell (Alexander). Gaimar and the Edgar–Ælfðryð story. Mod. Lang. Rev., 21, pp. 278–87. 1926.

1290 Beug (Kurt). Die Sage von König Athelstan. Arch. Stud. neueren Spr., Bd. 148, pp. 181–95. 1925.

1291 Brooks (W. M.). The battle of Brunanburgh. Antiquary, 12, pp. 168–71, *also* pp. 230–31. 1885.

1292 Bugge (Alexander). Havelok and Olaf Tryggvason. A contribution towards the further understanding of the Kings' sagas. Saga-Book V.C., 6, pp. 257–95. 1910.

1293 Campbell (Alistair). Two notes on the Norse kingdoms in Northumbria. –1. The Northumbrian kingdom of Rægnald. 2. The end of the kingdom of Northumbria. E.H.R., 57, pp. 85–97. 1942.

1294 Casson (T. E.). Horn Childe and the battle on Stainmoor. [?949–50.] Trans. Cumb. and Westm. Antiq. Soc., N.S. 37, pp. 30–39. 1937.

1295 Cellachan, *king of Cashel.* Caithréim Cellacháin Caisil : the victorious career of Cellachan of Cashel, or the wars between the Irishmen and the Norsemen in the middle of the 10th century. The original Irish text, edited with translation and notes by Alexander Bugge. *Norske Historiske Kildeskriftfond.* pp. xx, 171. 8° Christiania, 1905. [Gross, 1356a. Historical foundation. Cellachan, king of Munster, reigned c. 934–54.]

1296 Clift (J. G. Neilson). The mystery of Corfe. [Murder of Edward the Martyr.] Proc. Dorset Antiq. F.C., 33, pp. 50–69. 1912.

1297 Collingwood (William Gershom). Arthur and Athelstan. [Exploits of Athelstan's reign attributed to Arthur by Geoffrey of Monmouth.] Saga-Book V.C., 10, pp. 132–44. 1928.

1298 —— The battle of Stainmoor in legend and history. [c. 950–54 ?] Trans. Cumb. and Westm. Antiq. Soc., 2, p. 231–41. 1902.

1299 —— King Eirík of York. [i. Icelandic stories of Eirík Blódöx in England : ii. The Danish prince Hring : iii. The story of the times in English Chronicles : iv. Sidelights from legends– Egil, St. Cathroë, Stainmore and the Reycross.] Saga-Book V.C., 2, pp. 313–27. 1901.

1300 Conybeare (John William Edward). The Danes in Cambridgeshire. [Mostly 10th–c.] *Same jnl.*, 4, pp.127–31. 1905.

1301 Cremin (Cornelius). A landmark of time. [A *dallan* or uninscribed pillar stone to commemorate battle in 976 between Brian, king of Munster and the Eugenians : with history of the battle.] J. Cork Hist. Soc., 2nd S. 25, pp. 16–20, + 1 plate. 1919.

1302 Crow (Charles Langley). Malden and Brunnanburh, two Old English songs of battle. *Library of Anglo-Saxon poetry,* 4. pp. xxxvii, 47. 8° Boston, 1897.

1303 Freeman (Edward Augustus). The mythical and romantic elements in early English history. [Legends of drowning of the Ætheling Edwin, son of Edward the Elder ; and of Edgar the Peaceful and Ælfthryth.] Freeman (E. A.) : Historical essays, 3rd ed., series 1, pp. 1–39. (*and* Fort. Rev., May, 1866.) 1875.

1304 Gerould (Gordon Hall). Social and historical reminiscences in the Middle English *Athelstan*. [Sworn brotherhood of the four messengers, and relations between the king and Alryk, abp. of Canterbury.] Engl. Studien, 36, pp. 193–208. 1906.

1305 Goddard (A. R.). The Danish camp on the Ouse, near Bedford [921]. Saga-Book V.C., 3, pp. 326–37, + map. 1904.

1306 Gordon (Eric Valentine). The date of Ælthelred's treaty with the Vikings : Olaf Tryggvason and the battle of Maldon. [994 rather than 991.] Mod. Lang. Rev., 32. pp. 24–32. 1937.

1307 —— The date of Hǫfuðlausn. [? 936. Poem composed by Egill Skallagrimsson in praise of Eric Bloodaxe. Matter *re* Brunanburh.] Proc. Leeds Phil. and Lit. Soc., 1, pp. 12–14. 1925.

1308 Hailstone (E.). Traces of Danish conquest and settlement in Cambridgeshire. [Mostly 10th c.] Saga-Book V.C., 4, pp. 107–26, + map. 1905.

1309 Healy (W.). The battle of Ballaghmoon. [903 (F.M.), 908 (A.U.) between Munster and Leinster. ? site.] J. Waterford Archaeol. Soc., 2, pp. 162–69. 1896.

1310 Hollander (Lee M.). The battle on the Vin-heath [Brunanburh, 937] and the battle of the Huns. [With a ' note on the location of Brunanburh '.] J. Engl. and Germ. Phil., 32, pp. 33–43. 1933.

1311 Howorth (*Sir* Henry Hoyle). Ragnall Ivarson and jarl Otir. E.H.R., 26, pp. 1–19. 1911.

1312 Laborde (Edward Dalrymple). The Battle of Maldon. *Ph-D. Thesis, London.* 1931. [Apply Univ. Library.]

**1313 —— ** *ed.* Byrhtnoth and Maldon. pp. viii, 166, + map. 8° London, 1936. [With text of the poem. Attempt to identify personages in the poem by means of charters, wills, etc.]

1314 Lee (Timothy). The Northmen of Limerick. [Mostly 10th c.] J. Roy. Hist. and Arch. Assoc. Ireland, [19], 4th S. 9, pp. 227–31. 1889.

1315 Lees (Thomas). Something about the Reycross on Stainmore. Trans. Cumb. and Westm. Antiq. Soc., 9, pp. 448–57. 1888.

1316 Liebermann (Felix). Zur Geschichte Byrhtnoths, des Helden von Maldon. [Gross, 1529.] Arch. Stud. neueren Spr., Bd. 101, pp. 15–28. 1898.

1317 Lloyd (Howel William). Llywelyn ab Seisyllt and his times. Arch. Camb., 4th S. 13, pp. 176–96. 1882.

1318 Lloyd (*Sir* John Edward). Hywel Dda : the historical setting. Aberystwyth Stud., 10, pp. 1–4. 1928.

1319 Mawer (*Sir* Allen). The redemption of the Five Boroughs. E.H.R., 38, pp. 551–57. 1923.

1320 Miller (Samuel Henry). Ealdorman Brihtnoth buried at Ely. [991. Note in 4, p. 10 (1898) that his remains are in bp. West's chapel.] Fenland N. and Q., 3, p. 368. 1897.

1321 Moffat (Alexander G.). Palnatoki in Wales. [c. 930–990.] Saga-Book V.C., 3, pp. 163–73. 1903.

1321a Murch (Jerom). President's address, 1876. [' The coronation of king Edgar in Bath Abbey '.] [' The two chief questions to be dealt with are—the reality of the event, and how it came to be at Bath.'] Proc. Somerset Arch. Soc., 22 (1876), pp. 11–28, + frontispiece. 1877.

1322 Neuendorff (B.). Das Gedichte auf den Tod Eadweards des Märtyrers, 979. Arch. Stud. neueren Spr., Bd. 128, pp. 45–54. 1912.

1323 Owen (Thomas Morgan). King Edgar upon the river Dee. [? did 8 kings row him. Evidence.] Arch. Camb., 4th S. 8, pp. 237–39. 1877.

**1324 —— ** Legend or history ? [Refutes legend of Edgar being rowed on the Dee by eight kings.] Antiquary, 1, pp. 213–15. 1880.

1325 Parker (Charles Arundel). The story of Shelagh, Olaf Cuaran's daughter. A saga of the Northmen in Cumberland in the tenth century. pp. viii, 72, + 6 plates, + map. 8° Kendal, 1909.

1326 Poole (Reginald Lane). The Alpine son-in-law of Edward the Elder. (Burgundian notes–1). E.H.R., 26, pp. 310–17. 1911.

1327. Porter (William). The coronation of king Edgar, and the royal progress on the Dee. [Being a translation of vol. 3, chapter 7 of Johannes C. H. R. Steenstrup's Normannerne.] Walford's Antiquarian, 10, pp. 161–67. 1886.

1328 Ryan (John). The historical content of the ' Caithréim Ceallacháin Chaisil '. [Ceallachán, king of Cashel, 10th c.] J. Roy. Soc. Antiq. Ireland, 71 (7th S. 11), pp. 89–100. 1941.

1329 Stevenson (William Henry). The great commendation to king Edgar in 993. E.H.R., 13, pp. 505–7. 1898.

1330 Storm (Gustav). Havelok the Dane and the Norse king Olaf Kuaran. [Researches on the historical matter of the tradition. Havelok equated with Olaf Sihtricson, king of York and Welsh Abloc.] Engl. Studien, 3, pp. 533–35. 1880.

1331 Wainwright (Frederick Threlfall). The battles at Corbridge. [913/5, 918.] Saga-Bk. Viking Soc., 13, pp. 156–73. 1950.

1332 **Wainwright** (Frederick Threlfall). Ingimund's invasion. (Appendix: the story of Ingimund from Fragmenta tria annalium Hiberniae, fo. 33a–fo. 34b, Bibliothèque Royale, Brussels, MS. 5301–5320). [Norse settlement of Wirral from Ireland, 902, and attack on Chester, 907: with place-name evidence.] E.H.R., 63, pp. 145–69. 1948.

1333 —— The submission to Edward the Elder. [A.-S.C., A, sub anno 924 (=920). Scots and the north ' chose Edward for father and lord ' as strongest power against Norsemen. Their peaceful immigration into north as well as conquest.] History, N.S. 37, pp. 114–30. 1952.

1334 **Whistler** (Charles Watts). Brunanburh and Vinheith in Ingulf's chronicle and Egil's saga. Saga-Book V.C., 6, pp. 59–67. 1909.

1335 **Williams** (John). Observations on a passage in the Saxon Chronicle. [993. ' This year came Anlaff [i.e. Olaf Tryggvason] with 93 ships to Staines, which he plundered without, and went thence to Sandwich.'] Proc. Soc. Antiq., 4, pp. 261–64. 1859.

1336 **Woodruff** (Charles Eveleigh). The picture of queen Ediva [Eadgifu] in Canterbury cathedral. [Pp. 8–14, historical notice of Eadgifu, wife of Edward the Elder.] Arch. Cant., 36, pp. 1–14, + plate. 1923.

18. ELEVENTH CENTURY
(1000–1087)
§ a. General to 1066 (Anglo-Saxon)

1337 **Arnold** (Frederick H.). Fact and legend concerning Harold [II]. Sussex Archaeol. Collns., 19, pp. 71–82, + 1 plate. 1867.

1338 —— The nine months of Harold's reign. J. Brit. Archaeol. Assoc., 23, pp. 157–67. 1867.

1339 **Baring** (Hon. Francis Henry). Oxfordshire traces of the northern insurgents of 1065. E.H.R., 13, pp. 295–97. 1898.

1340 **Barkly** (Sir Henry). The earlier house of Berkeley. [Pp. 194–96, Roger de Berkeley (1), temp. Edward the Confessor.] Trans. Bristol and Glos. Arch. Soc., 8, pp. 193–223. 1884.

1341 **Bayley** (Arthur R.). Edward the Confessor and his Normans. N. and Q., 178, pp. 135–39. 1940.

1342 **Beltz** (G. F.). Observations on the coffin-plate and history of Gunilda, sister of the Saxon king Harold II. Archaeologia, 25, pp. 398–410, + 1 plate. 1834.

1343 **Boivin-Champeaux** (Louis). La reine Emma. pp. 39. 8° Rouen, 1885. [Gross, 1523.]

1344 **Boyle** (John Roberts). Who was Eddeva ? [Plea for identification of Ethitha Pulcra of Domesday with Edith Swanneck.] Trans. East Riding Antiq. Soc., 4, pp. 11–12. 1896.

1345 **Bryant** (Arthur). The end of the Saxon kingdom. [10th–11th c.] History today, 3, pp. 521–34. 1953.

1346 **Burrows** (John William). Where was the battle of Assandune fought ? [History of the campaign, 1016.] Trans. Southend Antiq. and Hist. Soc., 2, pp. 197–205. 1933.

1347 **Clay-Finch** (Mrs. —). 'A mother of men.' The countess Gytha. [Wife of Godwin.] Rept. and Trans. Devon. Assoc., 46, p. 346–58, + 1 plate. 1914.

1348 **Darlington** (Reginald Ralph). The last phase of Anglo-Saxon history. History, N.S., 22, pp. 1–13. 1937.

1349 **Dickins** (Bruce). The day of the battle of Æthelingadene (A.-S. C., 1001 A). [May 23, 1001, ' perhaps on or near the Hampshire border of Sussex '.] Leeds studies in English, 6, pp. 25–27. 1937.

1350 **Douglas** (David Charles). Edward the Confessor, duke William of Normandy, and the English succession. E.H.R., 68, pp. 526–45. 1953.

1351 **Encomium Emmae Reginae.** Edited . . . by Alistair Campbell. Camden series 3, 72. pp. lxix, 108. 8° London, 1949. [Text in Latin and English.]

1352 **Eyton** (Robert William). Robert FitzWimarch and his descendants. [Cousin of Edward the Confessor.] Trans. Shrop. Arch. Soc., 2, pp. 1–34. 1879.

F

1353 Fest (Sándor). The sons of Eadmund Ironside, Anglo-Saxon king, at the court of Saint Stephen. St. Margaret of Scotland. Archivum Europae Centro–Orientalis, 4, pp. 116–46. 1938.

1354 Fisher (J. L.). Thurstan, son of Wine. [Temp. Edward the Confessor : donor of manor of Harlowbury to abbey of Bury.] Trans. Essex Archaeol. Soc., N.S. 22, pp. 98–104. 1936.

1355 Fowler (George Herbert). The devastation of Bedfordshire and the neighbouring counties in 1065 and 1066. Archaeologia, 72, pp. 41–50, + 2 folding maps. 1922.

1356 Francis (Henry James). Hugh de Grentmesnil and his family. Part 1. Pre-Conquest : part 2. The Conquest and after. Trans. Leic. Archaeol. Soc., 13, pp. 155–98, + 5 plates. 1923–4.

1357 Freeman (Edward Augustus). History of earl Godwine. Rpt. of Trans. Archaeol. Inst., [9] (1853), pp. 5–9. 1856.

1358 —— On the life and death of earl Godwine. Archaeol. J., 11, pp. 236–52, 330–44 : 12, pp. 47–64. 1854–55.

1359 Gertz (M. Cl.). Kong Knuts Liv og Gerninger. *Skrifter Selskabet hist. kildeskrifters Oversærtelse, række* 2, 33. pp. 73. 8° København, 1896.

1360 Gray (Arthur). The massacre at the Bran ditch, A.D. 1010. Proc. Camb. Antiq. Soc., 31, pp. 77–87. 1931.

1361 Grierson (Philip). A visit of earl Harold to Flanders in 1056. E.H.R., 51, pp. 90–97. 1936.

1362 Hall (Hamilton). Earl Swegen and Hacon dux. Sussex Archaeol. Collns., 46, pp. 163–69 : 47, pp. 157–58, 1903–04.

1363 Harold II, *king*. Vita Haroldi. The romance of the life of Harold, king of England. From the unique manuscript [Harl. 3776] in the British Museum. Edited with notes and a translation by Walter de Gray Birch. pp. xv, 204. 8° London, 1885.

1364 Hartshorne (Charles Henry). The parliaments of Gloucester. [Witan at Gloucester, 1048, etc.] Archaeol. J., 17, pp. 201–217. 1860.

1365 Hogg (John). On two events which occurred in the life of king Canute the Dane. [Second is single combat with Edmund Ironside.] Trans. R. Soc. Lit., 2nd S. 5, pp. 169–86. 1856.

1366 Jones (Morris Charles), *etc.* Posterity of Harold II. N. and Q., 3rd S. 5, pp. 217–18, 246 : 6, pp. 318, 436–38. 1864.

1367 Larson (Laurence Marcellus). Canute the Great, 995 (circ.)–1035, and the rise of Danish imperialism during the Viking age. *Heroes of the Nations.* pp. xviii, 375. 8° New York, 1912. [Gross, 1528a.]

1368 —— The political policies of Cnut as king of England. A.H.R., 15, pp. 720–43. 1910.

1369 Leadman (Alexander D. H.). The battle of Stamford Bridge. Yorks. Archaeol. J., 11, pp. 131–39. 1891.

1370 Le Patourel (John Herbert). Geoffrey of Montbray, bishop of Coutances, 1049–1093. E.H.R., 59, pp. 129–161. 1944.

1371 Miller (Samuel Henry). Ælfred Ætheling. [Nothing new : bookwork only.] Fenland N. and Q., 3, pp. 179–80. 1896.

1372 Morley (Claude). Eadric of ' Laxfield ', the king's falconer. [Lord of Eye, temp. Edward the Confessor.] History Teachers' Miscellany, 1, pp. 113–16. 1923.

1373 Olrik (Áxel). Siward Digri of Northumberland. A Viking-saga of the Danes of England. Saga-Book V.C., 6, pp. 212–37. 1910.

1374 Petit-Dutaillis (Charles). The feudal monarchy in France and England from the tenth to the thirteenth century. *History of Civilization series.* pp. xx, 421. 8° London, 1936.

1375 Rason (Ernest). Thyra, the wife of Gorm the Old, who was she, English or Danish ? [? Daughter of Ethelred the Unready. If so, invasion of Svein and Cnut was no foreign conquest.] Saga-Book V.C., 8, pp. 285–301. 1914.

1376 Reichel (Oswald Joseph). The vicar of Pinhoe and the Danish raid of 1001 A.D., the story of the raid. [*See also* **3110.**] Devon and Cornwall N. and Q., 11, pp. 185–89. 1921.

1377 Round (John Horace). Feudal England. pp. xvi, 587. 8° London, 1895. [Gross, 1891. Pp. 3–146, Domesday; pp. 147–56, The Northamptonshire geld roll, 1066–75; pp. 317–31, Normans under the Confessor: pp. 332–98, Mr. Freeman and the battle of Hastings.]

1378 Stephens (George). Some account of Scandinavian runic stones which speak of Knut the Great, king of all the north. Archaeologia, 43, pp. 97–117. 1871.

1379 Stevenson (William Henry). An alleged son of king Harold Harefoot. E.H.R., 28, pp. 112–17. 1913.

1380 Surtees (Scott F.). Ancient battlefields in the southern portion of North Humberland; showing how Pontefract obtained its present name. pp. 31. 8° 1869. [Plea that battle of Stamford Bridge was fought at Pontefract.] Rpt. of Proc. Geol. Soc. W. Riding of Yorks., 5, pp. 57–85, + map. 1869.

1381 Whitelock (Dorothy). Archbishop Wulfstan, homilist and statesman. [Abp. of York, 1003–1023.] Trans. R.H.S., 4th S. 24, pp. 25–45. 1942.

1382 Wilkinson (Bertie). Freeman and the crisis of 1051. Bull. John Ryland's Library, 22, pp. 368–87. 1938.

1383 —— Northumbrian separatism in 1065 and 1066. *Same jnl.*, 23, pp. 504–26. 1939.

1384 Willis (—). Account of the battles between Edmund Ironside and Canute. Archaeologia, 8, pp. 106–10. 1787.

§ *b*. Edward the Confessor

(as saint and as king. Lives, etc.)

1385 Baker (A. T.). Fragment of an Anglo-Norman life of Edward the Confessor. Mod. Lang. Rev., 3, pp. 374–75. 1908.

1386 Browne (George Forrest), *bp. of Bristol.* St. Edward the Confessor and Westminster abbey. *Church Historical Pamphlets*, 1. pp. 15. 8° London, 1918.

1387 Clare (Osbert de). La vie de S. Édouard le Confesseur. [Pp. 5–63, introduction, by Marc Bloch: pp. 64–123, Latin text: pp. 124–31, appendices.] Anal. Boll., 41, pp. 5–131. 1923.

1388 Edward, *the Confessor*, *king*. La estoire de Seint Ædward le rei. The life of St. Edward the Confessor. Reproduced in facsimile from the unique manuscript (Cambridge University library Ee. 3.59) . . . with an introduction by M. R. James. *Roxburghe Club*. pp. 75, and 76 plates. 4° Oxford, 1920.

1389 —— Kong Edvard af England, udgivne af Jørgen Olrik. (En herlig ny historie om konning Edvardo aff Engeland, *etc.*, 1696.) *Danske folkebøger fra 16. og 17. aarhundrede*, 5, pp. xxxv–lxiii, 117–49, 218–28. 8° København, 1921.

1390 ––— La vie d'Eduard le Confesseur. Poème Anglo-Normand du 12e siècle. Publié avec introduction, notes et glossaire par Östen Södergard. pp. viii, 384, + 2 plates. 8° Uppsala, 1948.

1391 Heningham (Eleanor K.). The genuineness of the *Vita Æduuardi regis*. Speculum, 21, pp. 419–56. 1946.

1392 MacGregor (Cecilia). The life and times of S. Edward, king and Confessor. 16° London, 1873.

1393 Meyer (Paul). Notice du ms. Egerton 745 du Musée Britannique. Appendice: vie en prose de Saint Édouard, roi d'Angleterre. [Pp. 45–62, redaction complète de la version en vers: pp. 64–69, la vie de Saint Édouard d'après le MS. de Welbeck.] Romania, 40, pp. 41–69. 1911.

1394 Moore (Grace Edna). The Middle English verse life of Edward the Confessor. *Dissertation. Univ. Pennsylvania.* pp. xci, 142. 8° Philadelphia, 1942.

1395 Porter (Jerome). Edvardus redivivus. The life of St. Edward, king and Confessor. pp. 91. 12° London [?], 1710. Revised and corrected by a priest [?Charles J. Bowen.] 16° London, 1868.

1396 Rafn (Charles Christian) and **Sigurdson** (John), *ed.* The saga of St. Edward the king. [c. 1350. Introductory observations by the editors and translation from the Icelandic by Thorlief Gudmundson Repp.] Mém. Soc. roy. Antiq. Nord, 1845–49, pp. 265–86. 1849.

1397 Southern (Richard William). The first life of Edward the Confessor. E.H.R., 58, pp. 385–400. 1943.

1398 Tanner (Lawrence Edward). Some representations of St. Edward the Confessor in Westminster abbey and elsewhere. J. Brit. Archaeol. Ass., 3rd S., 15, pp. 1–12, + 4 plates. 1952.

1399 Waterton (Edmund). On a remarkable incident in the life of Saint Edward the Confessor, with notices of certain rings hallowed on Good Friday by the sovereigns of England. [Story of Edward's ring and St. John quoted from the Golden Legend with comments.] Archaeol. J., 21, pp. 103–13, + 1 plate. 1864.

§ *c*. Battle of Hastings

(See also **2621**, for plan.)

1400 Airy (*Sir* George Biddell). On the place of Julius Caesar's departure from Gaul for the invasion of Britain, and the place of his landing in Britain ; with an appendix on the battle of Hastings. [Pp. 246–88, appendix.] Archaeologia, 34, pp. 231–50, + map. 1852.

1401 Archer (Thomas Andrew) and **Norgate** (Kate). The battle of Hastings. E.H.R., 9, pp. 1–76, 602–11. 1894.

1402 Archer (Thomas Andrew). Mr. Freeman and the 'Quarterly Review'. [Problems of the battle of Hastings.] Contemp. Rev., 63, pp. 335–55. 1893.

1403 Baring (*Hon.* Francis Henry). The battle field of Hastings. E.H.R., 20, pp. 65–70. 1905.

1404 —— The Malfosse at the battle of Hastings. E.H.R., 22, pp. 69–72. 1907.

1405 Bmont (Charles). Wace et la bataille de Hastings. Correction au vers 7816 du Roman de Rou. [Palisades.] Romania, 39, pp. 370–73. 1910.

1406 Crawford (Osbert Guy Stanhope). Relics of the battle of Hastings. Antiquity, 2, pp. 213–14, + 1 plate. 1928.

1407 Creasy (*Sir* Edward Shepherd). The fifteen decisive battles of the world. pp. xv, 638. 8° London, 1853. [Pp. 257–313, no. 8, Hastings.]

1408 Cross (William) and **Hall** (A.). Roger de Montgomery at the battle of Hastings. Shrop. N. and Q., N.S. 4, pp. 106–07, 116. 1895.

1409 Duckett (*Sir* George Floyd), *bart.* The battle of Hastings. Sussex Archaeol. Collns., 42, pp. 73–74. 1899.

1410 Faulke-Watling (C.), *etc.* Did Harold die at Hastings ? N. and Q., 5th S. 3, pp. 53, 96. 1875.

1411 Freeman (Edward Augustus) and **Howorth** (*Sir* Henry Hoyle). Was Roger de Montgomery at Senlac ? Palatine Note-bk., 2, pp. 141–45. 1882.

1412 Johnston (Philip Mainwaring). Earl Roger de Montgomery and the battle of Hastings. Sussex Archaeol. Collns., 47, pp. 109–12, + 1 plate. 1904.

1413 Lower (Mark Antony). Observations on the landing of William the Conqueror and subsequent events. *Same jnl.*, 2, pp. 53–57. 1849.

1414 —— On the battle of Hastings. *Same jnl.*, 6, pp. 15–40, + 1 plate. 1853.

1415 Marshall (Edward). Landing-place of William the Conqueror. [?Bulverhythe or Pevensey.] N. and Q., 7th S. 1, p. 515. 1886.

1416 Matthews (H. J.). Some observations on the battle of Hastings. Sussex County Mag., 2, pp. 56–59. 1928.

1417 Neilson (George). Professor Freeman and the 'palisade' at the battle of Hastings. Antiquary, 27, pp. 167–68, 232. 1893.

1418 Raper (W. A.). The battle of Hastings. Sussex Archaeol. Collns., 42, pp. 64–72. 1899.

1419 Round (John Horace). Anglo-Norman warfare. [Tactics at the battle of Hastings.] The Commune of London and other studies, by J. H. Round, pp. 39–61. [=Study no. 3]. 1899.

1420 Round (John Horace). La bataille de Hastings. Rev. hist., 65, pp. 61–77. 1897.

1421 —— The battle of Hastings. National Review, 28, pp. 687–95. 1897.

1422 —— The battle of Hastings. [P. 63, bibliography of preceding controversy.] Sussex Archaeol. Collns., 42, pp. 54–63. 1899.

1423 —— Mr. Freeman and the battle of Hastings. E.H.R., 9, pp. 209–59. 1894.

1424 Rudkin (Ernest Horace). Where did William land ? [At a group of landing-places.] Sussex County Mag., 2, pp. 60–63. 1928.

1425 Shoosmith (Ernest). The battle of Hastings. Same jnl., 22, pp. 380–83. 1948.

1426 —— Notes on some events preceding the battle of Hastings. Same jnl., 2, pp. 549–50. 1928.

1427 Spatz (Wilhelm). Die Schlacht von Hastings. Historische Studien. Veröffentlicht von E. Ebering, Heft 3. pp. 69. 8° Berlin, 1896. [Gross, 3000.]

1428 Stevenson (William Henry). Senlac and the Malfossé. E.H.R., 28, pp. 292–303. 1913.

1429 Thierry (Jacques Nicolas Augustin). The battle of Hastings—through French eyes. Translated by John Blake. Sussex County Mag., 18, pp. 201–03. 1944.

1430 William I, *king.* The muster roll of the principal officers of the Norman army commanded by William the Conqueror ; with an historical account of the battle of Hastings. 12° London, 1799.

§ d. Bayeux Tapestry

(all aspects)

1431 Abraham (Jeanne) and **Letienne** (A.). Les bordures de la tapisserie-broderie de Bayeaux. Normannia, 2, pp. 483–518. 1929.

1432 Amyot (Thomas). A defence of the early antiquity of the Bayeux tapestry. Archaeologia, 19, pp. 192–208. 1821.

1433 Amyot (Thomas). Observations on an historical fact supposed to be established by the Bayeux tapestry. [Harold's visit to Normandy.] Same jnl., 19, pp. 88–95. 1821.

1434 Anquetil (Eugène). Antiquité de la tapisserie de Bayeux. pp. 9. Mém. Soc. Sciences . . . Bayeux, 12. [c. 1912?]

1435 —— La telle du conquest d'Angleterre. Tapisserie de la reine Mathilde. pp. 31. [Extrait de l'Annuaire de l'Association Normande.] 8° Caen, 1907.

1436 Bayeux Tapestry. Bibliothèque de Bayeux. . . . Tapisserie de la reine Mathilde. . . . Édition absolument complète, exécutée au moyen de photographies directes de l'original. Traduction littérale du texte brodé dans la tapisserie et notes historiques en anglais et en français, *etc.* Obl. fol., Bayeux, 1909.

1437 —— Notice historique sur la tapisserie brodée par la reine Mathilde, *etc.* pp. 20, + plates. 4° Paris, 1803. —. pp. 24. 12° Saint Lo, 1837.

1438 Belloc (Joseph Hilaire Pierre). The book of the Bayeux tapestry, presenting the complete work in a series of colour facsimiles ; the introduction and narrative by H.B. pp. xix, 76. 8° London, 1914.

1439 Birrell (Francis Frederick Locker). Guide to the Bayeux tapestry. 3rd edition. *South Kensington Museum.* pp. 135, + 12 plates. 8° London, 1931.

1440 Bruce (John Collingwood). The Bayeux tapestry elucidated. pp. 166, + 17 coloured plates. 4° London, 1856 [1855]. [Gross, 2139, note.]

1441 Chambers (B. M.). Symbolism in the Bayeux tapestry. [5 figures in text.] Sussex County Mag., 6, pp. 26–27, 113–15, 171–73. 1932.

1442 Chefneux (Helène). Les fables dans la tapisserie de Bayeux. Romania, 60, pp. 1–35, 153–94. 1934.

1443 Christie (Alexander). The Bayeux tapestry, and its uses and value as a national historical chronicle. Proc. Soc. Antiq. Scot., 1, pp. 122–24. 1852.

1444 Comte (Jules). La tapisserie de Bayeux. Reproduction phototypographique, avec un texte historique, descriptif et critique. pp. 64, + 79 plates. Obl. 4° Paris, 1878. [Gross, 2139. Based on Fowke's work.]

1445 Corney (Bolton). The Bayeux tapestry—Wadard. N. and Q., 3rd S. 11, pp. 316–17. 1867.

1446 —— Researches and conjectures on the Bayeux tapestry. 2nd edition, revised and enlarged. pp. 21. 8° Greenwich 1838. —. Traduites . . . par Victor Euremont Pillet. pp. 13. 8° Bayeux, 1841.

1447 Dawson (Charles). The Bayeux tapestry in the hands of ' restorers ', and how it fared. Antiquary, 43, pp. 253–58, 288–92 : 45, p. 470. 1907, 1909.

1448 —— The ' restorations ' of the Bayeux tapestry. pp. 14. 4° London, 1907. [7 figures in text.]

1449 Drake (H. H.). The Bayeux tapestry. N. and Q., 6th S. 4, pp. 245–46. 1881.

1450 Du Méril (Édélstand). Études sur quelques points d'archéologie. 8° Paris, 1862. [Gross, 2139, note. Pp. 384–426, De la tapisserie de Bayeux.]

1451 Fowke (Frank Rede). The Bayeux tapestry reproduced in autotype plates with historic notes. *Arundel Society.* 79 plates. 8° London, 1875.

1451a —— The Bayeux tapestry, a history and a description. pp. ix, 139, + 79 plates. 8° London, 1898. [Gross, 2139.]

1452 French (Gilbert). On the banners of the Bayeux tapestry, and the earliest heraldic charges. J. Brit. Archaeol. Assoc., 13, pp. 113–30, + 5 plates. 1857.

1453 Gurney (Hudson). Observations on the Bayeaux tapestry. [List of 72 inscriptions and subjects.] Archaeologia, 18, pp. 359–70. 1817.

1454 H. (B. B.). History of the Bayeux tapestry. pp. 8. obl. 16° London, [1922.]

1455 Hannah (Ian Campbell). The story of the Bayeux tapestry. [8 full-pages of figures in text.] Sussex County Mag., 6, pp. 14–25. 1932.

1456 Herrmann (Léon). Apologues et anecdotes dans la tapisserie de Bayeux. Romania, 65, pp. 376–82. 1939.

1457 Laffetay (Jacques), *abbé*. Notice historique et descriptive sur la la tapisserie dite de la reine Mathilde. pp. 75. 8° Bayeux, 1873.

1458 Lambert (Édouard). Réfutation des objections faites contre l'antiquité de la tapisserie de Bayeux à l'occasion de l'écrit de M. Bolton-Corney [**1446**]. pp. 26. 8° Bayeux, 1841.

1459 Lanore (M.). La tapisserie de Bayeux. Bibl. École des Chartes, 64, pp. 83–93. 1903.

1460 La Rue (Gervais de), *abbé*. Recherches sur la tapisserie, *etc.* pp. 114, + 8 plates. 8° Caen, 1841.

1461 —— Translation [by Francis Douce] of a memoir on the celebrated tapestry of Bayeux. Archaeologia, 17, pp. 83–109. 1814.

1462 Launey (H. Fr. de). Origine de la tapisserie de Bayeux, prouvée par elle-même. pp. 92. 4° Caen, 1824.

1463 Lefebvre de Noëttes (—), *commandant*. Nouvelles remarques sur la date probable de la tapisserie de Bayeux. Bull. monumental, 78, pp. 129–37, + 1 plate. 1914.

1464 —— La tapisserie de Bayeux datée par le harnachement des chevaux et l'equipement des cavaliers. [Dates to between 1120 and 1130.]. *Same jnl.*, 76, pp. 213–41, + 7 plates. 1912.

1464a Lejard (André). The Bayeux tapestry. 1947.

1465 Lethaby (William Richard). The perjury at Bayeux. [As represented on Bayeux tapestry.] Archaeol. J., 74, pp. 136–38. 1917.

1466 Lethieullier (Smart). A description of the Bayeux tapistry. pp. 329–404, + 8 plates. 4° Caen, 1767. [Being Appendix no. 1 to Ducarel (Andrew Coltee) : Anglo-Norman antiquities considered, *etc.*]

1467 —— Origine de la tapisserie de Bayeux. pp. 92, + 42 plates. 8° Caen, 1823.

1468 Levé (A. M.). Antériorité de la tapisserie de Bayeux sur la Chanson de Roland par le maniement de la lance. Bull. monumental, 77, pp. 129-35. 1913.

1469 —— La tapisserie de Bayeux, sa date, son auteur, son caractère français. Mém. Soc. roy. des Antiq. de France, 75, pp. 23-42. 1918.

1470 —— Tapisserie de la reine Mathilde, dite tapisserie de Bayeux. Réproduction integrale. Queen Matilda's tapestry, *etc.* 8 plates. Obl. fol. Paris, [1919]. [In French and English.]

1471 Loomis (Roger Sherman). The origin and date of the Bayeux embroidery. Art Bull., 6, pp. 3-7, + 2 plates. 1923.

1472 Maclagan (*Sir* Eric Robert Dalrymple). The Bayeux tapestry. *King Penguin books.* pp. 32, + plates. 8° London, 1943.

1473 Marignan (Albert). La tapisserie de Bayeux. Étude archéologique et critique. *Petite bibliothèque d'art et d'archéologie*, 26. pp. xxvi, 194. 12° Paris, 1902.

1474 Planché (James Robinson). On the Bayeux tapestry. J. Brit. Archaeol. Assoc., 23, pp. 134-56. 1867.

1475 Prentout (Charles). Essai d'identification des personnages inconnus de la tapisserie de Bayeux. [Ælgiva, Turold, Vital, Wadard.] Rev. hist., 176, pp. 14-23. 1935.

1476 Pryce (T. Davies). A note on the Bayeux tapestry. Antiquary, 43, pp. 346-47. 1907.

1477 Stothard (Charles Alfred). Some observations on the Bayeux tapestry. Archaeologia, 19, pp. 184-91. 1821.

1478 —— The tapestry of Bayeux. [Gross, 2139. 17 facsimile engravings.] Vetusta Mon., 6, plates 1-17. 1819-23.

1479 Tavernier (W.). The author of the Bayeux embroidery. [Case for Turold c. 1020- c. 1080.] Archaeol. J., 71, pp. 171-86, + 2 plates. 1914.

1480 Turgis (Suzanne). La très véridique histoire de la bonne Mathilde . . . auteur de la tapisserie-broderie de Bayeux. Origine et histoire de la célèbre tapisserie-broderie, avec l'explication de toutes les scènes, *etc.* pp. 134. 8° Paris, Bayeux, [1912].

1481 Verrier (Jean). La broderie de Bayeux. . . . Reproduction intégrale au cinquième de l'original accompagnée de huit planches en couleurs. Textes [in French and English] de Jean Verrier. pp. iv, 40, + 8 plates. Oblong fol. [Paris], 1946.

§ *e.* **William I—Lives of the King**

1482 [Anon.]. Brevis relatio de Willelmo, nobillissimo comite Normannorum, *etc.* Ab authore anonymo temp. Hen. primi. pp. 31. 8° Londini, 1663. [=pp. 180-211 of Silas Taylor's History of gavel-kind.]

1483 Abbott (Jacob). History of William the Conqueror. pp. 391. 12° New York, [1849]. [Popular.]

1484 Belloc (Joseph Hilaire Pierre). William the Conqueror. pp. 153. 8° London, 1938.

1485 Benton (Sarah Henry). From coronet to crown : or the life of William the Conqueror, from the early chronicles. pp. xix, 298, + 9 plates. 8° London, 1926.

1486 Bernau (Charles A.), *etc.* William the Conqueror's half brothers and sisters. N. and Q., 9th S. 8, pp. 199-200, 293-94, 525-26 : 9, pp. 36, 111. 1901-02.

1487 Birette (Charles Louis). La jeunesse de Guillaume le Conquérant. pp. 102. 8° Caen, 1933.

1488 Clarke (Samuel). The life and death of William, surnamed the Conqueror. pp. 36 [44]. 4° London, 1671.

1489 Coryn (Marjorie Stella). The Acquirer, 1027-1087. [A biography of William I.] pp. v, 287. 8° London, [1934.]

1490 Eudemare (François d'). Histoire excellente et héroique du roy Willaume le Bastard, *etc.* pp. 615. 8° Rouen, 1626. — 2e édition, augmentée. 12° Rouen, 1629.

1491 Francis (René). William the Conqueror. *Heroes of all time.* pp. 191. 8° London, 1915.

1492 Freeman (Edward Augustus). William the Conqueror. *Twelve English statesmen.* pp. viii, 200. 8° London, 1888. [Gross, 2814.]

1493 Guillemard (Julien). La vie prodigieuse de Guillaume le Conquérant. pp. 150. 4° Rouen, [1937].

1494 Guizot (François Pierre Guillaume). Guillaume le Conquérant. . . . 7e édition. pp. 148. 8° Paris, 1877.

1495 Hayward (*Sir* John). The lives of the III Normans, kings of England, *etc.* pp. viii, 314. 8° London, 1613. [Pp. 1–139, William I.]

1496 Henderson (Andrew). The life of William the Conqueror. pp. x, 290. 12° London, 1764.

1497 Holthausen (Ferdinand). Das altenglische Gedicht auf Wilhelm den Eroberer. Anglia, Beiblatt, 36, pp. 110–11. 1925.

1498 Koerting (Gustav). Willelm's von Poitiers Gesta Guilelmi ducis Normannorum et regis Anglorum. *Diss., Dresden. Programm der Kreuzschule zu Dresden,* 1875. pp. 41. 4° Dresden, 1875.

1499 La Dangie de Renchi (Mathieu de). Apologie pour Guillaume le Conquérant. *Société des Bibliophiles Normands.* pp. xxi, 123. 4° Rouen, 1919. [A reproduction of the edition published at Caen in 1610.]

1500 La Varende (Jean de). Guillaume le bâtard, conquérand. pp. 422. 8° Paris, 1946.

1501 Lomier (Eugène). L'étendard de Guillaume le Conquérant. pp. xxxi, 72. 8° Paris, 1932.

1502 Marx (Jean). Un nouveau récit de la mort de Guillaume le Conquérant. [Ms. Harl. 491 : De obitu Willelmi, ducis Normannorum regisque Anglorum, qui sanctam Ecclesiam in pace vivere fecit. Latin text.] Rev. hist., 111, pp. 289–91. 1912.

1503 Pauli (Reinhold). Bilder aus Alt-England. 2. Auflage. 8° Gotha, 1876. — Pictures of Old England, translated by E. C. Otté. pp. xii, 387. 8° London, [1906]. [Gross, 2805. ii. Die Politik Wilhelms des Eroberers.]

1504 Planché (James Robinson). The Conqueror and his companions. 2 vol. 8° London, 1874.

1505 Prentout (Henri). Histoire de Guillaume le Conquérant. Tome I. Le duc de Normandie. *Mém. Acad. Nat. des sciences,* . . . *Caen,* N.S., 8. 8° Caen, 1936.

1506 Richomme (Florent). La naissance de Guillaume-le-Conquérant à Falaise ; éclairissement historique. 8° Falaise, 1862.

1507 Roscoe (Thomas). The life of William the Conqueror. pp. xv, 415. 8° London, 1846.

1508 Russell (Phillips). William the Conqueror. pp. viii, 344. 8° New York, 1933.

1509 Stenton (Doris Mary), *Lady Stenton.* William the Conqueror. *Junior History series.* pp. 187, + 7 plates, + map. 8° London, 1927. [5 of the plates are scenes from the Bayeux tapestry.]

1510 Stenton (*Sir* Frank Merry). William the Conqueror. *Heroes of the Nations series.* pp. xi, 578, + 8 genealogical tables, + 22 plates, + 7 maps. 8° London, 1908. [Gross, 2828a.]

1511 Todière (Louis Phocion). Guilaume le Conquérant. *Bibliothèque des Écoles Chrétiennes.* 8° Tours, 1856.

1512 Vattelet (Hans). Der Konflikt Vilhelm des Eroberers mit seinem Sone [Sohn] Robert in 1087. pp. 64. 8° Zürich, 1874. [Gross, 2828b.]

1513 Vuilhorgne (L.). Guillaume le Conquérant et Robert Court-Heuse à Gerberoy, et à Auchy-en-Bray, . . . 1079. Étude critique. pp. 54. 8° Beauvais, 1898.

1514 William, *of Jumièges.* Gesta Normanorum ducum. Édition critique par Jean Marx. *Société de l'histoire de Normandie.* pp. xliv, 418. 8° Rouen et Paris, 1914. [Latin text.]

1515 William, *of Poitiers.* Histoire de Guillaume le Conquérant, éditée et traduite par Raymonde Foreville. *Classiques de l'histoire de France au moyen âge,* 23. pp. lxvi, 301, + map, + plan (of Hastings). 8° Paris, 1952. (Latin text, French translation, and notes.]

1516 Y. (E. H.). Sword [and coronation robes] of William the Conqueror. [At Battle abbey till Reformation : then taken to Cowdray and destroyed in its fire.] N. and Q., 1st S. 3, pp. 66. 1851.

§ f. William I—His Reign

(1066–87)

1517 [Anon.] The coming of Hugh Lupus, [earl of Chester]. Cheshire N. and Q., N.S. [3rd S.], 6, pp. 234–35. 1901.

1518 Adams (George Burton). The history of England from the Norman Conquest to the death of John. *Political History of England,* 2. pp. x, 473, + 2 maps. 8° London, 1905. [Gross, 2807a. Pp. 1–71, William I.]

1519 Alexander (John James). An Irish invasion of Devon. [1068.] Rept. and Trans. Devon. Assoc., 55 (1923), pp. 125–30. 1924.

1520 Baldricus, *abbot of Bourgueil, archbp. of Dol.* Les œuvres poétiques de Baudri de Bourgueil, 1046–1130. Étude critique, publiée d'après le manuscrit du Vatican par Phyllis Abrahams. pp. ix, 404. 8° Paris, 1926. [On course of events between the Norman council which decided on the invasion of England and the capture of a town after the battle of Hastings.]

1521 Baring (*Hon.* Francis Henry). The Conqueror's footprints in Domesday. E.H.R., 13, pp. 17–25. 1898.

1522 —— The making of the New Forest. E.H.R., 16, pp. 427–38. 1901. *Same title.* E.H.R., 27, pp. 513–15. 1912.

1523 —— William the Conqueror's march through Hampshire in 1066. Papers and Proc. Hants. F.C., 7 ii, pp. 33–39. 1915.

1524 Bartelot (R. G.) and **Beament** (W. O.). Wadard of Bayeux. [Retainer of bp. Odo. Plate shows Wadard in Bayeux tapestry. His acquisition of Ramesham (Rampisham) manor, in Upway, Dorset.] N. and Q. Som. and Dorset, 17, p. 105, + 1 plate : 172 73, 279–80. 1922–23.

1525 Bennett (James Arthur). Vestiges of the Norman conquest of Somerset. Proc. Somerset Arch. Soc., 25 (1879), pp. 21–28. 1880.

1526 Bishop (Terence Alan Martyn). The Norman settlement of Yorkshire. Studies pres. to F. M. Powicke, pp. 1–14. 1948.

1527 Boyce (R. A. M.). Ivo de Tail-Bois. [Leader of Angevin auxilliaries at Hastings.] Antiquary, 49, pp. 186–87, *also* p. 280 (note by John F. Curwen) : *also* p. 360 (reply by R. A. M. Boyce) : 50, pp. 137–41. 1913–14.

1528 Browne (A. L.). Robert de Todeni [Tosny] and his heirs. Trans. Bristol and Glos. Arch. Soc., 52, pp. 103–11. 1930.

1529 Bryant (Arthur). The founding of the Norman kingdom. History to-day, 3, pp. 591–602. 1953.

1530 Cooke (Edward). Argumentum anti-Normannicum ; or, An argument proving . . . that William, duke of Normandy, made no absolute conquest of England by the sword, in the sense of our modern writers, *etc.* pp. clxiv, + 1 plate. 8° London, 1682. — [A reissue]. A seasonable treatise . . . that king William . . . did not get the . . . Crown . . . by the sword, but by the election and consent of the people. pp. clxiv. 8° London, 1689.

1531 Corbett (William John). The development of the duchy of Normandy and the Norman conquest of England. Camb. Med. Hist., 5, pp. 481–520. 1926.

1532 Crow, *pseud.* The Norman earls of Chester : Introductory : Hugh Lupus, A.D. 1070–1101. Cheshire N. and Q., N.S. [3rd S.] 4, pp. 26–28, 84–87. 1899.

1533 Daniell (Francis Henry Blackburne). A pictorial record of the Conquest. [Poem of Baldric, abbot of Bourgueil, 1079–1107.] E.H.R., 7, pp. 705–08. 1892.

1534 David (Charles Wendell). Robert Curthose, duke of Normandy. *Harvard Historical Series*, 25. pp. xiv, 271, + map. 8° Cambridge, Mass., 1920.

1535 Davis (Henry William Carless). England under the Normans and Angevins. *History of England, ed. C. Oman*, 2. 13th edition. pp. xx, 591. 8° London, 1949. [Pp. 1–66, William I.]

1536 Dicker (Charles William Hamilton). The Normans in Dorset. [Including Conquest and Domesday material.] Proc. Dorset Antiq. F.C., 31, pp. 115–26, + 3 plates. 1910.

1537 Douglas (David Charles). The ancestors of William Fitz Osbern. [Arfast, etc.] E.H.R., 59, pp. 62–79. 1944.

1538 —— 'Companions of the Conqueror.' [27 provisional list, + ?5.] History, N.S., 28, pp. 129–47. 1943.

1539 —— The Norman Conquest. *Historical Association leaflet*, 73. pp. 16. 8° London, 1928.

1540 —— The Norman Conquest and British historians. *David Murray foundation lecture*, 13. *Glasgow Univ. Pubns.*, 67. pp. 40. 8° Glasgow, 1946.

1541 Dupont (Étienne). La participation de la Bretagne à la conquête de l'Angleterre par les Normands. pp. 50. 8° Paris, 1911.

1542 —— Recherches historiques et topographiques sur les compagnons de Guillaume le Conquérant. Répertoire de leurs lieux d'origine. 2 pts. 8° Saint-Servan, [1907–08?] [Gross, 2828b.]

1543 Ellis (Alfred Shelley) Gospatrick. N. and Q., 5th S. 3, pp. 131–32. 1875.

1544 —— Ivo Tailbois. [His parentage.] N. and Q., 6th S. 6, pp. 274, 395. 1882.

1545 Fox (Levi). The honor and earldom of Leicester: origin and descent, 1066–1399. E.H.R., 54, pp. 385–402. 1939.

1546 Freeman (Edward Augustus). The history of the Norman Conquest of England, its causes and results. 6 vol. 8° Oxford, 1867–79. — 3rd edition, revised, vol. 1–2. 8° Oxford, 1877. [Vol. 5, pp. 1–52, (chapter 22), Domesday.]

1547 Freeman (Edward Augustus). A short history of the Norman Conquest of England. pp. 156. 8° Oxford, 1880.

1548 Fry (—), *Miss*. Fragments concerning Eudo Dapifer and his family. Trans. Essex Archaeol. Soc., N.S. 1, pp. 33–44. 1878.

1549 Greswell (William Henry Parr). The Norman conquest of Somerset. Proc. Somerset Arch. Soc., 52 (1906), pp. 70–93. 1907.

1550 Grimes (Charles Hugh Duffy). In the steps of William the Conqueror, pp. 48, + plates. 8° [Le Havre, 1927].

1551 Haskins (Charles Homer). Normandy under William the Conqueror. A.H.R., 14, pp. 453–76. 1909.

1552 Hepple (Richard B.). Wife of Ivo Taillebois. N. and Q., 166, p. 462: 167, pp. 48, 86–87, 103–04, 119–20, 140, 173–74. 1934.

1553 Hill (Geoffry). The influence of the Norman Conquest upon the invasion of England. [Disunity in the island accounts for ease of the Conquest.] Antiquary, 40, pp. 208–12. 1904.

1554 Howorth (*Sir* Henry Hoyle). The first and second Roger de Montgomery. Palatine Note-Bk., 2, pp. 27–31. 1882.

1555 —— The family of De Montgomery. *Same jnl.*, 1, pp. 185–87. 1881.

1556 —— Roger of Poictou, [3rd son of Roger de Montgomery]. *Same jnl.*, 3, pp. 56–60. 1883.

1557 —— Roger the second de Montgomery. *Same jnl.*, 2, pp. 77–80. 1882.

1558 Hunter (Joseph). On the (so-called) roll of Battle abbey. [And on lists of families who came over with the Conqueror.] Sussex Archaeol. Collns., 6, pp. 1–14. 1853.

1559 Jewett (Sarah Orne). The story of the Normans told chiefly in relation to their conquest of England. *Story of the Nations*, 29. pp. xv, 373. 8° London, n.d. [Pp. 232–344, Normans and England to death of William I.]

1560 Lauer (Philippe). Le poème de Baudri de Bourgueil addressé à Adèle, fille de Guillaume le Conquérant, et la date de la tapisserie de Bayeux. [Latin text.] Mélanges . . . Bémont, pp. 43–58. 1913.

1561 Liebermann (Felix). The family of William the Conqueror, and the Church of Chartres. [Necrologium of 1027–1137. Gifts of William, Matilda, and their daughter Adeliza in 1070.] E.H.R., 16, pp. 498–99. 1901.

1562 Loyd (L. C.). The origin of the family of Warenne. Yorks. Archaeol. J., 31, pp. 97–113. 1934.

1563 Maclise (Daniel), *R.A.* The story of the Norman Conquest. 42 plates. Oblong folio, London, 1866.

1564 Magoun (Francis Peabody), *jr.* Norman history in the ' Lay of the Beach ' (Strandar ljóð). [Reflects campaign of William I, supported by an English army, against Maine in 1073.] Mod. Lang. Notes, 57, pp. 11–16. 1942.

1565 Marshall (George). The Norman occupation of the lands in the Golden Valley, Ewyas, and Clifford and their motte and bailey castles. [Pp. 157–58, table of summary of the holdings.] Trans. Woolhope N.F. Club, 1936–38, pp. 141–58, + coloured map. 1940.

1566 Miller (Edward). The Norman conquest. The heritage of early Britain, pp. 153–73. 1952.

1567 Parkin (Charles). An impartial account of the invasion under William, duke of Normandy, and the consequences of it. 4° London, 1756.

1568 Planché (James Robinson). On Raoul de Gael, the first earl of Norfolk. J. Brit. Archaeol. Assoc., 14, pp. 30–43. 1858.

1569 —— On the Norman earls of Shrewsbury. Coll. Archaeol., 1, pp. 67–78. 1861.

1570 Powell (Frederick York). A northern legend of the English conquest, [1066]. [Text in Orkneyinga Saga, vol. 1, Rolls Series.] E.H.R., 4, pp. 87–9. 1889.

1571 Ψ. Edgar Ætheling. N. and Q., 2nd S. 10, pp. 3–4. 1860.

1572 Round (John Horace). The attack on Dover, 1067. Antiquary, 12, pp. 49–53. 1885.

1573 —— Ingelric the priest and Albert of Lotharingia. The commune of London and other studies, by J. H. Round, pp. 28–38. [=study no. 2]. 1899.

1574 —— Is Mr. Freeman accurate ? [i.e. as a historian.] Antiquary, 13, pp. 239–42 : 14, pp. 150–54, 247–51. 1886.

1575 Rybot (N. V. L.). Duke Robert of Normandy and Edward the Atheling. Bull. Soc. Jersiaise, 12, pp. 529–30. 1935.

1576 Sedgefield (Walter John). Old English notes. [i. is on A.-S. C. (Laud MS.) sub anno 1086.] Mod. Lang. Rev., 18, pp. 471–72. 1923.

1577 Sparvel-Bayly (John Anthony). The Norman at Swanscombe. [Privileges granted by William I.] Antiquary, 20, pp. 111–13. 1889.

1578 Stapleton (Thomas). Observations on the history of Adeliza, sister of William the Conqueror. Archaeologia, 26, pp. 349–60. 1836.

1579 Tait (James). The first earl of Cornwall. [Brient or Brian of Brittany : ?temp. William I.] E.H.R., 44, p. 86. 1929.

1580 Taylor (Charles Samuel). The Norman settlement of Gloucestershire. [Includes (pp. 85–88) a list of ' Domesday owners and their predecessors in king Edward's time '.] Trans. Bristol and Glos. Arch. Soc., 40, pp. 57–88. 1917.

1581 Thierry (Jacques Nicolas Augustin). Histoire de la conquête de l'Angleterre par les Normands, avec ses causes. Nouvelle édition, revue et corrigée. 2 vol. 8° Paris, 1859. — History of the conquest of England . . . translated from the 7th Paris edition by W. Hazlitt. *Bohn's Standard Library*. 2 vol. 8° London, 1856. — Thierry's Norman Conquest. with an introduction by J. Arthur Price. *Everyman's Library*. 2 vol. 8° London, 1907.

1582 Tower (*Sir* Reginald). Odo, bishop of Bayeux and earl of Kent. Arch. Cant., 39, pp. 55–75. 1927.

1583 Tupper (Frederick), *jr.* The curse of Urse [d'Abetot, sheriff of Worcester]. [Inflicted by abp. Ealdred, c. 1069. 'Illustration of the gradual conversion of trustworthy history into irresponsible legend.' *See* Malmesbury, Gesta Pontificum, § 155.] J. Engl. and Germ. Philol., 11, pp. 100–103. 1912.

1584 Turner (G. J.). William the Conqueror's march to London in 1066. E.H.R., 27, pp. 209–25. 1912.

1585 Turner (Sharon). The history of England during the Middle Ages [William I to Henry VIII]. [=editions 2–5]. 8° London, 1825 (–1853).

1586 Ward (Gordon). Godfrey of Malling. [A Domesday tenant.] Sussex N. and Q., 5, pp. 3–6. 1934.

§ g. Hereward the Wake

1587 Bushnell (George Herbert), *etc.* Hereward the Wake. [In Lincs. Domesday, etc.] N. and Q., 159, pp. 346–47, 395. 1930.

1588 Foster (*Sir* William Edward). Hereward, the Fenman. pp. 40. 8° Leicester, 1914.

1589 Harward (Thomas Netherton). Hereward . . . a history of his life and character, with a record of his ancestors and descendants, A.D. 445–1896. pp. viii, 127. 4° London, 1896. [Gross, 1526a.]

1590 Lange (Joost de). The relation and development of English and Icelandic outlaw-traditions. *Diss., Utrecht.* pp. 138. 8° Haarlem, 1935. [Pp. 4–32, Hereward the Saxon.]

1591 Trollope (Edward). Hereward, the Saxon patriot. Assoc. Archit. Socs.' Rpts., 6, pp. 1–20. 1861.

1592 Waterton (Edmund), *etc.* Hereward le Wake. [Mostly genealogy.] N. and Q., 6th S. 4, pp. 9–10, 69–70, 456: 5, pp. 257, 313: 6, pp. 30–31, 196. 1881–82.

1593 Wright (Thomas). Essays on subjects connected with the literature, popular superstitions, and history of England in the Middle Ages. 2 vol. 8° London, 1846. [Vol. 2, pp. 91–120: Adventures of Hereward the Saxon.]

§ h. Earl Waltheof

1594 Imelmann (Rudolf Hans Robert). Vom romantischen und geschichtlichen Waldef. Engl. Studien, 53, pp. 362–69. 1920.

1595 Levien (Edward). The life and times of earl Waltheof. J. Brit. Archaeol. Assoc., 30, pp. 387–97. 1874.

1596 Miller (Samuel Henry). The grave of Waltheof. [Chapter-house, Crowland. Extract from Ordericus.] Fenland N. and Q., 2, pp. 37–39, 138. 1892.

1597 Scott (Forrest S.). Earl Waltheof of Northumbria. Arch. Æl., 4th S. 30, pp. 149–215, + map (of his possessions). 1952.

1598 —— Earl Waltheof of Northumbria in history and tradition. *M. Litt. Thesis, Cambridge,* 1950–51. [Apply University Library.]

1599 Sweeting (Walter Debenham). Waltheof's tomb. [His life, and miracles at his tomb at Crowland.] Fenland N. and Q., 7, pp. 53–59. 1907.

1600 White (G. H.). Waltheof, earl of Northumberland. [i. His wife; ii. His daughters: iii. His mother's family. Also his connection with Ralph de Toeni.] N. and Q., 10th S. 12, p. 447: 11th S. 1, pp. 32–33. 1909–10.

§ i. Celtic (1000–87)

1601 Anderson (Alan Orr). Macbeth's relationship to Malcolm II. Scot. H.R., 25, p. 377. 1928.

1602 Beveridge (Hugh). The battle of Carham [on Tweed, Nthb.], 1018. [Lothian ceded to Malcolm II. Preceded by a comet for 30 nights. Also sketch of Scottish history leading to it.] Scotia, 1, pp. 160–66. 1907.

1603 Chadwick (Nora Kershaw). The story of Macbeth. A study in Gaelic and Norse tradition. Scot. Gaelic Stud., 6, pp. 189–211 : 7, pp. 1–25. 1949–51.

1604 Dickins (Bruce). Orkney raid on Wales. [With help of expelled Gruffydd, king of Gwynedd, temp. William I.] Proc. Orkney Antiq. Soc., 8, pp. 47–48. 1930.

1605 Ferguson (Mary Catharine), *Lady*. The story of the Irish before the Conquest. 2nd edition, with maps, . . . enlarged. pp. xvi, 377. 8° Dublin, 1890. — New edition. 8° Dublin, 1903.

1606 Gering (Hugo). Die Episode von Rǫgnvaldr und Ermingerðr in der Orkneyinga Saga. Z. f. d. P., 43, pp. 428–34 ; 46, pp. 1–17. 1911–14.

1607 Goedheer (A. J.). Irish and Norse traditions about the battle of Clontarf. *Nederlandsche Bijdragen op het Gebiad van germaansche Philologie*, 9. pp. xi, 124. 8° Haarlem, 1938.

1608 Hamel (Anton Gerard van). Norse history in Hanes Gruffydd ap Cynan. [' Alyn ' = St. Olaf (died 1032).] Rev. celt., 42, pp. 336–44. 1925.

1609 Haugton (Samuel). On the time of high water in Dublin bay, on Good Friday, the 23rd April, 1014, the day of the battle of Clontarf. [*See also* **1631**.] Proc. R.I.A., 7 (1861), pp. 495–98. 1862.

1610 Johnston (Alfred Wintle). Some medieval house-burnings by the Vikings of Orkney. [' Account of some 11th and 12th century " burnings " in Orkney, Shetland, Caithness and Sutherland', etc.] Scot. H. R., 12 pp. 157–65. 1915.

1611 Jones (Arthur), *ed.* The history of Gruffydd ap Cynan. The Welsh text with translation, introduction and notes. pp. viii, 204, + map + 2 plates. 8° Manchester, 1910. [1055?–1137.]

1612 Keogh (Thomas M.). Clontarf. [Account of battle, 1014.] J. Ivernian Soc., 8, pp. 73–87. 1912.

1613 Linklater (Eric). The battle of Clontarf. Viking, 15, pp. 1–14. 1951.

1614 Lloyd (Howel William). The battle of Carno, A.D. 1077. Collns. hist. and archaeol. rel. to Montgom., 9, pp. 297–304. 1876.

1615 Lloyd (*Sir* John Edward). Wales and the coming of the Normans (1039–1093). Trans. Hon. Soc. Cymm., 1899–1900, pp. 122–79. 1901.

1616 Lockhart (William). Notices of Ethelred, earl of Fife and abbot of Dunkeld, and his place in the royal family of Scotland in the eleventh century. Proc. Soc. Antiq. Scot., 26 (3rd S. 2), pp. 104–13. 1892.

1617 M. (J.). Macbeth. (Was Macbeth a usurper?) (Macbeth : Malcolm Canmore). N. and Q., 2nd S. 3, pp. 241–42 : 11, pp. 24–26 : 3rd S. 10, pp. 201–03. 1857, 1861, 1866.

1618 Miller (Thomas). The palace of Birsay in Orkney. [Concerning Earl Thorfinn of Orkney.] Scot. H.R., 15, pp. 47–52, + plan. 1918.

1619 Mooney (John). St. Magnus, earl of Orkney. pp. xv, 324. 8° Kirkwall, 1935. [Died 1115.]

1620 D'Brien (*Hon.* Donough). History of the O'Briens from Brian Boroimhe, A.D. 1000 to A.D. 1945. pp. 302. 8° London, 1949. [Pp. 17–26, Battle of Clontarf, 1014.]

1621 O'Gorman (Thomas). On the site of the battle of Clontarf. J. Roy. Hist. and Arch. Assoc. Ireland, [15], 4th S. 5 (1879–82), pp. 168–82. 1882.

1622 O'Rahilly (Thomas Francis). Cúan ua Lothcháin and Corcrán Clérech. [Governed Ireland for 20 years (1022–42) according to Annals of Clonmacnoise : but?] Celtica, 1, pp. 313–17. 1950.

1623 Owen (Thomas Morgan). The battle of Rhyd y Groes, 1039, and its influence on that of Hastings. Collns. hist. and archaeol. rel. to Montgom., 7, pp. 163–172. 1874.

1624 —— The battles of Carno, A.D. 949 and 1077, with their causes and effects. *Same jnl.*, 9, pp. 287–96. 1876.

1625 Russell (Edward B.). The true Macbeth. Proc. Lit. and Phil. Soc. L'pool., 30, pp. 41–92. 1876.

1626 Ryan (John). The battle of Clontarf. [The sources, their value, and a reconstruction of events.] J. Roy. Soc. Antiq. Ireland, 68 (7th S. 8), pp. 1–50, + 2 maps. 1938.

1627 Smith (James A.). Banquo and Fleance. [?identity.] Antiq. Mag., 7, pp. 213–18; 8, pp. 12–19. 1885.

1628 Stephens (George). Macbeth, earl Siward and Dundee. A contribution to Scottish history from the rune-finds of Scandinavia. 4° London, 1876.

1629 Stopes (Charlotte Carmichael). The Scottish and English Macbeth. Trans. Roy. Soc. Lit., 2nd S. 18, pp. 235–84. 1897.

1630 Taylor (Alexander Burt). Karl Hundason, ' king of Scots '. Proc. Soc. Antiq. Scot., 71 (6th S. 11, 1936–37), pp. 334–42. 1937.

1631 Todd (James Henthorn). Some remarks on the history of the battle of Clontarf, in connection with Mr. Haughton's determination of the time of high water in Dublin bay on Good Friday, April 23, 1014. [*See also* **1609**.] Proc. R.I.A., 7 (1861), pp. 498–511. 1862.

1632 Westropp (Thomas Johnson). King Brian : the hero of Clontarf. 8° Dublin, 1914. [Reprinted from the Irish Monthly, 1914.]

19. FOREIGN RELATIONS

(Apart from Norse, for which see 11 and for cultural relations for which see 109. For trade relations, see 49.)

1633 Belaiew (Nikolai Timothyee-vich). Frisia and its relations with England and the Baltic littoral in the Dark Ages. [7 pp. of maps and illustrations in text. Also, in French, *in* Seminarium Kondakovianum, 4, Prag, 1931.] J. Brit. Archaeol. Assoc., N.S. 37, pp. 190–215. 1932.

1633a Bense (Johan Frederick). Anglo-Dutch relations from the earliest times to the death of William the Third. pp. xx, 293. 8° The Hague, 1935. [Ch. 1 (pp. 1–6), before the Conquest : pp. 7–13, William I.]

1634 Boissonnade (P.). Les relations entre l'Aquitaine, le Poitou, and l'Irlande du Ve au IXe siècle. [Kenney, 1, p. 157.] Bull. Soc. Antiquaires de l'Ouest, 3e S. 4, pp. 181–202. 1917.

1634a Borchling (Conrad) and **Muuss** (Rudolph). Die Friesen. pp. 200, + plates, + map. 8° Breslau, 1931.

1635 Buckler (F. W.). The *pallium* of Saint Cuthbert. [Thesis that it was a garment sent by Harun-al-Rashid to Charlemagne and transmitted to the shrine of St. Cuthbert through the royal house of Wessex.] Archaeol. Æl., 4th S. 1, pp. 199–123. 1925.

1636 Dawkins (*Sir* William Boyd). The place of the Welsh in the history of Britain. [A.-S. contacts, pp. 252–57.] Collns. hist. and archaeol. rel. to Montgom., 23, pp. 241–60. 1889.

1637 Deanesly (Margaret). Canterbury and Paris in the reign of Æthelberht. History, N.S. 26, pp. 97–104. 1941.

1638 Doble (Gilbert Hunter). Les relations durant les âges entre la Bretagne et le Cornwall. Bull. diocésain d'hist. et d'archéol. de Quimper et de Léon, 1924.

1639 Droegereit (Richard). Sachsen und Angelsachsen. [Wilfrid, Willibrord, Boniface, etc.] Niedersächsisches Jahrbuch f. Landesgeschichte, 21, pp. 1–62. 1949.

1640 Fenger (Helene). Friesland und England in ihren kulturellen und wirtschaftlichen Beziehungen. *Bonner Studien zur englischen Philologie*, 25. pp. 111. 8° Bonn, 1935. [Pp. 42–48, Die angelsächsischen Missionare Willibrord, Bonifaz, Luitger. Also archaeology, place-names, laws, etc.]

1641 Fowlis (*Sir* James), *of Colinton, bart*. Of the league said to have been formed between the emperor Charlemagne and the king of Scotland. Archaeol. Scot., 1, pp. 26–28. 1792.

1642 Grierson (Philip). The relations between England and Flanders before the Norman Conquest. [With sketch map of the county of Flanders at the close of the 10th c.] Trans. R.H.S., 4th S. 23, pp. 71–112, + map. 1941.

1643 Gwynn (Aubrey). Ireland and the continent in the eleventh century. Irish Hist. Stud., 8, pp. 193–216. 1953.

1644 Haff (Karl). Das Grosskirchspiel im nordischen und niederdeutschen Rechte des Mittelalters. [Pp. 28–31, der angelsächsische Einfluss auf die Kircheneinteilung in Norwegen.] Zeit. Rechtsges., 76, Kanon. Abt. 32, pp. 1–63. 1943.

1645 Howorth (*Sir* Henry Hoyle). The early intercourse of the Franks and Danes. Part 3. [Some A.-S. background, pp. 32–.] Trans. R.H.S., N.S. 1, pp. 18–61. 1883.

1646 —— The intercourse of the Danes with the Franks, etc. [In spite of title, deals largely with the wars of the Danes in Ireland.] *Same jnl.*, N.S. 2, pp. 302–34. 1885.

1647 Krappe (Alexander Haggerty). Spanish matter in British chronicles. [A.-S. stories in post-Conquest authors : i. Story of magician Pellitus and Edwin from Geoffrey of Monmouth : ii. Story of Buern Brucecarle, explaining the coming of the Danes to Northumberland from Gaimar.] Anglia, 58 (N.F. 46), pp. 358–67. 1934.

1648 Latham (Robert Gordon). The relation of the Lombards to the Angles. Trans. R. Soc. Lit., 2nd S. 6, pp. 416–47. 1859.

1649 Lindsay (Jack). Byzantium into Europe. pp. 485, + 9 plates. 8° London, 1952. [Pp. 291–94, links with Britain : Saxon art.]

1650 Lopez (Robert Sabatino). Le problème des relations anglo-byzantines du septième au dixième siècle. Byzantion, 18, pp. 139–62. 1948.

1651 Loth (Joseph). Bretons en Irlande. [Annals of Ulster, 822. ?a monastery of Breton origin.] Rev. celt., 28, p. 417. 1907.

1652 —— Bretons insulaires en Irlands. [Incursions and settlements of Bretons in Ireland.] Rev. celt., 18, pp. 304–09. 1897.

1653 Moore (Arthur William). The early connexion of the Isle of Man with Ireland. E.H.R., 4, pp. 714–22. 1889.

1654 Moran (Patrick Francis), *cardinal, abp. of Sydney*. On the early relations of Ireland with the Isle of Man. Irish Eccles. Rec., 5, pp. 241–61. 1869.

1655 Ratton (M. H.). The Saxon Borgo in Rome. Nat. Rev., 110, pp. 361–72. 1938.

1656 Salin (Éduard). Les traces d'industrie et de peuplement saxon ou anglo-saxon en Gaule mérovingienne. Rev. archéol., 6e S. 31–32, pp. 917–25. 1948.

1657 Sareatti (Mario). Influenza reciproca del diritto romano e del diritto anglosassone. Studi in memoria di A. Albertoni, pp. 563–75. 1938.

1657a Strasser (Karl Theodor). Sachsen und Angelsachsen. 2. Auflage. pp. 188. 8° Hamburg, 1935.

1658 Tesoroni (Domenico). The Anglo-Saxons at Rome. [Schola Saxonum, vicus Saxonum, Peter's pence, etc.] Archaeol. Rev., 4, pp. 32–50. 1889.

1659 Vasiliev (A. A.). The Anglo-Saxon immigration to Byzantium. Seminarium Kondakovianum (Prague), 9. 1937.

1660 Wallace-Hadrill (J. M.). The Franks and the English in the ninth century : some common historical interests. [Resistance to Norsemen : making of annals :—? for support of royal house.] History, N.S. 35, pp. 202–18. 1950.

1661 Williams (*Sir* Ifor). Wales and the North. [Connexions in early centuries.] Trans. Cumb. and Westm. Antiq. Soc., N.S. 51 (1951), pp. 73–88. 1952.

1662 Zimmer (Heinrich). Ueber die frühesten Berührungen der Iren mit den Nordgermanen. Sitzungsb. preuss. Akad. Wiss., 1891, pp. 279–317. 1891.

20. ANGLO-SAXON 'PROPAGANDA' IN NORMAN AND ANGEVIN TIMES

1663 Brown (Arthur Charles Lewis). A note on the *nugae* of G. H. Gerould's 'King Arthur and politics', [1665]. [Intrusion of the fairy Arthur into history by Geoffrey of Monmouth.] Speculum, 2, pp. 449–55. 1927.

1664 Chambers (*Sir* Edmund Kerchever). The date of Geoffrey of Monmouth's history. Rev. Engl. Studies, 1, pp. 431–36 : 3, pp. 332–3. 1925–27.

1665 Gerould (Gordon Hall). King Arthur and politics. [Geoffrey's Historia written to provide political prestige to be inherited by contemporary kings : Arthur legend created for purpose—also miraculous cures by Confessor.] Speculum, 2, pp. 33–51, 448. 1927.

1666 Giffin (Mary E.). Cadwalader, Arthur, and Brutus in the Wigmore manuscript. [re propaganda for royalty of Mortimer genealogy.] Speculum, 16, pp. 109–120. 1941.

1667 Hope (Henry G.), *etc.* King Arthur. [Angevin account of his grave at Camelford.] N. and Q., 6th S. 11, pp. 54–55. 1885.

1668 Jones (W. A.). On the reputed discovery of king Arthur's remains at Glastonbury. Proc. Somerset Archaeol. Soc., 9 (1859), pp. 128–41, +1 plate. 1860.

1669 Lewis (Timothy) and **Bruce** (J. Douglas). The pretended exhumation of Arthur and Guinevere. An unpublished Welsh account based on Giraldus Cambrensis. [With Irish text and English translation.] Rev. celt., 33, pp. 432–51. 1912.

1670 Loomis (Roger Sherman). Geoffrey of Monmouth and Arthurian origins. Speculum, 3, pp. 16–33. 1928.

1671 Loth (Joseph). Gaufrei de Monmouth et le Livre de Llandaf. (Remarques sur le Livre de Llandaf.) [Opposes theory of Gwenogfryn Evans that it was written by Geoffrey.] Rev. celt., 15, pp. 101–04, 369–70. 1894.

1672 Nitze (William Albert). The exhumation of king Arthur at Glastonbury. [1191. Angevin propaganda.] Speculum, 9, pp. 353–61. 1934.

1673 —— Geoffrey of Monmouth's king Arthur. Speculum, 2, pp. 317–21. 1927.

1674 Parry (John Jay). Geoffrey of Monmouth and the paternity of Arthur. Speculum, 13, pp. 269–77. 1938.

1675 Parsons (A. E.). The Trojan legend in England : some instances of its application to the politics of the times. Mod. Lang. Rev., 24, pp. 253–64, 394–408. 1929.

1676 Slover (Clark Harris). William of Malmesbury and the Irish. [Part played by Malmesbury in transmitting Celtic culture ' during his period of service as a writer of advertising propaganda for the great publicity campaign at Glastonbury Abbey.'] Speculum, 2, pp. 268–83. 1927.

1677 —— William of Malmesbury's Life of St. Patrick. [Principal versions in existence in William's time. Reconstruction of this lost life and its part in propaganda campaign of Glastonbury.] Mod. Philol., 24, pp. 5–20. 1926.

III. LOCAL HISTORY

21. DEVON AND CORNWALL

1677a [Anon.] The mythical history of Devon. ii. The legends of king Athelstan. (Barnstaple under king Athelstan). Devonian Y.B., 14, pp. 87–94 : 21, pp. 63–64. 1923, 1930.

1678 Alexander (John James). The beginnings of Ilfracombe. Rept. and Trans. Devon. Assoc., 65, pp. 207–12. 1933.

1679 —— The beginnings of Lifton. [A.-S. and Domesday.] *Same jnl.*, 63, pp. 349–58. 1931.

1680 —— The beginnings of Tavistock [i. Introduction : ii. The Celtic periods, 500 B.C.–A.D. 700 : iii. 8th and 9th centuries : iv. 10th c. : v. 11th c., *etc.*] *Same jnl.*, 74, pp. 173–202. 1942.

1681 —— Pilton with Barnstaple [in Anglo-Saxon times.] *Same jnl.*, 72, pp. 100–02. 1941.

1682 —— Second report on early history of Devon. [Includes ' chronological summary of events that occurred in Devon between 800 and 940.'] Third *ditto.* [*Ditto* . . . 940–1016.] Fourth *ditto.* [*Ditto* . . . 1016–69.] Seventh *ditto.* [i. Sub-Roman period : ii. West-Saxon bishoprics.] Tenth *ditto.* [I. C. Saxon conquest of east Devon : D. Early English place-names : II. A. Evolution of the hundred system : B. Statistical comparison of Domesday hundreds.] *Same jnl.*, 61, pp. 133–36 : 62, pp. 153–56 : 63, pp. 137–38 : 68, pp. 98–104 : 71, pp. 109–24. 1929–31, 1936, 1939.

1682a —— The Saxon conquest of Devon, [568–825]. Devonian Y.B., 8, pp. 82–91. 1917.

1683 —— Some notes on Tavistock history. Second series. [Pp. 372–75, A.-S. period.] Rept. and Trans. Devon. Assoc., 47, pp. 372–95. 1915.

G

1684 Alexander (John James). Werrington [in Anglo-Saxon times.] *Same jnl.*, 73, pp. 93–96. 1941.

1685 —— When the Saxons came to Devon. [i. Introductory : ii. The mid-Victorian writers : iii. The five conclusions : iv. The simultaneity of the conquest : v. The nature of the conquest : vi. 5th and 6th centuries : vii. 7th c. : viii. The limit of 710 : ix. The early inhabitants of Devon : x. The ancient name of Devon : xi. Phonology of the name : xii. A Wessex chronology : xiii. Wars of Ine : xiv. Charter of Athelhard : xv. Importance of place-names : xvi. Village names : xvii. Reign of Cuthred : xviii. Sigebert and Cynewulf : xix. End of 8th c. : xx. Boniface : xxi. Egbert : xxii. Gafulford : xxiii. Hengestesdun.] *Same jnl.*, 51, pp. 152–68 : 52, pp. 293–309 : 53, pp. 168–79 : 54, pp. 187–98. 1919–23.

1686 —— Wonford in early times. *Same jnl.*, 72, pp. 97–107. 1940.

1687 Amery (John Sparke). Address of the President, 1924 [to the Devonshire Association, on the history of Ashburton]. [Pp. 46–49, ' Saxon Ashburton,' and Domesday material.] *Same jnl.*, 56 (1924), pp. 43–102, + 2 plates. 1925.

1688 Appleton (Edward). Archaeological notes on Tavistock and neighbourhood. [Pp. 122–24, A.-S. period.] *Same jnl.*, 1, part 5, pp. 122–27, + 2 plates. 1866.

1689 Baring-Gould (Sabin). The early history of Cornwall. J. Roy. Inst. Cornwall, 13, pp. 368–86. 1898.

1690 Brushfield (Thomas Nadauld). Notes on the parish of East Budleigh. [Including Domesday material. *See also* **1716.**] Dept. and Trans. Devon. Assoc., 22, pp. 260–316, + map, + 1 plate. 1890.

1691 Carbonell (Barbara M. H.). The Nymet area. [?=' Sanctuary Land' in pagan times (the forest being pagan groves). Irish *nemed* = a sanctuary : Nimet or Limet in Domesday.] *Same inl.*, 63, pp. 297–99, + map. 1931.

1692 Chanter (John Frederick). The beginnings of Crediton (A.D. 550–780). *Same jnl.*, 54, pp. 138–45. 1923.

1693 —— Celtic Devon. [Pp. 53–66, ' Celtic Devon in post-Roman times '.] *Same jnl.*, 57 (1925), pp. 39–66. 1926.

1694 —— The parishes of Lynton and Countisbury. —1. Introductory, antiquities, historical sketch, and manors. [Pp. 121–22, place-names : pp. 122–24, 138–39, 150, 154, 160, 164, Domesday material.] *Same jnl.*, 38, pp. 114–68, + 6 plates. 1906.

1694a Chope (Richard Pearse). The early history of Devon as told in the Anglo-Saxon Chronicle, with notes from other sources. Devonian Y.B., 2, pp. 108–16. 1911.

1695 —— The early history of the manor of Hartland. [Pp. 418–21, A.-S. period and Domesday.] Rept. and Trans. Devon. Assoc., 34, pp. 418–54, + map. 1902.

1696 Crofts (C. B.). King Athelstan and the parish of St. Buryan. [Battle : grant to church.] Devon and Cornwall N. and Q., 23, pp. 337–42. 1949.

1697 Davidson (James Bridge). On the ancient history of Exmouth. [Pp. 144–57, A.-S. period.] Rept. and Trans. Devon. Assoc., 15, pp. 144–62, + map. 1883.

1698 —— On the early history of Dawlish. [A.-S. period, includes text in A.-S., Latin and English of charter of 1044, and of that of 1069 in Latin and English.] *Same jnl.*, 13, pp. 106–130, + map (1044). 1881.

1699 —— Seaton before the Conquest. *Same jnl.*, 17, pp. 193–98, + map. 1885.

1700 Duke (*Sir* Henry E.). The place of Damnonia in British history. *Same jnl.*, 54, pp. 43–60. 1923.

1701 Finberg (Herbert Patrick Reginald). The Castle of Cornwall. [Exchanged by Robert, count of Mortain, for manors of Benton and Haxton from the bishop of Exeter, between 1066 and 1086. ?= Launceston.] Devon and Cornwall N. and Q., 23, p. 123. 1947.

1702 —— The early history of Werrington, [Devon]. E.H.R., 59, pp. 237–251. 1944.

1703 Freeman (Edward Augustus). The place of Exeter in the history of England. [Pp. 307–18, A.-S.] Archaeol. J., 30, pp. 297–318. 1873.

1704 Greswell (William Henry Parr). Ancient Dumnonia. Proc. Somerset Arch. Soc., 47 (1901), pp. 175–88. 1902.

1705 Harris (S. G.). Notes on the state of Newton [Abbot] and its neighbourhood before the fifteenth century. [Pp. 217–21, Domesday material.] Rept. and Trans. Devon. Assoc., 18, pp. 215–28. 1886.

1706 Hoskins (William George). Devon. *A new survey of England.* pp. xx, 600. 8° London, 1954. [Pp. 39–56, ' the English settlement '—A.-S. 58 illustrations : 19 maps and plans.]

1707 —— The formation of parishes in Devonshire. [In Exe valley, 700–1200.] Devon and Cornwall N. and Q., 17, pp. 212–14, + map. 1933.

1708 Hutchinson (P. O.). Honey ditches. [Incursions of Danish chief, Hanna, in Axe valley.] Rept. and Trans. Devon. Assoc., 17, pp. 277–80, + map. 1885.

1709 Jenner (Henry). Who are the Celts and what has Cornwall to do with them ? pp. 42. 8° St. Ives, [19–?]

1710 Kerslake (Thomas). The Celt and the Teuton in Exeter. Archaeol. J., 30, pp. 211–25, + plan. 1873.

1711 King (Richard John). President's address [to the Devonshire Association]. [Largely on Devon in A.-S. times.] Rept. and Trans. Devon. Assoc., 7, pp. 25–49. 1875.

1712 Lega-Weekes (Ethel), *etc.* Ancient demesne or Cornwall fee. [Pre-Conquest status of South Tawton, Devon.] N. and Q., 9th, S. 10, pp. 443–44 : 11, pp. 153, 210–11, 449–50 : 12, pp. 72–73. 1902–03.

1713 Morshead (J. Y. A.). A history of Salcombe Regis. [Pp. 132–37, A.-S. and Domesday material.] Rept. and Trans. Devon. Assoc., 30, pp. 132–46, + plan. 1898.

1714 —— Our four parishes : Sidbury, Sidmouth, Salcombe Regis, and Branscombe. [Pp. 147–51, A.-S. period and Domesday. Map shows the four parishes ' at date of Domesday.'] *Same jnl.*, 35, pp. 146–55, + coloured folding map. 1903.

1715 Perry (Francis A.). Some literary associations of Celtic and Saxon Devon. [Aldhelm, Boniface, Leofric, bp. of Crediton, Exeter Book.] *Same jnl.*, 58 (1926), pp. 209–22. 1927.

1716 Phear (*Sir* John Budd). Additional notes [i.e. to those of T. N. Brushfield, *q.v.*, **1690**] on the parish of East Budleigh. [Including Domesday material.] *Same jnl.*, 23, pp. 203–14. 1891.

1716a Radford (Courtenay Arthur Ralegh). The Dumnonii. [Pp. 20–24, A.-S. period.] J. Roy. Inst. Cornwall, N.S. 2, pp. 12–24. 1953.

1717 Radford (*Mrs.* G. H.). Lydford town. [Plate shows ' pennies of Æthelred II struck at Lydford. Pp. 175–80, A.-S. period.] Rept. and Trans. Devon. Assoc., 37, pp. 175–87, + 1 plate. 1905.

1718 Reichel (Oswald Joseph). Hulham manor. A sketch, historical and economic. [Pp. 404–06, Domesday material.] *Same jnl.*, 27, pp. 404–36, + map. 1895.

1719 Rose-Troup (Frances). Holcombe by Dawlish [in A.-S. times]. [Pp. 266–67, ' translations of entries in the Sherborne cartulary, f. 14d.'] *Same jnl.*, 62, pp. 261–67. 1930.

1720 —— Newton St. Cyres and Norton. [A.-S. and Domesday material.] *Same jnl.*, 68, pp. 221–31. 1936.

1721 Rowe (J. Brooking). Presidential address [to the Devonshire Association, on the history of Crediton]. [Pp. 35–40, A.-S. period.] *Same jnl.*, 14, pp. 33–116. 1882.

1722 Skinner (Emily). Old Tiverton or Twyford. [Including A.-S. and Domesday material.] *Same jnl.*, 38, pp. 380–90. 1906.

1723 Smith (—), *Prebendary*. The early history of Crediton. [Pp. 192–95, A.-S. period, and St. Boniface.] *Same jnl.*, 14, pp. 191–98. 1882.

1724 Taylor (Thomas). St. Michael's mount and the Domesday survey. J. Roy. Inst. Cornwall, 17, pp. 230–35. 1908.

1725 Tuckett (John). [History of] Crediton. J. Brit. Archaeol. Assoc., 18, pp. 91–96. 1862.

1726 Varwell (P.). Notes on the ancient parish of Brixham, Devon, and on some of its ancient people. [Pp. 200–05, Brixham in Domesday.] Rept. and Trans. Devon. Assoc., 18, pp. 197–214, + 2 maps. 1886.

1727 Vidal (Robert Studley). An inquiry respecting the site of Kenwith or Kenwic castle in Devonshire. [See Asser, sub anno 878.] Archaeologia, 15, pp. 198–208. 1806.

1728 Watkin (Hugh Robert). Dittisham parish and church. [Pp. 37–39, A.-S. and Domesday period.] Rept. and Trans. Devon. Assoc., 50, pp. 37–50. 1918.

1729 Worth (Richard Nicholls). Beginnings of Plympton history. [Place-name and Domesday material.] *Same jnl.*, 19, pp. 363–76. 1887.

1730 —— Early days in South Molton. [Pp. 123–25, Domesday material.] *Same jnl.*, 26, pp. 122–32. 1894.

1731 —— Lydford and its castle. [Pp. 284–86, A.-S. period. *Same jnl.*, 11, pp. 283–302. 1879.

1732 —— Notes on the early history of Tavistock. *Same jnl.*, 21, pp. 132–37. 1889.

1733 Worth (Richard Nicholls) Okehampton beginnings. [Place-name and Domesday material.] *Same jnl.*, 27, pp. 93–112. 1895.

1734 —— Side lights on the early history of Torquay. [Domesday material, etc.] *Same jnl.*, 25, pp. 261–70. 1893.

22. EAST ANGLIA

(Norfolk, Suffolk, Essex, and Cambs.)

1735 Benham (*Sir* William Gurney). The reputed arms of the East Saxons. [3 *seaxes*, or Saxon swords. Quoting Verstegan (1605), and Speed (1611), also MSS. Stowe 670, fol. 110 and Harl. 1894, fol. 262.] Essex Rev., 24, pp. 161–68, + 1 plate. 1915.

1736 Bruce-Mitford (Rupert Leo Scott). Saxon Rendlesham: some preliminary considerations. [i. Royal associations : ii. Rendlesham and Sutton Hoo : iii. The status of the vicus regius at Rendlesham : iv. Church and temple : v. Physical character of the vicus regius : vi. General importance of the site : vii. Topography : viii. Site of the early church ; and a pagan cemetery on Hoo hill.] Proc. Suffolk Inst. Arch., 24, pp. 228–51, + 5 plates. 1948.

1737 Clarke (Roy Rainbird). Anglo-Saxon Norfolk. Archaeol. J., 106 (1949), p. 71. 1951.

1738 —— Norfolk in the Dark Ages, 400–800 A.D. Part 1. [Physical geography of Norfolk and it influence on the Anglian settlement : general character of the Anglian settlement, c. 450–550 : consolidation and expansion, c. 550–800 : A.-S. pottery of Norfolk, by J.N.L. Myres, *q.v.* **8591**.] Norfolk Archaeology, 27, pp. 163–249, + 12 plates. 1941.

1739 Clarke (William George). A brief survey of the history of Thetford. Eastern Counties Mag., 1, pp. 83–87, 175–78, 264–68. 1900–01.

1740 Conybeare (John William Edward). A history of Cambridgeshire. pp. xxviii, 307. 8° London, 1897. [Pp. 34–112, A.-S. period.]

1741 Cooke (William). Materials for a history of Hessett, [Suffolk]. [Pp. 301–03, A.-S. and Domesday.] Proc. Suffolk Inst. Archaeol., 4, pp. 301–32, + 2 plates. 1872.

1742 Cuming (Henry Syer). On the kings of East Anglia. J. Brit. Archaeol. Assoc., 21, pp. 22–31. 1865.

1743 Darby (Henry Clifford). The medieval fenland. pp. xvii, 200, + 11 plates. 8° Cambridge, 1940. [Pp. 1–20, the pre-Domesday fenland. With 5 maps, + 4 plates.]

1744 —— and **Miller** (E.). Political history [of Cambridgeshire]. [1. Anglo-Saxon settlement and Danish invasion: the Anglo-Norman settlement.] V.C.H., Cambs., 2, pp. 377–89. 1948.

1745 Deedes (Cecil). Little Cornard, Suffolk. [Domesday material.] East Anglian (N. and Q.), N.S. 1, pp. 302–05. 1886.

1746 Dunning (Gerald Clough). The Saxon town of Thetford. Archaeol. J., 106 (1949), pp. 72–73. 1951.

1747 Farrer (William). Feudal Cambridgeshire. pp. xii, 354. fol. Cambridge, 1920. [By hundred and place : including Domesday.]

1748 Freeman (Edward Augustus). Address to the Historical Section of the annual meeting of the [Royal Archaeological] Institute at Colchester, 1876. [Some material for history of East Saxon kingdom.] Archaeol. J., 34, pp. 47–75. 1877.

1749 Gray (Arthur). The dual origin of the town of Cambridge. *Cambridge Antiquarian Society, Quarto Publications,* N.S. 1. pp. 32, + map. 4° Cambridge, 1908.

1750 Green (W. C.). The Norsemen in Suffolk. Saga-Book V.C., 2, pp. 147–50. 1899.

1751 Harris (Harold Augustus). Thorndon before the Conquest. Trans. Suffolk Inst. Archaeol., 18, pp. 222–34, + map. 1924.

1752 Hore (S. Coode). Navestock in olden days ; stray notes, prehistoric, Saxon, and Norman. [Pp. 223–35, Navestock in Saxon times. Watch and ward.] Essex Nat., 8, pp. 220–44. 1894.

1753 Howard (Eliot). The place of Essex in early English history. Essex Rev., 18, pp. 1–13. 1909.

1753a Knocker (G. M.) and **Hughes** (R. G.). Anglo-Saxon Thetford. [Dating, house construction, industry, small finds, sites, etc.]. Archaeol. News Letter, 2, pp. 117–22; 3, pp. 41–46. 1950.

1754 Lethbridge (Thomas Charles). Anglo-Saxon Cambridgeshire. [Character of the country-side, houses of the pagan period, evidence of warfare in the pagan period, cemeteries of the pagan (–Christian) period, list of crosses of the late A.-S. period, list of objects of the Viking and late A.-S. periods, sites where pottery of the late A.-S. period have been found, the Viking age, the end of the A.-S. period in Cambs.]V.C.H. Cambs., 1, pp. 305–33, + map, + 12 plates. 1938.

1755 Miller (Samuel Henry). Henry of Huntingdon on the Fens. Fenland N. and Q., 3, pp. 216–18. 1896.

1756 —— Illustrations of the traces of the Romans and Saxons in the Fen district of the Isle of Ely (from notes by Marshall Fisher of Ely.) J. Brit. Archaeol. Assoc., 35, pp. 147–50. 1879.

1757 Morgan (Thomas). On East Anglian history in Saxon times. *Same jnl.*, 36, pp. 185–200. 1880.

1758 Morley (Claude). Freckenham, Suffolk : notes and theories on the village and its unrecorded castle [till 1086]. Proc. Suffolk Inst. Archaeol., 17, pp. 182–92, + map. 1921.

1759 —— A Norse camp at Brandon, Suffolk. [?relics of fight in 870.] Saga-Book V.C., 10, pp. 264–66. 1928.

1760 —— A Saxon village, visited 12th June, 1923 [by the Suffolk Institute of Archaeology]. [Haughley.] Trans. Suffolk Inst. Archaeol., 18, pp. 156–57. 1923.

1761 —— and **Cooper** (Ernest Read). The sea port of Frostenden. i. Its place in history : ii. The Danish quay discovered. *Same jnl.*, 18, pp. 167–79. 1924.

1762 Olerenshaw (J. R.). History of Soham, [Cambs.]. [Pp. 163–78, A.-S. period.] Fenland N. and Q., 1, pp. 163–72. 1890.

1763 Pollitt (William). The archaeology of Rochford hundred, south-east Essex. [Pp. 34–38, 60–63, + plates 13–14, A.-S.] Trans. Southend Antiq. Soc., 3, pp. 12–63, + 22 plates. 1935.

1764 —— Southend before the Norman Conquest : being the second (revised) edition of the archaeology of Rochford hundred and south east Essex. *Borough of Southend.* pp. 81, [22 plates in text]. 8° Southend, 1953. [Pp. 37–42, + 2 figures, A.-S.]

1765 Reaney (Percy Hide). The kings of Essex. Fact and fiction. [Correcting **1771**.] Essex Rev., 59, pp. 144–50. 1950.

1766 Redstone (Vincent Burrough). Notes on Suffolk castles. ii. Burgh. [Allusion in Bede, E.H.] Trans. Suffolk Inst. Archaeol., 11, pp. 308–14. 1903.

1767 Round (John Horace). An early reference to Domesday. [Re Chingford, Essex.] Domesday Studies, 2, pp. 539–59. 1891.

1768 —— The honour of Ongar. [Pp. 142–3, A.-S. and Domesday.] Trans. Essex Archaeol. Soc., N.S. 7, pp. 142–52. 1900.

1769 Rye (Walter). Traces of Norsk settlements in Norfolk. Norfolk Antiq. Misc., 1, pp. 184–94. 1873.

1770 Skeat (Walter William), *etc.* Ythancæster, Essex. [Cedd's church. St. Peter's, Bradwell-juxta-Mare.] N. and Q., 10th S. 4, pp. 90–91. 1905.

1771 Stewart (M. J.). The kings of Essex. [*But see* corrections in **1765**.] Essex Rev., 59. pp. 69–77. 1950.

1772 Stokes (Ethel) and **Round** (John Horace). Political history [of Essex]. [Pp. 204–10, A.-S. period.] V.C.H., Essex, 2, pp. 203–57. 1907.

1773 Whittingham (A. B.). The origins of Norwich. [Substance of lecture.] Archaeol. J., 106 (1949), pp. 74–75, + plan. 1951.

23. KENT

1774 Bosanquet (Geoffrey). Dover in 1066. Extracts translated from the Gesta Guillelmi ducis Normannorum by William of Poictou, archdeacon of Lisieux. Arch. Cant., 61 (1948), pp. 156–59. 1949.

1775 Box (E. G.). Notes on the history of Saxon Otford. Arch. Cant., 43, pp. 111–22, + plate. 1931.

1776 Curling (—) *Captain* and **Wright** (George). On the historical associations connected with the Reculver. J. Brit. Archaeol. Assoc., 9, pp. 391–98. 1854.

1777 Derham (Walter). The Fordwich stone and its legend. *Same jnl.*, N.S. 24, pp. 111–28, + 6 plates. 1918.

1778 Furley (Robert). The early history of Tenterden. [Pp. 38–41, A.-S. and Domesday, pannage, etc.] Arch. Cant., 14, pp. 37–60. 1882.

1779 Godfrey-Faussett (Thomas Godfrey). Canterbury till Domesday. Archaeol. J., 32, pp. 369–93, + 3 plans. 1875.

1780 Hardman (F. W.) and **Stebbing** (William Pinckard Delane). Stonar and the Wantsum channel. Part 1. Physiographical : Part 2. Historical, with an appendix on the [polychrome] pottery, by G. C. Dunning. Arch. Cant., 53, pp. 62–80, + plate, + map : 54, pp. 41–61, + plate. 1941–42.

1781 Jenkins (Robert Charles). The Saxon dynasty. Pedigree of the Kentish kings. pp. xx, 48, + 7 plates. 8° Folkestone, 1867. [Pp. 47–48, list of Kentish charters.]

1782 Jolliffe (John Edward Austin). Pre-feudal England : the Jutes. *Oxford Historical series.* pp. x, 122, + 2 maps. 8° London, 1933. [i. Kent : ii. The Jutish south-east : iii. The continental Jutes : iv. The hundred in Kent.]

1783 Jonas (Alfred Charles). Rochester, its castles and bridges. [*See also* note by W. F. Prideaux in 5, pp. 75–76, 1903.] Home Counties Mag., 4, pp. 261–67. 1902.

1784 Oman (*Sir* Charles William Chadwick). The kingdom of Kent. [To 859.] Archaeol. J., 86, pp. 1–19. 1929.

1785 Philip (Alexander John). The long ferry and its foundation. [Pp. 56–60, translations of the passages in Domesday relating to Gravesend, Milton, Denton, Northfleet, Southfleet and Higham.] Home Counties Mag., 14, pp. 56–66, + 1 plate. 1912.

1786 Philip (Alexander John) History of Gravesend and its surroundings. Vol. 1. pp. 151, + 18 plates. 8° London, 1914. [No more published. Pp. 83–98, + 5 plates, the Northmen in the Thames.]

1787 —— The Northmen in the Thames. [Remarks on Gravesend and district in A.-S. times.] Home Counties Mag., 13, pp. 217–22. 1911.

1788 Simkins (Maud E.). Political history [of Kent]. [Pp. 271–81, A.-S. period.] V.C.H., Kent, 3, pp. 271–317. 1932.

1789 Taylor (George Robert Stirling). The story of Canterbury. *Mediaeval town series.* pp. x, 390. 8° London, 1912. [Pp. 18–94, A.-S. period. Augustine, Saxon Canterbury, the Danes, at the Norman Conquest, Lanfranc.]

1790 Ward (Gordon). A note on the Mead Way, the street and Doddinghyrnan in Rochester. Arch. Cant., 62 (1949), pp. 37–44. 1950.

1791 —— The origins of Whitstable. Arch. Cant., 57 (1944), pp. 51–55. 1945.

1792 —— The Saxon history of the town and port of Romney. [With facsimile and translation of charter of 740 from Æthelbeorht II, king of Kent.] Arch. Cant., 65 (1952), pp. 12–25, + 1 plate. 1953.

1793 Ward (Gordon). The Saxon history of the Wantsum. [Between Thanet and mainland.] Arch. Cant., 56 (1943), pp. 23–27. 1944.

1794 —— Saxon Lydd. [p. 31, Sketch map.] Arch. Cant., 43, pp. 29–37, + plate. 1931.

1795 —— Saxon records of Tenterden. [i. The Heronden charter of 968, with identifications and map : ii. The charter of 833 : iii. The forming of the church of St. Mildred : iv. Place-names.] Arch. Cant., 49, pp. 229–46, + plate (facsimile of 968 charter). 1938.

1796 —— The Vikings come to Thanet. [753 : sack of Minster, 826.] Arch. Cant., 63 (1950), pp. 57–62. 1951.

24. LONDON

1797 Bromehead (Cyril Edward Nowill). The influence of its geography on the growth of London. [Pp. 130–31, A.-S. and Domesday.] Geog. J., 60, pp. 125–35. 1922.

1798 Gomme (*Sir* George Laurence). The making of London. pp. 255. 8° Oxford, 1912. [Pp. 96–125, A.-S. period.]

1799 Home (Gordon) and **Foord** (Edward). Mediaeval London. pp. 382, + map, + 19 plates. 8° London, 1927. [Pp. 17–67, A.-S. period.]

1800 Lethaby (William Richard). London before the Conquest. pp. ix, 217. 8° London, 1902. [Gross, 1009a. 43 figures in text.]

1801 Loftie (William John). London as the capital of Essex. [Kingdom of Essex, 5th–9th centuries.] Trans. Essex Archaeol. Soc., N.S. 1, pp. 220–31. 1878.

1802 London Museum. London and the Saxons, by R. E. M. Wheeler. *Catalogues*, 6. pp. 200. 8° London, 1935.

1803 —— London and the Vikings, by R. E. M. Wheeler. *Catalogues*, 1. pp. 55, + plates. 8° London, 1927.

1804 Myres (John Nowell Linton). Some thoughts on the topography of Saxon London. [Reply to Wheeler, 1812.] Antiquity, 8, pp. 437–42. 1934.

1805 Page (William). Notes on some early riverside settlements of London. [With discussion. Queenhithe, or Æthelred's Hithe, 9th c., etc.] Proc. Soc. Antiq., 2nd S. 31, pp. 125–27. 1919.

1806 Saunders (George). Results of an inquiry concerning the situation and extent of Westminster, at various periods. [Pp. 223–25, + first plan, A.-S. and Domesday period.] Archaeologia, 26, pp. 223–41, + 3 plans. 1836.

1807 Shore (Thomas William). Anglo-Saxon London and its neighbourhood. Trans. Lond. and Middsx. Archaeol. Soc., N.S. 1, pp. 366–91. 1905.

1808 —— Anglo-Saxon London and Middlesex. *Same jnl.*, N.S. 1, pp. 469–505. 1905.

1809 Shore (Thomas William). The Anglo-Saxon settlement round London, and glimpses of Anglo-Saxon life in and near it. pp. 36. 8° [1900].

1810 Spence (James Lewis Thomas Chalmers). Legendary London. Early London in tradition and history. pp. 286. 8° London, 1937.

1811 Stenton (*Sir* Frank Merry). Norman London. *Historical Association Leaflets*, 93–94. pp. 40, + plan. 8° London, 1934.

1812 Wheeler (*Sir* Robert Eric Mortimer). The topography of Saxon London. (Mr. Myres on Saxon London [1804] : a reply). Antiquity, 8, pp. 290–302, 443–47. 1934.

1812a Whitaker-Wilson (Cecil). Two thousand years of London. 2nd edition. pp. x, 330, + 20 plates. 8° London, 1933. [Pp. 18–69, A.-S.]

25. MERCIA

(between Thames and Humber)

1813 Allies (Jabez). On the ancient British, Roman and Saxon antiquities of Worcestershire. 2nd edition. pp. xv, 496, + 6 plates. 8° London, 1852.

1814 Andrews (Herbert C.). The six hills, Stevenage, [Herts.]. [? raised over Danes slaughtered on St. Brice's day, 1002.] East Herts. Archaeol. Soc., Trans., 3. ii. (1906), pp. 178–85, + 1 plate. 1907.

1815 Auden (George Augustus). Prehistory of the neighbourhood [of Birmingham]. [Pp. 17–28, outline of A.-S. period : history, cemeteries, crosses, etc.] Handbook for Birmingham (83rd meeting . . . B.A.), pp. 3–28. 1913.

1816 B. (R. W.). Herefordshire and its Welsh border during the Saxon period. Arch. Camb., 4th S. 13, pp. 19–40, + 1 map. 1882.

1817 Bannister (Arthur Thomas). Richard's Castle and the Normans in Herefordshire. Trans. Woolhope N.F.C., 1924–26, pp. 110–13. 1928.

1818 Bartleet (Samuel Edwin). History of the manor and advowson of Brockworth [Glos.]. [Pp. 132–35, A.-S. material, including entry in Domesday.] Trans. Bristol and Glos. Arch. Soc., 7, pp. 131–71. 1883.

1819 —— The manor and borough of Chipping Campden. [Contains (pp. 134–38, 354) place-name material, political history in A.-S. times and description in Domesday.] *Same jnl.*, 9, pp. 134–95, 354–55. 1885.

1820 Bazeley (William). Churchdown and Mattesdune before the Norman Conquest. Proc. Cottesw. Nat. F.C., 21, pp. 17–30. 1921.

1821 —— Notes on Buckland manor and advowson from A.D. 709 to A.D. 1546. [Includes description in Domesday, etc.] Trans. Bristol and Glos. Arch. Soc., 9, pp. 103–24. 1885.

1822 Bigsby (Robert). Historical and topographical description of Repton. pp. xxxiv, 410. 8° London, 1884. [Pp. 7–53, A.-S.]

1823 Binnall (Peter Blannin Gibbons). Descent of lands in East and West Barkwith, co. Lincoln. [i. Pre-Norman land-holders.] Lincs. Archit. and Archaeol. Soc., Rpts. 45 (N.S. 3), pp. 138–43. 1948.

1824 Brassington (William Salt). Historic Worcestershire. pp. xxiv, 328. 4° Birmingham, 1894. [Pp. 42–146, A.-S. Popular.]

1825 Braun (Hugh). Earliest Ruislip. Trans. Lond. and Middsx. Archaeol. Soc., N.S. 7, pp. 99–123, + 2 plans + 4 plates. 1937.

1826 Brooksbank (J. H.). Castleton [Derbs.]: its traditions, sayings, place-names, etc. (Further notes on Castleton and its neighbourhood). [Pp. 39–42, A.-S. period: kingdom of Orcoit or Argoed, etc.] Trans. Hunter Archaeol. Soc., 3, pp. 34–52: 4, pp. 306–08. 1929–37.

1827 Brown (Robert). Notes on the earlier history of Barton-on-Humber, [Lincs.]. 2 vol. 8° London [1906]. [Vol. 1, pp. 11–65, Anglo-Danish times.]

1828 Brownbill (John). A history of the old parish of Bidston, Cheshire [Part 1]. [Pp. 156–59 : chap. 2, 'Bidston in Domesday Book'. Map shows Wirral in 1086.] Trans. Hist. Soc. Lancs. and Ches., 87 (1935), pp. 133–99, + 2 plates, + folding map. 1936.

1829 Burbidge (Frederick Bliss). Old Coventry and Lady Godiva. pp. ix, 272. 8° Birmingham, [1952].

1830 Burgess (Joseph Tom). The Saxons in Warwickshire. pp. 11. 8° Warwick, 1877.

1831 Canham (A. S.). Notes on the history of Crowland : its charters and ancient crosses. J. Brit. Archaeol. Assoc., 46, pp. 116–29, + 3 plates (crosses, not A.-S.). 1890.

1832 Cardew (G. Arthur). Pre-Domesday Prestbury. Proc. Cheltenham Nat. Sci. Soc., 1896–7.

1833 Carlyle (E. I.). Political history [of Herefordshire]. [Pp. 347–57, A.-S. period.] V.C.H., Hereford, 1, pp. 347–405. 1908.

1834 Clark (George Thomas). Oswestry and Whittington. [And Domesday hundred of Mersete.] Arch. Camb., 4th S. 9, pp. 179–194. 1878.

1835 Cole (Robert Eden George). The royal burgh of Torksey [Lincs.], its churches, monasteries, and castle. [Pp. 451–60, A.-S. period.] Assoc. Archit. Socs'. Rpts., 28, pp. 451–530, + 3 plates. 1906.

1836 Collier (*Mrs.* B. F.). Historical notes on the town and priory of Stone [Staffs.]. J. Brit. Archaeol. Assoc., 52 (N.S. 2), pp. 75–79. 1896.

1837 Cottrill (Frank). Anglo-Saxon Leicestershire and Rutland. An illustrated catalogue. *City of Leicester Museum and Art Gallery*. pp. 24. 8° Leicester, 1946.

1838 Cracknell (F. K.). Grimsby before the Norman Conquest. Lincs. Mag., 3, pp. 106–09. 1937.

1839 Cronne (Henry Alfred). The borough of Warwick in the Middle Ages. *Dugdale Society, Occasional Papers*, 10. pp. 21. 8° Oxford, 1951. [pp. 8–14, A.-S. and Domesday.]

1840 Davies (Arthur Morley). Eleventh century Buckinghamshire. Rec. Bucks., 10, pp. 69–74. 1916.

1841 Davies (James). Herefordshire under the Britons, Romans and Anglo-Saxons. Arch. Camb., N.S. 5, pp. 91–107. 1854.

1842 Downs (R. S.). The Danes in Buckinghamshire. Rec. Bucks, 5, pp. 260–70. 1878.

1843 Edmonds (F. S.). Lyddington [Rutland] before the Norman Conquest. Rutland Mag., 3, pp. 9–12. 1907.

1844 Fletcher (A. W.). The parish of Eckington [Worcs.] : its church and records. [Pp. 147–48, A.-S. and Domesday.] Trans. Worcs. Archaeol. Soc., 2, pp. 146–63, + 5 plates. 1925.

1845 Fowler (William Warde). Kingham [Oxon.] old and new. pp. viii, 216, + 2 maps. 8° Oxford, 1913. [Pp. 1–24, A.-S. : pp. 25–34, Domesday.]

1846 Fox (Levi). The early history of Coventry. History, N.S. 30, pp. 21–37. 1945.

1847 Freeman (Edward Augustus). The early history of Chester. Archaeol. J., 43, pp. 250–72. 1886.

1848 Glover (Stephen). The history of the county of Derby. 2 vol. 8° Derby, 1829. [Vol. 1, pp. 317–71, A.-S.]

1849 Green (Emanuel). Nottingham castle. [Pp. 365–8, history of Nottingham in A.-S. period.] Archaeol. J., 58, pp. 365–97, + plan (1617), + 1 plate. 1901.

1850 Green (John Richard). The early history of Oxford. Oxford Hist. Soc., 41, pp. 1–24. 1901.

1851 Greene (Parnell). On the banks of the Dee : a legend of Chester concerning the fate of [king] Harold [II]. Preserved in the Harleian MS., British Museum. pp. x, 390. 8° London, 1886.

1852 Griffiths (R. G.). The early history of Clifton-on-Teme. [i. The tun and the hamme : ii. The vills. Appendix 1. The hide and plough of Domesday Book : Appendix 2. The will of Wulfgeat of Donnington, 1005.] Trans. Worcs. Archaeol. Soc., 6 (1929), pp. 68–91, + folding map of the parish in Norman times : 7 (1930), pp. 42–74, + 2 plates. 1930–31.

1852a Hallam (H. E.). The new lands of Elloe : a study of early reclamation in Lincolnshire. *Univ. Coll. Leicester, Dept. English local history, Occasional papers*, 6. pp. 42, + map. 8° Leicester, 1954. [Pp. 3–14, A.-S. settlement of Holland, Danish settlement of Holland, Domesday survey.]

1853 Harris (Mary Dormer). Life in an old English town. A history of Coventry from the earliest times compiled from official records. pp. xxiii, 391. 8° London, 1898. [Pp. 1–30, A.-S. (' i. Leofric and Godiva : ii. The Benedictine monastery.']

1854 Hawkes (Charles Francis Christopher). Anglo-Danish Lincolnshire and the deserted villages of the wolds. Archaeol. J., 103 (1946), pp. 100–01. 1947.

1855 Head (John Frederick). Buckinghamshire, A.D. 450–700. [Pp. 312–16, schedule of sites. 3 maps and 8 other figures in text.] Rec. Bucks., 14, pp. 301–40. 1946.

1856 Hill (James William Francis). Danish and Norman Lincoln. Assoc. Archit. Socs.' Rpts., 41 (1932), pp. 7–22. 1935.

**1857 —— ** Medieval Lincoln. pp. xvii, 487, + 23 plates. 8° Cambridge, 1948. [Pp. 15–63, English and Danish settlements : Norman Conquest.]

1858 Hipkins (Frederick Charles). Repton ; village, abbey, church, priory and school. pp. 64. 8° Derby, [1894]. [Pp. 4–14, A.-S. period.]

**1859 —— ** Repton and its neighbourhood. 2nd edition. pp. x, 142, + 22 plates. 8° Repton, 1899. [History, place-name, saints (Guthlac and Wystan, church, etc.]

1860 Historicus, *pseud.* Rutland, an old Mercian division. Leic. and Rutl. N. and Q., 1, pp. 73–76. 1891.

1861 Horwood (A. R.). Leicestershire in Anglo-Saxon times. Memorials of old Leicestershire, ed. Alice Dryden, pp. 88–101, + 2 plates. 1911.

1862 Hoskins (William George). The Anglian and Scandinavian settlement of Leicestershire. (Further notes, *etc.*). [Settlement of the county, 550–1000, A.D. with 5 pages of maps, and an appendix on the place-names of Leicestershire.] Trans. Leic. Archaeol. Soc., 18, pp. 109–47 : 19, pp. 93–109. 1935–36.

1863 Huyshe (Wentworth). The royal manor of Hitchin and its lords, [king] Harold [II] and the Balliols. pp. xiv, 197. 8° London, 1906.

1864 Hyett (F. A.). Incidents in the early history of Gloucester. [Roman period until 1100.]. Trans. Bristol and Glos. Arch. Soc., 26, pp. 83–107. 1903.

1865 Kerslake (Thomas). A Gloucestershire parish a thousand years ago. [Henbury and its charter of 883.] Antiq. Mag., 3, pp. 279–83, + map. 1883. *Reprinted in* : Glos. N. and Q., 6, pp. 101–04, 126–28. 1895.

1866 Kuhliche (F. W.). The Anglo-Saxons in Bedfordshire. Beds. Mag., 4, pp. 13–20. 1953.

1867 Langford (John Alfred). The Saxons in Warwickshire. B'ham and Midland Inst., Arch. Section, Trans., [10], pp. 70–84. 1881.

1868 Lawton (W. P.). Chester and the West Saxons. [c. 607–1066.] Wessex, 4, p. 183. 1938.

1869 McGovern (J. B.). Mercian origins. [i. Area : ii. Expansion to 704 : iii. Administration : iv. Lindsey bishopric.] N. and Q., 9th S. 9, pp. 1–3, 42–45. 1902.

1870 Madge (Sidney Joseph). The early records of Harringay alias Hornsey. From pre-historic times to 1216 A.D. *Hornsey Public Library.* pp. 99, + maps. 8° Hornsey, 1938.

1871 Mander (Gerald P.). Notes on Seisdon hundred, etc. [Hidation of Worfield—date of Kinver and Enville parishes, etc.] Collections for a history of Staffs., 1919, pp. 182–84. 1920.

1872 Mercier (Jerome). A history of Kemerton [Glos.]. [pp. 26–32, A.-S. and Domesday material.] Trans. Bristol and Glos. Arch. Soc., 19, pp. 24–40. 1895.

1873 Molyneux (William). A brief notice of the pre-Norman history of Repton, in Derbyshire. North Staffs. F.C. Ann. Rpt., [13], pp. 50–57. 1878.

1874 Morgan (Thomas). On the Briton, Roman, and Saxon, in Staffordshire. J. Brit. Archael. Assoc., 29, pp. 394–412. 1873.

1875 —— On the Wiccii and their territory. [Including as postscript : Grant from Offa, king of the Mercians, to Æthelmund, of land in Westbury, in the province of the Wiccas, A.D. 791–796. Text, transl. and 2 plates.] *Same jnl.*, 32, pp. 145–92, + 5 plates. 1876.

1876 Mortimer (William Williams). Memoir of the earls of Chester. Part I. On the Saxon earls. Hist. Soc. Lancs. and Ches., Proc., 2, pp. 215–25. 1850.

1877 Nevinson (Charles). Notes on the history of Stamford. [Pp. 160–63, A.-S. period.] J. Brit. Archaeol. Assoc., 35, pp. 159–68. 1879.

1878 Ormerod (George). Strigulensia. Archaeological memoirs relating to the district adjacent to the confluence of the Severn and the Wye. pp. viii, 118. 8° London, 1861. [Pp. 50–113, A.-S. and Norman period. All reprints from journals here listed, except pp. 73–77 : On the probable derivation and import of Estrighoiel, the name given to Chepstow in the Domesday survey.]

1879 Owen (Leonard Victor Davies). The borough of Nottingham, 1066–1284. [Including Domesday material.] Trans. Thoroton Soc., 49 (1945), pp. 12–27. 1946.

1880 —— The early history of Nottingham. [*i.e.* A.-S. period.] *Same jnl.*, 43 (1939), pp. 16–21. 1940.

1881 Palmer (Charles Ferrers). The history of the town and castle of Tamworth, in the counties of Stafford and Warwick. pp. xvi, 520, lxxvi, + plan. 8° Tamworth, 1845. [Pp. 8–55, A.-S. period.]

1882 Parker (James). The early history of Oxford to the close of the eleventh century. [Summary.] Proc. Oxford Archit. and Hist. Soc., N.S. 2, pp. 278–80. 1871.

1883 —— The early history of Oxford, 727–1100. *Oxford Historical Society*, 3. pp. xxxi, 420, + 2 maps. 8° Oxford, 1885. [Pp. 221–304, the description of Oxford in 1086, as given in the Domesday Survey.]

1884 —— On the history of Oxford during the tenth and eleventh centuries (912–1100): the material of a lecture delivered before the Oxford Architectural and Historical Society, Feb. 28, 1871. pp. 80, + map. 8° Oxford, 1871.

1885 Partington (S. W.). The Danes in Lancashire and Cheshire. pp. vi, 246. 8° London, 1909.

1886 Patrick (George). Some account of Peakirk, Northamptonshire. [St. Pega and her cell.] J. Brit. Archaeol. Assoc., 55 (N.S. 5), pp. 215–21. 1899.

1887 Pavey (A. K.). Some notes on the parochial history of Brixworth [Northants.]. (Further notes . . . field names, etc.). Assoc. Archit. Socs'. Rpts., 26, pp. 441–48, + 2 plans: 28, pp. 575–92. 1902, 06.

1888 Pearman (M. T.). The Chiltern hundreds in Oxon. Antiq. Mag., 3, pp. 293–96. 1883.

1889 Phillips (Charles William). Field archaeology in Lincolnshire. Lincs. Historian, no. 5, pp. 187–95. 1950.

1890 Phillips (William). Alcaston moat [Shropshire]. [Belonged to Edric Sylvaticus. Ædmundstun in Domesday.] Shropshire N. and Q., 3rd s. 3, pp. 106–07. 1913.

1891 Picton (*Sir* James Allanson). Notes on the city walls of Chester, historical and constructive. [Including notes on A.-S. Chester from the chroniclers.] J. Brit. Archaeol. Assoc., 44, pp. 135–63, + 5 plates. 1888.

1892 Prior (C. E.). Bedfordshire and its Danish period. Assoc. Archit. Socs.' Repts., 10, pp. 109–28, + 1 plate, + 3 plans. 1869.

1893 Robbins (Michael). Middlesex. *A new survey of England.* pp. xxiii, 456. 8° London, 1953. [Pp. 15–21, A.-S. 74 illustrations, + 11 maps and diagrams.]

1894 Ryder (Thomas Arthur). Gloucestershire through the ages. pp. 125, + 8 plates. 8° Worcester, 1950. [Pp. 29–42, A.-S. and Domesday.]

1895 Salter (Herbert Edward). Medieval Oxford. *Oxford Historical Society*, 100. pp. 160, + 2 maps. 8° Oxford, 1936. [Pp. 1–19, Saxon Oxford: pp. 20–39, Oxford in Domesday.]

1896 Sargant (W. L.). The Danes in Rutland. Ann. Rept. Rutland Archaeol. Soc., 45, pp. 7–10. 1947.

1897 —— Daneweed and the Danish vikings in Rutland and Kesteven. [Sambucus ebulus : ? introduced by Danes.] *Same jnl.*, 50, pp. 7–11, + map. 1952.

1898 Sharp (Samuel). On the Anglo-Saxon 'Hamtune', the Norman 'Northantone', Northampton castle, and the antiquities found on its site. Assoc. Archit. Socs'. Repts., 16, pp. 63–70. 1881.

1899 Sharpe (*Sir* Montagu). Four eras in the Middlesex area. [Pp. 202–8, + 6th map, 'Domesday Book'.] Trans. Lond. and Middsx. Archaeol. Soc., N.S. 7, pp. 193–209, + 7 maps. 1937.

1900 —— The making of Middlesex : its villages, fields and roads. [Pp. 249–55, the Saxon period.] *Same jnl.*, N.S. 5, pp. 237–55, + map. 1929.

1901 Stenton (*Sir* Frank Merry). Lindsey and its kings. Essays . . . presented to R. L. Poole, pp. 136–50. 1927.

1902 —— Pre-Conquest Herefordshire. Roy. Commission Hist. Mon., Hereford, 3, pp. lv–lxi. 1934.

1903 Stevenson (William). West Bridgford notes. Notts. and Derbs. N. and Q., 4, pp. 154–55. 1896.

1904 Stevenson (William Henry). The early history of Nottingham. Assoc. Archit. Socs.' Rpts., 19, pp. 8–21. 1887.

1905 Streatfeild (George Sidney). Lincolnshire and the Danes. pp. xiv, 386. 8° London, 1884. [Gross, 1536.]

1906 Sylvester (Dorothy). Rural settlement in Cheshire : some problems of origin and classification. [Figures 1–2, Domesday population and plough land.] Trans. Hist. Soc. Lancs. and Ches., 101 (1949), pp. 1–37, + map. 1950.

1907 Taylor (Charles Samuel). Cotswold in Saxon times. Trans. Bristol and Glos. Arch. Soc., 20, pp. 267–306. 1897.

1908 Thorpe (Harry). The growth of settlement [of the Birmingham district] before the Norman Conquest. [Pp. 100–12, A.-S. period : 3 maps in text.] B'ham., B.A., 1950, pp. 87–112. 1950.

1909 Trollope (Edward). The Danes in Lincolnshire. Assoc. Archit. Socs'. Rpts., 5, pp. 34–61. 1859.

1910 Tudor (Thomas L.). Repton, Northworthy (Derby), and Wirksworth. [Miscellaneous notes on St. Werburga, etc.] J. Derbs. Archaeol. Soc., 44, pp. 44–57, + 1 plate (of the Saxon stone in Wirksworth church). 1922.

1911 Vaughan (Henry F. J.). Oswestry [Salop], ancient and modern, and its local families. [Pp. 196–208, A.-S. period.] Arch. Camb., 5th S. 1, pp. 193–224, etc. 1884.

1912 Venables (Edmund). The Danish occupation of Lincolnshire illustrated by local names. Assoc. Archit. Socs'. Rpts., 16, pp. 151–58. 1882.

1913 Wainwright (Frederick Threlfall). Early Scandinavian settlement in Derbyshire. J. Derbs. Archaeol. Soc., 67, pp. 96–119. 1947.

1914 Walker (Benjamin). Birmingham from Domesday to the Stuart period. [Pp. 29–32, Domesday.] Handbook for Birmingham (83rd meeting . . . B.A.), pp. 29–36. 1913.

1915 Ware (E. M.). Pinner. [Under Offa, etc.] Trans. Lond. and Middx. Archaeol. Soc., N.S. 7, pp. 487–90. 1937.

1916 Webster (Graham). Chester in the dark ages. J. Chester and N. Wales Archit. Soc., 38, pp. 39–48. 1951.

1917 Wedgwood (Josiah C.). Early Staffordshire history (from the maps and from Domesday). [With ' note on prevalence of pre-Conquest personal names '.] Collectns. for a history of Staffs., 1916, pp. 138–205. 1918.

1918 Westell (William Percival). Historic Hertfordshire. pp. xiii, 198, + 8 plates, + map. 8° Hertford, 1931. [Pp. 55–91, A.-S. and Domesday.]

1919 Whatmore (A. W.). Flawford [Notts.]. Notts. and Derbs. N. and Q., 6, pp. 145–47, 170–72. 1898.

1920 —— Notintone in Domesday Book. [Anonymous comments on pp. 74–76.] Same jnl., 5, pp. 3–6, 17–22, 153–57. 1897.

1921 —— West Bridgford. Same jnl., 5, pp. 87–88. 1897.

1922 Wheeler (W. H.). The fens of south Lincolnshire : their early history and reclamation. [Pp. 28–31 : the Saxons, the Danes, the Normans.] Assoc. Archit. Socs.' Rpts., 20, pp. 24–34. 1889.

1922a Whitley (William Thomas). In the palmy days of Boston [Lincs.] . . . [Pp. 225–29, A.-S. period.] J. Brit. Archaeol. Assoc., N.S. 37, pp. 225–42. 1932.

1923 Willis-Bund (John William). The evolution of Worcester. Archaeol. J., 63, pp. 201–30, + 4 plans. 1906.

1924 Wilson (George Maryon). The manor of Hampstead : a sketch of copyholds. [Pp. 44–45, A.-S.] Trans. Hampstead Antiq. Soc., 1899, pp. 44–57. 1900.

1925 Wood (Alfred Cecil). A history of Nottinghamshire. *Thoroton Society.* pp. 314, + 13 plates. 8° Nottingham, 1947. [Pp. 9–43, the Anglian settlements, the end of Anglo-Danish Notts., the Norman settlement.]

1926 Wrottesley (F. J.). Our own county [Staffs.]. [Some A.-S. and Domesday material.] North Staffs. F.C., Trans., 36, pp. 129–41. 1902.

1927 Wyatt (James). A glance at ancient Bedford. Assoc. Archit. Socs'. Rpts., 8, pp. 145–64. 1865.

26. NORTHUMBRIA

(Humber to Forth)

1928 Baines (Thomas). Historical notes on the valley of the Mersey previous to the Norman Conquest. Hist. Soc. Lancs. and Ches., Proc., 5, pp. 131–41. 1853.

1929 Benson (George). York from its origin to the end of the eleventh century. pp. xii, 95. 8° York, 1911. [40 maps, plans and figures.]

1930 Blair (Peter Hunter). The *Moore Memoranda* on Northumbrian history. [Camb. Univ. Library, MS. Kk. 5.16.] Chadwick Mem. Stud., pp. 243–57, + 1 plate. 1950.

1931 —— The origins of Northumbria. pp. 62. 8° Gateshead, 1948.

1932 Blunt (J. H.). St. Cuthbert and his patrimony. J. Brit. Archaeol. Assoc., 22, pp. 420–42. 1866.

1933 Butler (George Grey). Yevering: the place and the name. [Claims as locality where Paulinus baptised people of Edwin : Glendale. = ' ad Gebrium ' of Bede, E.H. II. 14.] Hist. Berwick. Nat. Club, 25, pp. 574–91. 1925.

1934 Charlesworth (F.). Saxon Sheffield. Trans. Hunter Archaeol. Soc., 5 (1940), pp. 203–10. 1943.

1935 Clark (George Thomas). Bamburgh castle. Archaeol. J., 46, pp. 93–113, + plan and 3 plates. 1889.

1936 Colbeck (Alfred). The old kingdom of Elmet. [*See also* : 1, pp. 157, 197–98.] Yorks. N. and Q., 1, pp. 257–58. 1904.

1937 Collingwood (William Gershom). Angles, Danes and Norse in the district of Huddersfield. *Tolson Memorial Museum Publications*, Handbook 2. 2nd edition. pp. 62. 8° Huddersfield, 1929.

1938 —— The Angles in Furness and Cartmel. [Map on p. 289.] Trans. Cumb. and Westm. Antiq. Soc., N.S. 24, pp. 288–94. 1924.

1939 —— The Vikings in Lakeland : their place-names, remains, history. Saga-Book V.C., 1, pp. 182–96, + map + 2 plates. 1896.

1940 Creighton (—), *canon*. The Northumbrian border. [Pp. 46–52, A.-S. period.] Archaeol. J., 42, pp. 41–89. 1885.

1941 Crossman (*Sir* William). Holy Island. [Address at Society's meeting there.] Proc. Soc. Antiq. Newcastle, 2nd S. 7, pp. 73–82. 1895.

1942 Davis (Henry William Carless). Cumberland before the Norman conquest. E.H.R., 20, pp. 61–65. 1905.

1943 Demarest (E. B.). Inter Ripam et Mersham. [Late Saxon history of S. Lancashire.] E.H.R., 38, pp. 161–70. 1923.

1944 Edwards (William). The early history of the North Riding. pp. xvi, 267, + 32 plates, + map. 4° London, 1924. [Pp. 1–69, + 7 plates, Anglian kingdom of Northumbria, pre-conquest monasteries, the Northmen, Norman Conquest and settlement.]

1945 Ellwood (T.). The Landnama Book of Iceland, as it illustrates the dialect, place-names, folklore, and antiquities of Cumberland, Westmorland, and North Lancashire. With notes and additions by Eiríkr Magnússon. Trans. Cumb. and Westm. Antiq. Soc., 12, pp. 283–311. 1893.

1946 Federer (Charles Antoine). Excursion notes : Bardsey-with-Collingham. Bradford Antiquary, 3, pp. 103–11. 1900.

1947 Fell (T. K.). The Viking in Furness. Trans. Barrow Nat. F.C., 9, pp. 67–70. 1906.

1948 Ferguson (Robert). The Northmen in Cumberland and Westmorland. 8° London, 1856. [Gross, 1524. Popularisation of Worsaae, 754.]

1949 Freeman (Edward Augustus). The place of Carlisle in English history. Archaeol. J., 39, pp. 317–46. 1882. *Reprinted in* Trans. Cumb. and Westm. Antiq. Soc., 6, pp. 238–71. 1883.

1950 Graham (T. H. B.). Cumberland. [Pp. 274–80, its history in A.-S. period.] Trans. Cumb. and Westm. Antiq. Soc., N. S, 26, pp. 274–84. 1926.

1951 Gray (E. N. O.). Notes on the history of Lindisfarne and its place in the conversion of England to Christianity, *etc.* Hist. Berwick. Nat. Club, 31, pp. 98–109. 1948.

1952 Greenwell (William). The early history of Durham castle. Trans. Archit. Soc. Durham, 7 (1934–36), pp. 56–91. 1936.

1953 Hinde (John Hodgson). Lothian : its position prior to its annexation to Scotland. Archaeol. J., 14, pp. 301–19. 1857.

1954 —— On the early history of Cumberland. Archaeol. J., 16, pp. 217–35. 1859.

1955 —— On the state of the western portion of the ancient kingdom of Northumberland, down to the period of the Norman Conquest. Trans. Hist. Soc. Lancs. and Ches., 8, pp. 1–22. 1856.

1956 Hodgkin (Thomas). Inaugural address [to the British Archaeological Association], 1901 : the history of Northumberland. [ii. Chaos and the Northumbrian kingdom : iii. Danish devastations, or the migrations of the body of St. Cuthbert.] J. Brit. Archaeol. Assoc., 58 (N.S. 8), pp. 1–16. 1902.

1957 Hodgson (John). A history of Northumberland. Part I, containing the general history of the county . . . the Saxon and Danish kings of Northumberland, the official earldom, *etc. Soc. Antiq. Newcastle - upon - Tyne.* pp. x, 400 4°. Newcastle-upon-Tyne, 1858. [Pp. 57–200, A.-S.]

1958 Hollander (Lee M.). Some observations on the head-ransom episode in the Egilssaga. Acta Phil. Scand., 12, pp. 307–14. 1938.

1959 Hutchinson (W.). Howdenshire its rise and extension. Yorks. Archaeol. J., 11, pp. 361–71. 1891.

1960 Irving (George Vere). On the battle of Kaltraeth. [Fall of Strathclyde. ? date. Answering Beale Poste, 1975.] J. Brit. Archaeol Assoc., 16, pp. 277–85. 1860.

1961 Irving (George Vere) On the date of the battle of Kaltraez. [*See also* 1960 and 1975.] *Same jnl.*, 15, pp. 237–45. 1859.

1962 Jackson (Kenneth). The ' Gododdin ' of Aneirin. [With a Note on Cutraeth and Catterick.] Antiquity, 13, pp. 25–34. 1939.

1963 James (John). On the little British kingdom of Elmet and the region of Loidis. J. Brit. Archaeol. Assoc., 20, pp. 34–38. 1864.

1964 Just (John). The Danes in Lancashire. Hist. Soc. Lancs. and Ches., Proc., 4, pp. 121–30. 1852.

1964a Lamplough (Edward). Mediaeval Yorkshire. pp. viii, 188. 8° London, 1884. [Pp. 1–38, A.-S.]

1965 Leadman (Alexander D. H.). Proelia Eboracensia. Battles fought in Yorkshire : treated historically and topographically. pp. 192. 8° London, 1891. [Pp. 1–13, battles of Heathfield (i.e. Hatfield Chase), Winwæd, Stamford Bridge.]

1966 Lindkvist (Harald). A study on early medieval York. [Danish York : Danish element in its street-names, etc.] Anglia, 50 (N.F. 38), pp. 345–94. 1926.

1967 Longstaffe (William Hylton Dyer). Durham and Sadberge : pagan period : the early chronicles. Archael. Æl., N.S. 7, pp. 89–113, 196–203. 1876.

1968 —— Durham before the Conquest. [Divisions : the coast and streams : the forests and their tenants : weapons and implements : strongholds : transit : Roman commerce : sepulture : Saxon architecture.] Mems. Archaeol. Inst., [8 i.] (1852), pp. 41–96, + folding map. 1858.

1968a Lukis (William Collings). Ancient Ripon : an historical sketch, ecclesiastical and civil. pp. 36, + 2 plates. 8° Ripon, 1886.

1969 McIntire (W. T.). Historical relations between Dumfriesshire and Cumberland. [Pp. 72–74, A.-S. period.] Dumfries. Antiq. Soc., Trans., 3rd S. 21 (1936–38), pp. 70–89. 1939.

1970 Mawer (*Sir* Allen). The Scandinavian kingdom of Northumbria. Essays . . . presented to W. Ridgeway, pp. 306–14. 1914.

1970a Oliver (George). The history and antiquities of the town and minster of Beverley. pp. xxiii, 575. 4° Beverley, 1829. [Pp. 29–81, A.-S. period and Domesday : pp. 433–38, biography of St. John.]

1971 Oman (*Sir* Charles William Chadwick). The Danish kingdom of York, 576–954. [The two plates are of coins.] Archaeol. J., 91 (1934), pp. 1–21, + 2 plates. 1935.

1972 Page (William). Some remarks on the Northumbrian palatinates and regalities. [Pp. 143–46, A.-S. period : p. 155, 'pedigree of the house of Bamburgh'.] Archaeologia, 51, pp. 143–55. 1888.

1972a Pearson (Frederick Richard). Yorkshire. *Borzoi county histories.* pp. 173, + 8 plates. 8° London, 1928. [Pp. 41–63, Anglian and Danish Yorkshire : Domesday. P. 46, map of Deira.]

1973 Pease (Howard). Northumbria's decameron. pp. xii, 190. 8° London, 1927. [Pp. 14–80, + map ('days 3–5'), A.-S.]

1974 Picton (*Sir* James Allanson). Opening address at the Liverpool congress [of the British Archaeological Association], 1887. [Pp. 5–11, Brief sketch of Liverpool area in A.-S. period.] J. Brit. Archaeol. Assoc., 44, pp. 1–20. 1888.

1975 Poste (Beale). On the date of the battle of Kaltraeth, otherwise the battle of Gododin or Cor-eiddin. [*See also* 1960–61.] *Same jnl.*, 16, pp. 218–25. 1860.

1975a Poulson (George). Beverlac ; or, the antiquities and history of the town of Beverley. pp. xx, 816, 83, + plates. 2 vol. 8° London, 1829. [Pp. 20–47, A.-S. period (pp. 28–30, St. John) : pp. 687–88, fridstool.]

1975b Raine (James). York. *Historic towns.* pp. xi, 223, + plan. 8° London, 1893. [Pp. 24–56, A.-S.]

1976 Robertshaw (Wilfrid). The lost hamlet of Cockan. Bradford Hist. and Antiq. Soc. J., n.s. 6, pp. 289–309. 1938.

1977 Russell (—), *Miss.* The English claims to the overlordship of Scotland, in connection with the death of Thomas à Becket. [Relations of Cumbria to A.-S. kings, etc.] J. Brit. Archaeol. Assoc., 49, pp. 223–39, + 1 plate. 1893.

1978 Rylands (Thomas Glazebrook). Winwick and Culcheth in Lancashire, their place in history. Trans. Hist. Soc. Lancs. and Ches., 32, pp. 53–66. 1880.

1979 Saltmarshe (Philip). [Account of Howdenshire in Anglo-Saxon and later times]. [Pp. xxiv–xxvii, A.-S. period and Domesday.] Trans. East Riding Antiq. Soc., 12, pp. xxiv–xxxi. 1905.

1980 —— The river banks of Howdenshire, their construction and maintenance in ancient days. [Banks largely constructed before Conquest. Charter of Edgar relating to land boundaries of Howden, 959 : Domesday material.] *Same jnl.*, 23, pp. 1–15. 1920.

1981 Sewell (Augustus Bell). The ancient parish of Bradford, prefaced with observations on the formation of ancient parishes in England. Bradford Antiquary, 5 (N.S. 3). pp. 393–409, + map. 1911.

1982 Sheppard (Thomas). The Roman, Angle and Dane in East Yorkshire. Trans. Hull Sci. and F.N. Club, 4, pp. 1–21. 1907.

1983 Simpson (James). The present state of antiquarian research in Westmorland and Cumberland. [Pp. 9–12, the Northmen–runic inscriptions : pp. 12–15, incidents before the Conquest.] Trans. Cumb. and Westm. Antiq. Soc., 1, pp. 1–18. 1874.

1984 Sinclair (Clarence). Ruins adjoining Heysham church. (Singular coffins in the rock). Yorks. N. and Q., 1, pp. 32–33. 1904.

1985 Smith (Albert Hugh). Danes and Norwegians in Yorkshire. [Mostly linguistic evidence. Pp. 208–10, 'The extent of Danish and Norwegian settlements'.] Saga-Book V.C., 10, pp. 188–215. 1928.

1986 Smith (Albert Hugh) Some aspects of Irish influence on Yorkshire. [i. Historical: ii. Personal names—(a) names found in independent use and (b) names found as elements of place-names: iii. place-names showing Irish influence.] Rev. celt., 44, pp. 34–58, + map. 1927.

1987 Stenton (*Sir* Frank Merry). Pre-Conquest Westmorland. Roy. Commission on Hist. Mon., Westmorland, pp. xlviii–lv. 1936.

1988 —— York in the eleventh century. *York Minster Historical Tracts*, 8. pp. 16. 8° London, [1927].

1989 Thornber (William). The castle hill of Penwortham. [Pp. 69–73, its history during A.-S. period.] Trans. Hist. Soc. Lancs. and Ches., 9, pp. 61–76, + 2 plates. 1857.

1990 —— Traces of the Britons, Saxons and Danes in the Foreland of the Fylde. Hist. Soc. Lancs. and Ches., Proc., 4, pp. 100–18. 1852.

1991 Turner (Joseph Horsfall). Ancient Eccleshall, [Yorks.]. [Pp. 140–42, A.-S. and Domesday.] Bradford Antiquary, 3, pp. 137–58, etc. 1900.

1992 Wade-Evans (Arthur Wade). Prolegomena to a study of the Lowlands. [Till end of 7th c.] Trans. Dumfriesshire Antiq. Soc., 3rd S. 27 (1948–49), pp. 54–84. 1950.

1993 Wainwright (Frederick Threlfall). The Scandinavians in Lancashire. [10th c. —.] Trans. Lancs. and Ches. Antiq. Soc., 58 (1945–46), pp. 71–116. 1947.

1994 Warrilow (Joseph B.). Lindisfarne: a centenary. A.D. 635–A.D. 1935. Dublin Rev., 197, pp. 238–52. 1935.

1994a Waterman (Dudley M.). Viking and early medieval York. [Resumé of paper to York meeting of the Council for British Archaeology.] Archaeol. News Letter, 1 vi, pp. 12–13. 1948.

1995 Weston (G. F.). Crosby Ravensworth [Westmorland]. [Pp. 212–16, history during Danish period.] Trans. Cumb. and Westm. Antiq. Soc., 2, pp. 205–24. 1876.

1996 Wheater (W.). Yorkshire remote history. [Briton and Saxon in Yorkshire: the Dane in Wharfedale: the Norman and his conquest (Domesday extracts).] Old Yorkshire, ed. William Smith, vol. 3, pp. 212–33. 1882.

1997 Whitaker (Thomas Dunham). Loidis and Elmete: or an attempt to illustrate the districts described in those words by Bede, and supposed to embrace the lower portions of Aredale and Wharfdale [and the] vale of Calder. pp. 404, 80. fol. London, 1816.

1998 Williams (*Sir* Ifor). The problem of Catraeth. [? Catterick. ? desperate effort of a North Briton to recover a key position on Swale.] Yorks. Soc. Celtic Studies, Rept. for 1933–34, pp. 17–18. 1934.

1999 Wilson (James) and **Allison** (R. A.). Political history [of Cumberland]. [Pp. 221–36, A.-S. period.] V.C.H., Cumberland, 2, pp. 221–330. 1905.

2000 Wilson - Barkworth (Arthur Bromby). The composition of the Saxon hundred in which Hull and neighbourhood were situate, and as it was in its original condition. Pp. x, 97, + 2 maps. 4° Hull and London, [1920].

27. SUSSEX

2001 Baring (*Hon.* Francis Henry). Hastings castle, 1050–1100, and the chapel of St. Mary. Sussex Archaeol. Collns., 57, pp. 119–35. 1915.

2002 Cole (T. H.). Antiquities of Hastings. [Pp. 42–56, A.-S. and Domesday material, place-names, etc.] J. Brit. Archaeol. Assoc., 23, pp. 34–66. 1867.

2003 Freeman (Edward Augustus). The early history of Sussex. Archaeol. J., 40, pp. 335–67. 1883.

2004 Frost (Marian). The early history of Worthing. pp. vii, 99. 8° Hove, 1929. [Pp. 47–54, A.-S.]

2005 Griffith (A. F.). The Anglo-Saxons in Sussex. Abstract of Papers, Brighton and Hove N.H. and Phil. Soc., 2nd article. 1918.

2006 Homan (W. Mac Lean). The true romance of Hrammeslege. [Country between Rye bay and Sedlescombe in A.-S. times. Inaccuracies corrected in 2012.] Sussex County Mag., 13, pp. 674–80. 1939.

2007 Hudson (William). The manor of Eastbourne, its early history : with some notes about the honours of Mortain and Aquila. [Pp. 166–73 : i. Temp. Edward the Confessor : ii. Temp. William I.] Sussex Archaeol. Collns., 43, pp. 166–200. 1900.

**2008 —— The settlement of the East Sussex downs in Saxon times. [Distribution of hides, and distribution of the population.] Trans. Eastbourne N.H. Soc., N.S. 3, pp. 336–43. 1902.

2009 Maitland (George). Lindfield in pre-Saxon times. [i.e. Jutish.] Sussex N. and Q., 13, pp. 4–11. 1950.

2010 Medland (Thomas). Notices of the early history of Steyning and its church. [Pp. 111–19, A.-S. period.] Sussex Archaeol. Collns., 5, pp. 111–26. 1852.

2011 Mitchell (Henry). On the early traditions of Bosham, and the discovery of the stone coffin containing the remains of a daughter of king Canute, in the nave of Bosham church. *Same jnl.*, 18, pp. 1–9, + 3 plates. 1866.

2012 Ray (John E.). Ethelred [II]'s gift of Rammesleah to Fécamp. [Correcting 2006.] Sussex County Mag., 14, pp. 37–39. 1940.

**2013 —— Sussex and Normandy in Norman times. [Changes owing to the Conquest.] S.E. Naturalist, 52, pp. 10–15. 1947.

2014 Salzmann (Louis Francis). Political history [of Sussex]. [Pp. 481–90, A.-S. period. The plan is of the battle of Hastings, the 3 plates are of the Bayeux tapestry.] V.C.H., Sussex, 1, pp. 481–539, + 3 plates, + plan. 1905.

2015 Sawyer (Frederick Ernest). Traces of Teutonic settlements in Sussex as illustrated by land tenure and place-names. [' Physical features : grouping of settlements : surviving tribal names : territorial divisions : mark system :

Sussex marks : Sussex folk-moots : village community in Brighton : lot-lands and doles ; common flocks : inheritance customs in Sussex.'] Archaeol. J., 41, pp. 35–46, + map of Brighton, c. 1815. 1884.

2016 Smyth (C. Bohun). The first and last days of the Saxon rule in Sussex. Sussex Archaeol. Collns., 4, pp. 67–92. 1851.

2017 Wallis (W. Clarkson). The Brighton Steine and the Danes in Sussex. Brighton and Hove Archaeologist, 2, pp. 41–53. 1924.

2018 Ward (Gordon). Some eleventh century references to Sussex. [Sundry excerpts with notes from Domesday Book of Kent, Domesday Monachorum, etc.] Sussex N. and Q., 4, pp. 238–40. 1933.

28. WESSEX

2019 [Anon.] Corscombe [Dorset]. [In A.-S. times.] N. and Q. for Som. and Dorset, 23, p. 141. 1940.

2020 Anderson (John Corbet). Saxon Croydon. pp. 79–156, + 4 plates. 8° *n.p.*, 1877. [Pp. 115–56, A.-S. coins found in the parish of Croydon.]

2020a Baker (George Philip). The fighting kings of Wessex. A gallery of portraits. pp. xvi, 304, + plates, + maps. 8° London, 1931.

2021 Baring (*Hon.* Francis Henry). Concerning Farley Chamberlayne . . . [Slackstead—Torigleage in foundation charter of Newminster.] Papers and Proc. Hants. F.C., 6, p. 290. 1910.

**2022 —— Concerning Wonston in the 10th century. *Same jnl.*, 6, pp. 209–12. 1910.

2023 Barnes (William). Ancient Dorset. [Includes some A.-S. and some place-name material.] Archaeol. J., 22, pp. 278–94. 1865.

**2024 —— Notes on the history of Shaftesbury. Proc. Dorset Antiq. F.C., 3, pp. 27–33 : 4, p. 77. 1879, [82].

H

2025 Bennett (George J.). Wareham : its invasions and battles. [Pp. 90–96, A.-S. period.] *Same jnl.*, 13, pp. 82–114. 1892.

2026 Boger (Charlotte G.), *Mrs. E. Boger*. Myths, scenes, and worthies of Somerset. pp. xii, 666. 8° London, 1887. [Arthur ; Gildas ; Brithwald, abp. of Canterbury ; Ina ; St. Congar ; Alfred ; Dunstan ; Athelm, Wulfhelm, Ethelgar, Sigeric, Ælfeah, Æthelnoth, abps. of Canterbury ; etc.]

2027 Bond (Thomas). On the barony of the wife of Hugh Fitz Grip. [Domesday records her as holding 47 manors— 10 of which were in Purbeck.] Proc. Dorset Antiq. F.C., 14, pp. 114–18. 1893.

2028 Boston (Cecilia), *Lady*. The history of Compton in Surrey. pp. 228, + 28 plates. 4° London, 1933. [Pp. 127– 35, Church and A.-S. hermit's cell.]

2029 Brentnall (Harold Cresswell). Bedwyn in the tenth century. [i. Direction to the parish priest Ceolbeorht (Bern MS. 671) : ii. Rules of the local gild : iii. Two manumissions of women.] Wilts. Archaeol. Mag., 52, pp. 360–68. 1949.

2030 Brownbill (John). Hampshire : its formation. N. and Q., 11th S. 4, pp. 482–84. 1911.

2031 Browning (A. Giraud) and **Kirk** (R. E. G.). The early history of Battersea. Surrey Archaeol. Collns., 10, pp. 205–54. 1891.

2032 Cameron (C. Lovett). Mortimer in olden time : Saxon tombstone in S. Mary's church. [Here identified as that of Ædelward, ealdorman of Hampshire, (= Æthelweard I, ealdorman of Wessex) to whom Ælfric dedicated his Homilies. See also A.-S. C. under 994.] Berks, Bucks and Oxon Archaeol. J., 7, pp. 71–73. 1901.

2033 Clift (J. G. Neilson). Wareham. [Pp. 23–30, A.-S. period.] J. Brit. Archaeol. Assoc., 64 (N.S. 14), pp. 19– 44, + plan. 1908.

2034 Crawford (Osbert Guy Stanhope). The Anglo-Saxon bounds of Bedwyn and Burbage, [Wilts.]. Wilts. Archaeol. Mag., 41, pp. 281–301, + map. 1921.

2035 —— Anglo-Saxon bounds of land near Silchester. [Map on p. 252.] Antiquary, 51, pp. 250–56, *also* 318–20, 439, (note by James G. Wood), *also* pp. 359–60, (note by Albany F. Major), *also* p. 400 (note by Jessie C. Davis). 1915.

2036 —— Pre-historic, Roman and Saxon Nursling. Papers and Proc. Hants. F.C., 6 Supp., pp 36–41. 1913.

2037 Darby (Stephen). Cookham ; its name and history. Q.J. Berks. Archaeol. Soc., 2, pp. 134–37, + map. 1892.

2038 Ditchfield (Peter Hampson). The history of Wantage. Berks, Bucks and Oxon Archaeol. J., 6, pp. 46–51. 1900.

2039 Earle (John). An ancient Saxon poem of a city in ruins supposed to be Bath. Proc. Bath F.C., 2, pp. 259–70. 1872.

2040 —— Lecture on traces of the early history of Bath and its neighbourhood. Proc. Bath F.C., 1. ii, pp. 25–38. 1868.

2041 —— Traces of the Saxon period in Bath and the neighbourhood. Proc. Bath F.C., 6, pp. 153–67. 1887.

2042 Elliston - Erwood (Frank Charles) and **Mandy** (William H.). The history of the church, manor and parish of Plumstead [Surrey], with East Wickham, Kent, in the Middle Ages. [Pp. 11– 20, Saxon Plumstead : Plumstead and the Norman Conquest (with Domesday entries).] Woolwich Antiq. Soc., Ann. Rpt., 26, pp. 1–32. 1937.

2043 Elyard (S. John). Annals of Purton, [Wilts.]. Wilts. N. and Q., 1, pp. 242–45, 291–96, + 2 plates. 1894.

2044 Falconer (J. P. E.). The hundred of Bath Forum and the liberty of Hampton and Claverton, co. Somerset. N. and Q., 189, pp. 24–26, 76–81, etc. 1945.

2045 Field (John Edward). Benson, or Bensington. [A little A.-S. material.] Berks, Bucks and Oxon Archaeol. J., 2, pp. 44–50, 73–76 : 3, pp. 6–14. 1896–97.

2046 Finberg (Herbert Patrick Reginald). Sherborne, Glastonbury, and the expansion of Wessex. Trans. Roy. Hist. Soc., 5th S. 3, pp. 101–22. 1953.

2047 Finny (W. E. St. Lawrence). The kings and kingdom of Wessex [till 937.] S.E. Naturalist and Antiquary, 36, pp. 65–81. 1931.

2048 Fowler (Joseph). Mediaeval Sherborne. pp. 409, xvi, + 35 plates. 4° Dorchester, 1951. [Pp. 19–85, A.-S. St. Aldhelm: 26 A.-S. bishops: Bishop's hundred and manor in Domesday.]

2049 Fripp (—), *Mrs. Edward Fripp.* Political history [of Dorset]. [Pp. 224–31, A.-S. period.] V.C.H., Dorset, 2, pp. 123–74. 1908.

2050 Godwin (Henry). A brief sketch of the early history of Welford [Berks]. Trans. Newbury F.C., 2 (1872–75), pp. 80–87. 1878.

2051 —— Historical references to Lamborne [Berks.]. *Same jnl.,* 1 (1870–71), pp. 184–85. 1871.

2052 —— Inaugural address. [Pp. 14–17, Newbury district in A.-S. period.] *Same jnl.,* 1 (1870–71), pp. 9–20. 1871.

2053 Greenwood (A. D.). **Bartelot** (R. G.) and **Robinson** (Joseph Armitage). Cantuctun [Somerset]. [Identifies with Cannington. Occurs in Alfred's will.] N. and Q. for Som. and Dorset, 18, pp. 177–78. 1925.

2054 Grey (Gerald). Saxon and Norman Charlcombe. Proc. Bath branch, Somerset Archaeol. Soc., 1929, pp. 262–65. 1929.

2055 Grose (S.). The manor of Trowbridge. Wilts. N. and Q., 1, pp. 236–37. 1894.

2056 Head (J. Merrick). Portland. Historical notes : descent of manor, etc. [Pp. 115–17, A.-S. and Domesday.] Proc. Dorset Antiq. F.C., 12, pp. 115–31. 1891.

2057 Hicks (F. W. Potto). From Roman to Saxon Gloucestershire. Proc. Cotteswold N.F.C., 30 (1950), pp. 219–20. 1952.

2058 Hill (A. Du Boulay). The Saxon boundaries of Downton, Wilts. [Includes Carta regis Cynewalc de Duntune (Birch, 27) before 672 : in A.-S., Latin, and translation.] Wilts. Archaeol. Mag., 36, pp. 50–56, + map. 1910.

2059 Humpreys (Arthur Lee). The materials for the history of the town of Wellington, co. Somerset, collected and arranged. pp. xv, 308, + map. 8° London, 1889. [Pp. 17–24, the manor, Domesday, charter : text of grant by Edward the Elder to Asser, bp. of Sherborne.]

2060 J. (E.). Old Sarum. Wilts. N. and Q., 1, pp. 231–32. 1894.

2061 Jackson (John Edward). On the history of Chippenham. [Pp. 21–26, A.-S. and Danish period.] Wilts. Archaeol. Mag., 3, pp. 19–46. 1857.

2062 Jones (William Henry). Bradford-upon-Avon : general history of the parish. [Pp. 8–26, A.-S. period : pp. 247–52, + 5 plates, the Saxon church.] *Same jnl.,* 5, pp. 1–88, 210–55, + map (A.D. 1001) + 10 plates. 1859.

2063 —— Bradford-on-Avon : a history and description [from Wilts. Archaeol. Mag.] annotated and brought up to date by J. Beddoe. pp. xvi, 275. 8° Bradford-on-Avon, 1907. [Pp. 9–28, A.-S., + map of manor in 1001.]

2064 —— Early annals of Trowbridge. Wilts. Archaeol. Mag., 15, pp. 208–34, + 1 table, + 1 map. 1875.

2065 —— History of the parish of All Cannings [north Wilts.]. [Pp. 2–9, 176–78, A.-S. period and Domesday record.] *Same jnl.,* 11, pp. 1–40, 175–203. 1869.

2066 —— Potterne. [Pp. 247–54, notices in Domesday Book, etc.] *Same jnl.,* 16, pp. 245–86, + 3 plates, + 1 table. 1876.

2067 Kerslake (Thomas). Gyfla. [History of Yeovil in A.-S. times.] Proc. Somerset Arch. Soc., 32 (1886), pp. 16–23. 1887.

2068 Kerslake (Thomas). Saint Ewen, Bristol, and the Welsh border, circ. 577–926. (With a postscript : The Mercians in Cornwall and Devon). J. Brit. Archaeol. Assoc., 31, pp. 153–79. 1875.

2069 —— The Welsh in Dorset. Proc. Dorset Antiq. F. C., 3, pp. 74–103. 1879.

2070 Malden (Henry Elliot). Political history [of Surrey]. [Pp. 329–40, A.-S. period.] V.C.H., Surrey, 1, pp. 329–444. 1902.

2071 Maskelyne (T. S.). Ellendune and its ancient boundaries. [Evidence from charters and Domesday.] Wilts. N. and Q., 3, pp. 454–57. 1901.

2072 Meade-King (Richard Liddon). Taunton under the Normans. Proc. Somerset Arch. Soc., 83 (1937), pp. 107–12. 1938.

2073 Morgan (Thomas). On the West Saxons in Wiltshire. J. Brit. Archaeol. Assoc., 37, pp. 325–46. 1881.

2074 P. (C. R.). The Meonwaras. Hants. N. and Q., 4, p. 47. 1889.

2075 Palmer (Hurly Pring). Old Somerset. *Somerset Folk series*, 20. pp. 126. 8° London, 1925. [Pp. 1–40, Taunton in A.-S. times : pp. 41–69, Domesday Book : pp. 70–111, manorial system.]

2076 Parker (James). Historical notes on the Newbury district. Trans. Newbury F.C., 2 (1872–75), pp. 88–95. 1878.

2077 Poste (Beale). On old Winchester. J. Brit. Archaeol. Assoc., 15, pp. 268–71. 1859.

2078 Powell (J. U.). The early history of the upper Wylye valley. [Pp. 112–19, A.-S. period.] Wilts. Archaeol. Mag., 33, pp. 109–31. 1904.

2079 Pugh (R. B.). The early history of the manors in Amesbury. [Pp. 70–72, Amesbury before 1086.] *Same jnl.*, 52, pp. 70–110. 1947.

2080 Radford (W. Locke) and **Standerwick** (John W.). Caduc Bourn. [Boundary of Ilminster in charter of Ine, 725. ?=burn of St. Cadoc, 6th c. : or ?=Broadway river.] N. and Q. Som. and Dorset, 11, p. 128, 320–21. 1909.

2081 Reynolds (J. J.). Ancient history of Shaftesbury. Wilts. Archaeol. Mag., 7, pp. 250–71. 1862.

2082 Richardson (William H.). Notes on Blewbury. [Domesday material, etc.] Trans. Newbury F.C., 4 (1886–95), pp. 35–72, + plan, + 3 plates. 1895.

2083 Robinson (Joseph Armitage). Crucan or Cructan ? [Creechbury hill. Land between Tone and Blackbrook. Grant of Centwine to Glastonbury.] N. and Q. for Som. and Dorset, 17, pp. 43–44. 1921.

2084 —— Somerset historical essays. *British Academy*. pp. viii, 160. 8° London, 1921. [Pp. 1–53, i. William of Malmesbury, 'On the antiquity of Glastonbury' : ii. The Saxon abbots of Glastonbury. (Appendix A, the Liber terrarum of Glastonbury : Appendix B, the two earliest Glastonbury charters, 680, 670, with texts).]

2085 Russell (Constance), *Lady*. Swallowfield and its owners. [Pp. 82–84, A.-S. period.] Q. J. Berks. Archaeol. Soc., 1, pp. 82–85, *etc.* 1890.

2086 Sherwin (Gerald Ambrose). The Isle of Wight in the Saxon period. 4° *n.p.*, 1939. [MS. of notes, diagrams and photographs in the library of the Society of Antiquaries.]

2087 Shore (Thomas William). Annals of Barton Stacey. [Pp. 86–87, Saxon and Domesday records.] Hants. N. and Q., 8, pp. 84–90. 1896.

2088 —— The basis of Hampshire history. Hampshire Antiquary, 1, pp. 52–56. 1891.

2089 —— Hampshire Field Club : visit to . . . Odiham . . . Odiham manor. [Domesday account, etc.] *Same jnl.*, 1, pp. 7–10. 1891.

2090 —— The history and antiquities of Whitchurch, [Hants.]. [A.-S. and Domesday material.] Hants. N. and Q., 9, pp. 123–29. 1898.

2091 —— Kingsclere and its ancient tythings. [Pp. 184–86, A.-S. period and Domesday.] Papers and Proc. Hants. F.C., 3, pp. 183–99, + 1 plate. 1898.

2092 **Shore** (Thomas William) Micheldever. Hampshire Antiquary, 1, pp. 91–93. 1891.

2093 —— Notes on Wellow [Hants.] [A.-S. and Domesday material.] Hants. N. and Q., 9, pp. 63–66. 1898.

2094 —— Traces of the Jutes in Hampshire and the Isle of Wight. Antiquary, 29, pp. 100–04. 1894.

2095 —— Wonston [Hants]. [Domesday record, etc.] Hampshire Antiquary, 1, pp. 88–89. 1891.

2096 **Stenton** (*Sir* Frank Merry). The south-western element in the Old English Chronicle. Essays presented to T. F. Tout, pp. 15–24. 1925.

2097 **Taylor** (Charles Samuel). Banwell. [Includes A.-S. and Domesday material.] Proc. Somerset Arch. Soc., 51 (1905), pp. 31–76 + 3 plates. 1906.

2098 —— Bath, Mercian and West Saxon. [' History of the place and district in connection with the successive changes of ownership under West Saxon, Mercian and again West Saxon kings.] Trans. Bristol and Glos. Arch. Soc., 23, pp. 129–161. 1900.

2099 —— Bristol and its neighbourhood in Domesday. Proc. Clifton Antiq. Club, 2 (1888–93), pp. 67–82. 1893.

2100 —— The early history of the Bedminster churches. [Pp. 180–84, the Bedminster manors in Domesday.] *Same jnl.*, 2 (1888–93), pp. 179–213. 1893.

2101 —— The parochial boundaries of Bristol. [With plan of Westbury and Stoke, A.D. 883.] Trans. Bristol and Glos. Arch. Soc., 33, pp. 126–39, + map. 1910.

2102 **Taylor** (John). On the early history of Bristol. J. Brit. Archaeol. Assoc., 31, pp. 62–68. 1875.

2103 **Thomas** (J.). Shalfleet, I.W. [Includes Domesday entries.] Hampshire Antiquary, 1, pp. 110–11. 1891.

2104 **Treacher** (Llewellyn). The origin of the Berkshire villages. [Pp. 105–09, A.-S. period.] Berks, Bucks and Oxon Archaeol. J., 23, pp. 54–61, 105–09. 1917.

2105 **Turner** (A. G. C.). Some aspects of Celtic survival in Somerset. [Place-name evidence: dedications.] Proc. Som. Arch. Soc., 97, (1952), pp. 148–51. 1953.

2106 **Vivian-Neal** (A. W.). The arms of Wessex. [Heraldry attributed to West Saxon kings.] N. and Q. for Som. and Dorset, 22, p. 267. 1938.

2107 —— and **Gray** (Harold St. George). Materials for the history of Taunton castle. [Pp. 46–49, A.-S. period.] Proc. Somerset Arch. Soc., 86 (1940), pp. 45–78, + plan, + 2 plates. 1941.

2108 **Wade-Evans** (Arthur Wade). The origin of Glastonbury. N. and Q., 193, pp. 134–35. 1948.

2109 **Walters** (Alfred V.), **Benham** (W.), *etc*. The Meon valley and the Meonwaras. Hants. N. and Q., 2, pp. 3–11. 1884.

2110 **Ward** (Gordon). The manor of Lewisham and its wealden ' dens '. Trans. Greenwich Antiq. Soc., 4, pp. 112–17, + map. 1938.

2111 **Warne** (Charles). Ancient Dorset. The Celtic, Roman, Saxon, and Danish antiquities of the county, including the early coinage. Illustrated . . . Also, an introduction to the ethnology of Dorset . . . by T. W. W. Smart. fol. Bournemouth, 1872.

2112 —— Dorsetshire: its vestiges, Celtic, Roman, Saxon, and Danish. pp. vii, 56, + map. 8° London, 1865.

2113 **Weaver** (Frederic William). Geoffry, bishop of Coutances. [71 manors in Somerset (Domesday).] N. and Q. Som. and Dorset, 11, pp. 173–74. 1909.

2114 —— Traces of the Danes in Somerset. N. and Q., 6th S. 9, p. 265. 1884.

2115 **Whale** (Thomas William). Notes on the borough of Bath and the hundred of Bath Forinsecum. [Domesday material.] Proc. Bath F.C., 9, pp. 128–49. 1899.

2116 Whitehead (John Livesay). Bon-church parish [I.o.W.]. [Domesday material for manors of Luccombe and Bonchurch.] Papers and Proc. Hants. F.C., 5, pp. 65–81, + 1 plate, + 2 pedigrees. 1906.

2117 Wicks (A. T.). Leoman's grove—Lammas field. [*See* Grundy (G. B.) : Saxon charters of Somerset, p. 183.] N. and Q. Som. and Dorset, 21, pp. 78–79. 1933.

2118 Wildman (William Beauchamp). A short history of Sherborne from 705 A.D. 4th edition. pp. xv, 203. 8° Sherborne, 1930.

2119 Wilkinson (John). History of Broughton Gifford. [Pp. 270–80, ' Domesday notice and antiquities '.] Wilts. Archaeol. Mag., 5, pp. 267–341, + 2 plates, + table. 1859.

2120 Winton, *pseud.* The inroads of the Vikings. [?Invasion by valley of the Test. ?protected by Worlbury, Danebury and the Vanditch.] Hants. N. and Q., 5, pp. 49–50. 1890.

2121 Wise (John Richard). The New Forest, its history and its scenery. pp. xxv, 336. 4° London, 1863 [1862]. 5th edition. 8° London. 1895. [Gross, 927. Shows that chronicles have exaggerated desolation caused in its construction by William I.]

2122 Young (G. M.). Saxon Wiltshire. Wilts. Archaeol. Mag., 49, pp. 28–38. 1940.

2123 Young (*Sir* George), *bart.* Cookham church : a village lecture. [Pp. 108–09, Cookham in Domesday Book.] Berks, Bucks and Oxon Archaeol. J., 6, pp. 107–118, *etc.*, + plan. 1901.

29. IRELAND

2124 Brash (Richard Rolt). The antiquities of Cloyne [co. Cork]. [History, round tower, *etc.*] J. Kilkenny Archaeol. Soc., [5] N.S. 2, pp. 253–66. 1859.

2125 Canty (M.). Ardpatrick [co. Limerick]. [Pp. 187–94, St. Patrick's visit : pp. 196–98, round tower.] Irish Eccles. Rec., 4th S. 28, pp. 186–202. 1910.

2126 Comerford (Michael), *coadjutor bp. of Kildare.* Castledermot : its history and antiquities. J. co. Kildare Archaeol. Soc., 1, pp. 361–78, + 7 plates. 1895.

2127 Dobbs (Margaret E.) [Maighrēad Ni C. Dobs]. The Dál Fíatach. [Or Ulaid-population-group in N.E. Ireland, 3rd to 12th c.] Ulster J. Archaeol., 3rd S. 8, pp. 66–79. 1945.

2128 —— The History of the descendants of Ir. [Senchas Sil hIr, a compilation relating to the early population of N.E. Ireland and their colonies till 12th c. Irish text and English translation.] Zeit. celt. Phil., 13, pp. 308–59 : 14, pp. 44–144. 1921–23.

2129 —— On the graves of Leinster men. [Metrical tract on the traditions and topography of Leinster and incidents in sagas and annals : composed 972. Irish, and English translation.] *Same jnl.,* 24, pp. 139–53. 1953.

2130 —— The territory and people of Tethba. [co. Longford and half co. Westmeath.] J. Roy. Soc. Antiq. Ireland, 68 (7th S. 8), pp. 241–59 + map : 71, pp. 101–10 : 72, pp. 136–48. 1938, 1941–42.

2131 Fahey (Jerome). Galway and its surroundings in the pre-Norman period. J. Galway Archaeol. Soc., 1, pp. 51–58. 1900.

2132 —— The shrines of Inis-an-Ghoill, Lough Corrib. [History, architecture : also inscribed pillar-stones of Inchagoill (with 4 figures).] J. Roy. Soc. Antiq. Ireland, 31 (5th S. 11), pp. 236–45. 1901.

2133 Fee (Thomas). The kingdom of Airghialla and its sub-kingdoms before 1100. *M.A. Thesis, Univ. Coll., Dublin.* 1950. [Unpublished.]

2134 Ffrench (James F. M.). St. Mullins, co. Carlow. [St. Moling, his foundation and well.] J. Roy. Antiq. Ireland, 22 (5th S. 2), pp. 377–88. 1892.

2135 FitzGerald (*Lord* Walter). The ancient territories out of which the present county Kildare was formed, and their septs. J. co. Kildare Archaeol. Soc., 1, pp. 159–68, + table. 1893.

2136 FitzGerald (*Lord* Walter). The Curragh : its history and traditions. [Including its acquisition by S. Brigid.] *Same jnl.*, 3, pp. 1–32, + map. 1899.

2137 Flood (William Henry Grattan). Lismore in the sixth century. J. Waterford Archaeol. Soc., 3, pp. 152–59. 1897.

2138 —— Pre-Norman Lismore. *Same jnl.*, 5, pp. 78–88. 1899.

2139 Getty (Edmund). The island of Tory ; its history and antiquities. Part 3, ecclesiastical period. Ulster J. Archaeol., 1, pp. 142–58, + 2 plates. 1853.

2140 Hamilton (Gustavus E.). The kings of Leinster and their clans. J. co. Kildare Archaeol. Soc., 7, pp. 382–92, + table. 1914.

2141 Hayman (Samuel). The annals of Lismore, county of Waterford. [635 onwards.] Reliquary, 4, pp. 137–56, + 1 plate. 1864.

2142 Healy (John), *abp. of Tuam.* Tara [Meath], pagan and Christian. Irish Eccles. Rec., 4th S. 3, pp. 97–117. 1898.

2143 Hogan (James). The Ua Briain kingship in Telach Óc. [Events 1078–84.] Essays presented to E. MacNeill, pp. 406–44. 1940.

2144 Hore (Herbert Francis). The Scandinavians in Leinster. J. Kilkenny Archaeol. Soc., [4] N.S. 1, pp. 430–44. 1857.

2145 Lawless (Nicholas) [Enda, *pseud.*]. Louth, Armagh and Cloghar [co. Tyrone]. County Louth Archaeol. J., 7, pp. 324–29. 1920.

2146 —— Muirtheimhne. [' North Louth of to-day '.] *Same jnl.*, 3, pp. 156–66. 1913.

2147 Lawlor (Henry Cairnes). Dunluce [Antrim] and its owners prior to the Norman invasion. Proc. R.I.A., 43c, pp. 307–11. 1936.

2148 Lynch (J. Fetherston). Tullylease [co. Cork]. J. Cork Hist. Soc., 2nd S. 17, pp. 66–87. 1911.

2149 Macalister (Robert Alexander Stewart). The history and antiquities of Inis Cealtra. [Round tower, crosses, etc.] Proc. R.I.A., 33c, pp. 93–174, + 21 plates. 1916.

2150 McCarthy (S. T.). The Clann Carthaigh. [Pp. 166–79, 195–96, A.-S. period.] Kerry Archaeol. Mag., 1, pp. 160–79, 195–208. 1909–10.

2151 MacNeill (Eoin). Colonization under the early kings of Tara. (The colonial frontier of the kingdom of Tara.). J. Galway Archaeol. Soc., 16, pp. 101–24. 1935.

2152 MacNeill (John). Poems by Flann Mainistrech on the dynasties of Ailech, Mide and Brega. Archivium Hib., 2, pp. 37–47, + 3 gen. trees. 1913.

2153 Meyer (Kuno), *ed.* A poem by Dallán mac Móre. [Irish text, with English translation, from the Book of Leinster, p. 47a. Composed end of 9th c. Celebrates 40 battles fought by Cerball mac Muirecáin, king of Leinster, 887–909.] Rev. celt., 29, pp. 210–14. 1908.

2154 —— *ed.* The Song of the sword of Cerball. [Cerball mac Muirecáin, king of Leinster, 885–909. Text with English translation and introductory remarks.] Rev. celt., 20, pp. 7–12. 1899.

2155 Morris (Henry). Duleek [Meath] : the Cianachta [*fl.* 7th–9th c.] ; and the battle of Killineer [co. Louth, 868]. County Louth Archaeol. J., 1. i, p. 61. 1904.

2156 Mulchrone (Kathleen). Flannacán MacCellaich rí Breg hoc carmen. [Text of poem in Irish, with translation and notes. Flannacán, son of Cellach, king of Bregha was slain in 896 by the Norsemen.] J. Celtic Studies, 1, pp. 80–93. 1949.

2157 Murphy (Denis) and **Westropp** (Thomas Johnson). Notes on the antiquities of Tara [Meath]. [2 maps in text.] J. Roy. Soc. Antiq. Ireland, 24 (5th S. 4), pp. 232–42. 1894.

2158 Murray (Laurence P.). Danish Louth. [795–1014.] County Louth Archaeol. J., 2, pp. 72–77. 1908.

2159 —— Omeath [co. Louth]. [Pp. 213–17, Ancient history, ancient monasteries, Danish settlement, etc.] *Same jnl.*, 3, pp. 213–31. 1914.

2160 —— The Pictish kingdom of Conaille-Muirthemhne. Essays presented to E. MacNeill, pp. 445–53. 1940.

2161 Ó **Buachalla** (Liam). Contributions towards the political history of Munster, 450–800 A.D. J. Cork Hist. Soc., 2nd S. 56, pp. 87–90 : 57, pp. 67–86, + tree. 1951–52.

2162 —— Uí MacCaille [Imokilly] in pre-Norman times. *Same jnl.*, 2nd S. 50, pp. 24–27. 1945.

2163 O'Doherty (John K.). Aileach of the kings [Donegal] : a brief sketch of the history and traditions of the ancient northern residence of the Irish kings [O'Neills]. Irish Eccles. Rec., 4th S. 3, pp. 335–416. 1898.

2164 Ó **Dulgeannáin** (Mícheál). Notes on the history of the kingdom of Bréifne. J. Roy. Soc. Antiq. Ireland, 65 (7th S. 5), pp. 113–40, + map (c. 700 A.D.). 1935.

2165 Ó **Fiaich** (Tomás). Ui Cruinn, a lost Louth sept. [Kings of Aithir.] J. County Louth Archaeol. Soc., 12, pp. 105–12. 1951.

2166 O'Grady (John Sheil). History and antiquities of the Hill of Allen. J. co. Kildare Archaeol. Soc., 4, pp. 454–65. 1905.

2167 O'Mahony (John). The battle of Bealach Leachta [co. Cork] (978) and the events that led to it. J. Cork Hist. Soc., 2nd S. 17, p. 37. 1911.

2168 Omurethi. Knockaulin. [Dun of Aillinn (a hill N.W. of Old Kilcullen) and its appearance in Irish annals.] J. co. Kildare Archaeol. Soc., 4, pp. 359–65. 1904.

2169 Petrie (George). On the history and antiquities of Tara hill. Trans. R.I.A., 18 (Antiq.), pp. 25–232, + 2 maps, + 1 plate. 1839.

2170 Royal Society of Antiquaries of Ireland. Antiquarian handbook series. 7 vol. 8° Dublin, 1895–1916. [i. Dunsany, Tara, Glendalough : ii. Western islands, and the antiquities of Galway, Athenry, Roscommon, etc. : iii. Western islands, including the coasts of Clare, Kerry, Cork and Waterford, and the islands of Scattery and Shellig Michael, with notices of Cloyne and Lismore : iv. Western islands of Scotland, Orkney and Caithness, ed. R. Cochrane : v. Northern portion of co. Clare, by T. Johnson Westropp, ed. R. Cochrane : vi. Northern, western and southern islands and coast of Ireland : vii. Limerick and its neighbourhood, by T. J. Westropp, R.A.S. Macalister, etc.]

2171 Ryan (John). Pre-Norman Dublin. J. Roy. Soc. Antiq. Ireland, 79, pp. 64–83. 1949.

2172 Shearman (John Francis). The early kings of Ossory, etc. J. Roy. Hist. and Arch. Assoc. Ireland, [14], 4th S. 4 (1876–78), pp. 336–408, + 5 tables. 1879.

2173 Sherlock (William). Clondalkin [co. Dublin]. [7 figures in text—3 of the round tower.] J. co. Kildare Archaeol. Soc., 5, pp. 1–11. 1906.

2174 Stubbs (Francis William). Projected history of county Louth : the Danes. [Louth from 817 to 1041.] County Louth Archaeol. J., 5, pp. 66–68. 1921.

2175 Thunder (John M.) The kingdom of Meath. [Pp. 512–15, iv. Saint Patrick in Meath; v. The O'Melaghlins and the Danes.] J. Roy. Hist. and Arch. Assoc. Ireland, [18], 4th S. 8, pp. 507–25. 1887.

2176 Vogt (Lorents Juhl). Dublin som Norsk by . . . . Historisk fremstilling. pp. 407. 8° Christiania, 1896.

2177 Wakeman (William Frederick). Inis Muiredaich, now Inismurray, and its antiquities. [Off coast of Sligo. History, cashel, churches, inscriptions, sculptured crosses, holy wells, etc. 84 figures.] J. Roy. Hist. and Arch. Assoc. Ireland, [17] 4th S. 7, pp. 175–332, + map. 1885.

2178 —— A survey of the antiquarian remains on the island of Inismurray, [co. Sligo]. *Royal Society of Antiquaries of Ireland, extra vol. for 1892.* pp. xxvii, 163. 8° London, 1893. [84 plates and figures.]

2179 Walsh (Paul). Christian kings of Connacht. J. Galway Archaeol. Soc., 17, pp. 124–43, + 2 tables. 1939.

2180 —— Connacht in the Book of Rights. *Same jnl.*, 19, pp. 1–15. 1940.

2181 Walsh (Paul). The earliest records Fermanagh. ['Fir Manach occurs first in the Annals at 1009.'] Irish Eccles. Rec., 5th S. 24, pp. 344–55. 1924.

2182 —— Leinster states and kings in Christian times. *Same jnl.*, 5th S. 24, pp. 1–12 : 53, pp. 47–61. 1924, 1939.

2183 —— Meath in the Book of Rights. Essays presented to E. MacNeill, pp. 508–21. 1940.

2184 —— The Ua Maelechlainn kings of Meath. [Appendix of pedigrees, and genealogical table.] Irish Eccles. Rec., 5th S. 57, pp. 165–83. 1941.

2185 Westropp (Thomas Johnson), *etc.* Aran islands [Galway]. J. Roy. Soc. Antiq. Ireland, 25 (5th S. 5), pp. 250–78. 1895.

2186 —— Killaloe [co. Clare] : its ancient palaces and cathedral. *Same jnl.*, 22 (5th S. 2), pp. 398–410 : 23, pp. 187–201, + 1 plate. 1892–93.

2187 White (John Davis). Cashel of the kings. 2nd edition [Pt. 1]. 3 pts. 4° Cashel, 1876, 1866. [See founded 6th c.]

2188 —— A guide to the rock of Cashel. 3rd edition. 8° Cashel, 1883.

2189 Williams (Sterling de Courcy). The termon of Durrow [King's County]. [Termon=privileged area : c.f. terminus. Book of Durrow, crozier, etc.] J. Roy. Soc. Antiq. Ireland, 29 (5th S. 9), pp. 44–51, 219–32, + 3 plates. 1899.

30. ISLE OF MAN

2190 Cubbon (William). Our Norse heritage. [i. The antiquity of Tynwald : ii. The kingdom of Man and the Isles : iii. The four divisions of the Hebrides.] Isle of Man N.H. and Antiq. Soc., Proc., N.S. 5 (1942–46), pp. 1–15, + map. 1948.

2191 Cumming (Joseph George). The Isle of Man ; its history, physical, ecclesiastical, civil, and legendary. pp. xxxvi, 376, + maps. 12° London, 1848.

2192 Farrant (Reginald D.). The Norse occupation of Mann. [9th–13th c.] I.O.M. N.H. and Antiq. Soc., Proc., N.S. 4 (1937–39), pp. 287–90. 1941.

2193 Kermode (Philip Moore Callow) and **Herdman** (*Sir* William Abbott). Manks antiquities. 2nd edition. pp. 150. 8° Liverpool, 1914.

2194 Kinvig (Robert Henry). A history of the Isle of Man. pp. xv, 240, + 2 maps. 8° O.U.P. *for Manx Society*, 1944. —[2nd edition]. pp. viii, 180, + 31 plates. 8° Liverpool, 1950. [Pp. 54–107 (2nd ed., pp. 36–76, 7 maps in text) : early Christian period (450–800), Scandinavian period (800–1266), developments in the Scandinavian period.]

2195 Kneen (John Joseph). Before the Norsemen came. I.O.M. N.H. and Antiq. Soc., Proc., N.S. 4 (1935–37), pp. 209–18, + 4 plates (=8 maps). 1938.

2196 Marstrander (Carl Johan Sverstrup). Det norske landnåm på Man. (The Norwegian conquest of the Isle of Man). [Including linguistic and place-name evidence. English summary, pp. 333–55.] Norsk Tidsskr. Sprogvid., 6, pp. 40–386, + 3 charts, + 2 large folding maps. 1932.

2197 Moore (Arthur William). History of the Isle of Man. pp. 1044, + map. 2 vol. 8° London, 1900.

2198 Shimmin (Christopher R.). Mann and the Sudreys in the Norse sagas. [Synopsis of lecture : list of sagas concerned.] J. Manx Mus., 1, pp. 170–71. 1930.

2199 Vigfusson (Gudbrand). Northmen in the Isle of Man. E.H.R., 3, pp. 498–501. 1888.

2200 Walpole (Spencer). Some thoughts on the early history of the Isle of Mann. Manx Note Bk., 3, pp. 103–11. 1887.

31. SCOTLAND

2201 Balfour (John Alexander), *ed.* The book of Arran. . . . Archaeology. (Vol. 2, by W. M. Mackenzie. History and folklore). *Arran Society of Glasgow.* 2 vol. 4° Glasgow, 1910.

2202 Barron (James). The Celtic province of Moray. [Pictish history.] Trans. Gaelic Soc. Inverness, 8, pp. 64–76. 1879.

2203 Bremner (Robert Locke). Some notes on the Norsemen in Argyllshire and on the Clyde. Saga-Book V.C., 3, pp. 338–80, + map. 1904.

2204 Clouston (Joseph Storer). A history of Orkney. pp. xvi, 432, + map. 8° Kirkwall, 1932. [Pp. 1–60, A.-S. period.]

2205 Collingwood (William Gershom). Norse influence in Dumfriesshire and Galloway. [i. History : ii. Antiquities (monuments and place-names).] Trans. Dumfries. Antiq. Soc., 3rd S. 7, pp. 97–118, + map, + 2 plates. 1921.

2206 Fergusson (Charles). Sketches of the early history, legends, and traditions of Strathardle and its glens. [Pp. 298–302, A.-S. period.] Trans. Gaelic Soc. Inverness, 15, pp. 279–302. 1890.

2207 Galloway (Alexander). Notes relative to the district near Glasgow formerly known as the Levenachs or Lennox. [Pp. 101–04, ii. 450 to 1150.] Trans. Glasgow Archaeol. Soc., 2, pp. 99–113. 1883.

2208 Goodrich-Freer (Ada M.), *Mrs. H. H. Spoer.* The Norsemen in the Hebrides. Saga-Book V.C., 2, pp. 51–74. 1898.

2209 —— Outer isles. pp. xv, 448, + map. 8° Westminster, 1902. [Pp. 272–97, the Norsemen in the Hebrides.]

2210 Goudie (Gilbert). The Celtic and Scandinavian antiquities of Shetland. pp. xvi, 305. 8° Edinburgh, 1904. [Pp. 30–78, Celtic and Scandinavian periods : inscribed and sculptured monuments : religious foundations : Viking brooches, etc.]

2211 Gourlay (W. R.). Lochfergus and the lords of Galloway. [Pp. 349–52, early history of Galloway.] Trans. Dumfries. Antiq. Soc., 3rd S. 14 (1926–28), pp. 348–61. 1930.

2212 Gray (James). Sutherland and Caithness in saga-time . . . 870–1266. pp. xiv, 192, + map. 8° Edinburgh, 1922. [A history of the Norse occupation of Sutherland and Caithness from the Orkneyinga, St. Magnus, and Hakonar Sagas and from English and Scottish records. The succession to the Caithness earldom and the racial traits which were to leave the men of Orkney, Shetland, and Cat a strange mixture of Norse, Pict, and Gael.]

2213 Grieve (Symington). The book of Colonsay and Oronsay. 2 vol. 8° Edinburgh, 1923. [1, pp. 95–118, the Picts : pp. 189–220, A.-S. period (Dalriada and its rulers) : 2, Norsemen and Danes: saints and monks and their religious settlements.]

2214 Gunn (Adam). Durness [Sutherland] from the earliest times. [Pp. 269–73, the Culdee missionaries, the Norse invaion.] Trans. Gaelic Soc. Inverness, 17, pp. 266–82. 1892.

2215 Hamilton (John R. C.). Jarlshof, Shetland. *H.M.S.O.* pp. 39, + 8 plates, + plan. 8° Edinburgh, 1953. [Pp. 26–33, Viking settlement.]

2216 Hewison (James King). The isle of Bute in the olden time. 2 vol. 8° Edinburgh, 1893–95. [Vol. 1, Church history : crosses : Vikings, etc.]

2217 Johnston (Alfred Wintle). Orkney and Shetland folk, 880–1350. Saga-Book V.C., 9, pp. 372–408. 1925.

2218 —— Orkney and Shetland historical notes. *Same jnl.*, 8, pp. 211–63. 1914.

2219 Loth (Joseph). Persistance des institutions et de la langue des Brittons du nord (ancien royaume de Stratclut) au xiie. siècle. [History of Strathclyde and its institutions.] Rev. celt., 47, pp. 383–400. 1930.

2220 McKerlie (Peter Handyside). Galloway in ancient and modern times. pp. ix, 325. 8° Edinburgh, 1891. [Picts, Saxons, Angles, Jutes, Norse occupation, etc.]

2221 Macleod (R. C.). The Norsemen in the Hebrides. Scot. H.R., 22, pp. 42–50. 1925.

2222 MacRitchie (David). The Gael in Edinburgh. [Mostly before 1087.] Trans. Gaelic Soc. Inverness, 31 (1922–24), pp. 232–45. 1927.

2223 Marshall (David William Hunter). The Sudreys in early Viking times. pp. x, 49. 8° Glasgow, 1929.

2224 Marwick (Hugh). Antiquarian notes on Papa Westray. [Brochs, saga references, place-names, etc., 2 maps in text.] Proc. Orkney Antiq. Soc., 3, pp. 31–47. 1925.

2225 —— Antiquarian notes on Rousay. [Brochs, early Norse settlement, etc.] *Same jnl.*, 2, pp. 15–21. 1924.

2226 —— Antiquarian notes on Stronsay. [P. 63, map: pp. 65–66, The Norse period: pp. 73–83, Stronsay place-names.] *Same jnl.*, 5, pp. 61–83. 1927.

2227 —— Orkney. *The county books series.* pp. vii, 287, + map, + 35 plates. 8° London, 1951. [History, early church, topography, place-names.]

2228 Moore (Arthur William). The connexion between Scotland and Man. Scot. H.R., 3, pp. 393–409. 1906.

2229 Neilson (George). Annals of the Solway, until A.D. 1307. [Pp. 261–71, 'Legend, incidents, and law. A.D. 634 to 1292. —10. Saints' voyages, A.D. 661 and 684: 11. Norse memories: A.D. 875: 12. Traditions of the Scotiswath, A.D. 937.'] Trans. Glasgow Archaeol. Soc., N.S. 3, pp. 245–308, + 4 maps. 1899.

2230 Radford (Courtenay Arthur Ralegh). Hoddom [Dumfriesshire]. [St. Kentigern: British Church: Northumbrian Church: Viking age: great cross: smaller cross.] Antiquity, 27, pp. 153–60, + 4 plates [crosses]. 1953.

2231 —— and **Donaldson** (Gordon). Whithorn and Kirkmadrine, Wigtownshire. *H.M.S.O.* pp. 49, + 8 plates, + plan. 8° Edinburgh, 1953. [Ninian, early Christian inscriptions, Northumbrian supremacy, Viking age, Whithorn school of crosses, etc.]

2232 Russell (—), *Miss.* The name of Glasgow, and the history of Cumbria. J. Brit. Archaeol. Assoc., 46, pp. 43–52. 1890.

2233 Shearman (John Francis). The kingdom of Strathclyde. J. Roy. Hist. and Arch. Assoc. Ireland, [14], 4th S. 4 (1876–78), pp. 468–75. 1879.

2234 Simpson (William Douglas). The province of Mar. *Rhind Lectures*, 1941. *Aberdeen Univ. Studies*, 121. pp.

ix, 167, + 89 plates. 4° Aberdeen, 1943. [Pp. 84–106 + plates 42–60, the Celtic Church in Mar, and the origins of Pictish lapidary symbolism.]

2235 Skene (William Forbes). Extracts from the Norse sagas, illustrative of the early history of the north of Scotland, and of the influence of the northern pirates upon its inhabitants. Collectanea de rebus albanicis (Iona Club), v and xix. 1847.

2236 Smith (James Cromarty). Early Christian remains in Orkney and Shetland. Trans. Scot. Ecclesiol. Soc., 6, pp. 103–18. 1921.

2237 Torfaeus (Thormodus). Ancient history of Orkney, Caithness, and the north. Translated with copious notes, by Alexander Pope. pp. vi, 288. 12° Wick, 1866.

2238 Watson (William John). The Celts (British and Gael) in Dumfriesshire and Galloway. Trans. Dumfries. Antiq. Soc., 3rd S. 11 (1923–24), pp. 119–48. 1925.

2239 Wilkie (James). The history of Fife, from the earliest times to the nineteenth century. pp. xiv, 612. 8° Edinburgh, 1924. [Pp. 40–105, the coming of Christianity, the saints, the beginnings of St. Andrews and the Viking invasions, Malcolm Canmore and St. Margaret.]

32. WALES AND MONMOUTHSHIRE

2240 Banks (R. W.). On the early history of the land of Gwent. Arch. Camb., 5th S. 2, pp. 241–56. 1885.

2241 Bartrum (P. C.). Some studies in early Welsh history. [i. The chronology of the early kingdom of Glywysing: ii. Paul and Conigc, abbots of Llancarfan: iii. Rhieinwg: iv. The origin of some fictitious Welsh names.] Trans. Hon. Soc. Cymm., 1948, pp. 279–302. 1949.

2242 Corbett (John Stuart). Glamorgan. [Pp. 17–22, A.-S. period.] Cardiff Nat. Soc., Rpt. and Trans., 56 (1923), pp. 1–282, + map. 1925.

2243 —— Some notes as to Llantwit Major [Glamorgan]. *Same jnl.*, 38 (1906), pp. 49–62. 1907.

2244 Davies (Ellis W.). The Danes in Anglesey. Anglesey Ant. Soc., Trans., 1932, pp. 39–41. 1932.

2245 Dawson (M. L.). Caerwent [during A.-S. period]. Arch. Camb., 6th S. 4, pt. 239–46. 1904.

2246 Hillman (S.). Beachley and Buttington, 'twixt Severn and Wye. [Local notes, mostly A.-S. period.] Antiquary, 12, pp. 24–29, also 135. 1885.

2247 Howse (William Henry). Radnorshire. pp. 347, + 19 plates, + map. 8° Hereford, 1949. [Pp. 30–36, A.-S. period : Offa's dyke, etc.]

2248 Jones (Gwilym Peredur). Notes on the political history of early Powys. Arch. Camb., 85, pp. 131–41. 1930.

2249 Lloyd (—), *chevalier*. History of the lordship of Maelor Gymraeg or Bromfield, the lordship of Jal or Yale, and Chirkland, in the principality of Powis Fadog. [Pp. 284–94, A.D. 450–1087.] Arch. Camb., 4th S. 3, pp. 277–96. 1872.

2250 Lloyd (*Sir* John Edward). Bangor and its neighbourhood. Arch. Camb., 92, pp. 193–207. 1937.

2251 —— The story of Ceredigion, 400–1277. *Gregynog Lectures*, 1937. pp. viii, 105, + plates, + map. 8° Cardiff, 1937.

2252 Morgan (T. O.). On the history of the parish of Carno, Montgomeryshire. [Battles, 949 and 1077 or 1078.] Arch. Camb., N.S. 4, pp. 10–9. 1853.

2253 Owen (Robert). Welsh Pool and Powys-land. A history of the town and borough of Welsh Pool, and the surrounding district. [Pp. 178–224, A.-S. contacts.] Collns. hist. and archaeol. rel. to Montgom., 29, pp. 161–288. 1897.

2254 Palmer (Alfred Neobard). A history of the old parish of Gresford in

the counties of Denbigh and Flint. [Pp. 192–95, Domesday entries.] Arch. Camb., 6th S. 3, pp. 189–204, etc. 1903.

2255 Paterson (Donald Rose). Early Cardiff, with a short account of . . . surrounding place-names. [Pp. 15–21, Saxon influence, Scandinavian period, Norman occupation.] Cardiff Nat. Soc., Rpt. and Trans., 54 (1921), pp. 11–71. 1926.

2256 —— The pre-Norman settlement of Glamorgan. Arch. Camb., 77 (7th S. 2), pp. 37–60. 1922.

2257 Rees (William). Medieval Gwent. [7 maps in text.] J. Brit. Archaeol. Assoc., N.S. 35 (1929), pp. 189–207. 1930.

2258 —— The mediaeval lordship of Brecon. [Pp. 165–72, A.-S. period.] Trans. Hon. Soc. Cymm., 1915–16, pp. 165–224, + map. 1917.

2259 Sheppard (H. E.). Monmouth castle and Priory. [Pp. 66–71 : 5. Saxon and Norman conquests in Gwent. 6. William Fitz-Osbern. 7. Withenoc. 8. Questions as to the foundation of the priory. 9. The Domesday tenant of Monmouth.] Trans. Bristol and Glos. Arch. Soc., 20, pp. 59–75. 1897.

2260 Thomas (David Richard). The Ordovices and ancient Powys. Arch. Camb., 6th S. 6, pp. 1–16. 1906.

2261 Wakeman (Thomas). Caerleon. [Pp. 330–32, A.-S. period.] Arch. Camb., 3, pp. 328–44. 1848.

2262 Willis-Bund (John William). Early Cardiganshire. Arch. Camb., 6th S. 5, pp. 1–37. 1905.

2263 Wynne-Edwards (—), *canon*. History of the parish of Meifod. [Pp. 322–27, Saxon period.] Collns. hist. and archaeol. rel. to Montgom., 9, pp. 315–52, + 5 plates. 1876.

IV. CONSTITUTIONAL HISTORY AND LAW

33. GENERAL

2264 Campbell (Duncan). The imperial idea in early British history. [Especially relating to Arthur.] Trans. Gaelic Soc. Inverness, 14, pp. 276–97. 1889.

2265 Chadwick (Hector Munro). Studies on Anglo-Saxon institutions. pp. xiii, 422. 8° Cambridge, 1905. [Gross, 1489a. Deals with coinage, administrative system, territorial divisions, national council, nobility, royalty.]

2266 Deanesly (Margaret). Roman traditionalist influence among the Anglo-Saxons. [Bretwaldership, etc.] E.H.R., 58, pp. 129–46. 1943.

2267 Droegereit (Richard). Gab es eine angelsächsische Königskanzlei ? Arch. Urkundenforschung, 13, pp. 335–436, + 5 plates. 1935.

2268 Freeman (Edward Augustus). The English constitution of the tenth and eleventh centuries. Proc. Oxford Archit. and Hist. Soc., N.S.2, pp. 44–48. 1866.

2269 —— Four Oxford lectures. pp. 112. 8° London, 1888. [Gross, 1507. Pp. 61–112, Teutonic conquest in Gaul and Britain. 'Assails the theories of Celtic and Roman origins of English institutions.']

2270 Haskins (Charles Homer). The Norman ' consuetudines et iusticie ' of William the Conqueror. E.H.R., 23, pp. 502–08. 1908.

2271 Hoyt (Robert Stuart). The nature and origins of the ancient demesne. E.H.R., 65, pp. 145–74. 1950.

2271a —— The royal demesne in English constitutional history : 1066–1272. *American Historical Association.* pp. xii, 253. 8° Ithaca, N.Y., 1950. [Pp. 9–63, the royal demesne of the Norman settlement, 1066–1087—Domesday and related evidence, etc.]

2272 Hull (Vernam Edward). Cert Ríg Caisil : the Right of the king of Cashel. [With Irish text.] Med. Stud., 11, pp. 233–38. 1949.

2273 Jolliffe (John Edward Austin). The constitutional history of mediaeval England from the English settlement to 1485. 2nd edition. pp. 524. 8° London, 1948. [Pp. 1–138, A.-S. period.]

2274 —— Northumbrian institutions. [A.-S. and later]. E.H.R., 41, pp. 1–42. 1926.

2275 Lapsley (Gaillard Thomas). Mr. Jolliffe's construction of early constitutional history. History, N.S., 23, pp. 1–11. 1938.

2276 Maine (*Sir* Henry James Sumner). Lectures on the early history of institutions. 3rd edition. pp. ix, 412. 8° London, 1880. [Gross, 1394, lit. Ch. 1–2, Senchus Mor and Book of Aicill.]

2277 Maitland (Frederic William). The constitutional history of England. pp. xxviii, 548. 8° Cambridge, 1908. [Gross, 641a. Pp. 1–9, A.-S. period.]

2278 Murray (Katharine Maud Elizabeth). This constitutional history of the cinque ports. *Univ. Manchester, Hist. Series*, 68. pp. xvi, 282. 8° Manchester, 1935. [Pp. 8–27, origins. ' Domesday evidence shows that this organisation was the work of Edward the Confessor.']

2279 Petit-Dutaillis (Charles). Studies and notes supplementary to Stubbs' Constitutional history down to the Great Charter. pp. xv, 152. 8° Manchester, 1908.

2280 Pierquin (Hubert). Les institutions et les coutumes des Anglo-Saxons. pp. 234. 8° Paris, 1913.

2281 Pretyman (J. R.). Illustrations of English history. England under the Anglo-Saxon monarchy (ii. The Danes in England, *etc.*). ['A.-S. institutions and laws.'] Rec. Bucks., 4, pp. 128–47, 161–86. 1870.

2282 Stubbs (William), *bp. of Oxford.* The Anglo-Saxon constitution. Stubbs (W.) : Lectures on early English history, pp. 1–17. 1906.

2283 —— Constitutional history of England. 3 vol. 8° Oxford, 1874–78. Fifth edition of vol. 1. pp. viii, 692. 8° Oxford, 1891. [1, pp. 63–314, A.-S. period. 'Foundation of modern research in this field.'—Stenton.]

2284 Walter (Ferdinand). Das alte Wales : ein Beitrag zur Völker-, Rechts-, und Kirchen-Geschichte. pp. xiv, 535, + 1 plate. 8° Bonn, 1859. [Gross, 1118. Mainly legal and constitutional history. pp. 354–69, laws.]

34. ARMY, NAVY (Including Ships), DEFENCE, ETC.

2285 Brock (Edgar Philip Loftus). The discovery of an ancient ship at Brigg, Lincolnshire. [?A.-S.] J. Brit. Archaeol. Assoc., 42, pp. 279–86, + 1 plate. 1886.

2286 —— The discovery of an ancient war-ship near Botley, [Southampton Water]. [?Danish.] *Same jnl.,* 32, pp. 70–71. 1876.

2287 Broegger (Anton Wilhelm) and **Shetelig** (Haakon). Vikingeskipene, deres forgjengere och etterfølgere. pp. 296, + 12 plates. 8° Oslo, 1950. Viking ships, their ancestry and evolution : translated by Katherine John. pp. 248. 4° Oslo, 1953.

2288 Clapham (*Sir* John Harold). The horsing of the Danes. [Use of cavalry, 894–1016.] E.H.R., 25, pp. 287–93. 1910.

2289 Fox (C. Frederick). The Viking ship in the Hamble river. Papers and Proc. Hants. F.C., 16, pp. 163–65. 1945.

2290 Glover (Richard). English warfare in 1066. [Tactics, weapons, etc.] E.H.R., 67, pp. 1–18. 1952.

2291 Jaager (Werner). Zu ags.-lat. scapha—kleines Schiff. Archiv Stud. neueren Spr., Bd. 159, pp. 274–75. 1931.

2292 Liebermann (Felix). Matrosenstellung aus Landgütern der Kirche London um 1000. [Recruitment of sailors from estates belonging to the Church of London.] *Same jnl.,* Bd. 104, pp. 17–24. 1900.

2293 Manx Museum. A description of the model of the Gokstad ship, given by the friends of the museum. J. Manx Mus., 4, pp. 142–43, + 3 plates. 1939.

2294 Marwick (Hugh). Leidang in the West, or the Norse fleets of Orkney and the Isle of Man. [Provision of ships for defence : 10th c. →.] Proc. Orkney Antiq. Soc., 13 (1934–35), pp. 15–29. 1935.

2295 —— Naval defence in Norse Scotland. Scot. Hist. Rev., 28, pp. 1–11. 1949.

2296 Morgan (C. Octavius S.). Ancient Danish vessel discovered at the mouth of the Usk. Monmouth and Caerleon Antiq. Assoc., 1882, pp. 23–26. 1882.

2297 Oman (*Sir* Charles William Chadwick). A history of the art of war in the Middle Ages. 2nd edition. 2 vol. 8° London, 1924. [Vol. 1 (378–1278) : pp. 63–72, the Anglo-Saxons : pp. 89–115, the Vikings : pp. 149–68, + plan, Hastings.] —3rd edition. Revised and edited by John H. Beeler. pp. 176. 8° Ithaca, 1953.

2298 —— The old English army : the armies of the Danes. Social England, ed. Traill and Mann, 1, pp. 256–67. 1891.

2299 Pancoast (Henry S.). The origin of the long-bow. [?derived from Wales.] P.M.L.A., 44, pp. 217–28. 1929.

2300 Payn (Howard). Viking ships. Antiquary, 5, p. 87. 1882.

2301 Pratt (Fletcher). The cavalry of the Vikings. U.S. cavalry J., 42. 1933.

2302 Schnepper (Heinrich). Die Namen der Schiffe und Schiffsteile im Altenglischen. Eine kulturgeschichtlich-etymologische Untersuchung. *Diss., Kiel.* pp. xv, 87. 8° Kiel, 1908.

2303 Sølver (Carl V.). Leiðarsteinn, the compass of the Vikings. Old-Lore Misc., 10, pp. 293–321. 1946.

2304 Turner (William). Notes on a model of the Gokstadt Viking ship. Trans. Glasgow Archaeol. Soc., N.S. 1, pp. 121–29, + 1 plate. 1890.

2305 White (H. T.). The beacon system in Hampshire. [Used in A.-S. times according to Camden. Cf. *beacnian*, to beckon.] Papers and Proc. Hants. F.C., 10, pp. 252–78, + 1 plate, + sketch map. 1931.

35. CORONATION

2306 Browne (George Forrest), *bp. of Bristol*. An address on the Anglo-Saxon coronation forms, *etc.*, pp. 44. 8° London, 1902.

2307 —— President's address, 1903. [The earliest historical notices of Malmesbury, and the earliest beginnings of the services for the coronation of the sovereign.] Proc. Clifton Antiq. Club, 5 (1900–03), pp. 193–204. 1904.

2308 Estrich (Robert M.). The throne of Hrothgar :-Beowulf, ll. 168–169. [Sacredness of symbols of kingship in early A.-S. times, and their ritualistic importance.] J. Engl. and Germ. Phil. 43, pp. 384–89. 1944.

2309 Finny (W. E. St. Lawrence). The church of the Saxon coronations at Kingston [Surrey]. [Coronation service, Saxon church, Saxon cross (with plate), etc.] S.E. Naturalist., 46, pp. 1–46, + 1 plate. 1941. *Same title.* Surrey Archaeol. Collns., 48, pp. 1–7. 1943.

2310 Greenwell (William). The pontifical of Egbert, archbishop of York, A.D. 732–766. *Surtees Society*, 27. pp. xviii, 138. 8° Durham, 1853. [Gross, 1423. Pp. 100–05, coronation services.]

2311 Jones (Walter H.). The proclamation stone of the Connaught kings. [Hill of Carns, co. Roscommon. Used from time of St. Patrick.] J. Galway Archaeol. Soc., 12, p. 46. 1922.

2312 Jongs (William). Crowns and coronations. A history of regalia. pp. xxx, 551. 8° London, 1883. [Pp. 28–33, 103–07, 177–92, A.-S. period.]

2313 Legg (John Wickham). Three coronation orders. *Henry Bradshaw Society*, 19. pp. xliii, 191, + 3 plates. 8° London, 1900. [Pp. xxxviii–xliii, 53–64, 162–73, consecration of the Anglo-Saxon king.]

2314 Legg (Leopold George Wickham). English coronation records. pp. 502. fol. London, 1901. [Gross, 2218a. c. 700–1837.]

2315 Liebermann (Felix). Zum angel-sächsischen Krönungseid. Archiv Stud. neueren Spr., Bd. 109, pp. 375–76. 1902.

2316 O'Reilly (Patrick J.). Notes on the coronation stone at Westminster, and the *Lia Fail* at Tara. J. Roy. Soc. Antiq. Ireland, 32 (5th S. 12), pp. 77–92. 1902.

2317 Prideaux (W. F.), *etc.* Kingston-upon-Thames (coronation stone). N. and Q., 9th S. 2, pp. 232–33, 373–74, 516 : 5, pp. 391–92, 481. 1898, 1900.

2318 Robinson (Joseph Armitage). The coronation order in the tenth century. J. Theol. Stud., 19, pp. 56–72. 1918.

2319 Schramm (Percy Ernst). A history of the English coronation. Translated by Leopold G. Wickham Legg. pp. xv, 283. 8° Oxford, 1937. [Pp. 12–26, English origins : the king's accession under the Anglo-Saxons.]

2320 —— Die Krönung bei den West-franken und Angelsachsen von 878 bis um 1000. Zeit. Rechtsgesch., 67, Kanon. Abt., 23, pp. 117–242. 1934.

2321 —— Ordines-Studien III : Die Krönung in England. [Pp. 311–18, A.-S.] Archiv f. Urkundenforschung, 15, pp. 305–91. 1938.

2322 Silver (Thomas). The coronation service or consecration of the Anglo-Saxon [and later] kings, as it illustrates the origin of the constitution. 8° Oxford, 1831. [Gross, 675.]

2323 Skene (William Forbes). The coronation stone. [Scone a royal city of the Picts, and also of Kenneth Mac Alpin, Malcolm Canmore, etc.] Proc. Soc. Antiq. Scot., 8, pp. 68–99. 1871.

2324 Stuart (John). Note on the coronation stone. [Sculpture on stone pillar at Dunfallandy, in Athole,? showing inauguration of a Pictish chief.] *Same jnl.*, 8, pp. 99–105. 1871.

2325 Thomas (F. W. L.). Dunadd, Glassary, Argyllshire; the place of inauguration of the Dalriadic kings. *Same jnl.*, 13 (N.S. 1), pp. 28–47. 1879.

2326 Ward (Paul L.). The coronation ceremony in mediaeval England. [Edgar ordo, etc.] Speculum, 14, pp. 160–78. 1939.

2327 —— An early version of the Anglo-Saxon coronation ceremony. [With Ratold coronation text.] E.H.R., 57, pp. 345–61. 1942.

2328 Westropp (Thomas Johnson). Magh Adhair, co. Clare. The place of inauguration of the Dalcassian kings. Proc. R.I.A., 3rd S. 4, pp. 55–60, + 1 plate. 1896.

2329 Wilson (Henry Austin). The English coronation orders. [A.-S., pp. 482–89, Egbert, Dunstan, etc.] J. Theol. Stud., 2, pp. 480–504. 1901.

36. GOVERNMENT

§ *a*. Central

2330 Allen (John), *M.D.*, *master of Dulwich College.* Inquiry into the rise and growth of the royal prerogative in England; a new edition. To which is added an Inquiry into the life and character of king Eadwig. [Edited by B. Thorpe]. pp. xciv, 268. 8° London, 1849. [Gross, 661, 1521.]

2331 Baker (Imogene). The king's household in the Arthurian court from Geoffrey of Monmouth to Malory. A dissertation. *Catholic University of America.* pp. x, 166. 8° Washington, 1937. [A survey of the king's household in its Frankish and Saxon beginnings, etc.]

2332 Chrimes (Stanley Bertram). An introduction to the administrative history of mediaeval England. pp. xvi, 277. 8° Oxford, 1952. [Pp. 1–17, the king's household before the Norman Conquest.]

2333 Hallam (Henry). Dissertation on the Bretwaldas of the Saxon Chronicle. Proc. Soc. Antiq., 1, pp. 201–203. 1847.

2334 —— On the Anglo-Saxon kings denominated Bretwaldas. [The title and its significance.] Archaeologia, 32, pp. 245–54. 1847.

2335 Larson (Laurence Marcellus). The king's household in England before the Norman Conquest. Bull. Univ. Wisconsin: no. 100 (Hist. series, 1), pp. 55–211. 1904.

2336 Liebermann (Felix). The national assembly in the Anglo-Saxon period. pp. vii, 90. 8° Halle a. S., 1913.

2337 Maseres (Francis). A view of the ancient constitution of the English parliament [under William I]. (Observations, on the preceding paper, by Charles Mellish). Archaeologia, 2, pp. 301–40, 341–52. 1772.

2338 Mockler (J.). The kings of ancient Ireland: their number, rights, election and inauguration. J. Waterford Archaeol. Soc., 7, pp. 1–16, + 1 plate. 1901.

2339 Morris (William Alfred). The lesser Curia Regis under the first two Norman kings of England. A.H.R., 34, pp. 772–78. 1929.

2340 Purlitz (Friedrich). König und Witenagemot bei den Angelsachsen. pp. 66. 8° Bremen, 1892. [Gross, 1588.]

2341 Round (John Horace). The officers of Edward the Confessor. E.H.R. 19, pp. 90–92. 1904.

2342 —— The origin of the exchequer. [Domesday, etc.] The commune of London and other studies, by J. H. Round, pp. 62–96. [=study, no. 4]. 1899.

2343 Schuecking (Levin L.). Das Königsideal in Beowulf. Engl. Studien, 67, pp. 1–14. 1932.

2344 Steel (Anthony). The place of the king's household in English constitutional history, to 1272. History, N.S. 15, pp. 289–95. 1931.

2345 Williams (Benjamin). On the land of Ditmarsh, and the Mark Confederation. (On the house-marks of the Ditmarshers and Angeln). [Comparison of institutions, showing ' germ of our power of self-government and of our jury system.'] Archaeologia, 37, pp. 371–90, + 1 plate. 1857.

§ *b*. **Local (Trinoda Necessitas, etc.)**

2346 Boult (Joseph). Some of the ancient jurisdictions of South Britain. Proc. Lit. and Phil. Soc. L'pool., 29, pp. 299–340. 1875.

2347 Cam (Helen Maud). A comparison of the local administration and the law courts of the Carolingian empire with those of the West Saxon kings. *M.A. Thesis, London.* 1909. [Apply Univ. Library.]

2348 —— The king's government, as administered by the greater abbots of East Anglia. [A small amount of late A.-S. material, e.g. for Ely.] Proc. Camb. Antiq. Soc., 29, pp. 25–49. 1928.

2349 —— Local government in Francia and England. A comparison of the local administration and jurisdiction of the Carolingian empire with that of the West Saxon kingdom. pp. x, 156. 8° London, 1912. [Gross, 1563a. A.D. 768–1034. ' Discusses commitatus, shire, benefice, immunity and army.']

2350 Davis (Eliza Jeffries). Trinoda necessitas. (Historical revisions–xlv). History, N.S., 13, pp. 33–34, 337. 1928.

2351 Pollock (*Sir* Frederick). [Trinoda necessitas]. Law Q.R., 31, pp. 146–47. 1915.

2352 Rose-Troup (Frances). Devon charters and the threefold obligation. Rept. and Trans. Devon. Assoc., 65 pp. 393–404. 1933.

2353 Stevenson (William Henry). Trinoda necessitas. [Exemptions in A.-S. royal grants from military service and from repairs of bridges and fortresses.] E.H.R., 29, pp. 689–703. 1914.

2354 Stewart-Brown (R.). ' Bridgework ' at Chester. E.H.R., 54, pp. 83–87. 1939.

2355 Zoepfl (Heinrich). Alterthümer des deutschen Reichs und Rechts. 3 vol. 8° Leipzig, 1860–51. [Gross, 1586. i, pp. 170–239, jurisdiction of English barons in 11th–12th c.]

37. LAW, ANGLO-SAXON

§ *a*. General and Historical

2356 Adams (Henry). The Anglo-Saxon courts of law. Essays in A.-S. law, pp. 1–54. 1876.

2357 Bechert (Rudolf). Ein Einleitung des Rechtsgang nach angelsächsischem Recht. Zeit. Rechtsges., 60, German. Abt., 47, pp. 1–114. 1927.

2358 —— Recht oder Pflicht zur Beweisführung? unter Berücksichtigung der nordischen Rechte vornehmlich nach fränkischem und angelsächsischem untersucht. *Same jnl.*, 62, (German. Abt., 49), pp. 26–56. 1929.

2359 Bethurum (Dorothy). Stylistic features of the Old English laws. Mod. Lang. Rev., 27, pp. 263–79. 1932.

2360 Cherry (Richard Robert). Lectures on the growth of criminal law in ancient communities. pp. xi, 123. 8° London, 1890. [Gross, 687. Ch. i, Primitive custom as to crimes : Ch. ii, Ancient Irish law : ch. v–vi, Early English penal and criminal law.]

2361 Cook (Albert Stanburrough). Aldhelm's legal studies. J. Engl. and Germ. Phil., 23, pp. 105–13. 1924.

2362 Coote (Henry Charles). On the legal procedure of the Anglo-Saxons. Archaeologia, 41, pp. 207–18. 1867.

2363 Cowper (Henry Swainson). Law ting at Fell Foot, Little Langdale, Westmorland. Trans. Cumb. and Westm. Antiq. Soc., 11, pp. 1–6, + plan. 1890.

2364 Davis (Henry William Carless). The Anglo-Saxon laws. E.H.R., 28, pp. 417–30. 1913.

2365 Davoud-Oghlou (Garabed-Artin). Histoire de la législation des anciens Germains. 2 vol. 8° Berlin, 1843. [Gross, 1490. Vol. 2, pp. 271–765, A.-S. ' Of little value.']

I

2366 De Montmorency (James Edward Geoffrey). Danish influence on English law and character. Law Q.R., 40, pp. 324–43. 1924.

2367 Diamond (Arthur Sigismund). Primitive law. (2nd edition). pp. x, 451. 8° London, 1950. [Pp. 62–70, A.-S. laws.]

2368 Hazeltine (Harold Dexter). The laws of the Anglo-Saxons. Law Q.R., 29, pp. 387–98. 1913.

2369 Henderson (Ernest Flagg). Verbrechen und Strafen in England während der Zeit von Wilhelm 1 (1066–1087), bis Edward I (1272–1307). *Dissertation.* pp. 74. 8° Berlin, 1890.

2370 Holdsworth (*Sir* William Searle). History of English law. 3rd edition, rewritten. 12 vol. + index, 8° London, 1922–23, 1932. [Vol. 1, A.-S. and Norman feudalism, effects of the Norman Conquest, etc. : vol. 2, pp. 3–118, A.-S. antiquities.]

2371 Inderwick (Frederick Andrew). The king's peace : a historical sketch of the English law courts. pp. xxiv, 254. 8° London, 1895. [Pp. 1–44, A.-S. period.]

2372 Jenks (Edward). The development of Teutonic law. Select essays in Anglo-American legal history, 1, pp. 34–87. 1907.

2372a Jenks (Edward). A short history of English law. pp. xxxvi, 442. 8° London, 1912 (6th reprint, 1949). [Pp. 1–19, A.-S.]

2373 Jeudwine (John Wynne). Tort, crime and police in mediaeval England. A review of some early law and custom. pp. xix, 292. 8° London, 1917. [Including Celtic.]

2374 Lehmann (Karl). Abhandlungen zur germanischen insbesondere nordischen Rechtsgeschichte. pp. 215. 8° Berlin, 1888. [Gross, 1587. Pp. 74–78, Die angelsächsische *feorm.*]

2375 Liebermann (Felix). Zu den Gesetzen der Angelsachsen. Zeit. Rechtsgesch., 18 (German. Abt.), pp. 198–226. 1884.

2376 Logeman (Henri). On some cases of Scandinavian influence in English. iv. Danelaw and outlaw. [Danish law in force in that part of England. *See also* : Outlaw and Dane law, by F. Liebermann, *in* Bd. 118, pp. 130–32, 1907.] Archiv Stud. neueren Spr., Bd. 117, pp. 268–78. 1906.

2377 Maitland (Frederic William). The materials for English legal history. [Pp. 505–11, England before the Norman Conquest.] Pol. Sci. Q., 4, pp. 496–518, 628–47. 1889.

2378 —— Old English law. Social England, ed. Traill and Mann, 1, pp. 239–53. 1891.

2379 —— A prologue to a history of English law. [A.-S. and contemporary continental legislation.] Law Q.R., 14, pp. 13–33. 1898. *Same title.* Select essays in Anglo-American legal history, 1, pp. 7–33. 1907.

2380 Maurer (Konrad von). Angelsächsische Rechtsverhältnisse. Kritische Ueberschau d. deut. Gesetzgebung, i, pp. 47–120, 405–31 ; ii, pp. 30–68, 388–440 ; iii, pp. 26–61. 1853–56.

2381 Munford (George). Is the Dombec [in Laws of Edward the Elder] the Domesday [or Winchester Book] of Alfred ? N. and Q., 1st S. 1, p. 365. 1850.

2382 Olszewska (E. S.). Legal borrowings from Norse in Old and Middle English. [e.g. O.E. *niþing.* Mostly M.E.] Saga-Book V.C., 11 (1928–36), pp. 233–38. 1936.

2383 Palgrave (*Sir* Francis). The rise and progress of the English Commonwealth : Anglo-Saxon period. 2 pts. 4° London, 1832. [Gross, 1497. Largely on development of legal institutions.]

2384 Phillips (George). Versuch einer Darstellung des angelsächsischen Rechts. 8° Göttingen, 1825. [Gross, 1498. ' Now in large part antiquated '.]

2385 Pike (Luke Owen). A history of crime in England. 2 vol. 8° London, 1873–76. [Vol. 1, pp. 35–95, A.-S.]

2386 Plucknett (Theodore Frank Thomas). A concise history of the common law. 4th edition. pp. xxxiii, 707, 59. 8° London, 1948. [Pp. 7–13, A.-S., period, etc.]

2387 Pollock (*Sir* Frederick), *bart.* Anglo-Saxon law. E.H.R., 8, pp. 239–71. 1893.

2388 —— English law before the Norman Conquest. Law Q.R., 14, pp. 291–306. 1898. *Same title.* Select essays in Anglo-American legal history, 1, pp. 88–107. 1907.

2389 —— and **Maitland** (Frederic William). History of English law before the time of Edward I. 2nd edition. 2 vol. Cambridge, 1898. [Vol. 1, pp. 25–63, A.-S. law.]

2390 Seebohm (Frederic). Tribal custom in Anglo-Saxon law. pp. 554. 8° London, 1902. [Gross, 1553a. ' Devotes much attention to wergelds.']

2391 Senior (W.). England and the mediaeval Empire. [Pp. 483–88, ' Romanic legal influences during the Anglo-Saxon period.'] Law Q.R., 40, pp. 483–94. 1924.

2392 —— Roman law in England before Vacarius. Law Q.R., 46, pp. 191–206. 1930.

2393 Stubbs (William), *bp. of Oxford.* The laws and legislation of the Norman kings. Stubbs (W.) : Lectures on early English history, pp. 37–133. 1906.

2394 Tynan (Joseph). The growth of the Saxon laws. Irish Eccles. Rec., 3rd S. 11, pp. 19–29. 1890.

2395 Walker (Curtis H.). The date of the Conqueror's ordinance separating the ecclesiastical and lay courts. E.H.R., 39, pp. 399–400. 1924.

2396 Winfield (*Sir* Percy Henry). The chief sources of English legal history. pp. xviii, 374. 8° Cambridge, Mass., 1925. [Pp. 42–53 (Chapter 3), sources of A.-S. law.]

2397 Wuerdinger (Hans). Einwirkungen des Christentums auf das angelsächsische Recht. Zeit. Rechtsgesch., 68, Germ. Abt., 55, pp. 105–30. 1935.

2398 Zézas (Spyridion G.). Essai historique sur la législation d'Angle-terre . . . jusqu'au xii. siècle. pp. 336. 8° Paris, 1863. [Gross, 1504. 'A digest . . . of little value '.]

2399 Zinkeisen (Frank). The Anglo-Saxon courts of law. Pol. Sci. Q., 10, pp. 132–44. 1895.

§ *b.* Codes, Texts, etc.

2400 Attenborough (Frederick Levi). Laws of the earliest English kings. pp. xii, 256. 8° Cambridge, 1922. [To Athelstan. Text and translation, parallel.]

2401 Ballard (Adolphus). The law of Breteuil. [Including evidence from statements in Domesday Book.] E.H.R., 30, pp. 646–58. 1915.

2402 Bateson (Mary). The laws of Breteuil [Britolium]. E.H.R., 15, pp. 73–78, 302–18, 496–523, 754–57; 16, pp. 92–110, 332–45. 1900–01.

2403 Bethurum (Dorothy). Six anonymous Old English codes. [Geþycðo, Norðleóda laga, Mircna laga, Að, Hadbot, and Grið (Liebermann, 1, pp. 456–73) : all attributed to Wulfstan.] J. Engl. and Germ. Phil., 49, pp. 449–63. 1950.

2404 Cook (Albert Stanburrough). Extracts from the Anglo-Saxon laws. 8° New York, 1880.

2405 Kelham (Robert). A dictionary of the Norman or Old French language ; . . . to which are added the laws of William the Conqueror [and D. Wilkins' translation of them], with notes and references. 2 pt. 8° London, 1779. [Gross, 1407.]

2406 Kolderup-Rosenvinge (Jens Laurids Andreas). Legum regis Canuti Magni quas Anglis olim dedit versionem antiquam Latinam ex codibus Colbertino lectionibus atque observationibus additis, cum textu Anglo-Saxonico. pp. xii, 120. 4° Hauniae, 1826.

2407 Lambarde (William). Ἀρχαιο-νομία, sive de priscis Anglorum legibus libri, *etc.* pp. 18, + 141. 4° *n.p.*, 1568. —2nd edition [by Abraham Whelock, appended to his edition of Bede's Historia ecclesiastica, 2433]. pp. 16, 226, +9. fol. Cantabrigiae, 1644. [A.-S. and Latin, parallel. First published collection.]

2408 Liebermann (Felix). Die angelsächsische Verordnung über die Dunsæte. [Gross, 1400. Issued by Edgar. Herefordshire.] Archiv f.d. Studium neueren Spr., Bd. 102, pp. 267–96. 1899.

2409 —— Eine anglo-normannische Uebersetzung von Articuli Willelmi. [Gross, 2016 ' This translation, which is here printed in full, was made in 1192 or 1193.'] Zeit. roman. Philol., 19, pp. 77–84. 1895.

2410 —— *ed.* Consiliatio Cnuti, eine Übertragung angelsächsischer Gesetze aus dem zwölften Jahrhundert. pp. xx, 29. 8° Halle a. S., 1893.

2411 —— *ed.* Geréfa. [Gross, 1399. Introduction, A.-S. text, and German translation. MS. Camb. C.C.C. 383, fol. 102. Compiled early 11th c. Expounds duties of a reeve, and the management of a great estate.] Anglia, 9, pp. 251–66. 1886.

2412 —— *ed.* Die Gesetze der Angelsachsen. 3 vol. 4° Halle a. S., 1898–16. [Gross, 1391. Vol. 1, text and translation : Vol. 2, dictionary to Vol. 1 and citation to passages : vol. 3, introduction and commentary.]

2413 —— Das Handschriftenverhältnis in Cnuts Gesetzen. Archiv Stud. neueren Spr., Bd. 110, pp. 422–25. 1903.

2414 —— Ist Lambardes Text der Gesetze Æthelstans neuzeitliche Fälsehung? Anglia, Beiblatt, 35, pp. 214–18, 36, pp. 345–47. 1924–25.

2415 —— On the Instituta Cnuti aliorumque regum Anglorum. Trans. R.H.S., N.S., 7, pp. 77–107. 1893.

2416 —— *ed.* Quadripartitus, ein englisches Rechtsbuch von 1114. pp. viii, 168. 8° Halle, 1892. [Gross, 1409. Prologue gives account of English institutions, 1018–1110. ' Bk. i. contains a glossed translation of most of the A.-S. laws, those of Cnut being given first. . . . Some dooms of Athelstan, Edmund, and Ethelred are only known in the form of this Latin version.']

2417 —— Ueber die Gesetze Ines von Wessex. Mélanges d'histoire offerts à Charles Bémont, pp. 21–42. 1913.

2418 Liebermann (Felix). Über die Leges Edwardi Confessoris. pp. vii, 139. 8° Halle, 1896.

2419 —— Ueber die Leis Willelme. [Gross, 1407, note. Shows original text was in French and written in Mercia before 1150.] Arch. Stud. neueren Spr., Bd. 106, pp. 113–38. 1901.

2420 —— Über Pseudo-Cnuts Constitutiones de foresta. pp. iv, 55. 8° Halle a. S., 1894. [With the text.]

2421 —— Wulfstan und Cnut. [Gross, 1433, lit. Contends that Wulfstan's homilies were used in the Leges Cnuti. Evidence against Wulfstan's authorship of the Institutes of polity.] Archiv f.d. Stud. neueren Spr., Bd. 103, pp. 47–54. 1899.

2422 —— Zu Wihtræds Gesetz. *Same jnl.*, Bd. 146, p. 242. 1923.

2423 —— Zur Datierung von Ælfreds Gesetzgebung. *Same jnl.*, Bd. 119, pp. 175–76. 1907.

2424 March (F. A.) and **Child** (F. J.), *trans.* Select cases in Anglo-Saxon law. [35 cases. Latin, A.-S., and English translations.] Essays in A.-S. law, (Appendix), pp. 309–83. 1876.

2425 Matzke (John Ernst), *ed.* Lois de Guillaume le Conquérant en français et en latin. Textes et étude critique. *Collection de textes pour servir à l'étude de l'histoire.* pp. liv, 32. 8° Paris, 1899. [Gross, 1407.]

2426 Ritter (Otto). Zum ae. *Geréfa.* Archiv Stud. neueren Spr., Bd. 115, pp. 163–65. 1905.

2427 Robertson (Agnes Jane), *ed.* The laws of the kings of England from Edmund to Henry I. Edited and translated. pp. xiii, 426. 8° Cambridge, 1925.

2428 Schmid (Reinhold). Dir Gesetze der Angelsachsen. 2. Auflage. pp. lxxxiii, 680. 8° Leipzig, 1858. [Text, German translation, and glossary, etc.]

2429 Spelman (*Sir* Henry). Leges Anglo-Saxonicae, ecclesiasticae and civiles. Accedunt leges Edvardi Latinae, Guillielmi Conquestoris Gallo-Normanicae, *etc.* Cum codd. MSS. contulit . . . David Wilkins. pp. xxiv, 450. fol. Londini, 1721.

2430 Stearns (John M.). The germs and developments of the laws of England, embracing the Anglo-Saxon laws extant, . . . with notes and comments. pp. 370. 8° New York, 1889. [Gross, 1501. Largely a reprint of **2431**, with brief notes.]

2431 Thorpe (Benjamin), *ed.* Ancient laws and institutes of England, [with a translation from the Saxon.] *Record Commission.* pp. x, 548. fol. London, 1840. *Also in* 2 vols. 8° [London], 1840. [Gross, 1393.]

2432 Turk (Milton Haight). The legal code of Ælfred the Great, edited with an introduction. pp. viii, 147. 8° Boston, 1893.

2433 Whelock (Abraham), *ed.* Anglo-Saxonicae leges. pp. 16, 226 +9. fol. Cantabrigiae, 1644. [=vol. 2 of his edition of Bede's Historia ecclesiastica.]

2434 Whitelock (Dorothy). Wulfstan and the laws of Cnute. [i. The version of Cnut's laws in C.C.C.C. MS. 201. ii. The complete code.] E.H.R., 63, pp. 433–52. 1948.

2325 —— Wulfstan and the so-called laws of Edward and Guthrum. E.H.R., 56, pp. 1–21. 1941.

2436 Wilkins (David). Leges Anglo-Saxonicae ecclesiasticae et civiles, *etc.* fol. Londini, 1721. [Reprinted *in* Canciani (P.) : Barbarorum leges, 4, *and in* Hoüard (D.) : Traités sur les coutumes anglo-normandes, 1776.]

2437 Williams (Laurence Frederic Rushbrook). The status of the Welsh in the laws of Ine. E.H.R., 30, pp. 271–77. 1915.

2438 Wroblewski (Leonhard). Ueber die altenglischen Gesetze des Königs Knut. *Diss., Berlin.* pp. 60. 8° Berlin, 1901.

2439 Wuerdinger (A.). Gesetze der Angelsachsen. *Germanenrechte. Texte und Übersetzungen. Bd. 5. Schriften d. Akad. f. Recht. Gruppe Rechtsgeschichte.* 8° Weimar, 1935.

§ c. Law Terms

2440 Bellot (Hugh Hale Leigh). Hoke-day. [Low (?=Law) sunday. Not annual celebration of massacre of the Danes of 1002, but probably connected with *hocking* and A.-S. hundred court.] Law Q.R., 28, pp. 283–89. 1912.

2441 Brunner (Heinrich). Ae. *dryhtinbéag.* Archiv Stud. neueren Spr., Bd. 98, p. 398. 1897.

2442 Karaus (Arthur). Die Sprache der Gesetze des Königs Aethelred. *Diss., Berlin.* pp. 74. 8° Berlin, 1901.

2443 Liebermann (Felix). Angelsächsisch *boldgetæl* : Provinz. [In Laws of Alfred, 37.] Arch. Stud. neueren Spr., Bd. 123, pp. 400–01. 1909.

2444 —— Angelsächsish *drinclean.* [In Law of the Northumbrian priests, 67. 1.] *Same jnl.*, Bd. 127, p. 196. 1911.

2445 —— Ags. *rihthamscyld* : echtes Hoftor. [In Æthelberht's Laws, 32.] *Same jnl.*, Bd. 115, pp. 389–91. 1905.

2446 —— Ags. *teon* : erfolgreich verklagen, prozessual besiegen. *Same jnl.*, Bd. 144, p. 353. 1922.

2447 —— Altenglisch *homola* : verstümmelter ; *orige* unsichtbar. [In Laws of Alfred, 35.] *Same jnl.*, Bd. 98, pp. 127–28. 1897.

2448 —— *Borhtriming* 'Freibürgschaftsordnung'. *Same jnl.*, Bd. 151, p. 80. 1927.

2449 —— Kentish *hionne* : Hirnhaut. [In Æthelberht's Laws, 36.] *Same inl.*, Bd. 115, pp. 177–78. 1905.

2450 Stevenson (William Henry). *Burh-geat-setl.* [=house in the street of the settlement. In Law of Promotion, preserved in Textus Roffensis.] E.H.R., 12, pp. 489–92. 1897.

§ d. Penenden Heath Trial

(Inquiry in 1075 or 1076 before the shire court of Kent, owing to complaint by Lanfranc that Odo of Bayeaux had encroached on the estates of the see of Canterbury.)

2451 Cave-Browne (J.). Penenden heath. [Parish of Boxley, Kent.] J. Brit. Archaeol. Assoc., 47, pp. 260–67. 1891.

2452 Douglas (David Charles). Odo, Lanfranc, and the Domesday survey. Hist. essays in honour of J. Tait, pp. 47–57, + 1 plate. 1933.

2453 Le Patourel (John Herbert). The date of the trial on Penenden heath. [?1072, 1073 or 1076.] E.H.R., 61, pp. 378–88. 1946.

2454 —— The reports of the trial on Penenden heath. Studies pres. to F. M. Powicke, pp. 15–26. 1948.

2455 Levison (Wilhelm). A report on the Penenden trial. E.H.R., 27, pp. 717–20. 1912.

§ e. Wills

2456 Alexander (John James). The will of Alfred the Great. [A. the contents: B. The date (c. 881) : C. Bequests to Ethelweard : D. Bequests to Edward : E. The burghal hidage : F. Identifications of places mentioned.] Rept. and Trans. Devon Assoc., 70, pp. 106–14. 1938.

2457 Alfred, *king.* The will of Ælfred, king of the West Saxons. By Adwin Wigfall Green. pp. 24. 8° Dublin, 1944. [Commentary, with text and translation.]

2458 —— The will of King Alfred. pp. iii, 51. 4° Oxford, 1788. [A.-S. text, with English and Latin versions by Owen Manning and with notes by Thomas Astle.] —With a preface and additional notes. pp. xii, 32. 8° London, 1828.

2459 Bridgeman (Charles George Orlando). Will of Wulfric Spot. [Founder of Burton abbey. Includes text and translation.] Collectns. for a history of Staffs., 1916, pp. 1–66. 1918.

2460 Campbell (Alistair). An Old English will. [That of Badanoð Beotting in MS. Cotton Aug. II. 42. Kentish : 9th c. A.-S. text, translation, and notes.] J. Engl. and Germ. Phil., 37, pp. 133–52. 1938.

2461 Whitelock (Dorothy), *ed.* Anglo-Saxon wills. pp. xlvii, 244. 8° Cambridge, 1930. [A.-S. texts, translations and notes.]

2462 Wulfgeat, *of Donnington.* Wulfgeat's will. [A.-S. text from MS. Harl. Cart. 83. A.2, and English translation. c. 1005.] The Shrine, pp. 159–61. 1868–69.

§ f. Particular Law Themes

2463 Amira (Karl von). Erbenfolge und Verwandtschaftsgliederung nach den alt-niederdeutschen Rechten. pp. x, 225. 8° München, 1874. [Gross, 1541. Pp. 14–18, Das angelsächsische Recht.]

2464 Ashworth (Philip Arthur). Das Witthum, Dower, im englischen Recht. pp. 55. 8° Frankfurt, 1898. [Gross, 1553, note.]

2465 Baltensberger (Hermann). Eid, Versprechen und Treuschwur bei den Angelsachsen. *Diss., Zürich.* pp. vii, 70. 8° Zürich, 1920.

2466 Bonser (Wilfrid). Anglo-Saxon laws and charms relating to theft. Folklore, 57, pp. 7–11. 1946.

2467 Bridgeman (Charles George Orlando). The civil death of Wulfric Spot. Collectns. for a history of Staffs., 1919, pp. 127–28. 1920.

2468 Brunner (Heinrich). Sippe und Wergeld nach niederdeutschen Rechten. [Gross, 1542. Pp. 14–18, Das angelsächsische Recht.] Zeit. Rechtsgesch., 16, (Germ. Abt., 3), pp. 1–101. 1882.

2469 Buckstaff (F. G.). Married woman's property in Anglo-Saxon and Anglo-Norman law. [Gross, 1543.] Annals Amer. Acad. pol. and social sci., 4, pp. 33–64. 1893.

2470 Ellis (*Sir* Henry). Observations on some ancient methods of conveyance in England. [Including two from the Domesday survey concerning Evesham abbey.] Archaeologia, 17, pp. 311–19. 1814.

2471 Friedberg (Emil). Das Recht der Eheschliessung in seiner geschichtlichen Entwickelung. pp. xii, 827. 8° Leipzig, 1865. [Gross, 1545. Pp. 33–57, England]

2472 Gans (Eduard). Das Erbrecht in weltgeschichtlicher Entwickelung. 4 Bde. 8° Stuttgart, 1824–35. [Gross, 1546. 4, pp. 250–457, England to end of 15th c.]

2473 Gibson (William Sidney). On some ancient modes of trial, especially those in which appeal was made to the divine judgment through the ordeals of water, fire, or other judicia dei. [Laws of Ethelred, etc.] Archaeologia, 32, pp. 263–97. 1847.

2474 Goebel (Julius), *jr.* Felony and misdemeanour ; a study in the history of English criminal procedure. Vol. 1. pp. xxix, 455. 8° New York, 1937. [Up to year 1135. Pp. 336–440, Anglo-Saxon institutions and Norman justice.]

2475 Gomme (*Sir* George Laurence). On archaic conceptions of property in relation to the laws of succession ; and their survival in England. Archaeologia, 50, pp. 195–214. 1887.

2476 Haigh (Daniel Henry). The compensation paid by the Kentishmen to Ine for the burning of Mul. [A.-S. C., 687, 694.] Arch. Cant., 10, pp. 29–38. 1876.

2477 Harmer (Florence Elizabeth). Anglo-Saxon writs. pp. xxii, 604, + 2 plates. 8° Manchester, 1952. [Chronological and numerical lists of writs. Pt. 1, general introduction : Pt. 2, discussion and texts : Pt. 3, notes and appendices : Pt. 4, biographical notes.]

2478 —— Three Westminster writs of king Edward the Confessor. E.H.R., 51, pp. 97–103. 1936.

2479 Hazeltine (Harold Dexter). Zur Geschichte der Eheschliessung nach angelsächsischem Recht. pp. 38. [Gross, 1553, note.] Festgabe für Bernhard Hübler, pp. 249–84. 1905.

2480 Hermann (Franz Wilhelm Emil). Ueber die Entwicklung des altdeutschen Schöffengerichts. pp. vi, 264. 8° Breslau, 1881. [Gross, 1575. Pp. 227–39, Die Angelsachsen.]

2481 Hurnard (Naomi D.). The Anglo-Norman franchises. E.H.R., 64, pp. 289–327 : 433–60. 1949.

2482 Jastrow (Ignaz). Zur strafrechtlichen Stellung der Sklaven bei Deutschen und Angelsachsen. *Gierke* (D.) : *Untersuchungen zur deutschen Staats-und Rechtsgeschichte*, 2. pp. 83. 8° Berlin, 1878. [Gross, 1549. Pp. 38–83, Die Angelsachsen.]

2483 Laughlin (J. Laurence). The Anglo-Saxon legal procedure. Essays in A.-S. law, pp. 183–305. 1876.

2484 Lear (Floyd Seyward). Treason and related offenses in the Anglo-Saxon dooms. *Rice Institute Pamphlet.* 8° Houston, Texas, 1950.

2485 Liebermann (Felix). Angelsächsischer Protest gegen den Cölibat. Archiv f.d. Stud. neueren Sprachen, Bd. 109, p. 376. 1902.

2486 —— Die Friedlosigkeit bei den Angelsachsen. [Gross, 1576.] Festschrift Heinrich Brunner, pp. 17–37. 1910.

2487 —— Kesselfang bei den Westsachsen im siebenten Jahrhundert. [Gross 1576. *Ceace* (kettle) should be read for *ceape* in Ine's laws, cc. 37, 62 : hence ordeal then and not introduced 9th or 10th c., as most assert.] Sitzungsber. preuss. Akad. Wiss., 1896, ii, pp. 829–35. 1896.

2488 —— Zur angelsächsischen Exkommunikation. Archiv Stud. neueren Spr., Bd. 119, p. 176. 1907.

2489 —— Zwei Stellen über Ordal der Angelsachsen. *Same jnl.*, Bd. 151, p. 81. 1927.

2490 Lodge (H. Cabot). The Anglo-Saxon land-law. Essays in A.-S. law, pp. 55–189. 1876.

2491 Marquardsen (Heinrich). Ueber Haft und Bürgschaft bei den Angelsachsen. Vorstudie zu einer Geschichte des Habeas Corpus Rechts. pp. 70. 8° Erlangen, 1852. [Gross, 1577.]

2492 Maurer (Georg Ludwig von). Ueber die Freipflege (plegium liberale) und die Entstehung der grossen und kleinen Jury in England. pp. 60. 8° München, 1848. [Gross, 1578. ' Contends that the jury is derived from the frankpledge system.']

2493 Maurer (Konrad von). Das Gesetzsprecheramt in Dänemark. [Gross, 1568. Pp. 388–99, 'A.-S. *lahmen* of boroughs, *etc.*'] Sitzungsb. K. bayer. Akad. Wiss., Philos.-Philol. Klasse, 1887, ii. pp. 363–99. 1888.

2494 Maurer (Wilhelm). An inquiry into Anglo-Saxon mark-courts, and their relation to memorial and municipal institutions, and trial by jury. pp. 62. 8° London, 1855. [Gross, 1579. German version: Ueber angelsächsische Mark-verfassung: *in* Zeit. deutsches Recht, 16, pp. 201, *et seq.*, 1856. Much information re vills, 'but main conclusions untenable'.]

2495 Mezger (Fritz). Did the institution of marriage by purchase exist in Old Germanic law? [e.g. in Laws of Æthelberht, 77.] Speculum, 18, pp. 369–71. 1943.

2496 —— Self-judgment in OE documents. [Right granted by one party to another to terminate a feud or litigation.] Mod. Lang. Notes, 67, pp. 106–09. 1952.

2497 Miller (Edward). The Ely land pleas in the reign of William I. [i. The inquest of 1071–5: ii. The inquest of Hartford, April 1080: iii. The inquest of Kentford before bishop Geoffrey of Coutances: iv. The Conqueror's writs. etc.] E.H.R., 62, pp. 438–56. 1947.

2498 Morris (William Alfred). The frankpledge system. *Harvard Historical Studies*, 14. pp. xvi, 194. 8° New York, 1910. [Gross, 696a. Pp. 1–41, A.-S. origins (*borh* system, etc.).]

2499 Odegaard (Charles E.). Legalis homo. [In laws of Confessor—.] Speculum, 15, pp. 186–93. 1940.

2500 Opet (Otto). Erbrechtliche Stellung der Weibe in der Zeit der Volksrechte. pp. 86. 8° Breslau, 1888. [Gross, 1552. Pp. 75–82, Das angelsächsische Recht. 'Contends that no preference was shown to the sons in the inheritance of property.']

2501 —— Geschichte der Prozesseinleitungsformen. Abt. I. 8° Breslau, 1891. [Gross, 1580. Pp. 12–62, Das angelsächsische Recht.]

2502 Parker (F. H. M.). The forest laws and the death of William Rufus. E.H.R., 27, pp. 26–38. 1912.

2502a Pollock (*Sir* Frederick), *3rd bart*. The land laws. 3rd edition. pp. x, 233. 8° London, 1896. [Pp. 19–52, the Old English customary laws.]

2403 Puntschart (Paul). Über Gottesbürgschaft im angelsächsischen Recht. Festschrift zu Ehren Oswald Redlichs (Veröffentlichungen des Museums Ferdinandeum in Innsbruck, 8), pp. 501–32. 1928.

2504 Reinhard (J. R.). Burning at the stake in mediaeval law and literature. [Includes A.-S. penalties for adultery, etc., and Celtic material.] Speculum, 16, pp. 186–209. 1941.

2505 —— Setting adrift in mediæval law and literature. [Including Celtic and A.-S.] P.M.L.A., 56, pp. 33–68. 1941.

2506 Schlutter (Otto Bernhard). Zur Frage des keltischen Ursprungs von ae. *Gafol*. Anglia, 36 (N.F. 24), pp. 60, 377–80. 1912.

2507 Schmid (Reinhold). Rechtsbürgschaften. [Gross, 1581. *See also his* Gesetze der Angelsachsen, 1858, pp. 644–49, *also* 554, 564, 639, 641, 656, 660, etc.] Hermes, 32, pp. 232–64. 1829.

2508 Schwerin (Claudius), *Freiherr von*. Zur Entwicklung der Teilnahme im angelsächsischen Recht. Texte u. Forschungen: Festgabe für F. Liebermann, pp. 277–300. 1921.

2509 Scrutton (Thomas Edward). Land in fetters, or the history and policy of the laws restraining the alienation and settlement of land in England. pp. ix, 162. 8° Cambridge, 1886. [Gross, 736. A.-S. and feudal land laws, etc.]

2510 Stone (Gilbert). The transaction of sale in Saxon times. Law Q.R., 29, pp. 323–39. 1913.

2511 Vinogradoff (*Sir* Paul). Transfer of land in Old English law. Harvard Law Review, 20, pp. 532–48. 1907. *Reprinted in* Collected Papers of Vinogradoff, 1, pp. 149–67. 1928.

2512 Waitz (Georg). Deutsche Verfassungsgeschichte. 3. Auflage. 8 Bde. 8° Berlin, 1880–82. [Gross, 1582. Bd. 1, Appendix 1, A.-S. surety system.]

2513 Whitelock (Dorothy). Beowulf 2444–2471. [A.-S. law re executed criminals.] Medium Ævum, 8, pp. 198–204. 1939.

2514 Wilda (Wilhelm Eduard). Das Strafrecht der Germanen. 8° Halle, 1842. [Gross, 1583. Chap. 5, A.-S. wergeld, bots, etc.]

2515 Wuerdinger (Hans). Zum angelsächsischen Schuldrecht. 8° Köln, 1934.

2516 Young (Ernest). The Anglo-Saxon family law. Essays in A.-S. law, pp. 121–82. 1876.

38. LAW, CELTIC

§ *a*. General and Historical

2517 Allcroft (Arthur Hadrian). The Celtic circle-moot : some new facts and the inferences. Trans. Hon. Soc. Cymm., 1918–19, pp. 1–29. 1920.

2518 Byrne (Mary E.). On the punishment of sending adrift. Ériu, 11, pp. 97–102. 1930.

2519 Cameron (John). Celtic law : the Senchus Mór and the Book of Aicill, and the traces of an early Gaelic system of law in Scotland. pp. xvi, 272. 8° London, 1937.

2520 Dareste (Rodolphe). Études d'histoire du droit. pp. xii, 417. 8° Paris, 1889 [1888]. [Gross, 1394, lit. Pp. 356–81, Brehon and Welsh laws.]

2521 Loth (Joseph). Un genre particulier de compensation pour crimes et offenses chez les Celtes insulaires. Rev. celt., 48, pp. 332–51. 1931.

2522 Thurneysen (Rudolf). Das keltische Recht. Zeit. Rechtsges., 68, (Germ. Abt., 55), pp. 81–104. 1935.

2523 Valroger (Lucien Marie de). Les Celtes. La Gaule celtique. 8° Paris, 1879. [Gross, 1270. Pt. 4, Old Welsh and Irish law.]

§ *b*. Irish Law

2524 Arbois de Jubainville (Marie Henry d'). L'antiquité des compositions pour crime en Irlande. Nouvelle rev. hist. de droit, 11, pp. 66–69. 1887.

2525 —— L'antiquité des compositions pour crime en Irlande. Rev. celt., 8, pp. 158–61. 1887.

2526 Arbois de Jubainville (Marie Henry d'). Des attributions judiciaires de l'autorité publique chez les Celtes. Conséquences au double point de vue : 1. de l'organisation politique ; 2. de la procédure dans les contestations privées. [Pp. 11–37, La procédure irlandaise : le duel, la saisie mobilière, la saisie immobilière.] Rev. celt., 7, pp. 2–37. 1886.

2527 —— La clientèle en Irlande. Nouvelle rev. hist. de droit, 21, pp. 294–97. 1897.

2528 —— Le droit des femmes chez les Celtes. *Same jnl.*, 15, pp. 301–09. 1891.

2529 —— Le duel conventionnel en droit irlandais et chez les celtibériens. *Same jnl.*, 13, pp. 729–32. 1889.

2530 —— Du tarif de la composition pour meurtre en Irlande et dans la loi salique. Rev. celt., 8, p. 511. 1887.

2531 —— Études sur le droit celtique. *Cours de littérature celtique*, 7–8. 2 vol. 8° Paris, 1895. [Gross, 1394, lit. Vol. 1, pp. 332–84 and vol. 2, pp. 1–448, Senchus Mor.]

2532 —— Études sur le Senchus Mor. Nouvelle rev. hist de droit, 4, pp. 157–89, 513–34 : 5, pp. 1–19, 195–226. 1880–81.

2533 —— La *Gaisa* en Irlande. Rev. archéol., N.S. 18, pp. 192–94. 1877.

2534 —— L'homme de quarante nuit. [Senchus Mor : traité de la saisie mobilière.] Nouvelle rev. hist. de droit, 16, pp. 353–56. 1892.

2535 —— Le manuscrit cottonien Otho E XIII. La saisie irlandaise et galloise, la saisine bretonne. [10th–11th c.] Rev. celt., 7, pp. 238–40. 1886.

2536 —— La peine du vol en droit irlandais et en droit romain. Nouvelle rev. hist. de droit, 12, pp. 307–10. 1888.

2537 —— La *pignoris capio* avec enlèvement immédiat et sans commandement préalable en droit irlandais, d'après le *Senchus môr*. *Same jnl.*, 16, pp. 373–407. 1892.

2538 —— La procédure du jeûne en Irlande. Rev. celt., 7, pp. 245–49. 1886.

2539 —— La procédure du jeûne en Irlande d'après le Senchus Môr. Nouvelle rev. hist. de droit, 12, pp. 729–34. 1888.

2540 Arbois de Jubainvilla (Marie Henry d'). La puissance paternelle sur le fils en droit irlandais. Rev. celt., 7, pp. 91–96, 241. 1886.

2541 —— La saisie dans la loi salique et dans le droit irlandais. Nouvelle rev. hist. de droit, 12, pp. 303–06. 1888.

2542 —— Le Senchus Môr. *Same jnl.*, 8, pp. 33–44. 1884.

2543 Best (Richard Irvine) and **Thurneysen** (Rudolf). The oldest fragments of the Senchas Mār. From MS. H. 2.15 in the library of Trinity College, Dublin. With introduction. *Facsimiles in collotype of Irish MSS.–*1. pp. xiv, + 56 plates. fol. Dublin, 1931.

2544 Binchy (Daniel A.), *ed.* Studies in early Irish law. *Royal Irish Academy.* pp. viii, 286. 8° Dublin, 1936.

2545 Bryant (Sophie). Liberty, order and law under native Irish rule. A study in the Book of the ancient laws of Ireland. pp. xxiii, 398. 8° London, 1923.

2546 Clift (J. G. Neilson). Fasting. [In old Irish and in A.-S. laws.] J. Brit. Archaeol. Assoc., 65 (N.S. 15), pp. 157–70. 1909.

2547 Commissioners for Publishing the Ancient Laws and Institutes of Ireland. Ancient laws of Ireland. Edited . . . by W. N. Hancock, assisted by T. O'Mahony. 6 vol. 8° Dublin, 1865–1902. [Gross, 1394. Irish text and English translation. Vol. 1–3, Senchus Mor (vol. 3 also contains Book of Aicill) : vol. 4–5, various Brehon law tracts : vol. 6, Glossary, by Robert Atkinson.]

2548 Costello (John A.). The leading principles of the Brehon laws. Studies, 2, pp. 415–40. 1913.

2549 Ferguson (*Sir* Samuel). On the rudiments of the common law discoverable in the published portion of the Senchus Mor. Trans. R.I.A., 24 ii (Polite lit.), pp. 83–117. 1874.

2550 Ginnell (Laurence). The Brehon laws. A legal handbook. pp. vii, 249. 8° London, 1894. [Gross, 1394, lit. 'A popular account'. i. Ancient law : ii. Existing remains of Irish law ; iii.

Senchas Môr : iv. Legislative assemblies : v. Classification of society : vi. Law of distraining : vii. Criminal law : viii. Leges minores : etc.]

2551 Healy (Francis J.). The Scots of ancient Erin. [Mostly their laws.] J. Ivernian Soc., 1, pp. 35–47. 1908.

2552 Healy (John), *abp. of Tuam.* The Brehon laws. Irish Eccles. Rec., 3rd S. 9, pp. 673–82, 814–26. 1888.

2553 Hennessy (William Maunsell). On the forms of ordeal anciently practised in Ireland. [Forms extracted from Book of Ballymote, fol. 143–, with comments.] Proc. R.I.A., 10, pp. 34–43. 1870.

2554 Hogan (James). The Irish law of kingship, with special reference to Ailech and Cenél Eoghain. Proc. R.I.A., 40 c, pp. 186–254, + 7 tables. 1932.

2555 Hull (Vernam Edward). The ancient Irish practice of rubbing the earlap as a means of coercion. [*Brimon smetrach.*] Zeit. celt. Philol., 21, pp. 324–29. 1940.

2556 —— How St. Adamnan released the women of Ireland from military service. [Cáin Adamnáin. Irish text from Book of Lecan, fol. 166 r.–v.] *Same jnl.*, 21, pp. 335–38. 1940.

2557 Loth (Joseph). Le sens primitif de Bóroma. [=exact equivalent of A.-S. Rom-feoh. Bó originally=cow, then money.] Rev. celt., 17, pp. 428–30. 1896.

2558 Macauliffe (M. J.). The Berla laws ; or the ancient Irish common law. [Extracted from the Book of Aicill] by M. J. M. pp. 117. 8° Dublin, 1924.

[Reissued as]. The history of Aenach Tailtenn and the ancient Irish laws. pp. lxiv, 117. 8° Ennis, 1927. [Text, with an introduction.]

2559 MacCarthy (Charles J. F.). Some researches in ancient Irish law. A complementary note [to **2564**]. J. Cork Hist. Soc., 54, pp. 11–16. 1949.

2560 MacNeill (Eoin). Ancient Irish law. The law of status or franchise. Proc. R.I.A., 36 c, pp. 265–316. 1923.

2561 MacNeil (Eoin). Early Irish laws and institutions. New York Univ. Law Q.R., 7, pp. 149–265; 8, pp. 81–108, 271–84. 1930–31. *Same title.* pp. 152. 8° Dublin, 1935.

2562 —— The Irish law of dynastic succession. Studies, 8, pp. 367–82, 640–53. 1919.

2563 Meyer (Kuno), *ed. and trans.* Cáin Adamnáin. An Old-Irish treatise on the Law of Adamnan. pp. viii, 56. *Anecdota Oxoniensia*, 12. 8° Oxford, 1905. [Gross, 1394a. 697. Forbids women to take part in war. Notes and corrigenda *in* Arch. celt. Lexikog., 3, p. 108. 1906.]

2564 Ó Buachalla (Liam). Some researches in ancient Irish law. [A complementary note, by Charles J. F. MacCarthy, 54 (1949), pp. 11–16.] J. Cork Hist. Soc., 52, pp. 41–54; 135–48; 53, pp. 1–12, 75–81. 1947–48.

2565 O'Reilly (Edward). An essay on the nature and influence of the ancient Irish institutes, commonly called Brehon laws, and on the number and authenticity of the documents whence information concerning them may be derived; accompanied by specimens of translations from some of their most interesting parts, *etc.* Trans. R.I.A., 14 (Antiq.), pp. 141–226. 1825.

2566 Plummer (Charles). On the fragmentary state of the text of the Brehon laws. Zeit. celt. Philol., 17, pp. 157–66. 1928.

2567 Robinson (Fred Norris). Notes on the Irish practice of fasting as a means of distraint. Putnam anniversary vol., pp. 567–83. 1909.

2568 Ryan (John). The Cáin Adomnáin. Thurneysen (R.) *etc.*, Studies in early Irish law, pp. 269–76. 1936.

2569 Smith (Roland M.). The *Cach* formulas in the Irish laws. Zeit. celt. Philol., 20, pp. 262–77. 1936.

2570 —— Morand and the Ancient Laws of Ireland. *Same jnl.*, 16, pp. 305–09. 1927.

2571 —— Morand and the *Bretha Nemed*. [Law of the privileged classes.] *Same jnl.*, 17, pp. 407–11. 1928.

2572 Smith (Roland M.) On the unidentified passages in the Copenhagen fragment. [*See also* next entry.] *Same jnl.*, 19, pp. 111–16. 1933.

2573 Stokes (Whitley). On the Copenhagen fragments of the Brehon laws. *Same jnl.*, 4, pp. 221–33. 1903.

2574 Thurneysen (Rudolf). Aus dem irischen Recht I, II, III, IV, V (Nachtrag). [I. i. Das Unfrei-Lehen. Cain aigillne : Irish text with German translation and notes : II. ii. Das Frei-Lehen : iii. Das Fasten beim Pfändungsverfahren : III. iv. Die falschen Urteilssprüche Caratnia's : v. Zur Überlieferung und zur Ausgabe der Texte über das Unfrei-Lehen und das Frei-Lehen : IV. vi. Zu den bisheringen Ausgaben der irischen Rechts texte. (Nachträgliches.) : V (Nachtrag). vii. Zu Gūbretha Caratniad : viii. Zum ursprunglichen Umfang des Senchas Mār : ix. Zu der Etymologie von ir. *rāth* 'Bürgschaft' und zu der irischen Kanonensammlung und den Triaden : x. Nachträge zur Bürgschaft.] *Same jnl.*, 14, pp. 335–94 : 15, pp. 238–76 ; 15, pp. 302–761, 16, pp. 167–230, 406–10 ; 18, pp. 353–408 ; 19, pp. 346–51. 1923–33.

2575 —— Die Bürgschaft im irischen Recht. pp. 87. [Law of guarantee.] Abh. preuss. Akad. Wiss., Phil.-hist. Kl., 1928, no. 2. 1928.

2576 —— Cōic Conera Fugill. Die fünf Wege zum Urteil. Ein altirischer Rechtstext. Pp. 87. *Same jnl.*, 1925, no. 7. 1926.

2577 —— Irisches Recht. i. Dīre. ii. Zu den unteren Ständen in Irland. pp. 90. [A hitherto unpublished fragment of the Seneachus Mōr.] *Same jnl.*, 1931, no. 2. 1931.

2578 —— *etc.* Studies in early Irish law. *Royal Irish Academy.* pp. viii, 286. 8° Dublin, 1936.

2579 Vallancey (Charles). A critico-historical dissertation concerning the ancient Irish laws, *etc. Collectanea de rebus Hibernicis*, 3–4. 2 pts. 8° Dublin, 1774–75.

2580 Vallancey (Charles). Fragments of the Brehon laws of Ireland. *Collectanea de rebus Hibernicis*, *Vol.* 3 (*no.* 10). pp. 1–126. 8° Dublin, 1782. [Irish with English translation.]

§ c. Scottish Law

2581 Anderson (Alan Orr). Tanistry in united Scotland. Scot. H.R., 25, pp. 382–84. 1928.

2582 Elliot (Nenion). The early laws of Scotland. Trans. Hawick Archaeol. Soc., 11, 1872.

2583 Hibbert (Samuel). Memoir on the tings of Orkney and Shetland. [i. Evidence that the ting was, by our Gothic ancestors, either held on the site, or was made an appendage of the hof or temple, which had been dedicated to the rites of the Edda. ii. An inquiry into the more general forms and customs of the ting which existed previous to the introduction into Scandinavia of Christianity. iii. The changes which took place in the forms of customs of the ting after Christian churches had been established : *etc.*] Archaeol. Scot., 3, pp. 103–210. 1831.

2584 Johnston (Alfred Wintle). Óðal law in Orkney and Shetland. Old-lore Misc., 8, pp. 47–57. 1915.

2585 Stevenson (John Horne). The law of the throne—tanistry and the introduction of the law of primogeniture: a note on the succession of the kings of Scotland from Kenneth MacAlpin to Robert Bruce. Scot. H.R., 25, pp. 1–12. 1927.

§ d. Welsh Law

2586 Brynmôr-Jones (*Sir* David). The Brehon laws and their relation to the ancient Welsh institutes. Trans. Hon. Soc. Cymm., 1904–05, pp. 7–36. 1906.

2587 —— Foreign elements in Welsh mediaeval law. *Same jnl.*, 1916–17, pp. 1–51. 1918.

2588 Compton (C. H.). The ancient laws and statutes of Wales. J. Brit. Archaeol. Assoc., 34, pp. 436–59. 1878.

2589 Edwards (John Goronwy). Hywel Dda and the Welsh law books. pp. 27. 8° Bangor, 1929.

2590 Ellis (Thomas Peter). The Catholic Church in the Welsh laws. [Appendix of words and phrases of ecclesiastical import used in the Welsh laws.] Y Cymmrodor, 42, pp. 1–68. 1930.

2591 —— Hywel Dda : codifier. (Appendix : subjects dealt with in the Welsh laws). [Map shows ' interlaced character of the Welsh clan-occupation of land.'] Trans. Hon. Soc. Cymm., 1926–27, pp. 1–69, + sketch map. 1928.

2592 —— Legal references, terms and conceptions in the Mabinogion. Y Cymmrodor, 39, pp. 86–148. 1928.

2593 —— ' Mamwys '. Textual references. [Right of mamwys in Welsh tribal law acquired by a man through his mother (*mam*).] *Same jnl.*, 40, pp. 230–50. 1929.

2594 —— Welsh tribal law and custom in the Middle Ages. 2 vol. 8° Oxford, 1926.

2595 Hywel Dda, *king of Dyfed.* The laws of Howel the Good according to the Book of Blegywryd (the style of Dyfed). Critical edition by S. J. Williams and J. E. Powell. pp. xlvi, 281. 8° Caerdydd, 1942.

2595a —— The laws of Hywel Dda (The Book of Blegywryd). Translated by Melville Richards. pp. 149. 8° Liverpool, 1954.

2596 Jones (Owen), **Williams** (Edward) and **Pughe** (William Owen). The Myvyrian archaiology of Wales, collected out of the ancient manuscripts. To which has been added : additional notes upon the Gododin and an English translation of the laws of Howell the Good, also an explanatory chapter on ancient British music by John Thomas. 8° Denbigh, 1870. [Gross, 584a. Pp. 964–1070, laws of Hywel Dda, with a translation.]

2597 Levi (T. A.). The laws of Hywel Dda in the light of Roman and early English law. Aberystwyth Stud., 10, pp. 5–63. 1928.

2598 Lewis (Hubert). Ancient laws of Wales, viewed . . . in regard to the light they throw upon the origin of some English institutions. Edited by T. E. Lloyd. pp. xvi, 558. 8° London, 1889. [Gross, 641. ' Elaborate but not reliable '.]

2599 Lewis (Timothy). A bibliography of the laws of Hywel Dda. Aberystwyth Stud., 10, pp. 151–82. 1928.

2600 —— Copy of the Black Book of Chirk, Peniarth ms. 29, National Library of Wales, Aberystwyth. [Oldest Welsh ms. of laws of Hywel Dda. Welsh text only.] Zeit. celt. Philol., 20, pp. 30–96. 1935.

2601 —— *ed.* The laws of Howell Dda : a facsimile reprint of Llanstephan MS. 116 in the National Library of Wales. *University of Wales, Welsh texts, no.* 1. pp. xviii, 121, + plate. London, 1912. [Gross, 1396. Dimetian code : probably written in second half of 15th c.]

2602 Lloyd (*Sir* John Edward). Hywel Dda, 928–1928. 8° Cardiff, 1928.

2603 Loth (Joseph). L'étude et l'enseignement du droit dans le Pays de Galles du Xe. au XIIIe. siècle. Rev. celt., 48, pp. 293–311. 1931.

2604 Maitland (Frederic William). The laws of Wales : the kindred and the blood feud. [Gross, 1553a. Reprinted in his Collected papers, i, pp. 202–29.] Law Mag. and Rev., 4th S. 6, pp. 344–67. 1881.

2605 Owen (Aneurin), *ed.* Ancient laws and institutes of Wales : comprising laws supposed to be enacted by Howel the Good, *etc.* With an English translation, pp. xv, 1005. *Record Commission.* fol. London, 1841. *Also in* 2 vol. 8° London, 1841. [Gross, 1396. c. 928.]

2606 Parry-Williams (T. H.). The language of the laws of Hywel Dda. Aberystwyth Stud., 10, pp. 129–50. 1928.

2607 Probert (William), *trans.* The ancient laws of Cambria ; containing the institutional triads of Dyvnwal Moelmud, the laws of Howel the Good, *etc.* pp. 414. 8° London, 1823. [Gross, 1396. A translation of the triads, the laws of Howell the Good, etc.]

2608 Wade-Evans (Arthur Wade). Welsh medieval law : being a text of the laws of Howel the Good : namely the British Museum Harleian MS. 4353 of of the 13th century, with translation, introduction, glossary, etc. pp. xcvi, 395, + map. 8° Oxford, 1909. [Gross, 1396. Welsh and English.]

2609 Wotton (William). Leges Wallicae . . . Hoeli Boni et aliorum Walliae principum . . . notis et glossario illustravit G. Wottonus. [Edited by W. Clarke]. fol. Londini, 1730. [Gross, 1396. Welsh and Latin. Superseded by Owen's Ancient laws and institutes of Wales.]

39. GENERAL

§ *a.* Anglo-Saxon

2610 Addy (Sidney Oldall). The origin of the English coinage. [Ratio between size of A.-S. peasant's house and quantity of his arable land.] N. and Q., 9th S. 4, pp. 431–33, 504 : 5, pp. 29–32, 149–51, *also* pp. 85, 210–12, 271–72. 1899–1900.

2611 Anderson (Marjorie) and **Williams** (Blanche Colton). Old English handbook. pp. vii, 503. 8° New York, 1935.

2612 Anderson *afterwards* **Anderson-Arngart** (Olof Sigfrid). Some aspects of the relation between the English and the Danish element in the Danelaw. Stud. Neophilol., 20, pp. 73–87. 1947.

2613 Baxter (William). Old English village life as illustrated at Barrow and Twyford [Leicestershire.] [A.-S. and Domesday material.] J. Derbs. Archaeol. Soc., 26, pp. 153–67. 1904.

2614 Braude (Jakob). Die Familiengemeinschaften der Angelsachsen. pp. viii, 106. 8° Leipzig, 1932.

2615 Browne (George Forrest), *bp. of Bristol.* The importance of women in Anglo-Saxon times . . . and other addresses. pp. 194. 8° London, 1919.

2616 Brownlow (William Robert Bernard), *bishop of Clifton.* Life and labour in St. Marychurch in Saxon times. Rept. and Trans. Devon. Assoc., 18, pp. 429–41, + map. 1886.

2617 Chambers (Raymond Wilson). Everyday life of our Saxon forebears. [Revision of next entry.] Encylop. Mod. Knowledge, ed. J. A. Hammerton, 1, pp. 466–75, 506–17. 1936.

2618 —— The life of Saxon England. Universal hist. of the World, ed. J. A. Hammerton, 4, pp. 2444–70. 1928.

2619 Crawford (Samuel John). 'Ealuscerwen'. [Beowulf, 769. ?=deprivation of ale. Support from passage in Old Irish Life of St. Columba to indicate possibility that this was an A.-S. form of torture.] Mod. Lang. Rev., 21, pp. 302–03. 1926.

2620 Demarest (E. B.). 'Consuetudo regis' in Essex, Norfolk and Suffolk. [=Hundred-pennies.] E.H.R., 42, pp. 161–79. 1927.

2621 —— The firma unius noctis. [Annual render to Edward the Confessor from manors in Somerset.] E.H.R., 35, pp. 78–89. 1920.

2622 —— The hundred-pennies. [Edward the Confessor to 13th c.] E.H.R., 33, pp. 62–72. 1918.

2623 Ditchfield (Peter Hampson). Old village life. pp. xii, 253, + 8 plates. 8° London, 1920. [Pp. 55–79, 'the Saxon village'.]

2624 French (Richard Valpy). Nineteen centuries of drink in England : a history. pp. xxiv, 398. 8° London, 1884. [Pp. 10–54, Saxon and Danish periods.]

2625 Gomme (*Sir* George Laurence). Primitive folk-moots, or open-air assemblies in England. pp. xi, 316. 8° London, 1880. [Gross, 692.]

2626 Harris (George). Domestic everyday life, and manners and customs in this country from the earliest period to the end of the eighteenth century. [ii. From the coming of the Anglo-Saxons to the Norman Conquest ; iii. From the Norman Conquest to the end of the thirteenth century.] Trans. R.H.S., 6, pp. 86–130 ; 7, pp. 176–211. 1877–78.

2627 Hartley (Dorothy R.) and **Elliot** (Margaret Mary Victoria). Life and work of the people of England. A pictorial record from contemporary sources. Part I, A.D. 1000–1300. pp. 37, + 48 plates, + map. 8° London, 1925.

2628 Hodgetts (James Frederick). Anglo-Saxon dress and food. pp. 27. Anglo-Saxon dwellings, *etc.* pp. 28. *International Health Exhibition*, 1884. Lectures, *etc.* 8° London, 1884.

2629 Howard (George Elliott). A history of matrimonial institutions. 3 vol. 8° Chicago, 1904. [Gross, 1553, note. Deals with position of A.-S. women.]

2630 Hudson (William). Our pre-Conquest ancestors. [I. The land and its occupants. (West Norfolk before the Conquest). i. Freemen: ii. Sokemen. 2. Decay of the communal life and development of manorial control. iii. Villains. iv. Bordars. v. Serfs. Produce of land. Conclusion.] History Teachers' Miscellany, 4, pp. 199–24, 132–37. 1926.

2631 Johnson (Charles). The Danegeld in Norfolk. V.C.H., Norfolk, 2, pp. 204–11. 1906.

2632 Jolliffe (John Edward Austin). The era of the folk in English history. Oxford essays in medieval history presented to H. E. Salter, pp. 1–32. 1934.

2633 Kent (Charles William). Teutonic antiquities in Andreas and Elene. pp. 64. 8° Halle, 1887. [Gross, 1476. 'Attempts to form from these two poems a picture of the customs and manners of the Anglo-Saxons.']

2634 Kross (Theodor). Die Namen der Gefässe bei den Angel-Sachsen. *Diss., Kiel.* pp. xviii, 135. 1911.

2635 Lethbridge (Thomas Charles). Merlin's island and essays on Britain in the Dark Ages. pp. xi, 188, + 8 plates. 8° London, 1948.

2636 Liebermann (Felix). Zur Barttracht der Angelsachsen. Archiv Stud. neueren Spr., Bd. 112, p. 392. 1904.

2637 McLennan (John Ferguson). Studies in ancient history. Comprising a reprint of Primitive marriage. pp. xxx, 507. 8° London, 1876. [Pp. 453–507, divisions of the ancient Irish family.]

2638 Mann (A. H.). Old English social life. Social England, ed. Traill & Mann, 1, pp. 305–17. 1891.

2639 Maurer (Konrad von). Angelsächsische Rechtsverhältnisse. [Gross, 1494. 'Deals with the family, mark, hundred, tithing, shire, mutual suretyship, land-laws, classes of society, feud, and wergeld. Corrects many of Kemble's errors.'] Kritischer Ueberschau der deutschen Gesetzgebung, i. pp. 47–120, 405–31; ii. pp. 30–68, 388–440; iii. pp. 26–61. 1853–56.

2640 —— Ueber das Wesen des ältesten Adels der deutschen Stämme, *etc.* 8° München, 1846. [Gross, 1551. Pp. 123–95, Die Angelsachsen.]

2641 Mellor (J. E. M.). Falconry, with notes upon local [i.e. Herefordshire] records. [Pp. 14–15, A.-S. and Domesday references.] Trans. Woolhope Nat. F.C., 33 (1949), pp. 14–18. 1950.

2642 Meritt (Herbert). Old English entries in a manuscript at Bern. [Stadtbibliothek, MS. 671, ff. 75 v, 76r, 76v. 9th c. 'The first entry concerns the payment of tithes, the second the rules of a guild, the third and fourth are records of grants allowing freedom of going into a specified section of the country.' Transcript and notes.] J. Engl. and Germ. Phil., 33, pp. 343–51. 1934.

2643 Mezger (Fritz). Ae. *fæsl*, n. 'Nachkommenschaft' und ae. *cnósl* 'Nachkommenschaft, Geschlecht, Familie, Vaterland'. Archiv Stud. neueren Spr., Bd. 160, pp. 91–92. 1931.

2644 —— Ae. *forecynren*, n. 'Nachkommenschaft'— *mægcynren*, n. 'Familie, Linie'—*cynren*, n. 'Art, Gattung, Familie, Verwandschaft, Generation, Nachkommenschaft'. Same jnl., Bd. 161, pp. 228–29. 1932.

2645 Miller (Edward). The abbey bishopric of Ely. The social history of an ecclesiastical estate from the tenth century to the early fourteenth century. *Cambridge studies in medieval life and thought*, N.S. 1. pp. xiii, 313, + 2 maps. 8° Cambridge, 1951. [Pp. 8–74: ii. Origins: iii. The Old English estate and the Norman Conquest.]

2646 Peate (Iorwerth Cyfeiliog). The nine huntings. [Hunting customs among early Welsh.] Antiquity, 8, pp. 73–80. 1934.

2647 Pegge (Samuel). On the hunting of the ancient inhabitants of our island, Britons and Saxons. Archaeologia, 10, pp. 156–66. 1792.

2648 Pfaendler (Wilhelm). Die Vergnügungen der Angelsachsen. [i. Feasting and domestic amusements (dancing, music—profane and sacred, dice and board-games, etc.) : ii. Sport and outdoor entertainment (hunting of birds and animals, fishing, skating, riding, swimming, gymnastics, etc.) : iii. Children's games. Bibliography.] Anglia. 29 (N.F. 17), pp. 417–526. 1906.

2649 Phillpotts (*Dame* Bertha Surtees). Kindred and clan in the Middle Ages and after. A study in the sociology of the Teutonic races. Pp. xii, 302. 8° Cambridge, 1913. [Pp. 205–44, A.-S. Evidence from A.-S. laws.]

2650 Picton (*Sir* James Allanson). On social life among the Teutonic races in early times. Proc. Lit. and Phil. Soc. L'pool, 22, pp. 68–98. 1868.

2651 Powell (Frederick York). Britain under the English. Social England, ed. Traill and Mann, 1, pp. 175–205. 1891.

2652 —— The Danish invasion. *Same work*, 1, pp. 205–17, + 1 plate. 1891.

2653 Quennell (Marjorie *and* Charles Henry Bourne). Everyday life in Anglo-Saxon, Viking and Norman times. 3rd edition, revised. pp. 115. 8° London, 1952.

2654 Rhamm (Karl). Ethnologische Beiträge. I. Die Grosshufen der Nordgermanen. II. Urzeitliche Bauernhöfe in germanisch-slawischem Waldgebiet, 2 pts. 3 Bde., 8° Braunschweig, 1905–10. [Gross, 1552a. 'i, pp. 171–305, 669–834, deals in detail with the A.-S. hide, hundred, and classes of society'.]

2655 Ribton-Turner (Charles James). A history of vagrants and vagrancy and beggars and begging. pp. xxi, 720, + 19 plates. 8° London, 1887. [Pp. 1–20, A.-S. (laws, etc.).]

2656 Rickword (George). The East Saxon kingdom. [Social and economic : pp. 39–40, tables of ' statistics relating to the Domesday and tribal hundreds '.] Trans. Essex Archaeol. Soc., N.S. 12, pp. 38–50. 1913.

2657 Roeder (Fritz). Die Familie bei den Angelsachsen. Eine kultur- und literarhistorische Studie auf Grund gleichzeit. Quellen. 1. Mann und Frau. *Studien zur englischen Philologie*, 4. pp. ix, 183. 8° Halle, 1899. [Gross, 1553.]

2658 Seebohm (Frederic). Customary acres and their historical importance : being a series of unfinished essays. pp. xiii, 274. 8° London, 1914. [Gross, 736a. Welsh and Irish units of tribute and food-rent : units of tribute in Gaelic Scotland : units of tribute and assessment of the Domesday Survey : etc.]

2659 Slater (Gilbert). Social and economic history [of Kent]. [Pp. 319–38, A.-S. period.] V.C.H., Kent, 3, pp. 319–70. 1932.

2660 Smith (A. L.). The Norman conquest. Social England, ed. Traill and Mann, 1, pp. 335–40. 1891.

2661 Stenton (*Sir* Frank Merry). Documents illustrative of the social and economic history of the Danelaw. *British Academy : Records of the social and economic history of England and Wales*, 5. pp. cxliv, 554. 8° London, 1920.

2662 —— English families and the Norman conquest. Trans. R.H.S., 4th S., 26. pp. 1–12. 1944.

2663 —— Social and economic history [of Worcestershire] before 1086. V.C.H., Worcester, 4, pp. 435–42. 1924.

2664 Stephenson (Carl). The problem of the common man in early medieval Europe. A.H.R., 51, pp. 419–38. 1946.

2665 Strutt (Joseph). A complete view of the dress and habits of the people of England, from the establishment of the Saxons, *etc*. 2 vol. 4° London, 1796–99. Tableau complet, *etc*. vol. 1. 4° Londres, 1797. [No more published.]

2666 Strutt (Joseph). Glig-Gamena, or the sports and pasttimes of the people of England. A new edition, much enlarged and corrected by J. C. Cox. pp. lx, 322, + 41 plates. 4° London, 1903. [A little A.-S. material.]

2667 —— Porda Angel-cynnan, or a compleat view of the manners, customs, arms, habits . . . of the inhabitants of England from the arrival of the Saxons, *etc.* 3 vol. 4° London, 1775–76. Angleterre ancienne, ou tableau des moeurs, *etc.* Traduit [par A. M. H. Boulard], *etc.* 2 vol. 12° Paris, 1789. [Pp. 39–191, A.-S., pp. 192–211, Danes. 67 plates.]

2668 Stuart (Dorothy Margaret). The boy through the ages. pp. 288. 8° London, 1927. [Pp. 113–33, + 1 plate, the A.-S. boy.]

2669 Tankard (E.). Anglo-Saxon habitat group in the Liverpool free public museums. Mus. J., 36, pp. 1–4. 1936.

2670 Thrupp (John). The Anglo-Saxon home : a history of the domestic institutions and customs of England from the fifth to the eleventh century. pp. ix, 410. 8° London, 1862. [Gross, 1239.]

2671 Vinogradoff (*Sir* Paul). English society in the eleventh century. pp. xii, 599. 8° Oxford, 1908. [Gross, 1240a. i. Government and society : ii. Land and people.]

2672 —— Villeinage in England ; essays in English mediaeval history. pp. xii, 464. 8° Oxford, 1892. [i. The peasantry of the feudal age : ii. The manor and the village community.]

2673 Webb (Philip Carteret). A short account of Danegeld, with some further particulars relating to William the Conqueror's survey. *Society of Antiquaries.* pp. 33. 4° London, 1756. [Gross, 1590. 'A scholarly essay.']

2674 Whitelock (Dorothy). The beginnings of English society. *Penguin Books.* pp. 256. 8° Harmondsworth, 1952.

2675 Wright (Thomas). A history of domestic manners and sentiments in England during the Middle Ages. pp. xiv, 502. 8° London, 1862. [Pp. 1–79, A.-S. period. 54 figures in text.]

2676 Wright (Thomas). On the political condition of the English peasantry during the Middle Ages. [Pp. 209–37, A.-S. period.] Archaeologia, 30, pp. 205–44. 1844.

2677 —— Womankind in western Europe. pp. x, 340, + 9 plates. 8° London, 1869. [Pp. 52–80, A.-S. women. pp. 81–86, St. Boniface and the A.-S. nuns.]

§ b. Celtic

(*See also* **2637** and **2646**)

2678 Arbois de Jubainville (Marie Henry d'). La famille celtique. Rev. celt., 25, pp. 1–16, 181–207. 1904.

2679 —— La famille celtique. Étude de droit comparé. pp. xx, 221. 8° Paris, 1905.

2680 Brynmôr-Jones (*Sir* David). Early social life in Wales. Trans. Hon. Soc. Cymm., 1898–99, pp. 25–51. 1900.

2681 Fox (*Sir* Cyril and *Lady* Aileen Mary). Forts and farms on Margam Mountain, Glamorgan. [? 650–750. ' Social, cultural and economic life of South Wales in the Dark Ages.'] Antiquity, 8, pp. 395–413, + plate, + map. 1934.

2682 Hodges (John C.). The blood covenant among the Celts. [E.g., pp. 130–35, the races of Tadg and Eogan (6th c.), and Columcille and Cormac.] Rev. celt., 44, pp. 109–56. 1927.

2683 Jones (T. Gwynn). Social life as reflected in the laws of Hywel Dda. Aberystwyth Stud., 10, pp. 103–28. 1928.

2684 Joyce (Patrick Weston). A social history of ancient Ireland, treating of the government, military system, and law ; religion, learning, and art ; trades, industries, and commerce ; manners, customs, and domestic life of the ancient Irish people. 2nd edition. 2 vol. 8° London and Dublin, 1913. [Gross, 1231a.]

2685 O'Curry (Eugene). On the manners and customs of the ancient Irish. . . . Edited, with an introduction . . . by W. K. Sullivan. 3 vol. 8° London, 1873.

K

2686 Seebohm (Frederic).   The historical importance of the Cymric tribal system. Trans. Hon. Soc. Cymm., 1895–96, pp. 1–22. 1897.

2687 —— The tribal system in Wales : being part of an inquiry into the structure and methods of tribal society.   2nd edition, with an introductory note on the unit of family holding under earlier tribal custom. pp. xlvi, 238, 127, + 3 maps. 8° London, 1904. [Gross, 1116. Land system, bond of kindred, tribal development, etc.]

2688 Walsh (Paul).   Meath in the Book of Rights. Essays presented to Eoin MacNeill, pp. 508–21. 1940.

2689 Westropp (Hodder Michael). On the tribal system and land tenure in Ireland, under the Brehon laws.   J. Ethnol. Soc., N.S.2, pp. 342–51. 1870.

40. AGRICULTURE, MILLS, LIVESTOCK, ETC.

2690 Austin (William). The Domesday water mills of Bedfordshire. Pubs. Beds. Hist. Rec. Soc., 3, pp. 207–48. 1916.

2691 Barger (Evert).   The present position of studies in English field-systems. E.H.R., 53, pp. 385–411. 1938.

2692 Bennett (Richard) and **Elton** (John). History of corn milling. 4 vol. 8° London, 1898–1904. [Vol. 2, pp. 101–80, Domesday mills.]

2693 Blashill (Thomas).   Ancient methods of tillage. [Domesday, etc.] J. Brit. Archaeol. Assoc., 52 (N.S.2), pp. 218–23. 1896.

2694 Chope (Richard Pearse). Domesday mills in Devon and Cornwall. [With list of 104, of which 80 were situated on the rivers Axe, Otter and Exe, and only 6 in Cornwall.] Devon and Cornwall N. and Q., 12, pp. 21–23. 1922.

2695 Crawford (Osbert Guy Stanhope). A Saxon fish-pond near Oxford. [*Styrian pol* in bounds of Besselsleigh, 959 and of Eaton, 968.] Antiquity, 4, pp. 480–83. 1930.

2696 Curtis (Henry) *etc.*   Assart. [Forest land which has been converted into arable.] N and Q., 146, pp. 48–49. 1924.

2697 Duignan (Michael). Irish agriculture in early historic times. [8 figures in text.] J. Roy. Soc. Antiq. Ireland, 74 (7th S. 14), pp. 124–45. 1944.

2698 Ekwall (Eilert).   Old English *forræpe*. [= Assart-land. Occurs in a charter of 947 : grant of Eadred in Merstham, Surrey. Birch, 820.] Studia Neophil., 16, pp. 32–38. 1944.

2699 Finberg (Herbert Patrick Reginald).   The Domesday plough-team. E.H.R., 66, pp. 67–71. 1951.

2700 Fleming (Lindsay).   Pigs in Domesday Book. Sussex N. and Q., 11, pp. 32, 34. 1946.

2701 French (John). On the moated grange and mill at Waltham abbey. [? of early 11th c. origin.] Trans. Essex Archaeol. Soc., N.S 10, pp. 340–44. 1909.

2702 Graf (Leopold).   Landwirtschaftliches im altenglischen Wortschatze. *Diss., Breslau.* pp. 57. 8° Breslau, 1909.

2702a Gray (Howard Levi).   English field systems. *Harvard Historical Studies*, 22. pp. ix, 568. 8° Cambridge, Mass., 1915. [Pp. 50–82, A.-S.]

2703 Grube (F. W.). Cereal foods of the Anglo-Saxons. [Barley, oats, rye, wheat, other grains, farming, milling, meal, flour, baking.] Philol. Quart., 13, pp. 140–58. 1934.

2704 Hodgen (Margaret T.). Domesday water mills. [With 5 maps and 2 tables.] Antiquity, 13, pp. 261–79. 1939.

2705 Hutchinson (P.) *etc.*   Saxon spades. N. and Q., 3rd S. 12, pp. 509–10 : 4th S. 1, p. 84. 1867–68.

2706 Jenkins (J. Travis). Sturgeon in Anglo-Saxon times. [Rejoinder to **2695**.] Antiquity, 6, p. 93. 1932.

2706a Jessen (Knud) and **Helbaek** (Hans). Cereals in Great Britain and Ireland in prehistoric and early historic times. [26 figures in text. Series of tables comprising impressions of cereals identified on surfaces of hand-made pottery. Husked barley leads in A.-S. period.] K. Danske Vid. Selskab, Biol. Skrifter, 3, ii. pp. 68. 1944.

2707 Karslake (J. B.). The water mills of Hampshire. [318 in Hants., out of the 7,500 recorded in Domesday.] Papers and Proc. Hants. F.C., 14, pp. 3–8. 1938.

2708 Kennedy (Evory Hamilton). The Domesday mill at Betchworth. Surrey Archaeol. Collns., 40, pp. 120–22. 1932.

2709 Koebner (Richard). The settlement and colonisation of Europe. Cambridge Economic History, 1, Agrarian life of the Middle Ages, pp. 1–88. 1941.

2710 Lennard (Reginald). Domesday plough-teams : the south-western evidence. E.H.R., 60, pp. 217–33. 1945.

2711 Loth (Joseph). Les noms et les variétés du froment chez les celtes insulaires. Rev. celt., 81, pp. 193–203. 1924.

2712 Lucas (A. T.). The horizontal mill in Ireland. [Used for grinding corn for over 2,000 years. ? from Spain in pre-Viking times.] J. Roy. Soc. Antiq. Ireland, 83, pp. 1–36, + 5 plates. 1953.

2713 Orwin (Charles Stewart and Christabel Susan, *Mrs.*). The open fields. pp. xii, 332, + 29 plates, + 7 maps. 8° Oxford, 1938. [Especially pp. 21–29, + plate 6, before the Norman Conquest.]

2714 Payne (F. G.). The plough in ancient Britain. [Pp. 102–08, A.-S. period.] Archaeol. J., 104 (1947), pp. 82–111, + 7 plates. 1948.

2715 Richardson (H. G.). The medieval plough-team. (Historial revision.—c.). [Domesday →.] History, N.S., 26, pp. 287–94. 1942.

2716 Round (John Horace). Essex vineyards in Domesday. Trans. Essex Archaeol. Soc., N.S. 7, pp. 249–51. 1900.

2717 Seehohm (Frederic). Open-field system of agriculture traced to its source. [Synopsis of paper, with discussion.] Proc. Soc. Antiq., 2nd S. 8, pp. 88–91. 1879.

2718 Seebohm (Mabel Elizabeth) *Mrs. Christie.* The evolution of the English farm. pp. 376. 8° London, 1927. [Pp. 99–125, the Saxon period. 6 figures in text.]

2719 Size (Nicholas). Click mill at Buttermere. [Attributed to Shelagh of Eskdale, died 1000, whose cross still stands in Gosforth churchyard.] Old-lore Misc. V.C., 10, pp. 7–9. 1935.

2720 Slack (W. J.). The Shropshire ploughmen of Domesday Book. [Agricultural arrangements bearing on status of various classes—bovarii and servi.] Trans. Shrop. Arch. Soc., 50, pp. 31–35. 1939.

2721 Smith (Charles Roach). The archaeology of horticulture. [Pp. 93–96, documentary evidence from Domesday for 38 vineyards.] Collectanea Antiqua, 6, pp. 76–109, 269–74. 1868.

2722 Steensberg (Axel). North west European plough-types of prehistoric times and the Middle Ages. [Pp. 262–66, A.-S. period.] Acta Archaeol., 7, pp. 244–80. 1936.

2723 Stevens (Joseph). Hedges. [Use of in A.-S. times.] Q. J. Berks. Archaeol. Soc., 2, p. 48. 1891.

2724 Taylor (Isaac). The ploughland and the plough. Domesday Studies, 1, pp. 143–88. 1888.

2725 Trow-Smith (Robert). English husbandry from the earliest times to the present day. pp. 239, + 16 plates. 8° London, 1951. [Pp. 32–68, ii. The Saxon scene : iii. Domesday and manorial farming.]

2726 Warren F. C.). Long continuance of the common-field system : Sutton Waldron. Proc. Dorset Archaeol. Soc., 64 (for 1942), pp. 75–83. 1943.

41. BOROUGHS AND TOWNS

2727 Alexander (John James). The early boroughs of Devon. Rept. and Trans. Devon. Assoc., 58 (1926), pp. 275–87. 1927.

2728 Amery (P. F. S.). The ancient office of portreeve. *Same jnl.*, 21, pp. 300–04. 1889.

2729 Ashley (*Sir* William James). The Anglo-Saxon ' township '. [Gross, 1557. Discussion on significance of. Definition of *tun*, ham, vicus, villa, etc.] Q. J. Econ., 8, pp. 345–61. 1894.

2730 Ballard (Adolphus). The burgesses of Domesday. E.H.R., 21, pp. 699–709. 1906.

2731 —— The Domesday boroughs. pp. viii, 135. 8° Oxford, 1904. [Gross, 1563. *See also* **2745**.]

2732 Bateson (Mary). The burgesses of Domesday and the Malmesbury wall. E.H.R., 21, pp. 709–723. 1906.

2733 Cam (Helen Maud). The origin of the borough of Cambridge : a consideration of Professor Carl Stephenson's theories. [With 2 plans : one, ' the archaeology of pre-Norman Cambridge.'] Proc. Cambs. Antiq. Soc., 35, pp. 33–53. 1935.

2734 Carter (George Edward Lovelace). Anglo-Saxon Devon. [Mostly on ' The early boroughs of Devon '. Contains 3 tables—i. Burgage tenements, city of Exeter : ii. Ditto, the boroughs : iii. Castle service.] Rept. and Trans. Devon. Assoc., 64, pp. 519–38. 1932.

2735 —— Borough English and Burgage tenure. *Same jnl.*, 65, pp. 383–92. 1933.

2736 Darlington (Reginald Ralph). The early history of English towns. (Historical revision—lxxxvi.) History, N.S., 23, pp. 141–50. 1938.

2737 Dodds (Madeleine Hope). The bishop's boroughs [Durham]. [Pp. 82–86, ' the boroughs before the Norman Conquest '.] Archaeol. Æl., 3rd S. 12, pp. 80–185. 1915.

2738 Esdaile (George). Burghs in Chester. Trans. Lancs. and Ches. Antiq. Soc., 6 (1888). pp. 242–52. 1889.

2739 Fellows (G. E.). The Anglo-Saxon towns and their polity. 8° Berne, 1890. [Gross (1st ed. only), 1564. ' Unscholarly.']

2740 Hudson (William). Town life. [1. How Norwich began and grew. 2. Norwich after the Conquest.] History Teachers' Miscellany, 2, pp. 1–6, 19–24, + plan. 1923.

2741 Ladds (Sidney Inksip). The borough of Huntingdon and Domesday Book. Trans. Cambs. and Hunts.

Archaeol. Soc., 5, pp. 105–12, + plan. 1937.

2741a Lobel (Mary Doreen). The borough of Bury St. Edmund's. pp. xii, 203, + 2 plans. 8° Oxford, 1935. [Pp. 1–15, origin of the borough.]

2742 Maitland (Frederic William). The origin of the borough. E.H.R., 11, pp. 13–19. 1896.

2742a Mottram (Ralph Hale). Success to the mayor. A narrative of the development of local self-government in a provincial centre (Norwich) during eight centuries. pp. 280, + map (of A.–S. burgh), + 15 plates. 8° London, 1937. [Pp. 15–30, to 1066.]

2743 Oliver (Bruce W.). Barnstaple borough. Rept. and Trans. Devon. Assoc., 62, pp. 269–73. 1930.

2744 Pring (James Hurly). The ancient name and office of port-reeve. [*Also* (p. 328 of vol. 4) note by J. H. Round and reply by J. H. Pring (p. 107 of vol. 5, 1884) : Round (p. 162) ' deductions erroneous '. *Also* 6, pp. 254–55 (J.H.P.), pp. 299–300 (J.H.R.) : 7, p. 47 (J.H.P.), p. 94 (J.H.R.).] Antiq. Mag., 4, pp. 264–66 : 6, pp. 113–19. 1883–84.

2745 Reichel (Oswald Joseph). The Domesday boroughs. [Corrections of Ballard, **2731**, as regards Devon.] Devon N. and Q., 4, pp. 61–63. 1906.

2746 Round (John Horace). ' Port ' and ' port-reeve '. Antiq. Mag., 5, pp. 274–50, 282–87 : 6, pp. 23–24, 159–65. 1884.

2747 —— ' Shire-house ' and castle yard. [? castles (e.g. Cambridge) within jurisdiction of borough.] E.H.R., 36, pp. 210–214. 1921.

2748 Savage (*Sir* William). The making of our towns. pp. 189, + 6 plates. 8° London, 1952. [Pp. 42–49, towns in early A.–S. times.]

2749 Shore (Thomas William). Early boroughs in Hampshire. Archaeol. Rev., 4, pp. 286–91. 1889.

2750 Stephenson (Carl). The Anglo-Saxon borough. E.H.R., 45, pp. 177–207. 1930.

2751 Stephenson (Carl). Borough and town. A study of urban origins in England. *Mediaeval Academy of America, Monograph* 7. pp. xvi, 236. 8° Cambridge, Mass., 1933. [Pp. 47–72, the A.–S. borough: pp. 73–119, the Domesday borough: etc.]

2752 —— The origin of the English towns. A.H.R., 32, pp. 10–21. 1926.

2753 Tait (James). The firma burgi and the commune in England, 1066–1191. E.H.R., 42, pp. 321–60. 1927.

2754 —— The medieval English borough. *Pubns. Univ. Manch., Hist. ser.*, 70. pp. xx, 371. 8° Manchester, 1936. [Pp. 1–154, A.–S.]

2755 Wright (Thomas). The existence of municipal privileges under the Anglo-Saxons. Proc. Soc. Antiq., 1, pp. 169–70. 1847. *Same title.* Archaeologia, 32, pp. 298–311. 1847.

42. DOMESDAY

(*See also* contents (passim) and index.)

§ a. General Aspects

2756 [Anon.] Domesday Book. [Part 1, but not continued.] Walford's Antiquarian, 11, pp. 3–10. 1887.

2757 Allen (William Francis). Rural population of Domesday. Allen (W. F.): Essays and monographs (Boston), pp. 319–30. 1890.

2758 Ballard (Adolphus). The Domesday inquest. *Antiquary's Books.* pp. 283. 8° London, 1906. [Gross, 1884a.]

2759 Barber (Henry). British family names, their origin and meaning: with lists of Scandinavian, Frisian, Anglo-Saxon and Norman names. 2nd edition, enlarged. pp. xii, 286. 8° London, 1903. [Pp. 38–60, names of persons entered in Domesday Book as holding lands (T.R.E.): Names of tenants in chief in Domesday Book: Names of under tenants of lands at the time of the Domesday survey.]

2760 Baring (*Hon.* Francis Henry). Domesday and some thirteenth century surveys. E.H.R., 12, pp. 285–90. 1897.

2761 Barkly (*Sir* Henry). On an alleged instance of the fallibility of Domesday in regard to 'ancient demesne'. Domesday Studies, 2, pp. 471–83. 1891.

2762 Birch (Walter de Gray). Domesday Book: a popular account of the Exchequer manuscript so called. 2nd edition, revised. pp. viii, 328. 8° London, 1908. [Gross, 1885. Pp. 315–24, bibliography.]

2763 Bourrienne (Valentin Victor Arthur), *ed.* Antiquus cartularius ecclesiae Baiocensis [Bayeux].—Livre noir—publié . . . avec introduction par V.B. *Société de l'histoire de Normandie.* 2 vol. 8° Rouen et Paris, 1902–03.

2764 Clarke (Hyde). On the Turkish survey of Hungary, and its relation to Domesday Book. A study in comparative history. Domesday Studies, 1, pp. 37–46. 1888.

2765 Davies (Reginald Trevor). Documents illustrating the history of civilization in medieval England (1066–1500). pp. x, 413. 8° London, 1926. [Pp. 1–18, Domesday Book: motives, extracts, statistics.]

2766 Delisle (Léopold Victor). La commémoration du Domesday-Book. Charte normande de 1088. pp. 8. fol. Paris, 1886.

2767 Denne (Samuel). Doubts and conjectures concerning the reason commonly assigned for inserting or omitting the words ecclesia and presbyter in Domesday Book. Archaeologia, 8, pp. 218–38. 1787.

2768 Douglas (David Charles). The Domesday Survey. (Historical revision —lxxix.) History, N.S., 21, pp. 249–57. 1936.

2769 Ellis (*Sir* Henry). A general introduction to Domesday Book; accompanied by indexes. . . . Illustrated by notes and comments. *Record Commission.* 2 vol. 8° London, 1833. [Gross, 1886.]

2770 Eyton (Robert William). A key to Domesday, showing the method and exactitude of its mensuration, and the . . . meaning of its more usual formulae. . . exemplified by an analysis and digest of the Dorset survey. pp. iv, 176. 4° London, 1878. [Gross, 1897.]

2771 Eyton (Robert William). Notes on Domesday. Trans. Shropshire Arch. Soc., 1, pp. 99–118. 1878.

2772 Franklin (T. Bedford). Domesday—1(2). [Describes typical village.] Amateur Historian, 1, pp. 261–64, 297–300. 1954.

2773 Frost (Reuben Caesar). The Domesday Book and its times. Woolwich Antiq. Soc., Ann. Rpt., 12 (1906–07), pp. 67–71. 1907.

2774 Galbraith (Vivian Hunter). The making of Domesday Book. E.H.R., 57, pp. 161–77. 1942.

2775 —— Studies in the public records. pp. ix, 163. 8° London, 1948. [Pp. 89–121 (Chap. 4), Domesday Book.]

2776 Hofmann (Matthias). Die Französierung der Personenschatzes im Domesday Book der Grafschaften Hampshire und Sussex. *Dissertation.* pp. xv, 169. 8° Murnau, 1934.

2777 Hussey (Arthur). Notes on the churches in the counties of Kent, Sussex, and Surrey, mentioned in Domesday Book, *etc.* 8° London, 1852.

2778 Inman (Alfred H.). Domesday and feudal statistics, with a chapter on agricultural statistics. pp. xl, 161. 8° London, 1900. [Gross, 1887a.]

2779 —— Domesday and feudal statistics exemplified, with some observations on early knight service. 8° London, 1901.

2780 Kelham (Robert). Domesday Book illustrated, containing an account of the ancient record, as also of the tenants in capite or serjantry, *etc.* 8° London, 1788. [Gross, 1888. 'the best of the older works.' Pp. 145–369, glossary.]

2781 Léchaudé d'Anisy (Amédée Louis) and **Sainte Marie** (—de), *marquis.* Recherches sur le Domesday, ou Liber Censualis, d'Angleterre, *etc.* Tom. 1. pp. 282. 4° Caen, 1842.

2782 Maitland (Frederic William). Domesday Book and beyond. Three essays in the early history of England. pp. xiv, 527. 8° Cambridge, 1897. [Gross, 1493. i. Domesday Book : ii. England before the Conquest : iii. The hide.]

2783 Moore (Margaret F.). The feudal aspect of the Domesday survey of Somerset and Dorset in connection with the barony of Moiun (Dunster castle) and other analogous feudal estates. (Summaries of theses—lxxiii.) Bull. Inst. Hist. Res., 9, pp. 49–52. 1932.

2784 Moore (Stuart). On the study of Domesday Book. Domesday Studies, 1, pp. 1–36. 1888.

2785 Morgan (James F.). England under the Norman occupation. 8° London, 1858. [Gross, 2821. 'Containing the results of a careful perusal of Domesday Book.']

2786 Mostyn (John). *Haiae* in Domesday. Radnor. Soc. Trans., 3, p. 26. 1933.

2787 Page (William). The churches of the Domesday survey. [Printed in Archaeologia, **2788**. With discussion by G. F. Browne, W. A. Lindsay, J. D. Crace, C. Johnson, W. P. Baildon and A. F. Leach.] Proc. Soc. Antiq., 2nd S. 27, pp. 54–58. 1915.

2788 —— Some remarks on the churches of the Domesday survey. Archaeologia, 66, pp. 61–102. 1915.

2789 Pell (O. C.). Upon libere tenentes, virgatae, and carucae in Domesday, and in certain ancient mss. containing surveys of sixty manors in the counties of Hertford, Essex, Norfolk, Suffolk, Huntingdon and Cambridge ; and upon wara, what it probably meant or implied and the prevalent use of the word both here and on the continent in ancient times. Camb. Antiq. Commns., 6 (1884–88), pp. 17–40. 1891.

2790 Phillips (*Sir* Thomas), *bart.* Index to the genealogies of the tenants in capite in Domesday Book—by T. P. 4 pts. fol. [privately printed : Middle Hill, 1838–42].

2791 Pollock (*Sir* Frederick). A brief survey of Domesday. E.H.R., 11, pp. 209–30. 1896.

2792 Powell (Frederick York). Domesday Book. Social England, ed. Traill and Mann, 1, pp. 340–49. 1891.

2793 Reichel (Oswald Joseph). The leuca or lug of Domesday. Rept. and Trans. Devon. Assoc., 26, pp. 308–12. 1894.

2794 Reid (Herbert J.). Parish churches omitted in the survey. The presbyter. Domesday Studies, 2, pp. 433–46. 1891.

2795 Round (John Horace). The breviates of Domesday. [Gross, 1891.] Athenaeum, Sept., 15, 1900, pp. 346–47. 1900.

2796 —— Danegeld and the finance of Domesday. Domesday Studies, 1, pp. 77–142. 1888.

2797 — 'Domesday' and 'Doomsday'. E.H.R., 38, pp. 240–43. 1923.

2798 —— The Domesday 'ora'. E.H.R., 23, pp. 283–85. 1908.

2799 Rowe (Joseph Hambley). B and G [as initial letter] confused in Domesday and feudal aids. N. and Q., 11th S. 3, pp. 443–44. 1911.

2800 Russell (Josiah Cox). British medieval population. pp. xvi, 389. 8° Albuquerque, 1948. [Pp. 34–54, the Domesday survey. i. The agricultural population : ii. The clergy : iii. The boroughs : iv. Domesday population.]

2801 Sawyer (Frederick Ernest). The scope of local elucidations of the Domesday survey. Domesday Studies, 2, pp. 447–57. 1891.

2802 Stevenson (William Henry). A contemporary description of the Domesday survey. E.H.R., 22, pp. 72–84. 1907.

2803 Stubbs (William), *bp. of Oxford.* The Domesday and later surveys. Stubbs (W.) : Lectures on early English history. pp. 184–93. 1906.

2804 Taylor (Isaac). Domesday phonetics. [Every scribe a law unto himself : e.g. 15 ways (each) of spelling *-ley* and *burgh*.] N. and Q., 7th S. 8, p. 203. 1889.

2805 —— Domesday survivals. Domesday Studies, 1, pp. 47–66. 1888.

2806 Walker (J. K.), *M.D.* Churches in the Domesday survey. Gent. Mag., N.S. 19, pp. 485–89. 1843.

2807 Webb (Philip Carteret). A short account of some particulars concerning Domes-Day Book, with a view to promote its being published. *Society of Antiquaries.* 4° London, 1756.

2808 Whale (Thomas William). Date of the Domesday survey : and use of some of its terms. Rept. and Trans. Devon. Assoc., 35, pp. 156–66. 1903.

2809 —— Exchequer tax books and Domesday identification. *Same jnl.*, 29, pp. 216–24. 1897.

2810 —— Principles of the ' Domesday ' survey and ' feudal aids '. *Same jnl.*, 32, pp. 521–51. 1900.

2811 Wheatley (Henry Benjamin), *ed.* Domesday bibliography. Domesday Studies, 2, pp. 663–96. 1891.

2812 Williams J. F.). Local history and the Domesday Book. History Teachers' Miscellany, 7, pp. 137–40. 1929.

2813 Winters (William). Historical notes on Domesday Book. [Plate : ' facsimile of that part of Domesday Book which relates to Waltham Holy Cross, Essex.'] Reliquary, 21, pp. 209–14, + 1 plate. 1881.

§ b. Complete Document or two or more counties

2814 Domesday Book. Domesday Book : seu liber censualis, *etc.* [Edited by A. Furley.] 2 vol. fol. [London], 1783. [Title-pages issued in 1816 by the Record Commission, with two volumes containing indices and additamenta, edited by Sir H. Ellis. i. Kent–Lincolnshire : ii. Essex–Suffolk : iii. Indices : iv. Additamenta, viz. Exon Domesday, Inquisitio Eliensis, Liber Winton, Boldon Book.]

2815 —— Consuetudines et jura Anglo-Saxonica ex libro censuali, dicto Doomesday. *Rerum Anglicarum scriptorum veterum, tom.* 3. fol. Oxoniae, 1684.

2816 —— Facsimiles . . . photo-zincographed . . . at the Ordnance Survey Office, Southampton, under the direction of Sir H. James. [Edited by W. B. Sanders.] 35 pt., fol. and 4° Southampton, 1861–63. [Latin.]

2817 —— Index of counties in Domesday Book. pp. 6. 8° London, 1899.

2818 Domesday Book. Dom Boc ; . . . so far as relates to the counties of Middlesex, Hertford, Buckingham, Oxford and Gloucester ; by William Bawdwen. 4° Doncaster, 1812.

2819 —— Dom Boc. A translation . . . as relates to the county of York, including also Amounderness, Lonsdale and Furness in Lancashire, and such parts of Westmoreland and Cumberland as are contained in the survey, also the counties of Derby, Nottingham, Rutland and Lincoln, with an introduction, glossary and indexes by William Bawdwen. pp. 628, 62. 4° Doncaster, 1809.

2820 —— Dome-day ; or an actual survey of south Britain . . . translated with an introduction, notes and illustrations by Samuel Henshall and John Wilkinson. . . . Counties of Kent, Sussex, and Surrey. 4° London, 1799.

2821 —— Domesday tables for the counties of Surrey, Berkshire, Middlesex, Hertford, Buckingham and Bedford and for the New Forest. With an appendix on the battle of Hastings. Arranged with some notes by Hon. Francis Henry Baring. pp. xvi, 239, + plan [of battle of Hastings]. sm. fol. London, 1909. [Gross, 1884b.]

2822 —— A literal extension and translation of the portion of Domesday Book relating to Cheshire and Lancashire, and to parts of Flint and Denbighshire, Cumberland, Westmoreland, and Yorkshire ; with an introduction and notes, by William Beaumont. . . . 2nd edition. pp. xxi, 89. fol. Chester, 1882. [Latin and English.]

2823 Esdaile (George). Lancashire and Cheshire Domesday. [Description of 39 documents.] Trans. Lancs. and Ches. Antiq. Soc., 4 (1886), pp. 35–49. 1887.

2824 Farrer (William). The Domesday survey of north Lancashire and the adjacent parts of Cumberland, Westmorland, and Yorkshire. [First map shows : ' The land between the Esk and the Ribble, included in the survey under Euruicscire, showing the sub-division into Saxon manors before the Conquest.] *Same jnl.*, 18 (1900), pp. 88–113, + 2 folding maps, + 5 tables. 1901.

§ *c.* **By County**
(documents and comments)
(*i*) **Bedfordshire**

2825 Airy (William). A digest of the Domesday of Bedfordshire. . . . By William Airy. . . . With a preliminary note by . . . B. R. Airy. pp. 108. fol. Bedford, 1881. [Gross, 1892.]

2826 Fowler (George Herbert). Bedfordshire in 1086 : an analysis and synthesis of Domesday Book. pp. 118, + 9 plates. 4° Aspley Guise, 1922.

2827 —— Domesday notes, [Bedfordshire, 1], (2. Kenemondwick). Pubs. Beds. Hist. Rec. Soc., 1, pp. 63–73 : 5, pp. 61–73. 1913, 1919.

2828 Ragg (Frederick William). Translation of the Domesday text. [Bedfordshire.] (Index to Domesday of Bedfordshire). V.C.H. Bedford, 1, pp. 219–66, + map, 405–12. 1904.

2829 Round (John Horace). Introduction to the Bedfordshire Domesday. V.C.H. Bedford, 1, pp. 191–218, + map. 1904.

(*ii*) **Berkshire**

2830 [Anon.] Berkshire. Resumé of Domesday holders and holdings. Q. J. Berks. Archaeol. and Archit. Soc., 3, pp. 138–43, 167, 195–200 : Berks, Bucks and Oxon Archaeol. J., 1, pp. 26–28, 61, 75–78 : 2, pp. 19–22, 59–60, 86–89, 113–15. 1894–97.

2831 Field (John Edward). Some notes on the Domesday survey of Berkshire. Berks, Bucks and Oxon Archaeol. J., 10, pp. 81–86. 1904.

2832 Index to the Domesday of Berkshire. [i. Personal names : ii. Place names.] V.C.H., Berks., Index vol., pp. 115–21. 1927.

2833 Ragg (Frederick William). Translation of the Berkshire Domesday. V.C.H., Berkshire, 1, pp. 323–69, + map. 1906.

2834 Round (John Horace). Introduction to the Berkshire Domesday. V.C.H., Berkshire, 1, pp. 285–321. 1906.

(iii) Buckinghamshire

2835 Ragg (Frederick William). Text of the Buckinghamshire Domesday. V.C.H., Bucks., 1, pp. 229–77, + map. 1905.

2836 Round (John Horace). Introduction to the Buckinghamshire Domesday. V.C.H., Bucks., 1, pp. 207–28. 1905.

(iv) Cambridgeshire

2837 Darby (Henry Clifford). Social and economic history [of Cambridgeshire]. [Domesday Cambridgeshire. 7 figures in text, showing Domesday settlements, population, plough teams, mills, woodland, fisheries, meadow.] V.C.H., Cambs., 2, pp. 49–58. 1948.

2838 Domesday Book. The Cambridgeshire portion of the survey . . . The English translation of . . . W. Bawdwen, edited, with the original Latin text extended . . . by C. H. Evelyn-White . . . and H. G. Evelyn-White. pp. xxxviii, 174. 4° London, 1910.

2839 Evelyn-White (Hugh Gerard), *ed.* Domesday Book . . . Cambridgeshire. [Gross, 1892a. Extension of the text, with transcript of an unpublished translation made by William Bawdwen in 1869. Separately printed, 1910.] East Anglian (N. and Q.), N.S. 11, pp. 63–67, etc. *See* its index, N.S. 12, pp. 4–9, etc. 1905–08.

2840 Hamilton (Nicholas Esterhazy Stephen Armitage), *ed.* Inquisitio comitatus Cantabrigiensis, subjicitur Inquisitio Eliensis. *Royal Society of Literature.* 4° London, 1876. [Gross, 1893. Texts of Inquest and Domesday in parallel columns. Inquest of Ely relates to the lands of Ely abbey in Cambs., Herts., Essex, Norfolk, Suffolk and Hunts.]

2841 Otway - Ruthven (Jocelyn). Translation of the text of Cambridgeshire Domesday. Index to Domesday of Cambridgeshire. [P. 428, Lands, now in Cambs., entered in Domesday Book under other countries.] V.C.H., Cambs., 1, pp. 358–436. 1938.

2842 Salzman (Louis Francis). Introduction to the Cambridgeshire Domesday.

V.C.H., Cambs., 1, pp. 335–57, and map. 1938.

2843 Walker (Bryan). On the Inquisitio Comitatus Cantabrigiensis. [Gross, 1894. Seems to be a 12th c. copy of the original returns from which Domesday was compiled.] Camb. Antiq. Commns., 6, pp. 45–64. 1884.

2844 —— On the measurements and valuations of the Domesday of Cambridgeshire. [i. on hides and their size : ii. on caruca ex terra ad carrucam : iii. on Domesday acres : iv. on bovates : v. on hidation : vi. on the Domesday valuation (valet) of manors and holdings: vii. on the population of the county : viii. on the minor incidents of value.] *Same jnl.* 5, (1880–84), pp. 93–129, with an atlas of tables in folio. 1886.

(v) Cheshire

2845 Brownbill (John). Cheshire in Domesday Book. Trans. Hist. Soc. Lancs. and Ches., 51 (1899), pp. 1–26, + folding map. 1901.

2846 Domesday Book. The Domesday survey of Cheshire. Edited, with introduction, translation, and notes by James Tait. *Chetham Society : Remains hist. and lit. connected with Lancs. and Cheshire, N.S.*75. pp. xvii, 258, + map. 4° Edinburgh, 1916.

2847 Esdaile (George). Cheshire in Domesday and the Domesday of Cheshire. Cheshire N. and Q., 6 (N.S. 1), pp. 184–86. 1886.

2848 Irvine (William Fergusson). Notes on the Domesday survey, so far as it relates to the hundred of Wirral. J. Archit., Archaeol., and Hist. Soc. of Chester, N.S. 5, pp. 72–84, + map + table 1895.

2849 Leicester (*Sir* Peter), *bart.* Historical antiquities . . . whereunto is annexed a transcript of Domesday Book as far as it concerneth Cheshire, *etc.* pp. 437. fol. London. 1673.

(vi) Cornwall

2850 Couch (Jonathan). Translations from Domesday. Rept. and Trans., Penzance N.H. and Antiq. Soc., 2, pp. 110–25, 167–85, 244–69. c. 1883.

2851 Domesday Book. A literal extension of the text of Domesday Book in relation to...Cornwall. To accompany the facsimile copy photo-zincographed, *etc.* fol. London, 1861.

2852 —— A literal translation (by W. B. Sanders) of [ditto]. To accompany the facsimile, *etc.*, pp. 21. fol. Southampton, 1875.

2853 Picken (W. M. N.). The Domesday Book and East Cornwall. Old Cornwall, 2, pp. 24–27. 1936.

2854 Rutter (J. A.). Cornish [geld] acres in Domesday. N. and Q., 12th S. 7, pp. 392, 437, 471–72. 1920.

2855 Whitley (H. Michell). The Cornish Domesday and geld inquest. [i. The Inquisitio geldi from the Exeter Domesday Book, with translation and tabular statement of hides in each hundred. No more published.] J. Roy. Inst. Cornwall, 13, pp. 548–75. 1898.

(*vii*) Cumberland

2856 Wilson (James). Introduction to the Cumberland Domesday. V.C.H., Cumberland, 1, pp. 295–336, + 2 plates. 1901.

(*viii*) Derbyshire

2857 Domesday Book. Domesday Book of Derbyshire. . . . Extended Latin text; and literal translation. Edited with notes, glossary, indices . . . by L. Jewitt. fol. London, 1871.

2858 Statham (S. P. H.). Later descendants of Domesday holders of land in Derbyshire. [Includes the Domesday holdings.] J. Derbs. Archaeol. and N.H. Soc., N.S. 2 (1926–27), pp. 51–106, 233–328 ; N.S. 5 (1931), pp. 27–56. 1929–32.

2859 —— Notes on the Domesday tenants and under-tenants in Derbyshire. J. Derbs. Archaeol. and N.H. Soc., N.S. 1, pp. 152–199. 1925.

2860 Stenton (*Sir* Frank Merry). Introduction to (text of) the Derbyshire Domesday. V.C.H., Derbyshire, 1, pp. 293–355, + map, 427–35 (index). 1908.

2861 Yeatman (John Pym), *etc.* The feudal history of the county of Derby. 3 vol. [in 5 pts.], 8° London, [1886–95]. [Gross, 871. Contains translations of extracts from Domesday : also reprinted separately, pp. 88, 1886.]

(*ix*) Devon

2862 Baring (*Hon.* Francis Henry). The Exeter Domesday. E.H.R., 27, pp. 309–18. 1912.

2863 Devonshire Association. The Devonshire Domesday and geld inquest. Extensions, translations, and indices. pp. xlix, 1236. 8° Plymouth, 1884–92.

2864 Galbraith (Vivian Hunter). The date of the geld rolls in Exon Domesday. E.H.R., 65, pp. 1–17. 1950.

2865 Pollock (*Sir* Frederick). The Devonshire Domesday. Rept. and Trans. Devon. Assoc., 25, pp. 286–308. 1893.

2866 Reichel (Oswald Joseph). The Devonshire Domesday. [i. Some suggestions to aid in identifying the place-names : ii. The Devonshire Domesday and the Geldroll (1084) : iii. Berry Pomeroy and Stockleigh Pomeroy. A contribution to the economic history of the cultivating classes in Domesday : iv. The Domesday churches of Devon : v. The hundreds of Devon : vi. Domesday identifications.] *Same jnl.*, 26, pp. 133–67 : 27, pp. 165–98 ; 28, pp. 362–90, + 1 plate (2 maps) ; 30, pp. 258–315 ; 33, pp. 554–602, 603–39 ; 34, pp. 715–31. 1894–1902.

2867 —— Introduction to (translation of) the Devonshire Domesday. V.C.H., Devon, 1, pp. 375–549, + map. 1906.

2868 Whale (Thomas William) and **Reichel** (Oswald Joseph). Analysis of Exon. Domesday (Index to analysis). [Pp. 402–63, table showing 'Devon hundreds and Geldlist'.] Rept. and Trans. Devon. Assoc., 28, pp. 391–463 : 34, pp. 259–234. 1896, 1902.

2869 —— Analysis of the Exon. Domesday in hundreds (Supplement). *Same jnl.*, 35, pp. 662–712 : 36, pp. 156–72. 1903–04.

2870 —— History of the Exon Domesday. *Same jnl.*, 37, pp. 246–83. 1905.

(x) Dorset

2871 Moule (H. J.). Domesday return for Dorchester [Dorset]. N. and Q. Som. and Dorset, 2, p. 225. 1891.

(xi) Essex

2872 Christie (—) Mrs. *Archibald Christie*. The 'ings' and 'gings' of the Domesday survey especially Fryerning. [P. 99, 'table of suggested identifications', giving owner, hides, woodland, ploughs, value, etc., also.] Trans. Essex Archaeol. Soc., N.S. 12, pp. 94–100. 1913.

2873 Domesday Book. Domesday Book, relating to Essex : translated by T. C. Chisenhale-Marsh. 4° Chelmsford, 1864.

2874 Round (John Horace). The Domesday of Colchester. [*See also* 6, pp. 37–38, for note by John Fenton.] Antiquary, 5, pp. 244–50; 6, pp. 5–9, 95–100, 251–56. 1882.

2875 —— Introduction to (text of, index to) the Essex Domesday. V.C.H., Essex, 1, pp. 333–598, + map, + 1 plate. 1903.

2876 W. (W. C.). Essex Domesday. [Aluertuna = Alderton : Tippedana = Debden in Loughton.] N. and Q., 7th S. 10, p. 484. 1890.

(xii) Flint

2877 Tait (James). Flintshire in Domesday Book. Flintshire Hist. Soc. Pubs., 11, pp. 1–37, + map. 1925.

(xiii) Gloucestershire

2878 Ellis (Alfred Shelley). On the landholders of Gloucestershire named in Domesday Book. Trans. Bristol and Glos. Arch. Soc., 4, pp. 86–198, + table. 1879.

2879 Rudder (Samuel). A new history of Gloucestershire. . . . With a copy of Domesday-Book for Gloucestershire, *etc.* pp. x, 855, lxviii. fol. Cirencester, 1779.

2880 Taylor (Charles Samuel). An analysis of the Domesday Survey of Gloucestershire. pp. vi, 348. Trans. Bristol and Glos. Arch. Soc., Suppl., 1889.

2881 Taylor (Charles Samuel). Note on the entry in Domesday Book relating to Westbury-on-Severn. *Same jnl.*, 36, pp. 182–90. 1913.

(xiv) Hampshire

2882 Domesday Book. Hampshire extracted from Domesday Book; with an . . . English translation; a preface; and an introduction. To which is added a glossary . . . by R. Warner. 4° London, 1789.

2883 Domesday Book. Hampshire in 1086. An extension of the Latin text, and an English translation . . . with explanatory note by H. Moody. To accompany the facsimile copy photozincographed, *etc.* fol. Winchester, 1862. [Latin and English.]

2884 Round (John Horace). Introduction to (Text of, Index to) the Hampshire Domesday. V.C.H., Hampshire, 1, pp. 399–526 : Index vol., pp. 1–13. 1900–14.

2885 Y. (D.). Collections from the history of Hampshire and the bishopric of Winchester . . . with the original Domesday Book of the county, and an . . . English translation, preface, and . . . glossary. By Richard Warner, vol. 2. 5 vol. 4° London, [1795].

(xv) Herefordshire

2886 Galbraith (Vivian Hunter) and Tait (James), *ed.* Herefordshire Domesday, circa 1160–1170. Reproduced by collotype from facsimile photographs of Balliol College manuscript 350. *Publications of the Pipe Roll Society*, 63 (*N.S.* 25). pp. xxxii, 147, + 2 plates. [Contains pre-Conquest material. Significant variants from Domesday Book are recorded in the footnotes.] 8° London, 1950.

2887 Rennell of Rodd (Francis James Rennell Rodd), *2nd baron*. The Domesday manors in the hundreds of Hezetre and Elsedune in Herefordshire. Herefordshire : Centenary of Woolhope Club, pp. 130–58, + map. 1954.

2887a —— The manors of Rodd, Nash and Little Brampton, near Presteigne : a note on possible Domesday Book identification. Radnor. Soc. Trans., 14, pp. 24–29. 1944.

2888 Robinson (C. J.). The Domesday survey of Herefordshire. Trans. Woolhope N.F. Club, 1873, pp. 94–99. 1874.

2889 Round (John Horace). Introduction to (Translation of) the Hereford Domesday. V.C.H., Hereford, 1, pp. 263–345, 1 map. 1908.

(xvi) Hertfordshire

2890 Gould (Isaac Chalkley). Some notes on Wymondley in Domesday. East Herts Archaeol. Soc., Trans., 3, i (1905), pp. 12–13. 1906.

2891 Johnson (W. Branch). Hertfordshire nine hundred years ago. [Domesday. Population, c. 18,000 : 35,000 pigs : mills.] Herts. Countryside, 8, pp. 68, 95. 1953.

2892 Ragg (Frederick William). Text of (Index of) the Hertfordshire Domesday. V.C.H., Hertfordshire, 1, pp. 300–44, 387–93. 1902.

2893 Round (John Horace). Introduction to the Hertfordshire Domesday. V.C.H., Hertfordshire, 1, pp. 263–99, + map. 1902.

(xvii) Huntingdonshire

2894 Domesday Book. Translation of Domesday Book . . . with notes and explanations as far as it relates to Huntingdonshire. fol. Huntingdon, 1864.

2895 Stenton (*Sir* Frank Merry). Introduction to (Text of, Index to) the Huntingdonshire Domesday. V.C.H., Huntingdon, 1, pp. 315–55, 407–10, + map. 1926.

(xviii) Kent

2896 Domesday Book. The Domesday Book of Kent. With translation, notes, and appendix by Lambert Blackwell Larking. [Gross, 1902.] fol. London, 1869.

2897 Kirke (Edith M.). Index to the Kent Domesday and Domesday Monachorum. V.C.H., Kent, 3, pp. 437–52. 1932.

2898 Neilson (Nellie). The Domesday Monachorum. V.C.H., Kent, 3, pp. 253–69, 437–52 (index). 1932.

2899 —— Introduction to the Kent Domesday. V.C.H., Kent, 3, pp. 177–201, + map. 1932.

2900 Ragg (Frederick William). Text of the Kent Domesday. V.C.H., Kent, 3, pp. 203–52, + map. 1932.

(xix) Lancashire

2901 Farrer (William). Introduction to (Text of, Index to) the Lancashire Domesday. V.C.H., Lancs., 1, pp. 269–90, 377–81, + map. 1906.

2902 —— Notes on the Domesday survey of the land between Ribble and Mersey. Trans. Lancs. and Ches. Antiq. Soc., 16 (1898), pp. 1–38, + map, + 7 tables. 1899.

2903 Gray (Andrew Edward Phillimore). The Domesday record of the land between Ribble and Mersey. Trans. Hist. Soc. Lancs. and Ches., 39 (1887), pp. 35–48. 1889.

2904 Lumby (J. H.). The Domesday survey of south Lancashire. *Same jnl.*, 52 (1900), pp. 53–76, and folding map. 1902.

(xx) Leicestershire

2905 Domesday Book. A literal extension of the Latin text, and an English translation, of Domesday Book in relation to the country of Leicestershire (Rutland). To accompany the facsimile copy photo-zincographed, *etc.* 2 pts., fol. Leicester, 1864.

2906 Stenton (*Sir* Frank Merry). Introduction to (Translation of) the Leicestershire Domesday. V.C.H., Leicester, 1, pp. 277–338, + map. 1907.

(xxi) Lincolnshire

2907 Domesday Book. A translation of that portion of Domesday Book which relates to Lincolnshire and Rutlandshire. By C. G. Smith. 8° London, Manchester, [1870].

2908 Domesday Book. The Lincoln-shire Domesday and the Lindsey survey [1115–18]. Translated and edited by Charles Wilmer Foster and Thomas Longley. With an introduction by F. M. Stenton and appendices of extinct villages by C. W. Foster. *Lincoln Record Society*, 19. pp. cx, 315, + maps, + facsimile. 8° Horncastle, 1924.

2909 Welby (*Sir* Alfred Cholmeley Earle). Ulf of Lincolnshire, before and after the Conquest. [Domesday holdings of Ulf, the seneschal, and Madselm, his consort.] Lincs. N. and Q., 14, pp. 196–200. 1917.

(xxii) London and Middlesex

2910 Baylis (Charles F.). The omission of Edgware from Domesday Book. Trans. London and Mdx. Archaeol. Soc., N.S. 11, 62–66. 1952.

2911 Coote (Henry Charles). Notices of Deorman of London, a Domesday tenant in capite. *Same jnl.*, 3, pp. 153–56. 1870.

2912 Domesday Book. Facsimile of the original Domesday Book . . . with translation by General Plantagenet-Harrison. Pt. 1, Middlesex. fol. London, 1876. *No more published.*

2913 —— A literal extension of the Latin text; and an English translation of Domesday Book in relation to the county of Middlesex. To accompany the facsimile copy photo-zincographed, *etc.* fol. London, 1862. [Latin and English.]

2914 Griffith (Edward). Middlesex in the time of the Domesday survey. Trans. London and Middx. Archaeol. Soc., 1, pp. 175–82. 1860.

2915 Sharpe (*Sir* Montagu). The Domesday survey of Middlesex. Home Counties Mag., 10, pp. 315–16. 1908.

2916 —— Middlesex in Domesday Book. [2 figures in text. Scope of the Middlesex survey: rural economy: the hundred: land cultivation: carucated land: Danegeld from Middlesex: miscellaneous returns.] Trans. Lond. and Middsx. Archaeol. Soc., N.S. 7, pp. 509–27. 1937.

(xxiii) Norfolk

2917 Hoare (Christobel M.) [*Mrs. Ivo Hood*]. The history of an East Anglian soke. pp. 553, + 2 maps. 8° Bedford, 1918. [Gimingham. Pp. 6–14, Domesday.]

2918 Johnson (Charles). Introduction to (Translation of) the Norfolk Domesday. V.C.H., Norfolk, 2, pp. 1–203, + map. 1906.

2919 Munford (George). An analysis of the Domesday Book of the county of Norfolk. 8° London, 1858. [Gross, 1905.]

2920 Tingey (J. C.). Some notes on the Domesday assessment of Norfolk. Norfolk Archaeology, 21, pp. 134–42. 1923.

(xxiv) Northamptonshire

2921 Domesday Book. Domesday Book. The portion relating to Northamptonshire, extended and translated by S. H. Moore. fol. Northampton, 1863.

2922 Markham (Christopher A.). Domesday Book, Northamptonshire. Assoc. Archit. Soc's Rpts, 19, pp. 126–39, + 1 plate. 1887.

2923 Morton (John). The natural history of Northamptonshire; . . . to which is annexed a transcript of Domesday Book, so far as it relates to that county. pp. iv, 551–46. fol. London, 1712.

2924 Round (John Horace). Introduction to (Text of) the Northamptonshire Domesday (Domesday index). V.C.H., Northampton, 1, pp. 257–356, 423–36, + map. 1902.

(xxv) Nottinghamshire

2925 Stacye (John). Studies of the Nottinghamshire Domesday. 4° Worksop, 1904. *In* White (Robert), The Dukery records. pp. x, 452. 1904.

2926 Stenton (*Sir* Frank Merry). Introduction to (Text of) the Nottinghamshire Domesday. V.C.H., Nottingham, 1, pp. 207–88, + map. 1906.

2927 Stone Man, *pseud.* Notts. churches in Domesday. [List of 66.] Notts. and Derbs. N. and Q., 1, pp. 83–84. 1893.

(*xxvi*) Oxfordshire

2928 Lamborn (Edmund Arnold Greening). A problem of the Oxfordshire Domesday. [Chislehampton.] N. and Q., 187, pp. 203–05. 1944.

2929 Mowat (John Lancaster Gough). Notes on the Oxfordshire Domesday. pp. 31, + map. 8° Oxford, 1892. [Gross, 1908. Resumé of Domesday holders and holdings, etc.]

(*xxvii*) Radnorshire

2930 Howse (William Henry). Presteigne in Domesday. Radnor. Soc. Trans., 21, pp. 48–49. 1951.

2931 Venables - Llewelyn (*Sir* Charles). Domesday Book in Radnorshire and the Border. Radnor. Soc. Trans., 2, pp. 14–17. 1932.

(*xxviii*) Rutland

2932 Index to Domesday of Rutland. [i. Personal names : ii. Place names.] V.C.H., Rutland, Index vol., pp. 29–30. 1936.

2933 Stenton (*Sir* Frank Merry). Introduction to (Text of) the Rutland Domesday. V.C.H., Rutland, 1, pp. 121–42, + map. 1908.

(*xxix*) Shropshire

2934 Anderson (John Corbet). Shropshire : its early history and antiquities. Comprising a description of . . . its Saxon and Danish reminiscences : the Domesday Survey of Shropshire, *etc.* pp. viii, 491, + plates. 8° London, 1864. [Gross, 1066a. 'Based on Domesday : contains tables of Domesday hundreds.']

2935 Hartshorne (Charles Henry). Salopia antiqua. pp. xxii, 640, + 8 plates. 8° London, 1841. [Pp. 163–234, A.-S. period : pp. 284–91, places in Shropshire mentioned in Domesday Book.]

2936 'Juliana'. Shropshire churches in 1086. (Shropshire manors mentioned in the Domesday Book as possessing churches and priests). Shrop. N. and Q., N.S. 4, pp. 28–29. 1895.

(*xxx*) Somerset

2937 Bates (Edward Harbin). Omission in Eyton's Domesday studies— Somerset. [Manor of Milton (Clevedon).] N. and Q. Som. and Dorset, 5, pp. 346–50. 1897.

2938 —— Text of (Index to) the Somerset Domesday. (Geld Inquest : Exon. Domesday, fol. 75 seq.). V.C.H., Somerset, 1, pp. 433–537, and map; 2, pp. 603–16. 1906–11.

2939 Eyton (Robert William). Domesday studies : an analysis and digest of the Somerset survey (according to the Exon codex), and of the Somerset Gheld Inquiry of A.D. 1084, as collated with and illustrated by Domesday. [Gross, 1909.] 2 vol. 4° London, 1880.

2940 Harbin (E. H. Bates). Hescombe in Domesday and after. [Somerset manor of Geoffrey, bp. of Coutances.] N. & Q., Som & Dorset, 15, pp. 234–41. 1917.

2941 Hobhouse (Edmund), *bp. of Nelson, N.Z.* Domesday estates [in Somerset]. Proc. Somerset Arch. Soc., 35 (1889), pp. 22–23. 1890.

2942 —— On the devolution of Domesday estates in Somerset. *Same jnl.*, 36 (1890), pp. 32–35. 1891.

2943 —— Remarks on Domesday map. [Map of Somerset, shewing the chief estates as recorded in Domesday Book, + 2 pp. of explanation.] *Same jnl.*, 35 (1889), pp. ix–x + folding map, in colour. 1890.

2944 Lennard (Reginald). A neglected Domesday satellite. [Contained in 12th c. cartulary of priory of Bath. Deals with 7 Somerset manors. Relation to Exon Domesday.] E.H.R., 58, pp. 32–41. 1943.

2945 Round (John Horace). Introduction to the Somerset Domesday. V.C.H., Somerset, 1, pp. 383–432, + map. 1906.

2946 Whale (Thomas William). Analysis of Somerset Domesday, terrae occupatae and index. With reprint of [2947] and analysis in hundreds. pp. vi, 67, 48. 8° Bath, 1902.

2947 Whale (Thomas William). Principles of the Somerset Domesday. Trans. Bath F.C., 10, pp. 38–86. 1902.

(*xxxi*) Staffordshire

2948 Daniel (A. T.). Staffordshire Domesday Book. North Staffs. F.C., Trans., 37, pp. 37–60. 1903.

2949 Domesday Book. The Staffordshire Domesday. With an English translation. Edited by Henry Malcolm Fraser. pp. xii, 162. 8° Stone, 1936.

2950 Eyton (Robert William). Domesday studies : an analysis and digest of the Staffordshire survey, *etc.*, pp. vii, 135. 8° London, 1881. [Gross, 1910.]

(*xxxii*) Suffolk

2951 Bedell (Alfred J.), *etc.* Suffolk Domesday. East Anglian (N. and Q.). N.S. 3, pp. 12, 25–26, 97–98, 146–47, 215, 225–26, 311–12. 1889–90.

2952 Domesday Book. Suffolk Domesday. The Latin text extended and translated into English by [Lord John Hervey]. 2 vol. 8° Bury St. Edmunds, 1888–91. [Gross, 1910a.]

2953 Hervey (John William Nicholas), *baron Hervey*. Translation of the Suffolk Domesday. [Adapted from Lord Hervey's translation, **2952.**] V.C.H., Suffolk, 1, pp. 417–582, + map. 1911.

2954 Lees (Beatrice Adelaide). Introduction to the Suffolk Domesday. (The Danegeld and the leet system in Suffolk). V.C.H., Suffolk, 1, pp. 357–416, and map. 1911.

2955 Pearson (William C.). Notes on the Suffolk Domesday. East Anglian (N. and Q.), N.S. 4, pp. 233–38. 1892.

(*xxxiii*) Surrey

2956 Domesday Book. A literal extension of the Latin text, and an English translation, of Domesday Book in relation to the county of Surrey. To accompany the facsimile copy photozincographed, *etc.* fol. London, 1862. [Latin and English.]

2957 Malden (Henry Elliot). The Domesday survey of Surrey. Domesday Studies, 2, pp. 459–70. 1891.

2958 —— The text of (Index to) the Surrey Domesday. V.C.H., Surrey, 1, pp. 294–328, 445–49, + map. 1902.

2959 Manning (Owen) and **Bray** (William). The history and antiquities of the county of Surrey. . . . With a facsimile copy of Domesday. 3 vol. fol. London, 1804–14. [Gross, 1096. Domesday, 13 plates.]

2960 Round (John Horace). Introduction to the Surrey Domesday. V.C.H., Surrey, 1, pp. 275–93, + map. 1902.

(*xxxiv*) Sussex

2961 Domesday Book in relation to the county of Sussex. Edited by William Douglas Parish. *Sussex Archaeological Society.* pp. xiv, xxviii, 138. fol. Lewes, 1886. [Gross, 1911.]

2962 Harris (Emily). Doomsday or Domesday Book. [Especially relating to Sussex.] Sussex County Mag., 19, pp. 101–02. 1945.

2963 Napper (H. F.). Notes on [**2970.**] Sussex Archaeol. Collns., 36, pp. 239–40. 1888.

2964 Peckham (W. D.). Two Domesday Book freeholds. [At Ferring and Aldingbourne.] Sussex N. and Q., 2, p. 17. 1928.

2965 Round (John Horace). Introduction to the Sussex Domesday. V.C.H., Sussex, 1, pp. 351–85, + map. 1905.

2966 —— Note on the Sussex Domesday. Sussex Archaeol. Collns., 44, pp. 140–43. 1901.

2967 —— and **Howorth** (*Sir* Henry Hoyle). The Sussex rapes. [Criticism of **2970.**] Archaeol. Rev., 1, pp. 229–30. 1888.

2968 Salzmann (Louis Francis). Translation of (Index to) the Sussex Domesday. V.C.H., Sussex, 1, pp. 386–451, 541–54, + map. 1905.

2969 Sawyer (Frederick Ernest). Index of names of places in Domesday survey of Sussex. pp. 12. fol. [1880?].

2970 **Sawyer** (Frederick Ernest). Sussex Domesday studies.1. The rapes and their origins. Archaeol. Rev., 1, pp. 54–59. 1888.

(xxxv) Warwickshire

2971 **Carter** (William Fowler). Notes on the Domesday of Warwickshire. B'ham and Midland Inst., Arch. Section, Trans., 18, pp. 28–29. 1892.

2972 —— Text of (Index to) the Warwickshire Domesday. V.C.H., Warwick, 1, pp. 298–344, 407–15, + map. 1904.

2973 **Domesday Book.** Domesday Book for the county of Warwick, translated by William Reader. With a dissertation on Domesday Book, and biographical notices of the ancient possessors. 2nd ed., with a brief introduction by E. P. Shirley. pp. viii, 38. 4° Warwick, [1879].

2974 **Langford** (John Alfred). Birmingham, Aston and Edgbaston, as seen in Domesday Book. B'ham and Midland Inst., Arch. Section, Trans., [10], pp. 43–53. 1881.

2975 **Power** (C. J.). The Domesday Book and Birmingham, Erdington, Edgbaston, Aston and Witton. pp. 5. 8° Birmingham, 1929. [Domesday extract, with facsimile. Note on the manor.]

2976 **Renshaw** (T. Lloyd). Birmingham, its rise and progress. pp. 152, + map, + 8 plates. 8° Birmingham, 1932. [Pp. 6–22, Domesday Book entries.]

2977 **Round** (John Horace). Introduction to the Warwickshire Domesday. V.C.H., Warwick, 1, pp. 269–97, + map. 1904.

2978 **Walker** (Benjamin). Some notes on Domesday Book, especially that part of it which relates to the county of Warwick. [With lists of tenants-in-chief, hundreds, and of all places mentioned.] Birmingham Arch. Soc. Trans., pp. 33–80, + map. 1900.

(xxxvi) Wiltshire

2979 **Domesday Book.** Domesday for Wiltshire, extracted from accurate copies of the original records, accompanied with translations, illustrative notes, analysis of contents and general introduction. By William Henry Rich Jones. 4° Bath and London, 1865. [Gross, 1912.]

2980 —— Wiltshire, extracted from Domesday Book : to which is added a translation of the original Latin into English. With an index in which are adapted the modern names to the antient; and a preface by H. P. Wyndham. 8° Salisbury, 1788.

2981 **Finn** (Reginald Arthur Welldon). The making of the Wiltshire Domesday. Wilts. Archaeol. Mag., 52, pp. 318–27. 1948.

2982 **Jones** (William Henry). Gleanings from the Wiltshire Domesday. [i. Evidence as to the boundaries of the county being the same now as in the time of Domesday : ii. On the names of owners or occupiers still preserved in those of persons or places in Wiltshire.] Wilts. Archaeol. Mag., 10, pp. 165–73 ; 13, pp. 42–58. 1867, 1872.

2983 **Moody** (Henry). Notices on the Domesday Book for Wiltshire. Mems. Archaeol. Inst., [5] 1849, pp. 177–81. 1851.

(xxxvii) Worcestershire

2984 **Domesday Book.** A literal extension of the Latin text, and an English translation of Domesday Book, in relation to the county of Worcester [by W. B. Sanders], etc. fol. Worcester, 1864.

2985 **Nash** (Treadway Russell). The history and antiquities of Worcestershire. (Exact copy of Domesday as far as relates to Worcestershire). 13 plates [in black and red]. 2 vol. fol. London, 1781–99.

2986 **Round** (John Horace). Introduction to (Text of, Index to) the Worcestershire Domesday. V.C.H., Worcester, 1, pp. 235–323, 332–40, + map. 1901.

2987 **Willis-Bund** (John William). Domesday Book as far as it relates to Worcestershire. Assoc. Archit. Socs.' Rpts., 21, pp. 253–70. 1892.

(*xxxviii*) **Yorkshire**

2988 Atkinson (John Christopher). On the Danish aspect of the local nomenclature of Cleveland. [Domesday names of owners of land, etc.] J.R.A.I., 3, pp. 115–20. 1874.

2989 Beddoe (John) and **Rowe** (Joseph Hambley). The ethnology of West Yorkshire. [Appendix contains Domesday material. Table 8 : ' Names of proprietors and number of manors held by each of them in the West Riding, tempore regis Edwardi.' Table 9 : Landowners, tenants and population, temp. reg. Wilhelmi.' Also ' Domesday map of the West Riding,' showing holdings.] Yorks. Archaeol. J., 19, pp. 31–60, + folding map. 1907.

2990 Clapham (*Sir* John Harold). The Domesday survey of Yorkshire. Bull. Internat. Comm. Hist. Sciences, 40, pp. 511–13. 1938.

2991 Domesday Book for the East Riding of Yorkshire, excepting the lands in Holderness. Arranged under places . . . by A. B. Wilson-Barkworth. [With tables.] pp. iv, 66. 8° Scarborough, 1925.

2992 Ellis (Alfred Shelley). Biographical notes on Yorkshire tenants named in Domesday Book. Yorks. Archaeol. J., 4, pp. 114–57, 214–48, 384–415 : 5, pp. 289–330. 1877–79.

2993 Farrer (William). Introduction to (Translation of) the Yorkshire Domesday. V.C.H., York, 2, pp. 133–327, + 5 maps. 1912.

2994 Hornsby (William). The Domesday valets of the Langbargh wapentake. Yorks. Archaeol. J., 25, pp. 334–40. 1920.

2995 Index to Domesday of Yorkshire. [i. Personal names : ii. Place names.] V.C.H., Yorks, Index to General vols., pp. 67–100. 1925.

2996 Kendall (Hugh Percy). Domesday Book and after [for Halifax district.] Trans. Halifax Antiq. Soc., 1935, pp. 21–37. 1935.

2997 Skaife (Robert H.), *trans*. Domesday Book for Yorkshire. [Translation and notes.] Yorks. Archaeol. J., 13, pp. 321–52, 489–536 : 14, pp. 1–64, 249–312, 347–89. 1895–98.

2998 Taylor (Isaac). Note on the Domesday Book for Yorkshire. [Corrections of R. H. Skaife's translation, *q.v.* 2997.] *Same jnl.*, 14, pp. 242–43. 1898.

2999 Travis-Cook (J.). Fiscal areas ' for geld '. [Domesday : Yorks.] Antiquary, 47, pp. 468–69. 1911.

43. DRESS

3000 Cunnington (Cecil Willett *and* Phillis). Handbook of English mediaeval costume. pp. 192, + 3 coloured plates. 8° London, 1952. [Pp. 9–27, + 1 plate, A.–S.]

3001 Hansen (Auguste). Angelsächsische Schmucksachen und ihre Bezeichnungen. Eine kulturgeschichtlich-etymologische Untersuchung. *Diss., Kiel.* pp. xv, 59. 8° Kiel, 1913.

3002 McClintock (Henry Foster). Old Irish and Highland dress. . . . With chapters on pre-Norman dress as described in early Irish literature by F. Shaw. 2nd edition. pp. 141, 87. 4° Dundalk, 1950.

3003 Megaw (Basil R. S.) and **McClintock** (Henry Foster). The costume of the Gaelic peoples. [Plate 212 shows 10th c. Irish dress from Muiredach cross, and 9th c. dress from carving in the calf of Man.] J. Manx Mus., 5, pp. 149–60, + 2 plates. 1944.

3004 Planche (James Robinson). A cyclopoedia of costume, *etc*, pp. xi, 448. 4° London, 1876–79. [Pp. 25–47, A.D. 450–1066.]

3005 Stroebe (Lilly T.). Die altenglischen Kleidernamen. Eine kulturgeschichtlich-etymologische Untersuchung. *Diss., Heidelberg.* pp. vii, 85. 1904.

3006 Williams (John) *ab Ithel*. A glossary of terms used for articles of British dress and armour. [A–D only.] Arch. Camb., 4, pp. 9–12, 94–100, 160–67, 291–94. 1849. *Same title*. [Mabinogeon and laws of Howell Dda.] Arch. Camb., Suppl. 1850, pp. 111–80. 1851.

44. FEUDALISM

3007 Adams (George Burton). Anglo-Saxon feudalism. [Gross, 1555a. 'Contends that the feudal system did not exist in England in the A.-S. period, because the benefice and vassalage were not yet united.] A.H.R., 7, pp. 11–35. 1901.

3008 Dodwell (Barbara). East Anglian commendation. E.H.R., 63, pp. 289–306. 1948.

3009 Douglas (David Charles). The Norman Conquest and English feudalism. Econ. Hist. Rev., 9, pp. 128–43. 1939.

3010 Gibbs (Marion). Feudal order. A study of the origins and development of English feudal society. pp. vi, 149, + 5 plates. 8° London, 1949.

3011 Nichols (Francis Morgan). On feudal and obligatory knighthood. [A small amount of A.-S. and William I material.] Archaeologia, 39, pp. 189–244. 1860.

3012 Spelman (*Sir* Henry). Of feuds and tenures by knight service. fol. London, 1723. [Gross, 739. *In* his postumous works, pp. 1–46. Combats the view that feudal tenure existed among the A.-S.]

3013 Stenton (*Sir* Frank Merry). The first century of English feudalism, 1066–1166. *Ford Lectures for* 1928–29. pp. viii, 312. 8° Oxford, 1932.

3014 Stephenson (Carl). Commendation and related problems in Domesday. E.H.R., 59, pp. 289–310. 1944.

3015 —— Feudalism and its antecedents in England. A.H.R., 48, pp. 245–65. 1943.

3016 Stubbs (William), *bp. of Oxford*. Feudalism. Stubbs (W.) : Lectures on early English history, pp. 18–36. 1906.

3017 Zinkeisen (Frank). Die Anfänge der Lehngerichtsbarkeit in England. pp. 61. 8° Berlin, [1893]. [Gross, 1584. Feudal jurisdiction, especially in 11th and 12th c.]

45. FOREST AND WOODLAND

3018 Baring (*Hon.* Francis Henry). The making of the New Forest. Papers and Proc. Hants. F. C., 6, pp. 309–17, + map, + diagram. 1910.

3019 Burnard (Robert). The ancient population of the forest of Dartmoor. [Pp. 201–07, Domesday material.] Rept. and Trans. Devon. Assoc., 39, pp. 198–207. 1907.

3020 Coles (Rupert). The past history of the forest of Epping. [Pp. 123–28, + figures 4–5 (maps), A.-S.] Essex Nat., 24, pp. 115–33. 1934.

3021 Darby (Henry Clifford). The clearing of the English woodlands. [Place-names, Domesday woodland, etc.] Geography, 36, pp. 71–83. 1951.

3022 —— Domesday woodland. [10 maps in text. i. Domesday entries : ii. swine totals : iii. swine rents : iv. linear dimensions : v. measurement in acres : vi. miscellaneous entries : vii. the compilation of woodland maps : viii. forests.] Econ. Hist. Rev. 2nd S. 3, pp. 21–43. 1950.

3023 —— Domesday woodland in East Anglia. Antiquity, 8, pp. 211–5. 1934.

3024 —— Domesday woodland in Huntingdonshire. [2 maps in text.] Trans. Cambs. and Hunts. Archaeol. Soc., 5, pp. 269–73. 1935.

3025 —— Domesday woodland in Lincolnshire. [Map on p. 56.] Lincs. historian, 1, pp. 55–59. 1948.

3026 F. Forest laws and forest animals. in England. Antiquary, 10, pp. 21–24, 163–66, 255–58. 1884.

3027 Grundy (George Beardoe). The ancient woodland of Gloucestershire. Trans. Bristol and Glos. Arch. Soc., 58, pp. 65–155, + 3 maps : 59, pp. 205–09. 1936–37.

3028 —— The ancient woodland of Wiltshire. [Significant terms in place-names : Braydon, Chute, Clarendon, Grovely, Melksham and Selwood forests.] Wilts. Archaeol. Mag., 48, pp. 530–98, + map. 1939.

3029 Hart (Cyril E.). The metes and bounds of the forest of Dean. [P. 171, map 1, the forest at Domesday.] Trans. Bristol and Glos. Archaeol. Soc., 66 (1945), pp. 166–207. 1947.

3030 Kendall (Hugh Percy). The forest of Sowerbyshire. [Pp. 86*–87*, A.–S. and Domesday.] Papers, Reports, etc. Halifax Antiq. Soc., 1926, pp. 85*–107*. 1926.

3031 Leggatt (T. G.). The forest of Andérida : some of the scenes and history of the Weald. Brighton and Hove Archaeologist, [1], pp. 43–60. 1914.

3032 Lennard (Reginald). The destruction of woodland in the eastern counties under William the Conqueror. Econ. Hist. Rev., 15, pp. 36–43 ; 2nd S.1, p. 144. 1945, 1949.

3033 Moens (W. J. C.). The New Forest : its afforestation, ancient area, and law in the time of the Conqueror and his successors. Did William I devastate the New Forest district and destroy churches there, and had it been previously afforested as related by the early chroniclers ? Archaeol. J., 60, pp. 30–50, + coloured folding map. 1903.

3034 Morgan (F. W.). Domesday woodland in south-west England. [With 9 maps.] Antiquity, 10, pp. 306–24. 1936.

**3035 —— ** Woodland in Wiltshire at the time of the Domesday Book. [4 maps in text.] Wilts. Archaeol. Mag., 47, pp. 25–33. 1935.

3036 Neilson (H.). Early English woodland and waste. J. Economic Hist., 2, pp. 54–62. 1942.

3037 Nisbet (John) and **Lascelles** (Hon. Gerald W.). Forestry [in Hampshire] and the New Forest. V.C.H., Hampshire, 2, pp. 409–70. 1903.

3038 Nisbet (John). The history of the forest of Dean in Gloucestershire. [Domesday, etc.] E.H.R., 21, pp. 445–59. 1906.

3039 Sharpe (Sir Montagu). The forest of Middlesex. Home Counties Mag., 10, pp. 7–15, 93–100. 1908.

3040 Shenstone (J. C.). The woodlands of Essex. [Early history and Domesday material.] Essex Nat., 15, pp. 105–15, + map. 1907.

3041 Shore (Thomas William). Ancient Hampshire forests and the geological conditions of their growth. Papers and Proc. Hants. F.C., l. ii, pp. 40–60. 1888.

3042 Stokes (Henry Paine). Cambridgeshire forests. [Includes Domesday material : ' The Cambridgeshire woods and the pannage supply ', ' parks,' etc.] Proc. Camb. Antiq. Soc., 23, pp. 63–85. 1922.

3043 Terrett (Ian B.). The Domesday woodland of Cheshire. [2 figures in text.] Trans. Hist. Soc. Lancs. and Ches., 100 (1948), pp. 1–7. 1949.

3044 Wrottesley (Hon. George). The forest tenures of Staffordshire. [Including Domesday tenures.] Collectns. for a history of Staffs. (Wm. Salt Soc.), N.S. 10, i, pp. 191–243. 1907.

46. GUILDS

3045 Coornaert (Émile). Les ghildes médiévales (ve–xive siècles) : définition—évolution. [Pp. 35–41, les ghildes anglo-saxonnes.] Rev. hist., 199, pp. 22–55, 208–43. 1948.

3046 Gross (Charles). Gilda mercatoria. Ein Beitrag zur Geschichte der englischen Städteverfassung. pp. 109. 8° Göttingen, 1883. [Pp. 7–25, Die Gilden der Angelsachsen.]

3047 Hegel (Karl). Städte und Gilden der germanischen Völker im Mittelalter. 2 Bde., 8° Leipzig, 1891. [Bd. 1, pp. 19–35, Angelsächsische Gilden : pp. 35–42, Die Städte in der angelsächsischen Periode : pp. 42–57, Domesday.]

3048 Lambert (Joseph Malet). Two thousand years of gild life. pp. xi, 414. 8° Hull, 1891. [Pp. 36–60, A.–S.]

3049 Liebermann (Felix). Einleitung zum Statut der Londoner Friedensgilde unter Æthelstan. Mélanges H. Fitting (Montpellier), 2, pp. 77–103. 1908.

**3050 —— ** Die englische Gilde im achten Jahrhundert. [Gross, 1566. ' Deals with two of Alcuin's letters, which refer to " conjurationes " or " conventicula ".'] Arch. Stud. neueren Spr., Bd. 96, pp. 333–40. 1896.

3051 Unwin (George). The gilds and companies of London. pp. xvi, 397, + 19 plates. 8° London, 1908. [Pp. 15–29, A.-S. ' The frith gild and the cnihten gild '.]

3052 Walford (Cornelius). The history of gilds. [Chap. 14–15 (2, pp. 252–54, 298–301) 'Anglo-Saxon gilds (A.D. 827–1013) : Chap. 16 (3, pp. 28–29) ' Danish period (A.D. 1013–41),' and *passim.*] Antiq. Mag., 1, pp. 25–28, 54–58, 184–87, 246–49, 304–04 : 2, pp. 19–25, 78–83, 120–24, 173–78, 249–54, 298–301 : 3, pp. 28–31. *etc.* 1882–83.

47. HIDATION

§ *a.* **General**

3053 Anscombe (Alfred). *Aro-setna* in the Nomina Hidarum. [?scribal error for *Dor-sete.*] N. and Q., 10th S. 11, pp. 126–27. 1909.

3054 Baring (*Hon.* Francis Henry). The hidation of Northamptonshire in 1086. E.H.R., 17, pp. 76–83. 1902.

3055 —— The hidation of some southern counties. E.H.R., 14, pp. 290–99. 1899.

3056 —— The pre-Domesday hidation of Northamptonshire. E.H.R., 17, pp. 470–79. 1902.

3057 Bates (Edward Harbin). The five-hide-unit in the Somerset Domesday. Proc. Somerset Arch. Soc., 45 (1899), pp. 51–107 + map. 1899.

3058 Boult (Joseph). The *hide* of land. Trans. Hist. Soc. Lancs. and Ches., N.S. 12 [=24], pp. 1–24. 1872.

3059 Bridgeman (Charles George Orlando). The carucate in Staffordshire. Collectns. for a history of Staffs., 1919, pp. 144–51. 1920.

3060 —— The five-hide unit in Staffordshire. *Same jnl.*, 1919, pp. 134–44. 1920.

3061 —— The hides in Offlow hundred. *Same jnl.*, 1919, pp. 131–34. 1920.

3062 —— and **Mander** (Gerald P.). The Staffordshire hidation. [With tables showing modern name, Domesday name, T.R.E. tenant, Domesday tenant, hides.] *Same jnl.*, 1919, pp. 154–81. 1920.

3063 Brownbill (John). The Burghal hidage. [Comparison with corresponding Domesday hidages.] N. and Q., 11th S. 4, pp. 2–3. 1911.

3064 —— The hidage of Oxfordshire. N. and Q., 11th S. 5, pp. 444–45. 1912.

3065 Davies (Arthur Morley). The Domesday hidation of Middlesex. Home Counties Mag., 3, pp. 232–38, 330–31. 1901.

3066 Ellis (Alfred Shelley), **Round** (John Horace), *etc.* The carucate. N. and Q., 6th S. 6, pp. 41–42, 189–92, 229–30. 1882.

3067 Flower (Robin Ernest William). The text of the Burghal hidage. London mediæval studies, 1, pp. 60–64. 1937.

3068 Hollings (Marjory). The survival of the five hide unit in the western midlands. [Including A.-S. and Domesday material.] E.H.R., 63, pp. 453–87. 1948.

3069 Hornsby (William). A regrouping of the Domesday carucates in the Langbargh wapentake. (N. R. Yorks.) Yorks. Archaeol. J., 24, pp. 286–96. 1917.

3070 Jolliffe (John Edward Austin). The Domesday hidation of Sussex and the rapes. E.H.R., 45, pp. 427–35. 1930.

3071 —— The hidation of Kent. E.H.R., 44, pp. 612–18. 1929.

3072 Lennard (Reginald). The origin of the fiscal carucate. [Geld assessments.] Econ. Hist. Rev., 14, pp. 51–63. 1944.

3073 Pell (O. C.). On the Domesday geldable hide, what it probably was and what it certainly was not ; with an explanation of the Domesday terms terra ad carucam, carucata, and virgata from information contained in certain mss. of the 13th century, including the Hundred Rolls. Camb. Antiq. Commns., 6 (1884–88), pp. 65–176. 1891.

3074 Phear (*Sir* John Budd). The hide examined. Rept. and Trans. Devon. Assoc., 36, pp. 380–89. 1904.

3075 Round (John Horace). The Domesday hidation of Essex. E.H.R., 29, pp. 477–79. 1914.

3076 —— The hidation of Northamptonshire. [Domesday, etc.] E.H.R., 15, pp. 78–86. 1900.

3077 Salzmann (Lewis Francis). Hides and virgates in Sussex. E.H.R., 19, pp. 92–96. 1904.

3078 —— The rapes of Sussex. [Material on Domesday hidation.] Sussex Archaeol. Collns., 72, pp. 20–29. 1931.

3079 Tait (James). Hides and virgates at Battle Abbey. [Domesday material.] E.H.R., 18, pp. 705–08. 1903.

3080 —— Hides and virgates in Sussex. E.H.R., 19, pp. 503–06. 1904.

3081 —— Large hides and small hides. E.H.R., 17, pp. 280–82. 1902.

3082 Taylor (Charles Samuel). The pre-Domesday hide of Gloucestershire. Trans. Bristol and Glos. Arch. Soc., 18, pp. 288–319. 1894.

3083 Vinogradoff (*Sir* Paul). *Sulung* and hide. E.H.R., 19, pp. 282–86. 1904.

3084 Walker (Bryan). On the Inquisitio comitatus Cantabrigiensis. [With table showing ' hides in I. c. C.' and ' notes as to hides in Domesday, etc.'] Camb. Antiq. Commns., 6 (1884–88), pp. 45–64. 1891.

§ *b*. The Tribal Hidage

(?7th or 8th c.)

3085 Anscombe (Alfred), *etc*. Gifla [?=Gisla] : Isleworth : Islington. [In Tribal Hidage. Identifies Gislaland as West Middlesex.] N. and Q., 11th S. 4, pp. 43–44, 133–34, 196, 238. 1911.

3086 —— **Brownbill** (John), **Skeat** (Walter William), *etc*. Unecungga : Ynetunga. [In Tribal Hidage.] N. and Q., 11th S. 2, pp. 143–44, 211–13, 272, 332–33, 473–74. 1910.

3087 Anscombe (Alfred), *etc*. Wigesta. [In Tribal Hidage. ?location.] N. and Q., 11th S. 4, pp. 304–05 : 5, p. 18. 1911–12.

3088 Brooke (F. A.). Tribal Hidage. [7th c. Endeavour to show situation of the A.–S. tribes. With table of 36 tribes, also hides, counties, hundreds, etc.] J. Brit. Archaeol. Assoc., N.S. 35 (1929), pp. 273–76. 1930.

3089 Brownbill (John). The Chiltern dwellers in the Tribal Hidage. N. and Q., 154, pp. 75–76. 1928.

3090 Brownbill (John). The Tribal Hidage. E.H.R., 27, pp. 625–48. 1912. *Same title*. E.H.R., 40, pp. 497–503, + plate. 1925.

3091 Corbett (William John). The Tribal Hidage. [Gross, 1544. With coloured map and appendix giving list of the hundreds in the hidated counties.] Trans. R.H.S., N.S. 14, pp. 189–230. 1900.

3092 McGovern (J. B.). The Tribal Hidage. N. and Q., 9th S. 7, pp. 441–44, 99–100 : 8, pp. 272–73. 1901.

3093 Rickwood (George). The kingdom of the East Saxons and the Tribal Hidage. [Gross, 1544, note. With table of ' conjectural restoration of the ancient hundreds '. 'Attempt to show that the heavy hidation of Essex has been systematically reduced in Domesday.'] Trans. Essex Archaeol. Soc., N.S. 11, pp. 246–65 ; 12 pp. 38–50. 1910–11.

3094 Russell (Josiah Cox). The Tribal Hidage. Traditio, 5, pp. 192–209. 1947.

3095 —— Westerna in the Tribal Hidage. [?miswriting for West or Westan Hecan=Iceni.] N. and Q., 194, p. 228. 1949.

3096 Williamson (F.). The Tribal Hidage. N. and Q., 192, pp. 398–400, 423–26. 1947.

48. LAND AND PROPERTY

(*See also* sections 47, 52 and 53)

3097 Balfour-Melville (E. W. M.). A Northamptonshire estate of Malcolm Canmore. [Corby hundred : Northants Geld Roll, temp. William I.] Scot. Hist. Rev., 27, pp. 101–02. 1948.

3098 Baring (*Hon*. Francis Henry). Crundels. [A.–S. boundary term.] E.H.R., 24, pp. 300–03. 1909.

3099 Budgen (W.). Wists and virgates of land. [*Wist*=A.–S. for food, meal. Sussex term : ?=holding sufficient for sustenance of a household.] Sussex N. and Q., 10, pp. 73–76, 97–99, 121–25, + map. 1944–45.

3100 Crofton (Henry Thomas). Agrimensorial remains round Manchester. [Some A.-S. and Domesday material.] Trans. Lancs. and Ches. Antiq. Soc., 23 (1905), pp. 112–71, + map, + 2 plates. 1906.

3101 Curtler (William Henry Ricketts). The enclosure and redistribution of our land. pp. viii, 334. 8° Oxford, 1920. [Ch. 2–3, A.-S. period: ch. 4, The Norman Conquest and its effect on the manor.]

3102 Ellis (Thomas Peter). The land in ancient Welsh law. Aberystwyth Stud., 10, pp. 65–101. 1928.

3103 Farrant (Reginald D.). Manx land tenure. Law Q.R., 22, pp. 136–62. 1906.

3104 Fisher (Joseph). The history of landlording in England. [Pp. 108–32, 3. The Scandinavians (i.e. A.-S. and Danes): 4. The Normans.] Trans. R.H.S., 4, pp. 97–187. 1876.

3105 Garnier (Russell Montague). History of the English landed interest: its customs, laws, and agriculture. 2 vol. 8° London, 1892–93. [Gross, 728. Domesday, etc.]

3106 Hall (Hubert) and **Bird** (S. R.). Notes on the history of the crown lands. Parts 1 and 2. [' The folk-lands became crown-lands somewhere about the end of the 9th c.'] Antiquary, 13, pp. 1–6, 89–95, *also* 85–86 (note by J. H. Round). 1886.

3107 Jolliffe (John Edward Austin). Alod and fee. Camb. Hist. J., 5, pp. 225–34. 1937.

3108 —— English book-right. E.H.R. 50, pp. 1–21. 1935.

3109 Lapsley (Gaillard Thomas). The origin of property in land. [Pp. 443–48, Land-owning among the Anglo-Saxons.] A.H.R., 8, pp. 426–48. 1903.

3110 Lega-Weekes (Ethel), *etc.* The vicar of Pinhoe: origin of payments to. [*See also*, **1376**.] Devon and Cornwall N. and Q., 11, pp. 296–300: 12, pp. 14–16, 60–68, 116–17. 1921–22.

3111 McKerral (Andrew). Ancient denominations of agricultural land in Scotland: a summary of recorded opinions, with some notes, observations and references. [Celtic denominations: Saxon denominations: Celtic names for the ploughgate: its fractions: Norse denominations, etc.] Proc. Soc. Antiq. Scot., 78 (7th S. 6, 1943–44), pp. 39–80. 1944.

3112 Maitland (Frederic William). Domesday measures of land. Archaeol. Rev., 4, pp. 391–92. 1889.

3113 Page (Elwin Lawrence). The contributions of the landed man to civil liberty. *Williams College David A. Wells prize essays*, 1. pp. ix, 266. 8° Cambridge, Mass., 1905. [i. The Angles and Saxons on the continent: ii. The Anglo-Saxons in England: iii. The Norman conquest and feudalization.]

3114 Pell (O. C.). Domesday measures of land. Archaeol. Rev., 2, pp. 350–60. 1889.

3115 —— Domesday measures of land and modern criticism. Archaeol. Rev., 4, pp. 241–58. 1889.

3116 —— A new view of the geldable unit of assessment of Domesday: embracing the divisions of the libra or pound and the weights and measures of uncoined metal, flour, cloth, etc., as made by the Angli, Mercians, Danes, Normans, and Celts, and their connections with the true understanding of the words ' hida ', ' carucata ', ' virgata ', ' villanus ', ' anglicus numerus ', etc. (Summary [of above]). Domesday Studies, 1, pp. 227–385: 2, pp. 561–619. 1888–91.

3117 Phear (*Sir* John Budd). President's address [to the Devonshire Association, 1886]. [' Landholding of Norman and earlier times . . . and nature of the exigency which, arising therefrom, gave cause for the Domesday Survey.'] Rept. and Trans. Devon. Assoc., 18, pp. 33–54. 1886.

3118 Plucknett (Theodore Frank Thomas). Bookland and folkland. Econ. Hist. Rev., 6, pp. 64–72. 1935.

3119 Rose-Troup (Frances). Bookland and folkland. [Transforming of folkland into bookland shown in charter of Æthelwulf (846) whereby he grants land ' Om Homme ' in Devon to himself.] Devon and Cornwall N. and Q., 19, pp. 62–64. 1936.

3120 Round (John Horace). Archaic land tenure in Domesday. Antiquary, 5, pp. 104–06. 1882.

3121 —— Domesday measures of land. Archaeol. Rev., 1, pp. 285–95 : 4, pp. 130–40, 391. 1888–89.

3122 —— Notes on Domesday measures of land. Domesday Studies, 1, pp. 189–225. 1888.

3123 —— The words solinum and solanda. [Solanda=A.–S. *sulung*, plough land (Domesday).] E.H.R., 7, pp. 708–12. 1892.

3124 Saltmarshe (Philip). Ancient land tenures in Howdenshire. [Pp. 137–39, A.–S. period.] Trans. East Riding Antiq. Soc., 26, pp. 137–48. 1929.

3125 Shore (Thomas William). Boarhunt, and some of its early land tenures. Hants. Antiquary, 2, pp. 40–43. 1892.

3126 Skelton (Joseph). Anglo-Norman territorial claims in south Westmorland and north Lancashire. [Evolution from Anglo-Saxon occupation to feudal ownership.] Trans. Cumb. and Westm. Antiq. Soc., N.S. 42, pp. 159–69. 1942.

3127 Taylor (Isaac). The unit of Domesday land measures. [Wapentakes, etc.] N. and Q., 7th S. 2, pp. 405, 449, 481–82 ; 3, pp. 61–62, 92. 1886–87.

3128 Turner (G. J.). Bookland and folkland. Hist. essays presented to J. Tait, pp. 357–86. 1933.

3129 Vinogradoff (*Sir* Paul). Das Buchland. Vinogradoff (P.) Collected papers, 1, pp. 168–91. 1928.

3130 —— Folkland. E.H.R., 8, pp. 1–17. 1893.

3131 —— Folkland. Vinogradoff (P.) : Collected papers, 1, pp. 91–111. 1928.

3132 —— Romanistische Einflüsse im angelsächsischen Recht, das Buchland. [Gross, 1555, note.] Mélanges H. Fitting (Montpellier), 2, pp. 499–522. 1908.

3133 Vinogradoff (*Sir* Paul). Transfer of land in old English law. [Gross, 1555, note.] Harvard Law Rev., 20, pp. 532–48. 1907.

49. INDUSTRY AND TRADE

3134 Brasch (Carl). Die Namen der Werkzeuge im Altenglischen. Eine kulturhistorisch-etymologische Untersuchungen. *Diss., Kiel.* pp. 173. 8° Kiel, 1910.

3135 Cunningham (William). The growth of English industry and commerce during the early and middle ages. 4th edition. 8° Cambridge, 1915. pp. xxvi, 724. [Conquest of Britain, early changes in England, Danes, etc.]

3136 Fehr (Bernhard). Die Sprache des Handels in Altengland. Wirtschafts- und kulturgeschichtliche Beiträge zur englischen Wortforschung. pp. viii, 88. 8° St. Gallen, 1909.

3137 Harmer (Florence Elizabeth). *Chipping* and *market* : a lexicographical investigation. Chadwick Mem. Stud., pp. 333–60. 1950.

3138 Kletler (Paul). Nordwesteuropas Verkehr, Handel und Gewerbe in frühen Mittelalter. pp. 238, + map. 8° Wien, 1924. [Texts and remarks on travelling methods, with map of N.W. Europe, 600–900.]

3139 Klump (Wilhelm). Die altenglischen Handwerkernamen sachlich und sprachlich erläutert. *Anglistische Forschungen*, 24. pp. viii, 129. 8° Heidelberg, 1908.

3140 Leeds (Edward Thurlow). Anglo-Saxon exports : a criticism. [Evidence from brooches.] Antiq. J., 33, pp. 208–10. 1953.

3141 Lewis (E. A.). The development of industry and commerce in Wales during the Middle Ages. Trans. R.H.S., N.S. 17, pp. 121–73. 1903.

3142 Matzerath (Joseph). Die altenglischen Namen der Geldwerte. *Diss., Bonn.* pp. vii, 38. 8° Bonn, 1912.

3143 —— Die altenglischen Namen der Geldwerte, Masse und Gewichte, sachlich und sprachlich erläutert. pp. xvii, 128. 8° Bonn, 1913.

3144 Postan (Michael). The trade of medieval Europe : the north. [A.-S. merchants, trade, wool, etc.] Cambridge Economic History, 2, pp. 119–54. 1952.

3145 Simpson (Jesse James). The wool trade and the woolmen of Gloucestershire. [Pp. 65–67, A.-S. and Domesday.] Trans. Bristol and Glos. Arch. Soc., 53, pp. 65–97. 1931.

3146 Smirke (Edward). Tin trade between Britain and Alexandria in the seventh century [A.D.]. J. Roy. Inst. Cornwall, 2, pp. 283–91. 1867.

3147 Smith (A. L.). Trade and industry. Social England, ed. Traill and Mann, 1, pp. 294–304. 1901.

3148 Szogs (Arthur). Die Ausdrücke für 'Arbeit' und 'Beruf' im Altenglischen. *Anglistische Forschungen*, 73. pp. xv, 143. 8° Heidelberg, 1931. [Pp. 1–70, Kulturgeschichtlicher Teil.]

3149 Zimmer (Henrich). Über direkte Handelsverbindungen Westgalliens mit Irland im Altertum und frühen Mittelalter. [i. Zeugnisse für westgallisch-irischen Handelsverkehr von Giraldus Cambrensis (a. 1186) bis Tacitus (a. 98) : ii. Der Weinhandel Westgalliens im 1. bis 7. Jahrhundert a. Chr. und sein Niederschlag in irischer Sage und Sprache : iii. Galliens Anteil an Irlands Christianisierung im 4./5. Jahrhundert und altirischer Bildung.] Sitzungsber. k. preuss. Akad. Wiss., Hist.-phil. Cl., 1909, pp. 363–400, 430–76, 543–613 : 1910, 1031–1119. 1909–10.

50. SHIRES, SHERIFFS AND HUNDREDS

3150 Alexander (John James). Devonshire. [?division of England into shires in 9th and 10th c.] Devon and Cornwall N. and Q., 9, pp. 17–18. 1916.

3151 —— The hundred organization, [especially in Devon]. Rept. and Trans. Devon. Assoc., 72, pp. 107–14. 1940.

3152 —— The hundreds of Cornwall. Devon and Cornwall N. and Q., 18, pp. 177–82. 1934.

3153 Anderson, *afterwards* **Anderson-Arngardt** (Olof Sigfrid). The English hundred-names. [Yorks., Lancs. and Midlands]. pp. xlvii, 174. (The Southwestern counties, pp. xvii, 235. The south-eastern counties, with a survey of elements found in hundred-names and a chapter on the origin of the hundred. pp. xiii, 242). Lunds Univ. Årrskr., N.F., Avd. 1, 30, nr. 1 : 35, nr. 5 : 37, nr. 1. 1934, 1939, 1941.

3154 Anscombe (Alfred). The names of the Sussex hundreds in Domesday Book. Sussex Archaeol. Collns., 60, pp. 92–125. 1919.

3155 Barnes (William). On the origin of the hundred and tithing of English law. [Argument that Saxons found the hundred (*cantref*) as an institution of the Britons.] J. Brit. Archaeol. Assoc., 28, pp. 21–27. 1872.

3156 Braun (Hugh). The hundred of Gore and its moot-hedge. [Two maps in text. Domesday evidence.] Trans. Lond. and Middsx. Archaeol. Soc., N.S. 7, pp. 218–28, + 1 plate. 1937.

3157 Brentnall (Harold Cresswell). The hundreds of Wiltshire. [Including list of names in the Liber Exoniensis, (1083–4).] Wilts. Archaeol. Mag., 50, pp. 219–29. 1943.

3158 Cam (Helen Maud). Early groups of hundreds. [Domesday, etc.] Hist. essays in honour of J. Tait, pp. 13–25. 1938.

3159 —— The hundred outside the north gate of Oxford. Oxoniensia, 1, pp. 1113–28. 1936.

3160 —— The hundreds of Northamptonshire. J. Northants. Nat. Hist. Soc., 27, pp. 99–108, + 1 plate. 1934.

3161 Carter (George Edward Lovelace). History of the hundred in Devon. [i. Hundreds and hides : ii. Saxons and Danes in Devon : iii. Legislation of the 10th c. : iv. The royal power : v. New manors : vi. General conclusion, etc. Appendix—Danish names in the Devon Domesday.] Rept. and Trans. Devon. Assoc., 60, pp. 313–28, + map. 1928.

3162 Clarke (David K.). The Saxon hundreds of Sussex. Sussex Archaeol. Collns., 74, pp. 214–25. 1933.

3163 Davies (Arthur Morley). The ancient hundreds of Buckinghamshire. [Meaning of the order of sequence.—Names of the Domesday hundreds.—Origin of the county of Bucks.—Origin of detached parts.—Relation of hundreds to physical features. Map on p. 143.] Home Counties Mag., 6, pp. 134–44. 1904.

3164 —— The ancient hundreds of Buckinghamshire. [P. 115, map of Domesday hundreds.] Rec. Bucks., 9, pp. 104–19. 1909.

3164a —— The hundreds of Buckinghamshire and Oxfordshire. [Including Domesday material. 5 maps in text.] Rec. Bucks., 15, pp. 231–49. 1950.

3165 Farrer (William). The sheriffs of Lincolnshire and Yorkshire, 1066–1130. E.H.R., 30, pp. 277–85. 1915.

3166 Fry (*Sir* Edward). Somerset or Somersetshire. [? a 'shire' in A.-S. times.] Proc. Somerset Arch Soc., 49 (1903), pp. 1–11. 1904.

3166a Gomme (*Sir* George Laurence). Open-air courts of hundreds and manors. Proc. Soc. Antiq., 2nd S. 8, pp. 280–82. 1880.

3167 Great Britain, *Census.* Census, 1851. Population tables, vol. 1. fol. London, 1852. [Gross, 1564. Parl. papers, 85 (1852–53), pp. lvi–lxxxii, origin of shires, hundreds, etc.]

3168 Hudson (William). The hundred of Eastbourne and its six 'boroughs'. [Pp. 180–84 : i. Single-vill hundreds. ii. The hundred of Borne in Saxon times.] Sussex Archaeol. Collns., 42, pp. 180–208. 1899.

3169 Jenks (Edward). The problem of the hundred. [Criticism of Fustel de Coulanges' theories.] E.H.R., 11, pp. 510–14. 1896.

3170 Jolliffe (John Edward Austin). The origin of the hundred in Kent. Hist. essays in honour of J. Tait, pp. 155–68. 1933.

3171 Landon (L.). The sheriffs of Norfolk. [Pp. 148–50, A.-S. period.] Norfolk Archaeology, 23, pp. 147–65. 1929.

3172 Marshall (Edward). Hundred courts. [Omissions in **3166a**.] N. and Q., 6th S. 2, p. 203. 1880.

3173 Maurer (Konrad von). Das Vápnatak der nordischen Rechte. [Gross, 1569. Deals with the early history of the wapentake.] Germania, 16, pp. 317–33. 1871.

3174 Morris (William Alfred). The mediaeval English sheriff to 1300. pp. 309. 8° Manchester, 1927.

3175 —— The office of sheriff in the Anglo-Saxon period. E.H.R., 31, pp. 20–40. 1916.

3176 —— The office of sheriff in the early Norman period. E.H.R., 33, pp. 145–75. 1918.

3177 Reichel (Oswald Joseph). Barnstaple and its three sub-manors, part of the inland hundred of Braunton. [A little Domesday material.] Rept. and Trans. Devon. Assoc., 49, pp. 376–88. 1917.

3178 —— The Church and the hundreds in Devon. [Connection of Church organization with the hundred system.] *Same jnl.*, 71, pp. 331–42. 1939.

3179 —— The Domesday hundreds of Devon. 1. The hundred of Hartland and the Geldroll : 2. The hundred of Listone: 3. The hundred of North Tawton : [4, Apparently omitted] : 5. The hundred of Teignbridge : 6. The hundred of Witheridge (7 and 8. The hundreds of Bampton and Ufculm) : 9. The hundred of Budleigh in the time of Testa de Nevil, A.D. 1244 [but with Domesday evidence]: 10. The hundred of Haytor in the time of Testa de Nevil [but ditto] : 11. The hundred of Sulfretona or Hairidge in early times : 12. The early history of the hundred of Cadelintona or Colridge : 13. The Domesday hundred of Wenford or Wonford : [14 and 15 contain later material only.] *Same jnl.*, 26, pp. 416–18 : 28, pp. 464–93, + coloured folding map : 29, pp. 225–44, 245–74 : 30, pp. 391–457 : 35, pp. 279–317 : 40, pp. 110–37 : 42, pp. 215–57 : 43, pp. 190–236 : 44, pp. 278–311, 353–65 (index). 1894–1912.

3180 Reichel (Oswald Joseph). The hundred of Exminster in early times. [iv. Constituents of the Domesday hundred : v. The evidence of the Geldroll, 1084.] *Same jnl.*, 47, pp. 194–209, 237–47 (index). 1915.

3181 —— The hundreds of Devon (supplementary). *Devonshire Association.* pp. 584. 8° Plymouth, 1928–38.

3182 —— Index of personal and place-names in the hundreds of Devon. *Devonshire Association.* pp. 405. 8° Plymouth, 1942.

3183 —— The manor and hundred of Crediton. [ii Acquisition of the ownership by bishop Eadulf, (909–34) : iii. The hundred according to the Geldroll and the Great Survey.] Rept. and Trans. Devon. Assoc., 54, pp. 146–81. 1923.

3184 Rietschel (Siegfried). Untersuchungen zur Geschichte der germanischen Hundertschaft.—1. Die skandinavische und angelsächsische Hundertschaft. [Gross, 1569. 'Hundred originally comprised 100 hides.' *See also*, ibid., 42, pp. 261–304; 43, pp. 193–223.] Zeit. f. Rechtsgesch., 41, Germ. Abt., 28, pp. 342–434. 1907.

3185 Rose-Troup (Frances). Pre-Conquest hundreds of Devon. (Résumé). Rept. and Trans. Devon. Assoc., 70, pp. 146–49. 1938.

3186 Round (John Horace). The hundred of Swanborough [Sussex]. [Domesday, etc.] Archaeol. Rev., 4, pp. 223–25. 1889.

3187 Rowe (Joseph Hambley). The boundaries of hundreds [in Devon and Cornwall], ancient and modern. (The hundreds of Cornwall). Devon and Cornwall N. and Q., 11, pp. 256–57; 12, pp. 325–26. 1921–23.

3188 Schwerin (Claudius), *Frieherr von*. Die altgermanische Hundertschaft. *Untersuchungen zur deutschen Staats-und Rechtsgeschichte* (*v. Gierke*), 90. pp. viii, 215. 8° Breslau, 1907. [Gross, 1569. Including A.-S. hundreds.]

3189 Stephenson (Carl). The 'firma unius noctis' and the customs of the hundred. E.H.R., 39, pp. 161–74. 1924.

3190 Stevenson (William Henry). The hundreds of Domesday. 1. The hundred of land. E.H.R., 5, pp. 95–100. 1890.

3191 Taylor (Charles Samuel). The origin of the Mercian shires. Trans. Bristol and Glos. Arch. Soc., 21, pp. 32–57. 1898.

3192 Taylor (Isaac). Wapentakes and hundreds. Domesday Studies, 1, pp. 67–76. 1888.

3193 Tout (Thomas Frederick). The Welsh shires : a study in constitutional history. [Pp. 201–04, Domesday and pre-1087.] Y Cymmrodor, 9, pp. 201–26. 1888.

3194 Walker (Benjamin). The hundreds of Warwickshire. [P. 29, ' Diagram to show the positions of the hundreds, A.D. 1086.'] Trans. B'ham. Arch. Soc., 31, pp. 22–46. 1905.

3195 —— The hundreds of Warwickshire in the time of the Domesday survey. [With map.] Antiquary, 39, pp. 146–51, 179–84. 1903.

3196 Walters (H. B.). The Wiltshire hundreds. [Domesday, etc.] Wilts. Archaeol. Mag, 46, pp. 301–11, + map. 1933.

3197 Ward (Gordon). The lathe of Aylesford in 975. [=administrative district.] Arch. Cant., 46, pp. 7–26. 1934.

3198 Worth (Richard Nicholls). Domesday identifications—the hundreds. Rept. and Trans. Devon. Assoc., 27, pp. 374–403. 1895.

51. SOCIAL STATUS

3199 Alexander (John James) and **Finberg** (Herbert Patrick Reginald). Manumissions [of slaves] by Ordgar and others. [Quoted by Birch from pp. 3 and 6 of Leofric's Missal. (i) Queries date c. 970 : (ii) date is 1030–50, and manumissions are in different hands.] Devon and Cornwall N. and Q., 22, pp. 96–97, 135–36. 1942.

3200 Bjoerkmann (Erik). Die Festermen des Ælfric. Eine Namenliste aus York. [Ms. c. 1100, York Gospels.] Festschrift für L. Morsbach, pp. 1–19. 1913.

3201 Bromberg (Erik I.). Wales and the mediaeval slave trade. [Obtained in A.-S. border raids and sold by Gallo-Jewish merchants, and also obtained by Viking raiders for sale in Iceland, etc.] Speculum, 17, pp. 263–69. 1942.

3202 Brownrow (William Robert Bernard), *bishop of Clifton.* Were the Devonshire villani serfs? [Domesday material.] Rept. and Trans. Devon. Assoc., 19, pp. 438–50. 1887.

3203 Corner (George Richard). On the custom of Borough English, as existing in the county of Sussex. [Thesis that it was imposed by Norman lords as a mark of serfdom on their English vessels. Pp. 178–89, list of manors in Sussex in which the customary descent is to the youngest son, with possessors in Domesday Book.] Sussex Archaeol. Collns., 6, pp. 164–89. 1853.

3204 Devenish (W. H.). Widcombe Lyncombe's Anglo-Saxon Gospel Book. [5 manumissions on flyleaf from C.C.C.C., MS. 140, now in MS. 111.] N. and Q Som. and Dorset, 17, pp. 1–2, + 1 plate. 1923.

3205 Dodwell (Barbara). The free peasantry of East Anglia in Domesday. [Maps show: ' Distribution of free peasantry in 1066,' and ' Distribution of free peasantry, sheep, and woodland.'] Norfolk Archaeology, 27, pp. 145–57, + 2 maps. 1941.

3206 —— The sokemen of the southern Danelaw of the eleventh century. (Summaries of theses.–clv.) Bull. Inst. Hist. Res., 15, pp. 110–12. 1938.

3207 Elton (Charles). Villainage in England. Law Q.R., 8, pp. 117–28. 1892.

3208 Foerster (Max). Die Freilassungs-urkunden des Bodmin-Evangeliars. [With text in Latin and A.-S.] Grammatical miscellany offered to Otto Jespersen, pp. 77–99. 1930.

3209 Henning (R.). Ags. *birel.* [Occurs in laws of Æthelbirht (6th c.). Female servant of high status in household of *ceorl.*] Z.f.d.A., 37, pp. 317–19. 1893.

3210 Hermann (Franz Wilhelm Emil). Die Ständegliederung bei den alten Sachsen und Angelsachsen. *Gierke (Otto): Untersuchungen zur deutschen Staats-und Rechtsgeschichte*, 17. pp. v, 148. 8° Breslau, 1884. [Gross, 1547. Tries to prove ' laeti ' formed basis of wergeld system : unconvincing. Appendix deals with folkland and bookland.]

3211 Heywood (Samuel). A dissertation upon the distinctions in society, and ranks of the people, under the Anglo-Saxon governments. 8° London, 1818. [Gross, 1548.]

3212 Hudson (William). Status of villain and other tenants in Danish East Anglia in pre-Conquest times. Trans. R.H.S., 4th S., 4, pp. 23–48. 1921.

3213 Jenner (Henry). The manumissions in the Bodmin Gospels. J. Roy. Inst. Cornwall, 21, pp. 235–60. 1924.

3214 Lennard (Reginald). The economic position of the Domesday sokemen. Econ. J., 57, pp. 179–95. 1947.

3215 Liebermann (Felix). Die Abfassungszeit von Rectitudines singularum personarum und ags. *aferian.* [Gross, 1401, note. Temp. Cnut.] Arch. Stud. neueren Spr., Bd. 109, pp. 13–82. 1902.

3216 —— Angelsächsisch *færbena.* [Rusticus.] *Same jnl.*, Bd. 120, pp. 397–400. 1908.

3217 Lindkvist (Harald). Some notes on Elfric's festermen. [Place-name evidence to help in their identification.] Anglia, Beiblatt, 33, pp. 130–44. 1922.

3218 Little (Andrew George). Gesiths and thanes. E.H.R., 4, pp. 723–29. 1889.

3219 Loyn (H. R.). The term ealdorman in the translations prepared at the time of King Alfred. E.H.R., 68, pp. 513–25. 1953.

3220 Massingberd (W. O.). The Lincolnshire sokemen. [Domesday, etc.] E.H.R., 20, pp. 699–703. 1905.

3221 Pollock (*Sir* Frederick). Early English freeholders. Rept. and Trans. Devon. Assoc., 26, pp. 25–40. 1894.

3222 Reid (Rachel Robertson). Barony and thanage. E.H.R., 35, pp. 161–199. 1920.

3223 Round (John Horace). Molmen and Molland. [A.-S. rent.] E.H.R., 2, p. 103. 1887.

3224 Rowe (Joseph Hambley). Anglo-Saxon manumissions. [Inscribed on 8th leaf of Leofric's Missal, but omitted from Thorpe's Diplomatarium.] Devon and Cornwall N. and Q., 12, pp. 251–54. 1923.

3225 Rutter (J. A.) and **Reichel** (Oswald Joseph). Domesday and the geld inquests : villeins on the comital manors. N. and Q., 12th S. 9, pp. 65–7, 152, 192. 1921.

3226 Rutter (J. A.). Domesday : villeins on comital manors. [Returned as not paying geld.] Devon and Cornwall N. and Q., 11, pp. 310–15. 1921.

3227 Stenton (*Sir* Frank Merry). The free peasantry of the northern Danelaw. [Including Domesday material.] Bull. Soc. Roy. Lettres, Lund, 1925–26, pp. 72–185. 1926.

3228 Stevenson (William Henry). Molmen [rent]. E.H.R., 2, pp. 332–36. 1887.

3229 Stokes (Whitley). The manumissions [of slaves] in the Bodmin Gospels. [Corrections of Gilbert's published text : index of Celtic names. MS. B.M. Addit., 9067. 10th, or early 11th, c.] Rev. celt., 1, pp. 332–45. 1871.

3230 Vinogradoff (*Sir* Paul). Molmen and Molland. E.H.R., 1, pp. 734–7. 1886.

3231 Warren (Frederick Edward). Manumissions in the Leofric Missal. [A.-S. text and notes. Names of persons and places. Often done at cross-roads.] Rev. celt., 5, pp. 213–17. 1882.

3232 Wright (Joseph). On slavery, as it existed in England during the Saxon era, and the substitution of villenage after the Norman Conquest, until its gradual extinction. Trans. Hist. Soc. Lancs. and Ches., 10, pp. 207–30. 1858.

52. TENURE
§ *a.* Cornage

3233 Barnes (George Edward). The Pusey horn ; the Borstall horn. Oxfordshire Archaeol. Soc., Rpt. 38 (1899), pp. 28–31, + 1 plate. 1900.

3234 Borstal Horn. Of the Borstal horn. [Grant by Edward the Confessor to Nigel, a huntsman, of Derehyde, Hulewode, etc., per unum cornu.] Archaeologia, 3, pp. 15–18, + 1 plate. 1786.

3235 Bridge (Joseph C.). Horns. [Cornage. Pp. 119–121 + plate 6, on the horn of Ulphus.] J. Archit. and Hist. Soc. Chester, N.S. 11, pp. 85–166, + 13 plates. 1905.

3236 Brown (Robert), *jr.* The unicorn ; a mythological investigation. pp. vii, 97. 8° London, 1881. [Pp. 44–45, + frontispiece, the horn of Ulf.]

3237 Gale (Samuel). An historical dissertation upon the ancient Danish horn, kept in the cathedral church of York. [Horn of Ulphus. Figure on p. 202* shows runes. *See also* **11,450** and **11,453**]. Archaeologia, 1, pp. 187–202.* 1770.

3238 MacMichael (James Holden). The horn of Ulphus in York minster. J. Brit. Archaeol. Assoc., 48, pp. 251–62. 1892.

3239 Pegge (Samuel). Of the horn, as a charter or instrument of conveyance. Some observations on Samuel Foxlowe's horn ; as likewise on the nature and kinds of these horns in general. [Horn of Ulphus, etc.] Archaeologia, 3, pp. 1–12, + 1 plate. 1786.

3240 Pusey Horn. In the auction rooms : the Pusey horn, an Anglo-Saxon horn, with English fifteenth century mounts. [For £1,900, at Sotheby's.] Connoisseur, 96, pp. 53–54. 1935.

3241 —— Of the Pusey horn. ['The family of Pusey hold by a horn given to their ancestors by Canute.'] Archaeologia, 3, pp. 13–14, + 1 plate. 1786.

3242 Radnor (Jacob Pleydell-Bouverie), *6th earl.* Observations on the Pusey horn. Archaeologia, 12, pp. 397–400. 1796.

§ b. Other

3243 Coghlan (Daniel). The ancient land tenures of Ireland. pp. 311, vii. 8° Dublin, 1933.

3244 Couch (Thomas Quiller). Coliberti. [Tenure : in Cornish Domesday.] N. and Q., 3rd S. 5, p. 300. 1864.

3245 Dodwell (Barbara). East Anglian commendation. E.H.R., 63, pp. 289–306. 1948.

3246 Elton (Charles). Early English land tenures. ii. Domesday studies. Law Q.R., 4, pp. 276–85. 1888.

3247 Elton (Charles Isaac). The tenures of Kent. pp. xx, 424. 8° London, 1867. [Gavelkind : tenures in Kent before the Conquest : pp. 113–51, Domesday : tenure in burgage, etc.]

3248 Graham (T. H. B.). Border tenure. [A.-S. survivals : *noutgeld* and *endemot*.] Trans. Cumb. and Westm. Antiq. Soc., N.S. 25, op. 86–95. 1925.

3249 —— Servile tenures. [Including drengage under the Confessor and William I.] *Same jnl.*, N.S. 30, pp. 44–54. 1930.

3250 Hemmeon (Morley de Wolf). Burgage tenure in mediaeval England. *Harvard Historical Studies*, 20. pp. ix, 234. 8° Cambridge, Mass., 1914. [Gross, 728 b. Pp. 158–66, Burgage tenure in Domesday.]

3251 —— Burgage tenure in mediaeval England.-3. [Pp. 49–51, Burgage tenure in Domesday : pp. 51–53, Burgage tenure and the tenurial laws of Breteuil.] Law Q.R., 27, pp. 43–59. 1911.

3252 Kovalevsky (Maxime). Early English land tenures.—i. Mr. Vinogradoff's work. Law Q.R., 4, pp. 266–75. 1888.

3253 Mackay (Æneas James George). Notes and queries on the custom of gavel kind in Kent, Ireland, Wales, and Scotland. Proc. Soc. Antiq. Scot., 32 (3rd S. 8), pp. 133–58. 1898.

3254 O'Hanlon (John). Ancient Irish land tenures. Irish Eccles. Rec., 3rd S. 11, pp. 235–41. 1890.

3255 Pearce (Ernest Harold), *bp. of Worcester*. The tenure of Hartlebury. [A.-S. and Domesday material.] Trans. Worcs. Archaeol. Soc., 2 (1924–25), pp. 59–74. 1925.

3256 Round (John Horace). Military tenure before the Conquest. E.H.R., 12, pp. 492–94. 1898.

3257 Sandys (Charles). Consuetudines Kanciæ. A history of gavelkind and other remarkable customs in the county of Kent. pp. xvi, 352, + 4 plates. 8° London, 1851.

3258 Taylor (Silas). The history of gavel-kind. pp. xxv, 211. 8° London, 1663. [A.-S. passim.]

53. VILLAGE COMMUNITY AND MANOR

3259 Allen (William Francis). Essays and monographs. pp. vi, 392. 8° Boston, 1890. [Gross, 719. Pp. 240–56, Village community and serfdom : pp. 257–85, Manor, township, tithing, etc. : pp. 293–9, A.-S. ranks and classes : pp. 319–30, Rural population in Domesday : etc.]

3260 Andrews (Charles McLean). The old English manor. A study in English economic history. *Johns Hopkins University Studies in History, extra vol.* 12. pp. xiii, 291. 8° Baltimore, 1892. [Gross, 1556. Lands and tenants, agricultural arrangements, recreations, etc.]

3261 Ashbridge (Arthur). St. Marylebone and its Anglo-Saxon manors : an attempt to define their boundaries. Trans. Lond. and Middsx. Archaeol. Soc., N.S. 4, pp. 56–74, + plan. 1922.

3262 Ashley (*Sir* William James). An introduction to English economic history and theory. . . . The Middle Ages. 3rd edition. pp. xvi, 227. 8° London, 1894. [Gross, 1193. Bk. 1, Ch. 1, A.-S. manorial history.]

3263 Baildon (William Paley). Vinogradoff on the manor. Law Q.R., 21, pp. 294–300. 1905.

3264 Corbett (William John) and **Methold** (Thomas Tindal). The rise and devolution of the manors in Hepworth, Suffolk. [Pp. 19–23, Domesday material.] Proc. Suffolk Inst. Archaeol., 10, pp. 19–48. 1900.

3265 Drew (Charles D.). The manors of the Iwerne valley, Dorset. A study of early country planning. [With Domesday material.] Proc. Dorset Archaeol. Soc., 69 (1947), pp. 45–50. 1948.

3266 Earle (John). The villa and the manor. Econ. J., 2, pp. 744–77. 1892.

3267 Ellis (Alfred Shelley). On the manorial history of Clifton. [Domesday, etc.] Trans. Bristol. and Glos. Arch. Soc., 3, pp. 211–31. 1879.

3268 Evelyn-White (Charles Harold). The story of Cottenham, co. Cambridge. [Pp. 55–61, 'The manors in Domesday times'.] Trans. Cambs. and Hunts. Archaeol. Soc., 2 (1904–07), pp. 55–97. 1908.

3269 Gomme (*Sir* George Laurence). Chippenham as a village community. Archaeol. Rev., 1, pp. 102–08, 203–10. 1888.

3270 —— The history of Malmesbury as a village community. Archaeologia, 50, pp. 421–38. 1887.

3271 —— The village community at Aston and Cote in Oxfordshire. [Evidences of A.-S. origins.] Archaeol. Rev., 2, pp. 29–44. 1888.

3272 —— The village community, with special reference to the origin and form of its survivals in Britain. pp. xi, 299. 8° London, 1890. [Gross, 1558. Contends that it existed in Celtic as well as A.-S. England.]

3273 Hudson (William). The Anglo-Danish village community of Martham, Norfolk : its pre-Domesday tenants and their conversion into the customary tenants of a feudal manor in 1101. Norfolk Archaeology, 20, pp. 273–316, + 2 maps. 1921.

3274 —— Manorial life. [i. Agricultural tenants in pre-manorial days : ii. An Anglo-Saxon community (Mar-tham, Norfolk) at the time of the Conquest.] History Teachers' Miscellany, 1, pp. 97–100, 116–20. 1923.

3275 Huntbach (A.). Manors and the duchy of Lancaster. [Pp. 13–15, A.-S. period.] North Staffs. F.C., Trans., 74, pp. 13–21. 1940.

3276 Kenyon (R. Lloyd). The Domesday manors of Ruyton, Wikey and Felton. Trans. Shrop. Arch. Soc., 2nd S. 12, pp. 64–83. 1900.

3277 Leo (Heinrich), *ed.* Rectitudines singularum personarum, nebst einer einleitenden Abhandlungen über Landansidlung, Landbau, gutsherrliche und bauerliche Verhältnisse der Angelsachsen. 8° Halle, 1842. [Gross 349, 1401. Early 11th c. Exposition of the services rendered to the lord by various classes of persons on a manor. Pp. 1–104, Die angelsächsischen Ortsnamen.]

3278 Lipson (Ephraim). The economic history of England. Vol. 1, the Middle Ages. Seventh edition, revised and enlarged. pp. xii, 674. 8° London, 1937. [Pp. 1–87, the origin of the manor, the manor and the open field system : etc.]

3279 Maine (*Sir* Henry James Sumner). Village communities in the east and west. 3rd edition. pp. xii, 413. 8° London, 1876. [Gross, 1559. Chap. 3, the western village community ; chap. 5, the process of feudalisation.]

3280 Middleton (John Henry). Notes on the manor and parish church of Cheltenham. [Domesday entry in Latin and translation.] Trans. Bristol and Glos. Arch. Soc., 4, pp. 53–72. 1879.

3281 Pugh (R. B.). The early history of the manors in Amesbury. [Pp. 70–72, Amesbury before 1086.] Wilts. Archaeol. Mag., 52, pp. 70–110. 1947.

3282 Reichel (Oswald Joseph). The early history of the principal manors in Exminster hundred. [A little A.-S. and Domesday material.] Rept. and Trans. Devon. Assoc., 47, pp .210–247. 1915.

3283 Round (John Horace). The Domesday 'manor'. E.H.R., 15, pp. 293–302. 1900.

3284 **Rutton** (William Loftie). The manor of Eia, or Eye next Westminster. [Pp. 31–33, Domesday boundaries.] Archaeologia, 62, pp. 31–58, + map. 1910.

3285 **Scrutton** (Thomas Edward) Commons and common fields, or the history of the laws relating to commons and enclosures in England. pp. viii, 180. 8° Cambridge, 1887. [Gross, 735. Ch. 1, the early history of the manor.]

3286 **Seebohm** (Frederic). The English village community, examined in its relations to the manorial and tribal systems and to the common or open field system of husbandry. An essay in economic history. pp. xxii, 464, + 13 maps. 8° London, 1883. [Gross, 1222. 'Throws much light on the early agricultural system.' Pp. 82–104, Domesday Survey.]

3287 —— Serfdom in its relations to the open-field system. [Abstract of a paper ' to examine whether the English open-field system, in early Saxon times, was the shell of a free village community, or of a community in serfdom ' : with discussion.] Proc. Soc. Antiq., 2nd S. 8, pp. 355–58. 1880.

3288 **Sharpe** (*Sir* Montagu). Middlesex parishes and their antiquity. [Pp. 96–98 : tables of (1) 31 manors and vills mentioned in Saxon charters : (2) 22 Domesday manors and vills not mentioned in extant Saxon charters : (3) 12 Domesday and 5 charter vills subsequently merged in adjoining places.] Trans. Lond. and Middsx. Archaeol. Soc., N.S. 7, pp. 91–98. 1937.

3289 **Stenton** (*Sir* Frank Merry). Types of manorial structure in the northern Danelaw. *Oxford studies in social and legal history*, 2, *pp.* 3–96. 8° Oxford, 1910.

3290 **Vinogradoff** (*Sir* Paul). The growth of the manor. 2nd edition. pp. xi, 384. 8° London, 1911. [Bk. 2 (pp. 117–287), The Old English period. i. The English conquest : ii. The grouping of the folk : iii. The shares in the township : iv. The open field system : v. The history of the holding : vi. Manorial origins. Bk. 3, The feudal period. (pp. 291–365) The principles of the Domesday survey, etc.]

54. GENERAL

§ a. Anglo-Saxon

3291 Allison (Thomas). English religious life in the eighth century, as illustrated by contemporary letters. pp. xvi, 154. 8° London, 1929.

3292 Almack (A. C.). Wessex minsters. ['Reasons for considering the Wessex places which bear the suffix of "minster" to be the early stations of the missions of the Saxon Church, etc.'] Proc. Dorset Antiq. F.C., 38 (1916–17), pp. 59–67. 1918.

3293 Andrews (Herbert C.). Synod at Hertford [673]. East Herts Archaeol. Soc. Trans., 9, i (1934), pp. 24–32. 1935.

3294 Baron (J.). Report on the Anglo-Saxon documents in Wilkins's Concilia [3356]. pp. 40. 8° *for private circulation*, 1859.

3295 Boehmer (Heinrich). Kirche und Staat in England und in der Normandie im XI. und XII. Jahrhundert. pp. xii, 498. 8° Leipzig, 1899. [Pp. 42–79, Die englische Kirche im Jahre 1066 : pp. 79–126, Die Reform der englischen Kirche unter Wilhelm dem Eroberer und Lanfrank.]

3296 Bridgett (Thomas Edward). A history of the holy eucharist in Great Britain. With notes by Herbert Thurston. pp. xix, 325. fol. London, 1908. [Pp. 8–50, Picts and Scots, and A.-S. period.]

3297 Bright (William). Chapters of early English Church history. 3rd edition, revised, enlarged. pp. xx, 525, + map. 8° Oxford, 1897. [Gross, 1951. 597 to the death of Wilfrid. Ch. 1, ancient Celtic Church.]

3298 Browne (George Forrest), *bp. of Bristol*. The English Church in the eighth century : its influence on the continent of Europe. *Stafford House Lectures*, pp. 119. 8° London, 1897.

3299 Browne (George Forrest), *bp. of Bristol*. Lessons from early English Church history. pp. 115. 8° London, 1893.

3300 —— Theodore and Wilfrith. pp. 303. 8° London, 1897. [Gross, 1659.]

3301 Cabrol (Fernand). L'Angleterre chrétienne avant les Normands. *Bibliothèque de l'enseignement d'histoire écclesiastique.* pp. xxiii, 341. 8° Paris, 1909.

3302 Caraman (P. G.). The character of the late Saxon clergy. Downside Rev., 63, pp. 171–89. 1945.

3303 Chambers (John David). Anglo-Saxonica ; or animadversions on some positions . . . maintained in [3343]. pp. 66. 8° London, 1849.

3304 Chanter (John Frederick). Christianity in Devon before A.D. 909. Rept. and Trans. Devon. Assoc., 42, pp. 475–502. 1910.

3305 Churton (Edward). The early English Church. New edition. pp. xxiv, 404. 8° London, 1878. [Gross, 743. Popular : to Henry III.]

3306 Collingwood (William Gershom). Christian Vikings [in England]. Antiquity, 1, pp. 172–80. 1927.

3307 Cravens (Mary Joseph). Designations and treatment of the Holy Eucharist in Old and Middle English before 1300. A dissertation. *Catholic University of America.* pp. xi, 76. 8° Washington, 1932.

3308 Darlington (Reginald Ralph). Ecclesiastical reform in the late Old English period. E.H.R., 51, pp. 385–428. 1936.

3309 Deanesly (Margaret). Early English and Gallic minsters. [Appendix : The charters of King Aethelberht.] Trans. R.H.S., 4th S., 23, pp. 25–69. 1941.

3310 —— A history of the medieval Church, 590–1500. pp. 288, +2 maps. 8° London, 1925. [Connexion between English and continental movements.]

3311 Ebert (Adolf). Allgemeine Geschichte der Literatur des Mittelalters im Abandlande. (2. Auflage to Bd. 1, 1889.). 3 vol. 8° Leipzig, 1874–87. [Gross, 21. To beginning of 11th c. i, pp. 622–59, ii, pp. 12–36, Winfrid, Alcuin, Boniface : ii, pp. 387–91, iii, pp. 239–50, Nennius, A.-S. C., etc. : iii, pp. 3–96, 492–520, A.-S. poetry, lives of saints, homilies.]

3312 Fisher (D. J. V.). The Church in England between the death of Bede and the Danish invasions. Trans. Roy. Hist. Soc., 5th S. 2, pp. 1–19. 1952.

3313 Gage (John). The Anglo-Saxon ceremonial of the dedication and consecration of churches, illustrated from a pontifical in the public library at Rouen. Archaeologia, 25, pp. 235–74, + 3 plates. 1834.

3314 Gee (Henry) and **Hardy** (William John). Documents illustrative of English Church history, compiled from original sources. pp. xii, 670. 8° London, 1896. [Nos. 2–17, A.-S. period. In translation.]

3315 Greenwell (William). Durham cathedral. [Pp. 163–75, A.-S. ecclesiastical history : Cuthbert, Bede, etc.] Trans. Archit. Soc. of Durham, 2 (1869–79), pp. 163–234, + plan. 1883.

3316 Haddan (Arthur West) and **Stubbs** (William), *bp. of Oxford.* Councils and ecclesiastical documents relating to Great Britain and Ireland. 3 vol. [in 4], 8° Oxford, 1869–78. [Gross, 1424. A new ed. of Wilkins' Concilia. i. British Church, 200–681 : Wales, 681–1295 : ii. Cumbria and Scotland to 1188 and Ireland to 665 : iii. A.-S. to 870.]

3317 Haddan (Arthur West). Remains : edited by A. P. Forbes. 8° Oxford, 1876 [1875.] [Gross, 1592. ' Pp. 211–39, the Churches of the British confession ; pp. 258–94, Britons on the continent ; pp. 294–329, the early English Church.']

3318 Hamilton (Marie Padgett). The religious principle in *Beowulf.* [Assimilation of the Germanic tradition by the new theology.] P.M.L.A., 61, pp. 309–30. 1946.

M

3319 Hatch (Edwin). The growth of Church institutions. pp. xv, 227. 8° London, 1887. [Gross, 1593.]

3320 Hole (Charles). Early missions to and within the British islands. pp. xi, 244. 8° London, 1895.

3321 Howorth (*Sir* Henry Hoyle). The golden days of the early English Church, from the arrival of Theodore to the death of Bede. 2 vol. 8° London, 1917.

3322 Hunt (William). The English Church from its foundation to the Norman Conquest (597–1066). *A history of the English Church,* 1. pp. xix, 444, + 2 maps. 8° London, 1901. [Gross, 1594.]

3323 Joyce (James Wayland). England's sacred synods. A constitutional history of the convocations of the clergy . . . including a list of all councils, *etc.* pp. 751. 8° London, 1855. [Pp. 124–98, A.-S. synods and councils.]

3324 Keyser (Jacob Rudolph). The religion of the Northmen. Translated by B. Pennock. 8° London, 1854.

3325 Klaeber (Frederick). Die christlichen Elemente in Beowulf. Anglia, 35 (N.F.23), pp. 111–36, 249–70, 453–82 : 36, pp. 169–99. 1912–13.

3326 Latourette (Kenneth Scott). History of the expansion of Christianity. Vol. 2 The thousand years of uncertainty. A.D. 500–A.D.1500. 8° London, 1938.

3327 Levien (Edward). On unpublished Devonshire manuscripts in the British Museum [Cottonian Rolls, ii. 11]. [Pp. 135–36, days of indulgence obtained by Ethelgar, second bp. of Crediton, for benefactors of his church : c. 940. Translation.] J. Brit. Archaeol. Assoc., 18, pp. 134–45. 1862.

3328 Lightfoot (Joseph Barber), *bp. of Durham.* Leaders in the northern Church: sermons, *etc.* pp. xii, 203. 8° London, 1890.

3329 Lingard (John). The history and antiquities of the Anglo-Saxon church. Reprinted. 2 vols. 8° London, 1858. [Gross, 1595. Bishops, synods, monks, missions, religious practices, literature, etc.]

3330 MacCabe (William Bernard). A Catholic history of England. Part 1, England, its rulers, clergy, and poor, before the Reformation, as described by the monkish historians. 3 vol. 8° London, 1847–54.   [A.-S. period: no more published.]

3330a MacNeill (John) and **Carnoy** (Albert Joseph). Celtic and Teutonic religions. *Catholic Truth Society. Studies in comparative religion.* pp. 32. 8° London, 1935.

3331 Maude (J. H.). The English Church. Social England, ed. Traill and Mann, 1, pp. 224–39. 1891.

3332 Peake (Harold John Edward). Where were the councils of ' Chelsea ' held ? Antiquary, 39, pp. 363–69. 1903.

3333 Perry (George Gresley). A history of the English Church. 3rd edition. 3 vol. 8° London, 1887. [Vol. 1, pp. 18–175, A.-S. period.]

3334 Phillpotts (*Dame* Bertha Surtees). Wyrd and providence in Anglo-Saxon thought. Essays and studies (English Assocn.), 13, pp. 7–27. 1928.

3335 Pierquin (Hubert). Les annales et conciles de l'Église d'Angleterre pendant la période anglo-saxonne. pp. 595. 8° Paris, 1913. [Kenney, 1, p. 776.]

3336 Plummer (Alfred). The Churches in Britain before A.D. 1000. 2 vol. 8° London, 1911–12. [Gross, 1595a.]

3337 Rauschen (Gerhard). Eucharistie und Buszsakrament in den ersten sechs Jahrhundert der Kirche. 2. Auflage. pp. xi, 252. 8° Freiburg i. B., 1910. —. Traduit . . . par Michel Dicker et E. Ricard. pp. xi, 245. 8° Paris, 1910. [Kenney, 1, pp. 235–36.]

3338 Sansom (J.). Athelstane's form of donation [to church of High Bickington,Devon]—meaning of somagia. N. and Q., 1st S. 2, p. 120. 1850.

3339 Schubert (Hans von). Geschichte der christlichen Kirche im Frühmittelalter. pp. xxiv, 808. 8° Tübingen, 1921.   [Pp. 263–87, Die angelsächsische Kirche : pp. 288–305, Die Begründung der deutschen Kirche

durch Bonifatius : pp. 468–79, Die angelsächsische Kirche bis zu Alfred d. Grossen : etc.]

3340 Sheldon (Gilbert). The transition from Roman Britain to Christian England, A.D. 368–664. pp. xxiii, 219, + map. 8° London, 1932.

3341 Soames (Henry). The Anglo-Saxon Church : its history, revenues and general character. 4th edition, revised, *etc.* pp. 295. 8° London, 1856. [Gross, 1597.]

3342 —— An inquiry into the doctrines of the Anglo-Saxon Church. 8° Oxford, 1830. [Gross, 1596.]

3343 —— The Latin Church during Anglo-Saxon times. 8° London, 1848. [Gross, 1598.]

3344 Solloway (J.). The primate of England. [Pp. 657–61, A.-S. period. York *v.* Canterbury, claims for precedence.] Assoc. Archit. Socs'. Rpts., 30, pp. 655–64. 1910.

3345 Stapleton (Thomas). Historical details of the ancient religious community of secular canons in York prior to the Conquest. . . [i.e.] Holy Trinity otherwise called Christ Church ; . . . with biographical notices of the founder, Ralph Paynell, *etc.* Mems. Archaeol. Inst., [2] (1846), pp. 1–231, + 3 plates. 1848.

3346 Stevens (William Oliver). The cross in the life and literature of the Anglo-Saxons. *Yale Studies in English,* 23. pp. 105. 8° New York, 1904.

3347 Storm (A. V.). Early English influence on the Danish Church. [A.-S. Church and Denmark.] Saga-Book V.C., 7, pp. 220–31. 1912.

3348 Taranger (Absalon). Den angelsaksiske Kirkes. Inflydelse paa den Norske. *Norske Historisk Forening.* pp. xii, 459. 8° Christiania, 1890. [Gross, 1617b.]

3349 Thompson (Alexander Hamilton). The jurisdiction of the archbishops of York in Gloucestershire, with some notes on the history of the priory of St. Oswald at Gloucester. [Pp. 86–95, A.-S. period.] Trans. Bristol and Glos. Arch. Soc., 43, pp. 85–180. 1921.

3350 Timmer (Benno John). Heathen and Christian elements in Old English poetry. [Blending of ideas.] Neophilol., 29, pp. 180–85. 1944.

3351 —— Wyrd in Anglo-Saxon prose and poetry. Neophilol., 26, pp. 24–33, 213–28. 1941.

3352 Tupper (Frederick), *jr*. History and texts of the Benedictine reform of the tenth century. [Gross, 1440.] Mod. Lang. Notes, 8, pp. 344–67. 1893.

3353 Ussher (James), *abp. of Armagh*. Britannicarum ecclesiarum antiquitates. Editio secunda . . . aucta. 2 pts. fol. Londini, 1687. [Gross, 1599. Reprinted *in his* whole works, vols. 5–6. Dublin, 1847–64.]

3354 Varah (William Edward). Minsters. [Use of term in A.-S.C. 'Any church served by priests in common.'] N. & Q., 165, pp. 148–49. 1933.

3355 Watson (E. W.). The age of Bede. Bede : 12th centenary essays : ed. A. H. Thompson, pp. 39–59. 1935.

3356 Wilkins (David). Concilia Magnae Britanniae et Hiberniae, a Synodo Verolamiensi, A.D. 446 ad Londiniensem A.D. 1717. 4 vol. fol. London, 1737. [Gross, 631. *See also* **3294**. Earlier portions now superseded by Haddon and Stubbs, **3316**.]

§ b. Celtic

3357 [Anon.] The Celtic Church in Wales. Church Q. Rev., 45, pp. 130–51. 1898.

3358 [Anon.] The early Celtic Church. *Same jnl.*, 7, pp. 149–79. 1879.

3359 [Anon.] The origins of Irish Christianity. *Same jnl.*, 28, pp. 391–414. 1889.

3360 [Anon.] The position of the old Irish Church. *Same jnl.*, 21, pp. 89–96. 1886.

3361 Anderson (Joseph). Scotland in early Christian times. *Rhind Lectures*, 1879 (1880). 2 vol. 8° Edinburgh, 1881.

3362 Arbois de Jubainville (Marie Henry d'). Le jeûne du mercredi et du vendredi chez les irlandais du moyen âge. Rev. celt., 9, pp. 269–71. 1888.

3363 Balfour (John Alexander). Notice of a cashel, an early Christian settlement at Kilpatrick, Arran. [2 plans + 5 figures in text. ? constructed in 6th c.] Proc. Soc. Antiq. Scot., 44 (N.S. 8, 1909–10), pp. 90–101. 1910.

3364 Beaton (Donald). Ecclesiastical history of Caithness and annals of Caithness parishes. pp. vii, 344. 4° Wick, 1909. [Religious life of northern Highlands from earliest times.]

3365 Bellesheim (Alphons). Geschichte der katholischen Kirche in Irland, *etc*. 3 Bde. 8° Mainz, 1890–91.

3366 —— Geschichte der katholischen Kirche in Schottland. 2 Bde. 8° Mainz, 1883. History of the Catholic Church of Scotland . . . Translated by D. O. H. Blair. 4 vol. 8° Edinburgh, 1887–90. [Gross, 1600. Vol. 1, ch. 1–4, the early Irish Church, St. Columba, cloister-life in Iona, the Church in Northumbria, *etc.*]

3367 Best (W. Stuart). Some notes on the early British Church. Proc. Dorset Archaeol. Soc., 70, pp. 65–73. 1949.

3368 Bonwick (James). Irish druids and old Irish religions. pp. viii, 328. 8° London, 1894. [Bells, crosses, round towers, etc.]

3369 Brock (Edgar Philip Loftus). Historical and other evidence of the extent of the ancient British Church. J. Brit. Archaeol. Assoc., 41, pp. 53–64. 1885.

3370 Cathcart (William). The ancient British and Irish Churches, including the life and labors of St. Patrick. . . . With maps. pp. 347. 8° London, 1894. [Gross, 1601.]

3371 Chevalier (Jacques). L'Église celtique en Grande-Bretagne du IIIe au VIIe siècle. 8° Paris, 1914. [Printed under 'Angleterre' in A. Baudrillart's Dictionnaire d'histoire et de géographie écclesiastique, col. 145–56.]

3372 Chevlier (Jacques). Essai sur la formation de la nationalité et des réveils religieux du Pays de Galles, des origines à la fin du vi⁰ siècle. pp. xxxviii, 439. [Kenney, 1, p. 171.] Annales Univ. Lyon, N.S. 2 (droit, lettres), 34. 1923.

3373 Clerc (—). En quoi la tonsure irlandaise différait-elle de la forme générale des tonsures ? [Kenney, 1, p. 210.] Trav. Acad. Reims, 31, pp. 191–99. 1861.

3374 Collingwood (William Gershom) and **Rogers** (J.). Lost churches in the Carlisle diocese. [ii. Early Celtic Christianity in our district. iii. Irish Christianity among the Vikings.] Trans. Cumb. and Westm. Antiq. Soc., 15, pp. 288–302. 1899.

3375 Compton (C. H.). The ancient Church in Wales. J. Brit. Archaeol. Assoc., 49, pp. 129–37. 1893.

3376 Dawson (William). The Keltic Church and English Christianity. Trans. R.H.S., N.S. 1, pp. 376–84. 1884.

3377 Dowden (John), *bp. of Edinburgh*. The Celtic Church in Scotland. pp. ix, 338, + 1 plate + 1 map. 8° London, 1894.

3378 —— An examination of original documents on the question of the form of the Celtic tonsure. [5 figures in text.] Proc. Soc. Antiq. Scot., 30 (3rd S. 6), pp. 325–37. 1896.

3379 Duke (John Alexander). The Columban Church. pp. xii, 200. 8° Oxford, 1932.

3380 —— History of the Church of Scotland to the Reformation. pp. 293. 8° Edinburgh, 1937. [i. Beginnings of Christianity : ii. Columban Church : iii. Pictish Church and Picto-Scottish Church: iv. Romanization.]

3381 Ebrard (Johann Heinrich August). Die kuldeische Kirche der 7., 8., und 9. Jahrhunderte. [' The most misleading treatise on the matter '— Gougaud.] Zeit. hist. Theol., 32, pp. 504–624 ; 33, pp. 325–491. 1862–63.

3382 Edmonds (Columba). The early Scottish Church, its doctrine and discipline. pp. 326. 8° Edinburgh, 1906. [' Uncritical.']

3383 Fee (Thomas). The organisation of ecclesiastical life in Armagh before 1100. *M.A. Thesis, Univ. Coll., Dublin*, 1950. [Unpublished.]

3384 Flecker (William Herman). British Church history to A.D. 1000. pp. xiv, 159. 8° London, 1913.

3385 Flood (Joseph Mary). Ireland and the early Church. pp. 123. 8° London, 1920.

3386 Flower (Robin Ernest William). The two eyes of Ireland. Religion and literature in Ireland in the eighth and ninth centuries. The Church of Ireland : report of Church of Ireland Conference, ed. William Bell and N. O. Emerson, pp. 66–75. 1932.

3387 Funk (Franz Xaver von). Zur Geschichte der altbritischen Kirche. *Kirchengeschichtliche Abhandlungen und Untersuchungen*, 1. 8° Paderborn, 1897.

3388 Gaffney (James). The ancient Irish Church : was it catholic or protestant ? 8° Dublin, 1863. [Kenney, 1, p. 261.]

3389 Gougaud (Louis). Les Chrétientés celtiques. pp. xxxv, 410. 8° Paris, 1911. [Kenney, 1, p. 250. Pp. 267–78, good summary of Celtic canon law.]

3390 —— Christianity in Celtic lands a history of the Churches of the Celts, their origin, their development, influence and mutual relations ; translated . . . by M. Joynt. pp. lxii, 458, + 3 maps. 8° London, 1932.

3391 Gray (Andrew Edward Phillimore). Notes on the early history of the Church of Strathclyde, with special reference to the apostle of Lancashire. [i.e. St. Kentigern.] Trans. Hist. Soc. Lancs. and Ches., 40 (1888), pp. 77–92. 1890.

3392 Healy (John), *abp. of Tuam*. The ancient Irish Church. *Church History series*. pp. 192. 8° London, 1892. [Gross, 1603. 'A brief popular sketch.']

3393 Heron (James). The Celtic Church in Ireland. The story of . . . Irish Christianity . . . to the Reformation. pp. x, 430. 8° London, 1898 [1897]. [Gross, 949. Mainly early Irish Church.]

3394 Hewison (James King). Bute in early Christian times. Trans. Glasgow Archaeol. Soc., N.S. 2, pp. 158–60. 1896.

3395 Hogan (John). Did the ecclesiastics of ancient Ireland engage in mutual military warfare ? J. Roy. Hist. and Arch. Assoc. Ireland, [15], 4th S. 5 (1879–82), pp. 390–409. 1882.

3396 Howorth (*Sir* Henry Hoyle). The Columban clergy of north Britain and their harrying by the Norsemen. Trans. R.H.S., 7, pp. 395–444. 1878. *Also separately.* pp. 52. 8° London, 1879.

3397 Hughes (William). A history of the Church of the Cymry, from the earliest period to the present time. New edition, revised. pp. xv, 412. 8° London, 1916. [Gross, 1123. Pp. 78–130, A.-S. period.]

3398 Kattenbusch (Ferdinand). Irland in der Kirchengeschichte. *Theologische Studien und Kritiken,* 93. 8° Gotha, 1921. [Kenney, 1, p. 109.]

3399 Killen (William Dool). The ecclesiastical history of Ireland. 2 vol. 8° London, 1875.

3400 King (Robert). Memoir introductory to the early history of the primacy of Armagh, with some account of the ancient discipline, official persons, etc., of the Irish Church, previous to its subjugation to the see of Rome in the twelfth century. 2nd edition. pp. 112. fol. Armagh, 1854.

3401 Knight (George Alexander Franks). Archaeological light on the early Christianizing of Scotland. 2 vol. 8° London, 1933.

3402 Lanigan (John). An ecclesiastical history of Ireland from the first introduction of Christianity to the beginning of the thirteenth century. 2nd edition. 4 vol. 8° Dublin, 1829. [Gross, 951.]

3403 Leatham (Diana). Celtic sunrise. An outline of Celtic Christianity. pp. 191. 8° London, 1951.

3404 Lethbridge (Roper). The tithe in the ancient British Church of Wales. Church Q. Rev., 85, pp. 21–54. 1917.

3405 Loofs (Friedrich). Antiquae Britonum Scotorumque Ecclesiae, quales fuerint mores, quae ratio credendi et vivendi, quae controversiae cum Romana Ecclesia causa . . . quaesivit F. Loofs. pp. 120. 8° Lipsiae et Londinii, 1882. [Gross, 1604. Palladius and Patrick identified.]

3406 MacAndrew (—), *provost.* The early Celtic Church in Scotland. Trans. Gaelic Soc. Inverness, 12, pp. 15–28. 1886.

3407 MacCarthy (Bartholomew). The ancient Irish Church. [Criticism of Salmon : 3432.] Irish Eccles. Rec., 4th S. 2, pp. 166–70, 549–53 : 3, pp. 174–78. 1897–98.

3408 —— Professor Zimmer on the early Irish Church. [Chronology, Paschal question, cult of relics, St. Patrick, etc.] *Same jnl.,* 4th S, 14, pp. 385–411. 1903.

3409 McGregor (Duncan). Internal furnishings of an early Scottish church. Trans. Glasgow Ecclesiol. Soc., 3, pp. 1–15. 1901.

3410 Mackinnon (James). Culture in early Scotland. pp. xii, 239. 8° London, 1892. [Pp. 100–20, Ninian : pp. 145–239, Columba and Iona, Cuthbert, the Celtic monastery, etc.]

3410a MacNeil (John). Celtic religion. *Catholic Truth Society. Lectures on the history of religions,* 1. *iii.* pp. 32. 8° London, 1910.

3410b —— La religion des celtes. *Huby (Joseph) : Christus : manuel d'histoire des religions.* 6e édition (*pp. xx,* 1360). 8° Paris, 1934.

3411 Marstrander (Carl Johan Sverstrup). Treen og keeill. Et foernorsk orddelingsprinsipp paa de britiske oeyene. [Pp. 411–31, English summary. The treen was the smallest administrative unit : keeills are the primitive chapels dating to the Norwegian period.] Norsk Tidsskr. Sprogvidensk., 8, pp. 287–442. 1937.

3412 —— Was there a keeill in every treen division ? [Abstract.] J. Manx Mus., 4, pp. 3–5, + map, + 1 plate. 1938.

3413 Meissner (John Ludwig Gough). The Celtic Church in England after the synod of Whitby. pp. xii, 240. 8° London, 1929.

3414 Metcalfe (—). Notes on Celtic ecclesiology. Trans. Glasgow Ecclesiol. Soc., 2, pp. 19–25 : 3, pp. 19–26. 1898–1901.

3415 Mitchell (Anthony), *bp. of Aberdeen*. Biographical studies in Scottish Church history. *Hale Lectures*, 1913–4. pp. x, 302. 8° Milwaukee, 1914. [Pp. 1–33, + 1 plate, the Celtic period, St. Columba : pp. 35–69, + 1 plate, the transition from Celtic to Roman influence, St. Margaret.]

3416 Mitchell (Arthur). Vacation notes in Cromar, Burghead, and Strathspey. [Notes on St. Wallach, first bp. of Aberdeen, d. (?) 733 : objects found in Christian graves, e.g. inscribed stones and portable altars, etc.] Proc. Soc. Antiq. Scot., 10, pp. 603–89. 1875.

3417 Moran (Patrick Francis), *cardinal, abp. of Sydney*. Essays on the origin, doctrines, and discipline of the early Irish Church. 8° Dublin, 1864. [Gross, 1605. ' Devotes much attention to St. Patrick.']

3418 Murphy (J.). Professor [G. T.] Stokes on the early Irish Church. Irish Eccles. Rec., 3rd S. 11, pp. 1057–79 : 12, pp. 318–33. 1890–91.

3419 Newell (Ebenezer Josiah). A history of the Welsh Church to the dissolution of the monasteries. pp. xii, 435. 8° London, 1895.

3420 —— A popular history of the ancient British Church, with special reference to the Church in Wales. pp. 205, + map. 8° London, 1887.

3421 Ogilvie (George). Early progress of Christianity in Buchan. Being two papers read before the Club of Deir. pp. 6 + 52. 4° Aberdeen, 1873.

3422 Oliver (J. R.). Keeills and treen churches, Isle of Man. [5th c—.] Arch. Camb., 3rd S. 12, pp. 261–75, + 1 plate. 1866.

3423 Pender (Séamus). Coarbs, airchinnechs and the organization of Church lands. Irish Eccles. Rec., 5th S. 41, pp. 255–65. 1933.

3424 Phillips (Walter Alison), *ed.* History of the Church of Ireland from the earliest times to the present day. 3 vol. 8° London, 1933–34. [Vol. 1. The Celtic Church.]

3425 Power (Patrick). Early Christian Ireland. A manual of Irish Christian archaeology. pp. 113. 8° Dublin, 1925.

3426 Pryce (John). The ancient British Church. pp. xi, 292. 8° London, 1878. [Gross, 1606.]

3427 Reeves (William), *bp. of Down*. The ancient churches of Armagh. 8° Lusk, 1860. [Kenney, 1, p. 319.]

3428 —— The culdees of the British Islands, as they appear in history : with an appendix of evidences. 4° Dublin, 1864. *Also in* Trans. R.I.A., 24, pp. 119–263. 1873. [Gross, 792.]

3429 Richards (Robert). The vestiges of early Christianity in Gwynedd. Arch. Camb., 102, pp. 1–8. 1952.

3430 Ryan (John). Ecclesiastical relations between Ireland and England in the seventh and eighth centuries. St. Berchert of Tullylease. J. Cork Hist. Soc., 2nd S. 43, pp. 109–12. 1938.

3431 Salmon (John). The ancient Irish Church. [A reply to 3407.] Irish Eccles. Rec., 4th S. 2, pp. 402–13: 3, pp. 74–87, 264–71. 1897–98.

3432 —— The ancient Irish Church as a witness to Catholic doctrine. pp. xvi, 231. 8° Dublin, 1897. [Kenney, 1, p. 109.]

3433 Schoell (Earl Wilhelm). De ecclesiasticae Britonum Scotorumque historiae fontibus. pp. viii, 80. 8° Berolini, 1851. [Gross, 1355 : Lit. Pp. 20–28, deal with Book 1, of Bede's Historia ecclesiastica. Palladius and Patrick idenfied.]

3434 Scott (Archibald Black). The Brito-Celtic Church on the northern mainland and islands. [Ninianic foundations in Caithness and the northern isles : Colm, Cormac, etc.] Trans. Gaelic Soc. Inverness, 33 (1925–27), pp. 327–55. 1932.

3435 Scott (Archibald Black). The Celtic Church in Orkney. [Ninian and his foundations.] Proc. Orkney Antiq. Soc., 4, pp. 45–56. 1926.

3436 —— Early Christianity in Aberdeenshire and the north east : the chief mission centres. Trans. Scot. Ecclesiol. Soc., 8, pp. 139–59. 1927.

3437 —— The rise and relations of the Church of Scotland: early Brittonic period and S. Ninian's period, with supplement. pp. xv, 330. 8° Edinburgh, 1932.

3438 Simpson (William Douglas). The Celtic Church in Scotland. A study of its penetration lines and art relationships. *Aberdeen University Studies*, III. pp. 120. 8° Aberdeen, 1935.

3439 —— The origins of Christianity in Aberdeenshire. [Gist of forthcoming book.] Scot. N. and Q., 3rd S 3, pp. 43–46, + 1 plate. 1925.

3440 Skene (William Forbes). Notice of the early ecclesiastical settlements at St. Andrews. Proc. Soc. Antiq. Scot., 4, pp. 300–21. 1863.

3441 Snadden (James). Ancient chapels and religious sites of Liddesdale. Trans. Hawick Archaeol. Soc., 1921, pp. 7–14. 1921.

3442 Spence-Jones (H. D. M.), *dean of Gloucester*. The Celtic Church—a tragedy in history. [Its history, doctrines, organisation, buildings, liturgy.] Trans. Hon. Soc. Cymm., 1913–14, pp. 1–82. 1915.

3443 Stewart (Charles). The ancient Gaelic Church. Trans. Stirling Archaeol. Soc., 36. 1885.

3444 Stokes (George Thomas). Ireland and the Celtic Church to 1172. 7th edition, revised by H. J. Lawlor. pp. xvi, 384. 8° London, 1928. [Gross, 1607.]

3445 Stubbs (J. W.). On the early Irish Church. Irish Eccles. Rec., 3, pp. 198–206. 1867.

3446 Taylor (Thomas). The Celtic Christianity of Cornwall. Diverse sketches and studies. pp. xvi, 184. 8°

London, 1916. [Monastic bishoprics : evolution of the diocesan bishopric : saints : religious houses : hermits : etc.]

3447 Vaughan-Williams (*Sir* Roland Lomax). The ancient Church in Wales. [Pp. 8–9, A.-S. period.] Trans. Hon. Soc. Cymm, 1893–94, pp. 1–20, 1895.

3448 Wade-Evans (Arthur Wade). Welsh Christian origins. pp. 318. 8° Oxford, 1934.

3449 Warren (Frederick Edward). Conversion of the Kelts. [ii. Ireland : iii. Scotland.] Camb. Med. Hist., 2, pp. 502–13. 1913.

3450 Watt (Lauchlan MacLean). The Scottish Church's struggle with England for independence. Scot. Church Hist. Soc. Record, 5, pp. 185–95. 1935.

3451 Westropp (Thomas Johnson). The churches of county Clare, and the origin of the ecclesiastical divisions in that county. [Spread of Christianity, Danish wars, list of patrons, founders, types of the churches, relics, etc.] Proc. R.I.A., 3rd S. 6, pp. 100–80, + 6 plates. 1900.

3452 Williams (Hugh). Christianity in early Britain. pp. vii, 484. 8° Oxford, 1912. [Gross, 1609. Pp. 245–51, St. Patrick ; pp. 252–403, Monachism-Dubricius, Illtud, etc.]

3453 —— Some aspects of the Christian Church in Wales during the fifth and sixth centuries. [iii. End of century V to end of century VI : iv. Welsh monasticism.] Trans. Hon. Soc. Cymm., 1893–94, pp. 55–132. 1895.

3454 Williams (John) *ab Ithel.* The ecclesiastical antiquities of the Cymri ; or the ancient British Church, its history, doctrine, and rites. 15 nos. 8° London, 1844.

3455 Willis-Bund (John William). The Celtic Church of Wales. pp. vii, 533. 8°. London, 1897. [Gross, 1610.]

3456 Zimmer (Heinrich). The Celtic Church in Britain and Ireland. Translated by A. Meyer. pp. xiv, 131. 8° London, 1902. [Gross, 1610a. *From* Realencyklopädie für protestantische Theologie, 10, pp. 204–43, 1901. 'Contends that St. Patrick was an unimportant missionary in a limited field.']

55. SOCIAL AND ECONOMIC

3457 Boehmer (Heinrich). Das Eigenkirchentum in England. [History of patronage from Theodore to 11th c.] Festgabe für F. Liebermann, pp. 301–53. 1921.

3458 Chew (Helena Mary). The English ecclesiastical tenants-in-chief and knight service, especially in the 13th and 14th centuries. pp. xi, 203. 8° London, 1932. [The Conqueror's imposition of military service on the lands of bishops and abbots.]

3459 Cox (John Charles). The sanctuaries and sanctuary seekers of mediaeval England. pp. xx, 347, + 21 plates. 8° London, 1911. [Pp. 5–11, A.-S., and *passim* (St. Martin le Grand, Durham, Beverley, etc.)]

3460 —— The sanctuaries and sanctuary seekers of Yorkshire. [Privileges granted by Athelstan to Beverley, Ripon, *etc*.]. Archaeol. J., 68, pp. 273–99. 1911.

3461 Curtin (R.). The Domesday church and priest in Yorkshire. [List of 165 manors and their berewicks : of these 120 had both church and priest.] Antiquary, 26, pp. 197–200. 1892.

3462 Lega-Weekes (Ethel). The parish in England : its origin. N. and Q., 11th S. 3, pp. 381–83. 1911.

3463 Lloyd (Richard Duppa). The origin of the parish church buildings and institutions in Britain in the seventh century. J. Brit. Archaeol. Assoc., 50, pp. 235–47. 1894.

3464 Parker (James). The Church in Domesday, with especial reference to episcopal endowments. Domesday Studies, 2, pp. 399–432. 1891.

3465 Phear (*Sir* John Budd). Molland accounts. With an introductory note on the evolution of parishes. [Pp. 199–203, A.-S. administrative organisation.] Rept. and Trans. Devon. Assoc., 35, pp. 198–238. 1903.

3466 Reichel (Oswald Joseph). Churches and church endowments in the eleventh and twelfth centuries. [i. The term 'church' used in three senses : ii. Nature of the emoluments and profits usually described as a church : iii. The manner in which endowments were made : iv. The purposes for which endowments were given.]. *Same jnl.*, 39, pp. 360–93. 1907.

2467 —— The origin and upgrowth of the English parish. [Pp. 241–45 : 'The parish in Saxon England'.] *Same jnl.*, 52, pp. 239–62. 1920.

3468 —— The rise of the parochial system in England. Trans. Exeter Diocesan Archit. Soc., 12 (3rd S. 2), pp. 110–29. 1906.

3469 —— The treasury of God and the birthright of the poor : or facts illustrating the origin of 'parsons' and 'vicars' in England. [Church shot, tithes, etc.] Archaeologia, 60, pp. 391–410. 1907.

3470 Round (John Horace). 'Church-scot' in Domesday. E.H.R., 5, p. 101. 1890.

3471 Stoney (Constance B.). The English parish before the Norman Conquest. [Sundry remarks on A.-S. social and religious life.] Saga-Book V.C., 9, pp. 311–32. 1925.

3472 Thurston (Herbert). Clerical celebacy in the Anglo-Saxon Church. Month, no. 542, pp. 180–94. 1909.

56. PAGAN

(*See also* 118, 119 § d.)

3473 Akerman (John Yonge). The Saxon god Woden and his attributes. Proc. Soc. Antiq., 2, pp. 51–52. 1850.

3474 Anderson (Joseph). Notes on the survival of pagan customs in Christian burial ; with notices of certain conventional representations of 'Daniel in the den of lions', and 'Jonah and the whale', engraved on objects found in early Christian graves, and on the sculptured stones of Scotland, and crosses of Ireland. Proc. Soc. Antiq. Scot., 11, pp. 363–406, + 4 plates. 1876.

3475 Arbois de Jubainville (Marie Henry d'). L'anthropomorphisme chez les Celtes et dans la littérature homérique. Rev. celt., 19, pp. 224–35. 1898.

3476 Bannard (Henry E.). Some English sites of ancient heathen worship. [*Hearg, weoh, lundr.*—' Places identified with particular deities.'] Hibbert J., 44, pp. 76–79. 1945.

3477 Birch (Walter de Gray). A few notes on the gods of Britain. [Pp. 117–26, A.-S. paganism.] J. Brit. Archaeol. Assoc., 48, pp. 110–26. 1892.

3478 Blackburn (F. A.). The Christian coloring in the Beowulf. [Concludes that Beowulf once existed as a whole without the Christian allusions.] P.M.L.A., 12, pp. 205–25. 1897.

3479 Bonser (Wilfrid). Survivals of paganism in Anglo-Saxon England. Trans. B'ham. Arch. Soc., 56 (for 1932), pp. 37–70. 1934.

3480 Bouterwek (Carl Wilhelm). Cædmon's des Angelsachsen biblische Dichtungen. 2 Tl., 8° Gütersloh, 1854. [Teil 4, Einleitung : Die heidnischen Angelsachsen.]

3481 Brown (Arthur Charles Lewis). Barintus. [In Geoffrey of Monmouth's Vita Merlini ; the pilot who steered Arthur to the Fortunate Isles. Probably =a pagan sea-deity, later known as St. Barri, temp. St. David.] Rev. celt., 22, pp. 339–44. 1901.

3482 Christison (*Sir* Robert). On ancient wooden image, found . . . at Ballachulish peat-moss. [?from Norse galley where used as patron deity. Comparison with Holderness figures. 5 figures in text.] Proc. Soc. Antiq. Scot., 15 (N.S.3), pp. 158–78. 1881.

3483 Clarke (*Mrs.* Daisy Emily Martin). The office of thyle in *Beowulf*. [= poet, sage, or prophet.] Rev. Engl. Stud., 12, pp. 61–66. 1936.

3484 Cook (Arthur Bernard). The European sky-god. iv–viii. The Celts. Folk-lore, 17, pp. 27–71, 141–73, 308–48, 427–53 : 18, pp. 24–53. 1906–07.

3485 Cordner (W. S.). The cult of the holy well. [Pp. 34–36, correlation between well worship and other pagan cults.] Ulster J. Archaeol., 3rd s. 9, pp. 24–36, + 1 plate. 1946.

3486 Dalton (John P.). Cromm Cruaich of Magh Sleacht. [Idol demolished by St. Patrick.] Proc. R.I.A., 36c, pp. 23–67, + map. 1922.

3487 Dickins (Bruce). English names and Old English heathenism. Essays and studies (English Assocn.), 19, pp. 148–60. 1933.

3488 Donahue (Charles). The valkyries and the Irish war-goddesses. P.M.L.A., 56, pp. 1–12. 1941.

3489 Drake (O. S. T.). Merlin, the prophet of the Celts. Walford's Antiq. Mag., 12, pp. 9–14, 135–39. 1887.

3490 Du Bois (Arthur E.). *Beowulf*, 1107 and 2577 : hoards, swords and shields. [?connection of *icge* and *incge* with Ing. ?indications of a cult-war between shield-worshippers (Scyldings, etc.) and sword-worshippers.] Engl. Studien, 69, pp. 321–28. 1935.

3491 Hull (Eleanor). The development of the idea of Hades in Celtic literature. Folk-lore, 18, pp. 121–65. 1907.

3492 —— Pagan baptism in the west. [Pre-Christian baptism in Norse and Celtic lands.] Folk-lore, 43, pp. 410–18. 1932.

3493 Huntingford (George Wynn Brereton). Traces of ancient paganism in Berkshire. [Groves and temples : (1) *alh, ealh*, (2) *wih, weoh*, (3) *hearg*, (4) *vearo*, (5) *leáh* : mythology and place-names.] Berks. Archaeol. J., 37, pp. 17–22. 1933.

3494 Kermode (Philip Moore Callow). Traces of the Norse mythology in the Isle of Man. Yn Lioar Manninagh, 4, pp. 138–54. 1910.

3495 Loth (Joseph). Le sort chez les Germains et les Celtes. Rev. celt., 16, pp. 313–14. 1895.

3496 Magoun (Francis Peabody), *jr.* On some survivals of pagan belief in Anglo-Saxon England. [i. Mana in the Old-English charms : ii. Heavenly grace in Béowulf=Christianized personal mana: iii. Béowulf's funeral obsequies.] Harvard Theol. Rev., 40, pp. 33–46. 1947.

3497 Magoun (Francis Peabody) *jr.* Zum heroischen Exorzismus des Beowulfepos. Arkiv nord Filol, 54, pp. 215–28. 1939.

3498 Mann (A. H.). Old English paganism. Social England, ed. Traill and Mann, 1, pp. 217–24. 1891.

3499 Marstrander (Carl Johan Sverstrup). Thór en Irlande. Rev. celt., 36, pp. 241–53. 1916.

3500 Morgan (Thomas). On Odinism in Scandinavia, Denmark, and Britain. J. Brit. Archaeol. Assoc., 29, pp. 138–72. 1873.

3501 Munroe (Robert). Some traces of paganism in Gaelic words. Antiquary, 15, pp. 1–3. 1887.

3502 Ó Duígeannáin (Mícheál). On the medieval sources for the legend of Cenn (Crom) Cróich of Mag Slécht. [Chief idol of Ireland : overthrown by St. Patrick.] Essays presented to E. MacNeill, pp. 296–306. 1940.

3503 O'Laverty (James). Notes on pagan monuments in the immediate vicinity of ancient churches in the diocese of Down, and on peculiar forms of Christian interments observed in some of the ancient graveyards. J. Roy. Hist. and Arch. Assoc. Ireland, [15], 4th S. 5 (1879–82), pp. 103–08. 1882.

3504 Orpen (Goddard Henry). Aenach Carman : its site. [The great pagan festival of Leinster : held at Moy Liffey near Knockaulin.] J. Roy. Soc. Antiq. Ireland, 36 (5th S. 16), pp. 11–41. 1906.

3505 Philippson (Ernst Alfred). Germanisches Heidentum bei den Angelsachsen. *Kölner anglistische Arbeiten*, 4. pp. 239. 8° Leipzig, 1929.

3506 Piggott (Stuart). The name of the giant of Cerne. [Helith, and St. Augustine's visit.] Antiquity, 6, pp. 214–16. 1932.

3507 Ross (Alan Strode Campbell). OE. *wéofod, wibed, wígbed.* Leeds Studies in English, 3, pp. 2–6. 1934.

3508 Schuette (Gudmund). The cult of Nerthus. Saga-Book V.C., 8, pp. 29–43. 1913.

3509 Schulze (M.). Altheidnisches in den angelsächsischen Poesie, speziell im Beowulflede. *Programme, Berlin.* 8° Berlin, 1877.

3510 Smith (Albert Hugh). Old Scandinavian ' lundr '. [?=' wood offering sanctuary ' in A.-S. place-names : as need for places of refuge in Scandinavian England.] Leeds Studies in English, 2, pp. 72–74. 1933.

3511 Vendryes (Joseph). Imbolc. [Pagan festival of Feb. 1, absorbed in Christian festival of St. Brigid.] Rev. celt., 41, pp. 241–44. 1924.

3512 Watson (William John). The Celtic Church and its relations with paganism. Celtic Rev., 10, pp. 263–79. 1915.

3513 Westropp (Thomas Johnson). The marriages of the gods at the sanctuary of Tailltiu. Folk-lore, 31, pp. 109–41. 1920.

3514 Wise (Thomas Alexander). History of paganism in Caledonia, with an examination into the influence of Asiatic philosophy and the gradual development of Christianity in Pictavia. pp. xxvi, 259, 12, + 2 plates. 4° London, 1884. [Pp. 222–37, + 2 plates, sculptured crosses.]

3515 Wood-Martin (William Gregory). Traces of the elder faiths of Ireland, a folklore sketch. A handbook of Irish pre-Christian traditions. 2 vol. 8° London, 1902. [1, pp. 224–84, advent of St. Patrick, side-lights on paganism.]

3516 Wright (Arthur G.). The Dagenham idol. [?Viking relic, excavated 1922.] Trans. Essex Archaeol. Soc., N.S. 16, pp. 288–93. 1923.

57. CONVERSION AND EARLY HISTORY

3517 [Anon.] The planting of the English Church. Church Q. Rev., 45, pp. 1–25. 1897.

3518 Allcroft (Arthur Hadrian). The circle and the cross, a study in continuity. 2 vol. 8° London, 1927–30. [Vol. 2, Conversion of Ireland and England, Saxon paganism, Iona, first churches, etc.]

3519 Browne (George Forrest), *bp. of Bristol*. The conversion of the heptarchy. Revised edition. pp. 236. 8° London, 1906. [Gross, 1613. 'Seven popular lectures.']

3520 —— Inaugural address . . . as president of the [Wiltshire Archaeological] Society. [Early church in Wessex and Mercia: meeting at Augustine's Oak.] Wilts. Archaeol. Mag., 31, pp. 271–81. 1901.

3521 Crake (A. D.). Early Christian foundations in Berkshire. [*See also* p. 47, note signed J.E.F., under correspondence.] Q.J. Berks. Archaeol. Soc., 1, pp. 13–16, 47. 1890.

3522 Curtois (Huntley). Conversion of the English. pp. xii, 200. 8° London, 1927. [Substance of Bede's E.H., for the general reader.]

3523 Gray (Andrew Edward Phillimore). The origin of Christianity in Wirral. J. Brit. Archaeol. Assoc., 44, pp. 29–38. 1888.

3524 Hitchcock (Francis Ryan Montgomery). The Irish mission to England. Churchman, N.S. 3, pp. 189–200. 1938.

3525 Holmes (Thomas Scott). The conversion of Wessex. E.H.R., 7, pp. 437–43. 1892.

3526 Hope (*Mrs.* Anne). The conversion of the Teutonic race. . . . Conversion of the Franks and the English. . . . Edited by J. B. Dalgairns. . . . 2nd edition, revised and enlarged from the author's notes. pp. xi, 466. 8° London, [1892].

3526a Howorth (*Sir* Henry Hoyle). Saint Gregory the Great. pp. lvii, 340, + map. 8° London, 1912.

3527 Lach-Szyrma (Wladyslaw Somerville). Saint Chad and the conversion of the midlands. [No research.] J. Brit. Archaeol. Assoc., 52 (N.S. 2), pp. 130–35. 1896.

3528 Mason (J. Redfern). The conversion of East Anglia. Byegone Suffolk, ed. Cuming Walters, pp. 16–30. 1901.

3529 Pearson (Howard S.). The introduction of Christianity into Mercia. B'ham Hist. Soc., Trans., 1, pp. 25–42. 1881.

3530 Pennington (Edgar Legare). The planting of Christianity among the West Saxons. pp. vii, 69. 8° Windsor, 1951. [1952].

3531 Pring (Daniel James). Early Christianity in Somerset and how it has survived. pp. 20. 8° Taunton, 1936.

3532 Routledge (Charles Francis). The baptism of king Ethelbert [597]. [? by bishop Liudhard, not St. Augustine: ?in south porticus of church of St. Pancras, and not in St. Martin's.] Arch. Cant., 21, pp. 157–60. 1895.

3533 Seeley (*Sir* John Robert). Paul Ewald and pope Gregory I. [Contains: Liber beati . . . Gregorii . . . De vita atque eius virtutibus, which concerns his mission to England.] E.H.R., 3, pp. 295–310. 1888.

3534 Taylor (Charles Samuel). Early Christianity in Gloucestershire. Trans. Bristol and Glos. Arch. Soc., 15, pp. 120–38. 1891.

3535 Trollope (Edward). The introduction of Christianity into Lincolnshire during the Saxon period. Assoc. Archit. Socs'. Rpts., 4, pp. 1–8, + 2 plates. 1857.

3536 Venables (Edmund). St. Oswald, the patron saint of Bardney abbey, and the christianization of Lincolnshire. *Same jnl.*, 13, pp. 192–200. 1876.

3537 —— Traces of early Christianity in north Lincolnshire. *Same jnl.*, 19, pp. 318–25. 1888.

3538 Whitelock (Dorothy). The conversion of the eastern Danelaw. [c. 869–970.] Saga-Book V.C., 12, pp. 159–76. 1941.

3539 Whitney (J. P.). Conversion of the Teutons. [(1) The English. Augustine to Synod of Whitby.] Camb. Med. Hist., 2, pp. 515–32. 1913.

3540 Williams (Rowland). On the supposed reluctance of the West British Church to convert the Anglo-Saxons. Arch. Camb., 3rd S. 4, pp. 396–405. 1858.

3541 Williams (T.). The origin and first growth of Christianity in Bucks. Rec. Bucks., 7, pp. 343–61. 1897.

3542 Winmill (Joyce M.). The coming of Christianity to Essex. [Work of St. Cedd.] Essex Rev., 60, pp. 196–202. 1951.

58. RELATIONS WITH THE PAPACY

3543 Bethurum (Dorothy). A letter of protest from the English bishops to the pope. [Letter, by Wulfstan, in MS. Cotton Vesp. A XIV, ff. 178–79, re ordination of a bishop and simony.] Malone (K.): Philologica, pp. 97–104. 1949.

3544 Bright (William). The Roman see in the early Church, *etc.* pp. viii, 490. 8° London, 1896.

3545 Brooke (Zachary Nugent). The English Church and the papacy, from the Conquest to the reign of John. pp. xii, 260. 8° Cambridge, 1952. [Pp. 57–83, Lanfranc's Collection of canons : pp. 117–31, Lanfranc : pp. 132–46, William the Conqueror. The traditional outlook.]

3546 —— Pope Gregory VII's demand for fealty from William the Conqueror. E.H.R., 26, pp. 225–38. 1911.

3547 Dolan (Gilbert). Saint Gregory the Great and Ireland. Downside Rev., 23, N.S. 4, pp. 30–45. 1904.

3548 Greith (Carl Johann), *bp. of St. Gall*. Geschichte der altirischen Kirche und ihrer Verbindung mit Rom, Gallien und Allemannien (von 430–639) als Einleitung in die Geschichte des Stifts St. Gallen. pp. x, 462. 8° Freiburg im Breisgau, 1867. [Kenney, 1, p. 207.]

3549 Gwynn (Aubrey). Gregory VII [Hildebrand] and the Irish Church. [11th c.] Studi Gregoriani, 3, pp. 105–28. 1948.

3550 Gwynn (Aubrey). Ireland and Rome in the eleventh century. [Development of religious life in Norse-Irish settlement, 1028–74.] Irish Eccles. Rec., 5th S. 57, pp. 213–32. 1941.

3551 Gwynn (Aubrey). Pope Gregory VII and the Irish Church. *Same jnl.*, 5th S. 58, pp. 97–109. 1941.

3552 Holtzmann (Walther). Papst-urkunden in England. pp. 127, 488. 2 pts., 8° Berlin, 1936. [Gives texts of 292 papal letters, 1061–1198.]

3553 Jensen (O.). The 'denarius Sancti Petri' in England. [Pp. 171–83 : i. The relations between the papacy and England in the 7th and 8th c. : ii. The origin of Peter's pence in England. Pp. 190–98 : Appendix I : Ordinances relating to 'Romfeoh' in the A.-S. laws : collections of A.-S. coins found in Rome in 1843 and 1883. Appendix 2 : Ordinances relating to Peter's pence contained in the laws, mostly in the Anglo-Norman period.] Trans. R.H.S., N.S. 15, pp. 171–247. 1901.

3554 Kerr (William Shaw). The independence of the Celtic Church in Ireland. pp. 163. 8° London, 1931.

3555 Lunt (William Edward). Studies in Anglo-papal relations during the Middle Ages. 1. Financial relations of the papacy with England to 1327. *Mediæval Academy of America*, 33. pp. xv, 759. 8° Cambridge, Mass., 1939. [Pp. 3–30, Peter's pence, origin and development in the A.-S. period : pp. 88–90, Papal protection and exemption of A.-S. monasteries.]

3556 MacNaught (John Campbell). The Celtic Church and the see of St. Peter. pp. xv, 118. [Pascal controversy.] 8° Oxford, 1927.

3557 Maguire (R.). The early Irish Church independent of Rome until 1172, embodying a reply to Dr. Rock [3558]. 12°. 1853.

3558 Rock (Daniel). Did the early Church of Ireland acknowledge the Pope's supremacy ? 8° London, 1844. [Kenney, 1, p. 210. Reply by R. Maguire, 3557.]

3559 Todd (William Gouan). The Church of St. Patrick : an historical inquiry into independence of the ancient Church of Ireland. pp. ix, 153. 8° London, 1844. [Connections with the popes, 5th–12th c. : Paschal controversy: epistle of Cummian : testimony of Columbanus (his epistle to Boniface IV).]

59. PASCHAL CONTROVERSY

(Cycle of St. Hippolitus (16 years) used at Rome till end of 3rd c. That of Augustalis (84 years) substituted for it and remained in force till 457. That of Victorius of Aquitaine (532 years) was that introduced by Augustine, and not accepted by the Celts. That of Dionysius Exiguus, based on the Alexandrian cycle of 19 years (drawn up in 525) brought forward by Wilfrid at Whitby in 664. Iona adopted this orthodox Easter in 716).

3560 Anscombe (Alfred). The date of the obit of St. Columba. A vindication and refutation of those writers who would apply a cycle of 84 years to the computation of the British and Irish Easter. pp. 27. 8° Tottenham, 1893.

3561 —— The Paschal canon attributed to Anatolius. E.H.R., 10, pp. 531–33. 1895.

3562 C. (J.). The Irish paschal question. Irish Eccles. Rec., 11, pp. 445–58. 1874.

3563 Conybeare (Fred C.). The character of the heresy of the early British Church. Trans. Hon. Soc. Cymm., 1897–98, pp. 84–117. 1899.

3564 Corssen (P.). Das Osterfest. [Kenney, 1, p. 210.] Neue Jahrb., 20, pp. 170–. 1917.

3565 Fahey (J. A.). The Celtic paschal controversy. Irish Eccles. Rec., 3rd S. 10, pp. 303–13. 1889.

3566 Grosjean (Paul). Recherches sur les débuts de la controverse pascale chez les Celtes. [i. Dates de Pâques observées en Gaule par S. Colomban : ii. Date du Concile de Chalon-sur-Saône : iii. Dates trois premières lettres de S. Colomban : iv. S. Sillén, abbé de Bangor, et son disciple S. Mo-Chúaróc : v. Le réforme liturgique de Mo-Chúaróc : vi. Le faux de 606 provient -il de Cantorbéry ? Date de la lettre des SS. Laurent, Mellitus et Justus aux Irlandais : vii. Le faux de 606 ne provient ni de Gaule, ni de Grande-Bretagne, mais plutôt d'Irlande.] Anal. Boll., 64, pp. 200–44. 1946.

3567 Hay (Malcolm Vivian). A chain of error in Scottish history. pp. xx, 243. 8° London, 1927. [Disciplinary controversies.]

3568 Koch (H.). Pascha in den ältesten Kirche. [Kenney, 1, p. 210.] Zeit. wiss. Theol., 55, pp. 289–313. 1914.

3569 Krusch (Bruno). Die Einführung des griechischen Paschalritus im Abendlande. [Kenney, 1, p. 210.] Neues Archiv., 9, pp. 99–169. 1884.

3570 —— Studien zur christlich-mittelalterlichen Chronologie. Der 84–jährige Ostercyclus und seine Quellen. pp. viii, 349. 8° Leipzig, 1880. [Kenney, 1, p. 210.]

3571 O'Connell (Daniel J. K.). Easter cycles in the early Irish Church. [*See also* note by H. Morris, 67, pp. 131–32. 1937. 84 years cycle : cycle of Victorius : Munich computus (9th c.) : tables, etc.] J. Roy. Soc. Antiq. Ireland, 66 (7th S. 6), pp. 67–106. 1936.

3572 O'Hare (Charles M.). The paschal controversy in the Celtic Churches : a repudiation of papal supremacy ? Irish Eccles. Rec., 5th S. 40, pp. 337–49, 492–503 : 41, pp. 266–76, 615–29 : 42, pp. 365–77. 1943.

3573 Oulton (John Ernest Leonard). On a synod referred to in the De Controversia Paschali of Cummian [632]. [Held at Mag-Léna, southern Ireland.] Hermathena, 24 (no. 49), pp. 88–93. 1935.

3574 Poole (Reginald Lane). The earliest use of the Easter cycle of Dionysius. E.H.R., 33, pp. 57–62. 1918.

3575 Schmid (Joseph). Die Osterfestberechnung auf den britischen Inseln vom Aufgang des 4. bis zum Ende des 8. Jahrhunderts. pp. vii, 95 8° Regensburg, 1904. [Kenney, 1, p. 210.]

3576 —— Die Osterfestberechnung in den abendländischen Kirche . . . bis zum Ende des viii. Jahrhunderts. *Strassburger Theologische Studien*, 9 i. pp. ix, 111. 8° Freiburg i. Br., 1907. [Kenney, 1, p. 210.]

3577 Schwartz (E.). Christliche und jüdische Ostertafeln. [Kenney, 1, p. 210.] Abhand. k. Gesellsch. Wiss. Göttingen, phil.-hist. Kl., N.F. 8. 1905.

3578 Varin (Pierre Joseph). Mémoire sur les causes de la dissidence entre l'Église bretonne et l'Église romaine à la célébration de la fête de Pâques. *Mémoires présentés par divers savants à l'Académie des inscriptions et belles-lettres, séries 1, v. ii.* [Kenney, 1, p. 210.] 8° Paris, 1858.

60. MONASTIC HISTORY, ANGLO-SAXON

§ a. General

3579 Allison (Thomas). Benedict Biscop. [628–89 or 690.] Church Q. Rev., 107, pp. 57–79. 1928.

3580 Bateson (Mary). Origin and early history of double monasteries. [iv. (pp. 168–83): The double monastery in England.] Trans. R.H.S., N.S. 13, pp. 137–98. 1899.

3580a Benedict, *St., abbot of Monte Cassino.* Regularis Concordia Angliae Nationis Monachorum sanctimonialiumque (The monastic agreement, *etc.*) Translated from the Latin with introduction and notes by Thomas Symons. *Medieval Classics.* pp. lix, 77, + plate. 8° London, 1953. [Latin and English. English monastic revival of the 10th c., sources, *etc.*]

3581 Birch (Walter de Gray). Fasti monastici aevi Saxonici : or, an alphabetical list of the heads of religious houses in England previous to the Norman Conquest, to which is prefixed a chronological catalogue of contemporary foundations. pp. vii, 114. 8° London, 1873. [Gross, 1612.]

3582 Boot (Alfred). Northern monasticism. Archaeol. Æl., N.S. 17, pp. 91–100. 1895.

3583 Broughton (Richard). Monastichon Britannicum ; or, a historicall narration of the . . . monasteries . . . in the tymes of the . . . primitive Church of the Saxons, *etc.* pp. 416. 4° London, 1655.

3584 Burton (John). Monasticon Eboracense : and the ecclesiastical history of Yorkshire. Containing an account of the first introduction and progress of Christianity in that diocese until the end of William the Conqueror's reign, *etc.*, pp. xii, 481. fol. York, 1758.

3585 Ceolfrid, *abbot of Wearmouth and Jarrow.* The life of Ceolfrid . . . by an unknown writer of the eighth century. Translated from the original and edited . . . by Douglas Samuel Boutflower. . . . To which is added a reprint of an article on the Codex Amiatinus by J. L. Low, *etc.* pp. 120, + plate. 8° Sunderland, 1912.

3586 Cockayne (Oswald), *ed.* Eadgar's establishment of monasteries. *In his* Leechdoms . . . of early England [7410] vol. 3, pp. 406–18, 432–45. *Rolls series.* 8° London, 1866. [Gross, 1436. A.-S. and translation, and introduction. A.-S. fragment (in MS. Cotton Faustina, A.X., fol. 148a) of a postscript to Ethelwold's translation of St. Benedict's Rule.]

3587 Dugdale (*Sir* William). Monasticon Anglicanum. A new edition . . . by John Caley, *etc.* 6 vol. (in 8), fol. London, 1817–30. [A.-S., *passim.*]

3588 Eckenstein (Lina). Woman under monasticism. Chapters on saint-lore and convent life between A.D. 500 and A.D. 1500. pp. xv, 496. 8° Cambridge, 1896. [Gross, 783. Chiefly English and German.]

3589 Fisher (D. J. V.). The anti-monastic reaction in the reign of Edward the Martyr. Camb. Hist.J., 10, pp. 254–70. 1952.

3590 Fosbroke (Thomas Dudley). British monachism ; or, manners and customs of the monks and nuns of England. 3rd edition. pp. 428, +11 plates. 4° London, 1843. [Pp. 13–37, A.-S. : pp. 37–38, Rule of Fulgentius (Latin and A.-S.) : MS. Bodl. Archiv. Seld. D. 52.]

3591 Gee (Henry). Ecclesiastic history [of the county of Durham]. [Pp. 1–11, A.-S. period.] V.C.H., Durham, 2, pp. 1–77, + map. 1907.

3592 Goyau (Georges). La Norman-die bénédictine et Guillaume le Con-quérant. [Norman influence on English monasticism.] Rev. deux mondes, 48, pp. 337–55. 1938.

3593 Hirst (J.). On guildship in Anglo-Saxon monasteries. Archaeol. J., 49, pp. 107–119. 1892.

3594 Keim (H. W.). Aethelwold und die Mönchreform in England. Anglia, 41 (N.F. 29), pp. 405–43. 1917.

3595 Knowles (Michael David). Es-says in monastic history, 1066–1215. [i. Abbatial elections : ii. The Norman plantation : iii. The Norman monastic-ism : iv. The growth of exemption.] Downside Rev., 49, pp. 252–78, 441–56 : 50, pp. 33–48, 200–31, 396–436. 1931–32.

3596 —— The monastic order in England. A history of its development from the times of St. Dunstan to the fourth Lateran Council (943–1216). pp. xxi, 764. 8° Cambridge, 1949. [Pp. 31–82 ; Monastic revival under Dunstan ; English monasticism between Dunstan and the Conquest : pp. 695–704, Monastic bps., 960–1066, etc. : p. 721, derivation of 10th c. monasteries (tree).]

3597 —— The religious houses of medieval England. pp. viii, 167, + 5 maps. 8° London, 1940. [Pp. 11–20, the origins and development of the religious life in England (A.-S.).]

3598 Liebermann (Felix). Zur Kritik der Urkunden und Klosterreform-Liter-atur der Angelsachsen. [Sundry observ-ations on recent publications.] Arch. Stud. neueren Spr., Bd., 142 (N.S. 42), p. 250. 1921.

3599 Logeman (Willem S.). De consuetudine monachorum. [By Æthel-wold, bp. of Winchester. MS. Cotton Tib. A III, ff. 174a–176b (10th–11th c.). i. Text (A.-S. and Latin) : ii. Introduc-tion and notes.] Anglia, 13 (N.F. 1), pp. 365–454 : 15 (N.F. 3), pp. 20–40. 1891–93.

3600 Maclear (George Frederick) and **Merivale** (Charles). Conversion of the West. 5 vol. 8° London, [1878–79]. [Gross, 1616.]

3601 Montalembert (Charles Forbes René de), *count*. Les moins d'Occident depuis saint Benoît jusqu'à saint Bern-ard. 7 vol. 8° Paris, 1860–77. —. The monks of the West, *etc.* An authorised translation. 7 vol. 8° Edinburgh and London, 1861–79. [Gross, 791.]

3602 Robinson (Joseph Armitage). Lanfranc's monastic constitutions. J. Theol. Stud., 10, pp. 375–88. 1909.

3603 Ryan (Alice Mary). A map [and index] of Old English monasteries and related ecclesiastical foundations, A.D. 400–1066. *Cornell Studies in English*, 28. pp. vi, 33, + map. 8° Ithaca, 1939.

3604 Schmitz (Philibert). Geschichte des Benediktinerordens. 2 Bde. 8° Zürich, 1947–48. [Bd. 1, pp. 41–55, Gregor der Grosse—Die Benediktiner in England : pp. 56–72, Die Entfaltung des Ordens in Gallien, Belgien und Italien : pp. 23–84, *Ditto* in Friesland und Deutschland (Willibrord, Boniface, etc.) : pp. 85–110, Die Zeit der Karo-linger : pp. 190–205, Das benediktin-ische England (Dunstan, etc.).]

3605 Schroeer (Arnold). De consue-tudine monachorum. Engl. Studien, 9, pp. 290–96. 1886.

3606 Sumner (Oswald). The English Benedictine habit. [From time of St. Dunstan's reforms (10th c.).] Downside Rev., 61, pp. 105–14 : 62, pp. 24–33, 102–09. 1943–44.

3607 Symons (Thomas). The English monastic reform of the tenth century. *Same jnl.*, 60, pp. 1–22, 196–222, 268–79. 1942.

3608 ——The monastic observance of the Regularis Concordia. [10th c. code of observance.] *Same jnl.*, 44, pp. 157–71 : 45, pp. 146–64. 1926–27.

3609 —— The monastic reforms of king Edgar. *Same jnl.*, 39, pp. 38–51. 1921.

3610 —— Sources of the Regularis Concordia. [c. 970.] *Same jnl.*, 59, pp. 14–36, 143–70, 264–89. 1941.

3611 Taunton (Ethelred Luke). The English Black monks of St. Benedict ; a sketch of their history from the coming of St. Augustine to the present day. 2 vol. 8° London, 1897. [vol. 1, ch. 1, the coming of the monks ; ch. 2, the Norman Lanfranc. (pp. 1–30).]

3612 Taylor (Charles Samuel). The Benedictine revival in the Huiccian monasteries. Trans. Bristol and Glos. Arch. Soc., 18, pp. 107–33. 1894.

3613 Thompson (Alexander Hamilton). Northumbrian monasticism. Bede : 12th Centenary essays : ed. A. H. Thompson, pp. 60–101. 1935.

3614 Workman (Herbert Brook). The evolution of the monastic ideal from the earliest times down to the coming of the friars. 2nd edition. pp. xxi, 368. 8° London, 1927. [Chap. 4 : the ideals of monasticism in the Celtic Church.]

3615 Zupitza (Julius). Ein weiteres Bruchstück der Regularis Concordia in altenglischer Sprache. Archiv Stud. neueren Spr., Bd. 84, pp. 1–24. 1890.

§ b. Abingdon

3616 Crawford (Osbert Guy Stanhope). Abingdon. [*Abbendune* (between Bayworth and Pinsgrove) the original site of Hean's monastery in 675.] Antiquity, 4, pp. 487–89. 1930.

3617 Ditchfield (Peter Hampson). The history of Abingdon. [Pp. 73–77, A.-S. period.] J. Brit. Archaeol. Assec., 62 (N.S. 12), pp. 73–82, + 1 plate. 1906.

3618 Douglas (David Charles). Some early surveys from the abbey of Abingdon. [Domesday, etc.] E.H.R., 44, pp. 618–25. 1929.

3619 Field (John Edward). The beginning of Abingdon abbey. E.H.R., 20, pp. 693–97. 1905.

3620 —— Earmundslea at Appleton, Berks. [A.-S. property of the abbey of Abingdon, and its boundaries.] Berks, Bucks and Oxon Archaeol. J., 13, pp. 21–23, 41–48. 1907.

3621 Preston (Arthur E.). Sutton Courtenay and Abingdon abbey. [Pp. 23–32, A.-S. period.] *Same jnl.*, 25, pp. 23–38, etc. 1919.

3622 Stenton (*Sir* Frank Merry). The early history of the abbey of Abingdon. pp. vii, 52. 8° London, 1913.

3623 Townsend (James). A history of Abingdon. pp. 183, + 4 plates. 4° London, 1910. [Pp. 1–15, A.-S. and Domesday.]

§ c. Bury

3624 Douglas (David Charles), *ed.* Feudal documents from the abbey of Bury St. Edmunds. *British Academy* : *Records of the social and economic history of England and Wales*, 8. pp. clxxi, 247, + 3 plates. 8° London, 1932. [i. The Feudal Book of Baldwin, abbot, 1065–98 : ii. Royal charters, William I–Henry II : iii. Charters of the abbots, Baldwin, *etc.*]

3625 Galbraith (Vivian Hunter). The East Anglian see and the abbey of Bury St. Edmunds. [1070–1103.] E.H.R., 40, pp. 222–28. 1925.

3626 Goode (Frank B.). The shrine of the martyr-king. Byegone Suffolk, ed. Cuming Walters, pp. 79–92. 1901.

3627 Hervey (*Lord* Francis), *ed.* The history of king Eadmund the Martyr and of the early days of his abbey. (Corpus Christi College, Oxford, MS. 197.) pp. vii, 61, + 1 plate. 8° London, 1929.

3628 Hills (Gordon M.). The antiquities of Bury St. Edmunds. J. Brit. Archaeol. Assoc., 21, pp. 32–56, 104–40, + 2 plans and 1 plate. 1865.

3629 Morant (Alfred W.). On the abbey of Bury St. Edmunds. [Pp. 376–80, A.-S. period.] Proc. Suffolk Inst. Archaeol., 4, pp. 376–404, + plan, + 3 plates. 1872.

§ d. Canterbury

3630 Ballard (Adolphus), *ed.* An eleventh-century inquisition of St. Augustine's, Canterbury. *British Academy*, *Records of the social and economic history of England and Wales*, vol. 4, pt. 2. pp. xxvii, 33. 8° London, 1920. [Text (with parallels of Domesday Monachorum and Domesday Book), and introduction.]

3631 Boggis (Robert James Edmund). A history of St. Augustine's monastery, Canterbury. pp. 196, + 9 plates, + plan. [Pp. 1–45, A.-S.] 8° Canterbury, 1901.

3632 Boutemy (A.). Two obituaries of Christ Church, Canterbury. E.H.R., 50, pp. 292–99. 1935.

3633 Box (E. G.). Donations of manors to Christ Church, Canterbury and appropriation of churches. Arch. Cant., 44, pp. 103–19. 1932.

3634 Deanesly (Margaret). The familia at Christchurch, Canterbury, 597–832. Essays . . . presented to T. F. Tout, pp. 1–13. 1925.

3635 The Domesday Monachorum of Christ Church, Canterbury. Edited with an introduction by David C. Douglas. *Royal Historical Society.* pp. 127, + 16 plates (facsimiles). fol. London, 1944. [Pp. 77–110, text. Roughly coeval with the Domesday Survey whose entries are given in parallel columns.]

3636 Knowles (Michael David). The early community at Christ Church, Canterbury. [?monastic or not: sequel to 3638.] J. Theol. Stud., 39, pp. 126–31. 1938.

3637 Orger (J.). St. Augustine's abbey, Canterbury. J. Brit. Archaeol. Assoc., 40, pp. 15–27. 1884.

3638 Robinson (Joseph Armitage). The early community at Christ Church, Canterbury. [*See also* 3636.] J. Theol. Stud., 27, pp. 225–40. 1926.

3639 Symons (Thomas). The introduction of monks at Christ Church, Canterbury. [During archi-episcopate of Ælfric (995–1005).] *Same jnl.*, 27, pp. 409–11. 1926.

3640 Thorne (William). Chronicle of Saint Augustine's abbey, Canterbury, now rendered into English by A. H. Davis. pp. lxviii, 733. 8° Oxford, 1934. [Pp. 1–59, A.-S.]

3641 Walcott (Mackenzie Edward Charles). King Ethelbert's gifts to St. Augustine's, Canterbury, 605. Ecclesiologist, 29, pp. 355–56. 1868.

3642 Ward (Gordon). Domesday Monachorum. The Domesday Book of the monks of Canterbury. A short description, with lists of the churches mentioned, all of which were presumably Saxon foundations, and numbering over 200 in east Kent. pp. 12. 8° Canterbury, 1931.

N

3643 Woodruff (Charles Eveleigh) and **Danks** (William). Memorials of the cathedral and priory of Christ in Canterbury. pp. xxi, 490, + 33 plates. 8° London, 1912. [Pp. 1–35, the Roman-Saxon church: Lanfranc's Norman church.]

§ *e.* **Croyland**

3644 Canham (A. S.). Notes on the archaeology of Crowland. [Early history of the abbey.] J. Brit. Archaeol. Assoc., 47, pp. 286–300. 1891.

3645 English (Henry Scale). A light on the historians and on the history of Crowland abbey. pp. 232. 8° London, 1868. [Gross, 998.]

3646 Miller (Samuel Henry). Union of the convent of Peakirk with Crowland: the gift of Barnack to the latter. [Extract from Ordericus.] Fenland N. and Q., 2, pp. 318–19. 1894.

3647 Page (Frances Mary). The estates of Crowland abbey: a study in manorial organisation. pp. xiv, 462, + 5 plates, + table, + map. 8° Cambridge, 1934. [Including Domesday material.]

3648 Pegge (Samuel). Remarks on [3649]. Archaeologia, 5, pp. 101–05, + plate. 1779.

3649 Pownall (T.). On the boundary stone of Croyland abbey. [Early history of Croyland, quoting Ingulf, etc.] Archaeologia, 3, pp. 96–100. 1786.

3650 Searle (William George). Ingulf and the Historia Croylandensis. An investigation. *Cambs. Antiq. Soc.*, 8° *pubns.*, 27. pp. viii, 216, + 1 plate. 8° Cambridge, 1894.

§ *f.* **Evesham**

3651 Andrews (Francis Baugh). The Benedictine abbey of Evesham. [Pp. 35–39, A.-S. period.] B'ham Arch. Soc., Trans., 35, pp. 34–56. 1909.

3652 Batt (N. G.). The abbey of Evesham, illustrated by the lives of a triad of its abbots. J. Brit. Archaeol. Assoc., 32, pp. 193–202. 1876.

3653 Darlington (Reginald Ralph). Æthelwig, abbot of Evesham. [Last A.-S. abbot.] E.H.R., 48, pp. 1–22. 1933.

3654 Galton (Theodore H.). On the early history of Evesham abbey. [Charter of Ecgwine, 714, etc.] Assoc. Archit. Socs.' Rpts., 3, pp. 369–79. 1855.

3655 Stanbrook, *Benedictines of.* St. Egwin and the abbey of Evesham. By the Benedictines of Stanbrook [abbey, Worcester]. pp. v, 184. 8° London, 1904. [Gross, 1159a.]

3656 Tindal (William). The history and antiquities of the abbey and borough of Evesham. pp. viii, 363, + 6 plates. 4° Evesham, 1794. [Pp. 1–20, A.S.]

§ *g.* **Glastonbury**

3657 Freeman (Edward Augustus). President's inaugural address [on the early history of Glastonbury abbey.] Proc. Somerset Arch. Soc., 26 (1880), pp. 7–40. 1881.

3658 Green (J. R.). Dunstan at Glastonbury. *Same jnl.*, 11 (1861–2), pp. 122–42. 1863.

3659 Greswell (William Henry Parr). Chapters on the early history of Glastonbury abbey. pp. viii, 151, + 25 plates. 8° Taunton, 1909. [Gross, 1072a.]

3660 Lewis (Lionel Smithett). Glastonbury the mother of saints. Her saints, A.D. 37–1539. pp. iv, 72. 8° Bristol, 1925.

3661 Newell (William Wells). William of Malmesbury on the antiquity of Glastonbury, with especial reference to the equation of Glastonbury and Avalon. P.M.L.A., 18, pp. 459–572. 1903.

3662 Parker (James). Documentary evidence relating to the early history of Glastonbury. Proc. Somerset Arch. Soc., 26 (1880), pp. 40–43. 1881.

3663 Snow (T. B.). Glastonbury. Downside Rev., 9, pp. 186–212, + 2 plates, + plan. 1890.

3664 Watkin (Aelred). The Glastonbury ' pyramids ' and St. Patrick's ' companions '. [Which stood, according to William of Malmesbury, on either side of king Arthur's tomb : the names inscribed on them.] Downside Rev., 63, pp. 30–41. 1945.

3665 Whiting (Charles Edwin). Glastonbury. [Early history of the monastery.] Trans. Archit. Soc. Durham, 10, pp. 404–18. 1953.

3666 William, *of Malmesbury.* Glastonbury abbey before the Conquest. A translation by H. F. Scott Stokes . . . of William of Malmesbury's On the antiquity of the church of Glastonbury, . . . from Thomas Hearne's edition of Adam of Domesham . . . based on the . . . manuscript in the library of Trinity College, Cambridge. pp. 71, + map. 8° Glastonbury, 1932.

§ *h.* **Malmesbury**

3667 Akerman (John Yonge). Some account of the possessions of the abbey of Malmesbury, in north Wilts, in the days of the Anglo-Saxon kings ; with remarks on the ancient limits of the forest of Braden. [Charters, etc.] Archaeologia, 37, pp. 257–315, + 2 maps. 1857.

3668 Birch (Walter de Gray). On the succession of the abbots of Malmesbury. [Pp. 314–21, 446, A.-S. period.] J. Brit. Archaeol. Assoc., 27, pp. 314–42, 446–48. 1871.

3669 Brakspear (*Sir* Harold). Malmesbury abbey. [Pp. 458–60, history of the monastery, A.-S. period.] Wilts. Archaeol. Mag., 38, pp. 458–97, + 2 plans, + 26 plates. 1913.

3670 Jackson (John Edward). Malmesbury. [Pp. 16–28, 40–44, A.-S. period.] *Same jnl.*, 8, pp. 14–50, + 1 plate. 1864.

3671 Luce (*Sir* Richard Harman). Pages from the history of the Benedictine monastery of Malmesbury. pp. vi, 64, + 8 plates. 8° Devizes, 1929. [Pp. 1–15, before the Conquest.]

§ *i.* **Peterborough**

3672 English (Henry Scale). Crowland and Burgh. [Vol. 2–3 of **3645**], . . . Burgh (now Peterborough) in pre-Norman times, *etc.* 2 vol. 8° London, 1871. [Gross, 998.]

3673 Hugh, *Candidus, abbot of Peter-borough.* The chronicle of Hugh Candidus, a monk of Peterborough. Edited by W. T. Mellows. pp. xxxvi, 251. 8° London, 1949.

3674 —— The Peterborough chronicle of Hugh Candidus, translated by C. and W. T. Mellows, edited by W. T. Mellows. *Peterborough Natural History Society.* pp. 70. 8° Peterborough, 1941.

3675 Mellows (William Thomas). The estates of the monastery of Peterborough in the county of Lincoln. [Pp. 102–04, at Norman Conquest, etc.] Lincs. Historian, no. 3, pp. 100–14 : no. 4, pp. 124–66. 1948–49.

3676 Miller (Samuel Henry). Memorials of Leofric, abbot of Peterborough. [Nothing new.] Fenland N. and Q., 4, pp. 65–71. 1898.

3677 Poole (George Ayliffe). On the abbey church of Peterborough. ['Abbey of Medeshamstede founded : Burgh erected on the ruins : the site of Medeshamstede' : etc.] Assoc. Archit. Socs.' Rpts., 3, pp. 187–221. 1855.

3678 Stenton (*Sir* Frank Merry). Medeshamstede and its colonies. Hist. essays in honour of J. Tait, pp. 313–26. 1933.

3679 Stubbs (William), *bp. of Oxford.* On the foundation and early fasti of Peterborough. Archaeol. J., 18, pp. 193–211. 1861.

§ *j.* Tavistock

3680 Alexander (John James). Sihtric, fourth abbot of Tavistock. [Queries 1046 as his date of succession.] Devon and Cornwall N. and Q., 22, p. 101. 1942.

3681 Finberg (Herbert Patrick Reginald). Abbots of Tavistock. [First 5 in A.-S. period.] *Same jnl.,* 22, pp. 159–62. 1943.

3682 —— Childe's tomb. [Early history of Tavistock abbey, where Childe was buried.] Devonshire Studies, by W. G. Hoskins and H. P. R. Finberg, pp. 40–58. 1952.

3683 Finberg (Herbert Patrick Reginald). The house of Ordgar and the foundation of Tavistock abbey. [With text of charter.] E.H.R., 58, pp. 190–201. 1943.

3684 —— Tavistock abbey. A study in the social and economic history of Devon. *Cambridge studies in medieval life and thought,* N.S.2. pp. xii 320, + 2 plates, + map. 8° Cambridge, 1951. [Pp. 278–83, Latin text of the foundation charter, 981, from Ethelred II.]

3685 Radford (*Mrs.* G. H.). Tavistock abbey. [Pp. 120–24, A.-S. period.] Rept. and Trans. Devon. Assoc., 46, pp. 119–55, + 3 plates. 1914.

§ *k.* Other Monasteries

3686 Andrews (Francis Baugh). Pershore monastery : some chapters on its foundation and history. [Founded c. 689 by Oswald nephew of king Ethelred.] Laudate, 9, pp. 4–14, 89–98. 1931.

3687 Astley (Hugh John Dukinfield). The early history and associations of Lindisfarne, or Holy Island. J. Brit. Archaeol. Assoc., 58 (N.S. 8), pp. 115–28. 1902.

3688 Bazeley (William). The early days of the abbey of St. Peter, Gloucester. [Founded by Osric, 7th c.] Trans. Bristol and Glos. Arch. Soc., 13, pp. 155–61. 1889.

3689 Birch (Walter de Gray). Historical notes on the manuscripts belonging to Ramsey abbey [Hunts.]. [Pp. 229–31, early history of the abbey.] J. Brit. Archaeol. Assoc., 55 (N.S. 5), pp. 229–42. 1899.

3690 Boyle (John Roberts). On the monastery and church of St. Peter, Monkwearmouth. [Deals both with its history and architecture.] Archaeol. Æl., N.S. 11, pp. 33–51, + 4 plates. 1886.

3691 Brock (Edgar Philip Loftus). Winchcombe abbey. [Pp. 446–49, A.-S. period.] J. Brit. Archaeol. Assoc., 32, pp. 446–54. 1876.

3692 Chope (Richard Pearse). Hartland abbey. [Pp. 50–54, St. Nectan : Domesday material.] Rept. and Trans. Devon. Assoc., 57 (1926), pp. 49–112, + 4 plates. 1927.

3692a —— The religious houses of Devon. Devonian Y.B., 15, pp. 47–61. 1924.

3693 Clarke (Kate M.). The conventual houses of Exeter and the neighbourhood. [Pp. 129–33, A.-S. period.] Devon N. and Q., 3, pp. 129–51. 1905.

3694 Clutterbuck (R. H.). The story of Wherwell abbey. [Connections with Edred and Edgar : abbey founded by Ethelred II in 1002.] Hants. N. and Q., 4, pp. 85–96, + map. 1889.

3695 Compton (C. H.). The foundation of Waltham abbey. [Pp. 137–41, A.-S. period.] J. Brit. Archaeol. Assoc., 53 (N.S. 3), pp. 137–47. 1896.

3696 Cornford (Margaret E.). The religious houses of Durham. [Pp. 79–85, Saxon monasteries.] V.C.H., Durham, 2, pp. 78–131. 1907.

3697 Crawford (Osbert Guy Stanhope). Thunor's pit. [Boundaries of monastic ground in Thanet by course taken by tame doe : after murder of two grandsons of Ethelbert by Thunor (between 664 and 669).] Antiquity, 7, pp. 92–4, + 2 plates. 1933.

3698 Dowdeswell (E. R.). The monks of the monastery of St. Mary, at Tewkesbury. [Pp. 77–82, A.-S. period.] Trans. Bristol and Glos. Arch. Soc., 25, pp. 77–93. 1902.

3699 Ellis (Dorothy M. B.) and **Salzman** (Louis Francis). Religious houses [in Cambridgeshire]. [Pp. 199–202, Ely (A.-S. period) : pp. 210–12, Thorney (A.-S. period).] V.C.H. Cambs., 2, pp. 197–318. 1948.

3700 Emery (William). The priory and church of St. Neots, Huntingdonshire. [Pp. 11–13, A.-S. period.] Trans. Cambs. and Hunts. Archaeol. Soc., 2 (1904–07), pp. 11–24, + 2 plates. 1908.

3701 Eyton (Robert William). Wenlock priory [Shropshire]. [Pp. 99–105, A.-S. and Domesday.] Arch. Camb., N.S. 4, pp. 98–108. 1853.

3702 Freeman (Edward Augustus). The architecture and early history of Waltham abbey church. [Pp. 2–13, Early documentary history.] Trans. Essex Archaeol. Soc., 2, pp. 1–40, + 2 plates. 1863.

3703 Graham (Rose). The history of the alien priory of Wenlock. [Pp. 117–23, A.-S. period.] J. Brit. Archaeol. Assoc., 3rd S. 4, pp. 117–40, + plan + 6 plates. 1939.

3704 Haigh (Daniel Henry). Historical and descriptive notes relating to the ancient monasteries of St. Peter at Wearmouth, and St. Paul, at Jarrow. Trans. Brit. Archaeol. Ass. (2nd congress, Winchester, 1845), pp. 428–43, + 1 plate. 1846.

3705 —— Historical and descriptive notes relating to the ancient Saxon monastery at Repton, Derbyshire. *Same jnl.*, (2nd congress, Winchester, 1845), pp. 448–51. 1846.

3706 —— The monasteries of S. Heiu and S. Hild. Yorks. Archaeol. J., 3, pp. 349–91, 408, + 5 plates : 5, pp. 223–26, + 1 plate. 1875–79.

3707 Haigh (Gordon). The history of Winchcombe abbey. pp. 214. 8° London, 1947. [Pp. 11–30, A.-S.]

3708 Halliwell (James Orchard). On the history of the monastery of Ely, during the reign of William the Conqueror. Trans. R.Soc. Lit., 2nd s. 1, pp. 149–53. 1843.

3709 Hamilton (Adam). History of St. Mary's abbey of Buckfast, Devon. A.D. 760–1906. pp. xvi, 272, + 16 plates. [Gross, 878a. Pp. 1–36, A.-S. period.] 8° Buckfastleigh, 1907.

3710 Hind (G. E.). A Northumbrian monastery. [Lastingham, Yorks.] Irish Eccles. Rec., 4th S. 25, pp. 276–86. 1909.

3711 Hugo (Thomas). Athelney abbey. [Foundation by Alfred, etc.] Proc. Somerset Arch. Soc., 43 (1897), pp. 97–165. 1897.

3712 Hunt (William), *ed.* Two chartularies of the priory of St. Peter at Bath. *Somerset Record Society*, 7. pp. lxxx, 262. sm. 4° n.p., 1893. [Pp. 1–38, A.-S. period. A survey of seven Domesday manors.]

3712a Leach (Arthur Francis). Memorials of Beverley minster. vol. 1. *Surtees Socisty*, 98. pp. cxiv, 424. 8° Durham, 1898. [Pp. xv–xxxiii, monastery founded ? by St. John of Beverley, ? by Athelstan.]

3713 Levien (Edward). On early religious houses in Staffordshire. [Hanbury, etc.] J. Brit. Archaeol. Assoc., 29, pp. 325–37. 1873.

3714 —— On the early religious houses of Somersetshire. *Same jnl.*, 31, pp. 24–34. 1875.

3715 Low (John Low). Coldingham. [Pp. 186–90, history of Ebba's monastery.] Archaeol. Æl., N.S. 11, pp. 186–203. 1886.

3716 Lower (Mark Antony). The Chronicle of Battel abbey from 1066 to 1176, now first translated, with notes, *etc.* pp. xii, 227, + 2 plates. 8° London, 1851. [Pp. 1–42, under William I.]

3717 Martin (Alan R.). The alien priory of Lewisham. [Pp. 103–05, A.-S. period : pp. 125–26, on 5 A.-S. charters.] Trans. Greenwich Antiq. Soc., 3, pp. 103–27. 1927.

3718 Moule (H. J.). Abbotsbury abbey. [Pp. 38–39, A.-S. period.] Proc. Dorset Antiq. F.C., 8, pp. 38–48. 1887.

3719 Nightingale (J. E.). On the succession of the abbesses of Wilton, with some notice of Wilton seals. [Pp. 342–46, A.-S. period : 1st, abbess, Radegunde, 871.] Wilts. Archaeol. Mag., 19, pp. 342–62, + 1 plate. 1881.

3720 Page (William). St. Albans abbey before the Conquest. V.C.H., Herts., 4, pp. 367–72. 1914.

3721 Peers (*Sir* Charles Reed) and **Radford** (Courtenay Arthur Ralegh). The Saxon monastery at Whitby. [28 figures in text. History, sculptured stones, crosses, etc., and objects of metal, pottery, etc., excavated.] Archaeologia, 89, pp. 27–88, + 13 plates, + folding plan. 1943.

3722 Pocock (W. W.). Chertsey abbey. [Pp. 97–101, A.-S. period.] Surrey Archaeol. Collns., 1, pp. 97–114, + 7 plates, + plan. 1858.

3723 Roberts (R.). On Milton abbey church. [Pp. 78–80, its origin and foundation, c. 937.] Proc. Dorset Antiq. F.C., 4, pp. 78–90. 1882.

3724 Rose-Troup (Frances). The ancient monastery of St. Mary and St. Peter at Exeter, 680–1050. Rept. and Trans. Devon. Assoc., 63, pp. 179–220, + 6 plates. 1931.

3725 Savage (Henry Edwin). Abbess Hilda's first religious house. Archaeol. Æl., N.S. 19, pp. 47–75, + 1 plate. 1898.

3726 Simpson (William Douglas). Coldingham priory : a famous border monastery. [Pp. 69–76, A.-S. period.] Trans. Archit. Soc. Durham, 9, pp. 69–86, + 1 plate, + plan. 1939.

3727 Sisam (Kenneth). A secret murder. [Of Brihtnoth, abbot of Ely by king Edgar's widow Ælfthryth.] Medium Ævum, 22, p. 24. 1953.

3728 Smart (T. W. Wake). The ancient connection between Cranborne and Tewkesbury. Proc. Dorset Antiq., F.C. 8, pp. 29–37. 1887.

3728a Smith (Lucius), *bp. of Knaresborough*. The story of Ripon minster : a study in Church history, pp. 327, + plates. 4° Leeds, 1914. [Pp. 1–48, A.-S.]

3729 Stubbs (William), *bp. of Oxford*. Note on the date of the dedication of Waltham abbey church. [1060 : charter from Confessor, 1062.] Trans. Essex Archaeol. Soc., 2, pp. 59–60. 1863.

3730 Taylor (Charles Samuel). The church and monastery of Westbury-on-Trym. Proc. Clifton Antiq. Club, 4 (1897–99), pp. 20–42. 1900.

3731 —— Deerhurst, Pershore and Westminster. [Grant of Deerhurst and Pershore to Westminster by Edward the Confessor : estates belonging to them.] Trans. Bristol and Glos. Arch. Soc., 25, pp. 230–50. 1902.

3732 Thompson (Alexander Hamilton). The monastic settlement at Hackness and its relation to the abbey of Whitby. Yorks. Archaeol. J., 27, pp. 388–405. 1924.

3733 Thompson (Alexander Hamilton). Notes on the history of the abbey of St. Peter, St. Paul, and St. Oswald, Bardney. [Pp. 35–37, A.-S. period.] Assoc. Archit. Socs.' Rpts., 32, pp. 35–96, 351–402. 1913–14.

3734 Tooker (E. G.). Waltham abbey: its early history and architecture. J. Brit. Archaeol. Assoc., 63 (N.S. 13), pp. 1–28, + 2 plates, + plan. 1907.

3735 Ward (Gordon). The forgotten Saxon nunnery of St. Werburg at Hoo. Arch. Cant., 47, pp. 117–25. 1935.

3736 —— Saxon abbots of Dover and Reculver. Arch. Cant., 59 (1946), pp. 19–28. 1947.

3737 Way (Albert). The legend of Saint Werstan, and the first Christian establishment at Great Malvern. [Grant by Edward the Confessor.] Archaeol. J., 2, pp. 48–65. 1846.

3738 Wheeler (Lucy). Chertsey abbey. pp. xvi, 232. 8° London, 1905. [Pp. 1–62, A.-S. : Christianity in Wessex, Eorcenwald (founder), etc.]

3739 Williams (Laurence Frederic Rushbrook). History of the abbey of St. Alban. pp. xiii, 251, + plan. 8° London, 1917. [Pp. 17–32, the Saxon abbots : pp. 239–41, Foundation charter, 793 (MS. Cotton Nero, D. I. fol. 148) Latin text : pp. 242–43, second charter of Offa, 795 (ditto, fol. 148a–b, and 151 a-b) ; p. 245, St. Alban's land in Domesday.]

3740 Willis-Bund (John William). Worcestershire and Westminster. [A.-S. connections from time of Offa : Pershore, etc.] Assoc. Archit. Socs'. Rpts., 34, pp. 329–62. 1918.

3741 Winchester, *New Minster and Hyde abbey.* Liber vitae : register and martyrology of New Minster and Hyde abbey, Winchester. Edited by Walter de Gray Birch. pp. xcvi, 335. *Hampshire Record Society*, 5. 8° London and Winchester, 1892. [Appendices containing texts of charters to New Minster.]

3742 Young (George). A history of Whitby and Streoneshalh abbey. 2 vol. 8° Whitby, 1817. [Gross, 1191.]

61. MONASTIC HISTORY, CELTIC

§ *a.* General

3743 Albers (Bruno). Il monachismo nell' Irlanda e nell' Inghilterra. Riv. stor. benedettina, 10, pp. 183–203. 1915.

3744 Archdall (Mervyn). Monasticon Hibernicum ; or an history of the abbies, priories and other religious houses in Ireland. pp. xxiii, 820. 8° London, 1786. —. Edited, with many additional notes, by P. F. Moran. Vol. 1–2. *No more published.* 8° Dublin, 1873–76.

3745 —— Monasticon Hibernicum ... County of Antrim (of Armagh, Clare, Cork, Derry). [Text from Archdall : notes by the editors.] Irish Eccles. Rec., 5–8, *passim.* 1868–72.

3746 Baring-Gould (Sabin). The Celtic monasteries. Arch. Camb., 5th S. 17, pp. 249–76. 1900.

3747 Blair (David Hunter). The contributions of the monasteries to Scottish history. [Influence of the Columban monks.] Scot. H. R., 25, pp. 194–98. 1928.

3747a Duckett (Eleanor Shipley). The gateway to the Middle Ages. pp. xiii, 620. 8° New York, 1938. [Pp. 419–78, Celtic monasticism.]

3748 Fahey (J. A.). Primitive Irish monasteries. Irish Eccles. Rec., 3rd S. 4, pp. 80–88, 348–58, 508–17. 1883.

3749 Howorth (*Sir* Henry Hoyle). The Irish monks and the Norsemen. Trans. R.H.S., 8, pp. 281–330. 1880.

3750 Knox (R. B.). The decline of early Irish monasticism. Bull. Irish Committee of Historical Sciences, no. 39. 1945.

3751 Loth (Joseph). Le monachisme irlandais d'après un ouvrage récent [Ryan : Irish monasticism] et le monachisme britton.   1e partie, le monachisme irlandais. Ann. de Bretagne, 40, pp. 375–411, 661–80. 1933.

3752 MacBain (Alexander). The Culdees [in Scotland]. Trans. Gaelic Soc. Inverness, 23, pp. 146–53. 1902.

3753 MacNaught (John Campbell). Celtic monasticism. *Same jnl.*, 35 (1929–30), pp. 321–42. 1939.

3754 Martin (P. Harney). Life in an ancient Irish monastery. Historical Bull. (St. Louis), 27,pp. 3 *et seq.* 1948.

3755 Pflugk-Harttung (Julius von). Die Kuldeer. Zeit. Kirchengesch, 14, pp. 169–92. 1894.

3756 Pokorny (Julius). A. I. *montar, muinter.* [= the several foundations (familia) of an abbot.] Zeit. celt. Philol., 10, pp. 202–04. 1915.

3757 Reeves (William), *bp. of Down.* On the Céli-dé, commonly called Culdees. [9th c.→.] Trans. R.I.A., 24 iii (Antiq.), pp. 119–264. 1873.

3758 —— On the early system of abbatial succession in the Irish monasteries. [Trim, Armagh and Iona.] Proc. R.I.A., 6 (1857), pp. 447–51. 1858.

3759 Rushe (James Patrick). A second Thebaid : being a popular account of the ancient monasteries of Ireland. pp. xiii, 291. 8° Dublin, 1905. [Kenney, 1, p. 288.]

3760 Ryan (John). Irish monasticism. Origins and early development. pp. xv, 413, xiv. 8° London. 1921.

3761 —— Origins and ideals of Irish monasticism. Studies, 19, pp. 637–48. 1930.

3762 Willis-Bund (John William). The early Welsh monasteries. Arch. Camb., 5th S. 8, pp. 262–76 : 9, pp. 18–35. 1891–92.

3763 —— The religious houses in south Wales after 1066. [Founded from political rather than religious considerations. 6 founded between 1066 and 1100.] Arch. Camb., 5th S. 7, pp. 1–27. 1890.

§ *b.* Individual
(for others founded by St. Columba

See 69 § *c.*)

3764 Arnold (Thomas). An account of St. Columba's abbey, Inchcombe. [Pp. 45–49, early history of the island. Oratory, ? 9th c.] Archaeol. Scot., 5, pp. 45–70, + 3 plates. 1874.

3765 Brett (Thomas). Mayo of the Saxons. [Mayo abbey, founded by St. Colman, 668.] Irish Eccles. Rec., 5th S. 21, pp. 247–60. 1923.

3766 Carroll (Frederick M.). Some notes on the abbey and cross of Moone and other places in the valley of the Griese. J. co. Kildare Archaeol. Soc., 1, pp. 286–94, + 4 plates. 1895.

3767 Comey (Martin). The monastery at Slanore, [Cavan]. Breifny Antiq. Soc. J., 1, pp. 166–73. 1921.

3768 Doherty (William). The abbey of Fahan [co. Donegal]. [8 miles north of Derry. Founded by St. Mura, 6th c. Crozier and bell of St. Mura.] Proc. R.I.A., 2nd S. 2 (Antiq.), pp. 97–104. 1881.

3769 Fahey (J. A.). The sanctuaries of the Corrib : Inchiquin [co. Clare]. [Monastery founded by St. Brendan, c. 552 : St. Fursey.] Irish Eccles. Rec., 4th S. 12, pp. 193–212. 1902.

3770 Gwynn (Aubrey). The Irish monastery of Bangor. *Same jnl.*, 5th S. 74, pp. 388–97. 1950.

3771 Gwynn (Edward John) and **Purton** (W. J.). The monastery of Tallaght. [Teaching and practices of Maelruain, the founder and his disciple Maeldithruib (d. 840) : from MS. 3 B. 23 in R.I.A. library. Text in Irish, with translation and notes.] Proc. R.I.A., 29c, pp. 115–79. 1912.

3772 Healy (John), *abp. of Tuam.* An island shrine in the west. [Ardilaun, co. Galway. Founded by St. Fechin, 7th c.] Irish Eccles, Rec., 3rd S. 11, pp. 673–86. 1890.

3773 —— The monastic school of Ross [co. Cork]. [Founded by St. Fachtna, 6th c.] *Same jnl.*, 3rd S. 11, pp. 1–8. 1890.

3774 Henry (Françoise). The antiquities of Caher Island (co. Mayo). [Monastery flourishing (from evidence of the slabs) c. 7th c.] J. Roy. Soc. Antiq. Ireland, 77, pp. 23–38, + 6 plates. 1947.

3775 Kelly (Matthew J.). Three monasteries of Drogheda. County Louth Archaeol. J., 10, pp. 25–41, + 1 plate, + plan. 1941.

3776 Langan (Thomas). Clomacnoise. [St. Ciaran and his monastery.] J. Ardagh and Clonmacnoise Antiq. Soc., 1 i, pp. 71–85. 1926.

3777 Lawlor (Henry Cairnes). The monastery of Saint Mochaoi of Nendrum. *Belfast N.H. and Phil. Soc.* pp. xxviii, 187, + 19 plates, + plan. 8° Belfast, 1925. [Founded 445. Internal economy of a Hiberno-Celtic monastery : name and earliest history : St. Mochaoi, Danes, etc.]

3778 Macalister (Robert Alexander Stuart). The story of Clonmacnois. Proc. Belfast N.H. and Phil. Soc., 2nd S. 1, pp. 9–11. 1937.

3779 Macarthy (Charles J. F.). The Celtic monastery of Cork. [Founded by St. Finnbarr, c. 600.] J. Cork Hist. Soc., 2nd S. 48, pp. 4–8. 1943.

3780 Megaw (Basil R. S.). The monastery of St. Maughold. [Plates of inscribed stories.] I.O.M. Nat. Hist. and Antiq. Soc., Proc., N.S. 5, pp. 169–80, + 4 plates, + map. 1950.

3781 Monahan (John). Clonmacnoise, or the seven churches. Irish Eccles. Rec., 3rd S. 3, pp. 653–58, 718–23 ; 4, pp. 100–07. 1882–83.

3782 Murphy (Denis). Mungret abbey, county Limerick. J. Roy. Hist. and Arch. Assoc. Ireland, [19], 4th S. 9, pp. 171–81, + 1 plate. 1889.

3783 Murray (Laurence P.). Monasteries of Louth. Part 1—The pre-Norman monasteries. County Louth Archaeol. J., 1. i, pp. 23–36, + 2 plates. 1904.

3784 O'Reilly (Patrick). Drumlane abbey [co. Cavan]. [Founded by St. Mogue ?—or St. Columcille?] Breifny Antiq. Soc. J.,2, pp. 132–64. 1924.

3785 Palmer (Alfred Neobaud). Notes on the early history of Bangor Is y Coed [Monachorum]. [6th c. →.] Y Cymmrodor, 10, pp. 12–28. 1889.

3786 Price (Liam). Glendalough [co. Wicklow] : St. Kevin's road. [Died 618.] Essays presented to E. MacNeill, pp. 244–71, + 2 plates. 1940.

3787 Q. (J. C.). The early monastic associations of Spike Island and Cork harbour. J. Cork Hist. Soc., 2nd S. 41, pp. 47–48. 1936.

3788 Radford (Courtenay Arthur Ralegh). Celtic monastery on St. Helen's, Isles of Scilly. [Plan on p. 345.] Antiq. J., 41, pp. 344–46. 1941.

3789 —— Tintagel : the castle and Celtic monastery. Antiq. J., 15, pp. 401–19, + plan + 5 plates. 1935.

3790 Reade (George H.). Cill-Sleibhe-Cuillinn. Founded by St. Darerca, alias Moninne, about A.D. 518. [Kilslieve, co. Armagh. It is said she was brought up by St. Brigid.] J. Hist. Assoc. Ireland, [10] 3rd S. 1, pp. 93–102, + 2 plates. 1868.

3791 Ryan (John). The abbatial succession of Clonmacnoise, from the foundation of the monastery to the coming of the Norse, A.D. 545–799. Essays presented to Eoin MacNeill, pp. 490–507. 1940.

3792 Seymour (St. John Drelincourt). Liath-mor-Mochoemog. [Celtic monastery, co. Tipperary.] J. North Munster Archaeol. Soc., 2, pp. 127–33, + 1 plate. 1912.

3793 Simpson (William Douglas). The Celtic monastery and Cistercian abbey at Deer [Aberdeenshire]. [Founded by SS. Columba and Drostan.] Trans. Scot. Ecclesiol. Soc., 8, pp. 179–86. 1927.

3794 —— Coldingham priory. *Same jnl.*, 14, pp. 26–31. 1950.

3795 Stokes (George Thomas). Clane abbey [co. Kildare]. [Founded c. 520.] J. co. Kildare Archaeol. Soc., 3, pp. 101–06. 1899.

3796 Stuart (John). The monastery of St. Ebba. The priory of Coldingham. Hist. Berwick. Nat. Club, 5, pp. 207–29. 1865.

3797 Stuart (John). On the early history of the priory of Restennet. [Pp. 296–310: 'Report on the earlier part of the existing buildings,' begun by Nectan, king of the Picts. 8th c.] Archaeol. Scot., 5, pp. 285–316, + 6 plates. 1880.

3798 Stubbs (Francis William). Early monastic history of Dromiskin, in the county of Louth. J. Roy. Soc. Antiq. Ireland, 26 (5th S. 7), pp. 101–13. 1897.

3799 Tempest (H. G.). The monastery of Inis-mocht, [co. Meath]. [Island monastery plundered by Norsemen during great frosts, e.g. in 939 and 1026.] County Louth Archaeol. J., 10, pp. 342–45. 1944.

62. DIOCESAN HISTORY

§ a. Anglo-Saxon

3800 Alexander (John James). Bishops Tawton. [A mythical A.-S. see.] Rept. and Trans. Devon. Assoc., 72, pp. 98–100. 1941.

3801 Atkins (*Sir* Ivor). The Church of Worcester from the eighth to the twelfth century. [i. The constitution of the ' familia ' from the foundation of the see to St. Oswald : ii. The familia from the middle of the tenth to the beginning of the twelfth century. Appendix of charters and other documents.] Antiq. J., 17, pp. 371–91 : 20, pp. 1–38, 203–29, + 2 plates. 1937–40.

3802 Baber (Harry). Sketch of the parish of Ramsbury, Wiltshire. [Pp. 139–40, sketch of bishopric.] J. Brit. Archaeol. Assoc., 47, pp. 139–45. 1891.

3803 Barnes (W. Miles) *and others*. S. Birinus and the West Saxon bishopric. [Reasons for believing that the see of Birinus was at Dorchester (Dorset), not at Dorchester (Oxon). Refuted and discussed by W.B.W., H. J. Moule, Henry Symonds, etc.] N. and Q. Som. and Dorset, 2, pp. 98–103, 128–30, 171–75, 218–21, 281–83, 298–301 : 3, pp. 8–10, 45–47. 1891–92.

3804 Batson (Henrietta M.). The bishopric of Ramsbury. Q.J. Berks. Archaeol. Soc., 3, p. 206. 1895.

3805 Brownlow (William Robert Bernard), *bishop of Clifton*. The division of the bishoprics of Wessex. Proc. Somerset Arch. Soc., 44 (1898), pp. 149–57. 1898.

3806 Calthrop (M. M.). Ecclesiastical history [of Lincolnshire] to A.D. 1600. [Pp. 1–10, A.-S. period.] V.C.H., Lincoln, 2, pp. 1–58. 1906.

3807 Carne (John). The bishopric of Cornwall. Saxon period. J. Roy. Inst. Cornwall, 2, pp. 177–218. 1867.

3808 Chanter (John Roberts). Tawton—the first Saxon bishopric of Devonshire. Rept. and Trans. Devon. Assoc., 7, pp. 179–96. 1875.

3809 Cole (Robert Eden George). Notes on the ecclesiastical history of the deanery of Graffoe [Lincs.] to the close of the fourteenth century. [Pp. 384–89, A.-S. period : first plate is of A.-S. sculpture on Bassingham font.] Assoc. Archit. Socs.' Rpts., 24, pp. 381–448, + 2 plates. 1898.

3810 Cotton (Charles). The Saxon cathedral at Canterbury, and the Saxon saints buried therein. *Publications of the Univ. of Manchester*, 201. pp. xv, 111, + 10 plates. 8° Manchester, 1929.

3811 Cox (John Charles). Ecclesiastical history [of Hampshire]. [Pp. 1–10, A.-S. period.] V.C.H., Hampshire, 2, pp. 1–103. 1903.

**3812 —— ** Ecclesiastical history [of Suffolk]. [Pp. 1–11, A.-S. period.] V.C.H., Suffolk, 2, pp. 1–52. 1907.

3813 Craster (*Sir* Herbert Henry Edmund). The Red Book of Durham. [Contains history of sees of Lindisfarne, Chester-le-Street, and Durham : Book of High Altar of Durham.] E.H.R., 40, pp. 504–32. 1925.

**3814 —— ** Some Anglo-Saxon records of the see of Durham. Archaeol. Æl., 4th S. 1, pp. 189–98. 1925.

3815 Deanesly (Margaret). The archdeacons of Canterbury under archbishop Coelnoth (833–870). E.H.R., 42, pp. 1–11. 1927.

3816 Dickens (A. G.). The shire and privileges of the archbishop in eleventh century York. [A Domesday problem.] Yorks. Arch. J., 38, pp. 131–42. 1953.

3817 Fairbank (F. R.). York *versus* Canterbury. [Precedence owing to letter of Gregory to Augustine. Pp. 85–89, A.-S. period.] *Same jnl.*, 13, pp. 84–98. 1895.

3818 Godwin (Henry). Notes on the West Saxon bishoprics, more particularly that of Sherborne. J. Brit. Archaeol. Assoc., 28, pp. 313–27. 1872.

3819 Harrod (Henry). On the site of the bishopric of Elmham. Proc. Suffolk Inst. Archaeol., 4, pp. 7–13. 1864.

3820 Healy (John), *abp. of Tuam*. The Irish bishops of Lindisfarne. Irish Eccles. Rec., 3rd S. 8, pp. 289–302. 1887.

3821 Holmes (Thomas Scott). Ecclesiastical history [of Somerset]. [Pp. 1–10, A.-S. period.] V.C.H., Somerset, 2, pp. 1–67. 1911.

3822 Howlett (Richard). The ancient see of Elmham. Norfolk Archaeology, 18, pp. 105–28, + 3 plates (2 of plans). 1914.

3823 Jones (William Henry Rich). The bishops of Old Sarum, A.D. 1075–1225. [Herman, 1075–78 : Osmund, 1078–99.] Wilts. Archaeol. Mag., 17, pp. 161–91. 1878.

3824 —— Early annals of the episcopate in Wilts and Dorset. 8° London, 1871.

3825 Kemble (John Mitchell). A few notes respecting the bishops of East Anglia. [Pp. 51–54 : ' the will of bishop Deodred of London in Saxon and in English.'] Mems. Archaeol. Inst., [3] (1847), pp. 24–56. 1851.

3826 Livett (Grevile Mairis). Ecclesiastical history [of Kent] to the death of Lanfranc. V.C.H., Kent, 2, pp. 1–24. 1926.

3827 Longstaffe (William Hylton Dyer). The hereditary sacerdotage of Hexham. Archaeol. Æl., N.S. 4, pp. 11–28. 1860.

3828 Magoun (Francis Peabody), *jr.* Aldhelm's diocese of Sherborne *bewestan wuda*. Harvard Theol. Rev., 32, pp. 103–14. 1939.

2829 Miles (George). The bishops of Lindisfarne, Hexham, Chester-le-Street, and Durham, A.D. 635–1020. pp. xv, 311. 8° London, 1898. [Gross, 1618.]

3830 Moor (C.). The see of Lincoln. [The Conqueror's charter, etc.] Lincs. Archit. Soc. Rpts., 43 (N.S. 1, for 1937), pp. 121–26. 1939.

3831 Page (W. M.). The priory church of S. Andrew, Hexham. Trans. Scot. Ecclesiol. Soc., 9, pp. 97–106. 1929.

3832 Page (William). Ecclesiastical history [of Hertfordshire] before the Conquest. V.C.H., Herts., 4, pp. 282–94. 1914.

3833 Pedler (E. H.). The Anglo-Saxon episcopate of Cornwall ; with some account of the bishops of Crediton. 8° London, 1856. [Gross, 1617.]

3834 Risk (J. Erskine). The bishoprics and lands of the five western dioceses of Winchester, Ramsbury, Sherborne, Wells, and Crediton, and their division. Rept. and Trans. Devon. Assoc., 29, pp. 510–13. 1897.

3835 Sheehy (Stephen). The manner of appointing bishops in England. Its origin, growth and later developments. Part 1. [Pp. 529–33, A.-S.] Downside Rev., 54, pp. 528–40. 1936.

3836 Smith (Martin Linton), *bp. of Rochester*. The early succession of the see of Hereford. [Evidence from the Textus Roffensis.] Trans. Woolhope N.F.C., 1930–32, pp. 141–44. 1935.

3837 Smith (Reginald Anthony Lendon). The early community of St. Andrew at Rochester, 604—c. 1080. [Argument that ' the community was secular in origin and continued to be so without interruption until the Norman Conquest.'] E.H.R., 60, pp. 289–99. 1945.

3838 Stephens (William Richard Wood). Memorials of the South Saxon see and cathedral church of Chichester. 8° London, 1876. [Gross, 1109.]

3839 Stephens (William Richard Wood). The South-Saxon diocese, Selsey-Chichester . . . with map and plan. *Diocesan Histories*. pp. vii, 282. 8° London, 1881.

3840 Stevenson (Francis Seymour). The present state of the Elmham controversy. Proc. Suffolk Inst. Archaeol., 19, pp. 110–16. 1926.

3841 Stubbs (William), *bp. of Oxford*. The cathedral, diocese, and monasteries of Worcester in the eighth century. Archaeol. J., 19, pp. 236–52. 1862.

3842 —— Registrum sacrum Anglicanum : an attempt to exhibit the course of episcopal succession in England from the records and chronicles of the Church. 2nd edition. pp. xvi, 248. 4° Oxford, 1897. [Gross, 814. Pp. 1–39, A.-S. period.]

3843 Tait (James). Ecclesiastical history [of Lancashire] to the Reformation. [Pp. 1–11, A.-S. period.] V.C.H., Lancs., 2, pp. 1–40. 1908.

3844 Taylor (Thomas). Evolution of the diocesan bishopric from the monastery bishoprics of Cornwall. Rev. celt., 35, pp. 301–16. 1914. *Also in* J. Roy. Inst. Cornwall, 19, pp. 416–32. 1914.

3845 —— The monastery bishoprics of Cornwall. Rev. celt., 35, pp. 193–202. 1914. *Also in* J. Roy. Inst. Cornwall, 19, pp. 406–15. 1914.

3846 Thompson (Alexander Hamilton). Ecclesiastical history [of Yorkshire]. [Pp. 1–12, A.-S. period.] V.C.H., York, 3, pp. 1–88. 1913.

3847 Walcott (Mackenzie Edward Charles), *etc.* Ancient English episcopal sees. [And titles of A.-S. bps.] N. and Q., 5th S. 2, pp. 117, 291. 1874.

3848 —— Catalogue of bishops of Selsey and Chichester. 8° [London, 1866].

3849 Whiting (Charles Edwin). The Anglian bishops of Hexham. [A life of Wilfrid, followed by a chronicle of the kingdom and Church of Northumbria (including the bishopric of Hexham), 604–820.] Arch. Æl., 4th S. 24, pp. 119–56. 1946.

3850 Woodruffe (Charles Eveleigh). Some early professions of canonical obedience to the see of Canterbury. Trans. St. Paul's Ecclesiol. Soc., 7, pp. 161–76, + 1 plate. 1915.

§ b. Celtic

3851 [Anon.] The antiquity of Bangor, Carnarvonshire. [See founded by St. Deiniol, 6th c.] Antiquity, 26, pp. 145–47. 1952.

3852 Brady (John). The original growth of the diocese of Meath. [From Clonard and Duleek.] Irish Eccles. Rec., 5th S. 72, pp. 1–13. 1949.

3853 Callary (Philip). History of Trim, [Meath], as told in her ruins. [See founded by St. Patrick.] *Same jnl.*, 4th S. 2, pp. 442–49. 1897.

3854 Cooke (Edward Alexander). The diocesan history of Killaloe [co. Clare], Kilfenora [co. Clare], Clonfert [co. Galway], and Kilmacduagh, [co. Galway]. A.D. 639—A.D. 1886. pp. viii, 140. 8° Dublin, 1886.

3855 Cotton (Henry). Fasti ecclesiae Hibernicae. The succession of the prelates and members of the cathedral bodies of Ireland. 5 vol. 8° Dublin, 1851–60.

3856 Flood (William Henry Grattan). The episcopal city of Ferns [co. Wexford]. [See founded 6th c.]. Irish Eccles. Rec., 4th S. 2, pp. 350–63, 1897.

3857 Gogarty (Thomas). The boundaries of some Irish dioceses. Irish Theol. Q., 4, pp. 275–303. 1909.

3858 Gwynn (Aubrey). The origins of the see of Dublin. [Diocese first organized in the reign of Sitric Silkbeard, king of Dublin (989–1036).] Irish Eccles. Rec., 5th S. 57, pp. 40–55, 97–112. 1941.

3859 Kermack (W. R.). Trumwine's diocese. [That of the Picts.] Antiquity, 17, pp. 212–13. 1943.

3860 Kolsrud (Oluf). The Celtic bishops in the Isle of Man, the Hebrides and Orkneys. Zeit. celt. Phil., 9, pp. 357–79. 1913.

3861 Long (R. H.). Cashel and Emly. [History of diocese to 1142.] J. Cork Hist. Soc., 2nd S. 4, pp. 170–85 ; 6, pp. 21–32. 1898, 1900.

3861a Newell (Ebenezer Josiah). Supremacy of the see of Canterbury. [Consecration of Welsh bps. by abp.] Cymru Fu, 1, pp. 173–75. 1888.

3862 O'Doherty (John K.). The see of St. Eugene at Ardstraw [co. Tyrone], together with a sketch of the history and the antiquities of its neighbourhood. [Founded c. 602. Later removed to Derry.] Irish Eccles. Rec., 4th S. 4, pp. 385–410. 1898.

3863 Power (Patrick). The early bishops of Lismore. Same jnl., 5th S. 68, pp. 42–52. 1946.

3864 Ronan (Myles V.). The diocese of Dublin in its beginnings. [i. Kings of Dublin : ii. Bishops of Dublin.] Same jnl., 5th S. 42, pp. 471–87 ; 43, pp. 12–26, 137–54. 1934.

3865 Webster (Charles A.). The diocese of Ross and its ancient churches. [The coming of Christianity : St. Fachtna and his house at Ross Ailithir : The coming of the Norsemen, etc.] Proc. R.I.A., 40 c., pp. 255–95, + 2 plates. 1932.

3866 Willis-Bund (John William). The Teilo churches. [Claim of jurisdiction by bishops of Llandaff, 10th–12th c.] Arch. Camb., 5th S. 10, pp. 193–217. 1893.

64. HISTORIES OF INDIVIDUAL CHURCHES

§ a. Anglo-Saxon

3867 Barns (Thomas). The seven churches of Oxford. Berks, Bucks and Oxon Archaeol. J., 15, pp. 120–25. 1910.

3868 Butterworth (George). Notes on the early history of Deerhurst. Proc. Clifton Antiq. Club, 1 (1884–88), pp. 22–26. 1888.

3869 Cash (J. O.). The Saxon church at Glastonbury. St. Dunstan's tower. N. and Q., Som. and Dorset, 20, pp. 193–97. 1932.

3870 Cater (W. A.). The date of the foundation of the church of St. Alphage, London Wall. Trans. Lond. and Middsx. Archaeol. Soc., N.S. 4, pp. 179–80. 1922.

3871 Cave-Browne (J.). Minster in Sheppey. [Pp. 144–47, foundation of the church by Sexburga, 675.] Arch. Cant., 22, pp. 144–68. 1897.

3872 Clarke (Daisy Emily Martin). Two Exeter churches and the Vikings. [St. Edmund and St. Olave and their connection with Gytha, wife of God-wine.] Devon and Cornwall N. and Q., 15, pp. 374–79 ; 16, p. 255. 1929–31.

3873 Clifford (H.). St. Andrew's church, Greensted, Essex. Home Counties Mag., 14, pp. 274–79. 1912.

3874 Davidson (James Bridge). On some ancient documents relating to Crediton minster. [4 documents (indulgences, etc.) in A.-S., with translations. See also note by O. J. Reichel on document 4 in Devon and Cornwall N. and Q., 10, pp. 120–21, 1918.] Rept. and Trans. Devon. Assoc., 10, pp. 237–54. 1878.

3875 Dickins (Bruce). The dedication stone of St. Mary-le-Wigford, Lincoln. Archaeol. J., 103 (1946), pp. 163, 165. 1947.

3876 Dodds (George). Observations on the origin of St. Mary-Stow, in the county of Lincoln. [Shows Stow church was never a cathedral, or mother of that of Lincoln. Built c. 673, destroyed by Danes, c. 873, rebuilt c. 1010 for secular priests by Eadnoth, bp. of Dorchester, etc.] Reliquary, 12, pp. 239–44; 13, pp. 29–34. 1872.

3877 Dowker (George). Reculver church. Arch. Cant., 12, pp. 248–68, + 2 plates. 1878.

3878 Finny (W. E. St. Lawrence). The Saxon church at Kingston-upon-Thames. J. Brit. Archaeol. Assoc., N.S. 32, pp. 253–64, + 1 plate, and plan. 1926.

3879 Fishwick (H.). Pre-Norman churches in Lancashire. Same jnl., 51 (N.S. 1), pp. 154–60. 1895.

3880 Forster (R. H.). Wilfrid's church at Hexham. [Plate shows foundations of 7th c. apse.] *Same jnl.*, 64 (N.S. 14), pp. 185–92, + 1 plate. 1908.

3881 Fowler (Joseph Thomas). The Church in Ripon. [Pp. 1–7, A.-S. period.] Yorks. Archaeol. J., 22, pp. 1–15. 1913.

3882 Hodgson (J. F.). Hartlepool church. [Work of Hilda, etc.] Archaeol. Æl., N.S. 17, pp. 201–43, + 7 plates. 1895.

3883 Hope (*Sir* William Henry St. John). The site of the Saxon cathedral church of Wells. Archaeol. J., 67, pp. 223–34, + 2 plans. 1910.

3884 Jenkins (Robert Charles). The basilica of Lyminge : Roman, Saxon, and mediæval. Arch. Cant., 9, pp. 205–23. 1874.

3885 —— Historical notes relating to the church or minster of St. Mary and St. Eadburg, in Lyminge, co. Kent. J. Brit. Archaeol. Assoc., 43, pp. 363–69. 1887.

3886 —— St. Mary's Minster in Thanet, and St. Mildred. Arch. Cant., 12, pp. 177–96. 1878.

3887 Jones (William Henry). On the finding of the Saxon church of St. Laurence at Bradford-on-Avon. J. Brit. Archaeol. Assoc., 31, pp. 143–52, + 2 plates. 1875.

3888 Middleton (John Henry). Newly-discovered Saxon church [Odda's] at Deerhurst, Gloucestershire [and plans for its restoration]. Proc. Soc. Antiq., 2nd S. 11, pp. 15–19, 155. 1885–86.

3889 Morley (Claude). A check-list of the (1001) sacred buildings of Suffolk to which are added gilds. [Including the few A.-S., and those mentioned in Domesday.] Proc. Suffolk Inst. Archaeol., 19, pp. 168–211. 1926.

3890 Morris (Joseph E.). Saxon churches in old London. [Records of All Hallow's, Lombard St. (1053) : St. Michael's, Cornhill (1055) : St. Helen's, Bishopsgate (1010).] N. and Q., 172, pp. 156–57. 1937.

3891 Peers (*Sir* Charles Reed). The earliest Christian churches in England. [With 6 ground plans.] Antiquity, 3, pp. 65–74. 1929.

3892 Potts (Robert Ullock). St. Mildred's church, Canterbury. Further notes on the site. [Map of island of Binnewith on p. 21.] Arch. Cant., 56 (1943), pp. 19–22. 1944.

3893 Rawson (J.). The mother church of the Saxons. [St. Martin's, Canterbury ; re-dedicated to him.] N. and Q., 1st S. 3, pp. 90–91. 1851.

3894 Routledge (Charles Francis). The history of St. Martin's church, Canterbury. *Bell's cathedral series.* pp. xiv, 189, + 2 plates. 8° London, 1891.
—— 2nd edition. 8° London, 1901.

3895 Shore (Thomas William). Saxon and Norman churches in Hampshire and the Isle of Wight. [Including a list of those mentioned in Domesday.] Hants. N. and Q., 6, pp. 135–37. 1892.

3896 Smith (Henry Ecroyd). Reliques of the Anglo-Saxon churches of St. Bridget and St. Hildeburga, West Kirby, Cheshire. [Miscellaneous information : plates 1–4 show A.-S. sculpture fragments : pp. 33–42, ' Island of St. Hildeburghe, Anglo-Saxon period.'] Trans. Hist. Soc. Lancs. and Ches., N.S., 11 [=23], pp. 13–46, + 5 plates. 1871.

3897 Stevenson (William). The early churches of Nottinghamshire. Trans. Thornton Soc., [1], 1897, pp. 41–46. 1898.

3898 Tupling (G. H.). The pre-Conquest and Norman churches of Lancashire. Trans. Lancs. and Ches. Antiq. Soc., 60 (1948), pp. 1–28, + 6 plates. 1949.

3899 Ward (Gordon). The age of Saint Mildred's church, Canterbury. Arch. Cant., 54, pp. 62–68. 1942.

3900 —— The list of Saxon churches in the Textus Roffensis. Arch. Cant., 44, pp. 39–59. 1932.

3901 —— The lists of Saxon churches in the Domesday Monachorum and White Book of St. Augustine. Arch. Cant., 45, pp. 60–89. 1933.

3902 Williams (Geoffrey S.). The site of S. Aldhelm's church 'juxta Werham'. Proc. Dorset Archaeol. Soc., 64 (for 1942), pp. 60–67. 1943.

3903 Woodruff (Charles Everleigh). Church of SS. Mary and Ethelburga, Lyminge. J. Brit. Archaeol. Assoc., 70 (N.S. 20), pp. 192–95. 1914.

b. Celtic

3904 Clinnick (Anthony Allen). The story of the three churches of St. Piran (the miners' patron saint of Cornwall). pp. 16. 8° Truro, 1936. [i. How Christianity came to Cornwall : ii. St. Piran's oratory, etc.]

3904a Cochrane (Robert). Ancient monuments in the county of Cork. viii. List of some of the abbeys so called, and unclassified churches of early date. J. Cork Hist. Soc., 2nd S. 18, pp. 129–31. 1912.

3905 Dagg (George A. de M. Edwin). The old church of Aghalurcher, county Fermanagh. J. Roy. Soc. Antiq. Ireland, 24 (5th S. 4), pp. 264–70, + 1 plate. 1894.

3906 Dexter (Thomas Francis George). St. Piran's oratory : an attempt to trace its history and to show that it was a mediaeval pilgrim shrine. [Built 6th or 7th c.] J. Roy. Inst. Cornwall, 20, pp. pp. 358–73. 1919.

3907 MacDonald (James). Burghead [Moray] as the site of an early Christian church ; with notices of the incised bulls and the burning of the clavie. Trans. Glasgow Archaeol. Soc., N.S. 2, pp. 63–115, + map, + 6 plates. 1896.

3908 Olden (Thomas). The oratory of Gallerus. [At Kilmal Kedar, Kerry.] Proc. R.I.A., 3rd S. 3, pp. 564–69. 1895.

3909 Reeves (**William**), *bp. of Down*. The ancient churches of Armagh. Ulster J. Archaeol., 2nd S. 2, pp. 194–204 ; 3, pp. 193–95 ; 4, pp. 205–28 ; 5, pp. 220–27 ; 6, pp. 24–33. 1896–1900.

3910 Westropp (Thomas Johnson). A survey of the ancient churches in the county of Limerick. [Notes on the history : patrons and church names : survey of the churches.] Proc. R.I.A., 25C, pp. 327–480, + 9 plates. 1905.

64. LIVES OF ANGLO-SAXON ARCHBISHOPS AND BISHOPS

§ a. Aldhelm, Abbot of Malmesbury and 1st Bishop of Sherborne (705–09)

(*See also* Sherborne, in index, and **119** § *g.* for his riddles.)

3911 [Anon.] Somersetshire saints.— St. Aldhelm. Downside Rev., 5, pp. 244–51. 1886.

3912 Aldhelm, *St., bp. of Sherborne.* Opera. Edidit Rudolfus Ehwald. *Monumenta Germaniae historica. Auctorum antiquissimorum tomi primi pars prior,* 15. pp. xxv, 765, + 5 plates. 4° Berolini, 1913–19.

3913 Alexander (John James). Sherborne and its first bishop. Devon and Cornwall N. and Q., 16, pp. 26–31. 1930.

3914 Barnes (William). Ealdhelm and the meeting of the English and Britons, and their two Churches in Wessex. Proc. Somerset Arch. Soc., 20 (1874), pp. 85–97. 1875.

3915 Boenhoff (Leo). Aldhelm von Malmesbury : ein Beitrag zur angelsächsischen Kirchengeschichte. *Diss., Dresden.* 8° Dresden, 1894. [Gross, 1631.]

3916 Browne (George Forrest), *bp. of Bristol.* St. Aldhelm : his life and times. pp. 366. 8° London, 1903.[Gross, 1631a.]

3917 Cook (Albert Stanburrough). Aldhelm at the hands of Sharon Turner. Speculum, 2, pp. 201–03. 1927.

3918 —— Sources of the biography of Aldhelm. [Kenney, 1, p. 776.] Trans. Conn. Acad. Arts and Sci., 28, pp. 273–93. 1927.

3919 —— Who was the Ehfrid of Aldhelm's letter ? [? Eadfrith, bp. of Lindisfarne or four others.] Speculum, 2, pp. 363–73. 1927.

3920 Dolan (John Gilbert) and **Horne** (Ethelbert). St. Aldhelm. pp. 16. 8° London, [1909]. —Re-issue. *Catholic Biographies,* 21. 8° London, 1912.

3921 Ehwald (Rudolf). Aldhelm von Malmesbury. Jahrbücher k. Akad. gemeinütziger Wiss., Erfurt, N.F. 33, pp. 91–116. 1907.

3922 Fowler (Joseph). Saint Aldhelm. pp. 28. 8° *n.p.*, 1947.

3923 Furst (Clyde). A group of old authors. 8° Philadelphia, 1899. [Pp. 131 *et seq.*, Aldhelm.]

3924 Hausknecht (Emil). Die altenglischen Glossen des Codex Ms. 1650 der Kgl. Bibliothek zu Bruessel. [Aldhelm's De laudibus virginitatis sive de virginitate sanctorum.] Anglia, 6, pp. 96–103. 1883.

3925 Jones (William Henry Rich). The life and times of Aldhelm. Wilts. Archaeol. Mag., 8, pp. 62–81. *Same title. Society for Promoting Christian Knowledge.* 16° London, [1874].

3926 Logeman (Henri). New Aldhelm [De laude virginitatis] glosses. [*See also* **5832**.] Anglia, 13 (N.F.1), pp. 26–41. 1891.

3927 Manitius (Maximilian). Zu Aldhelm und Beda. pp. 102. 8° Wien, 1886. [Gross, 1632. 'Deals mostly with Aldhelm's literary works.' *Also in* Sitzungsb. k. Akad. Wiss., Wien, Phil.-hist. Kl., 112, pp. 535–637. 1886.

3928 Mazzoni (D.). Aldhelmiana. Studio critico letterario su Aldhelmo di Sherborne. [Kenney, 1, p. 226.] Riv. storica benedittina, 6, 1915. *Also separately*, Roma, 1916.

3929 Meade (R. J.). A short memoir of bishops Aldhelme and Athelme or Adelme [of Wells]. Proc. Somerset Arch. Soc., 20 (1874), pp. 74–84. 1875.

3930 Mueller (Lucian). Zu Aldhelmus. Rhein. Mus., N.F. 22, pp. 150–51. 1867.

3931 Napier (Arthur Sampson). Collation der altenglischen Aldhelmglossen des Codex 38 der Kathedral-Bibliothek zu Salisbury. Anglia, 15 (N.F. 3), pp. 204–09. 1893.

3932 Schlutter (Otto Bernhard). Zu den Brüsseler Aldhelmglossen. [Ms. 1650.] Anglia, 33 (N.F. 21), pp. 232–38. 1910.

3933 Wildman (William Beauchamp). Life of S. Ealdhelm. pp. 134. 8° London, 1905. [Gross, 1632*a*.]

3934 Zupitza (Julius). Eine Conjectur zu Aldhelm. Romanische Forschungen, 3, p. 280. 1887.

§ *b*. Augustine, 1st Archbishop of Canterbury (597–604)

3935 [Anon.] Was St. Augustine of Canterbury a Benedictine ? Downside Rev., 3, pp. 45–61, 223–40. 1884.

3936 Auden (H. M.). Did Augustine come to Cressage ? Trans. Shrop. Arch. Soc., 3rd S. 4, p. xvi (at end). 1904.

3937 Bassenge (F. E.). Die Sendung Augustins zur Bekehrung der Angelsachsen, A.D. 596–604. *Dissertation*. pp. iv, 75. 8° Leipzig, 1890. [Gross, 1633.]

3938 Bing (Harold F.). St. Augustine of Canterbury and the Saxon Church in Kent. [Sources : story of Augustine : landing-place : religious conditions on arrival : attitude to paganism : his influence on Kentish church architecture : his influence on church organization : burial place : character.] Arch. Cant., 62 (1949), pp. 108–29. 1950.

3939 Brou (Alexandre). Saint Augustine of Canterbury and his companions. From the French. pp. viii, 188. 8°. London, 1897. [Gross, 1634.]

3940 Browne (George Forrest), *bp. of Bristol*. Augustine and his companions. 4th edition. pp. vi, 205. 8° London, 1910. [Gross, 1635.]

3941 —— The St. Augustine commemoration. A sermon, etc. pp. 31. 8° London, 1897.

3942 Collins (William Edward). The beginnings of English Christianity, with special reference to the coming of St. Augustine. pp. 209. 8° London, 1898 [1897.] [Gross, 1614.]

3943 Cooper (James). The commemoration of the coming of S. Augustine at Ebbs fleet, Richborough and Canterbury, July 2nd and 3rd, 1897. Trans. Aberdeen Ecclesiol. Soc., 4 (1897), pp. 57–76. 1901.

3944 Cox (John Charles). [Exhibition of] a wooden chair from the church of Stanford Bishop, Herefordshire, traditionally assigned to St. Augustine : [also of the 'Bede chair' from Jarrow]. [Figures of both chairs in text.] Proc. Soc. Antiq., 2nd S. 17, pp. 234–38. 1898.

3945 Cutts (Edward Lewes). Saint Augustine. *The Fathers for English Readers.* pp. 239. 8° London, 1881. [Gross, 1636]—.Augustine of Canterbury. *Leaders of Religion.* pp. xii, 207. 8° London, 1895.

3946 Doble (Gilbert Hunter). Saint Augustine of Canterbury in Anjou. pp. 8. 8° Truro, 1932.

3947 Dowker (George). On the landing-place of St. Augustine. [Argument for Stonar-in-Thanet.] Arch. Cant., 22, pp. 123–39, + 2 maps. 1897.

3948 Dudden (Homes). Zur Frage nach der Echtheit und Abfassungszeit des ' Responsum b. Gregorii ad Augustinum episcopum '. Theologische Quartalschrift, 113, pp. 94–118. 1932.

3949 Gasquet (Francis Aidan), *cardinal.* The mission of St. Augustine, and other addresses. pp. viii, 209. 8° London, 1924. [i. The mission of St. Augustine : ii. The story of St. Bede (pp. 1–51).]

3950 —— St. Gregory's responsiones ad interrogationes B. Augustini. Miscellanea Amelli (Montecassino), pp. 1–16. 1920.

3951 —— St. Gregory's responsions to St. Augustine. Downside Rev., 23, N.S. 4, pp. 2–14. 1904.

3952 Harcourt (Charles George Vernon). Legends of St. Augustine, St. Anthony, and St. Cuthbert, painted on the back of the stalls in Carlisle cathedral. 8° Carlisle, 1868.

3953 Hedley (John Cuthbert), *bp. of Newport.* The apostle of England. A sermon preached at the centenary celebration, Ebbs Fleat, Sept. 14, 1897. pp. 19. 8° London, 1897.

3954 Hennon (C.) and **Bernard** (A.). The consecration of Saint Augustine at Arles. pp. 28. 8° Aix, 1888.

3955 Howorth (*Sir* Henry Hoyle). The birth of the English Church. Saint Augustine of Canterbury. pp. xcix, 451, + 14 plates, + maps and tables. 8° London, 1913.

3956 Johnston (James). The finding of Saint Augustine's chair. pp. iv, 98. 8° Birmingham, 1898.

3957 Levêque (Louis). St. Augustin de Cantorbéry, première mission bénédictine. [Gross, 1637. Deals especially with his activity as a monk and a missionary.] Rev. questions hist., 65 (N.S. 21), pp. 353–423. 1899.

3958 Lynn (William Thynne). The landing-place of St. Augustine in England. [? Richborough.] N. and Q., 8th S. 12, pp. 245–46. 1897.

3959 Marshall (George). The authenticity of the so-called chair of St. Augustine, at Stanford Bishop, from the historical standpoint. [Stanford Bishop not to be identified with Augustine's Oak.] Trans. Woolhope N.F. Club, 31, pp. 179–82, + 1 plate. 1947.

3960 Mason (Arthur James), *ed.* The mission of St. Augustine to England, according to the original documents, being a handbook for the thirteenth centenary. pp. xix, 252. 8° Cambridge, 1897. [Gross, 1638. Pp. 1–160, letters of Gregory the Great and extracts from Bede, with a translation : pp. 161–83, political outlook of Europe in 597, by C. W. C. Oman : pp. 184–208, mission of Augustine, by A. J. Mason : pp. 209–34, landing-place of Augustine, by T. M. Hughes : pp. 235–52, liturgical questions, by H. A. Wilson.]

3961 Oakeley (Frederick). The life of St. Augustine. *Lives of the saints.* pp. iv, 266. 8° London, 1844. [*Also in* Newman (J. H.) : The lives of the English saints, vol. 3, 1901.]

3962 O'Hare (Charles M.). St. Augustine and the conversion of England. Irish Eccles. Rec., 5th S. 38, pp. 124–41, 285–99. 1931.

3963 Saxton (Austin J.). St. Augustine, apostle of the English. pp. 28. 8° London, [1890].

3964 Smith (Sydney Fenn). The landing of St. Augustine. *Catholic Truth Society, Historical Papers*, 24. pp. 24. 8° London, [1897].

3965 Stanley (Arthur Penrhyn), *dean of Westminster*. Historical memorials of Canterbury. 5th edition, with the author's final revision. pp. [45], 540. 8° London, 1883. [Gross, 979. Ch. 1, the landing of Augustine.]

3966 Surtees (Frederic R.). Saint Augustine, and Augustine the monk and archbishop. [Augustine of Canterbury not canonized.] J. Brit. Archaeol. Assoc., 40, pp. 295–96. 1884.

3967 Taylor (Charles Samuel). Aust and St. Austin. [Summary of evidence.] Proc. Clifton Antiq. Club, 4 (1897–99), pp. 43–47. 1900.

3968 —— Aust, the place of meeting. [i.e. between Augustine and the British bishops.] Trans. Bristol and Glos. Arch. Soc., 24, pp. 159–71. 1901.

3969 Wood (James George). St. Augustine's oak. [Argument for Broadoak, near Westbury-on-Severn.] Trans. Woolhope N.F. Club, 1905–07, pp. 344–49. 1911.

§ *c*. **Dunstan, Archbishop of Canterbury (960–88)**

3970 Crippen (T. G.). A light in the Dark Ages. Glastonbury Antiq. Soc. Proc., [2] (1904), pp. 76–96. 1906.

3971 Pontifex (Dunstan). St. Dunstan and his first biography. Downside Rev., 51, pp. 20–40, 309–25. 1933.

3972 R. (W.), *LL.D.* The life of Saint Dunstan. 8° Tottenham, 1844.

3973 Robinson (Joseph Armitage), *dean of Wells*. Memoirs of Saint Dunstan in Somerset. Proc. Somerset Arch. Soc., 62 (1916), pp. 1–25, + 1 plate. 1917.

3974 —— Saint Dunstan. Somerset Year Book, 16th Ann. Rpt. 1918.

3975 —— Some memories of Saint Dunstan in Somerset : Presidential address, 1916. Proc. Somerset Arch. Soc., 62 (1916), pp. xxvii–xxxii. 1917.

3976 —— The times of St. Dunstan. *Ford Lectures*, 1922. pp. 188. 8° Oxford, 1923.

O

3977 Toke (Leslie Alexander St. Lawrence). Some notes on the accepted date of St. Dunstan's birth. 8° London, [1908]. [Reprinted from the appendix to Gasquet and Bishop : The Boswoth Psalter.]

§ *d*. **Lanfranc, Archbishop of Canterbury (1070–89)**.

3978 Boehmer (Heinrich). Die Fälschungen Erzbischof Lanfranks von Canberbury. *Studien zur Geschichte der Theologie und der Kirche*, 8. *i*. pp. viii, 175. 8° Leipzig, 1902. [Charge of forgery unqualified—Stenton.]

3979 Brooke (S. N. L.). The Canterbury forgeries and their author. [Not Lanfranc. ? work of monk Guerno, c. 1070.] Downside Rev., 68, pp. 462–76 ; 69, pp. 210–31. 1950–51.

3980 Charma (Antoine). Lanfranc, notice biographique, littéraire et philosophique. *Méms. Soc. Antiquaires Normandie*, 17. pp. 160. 8° Paris, 1849. [Gross, 3138.]

3981 Crozals (Jacques Marie Ferdinand Joseph de). Lanfranc. . . . Sa vie, son enseignement, sa politique. pp. 270. 8° Paris, 1877. [Gross, 3139.]

3982 Dell'Acqua (Carlo). Di Lanfranco da Pavia, maestro di S. Anselmo e delle sue memorie. Riv. stor. benedettina, 4, pp. 455–84. 1909.

3983 Du Boys (Albert). L'église et l'état en Angleterre depuis la conquête des Normands, jusqu'à nos jour [*sic*]. pp. vii, 414. 8° Lyons, 1887. [Gross, 3079. Lanfranc, etc.]

3984 Endres (J. A.). Lanfrancs Verhältnis zur Dialektik. Katholik, 82, 1902.

3985 Gwynn (Aubrey). Lanfranc and the Irish Church. Irish Eccles. Rec., 5th S. 57, pp. 481–500 : 58, pp. 1–15. 1941.

3986 Kissan (B. W.). Lanfranc's alleged division of lands between archbishop and community. E.H.R., 54, pp. 285–93. 1939.

3987 Lanfranc, *abp. of Canterbury*. Decreta Lanfranci monachis Cantuariensis transmissa. (The monastic constitutions of Lanfranc) translated . . . with introduction and notes by David Knowles. *Medieval Classics.* pp. xl, 157. 8° London, 1951. [Latin and English. Also text and translation of the anonymous Instructio noviciorum secundum consuetudinem ecclesiae Cantuariensis.]

3988 Liebermann (Felix). Lanfranc and the antipope. [Wibert : Clement III.] E.H.R., 16, pp. 328–32. 1901.

3989 Longuemare (Élie). L'église et la conquête de l'Angleterre. Lanfranc ...conseiller politique de Guillaume le Conquérent. pp. xix, 225. 8° Paris, 1902. [Gross, 3139 a. Pp. xiii–xix, Bibliography ; 'and bibliographical appendixes '.]

3990 MacDonald (Allan John Macdonald). Eadmer and the Canterbury privileges. [?documents copied by Eadmer and William of Malmesbury were not those produced by Lanfranc in 1072, but later and extensive forgeries.] J. Theol. Stud., 32, pp. 39–55, + 1 plate. 1931.

3991 —— Lanfranc. A study of his life, work and writing. (Second edition) pp. vii, 1–296, 296A–T, 297–307. 8° London, 1944.

3992 —— Lanfranc of Canterbury. Church Q. Rev., 120, pp. 241–56. 1935.

3993 Moiraghi (Pietro). Lanfranco di Pavia. pp. 27. 8° Padova, 1889. [Gross, 3140.]

3994 Southern (Richard William). Lanfranc of Bec and Berengar of Tours. Studies pres. to F. M. Powicke, pp. 27–48. 1948.

3995 Tamassia (Nino). Lanfranco, arcivescovo di Canterbury, e la scuola Pavese. Mélanges H. Fitting, 2, pp. 189–201. 1908.

3996 White (Robert). The Epistolae Lanfranci. Proved a forgery. pp. 22. 8° Tamworth, 1913.

3997 Wigmore (John H.). Lanfranc, the prime minister of William the Conqueror : was he once an Italian professor of law ? Law Q.R., 58, pp. 61–81. 1942.

§ e. Swithun, Bishop of Winchester (852–62)

3998 Earle (John). Gloucester fragments. I. Facsimile of some leaves in Saxon handwriting on St. Swithun . . . with elucidations and an essay [on St. Swithun], *etc.* 4° London, 1861. [Gross, 1658. Pp. 21–56, essay on his life and times ; pp. 67–81, Vita S. Swithuni auctore Gotzelino (11th c.), and 2 other lives.]

3999 Gerould (Gordon Hall). Ælfric's Legend of St. Swithin. [What original and what derived from Lantfred.] Anglia, 32 (N.F. 20), pp. 347–57. 1909.

4000 Goscelin, *monk of Canterbury*. Vita Sancti Swithuni, Wintonensis episcopi, ex Ebroicensi codice nunc primum edidit E. P. Sauvage. Anal. Boll., 7, pp. 373–80. 1888.

4001 Lantfred, *monk of Winchester*. Sancti Swithuni, Wintonienis episcopi translatio et miracula. Ex codice olim Gemeticensi, jam Rotomagensi, nunc primum edidit E. P. Sauvage. Anal. Boll., 4, pp. 367–410. 1885.

4002 Vaughan (John). St. Swithun. A sermon. pp. 11. 8° Winchester, [1918].

4003 Wulfstan, *monk of St. Swithun's, Winchester* (*fl.* 1006). Narratio metrica de sancto Swithuno. Edidit Alistair Campbell. pp. 63–183. 8° Turici, 1950. [In the same volume as **4012.**]

4004 —— S. Swithunus, miracula metrica auctore Wulfstano monacho. Beitrag zur altenglischen Geschichte und Literatur von P. Michael Huber. 8° Landshut, 1906. [With text.]

§ f. Wilfrid, Bishop of York (664–78)

4005 Bailey (A. C.). St. Wilfred of Sussex. Sussex County Mag., 18, pp. 278–80. 1944.

4006 Dann (M. E.). St. Wilfrid in Sussex. [With description of Sompting church and the carved fragment representing St. Wilfrid.] Buckfast Abbey Chronicle, 7, pp. 244–52. 1937.

4007 Eddius, *Stephanus.* Het Leven van Sint Wilfrid. Ingeleid, vertaald en van aanteekeningen voorzien door Honorius Moonen. pp. ix, 440. 8°'s-Hertogenbosch, 1946.

4008 —— Life of bishop Wilfrid. Text, translation and notes, by B. Colgrave. pp. xix, 192. 8° Cambridge, 1927.

4009 —— Vita Wilfridi I episcopi Eboracensis, edidit Wilhelm Levison. *Monumenta Germaniae Historica, Script. rerum Merovingicarum,* 6 : *Passiones vitaeque sanctorum aevi Merovingici.* pp. 163–263. 4° Hannoverae, 1913.

4010 Faber (Frederick William). Lives of the English saints : Wilfrid, bishop of York. pp. 209. 8° London, 1844. [Gross, 1660. *Also in* Newman (J.H.) : The lives of the English saints, vol. 1, 1900.]

4011 Fletcher (Joseph Smith). The life and work of St. Wilfrid of Ripon. A lecture. pp. 63. 8° Chichester, 1925.

4012 Frithigodus. Breuiloquium vitae beati Wilfredi : et Wulfstani cantoris Narratio metrica de sancto Swithuno, edidit Alistair Campbell. pp. xi, 183. 8° Turici, 1950.

4013 Housman (Henry). Saint Wilfrith and the conversion of Sussex. A sermon. pp. 8. 8° Wilmshurst, Chichester, 1889.

4014 Hutton (William Holden). St. Wilfrid. *York minster historical tracts,* 5. pp. 16. 8° *n.p.,* [1927].

4015 l'Anson (J.). St. Wilfrid. J. Brit. Archaeol. Assoc., 43, pp. 275–90. 1887.

4016 Ignatius, *pseud.* St. Wilfrid. [Bibliography.] N. and Q., 3rd S. 9, pp. 323–24. 1866.

4016a Mitchell (Gordon). Saint Wilfred's chapel. [Selsey.] Sussex County Mag., 22, pp. 108–09. 1948.

4017 Obser (Karl). Wilfrid der ältere, Bischof von York. pp. 103. 8° Karlsruhe, 1884. [Gross, 1661.]

4018 Poole (Reginald Lane). St. Wilfrid and the see of Ripon. [With appendix : the date of Wilfrid's death.] E.H.R., 34, pp. 1–24. 1919.

4019 Sawyer (Frederick Ernest). S. Wilfrith's life in Sussex and the introduction of Christianity. Sussex Archaeol. Collns., 33, pp. 101–28. 1883.

4020 Streeter (A.). St. Wilfrid, with an introductory essay by . . . L. Rivington. *Catholic Truth Society.* pp. iv, 89. 8° London, 1897. [Gross, 1662.]

4021 Two Sisters of Notre Dame of Namur. St. Wilfrid, 633–709. pp. 240, + plates. 8° London, [1928].

4022 Van Tromp (Harold). Saint Wilfrid in Sussex. Sussex County Mag., 6, pp. 812–16. 1932.

4023 Walbran (John Richard). On St. Wilfrid, and the Saxon church of Ripon. Assoc. Archit. Socs.' Rpts., 5, pp. 63–96(g.). 1859.

4024 Wells (Benjamin W.). Eddi's life of Wilfrid. E.H.R., 6, pp. 535–50. 1891.

4025 Whiting (Charles Edwin). St. Wilfrid of York. Durham Univ. J., 25, pp. 242–57. 1927.

§ g. **Wulfstan (II), Bishop of Worcester (1062–95)**

4025a Browne (E. O.). St. Wulfstan and Gloucestershire. Glos. Countryside, 1, pp. 58–59. 1932.

4026 Church (Richard William). Life of St. Wulstan. pp. 46. 8° London, 1844. [*Also in* J. H. Newman : The lives of the saints, 5, 1900.]

4027 Flower (Robin Ernest William). A metrical life of St. Wulfstan of Worcester. [Peniarth MS. 386 (formerly Hengwrt MS. 362).] Nat. Lib. Wales J., 1, pp. 119–30, + 2 plates. 1940.

4028 Henderson (F. B.) *Mrs.* St. Wulstan and his connection with St. Alban's abbey. Trans. St. Albans Archit. Soc., N.S. 2, pp. 11–29. 1903.

4029 Hook (Walter Farquhar), *dean of Chichester.* The life and times of Wulfstan. Archaeol. J., 20, pp. 1–28. 1863.

4030 Lamb (John William). Saint Wulfstan, prelate and patriot. A study of his life and times. *Church Hist. Soc.,* N.S. 16. pp. xiii, 218. 8° London, 1933.

4031 William, *of Malmesbury.* Life of St. Wulfstan . . . rendered into English by James Hamilton Francis Peile. pp. 103. 8° Oxford, 1934.

4032 —— The Vita Wulfstani. To which are added the extant abridgments of this work and the Miracles and translation of St. Wulfstan. Edited by R. R. Darlington. *Camden Society, 3rd Series,* 40. pp. lii, 204. 8° London, 1928.

§ *h.* Others

4033 Adams (J.). St. Birinus, bishop of Dorchester. Trans Newbury F.C., 3 (1875–86), pp. 9–13. 1886.

4033a Bede. The story of St. John of Beverley, bishop of Hexham, fifth bishop of York. pp. 15. 8° Beverley, 1951. [Extracts from E.H., etc.]

4034 Beloe (Edward Milligen). Herbert de Lozinga : an inquiry as to his cognomen and birthplace. Norfolk archaeology, 8, pp. 282–302, + map. 1879.

4035 Bishop (Herbert Eustace) and **Rose-Troup** (Frances). Bishop Leofric's burial places. (Leofric's stone.) Devon and Cornwall N. and Q., 15 pp, 53–54, 107–08, 266–67. 1928–29.

4036 Bolton (Charles A.). Centenary of St. Aidan, Irish apostle to the Anglo-Saxons. [Brief life.] Irish Eccles. Rec., 5th S. 76, pp. 105–10. 1951.

4037 Bushell (William Dene). St. Chad and St. Cedd : two brother bishops. Arch. Camb., 6th S. 16, pp. 141–51, + 3 plates. 1916.

4038 Cassan (Stephen Hyde). The lives of the bishops of Winchester. 2 vol. 8° London, 1827. [Vol. 1, pp. 97–141, A.-S.]

4039 Collins (James T.). Life of St. Chad. pp. 19. 8° Birmingham, 1919.

4040 Cook (Albert Stanburrough). The Old-English Andreas and bishop Acca of Hexham. Trans. Conn. Acad. Arts and Sci., 26, pp. 245–332. 1924.

4041 —— Theodore of Tarsus and Gislenus of Athens. [i. England's earliest hellenizer : ii. Greek writings in 7th c. England : iii. Theodore's pupils, etc.] Philol. Q., 2, pp. 1–25. 1923.

4042 Crawford (Samuel John). Byrhtferth of Ramsay and the Anonymous life of St. Oswald [bp. of York]. [MS. Cotton Nero E.1,— 11th c. ? written by Byrhtferth.] Speculum religionis, essays presented to C. G. Montefiore, pp. 99–111. 1929.

4043 Cuming (Henry Syer). The early saints of Worcester. [Egwin, Dunstan, Oswald, Wulfstan.] J. Brit. Archaeol. Assoc., 32, pp. 321–29. 1876.

4044 —— St. Felix, bishop of Dunwich. *Same jnl.*, 36, pp. 334–35. 1880.

4045 Dixon (William Henry). Fasti Eboracenses : lives of the archbishops of York. Edited and enlarged by James Raine. Vol. 1, pp. xxiv, 496. 8° London, 1863. [Gross, 1171. *No more published.* Pp. 1–158, A.-S. period.]

4046 Field (John Edward). Saint Berin, the apostle of Wessex. The history, legends and traditions of the beginning of the West Saxon Church. pp. 248. 12° London, 1902. [Gross, 1638a.]

4047 Fisher (D. J. V.). The early biographies of St. Ethelwold. E.H.R., 67, pp. 381–91. 1952.

4048 Fryer (Alfred Cooper). Aidan, the apostle of the north. pp. x, 117. 8° London, [1884]. — New edition. Aidan, the apostle of England. pp. 96. 8° London, 1902. [Gross, 1623.]

4049 Green (J. R.). Earl Harold and bishop Giso [of Wells]. Proc. Somerset Arch. Soc., 12 (1863–4), pp. 148–57. 1865.

4050 Hall (Hamilton). Stigand, bishop of Chichester. A note on the date at which the seat of the Sussex diocese was removed from Selsey to Chichester. [Bp. of Selsey, 1070–75 : of Chichester, 1075–87. *See also* note by J. H. Round, **4068.**] Sussex Archaeol. Collns., 43, pp. 88–104 : 47, p. 158. 1900–04.

4051 Hepple (Richard B.). Tailbois : an illustrative mediaeval pedigree. [Aldhun, bp. of Chester-le-Street, 990–96, and then of Durham : married A.-S. clergy.] N. and Q., 180, pp. 308–11, 314–15 : 181, pp. 30–33. 1941.

4052 Hook (Walter Farquhar), *dean of Chichester*. Gundulf, bishop of Rochester. [1023–1108.]   Archaeol. J., 21, pp. 1–28. 1864.

4053 —— Lives of the archbishops of Canterbury. 12 vols. 8° London 1860–76. [Gross, 974. Vol. 1, A.-S. period. 4th edition, 1882. pp. xx, 532.]

4054 Hugo (Thomas). A memoir of Gundulf, bishop of Rochester, (1077–1108). With notices of the other ecclesiastical founders of that church and monastery. J. Brit. Archaeol. Assoc., 9, pp. 231–70, + 1 plate. 1854.

4055 Marshall (Edward), *etc*.   St. Felix place-names [and dedications]. N. and Q., 7th S. 8, pp. 312–13. 1889.

4056 Napier (Arthur Sampson). Ein altenglisches Leben des heiligen Chad. [Introduction, A.-S. text, and notes. MS. Bodley, Junius 24.] Anglia, 10, pp. 131–56. 1888.

4057 Offler (H. S.).   William of St. Calais, first Norman bishop of Durham. Trans. Archit. Soc. Durham, 10, pp. 258–79. 1950.

4058 Pearce (Ernest Harold), *bp. of Worcester*. St. Oswald of Worcester and the Church of York. *York minster historical tracts*, 7. pp. 16. 8° *n.p.*, [1927].

4059 Philpot (W. B.). On Grimketel, bishop of Selsey.   [Temp. Canute.] Sussex Archaeol. Collns., 36, pp. 250–51. 1888.

4060 Potts (Robert Ullock). The tombs of the kings and archbishops in St. Austin's abbey.   Arch Cant., 38, pp. 97–112, + 2 plates. 1926.

4061 Raine (James), *ed*. Historians of the Church of York and its archbishops. *Rolls series*. 3 vol. 8° London, 1879–94. [Gross, 1441. Contains lives of bps. Oswald and Wilfrid, St. John of Beverley, *etc*.]

4062 Reany (William). St. Theodore of Canterbury. pp. ix, 227. 8° St. Louis, Mo. and London, 1944.

4063 Robertson (William Archibald Scott). Burial places of the archbishops of Canterbury. [Pp. 277–79; of A.-S. archbishops; 11 buried at St. Augustine's and 19 at Christ Church, Canterbury: 2 at Winchester and one at Jumièges.] Arch. Cant., 20, pp. 276–94. 1893.

4064 Robinson (Joseph Armitage), *dean of Wells*. Effigies of Saxon bishops at Wells. Archaeologia, 65, pp. 95–112, + 5 plates, + plan. 1914.

4065 —— St. Oswald and the Church of Worcester. *British Academy, Supplemental papers*, 5. pp. 51. 8° London, 1919. [Pp. 22–33, Appendix of Worcester charters of St. Mary's before St. Oswald's time.]

4066 —— The Saxon bishops of Wells, a historical study in the tenth century. *British Academy, Supplemental papers*, 4. pp. 70. 8° London, 1918.

4067 Rose-Troop (Frances Batchelder). Leofric the first bishop of Exeter. Rept. and Trans. Devon. Assoc., 74, pp. 41–66. 1942.

4068 Round (John Horace). Stigand, bishop of Chichester. [Note on **4050**.] Sussex Archaeol. Collns., 46, pp. 234–35. 1903.

4069 Rowe (Joseph Hambley). Date of bishop Leofric's death. [? 1071, 1072, or 1074.] Devon and Cornwall N. and Q., 12, pp. 318–19. 1923.

4070 Rye (Walter).   The alleged identity of bishop William de Bellafago of Thetford with bishop Herbert de Losinga of Norwich. [Nominated to Thetford, Christmas 1085.]   Norfolk Antiq. Misc., 1, pp. 413–19, + table. 1877.

4071 Savage (Henry Edwin). St. Chad. *York Minster historical tracts*, 4. pp. 16. 8° *n.p.*, [1927].

4072 Smith (Reginald Anthony Lendon). The place of Gundulf in the Anglo-Norman church. E.H.R., 58, pp. 257–72. 1943.

4073 Stephens (William Richard Wood).   The bishops of Winchester. 2 pt. 4° Winchester, 1907. [Pt. 1, Birinus to Stigand.]

4074 Stuart-Douglas (J. A.).   St. Aidan.   Ampleforth J., 44, pp. 1–15. 1938.

4075 Varley (Telford).   St. Birinus and Wessex. From Odin to Christ. pp. 80. 8° Winchester, 1934.

4076 Venables (Edmund). St. John of Beverley, his miracles and his minster. Assoc. Archit. Socs'. Repts., 17, pp. 229–35. 1884.

4077 Vleeskruyer (Rudolf). The life of St. Chad. An Old English homily, edited with introduction, notes, illustrative texts and glossary. *Acad. Proefschrift, Amsterdam.* pp. 248, + plate. 8° Amsterdam, 1953. [MS. Bodl., Hatton 116, formerly Junius, 24.]

4078 Warner (Richard Hyett). Life and legends of Saint Chad. With extracts from un-edited MSS. 4° Wisbech, [1871].

4079 Wheatley (Sydney Williams). St. Justus, first bishop of Rochester, fourth archbishop of Canterbury, died Nov. 10, 627. pp. 22, + 3 plates. 8° Chatham, 1927.

4080 Wright (Thomas). The romantic materials of history, illustrated from the autobiography of Egwin, bishop of Worcester. Rept. of Proc. Brit. Archaeol. Assoc., 5 (Meeting at Worcester, 1848), pp 65–86. 1851.

65. HAGIOLOGY

§ *a*. General

4081   Arnold-Forster (Frances). Studies in church dedications, or England's patron saints. 3 vol. 8° London, 1899. [Abps. of Canterbury and York, English bps., apostles of Ireland and Scotland, SS. Bridget and David, Celtic royalties, Irish and Welsh saints in Cornwall, Saxon ladies of high degree, etc.]

4082 Baring-Gould (Sabin). The lives of the saints. New edition. 16 vol. 8° London, 1897–98.

4083   Bollandus (Joannes) and **Henschenius** (Godefridus). Acta sanctorum. Editio novissima, *etc.* 64 [+] vol. fol. Parisiis, etc., 1861–.

4084 Bull (Edvard). The cultus of Norwegian saints in England and Scotland. Saga-Book, V.C., 8, pp. 133–48. 1914.

4085 Dunbar (Agnes B. C.). A dictionary of saintly women. 2 vols. 8° London, 1904–05.

4086 Englebert (Omer). The lives of the saints. pp. xi, 532. 8° London, 1951. [c. 2,300 entries and biographies.]

4087 Hewins (WilliamAlbert Samuel). The royal saints of Britain from the latter days of the Roman Empire : showing their genealogical connections ; the relation of the early saints to the story of Glastonbury, and some of the characters in the Arthurian romances. pp. 70. fol. London, 1929.

4088 Holt (P.). Die Sammlung von Heiligenleben des Laurentius Surius [6 v., Cologne, 1570–75 ; new ed., 13 v. Turin, 1875–80]. [Kenney, 1, p. 289.] Neues Archiv, 44, pp. 341–64. 1922.

4089 Horstman (Carl). Nova legenda Anglie, as collected by John of Tynemouth, John Capgrave, and others, and first printed, with new lives by Wynkyn de Worde A.D. mdxvi. 2 vol. 8° Oxford, 1901. [Arranged alphabetically : A.-S. and Celtic.]

4090 St. Augustine's Abbey, Ramsgate, *Monks of.* The book of saints. A dictionary, *etc.* 4th edition. pp. xviii, 707. 8° London, 1947.

4091 Schenkl (H.). Bibliotheca patrum latinorum Britannica. Sitz. Akad. Wiss. Wien, Phil.-hist. Kl., 121–27, 131, 133, 136–37, 139, 143, 150. 1890–1905.

4092 Smedt (Charles de). Introductio generalis ad historiam ecclesiasticam critice tractandam. 8° Gandavi, 1876. [Gross, 26. Pp. 111–97, Bibliography of lives of saints : pp. 337–46, Church history (Great Britain).]

4093 Stanton (Richard). A menology of England and Wales : or, brief memorials of the ancient British and English saints arranged according to the calendar. pp. xix, 811. 8° London, 1892.

4094 Wright (Thomas). On monkish miracles as illustrative of history. Trans. Brit. Archaeol. Assoc., 3rd Congress (Gloucester) 1846, pp. 58–65. 1848.

§ *b*. Asceticism

4095 Bishop (Edmund). The method and degree of fasting and abstinence of the Black monks in England before the Reformation. [Pp. 184–90, 212–16 (references), A.-S.] Downside Rev., 43, pp. 184–237. 1925.

4096 Bonser (Wilfrid). Praying in water. [A.-S. and Celtic.] Folk-lore, 48, pp. 385–88. 1937.

4097 Clay (Rotha Mary). The hermits and anchorites of England. *Antiquary's Books.* pp. xx, 272. 8° London, 1914. [A.-S., passim.]

4098 Gougaud (Louis). Anciennes traditions ascétiques. 1.—L'usage de voyager à pied. Revue d'ascétique et de mystique, 3, pp. 56–59. 1922.

4099 —— Devotional and ascetic practices in the Middle Ages. English edition. pp. xiii, 237. 8° London, 1927. [E.g., fasting (in Ireland), ascetic immersions (pp. 159–78), *etc.*]

4100 —— Ermites et reclus. Études sur d'anciennes formes et vie religieuse. pp. iii, 144. 8° Liguge, 1928.

4101 —— La mortification par les bains froids, spécialement chez les ascétiques celtiques. Bull. anc. litt. et d'archéol. chrét., 4, pp. 96–108. 1914.

4102 —— Some liturgical and ascetic traditions of the Celtic Church : 1. Genuflexion. J. Theol. Stud., 9, pp. 556–61. 1908.

§ c. Relics

(*see also* **66** § c. for relics of St. Cuthbert : also index. For reliquaries—as art—*see* **202.**)

4103 [Anon.] Discovery of the supposed remains of St. Eanswith at Folkestone. [7th c.] Reliquary, 26, pp. 55–56. 1885.

4104 [Anon.] The relics of St. Eanswith. Illust. Archaeologist, 2, pp. 47–48. 1894.

4105 Bartholomew (Maude H.). The translations of Edward the Confessor['s body]. N. and Q., 9th S. 6, pp. 321–22. 1900.

4106 Chadwick (H.). The arm of St. Ninian. [Its history, including certificate of genuineness by bishop of Arras, 1627.] Trans. Dumfries. Antiq. Soc., 3rd S. 23 (1940–44), pp. 30–35. 1946.

4107 Foerster (Max). Zur Geschichte des Reliquienkultur in Altengland. Sitzungsb. bayerischen Akad. Wiss., Phil.-hist. Abt., Heft 8. 1943.

4108 G. (W. S.) *etc.* Black rood of Scotland. N. and Q., 1st S. 2, pp. 308–09, 409–10 : 3, pp. 105–05. 1850–51.

4109 Gwynn (Lucius). The reliquary of Adamnan. [Irish text and translation of a poem by Adamnan enumerating relics assembled by him in a single shrine which was used to make an intercession of peace in 727.] Archivium Hib., 4, pp. 199–214. 1915.

4110 Hems (Harry). St. Eanswith. [Discovery of her relics in 1885, with bibliography (in newspapers).] N. and Q., 9th S. 4, pp. 460–61 : 5, p. 74. 1899–1900.

4111 Hewitt (John). The ' keeper of St. Chad's head ' in Lichfield cathedral, and other matters concerning that minster in the fifteenth century. [Concerning relics of St. Chad in post A.-S. period.] Archaeol. J., 33, pp. 72–82. 1876.

4112 Loomis (Laura Hibbard). The Athelstan gift story ; its influence on English chronicles and Carolingian romances. [Hoard of relics received from France.] P.M.L.A., 67, pp. 521–37. 1952.

4113 —— The holy relics of Charlemagne and king Athelstan : the lances of Longinus and St. Mauricius. Speculum, 25, pp. 437–56. 1950.

4114 Loth (Joseph). Saint Branwalatr. [Or Brelade. Relics at Milton abbey, Dorset.] Rev. celt., 11, pp. 490–92. 1890.

4115 Micklethwaite (John Thomas). Notes on the Saxon crypt of Ripon minster. [Plan on p. 193. List of bones found Dec. 1, 1891. ? relics stowed there at Reformation.] Proc. Soc. Antiq., 2nd S. 14, pp. 191–96. 1892.

4116 Miller (Samuel Henry). The remains of St. Neot removed to Whittlesea from Crowland. [End of 10th c. From Ordericus.] Fenland N. and Q., 4, pp. 72–73. 1898.

4117 Rasmussen ( ), *headmaster at Odense.* St. Alban and Odense. [Note in 10, p. 77, 1908.] Home Counties Mag., 9, pp. 313–14. 1907.

4118 Rundle (S.).   Relics of the Cornish saints. J. Roy. Soc. Cornwall, 14, pp. 74–78. 1900.

4119 S. (J. J.).   Sainted kings incorruptible. [i.e. their bodies. Edward the Confessor and Edgar.] N. and Q., 1st S. 5, pp. 223–24. 1852.

4120 Storm (A. V.) and **Collins** (William Edward).   St. Alban and Odense. [Answers to query in 5, pp. 310–11, 1903. *But see* Walsingham: Gesta abbatum S. Albani, 1, pp. 12–18. *Rolls Series.* Another (extraneous) answer in 6, pp. 246–47, 1904.] Home Counties Mag., 6, pp. 79–81. 1904.

4121 Sweeting (Walter Debenham). St. Neot's body at Crowland. [11th c. Stolen from Cornwall by monks of Eynesbury, Hunts.   To Crowland in 1003 on Sweyn's invasion.   Restored to Eynesbury, but Crowland pretended still to possess the body, which testified by Anselm, 1078–9.] Fenland N. and Q., 6, pp. 242–43. 1905.

4122 Varah (William Edward). Translation of the bones of king Edwin and king Oswald. [To Whitby and to Bardney: related by anon. monk of Whitby in Life of Gregory, and by Bede.] N. and Q., 178, pp. 187–88. 1940.

4123 Watson (George).   The black rood of Scotland. [Gifted by St. Margaret to Dunfermline. ? formed out of piece of the ' true cross ' given by pope Marinus to king Alfred.] Trans. Scot. Ecclesiol. Soc., 2, pp. 27–46. 1907.

66. HAGIOLOGY, ANGLO-SAXON

§ *a*. General

4124 Adams (David Charles Octavius). The saints and missionaries of the Anglo-Saxon era. 2 series, 8° Oxford, [1897–1901]. [Gross, 1617 c. ' Popular account.']

4125 Allen (John Romilly). List of dedication stones still existing in England . . . with the positions they now occupy. [9 of Saxon period.] Proc. Soc. Antiq., 2nd S. 19, pp. 93–95. 1902.

4126 Almond (T. Leo). Whitby life of Gregory. [?c. 700. With Latin text and English translation.] Downside Rev., 23, N.S. 4, pp. 15–29. 1904.

4127 Bishop (Edmund).   English hagiology. Dublin Rev., 3rd S. 13, pp. 123–54. 1885.

4128 Brownbill (John).   Ancient church dedications in Cheshire and south Lancashire. ['Dedications often preserve the sites and labours of the early missionaries ', e.g. Wilfrid and Chad, etc.] Trans. Hist. Soc. Lancs. and Ches., 54 (1902), pp. 19–44. 1904.

4129 Chanter (John Frederick). The saints of Devon. Devonian Y.B., 6, pp. 86–109 : 7, pp. 77–105. 1915–16.

4130 Cuming (Henry Syer). A glance at the saints of Staffordshire. J. Brit. Archaeol. Assoc., 29, pp. 337–41. 1873.

4131 Doble (Gilbert Hunter).   Some remarks on the Exeter martyrology. (Exeter Chapter MSS. 3518.) pp. 20. [11th c. hand.] 8° Bristol, 1933.

4132 Duckett (Eleanor Shipley). Anglo-Saxon saints and scholars. pp. x, 488. 8° New York, 1947. [Aldhelm of Malmesbury, Wilfrid of York, Bede of Jarrow, Boniface of Devon.]

4133 Graham (T. H. B.) and **Collingwood** (William Gershom). Patron saints of the diocese of Carlisle. [Pp. 12–15, Anglian saints.] Trans. Cumb. and Westm. Antiq. Soc., N.S. 25, pp. 1–27. 1925.

4134 Grierson (Elizabeth Wilson). The story of Northumbrian saints. S. Oswald, S. Aidan, S. Cuthbert. pp. x, 131. 8° London, 1913.

4135 Grosjean (Paul).   De codice hagiographico Gothano. (Codicis Gorhani appendix.) [Latin texts in appendix. i. Annotationes de translatione S. Edmundi regis : ii. Vita S. Aelkmundi regis : iii. Passio SS. Vulfadi et Ruffini : iv. Miracula S. Swithuni : v. Translatio S. Swithuni : vi. Vita S. Cuthmanni : vii. Translatio S. Helenae : viii. Legenda S. Sativolae.] Anal. Boll., 58, pp. 90–103, 177–204. 1940.

4136 Hardman (J. W.). The hagiology of Somerset. Proc. Somerset Arch. Soc., 32 (1886), pp. 59–67. 1887.

4137 Hutton (William Holden). The influence of Christianity upon national character, illustrated by the lives and legends of the English saints. *Bampton Lectures*, 1903. pp. xiv, 385. 8° London, 1903. [Background to A.-S.]

4138 Imelmann (Rudolf Hans Robert). Das altenglische Menologium. *Diss., Berlin.* pp. 64. 8° Berlin, 1902. [With A.-S. text. *See also* note on this thesis by F. Liebermann *in* Archiv Stud. neueren Spr., Bd. 110, pp. 98–99. 1903.]

4139 Jameson (Anna Brownell). Legends of the monastic orders, as represented in the fine arts. 7th edition. pp. xlvii, 461, + 11 plates. 8° London, 1888. [Pp. 39–112, the Benedictines in England and Germany.]

4140 King (Richard John). The great shrines of England. [Reprinted from Quart. Rev., 133, 1872.] King (R. J.): Sketches and Studies, pp. 197–265. 1874.

4141 Liebermann (Felix). Die Heiligen Englands (*þa halgan on Angelcynne*). Angelsächsisch und Lateinisch, herausgegeben von F.L. pp. ix, 23. 8° Hannover, 1889.

4142 Long (Edward T.). Dorset church dedications. [Largely to A.-S. saints.] Proc. Dorset Archaeol. Soc., 52, pp. 30–58. 1931.

4143 Loomis (Charles Grant). King Arthur and the saints. [Summary of 'fragments of Arthurian legend such as they appear in various hagiological documents'.] Speculum, 8, pp. 478–82. 1933.

4144 Loomis (Grant). Further sources of Ælfric's saints' lives. Harvard Stud. and notes in Phil. and Lit., 13, pp. 1–8. 1931.

4145 Ott (J. Heinrich). Über die Quellen der Heiligenleben in Ælfrics Lives of Saints, I. *Diss., Halle.* pp. 60. 8° Halle, 1892.

4146 Piper (Ferdinand). Die Kalendarien und Martyrologien der Angelsächsen, *etc.* pp. xii, 180. 8° Berlin, 1862. [Pp. 40–116, Die Kalendarien und die Fest-Ordnung der Angelsachsen.]

4147 Prins (A. A.). Some remarks on Ælfric's Lives of Saints and his translations from the Old Testament. Neophil., 25, pp. 112–22. 1940.

4148 Sisam (Celia). An early fragment of the Old English martyrology. [B.M., MS. Addit. 40165A. Mercian, 9th c. With A.-S. text.] Rev. Engl. Stud., N.S. 4, pp. 209–20. 1953.

4148a Smith (Albert Hugh), *ed.* Three Northumbrian poems, Caedmon's Hymn, Bede's Death Song and the Leiden riddle. pp. x, 54. 8° London, 1933. [Leiden riddle : the O.E. version of the Lorica, one of the Ænigmata of Aldhelm.]

4149 Stoughton (John). Golden legends of the olden time. pp. xvi, 365. 8° London, 1885. [Pp. 143–68, A.-S. saints.]

4150 Venables (Edmund). The dedications of the churches of Lincolnshire, as illustrating the history of the county. [Many A.-S. Pp. 381–90, list of dedications.] Archaeol. J., 38, pp. 365–90. 1881.

4151 Wilmart (André). Un témoin Anglo-Saxon du calendrier métrique d'York. Rev. Bénédictine, 46, pp. 41–69. 1934.

4152 Wormald (Francis). The English saints in the litany in Arundel MS. 60. [11th c. Footnotes on the English saints in the 173 listed.] Anal. Boll., 64, pp. 72–86. 1946.

4153 Zupitza (Julius). Bemerkungen zu Älfric's Lives of saints (I) ed. Skeat. [Textual emendations, etc.] Z.f.d.A., 29, pp. 269–96. 1885.

§ *b*. **Bede**

i. **Historical Works** (and notes on them).

4154 Anderson *afterwards* **Anderson-Arngart** (Olof Sigfrid), *ed.* Old English material in the Leningrad manuscript of Bede's Ecclesiastical History. *Skrifter utgivna av K. hum. Vetenskapssamfundet i Lund*, 31. pp. vii, 165, + 3 plates. 8° Lund, 1941.

4155 Bede, *Venerable.* Opera historica, instruxit Carolus Plummer. 2 vol. 8° Oxford, 1896. [Historia ecclesiastica, Historia abbatum, Epistola ad Ecgberctum, una cum Historia abbatum auctore anonymo. Vol. 2, pp. 57–60, A.-S. references to Æsir.]—[in one vol.] 8° Oxford, 1946.

4156 —— Opera historica, with an English translation by J. E. King. *Loeb Library.* 2 vol. 8° London, 1930.

4157 —— Ecclesiastical history . . . with introduction by Vida D. Scudder. *Everyman's Library.* pp. xxxiv, 370. 8° London, [1910].

4158 —— Ecclesiastical history of England. A revised translation, with introduction, life and notes by A. M. Sellar. *Bohn's Antiquarian Library.* pp. xliii, 439. 8° London, 1907 (reissued 1912).

4159 —— The History of the Church of Englande, translated out of Latin into English by Thomas Stapleton. [Edited by Philip Hereford.] pp. xx, 479. fol. Oxford, 1930.

4160 —— The Ecclesiastical history. . . . Translated . . . by Thomas Stapleton. . . . Edited by Philip Hereford, *etc.* pp. lxiii, 372, + map. 8° London, 1935.

4161 —— Ecclesiastical history of the English nation, books 1–2 ; newly translated into English with notes and introduction, by Michael Maclagan. pp. iii, 195. 8° Oxford, 1949.

4162 —— Selections from the Old English Bede, with text and vocabulary on an early West Saxon basis . . . by W. J. Sedgefield. *Univ. Manchester Publns.*, 110. 2nd edition. pp. viii, 110. 8° Manchester, 1937.

4163 —— Interpolations in Bede's Ecclesiastical history and other ancient annals affecting the early history of Scotland and Ireland. pp. 84. 8° Peebles, 1883.

4164 —— Lives of the first five abbots of Wearmouth and Jarrow : Benedict, Ceolfrid, Eosterwine, Sigfrid and Huetbert. Translated from the Latin. To which is prefixed a life of the author. By Peter Wilcock. pp. iii, 115. 8° Sunderland, 1910.

4165 Bede, *Venerable.* Bedas metrische Vita sancti Cuthberti. [Edited by Werner Jaeger.] *Palaestra*, 198. pp. xi, 136. 8° Leipzig, 1935.

4166 Campbell (J. J.). The O E Bede : book III, chapters 16 to 20. [Two renderings of the Latin.] Mod. Lang. Notes, 67, pp. 381–86. 1952.

4167 Hahn (Heinrich). Die Continuatio Bedae. [Gross, 1361 note. 731–66, mostly Northumbria.] Forsch. z. deut. Gesch., 20, pp. 553–69. 1880.

4168 Hempl (George). The misrendering of numerals, particularly in the Old-English version of Bede's History. Mod. Lang. Notes, 11, col. 402–04. 1896.

4169 Holthausen (Ferdinand). Die altenglischen Beda-Glossen. [9–10 c. hand. At end of MS. Cotton Tib. C. II. E. H. 1, cap. 10–22.] Arch. Stud. neueren Spr., Bd. 136, pp. 290–92. 1917.

4170 Jones (Putnam Fennell). Concordance to the Historia ecclesiastica of Bede. *Medieval Academy of America*, 2. pp. ix, 585. 8° Cambridge, Mass., 1929.

4171 Klaeber (Frederick). Zur altenglischen Bedaübersetzung. [Critical examination of the A.-S. text.] Anglia, 25 (N.F. 13), pp. 257–315 : 27 (N.F. 15), pp. 243–82, 399–435. 1902–04.

4172 Koehler (Theodor). Die altenglischen Namen in Baedas Historia Ecclesiastica und auf den altnorthumbrischen Münzen. *Diss., Berlin.* pp. 44. 8° Berlin, 1908.

4173 Levison (Wilhelm). Bede as historian. [i. Chronology and chronicles : ii. Hagiography and biography : iii. The Ecclesiastical history (Bede's sources, analysis, etc.).] Bede : 12th centenary essays, ed. A. H. Thompson, pp. 111–51. 1935.

4174 Lowe (Elias Avery). A new manuscript fragment of Bede's ' Historia Ecclesiastica '. [Leaf containing part of letter of Vitalian to Oswy, III. 29.] E.H.R., 41, pp. 244–46. 1926.

4175 Meyer (Kuno). Eine irische Version von Beda's Historia. [Irish text of fol. 87a of Bodl. MS. Laud 610.] Zeit. celt. Phil., 2, pp. 321–22. 1899.

4176 Pearce (J. W.). Did king Alfred translate the *Historia Ecclesiastica* ? P.M.L.A., 8, pp. vi–x. 1893.

4177 Potter (Simeon). On the relation of the Old English Bede to Werferth's Gregory and to Alfred's translation. Mém. Soc. roy. Sc. Bohême, 1930.

4178 Schipper (Jacob). Die Geschichte und der gegenwärtige Stand der Forschung über König Alfreds Übersetzung von Bedas Kirchengeschichte. pp. 13. Sitzungsb. k. Akad. Wiss. Wien, phil.-hist. Kl., 138, Abt. 7. 1898.

4179 Schmidt (Ludwig). Ravennatische Annalen bei Beda. [Years 525–26.] Neues Archiv, 9, pp. 197–200. 1884.

4180 Thum (B.). S. Beda in Historia ecclesiastica Angliae. Commentarii pro religiosis, 17, pp. 30–36. 1936.

4181 Van Draat (P. Fijn). The authorship of the Old English Bede. A study in rhythm. [Translations of the Pastoral Care and Ecclesiastical History not by the same hand.] Anglia, 39 (N.F. 27), pp. 319–46. 1916.

4182 Zupitza (Julius). Altenglische Glossen zu Beda. [To E.H.] Z.f.d.A., 31, pp. 28–31. 1887.

ii. Scientific Works (and notes on them)

4183 Bede, *Venerable*. Opera de temporibus ; edited by Charles Williams Jones. *Medieval Academy of America*, 41. pp. xiii, 416. 4° Cambridge, Mass. 1943. [De temporum ratione, De temporibus, Epistola ad Pleguinam, Epistola ad VVicthedum.]

4184 —— Bedae pseudepigraphica : scientific writings falsely attributed to Bede ; edited by Charles W. Jones. pp. xvi, 154. 8° Oxford, 1939.

4185 Cordoliani (A.). A propos du chapitre premier du De temporum ratione, de Bède. Moyen âge, 54, pp. 209–23. 1948.

4186 Fordyce (C. J.). A rhythmical version of Bede's De ratione temporum. Archivum Lat. Med. Aevi, 3, pp. 59–73, 129–41. 1927.

4187 Henel (Heinrich). The new edition of Bede's computistical treatises. J. Engl. and Germ. Philol., 43, pp. 411–16. 1944.

4188 Jones (Charles Williams). Bede and Vegetius. [Quotes from Vegetius' Epitoma rei militaris in De temporum ratione, 28.] Class. Rev., 46, pp. 248–49. 1932.

4189 —— A note on concepts of the inferior planets in the early Middle Ages. [On two Bede MSS. : Codex Mellicensis, 370 (De temporum ratione) 9th c., and Karlsruhe MS. (Reichenau, 167), Irish hand, 836–48.] Isis, 24, pp. 397–99. 1936.

4190 Strachan (John). The Vienna fragment of Bede. [De temporum ratione. i. Readings of glosses already published : ii. New glosses.] Rev. celt., 23, pp. 40–49. 1902.

4191 Welzhofer (Karl). Beda's Citate aus der Naturalis historia de Plinius. Abhandlungen . . . Wilhelm von Christ zum 60. Geburtstag, pp. 25–41. 1891.

iii. Liturgical works (and notes on them).

4192 Bede, *Venerable*. Be Dōmes Dæge. Herausgegeben und erläutert von Hans Löhe. *Bonner Beiträge zur Anglistik*, 22. pp. 106. 8° Bonn, 1907. [Latin text and German translation.]

4193 —— Expositio actuum apostolorum et retractatio. Edited by M. L. W. Laistner. *Medieval Academy of America*, 35. pp. xlv, 176. 8° Cambridge, Mass., 1939.

4194 —— The four Gospels in epitome. Transcribed by the disciples of the Venerable Bede's school. Extracted and translated from Bede's own Gospel-Book. Latin and English. 8° 1930.

4195 Elder (J. P.). Did Remigius of Auxerre comment on Bede's *De schematibus et tropis* ? Med. Stud., 9, pp. 141–50. 1947.

4196 Hablitzel (Johann). Bedas Expositio in Proverbia Solomonis und seine Quellen. Biblische Zeit., 14, pp. 357–59. 1939.

4197 Hull (Vernam Edward). The Middle Irish version of Bede's *De locis sanctis*. [Introduction, text and translation.] Zeit. celt. Philol., 17, pp. 225–40. 1928.

4198 Lehmann (Paul). Die Erstveröffentlichungen von Bedas Psalmen-Gedichten. Zeit. Kirchenges., 34, pp. 89–92. 1913.

4199 —— Wert und Echtheit einer Beda abgesprochenen Schrift (Liber quaestionum). Sitzungsb. bayer. Akad. Wiss., Philos.-philol. Kl., 1919, Abt. 4. 1919.

4200 Meyer (Wilhelm). Bedas oratio ad Deum. Nachr. kgl. Ges. Wiss., Göttingen, Phil.-hist. Kl., 1912, pp. 228 *et seq.* 1912.

4201 Morin (Germain). Le Pseudo-Bède zur les Psaumes et l'Opus super Psalterium de Maître Manigold de Lautenbach. Rev. Bénédictine, 28, pp. 331 *et seq.* 1911.

4202 —— Le recueil primitif des homélies de Bède sur l'Évangile. *Same jnl.*, 9, pp. 316–26. 1892.

4203 Ogilvy (Jack David Angus). A noteworthy contribution to the study of Bede. [Appearance of Laistner's edition of Expositio in Actuum Apostolorum & Retractatio.] Univ. Colorado Stud., B, 1, pp. 261–64. 1941.

4204 Plaine (Franciscus Beda). Le vénérable Bède docteur de l'église. [On his liturgical writings.] Rev. anglo-romaine, 3, pp. 49–96. 1896.

4205 Schoenbach (A. F.). Über einige Evangelienkommentare des Mittelalters. Sitzungsb. k. Akad. Wiss., Wien, phil.-hist. Kl., 147, iv. 1903.

4206 Sutcliffe (E. F.). Quotations in the Venerable Bede's Commentary on St. Mark. Biblica, 7, pp. 428–39. 1926.

4207 Whitbread (L.). A study of Bede's *Versus de die iudicii*. [i. Popularity : ii. Authorship : iii. Character and purpose of the poem.] Philol. Quart., 23, pp. 193–221. 1944.

4208 Wilmart (André). La collection de Bède le Vénérable sur l'Apôtre. Rev. Bénédictine, 38, pp. 16–52. 1926.

iv. Bede's Death Song

4209 Bischoff (Dietrich). Das Philosophische im Sterbegesang des Ehrwürdigen Beda, 673–735. Die Sammlung, 2, pp. 545–55. 1947.

4210 Bulst (Walther). Bedas Sterbelied. [Considers Bede not to have been the author.] Z.f.d.A., 75, pp. 11–14. 1938.

4211 D'Evelyn (Charlotte). Bede's death song. [Stonyhurst MS. lxix, fol. 15a.] Mod. Lang. Notes, 30, p. 31. 1915.

4212 Foerster (Max). Paläographisches zu Bedas Sterbespruch und Cædmons Hymnus. Arch. Stud. neueren Spr., Bd. 135, pp. 282–84. 1916.

v. Manuscripts of Bede

4213 Anderson, *afterwards* **Arngart** (Olof Sigfrid), *ed.* The Leningrad Bede. An eighth century manuscript of the Venerable Bede's Historia Ecclesiastica gentis Anglorum in the Public Library, Leningrad. *Early English Manuscripts in facsimile*, eds. B. Colgrave, Kemp Malone, Knud Schibsbye, 2. pp. 36, + 322 plates. 4° Copenhagen, 1952.

4214 Beeson (Charles H.). The manuscripts of Bede. [Especially Bern 207 ; Paris 4841, 14088, 13025 ; Naples IV, A.34. Also general description and an appreciation of Laistner's work.] Classical Philology, 42, pp. 73–87. 1947.

4215 Brotanek (Rudolf). Nachlese zu den Hss. der *Epistola Cuthberti* und des *Sterbespruches Bedes*. Anglia, 64 (N.F. 52), pp. 159–90. 1940.

4216 Colgrave (Bertram). The history of British Museum additional MS. 39943. [Late 12th c. : consists of ' Bede's Prose life of St. Cuthbert and a series of anonymous miracles relating to the same saint.'] E.H.R., 54, pp. 673–77. 1939.

4217 —— The new Bede MS. [12th c. Lives of SS. Cuthbert, Aidan, Oswald. Bought by Durham, 1927.] Durham Univ. J., 30, pp. 1–5. 1936.

4218 Dobbie (Elliott van Kirk). Manuscripts of Caedmon's Hymn and Bede's Death song ; with a critical text of the Epistola Cuthberti de obitu Bedae. *Columbia Univ. Studies in English*, 128. pp. xi, 129. 8° New York, Oxford, 1937.

4219 Harrison (James Park). On an early illuminated manuscript at Cambridge. [16th c. Bede's Life of Cuthbert in Corpus Christi College.] Archaeologia Oxon., pp. 165-70. 1895.

4220 Inguanez (Mauro). Il Venerabile Beda nei codici e negli scrittori cassinesi medievali. Studia Anselmiana, 6, pp. 41-50. 1936.

4221 James (Montague Rhodes). The manuscripts of Bede. Bede, 12th centenary essays, ed. A. H. Thompson, pp. 230-36. 1935.

4222 Jones (Charles Williams). The ' lost ' Sirmond manuscript of Bede's ' Computus '. E.H.R., 52, pp. 204-19. 1937.

4223 —— Manuscripts of Bede's De natura rerum. [With list of 66 mss.] Isis, 27, pp. 430-40. 1937.

4224 Ker (Neil Ripley). The Hague manuscript of the Epistola Cuthberti de obitu Bedæ with Bede's song. [Early 10th c. Text of ff. 42-45, Epistola de obitu Bedæ, transcribed.] Medium Ævum, 8, pp. 40-44. 1939.

4225 Laistner (Max Ludwig Wolfram) and **King** (Henry Hall). A hand-list of Bede manuscripts. pp. 168. 8° Oxford, 1943.

4226 Laistner (Max Ludwig Wolfram). Source-marks in Bede manuscripts. [i.e Bede's ' notation of those names which have been placed above in the margin '.] J. Theol. Stud., 34, pp. 350-54. 1933.

4227 Miller (Thomas). Place-names in the English Bede and the localisation of the manuscripts. *Quellen und Forschungen*, 78. pp. 80. 8° Strassburg, 1896.

4228 Morin (Germain). Le manuscrit namurois du Liber de locis sanctis de Bède. Rev. Bénédictine, 16, pp. 210-11. 1899.

4229 Potter (Simeon). The Winchester Bede. [The ms., with facsimile of f.81.] Wessex, 3, pp. 39-45, + 1 plate. 1935.

4230 Weisweiler (H.). Die handschriftlichen Vorlagen zum Erstdruck von Pseudo-Beda, in Psalmorum librum Exegesis. Biblica, 18, pp. 197-204. 1937.

vi. Lives of Bede and miscellaneous Bede Material

4231 [Anon.] The father of English history. Church Q. Rev., 43, pp. 112-32. 1896.

4232 [Anon.] The Venerable Bede : Ascension eve, 735-1935. Times Lit. Supp., 34, pp. 317-18. 1935.

4233 Abbott (Wilbur Cortez). An uncanonized saint : the Venerable Bede. *In his* Conflicts with oblivion, pp. 243-70. 1924.

4234 Boult (Joseph). The credibility of Venerable Bede, . . . and of his followers. Proc. Lit. and Phil. Soc., L'pool., 32, pp. 127-50. 1878.

4235 Brown (Robert). An inquiry into the origin of the name ' Sunderland ' ; and as to the birth place of the Venerable Bede. Archaeol. Æl., [1st S.] 4, pp. 277-83. 1855.

4236 Browne (George Forrest), *bp. of Bristol*. The Venerable Bede. pp. 192. 8° London, 1879.

4236 a —— The Venerable Bede, his life and writings. pp. xiii, 327 + 20 plates. 8° London, 1919. [Gross, 1355 : Lit.]

4237 Carelle (Bernard). Le rôle théologique de Bède le Vénérable. Studia Anselmiana, 6, pp. 1-40. 1936.

4238 Carroll (Mary Thomas Aquinas). The Venerable Bede : his spiritual teachings. A dissertation. *Catholic Univ. America, Stud. med. hist.*, N.S. 9. pp. ix, 270. 8° Washington, 1946.

4239 Chambers (Raymond Wilson). Bede. (Annual lecture on a master mind). Proc. Brit. Acad., 22, pp. 129-56. 1936.

4240 Colgrave (Bertram). Bede's miracle stories. Bede, 12th centenary essays, ed. A. H. Thompson, pp. 201-29. 1935.

4241 Condamine (Albert). L'inerrance biblique d'après saint Bède. Recherches de science relig., 4, pp. 73–75. 1913.

4242 Cook (Albert Stanburrough). Bede and Gregory of Tours. [Acquaintance with, and borrowing from.] Philol. Quart., 6, pp. 315–16. 1927.

4243 —— Bede and Homer. [Not necessarily acquainted with the original.] Arch. Stud. neueren Spr., Bd. 147, pp. 93–94. 1924.

4244 Davis (Ruby). Bede's early reading. Speculum, 8, pp. 179–95. 1933.

4245 Foggon (J.). The Venerable Bede. Reliquary, 22, pp. 145–51. 1882.

4246 Gehle (Henrik). Disputatio historico-theologica de Bedæ Venerabilis . . . vita et scriptis. pp. 113. 8° Lugduni Batavorum, 1838. [Gross, 1355 : Lit.]

4247 Gillett (Henry Martin). St. Bede the Venerable. pp. x, 111. 8° London, 1935.

4248 Gladysz (Bronislas). Éléments classiques et post-classiques de l'oeuvre de Bède. Eos, 34, pp. 319–42. 1933.

4249 Goodier (Alban). St. Bede the Venerable. Month, 165, pp. 205–14. 1935.

4250 Hart (James Morgan). Rhetoric in the translation of Bede. English miscellany presented to F. J. Furnivall, pp. 150–54. 1901.

4251 Hill (Elspeth). The Venerable Bede. pp. 8. 8° London, [1935].

4252 Holland (Thomas). St. Bede the theologian. Beda Rev., 3, pp. 16–20. 1935.

4253 Home (Gordon). Bede, Durham and Northumbria. Geog. Mag., 1, pp. 299–300. 1935.

4254 Jenkins (Claude). Bede as exegete and theologian. Bede, 12th centenary essays, ed. A. H. Thompson, pp. 152–200. 1935.

4255 Jones (Charles Williams). Bede as early medieval historian. Medievalia et Humanistica, fasc. 4, pp. 26–36. 1946.

4256 Jones (Thomas). [Bibliothecar. Chetham., *pseud.*] A general literary index : index of authors : Venerable Bede. [A bibliography of Bede's works (to 1872).] N. and Q., 4th S., 9 pp. 193–95, 529–31 : 10, pp. 269–71. 1872.

4257 Laistner (Max Ludwig Wolfram). Bede as a classical and patristic scholar. Trans. R.H.S., 4th S. 16, pp. 69–94. 1933.

4258 Le Bachelet (X.). Bède et l'eucharistie. Études, 118, pp. 493–504. 1909.

4259 Levison (Wilhelm). Modern editions of Bede. Durham Univ. J., 37, pp. 78–85. 1945.

4260 Manser (Anselm). Von Bedas früher Verehrung auf deutschem Boden. Zeit. deut. Geistesgesch., 1, pp. 298–303. 1936.

4261 Maycock (A. L.). Bede and Alcuin (735–1935). Hibbert J., 33, pp. 402–12. 1935.

4262 Mommsen (Theodor). Die Papstbriefe bei Beda. Neues Archiv, 17, pp. 387–96. 1892.

4263 Morin (Germain). Notes sur plusieurs écrits attribués à Bède le Vénérable. Rev. Bénédictine, 11, pp. 289–95. 1894.

4264 Northbourne (Walter Charles (James)) *baron.* The birthplace of Bede. A lecture. pp. 28. 8° London, [1866].

4265 Orchard (Bernard). Bede the Venerable. Downside Rev., 53, pp. 344–68. 1935.

4266 Patterson (James). The birthplace of the Venerable Bede. [?Wearmouth.] Antiq. Sunderland, 12 (1911), pp. 41–50. 1912.

4267 Raby (F. J. E.). Bede, 735–1935. Laudate, 13, pp. 140–55. 1935.

4268 Rawnsley (Hardwicke Drummond). The Venerable Bede : his life and work. A lecture . . . with an appendix, giving account of Anglian art in northern Britain. pp. 64, + 6 plates. 8° Sunderland, 1904.

4269 Redlich (P. Virgil). Beda und die deutsche Geistesgeschichte. Zeit. deut. Geistesgesch., 1, pp. 273–77. 1935.

4270 ' **Rupicastrensis** ', *and others.* The dying words of the Venerable Bede. [Meaning of tempera (dilute?) in 'Accipe tuum calamum, tempera et scribe velociter.'] N. and Q., [1st S.] 10, pp. 139–40, 229–30, 329–31, 494 : 11, pp. 132, 373 : 12 pp. 306–07, 242. 1854–55.

4271 Sarabia (José M.). La romanidad de S. Beda el Venarable. Estudios eclesiásticos, 14, pp. 51–74. 1935.

4272 Schreiber (Heinrich). Beda in Buchgeschichtlicher Betrachtung. Zent. Bibliothekswesen, 53, pp. 635–52. 1936.

4273 —— Beda Venerabilis und die mittelalterliche Bildung. Stud. u. Mitteil. Gesch. Benediktiner-Ordens, 55, i. 1937.

4274 Sutcliffe (E. F.). Some footnotes to the Fathers. [Bede.] Biblica, 6, pp. 205– . 1925.

4275 —— The Venerable Bede's knowledge of Hebrew. Biblica, 16, pp. 301–06. 1935.

4276 Werner (Karl). Beda der Ehrwürdige und seine Zeit. Neue Ausgabe. pp. viii, 236. 8° Wien, 1881. [Gross, 1355, lit.]

4277 Whiting (Charles Edwin). Bede in after history. Trans. Archit. Soc. of Durham, 7 (1934–36), pp. 178–99. 1936.

4278 —— The life of the Venerable Bede. Bede : 12th centenary essays : ed. A. H. Thompson, pp. 1–38. 1935.

4279 Winmill (Joyce M.). The Venerable Bede. Irish Eccles. Rec., 5th S. 75, pp. 445–52. 1951.

§ *c.* Cuthbert

(*See also under* Textiles, **203**, for his stole and maniple.)

4280 Bates (Cadwallader John). The names of persons and places mentioned in the early lives of St. Cuthbert. Archaeol. Æl., N.S. 16, pp. 81–92. 1892.

4281 Battiscombe (C. F.). The relics of St. Cuthbert—some notes on recent research into their provenance and on the measures taken for their preservation. [i. 3 coffins : ii. linen winding sheet : iii. 5 robes : iv. ivory comb : v. small portable altar : vi. burse : vii. stole, maniple,

girdle, and 2 bracelets given by Athelstan and another maniple : viii. pectoral cross (5th c.).] Trans. Archit. Soc. of Durham, 8, pp. 43–79, + 6 plates. 1937.

4282 Blane (Henry). On Chester-le-Street. [Its story in relation to St. Cuthbert, etc.] J. Brit. Archaeol. Assoc., 22, pp. 22–30, + plan. 1866

4283 Boyd (Halbert J.). Saint Cuthbert. [Sketch of life.] Hist. Berwick Nat. Club, 30, pp. 84–91. 1938.

4284 Brown (William). Where is St. Cuthbert buried? pp. 80, + plates. 8° Durham, 1897. [Reprinted, with additions and corrections, from the Ushaw magazine.]

4285 Butler (Dugald). Saint Cuthbert of Melrose. *Iona Books*, 9. pp. 51. 8° Edinburgh, 1913.

4286 Catcheside (F. L.). Life of S. Cuthbert. Second edition. pp. xii, 57, + plates. 8° London, [1879].

4287 Cheetham (F. H.). Notes on North Meols [Lancs.]—1. Did St. Cuthbert's body rest there? Trans. Hist. Soc. Lancs. and Ches., 76 (1924), pp. 71–80. 1925.

4288 Colgrave (Bertram) and **Crawford** (Osbert Guy Stanhope). The anonymous life of St. Cuthbert. Antiquity, 8, pp. 97–100. 1934.

4289 Colgrave (Bertram). The post-Bedan miracles and translations of St. Cuthbert. Chadwick Mem. Stud., pp. 305–32. 1950.

4290 —— The St. Cuthbert paintings on the Carlisle cathedral stalls. [15th c.] Burl. Mag., 73, pp. 16–21, 2 plates. 1938.

4291 —— Two lives of St. Cuthbert ; a life by an anonymous monk of Lindisfarne and Bede's prose life. Texts, translation, and notes. pp. xiii, 375. 8° Cambridge, 1940.

4292 Colgrave (Hilda). St. Cuthbert of Durham. pp. 51, + plates. 8° Durham, 1947.

4293 Consitt (Edward). Life of Saint Cuthbert. pp. xv, 254. 8° London and New York, 1887.

4294 Craster (*Sir* Herbert Henry Edmund). The miracles of Farne. Arch. Æl., 4th S. 29, pp. 93–107. 1951.

4295 —— The miracles of St. Cuthbert at Farne. [With Latin text of MS. Harl. 4843, by William Tode, a monk of Durham, 1528.] Anal. Boll., 70, pp. 5–19. 1952.

4296 Cummins (J. I.). Saint Cuthbert. Ampleforth J., 41, pp. 126–37. 1936.

4297 Cuthbert, *St.* Sainct Cudberht hys hatrid that he bare vnto women, *etc.* pp. 24. 8° Nevv Castell, 1844. [Pp. 14–17, passages from Symeon of Durham.]

4298 Dodds (Madeleine Hope). The little book of the birth of St. Cuthbert, commonly called the Irish life of St. Cuthbert. Translated with notes. Archaeol. Æl., 4th S. 6, pp. 52–94, + 1 plate. 1929.

4299 Eyre (Charles), *abp. of Glasgow.* The history of S. Cuthbert; or an account of his life, decease, and miracles; of the wandering of his body at intervals during 124 years; and of the state of his body from his decease until A.D. 1542, and of the various monuments erected to his memory. 3rd edition. pp. xvi, 363. 8° London, 1887. [Gross, 1649.]

4300 —— St. Cuthbert's ring. [With figure.] Archaeol. Æl., N.S. 2, pp. 66–68. 1858.

4301 F. (H. L.). St. Cuthbert of Lindisfarne. pp. 30. 12° London, 1848.

4302 F. (P. A.) *etc.* St. Cuthbert's remains. [? exhumation in reign of Mary.] N. and Q., [1st S.] 11, pp. 173, 255, 272, 304–05 : 12, p. 519. 1855.

4303 Fowler (Joseph Thomas). Haliwerfolk. ['They were in the first instance the people who went about with the body of St. Cuthbert in its wanderings.'] Yorks. Archaeol. J., 17, p. 127. 1903.

4304 —— On an examination of the grave of St. Cuthbert in Durham cathedral church, in March 1899. [With 'note on traditions as to the removal of St. Cuthbert's body' : 'note on the bones—St. Cuthbert—St. Oswald' [plate shows skulls of both saints.] Archaeologia, 57, pp. 11–28, + 1 plate. 1900.

4305 —— On the St. Cuthbert window in York minster. (—. Additional notes). Yorks. Archaeol. J., 4, pp. 249–376, + 10 plates ; 11, pp. 486–501. 1877, 1891.

4306 —— St. Cuthbert. A sermon. pp. 12. 8° York. 1887.

4307 Fryer (A.). Wrangham, near Melrose, the supposed birthplace of St. Cuthbert. J. Brit. Archaeol. Assoc., 36, pp. 358–59. 1880.

4308 Fryer (Alfred Cooper). Cuthbert of Lindisfarne : his life and times. pp. 215. 8° London, 1880. [Gross, 1650. Popular.]

4309 Healy (John), *abp. of Tuam.* Was St. Cuthbert an Irishman ? Irish Eccles. Rec., 3rd S. 9, pp. 1–16, 110–18. 1888.

4310 Hegge (Robert). The legend of Saint Cuthbert, or the histories of his churches at Lindisfarne, Cunecascestre, and Dunholm. pp. xv, v, 67. 4° Sunderland, 1816.

4311 Hutcheson (Alexander). Notice of the discovery of an inscribed stone at Weem, near Aberfeldy, Perthshire, with some account of St. Cuthbert's connection with Weem. Proc. Soc. Antiq. Scot., 50 (5th S. 2, 1915–16), pp. 288–302. 1916.

4312 Jaager (Werner), *ed.* Bedas metrische Vita Sancti Cuthberti. *Palaestra*, 198. pp. xi, 136. 8° Leipzig, 1935.

4313 Kerr (—), *Mrs. Francis Kerr.* St. Cuthbert. pp. 24. 8° London, [1892].

4314 Kitchin (George William). The contents of St. Cuthbert's shrine, preserved in the Dean and Chapter library, Durham. [4 plates interpaginated.] V.C.H., Durham, 1, pp. 241–58, + 3 plates. 1905.

4315 Kitzinger (Ernst). The coffin of Saint Cuthbert, drawn by Donald MacIntyre, introduction by E. Kitzinger. pp. 6 + 5 plates. 4° Oxford, 1950. [5 drawings.]

4316 Lees (Thomas). An attempt to trace the translation of Saint Cuthbert through Cumberland and Westmorland. Trans. Cumb. and Westm. Antiq. Soc., 2, pp. 14–20. 1875.

4317 Longstaffe (William Hylton Dyer). Unused evidences relating to SS. Cuthbert and Bede. Archaeol. Æl., N.S. 13, pp. 278–83. 1889.

4318 Low (John Low). On the authorities for the life of St. Cuthbert. Archaeol. Æl., N.S. 11, pp. 18–26. 1886.

4319 Murray (*Sir* James Augustus Henry). Sanct Cuthbert's chapelle by ye Slitrith. A legend of old Hawick. Trans. Hawick Archaeol. Soc., 1925, pp. 23–27. 1925.

4320 Plummer (Selby Wetherell). Notes on the examination of St. Cuthbert's remains. [1899 exhumation.] Northumberland and Durham Med. J., 7, pp. 231–45. 1899.

4321 Raine (James), *the elder*. Saint Cuthbert, with an account of the state in which his remains were found . . . in 1827. pp. iv, 228, 15. 4° Durham, 1828. [Gross, 1651.]

4322 Richmond (Ian Archibald). Saint Cuthbert's dwelling on Farne. Antiquity, 15, pp. 88–89. 1941.

4323 Taylor (Edward James). Re-opening of St. Cuthbert's tomb. [On May 1, 1899.] Proc. Soc. Antiq. Newcastle, 2nd S. 9, pp. 18–21. 1899.

4324 Thompson (Alexander Hamilton). The ms. list of churches dedicated to St. Cuthbert, attributed to prior Wessyngton. Trans. Archit. Soc. of Durham, 7 (1934–36), pp. 151–77. 1936.

4325 Watkin (Aelred). Farne island and St. Cuthbert. Downside Rev., 70, pp. 292–307. 1952.

§ *d*. **Edmund, King of East Anglia**
(*See also* **60**§c for Bury)

4326 Astley (Hugh John Dukinfield). Bury St. Edmunds : notes and impressions. [Pp. 263–4 : ' note on St. Edmund the king '.] Antiquary, 43, pp. 210–16, 258–64, 280. 1907.

P

4327 Gould (Isaac Chalkley). Greenstead and the course of St. Edmund's translation [1013]. Trans. Essex Archaeol. Soc., N.S. 10, pp. 104–07. 1909.

4328 Leonard (George Hare). St. Edmund in stained glass. Proc. Clifton Antiq. Club, 6 (1904–08), pp. 13–21, + 1 plate. 1908.

4329 Loomis (Grant). The growth of the Saint Edmund legend. Harvard Stud. and Notes in Phil. and Lit., 14, pp. 83–113. 1932.

4330 McKeehan (Irene Pettit). St. Edmund of East Anglia, the development of a romantic legend. Univ. Colorado Stud., 15, pp. 13–74. 1925.

4331 Mackinlay (J. Boniface). St. Edmund, king and martyr : a history of his life and times, with an account of the translations of his incorrupt body. pp. xvii, 435. 8° London, 1893. [Gross, 1530.]

4332 Page (John T.), *etc*. St. Edmund. [?relics from Rome to Arundel (for Westminster).] N. and Q., 9th S. 8, pp. 103, 193–94, 227. 1901.

4333 Smylie (R. Stewart). St. Edmund of East Anglia. [Popular account.] Eastern Counties Mag., 1, pp. 257–60. 1901.

4334 ' Vebna.' St. Edmund of East Anglia. [Tradition that body was taken to Toulouse by Louis, son of Philip II in 1216.] N. and Q., 6th S. 5, p. 137. 1882.

4335 Whitbread (L.). The death of St. Edmund. [Translation of East Anglian version of O. E. homily in MS. Bodley 343.] N. and Q., 192, pp. 253–54. 1947.

Edward the Confessor
See 1385–99

§ *e*. **Guthlac**

4336 Birch (Walter de Gray), *ed*. Memorials of St. Guthlac of Crowland. Collected from the original manuscripts, etc. pp. liv, 80. 8° Wisbech, 1881. [Latin text.]

4337 Birch (Walter de Gray). On the roll containing illustrations of the life of Saint Guthlac in the British Museum. Trans. Roy. Soc. Lit., 2nd S. 12, pp. 640–64, + 4 plates. 1882.

4338 Forstmann (Hans). Das altenglische Gedicht Guthlac der Einsiedler und die Guthlac-Vita des Felix. *Dissertation, Bonn.* pp. 23. 8° Halle, 1901.

4339 —— Untersuchungen zur Guthlac-Legende. *Bonner Beiträge zur Anglistik*, 12 *i.* pp. 1–40. 8° Bonn, 1902.

4340 Gerould (Gordon Hall). The Old English poems on St. Guthlac and their Latin source. [i. Guthlac the hermit: ii. Guthlac's death.] Mod. Lang. Notes, 32, pp. 77–89. 1917.

4341 Gonser (Paul), *ed.* Das angelsächsische Prosa-Leben des heilige Guthlac. *Anglistische Forschungen*, 27. pp. vii, 200, + 9 plates. 8° Heidelberg, 1909.

4342 Guthlac, *St.* The Guthlac roll. Scenes from the life of St. Guthlac of Crowland by a twelfth-century artist reproduced from Harley roll Y.6 in the British Museum, with introduction by Sir George Warner. *Roxburghe Club.* pp. 23, + 25 plates. 4° Oxford, 1928.

4343 Jones (Charles Williams). Romanesque literature, vol. 1. Saints' lives and chronicles of early England ; together with first English translations of the Oldest life of pope St. Gregory the Great, by a monk of Whitby and the Life of St. Guthlac of Crowland, by Felix. pp. xiii, 232, + 1 plate. 8° Ithaca, N.Y., 1947.

4344 Kurtz (Benjamin P.). From St. Antony to St. Guthlac. A study in biography. [Comparison of Latin version of Antonius of Evagrius and Felix's Life of Guthlac.] Univ. California, Pubns. in Mod. Philol., 12, pp. 103–46. 1926.

4345 Moore (Edwin). St. Guthlac of Croyland. [Plan is of ' foundations on site of St. Cuthlac's cell.'] J. Brit. Archaeol. Assoc., 35, pp. 132–34, + plan. 1879.

4346 Vassall (H.). The vignettes of St. Guthlac, as reproduced in the windows of Repton School library. [Drawings late 12th c. work.] J. Derbs. Archaeol. Soc., 35, pp. 247–56, + 9 plates. 1913.

§ f. Oswald, King of Northumbria

(*See also* 15 § **a** for king Oswald in history.)

4347 Baker (Eric Paul). The cult of St. Oswald in northern Italy. Archaeologia, 94, pp. 167–94, + 6 plates. 1951.

4347a —— St. Oswald and his church at Zug. [Pp. 121–22, Swiss dedications of St. Oswald.] Archaeologia, 93, pp. 103–23, + 5 plates. 1949.

4348 Berger (A.). Die Oswaldlegende in der deutschen Literatur, ihre Entwicklung und ihre Verbreitung. P.B.B., 11, pp. 365–469. 1886.

4349 Bonser (Wilfrid). The magic of St. Oswald. [Cures by means of his relics.] Antiquity, 9, pp. 418–23. 1935.

4350 Braendl (Matthaeus). Kurtze Lebens-Verfassung des heiligen Oswaldi Königs in Engelland. pp. 120. 8° Saltzburg, 1719.

4351 Champneys (Arthur Charles). Saint Oswald. pp. 52. 8° London, 1911.

4352 Curtoys (William Francis Denny). A short life of St. Oswald. pp. 8. 8° Gloucester, 1913.

4353 Edzardi (Anton). Untersuchungen über das Gedicht von St. Oswald. 8° Hannover, 1876.

4354 Fabbrovitch (E.). Un santo inglese venerato in Carnia. 8° Udine, 1932.

4355 Gill (William). St. Oswald's well, Winwick [Lancs.]. Antiquary, 3, pp. 260–62. 1881.

4356 Haupt (Moriz), *ed.* Oswalt. [Von sand Oswolds Leben. Aus MS. Germ. Oct. 288 der Königlichen Bibliothek in Berlin, aus dem 15n Jahrhunderte.] Z.f.d.A., 13, pp. 466–91. 1867.

4357 Hodgson (J. Crawford). Silver gilt reliquary of the tenth century containing the head of St. Oswald, in the cathedral church of Hildesheim, Hanover. [Illustration.] Proc. Soc. Antiq. Newcastle, 2nd S. 8, pp. 170–71. 1898.

4358 Lucchini (L.). Memorie del sanctuario di S. Osvaldo in Sauris arcidiacesi di Udine. 8° Udine, 1880. [Protector against plague and contagious epidemics as early as 1348.]

4359 MacKinlay (James Murray). Saint Oswald of Northumbria. Trans. Scot. Eccles. Soc., 2, pp. 262–74. 1908.

4360 Manzoni (G.). Orazione panegirica in onore di S. Osvaldo re di Northumberland, *etc.* 8° Ferrara, 1774.

4361 Marzuttini (G. D.). Sermone al popolo in onore di S. Osvaldo re e martire, *etc.* 8° Udine, 1827.

4362 Oswald, *St., king of Northumbria.* Der Münchener Oswald. Text und Abhandlungen von Georg Baesecke. *Germanistische Abhandlungen*, 28. pp. xviii, 445. 8° Breslau, 1907.

4363 —— Sant Oswaldes Leben. Ein Gedicht aus dem zwölften Jahrhundert. Herausgegeben von L. Ettmüller. 8° Zürich, 1835.

4364 —— Der Wiener Oswald. Herausgegeben von Georg Baesecke. *Germanische Bibliothek*, 3 *ii.* pp. cx, 67. 8° Heidelberg, 1912. [Text.]

4365 —— Der Wiener Oswald, herausgegeben von Gertrud Fuchs. *Germanistische Abhandlungen*, 52. pp. xxxiii, 64. 8° Breslau, 1920.

4366 Pace (S.). Vita di S. Osvaldo, re di Northumbria. 8° Bassano, 1712.

4367 Pfeiffer (Franz), *ed.* Sanct Oswalds Leben. [Text. ' Aus der Wiener Handschrift 3007, früher N. 297, pap. vom j. 1492 ; vergl. Hoffmanns Verzeichnis s. 180.'] Z.f.d.A., 2, pp. 92–130. 1842.

4368 Schell (Paulus). Historia von S. Oswaldi leben, unnd wunderwercken. 8° Costantz am Bodensee, 1617.

4369 Schiavo (Alessandro). Di S. Osvaldo M. re della Northumbria et Bretwalda degli Angli. Orazione panegirica, *etc.* 8° Vicenza, 1857.

4370 Soardo (P. C.). Vita di S. Osvaldo re di Northumbria, *etc.* 8° Udine e Bassano, 1689.

4371 Stua (Giovanni Pietro della). Vita di S. Osvaldo re di Northumberland e martire colla storia del suo culto. 8° Udine, 1769.

4372 Winmill (Joyce M.). Iona and Lindisfarne. [Work of St. Oswald.] Irish Eccles. Rec., 5th. S. 80, pp. 106–14. 1953.

4372a Zingerle (Ignaz Vincenz). Die Oswaldlegende und ihre Beziehung zur deutschen Mythologie. pp. viii, 104. 8°. Stuttgart, München, 1856.

§ g. Sidwell (Sativola)

(Virgin beheaded with a scythe and buried at St. Sidwell's, near Exeter, 740 A.D.)

4373 Alexander (John James), **Lega-Weekes** (Ethel), *etc.* St. Sidwell. Devon and Cornwall N. and Q., 12, pp. 248, 302–03, 352 : 13, pp. 18–23, 65–69, 104–06. 1923–24.

4374 Bishop (Herbert Eustace). The legend of St. Sativola. *Same jnl.*, 17, pp. 247–49. 1933.

4375 Doble (Gilbert Hunter). The Vita of St. Sativola. *Same jnl.*, 17, pp. 245–47. 1933.

4376 Grosjean (Paul). Legenda S. Sativolae Exoniensis. [With Latin text.] Anal. Boll., 53, pp. 359–65. 1935.

4377 Lethaby (William Richard). St. Sidwell and Exeter. Devon N. and Q., 4, pp. 190–91. 1907.

4378 Rose-Troup (Frances). St. Sativola. Devon and Cornwall N. and Q., 17, pp. 256–57. 1933.

4379 Rushforth (G. McN.). The iconography of St. Sidwell. *Same jnl.*, 17, pp. 249–53, + 1 plate. 1933.

4380 Simpson (William John Sparrow). St. Sidwell. N. and Q., 8th S. 5, p. 357. 1894.

4381 Weaver (Frederic William). St. Sidwell. N. and Q. Som. and Dorset, 3, pp. 47–48. 1892.

§ h. Other Anglo-Saxon Saints

4382 Armstrong (T. Percy), *etc.* St. Osyth. [9th c.] N. and Q., 157, pp. 83–84. 1929.

4383 Armstrong (T. Percy), *etc.* St. Rumbald. [Grandson of Penda.] N. and Q., 159, pp. 155– 56. 1930.

4384 Baker (A. T.). An Anglo-French life of St. Osith. Mod. Lang. Rev., 6, pp. 476–502. 1911.

4385 Bannister (Arthur Thomas). Sutton Walls, and the legend of St. Ethelbert. Trans. Woolhope N.F. Club, 1914–17, pp. 221–26. 1918.

4386 Barber (Edward). St. Plegmund; and his connection with Cheshire. [9th c.] J. Archit. and Hist. Soc. of Chester, N.S. 16, pp. 54–69, + 1 plate. 1909.

4386a —— St. Werburgh and her shrine. *Same jnl.*, N.S. 10, pp. 68–85, + 5 plates. 1904.

4387 Baring-Gould (Sabin). The life of S. Germanus by Constantius. [? 5th c. or forgery of 6th c.] Y Cymmrodor, 17, pp. 65–81. 1904.

4388 Blaauw (William Henry). On the translation of Saint Lewinna from Seaford, in 1058. Sussex Archaeol. Collns., 1, pp. 46–54. 1848.

4389 Bott (D. J.). The murder of St. Wistan. [849: ? at Wistow, Leics. Son of Wimund, king of Mercia.] Trans. Leic. Arch. Soc., 29, pp. 30–41. 1953.

4390 Boyle (John Roberts). A fragment of the early history of Spurn. [On Wilgils (father of Wilbrord). From Monumenta Alcuiniana.] Trans. Hull Sc. F.C., 1, p. 69. 1899.

4391 Brown (Carleton Fairchild). The autobiographical element in the Cynewulfian rune passages. [Cynewulf a Northumbrian ecclesiastic. ? to be identified with the bishop of Lindisfarne, 740–780.] Engl. Studien, 38, pp. 196–233. 1907.

4391a Brown (Philip William French). St. Clement's day celebrations and the blacksmiths.—4. [King Alfred and St. Clement: ? a Danish patron saint: 32 dedications to him in the Danelaw. List of dedications on pp. 229–30.] N. and Q., 196, pp. 71–73. 1951.

4392 Brushfeld (Thomas Nadauld). President's address [to the Devonshire Association: on Devonshire literature]. [Pp. 26–29, 'first period,—1087.'—Winfrith; Willibald; Alfredus, Lyfing, Leofric, bishops of Crediton.] Rept. and Trans. Devon. Assoc., 25, pp. 25–158. 1893.

4393 Buchannan (George). The feast days of St. Hilda. Yorks. Archaeol. J., 17, pp. 249–53. 1903.

4394 Cook (Albert Stanburrough). Hadrian of Africa, Italy, and England. Philol. Quart., 2, pp. 241–58. 1923.

4395 —— King Oswy and Cædmon's hymn. [Oswy's influence on religion and relations with Hild.] Speculum, 2, pp. 67–72. 1927.

4396 Cox (Ernest W.). St. Cuthman. What is known of him? Sussex N. and Q., 4, pp. 204–07, + 1 plate. 1933.

4397 Cuming (Henry Syer). On effigies of St. Etheldreda. J. Brit. Archaeol. Assoc., 29, pp. 423–25. 1873.

4398 —— St. Milburga, abbess of Wenlock. *Same jnl.*, 41, pp. 86–90, + 1 plate. 1885.

4399 Dalton (J.). St. Withburge's well, East Dereham, Norfolk. [Youngest daughter of Anna, king of the East Angles, d. 743. Body 'stolen' from Dereham by Ely, 974.] N. and Q., 3rd S. 6, pp. 29–30, 71 : 8, p. 247. 1864–65.

4400 Deedes (Cecil). St. Aldate, bishop of Gloucester. [An unidentified saint to whom churches in Oxfordshire and Gloucestershire are dedicated. Often identified (as here) with St. Eldad, *fl.* 490.] Glos. N. and Q., 3, pp. 404–05. 1887.

4401 Dickins (Bruce). The cult of St. Olave in the British Isles. [i.e. Olaf Haraldsson, died 1030.] Saga-Book V.C., 12 (1937–38), pp. 53–80, + 4 plates. 1940.

4402 Fletcher (James Michael John). The marriage of St. Cuthburga, who was afterwards foundress of the monastery of Wimborne. [Includes Latin text with translation of Lansdowne MS. 436, ff. 38*b*–41*b*.] Proc. Dorset Antiq. F.C., 34, pp. 167–85. 1913.

4403 Fletcher (James Michael John). St. Edwold. [Died 871. Brother to St. Edmund of E. Anglia.] N. and Q. Som. and Dorset, 22, pp. 32–34. 1936.

4404 —— Some Saxon saints of Wimborne. [SS. Cuthburga, Tetta, Lioba, Walpurga, Tecla, etc.] Proc. Dorset Antiq. F.C., 32, pp. 199–212. 1911.

4405 Fowler (Joseph Thomas). St. Etheldreda at West Halton, c. A.D. 671. Lincs. N. and Q., 2, pp. 176–77. 1891.

4406 Goscelin, *monk of Canterbury*. La vie de Sainte Vulfhilde [ed. Mario Esposito]. [Abbess of Barking : died c. 1000. Latin text.] Anal. Boll., 32, pp. 10–26. 1913.

4407 Gray (Arthur). The coffin stone of Etheldreda. [Found by the Ely brethren ' in a place which to the present day is called Aermeswerch ' : ? = Granchester.] Fasciculus Ioanni Willis Clark dicatus, pp. 254–64. 1909.

4408 H. (C.), *etc*. St. Botolph. [A.-S. C., 654.] N. and Q., 1st S. 5, pp. 566–67. 1852.

4409 H. (H. de B.). The various St. Ediths in the western calendar. [St. Edith, abbess of Wilton. Died 974.] N. and Q. ,7th S. 7, pp. 163–64. 1889.

4410 Hartland (Edwin Sidney). The legend of St. Kenelm. Trans. Bristol and Glos. Arch. Soc., 39, pp. 13–65, + plate. 1916.

4411 Heather (Percy J.). Three lives of saints : their bearing on folk-lore. [St. Edmund, Edward the Martyr and Becket : notes on the Early South English Legendary.] Folk-lore, 27, pp. 279–97. 1916.

4412 Herzfeld (Georg). Zu [Cockayne :] Leechdoms III, 428 ff. [MS. Lambeth, 427 : end of 10th c. On two fragments in A.-S. concerning St. Mildred.] Engl. Studien, 13, pp. 140–42. 1889.

4413 James (Montague Rhodes). Two lives of St. Ethelbert, king [of the East Angles] and martyr. [With texts : i. by Giraldus ; ii. Passio in C.C.C.C. MS. 308.] E. H. R., 32, pp. 214–44. 1917.

4414 Kerry (Charles). S. Modwen and ' the devill of Drakelowe '. [Temp. Æthelwulf.] J. Derbs. Archaeol. Soc., 17, pp. 49–59. 1895.

4415 Kid Ner Tarw. Alkmund, Alcmund, or Alkmond. Shrop. N. and Q., N.S. 1, pp. 99, 101. 1892.

4416 Lamborn (Edmund Arnold Greening). The shrine of St. Edburg [Stanton Harcourt]. Rpt. Oxford Archaeol. Soc., 80 (1934), pp. 43–52. 1935.

4417 Leadman (Alexander D. H.). St. Hilda. Yorks. Archaeol. J., 17, pp. 33–49, + 1 plate. 1903.

4418 Lees (Thomas). S. Herbert of Derwentwater. [d. 687?] Trans. Cumb. and Westm. Antiq. Soc., 6, pp. 338–43. 1883.

4419 Levison (Wilhelm). St. Alban and St. Albans. Antiquity, 15, pp. 337–59. 1941.

4420 Lindley (E. S.). St. Arild of Thornbury. [Martyred at Kington, near Thornbury, Glos. Relics at St. Peter's abbey, Gloucester.] Trans. Bristol and Glos. Arch. Soc., 70 (1951), pp. 152–53. 1952.

4421 Mitchell (T. Carter). S. Alkelda of Middleham. Yorks. Archaeol. J., 12, pp. 83–86. 1893.

4422 Neot, *St.* Life of St. Neot. [A.-S. text from MS. Cotton Vesp. D. XIV, fol. 142 *b*, and English translation.] The Shrine, pp. 12–22. 1864.

4423 Palgrave (*Sir* Francis). Observations on the history of Caedmon. Archaeologia, 24, pp. 341–43. 1832.

4424 Povey (Kenneth). Saint Lewinna, the Sussex martyr, [and her relics]. Sussex County Mag., 2, pp. 280–91. 1928.

4425 Robertson (William Archibald Scott). St. Eanswith's reliquary in Folkestone church. Arch. Cant., 16, pp. 322–26. 1886.

4426 Rodwell (G. E. C.). The flight of St. Frideswide. [? to Bampton.] J. Brit. Archaeol. Assoc., 72 (N. S. 22), pp. 85–89. 1916.

4427 Rye (Henry A.). Saint Modwen. Trans. Burton Archaeol. Soc., 4. ii, pp. 37–48. 1901.

4428 Serjeantson (Robert Meyricke). A mediaeval legend of St. Peter's, Northampton. [Story of 'St. Ragener, soldier and martyr, kinsman of St. Edmund', from MS. Trin. Coll. Dublin, B.2.] Assoc. Archit. Socs'. Repts., 29, pp. 113–20. 1907.

4429 Sharp (Arthur D.). Saint Alphege [Ælfheah]. [With history of Deerhurst priory, and note on 15th c. window representing saint there.] Trans. Greenwich and Lewisham Antiq. Soc., 4, pp. 6–16, + 1 plate. 1936.

4430 Sieveking (I. Giberne). St. Hild and her abbey at Whitby. Antiquary, 40, pp. 327–30. 1904.

4431 Singer (Charles Joseph). Some early versions of the Bible in English. 1. The life of Caedmon. [From Bede.] Liberal Jewish Monthly, 1, pp. 46–47. 1929.

4432 Smith (Henry Ecroyd). Notice of a mediaeval signaculum of the Anglo-Saxon saints, Edwyn and Ecgwyn (+ supplemental and correctional note). [Includes information *re* King Edwyn and Ecgwyn, bp. of Mercia (died c. 718).] Trans. Hist. Soc. Lancs. and Ches., N.S. 9 [= 21], pp. 165–80, + 1 plate; pp. 253–56. 1869.

4433 Smith (Hubert). Bridgnorth hermitage. [? first inhabited by brother of Athelstan.] Trans. Shropshire Arch. Soc., 1, pp. 159–72, + plan, + 2 plates. 1878.

4434 Smith (O. King). St. Cuthman. N. and Q, 12th S. 5, pp. 76–77. 1919.

4435 Stenton (*Sir* Frank Merry). St. Frideswide and her times. Oxoniensia, 1, pp. 103–112. 1936.

4436 Stephens (G. R.) and **Stephens** (W. D.). Cuthman: a neglected saint. Speculum, 13, pp. 448–53. 1938.

4437 Stevenson (Francis Seymour). St. Botolph (Botwulf) and Iken. Trans. Suffolk Inst. Archaeol., 18, pp. 29–52. 1922.

4438 Taylor (Charles Samuel). Osric of Gloucester. [Founder of St. Peter's minster : probably to be identified with Osric, king of Northumbria, d. 729.] Trans. Bristol and Glos. Arch. Soc., 26, pp. 308–25. 1903.

4439 Tempest (B. C.) and **Rowe** (Joseph Hambley). The chapel of St. Sitha at Bradford : who was St. Sitha ? [? St. Osyth. *But see* article 'St. Sitha', by W. H. Barraclough, 5, pp. 381-92, identifying her with St. Zita, of Lucca, born 1218.] Bradford Antiquary, 5 (N.S. 3), pp. 250–54. 1909.

4440 W. (T.). St. Oswyth. [Daughter of Frithewald, sub-king of Surrey, 7th c.] N. and Q., 8th S. 5, pp. 257, 337–38. 1894.

4441 Whitbread (L.). An analogue of the Cædmon story. Rev. Engl. Stud., 15, pp. 333–35. 1939.

4442 Williams (Emily Octavia). St. Germanus, or Garmon, bishop of Auxerre. Arch Camb., 3rd S. 5, pp. 57-66. 1859.

4442a Wilmart (André). La légende de Ste. Édith en prose et vers par le moine Goscelin. [With Latin text.] Anal. Boll., 56, pp. 5–101, 265–307. 1938.

4443 Wood (—) *canon*. A forgotten saint [Fremund, son of Offa]. [Connection with Cropredy.] Antiquary, 27, pp. 202-07, 247-53 : 28, p. 246. 1893.

4444 Wood (James George). 'Fernley', and the burials of St. Ethelbert. Trans. Woolhope N.F. Club, 1914–17, pp. 235–38. 1918.

4445 Wuelcker (Richard). Ein angelsaechsisches Leben des Neot. [MS. Cotton Vesp. D. XIV. Includes A.-S. text.] Anglia, 3, pp. 104–14. 1880.

67. HAGIOLOGY, CELTIC : GENERAL

4446 Baring-Gould (Sabin). The Celtic saints. [i. Political and social organization : ii. Ecclesiastical organisation. Education in ancient Celtic lands.] J. Roy. Inst. Cornwall, 14, pp. 11–47. 1900.

4447 Jones (Griffith Hartwell). Primitive magic in the lives of the Celtic saints. Trans. Hon. Soc. Cymm., 1936, pp. 69–96. 1937.

4448 Knight (George Alexander Frank). The influence on Scotland of the twelve apostles of Ireland. Trans. Scot. Ecclesiol. Soc., 8, pp. 202–28. 1927.

4449 Mackinlay (James Murray). ' In oceano desertum '—Celtic anchorites and their island retreats. Proc. Soc. Antiq. Scot., 33 (3rd S. 9), pp. 129–33. 1899.

4450 Rees (Alloyn D.). The divine hero in Celtic hagiology. [19 points for comparative study illustrated by lives of SS. David, Cadoc, Patrick.] Folk-lore, 47, pp. 30–41. 1936.

4451 Rhys (*Sir* John). Gleanings in the Italian field of Celtic epigraphy. [Pp. 329–31, on forms of names of S. Illtud : Elltud, etc.] Proc. Brit. Acad., [6] 1933–34, pp. 315–69, + 7 plates. 1914.

4452 Shearman (John Francis). On the Celtic races of Great and lesser Britain. [' St. Ninian . . . Candida casa . . . The Seminary of the Patrician missionaries SS. Ibhar, Benignus, etc., Ninnio . . . his monastery . . . pupils . . . its early history attributed to Glastonbury, etc.'] J. Roy. Hist. and Arch. Assoc. Ireland, [16] 4th S. 6 (1883–84), pp. 250–78, + 2 tables. 1884.

4453 Willis-Bund (John William). Some characteristics of Welsh and Irish saints. Arch. Camb., 5th S. 11, pp. 276–91. 1894.

68. HAGIOLOGY : IRISH
§ *a*. General

4454 Anscombe (Alfred). The great ages assigned to certain Irish saints. [Of vth, vith and viith centuries.] Ériu, 5, pp. 1–6. 1911.

4455 Barrett (M.). Irish saints honoured in Scotland. [Kenney, 1, p. 446.] Am. Cath. Q. Rev., 44, pp. 331–43. 1919.

4456 Colgan (John). Acta Sanctorum Hiberniae. Reproduced [from the 1645, Louvain, edition] . . . with introduction by Brendan Jennings. *Irish Manuscripts Commission, Reflex facsimiles*, 5. pp. 906. fol. Dublin, 1948.

4457 Curtayne (Alice). Five Irish saints. [SS. Patrick, Columcille, Brendan, Ita, Columbanus.] Capuchin Annual, 1945, pp. 269–76. 1945.

4458 Cusack (Mary Francis). The Trias Thaumaturgica, or three wonderworking saints of Ireland, St. Patrick, St. Bridget, and St. Columba. [With the Tripartite Life of St. Patrick, translated from the Irish of Saint Evin by William M. Hennessy.] pp. xvi, 10–959. 4° London, [1877].

4459 Donatus (*Sister* Mary). Beasts and birds in the lives of the early Irish saints. *Thesis, University of Pennsylvania.* pp. 255. 8° Philadelphia, 1934. [Domestic, wild, fabulous, supernatural, animals.]

4460 Footprints of the Irish saints. 23 nos., 8° Dublin, n.d.

4461 Gougaud (Louis). Les conceptions du martyre chez les Irlandais. [Kenney, 1, p. 291.] Rev. Bénédictine, 24, pp. 360–73. 1907.

4462 Gougaud (Louis). Les saints irlandais dans les traditions populaires des pays continentaux. [i. Les trois grands saints nationaux-Patrice, Brigide, Columcille : ii. Saint Brendan le navigateur : iii. Les moines missionnaires : Saint Colomban et Saint Gall : iv. Saints spécialement honorés en Belgique et en France—Fursy, Fiacre, etc. : v. Saints spécialement honorés dans les pays germaniques—Kilian, Fridolin, Monus, Coloman : vi. Notes additionnelles.] Rev. celt., 39, pp. 199–226, 355–58. 1922.

4463 Grosjean (Paul). Catalogus codicum hagiographicorum Latinorum bibliothecarum Dubliniensium. Anal. Boll., 45, pp. 81–148. 1927.

4464 —— Édition du Catalogus praecipuorum sanctorum Hiberniae de Henri Fitzsimon. Essays presented to E. MacNeill, pp. 335–93. 1940.

4465 Grosjean (Paul). Hagiographia Celtica, 4. Sancti Hiberni septem nunquam morituri. Anal. Boll., 55, pp. 287–95. 1937.

4466 —— Le Martyrologe de Tallaght. Anal. Boll., 51, pp. 117–30. 1933.

4467 —— Notes d'hagiographie celtique. [i. La prétendue fête de la Conception de la Sainte Vierge dans les églises celtiques : ii. Les douze évêques de Cell Achaid et les listes anciennes d'évêques irlandais : iii. Le Liber de Gradibus Caeli attribué à S. Grégoire le Grand : iv. Une invocation des saintes Brigides : v. S. Domangort de Slíab Slainge : vi. La patrie de S. Patrice : vii. Notes chronoligiques sur le sejour de S. Patrice en Gaul : viii. Les périodes de 30 ans dans la chronologie de S. Patrice : ix. S. Patrice et S. Vietrice : x. Quand fut composé la Confession de S. Patrice ? : xi. La source britannique des Vies de S. Patrice : xii. La mort de S. Columba, celle de S. Donnan et le cycle pascal celtique : xiii. Relations mutuelles de Vies latines de S. Cáemgen de Glenn Dà Loche : xiv. Le sigle z dans les manuscrits insulaires.] Anal. Boll., 61, pp. 91–107 : 63, pp. 65–130. 1943, 1945.

4468 Gwynn (Edward John). Some saints of Ireland. Church Q. Rev., 74, pp. 62–81. 1912.

4469 Hennig (John). The Irish counterparts of the Anglo-Saxon Menologium. Med. Stud., 14, pp. 98–106. 1952.

4470 —— A list of Irish saints in Rawl, 484. Eigse, 6, pp. 50–55. 1949.

4471 Hogan (Edmund Ignatius), *ed.* The Latin lives of the saints as aids towards the translation of the Irish texts and the production of an Irish dictionary. *Royal Irish Academy*, *Todd Lecture series*, 5. pp. xii, 140. 8° Dublin, 1894. [Patrick, Brigit, Columba, etc.]

4472 Hogan (John). Patron days and holy wells in Ossory. J. Roy. Hist. and Arch. Assoc. Ireland, [12], 4th S. 2 (1872–73), pp. 261–81. 1874.

4473 Hull (Vernam Edward). Keating, Colgan, and the *Saltair na Rann*. [On the guardian saints of the tribes of Ireland.] Zeit. celt. Philol., 16, pp. 453–57. 1927.

4474 Kelly (James J.). Patron saints of the parishes of the diocese of Elphin. Irish Eccles. Rec., 4th S. 16, pp. 43–58. 1904.

4475 Kelly (Matthew). Calendar of Irish saints, the Martyrology of Tallaght. With notices of the patron saints of Ireland. pp. xlii, 189. 8° Dublin, 1857.

4476 Lismore, *Book of.* The Book of MacCarthaigh Riabhach, otherwise the Book of Lismore. Collotype facsimile, with descriptive introduction and indices by R. A. S. Macalister. pp. xxxvii, + 198 plates. fol. Dublin, 1950. [MS., 15th c.]

4477 MacCaffrey (James). Lives of the Irish saints. Irish Theol. Q., 5, pp. 334–47. 1910.

4478 MacCarthy (Charles J. F.). Early Christian foundations of Imokilly. [And the saints who founded them.] J. Cork Hist. Soc., 2nd S. 50, pp. 28–30. 1945.

4479 Moran (Patrick Francis), *cardinal*, *abp. of Sydney.* Irish saints in Great Britain. pp. viii, 336. 8° Dublin, 1879. [Gross, 1619. Early Irish missions.]

4480 Morris (Henry). O Gorman's martyrology. [3,000 saints—A.-S., Irish, etc.] County Louth Archaeol. J., 6, pp. 28–31. 1925.

4481 Ó Briain (Felim). The hagiography of Leinster. Essays presented to E. MacNeill, pp. 454–64. 1940.

4482 —— Miracles in the lives of the Irish saints. Irish Eccles. Record, 5th S. 66, pp. 331–42. 1945.

4483 —— Saga themes in Irish hagiology. Essays presented to . . . Torna, pp. 33–42. 1947.

4484 O'Brien (Sylvester). Irish hagiography : historiography and method. 8° Dublin, 1944.

4485 O'Grady (Standish Hayes), *ed. and trans.* Silva Gadelica (i–xxxi). A collection of tales in Irish. Vol. 1, Irish text. Vol. 2, translation and notes. pp. xxxii, 604. 2 vol. 8° London, 1892. [Vol. 2. pp. 1–69, lives of SS. Kieran of Saighir, Molasius of Devenish, Magnenn of Kilmainham, Cellach of Killala.]

4486 O'Hanlon (John). Lives of the Irish saints. 10 vol. 8° Dublin, 1875–1903. [Kenney, 1, p. 290.]

4487 Olden (Thomas). On the *consortia* of the first order of Irish saints. [First order, to 543 A.D., of superior sanctity as ' they rejected not the service and consortia of women.'] Proc. R.I.A., 3rd S. 3, pp. 415–20. 1894.

4488 Plummer (Charles), *ed.* Bethada náem nÉrenn : lives of Irish saints. Edited from the original mss., with introduction, translations, notes, glossary and indexes. 2 vol. 8° Oxford, 1922. [Lives of Abban, Bairre [Finbar] of Cork, Berach, Brendan of Clonfert, the 12 apostles of Ireland, Ciaran of Saigir, Coemgen, Colman Ela, Máedóc of Ferns, Mochuda, sons of Ua Guanaig, Ruadan.]

4489 —— A tentative catalogue of Irish hagiography. [List of mss. : i. Irish lives of Irish saints : ii. Shorter tracts and anecdotes : iii. Tracts on Irish hagiography, martyrologies, calendars, etc. : iv. Historical poems and hymns : v. Latin lives of Irish saints : vi. Irish lives, passions, etc., of non-Irish saints. Indices of place-names and persons.] Subsidia hagiographica, (Soc. Boll.), 15, pp. 171–285. 1925.

4490 —— On two collections of Latin lives of Irish saints in the Bodleian Library, Rawl. B. 485 and Rawl. B. 505. Zeit. celt. Phil., 5, pp. 429–54. 1905.

4491 ——, *ed.* Vitae sanctorum Hiberniae partim hactenus ineditae. 2 vol., 8° Oxford, 1910. [Gross, 1442a. 32 lives, chiefly from Dublin and Oxford mss.]

4492 Power (Patrick). The ' Lives ' of the Irish saints. [And difficulty of interpreting the material.] Irish Eccles. Rec., 5th S. 24, pp. 592–602. 1924.

4493 Ryan (John), *ed.* The hagiography of Leinster. 8° Dublin, 1940.

4494 Smedt (Charles de) and **Backer** (Joseph de), *ed.* Acta sanctorum Hiberniae ex Codice Salmanticensi, *etc.* pp. iv, col. 975. 4° Edinburgi & Brugis, 1888. [Gross, 607.]

4495 Snieders (Irène). Influence de l'hagiographie irlandaise sur les Vitae des saints irlandais de Belgique. Rev. hist. ecclés., 24, pp. 596–627, 828–67. 1928.

4496 Stokes (Whitley), *ed.* Lives of [Irish] saints from the Book of Lismore, edited with a translation, notes and indices by W. S. *Anecdota Oxoniensia.* pp. cxx, 411, + 1 plate. 8° Oxford, 1890. [Gross, 609. Irish text and translation. Lives of Patrick, Colom-Cille, Brigit, Senán, Findian of Clonard, Findchua of Brigown, Brenainn, Ciarán of Clonmacnois, Mochua of Balla.]

4497 Stubbs (Francis William). Holy wells in county Louth. County Louth Archaeol. J., 2, p. 40. 1908.

4498 Tallaght, *abbey.* The Martyrology of Tallaght, from the Book of Leinster and MS. 5100–4 in the Royal Library, Brussels. Edited with introduction, translations, notes and indices by Richard Irvine Best and Hugh Jackson Lawlor. *Henry Bradshaw Society*, 68. pp. xxviii, 262. 8° London, 1931. [c. 800 A.D.]

4499 Tatlock (John Strong Perry). Greater Irish saints in Lawman and in England. Mod. Philol., 43, pp. 72–76. 1945.

4500 Térilis (J.), *pseud.* [i.e. Jérôme Buléon]. Saints d'origine irlandaise particulièrement populaires chez les Bretons de France. Semaine religieuse du diocèse de Vannes, 11 juin, 1932, pp. 379–81, 18 juin, pp. 404–06. 1932.

4501 Thurneysen (Rudolf). Die Abfassung des Félire von Óengus. [A metrical martyrology composed at Tallaght between 797 and 808.] Zeit. celt. Philol., 6, pp. 6–8. 1901.

4502 Tyler (F. C.), *etc.* Irish saints and their lechs [(with, or on) flat stones]. [? connection with megalith builders.] Devon and Cornwall N. and Q., 15, pp. 101, 159–60. 1928.

4503 Vendryes (Joseph). L'épisode du chien ressuscité dans l'hagiographie irlandaise. Rev. celt., 35, pp. 357–60. 1914.

4504 Waddell (Helen Jane). Beasts and saints. Translations. pp. xx, 151. 8° London, 1934. ['Stories of the mutual charities between saints and beasts from the end of the 4th to the end of the 12th c.' Pp. 41–147, saints of the west, and of Ireland.]

§ *b*. Brigid, Abbess of Kildare

(c. 453–523. For her mantle, at Bruges, *see* section **203**)

4505 Atkinson (Sarah). St. Brigid. pp. 48. 8° London, [1908]. [Reprinted from Irish Monthly and abridged.]

4506 Carey (Francis Patrick). Fanghart of St. Brigid. An ancient Irish pilgrimage shrine. pp. 20. 8° Dublin, 1950.

4507 Certani (Giacomo). La sanità prodigiosa, vita di S. Brigida ibernese. pp. 567. 4° Venetia, 1677. — Di nuouo fatta ristampare da un diuto di detta S. Brigida. pp. 319. 4° Bologna, 1695.

4508 Cowell (George Young). St. Brigid and the cathedral church of Kildare. J. co. Kildare Archaeol. Soc., 2, pp. 235–52. 1897.

4509 Curtayne (Alice). St. Brigid. The Mary of Ireland. pp. 31. 8° Dublin, [1933]. St. Brigid of Ireland. pp. 162. 8° [Dublin, 1933].

4510 FitzGerald (*Lord* Walter). The erection of a church to St. Brigid at Kildare in A.D. 868. J. co. Kildare Archaeol. Soc., 4, p. 65. 1902.

4511 Herbert (*Hon.* Algernon). St. Brighid and her times. According to the account of Hon. A. H. By Christopher Irvine. pp. vi, 101. 8° Dublin, 1903.

4512 Knowles (Joseph A.). St. Brigid, patroness of Ireland. pp. xiv, 292. 8° Dublin, 1907.

4513 Lynch (Maud). St. Brigid of Ireland. pp. 24. 8° Dublin, [1940].

4514 Meraude (Noel de). La vie admirable de S. Brigide vierge taumaturgue. pp. 400. 8° Tournaay, 1652.

4515 Murphy (Denis). St. Brigid of Kildare. J. co. Kildare Archaeol. Soc., 1, pp. 169–76. 1893.

4516 O'Brien (M. A.). The Old Irish life of St. Brigit. Irish Hist. Stud., 1, pp. 119–34, 343–53. 1938–39.

4517 Pfleger (Luzian). Le culte d'une sainte irlandaise en Alsace : Ste. Brigide. [Kenney, 1, p. 356.] Bull. ecclés de Strasbourg, 42, pp. 51–55. 1923.

4518 Robinson (John L.). St. Brigid and Glastonbury. [Visit in 488.] J. Roy. Soc. Antiq. Ireland, 83, pp. 97–99. 1953.

4519 Schmid (Toni). Le culte en Suède de Sainte Brigide l'irlandaise. Anal. Boll., 61, pp. 108–15. 1943.

4520 Sherlock (William). St. Brigid and Clane. J. co. Kildare Archaeol. Soc., 3, p. 269. 1900.

4521 Stubbs (Francis William). The birthplace and life of St. Brigit of Kildare. *Same jnl.*, 3, pp. 216–28. 1900.

4522 Wilkie (James). Saint Bride, the greatest woman of the Celtic Church. *Iona Books*, 5. pp. 53. 8° London, 1913.

§ *c*. Fechin, Abbot of Fore

(7th c.)

4523 Gunning (John). Saint Féchin, his life and times. *Catholic Truth Society*, *no.* 736. 8° Dublin, n.d.

4524 Smith (P. G.). Cong of Saint Féchin. *Catholic World*, 84, *no.* 503. 1907.

4525 Stokes (George Thomas). St. Fechin of Fore and his monastery. [Fore, co. Westmeath, founded 630.] J. Roy. Soc. Antiq. Ireland, 22 (5th S. 2), pp. 1–12. 1892.

4526 Stokes (Whitley). Life of S. Féchin of Fore. [Irish from MS. Phillips, 9194, with English translation.] Rev. celt., 12, pp. 318–53. 1891.

4527 Thunder (John M.). Saint Fechin of Fore. Irish Eccles. Rec., 3rd S. 9, pp. 437–41. 1888.

§ *d.* **Finbar, Bishop of Cork**
(died 630)

4528 Caulfield (Richard). The life of Saint Fin Barre, first bishop and founder of the see of Cork. Edited with notes from mss. in the Bodleian library, Oxford, [MS. Z. 3. I. 5 of] archbishop Marsh's library, and Trinity College, Dublin. pp. 23. 8° London, 1864. [Latin texts.]

4529 Grosjean (Paul). Les vies de S. Finnbarr de Cork, de S. Finnbarr d'Écosse et de S. Mac Cuilinn de Lusk. Anal. Boll., 69, pp. 324–47. 1951.

4530 Lunham (T. A.). The life of Saint Fin Barre. Translated and annotated [from the Codex Kilkenniensis, Marsh's Library, Dublin]. J. Cork Hist. Soc., 2nd S. 12, pp. 105–20. 1906.

4531 MacCarthy (Charles J. F.). St. Finbar and his monastery. *Same jnl.*, 2nd S. 40, pp. 57–62 : 41, pp. 13–19, 85–91 : 42, pp. 16–24, 96–110. 1935–37.

4532 —— Saint Finnbarr of Cork. *Same jnl.*, 2nd S. 48, pp. 1–4. 1943.

4533 Murphy (Michael). St. Finnbarr's itinerary. Irish Eccles. Rec., 5th S. 4, pp. 43–60. 1914.

4534 Ó Foghludha (Risteárd). Footprints of Finbar. *Same jnl.*, 5th S. 74, pp. 242–50. 1950.

4535 Stanton (Patrick), *trs.* The life of St. Finbar of Cork. [Kenney, 1, p. 402. Irish text, and trans. Written by Michael O'Clery in 1629. Burgundian Library, Brussels.] J. Cork Hist. Soc., 2, pp. 61–69, 87–94. 1893.

§ *e.* **Moling, Bishop of Ferns**
(7th c.)

4536 Grosjean (Paul). Further reflections on Mo-lling. [On 4737.] Zeit. celt. Philol., 18, pp. 231–32. 1930.

4537 Hull (Vernam Edward). Two anecdotes concerning St. Moling. [Irish texts with English translation.] *Same jnl.*, 18, pp. 90–99. 1930.

4538 Meyer (Kuno), *ed.* Anecdotes of St. Moling. [Book of Leinster, pp. 283b, 285a. Irish text and English translation.] Rev. celt., 14, pp. 188–94. 1893.

4539 Stokes (Whitley), *ed.* The birth and life of St. Moling. [Irish text and English translation.] Rev. celt., 27, pp. 257–312 : 28, pp. 70–72. 1906–07.

4540 —— The birth and life of St. Moling. A new edition. Edited from a ms. in the Royal Library, Brussels, with a translation and glossary, by Whitley Stokes. pp. 68. 8° London, 1907.

§ *f.* **Patrick**
i. **His writings and notes on them**

4541 Bieler (Ludwig). Codices Patriciani Latini. A descriptive catalogue of Latin manuscripts relating to St. Patrick. *Dublin Institute for advanced studies.* pp. xvii, 72. 8° Dublin, 1942.

4542 —— Libri epistolarum Sancti Patricii episcopi. Introduction, text, and commentary. Classica et Mediaevalia, 11, pp. 1–150 (text) : 12, pp. 79–214. 1950–51.

4543 Bolton (Charles A.). St. Patrick's breastplate. A new interpretation. Irish Eccles. Rec., 5th S. 75, pp. 226–31. 1951.

4544 —— St. Patrick's pastoral testament. [Dicta Patricii in the Book of Armagh.] *Same jnl.*, 5th S. 74, pp. 234–41. 1950.

4545 Dottin (Georges). Les livres de S. Patrice. 8° Paris, 1909. [Kenney, 1, p. 166.]

4546 Esposito (Mario). Notes on the Latin writings of St. Patrick. J. Theol. Stud., 19, pp. 342–46. 1918.

4547 Ferguson (*Sir* Samuel). On the Patrician documents. [With translations of the ' Confessio ' of St. Patrick and the ' Coroticus ' epistle.] Trans. R.I.A., 27, pp. 67–134. 1882.

4548 Healy (John), *abp. of Tuam.* The life and writings of St. Patrick. pp. xi, 754. 8° Dublin, 1905. [Gross, 1653a. Including the text of Patrick's writings, with a translation.]

4549 Hitchcock (Francis Ryan Montgomery). The Confession of St. Patrick. ['Light on four . . . passages . . . connected with the life and mission of the saint.' (389–461).] J. Theol. Stud., 8, pp. 91–95. 1907.

4550 —— Notes and emendations on the Latin writings of St. Patrick. Hermathena, no. 51, pp. 65–76. 1938.

4551 Nerney (D. S.). A study of St. Patrick's sources. [i. Relation of Scripta S. Patricii to the Corinthian epistles : ii. Doctrine of divine vocation : iii. His theology contrasted with the errors of Pelagius and the Massilienses : iv. Proof of divine vocation.] Irish Eccl. Rec., 5th S. 71, pp. 497–507 : 72, pp. 14–26, 97–110, 265–80. 1949.

4552 Oulton (John Ernest Leonard). The credal statements of St. Patrick as contained in the fourth chapter of his Confession. A study of their sources. pp. 36. 8° Dublin, 1940.

4553 Patrick, *Saint*. Das Bekenntnis des heiligen Patrick und sein Brief an die Gefolgsleute des Coroticus. Eingeleitet und übersetzt von F. Wotke. pp. 53. 8° Freiburg, 1940.

4554—— The breastplate of St. Patrick. [English translation.] J. Ardagh and Clonmacnoise Antiq. Soc, 1 iii, pp. 84–87. 1932.

4555—— The Latin writings. Being his Confession and the Epistle to Coroticus. Translated by Delphis Gardner. 2 pt. 4° Maidenhead, 1932.

4556 —— Libri epistolarum Sancti Patricii episcopi, *etc*. [Edited by Ludwig Bieler]. Pt. 1, Introduction and text. *Irish MSS. Commission*. 8° Dublin, 1952— [Pt. is reissue of 1950 ed.]

4557 —— Libri Sancti Patricii : the Latin writings of Saint Patrick. Edited, with introduction, translation and notes, by Newport J. D. White. Proc. R.I.A., 25c, pp. 201–326. 1905.

4558 —— Libri Sancti Patricii : the Latin writings of St. Patrick. A revised text, with a selection of various readings, based on all known manuscripts. Edited by Newport J. D. White. pp. 32. 8° London, 1918.

4559 Patrick, *Saint*. St. Patrick, his writings and life. [Translations with introductions and notes] by Newport J. D. White. *Translations of Christian Literature, series 5, lives of the Celtic saints*. pp. v, 142. 8° London, 1920.

4560 —— St. Patrick's breastplate. pp. 16. 8° London, [1902]. [His Lorica : Irish, with the translations of Whitley Stokes and others.] —. The breastplate of St. Patrick. [With extracts from his other works and a commentary]. By J. G. Maynard. pp. 23. 8° London, [1909].

4561 —— St. Patrick's breastplate. Adapted by Katherine M. Buck. pp. 7. 8° London, 1926.

4562 —— Works [and] St. Secundinus' Hymn on St. Patrick. Translated and annotated by Ludwig Bieler. *Ancient Christian Writers, ed. J. Quasten and J. C. Plumpe*, 17. pp. 121. 8° London, 1953.

4563 —— The writings of St. Patrick. Translated by Newport J. D. White. . . . Together with the Hymn in Patrick's praise, by St. Sechnall. pp. 41. 8° London, 1932.

4564 Pflugk-Harttung (Julius von). Die Schriften S. Patricks. [Against authenticity of the Confessio.] Neue Heidelberger Jahrbücher, 3i, pp. 71–87. 1893.

4565 Ryan (John). A difficult phrase in the Confession of St. Patrick : reppuli sugere mammellas eorum, § 18. Irish Eccles. Rec., 5th S. 52, pp. 293–99. 1938.

4566 White (Newport John Davis). The Paris manuscript of St. Patrick's Latin writings. [Sequel to 4557.] Proc. R.I.A., 25c, pp. 542–52. 1905.

ii. The Lives, and notes on them

4567 Armagh, *Book of*. Book of Armagh, the Patrician documents. With an introduction by Edward Gwynn. *Irish Manuscripts Commission, Facsimiles in collotype of Irish manuscripts*, 3. pp. iv, + 48 plates. 4° Dublin, 1937.

4568 Armagh, *Book of*. Liber Ardmachanus, the Book of Armagh. Edited . . . by John Gwynn. *Royal Irish Academy*. pp. ccxc, 503, with facsimiles. 4° Dublin, 1913.

4569 Bieler (Ludwig). Studies on the text of Muirchú. [MS. Novara 77. Last eight leaves, a life of St. Patrick. Latin text and notes.] Proc. R.I.A., 52c, pp. 179–220. 1950.

4570 Bury (John Bagnell). Sources of the early Patrician documents. E.H.R., 19, pp. 493–503. 1904.

4571 —— Tírechán's Memoir of St. Patrick. [7th c.] E.H.R., 17, pp. 235–67, 700–04. 1902.

4572 —— The tradition of Muirchu's text. Hermathena, 12, pp. 172–207. 1902.

4573 Esposito (Mario). Notes on a Latin life of St. Patrick. [Included in vol. 3 of Johannes Herwagen's edition of Bede, Bâle, 1563.] Classica et Mediaevalia, 13, pp. 59–72. 1952.

4574 Fiecc, *St.* St. Fiecc's poem on the life of St. Patrick. [Irish text with English translation.] Irish Eccles. Rec., 4, pp. 269–93. 1868.

4575 Gaidoz (Henri). La Vie Tripartite de Saint Patrice. [Bibliography.] Rev. celt., 8, p. 164. 1887.

4576 Graves (Charles), *bp. of Limerick.* Some notices of the Acts of St. Patrick, contained in the Book of Armagh. [Concerning Muirchu Maccumachteni, author of the life of St. Patrick in the Book of Armagh and his father Cogitosus—died c. 670.] Proc. R.I.A., 8 (1863), pp. 269–71. 1864.

4577 Grosjean (Paul). Notes sur les documents anciens concernant S. Patrice. Anal. Boll., 62, pp. 42–73. 1944.

4578 Hogan (Edmund Ignatius). Patrician documents. [Textual queries. Book of Armagh, etc.] Irish Eccles. Rec., 3rd S. 8, pp. 229–42. 1887.

4579 Lawlor (Henry Cairnes). Saint Patrick : our sources of knowledge concerning him. Proc. Belfast N.H. and Phil. Soc., 1931–2, pp. 51–55. 1933.

4580 Lot (Ferdinand). La date de la Vie Tripartite de Saint Patrick. [Kenney, 1, p. 342.] Ann. de Bretagne, 11, pp. 360–61. 1896.

4581 MacCarthy (Bartholomew). The Tripartite life of St. Patrick : new textual studies. Trans. R.I.A., 29, pp. 183–206. 1889.

4582 MacNeill (Eoin). Dates of texts in the Book of Armagh relating to St. Patrick. J. Roy. Soc. Antiq. Ireland, 58 (6th S. 18), pp. 85–101. 1928.

4583 —— The earliest lives of St. Patrick. *Same jnl.*, 58 (6th S. 18), pp. 1–21. 1928.

4584 —— The origin of the Tripartite life of Saint Patrick. *Same jnl.*, 59 (6th S. 19), pp. 1–15. 1929.

4585 —— The Vita Tripartita of St. Patrick. [i. Later accretions. ii. Topographical importance.] Ériu, 11, pp. 1–41. 1930.

4586 Meissner (John Ludwig Gough). The British tradition of St. Patrick's life. [Sources used by Muirchu for his life : ?when composed.] Proc. R.I.A., 40 c, pp. 356–84. 1932.

4587 Muirchu Maccumachtheni. Vita Sancti Patricii Hibernorum apostoli auctore M.M., et Tirechani Collectanea de S. Patritio, nunc primum integra ex libro Armachano ope codicis Bruxellensis, edidit Edmundus Hogan. Anal. Boll., 1, pp. 531–85. 1882.

4588 Mulchrone (Kathleen). Die Abfassungszeit und Überlieferung der Vita Tripartita. Zeit. celt. Philol., 16, pp. 1–94. 1927.

4589 —— *ed.* Bethu Phátraic. The Tripartite life of Patrick. Edited with translation and indexes. 1. Text and sources. *Royal Irish Academy.* pp. ix, 158. 8° Dublin, 1939. [Pp. 156–58, Irish text of Lorica Sancti Patricii.]

4590 —— Tírechán and the Tripartite life. Irish Eccles. Rec., 5th S. 79, pp. 186–93. 1953.

4591 —— The Tripartite life of Patrick. Fragments of Stowe copy found. [With Irish text.] J. Galway Archaeol. Soc., 20, pp. 129–44. 1943.

4592 —— The Tripartite life of Patrick. Lost fragment discovered. [With Irish text and translation.] *Same jnl.*, 20, pp. 39–53, + 1 plate. 1942.

4593 Mulchrone (Kathleen). What are the Armagh notulae ? [Book of Armagh, ff. 18 b–19b. Abbreviated names of persons and places associated with St. Patrick. In 9th c. hand.] Ériu, 16, pp. 140–44. 1952.

4594 Patrick, *St.* A life of St. Patric (Colgan's Tertia vita). Edited by J. B. Bury. [Latin text and notes.] Trans. R.I.A., 32 c., pp. 199–262. 1904.

4595 Stokes (Whitley). Glossed extracts from the Tripartite life of S. Patrick. Archiv f. celt. Lexik., 3, pp. 8–38. 1907.

4596 Tirechán, *bishop.* Collectanea de Sancto Patricio ex Libro Armachano. (Additamenta ad collectanea.). Anal. Boll., 2, pp. 35–68, 213–38. 1883.

4597 Walsh (Paul). Recent studies on the Patrician documents. Irish Eccles. Rec., 5th S. 39, pp. 232–42. 1932.

iii. Biographies and incidents in his life

4598 [Anon.] Notes on the life of St. Patrick. i. Where and by whom was St. Patrick consecrated bishop ? (ii. St. Patrick at Tours). Irish Eccles. Rec., 3, pp. 7–18, 191–97. 1867.

4599 Barry (Albert). Chronology of St. Patrick. *Same jnl.*, 3rd S. 16, pp. 751–58. 1895.

4600 Bieler (Ludwig). The life and legend of St. Patrick. *Same jnl.*, 5th S. 70, pp. 1087–91. 1948.

4601 —— The life and legend of St. Patrick : problems of modern scholarship. pp. 146. 8° Dublin, 1949. [The real St. Patrick : sources : the saint's testimony about himself : chronology and St. Patrick and the Irish annals : evidence of the Lives.]

4602 —— The ordination of St. Patrick. Scriptorium, 2, pp. 286–87. 1948.

4603 —— Sidelights on the chronology of St. Patrick. [Patrician dates in the Ulster Chronicle : The Annals in the Book of Leinster, and the list of coarbs of Patrick.] Irish Hist. Stud., 6, pp. 247–60. 1949.

4604 Bolton (Charles A.). The saint on Croach Patrick. [Cruachan Aigli (hill of the eagles) to which St. Patrick retreated.] Irish Eccles. Rec., 5th S. 70, pp. 680–86. 1948.

4605 —— St. Patrick and the Easter fire. [Lighted on Slane hill, Tara. ? connection with Beltine fires.] *Same jnl.*, 5th S. 69, pp. 215–20. 1947.

4606 Bury (John Bagnell). Life of St. Patrick and his place in history. pp. xv, 404, + 2 maps. 8° London, 1905. [Gross, 1651a. Critical appendix of the sources.]

4607 Certani (Giacomo). Il Mosè dell' Ibernia. Vita del glorioso S. Patrizio, *etc.* pp. 519. 4° Bologna, 1686. —— pp. 332. 8° Venezia, 1757.

4608 Chamberlain (George Ashton). St. Patrick : his life and work. pp. 122. 8° Dublin. 1932.

4609 Concannon (Helena). Saint Patrick : his life and mission. pp. xxxiv, 260, + plates. 8° London, 1931.

4610 Cusack (Mary Frances). The life of Saint Patrick. [With the Tripartite life of St. Patrick, translated from the Irish of Saint Evin by William M. Hennessy]. pp. xii, 656. 4° London, 1871. [Gross, 1652.]

4611 D'Alton (E. A.). A new word on St. Patrick. [Brief life.] Irish Eccles. Rec., 4th S. 4, pp. 343–53. 1898.

4612 Dillon (John). Observations on the accounts given of the life and acts of Saint Patrick. Archaeol. Scot., 2, pp. 213–52. 1822.

4613 Fleming (William). The life of St. Patrick. pp. xiii, 178. 8° London, 1905.

4614 Gaffney (John). Life of St. Patrick, . . . with novena and other prayers in honour of St. Patrick. pp. 108. 16° Dublin, [1932].

4615 Gargan (Denis). The ancient Church of Ireland : a few remarks on Todd's Memoir of the life and mission of St. Patrick, [**4630**]. 8° Dublin, 1864.

4616 Gradwell (Robert), *bp. of Lydda.* Suceat : the story of sixty years of the life of St. Patrick, A.D. 373–433. pp. xxiv, 305. 8° London, [1891]. [Gross, 1653. Popular.]

4617 Grosjean (Paul). Recent research on the life of St. Patrick. Thought, 5, pp. 22–41. 1930.

4618 Lynch (Patrick). The life of St. Patrick . . . to which is added St. Frech's Irish hymn. 12° Dublin, 1828. [Hymn in Irish, Latin and English.]

4619 Malone (Sylvester). The ancient Irish scholiast. [Deals with St. Patrick : place of his capture and birth, of his consecration and of his death.] Irish Eccles. Rec., 3rd S. 9, pp. 519–27. 1888.

4620 —— Chapters towards a life of St. Patrick. pp. viii, 226. 8° Dublin, 1892.

4621 —— Nomina Patriciana. [Ordained by Paulinus of Nola under Mt. Sarnus ; consecrated by Amatus, abbot-bp. of Eburo-briga (now St. Florentine, N.N.E. of Auxerre).] Irish Eccles. Rec., 3rd S. 8, pp. 385–99, 886–904. 1887.

4622 Moran (Patrick Francis), *cardinal, bp. of Ossory*. Some strictures on Bury's Life of St. Patrick. Irish Theol. Q., 2, pp. 151–75. 1907.

4623 Morris (William Bullen). The life of St. Patrick . . . with a preliminary enquiry into the authority of the traditional history of the saint. 4th edition. pp. xviii, 303. 8° London, 1890. [Gross, 1654.]

4624 Newell (Ebenezer Josiah). St. Patrick : his life and teaching. 2nd edition, revised. pp. viii, 237. 8° London, 1907.

4625 Patrick, *St.* The life of Saint Patrick. . . . To which is added . . . the celebrated hymn . . . by Saint Fiech, comprehending a . . . history of his life, *etc.* pp. 350. 12° Dublin, 1810.

4626 —— St. Patrick. *Notre Dame series of the lives of the saints.* pp. xi, 274. 8° London, 1911.

4627 Robert (Benjamin). Étude critique sur la vie et l'oeuvre de Saint Patrick. *Thèse, Paris*, 1883. pp. 133. 8° Paris, 1883. [Gross, 1656. ' Devotes much attention to the mediaeval lives '.]

4628 Sanderson (Joseph). The story of Saint Patrick. Embracing a sketch of the condition of Ireland . . . during his life, at his death, and immediately after it. pp. 286. 8° New York, 1902.

4629 Stevenson (John Sinclair). The story of Saint Patrick. With the hymn of the saint in modern Irish. pp. 39. 8° London, 1932.

4630 Todd (James Henthorn). St. Patrick . . . a memoir of his life and mission. With an introductory dissertation on some early usages of the Church in Ireland, *etc.* pp. xii, 538. 8° Dublin, 1864.

4631 Wells (Benjamin W.). St. Patrick's earlier life. E.H.R., 5, pp. 475–85. 1890.

iv. **Birthplace and burial place**

4632 Ardill (John Roche). St. Patrick: Where was he born ? pp. 29. 8° Dublin, 1934.

4633 Barry (Albert). The birthplace of St. Patrick. [North Wales.] Irish Eccles. Rec., 3rd S. 14, pp. 1122–31. 1893.

4634 Bigger (Francis Joseph). The grave of St. Patrick. [Monument over reputed grave at Downpatrick.] Ulster J. Archaeol., 2nd S. 6, pp. 61–64. 1900.

4635 Courtois (R.). Saint Patrice est-il né à Boulogne-sur-mer? pp. 23. 8° Arras, 1933.

4636 Dickinson (Francis Henry). St. Patrick. [Born at Bonavem Taberniae. ? = Glastonbury.] Glastonbury Antiq. Soc. Proc., 1 (1886), pp. 17–19. 1887.

4637 Gógan (Liam S.). The home of St. Patrick. [Manavia=Manau=Anglesea.] Irish Eccles. Rec., 5th S. 75, pp. 193–204. 1951.

4638 Haverfield (Francis John). English topographical notes.—2. Bannavem Taberniae [home of St. Patrick's father.] E.H.R., 10, pp. 711–12. 1895.

4639 Healy (John), *abp. of Tuam*. The burial-place of St. Patrick. [Downpatrick cathedral ? also of SS. Brigid and Columcille.] Irish Eccles. Rec., 3rd S. 15, pp. 1–17, 303–15. 1894.

4640 Leigh (Stephen de). St. Patrick in Britain. [Catalogue of localities assigned as his birthplace.] Tablet, Mch. 14, 1925, pp. 340–41. 1925.

4641 Macgregor (D. Mackintosh). Where was St. Patrick born ? 8° [n.p.], 1910.

4642 MacNab (Duncan). The birthplace of St. Patrick. 8° Dublin, 1866.

4643 MacNeill (Eoin). The native place of St. Patrick. Proc. R.I.A., 37 c., pp. 118–40. 1926.

4644 MacSweeney (Michael T.). The birthplace of St. Patrick : its solution and consequences. Irish Eccles. Rec., 5th S. 11, pp. 265–85. 1918.

4645 Malone (Sylvester). The birthplace of St. Patrick. [Usktown, S. Wales. Answer to O'Brien, 4649.] *Same jnl.*, 4th S. 6, pp. 97–113 ; 7, pp. 229–40, 342–56. 1899–1900.

4646 —— Mistaken identity as to St. Patrick's birth-place. J. Roy. Hist. and Arch. Assoc. Ireland, [19], 4th S. 9, pp. 49–52. 1889.

4647 —— St. Patrick's burial-place. [Saul, co. Down.] Irish Eccles. Rec., 3rd S. 15, pp. 341–51. 1894.

4648 —— St. Patrick's native town and street. ['Vio Bannavem Taberniae' (Bk. of Armagh).] *Same jnl.*, 3rd S. 10, pp. 385–94. 1889.

4649 O'Brien (Edward). The birthplace of St. Patrick. [? Cantabria.] *Same jnl.*, 4th S. 5, pp. 491–507 : 6, pp. 11–26, 237–42. 1899.

4650 Olden (Thomas). On the burial-place of St. Patrick. [Armagh.] Proc. R.I.A., 3rd S. 2, pp. 655–66. 1893.

4651 O'Regan (Patrick J.). St. Patrick's boyhood home was in Inverness-shire at Banavie, Lochaber. pp. 38. 8° Oban, [1948].

4652 Quine (John). The birthplace of St. Patrick. [In Isle of Man.] J. Waterford Archaeol. Soc., 14, pp. 169–76. 1911.

4653 Scott (A. Boyd). The birthplace of St. Patrick. [Argument for Nemthur, near Old Kilpatrick, on the Clyde.] Rec. Scot. Church Hist. Soc., 1, pp. 161–72. 1926.

4654 Sexton (John E.). The birthplace of St. Patrick, an essay in textual criticism. [Locates outside Rome.] Cath. Hist. Rev., 17, pp. 131–50. 1931.

4655 Stack (Gerald). St. Patrick's birthplace : the voice of the Irish. [Dumbarton.] Irish Eccles. Rec., 4th S. 6, pp. 341–58, 444–55, 521–41 : 7, pp. 122–47. 1899–1900.

4656 Turner (J. H.). An enquiry as to the birthplace of St. Patrick. Archaeol. Scot., 5, pp. 261–84. 1874.

4657 Wheeler (G. H.). St. Patrick's birthplace. E.H.R., 50, pp. 109–13. 1935.

v. Place of captivity (Silva Focluti)

4658 Bieler (Ludwig). The problem of 'Silua Focluti'. Irish Hist. Stud., 3, pp. 351–64. 1943. (*Also* Correspondence. 4, pp. 103–05, 1944).

4659 Concannon (Helena). Silva Focluti, silva Illuti, or silva virgulti ? Essays presented to E. MacNeill, pp. 282–85. 1940.

4660 Goldrick (P. J.) and **O'Doherty** (John F.). The place of St. Patrick's captivity. [Boultypatrick, Donegal.] Irish Eccles. Rec., 5th S. 51, pp. 314–15, 430–31 : 54, pp. 420–30. 1938–39.

4661 Macalister (Robert Alexander Stewart). Silva Focluti. [Passage in Confessio Patricii. Shows how original 'Macedoniā' came to be written 'silvā Focluti' in the Book of Armagh.] J. Roy. Soc. Antiq. Ireland, 62 (7th S. 2), pp. 19–27, 225. 1932.

4662 MacErlean (John). Silva Focluti. Anal. Boll., 57, pp. 334–63. 1939.

4663 MacNeill (Eoin). Silva Focluti. [In St. Patrick's account of his vision. ?=Silua Uluti.] Proc. R.I.A., 36 c., pp. 249–55. 1923.

4664 MacNeill (Patrick). The identification of Foclut. [Faughal (Fachoill) between Cushendall and the sea, co. Antrim.] J. Galway Archaeol. Soc., 22, pp. 164–73. 1947.

4665 Meissner (John Ludwig Gough). The place of St. Patrick's captivity. Proc. R.I.A., 41 c., pp. 131–40. 1932.

4666 Murray (Laurence P.). The wood of Forclut. County Louth Archaeol. J., 9, pp. 166–68. 1938.

4667 Thurneysen (Rudolf). Silva vocluti. Zeit. celt. Philol., 19, pp. 191–92. 1933.

vi. Itineraries

4668 Bairead (Fearghus). St. Patrick's itinerary through county Limerick. N. Munster Antiq. J., 4, pp. 68–73. 1944.

4669 Barry (James Grene). Carnarry. The itinerary of St. Patrick through N.E. Limerick. J. North Munster Archaeol. Soc., 1, pp. 213–18. 1911.

4670 Begley (John). Local traces of St. Patrick. Irish Eccles. Rec., 3rd S. 17, pp. 317–24. 1896.

4671 Brophy (Patrick J.). St. Patrick's other island. [Lerins.] *Same jnl.*, 5th S. 75, pp. 243–46. 1951.

4672 Bury (John Bagnell). The itinerary of Patrick in Connaught, according to Tírechán. Proc. R.I.A., 24 c., pp. 153–68. 1903.

4673 Connellan (M. J.). St. Patrick's two crossings of the Shannon. J. Ardagh and Clonmacnoise Antiq. Soc., 2 xii, pp. 78–84. 1951.

4674 Dawson (Abraham). St. Patrick's view of the Braid valley, and the burning of Milchu's homestead. Ulster J. Archaeol., 2nd S. 3, pp. 112–19. 1897.

4675 Gogarty (Oliver St. John). I follow St. Patrick. pp. xi, 336, and 4 maps. 8° London, 1938. (reprinted, 1950). [Follows the journeys of St. Patrick.]

4676 Grosjean (Paul). S. Patricius in monte Cruachan Aighle. [With Irish text, and Latin translation.] Anal. Boll., 50, pp. 346–57. 1932.

4677 Hanna (J. W.). An inquiry into the true landing place of St. Patrick in Ulster. [Kenney, 1, p. 321. Ringbune, in 432. Reprinted from a tract dated Downpatrick, 1858.] Ulster J. Archaeol., 2nd S. 11, pp. 9–14, 71–76. 1905.

4678 Healy (John), *abp. of Tuam*. St. Patrick in Tirawley [co. Mayo]. Irish Eccles. Rec., 3rd S. 10, pp. 673–81, 906–14. 1889.

4679 Horne (Ethelbert), *abbot of Downside*. St. Patrick in Somerset. N. and Q. Som. and Dorset, 24, pp. 79–80. 1944.

4680 Howorth (*Sir* Henry Hoyle) and **McGovern** (J. B.). Heysham and St. Patrick (Heysham antiquities). [?Its church dedicated to him, as Heysham was included in his itinerary.] N. and Q., 9th S. 2, pp. 281–82, 409–11, 469–70 ; 3, pp. 169–70. 1898–99.

4681 Lonergan (P.). St. Patrick in Munster. J. Waterford Archaeol. Soc., 2, pp. 37–44, 104–11. 1896.

4682 Louis (René). Le séjour de Saint Patrice à Auxerre. Mélanges d'histoire au moyen âge, dediés à la mémoire de Louis Halphen, pp. 445–51. 1951.

4683 Morris (William Bullen). The footprints of St. Patrick. Irish Eccles. Rec., 3rd S. 6, pp. 180–91. 1885.

4684 Murray (Laurence P.). St. Patrick and Louth. County Louth Archaeol. J., 2, pp. 213–36. 1910.

4685 Pooler (Lavis Arthur Hill Trevor). St. Patrick in co. Down : a reply to Professor Zimmer. pp. 12. 8° Dublin, 1904.

4686 Shearman (John Francis). Loca Patriciana : an identification of localities, chiefly in Leinster, visited by St. Patrick. . . . With an essay on the three Patricks, Palladius, Sen Patrick and Patrick Mac-Calphurn, apostles of Ireland in the fifth century. 2nd edition. pp. xiii, 495. 8° Dublin, 1882. [Kenney, 1, p. 320.]

4687 Thompson (E. A.). A note on St. Patrick in Gaul. Hermathena, 79, pp. 22–29. 1952.

vii. The Two Patricks

4688 Arbois de Jubainville (Marie Henry d'). Saint Patrice et Sen Patrice, Rev. celt., 9, pp. 111–16. 1888.

4689 Barry (Albert). Sen Patrick. [St. Patrick as founder of Glastonbury. Answered by S. Malone, **4697**.] Irish Eccles. Rec., 3rd S. 14, pp. 627–35. 1893.

4690 Croke (William J. D.). The double personality of St. Patrick. [Answered by S. Malone, **4694**.] *Same jnl.*, 4th S., 12, pp. 442–50. 1902.

4691 Grosjean (Paul). S. Patrice d'Irlande et quelques homonymes dans les anciens martyrologes. J. eccles. hist., 1, pp. 151–71. 1950.

4692 MacCaffrey (James). Rome and Ireland. Pre-Patrician Christianity. [Palladius, etc.] Irish Theol. Q., 1, pp. 47–68. 1907.

4693 MacNeill (Eoin). 'The other Patrick.' Studies, 32, pp. 308–14. 1943.

4694 Malone (Sylvester). The individuality and work of our national apostle. [Answering W. J. D. Croke. **4690**.] Irish Eccles. Rec., 4th S. 13, pp. 212–27. 1903.

4695 —— Sen (old) Patrick, who was he ? *Same jnl.*, 3rd S. 12, pp. 800–09. 1891.

4696 —— A sketch of Palladius. *Same inl.*, 3rd S., 10, pp. 121–33. 1889.

4697 —— Who Sen Patrick was not. [Answer to A. Barry, **4689**.] *Same jnl.*, 3rd S. 14, pp. 815–20. 1893.

4698 Mulchrone (Kathleen). The old-Irish form of *Palladius*. J. Galway Archaeol. Soc., 22, pp. 34–42. 1946.

4699 Murphy (Gerard). The two Patricks. Studies, 32, pp. 297–307. 1943.

4700 O'Brien (Edward). St. Patrick and Palladius. Was St. Patrick and the Palladius mentioned by St. Prosper and the Venerable Bede one and the same ? Irish Eccles. Rec., 3rd S. 8, pp. 723–31. 1887.

4701 O'Rahilly (Thomas Francis). The two Patricks. *Dublin Institute of Advanced Studies*. pp. 83. 8° Dublin, 1942. [Ireland converted by 2 workers , Palladius, sent by Pope Celestine in 431, d. 461, and Patrick, who succeeded him in 461 and died c. 492. Acta mingled and result one synthetic product, St. Patrick.]

4702 Ryan (John). The two Patricks. [Arising from **4701**.] Irish Eccles. Rec., 5th S. 60, pp. 241–52. 1942.

4703 Snx, P. St. Palladius and the diocese of Ferns. [Short account of Palladius.] The Past (Ui Ceinnsealaigh Historical Society), 2, pp. 100–12. 1921.

4704 Zimmer (Heinrich). Pelagius in Irland. Texte und Untersuchungen zur patristischen Litteratur. pp. viii, 450. 8° Berlin, 1901. [i. Beiträge aus altirischen Handschriften zum unverstümmelten Pelagiuskommentar und zur Kenntniss der patristischen Litteratur des 4. Jahrhunderts : ii. Die *Expositio Pelagii super omnes epistolas Pauli* nach St. Gallensis 73 S. ix.]

viii. Miscellaneous

4705 Ardill (John Roche). The date of St. Patrick. A reply to N. J. D. White [**4760**]. 3rd issue, revised. pp. 19. 8° Dublin, 1932.

4706 —— St. Patrick A.D. 180. pp. ix, 221. 8° London, [1931].

4707 Baggi (Giovanni Battista). S. Patrizio vescovo. Apostolo taumaturgo dell' Irlanda. Speciale protettore di Vertova-Bergamo. pp. 246, + plates. 8° Bergamo, 1928.

4708 Barsanti (Ottavio). St. Patrick's apostleship. A lecture, *etc.* pp. 31, v. 8° Melbourne, 1871.

4709 Bieler (Ludwig). O'Sullevan Beare's Patriciana decas. A modern Irish adaptation. J. Galway Archaeol. Soc., 22, pp. 19–33. 1946.

4710 Blacam (Hugh de). Saint Patrick. pp. 176. 8° Milwaukee, 1941.

4711 Connellen (M. J.). Three Patrician bishops and their seats in Airteach. [Identification of sees of Telach / Tulach na gCloch, Telach / Tulach Liag and Cúil Conalto.] J. Galway Archaeol. Soc., 24, pp. 125–29. 1951.

4712 Culhane (Robert). St. Patrick and Italy. Irish Eccles. Rec., 5th S. 72, pp. 308–20. 1949.

4713 Curtayne (Alice). St. Patrick. pp. 32. 8° Dublin, [1931].

4714 Czarnowski (Stefan Zygmunt). Le culte des héros et ses conditions sociales. Saint Patrick. pp. xciv, 369. 8° Paris, 1919. [Kenney, 1, p. 167. Accredits him with supernatural and magical powers.]

4715 Diamond (Lucy). St. Patrick. pp. 48. 16° London, 1948.

4716 Dobbs (Margaret E.). [Maighréad Ní C. Dobs]. Altrourh Tighi da Medar. [The fosterage of the house of the two goblets]. [Irish text and English translation. Concerns St. Patrick.] Zeit. celt. Philol., 18, pp. 189–230. 1930.

4717 Gannon (Patrick Joseph). St. Patrick and the Irish Church . . . Sermon, *etc.* pp. 20. 8° Dublin, 1932.

4718 Gogarty (Thomas). St. Patrick's church at the ford of the two forks. [Carntown under Sliabh Breg.] Irish Eccles. Rec., 4th S. 23, pp. 473–80. 1908.

4719 Gougaud (Louis). Les plus anciennes attestations du culte de Saint Patrice. [A collection of all literary practical and liturgical testimonies on the devotion to St. Patrick going back to 5th c.] Ephemerid. liturgic. 35, pp. 182–85. 1931.

4720 —— Le scribe aux doigts lumineax. Bull. écrivains cathol., 1923, pp. 151–54. 1923.

4721 Grosjean (Paul). Patriciana. [Various questions discussed : in Latin.] Anal. Boll., 43, pp. 241–60. 1925.

4722 —— Les Vies latines de S. Cáemgen et de S. Patrice du manuscrit 121 des Bollandistes. (Les Leçons du Bréviaire des chanoines réguliers de Sion sur S. Patrice.) (Paladius episcopus . . . qui Patricius.) Anal. Boll., 70, pp. 313–26. 1952.

4723 Healy (John), *abp. of Tuam.* St. Patrick. *Assoc. for prom. Christian knowledge. Lectures on Irish Church history,* 1. pp. 36. 8° Dublin, 1897.

4724 Hennig (John). The literary tradition of Moses in Ireland. [Parallel of Moses and St. Patrick.] Traditio, 7, pp. 233–61. 1951.

4725 Herrmann (Léon). Du nouveau sur saint Patrick ? [i. Vers sur des prodiges : ii. L'épithalame d'Auspicius : iii. Hypothèse sur les débuts de S. Patrick.] Rev. belge Philol., 30, pp. 805–12. 1952.

4726 Hitchcock (Francis Ryan Montgomery). St. Patrick and his Gallic friends. pp. 164. 8° London, 1916. [Kenney, 1, p. 166.]

4727 Hogan (Edmund Ignatius). New lights on St. Patrick. Irish Eccles. Rec., 3rd S. 7, pp. 511–19. 1886.

4728 Hurley (Timothy). St. Patrick and the parish of Kilkeevan. vol. 1. pp. xxvii, 618. 8° Dublin, 1944.

4729 Kelly (James J.). Ethne and Fedelm : the white rose and the red. [2 daughters of king Laeghaire : baptised by St. Patrick on the slope of Cruachain.] Irish Eccles. Rec., 3rd S. 9, pp. 31–39. 1888.

4730 Krappe (Alexander Haggerty). St. Patrick and the snakes. Traditio, 5, pp. 323–30. 1947.

4731 Laheen (Kevin). St. Patrick. pp. 24. 8° London, 1945.

4732 Lawlor (Hugh Jackson) and **Best** (Richard Irvine). The ancient list of the coarbs of Patrick. Proc. R.I.A., 35 c., pp. 316–62. 1919.

4733 MacNeill (Eoin). The fifteenth centenary of St. Patrick. A suggested form of commemoration [by publication of unpublished documents]. [Pp. 189–200, Comments by Paul Walsh, Daniel A. Binchy, Brendan Jennings, Louis Gougaud, Thomas F. O'Rahilly.] Studies, 13, pp. 177–200. 1924.

4734 —— The hymn of St. Secundinus in honour of St. Patrick. Irish Hist. Stud., 2, pp. 129–53. 1940.

4735 —— St. Patrick. pp. viii, 122. 8° London, 1934.

4736 MacSweeney (Michael T.). The genealogy of St. Patrick. Irish Eccles. Rec., 5th S. 19, pp. 476–92. 1922.

4737 Malone (Sylvester). The genesis of Patrick. [His name.] *Same jnl.*, 3rd S. 11, pp. 543–52. 1890.

**4738 —— Was St. Patrick a hymnographer ? *Same jnl.*, 3rd S. 7, pp. 707–15. 1886.

4739 Morris (Henry). The iconography of St. Patrick. Down and Connor Hist. Soc. J., 7. 1936.

4740 —— St. Patrick and the politics of his day. Studies, 21, pp. 7–19. 1932.

4741 Morris (William Bullen). The apostle of Ireland and his modern critics. [Reprinted, with an introductory letter by Aubrey de Vere. pp. 39. 8° London, 1881 [1880].] Dublin Rev., 3rd S. 4, pp. 59–87. 1880.

4742 —— Ireland and Saint Patrick. pp. xxxi, 307. 8° London, 1891.

4743 Mueller (K.). Der hl. Patrick. [His mission and writings, with special reference to views of Zimmer and Bury.] Nachrichten Gesell. Wiss. Göttingen, Phil. hist. Kl., 82, pp. 62–116. 1931.

4744 Mulcahy (C.). The hymn of St. Secundinus in praise of St. Patrick. [Latin text and English translation.] Irish Eccles. Rec., 5th S. 65, pp. 146–49. 1945.

4745 Murphy (Gerard). St. Patrick and the civilizing of Ireland. *Same jnl.*, 5th S. 79, pp. 194–204. 1953.

4746 Nicholson (R. Steele). St. Patrick, apostle of Ireland in the third century ; the story of his mission to pope Celestine in A.D. 431 . . . proved to be a mere fiction, *etc*. 8° Dublin, 1868. [Gross, 1655.]

4747 Ó Ceallaigh (Seán). Ireland's spiritual empire. St. Patrick as a world figure. pp. 318. 8° Dublin, 1952.

4748 O'Keeffe (C. M.). Saint Patrick and the serpents. *Catholic World*, 47, *no.* 277. 1888.

4749 O'Riordan (Michael). The mission of St. Patrick, a witness to the supernatural. A sermon. pp. 41. 8° Dublin, 1918.

4750 Patrick, *St*. St. Patrick and the saints of Ireland. From authoritative sources. *The Irish Library*, 3. pp. 94. 8° London, 1908.

4751 Riguet ( ) *abbé*. Saint Patrice (vers 389–461). *Les saints*. pp. vii, 203. 8° Paris, 1911. — Saint Patrick (about 389–461). *The Saints*. pp. iv, 163. 8° London, 1912. [Kenney, 1, p. 320.]

4752 Ryan (John). St. Patrick and the Roman see. pp. 32. 8° Dublin, 1932.

4753 Shahan (Thomas Joseph). St. Patrick in history. pp. 77. 8° New York, 1904. [Gross, 1656a.]

4754 Sullivan (Joseph M.). Saint Patrick as a lawgiver. *Catholic World*, 78, *no.* 468. 1904.

4755 Teufelsbauer (Leopold). Die Verehrung des hl. Patristius in der Oststeiermark und im angrenzenden Nieder-Oesterreich. Wiener Zeit. f. Volkskunde, 34, pp. 83–94. 1934.

4756 Todd (James Henthorn). On the name said to have been given to St. Patrick, when a captive in Ireland, by his heathen masters. [*Cothraighe.*] Proc. R.I.A., 6 (1856), pp. 292–98. 1858.

4757 Todd (William Gouan). The patrons of Erin ; or some account of St. Patrick and St. Brigid. 8° London, 1859.

4758 Walker (John Cotton). Letters on Saint Patrick, and the ancient Catholic Church of Ireland. 3rd edition. pp. 63. 8° Dublin, 1874.

4759 Walsh (Paul), *ed*. Saint Patrick, A.D. 432–1932. A fifteenth century memorial book. pp. 128, + 34 plates. Fol. Dublin, [1932].

4760 White (Newport John Davis). The date of St. Patrick. The internal evidence of his Latin writings. pp. 11. 8° Dublin, 1932.

§ *g*. Others

4761 [Anon.] Iseal Chiarain, the low place of St. Ciaran, where was it situated ? J. Ardagh and Clonmacnoise Antiq. Soc., 2 xii, pp. 52–65. 1951.

4762 [Anon.] The life and works of St. Ængusius Hagiographus, or St. Ængus the Culdee, bishop and abbot at Clonenagh and Dysartenos, Queen's County. [8th c.] Irish Eccles. Rec., 5, pp. 1–20, 73–81, 97–108. 1868.

4763 [Anon.] St. Blaitmaic, of Iona, martyr. [9th c.] *Same jnl.*, 9, pp. 502–08. 1873.

4764 [Anon.] St. Munchin, patron of Limerick city and diocese. [?identity.] *Same jnl.*, 9, pp. 569–78. 1873.

4765 [Anon.] A visit to the Aranmore of St. Enda. [6th c.] *Same jnl.*, 7, pp. 19–31, 105–23. 1870.

4766 Anscombe (Alfred). The Longobardic origin of St. Sechnall. [With postscript : ' the area of the Hwiccas.'] Ériu, 4, pp. 74–90. 1908.

4767 Arbois de Jubainville (Marie Henry d'). La conversion de Maelsuthain. [11th c. Confessor to Brian Boroimhe.] Rev. celt., 11, pp. 492–93. 1890.

4768 Bigger (Francis Joseph). Inis-Mahee [co. Down] of the saints and scholars. [St. Mochai, etc., 5th c.] Antiquary, 51, pp. 295–97. 1915.

4769 Bruyne (Donation de). La vie de S. Idunet. [Kenney, 1, p. 180.] Bull. Soc. archéol. Finistère, 1916, pp. 178–79. 1916.

4770 C. (B. M.). St. Ciaran of Ossory and our correspondents. [6th c.] Irish Eccles. Rec., 3, pp. 25–35. 1867.

4771 Cainneach [Canice], *St., of Kilkenny*. Vita Sancti Kannechi a codicibus in Bibliotheca Burgundiana extante Bruxellis transcripta et cum codice in Bibliotheca Marsiana Dublinii adservato collata. [Edited with an introduction, by James Butler, 6th marquis of Ormonde.] *Kilkenny Archaeological Society*. pp. xxv, 47. 4° [London], 1853. [From Cod. Salmanticensis, with variants from MS. Z. 3, I. 5 of Marsh's Library, Dublin.]

4772 Cellach, *St., bp. of Killala*. Caithréin Cellaig. Edited by Kathleen Mulchrone. *Mediaeval and Modern Irish Series*, 4. pp. xix, 55. 8° Dublin, 1933.

4773 Coleman (James). St. Beretchert, the Saxon saint of Tullylease, county Cork. J. Cork Hist. Soc., 2nd S. 1, pp. 61–68. 1895.

4774 —— St. Colman of Cloyne. [522–600.] *Same jnl.*, 2nd S., 16, pp. 132–42. 1910.

4775 Conchubranus. Conchubrani vita Santae Monennae, edited with an introduction by Mario Esposito. [MS. Cotton Cleopatra A. II. Author lived not earlier than 11th c.] Proc. R.I.A., 28 c., pp. 202–51, + 2 plates. 1910.

4776 Connellan (M. J.). St. Brocaidh of Imliuch Brocadha. [Contemporary of St. Patrick.] J. Galway Archaeol. Soc., 23, pp. 138–46. 1949.

4777 —— St. Muadhnat [Mónath] of Kill Muadhnat. [6th c.] *Same jnl.*, 21, pp. 56–62. 1944.

4778 —— St. Raoilinn of Teampal Raoileann. *Same jnl.*, 20, pp. 145–50. 1943.

4779 Cox (Liam F.). Parentage, birth, and early years of St. Ciaran [of Clonmacnoise]. J. Ardagh and Clonmacnoise Antiq. Soc., 2 xi, pp. 52–63. 1946.

4780 Cullen (John B.). A bardic-saint of Ireland. [St. Fiacc of Slotty, bp. of Hy-Kinsellagh, Leinster, 5th c.] Irish Eccles. Rec., 5th S. 18, pp. 506–14. 1921.

4781 —— Finglas and its patron. [St. Canice, 6th c.] *Same jnl.*, 5th S. 21, pp. 164–73. 1923.

4782 —— A missionary nun of early Christian Ireland. [St. Mo-Edana or Modenna : d. 516.] *Same jnl.*, 5th S. 19, pp. 36–42. 1922.

4783 —— A pre-Patrician saint of Ireland. [St. Ibar, patron of Wexford. Died 500.] *Same jnl.*, 5th S. 18, pp. 374–83. 1921.

4784 —— St. Abban of Hy-Kinsellagh. [5th c. 2nd abbot of island monastery of Lough Garman, co. Wexford.] *Same jnl.*, 5th S. 22, pp. 292–304. 1923.

4785 Esposito (Mario). The sources of Conchubranus' Life of St. Monenna. E.H.R., 35, pp. 71–78. 1920.

4786 Fahey (J. A.). Saint Colga of Kilcolgan. [Founder and abbot of Kilcolgan, co. Galway. 6th c.] Irish Eccles. Rec., 3rd. S. 6, pp. 525–32. 1885.

4787 Flood (William Henry Grattan). St. Carthage of Lismore. J. Waterford Archaeol. Soc., 4, pp. 228–37. 1898.

4788 Ganly (William). The holy places of Connemara. [St. Caillin (5th c.).] Irish Eccles. Rec., 3rd S. 10, pp. 432–40. 1889.

4789 —— Mayo of the Saxons. [On St. Colman of Mayo, 7th c.]. *Same jnl.*, 3rd S. 9, pp. 211–19, 318–29. 1888.

4790 Gogarty (Thomas). The burial place of St. Fancheer. [Argument for Kilslattery.] County Louth Archaeol. J., 1, iv, pp. 34–46 : 2, pp. 382–86, + 1 plate. 1907, 1911.

4791 —— The footsteps of St. Feighin in co. Louth. [7th c.] *Same jnl.*, 2, pp. 14–18. 1908.

4792 Grosjean (Paul). Élégie de S. Cíarán de Clúain Moccu Nois. Anal. Boll., 69, pp. 102–06. 1951.

4793 —— Un miracle postume de S. Cíarán de Clúain en faveur du roi Diarmait mac Cerrbéoil. Anal. Boll., 69, pp. 96–102. 1951.

4794 —— S. Comgalli vita latina : accedunt duae narrationes gadelicae. [Abbot of Bangor (Ireland). Latin text. Narrationes : i. Comgallus et monachus Britannus : ii. Comgallus et Mochoemoc: Irish texts with Latin translations.] Anal. Boll., 52, pp. 343–56. 1934.

4795 —— S. Fintán Máeldub. Anal. Boll., 69, pp. 77–88 : 70, pp. 312–13. 1951–52.

4796 —— Une vie de Saint Secundinus, disciple de Saint Patrice. [With Latin text from Bibl. roy. de Belgique, Ms. 8957–58, ff. 25–27 v.] Anal. Boll., 60, pp. 26–34. 1942.

4797 —— Vita Sancti Ciarani, episcopi de Saigir, ex codice hagiographico Gothano. [With Latin text.] Anal. Boll., 59, pp. 217–71. 1941.

4798 Harris (Dorothy C.). Saint Gobnet, abbess of Ballyvourney. [6th–7th. c.] J. Roy. Soc. Antiq. Ireland, 68 (7th S. 8), pp. 272–77, + 2 plates. 1938.

4799 Healy (John), *abp. of Tuam.* Marianus Scotus, the chronicler. [1028–1112.] Irish Eccles. Rec., 3rd S. 5, pp. 420–30. 1884.

4800 Healy (John). St. Cummain the tall, bishop of Clonfert. [7th c.] *Same jnl.*, 3rd S. 7, pp. 1–16. 1886.

4801 —— The school of Bangor—St. Comgall. [c. 520–600 or 601.] *Same jnl.*, 3rd S. 5, pp. 749–55. 1884.

4802 Hennig (John). A note on the Calendar of Cashel. [Concerning Gormgal, abbot of 'Ard-oilén (died 1018).] Scriptorium, 6, pp. 101–02. 1952.

4803 Hogan (J. F.). St. Dympna of Gheel. [6th c.] Irish Eccles. Rec., 3rd S. 14, pp. 577–89. 1893.

4804 Hogan (John). St. Ciaran, patron of Ossory. 8° Kilkenny, 1876. [Kenney, 1, p. 316.]

4805 Howlett (J. A.). St. Aidan, or Maidoc, bishop of Ferns. [6th–7th c.] Irish Eccles. Rec., 3rd S. 12, pp. 673–92. 1891.

4806 Hynes (John). St. Caillin [?7th c. Pp. 51–53, + 2 plates, St. Caillin's bell, or Clog-na-righ.] J. Roy. Soc. Antiq. Ireland, 61 (7th S. 1), pp. 39–54, + 5 plates. 1931.

4807 Hynes (S. B. E.). Legends of Saint Kevin. *Catholic Truth Society, no.* 959. 8° Dublin, 1927. [St. Coemgen, founder of Glendalough. Died 618 or 622.]

4808 Kelly (James J.). St. Assicus, first bishop and patron of the diocese of Elphin [co. Roscommon]. Irish Eccles. Rec., 4th S. 11, pp. 289–309, 400–12. 1902.

4809 Kelly (M. T.). A bishop-king of Cashel. [Cormac McCullinan.] J. Cork Hist. Soc., 2nd S. 1, pp. 193–200. 1895.

4810 —— Saint Gobnata, and her hive of bees. [6th c.] *Same jnl.*, 2nd S. 3, pp. 100–06. 1897.

4811 Kelly (Richard J.). St. Jarlath of Tuam. [1st bishop : 6th c.] J. Galway Archaeol. Soc., 1, pp. 90–108, + 1 plate. 1901.

4812 Knox (Hubert Thomas). The two saints Benen. J. Roy. Soc. Antiq. Ireland, 32 (5th S. 12), pp. 187–88. 1902.

4813 Lawless (Nicholas) [Enda, *pseud.*] Killaine in Stieve Breagh. [Argument that St. Fanchea was buried at Fuinseog (Funshog). Her monastery founded 5th–6th c., in co. Louth.] County Louth Archaeol. J., 1, iii, pp. 54–58 : 2, pp. 27–28, 375–81. 1906, 1908, 1911.

**4814 —— St. Sillan of Imbluich in Cooley [Louth]. [7th c.] *Same jnl.*, 4, pp. 298–99, 330–32. 1920.

4815 Lawlor (Henry Cairnes). Degen of Kilconriola. [Irish bishop, died 639. ?=Bede's Dagan. Figure of his slab cross, now at Ballymena.] Ulster J. Archaeol., 3rd S. 1, pp. 32–35. 1938.

4816 Loth (Joseph). Saint Doccus et l'hagio-onomastique. [Wrongly called Cadocus. 6th c.] Mém. Soc. d'hist. et d'archéol. Bretagne, 10, pp. 1–12. 1929.

4817 Luasa (Máire ní), *ed.* Carthage of Lismore : two fragmentary lives. [St. Mochuda. Irish, and English translation. Incomplete.] J. Waterford Archaeol. Soc., 19, pp. 20–29. 1920.

4818 Lynch (J. Fetherston). Lugaid Mac Maenaich : an old Munster saint. [6th c.] J. Cork Hist. Soc., 2nd S. 19, pp. 191–97. 1913.

4819 Macalister (Robert Alexander Stewart). Beg-Eire. [Island in Wexford harbour. St. Ibar, founder of its monastery, 5th c.] The Past, 1, pp. 5–14. 1921.

**4820 —— The Latin and Irish lives of Ciaran [of Clonmacnois]. *Translations of Christian literature, series 5, lives of the Celtic saints.* pp. 190. 8° London, 1921.

**4821 —— The life of Saint Finan. [Irish text and English translation (with notes) of a fragment of a life in a ms. in the possession of F. A. MacCollum.] Zeit. celt. Phil., 2, pp. 545–65. 1899.

4822 MacCabe (William Bernard), *etc.* An Irish saint and an English minister. A legend. [St. Senan. Legend quoted from Albert Le Grand.] N. and Q., 4th S. 8, pp. 219–20, 265–67. 1871.

4823 MacErlean (John). The Acta Sanctorum and three Irish saints. [St. Benignus of Armagh (died 467) : St. Grellan (year unknown) : Ædh Mac Bric (died 589 or 595).] Studies, 15, pp. 660–64. 1926.

**4824 —— St. Rynagh. [Mother of St. Colman of Clonard.] J. Ardagh and Clonmacnoise Antiq. Soc., 1 iii, pp. 70–71. 1932.

4825 MacInerny (M. H.). St. Mochta and Bachiarius. [1st bp. of Louth, 5th c. Wrongly identified with Bacchiarius.] Irish Eccles. Rec., 5th S. 21, pp. 468–80, 618–32, 22, pp. 153–65, 573–91. 1923.

4826 MacKenna (James Edward). Inismacsaint, [co. Fermanagh, and bishop Ninnidh]. Ulster J. Archaeol., 2nd S. 10, pp. 113–17. 1904.

4827 Maguire (Edward). St. Naal of Inver-naile. [Died 563 (F. M.).] Irish Eccles. Rec., 3rd S. 16, pp. 520–28. 1895.

4828 Malone ( ). Life of St. Flannan [of Killaloe]. 8° Dublin, 1902. [Kenney, 1, p. 405. 7th c.]

4829 Malone (Sylvester). Killaloe's [co. Clare] patron and titular saints. [St. Flannan, 7th c.] Irish Eccles. Rec., 3rd S. 10, pp. 1057–66. 1889.

4830 Masterson (M. J.). St. Fraech, founder of Cloone Abbey. [6th c.] J. Ardagh and Clonmacnoise Antiq. Soc., 1 vi, pp. 74–75. 1937.

4831 Mescal (Daniel). The story of Inis Cathaigh (Scattery island) [co. Clare]. pp. 88. 8° Dublin, 1902. [With life of St. Senan, 6th c. : pp. 67–72, his bell, the Clog-oir.]

4832 Meyer (Kuno). Aed Dub Mac Colmáin, bishop-abbot of Kildare. [Died 639.] Zeit. celt. Phil., 9, pp. 458–60. 1913.

**4833 ——, *ed.* Betha Colmáin Maic Lúacháin. Life of Colmán son of Lúachan. Edited from a manuscript in the library of Rennes, with translation, introduction, notes and indices. *Royal Irish Academy, Todd Lecture Series*, 17. pp. xviii, 186. 8° Dublin, 1911. [7th c. saint. Founder of church of Lann Llynn, co. Westmeath.]

4834 Meyer (Kuno). Orthanach ūa Cōillāma cecinit. [Bishop of Kildare, died 840. Irish text and German translation.] Zeit. celt. Phil., 11, pp. 107–13. 1917.

4835 Monahan (John). St. Manchan : his church and shrine. [Died 664 (Four Masters) of Yellow Plague. Founded Lemanaghan monastery, King's County, 7th c.] Irish Eccles. Rec., 3rd S. 7, pp. 203–13. 1886.

4836 Moore (Courtenay). The ecclesiastical antiquities of Brigown (Mitchelstown), with a sketch of the life of Saint Findchua. [6th c.] J. Cork Hist. Soc., 2nd S. 4, pp. 20–32. 1898.

4837 Moran (Patrick Francis), *cardinal, bp. of Ossory*. Inaugural address . . . at the first meeting of the Ossory Archaeological Society. [On SS. Kieran (5th c.), Cainneach (Canice, 6th c.) and Scothin (6th c.).] Irish Eccles. Rec., 10, pp. 141–60. 1874.

4838 —— St. Aidan, bishop and patron of Ferns. [Died 632.] *Same jnl.*, pp. 312–25, 361–69, 393–407. 1871.

4839 Mulcahy (David B.), *ed.* Life of S. Kiaran (the elder) of Seir. The Gaelic text ; edited with literal English translation, notes, etc. pp. vi, 90. 8° Dublin, 1895. [Translation from Celtic of life of 5th c. Irish saint.]

4840 Murphy (N.). St. Canice, abbot and confessor, patron of the city of Kilkenny. Irish Eccles. Rec., 3rd S. 15, pp. 925–38. 1894.

4841 —— St. Kieran of Saigher, B.C., patron of Ossory. *Same jnl.*, 3rd S. 15, pp. 351–61. 1894.

4842 Murray (Desmond P.). A forgotten saint. [St. Monenna or Modwenna of Killevy, 6th c.] County Louth Archaeol. J., 5, pp. 154–60. 1923.

4843 Murray (Laurence P.). The burial-place of St. Fanchea : Fuinsheog, Kilslaughtery, or Killany ? [Argument for Killany (Killaine).] *Same jnl.*, 2, pp. 275–84, + map : 431–33. 1910–11.

4844 O'Daly (B.). St. Damhnat. [Her crozier, 11th c., with interlaced ornament preserved by R.I.A.] *Same jnl.*, 11, pp. 243–51. 1949.

4845 O'Hanlon (John). St. Berach or Berachius, abbot, patron of Kilbarry, county of Roscommon. [6th on 7th c.] J. Ardagh and Clonmacnoise Antiq. Soc., I v, pp. 17–35. 1935.

4846 Ó hÉaluighthe (D.). St. Gobnet of Ballyvourney. [6th c.] J. Cork Hist. Soc., 57, pp. 43–61. 1952.

4847 Olsen (Magnus). Runerne i St. Molaise's celle paa Holy Island, Arran, Skotland. [With English summary.] Skr. Videnskapsselskapet, Kristiania. Hist.-filos. Kl., 1912, no. 1. pp. 24. 1912.

4848 O'Shaughnessy (D. F.). St. Molua's well—Emlygrennan. [Born 534.] J. Cork Hist. Soc., 2nd S. 37, pp. 90–92, + 1 plate. 1932.

4849 Parlin (Henry). St. Fintan, abbot of Dromin [co. Louth]. [?=Finnian, contemporary of St. Columba : ? ever existed.] County Louth Archaeol. J., 4, pp. 341–43. 1920.

4850 —— St. Fintan, abbot of Dromin. [5th c.] Irish Eccles. Rec., 5th S. 26, pp. 248–57. 1925.

4851 Patterson (William Hugh). Cross, relig, and holy well of St. Conall, co. Donegal. [Died c. 590.] J. Roy. Hist. and Arch. Assoc. Ireland [11], 4th S. 1 (1870–71), pp. 466–70. 1878.

4852 Philippen (L. J. M.). Saint Rombaut. Sa patrie. Son épiscopat. [Insufficient evidence that he was Irish by birth, 6th–8th c.] Revue d'hist. ecclés., 29, pp. 365–67. 1933.

4853 Plummer (Charles). Life of Cranat. [6th c. With Irish text and English translation.] Subsidia hagiographica, (Soc. Boll.), 15, pp. 157–69. 1925.

4854 —— Life of MacCreiche. [5th–6th c. With Irish text and English translation.] *Same work*, 15, pp. 7–96. 1925.

4855 —— Life of Naile. [6th c. With Irish text and English translation.] *Same work*, 15, pp. 97–155. 1925.

4856 Power (Patrick). Life of St. Declan of Ardmore (edited from a MS. in the Bibliothèque royale, Bruxelles) and Life of St. Mochuda of Lismore (edited from a MS. in the library of the Royal Irish Academy). With introduction, translation, and notes. *Irish Texts Society*, 16. pp. xxxi, 202. 8° London, 1914.

4857 Reeves (William), *bp. of Down*. St. Beretchert of Tullylease, [co. Cork]. [9th c.] Ulster J. Archaeol., 6, pp. 267–75, + 1 plate. 1858.

4858 —— St. Moedoc, vulgarly called St. Mogue. [Born c. 555.] Proc. R.I.A., 8, pp. 446–50. 1864.

4859 —— Saint Mura. [7th c.] Ulster J. Archaeol., 1, pp. 271–73. 1853.

4860 Reynolds (D.). St. Manchan (Managhan) of Mohill and Lemanaghan (Offaly). [7th c.] J. Ardagh and Clonmacnoise Antiq. Soc., 1 iii, pp. 65–69. 1932.

4861 Ross (W. J. Calder), **Gammack** (James), *etc.* St. Molio. [?companion of S. Columba. ?=S. Molaise.] Scot. N. and Q., 2, p. 95 : *see also* pp. 80, 109. 1888.

4862 Spence (Andrew). The antiquities of Fahan in Inis-Eoghan. [Cross, bell, etc. of St. Mura. ? 7th c.] Ulster J. Archaeol., 2nd S. 17, pp. 17–31. 1911.

4863 Stokes (George Thomas). St. Hugh of Rahue : his church, his life, and his times. [Friend of Columba.] J. Roy. Soc. Antiq. Ireland, 26 (5th S. 6), pp. 325–35. 1896.

4864 Stokes (Margaret MacNair). St. Beoc of Wexford, and Lan Veoc in Brittany, June 15. (Died 585). [Two figures of his oratory in text.] *Same jnl.*, 23 (5th S. 3), pp. 380–85. 1893.

4865 Thunder (John M.). St. Finnian of Clonard. [6th c.]. Irish Eccles. Rec., 3rd S. 13, pp. 810–15. 1892.

4866 Thurneysen (Rudolf). Colmán mac Lēnēni und Senchān Torpēist. [Colman, of Cloyne, died 604.] Zeit. celt. Philol., 19, pp. 193–209. 1933.

4867 Urwalek (J.). Der königliche Pilger St. Colomann. *Programm, Wien,* 1880. 8° Wien, 1880. [Kenney, 1, p. 613. Irish saint, murdered at Stockerau, near Vienna, in 1012, when on pilgrimage to Jerusalem.]

4868 Vendryes (Joseph), *ed.* Betha Grighora (Vie de Saint Grégoire). [Irish text and French translation. Gregory the Great in Irish hagiography.] Rev. celt., 42, pp. 119–53. 1925.

4869 Walker (R. V.). The birth place of Saint Mogue. [=St. Aidan of Ferns. c. 560–632.] Breifny Antiq. Soc. J., 1, pp. 204–06. 1921.

4870 Westropp (Thomas Johnson). St. Mochulla of Tulla, county Clare : his legend and the entrenchments and remains of his monastery. [7th c.] J. Roy. Soc. Antiq. Ireland, 41 (6th S. 1), pp. 5–19, + 1 plate. 1911.

4871 Zimmer (Heinrich). Blaithmaic. Moengal. [St. Blaithmac, of Iona, d. 823 (F. M.) : St. Moengal, abbot of Bangor, d. 869 (F.M.) ; 871 (A.U.).] Neues Archiv, 17, pp. 209–11. 1891.

69. HAGIOLOGY, SCOTTISH

§ *a*. General

4872 Forbes (Alexander Penrose), *bp. of Brechin*. Kalendars of Scottish saints. With personal notices of those of Alba, Landonia, and Strathclyde. An attempt to fix the districts of their several missions, *etc.* pp. lxv, 468. 4° Edinburgh, 1872. [Kenney, 1, p. 367. Pp. 261–468, alphabetical list of saints.]

4873 Gammack (James). The patron saints of Scotland, with dedications. Scot. N. and Q., 3rd S. 1, pp. 83–85, 102–04, 118–20. 1923.

4874 Grierson (Elizabeth Wilson). Early light-bearers of Scotland. pp. 255. 8° Edinburgh, 1937.

4875 Mackinlay (James Murray). Ancient church dedications in Scotland —non-scriptural dedications. pp. xxxvi, 552. 8° Edinburgh, 1914. [Irish, Cymric, Pictish, Northumbrian and other English, saints.]

4876 Maclagan (Robert Craig). Religio Scotica : its nature as traceable in Scotic saintly tradition. pp. viii, 233. 8° Edinburgh, 1909. [Columba, Adamnan, Brigit, etc.]

4877 Pinkerton (John). Vitae antiquae sanctorum qui habitaverunt in ea parte Britanniae nunc vocato Scotia, vel in ejus insulis. pp. xx, 470. 8° Londini, 1789. —Lives of the Scottish saints, revised and enlarged by W. M. Metcalfe. 2 vol. 8° Paisley, 1889. [i. Ninian, Columba : ii. Kentegern, Servanus, Margaret, Magnus, David.]

4878 Russell (H.). The early church dedications of the south of Scotland. Archaeol. Rev., 3, pp. 164–74. 1889.

§ b. Adamnan, 9th Abbot of Hy
(624–704)

(for his visions, see 66§c)

4879 Geyer (Paul). Adamnus, Abt von Jona. I. Teil, Sein Leben, seine Quellen, sein Verhältnis zu Pseudoeucherius de locis sanctis, seine Sprache. *Programm . . . Augsburg*, 1895. pp. 47. 2. Teil, Die handschriftliche Überlieferung der Schrift De locis sanctis. *Programm . . . Erlangen*, 1897. 8° Augsburg, Erlangen, 1895–97. [Kenney, 1, p. 283.]

4880 Healy (John) *abp. of Tuam*. St. Adamnan, ninth abbot of Hy. Irish Eccles. Rec., 3rd S. 3, pp. 408–19. 1882.

4881 Joynt (Maud) *trs.* The Life of Adamnan (translated from the *Betha Adamnáin*, printed in Anecdota from Irish MSS., no. 2, from MS. no. 4190–4200, fol. 29–33, Bibliothèque Royale, Brussels). Celtic Rev., 5, pp. 97–107. 1908.

4882 Maguire (Edward). Life of St. Adamnan, patron of Raphoe. pp. 134. 8° Dublin, 1917. [Kenney, 1, p. 443.]

4883 —— St. Adamnan or Eunan, patron of Raphoe. [Identified with Adamnan, 9th abbot of Iona.] Irish Eccles. Rec., 4th S. 9, pp. 113–34. 1901.

§ c. Columba (Columcille)
(521–97)

(Trained at Moville and Clonard. Founded monasteries of Derry, Durrow and Iona (Hy). For his Cathach, see

112 § a.)

i. Documents and commentaries on them

4884 Adamnan, *St., 9th abbot of Hy*. The life of St. Columba. Edited . . . by J. T. Fowler. . . . New edition, revised. pp. 280. 8° Oxford, 1920.

4885 Albers (Bruno). Zu den beiden ersten Lebensbeschreibungen des Abtes Columba von Iona. [Kenney, 1, p. 428.] Studien u. Mitt. z. Gesch. d. Benediktinerordens, 33, pp. 405–20. 1912.

4886 Boulton (*Sir* Harold Edwin), *bart.* An unrecorded miracle of St. Columba. With a Gaelic translation by Archibald McDonald. pp. 41. 8° London, [1930].

4887 Bruening (Gertrud). Adamnans Vita Columbae und ihre Ableitungen. [MSS., sources, etc.] Zeit. celt. Phil., 11, pp. 213–304. 1917.

4888 Grosjean (Paul). Hagiographia Celtica. 1. Narratiuncula de S. Columba Hiensi. Anal. Boll., 55, pp. 96–108. 1937.

4889 —— The life of St. Columba from the Edinburgh MS. (supplementary note). [Nat. Lib. Scot., MS. Gaelic XL. Text and translation.] Scot. Gaelic Stud., 2, pp. 111–71 : 3, pp. 84–85. 1927–31.

4890 —— S. Columbae Hiensis cum Mongano heroe colloquium. [With two Irish texts, and Latin translation, ' Colloquium Columbae et juvenis in loco dicto Carn Eolairg.'] Anal. Boll., 45, pp. 75–83. 1927.

4891 —— A tale of Doomsday Colum Cille should have left untold. (Addenda et corrigenda). [Text and translation from R.I.A. ms.] Scot. Gaelic Stud., 3, pp. 73–83, 188–99. 1931.

4892 Henebry (Richard) and **O'Kelleher** (Andrew). The life of Columb Cille. (Betha Coluimb Chille). [Irish text with English translation from a MS. in Rawlinson collection.] Zeit. celt. Phil., 3, pp. 516–71 : 4, pp. 276–331 : 5, pp. 26–87 : 9, pp. 242–87 : 10, pp. 228–65 : 11, pp. 114–47. 1901–03, 1913–17.

4893 Kenney (James Francis). The earliest life of St. Columcille. [Adamnan and Cuimine.] Cath. Hist. Rev., 11 (N.S. 5), pp. 636–44. 1926.

4894 Lawlor (Hugh Jackson). The tract ' De causa peregrinationis S. Columbae '. [MSS. Rawlinson B. 485, B. 505. Latin text.] Proc. R.I.A., 33c, pp. 408–12. 1916.

4895 Meyer (Kuno) and **Nutt** (Alfred). The colloquy of Colum Cille and the youth at Carn Eolairg. [Original not later than 9th c. Irish text and English translation, and notes.] Zeit. celt. Phil., 2, pp. 313–20. 1899.

4896 O'Donnell (Manus), *earl of Tyrconnell* (1491–1564). Betha Colaim chille, Life of Columcille ; edited and translated from manuscript Rawlinson B. 514 in the Bodleian Library, Oxford, with introduction, glossary, notes and indices by Andrew O'Kelleher and Gertrude Schoepperle. *Bulletin Univ. Illinois*, 15 (*no.* 48). pp. lxxviii, 516. fol. Urbana, 1918. [Kenney, 1, p. 442. Irish and English.]

4897 O'Kearney (Nicholas), *ed. and trans.* The prophesies of St. Columbkille. As compiled, translated and annotated by . . . N. O'Kearney. pp. xii, 137. 8° Dublin, 1925.

4898 Shaw (Thomas J.). The Amra Choluim Chille, or Eulogy of St. Columbkille. [With translation, from that of W. Stokes, **4901.**] Irish Eccles. Rec., 5th S. 9, pp. 118–29. 1917.

4899 Stokes (Whitley), *ed.* The Adventure of St. Columba's clerics. [Incident from mid 7th c. Tale from 14th c. Yellow Book of Lecan, col. 707–15. Irish text and English translation.] Rev. celt., 26, pp. 130–70. 1905.

4900 Stokes (Whitley). The Adventure of St. Columba's clerics. From W. Stokes' translation [**4899.**] County Louth Archael. J., 3, pp. 16–17. 1912.

4901 —— *ed.* The Bodleian Ambra Choluimb Chille. [Ms. Rawlinson B. 502. Text with English translation and introductory remarks.] Rev. celt., 20, pp. 30–55, 132–83, 248–89, 400–37 ; 21, p. 133. 1899–1900.

4902 Strachan (John). The date of the Amra Choluimb Chille. [Assigns to early 9th c.] Rev. celt., 17, pp. 41–44. 1896.

4903 Vendryes (Joseph). Une anecdote sur Saint Columba. [From Ms. Bibl. Nat., Paris, fonds celt., no. 1. f. 56v. Irish text and French translation.] Rev. celt., 33, pp. 354–56. 1912.

4904 —— A propos d'un quatrain annonçant la naissance de Colum Cille. [In the Betha Coluim Chille.] Rev. celt., 45, pp. 93–101. 1928.

ii. Biographies—Iona—Work of his monks

4905 [Anon.] A day in Iona : recollections of Saint Columba. Irish Eccles. Rec., 2, pp. 108–23. 1866.

4906 Andrews (Elizabeth). Some Ulster memories of St. Columkille (St. Columba). Antiquary, 51, pp. 210–15. 1915.

4907 Argyll (George Douglas Campbell), *8th duke*. Iona. New edition. pp. 142, + plates. 8° Edinburgh, 1889.

4908 Banks (*Mrs.* Mary MacLeod). A Hebridean version of Colum Cille and St. Oran. [Foundation sacrifice theme : absent from Adamnan's Life.] Folk-lore, 42, pp. 55–60. 1931.

4909 Branford (Victor Verasis). St. Columba. A study of social inheritance. Utopian papers, ed. Dorothea Hollins, pp. 52–101. 1908.

4910 —— St. Columba : a study of social inheritance and spiritual development. pp. 83. 8° Edinburgh. 1913.

4911 Buckler (John Chessell *and* Charles Alban). The cathedral, or abbey church of Iona. A series of drawings . . . and some account of the early Celtic Church, and of the mission of St. Columba. By [Alexander Ewing], bishop of Argyll. pp. 78. 4° London, 1866.

4912 Burton (Philip). St. Columba, metropolitan of Caledonia. [*See also* 5, pp. 465–66.] Irish Eccles. Rec., 4th S. 5, pp. 229–37. 1899.

4913 Chisholm (Colin). The monks of Iona. [Pp. 58–60, list of localities in Scotland where they ' planted religion '.] Trans. Gaelic Soc. Inverness, 8, pp. 56–63. 1879.

4914 Coffey (Peter). Columcille, his life and labors. *Catholic Truth Society.* 8° Dublin, 1926.

4915 Colum (Padraic). The legend of Saint Columba. pp. 156. 8° London, 1936.

4916 Cooke (Edward Alexander). Saint Columba, his life and work. 2nd edition, pp. x, 153. 8° Edinburgh, 1893. [Pp. 141–43, text of his Rule.]

4917 Crawford (Osbert Guy Stanhope). Iona. [Where did Columba land ? Was Iona inhabited before Columba's time ? Where was the earliest monastery ? The name Iona : the legend of Oran : bibliography.] Antiquity, 7, pp. 453–67 + 4 plates. 1933.

4918 —— The magic of Columba. [With list of his miracles.] Antiquity, 8, pp. 168–75 + 2 plates. 1934.

4919 Curtayne (Alice). Saint Columcille, the dove of the Church. pp. 32. 8° Dublin, [1934].

4920 Drummond (James). Notice of one of the supposed burial-places of St. Columba. Proc. Soc. Antiq. Scot., 10, pp. 613–17. 1875.

4921 Ewing (Alexander), *bp. of Argyll.* The cathedral or abbey church of Iona, and the early Celtic church and mission of St. Columba. pp. viii, 120, + 12 plates. 8° Edinburgh, 18—.

4922 Ferguson (A. B. Ochiltree). Saint Columba. pp. 84, + plates. 8° Dublin. 1920.

4923 Forbes (Frances Alice Monica). The life of Saint Columba. pp. 126. 8° London, 1914. [For children.]

4924 Gunn (John). Iona, S. Columba, and the Western Highlands. Irish Eccles. Rec., 3rd S. 6, pp. 463–72. 1885.

4925 Gwynn (Denis Rolleston). St. Columba. pp. 24. 8° London, 1928.

4926 Iona, *pseud.* The story of Saint Columba. pp. vii, 72. 8° Dublin, 1928.

4927 Jamieson (John). An historical account of the ancient culdees of Iona, and of their settlements in Scotland, England and Ireland. pp. 257. 8° Glasgow, 1890.

4928 Keegan (James). Saint Columcille and the mower. Catholic World, 41, no. 243. 1885.

4929 Kelly (James J.). The Columbian monasteries and rule. Irish Eccles. Rec., 3rd S. 2, pp. 467–78 : 3, pp. 23–35. 1881–82.

4930 —— St. Columba at Boyle. *Same jnl.*, 3rd S. 1, pp. 391–401. 1880.

4931 Keyworth (Samuel). St. Columba. The story of his life. pp. x, 201. 8° London, 1895.

4932 Kirwan (W. H.). Some Celtic missionary saints. St. Columba. Irish Eccles. Rec., 4th S. 30, pp. 598–608. 1911.

4933 La Borderie (Louis Arthur Le Moyne de). Les monastères celtiques aux VIe et VIIe siècles d'après les usages de l'ile d'Iona. (Le monastère d'Iona et la règle de saint Columba). Ann. de Bretagne, 9, pp. 183–209, 379–94. 1894.

4934 Ludwig (Gottfried). Das Leben des Heiligen Columba. 16° Bern, 1861.

4935 Lynch (Patrick). Life of Columcille. pp. viii, 151. 8° Dublin, 1914.

4936 MacCorry (John Stewart). The monks of Iona ; in reply to ' Iona ' by the Duke of Argyll [**4907**]. With a review of ' The cathedral and abbey church of Iona ', by . . . the Bishop of Argyll [**4921**.] 8° London, 1871.

4937 MacGregor (D.). St. Columba. 8° Aberdeen, 1897. [Kenney, 1, p. 263.]

4938 McNeill (Florence Marian). Iona : a history of the island. pp. 105, + maps. 8° London, 1920. [Kenney, 1, p. 423.]

4939 Macphail (James Calder). Columba. [A biography]. 8° Edinburgh, 1882.

4940 Menzies (Lucy). St. Columba of Iona. pp. 150. 8° Glasgow, 1949.

4941 Milligan (Seaton Forrest). Ireland and the Scottish isles ; ancient connexions and intercourse. (Abstract). [Pp. 34–36, Columba.] Rpt. and Proc. Belfast N.H. and Phil. Soc., 1899–1900, pp. 34–40. 1900.

4942 Morrison (George Herbert). St. Columba. His life and times. pp. 24. 8° Edinburgh, 1903.

4943 Muir (William). The life of St. Columba. pp. 52. 8° Iona, 1889.

4944 Murray (Laurence P.). St. Columba in Louth. [i. Columban monasteries in Louth (Clonmore, Monasterboice, Louth) : ii. Visions of Columcille relating to people in Louth : iii. Causes of the battle of Culdremhne.] County Louth Archaeol. J., 2, pp. 337–46. 1911.

4945 Olden (Thomas). St. Columba. *Lectures on Irish Church History*—2. pp. 24. 8° London, 1897.

4946 O'Mahony (Michael). St. Columba. pp. 19. 8° Liverpool, 1926.

4947 O'Reilly (Patrick J.). The site of Columb's monastery on Iona. J. Roy. Soc. Antiq. Ireland, 30 (5th S. 10), pp. 334–42. 1900.

4948 Parlin (Henry). The bookowner in the Columban transcript legend. [i.e. of the book from which St. Columba copied the Cathach. Fionntain=? St. Fintan of Dromin.] Irish Eccles. Rec., 5th S. 28, pp. 181–90. 1926.

4949 —— Dates of St. Columba's birth, exile and death. [521, 563, 597.] County Louth Archaeol. J., 6, p. 3. 1925.

4950 Piercy (William Coleman). St. Columba. pp. 23. 12° London, 1925.

4951 Ψ. Saint Columba. Ulster J. Archaeol., 6, pp. 1–26. 1858.

4952 Reeves (William), *bp. of Down.* The island of Tiree. [=Ethica insula, in Adamnan's life of Columba.] *Same jnl.*, 2, pp. 233–44, + map. 1854.

4953 Richomme (Florent). Histoire de S. Columb. 12° Paris, 1861.

4954 Ritchie (Alexander *and* Euphemia). Map of Iona : with a sketch historical and geological of the island. pp. 35, + 2 maps. 8° Edinburgh, 1928. —Iona past and present. 3rd edition [*of above*]. pp. 43, + maps. 8° Edinburgh, 1934.

4955 Scott (Archibald Black). St. Columba (Columcille), the Gaidheal : his relations with the Picts, and how they developed. Trans. Gaelic Soc. Inverness, 28 (1912–14), pp. 15–66. 1918.

4956 Simpson (William Douglas). The historical Saint Columba. 2nd edition. pp. xxxiii, 177. 4° Aberdeen, 1927. [78 figures at end.]

4957 Skene (William Forbes). Notes on the history and probable situation of the earlier establishments at Iona, prior to the foundation of the Benedictine monastery in the end of the twelfth century. Proc. Soc. Antiq. Scot., 11, pp. 330–49. 1876.

4958 Smith (John), *D.D., minister of Campbeltown.* Life of St. Columba. pp. ix, 168. 8° Edinburgh, 1798.

4959 Spence (James). St. Columba. Trans. Buchan F.C., 3. 1892.

4960 Storer (Agnes C.). Iona the isle of Columba's cell. *Catholic World*, 73, *no.* 438. 1901.

4961 Thomson (T. Harvey). The ancient churches and chapels of Kintyre. [52, + crosses, slabs and relics, connected with Columba.] Trans. Scot. Ecclesiol. Soc., 11, pp. 74–91, + 3 plates. 1935.

4962 Thomson (William), *etc.* St. Columba's birthplace. Scottish N. and Q., 4, pp. 59, 77. 1890.

4963 Thunder (John M.). St. Columba's churches. Irish Eccles. Rec., 3rd S. 11, pp. 821–27. 1890.

4964 Trenholme (Edward Craig). The story of Iona. pp. xv, 173, + maps. 8° Edinburgh, 1909. [Kenney, 1, p. 423.]

4965 Walker (Thomas Henry). Saint Columba. pp. 120. 8° Paisley, 1923.

4966 Watt (Louchlan Maclean). Columba : saint, statesman, and poet. 521–1921. Hibbert J., 20, pp. 236–50. 1922.

§ *d.* **Margaret, Queen of Scotland**

4967 Bryce (William Moir). St. Margaret of Scotland and her chapel in the castle of Edinburgh. pp. 66, + 6 plates. 4° Edinburgh, 1914.

4968 Chalmers (Peter). St. Margaret. [Her relics.] N. and Q., 2nd S. 4, pp. 476–77. 1857.

4969 Fest (Sándor). The Hungarian origin St. Margaret of Scotland. 8° Debrecen, 1940. [Throws light on the marriage of Edward the Ætheling.]

4970 Gordon (Margaret). St. Margaret, queen of Scotland. 2nd edition. pp. xv, 229. 8° Edinburgh, 1934.

4971 Griffinhoofe (H. G.), *etc.* Remains of St. Margaret. N. and Q., 7th S. 11, pp. 209–10, 252–53. 1891.

4972 Henderson-Howat (Agatha Mary Dorothea). Royal pearl : the life and times of Margaret, queen of Scotland. pp. xii, 146. 8° London, 1949.

4973 Menzies (Lucy). St. Margaret, queen of Scotland. pp. 219. 8° London, 1925. [With bibliography.]

§ *e.* **Ninian, Bishop of Galloway**
(c. 360–432)
and the Ninian-Columba Controversy

4974 Barrow (John). Life of Ninian. *Lives of the English saints.* pp. vi, 148. 8° London, 1845. [*Also in* J. H. Newman's Lives of the English saints, vol. 5, 1901.]

4975 Beaton (Donald). The Ninian-Columba controversy. [?first to evangelise Scotland.] Rec. Scot. Church Hist. Soc., 5, pp. 196–207. 1935.

4976 Chadwick (*Mrs.* Nora Kershaw). St. Ninian : a preliminary study of sources. Trans. Dumfriesshire Antiq. Soc., 3rd S. 27 (1948–49), pp. 9–53. 1950.

4977 Chalmers (P. MacGregor). Saint Ninian's Candida casa. [Site at Whithorn. Comparisons with Monkwearmouth, Jarrow, St. Andrews, etc., as regards probable plan.] Scots lore, 1, pp. 192–210. 1895.

4978 Davidson (J.). St. Ninian. I.O.M., N.H. and Antiq. Soc., Proc., N.S. 2 (1923–26), pp. 417–25. 1926.

4979 Galloway (William). St. Ninian and the early Christianisation of Scotland. Trans. Stirling Archaeol. Soc., 12 (1889–90). 1890.

4980 Levison (William). An eighth century poem on St. Ninian. Antiquity, 14, pp. 280–91. 1940.

4981 Luff (S. G. A.). *Ad Candidam Casam* : an examination of St. Ninian's position as a father of British monasticism. Irish Eccles. Rec., 5th S. 80, pp. 17–27. 1953.

4982 Mackie (J. D.). St. Ninian and the Picts. Trans. Dumfries. Antiq. Soc., 3rd S. 30 (1951–52), pp. 17–37. 1953.

4983 Mackinnon (James). Ninian und sein Einfluss auf die Ausbreitung des Christenthums in Nord-Britannien. pp. 39. 8° Heidelberg, 1891.

4983a Maxwell (*Sir* Herbert Eustace), *7th bart.* St. Ninian and Whithorn. pp. 14. 8° n.p., 1932.

4984 Maxwell (William Delbert). St. Ninian. pp. 47. 16° London, 1948.

4985 Murrin (D.). St. Ninian of Candida Casa. Irish Eccles. Rec., 5th S. 40, pp. 397–404. 1932.

4986 Ninian, *St., bp. of Galloway.* The legends of SS. Ninian and Machor. From a unique MS. in the Scottish dialect of the fourteenth century. Edited . . . by W. M. Metcalfe. pp. 237. 8° Paisley, 1904.

4987 Radford (Courtenay Arthur Ralegh). St. Ninian's cave (Whithorn). Trans. Dumfriesshire Antiq., Soc. 3rd S. 28 (1949–50), pp. 96–98. 1951.

4988 Radford (E.). St. Ninian. 8° Edinburgh, 1940.

4989 Sands (Christopher Nicholson Johnston), *Lord.* Candida Casa. Trans. Scot. Ecclesiol. Soc., 10, pp. 75–85. 1932.

4990 Scott (Archibald Black). Continuity and contacts of the Brito-Celtic Church. [History of Candida Casa.] *Same jnl.*, 10, pp. 169–84. 1933.

4991 —— Nynia [Ninian] in northern Pictland. Scot. H.R., 2, pp. 378–88. 1905.

4992 —— St. Ninian, apostle of the Britons and Picts : a research study of the first founding of the Church in Britain. pp. 167. 8° London, 1917.

4993 Simpson (William Douglas). New light on St. Ninian. Archaeol. Æl., 4th S. 23, pp. 78–95, + map. 1945.

4994 —— The Ninianic controversy. [Excavations at Whithorn. Ninianic mission in Cumbria.] Trans. Dumfries. Antiq. Soc., 3rd S. 27 (1948–49), pp. 155–62. 1950.

4995 —— Saint Ninian and the origins of the Christian Church in Scotland. pp. xii, 112, + 12 plates, + 2 maps. 8° Edinburgh, 1940.

4996 —— Some thoughts on the Celtic Church in Scotland. [Ninian-Columba controversy.] Scot. Gaelic Stud., 5, pp. 169–82. 1942.

4997 Strecker (Karl). Zu den Quellen für das Leben des hl. Ninian. Neues Archiv, 43, pp. 1–26. 1922.

4998 Wade-Evans (Arthur Wade). Who was Ninian ? Trans. Dumfries. Antiq. Soc., 3rd S. 28 (1949–50), pp. 79–91. 1951.

4999 Watson (William John). Notes on St. Ninian. Evangel. Rev., 5, pp. 21–32.

§ f. Others

5000 [Anon.]. St. Donnan the great. [Missionary to Picts, sent out by St. Columba.] Scot. N. and Q., 3rd S. 13, pp. 161–65, 177–80. 1935.

5001 Balfour (John Alexander). The ecclesiastical remains on the Holy Isle, Arran. [Cell of St. Molaise (7th c.), etc.] Proc. Soc. Antiq. Scot., 43 (4th S. 7, 1908–09), pp. 147–58. 1909.

5002 Campbell (Niall D.). Saint Maolrubha. [642–722. Missionary to the Picts.] Scot. H.R., 6, pp. 442–43. 1909.

5003 Colquhoun (F. Mary). Saint Kessog. [Missionary to Scotland. ? 6th c.] Highland Monthly, 1, pp. 680–88, + 1 plate. 1890.

5004 Cooper (James). Saint Gerardine. A chapter in the ecclesiastical history of Moray. [10th c.] Trans. Aberdeen Ecclesiol. Soc., 2, pp. 105–16. 1895.

5005 Curlew, *pseud.* Saint Conan. [8th c.] Highland Monthly, 2, pp. 363–75. 1890.

5006 Gammack (James). S. Machar, patron saint of Old Aberdeen. [Temp. Columba.] Scot. N. and Q., 1, pp. 66–68 : *see also* pp. 109–10. 1887.

5007 Harper (J. W.). The problem of S. Serf, and his muinntir at Culross : a proposed reconstruction. [Two S. Serfs, (5th–6th c., and 7th–8th c.), both buried there.] Trans. Scot. Ecclesiol. Soc., 10, pp. 54–65. 1931.

5008 Johnston (Alfred Wintle). Modan, Moddan, Maddan, or Maddad. [St. Modan, abbot of Mailros, lived early 6th c. Survival of name.] Old-lore Misc. V.C., 3, pp. 71–72. 1910.

5009 Lees (Thomas). S. Kentigern and his dedications in Cumberland. Trans. Cumb. and Westm. Antiq. Soc., 6, pp. 328–37. 1883.

5010 Mackay (William). Saints associated with the valley of the Ness. [i. Ninian : ii. Erchard : iii. Drostan : iv. Columba : v. Baithan : vi. Donnan : vii. Moluac : viii. Cumine : ix. Adamnan ; x. Curadan : xi. Gorman : xii. Cyril : xiii. Michael.] Trans. Gaelic Soc. Inverness, 27 (1908–11), pp. 145–62. 1915.

5011 Mackinlay (James Murray). St. Kessog and his cultus in Scotland. [Died 520.] Trans. Glasgow Archaeol. Soc., N.S. 3, pp. 347–59. 1899.

5012 Mackinlay (James Murray). Some notes on St. Baldred's country. [Died c. 606–8. Around Bass rock.] Proc. Soc. Antiq. Scot., 28 (3rd S. 4), pp. 78–83. 1894.

5013 —— Traces of the cultus of St. Fergus in Scotland. *Same inl.*, 38 (4th S. 2, 1903–04), pp. 445–53. 1904.

5014 —— Traces of the cultus of St. Fillan at Killallan, Renfrewshire. *Same jnl.*, 29 (3rd S. 5), pp. 251–55. 1895.

5015 —— Traces of the cultus of the Nine Maidens in Scotland. [Sisters, daughters of St. Douevald, early 8th c., living in parish of Glamis.] *Same jnl.*, 40 (4th S. 4, 1905–06), pp. 255–65. 1906.

5016 Maclean (Arthur John), *bp. of Moray and Ross.* The effect of the work of S. Ninian, S. Mungo, S. Columba, and St. Margaret on Scottish history. Trans. Gaelic Soc. Inverness, 27 (1908–11), pp. 291–309. 1915.

5017 McMillan (W.). St. Conal : the patron saint of Kirkconnell. [Temp. S. Mungo.] Trans. Dumfries. Antiq. Soc., N.S. 21 (1908–09), pp. 19–24. 1910.

5018 Reeves (William), *bp. of Down.* Saint Maelrubha : his history and churches. pp. 41. 8° Edinburgh, 1861. *Same title.* Proc. Soc. Antiq. Scot., 3, pp. 258–96. 1862.

5019 Scott (Archibald Black). St. Donnan the Great, and his muinntir [associates]. [Missionary sent out by Columba to Picts.] Trans. Scot. Ecclesiol. Soc., 1, pp. 256–67. 1906.

5020 —— S. Drostan of Buchan and Caithness. [6th c.] Trans. Gaelic Soc. Inverness, 27 (1908–11), pp. 110–25. 1915.

5021 —— S. Finbarr of Caithness and Ulster. [c. 500–?578.] *Same jnl.*, 27 (1908–11), pp. 20–30. 1915.

5022 —— Saint Maolrubha. Scot. H.R., 6, pp. 260–80. *See also* pp. 442–43. 1909.

5023 —— S. Moluag and his work. [c. 530–92.] Trans. Gaelic Soc. Inverness, 27 (1908–11), pp. 310–23. 1915.

5024 Scott (Archibald Black). S. Moluag, his work and influence. [c. 520–592.] Trans. Scot. Ecclesiol. Soc., 3, pp. 294–309. 1912.

5025 Stevenson (William). The legends and commemorative celebrations of St. Kentigern, his friends and disciples. Translated from the Aberdeen Breviary and the Arbuthnott Missal. pp. xi, 133. 4° Edinburgh, 1874.

5026 Stuart (John). Notices of the early ecclesiastical history of East Lothian and the Bass, and of caves as the retreats of the early saints. [St. Baldred of East Lothian, 6th–7th c., etc.] Hist. Berwick. Nat. Club, 7, pp. 86–90. 1873.

5027 Turnbull (John). St. Bathan. [Baithen (son of Brendan), successor to Columba as abbot of Iona.] *Same jnl.*, 4, pp. 194–205. 1860.

5028 Watson (William John). Saint Cadoc. [c. 500–c. 570.] Scot. Gaelic Stud., 2, pp. 1–12. 1927.

70. HAGIOLOGY, WELSH AND CORNISH

§ *a*. General

See also 5184

5029 Adams (John). Chronicles of Cornish saints. [i. S. Cuby : ii. S. Petrock : iii. S. Constantine : iv. S. Samson : v. S. David : vi. S. Burian : vii. S. Crantock : viii. S. Gunwallo.] J. Roy. Inst. Cornwall, 2, pp. 314–23 : 3, pp. 1–9, 82–88, 89–98, 155–61 : 4, pp. 140–43, 272–77 : 5, pp. 145–47. 1867–75.

5030 Baring-Gould (Sabin). A catalogue of saints connected with Cornwall, with an epitome of their lives, and list of churches and chapels dedicated to them. [In 8 parts.] *Same jnl.*, 13, pp. 439–532 (A–C) : 14, pp. 85–172 (D–G), 260–313 (H–Ke) : 15, pp. 17–53 (Ki–Ma), 347–66 (Me–Mor) : 16, pp. 144–58 (Na–Non), 279–91 (Od–Pa), 395–422 (Si–W) : 17, pp. 155–69 (Pa–Se), + map, + 1 plate. 1898–1907.

5031 —— and **Fisher** (John). Lives of the British Saints [Wales and Cornwall]. *Hon. Society of Cymmrodorion.* 4 vol. 8° London, 1907–13. [Gross, 601a.]

5032 Borlase (William Copeland). The age of the saints, a monograph of early Christianity in Cornwall. [Authorities: legendary lives and their value: Irish saints in Cornwall (450–550): oriental element: Welsh saints in Cornwall (520–682): Breton influence: Christian archaeology of Cornwall (6th–9th c.).] J. Roy. Inst. Cornwall, 6, pp. 9–119. 1878.

5033 —— The age of the saints, *etc.* pp. xxxi, 208, + 5 plates. 8° Truro, 1893. [An expansion of **5032** including, e.g. a chapter on St. Patrick.]

5034 Bowen (Emrys George). The Celtic saints in Cardiganshire. [5 maps in text.] Ceredigion, 1, pp. 3–17. 1950.

5035 —— The saints of Gwynedd. [6 maps in text.] Caernarvonshire Hist. Soc., Trans., 9, pp. 1–15. 1948.

5036 —— The settlements of the Celtic saints in south Wales. [10 maps in text showing distribution of dedications to SS. Dubricius, Cadoc, Illtud, Brychan, Teilo and David, culture areas in Roman times, ogam inscribed stones, etc.] Antiquity, 19, pp. 175–86. 1945.

5036a —— The settlements of the Celtic saints in Wales. pp. x, 175. 8° Cardiff, 1954. [53 figures in text. Cults and distribution.]

5037 Davies (J. Conway). Vitae sanctorum Britanniae. [On Wade-Evans, **5054**.] J. Hist. Soc. Church in Wales, 1, pp. 141–53. 1947.

5038 Davies (James). On parochial churches in Herefordshire dedicated to Cambro-British saints. Arch. Camb., 3rd S. 7, pp. 111–19, + map. 1861.

5039 Doble (Gilbert Hunter). Celtic hagiography and the sources for the early history of Cornwall. Yorks. Soc. Celtic Stud., Rpt. for 1935–36, pp. 10–17. 1936.

5040 —— Cornish saints. 46 parts, 8° Helston, 19[3–]–41.

5041 —— St. Nectan, St. Keyne, and the children of Brychan in Cornwall. Downside Rev., 48, pp. 217–36; 49, pp. 149–72. 1930–31.

R

5042 Doble (Gilbert Hunter). Les saints du Cornwall. Mém. Assoc. bretonne, congrès de Quimperlé, 1928. pp. 13. 1929.

5043 —— The Welsh saints, parts 1–4. 8° Helston, 1942–43. [i. St. Paulinus of Wales. pp. 20. 1942: ii. St. Dubricius. pp. 36. 1943: iii. St. Teilo. pp. 48. 1942; iv. St. Oudoceus. 1943.]

5044 Fisher (John). Montgomeryshire saints. [Pts. 1 and 2: apparently not continued.] Collns. hist. and archaeol. rel. to Montgom., 25, pp. 133–47, 235–52. 1891.

5045 —— Welsh church dedications. [7 figures of saints in text.] Trans. Hon. Soc. Cymm., 1906–07, pp. 76–108, + plate. 1908.

5046 Loth (Joseph). Quelques victimes de l'hagio-onomastique en Cornwal: saint Péran, saint Kéverne, saint Achebran. Mém. Soc. d'hist. et d'archéol. Bretagne, 11, pp. 157–72. 1930.

5047 Meyer (Kuno). A collation of Rees' Lives of the Cambro-British saints. Y Cymmrodor, 13, pp. 76–96. 1900.

5048 Nedeles (Louis). Cambria sacra, or, the history of the early Cambro-British Christians. pp. xxxi, 584. 8° London, 1879. [Uncritical.]

5049 Newell (Ebenezer Josiah). Celtic saints and Celtic symbols. [iv. The crosses at Llantwit Major: v. The struggle with paganism: vi. Relics of paganism: vii. Well worship: viii. Stone worship.] Cymru Fu, 1, pp. 375–77, 380–82, 385–87, 401–02, 407–09. 1889.

5050 Rees (Rice). An essay on the Welsh saints. pp. xiv, 358. 8° London, 1836. [Gross, 1620. To the end of 7th c.]

5051 Rees (William Jenkins). Lives of the Cambro-British saints of the fifth and immediately succeeding centuries, *etc.* with English translations, and notes. *Society for the Publication of ancient Welsh manuscripts.* pp. xxiii, 636, 20. 8° Llandovery, 1853. [Gross, 606.]

5052 Tatlock (John Strong Perry). The dates of the Arthurian saints' legends. [SS. Cadoc, Gildas, Illtud, etc.] Speculum, 14, pp. 345–65. 1939.

5053 Wade-Evans (Arthur Wade). Bonedd y Saint, E [Descent of the saints]. [Text (of 1458) in Welsh, and notes.] Arch. Camb., 86, pp. 158–75. 1931.

5054 —— *ed.* Vitae sanctorum Britanniae et genealogiae. *Board of Celtic Studies, University of Wales, History and law series,* 9. pp. xx, 336. 8° Cardiff, 1944.

5055 Williamson (Edward William), *bp. of Swansea.* Vespasian A XIV. [Collection of lives of Welsh (and Celtic) saints.] Arch. Camb., 101, pp. 91–105. 1951.

5056 Willis-Bund (John William). Welsh saints. Trans. Hon. Soc. Cymm., 1893–94, pp. 21–54. 1895.

§ b. David, Bishop of Menevia
(5th–6th c.)

5057 [Anon.] The origin of the Annales Cambriae : the true date of St. David's death. [544.] Arch. Camb., 6th S. 10, pp. 473–79. 1910.

5058 D. (A.). The life of S. David. [With a preface by Sir George Prevost]. pp. 23. 12° London, 1870.

5059 Dawson (M. L.). St. David. pp. 19. 8° Carmarthen, [1920?].

5060 Leatham (Diana). The story of St. David of Wales. pp. viii, 108. 8° London, 1952.

5061 Lloyd (Howel William). Notes on the life of St. David. Y Cymmrodor, 8, pp. 25–40. 1887.

5062 Newell (Ebenezer Josiah). Date of the birth of St. David. Cymru Fu, 1, p. 32. 1887.

5063 Phillips (James). The history of Pembrokeshire. pp. viii, 592. 8° London, 1909. [Pp. 43–93, St. David, early Christianity and the apostles of Wales, 600–1000, 11th c.]

5064 Rhygyfarch. Life of St. David. [With selections from other lives. Edited by A. W. Wade-Evans. *Translations of Christian Literature, Series* 5. pp. xx, 124. 8° London, 1923.

5065 Rhys (Ernest). The life of St. David. [Compiled from the life by Rhygyfarch and other sources]. pp. 41. 4° Gregynog, 1927.

5066 Vaughan (Herbert M.). St. David and the early Welsh saints. Church Q. Rev., 64, pp. 277–300. 1907.

5067 Vendryes (Joseph). Saint David et le roi Boia. Rev. celt., 45, pp. 141–72. 1928.

5068 Wade-Evans (Arthur Wade), *trs.* Life of St. David. pp. xx, 124. 8° London, 1923. [Kenney, 1, p. 178. Life by Rhygyfarch, c. 1090.]

5069 —— Rhygyvarch's Life of St. David. Y Cymmrodor, 24, pp. 1–73. 1913.

5070 —— St. David and Glastonbury. Arch. Camb., 80 (7th S. 5), pp. 365–71. 1925.

§ c. Others

5071 Alexander (John James), *etc.* St. Rumon. [Patron saint of Tavistock abbey. ? identity. ? Celtic bishop. ? 5th to 9th c. *See also,* 22, pp. 281–85, 331–32. 1945.] Devon and Cornwall N. and Q., 19, pp. 345–50. 1937.

5072 Armstrong (T. Percy). St. Daniel. [Deiniol, hermit on Lough Ree, and bp. of Gwynedd. 6th c.] N. and Q., 175, p. 443. 1938.

5073 Baring-Gould (Sabin). St. Brychan, king, confessor. Arch. Camb., 6th S. 3, pp. 345–70. 1903.

5074 —— Saint Carannog. Y Cymmrodor, 15, pp. 88–99. 1902.

5075 —— S. Petroc. Devon N. and Q., 1, pp. 6–13. 1900.

5076 —— S. Petroc in Devon. *Same jnl.,* 2, pp. 58–59. 1902.

5077 —— Vita Sancti Kebie [Cybi or Cuby.] [Cousin of St. David.] Y Cymmrodor, 14, pp. 86–95. 1900.

5078 Bayley (Arthur R.), and **Strachan** (Lionel Richard Mortimer), *etc.* St. Endellion. [Cousin of St. David.] N. and Q., 180, pp. 12–14, 63–65, 196–97. 1941.

5079 Brioc, *St.*, *bishop and confessor.* Vita S. Brioci episcopi et confessoris ab anonymo Suppari conscripta, edita studio et opera Fr. Plaine. (Epilogus vitae S. Briomagli.) [440–530.] Anal. Boll., 2, pp. 161–90 ; 23, pp. 264–65. 1883, 1904.

5080 Chanter (John Frederick). St. Urith of Chittlehampton : a study in an obscure Devon saint. [Celtic?] Rept. and Trans. Devon Assoc., 46, pp. 290–308. 1914.

5081 Chope (Richard Pearse). St. Nectan. [3 (unanswered) queries.] Devon and Cornwall N. and Q., 12, pp. 312–14, + 1 plate. 1923.

5082 Clark (Joseph). St. Gildas. [A construction of his life.] Glastonbury Antiq. Soc. Proc., [2] (1904), pp. 35–48. 1906.

5083 Collier ( ), *Mrs.* St. Clether : his chapel and holy wells. J. Brit. Archaeol. Assoc., 62 (N.S. 12), pp. 83–90, + 1 plate. 1906.

5084 Doble (Gilbert Hunter). The Celtic saints in the Glastonbury relic lists. N. and Q. Som. and Dorset, 24, pp. 86–89, 128. 1944.

5085 —— Four saints of the Fal. St. Gluvias, St. Kea, St. Fili, and St. Rumon. Downside Rev., 47, pp. 1–32. 1929.

5086 —— Saint Branwalader. [His relics given by Athelstan to Milton abbey, Dorset.] Laudate, 23, pp. 23–33. 1945.

5087 —— St. Congar. [Eponym of Congresbury.] Antiquity, 19, pp. 32–43, 85–95. 1945.

5088 —— St. Dubricius. [*See also* 21, pp. 50–51, for note by S. M. Harris.] Laudate, 19, pp. 98–109 : 20, pp. 50–59, 105–14. 1941–42.

5089 —— Un saint du Cornwall dans le Morbihan. [St. Gwinear.] Mém. Assoc. bretonne, Congrès de Vannes, 1931. pp. 19. 1932.

5090 —— Saint Iltut. pp. 52. 8° Cardiff, 1944.

5091 —— Saint Indract and Saint Dominic. [Died temp. Ina, early 8th c. Includes transcript, in translation, of the Digby MS. 112. (Life of S. Indract).] Somerset Record Soc., 57 (Collectanea, 3), pp. 1–24. 1942.

5092 Doble (Gilbert Hunter). Saint Oudoceus. [Third saint in Liber Landavensis.] J. Theol. Stud., 43, pp. 204–16 : 44, pp. 59–67. 1942–43.

5093 —— Saint Sulian and Saint Tysilio. [Sulian : Welsh by birth (530) ; founded churches in Britanny.] Laudate, 13, pp. 217–38 : 14, pp. 46–53. 1935–36.

5094 Fleetwood (William), *bp. of St. Asaph, Ely.* The life and miracles of St. Wenefrede [by Robert, prior of Shrewsbury, *q.v.* **5111**], together with her litanies ; with some historical observations made thereon. 2nd edition. pp. 128. [7th c.] 8° London, 1713.

5095 Grosjean (Paul). Cyngar Sant. [Who was St. Congar, or Cungar, who gave his name to Congresbury?] Anal. Boll., 42, pp. 100–20. 1924.

5096 —— Trois pièces sur S. Senán. Anal. Boll., 66, pp. 199–230. 1948.

5097 —— Vie de Saint Cadoc, par Carodoc de Llancarfan. [With Latin text from MS. Gotha, I. 81, ff. 156–61.] Anal. Boll., 60, pp. 35–67. 1942.

5098 —— Vie de S. Rumon [de Tavistock]. Vie, invention et miracles de S. Nectan [de Hartland.] [Eldest child of St. Brychan. With Latin text, ex codice Gothano, fol. 148v–150r, fol. 52–55 v.] Anal. Boll., 71, pp. 359–414. 1953.

5099 James (John). St. Briavel— may he not be identified with S. Ebrulfus ? [Evroult : died 596 or 600.] Trans. Bristol and Glos. Arch. Soc., 8, pp. 149–52, 342. 1884.

5100 Johnstone (P. K.). Dual personality of Saint Gildas. [' Gildas, son of Caw, founder of Rhuys, was not the writer of the De Excidio, but his namesake.'] Antiquity, 20, pp. 211–13 : 22, pp. 38–40. 1946, 1948.

5101 Lloyd (Howel William). The legend of St. Curig. [St. Cyr. ? 7th c.] Arch. Camb., 4th S. 6, pp. 145–64. 1875.

5102 Lloyd (William Valentine). St. Germanus's blessing or prophecy of perpetual sovereignty to the family of Cadeth Dyrnllwg, king of old Powys. [Nennius.] Collns. hist. and archaeol. rel. to Montgom., 4, pp. 35–39. 1871.

5103 Loth (Joseph). Le nom de Gildas dans l'île de Bretagne, en Irlande, et en Armorique. Rev. celt., 46, pp. 1–15. 1929.

5104 —— Un phénomène linguistique: Saint Budoc devenu Saint André : Saint André et la coqueluche. Rev. celt., 46, pp. 118–19. 1929.

5105 —— La vie de saint Teliau [Teilo] d'après le Livre de Llandaf. [Died c. 580. Founder and abbot-bp. of Llandaff monastery (Llandeilo Fawr), Carmarthenshire.] Ann. Bretagne, 9, pp. 81–85, 277–86, 438–46 : 10, pp. 66–77. 1893–94.

5106 M. (G. W.). St. Decuman. [D. 706.] N. and Q., 4th S. 2, p. 299. 1868.

5107 Meyrick (Thomas). Life of St. Wenefred, . . . patroness of North Wales and Shrewsbury. 8° London, 1878.

5108 O'Donoghue (Denis). Mor, sister of St. David of Menevia, patron of Wales, the mother of Kerry saints. J. Roy. Soc. Antiq. Ireland, 21 (5th S. 1. ii), pp. 703–11. 1891.

5109 Platts (C.), *trs.* The martyrdom of St. Indract. [c. 700. Translated from MS. Digby 112 in the Bodleian Library.] N. and Q. for Somerset and Dorset, 17, pp. 17–23. 1921.

5110 Plummer (Charles). The miracles of Senan. [Irish text, with English translation, and notes. Edited from two MSS. in the Royal Library of Brussels.] Zeit. celt. Phil., 10, pp. 1–35. 1915.

5111 Robert, *prior of Shrewsbury*. The admirable life of St. Wenefrede, written [in Latin] by Robert, monke and priour of Shrewsbury : [translated into English] by J. F. [John Falconer or Falkner]. pp. 88. 8° [St. Omer], 1635.

5112 Robinson (Joseph Armitage). A fragment of the Life of St. Cungar. [Son of Geraint, 6th c., Welsh.] J. Theol. Stud., 20, pp. 97–108. 1919.

5113 —— The Lives of St. Cungar and St. Gildas. *Same jnl.*, 23, pp. 15–22. 1922.

5114 —— St. Carantoc in Somerset. [5th c.] Downside Rev., 46, pp. 234–43. 1928.

5115 Robinson (Joseph Armitage). St. Cungar and St. Decuman. J. Theol. Stud., 29, pp. 137–40. 1928.

5116 Rose-Troup (Frances). Saint Carantoc. Devon and Cornwall N. and Q., 15, p. 171. 1928.

5117 —— Saint Melor. *Same jnl.*, 15, p. 118. 1928.

5118 Rowe (Joseph Hambley). St. Laluwy. Another Cornish saint : the dedication of Menheniot church. [?= St. Ladislas of Hungary : ? connection with St. Neot.] *Same jnl.*, 6, pp. 3–7. 1910.

5119 Rushforth (G. McN.). St. Urith [of Chittlehampton]. *Same jnl.*, 17, pp. 290–91, + 1 plate. 1933.

5120 Schubel (Friedrich). Die heilige Pinnosa. [Supplants Ursula as leader of the 11,000 virgins in middle of 10th c. Here identified with Cornish Winnosa or Winnoc.] Anglia, 65 (N.F. 53), pp. 64–80. 1941.

5121 Stokes (Whitley). Amra Senáin. [Eulogy of S. Senán of Inis Cathaig, ascribed to Dallán, alleged author of eulogy of St. Columba. Irish, with English translation.] Zeit. celt. Phil., 3, pp. 220–25. 1901.

5122 Stonor (Julian). Saint Petroc's cell on Bodmin moor. Downside Rev., 66, pp. 64–74. 1948.

5123 Swift (Thomas). The life of Saint Winefride, virgin and martyr. Based on the Acts compiled by the Bollandist Fathers. pp. x, 116. [7th c.] 8° Holywell, 1906.

5124 Thompson (Kate). St. Winefred. [With bibliography.] N. and Q., 6th S. 10, pp. 374–76, 415. 1884.

5125 Vivian-Neal (A. W.). St. Carantoc at Carhampton. Proc. Somerset Arch. Soc., 83 (1937), pp. 211–14. 1938.

5126 Wade-Evans (Arthur Wade). Beuno Sant. [?died 660.] Arch. Camb., 85, pp. 315–41. 1930.

5127 —— St. Paulinus of Wales. Arch. Camb., 75 (6th S. 20), pp. 159–78. 1920.

5128 Williams (W.). St. Dubricius, [bp. of Llandaff]. N. and Q., 5th S. 7, pp. 432–33 : 8, pp. 278–79. 1877.

71. MISSIONARIES TO THE CONTINENT

1. GENERAL

5129 Cahill (E.). Influence of Irish on medieval Europe. [Missionaries and scholars in France and Germany.] Irish Eccles. Rec., 5th S. 46, pp. 464–76. 1935.

5130 Campenhausen (Hans von), *Baron*. Die asketische Heimatlosigkeit im altkirchlichen und frümittelalterlichen Mönchtum. *Sammlung Gemeinverständlicher Vorträge und Schriften a. d. Gebiet der Theologie*, 149. 8° Tübingen, 1930. [' Peregrinatio ' :=voluntary expatriation for leading a life of austerity.]

5131 Dunn (John Joseph). Irish monks on the continent. [i. St. Columbanus : ii. St. Gall : iii. Irish monks of Reichenau.] Cath. Univ. Bull., 10, pp. 307–28. 1904.

5132 Ebrard (Johann Heinrich August). Die iroschottische Missionskirche des sechsten, siebenten, und achten Jahrhunderts. Mit einem Kärtchen. 8° Gütersloh, 1873. [Gross, 1602. ' Full of erroneous opinions '.—Gougaud.]

5133 Esposito (Mario). The poems of Colmanus [episcopus] ' nepos Cracavist ', and Dungalus ' praecipuus Scottorum '. [Diffusion of story of St. Brigid in Italy by labours of 2 emigrant Irish (Scotti)—Colmanus who sojourned at Rome early 9th c., and Donatus, bp. of Fiesole (c. 829–76).] J. Theol. Stud., 33, pp. 113–31. 1932.

5134 Fuhrmann (Joseph Paul). Irish medieval monasteries on the Continent. *Catholic University of America.* pp. xiii, 121, + map. 8° Washington, D.C., 1927.

5135 Gougaud (Louis). The achievement of the influence of Irish monks. Studies, 20, pp. 195–208. 1931.

5136 —— Gaelic pioneers of Christianity : the work and influence of Irish monks and saints in continental Europe, VIth–XIIth century. Translated by Victor Collins. pp. xxiii, 166. 8° Dublin, 1923. [Kenney, 1, p. 186. Cult of SS. Columban and Gall in Europe.]

5137 Gougaud (Louis). L'oeuvre des *Scotti* dans l'Europe continentale (fin Ve–fin XIe siècles). [Kenney, 1, p. 486.] Rev. hist. ecclés., 9, pp. 21–37, 255–77. 1908.

5138 —— Les saints irlandais hors d'Irlande, étudiés dans le culte et dans la dévotion traditionelle. *Bibl. de la Revue d'hist. ecclésiastique*, 16. pp. xiii, 219, + 1 plate. 8° Louvain and Oxford, 1936.

5139 Goyan (Georges). Missionaires d'Irlande dans l'Europe mérovingienne. Revue générale (Bruxelles), 120, pp. 129–46. 1928.

5140 Hennig (John). Irish monastic activities in eastern Europe. Irish Eccles. Rec., 5th S. 65, pp. 394–400. 1945.

5141 Hennig (John). Irish saints in the liturgical and artistic tradition of central Europe. [i. Switzerland, Bavaria, Austria : ii. Belgium and Holland.] *Same jnl.*, 5th S. 60, pp. 181–92. 1942.

5142 Jones (Griffith Hartwell). Early Celtic missionaries. Y Cymmrodor, 39, pp. 39–67. 1928.

5143 MacDonnell (Charles P.). Notice of a lost work of Colgan, author of the Acta sanctorum Hiberniae, on the early evangelical labours and monastic foundations of the Irish abroad. Proc. R.I.A., 6 (1854), pp. 103–12. 1858.

5144 Mayer (Anton). Die Iren auf dem Kontinent im Mittelalter. [Kenney, 1, p. 486.] Hochland, 13, pp. 605–14. 1916.

5145 O'Briain (Felim). The expansion of Irish Christianity to 1200 : an historiographical survey. Irish Hist. Stud., 3, pp. 241–66 ; 4, pp. 131–63. 1943–44.

5146 —— Irish missionaries and medieval Church reform. Miscellanea historica in honorem Alberti de Meyer (Louvain), 1, pp. 228–54. 1946.

5147 Olden (Thomas). St. Aidan and Irish missions abroad. *Lectures on Irish Church History*–2. pp. 24. 8° London, 1897.

5148 Pflugk-Harttung (Julius von). The Old Irish on the continent. Trans. R.H.S., N.S., 5, pp. 75–102. 1891.

5148a Robinson (Charles Henry). The conversion of Europe. pp. xxiii, 640, + 6 maps. 8° London, 1917. [Pp. 46–161, A.–S. : and *passim*, e.g. pp. 356–80, ' The work of Boniface '.]

5149 Schultze (Walther). Die Bedeutung der iroschottischen Mönche für die Erhaltung und Fortflanzung der mittelalterlichen Wissenschaft (mit besonderer Rücksicht auf die noch vorhandenen irischen Handschriften in Bibliotheken des Continents). [117 Irish mss. older than 11th c. in continental libraries. (Kenney, 1, p. 92).] Cent. Bibliothekswesen, 6, pp. 185–98, 233–41, 281–98. 1889.

5150 Scott (Archibald Black). Celtic missionaries on the continent–[3]. Cadoc, Gildas, Samswn, and others. Trans. Gaelic Soc. Inverness, 32 (1924–25), pp. 337–60. 1929.

5151 Timerding (Heinrich), *ed.* Die christliche Frühzeit in den Berichten über die Bekehrer. 8° Jena, 1929.

72. MISSIONARIES TO THE CONTINENT
2. IN FRANCE
§ *a.* General

(for work of Columban at Brie and at Luxeuil, *see* 74 § b.)

5152 Bittermann (Helen Robbins). The influence of Irish monks on Merovingian diocesan organization. A.H.R., 40, pp. 232–45. 1935.

5153 Boll (Franz), *ed.* Perrona Scottorum. [Kenney, 1, p. 500. History of the Irish colony at Péronne (8th c.), and some questions of Irish palaeography.] Traube (L.) : Vorlesungen und Abhandlungen, 3, pp. 95–119. 1920.

5154 Cuvillier (Alfred). Histoire de S. Kilien, évêque missionaire de l'Artois au VIIe siècle. 12° Lille, 1861. [Kenney, 1, p. 492. Killian, a 7th c. Irish hermit, settled by St. Columban at Aubigny near Arras. Body at Montreuil.]

5155 Finsterwalder (Paul Willem). Wege und Ziele der irischen und angelsächsischen Mission im fränkischen Reich. [Kenney, 1, p. 783.] Zeit. Kirchengesch., 47 (N.F. 10), pp. 203–26. 1928.

5156 Levison (Wilhelm). Die Iren und die fränkische Kirche. [Kenney, 1, p. 486.] Hist. Zeit., 109, (3. F., 13), pp. 1–22. 1912.

5157 Moran (Patrick Francis), *cardinal, bp. of Ossory*. St. Fiacre. [Of Connaught, 7th c.] Irish Eccles. Rec., 12, pp. 361–68. 1875.

5158 Perret (A.). Histoire de saint Kilien d'Aubigny, sa vie et son culte. 8° Calais, 1920.

5159 Poncelet (Albert), *ed.* Vita S. Killiani [Chillien] confessoris Albiniacensis. [Latin text.] Anal. Boll., 20, pp. 432–44. 1901.

5160 Stokes (Margaret MacNair). Three months in the forests of France. A pilgrimage in search of vestiges of Irish saints in France. pp. li, 291. 8° London, 1895. [Kenney, 1, p. 183. ' Uncritical '.]

5161 Traube (Ludwig). Perrona Scottorum, ein Beitrag zur Ueberlieferungsgeschichte und zur Palaeographie des Mittelalters. [Kenney, 1, p. 500. Irish colony at Péronne.] Sitgungsb. K. bayer. Akad. Wiss., philos.-philol. Kl., 1900 (Heft 4), pp. 469–538. 1900.

5162 Vendryes (Joseph). Saints Lugle et Luglien, patrons de Montdidier. [Two 7th c. martyrs, localized at Thérouanne on the Lys. Sons of Irish king Dodanus.] Rev. celt., 44, pp. 101–08. 1927.

§ *b.* **Brittany**
i. **General**

5163 Buléon (Jérome). La légende de saint Cornély. Ann. Bretagne, 14, pp. 632–41. 1899.

5164 Couffon (R.). Les pagi de la Dumnonée au IXe siècle d'après les hagiographes. Mém. Soc. d'hist. et d'archéol. Bretagne, 24, pp. 1–23, + map. 1944.

5165 Doble (Gilbert Hunter). Saint Paulinus of Wales. A recent discovery about the founder of St. Pol-de-Léon. Laudate, 19, pp. 28–45. 1941.

5165a —— and **Kerbiriou** (L.). Les saints bretons. pp. 35. 4° Brest, 1933.

5166 Duchesne (Louis). La vie de Saint Malo. Étude critique. [9th c. 2 versions, one by Bili of Alet, the other anonymous, from Saintes.] Rev. celtique, 11, pp. 1–22. 1890.

5167 Duine (François), *pseud.* [Henri de Kerbeuzec]. Catalogue des sources hagiographiques pour l'histoire de Bretagne jusqu'à la fin du XIIe siècle. pp. 62. 8° Paris, 1922.

5168 —— Inventaire liturgique de l'hagiographie bretonne. pp. ix, 291. 8° Paris, 1922.

5169 —— Memento des sources hagiographiques de l'histoire de Bretagne, Ve–Xe siècles. pp. 214. 8° Rennes, 1918.

5170 Edwards (W.). The settlement of Brittany. Y Cymmrodor, 11, pp. 61–101. 1892.

5171 Fonsagrives (J.). Saint Gildas de Ruis et la société bretonne au VIe siècle. 8° Paris, 1908.

5172 Gougaud (Louis). Le Chrétienté bretonne des origines à la fin du XIIe siècle. [Causes et date de l'émigration, etc.] Mém. Soc. d'hist. et d'archéol. Bretagne, 13, pp. 1–38. 1932.

5173 —— Mentions anglaises de saints bretons et de leurs reliques. Ann. de Bretagne, 34, pp. 273–77. 1920.

5174 —— Notes sur le culte des saints bretons en Angleterre. *Same jnl.*, 35, pp. 601–09. 1923.

5175 Gruyer (Paul). Les saints bretons. pp. 64. 8° Paris, 1926.

5176 Guénin (G.). L'évangélisation du Finistère (VIe siècle). [By St. Paul Aurelian, a native of S. Wales : 6th c.] Bull. Soc. académique de Brest, 2e S. 32 (1906–07), pp. 29–82, + map. 1908.

5177 La Borderie (Louis Arthur le Moyne de). Les Bretons insulaires et les Anglo-Saxons du Ve au VIIe siècle. 12° Paris, 1873. [Gross, 1515. 'Migration of Celts of Britain to Armorica during period of the Germanic conquest of Britain.']

5178 —— Études historiques bretonnes. L'Historia Britonum attribuée à Nennius, et l'Historia Britannica avant Geoffroi de Monmouth. pp. vii, 132. 8° Paris, 1883.

5179 La Borderic (Louis Arthur le Moyne de). Histoire de Bretagne. 3 vol. 4° Rennes, 1896–99.

5180 —— *ed.* Saint Tudual. Texte des trois vies les plus anciennes, *etc.* [Composed 6th, 9th and 11th c. Latin texts. First abbot and bp. of Tréguer.] Mém. Soc. archéol. Côtes-du-Nord, 2e S. 2, pp. 77–122. 1886.

5181 Largillière (René). Mélanges d'hagiographie bretonne. pp. 45. 8° Brest, 1925.

5182 —— Les saints et l'organisation chrétienne primitive dans l'Armorique bretonne. 8° Rennes, 1925.

5183 —— La topographie du culte de saint Gildas. Mém. Soc. d'hist. et d'archéol. Bretagne, 4, pp. 1–25. 1924.

5184 Latouche (Robert). Mélanges d'histoire de Cornouaille (Ve–XIe siècle). *Bibl. École des Hautes Études*, 192. pp. 123. 8° Paris, 1911.

5185 Le Grand (Albert). Les vies des saints de la Bretagne-Armorique. . . . 5e édition. pp. xxvi, 806, 344. 8° Quimper, 1901. [Aim : ' Moral edification of the reader.']

5186 Lobineau (Gui Alexis). L'histoire de Bretagne composée sur les actes et auteurs originaux. 2 vol. fol. Paris and Rennes, 1707.

5187 —— Les vies des saints de Bretagne. . . . Nouvelle édition . . . augmentée par l'Abbé Tresvaux. 6 vol. 8° Paris, 1836–39.

5188 Lot (Ferdinand). Mélanges d'histoire bretonne. pp. 478. 8° Paris, 1907. [Pp. 97–206, 287–430 (texts), les divers rédactions de la Vie de saint Malo : pp. 207–83, 431–76 (text), La Vie de saint Gildas.]

5189 Loth (Joseph). L'émigration bretonne en Armorique du Ve au VIIe siècle de notre ère. pp. 260. 8° Paris, 1883.

5190 —— Les saints et l'organisation chrétienne primitive dans l'Armorique bretonne d'après un livre récent [par René Largillière]. Mém. Soc. d'hist. et d'archéol. Bretagne, 7, pp. 1–24. 1926.

5191 Morice de Beaubois (Pierre Hyacinthe). Histoire ecclésiastique et civile de Bretagne. 2 vol. fol. Paris, 1750–56.

5192 —— Mémoires pour servir de preuves à l'histoire ecclésiastique et civile de Bretagne. 3 vol. fol. Paris, 1742–46.

5193 Mottay (J. Gaultier du). Essai d'iconographie et d'hagiographie bretonne. [Alphabetical.] Mém. Soc. archéol. Cotes-du-Nord, 3, pp. 112–44, 205–66. 1869.

5194 Oheix (André). Notes sur la Vie de S. Gildas. 8° Nantes, 1913.

4195 —— Vie inédite de S. Cunwal. [Vita Cunuali : bp. of Tréguier.] Rev. celt., 32, pp. 154–83. 1911.

5196 —— and **Fawtier-Jones** (Ethel C.). La Vita ancienne de saint Corentin. [First bishop of Quimper. ?5th c.] Mém. Soc. d'hist. et d'archéol. Bretagne, 6, pp. 3–56. 1925.

5197 Plaine (Bède). La colonisation de l'Armorique par les Bretons insulaires. 8° Paris, 1899. [Gross, 1515, note.]

5198 Shearman (John Francis). The Celto-Britons of Armorica.... Armorican saints and ecclesiastics ; their connexions with Great Britain and Ireland in the fifth and sixth centuries. J. Roy. Hist. and Arch. Assoc. Ireland, [15], 4th S. 5 (1879–82), pp. 597–630, + 2 tables. 1882.

5199 Wrdisten, *abbot of Landévennec.* Vita S. Winwaloei, primi abbatis Landevenecensis, auctore Wurdestino, nunc primum integre edita. [Winwalloc or Guénolé, 5th c. Latin text, composed c. 880.] Anal. Boll., 7, pp. 167–264. 1888.

5200 Wrmonoc, *of Landévennec.* Vie de S. Paul de Léon en Bretagne, d'après un manuscrit de Fleury-sur-Loire, conservé à la bibliothèque publique d'Orléans. [6th c. Latin text.] Rev. celt., 5, pp. 413–60. 1883.

5201 Wrmonoc, *of Landévennec.* Vita Sancti Pauli episcopi Leonensis . . . edita studio et opera Fr. Plaine. [Paul Aurelian, a native of South Wales, first bp. of Léon : c. 530.] Anal. Boll. 1, pp. 208–58. 1882.

ii. Samson, bishop of Dol.

(c. 485–c. 565)

5202 Burkitt (Francis Crawford). St. Samson of Dol. J. Theol. Stud., 27, pp. 42–57. 1926.

5203 Bushell (William Dene). The early life of St. Samson of Dol. Arch. Camb., 6th S. 3, pp. 319–38. 1903.

5204 Duine (François), *pseud.* [Henri de Kerbeuzec]. Culte de saint Samson à la fin du Xe siècle. [Kenney, 1, p. 174.] Ann. Bretagne, 17, pp. 425–32. 1902.

5205 —— Questions d'hagiographie et vie de S. Samson. pp. 66. 8° Paris, 1914. [Kenney, 1, p. 174.]

5206 —— S. Samson et sa légende. 8° Paris, 1900. [Kenney, 1, p. 174.]

5207 —— S. Samson, évêque de Dol. Quelques objections à une réponse [5209]. Ann. Bretagne, 35, pp. 171–86. 1922.

5208 —— La vie de S. Samson à propos d'un ouvrage récent [Fawtier's Vita I.] [Kenney, 1, p. 174.] *Same jnl.,* 28, pp. 332–56. 1913.

5209 Fawtier (Robert). S. Samson, abbé de Dol. Réponse à quelques objections [5208]. Ann. Bretagne, 35, pp. 137–70. 1922.

5210 —— La vie de Saint Samson : essai de critique hagiographique. *Bibliothèque de l'Ecole des Hautes Etudes,* 197. pp. 180. 8° Paris, 1912. [Kenney, 1, p. 173. Contains earliest life. Latin text, with introduction and commentary.]

5211 Loth (Joseph). La vie la plus ancienne de Saint Samson de Dol, d'après des travaux récents : remarques et additions. Rev. celt., 35, pp. 269–300 : 39, pp. 301–33 : 40, pp. 1–50. 1914, 1922–23.

5212 Samson, *St., abbot of Llantwit and bp. of Dol.* Vita antiqua Sancti Samsonis, Dolensis episcopi, edidit Fr. Plaine. Anal. Boll., 6, pp. 77–150. 1887.

5213 Simpson (William John Sparrow), *etc.* St. Sampson. N. and Q., 8th S. 9, p. 16. 1896.

5214 Taylor (Thomas), *trs.* Life of St. Samson of Dol. *Translations of Christian literature, series 5, lives of Celtic saints.* pp. 124. 8° London, 1925.

§ *c.* **Fursa (Fursey), Abbot of Lagny**

(Founded monastery of Cnoberesburgh (Burgh castle), Suffolk, c. 630. Migrated to Gaul, c. 641 and founded monastery of Lagny in Brie. Died ?649 : buried at Péronne—called Perrona Scottorum since its abbots were Irishmen for more than a century.)

5215 Dahl (Louis Harold). The Roman camp and the Irish saint [i.e. St. Fursey] at Burgh castle with local history. pp. xii, 248. 8° London, 1913.

5216 Davila (Thomas). Historia y vida del admirable . . . San Furseo. pp. 360. 4° Madrid, 1699.

5217 Friart (Norbert). Histoire de saint Fursy et des ses deux frères saint Feuillien, évêque et martyr, et saint Ultain. pp. 471. 8° Lille, 1913. [Kenney, 1, p. 500.]

5218 Fursey, *St., abbot of Lagny.* The life of Fursa. Edited and translated from the ms. in the handwriting of M. O'Clery in the Royal Library, Brussels, [MS. 2324], by Whitley Stokes. 8° Paris, 1904. [Irish and English.]

5219 Fursey, *St., abbot of Lagny.* Vita virtutesque Fursei abbatis Latiniacensis et de Fuilano additamentum Nivialense. *Monumenta Germaniae historica, script. rerum Merovingicarum,* 4. *Passiones vitaeque sanctorum,* pp. 423–51 : 7, pp. 837–42. 4° Hannoverae, 1902, 1920.

5220 Gruetzmacher ( ), *Prof., Heidelberg.* Die Viten des heiligen Furseus. Zeit. Kirchengesch., 19, pp. 190–96. 1899.

5221 Hennig (John). The Irish background of St. Fursey. Irish Eccles. Rec., 5th S. 77, pp. 18–28. 1952.

5222 Kirwan (W. H.). Some Celtic missionary saints.—St. Fursey. *Same jnl.,* 4th S. 32, pp. 170–87. 1912.

5223 Stokes (Whitley), *ed.* Betha Fursa, the Life of Fursa. [Irish text and English translation from MS. 2324 in the Royal Library, Brussels.] Rev. celt., 25, pp. 385–404. 1904.

5224 Warren (Frederick Edward). St. Fursey. Proc. Suffolk Inst. Archaeol., 16, pp. 252–77. 1918.

73. MISSIONARIES TO THE CONTINENT
3. IN GERMANY AND AUSTRIA
§ *a.* General

5225 Aufhauser (Johann Baptist). Bayerische Missionsarbeit im Osten während des 9. Jahrhundert. [Salzburg (bp. Virgil), *etc.*] Festgabe Alois Knöpfler zur Vollendung des 70. Lebenjahres, pp. 1–17. 1917.

5226 Bauerreiss (P. Rumuald). Irische Frühmissionäre in Sudbayern. Wiss. Festgabe zum 1200. Jubiläum des hl. Corbinian (München), hrsg. von J. Schlecht, pp. 43–60. 1924.

5227 Beyerle (Konrad), *ed.* Die Kultur der Abtei Reichenau. Erinnerungsschrift zur 1200. Wiederkehr des Gründungsjahres des Inselklosters 724–1924. 2 Bde. 4° München, 1925.

5228 Bigelmair (Andreas). Die Anfänge des Christentums in Bayern. Festgabe A. Knöpfler (60. Lebensjahr), pp. 1–24. 1907.

5229 Brownlow (William Robert Bernard), *bp. of Clifton.* The brother and sister of Saint Willibald. [Wunebald and Walburga. Missionaries among the Germans.] Rept. and Trans. Devon. Assoc., 23, pp. 225–38. 1891.

5230 —— St. Willibald : a west-country pilgrim of the eighth century. [Bp. of Eichstädt.] *Same jnl.,* 22, pp. 212–28. 1890.

5231 Doerries (Hermann). Germanische Religion und Sachsenbekehrung. 3. Auflage. pp. 37. 8° Göttingen, 1935.

5232 Falk (Franz). Die irischen Mönchen in Mainz. [Grant, c. 817, to Fulda for an Ecclesia Scottorum in Mainz.] Katholik, N.S. 20, pp. 311–16. 1868.

5233 Fischer (J.). Kann Bischof Johannes aus Irland mit Recht als erster Märtyrer Amerikas bezeichnet werden? [Martyred at Mecklenburg in 1066.] Zeit. kathol. Theol., 24, pp. 746–58. 1900.

5234 Flaskamp (Franz). Die Anfänge friesischen und sächsischen Christentums. *Geschichtliche Darstellungen und Quellen,* 9. pp. xvi, 81, + 2 plates. 8° Hildesheim, 1929.

5235 —— Die beiden Ewalde. 8° Münster, 1930. [Extracted from Westfälische Lebensbilder.]

5236 —— Das Hessen-Bistum Buraburg. Festgabe für L. Schmitz-Kallenberg, pp. 1–55, + 1 plate. 1927.

5237 —— Suidbercht, Apostel der Brukterer, Gründer von Kaiserwerth. pp. 30. 8° Duderstadt, 1930.

5238 Hauck (Albert). Kirchengeschichte Deutschlands. 5 Bde. 8° Leipzig, 1911–25. [Bd. 1 (1922), pp. 389–52, Die Thätigkeit der angelsächsischen Missionare in Deutschland und das Verhältnis zu Rom (Mission in Friesland, Bonifatius, etc.) : Bd. 2 (1912), Alkuin (passim), etc.] —Bd. 1, 7. Auflage. pp. viii, 584 : Bd. 2, 6. Auflage. pp. viii, 859. [Announced].

5239 Heber (   ). Die neun vormaligen Schottenkirchen in Mainz und in Oberhessen. Archiv hessische Geschichte, 9, pp. 193–348. 1860.

5240 Hogan (J. F.). Irish bishops of Strasburg. [SS. Arbogast, Florentius : 673–93]. Irish Eccles. Rec., 4th S. 12, pp. 481–90. 1902.

5241 —— Irish monasterias in Germany—Cologne. *Same jnl.,* 4th S. 3, pp. 526–35. 1898.

5242 —— Irish monasteries in Germany—Honau. [Founded 724 by abbot Tubanus.] *Same jnl.,* 4th S. 4, pp. 265–69. 1898.

5243 —— Irish monasteries in Germany. [Metz (7th c), Mainz (9th c.), etc.] *Same jnl.,* 4th S. 21, pp. 507–17. 1907.

5244 —— St. Colman, patron of Lower Austria. [11th c.] *Same jnl.* 3rd S., 15, pp. 673–81. 1894.

5245 Huber (Altons). Geschichte der Einführung und Verbreitung des Christentums in Sudöstdeutschland. 8° Salzburg, 1875.

5246 Juhasz (Koloman). St. Koloman der einstige Schutzpatron Nieder-Österreichs. 8° Linz, 1916. [Colman, d. 1014, buried at Melk on the Danube.] Theol. prakt. Quartalschrift, 69, pp. 552 *et seq.* 1916.

5247 Law (Hermann). Die angelsächsische Missionsweise im Zeitalter des Bonifaz. 8° Kiel, 1909.

5248 Morin (Germain). D'où est venu Saint Pirmin ? [Died c. 753. Founder of Reichenau. Probably a Scot.] Revue Charlemagne, 1, pp. 1–8. 1911.

5249 Neuss (Wilhelm). Die Anfänge des Christentums im Rheinlande. pp. 90. 8° Bonn, 1923.

5250 Pfleger (Lucien). Eine neue Interpretation der Urkunde des Abtes Beatus von Honau von Jahre 810. Archiv elsässische Kirchengesch., 7, pp. 375–77. 1932.

5251 Reeves (William), *bp. of Down.* On SS. Marinus and Anianus, two Irish missionaries of the seventh century. [Patron saints of the Benedictine monastery of Rot, on the Inn.] Proc. R.I.A., 8 (1863), pp. 295–300. 1864.

5252 —— On the Irish abbey of Honau on the Rhine. [Founded 724 by Tubanus or Benedict. Five miles below Strassburg : since submerged by the river.] Proc. R.I.A., 6 (1857), pp. 452–61. 1858.

5253 Ryan (John). Early Irish missionaries on the continent and St. Vergil of Salzburg. *Sheaf mission series,* 5. pp. 24. 8° Dublin, 1924.

5254 Sauer (Joseph). Die Anfänge des Christentums und der Kirche in Baden. pp. 130. 8° Heidelberg, 1911.

5255 Schieffer (Theodor). Angelsachsen und Franken. Zwei Studien zur Kirchengeschichte des 8. Jahrhunderts. [i. Bonifatius und Chrodegang : ii. Erzbischof Lull und die Anfänge des Mainzer Sprengels.] Akad. Wiss., Mainz: Abh. Geistes-u. Sozialwiss. Kl., 1 (no. 20), pp. 1427–1539. 1950.

5256 Scholle (J.). Das Erfurter Schottenkloster. 8° Dusseldorf, 1932.

5257 Schreiber (Georg). Iroschott-ische und angelsächsische Wanderkulte in Westfalen mit Ausblicken auf den gesamtdeutschen Raum. Westfalia sacra, 2 ii, pp. 1–132. 1951.

5258 Stenzel ( ), *Prof. in Breslau.* Ueber Marianus Scottus. [Monk of Fulda, d. 1086.] Archiv Gesell. ältere-deut. Geschichtskunde, 5, pp. 768–79. 1824.

5259 Sullivan (Richard G.). The Carolingian missionary and the pagan. Speculum, 28, pp. 705–40. 1953.

5260 Voigt (H. G.). Von der iroschott-ischen Mission in Hessen und Thürin-gen und Bonifatius' Verhältnis zu ihr. Theol. Stud. u. Kritiken, 103, pp. 254–60. 1931.

5261 Walderdoff (Hugo von). St. Mercherdach und St. Marian [Marianus Scottus] und die Anfänge des Schotten-klöster zu Regensburg. [Abbey of St. James founded 1090.] Verh. hist. Vereins von Oberpfalz u. Regensburg, 39, pp. 189–232. 1878.

5262 Wattenbach (Wilhelm). The Irish monasteries in Germany. [Trans-lated from **5263** and edited by William Reeves.] Ulster J. Archaeol., 7, pp. 227–47, 295–313. 1859.

5263 —— Die Kongregation der Scott-enklöster in Deutschland. Zeit. christl. Archäologie, 1, pp. 21–30, 49–58. 1856.

5264 Wiedemann (H.). Die Sachsen-bekehrung. *Veröffentlichungen Inst. mis-sionswiss. Forschung*: Missionswiss. Stud-ien, *n.R.*, 5. 8° Münster i. W., 1932.

5265 Wieland (M.). Das Schotten-kloster zu St. Jakob in Würzburg. Archiv hist. Vereins Unterfranken, 16, pp. 1–182. 1863.

§ *b*. **Boniface, Archbishop of Mainz**
(d. 755)
i. **His Works, and notes on them**

5266 Boniface, *St., abp. of Mainz.* Die Briefe des heiligen Bonifatius, her-ausgegeben von Michael Tangl. *Die Geschichtschreiber der deutschen Vorzeit*, 92. 8° Berlin, 1912.

5267 Boniface, *St., abp. of Mainz.* Die Briefe der heiligen Bonifatius und Lullus. Herausgegeben van Michael Tangl. (Epistolae selectae in usum schola-rum ex Monumentis Germaniae his-toricis separatim editae, fasc. 1). pp. xi, 321, + 3 plates. 8° Berlin, 1916. [Kenney 1, p. 520.]

5268 —— The English correspondence of Saint Boniface . . . translated and edited with . . . life by Edward Kylie. *King's classics.* pp. xiv, 212. 8° London, 1911.

5269 —— The letters of Saint Boniface. Translated, with an introduction by Ephraim Emerton. [Edited by George La Piana]. *Records of Civilization. Sources and studies*, 31. pp. 204. 8° New York, 1940.

5270 Fickermann (Norbert). Der Widmungsbrief des hl. Bonifatius. Neues Archiv, 50, pp. 210–21. 1935.

5271 Hahn (Heinrich). Bonifaz und Lul : ihre angelsächsischen Korres-pondenten. Erzbischof Luls Leben. pp. xii, 351. 8° Leipzig, 1883. [Gross, 1642. Much concerning Aldhelm, Egbert, abp. of York, etc.]

5272 La Piana (George). A note on chronology in the letters of St. Boniface. Speculum, 17, pp. 270–72. 1942.

5273 Loofs (Friedrich). Zur Chrono-logie der auf die fränkischen Synoden des hl. Bonifatius bezüglichen Briefe. 1881.

5274 Nuernberger (August Josef). Aus der litterarischen Hinterlassenschaft des hl. Bonifatius und des hl. Burchardus. Ber. Wiss. Gesell. Phil. in Neisse, 24, pp. 133–81. 1888.

5275 —— Dicta Bonifatii. Theol. Quartalschrift, 70, pp. 287 *et seq.* 1888.

5276 —— Verlorene Handschriften der Briefe des hl. Bonifatius. Neues Archiv, 7, pp. 355–81. 1881.

5277 Perels (Ernst). Hinkmar von Reims und die Bonifatiusbriefe. Neues Archiv, 48, pp. 156–60. 1930.

5278 Robinson (George Washington). Letters of Saint Boniface to the popes and others : first English translation. Papers Amer. Soc. Church Hist., 2nd S. 7, pp. 163 *et seq.* 1923.

5279 Tangl (Michael). Studien zur Neuausgabe der Bonifatius-Briefe [M.G.H.]. Neues Archiv, 40, pp. 641–790 : 41, pp. 23–101. 1916–19.

5280 Traube (Ludwig). Die älteste Handschrift der Aenigmata Bonifatii. (Anhang von E. Dümmler). Neues Archiv, 27, pp. 211–16. 1902.

ii. Lives

(By Willibald, etc.), **and notes on them**

5281 Levison (Wilhelm), *ed.* Vita Sancti Bonifatii. *Pertz (G. H.) : Scriptores rerum Germanicarum.* pp. lxxxvi, 241. 8° Hannoverae, 1905.

5282 Mueller (Karl Otto). Eine neue Handschrift (Bruchstück) der Vita s. Bonifatii von Otloh. Neues Archiv, 41, pp. 691–704. 1919.

5283 Tangl (Michael). Leben des hl. Bonifazius von Wilibald bis Otloh, der hl. Leoba von Rudolf von Fulda, des Abtes Sturmi von Eigil. Nach den Ausgaben der Monumenta Germaniae übersetzt. 3. vollständig neubearbeitete Auflage. pp. xxix, 144. 8° Leipzig, 1920.

5284 Waitz (Georg). Ueber eine Bearbeitung der Vita Bonifatii des Willibald. [In Brussels, MS. 18644, 12th c. *See* **5287.**] Neues Archiv, 8, pp. 169–71. 1883.

5285 Willibaldus, *presbyter.* The life of Saint Boniface. . . . Translated . . . for the first time, with introduction and notes by George Washington Robinson. *Harvard Translations.* pp. 114. 8° Cambridge, *Mass.,* 1916.

5286 —— La recension abrégée de la vie de S. Boniface par Willibald. Anal. Boll., 15, pp. 268–70. 1896.

5287 —— Vita Sancti Bonifacii . . . secundum priorem, ut videtur, conscriptionem, nunc primum edita. [MS. Bibl. Reg. Brux., 18644–52.] Anal. Boll., 1, pp. 49–72. 1882.

5288 —— *etc.* Vitae sancti Bonifatii archiepiscopi Moguntini. Recognovit W. Levison. *Script. rerum Germ.,* 48. pp. lxxxvi, 241. 8° Hannoverae, 1905.

5289 Woelbing (Gustav). Die mittelalterlichen Lebensbeschreibung des Bonifatius, ihrem Inhalte nach untersucht, verglichen und erläutert. pp. viii, 160. 8° Leipzig, 1892.

iii. Miscellaneous

5290 Barber (Henry). The shrine of St. Boniface at Fulda. Western Antiquary, 9, pp. 146–49. 1890.

5291 Betten (Francis Sales). St. Boniface and St. Virgil : a study from the original sources of two supposed conflicts ; a contribution to the history of the eighth century. *Benedictine historical monographs,* 2. pp. 76. 8° Brookland, D.C., 1927.

5292 Bishop (Edmund). St. Boniface and his correspondence. Rept. and Trans. Devon. Assoc., 8, pp. 497–516. 1876.

5293 Boehmer (Heinrich). Zur Geschichte des Bonifatius. [Pp. 210–15, Chronological table of his life.] Zeit. Vereins hess. Gesch., 50 (N.F. 40), pp. 171–215. 1917.

5294 Browne (George Forrest), *bp. of Bristol.* Boniface of Crediton and his companions. pp. x, 372. 8° London, 1910. [Gross, p. 321.]

5295 Brownlow (William Robert Bernard), *bp. of Clifton.* St. Boniface and St. Virgilius. [Reply by B. MacCarthy, pp. 205–06, on identity of Virgilius.] Irish Eccles. Rec., 3rd S. 6, pp. 53–59. 1885.

5296 —— Saint Boniface in England. Rept. and Trans. Devon. Assoc., 24, pp. 151–62. 1892.

5297 —— Was St. Boniface an Irishman ?—Saint Boniface in his relations with the Irish. *Same jnl.,* 16, pp. 581–89. 1884.

5298 Buss (Franz Joseph von). Winfrid-Bonifacius. Herausgegeben von Rudolf, Ritter von Scherer. pp. viii, 396. 8° Graz, 1880. [Gross, 1639.]

5299 Cox (*Sir* George William), *bart.* The life of Saint Boniface. pp. viii, 165. 8° London, 1853.

5300 Ebrard (Johann Heinrich August). Bonifatius der Zerstörer des columbanischen Kirktums auf dem Festlande : ein Nachtrag zu dem Werke : Die iroschottische Missions Kirche [**5132**]. pp. viii, 258. 8° Gütersloh, 1882. [Gross, 1640.]

5301 Erdmann (Christian Friedrich David). Winfried oder Bonifacius. 8° Berlin, 1855.

5302 Fabricus (Rudolphus Antonius), *resp.* Observationes miscellaneae ex historia Bonifacii selectae. *Praes.* H. P. Gudenio. 4° Helmstadii, [1720].

5303 Fischer (Otto). Bonifatius. Nach den Quellen dargestellt. pp. 295. 8° Leipzig, 1881. [Gross, 1641.]

5304 Flaskamp (Franz). Auf hessischen Bonifatiuspfaden. pp. 29. 8° Münster, 1924.

5305 —— Bonifatius und die Sachsenmission. Zeit. Missionswiss., 6, 1916.

5306 —— Das Geburtsjahr des Wynfrith-Bonifatius. Zeit. Kirchengesch., 45 (N.F. 8), pp. 339–44. 1927.

5307 —— Das hessische Missionswerk des heiligen Bonifatius. 2. Auflage. pp. xxiv, 143. 8° Duderstadt, 1926.

5308 —— Die homilitische Wirksamkeit des hl. Bonifatius. *Geschichtliche Darstellungen und Quellen*, 7. pp. xxiii, 40. 8° Hildesheim, 1926.

5309 —— Die Missionsmethod des hl. Bonifatius. Zeit. Missionswissenschaft, 15, pp. 89–93. 1925. *Same title*, 2. Auflage. *Geschichtliche Darstellungen und Quellen*, 8. pp. xviii, 62. 8° Hildesheim, 1929.

5310 —— Das Todesjahr des heiligen Bonifatius. Hist. Jb., 27 (Bd. 47), pp. 473–88. 1927.

5311 —— Zur Hessenbekehrung des Bonifatius. Zeit. Missionswiss., 13, pp. 135–52. 1923.

5312 Goodchild (W.). St. Boniface and Somerset. [? born near Weston-super-Mare, not Crediton. Evidence from charter of Forthere, 2nd bp. of Sherborne to monastery at Bleadon.] N. and Q. Som. and Dorset, 11, pp. 172–73. 1909.

5313 Hahn (Heinrich). Die Namen der Bonifazischen Briefe in Liber Vitae ecclesiae Dunelmensis. Neues Archiv, 12, pp. 111–27. 1886.

5314 Harrison (Henry). The vernacular form of abjuration and of confession of faith used by the 8th century German converts of the Devonian Wynfrith, St. Boniface. pp. 7. 8° London, 1914.

5315 Healy (John), *abp. of Tuam,* and **Brownlow** (William Robert Bernard), *bp. of Clifton.* The nationality of St. Boniface. Irish Eccles. Rec., 3rd S. 5, pp. 115–21, 190–91, 259–64. 1884.

5316 Heinrich (J. B.). Das Leben und Wirken des heiligen Bonifacius. 8° Mainz, 1855.

5317 Hess (Heinrich Maria von). Vie de saint Boniface. Douze planches gravées d'après les fresques peintes par H. dans l'église Saint-Boniface, à Munich. Texte par M. Bathild Bouniol. Oblong fol. Paris, [1869].

5318 Hoefler (Constantin), *Ritter von.* Bonifatius . . . und die Slavenapostel Konstantinos (Cyrillus) und Methodius. pp. 64. 8° Prag, 1887.

5319 Hope (*Mrs.* Anne). The conversion of the Teutonic race. . . . S. Boniface and the conversion of Germany. Revised edition. pp. xxiv, 313. 8° London, [1892]. [Gross, 1643.]

5320 Keitz (A. von). Die Codices Bonifationi in der Landesbibliothek zu Fulda. *Hessenland*, 4. 1890.

5321 Koch (H.). Die Stellung des Heiligen Bonifatius zur Bildung und Wissenschaft. 8° Braunsberg, 1905. [Gross, p. 321.]

5322 Koehler (Walther). Bonifatius in Hessen und das hessische Bistum Buraburg. Zeit. Kirchengesch., 25, pp. 197–232. 1904.

5323 —— Dettic und Deorulf, die ersten von Bonifaz belehrten hessischen Christen. Mitteil. oberhess. Geschichtsvereins, N.F. 10, pp. 120–24. 1901.

5324 Kuhlmann (Bernhard). Der heilige Bonifatius. pp. xiv, 504. 8° Paderborn, 1895. [Gross, 1644.]

5325 Kurth (Godefroid Joseph François). Saint Boniface, 680–755. 2e édition. (Appendice.—Bibliographie critique de saint Boniface). *Les saints.* pp. iv, 195. 8° Paris, 1902.

5326 —— Saint Boniface, 680–755, translated by Victor Day and with insertions from the latest historical findings by F. S. Betten. pp. xiii, 178. 8° Milwaukie, 1935. [Gross, p. 321.]

5327 Kylie (Edward J.). The condition of the German provinces as illustrating the methods of St. Boniface. J. Theol. stud., 7, pp. 29–39. 1906.

5328 Lampen (Willibrord). Willibrord en Bonifatius. *Patria,* 16. pp. 159, + plates. 8° Amsterdam, 1939. —Winfried-Bonifatius. 2e druk. *Patria,* 45. pp. 144, + plates. 8° Amsterdam, 1949.

5329 Laux (Johann Joseph). Der heilige Bonifatius. pp. xii, 307. 8° Freiburg i. Br., 1922.

5330 —— Two early medieval heretics : an episode in the life of St. Boniface. [Aldebert and Clement.] Cath. Hist. Rev., 21, pp. 190–95. 1935.

5331 Loeffler (Josias Friedrich Christian), *ed.* Bonifacius, oder Feyer des Andenkens an die erste christliche Kirche in Thüringen, bey Altenberga. —Nebst einer historischen Nachricht von seinem Leben. 8° Gotha, 1812.

5332 Luebeck (Konrad). Das Bonifatiusgrab zu Fulda. pp. 152. 8° Fulda, 1947.

5333 Merivale (Charles), *dean of Ely.* President's address [to the Devonshire Association, on St. Boniface]. Rept. and Trans. Devon. Assoc., 15, pp. 33–51. 1883.

5334 Mitterer (P. Sigisbert). Die Bedeutung des hl. Bonifazius für das bayerische Klosterwesen. Stud. u. Mitt. z. Gesch. d. Benediktiner Ordens, 46 (N.F. 15), pp. 333–60. 1928.

5335 —— Die bischöflichen Eigenklöster in den von hl. Bonifazius 739 gegründeten bayerischen Diözesen. *Studien und Mitteilungen zur Geschichte des Benediktiner-Ordens. Ergänzungsheft* 2. pp. 158. 8°. München, 1929.

5336 Moran (Patrick Francis), *cardinal, abp. of Sydney.* Was St. Boniface an Irishman ? Irish Eccles. Rec., 3rd S. 5, pp. 181–190. 1884.

5337 Mueller (Johan Peter). Bonifacius : eene kerkhistorische studie. 2 pts. 8° Amsterdam, 1869–70. [Gross, 1645.]

5338 Nuernberger (August Josef). Die angebliche Unechtheit der Predigten des h. Bonifatius. Neues Archiv, 14, pp. 109–34. 1888.

5339 —— Die Bonifatius-Litteratur der Magdeburger Centuriatoren. Neues Archiv, 11, pp. 9–41. 1886.

5340 Pfahler (Georg). St. Bonifacius und seine Zeit. pp. vi, 396. 8° Regensburg, 1880. [Gross, 1646.]

5341 Preisinger (Werner). Die Weltanschauung des Bonifatius. Eine Untersuchung sur Überfremdung deutschen Wesens durch die christliche Mission. pp. 126. 8° Stuttgart, 1939.

5342 Reinerding (Franz Heinrich). Der heil. Bonifazius als Apostel der Deutschen mit Bezugnahme auf sein Verhältniss zu Fulda, *etc.* 8° Würtzburg, 1855.

5343 Richter (Gregor) and **Scherer** (Karl). Festgabe zum Bonifatius-Jubiläum, 1905. i. Beiträge zur Geschichte der Grabeskirche des hl. Bonifatius in Fulda, von G. Richter. ii. Die Codices Bonifatiani in der Landesbibliothek zu Fulda, von Karl Scherer. pp. vi, lxxvi, iv, 37, + 4 plates. 8° Fulda, 1905.

5344 S. (C.) and **B.** (C. C.). St. Boniface at Nursling. Hampshire Antiquary, 1, pp. 132–33, 136. 1891.

5345 Sante (Georg Wilhelm). Bonifatius und die Begründung des Mainzer Erzbistums. Hist. Jb. 57, pp. 157–79. 1937.

5345a Schieffer (Theodor). Winfrid-Bonifatius und die christliche Grundlegung Europas. pp. xii, 326, + 2 maps. [Announced].

5346 Schmerbauch (Moritz). Bonifacius, . . . mit besonderer Berücksichtigung der Geschichte des heiligen Kilianus, des heiligen Ruprecht, des Abtes Lullus und anderer Mitarbeiter dieses Apostels. 2. Ausgabe. 8° Fulda, 1829.

5347 Schmidt (K. Dietrich). Boniface, founder of spiritual unity in the west. Church Q. Rev., 154, pp. 269–81. 1953.

5348 Schnuerer (Gustav). Bonifatius. Die Bekehrung der Deutschen zum Christentum. pp. viii, 110. 8° Mainz, 1909.

5349 Schwarz (Ignaz). Der heilige Winfried Bonifacius. 8° Fulda, 1855. [Life, in verse.]

5350 Seiters (J. Ch. A.). Bonifacius, *etc.* 8° Mainz, 1845.

5351 Serland (F. S.). The controversy concerning baptism under St. Boniface. [Kenney, 1, p. 520.] Am. Cath. Q. Rev., 42, pp. 270–75. 1917.

5352 Smith (Isaac Gregory). Boniface. *The Fathers for English readers.* pp. 106. 8° London, 1896.

5353 Stephan (John). Some notes on Saint Boniface. [i. Birthplace : ii. What sort of man was St. Boniface ? iii. Veneration in England.] Rept. and Trans. Devon. Assoc., 83, pp. 259–66. 1951.

5354 Tangl (Michael). Bonifatiusfragen. pp. 41. Abh. preuss. Akad. Wiss., Phil.-hist. Kl., 1919 ii. 1919.

5355 —— Das Todesjahr des Bonifatius. Zeit. Vereins hess. Gesch., 37 (N.F. 27), pp. 223–50. 1903.

5356 Traub (Gottfried). Bonifatius : ein Lebensbild. pp. vii, 223. 8° Leipzig, 1894. [Gross, 1647. 'A popular account.']

5357 Werner (August). Bonifacius . . . und die Romanisierung von Mitteleuropa. 8° Leipzig, 1875. [Gross, 1648.]

5358 Williamson (James Mann). The life and times of St. Boniface. pp. iv, 137. 8° Ventnor, 1904. [Gross, p. 321.]

5359 Wissig (Otto). Iroschotten und Bonifatius in Deutschland. pp. 255. 8° Gütersloh, 1932.

5360 —— Wynfrid, Bonifatius, ein Charakterbild nach seinen Briefen gezeichnet. 8° Gütersloh, 1929.

5361 Zehetbauer (Fritz). Das Kirchenrecht bei Bonifatius. Nach den Quellen bearbeitet. pp. vii, 140. 8° Wien, 1910.

5362 Zehrs (C.). Die Einführung des Christenthums auf dem Eichsfelde durch den Hl. Bonifacius. 8° 1847.

§ *c.* Fulda

(Benedictine abbey, founded in 744 at the instigation of St. Boniface by his pupil Sturm, who became its first abbot. Reformed by monks from Scotland, early 10th c. Alcuin was among its teachers.)

5363 Beumann (Helmut) and **Grossman** (Dieter). Das Bonifatiusgrab und die Klosterkirchen zu Fulda. Marburger Jb. Kunstwiss., 14, pp. 17–56. 1949.

5364 Beumann (Helmut). Eigils Vita Sturmi und die Anfänge der Klöster Hersfeld und Fulda. [*See also* pp. 193–94 (D. Heller : Entgegnung und H. Beumann : Schlusswort).] Hessisches Jb. f. LG., 2, pp. 1–15. 1952.

5365 —— Zur Fuldaer Geschichte, Literaturbericht. *Same jnl.*, 1, pp. 211–17. 1951.

5366 Dronke (E. F. J.). Bemerkungen über die ältesten Fuldaer Privilegien and Immanitätsurkunden. Zeit. Vereins hessische Gesch., 4, pp. 360–82. 1847.

5367 —— Zur Chronologie der Fuldaer Aebte von Sturmi bis Marcward I, [744–1165]. *Same jnl.*, 5, pp. 29–38. 1850.

5368 Flaskamp (Franz). Zum Leben Sturms von Fulda. Ein Desiderat. Zeit. Kirchengesch., 44 (N.F. 7), pp. 486–88. 1925.

5369 Fulda, *Abbey.* Urkundenbuch des Klosters Fulda, . . . 1. Bd., 1. Hälfte (Die Zeit des Abtes Sturmi.) Bearbeitet von E. E. Stengel. *Veröffentlichungen des Historischen Kommission für Hessen,* 10. pp. ix, 202. 8° Marburg, 1913.

5370 Gegenbaur (J.). Das Kloster Fulda in Karolinger Zeitalter. Erstes Buch. 3 pt. 8° Fulda, 1871–74.

5371 Goetting (Hans). Die Anfänge des Reichsstifts Gandersheim 2 : Die Frage der Fuldaer Mission nördlich des Harzes und das Bonifatiuskloster Brunshausen, Braunschweig. Marburger Jb. Kunstwiss., 31, pp. 11–27. 1950.

5372 Heller (Dominikus). Quellen-studien zur Frühgeschichte des Klosters Fulda. pp. 131. 8° Fulda, 1949.

5373 Hellmann (Siegmund). Die Annales Fuldenses. [*See also* : pp. 778–85, reply by its editor, Friedrich Kurze.] Neues Archiv, 37, pp. 53–65. 1912.

5374 —— Die Entstehung und Ueber-lieferung der Annales Fuldenses. Neues Archiv, 33, pp. 695–742 : 34, pp. 15–66. 1909.

5375 Kurze (Friedrich). Die Annales Fuldenses. (Entgegnung). Neues Ar-chiv, 17, pp. 83–158 : 36, pp. 343–93 : 37, pp. 778–85. 1891, 1911–12.

5376 Luebeck (Konrad). Der erste Diözesanbischof des Klosters Fulda. Zeit. Rechtsges., 81, Kanon. Abt., 37, pp. 360–76. 1951.

5377 —— Die Fuldaer Abtswahl-privilegien. *Same jnl.*, 79, Kanon. Abt., 35, pp. 340–89. 1948.

5378 —— Fuldaer Heilige. pp. 239. 8° Fulda, 1947.

5379 —— Fuldaer Nebenklöster in Mainfranken. Mainfrank. Jb., 2, pp. 1–52. 1950.

5380 —— Fuldaer Studien, Geschicht-liche Abhandlungen 1 und 2. pp. 208, 258. 8° Fulda, 1949–50.

5381 —— Der Hofämter der Fuldaer Äbte im frühen Mittelalter. Zeit. Rechts-ges, 78, Germ. Abt., 65, pp. 177–207. 1947.

5382 —— Eine iroschottische Mis-sionsstation in Fulda. Fuldaer Studien, 2, pp. 85–112. 1950.

5383 —— Das Kloster Fulda und die Päpste in den Jahren 1046–1075. Studi Gregoriani, 1, pp. 459–89. 1947.

5384 —— Die Ministerialen der Reichs-abtei Fulda. Zeit. Rechtsgesch., 79, Kanon. Abt., 35, pp. 201–33. 1948.

5385 —— Die Reichsabtei Fulda im Investiturstreite. Studi Gregoriani, 4, pp. 149–69. 1952.

5386 Maurer (Karl). 1200 Jahre Fulda, 744–1944. pp. 63, + 16 plates. 8° Fulda, 1944.

5387 Muegge (Helmut). Studien zur Geschichte der fuldisch-mainzischen Beziehungen von 8. bis 11. Jahrhundert. *Diss. Marburg.* pp. 179. 8° Marburg, 1951.

5388 Richter (Gregor), *ed.* Quellen und Abhandlungen zur Geschichte der Abtei und der Diözese Fulda. 8° Fulda, 1904.

5389 Schannat (Johann Friedrich). Corpus traditionum Fuldensium . . . complectens omnes . . . donationes in ecclesiam Fuldensem, *etc.* pp. 440. fol. Lipsiae, 1724.

5390 —— Historia Fuldensis. 2 vol. fol. Frankfurti ad Moenum, 1729.

5391 Schneider (Joseph). Nachträge zur Fuldaischen Geschichte. Zeit. Ver-eins hess. Gesch., 2, pp. 188–216. 1840.

5392 Sepp (Bernhard). Zur Fuldaer Privilegienfrage. pp. 22. 8° Regensburg, 1908.

5393 Stengel (Edmund Ernst). Fuld-ensia. [5, pp. 54–77, Die Umgrenzungs-urkunde des Erzbischofs Bonifatius : pp. 141–47, Rudolf von Fulda und die karolinischen Cartulare des Klosters Fulda.] Arch. Urkundenforschung, 5, pp. 41–152 : 7, pp. 1–46. 1914, 1921.

5394 —— Die Reichsabtei Fulda in der deutschen Geschichte. pp. 38. 8° Weimar, 1948.

5395 —— Zur Frühgeschichte der Reichsabtei Fulda. Zugleich ein Liter-aturbericht, [here abstracted]. Deut. Archiv Erforschung Mittelalters, 9, pp. 513–34. 1952.

5396 Tangl (Michael). Die Urkunde Ludwig d. Fr. für Fulda von 4. August 817. Mühlbacher 656 (642). [Latin text.] Neues Archiv, 27, pp. 11–34. 1902.

5397 Vonderau (Joseph). Die Gründ-ung des Klosters Fulda und seine Bauten bis zum Tode Sturms. pp. 48, + 28 plates. 8° Fulda, 1944.

5398 Waitz (Georg). Hersfelder An-nalen. 2. Annales Fuldenses, Lobienses, Monasterienes, Marianus Scotus. Ar-chiv Gesellschaft ältere deut. Geschichts-kunde, 6, pp. 670–75. 1838.

§ *d.* **Kilian, Apostle of Franconia**
(Born in Ireland, d. 689)

5399 Bischoff (Bernhard) and **Hofmann** (J.). Libri Sancti Kyliani : die Würzburger Schreibschule und die Dombibliothek im viii. und ix. Jahrhundert. *Quellen und Forschungen zur Geschichte des Bistums und Hochstifts Würzburg*, 6. 8° Würzburg, 1952.

5400 Douai, *Public Library*. Catalogus codicum hagiographicorum latinorum bibliothecae publicae Duacenis. Appendix 5. Vita S. Killiani confessoris Albiniacensis. [MSS. 857 and 840.] Anal. Boll., 20, pp. 432–44. 1901.

5401 Emmerich (Franz). Der heilige Kilian . . . historisch-kritisch dargestellt. pp. xii, 134. 8° Würzburg, 1896.

5402 Goepfert (Fritz Adam). St. Kilianus-Büchlein. 2. Auflage. pp. 182. 8° Würzburg, 1902. [Kenney, 1, p. 512.]

5403 Hennig (John). Ireland and Germany in the tradition of St. Kilian. Irish Eccles. Rec., 5th S. 78, pp. 21–33. 1952.

5404 Hogan (J. F.). St. Killian of Würzburg. Irish Eccles. Rec., 3rd S. 11, pp. 385–98. 1890.

5405 Riezler (S.). Die Vita Kiliani. [Kenney, 1, p. 512.] Neues Archiv, 28, pp. 232–34. 1903.

74. MISSIONARIES TO THE CONTINENT
4. IN ITALY
§ *a.* **General**

(Cataldus, bp. of Taranto, 6th or 7th c. : Frediano, bp. of Lucca, c. 560–588 ; etc.)

5406 Brown (J. Wood). San Viano : a Scottish saint. [Cult in the Garfagnana. ?=Italian rendering of Celtic Fian. ' Probably belonged to the movement associated with the greater name of Columbanus.' Scot. H.R., 9, pp. 387–89. 1912.

5407 Fanucchi (Giuseppe). Vita di S. Frediano, vescovo di Lucca, e notizie dei suoi tempi. 8° Lucca, 1870. [Kenney, 1, p. 185. Bp., c. 560–88.]

S

5408 Hoerle (G. H.). Frühmittelalterliche Mönchs- und Klerikerbildung in Italien. 8° Freiburg-in-Br., 1914.

5409 Hogan (J. F.). Irish saints in Italy. [St. Frigidian (i.e. Frediano), bp. of Lucca (6th c.) : Sillan and Mingarda (his contemporaries there) : St. Donatus, bp. of Fiesole (8th c.), etc.] Irish Eccles. Rec., 4th S. 13, pp. 406–17. 1903.

5410 —— St. Cathaldus of Taranto. *Same jnl.*, 3rd S. 17, pp. 403–16. 1896.

5411 Le Schonix (Roach). Irish saints in Italy. Antiquary, 26, pp. 65–69. 1892.

5412 Mercati (Angelo). San Pellegrino delle Alpi in Garfagnana. 8° Roma, 1926.

5413 Pettito (Remo Renato). Santi irlandesi in Italia. Report of the 31st Eucharistic Congress, Dublin, 2. 1934.

5414 Stokes (Margaret MacNair). Six months in the Apennines, or a pilgrimage in search of vestiges of the Irish saints in Italy. pp. xiv, 313. 8° London, 1892. [Kenney, 1, p. 183. ' Uncritical.']

5415 Tommasini (Anselmo Maria). I santi irlandesi in Italia. pp. 443. 8° Milano, 1932. —. Irish saints in Italy. Translated, with some additional notes, by J. F. Scanlon. pp. 532. 8° Edinburgh, 1937.

5416 Tononi (A. Gaetano). Ospizio pei pelligrini irlandesi. 8° Strenna Piacentina, 1891. [Kenney, p. 602. Church in district of Piacenza granted by (Irish) Donatus, bp. of Fiesole in 850 to monastasy of Bobbio : hospice afterwards added.]

§ *b.* **Columban** (543–615)
i. **His works (Rule, etc.) and notes on them**

5417 Ascoli (Graziadio Isaia). Il codice Irlandese dell' Ambrosiana. [Kenney, 1, p. 200. Reproduction of text of c. 301 inf. (8th–9th c.), a commentary on the psalms attributed to Columbanus.] Archivio glottologico Ital., 5, pp. 1–610. 1878.

5418 Bieler (Ludwig). Versus Sancti Columbani. Irish Eccles. Rec., 6th S. 76, pp. 376–82. 1951.

5419 Domenici (G.). San Colombano, il testa della ' Regula monachorum', del ' Ordo de vitas et actione monachorum ' e dell' ' Oratio '. [Kenney, 1, p. 187.] Riv. Stor. benedittina, 11, pp. 185–202. 1920.

5420 Gundlach (Wilhelm). Ueber die Columbanus-Briefe. [Kenney, 1, p. 189.] Neues Archiv, 15, pp. 497–526 : 17, pp. 425–29. 1890–92.

5421 Hay (Malcolm Vivian). Columbanus and Rome. [Errors arising from Skene's mistranslation (in Celtic Scotland, vol. 2, p. 7) of Columbanus' letter to the pope (in Migne's Patrologia, 80, col. 275) re attitude of Celtic Church on Easter controversy.] Rev. celt., 38, pp. 315–18. 1921.

5422 Hertel (G.). Über des heiligen Columban Leben und Schriften, besonders über seine Klosterregel. [Kenney, 1, p. 186.] Zeit. hist. Theol., 45, pp. 396–454. 1875.

5423 Krusch (Bruno). Zur Mönchsregel Columbans. Neues Archiv, 44, pp. 148–55. 1926.

5424 Laux (John Joseph), [**Metlake** (George), *pseud.*] Saint Columban and the penitential discipline. [Kenney, 1, p. 200.] Ecclesiastical Rev., 50, pp. 663–73. 1913.

5425 Mitchell (Gerard). St. Columbanus on penance. Irish Theol. Q., 18, pp. 43–54. 1951.

5426 Morin (Germain). Explication d'un passage de la règle de S. Colomban relatif à l'office des moines celtique. [Kenney, 1, p. 197.] Rev. Bénédictine, 12, pp. 200–01. 1895.

5427 —— Le Liber S. Columbani in Psalmos et le MS. Ambros. c. 301 inf. *Same jnl.*, 38, pp. 164–77. 1926.

5428 Pellizzari (A.). S. Colombano e le lettere. Scuola cattolica, 1923, pp. 524 *et seq.* 1923.

5429 Roche (Thomas). The Rule of St. Columbanus. Irish Theol. Q., 13, pp. 220–32. 1918.

5430 Seebass (Otto). Ein Beitrag zur Rekonstruktion der Regel Columbas des Jüngeren. Zeit. Kirchengesch., 40 (N.F. 3), pp. 132–37. 1922.

5431 Seebass (Otto). Ordo sancti Columbani abbatis de vita et actione monachorum. [With Latin text.] *Same jnl.*, 14, pp. 77–92. 1894.

5432 —— Das Poenitantiale Columbani. [With Latin text.] *Same jnl.*, 14, pp. 430–48. 1894.

5433 —— Regula coenobialis S. Columbani abbatis. [With Latin text.] *Same jnl.*, 17, pp. 215–34. 1897.

5434 —— Regula monachorum sancti Columbani abbatis. [With Latin text.] *Same jnl.*, 15, pp. 366–86. 1895.

5435 —— Über Columba von Luxeuils Klosterregel und Bussbuch. *Diss.*, Dresden, 1883. pp. 66. [Kenney, 1, p. 197.] 8° Dresden, 1883.

5436 —— Über die beiden Columba Handschriften der Nationalbibliothek in Turin. [Kenney, 1, p. 196.] Neues Archiv, 21, pp. 739–46. 1896.

5437 —— Über die Handschriften der Sermonem und Briefe Columbas von Luxeuil. [Kenney, 1, p. 189.] Neues Archiv, 17, pp. 245–59. 1892.

5438 —— Über die sogennanten Instructiones Columbani. [Kenney, 1, p. 196.] Zeit. Kirchengesch., 13, pp. 513–34. 1892.

5439 —— Über die sogennanten Regula coenobialis Columbani und die mit dem Pönitential Columbas verbundenen kleineren Zusätze. [Kenney, 1, p. 199.] *Same jnl.*, 18, pp. 58–76. 1898.

5440 —— Zu Columba von Luxeuils Klosterregel und Bussbuch. [Kenney, 1, p. 197.] *Same jnl.*, 8, pp. 459–65. 1886.

ii. Life (Jonas) and notes on it.

5441 Concannon (Helena). Jonas of Bobbio, biographer of St. Columban. Studies, 39, pp. 301–06. 1950.

5442 Jonas, *abbas Elnonensis*. Vitae Columbani abbatis discipulorumque eius libri duo auctore Iona. *Monumenta Germaniae historica, script. rerum Merovingicarum*, 4. *Passiones vitaeque Sanctorum*, pp. 1–156 : 7, pp. 822–27. 4° Hannoverae, 1902, 1920.

5443 Jonas, *abbas Elnonensis*. Vitae sanctorum Columbani, Vedastis, Iohannis. Recognovit Bruno Krusch. *Scriptores rerum Germ.*, 25. ˙pp. xii, 366. 8° Hannoverae, 1905. [Pp.1–294, Columbanus.]

5444 Krusch (Bruno). Eine englische Studie über die Handschriften der Vita Columbani. [Kenney, 1, p. 204.] Neues Archiv, 29, pp. 445–63. 1904.

5445 Lawlor (Hugh Jackson). The manuscripts of the Vita S. Columbani. Trans. R.I.A., 32c, pp. 1–32, + 18 plates. 1903.

iii. In France (Brie, Luxeuil : 590–610)

5446 Baumont (Henri). Étude historique sur l'abbaye de Luxeuil, 590–1790. pp. ii, 114. 8° Luxeuil, 1895. [Kenney, 1, p. 186.]

5447 Beauséjours (E. de). Les moines de Luxeuil et les forêts des Vosges. Mém. Académie sc. Besançon, 93, pp. 184–204. 1892.

5448 —— Le monastère de Luxeuil. 8° Besançon, 1901.

5449 Bonet-Maury (Gaston). Saint Colomban et la fondation des monastères irlandaises en Brie au viie siècle. Rev. hist., 83, pp. 277–99. 1903.

5450 Digot (Auguste). St. Columban et Luxeuil. 1840. [Kenney, 1, p. 186.]

5451 Gougaud (Louis). Un point obscur de l'itinéraire de Saint Colomban venant en Gaule. [Translated in Celtic Rev., 5, pp. 171–85, 1908.] Ann. Bretagne, 22, pp. 327–43. 1907.

5452 Holmes (Thomas Scott). The origin and development of the Christian Church in Gaul during the first six centuries of the Christian era. *Birkbeck Lectures, Cambridge,* 1907 *and* 1908. pp. xiv, 584. 8° London, 1911. [Pp. 540–67, St. Columbanus.]

5453 Malnory (A.). Quid Luxovienses monachi discipuli Sancti Columbani, ad regulam monasteriorum atque ad communem ecclesiae profectum contulerint. *Thesis.* 8° Parisiis, 1894. [Kenney, 1, p. 187.]

5454 Mériot ( ). Colomban ou le Christianisme dans l'Est. [Kenney, 1, p. 775.] Mém. Soc. d'Émulation de Montbéliard, pp. 113–264. 1923.

5455 O'Carroll (James). The Luxeuil congress in honour of the fourteenth centenary of St. Columban, July, 1950. Irish Eccles. Rec., 5th S. 75, pp. 490–98 : 76, pp. 37–43. 1951.

5456 Roussel (J.). Le Monasterium Salicis et son identification. [Mentioned by Jonas as close to Luxeuil and founded at end of 6th c. as that abbey expanded]. Rev. Charlemagne, 1, pp. 65–80. 1910.

5457 Shahan (Thomas Joseph). Saint Columbanus at Luxeuil. [Kenney, 1, p. 186.] Amer. Cath. Q.R., 127, pp. 54–78. 1902.

iv. Bobbio

(for Bobbio Library and manuscripts, *see* **110§bi.**)

5458 Bertacchi (Daniele). Monografia di Bobbio, ovvero cenni storici, statistici, topografici ed economici. pp. viii, 275. 8° Pinerolo, 1859. [Kenney, 1, p. 186.]

5459 Cambiaso (Domenico). San Colombano, sua opera e suo culto in Liguria. [Kenney, 1, p. 186.] Riv. diocesana Genovese, 6, pp. 121–25. 1916.

5460 Chute (Desmond). On St. Columban of Bobbio. [i. Bobbio : an Irish monastery ? ii. Did St. Columban pass through Britain ?] Downside Rev., 67, pp. 170–82, 304–12. 1949.

5461 Cipolla (Carlo), *count*. Una 'adbreviatio' inedita dei beni dell' abbazia di Bobbio. [9th c.] Riv. stor. benedettina, 1, pp. 14–30. 1906.

5462 Curti-Pasini (G. B.). Il culto di San Colombano in San-Colombano al Gambro. 8° Lodi, 1923. [Kenney, 1, p. 775.]

5463 Hartmann (Ludo Moritz). Zur Wirtschafts des Klosters Bobbio im 9. Jahrhunderts. *In his* Zur Wirtschaftsgeschichte Italiens im frühen Mittelalter. 8° Gotha, 1904.

5464 Martin (Léon Eugène). Bobbio. L'ombre d'un grand nom. [Account of the foundation of the monastery.] Mémoires de l'Académie de Stanislas (Nancy), série 6, 3, pp. 260–329. 1906.

5465 Rossetti (Benedetto). Bobbio illustrato. 3 vol. 8° Torino, 1795. [Kenney, 1, p. 186.]

5466 Stafford (L. J.). Ireland at Bobbio. Irish Eccles. Rec., 5th S. 22, pp. 449–58. 1923.

5467 Uhlirz (Mathilde). Das Kloster Bobbio im Zeitalter der Ottonen. Zeit. hist. Vereins Steiermark, 26, pp. 20–35. 1931.

v. Miscellaneous

5468 [Anon.] An Irish missionary of the sixth century and his work. Irish Eccles. Rec., 5, pp. 408–33. 1868.

5469 Albers (Bruno). S. Colombano —sue fondazioni e sua regola. Riv. stor. benedettina, 10, pp. 38–49. 1915.

5470 Besser (Wilhelm Friedrich). Der heilige Columban. Ein Lebensbild aus der alten Kirche. pp. 87. 16° Leipzig, 1857.

5471 Bispham (Clarence Wyatt). Columban, saint, monk, and missionary, 539–615 A.D. : notes concerning his life and times. pp. 63. 8° New York, 1903. [Gross, 1648a, note. With a bibliography.]

5472 Concannon (Helena). The date of St. Columban's birth. [Reply to Aubrey Gwynn, **5478.**] Studies, 8, pp. 59–68. 1919.

5473 —— The life of St. Columban, a study of ancient Irish monastic life. 8° Dublin, 1915. [Kenney, 1, p. 186.]

5474 —— Saint Columban : apostle of peace and penance. Studies, 4, pp. 513–26. 1915.

5475 Dedieu (L.). Columban, législateur de la vie monastique. pp. 70. 8° Cahors, 1901.

5476 Domenici (G.). San Colombano (543–615). [Kenney, 1, p. 186.] Civiltà Cattolica, 1916. 1916.

5477 Gianelli (Antonio Maria), *bp. of Bobbio*. Vita di S. Colombano abate, irlandese, protettore della città e diocesi di Bobbio. 8° Torino, 1844. —. Ed. 2e. 1894. [Kenney, 1, p. 186.]

5478 Gwynn (Aubrey). The date of St. Columban's birth. [?540 : ?559–60. *See also* **5472** and Gwynn's reply to it on pp. 67–68 of Studies, 8.] Studies, 7, pp. 474–84. 1918.

5479 Healy (John), *abp. of Tuam*. The school of Bangor—St. Columbanus. Irish Eccles. Rec., 3rd S. 6, pp. 209–19. 1885.

5480 Hennig (John). St. Columbanus in the liturgy. *Same jnl.*, 5th S. 62, pp. 306–12. 1943.

5481 Hertel (G.). Anmerkungen zur Geschichte Columba's. [Kenney, 1, p. 186.] Zeit. Kirchengesch., 3, pp. 145–50. 1879.

5482 Kirwan (W. H.). Some Celtic missionary saints.—St. Columbanus. Irish Eccles. Rec., 4th S. 32, pp. 60–75. 1912.

5483 Laux (Johann Joseph) [Metlake (George), *pseud.*]. Der heilige Kolumban, sein Leben und seine Schriften. pp. xvi, 290, + 7 plates. 8° Freiburg i. B., 1919. [Kenney, 1, p. 186.]

5484 —— The life and writings of St. Columban, 542–615. 8° Philadelphia, 1914. [Kenney, 1, p. 186.]

5485 Lugnano (Placido). San Colombano, monaco e scrittore (542–615). [Kenney, 1, p. 186.] Riv. stor. benedettina, 11, pp. 5–46. 1916.

5486 MacCarthy (Bartholomew). The death of St. Columbanus. [Sunday, Nov. 23, 615.] Irish Eccles. Rec., 3rd S. 5, pp. 771–80. 1884.

5487 McCarthy (E. J.). Portrait of St. Columban. *Same jnl.*, 5th S. 74, pp. 110–15. 1950.

5488 Martin (Léon Eugène). St. Colomban. *Les saints*. pp. vi, 198. 8° Paris, 1905. [Gross, 1648a.] —3e édition. 8° Paris, 1921.

5489 O'Doherty (John F.). St. Columbanus and the Roman see. Irish Eccles. Rec., 5th S. 42, pp. 1–10. 1933.

5490 O'Gorman (J. J.). St. Columban. 8° Ottawa, 1915. [Kenney, 1, p. 186.]

5491 O'Riordan (J. B.). Saint Columbanus. *Catholic Truth Society, no.* 174. 8° Dublin, n.d.

5492 Rivière (Jean). Saint Columban et le jugement du pape hérétique. Rev. sciences religieuses, 3, pp. 277–82. 1923.

5493 Schmidlin (J.). St. Kolumban in Sundgau. Strassburger Diözenblatt, 19, pp. 165–73. 1900.

5494 Scott (Archibald Black). The Celtic missionaries on the continent.—1. St. Columbanus. Trans. Gaelic Soc. Inverness, 29 (1914–19), pp. 47–67. 1922.

5495 Stokes (George Thomas). Ancient Celtic expositors. Columbanus and his teaching. Expositor, 3rd S. 10, pp. 136–50. 1889.

5496 Torre (Pietro Luigi della). Vita di S. Colombano. . . . Accrescintasi in questa edizione ii d'un compendio storico della traslazione del di lui santo corpo da Bobio a Pavia, sequita e scritta nel x. secolo. 8° Milano, 1728.

5497 Vinay (G.). Interpretazione di S. Colombano. Bollettino storico-bibliografico subalpino, 46, pp. 5–30. 1948.

5498 Zimmermann (J. A.). Die Heiligen Columban und Gallus nach ihrem Leben und Wirken geschildert. pp. xxiii, 264. 8° St. Gallen, 1865. [Kenney, 1, p. 186.]

75. MISSIONARIES TO THE CONTINENT

5. IN THE LOW COUNTRIES

§ a. General

5499 Bellesheim (Alphons). Über einiger Beziehungen Irlands zur Reichsstadt Aachen und Diözese Lüttich. Zeit. Aachener Geschichtsvereins, 14, pp. 38–53. 1892.

5500 Crépin (Joseph). Le monastère des Scots de Fosse. Terre wallonne, 8, pp. 357–85 : 9, pp. 16–26. 1923–24.

5501 —— Notice historique sur le culte de Sainte Brigide à Fosses. 8° Fosses, 1905.

5502 Cullen (John B.). St. Rumoldus of Dublin—bishop and martyr. [Bp. of Mechlin. 8th c.] Irish Eccles. Rec., 5th S. 20, pp. 54–64. 1922.

5503 Essen (Léon van der). Étude critique et littéraire sur les Vitae des saints mérovingiens de l'ancienne Belgique. *Univ. de Louvain, Recueil de travaux,* 17. pp. xx, 447. 8° Louvain and Paris, 1907.

5504 Gabbema (Simon Abbes). Nederlandse watervloeden. . . . Hieragter sijn bygevoegt de Leevens van Willibrord en Bonifaas. 2 pt. 8° Franeker, 1703.

5505 Grosjean (Paul), *ed.* Un poème latin du xviie siècle sur les saints irlandais honorés en Belgique. Anal. Boll., 43, pp. 115–21. 1925.

5506 Healy (John), *abp. of Tuam.* St. Livinus, bishop and martyr. [Died 656.] Irish Eccles. Rec., 3rd S. 7, pp. 289–301. 1886.

5507 Hogan (J. F.). St. Livinus of Ghent. *Same jnl.,* 3rd S. 13, pp. 961–78. 1892.

5508 —— St. Rumold of Mechlin. [8th c.] *Same jnl.,* 3rd S. 14, pp. 58–77. 1893.

5509 Jung-Diefenbach (Josef). Die Friesenbekehrung bis zum Martertode des hl. Bonifatius. *Veröffentlichungen internat. Inst. missionswiss. Forschungen : Missionswiss. Forschungen,* N.R. 1. pp. viii, 118. 8° Wien, 1931.

5510 Lahaye (Léon). Étude sur l'abbaye de Waulsort. pp. 296. 8° Liége, 1890. [On Meuse. Reserved by charter of Otto I (946) for *pelegrini* from Ireland.]

5511 Moreau (Édouard de). Histoire de l'église en Belgique. Tome 1, La formation de la Belgique chrétienne des origines au milieu du xe siècle. 2e édition, revue et corrigée. pp. xix, 388, + 9 plates. 8° Bruxelles, 1945.

5512 Vernulaeus (Nicolaus). De propagatione fidei christianae in Belgio per sanctos ex Hibernia viros liber. pp. 90. 8° Lovanii, 1639. [Kenney, 1, p. 486.]

5513 Walsh (T. A.). Irish saints in Belgium. [Kenney, 1, 486.] Ecclesiastical Rev., 39, pp. 122–40. 1908.

§ *b*. Willibrord

(first bishop of Utrecht, 695–739. *See also* bibliography in **5549**.)

5514 Alberdingk-Thijm (Petrus Paul Maria). Willibrordus, Apostel der Nederlanden. 8° Amsterdam, 1861. Der heilige Willibrord . . . Erweiterte deutsche Ausgabe. pp. viii, 230. 8° Münster, 1863. [Gross, 1663.]

5515 Alcuin. Vita Willibrordi archiepiscopi Traiectensis, edidit Wilhelm Levison. *Monumenta Germaniae historica, script. rerum Merovingicarum,* 7. *Passiones vitaeque sanctorum,* pp. 81–141. 4° Hannoverae, 1919.

5516 Attwell (Henry). The Echternach Whitsuntide dancers [to the shrine of St. Willibrord]. N. and Q., 7th S. 9, pp. 381–82, 511. 1890.

5517 Bannenberg (G. P. J.). Sint Willibrord in Waalro en Valkenswaard. pp. vi, 100, + plates, + map. 8° Nijmegen, 1948.

5518 Boniface, *St., abp. of Mainz.* The Calendar of St. Willibrord from Ms. Paris Lat. 10837. A facsimile and transcription, introduction and notes. *Henry Bradshaw Society,* 55. pp. xxiv, xiii, 49. 4° London, 1918.

5519 Engling (Johann). Apostolat des heiligen Willibrod im Lande der Luxemburger, durch Geschichte und Tradition aufgefasst. 12° Luxemburg, 1863.

5520 Essen (Léon van der). De heilige Willibrordus en zijne levens beschrijvingen. Geschiedkundige bladen, 1. 1905.

5521 Etten (F. J. P. van). Het leven van den H. Willebrord of vestiging van het Christendom in Noordelijk-Nederland. pp. 375. 8° Rotterdam, 1881.

5522 Goetzinger (Nikolaus). Willibrordus, Echternacher Festschrift zur 12. Jahrhundertfeier des hl. Willibrord. 8° Luxemburg, 1940.

5523 Grieve (Alexander). Willibrord, missionary in the Netherlands, 670–739, including a translation of the Vita Willibrordi by Alcuin of York. pp. 139. 8° Westminster, 1923.

5524 Hau (J.). Sankt Willibrord. 8° Saarbrucken, 1932.

5525 Heusgen (Paul). St. Willibrords Wirken in der Nordeifel. Hist. Archiv des Erzbistums Köln, 1, pp. 83–89. 1928.

5526 Hordijk (C. Pijnacker). Bisschoppen van Utrecht. 695–1301. [Pp. 23–24, Willibrord (695–739), etc.] Nederlandsch Archievenblad, 20 (1911–12), pp. 23–56. 1912.

5527 Janssens (Hubert). St. Willibrord and Ireland. Irish Eccles. Rec., 5th S. 77, pp. 356–65. 1952.

5528 Krier (J. Bernhard). La procession dansante, ou le pélerinage au tombeau de St. Willibrord à Echternach. Petit manual à l'usage des pélerins. 12° Luxembourg, 1870. —Die Spring prozession und die Wallfahrt zum Grabe des heiligen Willibrord in Echternach. (Leben des hl. Willibrord). 12° Luxemburg, 1870.

5529 Laenen (J.). St. Willibrordus en St. Amandus te Antwerpen. Collectanea Mechlin, N.S.5, 1931.

5530 Lampen (Willibrord). De abdij Sint-Willibrord te Echternach. Katholik, 157, pp. 257–74. 1920.

5531 —— De Kalender van St. Willibrord. Tijdschrift voor Liturgie, 11, 1931.

5532 —— Sint Willibrord. 8° Utrecht, 1916.

5533 —— Willibrordiana. Hist. Tijdschrift, 10, pp. 126–38. 1931.

5534 Levison (Wilhelm). À propos du Calendrier de S. Willibrord. Rev. Bénédictine, 50, pp. 37–41. 1938.

5535 —— Eine neue Vita Willibrordi. Neues Archiv, 29, pp. 255–61. 1904.

5535 Levison (Wilhelm). St. Willibrord and his place in history. Durham Univ. J., 32 (N.S. 1), pp. 23–41. 1940.

5537 —— Willibrordiana. Neues Archiv, 33, pp. 517–30. 1908.

5538 Liebermann (Felix). Alcvins Willibrord-Biographie. Arch. Stud. neueren Spr., Bd. 142 (N.S. 42), pp. 126–27. 1921.

5539 Lindeboom (Johannes). St. Willibrord's Roomsche reizen. pp. 13. Mededelingen k. Ned. Akad. Wet., Afd. Let., N. Reeks, 11, no. 5. 1948.

5540 Muellendorff (Julius). Leben des hl. C. Willibrord. 12° Luxemburg, 1868.

5541 —— Leben des hl. Clemens Willibrord, Apostel der Niederlande und Gründer der Abtei Echternach. 8° Regensburg, 1898.

5542 Poncelet (Albert). Les miracles de S. Willibrord, B.H.L., 8943. Anal. Boll., 26, pp. 73–77. 1907.

5543 —— Le ' testament ' de Saint Willibrord. [Including Latin text.] Anal. Boll., 25, pp. 163–76. 1906.

5544 —— La vie de S. Willibrord, par le prétre Egbert. Anal. Boll., 22, pp. 419–22. 1903.

5545 Rushton (Gerald Wynne). The dancing procession at Echternach. [Annual ceremony after cattle pestilence of 1347 had ceased through prayers of St. Willibrord.] Irish Eccles. Rec., 5th S. 55, pp. 274–81. 1940.

5546 Tenhaeff (Nicolaas Bernardus). De oorkonden-schat van den heiligen Willebrord. 8° Groningen, 1929.

5549 Verbist (Gabriël H.). Saint Willibrord, apôtre des Pays Bas et fondateur d'Echternach. pp. xxxiv, 352, + 11 plates. 8° Bruges, 1939. [With a bibliography.]

5550 Weerd (Hubert van de). De H. Willibrordus onder de Vlamingen. Dietsche Warande en Belfort, 21. 1921.

5551 —— Limburg in het testament van H. Willibrordus. Limburg, 16. 1934–5.

5552 —— Saint Willibrord en Campine. 1914.

76. MISSIONARIES TO THE CONTINENT
6. IN SWITZERLAND
§ a. General

5553 Benziger (Carl Josef). Die Fridolinslegende nach einem Ulmer Druck des Johann Zainer. Studien zur deutschen Kunstgeschichte, 166. pp. 30. 8° Strassburg, 1913. [37 figures.]

5554 Blanke (Fritz). Columban und Gallus. Urgeschichte des schweizerischen Christentums. pp. 235. 8° Zürich, [1940].

5555 Heer (Gottfried). St. Fridolin, der Apostel Alamanniens. Vortrag, etc. pp. 64. 8° Zürich, 1889.

5556 Hogan (J. F.). St. Fintan of Rheinau. [c. 800.] Irish Eccles. Rec., 3rd S. 14, pp. 385–96. 1893.

5557 —— St. Fridolin of Seckingen. [?6th c.] Same jnl., 3rd S. 14, pp. 193–213. 1893.

5558 —— St. Pirminius of Reichenau. [Founded 724.] Same jnl., 3rd S. 15, pp. 403–17. 1894.

5559 Meyer von Knonau (Gerold). Die Anfänge des Klosters Rheinau. [Founded by Wolvene, 858.] Neues Archiv, 10, pp. 375–77. 1885.

§ b. Gall

(For the abbey of St. Gall, see also Kenney, vol. 1, pp. 594–600)

5560 Baesecke (Georg). Der Vocabularius Sti. Galli in der angelsächsischen Mission. pp. x, 171, + 44 plates. 4° Halle, 1933.

5561 Egli (Emil). Eine neue Recension der Vita s. Galli. [Paul Schweizer]. Neues Archiv, 21, pp. 361–71. 1896.

5562 Gall, St. Vita Galli confessoris triplex. (i. Vitae vetissimae fragmentum : ii. Vita auctore Wettino : iii. Vitae auctore Walahfrido). Monumenta Germaniae historica : script. rerum Merovingicarum, 4. Passiones vitaeque sanctorium, pp. 229–337 ; 7, pp. 834–35. 4° Hannoverae, 1902, 1920.

5563 Gmuer (Theo). St. Gall : its Irish founder and his successors. J. Ivernian Soc., 6, pp. 24–35. 1913.

5564 Greith (Carl Johann), *bp. of St. Gall.* Der heilige Gallus, der Apostel Alemanniens und seine Glaubenslehre, gegenüber den Deutschkirchlern und ihren Irrthümern. Predigt. 8° St. Gallen, 1845. [Kenney, 1, p. 207.]

5565 —— Die heiligen Glaubensboten Kolumban und Gall und ihre Stellung in der Urgeschichte St. Gallens, nach den ältesten Quellen und den neuesten Fabeln. pp. 58. 8° St. Gallen, 1865. [Kenney, 1, p. 186.]

5566 Hogan (J. F.). The monastery and library of St. Gall. [Kenney, 1, p. 594. 9th c.] Irish Eccles. Rec., 3rd S. 15, pp. 35–54. 1894.

5567 —— St. Gall, apostle of Allemania. *Same jnl.*, 3rd S. 14, pp. 1057–73. 1893.

5568 Knappert (Laurentius). La vie de S. Gall et le paganisme germanique. [Kenney, 1, p. 207.] Rev. hist. religions, 29, pp. 259–95. 1894.

5569 Munding (Emmanuel), *ed.* Die Kalendarien von St. Gallen aus XXI Handschriften neuntes bis elftes Jahrhundert. pp. 114. 8° Beuron, 1948.

5570 Scott (Archibald Black). The Celtic missionaries on the continent. —[2.] S. Gall, 'the apostle of the Rhine'. Trans. Gaelic Soc. Inverness, 32 (1924–25), pp. 105–39. 1929.

5571 Sickel (Theodor). St. Gallen unter den ersten Karolingern. [Kenney, 1, p. 207.] Mitth. vaterländ. Gesch., 1865, pp. 1–21. 1865.

5572 Strabo (Walafridus). The life of St. Gall. [Translated] by M. Joynt. *Translation of Christian literature. Series 5 : lives of Celtic Saints.* pp. 168, + 1 plate. 8° London, 1927. [Kenney, 1, p. 776. 6th c.]

5573 Strecker (Karl). Notkers Vita s. Galli. Neues Archiv, 38, pp. 57–93. 1913.

5574 Winterfeld (Paul von). Nochmals Notkers Vita s. Galli. Neues Archiv, 28, pp. 63–76. 1903.

5575 —— Zur metrischen Vita s. Galli confessoris. Neues Archiv, 28, pp. 507–09. 1903.

77. ECCLESIASTICAL LAW, CANONS AND PENITENIALS

§ *a.* Anglo-Saxon and General

5576 Bateson (Mary). Rules for monks and secular canons after the revival under king Edgar. E.H.R., 9, pp. 690–705. 1894.

5577 —— The supposed Latin penitential of Egbert and the missing work of Halitgar of Cambrai. E.H.R., 9, pp. 320–26. 1894.

5578 Birch (Walter de Gray). MSS. and charters in the possession of the dean and chapter of Wells.—On the Wells fragment of the Old English version of the Benedictine Rule. J. Brit. Archaeol. Assoc., 38, pp. 384–85. 1882.

5579 Caro (G.). Die Varianten der Durhamer Hs. und des Tiberius-Fragments der ae. Prosa-Version der Benedictinerregel und ihr Verhältniss zu den übrigen HSS. Engl. Studien, 24, pp. 161–76. 1898.

5580 Egbert, *St., abp. of York.* Das altenglische Bussbuch, sog. Confessionale pseudo-Egberti. Ein Beitrag zu den kirchlichen Gesetzen der Angelsachsen. Kritische Textausgabe nebst Nachweis der mittellateinischen Quellen . . . von Robert Spindler. pp. xii, 210. 8° Leipzig, 1934.

5581 Finsterwalder (Paul Willem), *ed.* Die canones Theodori Cantuariensis und ihre Ueberlieferungsformen. pp. xx, 234. 8° Weimar, 1929.

5582 Fournier (Paul) and **Le Bras** (Gabriel). Histoire des collections canoniques . . . en occident, depuis les Fausses décretales jusqu'un Décret de Gratien [860–1142]. 2 vol. 8° Paris, 1931–32.

5583 Kunstmann (Friedrich), *ed.* Die lateinischen Pönitentialbücher der Angelsachsen, mit geschichtlicher Einleitung. 8° Mainz, 1844. [Gross, 1425. Edits spurious texts of Theodore and Bede, etc.]

5584 Liebermann (Felix). Aethelwolds Anhang zur Benediktinerregel. Archiv Stud. neueren Sprachen, Bd. 108, pp. 375–77. 1902.

5585 Liebermann (Felix). Zu Bussbüchern der lateinischen Kirche. [Pp. 297–98, Theodori poenitentiale Umbrense; pp. 298–301, Zu Egberti Eboracensis poenitentiale.] Zeit. Rechtsgesch., 54, (Kanon. Abt. 10), pp. 292–301. 1920.

5586 —— Zum Poenitentiale Arundel [65]. [Schmitz (1883), pp. 432–65.] *Same jnl.*, 59, (Kanon. Abt. 15), pp. 531–32. 1926.

5587 Mone (Franz Joseph). Quellen und Forschungen der teutschen Literatur und Sprache. Bd. 1. 8° Aachen und Leipzig, 1830. [No more published. Gross, 1426. Pp. 482–548, Zur Kritik der angelsächsischen Gesetze. Treats mainly of penitentials.]

5588 Morin (Jean). Commentarius historicus de disciplina in administratione Sacramenti poenitentiae, tredecim primis seculis . . . observata, *etc.* 2 pt. fol. Parisiis, 1651. [Kenney, 1, p. 235.]

5589 Napier (Arthur Sampson), *ed.* The Old English version of the enlarged rule of Chrodegang together with the Latin original. An Old English version of the Capitula of Theodulf together with the Latin original. An interlinear Old English rendering of the Epitome of Benedict of Aniane. *Early English Text Society*, O.S. 150. pp. xi, 131, + 3 plates. 8° London, 1916.

5590 —— The Rule of Chrodegang in Old English. [Sources of De ebrietate and De clericis.] Mod. Lang. Notes, 18, p. 241. 1903.

5591 Oakley (Thomas Pollock). The co-operation of mediaeval penance and secular law. [Includes A.-S. and Hoël the Good.] Speculum, 7, pp. 515–24. 1932.

5592 —— English penitential discipline and Anglo-Saxon law in their joint influence. *Columbia University, Studies in History*, 107, ii. (no. 242). pp. 226. 8° New York, 1923.

5593 —— The penitentials as sources for mediaeval history. Speculum, 15, pp. 210–23. 1940.

5594 —— Some neglected aspects in the history of penance. Cath. Hist. Rev., 24, pp. 293–309. 1938.

5595 O'Carroll (James). Monastic Rules in Merovingian Gaul. [Columbanus, etc.] Studies, 42, pp. 407–19. 1953.

5596 Petau (Denis) [Petavius]. De poenitentia vetere. 8° Paris, 1624. [Kenney, 1, p. 235.]

5597 Poschmann (Bernhard). Die abenländische Kirchenbusse im frühen Mittelalter. *Breslauer Studien zur historischen Theologie*, 16. pp. 244. 8° Breslau, 1930.

5598 Schmitz (Hermann Joseph). Die Bussbücher und die Bussdisciplin der Kirche. Nach handschaftlichen Quellen dargestellt H.J.S. pp. xvi, 864. (Bd. 2, Die Bussbücher und das kanonische Bussverfahren. pp. xii, 741). 8° Mainz, 1883 (Düsseldorf, 1898). [Kenney, 1, p. 235.]

5599 Wasserschleben (F. W. Hermann). Die Bussordnungen der abenländischen Kirche nebst einer rechtsgeschichtlichen Einleitung. pp. xvi, 727. 8° Halle, 1851. [Gross, 1428. Pp. 101–352, old British, Irish and A.-S. penitentials. 'A valuable collection, well edited.']

5600 Watkins (Oscar Dan). A history of penance : being a study of the authorities. 2 vol. 8° London, 1920. [Kenney, 1, pp. 200, 236. Vol. 2, the Western Church : A.D. 450–1215. pp. 295.]

§ *b.* Celtic

(For the Rule of Columbanus, *see* 74§b*i.*)

5601 Berger (Samuel). Confession des péchés attribuée à Saint Patrice. [Latin text, from 9th c. MS. Angers 14.] Rev. celt., 15, pp. 155–59. 1894.

5602 Bradshaw (Henry). The early collection of canons known as the Hibernensis. pp. viii, 64. 8° Cambridge, 1893. [Gross, 1429, note.]

5603 Fahey (J. A.). Canon Bourke and our primitive Irish monastic rules. Irish Eccles. Rec., 3rd S. 2, pp. 189–200. 1881.

5604 Fournier (Paul). De l'influence de la collection canonique irlandaise sur la formation des collections canoniques. [Gross, 1429, note.] Nouv. Rev. hist. droit, 23, pp. 27–78. 1899.

5605 Fournier (Paul). Études sur les pénitentials. [Kenney, 1, p. 236. Cummean, etc.] Rev. d'hist. et de litt. relig., 6, pp. 289–317 : 7, pp. 59–70, 121–27 : 8, pp. 528–53 : 9, pp. 97–103. 1901–04.

5606 —— Le Liber ex lege Moysi et les tendances bibliques du droit canonique irlandais. [Texts from the Pentateuch. Compiled in Ireland, 8th c.] Rev. celt., 30, pp. 221–34. 1909.

5607 Gougaud (Louis). Inventaire des régles monastiques irlandaises. [Kenney, 1, p. 288.] Rev. Bénédictine, 25, pp. 167–84, 321–33 : 28, pp. 86–89. 1908, 1911.

5608 Lugnano (Placido). Il testo della Regula monachorum dell' Ordo de vita et actione monachorum e dell Oratio di S. Colombano. Rev. stor. benedettina, 11, pp. 185–202. 1916.

5609 MacEclaire (—). The rule of St. Carthage. [Irish and English translation.] Irish Eccles. Rec., 4th S. 27, pp. 495–517. 1910.

5610 MacNeill (John Thomas). The Celtic penitentials. [i. Survey of literary sources. Canons of St. Patrick, Canones Hibernenses, of SS. Gildas and Finnian, connected with St. David, Columbani, Canones Wallici, Adamnani, related A.–S. penitentials (Theodori, Bedae, Egberti), related Frankish : ii. Relation of the Celtic penitentials to the penitential discipline of the ancient Catholic Church : iii. Relation of Celtic penance to pre-Christian Celtic customs : iv. Special features as affected by pre-Christian customs—composition and commutation, fasting, etc.] Rev. celt., 39, pp. 257–300 ; 40, pp. 51–103, 320–41. 1922–23.

5611 —— The Celtic penitentials and their influence on continental Christianity. *Diss.* pp. vi, 199. 8° Paris, 1923. [Chap. 1–4, *in* Rev. celtique, 39, pp. 257–300 : 40, pp. 320–41. 1922–23.]

5612 —— and **Gamer** (Helena Margaret). Medieval handbooks of penance. A translation of the principal libri poenitentiales and selections from related documents. *Records of Civilization,* 29.

pp. xiv, 476. 8° New York, 1938. [Pp. 75–168, Irish ; pp. 169–78, Welsh ; pp. 179–248, A.–S.; pp. 249–70, Continental Irish.]

5613 MacNeill (John Thomas). Note on Cummean the Long and his penitential. [592–662.] Rev. celt., 50, pp. 289–91. 1933.

5614 Mitchell (Gerard). Commutation of penances in the Celtic penitentials. Irish Éccles. Rec., 5th S. 40, pp. 225–39. 1932.

5615 Nicholson (Edward Williams Byron). The origin of the ' Hibernian ' collection of canons. [Probably collected by Adamnan, before 726, at Iona.] Zeit. celt. Philol., 3, pp. 99–103. 1901.

5616 Oakley (Thomas Pollock). Celtic penance : its sources, affiliations, and influences. Irish Eccles. Rec., 5th S. 52, pp. 147–64, 581–601. 1938.

5617 —— Cultural affiliations of early Ireland in the penitentials. Speculum, 8, pp. 489–500. 1933.

5618 —— A great Irish penitential and its authorship. [Paenitentiale Cummeani.] Romanic Rev., 25, pp. 25–33. 1934.

5619 —— The origins of Irish penitential discipline. Cath. Hist. Rev., 19, pp. 320–32. 1933.

5620 O'Donnell (M. J.). Penance in the early Church. pp. viii, 151. 8° Dublin, 1907. [Kenney, 1, p. 236.]

5621 O'Keeffe (J. G.). The Rule of St. Patrick. [Text in Irish and in English, with notes.] Ériu, 1, pp. 216–24. 1904.

5621a O'Neill (Joseph). The Rule of Ailbe of Emly. [Abbot of Emly, Munster, contemp. with St. Patrick. Irish text and translation.] Ériu, 3, pp. 92–115. 1907.

5622 Reeves (William), *bp. of Down.* On the Céli-Dé, commonly called Culdees. [Pp. 200–01, Rule of Fothad : pp. 202–15, Rule of the Céli Dé, with translation.] Trans. R.I.A., 24, pp. 119–264. 1873.

5622a Strachan (John). Cormac's Rule. [9th c. Irish text and translation.] Ériu, 2, pp. 62–68. 1905.

5622b Strachen (John). Two monastic Rules. [From R.I.A., MS. 23 P. 3. Irish texts.] Ériu, 2, pp. 227–29. 1905.

5623 Tallaght, *abbey.* The Rule of Tallaght. Edited by Edward John Gwynn. pp. xxvi, 109. [Irish and English.] Hermathena, no. 44, 2nd suppl. 1927.

5624 Thurneysen (Rudolf). Zur irischen Kanonensammlung. Zeit. celt. Phil., 6, pp. 1–5, 556. 1908.

5625 Wasserschleben (F. W. Hermann), *ed.* Die irische Kanonensammlung. 2. Auflage. pp. xii, 243. 8° Leipzig, 1885. [Gross, 1429. Latin collection of canons, probably compiled in Ireland, early in 8th c., by Rubin of Dairinis (d. 725) and Cuchuimne of Iona (d. 747). Usually known as ' The Hibernensis.']

5626 Zettinger (J.), *ed.* Das Paenitentiale Cummeani. [Died 662.] Archiv kathol. Kirchenrecht, 82, pp. 501–40. 1902.

78. RELIGIOUS LITERATURE
§ *a.* Ælfric

(for his Lives of the saints, *see* 66§a)

5627 Ælfric, *abbot of Eynsham.* Ælfric's Colloquy. Edited by G. N. Garmonsway. *Old English Library,* ser. B, 2. pp. ix, 65. 8° London, 1939.

5628 —— De temporibus anni, edited . . . with an introduction, sources, parallels, and notes by Heinrich Hemel. *Early English Text Society,* O.S. 213. pp. lviii, 106, + 2 plates. 8° London, 1942.

5629 —— An English-Saxon homily on the birthday of St. Gregory . . . giving an account of the conversion of the English. . . . Translated . . . with notes by Elizabeth Elstob. New edition with a preface containing some account of Mrs. Elstob. pp. xxxvi, 75. 8° London, 1839.

5630 —— Exameron Anglice, or the Old English Hexameron. Edited . . . by S. J. Crawford. *Bibliothek der angelsächsischen Prosa,* 10. pp. 85. 8° Hamburg, 1921.

5631 Ælfric, *abbot of Eynsham.* Fragment of Ælfric's translation of Æthelwold's De consuetudine monarchorum and its relation to other mss., critically edited from the MS. Cotton Tib. A. III. . . by Edward Breck. *Dissertation,* *Leipsic.* pp. 38. 8° Leipsic, 1887. [Gross, 1435.]

5632 —— Die Hirtenbriefe Ælfrics in altenglischer und lateinischer Fassung. Herausgegeben und mit Übersetzung und Einleitung versehen von Bernhard Fehr. *Bibliothek der angelsächsischen Prosa,* 9. pp. cxxvi, 269. 8° Hamburg, 1914.

5633 —— Selected homilies. Edited by Henry Sweet. Second edition. pp. 80. 8° Oxford, 1922.

5634 Assmann (Bruno). Abt Ælfric's angelsächsische Bearbeitung des Buches Esther. [A.–S. text and notes.] Anglia, 9, pp. 25–38. 1886.

5635 —— Abt Ælfric's angelsächsische Bearbeitung des Buches Hiob, Druck mit der Handschrift verglichen. [Text in Grein's Prosa, 1.] Anglia, 9, pp. 39–42. 1886.

5636 —— Abt Ælfric's angelsächsische Homilie über das Buch Judith. [Introduction, A.–S. text, and notes.] Anglia, 10, pp. 76–104. 1888.

5637 Barrett (Charles Robin). Studies in the word-order of Ælfric's Catholic homilies and lives of the saints. *Diss.,* *Bern.* Occas. Papers, Dept. A.–S., Camb., 3. pp. ix, 135. 1953.

5638 Brotanek (Rudolf). Texte und Untersuchungen zur altenglischen Literatur und Kirchengeschichte. Zwei Homilien des Ælfric.—Synodalbeschlüsse.—Ein Briefentwurf.—Zur Überlieferung des Sterbegesanges Bedas. pp. viii, 203. 8° Halle, 1913.

5639 Davis (Charles Rexford). Two new sources for Ælfric's ' Catholic Homilies '. J. Eng. and Germ. Phil., 41, pp. 510–13. 1942.

5640 Dietrich (Eduard F.). Abt Ælfrik. [Gross, 1621. Account of his life and writings.] Zeit. hist. Theol., 25, pp. 487–594 : 26, pp. 163–256. 1855–56.

5641 Du Bois (Marguerite Marie). Ælfric ; sermonnaire, docteur et grammairien ; contribution à l'étude de la vie et de l'action bénédictines en Angleterre au 10e siècle. pp. viii, 419, + 4 plates. 8° Paris, 1943.

5642 Elstob (Elizabeth). Some testimonies . . . in favour of the intended edition of the Saxon homilies. Concerning the learning of the author of those homilies [i.e. Ælfric], etc. 8° London, 1713.

5643 Fehr (Bernhard). Über einige Quellen zu Ælfrics Homiliae catholicae. Archiv Stud. neueren Spr., Bd. 130, pp. 378–81. 1913.

5644 Foerster (Max). Ælfric's s.g. Hiob-Übersetzung. Anglia, 15 (N.F. 3), pp. 473–77. 1893.

5645 —— Über die Quellen von Ælfric's exegetischen Homilae catholicae. Anglia, 16 (N.F. 4), pp. 1–61. 1894.

5646 —— Über die Quellen von Ælfric's Homiliae catholicae I. Legenda. Diss. pp. 49. 8° Berlin, [1892].

5647 Gem (Samuel Harvey). An Anglo-Saxon abbot : Ælfric of Eynsham. pp. xvi, 200. 8° Edinburgh, 1912.

5648 Jost (Karl Theodor). Unechte Ælfrictexte. Anglia, 51 (N.F. 39), pp. 81–103, 177–219. 1927.

5649 MacLean (George Edwin). Ælfric's version of Alcuini Interrogationes Sigeuulfi in Genesin. [Authors : analysis : on the texts (A.–S. and Latin) : on the mss. : question of authorship of A.–S. version : parallel A.–S. and Latin texts with their variations.] Anglia, 6, pp. 425–73 : 7, pp. 1–57, + 1 plate. 1883–84.

5650 Reum (A.). De temporibus, ein echtes Werk des Abtes Aelfric. Anglia, 10, pp. 457–98. 1888.

5650a Singer (G. W.), **Thorpe** (Benjamin), etc. Ælfric's Colloquy. [Sprote (fish) etc.] N. and Q., 1st S. 1, pp. 168, 197–98, 232, 248–49, 278. 1850.

5651 Stephan (Adalbert). Eine weitere Quelle von Ælfric's Gregorhomilie. Anglia, Beiblatt, 14, pp. 315–20. 1903.

5652 Thompson (Sir Edward Maunde). Ælfric's vocabulary. J. Brit. Archaeol. Assoc., 41, pp. 144–52. 1885.

5653 Whitbread (L.). Notes on Ælfric's Colloquy. N. and Q., 184, pp. 69–71. 1943.

5654 White (Caroline Louisa). Ælfric : a new study of his life and writings. Yale Studies in English, 2. pp. 218. 8° Boston, 1898. [Gross, 1622. Pp. 199–212, bibliography. Largely based on **5640**.]

5655 Whitelock (Dorothy). Two notes on Ælfric and Wulfstan. [i. The date of Ælfric's death. ii. Gildas, Alcuin, and Wulfstan.] Mod. Lang. Rev., 38, pp. 122–26. 1943.

5656 Zimmermann (Otto). Die beiden Fassungen des dem Abt Ælfrics zugeschriebenen Traktats über die 7 Gaben des heiligen Geistes. Diss., Leipzig, 1888. 8° Leipzig, 1888.

5657 Zupitza (Julius). Die ursprüngliche Gestalt von Älfrics Colloquium. Z.f.d.A., 31, pp. 32–45. 1887.

§ b. Alfred

5658 Alfred, king. Blooms by king Ælfred. [From Flores Soliloquiorum of S. Augustinus. A modern version. A.–S. text from MS. Cotton Vitellius A. XV, fol. 1a.] The Shrine, pp. 163–205. 1869–70.

5659 Cockayne (Oswald). King Ælfred's Book of martyrs. [A.–S. text.] The Shrine, pp. 44–158. 1867–68.

5660 Flasdieck (Hermann M.). Das Kasseler Bruchstück der Cura Pastoralis. (Weiteres . . .). [Note in 63, p. 87.] Anglia, 62 (N.F. 50), pp. 193–233 : 66, pp. 56–58. 1938, 1942.

5661 Hartmann (K. A. Martin). Ist Koenig Aelfred der Verfasser der alliterierenden Uebertragung der Metra des Boetius ? Anglia, 5, pp. 411–50. 1882.

5662 Kern (J. H.). Zur Cura Pastoralis. Anglia, 33 (N.F. 21), pp. 270–76. 1910.

5663 Klaeber (Frederick). Zu König Ælfred's Vorrede zu seiner Übersetzung der Cura Pastoralis. Anglia, 47 (N.F. 35), pp. 53–65. 1923.

5664 Leicht (Alfred). Ist Koenig Aelfred der Verfasser der alliterierenden Metra des Boetius ? Anglia, 6, pp. 126–70. 1883.

**5665 —— Zur angelsächsischen Bearbeitung des Boethius. Anglia, 7, pp. 178–202. 1884.

5666 Potter (Simeon). The Old English ' Pastoral Care '. Trans. Philol. Soc., 1947, pp. 114–25. 1948.

5667 Wichmann (Johannes). König Aelfred's angelsächsische Übertragung der Psalmen i–li excl. Anglia, 11, pp. 39–96. 1889.

§ *c.* **Bible (Vulgate, Etc.)**

(for Codex Amiatinus, *see* **111** § a)

5668 Berger (Samuel). Histoire de la Vulgate pendant les premiers siècles du moyen âge. pp. xxiv, 443. 8° Paris, 1893. [Kenney, 1, p. 623. Pt. 1, chap. 3, les textes irlandais et anglo-saxons ; chap. 4, les Irlandais en Europe.]

5669 Bible—*Heptateuch.* The Old English version of the Heptateuch. Aelfric's Treatise on the Old and New Testament and his preface to Genesis. Edited . . . by S. J. Crawford. *Early English Text Society*, *O.S.*, 160. pp. xi, 442, + 3 plates. 8° London, 1922.

5670 Burkitt (Francis Crawford). The Bible of Gildas. [State of Bible in pre-Saxon Britain conjectured from his quotations.] Rev. Bénédictine, 46, pp. 206–15. 1934.

5671 Chase (Frank Herbert). A new text of the Old English prose Genesis. [With parallel A.–S. texts of 6 chapters from MSS. A. and C. Cotton Claudius B. IV and Camb. Univ. Library, Ii. 1.33.).] Archiv Stud. neueren Spr., Bd. 100, pp. 241–66. 1898.

5672 Glunz (Hans Hermann). Britannien und Bibeltext : der Vulgatetexte der Evangelien in seinem Verhältnis zur irisch-angelsächsischen Kultur des Frühmittelalters. *Kölner Anglistische Arbeiten*, 12. pp. 187, + 4 plates. 8° Leipzig, 1930.

5673 Glunz (Hans Hermann). History of the Vulgate in England from Alcuin to Roger Bacon. Being an inquiry into the text of some English manuscripts of the Vulgate Gospels. pp. xx, 383. 8° Cambridge, 1933.

5674 Hoenncher (Erwin). Über die Quellen der angelsächsischen Genesis. Anglia, 8, pp. 41–84. 1885.

**5675 —— Zur Interpolation der angelsächsischen Genesis. Vers. 235–851. Anglia, 7, pp. 469–96. 1884.

5676 Moore (Samuel). On the sources of the Old-English *Exodus*. Mod. Phil., 9, pp. 83–108. 1911.

5677 Thompson (S. Harrison). Bishop Gundulph of Rochester and the Vulgate. [Lanfranc's collation of text— ' non-tantum per se, sed etiam per discipulos suos '—esp. Gundulph.] Speculum, 6, pp. 468–70. 1931.

§ *d.* **Gospels**

5678 Abraham (Charles John), *bp. of Wellington.* A collation of St. Chad's Gospels at Lichfield. Reliquary, 17, pp. 1–2, 129 + 1 plate. 1876–77.

5679 Bible.—*Gospels* : *Latin.* Evangeliorum versio antehieronymiana ex Codice Usseriano-Dublinensi, adjecta collatione Codicis Usseriani alterius. Accedit versio vulgata sec. Cod. Amiatinum, cum varietate Cod. Kenanensis—Book of Kells, et Cod. Durmochensis—Book of Durrow. Edidit et praefatus est Thomas Kingsmill Abbott. 2 pt. 8° Dublini, 1884.

**5680 —— —— The oldest manuscript of the Vulgate Gospels (St. Gall MS. 1395). Deciphered and edited with an introduction and appendix by Cuthbert Hamilton Turner. (Completed by A. Souter). pp. lxiii, 216. 8° Oxford, 1931.

5681 Chapman (John). Notes on the early history of the Vulgate Gospels. pp. xi, 299. 8° Oxford, 1908. [Kenney, 1, p. 623. ' Holds that the " Irish " type of Gospel text is fundamentally old Latin, modified by the Vulgate.]

5682 Foerster (Max). Zum altenglischen Nicodemus-Evangelium. Archiv Stud. neueren Spr., Bd. 107, pp. 311–21. 1901.

5683 Hopkin-James (Lemuel John). The Celtic Gospels, their story and their text. [With facsimiles.] pp. lxx, 278, + 4 plates. 8° London, 1934. [Latin text from Chad Gospels (down to Luke, iii, 8), and from the Hereford Gospels : with an introduction.]

5684 Hoskier (Herman Charles). Concerning the genesis of the versions of the New Testament Gospels. pp. 470, 325. 2 vol. 8° London, 1910. [Kenney, 1, p. 623. 'Particular attention given to Irish mss.']

5685 Hulme (William H.). The Old English Gospel of Nicodemus. [i. Ms. Cotton Vesp. D XIV, ff. 87b–100 : ii. Homily from Ms. C.C.C.C. 41, pp. 295–30 : iii–iv. The O.E. texts of i and ii.] Mod. Phil., 1, pp. 579–614. 1904.

5686 Jenner (Henry). The Bodmin Gospels. [MS. B.M. Add. 9381. 9th or 10th c.] J. Roy. Inst. Cornwall, 21, pp. 113–45. 1923.

5687 Koeberlin (K.). Eine Würzburger Evangelienhandschriften. *Programm, Augsburg,* 1891. Augsburg, 1891. [Kenney, 1, p. 636. Gospel of St. Matthew. Semi-uncial scripts, A.-S.—or Irish ? Irish text of 8th c., glosses of 9th c.]

5688 Lawlor (Hugh Jackson). Chapters on the Book of Mulling. pp. 208. 8° Edinburgh, 1897. [7th c.]

**5689 —— Notes on some non-biblical matter in the ms. of the four Gospels known as the Book of Mulling. [c. 800.] Proc. Soc. Antiq. Scot., 29 (3rd S. 5), pp. 11–45. 1895.

**5690 —— Notes on the biblical text of the Book of Mulling. *Same inl.,* 31 (3rd S. 7), pp. 7–64. 1897.

5691 Luce (A. A.). The Book of Kells and the Gospels of Lindisfarne—a comparison. Hermathena, 79, pp. 61–74 : 80, pp. 12–25. 1952.

5692 Mincoff (Marco Konstantinos). Zur Altersfrage der Lindisfarner Glosse. Archiv Stud. neueren Spr., Bd. 173, pp. 31–43. 1938.

5693 Morin (Germain). La Liturgie de Naples au temps du S. Grégoire, d'après deux évangéliaires du septième siècle. [Évangéliaire de S. Cuthbert, MS. Cotton Nero D IV, and MS. Royal I B. VII.] Rev. Bénédictine, 8, pp. 481–93, 529–37. 1891.

5694 Napier (Arthur Sampson). Bruchstücke einer altenglischen Evangelienhandschrift. [St. John's Gospel found in the cover of a Court Book at Flixton Hall, Suffolk. 11th c. A.–S. text.] Archiv Stud. neueren Spr., Bd. 87, pp. 255–65. 1891.

5695 Ross (Alan Strode Campbell). The errors in the Old English gloss to the Lindisfarne Gospels. Rev. Engl. Stud., 8, pp. 385–94. 1932.

5696 Savage (Henry Edwin). St. Chad's Gospels. pp. 31, + 2 plates. 8° Litchfield, 1931.

5697 Turner (Cuthbert Hamilton). The oldest manuscript of the Vulgate Gospels, deciphered and edited, with introduction. pp. lxiii, 217, + 1 plate. 8° Oxford, 1931. [St. Gall. MS. 1395. c. 500. Italian script. Property of St. Gall's monastery from c. 600.]

5698 Urry (William). An eighth-century fragment of the Gospels in the chapter library, [Canterbury]. Friends of Canterbury Cathedral, Ann. Rept., 21, pp. 33–35, + 1 plate. 1948.

§ *e.* **Psalter**

(for Utrecht Psalter, *see* **111** § **b**)

5699 Bannister (Henry Marriott). Irish psalters. J. Theol. Stud., 12, pp. 280–84. 1911.

5699a Bible—*Psalms.* Der altenglische Arundel-Psalter. Eine Interlinearversion in der Handschrift Arundel 60. Herausgegeben von Guido Oess. *Anglistische Forschungen,* 30. pp. vii, 255. 8° Heidelberg, 1910.

**5700 —— Der altenglische Junius-Psalter. Die Interlinearglosse des Handschrift Junius 27. Herausgegeben von Eduard Brenner. *Anglistische Forschungen,* 42. pp. xlii, 194. 8° Heidelberg, 1908.

5701 **Bible** Der altenglische Regius-Psalter. Eine Interlinearversion in Hs. royal 2. B.5 des Brit. Mus. . . . Herausgeben von Fritz Roeder. *Studien zur englischen Philologie*, 18. pp. xxii, 305. 8° Halle, 1904.

5702 —— Der Cambridger Psalter (Hs. Ff1. 23). Zum ersten Male herausgegeben von Karl Wildhagen. 1. Text mit Erklärungen. *Grein (C.W.M.)* : *Bibliothek der angelsächsischen Prosa*, 7. pp. xxiii, 416. 8° Hamburg, 1910.

5703 —— Liber Psalmorum. The West Saxon Psalms. Being the prose portion, or the 'first fifty' of the so-called Paris Psalter. Edited . . . by James Wilson Bright . . . and Robert Lee Ramsay. pp. vi, 156. 8° London, 1907.

5704 —— The Paris Psalter and the meters of Boethius. Edited by George Philip Krapp. *Anglo-Saxon Poetic records*, 5. pp. lv, 239. 8° New York, 1932. [A.-S. text and notes.]

5705 **Bright** (James Wilson) and **Ramsay** (Robert Lee). Notes on the ' introductions ' of the West-Saxon psalms. J. Theol. Stud., 13, pp. 520–58. 1912.

5706 **Bromwich** (J. I'A.). Who was the translator of the prose portion of the Paris Psalter? Chadwick Mem. Stud., pp. 289–303. 1950.

5707 **Brou** (Louis), *ed*. The psalter collects from V–VIth century sources (Three series). Edited with introduction, apparatus criticus and indexes by L. Brou from the papers of André Wilmart. *Henry Bradshaw Society*, 83. pp. 283. 8° London, 1949.

5708 **Bruce** (James Douglas). The Anglo-Saxon version of the Book of Psalms commonly known as the Paris Psalter. [MS. Bibl. Nat., Fonds latin, 8824. 9th–10th c.] P.M.L.A., 9, pp. 43–164. 1894.

5709 —— Immediate and ultimate source of the rubrics and introductions to the psalms in the Paris Psalter. Mod. Lang. Notes, 8, cols. 72–82. 1893.

5710 **Foerster** (Max). Die altenglischen Beigaben des Lambeth-Psalters. [i. Gebete ; ii. Hagiologisches (a) St. Mildryð, (b) St. Seaxburh.] Arch. Stud. neueren Spr., Bd. 132, pp. 328–35. 1914.

5711 —— Eine neue altenglische Psalter-Glosse. [Psalms 131–33.] *Same jnl.*, Bd. 122, pp. 96–98. 1909.

5712 **Heinzel** (Otto). Kritische Entstehungsgeschichte des ags. Interlinear-Psalters. *Palaestra*, 151. pp. 119. 8° Leipzig, 1926.

5713 **James** (Montague Rhodes). The Canterbury Psalter and its parent, the Utrecht Psalter. Friends of Canterbury Cathedral, Ann. Rep, 6, pp. 46–52, + 1 plate. 1933.

5714 **Lindeloef** (Uno). Die altenglischen Glossen im Bosworth-Psalter (Brit. Mus. MS. Addit. 37517). [Text, A.-S. and Latin.] Méms. Soc. néophilol. Helsingfors, 5, pp. 137–231. 1909.

5715 —— Der Lambeth-Psalter, eine altenglische Interlinearversion des Psalters in der Hs. 427 der erzbischöflichen Lambeth Palace library zum ersten Male hrsg. Acta Soc. Sc. Fennicae, 35 i (Text und Glossar), pp. 323 : 43 iii (Beschreibung und Geschichte der Hs.), pp. iv, 104. 1909–14.

5716 —— Studien zu altenglischen Psalterglossen. *Bonner Beiträge zur Anglistik*, 13. pp. 123. 8° Bonn, 1904.

5717 **Oess** (Guido). Untersuchungen zum altenglischen Arundel-Psalter. *Diss. Heidelberg*. pp. 38. 8° Heidelberg, 1908. [With A.-S. and Latin text.]

5718 **Ramsay** (Robert Lee). The Latin text of the Paris Psalter : a collation and some conclusions. [Comparison with A.-S. text, etc.] Am. J. Philol., 41, pp. 147–76. 1920.

5719 —— Theodore of Mopsuestia and St. Columban on the psalms. [Theodore is source of an A.-S. version.] Zeit. celt. Phil., 8, pp. 421–51. 1912.

5720 **Wichmann** (Johannes). König Aelfreds angelsächsische Übertragung der Psalmen i–li excl. 8° Halle, 1888.

5721 **Wildhagen** (Karl). Der Psalter des Eadwine von Canterbury. *Studien zur englischen Philologie*, 12. pp. xv, 257, + 2 plates. 8° Halle, 1905.

5722 Wildhagen (Karl). Das Psalterium Gallicanum in England und seine altenglischen Glossierungen. Engl. Studien, 54, pp. 35–45. 1920.

5723 —— Über die in Eadwine's Canterbury Psalter (Trinity College, Cambridge) enthaltene, altenglische Psalter-Interlinearversion. *Diss. Göttingen.* pp. 35. 8° Halle a.d.S., 1903.

5724 Wilmart (André). The prayers of the Bury Psalter. [MS. Vatican, Regina 12. 11th c. Latin text.] Downside Rev., 48, pp. 198–216. 1930.

5725 Wuelcker (Richard Paul). Aus englischen Bibliotheken. [Pp. 354–74, 1. Salisbury und London : A.S. glosses on the Psalter.] Anglia, 2, pp. 354–87. 1879.

79. MISSALS
(and the Mass)
§ *a.* Bobbio Missal

(8th c. MS. Paris, Bibl. Nat. Latin 10837)

5726 Bobbio Missal. The Bobbio Missal. *Henry Bradshaw Society,* 53, 58, 61. 3 vol. 8° London,1917–24. [i. Facimiles : ii. Text,edited by E. A. Lowe : iii. Notes and studies, by André Wilmart, E. A. Lowe and H. A. Wilson.]

5727 Burkitt (Francis Crawford). The Bobbio Missal. J. Theol. Stud., 26, pp. 177–79. 1925.

5728 Morin (Germain). D'où provient le Missel de Bobbio ? Rev. Bénédictine, 31, pp. 326–32. 1914.

5729 Wilmart (André). Une curieuse instruction liturgique du Missel de Bobbio. [7th–8th c. Bib. Nat., MS. 13, 246.] Rev. Charlemagne, 2, pp. 1–16, + 1 plate. 1912.

5730 —— Le palimpseste du Missel de Bobbio. [Kenney, 1, p. 690. St. Ambrose's commentary on Luke, in semiuncials of the 5th or 6th c.] Rev. Bénédictine, 33, pp. 1–18. 1921.

§ *b.* Stowe Missal

(Probably composed for the abbey of Tallaght in first decade of 9th c. Belonged to duke of Buckingham (at Stowe House), then to earl of Ashburnham, and now in R.I.A., Dublin. Irish minuscule. Text in 5 hands.)

5731 **Baeumer** (Suitbert). Das Stowe-Missale neue untersucht. [Kenney, 1, p. 692. Text of mass, based on MacCarthy, and comment.] Zeit. kathol. Theologie, 16, pp. 446–90. 1892.

5732 Bishop (Edmund). The litany of saints in the Stowe Missal. [Reprinted in his Liturgica historica, pp. 137–64. 1918.] J. Theol. Stud., 7, pp. 122–36. 1906.

5733 Bishop (W. C.). The Stowe Missal. Church Q. Rev., 85, pp. 302–14. 1918.

5733a Charleson (John). Stowe Missal. [Plates show its shrine.] Trans. Glasgow Eccles. Soc., 2, pp. 57–67, + 2 plates. 1898.

5734 Grisar (Hartmann). Das gelasianische Messcanon. [Kenney, 1, p. 692. Text of the Stowe Canon, based on Warren.] Zeit. kathol. Theologie, 10, pp. 1–35. 1886.

5735 Healy (John), abp. of Tuam. The Stowe Missal. [*See also* pp. 370–4, reply by B. MacCarthy.] Irish Eccles. Rec., 3rd S., 12, pp. 97–108. 1891.

5736 MacCarthy (Bartholomew). On the Stowe Missal. [With Latin text and notes.] Trans. R.I.A., 27, pp. 135–268, + 1 plate. 1886.

5737 —— The Stowe Missal. [Corrections to Probst : Die abenländische Messe, 5756.] Irish Eccles. Rec., 3rd S. 17, pp. 1132–38. 1896.

5738 Malone (Sylvester). The Stowe Missal. Irish Eccles. Rec., 3rd S., 13, pp. 842–48. 1892.

5739 O'Rahilly (Thomas Francis). The history of the Stowe Missal. Ériu, 10, pp. 95–109. 1926.

5740 Plummer (Charles). Notes on the Stowe Missal. [Kenney, 1, p. 693.] Zeit. vergl. Sprachforschung, 27, pp. 441–48. 1884.

5741 Stokes (Whitley). The Irish passages in the Stowe Missal. pp. 20. 8° Calcutta, 1881. — Revised ed. *in* Zeit. vergl. Sprachforschung, 26, pp. 497–519. 1882 [Kenney, 1, p. 688. Both with Irish and transl.]

5742 Todd (James Henthorn). On the ancient Irish missal, and its silver box, described by Dr. O'Conor in his catalogue of the Stowe MSS., etc. Trans. R.I.A., 23 (Antiq.), pp. 3–37. 1856.

5743 Warren (Frederick Edward). [On] the Stowe Missal. [Question as to which was the earliest form of liturgy in use in the Irish Church.] Proc. Soc. Antiq., 2nd S. 8, pp. 419–24. 1880.

5744 Zimmer (Heinrich). Zum Stowe Missal. [Kenney, 1, p. 693.] Zeit. vergl. Sprachforschung, 28, pp. 376–81. 1886.

§ c. Others

5745 Bannister (Henry Marriott). Fragments of an Anglo-Saxon sacramentary. [' 4 Bll. aus dem Sacramentarium Gelasianum,' found in Cologne City archives.] J. Theol. Stud., 12, pp. 451–54. 1911.

5746 —— Some recently discovered fragments of Irish sacramentaries. *Same jnl.*, 5, pp. 49–75. 1903.

5747 Fierville (Charles). Les préfaces du Missal de Winchester, avec introduction et notes. *Recueil des publications de la Société havraise d'études diverses*, 1880–81, pp. 402–56. 8° Havre, 1882.

5748 Forbes (George Hay), *ed.* Missale Drummondiense : the ancient Irish missal in the possession of Baroness Willoughby de Eresby, Drummond Castle, Perthshire. pp. xxvi, 91, 44, xv. 8° Burntisland, 1882. [Kenney, 1, p. 705. Irish minuscule, 11th c.].

5749 Gougaud (Louis). Les rites de la consécration et de la fraction dans la liturgie celtique de la messe. Report : 19th Eucharistic Congress (London), pp. 348–61. 1908.

5750 Jenner (Henry). The Lannaled mass of St. Germanus in Bodl. MS. 572. [10th–11th c. ms. and its contents.] J. Roy. Inst. Cornwall, 23, pp. 477–92. 1932.

5751 Leofric Missal. The Leofric Missal as used in the cathedral of Exeter . . . 1050–1072 ; together with some account of the Red Book of Derby, the Missal of Robert of Jumièges, and a few other early . . . books of the English Church. Edited . . . by F. E. Warren. pp. lxvi, 344, + 1 plate. 4° Oxford, 1883. [Latin text.]

5752 Leroquais (Victor). Les sacramentaires et les missels manuscrits des bibliothèques publiques de France. 4 vol. 4° Paris, 1924. [Vol. 4, planches. i. Bobbio Missal (7th c.) : Missal of Robert of Jumièges (11th c.), etc.]

5753 Loisel (——), *abbé*. Un missel et un bénédictionnaire anglo-saxons de la Bibliothèque de Rouen. [Both of abp. Robert of Jumièges.] Amis des monuments rouennais, Bull., 1911, pp. 119–33, + 1 plate. 1911.

5754 McCarthy (Bartholomew). Ancient Irish missals. [Corpus, Oxford, missal. Between 1002 and 1014.] Irish Eccles. Rec., 3rd S. 1, pp. 505–14. 1880.

5755 Power (Patrick). The Mass in the early Irish Church. *Same jnl.*, 5th S. 60, pp. 197–206. 1942.

5756 Probst (Ferdinand). Die abenländische Messe vom fünften bis zum achten Jahrhundert. pp. xv, 444. 8° Münster, 1896. [3 chapters on the Irish liturgy (pp. 40–99, the Stowe Missal : corrections by B. MacCarthy, 5737).]

5757 Quigley (E. J.). The Clones missal. [?date. 800–900 (Madan) : 11th–12th c. (Lowe) : 1002–14 (B. McCarthy). At Corpus Christi, Oxford.] Irish Eccles. Rec., 5th S. 17, pp. 381–89, 496–503, 603–09. 1921.

5758 Wilson (Henry Austin). English mass-books in the ninth century. J. Theol. Stud., 3, pp. 429–33. 1902.

80. OTHER SERVICE BOOKS

(*See also* 111 and 204)

5759 Atkins (*Sir* Ivor). An investigation of two Anglo-Saxon kalendars (Missal of Robert of Jumièges and St. Wulfstan's Homiliary). Archaeologia, 78, pp. 219–54, + 2 plates. 1928.

T

5760 Benedict, *St.* Das Benediktiner-Offizium, ein altenglisches Brevier aus dem 11. Jahrhundert. Ein Beitrag zur Wulfstanfrage von Emil Feiler. *Anglistische Forschungen*, 4. pp. viii, 81. 8° Heidelberg, 1901. [Teil I, Einleitung. *Diss., Heidelberg.* pp. 48. *Published separately.* 8° Heidelberg, 1900.]

5761 Bishop (W. C.). A service book of the seventh century. [Kenney, 1, p. 197. Antiphony of Bangor. At Bobbio till 1606, when transferred to Ambrosian Library, Milan.] Church Q. Rev., 37, pp. 337–63. 1894.

5762 Canterbury Benedictional. The Canterbury Benedictional (British Museum, Harl. MS. 2892). Edited by Reginald Maxwell Woolley. *Henry Bradshaw Society*, 51. pp. xxvi, 178, + 3 plates. [?Second quarter of 11th c.] 8° London, 1917.

5763 Cook (Albert Stanburrough). The Old English glosses of the *Te Deum*. Arch. Stud. neueren Spr., Bd. 122, pp. 263–68. 1909.

5764 Culhane (Robert). The Bangor hymn to Christ the king. [In Antiphony of Bangor (680–91): did St. Hilary write the hymn?] Irish Eccles. Rec., 5th S. 74, pp. 207–19. 1950.

5765 Doble (Gilbert Hunter). The Lanalet Pontifical. (Bibliothèque de la ville de Rouen, A. 27). pp. 19. 8° Bristol, 1934. [Formerly belonged to Jumièges. Compilation of an English bishop, probably of Wells. 10th c.]

5766 Durham, *Monastery.* Rituale ecclesiae Dunelmensis. The Durham Collectar. A new and revised edition of the Latin text with the interlinear Anglo-Saxon version. *Surtees Society*, 140. pp. lxxxi, 221, + 3 plates. 8° Durham, 1927.

5767 Fehr (Bernhard). Altenglische Ritualtexte für Krankenbesuch, heilige Ölung und Begräbnis. Texte u. Forschungen. Festgabe für F. Liebermann, pp. 20–67. 1921.

5768 Leofric Collectar. The Leofric Collectar (Harl. MS. 2961), with an appendix containing a litany and prayers from Harl. MS. 863. (The Leofric Collectar compared with the Collectar of St. Wulfstan, together with kindred documents of Exeter and Worcester). *Henry Bradshaw Society*, 45, 56. 2 vol. 4° London, 1914–21.

5769 Morin (Germain). Le Collectaneum de Léofric et le Liber capitularis d'Étienne de Liège. [MS. Harl. 2961. 11th c.] Rev. Bénédictine, 12, pp. 196–98. 1895.

5770 Robinson (Stanford Frederick Hudson). On a fragment of an Anglo-Saxon benedictional preserved at Exeter cathedral. Trans. St. Paul's Ecclesiol. Soc., 5, pp. 221–28. 1904.

5771 Rock (Daniel). The Church of our fathers, as seen in St. Osmund's rite for the cathedral of Salisbury, with dissertations on the belief and ritual in England before and after the coming of the Normans. 3 vol. [in 4]. 8° London, 1849. [Temp. William I.]

5772 Skeat (Walter William). Collation of the Durham Ritual, with notes, etc. Trans. Philol. Soc., 1877–79, pp. 51*–72*. 1879.

5773 Williams (B.), *ed.* Anglo-Saxon calendar of the early part of the eleventh century from a missal preserved in the public library of Rouen, marked MS. Y$\frac{34}{22}$ bis. pp. 23. 8° London, 1851.

5774 Wilson (Henry Austin), *ed.* The Benedictional of archbishop Robert [of Jumièges, at Rouen]. *Henry Bradshaw Society*, 24. pp. xxii, 210, + 6 plates (facsimiles). 8° London, 1903. [Gross, 1429a. A pontifical written at Winchester late in 10th c.].

5775 Wormald (Francis), *ed.* English kalendars before A.D. 1100. vol. 1, texts. *Henry Bradshaw Society*, 72. pp. xv, 265. 8° London, 1934.

81. DEVOTIONAL BOOKS, PRAYERS, LORICAS, ETC.

5776 Byrne (Mary E.). Feilire Adamnáin. [Prayer to saints who preside over different seasons. Irish text and translation.] Ériu, 1, pp. 225–28. 1904.

5776a Cabrol (Fernand). Le Book of Cerne et les liturgies celtiques. [Kenney, 1, p. 721.] Rev. quest. hist., 76, pp. 210–22. 1904.

5777 Cerne, *Book of.* The Prayer Book of Ædeluald the bishop, commonly called the Book of Cerne. Edited by Arthur Benedict Kuypers. pp. xxxvi, 286, + 2 plates. 4° Cambridge, 1902. [Kenney, 1, p. 720. MS. Camb. Univ. Lib., Ll. I. 10. 8th–9th c.]

5778 Esposito (Mario). The Lorica of Lathcen. J. Theol. Stud., 30, pp. 289–91. 1929.

5779 Friedel (Victor H.). La lorica de Leyde. [MS. of 9th or 10th c. Latin text and French translation, and notes.] Zeit. celt. Phil., 2, pp. 64–72, + 1 plate. 1899.

5780 Gildas. Der Lorica-Hymnus mit der angelsächsischen Glossierung nebst einer Abhandlungen über Text und Sprache des Denkmals. (Das Lorica-Gebet und die Lorica-Namen). Herausgegeben von Günther Leonhardi. *Bibliothek der angelsächsischen Prosa (W. M. Grein und R. P. Wülker)*, Bd. 6, pp. 175–243. 8° Hamburg, 1905.

5781 Gougaud (Louis). Étude sur les *loricae* celtiques et sur les prières qui s'en rapprochent. [Kenney, 1, p. 251. List with bibliographies and commentary.] Bull. d'ancienne litt. et d'archéol. chrét., 1, pp. 265–81; 2, pp. 33–41, 101–27. 1911–12.

5782 Holthausen (Ferdinand). Eine altenglische Aufforderung zum Gebet um Fürbitte. [Reconstruction of text in A.–S. and Latin.] Engl. Studien, 75, pp. 284–86. 1943.

5783 —— Altenglische Interlinearversionen lateinischer Gebete und Beichten. [From Arundel MS. 155. With A.–S. and Latin texts.] Anglia, 65 (N.F. 53), pp. 230–54. 1941.

5784 Leofric Missal. Prière tirée du Missel de Léofric. [Latin text only.] Rev. anglo-romaine, 1, p. 321. 1895.

5785 Leonhardi (Günther). Die Lorica des Gildas. *Diss., Leipzig.* pp. 50. 8° Leipzig, 1905.

5786 Long (Edward T.). The Book of Cerne. Proc. Dorset Archaeol. Soc., 53 (for 1931), pp. xli–xliii. 1932.

5787 Meyer (Kuno). An Old Irish prayer for long life. [8th c. Poem: 'I invoke the seven daughters of the sea', with translation, from MS. Laud 610 and Book of Ballymote, 340a.] Miscellany pres. J. M. Mackay, pp. 226–32. 1914.

5788 Meyer (Wilhelm). Gildae oratio rythmica. Nachrichten K. Gesell. Wiss. Göttingen, Philol.-hist. Kl., 1912, pp. 48–108. 1912.

5789 —— Poetische Nachlese aus dem sogenannten Book of Cerne in Cambridge und aus dem Londoner Codex Regius 2A. xx. *Same jnl.*, 1917, pp. 597–625. 1917.

5790 Nunnaminster, *Book of.* An ancient manuscript of the eighth or ninth century: formerly belonging to St. Mary's abbey, or Nunnaminster, Winchester. Edited by Walter de Gray Birch. *Hampshire Record Society*, 1. pp. 152, + 1 plate. 8° London and Winchester, 1889. [Latin text of MS. Harley 2965, with introduction on history of the abbey and of the ms., and appendices.]

5791 Singer (Charles Joseph). The Lorica of Gildas the Briton (?547). A magico-medical text containing an anatomical vocabulary. [With Latin text and translation.] Proc. Roy. Soc. Med. (Hist. med. section), 12, pp. 124–44. 1919.

5792 —— The Lorica of Gildas the Briton. A magical text of the sixth century. [A fuller version of **5791.**] Singer (C.): From magic to science, pp. 111–32, + 1 plate. 1928.

5793 Wilson (Henry Austin). On a rhythmical prayer in the Book of Cerne. [Mercian, first half of 9th c.] J. Theol. Stud., 5, pp. 263–65. 1904.

5794 Zupitza (Julius). Eine weitere Aufzeichnung der Oratio pro peccatis. [A.–S. text.] Arch. Stud. neueren Spr., Bd. 84, pp. 327–29. 1890.

82. HOMILIES

§ *a*. The Blicking Homilies

5795 Foerster (Max). Zu den Blickling Homilies. [*See also* Bd. 92 (1894), p. 413 for a comment by F. Holthausen.] Arch. Stud. neueren Spr., Bd. 91, pp. 179–206. 1893.

5796 —— Zur vierten Blickling Homily. [Cf. Visio Pauli, § 35.] *Same jnl.*, Bd. 103, p. 149. 1899.

5797 Holthausen (Ferdinand). Zur 14. Blickling homily. *Same jnl.*, Bd. 123, p. 401. 1909.

5798 Willard (Rudolph). The Blickling-Junius tithing homily and Caesarius of Arles. Malone (K.): Philologica, pp. 65–78. 1949.

5799 —— On Blickling homily XIII; *the Assumption of the Virgin*: the source and the missing passages. Rev. Engl. Stud., 12, pp. 1–17. 1936.

5800 —— The two accounts of the Assumption in Blickling homily XIII. *Same jnl.*, 14, pp. 1–19. 1938.

§ *b*. Wulfstan, Homilist

(archbishop of York, 1003–23)

5801 Becher (Christian Felix Richard). Wulfstans Homilien. *Diss.*, *Leipzig*. pp. 106. 8° Leipzig, 1910.

5802 Bethurum (Dorothy). Archbishop Wulfstan's commonplace book. [Largely liturgical matter.] P.M.L.A., 57, pp. 916–29. 1942.

5803 Jost (Karl Theodor). Einige Wulfstantexte und ihre Quellen. Anglia, 56 (N.F. 44), pp. 265–315. 1932.

5804 —— Wulfstanstudien. *Schweitzer anglistische Arbeiten*, 23. pp. 271. 8° Bern, 1950.

5805 Kinard (James Pinckney). A study of Wulfstan's homilies, their style and sources. A dissertation. pp. 60. 8° Baltimore, 1897. [Gross, 1433, lit.]

5806 McIntosh (Angus). Wulfstan's prose. Proc. Brit. Acad., 35, pp. 109–42. 1949.

5807 McLachlan (*Dame* Laurentia)˙ St. Wulfstan's prayer book. [MS. C.C.C.C. 391, 11th c. Formerly known as Portiforium (or Breviarium) Oswaldi.] J. Theol. Stud., 30, pp. 174–77. 1929.

5808 Napier (Arthur Sampson). Über die Werke des altenglischen Erzbischofs Wulfstan. *Diss.*, *Göttingen*, 1882. pp. 71. 8° Weimar, 1882. [Gross, 1433, lit.]

5809 Priebsch (Robert Charles). The chief sources of some Anglo-Saxon homilies. [Wulfstan xlv, xliii, lvii. Latin and A.-S. texts.] Otia Merseiana, 1, pp. 129–47. 1899.

5810 Whitelock (Dorothy). A note on the career of Wulfstan the homilist. E.H.R., 52, pp. 460–65. 1937.

5811 Wulfstan, *II, abp. of York, St. and homilist.* Sammlung der ihm zugeschriebenen Homilien, herausgegeben von A. S. Napier, nebst Untersuchungen über ihre Echtheit. Abt. 1, Text und Varianten. pp. x, 318. 8° Berlin, 1883. [Gross, 1433.]

5712 —— Sermo Lupi ad Anglos, edited by Dorothy Whitelock. *Methuen's Old English Library*, B.3. pp. viii, 63. 8° London, 1939.

§ *c*. Other Anglo-Saxon Homilies

5813 Crawford (Samuel John). Beowulfiana. [i. Beowulf, 1724–1768. Comparison of 'Hrothgar's sermon', with letter of St. Boniface to Æthilbald of Mercia (Monumenta Moguntina ed. Jaffé), Ep. 59, pp. 168–77.] Rev. Eng. Stud., 7, pp. 448–50. 1931.

5814 Foerster (Max). Altenglische Predigtquellen. [I. i. Pseudo-Augustin und die 7. Blickling Homily: ii. Pseudo-Augustin und Ælfric: iii. Adso und Wulfstan: iv. Anselm von Canterbury: v. Honorius' Elucidarium: II. vi. Petrus Chrysologus und die 14. Blickling Homily: vii. Augustin und *Be Gecyrrednysse*: viii. Defensor und *Be þurhwununge*: ix. Martin vaa Braga und Ælfrics De falsis deis.] Arch. Stud. neueren Spr., Bd. 116, pp. 301–14; 122, pp. 246–62. 1906–09.

5815 Foerster (Max). Der Inhalt der altenglischen Handschrift Vespasianus D. XIV. [Supplementary to **5818**.] Engl. Studien, 54, pp. 46–68. 1920.

5816 —— Der Vercelli-Codex CXVII nebst Abdruck einiger altenglischer Homilien der Handschrift. Festschrift für L. Morsbach, pp. 20–180. 1913.

5817 Napier (Arthur Sampson). Contributions to Old English literature : 1. An Old English homily on the observance of Sunday. English miscellany presented to F. J. Furnivall, pp. 355–61. 1901.

5818 Warner (Rubie D.-N.). Early English homilies, from the twelfth century MS. Vesp. D. XIV. *Early English Text Society*, O.S. 152. pp. viii, 149. 8° London, 1917. [*See also* **5815**].

5819 Willard (Rudolph). Two Apocrypha in Old English homilies. *Beiträge zur englischen Philologie*, 30. pp. viii, 149. 8° Leipzig, 1935. [The Apocryphon of the Seven Heavens, and The three utterances of the soul.]

5820 —— Vercelli homily VIII and the *Christ*. [A.–S. text of homily given : = sermon on penance and the Last Judgement.] P.M.L.A., 42, pp. 314–30. 1927.

5821 —— Vercelli homily XI and its sources. [First of three for Rogationtide. Text in Latin and A.–S., with English translation.] Speculum, 24, pp. 76–87. 1949.

83. MISCELLANEOUS LITUR-
GICAL TEXTS, ETC.

§ *a*. Anglo-Saxon

5822 [Anon.] The liturgy and ritual of the Anglo-Saxon Church. Church Q. Rev., 14, pp. 276–94. 1882.

5823 Foerster (Max). Die altenglischen Bekenntnisformeln. Engl. Studien, 75, pp. 159–69. 1943.

5824 —— Das lateinisch-altenglische Fragment der Apokryphe von Jamnes und Mambres. Archiv Stud. neueren Spr., Bd. 108, pp. 15–28. 1902.

5825 —— Zu den ae. Texten aus Ms. Arundel 155. [*See also* p. 168, note by Holthausen.] Anglia, 66 (N.F. 54), pp. 52–55. 1942.

5826 Foerster (Max). Zur Liturgik der angelsächsischen Kirche. [i. Altenglische *Confiteor*-Texte : ii. Altenglische Achtloster-Reihen : iii. Ein ae. Apostelgebet.] Anglia, 66 (N.F. 54), pp. 1–51. 1942.

5827 Holthausen (Ferdinand). Eine altenglische Interlinearversion des Athanasianischen Glaubensbekenntnisses. [A.–S. and Latin text from MS. Harl. 863, fol. 107–08, 10th c.] Engl. Studien, 75, pp. 6–8. 1942.

5828 Koelbing (Eugen). Zur altenglischen Glossen-Literatur. *Same jnl.*, 3, pp. 469–72. 1880.

5829 Lindeloef (Uno). A new collation of the gloss of the Durham Ritual. Mod. Lang. Rev., 18, pp. 273–80. 1923.

5830 Logeman (Henri). Anglo-Saxonica minora. [A.–S. texts–penitentials, prayers, confessions, homilies, etc.] Anglia, 11, pp. 97–120 : 12, pp. 497–518. 1889.

5831 Shepherd (Geoffrey). The sources of the O.E. *Kentish hymn*. [MS. Cotton Vesp. D.VI.] Mod. Lang. Notes, 67, pp. 395–97. 1952.

5832 Sievers (Eduard). Zu den angelsächsischen Glossen. [i. Aldhelm (Anglia 13, [**3926**]) : ii. Zu Ælfric's Glossar : iii. Zu den Glossae Harleianae : iv. Zu den Prosperglossen : v. Zu den Cleopatraglossen.] Anglia, 13 (N.F. 1), pp. 309–32. 1891.

5833 Turner (Cuthbert Hamilton). The Churches at Winchester in the early eleventh century. [A liturgical text in MS. F. 173 in Worcester Cathedral Library, written at Winchester.] J. Theol. Stud., 17, pp. 65–68. 1916.

§ *b*. Celtic

5834 [Anon.] Ancient Irish hymn of St. Brogan-Cloen in praise of St. Brigid. [Irish and Latin text.] Irish Eccles. Rec., 4, pp. 221–37. 1868.

5835 [Anon.] Ancient Irish poem by Saint Colman Uacluasaigh. [7th c. Irish text and English translation.] *Same jnl.*, 4, pp. 402–09. 1868.

5836 [Anon.] Fragments from the early Irish Church. [Prayer of St. Molaissi, abbot of Devenish : Hymn to St. Molaissi : Sermon on St. Brigid.] *Same jnl.*, 5, pp. 224–29. 1869.

5837 [Anon.] Liturgical fragments from the early Celtic Church. [i. The Book of Deer : ii. The Stowe Missal.] *Same jnl.*, 6, pp, 549–59, 645–58. 1870.

5838 [Anon.] The liturgy and ritual of the Celtic Church. Church Q. Rev., 10, pp. 50–84. 1880.

5839 Anderson (Alan Orr), *ed.* Peannaid Adaim, ' The penance of Adam '. [Irish text from MS. XL, Advocates Library, and English translation.] Rev. celt., 24, 99. 243–53. 1903.

5840 Bernard (J. H.). i. On the Stowe St. John : and ii. On the citations from scripture in the Leabhar Breac. Trans. R.I.A., 30, pp. 313–24. 1893.

5840a Best (Richard Irvine). The canonical hours. [Irish text and translation from T.C.D., Ms. H. 3. 17, col. 675. Ériu, 3, p. 116. 1907.

5841 Blume (Clemens). Hymnodia Hiberno-Celtica, sæc. v–ix. Dreves : Analecta hymnica, 51, pp. 257–372. 1908.

5842 Gougaud (Louis). The Celtic liturgies historically considered. Cath. Hist. Rev., 16, pp. 175–82. 1930.

5843 —— Liturgies et arts celtiques : 1. Les liturgies celtiques. Rev. celt., 32, pp. 245–50. 1911.

5844 —— Sur trois anciennes fêtes de Notre-Seigneur. [In Martyrology of Oengus, etc., 9th c. Return from Egypt, presentation in the temple, and victory over the devil.] Bull. anc. litt. et archéol. chrét., 4, pp. 208–10. 1914.

5845 Hennig (John). Studies in the liturgy of the early Irish Church. Irish Eccles. Rec., 5th S. 75, pp. 318–33. 1951.

5846 James (Montague Rhodes). Irish apocrypha. J. Theol. Stud., 20, pp. 9–16. 1919.

5847 —— Syriac apocrypha in Ireland. [?Obligation on the part of an Irish writer to an Oriental text.] *Same jnl.*, 11, pp. 290–91. 1910.

5848 Knott (Eleanor). An index to the proper names in Saltair na Rann. Ériu, 16, pp. 99–122. 1952.

5849 MacGregor (Duncan). An ancient Gaelic treatise on the symbolism of the Eucharist, with translation and notes. [Two forms : i. in Lebar Brecc—Irish text and English translation here, with additions from ii. Stowe Missal version.] Trans. Aberdeen Ecclesiol. Soc., 3 (1896), pp. 293–340. 1898.

5850 Meyer (Wilhelm), *ed.* Das turiner Bruckstück der ältesten irischen Liturgie. [Kenney, 1, p. 712. Turin, MS. F. IV. 1 ; from Bobbio. *See also* **5863**.] Nachrichten K. Gesell. Wiss. Göttingen, philol.-hist. Kl., 1903, pp. 163–214. 1903.

5851 Milne-Home (Grace). On the Gallican liturgy. Trans. Aberdeen Ecclesiol. Soc., 4 (1897), pp. 100–08. 1901.

5852 Morin (Germain). Destination de la formule ' ad pacem celebrandam ' dans l'Antiphonaire de Bangor. [Kenney, 1, p. 707. 7th c.] Rev. Bénédictine, 12, pp. 201–02. 1895.

5853 Mulcahy (C.). The Irish Latin hymns : Sancti venite of St. Sechnall (d. *cir.* 447) and Altus prosator of St. Columba (521–597). [With Latin text and translations.] Irish Eccles. Rec., 5th S. 57, pp. 385–405. 1941.

5854 Nerney (D. S.). The Bangor [baptismal] Symbol. Irish Theol. Q., 19, pp. 369–85 : 20, pp. 273–86, 389–401. 1952–53.

5855 O'Curry (Eugene). The mss. remains of Prof. O'Curry in the Catholic University. 1. The prayer of St. Colga of Clonmacnoise. (2. Prayer of St. Aireran the Wise, ob. 664 : 3. The rule of St. Carthach (ob. A.D. 636). Irish Eccles. Rec., 1, pp. 63–64, 112–18. 1864.

5856 O'Mahony (T. J.). The Alleluiatic hymn of St. Cummain Fota. (A postscript to remarks on St. Cummain Fota's hymn.) [Bp. and abbot of Clonfert, 7th c.] *Same jnl.*, 4th S. 1, pp. 441–48 : 2, pp. 152–59. 1897.

5857 Plummer (Charles), *ed.* Irish litanies. Text and translation. Edited from the manuscripts. *Henry Bradshaw Society*, 62. pp. xxiv, 140. 8° London, 1925. [Kenney, 1, p. 729. Irish and English.]

5858 Priebsch (Robert Charles). Quelle und Abfassungszeit der Sonntagsepistel in der irischen Cáin Domnaig. [9th c.] Mod. Lang. Rev., 2, pp. 138–54. 1907.

5859 Sanctain, St. Hymn of St. Sanctain. [5th c. Irish text, and English translation.] Irish Eccles. Rec., 4, pp. 317–25. 1868.

5860 Seymour (St. John Drelincourt). Notes on Apocrypha in Ireland. Proc. R.I.A., 37c, pp. 107–17. 1926.

5861 Stokes (Whitley). The Lebar Brecc Tractate on the consecration of a church. [15th c., but treatise dates (on linguistic grounds) from 11th c.] Miscellanea linguistica in onore di G. Ascoli, pp. 363–87. 1901.

5862 ——, *ed.* Tidings of the Resurrection. [Irish text and English translation, from Book of the Dun Cow (Leabhar na Huildhre), pp. 34a–37b, of end of 12th or beginning of 13th c.] Rev. celt., 25, pp. 232–59. 1904.

5863 Warren (Frederick Edward). An early Irish liturgical fragment. [7th c.? From Turin MS. F. IV. 1. Published with notes by W. Meyer, **5850.**] J. Theol. Stud., 4, pp. 610–13. 1903.

5864 —— The liturgy and ritual of the Celtic church. pp. xix, 291. 8° Oxford, 1881. [Gross, 1608.]

5865 —— Un monument inedit de la liturgie celtique. [Latin text. At end of a 10th c. psalter in Salisbury Cathedral Library.] Rev. cclt., 9, pp. 88–96. 1888.

84. GEOGRAPHY, GENERAL

§ *a.* Anglo-Saxon

5866 Arkell (William Joscelyn). Place-names and topography in the upper Thames country: a regional essay. Oxoniensia, 7, pp. 1–23. 1942.

5867 Bowen (Emrys George). Early Christianity in the British Isles—a study in historical geography. Geography, 17, pp. 267–76. 1932.

5868 Coote (Henry Charles). Notes on the district of the Magesætas, and on the topography generally referred to in the charter of king Eadgar, described by Mr. de Gray Birch [299]. Proc. Soc. Antiq., 2nd S. 8, pp. 273–75. 1880.

5869 Crawford (Osbert Guy Stanhope). Map of Britain in the Dark Ages. *Ordnance Survey.* 2 sheets, Southampton, 1935–38. [South sheet to 871 : North sheet to c. 850.]

5870 Darby (Henry Clifford). The economic geography of England, A.D. 1000–1250. [With 8 figures in text, Waste and forest : colonisation : the English village : towns and commerce.] Hist. geog. of England, ed. H. C. Darby, pp. 165–229. 1936.

5871 ——, *ed.* An historical geography of England before A.D. 1800 ; fourteen studies. pp. xii, 568. 8° Cambridge, 1936. [87 maps. *See also* under individual authors.]

5872 —— The human geography of the Fenland before the drainage. [A.–S. (Ingulf) and Domesday evidence. P. 422, map of ' surface deposits of the Fenland and distribution of Domesday vills.'] Geog. J., 80, pp. 420–35. 1932.

5873 Evans (E. Estyn). An essay on the historical geography of the Shropshire-Montgomeryshire borderland. Collns. hist. and archaeol. rel. to Montgom., 40, pp. 242–70, + map. 1928.

5874 Fullbrook-Leggatt (L.E.W.O.) Saxon Gloucestershire. [County boundaries and hundreds—Place- and personal-names—Trackways and saltways—Index to map.] Trans. Bristol and Glos. Arch. Soc., 57, pp. 110–35 + folding map. 1935.

5875 G. (R. M.). Whittlesey meer [Cambs.]. [A fourth part bought by Ælfsius, abbot of Burgh (1006–55) : description of its boundaries and rights of the abbot over it. Translated from Chronicon Petroburgense.] Fenland N. and Q., 3, pp. 2–4. 1895.

5876 Irving (George Vere). On the geography of the wars between the Saxons of Northumberland, and the northern Britons, from the battle of Menno to that of Kaltraez. J. Brit. Archaeol. Assoc., 11, pp. 40–56, 117–28, + 1 plate. 1855.

5876a Jackson (J. N.). The historical geography of Herefordshire, from Saxon times to the Act of Union, 1536. Herefordshire : Centenary of Woolhope Club, pp. 180–90, + 6 maps. 1954.

5877 Lach-Szyrma (Wladyslaw Somerville). The site of London beyond the border a thousand years ago. [The forest of Essex, with the vills of Barking, Stratford, etc., in the clearings.] *Same jnl.,* 57 (N.S. 7), pp. 39–46. 1901.

5878 Major (Albany Featherstonehaugh). The geography of the lower Parrett in early times and the position of Cruca. Proc. Somerset Arch. Soc., 66 (1920), pp. 56–65. 1921.

5879 Mohr (W.). Die geographische Beschreibung Englands in Bedas Kirchengeschichte. Zeit. deut. Geistesgesch., 1, pp. 322–24. 1936.

5880 Myres (John Nowell Linton). Britain in the Dark Ages. [The Dark Ages map : place-names, etc.] Antiquity, 9, pp. 455–64. 1935.

5881 Ormerod (George). An account of some ancient remains existing in the district adjacent to the confluence of the Wye and the Severn . . . and an identification of the Estriyhoiel of Domesday. Archaeologia, 29, pp. 5–31, + map, + 1 plate. 1842.

5882 Page (William). Notes on the types of English villages and their distribution. [Nucleated settlements, including their A.–S. cemeteries.] Antiquity, 1, pp. 447–68. 1927.

5883 —— The origins of forms of Hertfordshire towns and villages. [9 plans in text. *See also* Proc. Soc. Antiq., 2nd S. 30, pp. 219–21, 1918 : Discussion.] Archaeologia, 69, pp. 47–60. 1920.

5884 Peake (Harold John Edward). Roeburgh hundred [Berkshire] and its associations. Trans. Newbury District F.C., 8, pp. 63–70. 1938.

5885 Smith (Reginald Allender). Roman roads and the distribution of Saxon churches in London. [7 plans and 3 figures in text.] Archaeologia, 68, pp. 229–62. 1917.

5886 Somersetshire Archæological Society. Alfred the Great's millenary. Visit to Alfred's country. [Including Lyng, Athelney, Boroughbridge, and Aller.] Proc. Somerset Arch. Soc., 47 (1901), pp. 67–81. 1902.

5887 Walker (George P.). The lost Wantsum Channel : its importance to Richborough castle. [Pp. 102–08, Saxon period : with map.] Arch. Cant., 39, pp. 91–111. 1927.

5888 Ward (Gordon). The river Limen at Ruckinge. [' To show that in A.D. 724 it passed through the southern part of the parish of Ruckinge. With map.] Arch. Cant., 45, pp. 129–32. 1933.

5889 —— The topography of some Saxon charters relating to the Faversham district. Arch. Cant., 46, pp. 123–36, + map. 1934.

5890 Wooldridge (Sidney William). The Anglo-Saxon settlement. [With 7 figures in text. Physique of Saxon England : on the nature of the conquest : the entrance phase, archaeological evidence : the entrance phase, evidence of place-names : the emergence of the kingdoms : the later A.–S. period.] Hist. geog. of England, ed. H. C. Darby, pp. 88–132. 1936.

5891 —— and **Linton** (D. L.). Some aspects of the Saxon settlement in south-east England considered in relation to the geographical background. Geography, 20, pp. 161–75. 1935.

5892 —— and **Smetham** (D. J.). The glacial drifts of Essex and Hertfordshire, and their bearing upon the agricultural and historical geography of the region. [Pp. 259–64 deal with the geography of the Saxon settlement. Fig. 9 : distribution of Saxon place-names, fig. 10 : distribution of manors noted in the Domesday Book.] Geog. J., 78, pp. 243–69. 1931.

§ b. Viking

5893 Bugge (Alexander). Seafaring and shipping during the Viking ages. Saga Book V.C., 6, pp. 13–27. 1909.

5894 Downes (George). On the Norse geography of ancient Ireland. Trans. R.I.A., 19 (Antiq.), pp. 84–96. 1843. *Same title.* Proc. R.I.A., 2 (1841), pp. 87–89. 1844.

5895 Du Chaillu (Paul Belloni). Scandinavia : the Vikings and the geography of their times. [A small amount of A.–S. background.] Scot. Geog. Mag., 6, pp. 225–34. 1890.

5896 Ekwall (Eilert). The Scandinavian settlement. [The northern Danelaw : the Danish midlands : Danish East Anglia : Norwegian settlements in the west : the Danish settlers.] Hist. geog. of England, ed. H. C. Darby, pp. 133–64. 1936.

5897 Eminson (Thomas Benjamin Franklin). The holmes of the manor of Scotter [Lincs.], in the Lindsey vale of the Trent. [To show, by a description of the holmes of the open country, how complete was the Danish dominance of the valley.] Antiquary, 47, pp. 101–9. 1911.

5898 Kendrick (*Sir* Thomas Downing). Maps illustrating the Viking invasions of England. [5 maps in text : i. Exploratory invasions : ii. Conquest of the east and the attack on Wessex : iii. The three years' war : iv. The second invasion : v. Svein's conquest.] Saga-Book V.C., 11 (1928–33), pp. 61–70. 1934.

5899 McIntire (W. T.). The historical connection between Mann, Cumberland and Westmorland. [Synopsis of a lecture. Evidence of identity of Viking settlements from crosses.] J. Manx Mus., 2, pp. 46–48. 1932.

5900 Mawer (*Sir* Allen). The Viking age. Newton (A. P.) : Travel and travellers of the Middle Ages, pp. 70–87. 1926.

5901 O'Dell (Andrew C.). The Norse setttlement of north Scotland in its geographical setting. Saga-Book V.C., 11 (1928–36), pp. 252–59. 1936.

5902 Smith (Joseph Huband). On the ancient Norse and Danish geography of Ireland. Proc. R.I.A., 7 (1861), pp. 390–92. 1862.

§ *c*. Celtic

5903 Crawford (Osbert Guy Stanhope). Early Scotland. Map of Britain in the Dark Ages, north sheet. [450–850]. Antiquity, 13, pp. 53–57. 1939.

5904 Fitzgerald (*Lord* Walter). The historical geography of early Ireland. *Geographical Teacher, supplement*, 1. pp. vii, 94. 8° London, 1926. [Kenney, 1, p. 100. Map on p. 86.]

5905 Kerslake (Thomas). Traces of the ancient kingdom of Damnonia outside Cornwall. [Dedications to Celtic saints.] J. Brit. Archaeol. Assoc., 33, pp. 411–31. 1877.

5906 Lawlor (Henry Cairnes). The circuit of Muirchertach [941]. [Comments on **5910**.] J. Roy. Soc. Antiq. Ireland, 67 (7th S. 7), pp. 128–30. 1937.

5907 Lithgow (Robert Alexander Douglas). Saul, in Ulster, [co. Down], and its locality, with especial reference to St. Patrick. J. Brit. Archaeol. Assoc., 40, pp. 72–90. 1884.

5908 Mackinnell (W. A.). The Isle of Saints. Lantern lecture. [Off coast of Argyllshire.] Trans. Dumfries. Antiq. Soc., N.S. 23, pp. 302–05, + 2 plates. 1911.

5909 Milman (Henry Salusbury). The political geography of Wales. [Pp. 19–24, A.-S. period.] Archaeologia, 38, pp. 19–36. 1860.

5910 Morris (Henry). The circuit of Ireland : by Muirchertach na gCochall gCroiceann, A.D. 941. [Identification of 32 camping places. *See also* **5906**.] J. Roy. Soc. Antiq. Ireland, 66 (7th S. 6), pp. 9–31 : 68, pp. 291–93. 1936, 1938.

5911 —— From ' The Triads of Ireland '. [9th c. 12 topographical triads with notes.] County Louth Archaeol. J., 5, pp. 35–36. 1921.

5912 Munch (Peter Andreas). Geographical elucidations of the Scottish and Irish local names occurring in the sagas. [i. The Orkneys : ii. Katones (Caithness) and its adjoining districts : iii. Shetland (Hjatlland).] Mém. Soc. roy. Antiq. Nord, 1845–49, pp. 208–65 : 1850–60, pp. 61–134. 1849–60.

5913 Murray (Laurence P.). The ancient territories of Oirghialla, Uladh and Conaille Muirthemhne. [West, east, and north Ulster.] County Louth Archaeol. J., 3, pp. 52–65. 1912.

5914 Olden (Thomas). On the geography of Ros Ailithir. [=Rosscarbery, co. Cork. Monastery and School founded by St. Fachtna. Treatise, 10th c.] Proc. R.I.A., Ser. 2. 2, pp. 219–52. 1884.

5915 Owen (Thomas Morgan). Historic places on the Welsh borders. [Buttington, Rhyd y Groes, Carno, *etc.*). Antiq. Mag., 5, pp. 185–9. 1884.

5916 Palmer (Alfred Neobard). Welsh settlements, east of Offa's dyke, during the eleventh century. Y Cymmrodor, 10, pp. 29–45. 1889.

5917 Rees (William). An historical atlas of Wales. pp. 71, + 70 maps. 4° Cardiff, 1951. [Pp. 14–25, + maps 17–29, A.-S. period.]

5918 Rose-Troup (Frances). Wealcynne : the land of the Britons. [In Alfred's will. ?=Wilts, Dorset and Somerset, or ?=Devon and Cornwall.] Devon and Cornwall N. and Q., 20, pp. 10–15. 1938.

5919 Walsh (Paul). The topography of *Betha Colmáin.* [Colman was a Westmeath saint.] Zeit. celt. Phil., 8, pp. 568–82. 1912.

5920 Worth (Richard Nicholls). Notes on the ancient topography of Cornwall. [Including 7th c. Ravennat's list.] J. Roy. Inst. Cornwall, 8, pp. 343–53, + map. 1885.

5921 Young (J. L.). Olaf Peacock's journey to Ireland. [Laxdæla Saga, 21. In 955–58.] Acta phil. Scand., 8, pp. 94–96. 1933.

85. FRONTIERS AND BOUNDARIES OF KINGDOMS AND SHIRES

(*See also* **121 § b** for Offa's dyke)

5922 Alexander (John James). The Devon-Cornwall boundary. [Including pre-Conquest.] Devon and Cornwall N. and Q., 15, pp. 270–74. 1929.

5923 Bates (Cadwallader John). The Beornicas and the Deras. [Limits of Bernicia and Deira, and the two royal families.] Archaeol. Æl., N.S. 19, pp. 147–54. 1898.

5924 Beresford (W.). The ' mark ' of the Mercians. Antiquary, 38, pp. 262–64. 1902.

5925 Blair (Peter Hunter). The boundary between Bernicia and Deira. Arch. Æl., 4th S. 27, pp. 46–59. 1949.

5926 —— The Northumbrians and their southern frontier. Arch. Æl., 4th 26, pp. 98–126. 1948.

5927 Darby (Henry Clifford). The fenland frontier in Anglo-Saxon England. [With 2 maps.] Antiquity, 8, pp. 185–201. 1934.

5928 Davidson (James Bridge). Notes on part of the county boundary between Somerset and Devon. [Largely A.–S. masterial.] Proc. Somerset Arch. Soc., 28 (1882), pp. 1–27, + 2 maps. 1883.

5929 Davidson (James Bridge). Some Anglo-Saxon boundaries, now deposited at the Albert Museum, Exeter. [Ashburn, etc.] Rept. and Trans. Devon. Assoc., 8, pp. 396–419, + 1 plate. 1876.

5930 Dickinson (Francis Henry). The boundaries of the county of Somerset [in Anglo-Saxon times]. N. and Q. Som. and Dorset, 1, pp. 2–6, 44–46. 1890.

5931 Evans (J. Wilson). The boundaries of the three principalities of Wales. [Gwynedd, Dyfed and Ceredigion, Powys, 9th c.] Cymru Fu, 2, pp. 92–94. 1889.

5932 Fenning (W. D.). Elbow lane. [' Boundary between East Saxons and Mercians. '] East Herts Archaeol. Soc., Trans., 6 (1921–22), pp. 68–71, + folding map. 1923.

5933 Finberg (Herbert Patrick Reginald). The Devon-Cornwall boundary. [Question of Werrington.] Devon and Cornwall N. and Q., 23, pp. 104–07. 1947.

5934 —— The making of a boundary [between Devon and Cornwall]. Devonshire Studies, by W. G. Hoskins and H. P. R. Finberg, pp. 19–39, + map. 1952.

5935 Fox (*Sir* Cyril). The western frontier of Mercia in the viiith century. Yorkshire Celtic Studies, 1, pp. 3–10, + 2 plates, + 3 maps. 1938.

5936 Greene (W. H.). The boundaries of the ancient kingdom of Ergyngfield, on the Wye. Cymru Fu, 2, p. 4. 1889.

5937 Guest (Edwin). On the boundaries that separated the Welsh and English races during the 75 years which followed the capture of Bath, A.D. 577, with speculations as to the Welsh princes, who during that period were reigning over Somersetshire. Archaeol. J., 16, pp. 105–31, + map. 1859. *Also in* Arch. Camb., 3rd S. 7, pp. 269–92, + map. 1861.

5938 Marks (Arthur W.) and **Drew** (Charles D.). The Saxon mark [*mearc*] in Dorset. N. and Q. Som. and Dorset, 25, pp. 89–90, 162, 184, 215–16. 1948–49.

5939 Oman (*Sir* Charles William Chadwick). Concerning some Gloucestershire boundaries. [Boundaries of the Hwiccas.] Essays . . . presented to R L. Poole, pp. 86–97, + map. 1927.

5940 Savage (Henry Edwin), *dean of Lichfield*. The boundary between Bernicia and Deira. Archael. Æl., N.S. 19, pp. 75–88. 1898.

5941 Taylor (Charles Samuel). The northern boundary of Gloucestershire. ['Probably laid down during the reign of king Ethelred.' With a table of names of Domesday owners of estates in north of the shire and reference to page of Domesday : also table of grantors and grantees and references to Kemble and Birch.] Trans. Bristol and Glos. Arch. Soc., 32, pp. 109–39. 1909.

86. DOMESDAY GEOGRAPHY, GENERAL

5942 Bayley (C. P.). The Domesday geography of Northamptonshire. [14 maps in text.] J. Northants, N.H.Soc., 29, pp. 1–22. 1938.

5942a Buchanan (Keith McPherson). Worcestershire. *The land of Britain ; the report of the Land Utilisation Survey of Britain, edited by L. Dudley Stamp, part 68.* 4° London, 1944. [Pp. 486–90, with figures 68–74, pre-Domesday period, land utilisation in Domesday Worcestershire.]

5943 Darby (Henry Clifford). The Domesday geography of Cambridgeshire. [With 10 maps.] Proc. Camb. Antiq. Soc., 36 pp. 35–57. 1936.

5944 —— The Domesday geography of eastern England. pp. xiv, 400, + 1 plate. 8° Cambridge, 1952. [109 maps in text.]

5944a —— and **Terrett** (Ian B.). The Domesday geography of Midland England. pp. xvi, 482, + plate. 8° Cambridge, 1954. [159 maps in text.]

5945 Darby (Henry Clifford). The Domesday geography of Norfolk and Suffolk. [With 8 figures. i. Settlements : ii. Danegeld : iii. Recorded adults in 1086 : iv. Plough-teams in

1066 : v. Distribution of woodland in 1066 : vi. Distribution of sheep in 1066 : vii. Domesday acres of meadow in 1066 : viii. Domesday saltpans.] Geog. J., 85, pp. 432–52. 1935.

5945a Gaut (Robert Charles). A history of Worcestershire agriculture and rural evolution. pp. xvi, 490. 8° Worcester, 1949. [Chap. 3 is concerned with Domesday statistics.]

5946 Holly (D.). The Domesday geography of Leicestershire. [With 17 maps in the text.] Trans. Leic. Archaeol. Soc., 20, pp. 167–202. 1938.

5946a Howell (Emrys Jones). Shropshire. *The land of Britain . . . part 66.* 4° London, 1941. [Pp. 278–82, with figures 20 and 21, Domesday.]

5947 Kinvig (Robert Henry). The Birmingham district in Domesday times. [i. General picture : ii. administrative geography : iii. Domesday analysis (woodland, etc.) : iv. regional summary. 3 maps in text.] B'ham., B.A. 1950, pp. 113–34. 1950.

5947a Maxwell (I. S.). The geographical identification of Domesday vills. [10 figures in text.] Institute of British Geographers, Trans. and Papers, 16 (1950), pp. 97–121. 1952.

5948 Morgan (F. W.). The Domesday geography of Berkshire. [With 7 diagrams.] Scottish geog. Mag., 51, pp. 353–63. 1935.

5949 —— The Domesday geography of Devon. [17 maps in text.] Rept. and Trans. Devon. Assoc., 72, pp. 305–31. 1940.

5950 —— The Domesday geography of Somerset. Proc. Somerset Arch. Soc., 84 (1938), pp. 139–55 + 4 plates (maps). 1939.

5951 —— The Domesday geography of Wiltshire. [4 maps in text.] Wilts. Archaeol. Mag., 48, pp. 68–81. 1937.

5952 Nicklin (Phyllis Amelia). The early historical geography of the forest of Arden. [With Domesday evidence of life in forest region and map showing distribution of population.] Trans. B'ham. Archaeol. Soc., 56 (for 1932), pp. 71–76. 1934.

5952a Pounds (Norman John Greville). The Domesday geography of Cornwall. Ann. Rep. Roy. Cornwall Polytechnic Soc., 1942, pp. 1–15. 1942.

5953 Sheppard (Thomas). Changes on the east coast of England within the historical period. 1. Yorkshire. [Pp. 505–07, Domesday evidence.] Geog. J., 34, pp. 500–13. 1909.

5953a Stamp (Laurence Dudley). Devonshire. *The land of Britain . . . part* 92. 4° London, 1941. [Pp. 499–500, with figures 16–19, Domesday.]

5954 Sylvester (Dorothy). Rural settlement in Domesday Shropshire : a geographical interpretation. [5 maps in text.] Sociol. Rev., 25, pp. 244–57. 1933.

87. IDENTIFICATION OF SITES, ANGLO-SAXON

§ *a.* Arthurian Sites

5955 Airy (*Sir* George Biddell), *etc.* On the locality of the Mons Badonicus. Athenæum, 1885 ii, pp. 507, 537, 570. 1885.

5956 Anscombe (Alfred). Local-names in the 'Arthuriana' in the 'Historia Brittonum'. [The 12 battles located in the Midlands.] Zeit. celt. Philol., 5, pp. 103–23. 1904.

5957 —— Sir Lancelot du Lake and Vinovia [8th victory]. [Argument that Vinovia=early Welsh Guinui-on=Castellum Guinnion of Nennius=Binchester near Catterick.] Celtic Rev., 9, pp. 77–80. 1913.

5958 Birley (Robert). The battle of Mount Badon. [Argument for Whitsbury camp above Charford.] Antiquity, 6, pp. 459–63. 1932.

5959 Burne (Alfred H.). The battle of Badon—a military commentary. [Argument for Badbury, Wilts.] History, N.S. 30, pp. 133–44. 1945.

5960 Chancellor (E. C.). Badbury rings reviewed. Proc. Dorset Archaeol. Soc., 66 (for 1944), pp. 19–30. 1945.

5961 Collingwood (William Gershom). Arthur's battles. [Argument for sites in Kent and Sussex. With map and text of Nennius, cap. 56.] Antiquity, 3, pp. 292–98. 1929.

5962 Curwen (Eliot Cecil). Sussex and king Arthur. Sussex County Mag., 3, pp. 752–53. 1929.

5963 Dobson (Dina Portway). Mount Badon again. [Argument for Brent Knoll.] Antiquity, 22, pp. 43–45. 1948.

5964 Earle (John), *etc.* Baddanbyrig, Badbury near Wimborne. [A.-S. C., 901 : ? equate with Mons Badonicus.] N. and Q. Som. and Dorset, 1, pp. 42–44, 152. 1890.

5965 Glennie (John Stuart Stuart). Arthurian localities ; their historical origin, chief country, and Fingalian relations ; with a map of Arthurian Scotland. pp. vii, 140. 8° Edinburgh, 1869. [*Also in* Early English Text Society, O.S. 36, pp. xvii–clvi, + map. 1869.]

5966 Hallett (Shackleton), **Hughes** (Jonothan), *etc.* Celliwig. [Identifies Arthur's principal coronation city with Silchester, etc.] N. and Q., 8th S. 6, pp. 67, 292, 474–75 : 7, pp. 90–91, 232–33. 1894–95.

5967 Jackson (Kenneth). Arthur's battle of Breguoin. ['Mount Agned.' Argument for identification with Bremenium, High Rochester on the Border.] Antiquity, 23, pp. 48–49. 1949.

5968 Johnstone (P. K.). Kelliwic in Cornwall. [King Arthur's *llys* identified with Callington.] Antiquity, 19, pp. 156–57. 1945.

5969 —— Mount Badon—a topographical clue ? [Passage from life of St. Finnian of Clonard in the Book of Lismore, which suggests that he was present at the siege of Mont Badon.] Antiquity, 20, pp. 159–60. 1946.

5970 —— *etc.* The victories of Arthur. [Sites of battles on Roman highways.] N. and Q., 166, pp. 381–82, 425–27, 466 : 167, p. 65. 1934.

5971 Lot (Ferdinand). Nouvelles études sur le cycle arthurien. [Pp. 40–42, iv. Camlann.] Romania, 46, pp. 39–45 1920.

5972 Loth (Joseph). Les deux Mano irlandais et les deux Manaw Brittons. L'énigme de Vervyn Vrych : le lieu de la bataille de Catraeth. [Caer Iudeu, on the Firth of Forth. Arthur's tenth battle.] Rev. celt., 51, pp. 185–95. 1934.

5973 Nitze (William Albert). More on the Arthuriana of Nennius. [Sites of Arthur's battles.] Mod. Lang. Notes, 58, pp. 1–8. 1943.

5974 Rowe (Joseph Hambley). Tristram, king Rivalen and king Mark. (King Arthur's territory). [Geography of king Arthur, but in romance, rather than history.] J. Roy. Inst. Cornwall, 22, pp. 445–64 ; 23, pp. 48–69. 1928–29.

5975 Stephens (George Arbour). New light on the Arthurian battlefields. pp. 12. 8° Haverfordwest, 1938. [Locates in South Wales. Equates Mt. Badon with Llanbadarn Fynydd, north Radnorshire.]

5976 Tydecho. Site of the battle of Camlan. Arch. Camb., 4th S., 3, pp. 266–67. 1872.

§ *b*. **Battle of Ashingdon**

(1016. Between Edmund Ironside and Cnut. *See also* Place-names of Essex (Place-name Society), p. 177.)

5977 Brocklebank (C. Gerald). Notes on the battle of Assandun. [Against **5979.**] J. Brit. Archaeol. Assoc., N.S. 32, pp. 123–25. 1926.

5978 Burrows (John William). Notes on the battle of Assandune. The battle over a battle. [Against **5979.**] *Same jnl.*, N.S. 32, pp. 125–28. 1926.

5979 Christy (Miller). The battle of Assandun : where was it fought ? [Arguments for Ashdon, near Hadstock, north Essex. *But see* **5977—78.**] *Same jnl.*, N.S. 31, pp. 168–90, + 2 maps. 1925.

5980 Heygate (W. E.). The Danish camps at Bemfleet and Shoebury, and the battle of Ashingdon. Trans. Essex Archaeol. Soc., 2, pp. 75–81. 1863.

5981 Steer (Francis W.). The site of the battle of Assandun or Assingdon. [Map on p. 81. Ashingdon.] Essex Rev., 46, pp. 80–84. 1937.

5982 Swete (Henry Barclay). On the identification of Assanduna with Ashdon. Trans. Essex Archaeol. Soc., N.S. 4, pp. 5–10. 1893.

§ *c*. **Battle of Brunanburh**

(937. Between Athelstan and Olaf of Dublin, with Scotland and Strathclyde. *See also* Section 17.)

5983 Alexander (John James). The battle of Brunanburh. [Millenary year. Discusses site : probably not Axminster.] Devon and Cornwall N. and Q., 19, pp. 303–07. 1937.

5984 Angus (W. S.). The battlefield of Brunanburh. [Case for Burnswark, Dumfriesshire.] Antiquity, 11, pp. 283–93. 1937.

5985 Broadmead (W. B.). The battle of Brunanburh. [Not in Somerset, but in north of England.] N. and Q., Som. and Dorset, 1, pp. 137–38. 1890.

5986 Bulleid (C.). Battle of Brunanburh at Breandune. [Somerset.] *Same jnl.*, 5, p. 286. 1897.

5987 Cockburn (John Henry). The battle of Brunanburh and its period elucidated by place-names. pp. xiv, 300. 8° London, 1931. [Plea for Templeborough site, etc.]

5988 Crawford (Osbert Guy Stanhope). The battle of Brunanburh. [?Brown Moor, Dumfriesshire.] Antiquity, 8, pp. 338–39. 1934.

5989 Dickinson (Francis Henry). The site of the battle of Brunanburh. [Argument for Bromfield, Somerset.] N. and Q., Som. and Dorset, 1, pp. 52–53. 1890.

5990 Hampson (Charles Phillips). New light on the battle of Brunanburh, A.D. 937. [Argument for the plain of the Fylde, and near the rock called Bronneberh in an indenture of 1250, two miles south of Heysham.] Trans. Lancs. and Ches. Antiq. Soc., 58 (1945–46), pp. 269–88. 1947.

5991 Hesleden (William). Account of ancient earth works at Barton-upon-Humber, and conjectures relating to the site of the battle of Brunanburh. Trans. Brit. Arch. Assoc., 2nd annual congress (Winchester, 1845), pp. 221–34. 1846.

5992 Hogarth (Frederick Whewell). Further views on the site of Brunanburh. [P. 291=plate. Argument for plain of the Fylde. ?Thorold's tomb= barrow in grounds of Heysham hall. ?Cuerdale hoard=treasure chest of Constantine, king of Scots.] Trans. Lancs. and Ches. Antiq. Soc., 58 (1945–46), pp. 289–94. 1947.

5993 Holderness (Thomas). The battle of Brunanburh: an attempt to identify the site. pp. 55. 8° Driffield, 1888. [Grosse, 1527.]

5994 Home (Robert). The battle of Brunanburg. [Plea for Bromeridge, Northumberland.] Hist. Berwick. Nats.' Club, 2, pp. 115–16. 1845.

5995 Hunt (Alfred). Brunanburh: A.D. 937. Identification of this battle site in north Lincolnshire. [Evidence for Burnham.] Assoc. Archit. Socs.' Rpts., 28, pp. 28–43, + 4 plates, + 5 maps. 1905. *See also* Saga-Book V.C., 4, pp. 18–20. 1905.

5996 Law (Alice). Burnswork and Brunanburh. Scot. H. R., 7, pp. 431–36. 1910.

5997 McGovern (J. B.). The battle of Brunanburh. [i. The question: ii. The claims: iii. Value of the claims.] Trans. Lancs. and Ches. Antiq. Soc., 38 (1920), pp. 112–37. 1922.

5998 Marquis (James T.). Brunanburh. [Case for Burnley, Lancs.] *Same jnl.*, 26 (1908), pp. 35–52, + 2 maps. 1909.

5999 —— Burnley . . . reputed site of the battle of Brunanburgh, A.D. 937. *Same jnl.*, 27 (1909), pp. 178–82. 1910.

6000 Napper (H. F.). The battle of Brunanburh (A.D. 938). [Argument for Burnby, near Weighton, Yorks.] N. and Q. Som. and Dorset 5, pp. 294–96. 1897.

6001 Neilson (George). Brunanburh and Burnswork [Dumfriesshire.] Scot. H.R., 7, pp. 37–55, + plan. *See also* pp. 212–14, 431–36. 1909–10.

6002 Smith (Albert Hugh). The site of the battle of Brunanburh. [Plea for Bromborough in the Wirral.] London Mediaeval Studies, 1, pp. 56–59. 1937.

6003 Thompson (Pishey). Battle of Brunnanburg. [Argument for Burnham (on Humber).] N. and Q., 2nd S. 2, pp. 277, 295. 1856.

6004 Thurnam (John), *etc.* Battle of Brunanburgh. [On north side of Humber.] N. and Q., 1st S. 4, pp. 249–50, 327. 1851.

6005 Turner (J. H.). On the Northumbrian names of Brunanburh and Berwick. N. and Q., 4th S. 8, pp. 179–81. 1871.

6006 ——, Ellis (Alfred Shelley), *etc.* Site of Brunanburgh. [?Aldborough, Yorks.] N. and Q., 9th S. 8, pp. 100, 253–54. 1901.

6007 Varah (William Edward). The battlefield of Brunan-burh. [Argument for Burnham Hill, Lincs., 3 miles from Humber.] N. and Q., 173, pp. 434–36. 1937.

6008 Wake (Charles Staniland). The battle of Brunanburgh. [Plea for Brough, Yorks., Humber mouth.] Antiquary, 12, pp. 206–07. 1885.

6009 Welby (E. M. E.). Battle of Brunnanbyrig. [Plea for Flamborough.] Antiquary, 11, pp. 68–69. 1885.

6010 Whistler (Charles Watts). Battlefield of Brunanburh. [?Milton Hill, Dorset.] Saga-Book V.C., 3, pp. 324–25. 1904.

6011 Wilkinson (Thomas Turner). Battle of Brunnaburh. [Case for Burnley, Lancs.] N. and Q., 3rd S. 6, pp. 342–43. 1864.

6011a —— On the battle of Brunanburgh; and the probable locality of the conflict. (Appendix. On some funeral urns found at Catlow, etc.). [Argument for Burnley, Lancs.] Trans. Hist. Soc. Lancs. and Ches., 9, pp. 21–42, + map + 1 plate. 1857.

6012 Wilson (James). The site of the battle of Brunanburh. Scot. H. R., 7, pp. 212–14. 1910.

§ *d*. Domesday Sites

6013 Adams (J. H.). Landelech in Domesday. [Identifies with Landulph, rather than V.C.H. identification with Landlake in South Petherwin.] Devon and Cornwall N. and Q., 18, pp. 196–98. 1935.

6014 Anscombe (Alfred). 'Segnes-come'. [Queried location of a Domesday site.] Sussex N. and Q., 2, pp. 236–37. 1929.

6015 B. (R. W.). The Golden valley, Herefordshire. [?to be identified with the valley of Stradelei of Domesday Book.] Arch. Camb., 3rd S. 13, pp. 299–300 : 15, p. 412. 1867–69.

6016 Bridgeman (Charles George Orlando). Some unidentified Domesday vills [in Staffordshire.] Collectns. for a history of Staffs, 1923, pp. 23–44. 1924.

6017 Bryan (Benjamin). The lost manor of Mestesforde. [Present boundaries of Matlock coterminous with those of Mestesforde of Domesday, and its berewick of Meslach.] J. Derbs. Archaeol. Soc., 23, pp. 77–82. 1901.

6018 Burne (Sambrooke Arthur Higgins). A note on the Domesday 'Niwetone'. [Identification with Draycott-in-the-Moors.] North Staffs. F.C., Trans., 50, pp. 90–91. 1916.

6019 Cam (Helen Maud). The English lands of the abbey of St. Riquier. [8 villages identifiable in the Norfolk Domesday.] E.H.R., 31, pp. 443–47. 1916.

6020 Carne (John). An attempt to identify the Domesday manors in Cornwall. (Some notes and corrections). J. Roy. Inst. Cornwall, 1. iv, pp. 11–59: 2, pp. 219–22. 1865–67.

6021 Carter (William Fowler). A note on the identification of the place named Monetville, in the Domesday survey of Staffordshire. Collectns. for a history of Staffs. (Wm. Salt Soc.), N.S. 11, pp. 227–30. 1908.

6022 Chippindall (W. H.). The lost [Domesday] manor of Thirnby. [Lancs., near Kirby Lonsdale.] Trans. Hist. Soc. Lancs. and Ches., 73 (1921), pp. 225–27. 1922.

6023 Cossons (Arthur). East Chilwell or Keighton. [?identification of Domesday Estrecilleuelle.] Trans. Thoroton Soc., 33 (1929), pp. 1–9. 1930.

6024 Dare (M. Paul). 'Aldeby' : a suggested identification in the Leicestershire Domesday, with a note on the site and church. Trans. Leic. Archaeol. Soc., 15, pp. 333–36. 1927–8.

5025 Drinkwater (C. H.). Unidentified places in Domesday. [19 names from Shropshire.] Trans. Shrop. Arch. Soc., 3rd S. 2, pp. 158–60. 1902.

6026 Finberg (Herbert Patrick Reginald). A Domesday identification. [Elent in Cornish Domesday, identified with Heli.] Devon and Cornwall N. and Q., 22, p. 95. 1942.

6027 Gowland (Tom S.). Some Yorkshire field names. [With identifications of 4 lost Domesday sites.] Yorks. Archaeol. J., 30, pp. 225–30. 1931.

6028 Greswell (William Henry Parr). The 'Cantoche' of Domesday (1086). [Where was the original Domesday settlement of Cantoche or Quantock ?] Proc. Somerset. Arch. Soc., 56 (1910), pp. 79–84. 1911.

6029 Hoskins (William George). A Domesday identification (Leigh Barton, Silverton). [Estochelia or Stochelie, between Chederlia and Bichelia.] Devon and Cornwall N. and Q., 24, pp. 111–12. 1950.

6030 Malden (Henry Elliot). Kingsland in Newdigate and Newdigate in Copthorne hundred. [Identification of 2 Domesday hides held by one Orcus.] Surrey Archaeol. Collns., 39, pp. 147–49. 1931.

6031 Picken (W. M. M.). Charaton and Penhawger. [Two Cornish Domesday manors.] Devon and Cornwall N. and Q., 23, pp. 202–05. 1948.

6032 Reaney (Percy Hide). Some identifications of Essex place-names. [Identification of places mentioned in Domesday, etc.] Trans. Essex Archaeol. Soc., N.S. 21, pp. 56–72. 1937.

6033 Reichel (Oswald Joseph). Some doubtful and disputed 'Domesday' identifications [in Devon]. Rept. and Trans. Devon. Assoc., 36, pp. 347–79. 1904.

6034 Reichel (Oswald Joseph). Wreyland documents by Cecil Torr. [Discussion on manor of Wray (Moreton Hampstead), and Domesday manor of Wergi or Wereia. *See also* replies by C. Torr, **6042**.] Devon and Cornwall N. and Q., 6, pp. 189–90, 202–06, 228–30. 1911.

6035 Robson (John). On the Walintune [S. Lancs.] of Domesday Book. Trans. Hist. Soc. Lancs. and Ches., 3rd S. 3 [=27], pp. 180–83. 1875.

6036 Rowe (Joseph Hambley). Alured the Marshall. [List of manors in N.E. Cornwall held by him in the Exon Domesday Book, with identifications.] Devon and Cornwall N. and Q., 13, pp. 126–30. 1924.

6037 —— Cheldis: a Domesday manor in Craven, and its identification. [Identified with Keltus, formerly in modern township of Crosshills.] Bradford Antiquary, 5 (N.S. 3), p. 246. 1909.

6038 —— Domesday manors in Cornwall. [Boten, Polscat and Carbihan.] Devon and Cornwall N. and Q., 12, pp. 135–36. 1922.

6039 Sayers (Edward). The manor of 'Dentune'. [Identification of Domesday Dentune with Dankton farm, Sompting.] Sussex Archaeol. Collns., 50, p. 176. 1907.

6040 Shrubsole (George W.). The Castreton of Attis-cross hundred in *Domesday* identified with the town of Flint. Arch. Camb., 5th S. 8, pp. 17–22. 1891.

6041 Skinner (Emily). Cillitona: the land of the wife of Hervius. ['Which she held in the Domesday hundred of Tiverton'.] Rept. and Trans. Devon. Assoc., 42, pp. 420–22. 1910.

6042 Torr (Cecil). Wreyland documents. [Discussion with O. J. Reichell, *q.v.*, **6034**, on manor of Wray (Moreton Hampstead), and Domesday manor of Wergi or Wereia.] Devon and Cornwall N. and Q., 6, pp. 190–91, 206–07: 7, pp. 34–37. 1911–12.

6043 Ward (Gordon). A suggested identification of Berts. [A Domesday manor in the rape of Lewes.] Sussex N. and Q., 5, pp. 111–12. 1934.

U

6044 Watkin (Hugh Robert). Little Hempston manor and parsonage. [3 Domesday manors of Hemistona in Devon.] Devon and Cornwall N. and Q., 14, pp. 33–45. 1926.

6045 Wood (James George). Some Domesday place-names in the neighbourhood of Dean forest. Trans. Woolhope N.F. Club, 1905–07, pp. 244–50. 1911.

6046 Worth (Richard Nicholls). The identifications of the Domesday manors of Devon. Rept. and Trans. Devon. Assoc., 25, pp. 309–42. 1893.

§ e. Battle of Ethandun

(878. Between Alfred and Guthrum)

6047 Alexander (R. C.). Edington or Yatton the Ethandun of Alfred's victory? Wilts. Archaeol. Mag., 5, pp. 193–207, 392. 1859.

6048 Clifford (William Joseph Hugh), *bp. of Clifton*. Site of the battle of Aethan-dune, and of other localities mentioned by Asser . . . in . . . 878. Proc. Somerset Arch. Soc., 21 (1875), pp. 1–27 + map. 1876.

6049 Dowding (William). The battle of Ethandune. [Argument for Yatton, 5 miles N.W. of Chippenham.] Wilts. N. and Q., 1, pp. 367–68. 1894.

6050 Major (Albany Featherstonehaugh). A reply to Mr. Rawlence's paper on the battle of Ethandun [**6054–55**]. Antiq. J., 1, pp. 118–21. 1921.

6051 Money (Walter). The battle of Ethandune. [Argument for Eddington, near Hungerford, Berks.] Antiquary, 27, pp. 146–48. 1893.

6052 —— The battle of Ethandune. [Argument as last.] Wilts. Archaeol. Mag., 27, pp. 109–13. 1894.

6053 Radford (W. Locke). Æthandune. Proc. Somerset Arch. Soc., 51 (1905), pp. 169–80. 1906.

6054 Rawlence (E. A.). On the site of the battle of Ethandun. [Summary; with discussion by G. F. Browne, etc.] Proc. Soc. Antiq., 2nd S. 31, pp. 163–64. 1919.

6055 Rawlence (E. A.). On the site of the battle of Ethandun. [Argument for Edington, near Westbury, Wilts.] Antiq. J., 1, pp. 105–117. 1921.

6056 Trethowan (Illtyd). Alfred and the great white horse of Wiltshire. Downside Rev., 57, pp. 340–59. 1939.

6057 Whatmore (A. W.). The battle of Ethandune. [Case for Edington, Somerset.] Wilts. N. and Q., 2, pp. 476–78. 1898.

6058 Whistler (Charles Watts). The battlefield of Ethandune. [Case for Edington on Poldens.] Antiquary, 37, pp. 170–75, 200–205 : (Correspondence, 224.) 1901.

§ f. Moot Sites

6059 Budgen (W.). Two probable hundred moot sites. [i. Willingdon hundred : ii. Totnore hundred.] Sussex N. and Q., 2, pp. 210–14 : 242–43. 1929.

6060 Christy (Miller). The Essex hundred-moots : an attempt to identify their meeting-places. [i.e. during A.–S. period ; became peripatetic after the Conquest.] Trans. Essex Archaeol. Soc., N.S. 18, pp. 172–97. 1928.

6061 Cole (Edward Maule). The Driffield moot-hill. Trans. East Riding Antiq. Soc., 3, pp. 13–16. 1895.

6062 Cragg (William A.). Aveland [Lincs.]. [Site of A.–S. *gemote*. With note on the place name by F. M. Stenton.] Lincs. N. and Q., 22, pp. 66–69. 1933.

6063 Crawford (Osbert Guy Stanhope). A Saxon moot. [At Calbourne, I.o.W.] Papers and Proc. Hants. F. C., 17, pp. 138–39. 1951.

6064 Emmison (F. G.). The meeting places of Stodden and Redbournstoke hundreds. Pubs. Beds. Hist. Rec. Soc., 12, pp. 93–96. 1928.

6065 Fowler (George Herbert). The meeting-place of Manshead hundred. *Same inl.*, 8, pp. 174–75. 1924.

6066 Joce (T. J.). A Saxon moot hill ? [Moot hill, Downton, Devon, for hundred of Wonford.] Devon and Cornwall N. and Q., 15, pp. 75–76. 1928.

6067 Mortimer (John Robert). On nine embankment crosses believed by him to be early Christian folk moots. [Use of British barrows, e.g. at Fimber and Sledmere, by Anglo-Saxons as graveyards, and also as folk moots.] Proc. Soc. Antiq., 2nd S. 16, pp. 278–87. 1897.

6068 Nicholson (John). The moot hill at Driffield, East Yorks. N. and Q., 6th S. 9, p. 205. 1884.

6069 Tomkins (Henry George). King Alfred's moot-places of Swinborg and Langandene [Wilts.] Wilts. N. and Q., 1, pp. 562–64. 1895.

6070 —— The Langandene of King Alfred's will. [A dean on the Marlborough downs about three miles from Swanborough Tump.] Academy, 27, p. 422. 1885.

6071 —— The Swinbeorg of King Alfred's will. [=Swanborough Tump, Wilts.] Academy, 25, pp. 368–69. 1884.

6072 —— Where was the moot-place, Swinbeorh, of King Alfred's will ? Wilts. N. and Q., 2, pp. 183–90. 1896.

6073 Westropp (Thomas Johnson). The ancient places of assembly in the counties of Limerick and Clare. [Oenach sites.] J. Roy. Soc. Antiq. Ireland, 48 (6th S. 9), pp. 1–24. 1919.

§ g. Other Anglo-Saxon Sites

6074 [Anon.] The battle of Sceorstan, A.D. 1016. [Argument for Sarson, near Andover.] Hants. N. and Q., 5, pp. 125–34. 1890.

6075 Alexander (John James) and **Carter** (George Edward Lovelace). Arx Cynuit. [Scene of defeat of brother of Ingwar and Halfdane in 878. A site in N. Devon. ?=Countisbury.] Devon and Cornwall N. and Q., 16, pp. 310–13, 351–52. 1931.

6076 Alexander (John James). Creodantreow. [Site, near Crediton.] Rept. and Trans. Devon. Assoc., 72, pp. 96–98. 1941.

6077 Anscombe (Alfred). The site of Oswy's victory over Penda [655]. [Argument for Winskill Moor, Leath, Cumberland. Regio Loidis=the region of Loidēs=the ward of Leath in Cumberland. Edenhall in Leath=Giudan-heall, and is the Urbs Iudeu of Nennius, cap. 64. In campa gai=Maes Guin, i.e. Winfield, near Edenhall. Winwaed=*win* (war) and *wæð* (ford) over the swollen river Eden, now spanned by stone bridge of two arches.] Anglia, 33 (N.F. 21), pp. 523–26. 1910.

6078 —— Where was Leonaford ? [Visit of Asser to Alfred at royal vill of Leonaford in 887.] Sussex N. and Q., 1, pp. 234–37. 1927.

6079 Atkinson (John Christopher). A study of some archaic place-names. (A further study . . . where and what was Camisedale ?) [Domesday, etc., evidence. Argument for Greenhow, Yorks.] Reliquary, N. [2nd] S. 5, pp. 147–53 ; 6, pp. 70–77. 1891–92.

6080 Auden (Thomas). Where was Fethanleag ? [A.-S.C., under 584 : 'In this year Ceawlin and Cutha fought against the Britons at . . . Fethanleag, and Cutha was there slain.' Argument for Fotherley, 4 miles S.W. of Lichfield.] Trans. Shrop. Arch. Soc., 3rd S., 1, pp. 147–50, 282. 1901.

6081 Baring (*Hon.* Francis Henry). The Aclea[h].—i. of the battle in 851 : ii. of the synods in 782, etc. [Plea for identification with Oakley in Hants.] Papers and Proc. Hants. F.C., 8, pp. 95–99. 1917.

6082 Bates (Cadwallader John). The home of St. Cuthbert's boyhood. [Identification of Hruringaham with Wrangham, near Doddington, rather than Wrangholm, near Melrose.] Archaeol. Æl., N.S. 19, pp. 155–59. 1898.

6083 Burne (Alfred H.). Ancient Wiltshire battlefields. [Mount Badon, c. 500 : ii. Beranburh, 556 : iii. Wodnesbeorh, 592 and 715 : iv. Bedwyn, 675 : v. Ellandun, 825 : vi. Ethandun, 878 (with plan and plate) : vii. Cynete, 1006.] Wilts. Archaeol. Mag., 53, pp. 397–412, + 1 plate. 1950.

6084 Cooksey (Charles Frederick). On the site of the battle of Aclea, A.D. 851. [Plea for Oakley, near Basingstoke.] Papers and Proc. Hants. F.C., 5, pp. 26–35, + 1 plate. 1906.

6085 Coulson (William). The site of the battle of Denisesburn [634]. [Oswald defeats Cadwallon.] Archaeol. Æl., N.S. 5, pp. 103–08. 1861.

6086 Crawford (Osbert Guy Stanhope). Coludes burh. [On St. Abb's head, Berwickshire.] Antiquity, 8, pp. 202–04 + 2 plates. 1934.

6087 Davies (James). Ancient battlefield near Hereford. [At Pipe, 3 miles north of Hereford. ?site of battle between Gruffyd and Randulph, 1054.] Arch. Camb., 3rd S. 4, pp. 207–08. 1858.

6088 Dymond (Charles W.). On the identification of the site of 'Buttingtune' of the Saxon Chronicle, anno 894. Collns. hist. and archeol. rel. to Montgom., 31, pp. 337–46. 1900.

6089 Graves (Philip P.). Wallop, Guollopum and Catguoloph. [Site of 'discordia' between Guitolinus and Ambrosius in Historia Britonum.] Antiquity, 12, pp. 474–76. 1938.

6090 Grinsell (Leslie Valentine). Wayland's smithy, Beahhild's byrigels, and Hwittuc's hlaew. [Evidence of A.-S. charters, etc.] Trans. Newbury F.C., 8, pp. 136–39. 1939.

6091 Gurney (Frederick G.). Yttingaford and the tenth-century bounds of Chalgrave and Linslade. [Identification of ford=scene of peace negotiations between Edward the Elder and Guthrum Echricsson.] Pubs. Beds. Hist. Rec. Soc., 5, pp. 163–179 + map. 1920.

6092 Harris (Harold Augustus). Clovesho disclosed (?) Trans. Suffolk Inst. Archaeol., 18, pp. 77–78. 1922.

6093 Hunt (Alfred). Maserfield A.D. 642. Identification of site in north west Lincolnshire. [Argument for Epworth, Isle of Axholme. Plate shows Saxon stone in Crowle St. Oswald church.] Lincs. N. and Q., 18, pp. 78–88, + 1 plate. 1925.

6094 Hunt (Alfred). Maserfield battle, A.D. 642. Battlefields of Lincolnshire. Identification of site in north west Lincolnshire. J. Brit. Archaeol. Assoc., N.S. 30, pp. 107–19, + 1 plate. 1924.

6095 Huntingford (George Wynn Brereton). Ashdown. [1871]. Berks. Archaeol. J., 39, pp. 145–50, + sketchmap. 1935.

6096 Hussey (Arthur). An inquiry after the site of Anderida or Andredesceaster. [And its overthrow by Ælla.] Sussex Archaeol. Collns., 6, pp. 90–106. 1853.

6097 Kerslake (Thomas). Codex Diplomaticus, no. DXXIV, Eadgar, A.D. 967. [Identification of Lesmanaoc and Pennarth with localities in Glamorgan.] N. and Q., 5th S. 9, pp. 351. 1878.

6098 Laborde (Edward Dalrymple). The site of the battle of Maldon [991–3]. E.H.R., 40, pp. 161–73. 1925.

6099 Lethbridge (Thomas Charles). An attempt to discover the site of the battle of Aldreth. [Temp. William I versus Hereward.] Proc. Camb. Antiq. Soc., 31, pp. 155–56. 1931.

6100 Manning (Charles Robertson). Discovery of the site of Clovesho at Mildenhall, Suffolk. East Anglian (N. and Q.), N.S. 2, pp. 69–70, 112–14, 208. 1887–88.

6101 Martin (John May). The Camelford of the Anglo-Saxon Chronicle: where was it? [A.-S. C. 823: 'Her wæs Weala gefeoht and Defna at Gafulforda.' ?Kembleford, between Crediton and Coplestone Cross; but not Camelford in Cornwall.] Rept. and Trans. Devon. Assoc., 29, pp. 275–85. 1897.

6102 Maskelyne (T. S.). Ellandune. [823. North Wilts. site.] Wilts. N. and Q., 3, pp. 328–33. 1900.

6103 —— Ellandune identified. [823. Case for Wroughton.] Wilts. Archaeol. Mag., 31, pp. 241–43. 1901.

6104 Mawer (*Sir* Allen). Some place-name identifications in the Anglo-Saxon Chronicles. [Streoneshal (680), argument for Strensall, 6 miles N.E. of York rather than Whitby: and 41 other names.] Anglica [für A. Brandl], Bd. 1: Palaestra, **147**, pp. 41–54. 1925.

6105 Morley (Claude), **Harris** (Harold Augustus), and **Stevenson** (Francis Seymour). Clovesho. i. The councils and the locality: ii. Clovesho disclosed: iii. The witan of Godmundesley: an evidence of location. [Identified with Mildenhall.] Trans. Suffolk Inst. Archaeol., 18, pp. 91–122. 1923.

6106 Morrison (Walter). On the site of the battle of Ashdown [871]. (Addendum, by the editor [Walter Money]). Trans. Newbury F.C., 4 (1886–95), pp. 87–95, + 3 maps. 1895. — *Same title. Newbury Field Club*, pp. 9. 8° Newbury, 1893.

6107 Napper (H. F.). Towercreep: is it Mercredsburn? [Penhurst, near Battle. Site of battle between Ælla and Britons, 485 ?] Sussex Archaeol. Collns., 39, pp. 168–74. 1894.

6108 Pollard (H. P.). Danesfield, Watton. [?site of slaughter of Danes in 1002 or 1016.] East Herts Archaeol. Soc., Trans., 3. ii (1906), pp. 175–77. 1907.

6109 Poole (E. H. Lane). The battle of Meretune, 871. [Martin, Hants.] Wilts. Archaeol. Mag., 54, pp. 36–40. 1951.

6110 Poole (Reginald Lane). Monasterium Niridanum. [Home of abbot Hadrian, companion of Theodore.] E.H.R., 36, pp. 540–45. 1921.

6111 Rose-Troup (Frances). Brihtricestan, a lost manor. [Listed among Leofric's donations to his cathedral. ?Change of name to Clyst Hyneton.] Devon and Cornwall N. and Q., 18, pp. 152–59. 1934.

6112 Skene (William Forbes). Notice of the site of the battle of Ardderyd or Arderyth. [577. Arthuret on the Esk.] Proc. Soc. Antiq. Scot., 6, pp. 91–98. 1868.

6113 Smith (Martin Linton), *bp. of Rochester*. A Lancashire parish [Winwick] in life and history. 8° Warrington, 1920. [?Winwick or Oswestry scene of Oswald's death discussed.]

6114 Stephens (Thomas). The Godo-din. [Battle of Cattraeth (603) equated with that of Degstan (Dægsanstane) or Egesanstana and identified with Sigges-ton near Catterick, Yorks. Aneurin there taken prisoner.] N. and Q., 1st S. 4, pp. 468–70. 1851.

6115 Stevenson (William Henry). Notes on Old-English historical geo-graphy. 1. The battle of Ringmere [Florence of Worcester, under 1010]. 2. The site of Brunemue [Chronicle, under 1066]. E.H.R., 11, pp. 301–4. 1896.

6116 Sympson (Edward Mansel). Where was Sidnacester ? [Argument for Stow in Lindsey as site of see of the bishops of Lindsey.] Assoc. Archit. Socs'. Rpts., 28, pp. 87–94. 1905.

6117 Thorpe (Benjamin). On the locality of Biohchandoune. [*See also* Blaauw (W. H.). Buncton [304]. Thorpe identifies with Bucham hill rather than with Buncton.] Sussex Archaeol. Collns., 21, p. 222. 1869.

6118 Wallenberg (Johannes Knut). Studies in Old Kentish charters. [*Hyr-ingdænn*=Heronden in Tenterden (Birch identifies with Heronden near Eastry–968 BCS 1212.)] Studia neophil., 1, pp. 34–44. 1928.

6119 Ward (Gordon). The wi-wara-wics. ['Dairy farms of the men of Wye' in charter of 858 (Birch, 496), and their identification.] Arch. Cant., 53, pp. 24–28. 1941.

6120 Watkin (Hugh Robert). Caell-wic, Cornwall. [Identification of a manor granted by Egbert to the bp. of Sherborne between 810 and 840.] Devon and Cornwall N. and Q., 11, pp. 153, 203–04. 1920–21.

6121 Watson (John). A mistaken passage in Bede's Ecclesiastical History explained. ['In Campodono . . . fecit (Paulinus) basilicam . . .' Argument that Paulinus built this church at Doncaster, not Catarick : Campodonum = Dona-felda (A.-S. translation) = Doncaster.] Archaeologia, 1, pp. 242–47. 1770.

6122 Whitley (William Thomas). Botulph's Ycean-ho. [=Iken, Suffolk. Mostly on St. Botulph and place-names attributed to him. With sketch-map.] J. Brit. Archaeol. Assoc., N.S. 36 (1930), pp. 233–38. 1931.

6123 Williams (Benjamin). An at-tempt to identify the ' Kingston ' of the Saxon Chronicle and the ' Weorthig ' of the Witenagemot of 931. [=Longworth, near Kingston Bagpuze, Berks.] Proc. Soc. Antiq., 2, pp. 38–39, 76. 1850.

6124 —— Identification of the ' Stane ' of the Saxon Chronicle. [Concerning Allhallows-Staining, London.] *Same jnl.*, 2nd S. 1, pp. 53–54. 1860.

6125 —— Localities mentioned in Anglo-Saxon charters. [Identification of 29 place-names.] N. and Q., 1st S. 7, p. 473. 1853.

6126 X. The battle of Ockley, A.D. 852. [Case for 'Aclea '=Ockley wood, Merst-ham.] Surrey Archaeol. Collns., 25, pp. 136–38. 1912.

88. IDENTIFICATION OF SITES, CELTIC

6127 Anderson (John). On the site of Macbeth's castle at Inverness. Ar-chaeol. Scot., 3, pp. 234–44. 1831.

6128 Hanna (J. W.). The battle of Magh Rath : its true site determined. [Near Crown Rath beside Newry.] Ulster J. Archaeol., 4, pp. 53–61. 1856.

6129 Hogg (Alexander Hubert Ar-thur). Llwyfenydd. [Home of Urien of Reged : 6th c. Equation with Lyvennet Beck in Westmorland.] Antiquity, 20, pp. 210–11. 1946.

6130 Jones (*Sir* Evan D.), *bart*. The locality of the battle of Mynydd Carn, A.D. 1081. [Argument for near Fish-guard, Pembrokeshire.] Arch. Camb., 77 (7th S. 2), pp. 181–97, + map. 1922.

6131 Knox (Hubert Thomas). An identification of places named in Tire-chan's collections [and in the Tripartite Life of St. Patrick.] J. Roy. Soc. Antiq. Ireland, 31 (5th S. 11), pp. 24–39, 432–33. 1901.

6132 Lawless (Nicholas) **[Enda,** *pseud.*] Rathcoole, Ui-Segain, Leire. [Argument that these 3 places mentioned in 7th life of St. Patrick are in Louth, not in Meath]. County Louth Archaeol. J., 3, pp. 31–35. 1912.

6133 Llallawg, *pseud.* Battle of Penletheru. [Annales Cambriae, 1087. Between Rhys ab Tewder and the sons of Bleddyn ab Cynvyn. ?locality.] Arch. Camb., 4th S. 3, pp. 149–51. 1872.

6134 Lloyd (Joseph H.). The identification of the battlefield of Glenn Mama, A.D. 1000. J. co. Kildare Archaeol. Soc., 7, pp. 365–72. 1914.

6135 Loth (Joseph). La patrie de Tristan. [Almain and Ermonie : ? in Munster.] Rev. celt., 18, pp. 315–17. 1897.

6136 McLeod (John N.). Remarks on the supposed site of Delgon or Cindelgen, the seat of Conall, king of Dalriada, A.D. 563. [Argument for island of Ealain da Ghallagan.] Proc. Soc. Antiq. Scot., 28 (3rd S. 4), pp. 13–18. 1894.

6137 Miller (Peter). Suggestions respecting the site of Bede's ancient city, Giudi. (Additional notes, etc.) [Argument for castle of Blackness, on Firth of Forth.] *Same jnl.*, 19 (N.S. 7), pp. 54–62 : 29 (3rd S. 5), pp. 55–58. 1885, 1895.

6138 Morris (Henry). Ath Da Ferta [Ford of the grave]. [Identification of a ford mentioned in most Irish annals as place where Aedh Oirnidhe, king of Ireland, died in 816, 817, 818 or 819 as the Fort Field, near Louth.] County Louth Archaeol. J., 6, pp. 61–76. 1926.

6139 Murray (Alexander D.). A famous old battlefield. [Dawston Rigg =Daegsastan, 603.] Trans. Dumfries. Antiq. Soc., 11 (1894–95), pp. 89–96. 1896.

6140 O'Leary (E.). Notes on the place of king Laoghaire's death. [438. Locality on the bog of Allen.] J. co. Kildare Archaeol. Soc., 5, pp. 193–99. 1907.

6141 Orpen (Goddard Henry). Site of the battle of Glen-Mama [A.D. 1000].

[Brian v. Leinstermen and Danes. Probably near Newcastle-Lyons rather than Dunlavin.] J. Roy. Soc. Antiq. Ireland, 36 (5th S. 16), pp. 78–80. 1906.

6142 Seyler (Clarence A.). ' Clede Mutha '. [*Burh* built by Edward the Elder in 921 (A.-S.C.). Identified here with Dunglas castle on the Clyde.] Arch. Camb., 76 (7th S. 1), pp. 253–64. 1921.

6143 Skene (William Forbes). Observations on Forteviot, the site of the ancient capital of Scotland. [Argument for Fortren. Abernethy not ancient Pictish capital.] Archaeol. Scot., 4, pp. 271–79. 1857.

6144 Wade-Evans (Arthur Wade). Is ' Porth-Kerdin ' in Moylgrove [north Pembrokeshire]? [In story of Kulhwch.] Arch. Camb., 6th S. 4, pp. 33–48. 1904.

6145 Wainwright (Frederick Threlfall). Cledemutha. [A.-S. C., A.D. 921. Fortress built by Edward the Elder : ? at the mouth of the Clwyd : ? Rhuddlan.] E.H.R., 65, pp. 203–12. 1950.

89. KING ALFRED'S GEOGRAPHY

(for older texts and translations of the voyages of Ohthere and Wulfstan, *see also* Wülker (Richard) : Grundriss zur Geschichte der angelsächsischen Litteratur, 1885, pp. 407–10.)

6146 Alfred, *king.* A description of Europe, and the voyages of Ohthere and Wulfstan . . . With . . . a facsimile copy of the whole Anglo-Saxon text . . . and notes by Joseph Bosworth. [With map.] pp. iv, 8, 4, 26, 63, + 5 plates. 8° London, 1855.

6147 —— Ottars og Ulfstens korte Rejseberetainger med dansk Oversættelse, kritiske Anmærkninger og andre Oplysninger, af R. Rask. pp. 132. 12° Kiöbenhavn, 1816. [A.-S. and Danish.]

6148 Boer (Richard Constant). Wulfstáns Beschreibung der Weichselmündung. Festschrift Vilhelm Thomsen, pp. 56–58. 1912.

6149 Bosworth (Joseph). King Alfred's Orosius. N. and Q., [1st S.] 12, pp. 179–80. 1855.

6150 Craigie (*Sir* William Alexander). 'Iraland' in king Alfred's 'Orosius'. Mod. Lang. Rev., 12, pp. 200–01 (and 494). 1917.

6151 —— The nationality of king Alfred's Wulfstan. [An Angle.] J. Engl. and Germ. Phil., 24, pp. 396–97. 1925.

6152 Cross (Samuel H.). Notes on king Alfred's north : Osti, Este. Speculum, 6, pp. 296–99. 1931.

6153 Ekblom (Einar). Der Volksname *Osti* in Alfreds des Grossen Orosius-Übersetzung. [*See also* note by Kemp Malone in 15, p. 410.] Studia Neophil., 13, pp. 161–73. 1941.

6154 Ekblom (R.). Alfred the Great as geographer. *Same jnl.*, 14, pp. 115–44. 1942.

6155 —— Alfred's geography of north and central Europe. A philological miscellany presented to Eilert Ekwall, pp. 115–44. 1942.

6156 —— Den Forntida nordiska orienteringen von Wulfstans resa till Truso. [With English summary, 5 maps in text.] Fornvännen, 33, pp. 49–68. 1938.

6157 —— Ohthere's voyage from Skiringssal to Hedeby. Studia Neophil., 12, pp. 177–90. 1940.

6158 Emerson (Oliver Farrar). 'Iraland' (Alfred's 'Orosius', I. 1). Mod. Lang. Rev., 11, pp. 458–59. 1911.

6159 Geidel (Heinrich). Alfred der Grosse als Geograph. *Münchener geographische Studien*, 8. pp. vii, 105. 8° München, 1904.

6160 Hampson (R. T.), **Singer** (S. W.), *etc.* King Alfred's geography of Europe. N. and Q. [1st S.], 1, pp. 257–8, 313–14 : 2, pp. 177–79. 1850.

6161 Huebener (Gustav). König Alfred und Osteuropa. [Maegþas, Ohthere und Wulfstan, Truso, Sitten der Esthen.] Engl. Studien, 60, pp. 37–57. 1925.

6162 —— Koenig Alfred's Geografie. Speculum, 6, pp. 428–34. 1931.

6163 Ingram (James). An inaugural lecture on the utility of Anglo-Saxon literature ; to which is added the geography of Europe by King Alfred, including his account of the discovery of the North Cape in the ninth century. pp. viii, 112. 4° Oxford, 1807. [Pp. 90–112, notes by John Reinhold Foster.]

6163a Jansson (Valter). Bjarmaland. Ortnamnssälskapets . . . årsskr., 1, pp. 33–50. 1936.

6164 Koutaissoff (Elisabeth). Ohtheriana, 1 : Kuznetsov on Biarmia. [?=Murman coast. *See also* **6165**.] Engl. and Germ. Stud., 2, pp. 20–33. 1949.

6165 Kuznetsov (S. K.). K voprosu o Biarmii [On the problem of Biarmia.] [Russian translations of passages on Biarmia from the sagas : information from Icelandic geographical works. Concludes that Biarmia and Perm were different places.] Etnograficheskoe Obozrenie, 65–66, pp. 1–95. 1905.

6166 Laborde (Edward Dalrymple). King Alfred's system of geographical description in his version of Orosius. [Map and 4 figures in text.] Geog. J., 62, pp. 133–38. 1923.

6167 Logeman (Henri). The *mægð* that Wulfstan found among the Esthonians. [? *mægð*=power, not tribe. '*And þær is mid Estum án mægð þæt hi magon cyle gewyrcan*'=' There is with the Esthonicus a " power " that they can " cause cold ",' i.e. possess the art of refrigeration.] Engl. Studien, 40, pp. 464–65. 1909.

6168 Macdonald (A.). Wulfstan's voyage and freezing. [As seen in Esthonia for bodies and ale. Compares passage in Stein's Ancient Khotan.] Mod. Lang. Rev., 43, pp. 73–74. 1948.

6169 Malone (Kemp). The date of Ohthere's voyage to Hæthum. Mod. Lang. Rev., 25, pp. 78–81. 1930.

6170 —— King Alfred's 'Geats'. *Same jnl.*, 20, pp. 1–11. 1925.

6171 —— King Alfred's 'Götland'. *Same jnl.*, 23, pp. 336–39. 1928.

6172 —— King Alfred's north : a study in mediaeval geography. [Meaning of terms for cardinal points in first chapter of Alfred's Orosius.] Speculum, 5, pp. 139–67, + 5 'maps'. 1930.

6173 Malone (Kemp). On Alfred's Osti. Stud. Neophil., 15, p. 410. 1943.

6174 —— On king Alfred's geographical treatise. [i. Ests and *Osti* : 2. Identity of the *Osti* : 3. The *Eastfrancan* : 4. *Iraland*.] Speculum, 8, pp. 67–78. 1933.

6175 —— On Wulfstan's Scandinavia. Stud. in Philol., 28, pp. 574–79. 1931.

6176 Porthan (Henricus Gabriel). Försök at uplysa Konung Ælfreds Geographiska Beskrifning öfver den Europeiska Norden. [A.–S. text : Swedish transl. and commentary.] K. Vitterhets Hist. och Antiq. Acad. Handlingar, 6. Delen, pp. 37–106. 1800.

6177 Rask (Rasmus Christian Nielsen). Ottars og Ulfsteens korte Reiseberetninger med dansk Oversættelse, kritiske Anmærkninger og andre Oplysninger. Skandinav. Litteraturselskabs Skrifter, 11, pp. 1–132. 1815.

6178 Ross (Alan Strode Campbell). The Terfinnas and Beormas of Ohthere. *Leeds School of English Language* : *Texts and monographs*, 7. pp. 63. 8° Leeds, 1940. [Text and translation. Both peoples lived on Kendalaks Bay, White Sea.]

6179 Skeat (Walter William). Ohthere's voyage. [Explains killing of 60 ' whales' in two days by translating ' walruses'.] N. and Q., 7th S. 6, p. 44. 1888.

6180 Spelman (*Sir* John). Periplus Ohtheri . . . et Wulfstani . . . cum J. Spelmanni vita Ælfredi Magni, e veteri codice manuscripto Bibliothecae Cottonianae editus ; . . . repetitus ac brevibus notis adauctus ab A. Bussaeo. *In* Arii Thorgilis filii . . . Schedae, seu libellus de Is-landia, *etc.* : pt. 2. 3 pts., 4° Havniae, 1733.

6181 Tallgren (A. M.). Biarmia. Eurasia Septentrionalis Antiqua, 6, pp. 100–20. 1931.

6182 Vasmer (Max). Zum Namen der Terfinnas in König Ælfreds Orosius-Uebersetzung. Engl. Studien, 56, pp. 169–71. 1922.

6183 Waterhouse (G.). Wulfstan's account of the Esthonians. Mod. Lang. Rev., 25, p. 326. 1930.

6184 Whitbread (L.). Old English whale-hunting. [Light on Ohthere's account.] *Same jnl.*, 41, p. 196. 1946.

6185 Whiting (B. J.). Óhthere (Óttar) and *Egils Saga*. Philol. Quart., 24, pp. 218–26. 1945.

90. ROADS

6186 Boyle (John Roberts). On roads and boundaries. [Attempt to 'allocate to one or other of seven periods ' of which iii is A.–S., and iv is Danish.] Antiquary, 29, pp. 57–60, 197–99. 1894.

6187 Copley (Gordon J.). Stane Street in the Dark Ages. [Map on p. 99. The road and cemeteries, etc., along it.] Sussex Archaeol. Collns., 89, pp. 98–104. 1950.

6188 Grundy (George Beardoe). The ancient highways and tracks of Wiltshire, Berkshire and Hampshire, and the Saxon battlefields of Wiltshire. [Details of 79 roads in Wilts., of 58 in Berks, and of 56 in Hants. : battle-sites of Wodnesbeorh, Ethandun, Ellandun, Beranburh, campaign of 871, Wiltun, and Cynete.] Archaeol. J., 75, pp. 69–194. 1918.

6189 —— The ancient highways and tracks of Worcestershire and the middle Severn basin. Archaeol. J., 91 (1934), pp. 66–96, 241–68 : 92 (1935), pp. 98–141, + 6 maps. 1935–36.

6190 —— Ancient highways of Cornwall. Archaeol. J., 98 (1941), pp. 165–180, + 1 map (opposite p. 162). 1942.

6191 —— Ancient highways of Devon. Archaeol. J., 98 (1941), pp. 131–64, + 1 map. 1942.

6192 —— The ancient highways of Dorset, Somerset, and south-west England. Archaeol. J., 94 (1937), pp. 257–90 : 95 (1938), pp. 174–222 : + 1 map. 1938–39.

6193 —— The ancient highways of Somerset. Archaeol. J., 96 (1939), pp. 226–97, + 1 map. 1940.

6194 —— The evidence of Saxon land charters on the ancient road-system of Britain. Archaeol. J., 74, pp. 79–105. 1917.

6195 Houghton (Frederick Tyrie Sidney). Salt-ways. [Including A.–S. and Domesday evidence, and maps.] Trans. B'ham. Arch. Soc., 54 (for 1929–30), pp. 1–17, + 4 maps. 1932.

6196 Margary (Ivan D.). The early development of tracks and roads in and near East Grinstead. [Fig. 2, 'early Saxon tracks'.] Sussex N. and Q., 11, pp. 77–81. 1946.

6197 Morris (Henry). The Slighe Cualann. [=high road where king Laeghaire was killed.] J. Roy. Soc. Antiq. Ireland, 68 (7th S. 8), pp. 113–23. 1938.

6198 O Loghlainn (Colm). Roadways in ancient Ireland. Essays presented to E. MacNeill, pp. 465–74, + folding map. 1940.

6199 Peake (Harold John Edward). The Ridgeway and the Icknield Way in Berkshire. [Evidence from charters of course of both roads in A.–S. times.] Trans. Newbury F.C., 6, pp. 51–65. 1931.

6200 Power (Patrick). The 'Rian Bo Phadraig' (The ancient highway of the Decies). [The track of St. Patrick's cow between Cashel and Ardmore.] J. Roy. Soc. Antiq. Ireland, 35 (5th S. 15), pp. 110–29, + 4 maps. 1905.

6201 Shore (Thomas William). Old roads and fords of Hampshire. Archaeol. Rev., 3, pp. 88–98. 1889.

6202 Stenton (Sir Frank Merry). The road system of medieval England. [A small amount of A.–S. material.] Econ. Hist. Rev., 7, pp. 1–21. 1936.

6203 Whitley (W. T.). Saltways of Droitwich district. [Including A.–S. and Domesday information.] B'ham. Arch. Soc., Trans., 49, pp. 1–15. 1923.

91. TRAVEL

§ *a.* **Pilgrimages, Etc.**

6204 Adamnan, St., *9th abbot of Hy.* The pilgrimage of Arculfus in the Holy-Land about the year A.D. 670. Translated and annotated by J. R. Macpherson. pp. xx, 91. 8° London, 1889.

6205 Beazley (Sir Charles Raymond). The dawn of modern geography. Vol. 1. pp. xvi, 538. 8° London, 1897. [Pp. 125–57, Anglo-Frankish pilgrims, c. 680–870. i. Arculf, ii. Willibald: pp. 224–42, Irish missionary travel: Brandan.]

6206 Cook (Albert Stanburrough). Augustine's journey from Rome to Richborough. Speculum, 1, pp. 375–97. 1926.

6207 Gougaud (Louis). Sur les routes de Rome et sur le Rhin avec les Peregrini insulaires. Rev. d'hist. ecclés., 29, pp. 253–71. 1933.

6208 Hahn (Heinrich). Die Reise des heiligen Willibald nach Palästina. pp. 25. 4° Berlin, 1856.

6209 Jenkins (Claude). Christian pilgrimages, A.D. 500–800. Newton (A.P.): Travel and travellers of the Middle Ages, pp. 39–69. 1926.

6210 Jones (Griffith Hartwell). Celtic Britain and the pilgrim movement. *Y Cymmrodor,* 23. pp. xii, 581. 8° London, 1912. [Especially Cornish, Welsh, Irish and Scottish pilgrims.]

6211 Jung (J.). Das Itinerar [990–94] des Erzbischofs Sigeric von Canterbury und die Strasse vom Rom über Siena nach Lucca. Mitt. Inst. oesterreichische Geschichtsforschung, 25, pp. 1–90. 1904.

6212 Magown (Francis Peabody) *jr.* An English pilgrim—diary of the year 990. [Associated with Sigeric, abp. of Canterbury (990–94). 'The only complete itinerary of an A.–S. pilgrim to Rome.' Catalogue of 23 Roman churches and list of 79 stopping places between Rome and the channel: with notes on them.] Med. Stud., 2, pp. 231–52. 1940.

6213 Meyrick (Thomas). The life of St. Walburge, with the Itinerary of St. Willibald. 8° London, 1873.

6214 Moore (Wilfred J.). The Saxon pilgrims to Rome and Schola Saxonum. *Diss., Fribourg,* 1937. pp. 140. 8° Fribourg, 1937. [List of A.–S. pilgrims, 7th–8th c.]

6215 Pesci (Benedetto). L'itinerario romano di Sigerico archivescovo di Canterbury e la lista dei Papi da lui portata in Inghilterra (anno 990). Riv. Archaeol. Cristiani, 13, pp. 43–60. 1936.

6216 Thrall (William Flint). Clerical sea pilgrimages and the 'Imrama'. ['Tale from which the *filid* could take subject-matter for an epic.'] Manley anniversary studies (Chicago), pp. 276–83. 1923.

6217 Willibald, *St., bp. of Eichstadt.* Hodoeporicon S. Willibaldi, oder S. Willibalds Pilgerreise, geschrieben von der Heidenheimer Nonne. Uebersetzt und erläutert von J. Brückl. *Programm, etc.* pp. xvi, 78. 8° Eichstätt, [1880]. [Latin and German.]

6217a Wright (Thomas), *ed.* Early travels in Palestine. *Bohn's Antiquarian Library.* pp. xxxi, 517. 8° London, 1848. [Pp. 1–12, Arculf: pp. 13–22, Willibald.]

§ *b.* Travels of Celtic Saints

6218 Bowen (Emrys George). Carmarthenshire and the wanderings of the Celtic saints. Trans. Carmarthen Antiq. Soc., 26, pp. 42–45. 1936.

6219 —— The travels and settlements of the Celtic saints. [Grouping of influence from church dedications.] Wales, 24, pp. 100–03. 1946.

6220 —— The travels of St. Samson of Dol. Aberystwyth Stud., 13, pp. 61–67, + 1 map. 1934.

6221 —— The travels of the Celtic saints. [With 5 maps to show relation of cults of SS. Columba, Chattan, Braec and Sampson to the distribution of megaliths.] Antiquity, 18, pp. 16–28. 1944.

6222 Crawford (Osbert Guy Stanhope). Western seaways. [2 maps shewing England and Brittany, and South Wales to illustrate travels of Celtic saints, etc.] Custom is king: essays presented to R. R. Marett, pp. 179–200. 1936.

6223 Gerville (-de). Lettres sur la communication entre les deux Bretagnes. [With biographies of various Celtic saints: St. Germanus of Auxerre, St. Iltut, St. Dubricius, *etc.*] Rept. of Proc., Brit. Archaeol. Assoc., 5 (Meeting at Worcester, 1848), pp. 429–54. 1848.

6224 —— On the communications between Brittany and Wales, from the times of the Romans down to the present time. [Travels of Celtic saints.] J. Brit. Archaeol. Assoc., 4, pp. 229–45. 1849.

6225 Lot (Ferdinand). Le curagh et les pélerinages par mer. [Kenney, 1, p. 407. Dates back to 9th c.] Ann. de Bretagne, 11, pp. 362–63. 1896.

6226 Meyer (Kuno). Early relations between Gael and Brython. [Wanderings of saints, place-names, ethnology, etc.] Trans. Hon. Soc. Cymm., 1895–96, pp. 55–86. 1897.

§ *c.* Celtic Exploration (General and Miscellaneous)

6227 Babcock (William Henry). Legendary islands of the Atlantic. *American Geographical Society, Research Series,* 8. pp. 196, + maps. 8° New York, 1922.

6228 Gaffarel (Paul). Les explorations maritimes des Irlandais au moyen âge. [Kenney, p. 408.] Rev. politique et litt., Jan. 1875.

6228a Joyce (Patrick Weston). The voyage of Maildun. An account of the adventures of Maildun and his crew, and of the wonderful things they saw during their voyage of three years and seven months, in their curragh, on the western sea. Joyce (P. W.): Old Celtic romances, pp. 112–76. 1920.

6229 Lethbridge (Thomas Charles). Herdsmen and hermits, Celtic seafarers in the northern seas. pp. xix, 146. 8° Cambridge, 1950. [Chap. 5, Saxon, Scot and Pict: Chap. 6, The Celts in Iceland.]

6230 Marcus (G. J.). Irish pioneers in ocean navigation of the Middle Ages. Irish Eccles. Rec., 5th. S 76, pp. 353–63, 469–79. 1951.

6231 Marcus (G. J.). The Scotic curach. [4th–7th c. Used by Maíl Dúin, etc.] Scot. Gaelic Stud., 7, pp. 105–14. 1953.

6232 Nutt (Alfred). Notes sur le voyage de Mael Duin. Rev. celt., 10, pp. 347–48. 1889.

6233 O'Neill (Seamus). Irish maritime history : early period to Norse invasions. Studies, 34, pp. 404–11. 1945.

6234 Stokes (Whitley). The voyage of Mael Duin. [Irish text and English translation.] Rev. celt., 9, pp. 447–95 : 10, pp. 50–95. 1888–89.

6235 —— The voyage of Snedgus and Mac Riagla. [Text in Irish and English. Story contains historical characters of 7th c.] Rev. celt., 9, pp. 14–25. 1888.

6236 Thrall (William Flint). The historical setting of the legend of Snedgus and Mac Riagla. Stud. in Philol., 22, pp. 347–82. 1925.

6237 Westropp (Thomas Johnson). Brasil and the legendary islands of the north Atlantic : their history and fable. A contribution to the 'Atlantis' problem. [i. The Irish sea beliefs : ii. Early *Imrama* or sea tales : iii. The Norse sagas and Ireland, etc.] Proc. R.I.A., 30c, pp. 223–60, + 3 plates. 1912.

§ *d.* **St. Brendan**

i. **Texts and notes on them.**

6238 Baelz (Martha). Die me. Brendanlegende des Gloucesterlegendars, kritisch herausgegeben mit Einleitung. *Diss.* pp. xxxii, 70. 8° Berlin, 1909. [From MS. Tours, Bibl. Munic., no. 1008.]

6239 Brendan, *St., abbot of Clonfert.* De Reis van Sinte Brandaan. Uitgave, inleidung en commentaar door Maartje Draak. Herdicht door Bertus Aafjes. pp. 245, 24. 8° Amsterdam, 1948. [Middle Dutch text, combined with the versions of the Hulthem and Comburg mss.]

6240 Grosjean (Paul). Vita S. Brendani Clonfertensis e codice Dubliniensi. [With Latin text.] Anal. Boll., 48, pp. 99–123. 1930.

6241 Horstmann (Carl), *ed.* Die altenglische Legende von St. Brendan aus MS. Ashmol, 43, fol. 716. Archiv Stud. neueren Spr., Bd. 53, pp. 17–48. 1874.

6242 Meyer (Kuno). Ein mittelirisches Gedicht auf Brendan der Meerfahrer. Sitzungsb. k. preuss. Akad. Wiss., 25, pp. 436–43. 1912.

6243 Meyer (Wilhelm). Die Überlieferung der deutschen Brendanlegende. *Dissertation.* 1. Der Prosatext. pp. 125. 8° Göttingen, 1918. *No more published.*

6244 Moltzer (Henri Ernest). Levens en legenden van heiligen. I. Brendaen en Panthalioen, naar het Utrechtsche handschrift. pp. xvi, 70. 8° Groningen, 1891.

6245 Moran (Patrick Francis), *carinal, abp. of Sydney, ed.* Acta Sancti Brendani : original Latin documents connected with the life of Saint Brendan. pp. viii, 144. 8° Dublin, 1872. [Kenney, 1, p. 729.]

6246 Plummer (Charles). De Vita Gadelica Cantabrigiensi ex schedis C. Plummer. [On life of Brendan in MS. McClean, 187 in Fitzwilliam Museum.] Anal. Boll., 48, pp. 121–23. 1930.

6247 Schroeder (Carl). Sanct Brandan. Ein lateinischer und drei deutsche Texte. pp. xix, 196. 8° Erlangen, 1871.

6248 Steinweg (C.). Die handschriftlichen Gestaltung der lateinischen Navigatio Brendani. *Diss., Halle,* 1891. 8° Halle, 1891. [Kenney, 1, p. 415. *Also in* Roman. Forsch., 7, pp. 1–48.]

6249 Thurneysen (Rudolf). Eine Variante der Brendan-Legende. Zeit. celt. Phil., 10, pp. 408–20. 1915.

6250 Vendryes (Joseph). Trois historiettes irlandaises du manuscrit de Paris. [Bibl. Nat., fonds celtique, no. 1. iv. Historiette zur saint Brendan, Irish text and French translation.] Rev. celt., 31, pp. 300–11. 1910.

6251 Wahlund (Carl). Eine altprovenzalische Prosaübersetzung von Brendans Meerfahrt. Festgabe Wendelin Foerster, pp. 175–98. 1902.

6252 Waters (Edward George Ross), *ed.* The Anglo-Norman voyage of St. Brendon by Benedeit. pp. cii, 211. 8° Oxford, 1928.

6253 ——, *ed.* An Old Italian version of the Navigatio Sancti Brendani. *Publications of the Philological Society*, 10. pp. 86, + 1 plate. 8° Oxford, 1931. [From MS. Tours, Bibl. Mun., 1008.]

ii. Miscellaneous

6254 Babcock (William Henry). St. Brendan's explorations and islands. [Kenney, 1, p. 408.] Geog. Rev., 8, pp. 37–46. 1919.

6255 Benedict (Robert Dewey). The Hereford map and the legend of Saint Brandan. Bull. Amer. Geog. Soc., 24, pp. 321–65. 1892.

6256 Benz (Richard). Meerfahrt sanct Brendans. 8° Jena, 1927.

6257 Bonnebakker (E.). Sente Brendane. 2 vol. 8° Amsterdam, 1894.

6258 Bute (John Patrick (Crichton-Stuart)) *3rd marquis.* Brendan's fabulous voyage. County Louth Archaeol. J., 2, pp. 109–23. 1909.

6259 Claussen (Bruno). Van Sunte Brendanus. Nordisk Tidsskrift för Bok-och Biblioteksväsen, 1, pp. 33 *et seq.* 1914.

6260 Dunn (Joseph). The Brendan problem. [General survey and problems awaiting solution concerning life, work and legends. With bibliography.] Cath. Hist. Rev., 6, pp. 395–477. 1921.

6261 Goeje (Michiel Johannes de). La légende de Saint Brendan. pp. 36. 8° Leide, 1890. Actes 8e Congress internat. Orientalistes, Leide, 1889. 1. i.

6262 Grotefend ( ). Das Fest des heiligen Brandanus. Korrespondenzblatt Gesammtvereins deut. Geschichts-und Altertumsvereine, 57, cols. 395–97. 1909.

6263 Hennig (John). A note on Ireland's place in the literary tradition of of St. Brendan. Traditio, 8, pp. 397–402. 1952.

6264 Huet (G. Busken). Van sinte Brandane, vs. 137–260. Tijdschr. Ned. Taal-en Lettk., 7, pp. 85–92. 1887.

6265 Jubinal (Achille). La légende latine de S. Brandaines. 8° Paris, 1836.

6266 Kenney (James Francis). The legend of St. Brendan. [Kenney, 1, p. 407.] Trans. Roy. Soc. Canada, 1920, sect. ii, pp. 51–67. 1920.

6267 Little (George Aloysius). Brendan the navigator. An interpretation. pp. xix, 253, + plates. 8° Dublin, 1945.

6268 Loewenberg (J.). Notes on the life of St. Brendan. [Kenney, 1, p. 407.] Irish Eccles. Rec., 8, pp. 17–25, 79–86, 178–90, 193–208. 1871–72.

6269 MacDermott (Anthony). St. Brandan the navigator. Mariner's Mirror, 30, pp. 73–80. 1944.

6270 O'Donoghue (Denis). Brendaniana. St. Brendan the voyager in story and legend. pp. xxviii, 399, + 5 plates. 8° Dublin, 1893. [Kenney, 1, p. 407.]

6271 Olden (Thomas). The voyage of St. Brendan. J. Roy. Soc. Antiq. Ireland, 21 (5th S. 1. ii), pp. 676–84. 1891.

6272 O'Riordan (J. B.). Saint Brendan, saint and navigator. *Catholic Truth Society, no.* 522. 8° Dublin, n.d.

6273 Peschel (O. F.). Der Ursprung und die Verbreitung einiger geographischen Mythen im Mittelalter : Die Legende von den Schiffahrten des heil. Brandan. [Kenney, 1, p. 407.] Deutsche Vierteljahrsschrift, lxxvi, pp. 242–50. 1854.

6274 Plummer (Charles). Some new light on the Brendan legend. Zeit. celt. Phil., 5, pp. 124–41. 1904.

6275 Schirmer (Gustav). Zur Brendanus-Legende. pp. 75. 8° Leipzig, 1888. [Kenney, 1, p. 407.]

6276 Schulze (Alfred). Zur Brendanlegende. [Kenney, 1, p. 407.] Zeit. roman. Phil., 30, pp. 257–79. 1906.

6277 Selmer (Carl). The Irish St. Brendan legend in lower Germany and on the Baltic coast. Traditio, 4, pp. 408–13. 1946.

6278 —— On the beginnings of the St. Brendan legend on the continent. Cath. Hist. Rev., 29, pp. 169–76. 1943.

6279 —— The St. Brendan-legend in Old German literature. J. Am. Irish Hist. Soc., 32, pp. 161–69. 1941.

6280 Tuffrau (Paul). Le merveilleux voyage de Saint Brandan à la recherche du Paradis. Légende latine . . . renouvelée par P. T. pp. 195. 8° Paris, 1925.

6281 Wilkie (James). St. Brendan the voyager and his mystic quest. pp. 73. 8° London, 1916.

6282 Zimmer (Heinrich). Keltische Beiträge. 2. Brendans Meerfahrt. [i. In des mittelirischen Literatur : ii. Im Lichte irischer Schiffersagen : iii. Die Terra repromissionis im Lichte der irischen Sage : iv. Betrachtungen und Schlussfolgerungen.] Z.f.d.A., 33, pp. 129–220, 257–338. 1889.

92. PLACE-NAMES

(All place-name material included as relevant—or background—unless referring to foreign elements or obviously more modern names.)

§ a. General

6283 Birch (Walter de Gray). An unpublished manuscript list of some early territorial names in England. [MS. Harl. 3271, f. 6b. 10th–11th c.] J. Brit. Archaeol. Assoc., 40, pp. 28–46. 1884.

6284 Bradley (Henry). English place-names. Essays and studies (English Assn.), 1, pp. 7–41. 1910.

6285 —— Some place-names in Sweet's Anglo-Saxon reader. [Baddanburh, etc.] Archiv Stud. neueren Spr., Bd. 131, pp. 427–28. 1913.

6286 Browne (Walter Raleigh). On the distribution of English place names. Trans. Philol. Soc., 1880–81, pp. 86–98, and folding chart. [1881.]

6287 Crawford (Osbert Guy Stanhope). Place-names. Archaeol. J., 78, pp. 31–46. 1921.

6288 Edmunds (Flavell). Traces of history in the names of places. With a vocabulary of the roots out of which names of places in England and Wales are formed. New edition. 8° London, 1872.

6289 Ekwall (Eilert). The concise Oxford dictionary of English place-names. 3rd edition. pp. xlvii, 530. 8° Oxford, 1947.

6290 —— Early names of Britain. [Including A.-S. *England*, etc.] Antiquity, 4, pp. 149–56. 1930.

6291 —— Names of trades in English place-names. Hist. essays in honour of J. Tait, pp. 79–89. 1933.

6292 —— An Old English sound-change and some English forest names. Anglia, Beiblatt, 36, pp. 146–51. 1925.

6293 —— Some notes on English place-names containing names of heathen deities. [i. Tysoe : ii. Place-names containing the names Frig (Frēo)—Fretherne, Glos., Fryup, Yorks., Freefolk and Froyle, Hants.] Engl. Studien, 70, pp. 55–59. 1935.

6294 —— Studies on English place-names. K. Vitt. hist. och Antik. Akad. Handl., 42, pp. 1–221. 1936.

6295 Eminson (Thomas Benjamin Franklin). Some deceptive place-names of England and Normandy. Antiquary, 51, pp. 100–05, 173–78. 1915.

6296 Forsberg (Rune). A contribution to a dictionary of Old English place-names. *Nomina Germanica*, 9. pp. xlvi, 225. 8° Uppsala, 1950.

6297 Gelling (Margaret). Place-names as clues to history. (Common elements in English place-names). Amateur historian, 1, pp. 51–59. 1952.

6298 Gevenich (Olga). Die englische Palatisierung von K>č im Lichte der englischen Ortsnamen. *Studien zur englischen Philologie* (*Morsbach*), 57. pp. xvi, 168. 8° Halle, 1918.

6299 Guest (Edwin). On certain Welsh names of places preserved in English compounds. Proc. Philol. Soc., 1, pp. 9–12. 1842.

6300 Haverfield (Francis John). The antiquity of place-names. [Includes a letter from W. H. Stevenson ' on the forms of the name of the Magesaete.'] J. Archit. Soc. of Chester, N.S. 6, pp. 36–41. 1897.

6301 Haverfield (Francis John). English topographical notes. —1. Some place-names in Bede. E.H.R., 10, pp. 710–11. 1895.

6302 Hope (Robert Charles). A glossary of dialectal place-nomenclature. 2nd edition. pp. xii, 159. 8° London, 1883. [1st edition reads : A provisional glossary, etc. pp. 22. 12° Scarborough, [1882].]

6303 Johnston (James Brown). Place-names of England and Wales. pp. 540. 8° London, 1915.

6303a Koekeritz (Helge). Vad engelska ornamn berätta. Ortnamnssäll-skapets . . . årsskr., 1939–40, pp. 1–32. 1941.

6304 Langenfelt (Gösta). Toponymics, or derivations from local names in English. *Diss., Uppsala.* pp. xvi, 252. 8° Uppsala, 1920. [Pp. 36–104, OE toponymics.]

6305 Leo (Heinrich). Treatise on the local nomenclature of the Anglo-Saxons, as exhibited in the Codex diplomaticus aevi Saxonicae, translated from the German [of §1, Die angelsächsischen Ortsnamen *in* Rectitudines singularum personarum] . . . with additional examples and explanatory notes [by B. Williams]. pp. xviii, 131. 12° London, 1852. [Gross, 349.]

6306 Lyons (Jessie M.). Frisian place-names in England. P.M.L.A., 33, pp. 644–55. 1918.

6307 McClure (Edmund). British place-names in their historical setting. pp. 349. 8° London, 1910. [Pp. 119–304, A.-S. and Norse.]

6308 Magown (Francis Peabody) *jr.* Territorial, place-, and river-names in the Old-English Chronicle, A-text (Parker MS.), (—D-text (MS. Cotton Tiberius B. IV).) [Alphabetical index : place-names by counties, etc.] Harvard Stud. and Notes, 18, pp. 69–111 ; 20, pp. 147–80. 1935, 1938.

6309 Mawer (*Sir* Allen). Animal and personal names in O.E. place-names. Mod. Lang. Rev., 14, pp. 233–44. 1919.

6310 Mawer (*Sir* Allen). English place-names and English philology. Trans. Philolog. Soc., 1937, pp. 120–33. 1937.

6311 —— and **Stenton** (*Sir* Frank Merry), *ed.* Introduction to the survey of English place-names. *English Place-name Society*, 1. i. pp. 201. 8° Cambridge, 1924.

6312 Mawer (*Sir* Allen). Place-names and archaeology. Antiquity, 1, pp. 151–58 + 1 plate. 1927.

6313 —— Place-names and history. pp. 38. 8° Liverpool, 1922.

6314 —— The Scandinavian settlements in England as reflected in English place-names. Acta phil. Scand., 7, pp. 1–30. 1932.

6315 —— Some unconsidered elements in English place-names. Essays and Studies (English Assn.), 4, pp. 55–71. 1913.

6316 Mezger (Fritz). Die angelsächsischen Völker-und Ländernamen. *Diss., Berlin.* pp. 60. 8° Berlin, 1921.

6317 Moorman (Frederick William). English place-names and Teutonic sagas. Essays and Studies (English Assn.), 5, pp. 75–103. 1914.

6318 Nicolson (John). History from place-names. [Summary.] Word-lore, 1, pp. 97–99. 1926.

6319 Oliver (Walter). Links with our old Norse ancestors, the Scandinavian descent of the borderers, *etc.* Trans. Hawick Archaeol. Soc., 1927, pp. 61–70. 1927.

6320 Phillipps (*Sir* Thomas), *bart.* Letter to W. R. Hamilton, Esq., on the Saxon names of places. Trans. Roy. Soc. Lit., 3, pp. 97–104. 1839.

6321 Picton (*Sir* James Allanson). The system of place-names in Wales compared with that of England. Arch. Camb., 4th S. 12, pp. 125–37. 1881.

6322 Ritter (Otto). Kritische Notizen zur englischen Namenkunde. [Personal names : Ecga, Friðburh (Friðhild), Sidwell (Sativola) : the rest place-names.] Anglia, 69 (N.F. 57), pp. 172–203. 1950.

6323 Skeat (Walter William). Vowel-shortening in English place-names. N. and Q., 7th S. 7, pp. 321, 430, 473. 1889.

6324 Smith (Albert Hugh). Stress-shifting in place-names. London mediaeval studies, 1, pp. 48–55. 1937.

6325 Stenton (*Sir* Frank Merry). The historical bearing of place-name studies. [i. England in the sixth century : ii. The English occupation of southern Britain : iii. Anglo-Saxon heathenism (with map) : iv. The Danish settlement of eastern England : v. The place of women in Anglo-Saxon society.] Trans. Roy. Hist. Soc., 4th S. 21, pp. 1–19 : 22, pp. 1–22 : 23, pp. 1–24 : 24, pp. 1–24 : 25, pp. 1–13. 1939–43.

6326 —— Place-names as evidence of female ownership of land in Anglo-times. [E.g. Adderbury, Oxon. (Eadburh) : Kenilworth, Warw. (Cynehild) : Chellington, Beds. (Ceolwynn) : Kemerton, Glos. (Cyneburh) : Eddington, Berks. (Eadgifu).] Academy, 71, p. 21. 1906.

6327 Stevenson (William Henry). The derivation of place-names. Archaeol. Rev., 2, pp. 104–07. 1888.

6328 Stokes (H. G.). English place-names. 2nd edition, revised. *British heritage series.* pp. 120, + 32 plates. 8° London, 1949.

6329 Stolze (Max). Zur Lautlehre der altenglischen Ortsnamen in Domesday Book. pp. iii, 50. 8° Berlin, 1902.

6330 Sydow (Carl Wilhelm von). Grendel i anglosaxiska ortsnamn. Namn och Bygd (Tidskrift för nordisk Ortsnamnsforskning), 2, pp. 160–64. 1914.

6331 Taylor (Isaac). Names and their histories, alphabetically arranged, *etc.* pp. v, 392. 8° London, 1896 [1895].

6332 —— Words and places. Edited with corrections and additions by A. Smythe Palmer. pp. 464. 8° London, 1909. —*Everyman's Library.* pp. xx, 417. 8° London, 1911.

6333 Tengstrand (Erik). A contribution to the study of genitival composition in Old English place-names. *Diss., Uppsala. Nomina Germanica,* 7. pp. lxvii, 354. 8° Uppsala, 1940.

6334 Watkins (Alfred). A neglected factor in place-names. [From characteristic of road or track on which it is placed, goods carried or makers and users. i. Salt-roads : ii. Hill names : iii. Trading names : iv. Track maker : v. Generic names : vi. Seasonal names : vii. Terminals.] N. and Q., 153, pp. 311–15, 327–30, 354, 409–10 : 154, pp. 455–58 : 155, pp. 4–7, 60–62, 70, 159. 1927–28.

6335 Westphal (Johannes). Englische Ortsnamen im Altfranzösischen. pp. 39. 8° Strasburg, 1891. [Gross, 352.]

6336 Zachrisson (Robert Eugen). Engelska ortnamn och englesk historia. [Keltiska ortnamn : Latinska ortnamn : Anglosaxiska ortnamn : Nordiska ortnamn : Anglofranska namn.] Ortnamnssällskapets . . . årsskr., 1, pp. 21–32. 1936.

6336a —— English place-name puzzles. A methodical investigation into the question of personal names or descriptive words in English place-names. Studia Neophil., 5, pp. 1–69. 1933. *Also separately.* pp. 69. 8° Uppsala, 1932.

6337 —— Full-names and short-names in Old English place-names. A reply to Professor Eilert Ekwall (MLN. 1935 [pp. 535–42]). [Reply to review by Ekwall of **6336a** and **6338** by Zachrisson.] *Same jnl.,* 8, pp. 82–98. 1936.

6338 —— The meaning of English place-names in the light of the terminal theory. [O.E. charters as sources of place-names, etc.] *Same jnl.,* 6, pp. 25–89, 150–51. 1934–35.

6339 —— Some English place-name etymologies. [By county.] Studier mod. Språkvetenskap, 9, pp. 113–46. 1924.

§ *b*. Individual Names, Miscellaneous

6340 [Anon.] Cold Harbour. N. and Q., 1st S. 2, pp. 340–41. 1850.

6341 Anscombe (Alfred). The etymon of Portslade and Portsmouth. [Argues that ' Port is a genuine personal name.'] Anglia, 46 (N.F. 24), pp. 383–84. 1922.

6342 Bradley (Henry). Two place-names in Nennius. [Cair Guin Truis= Burford or Bourton-on-the-Water (guin truis = gwyn-drwys = Windrush) : Cair Luit Coit=Lichfield.] Academy, 16, p. 269. 1879.

6343 Ekwall (Eilert). Etymological notes. [i. Waltham : ii. Malton, Y. (N.R.): iii. Some Lincolnshire place-names.] Studia Neophil., 1, pp. 97–108 ; 2, pp. 28–40. 1928–29.

6344 —— Some English place-name etymologies. [i. Navisford, Naveslund, Northants : ii. Acklam, Yorks. : iii. Withernsea, Withernwick, Yorks.]. *Same jnl.*, 8, pp. 103–18. 1938.

6345 Ellison (Ralph Carr). Saxon names of certain Roman roads. [Waetlinga-strete—'Gwatling-Street'—Watling street : Maiden way.] Archaeol. Æl., N.S. 9, pp. 49–51. 1883.

6346 Foerster (Max). Englisch-keltisches. [ii. Nith (Dumfriesshire) and *Νοουιος* : iii. Aberystwyth and *Στουκκία* : iv. Loidis, Leeds and Lothian : v. *Peanfāhel, Penneltūn* and Kinnell.] Englische Studien, 56, pp. 204–39. 1922.

6347 Freer (A. S. B.) and **Robinson** (Joseph Armitage). Origin of the name Gussage. [A.-S. *Geotan*, to pour out.] N. and Q. Som. and Dorset, 19, pp. 275–76. 1929.

6348 Karlstroem (Sigurd). Kilvington and some related English place-names. Studia Neophil., 4, pp. 120–40. 1932.

6349 Malone (Kemp). A note on *Brunanburh*. [On the variant spellings of the name ; Brown's castle]. Mod. Lang. Notes, 42, pp. 238–39. 1927.

6350 Mansel-Pleydell (J. C.). Coal Harbour or Cold Harbour. [Attributes A.-S. etymology. *But see* English Place-name Society, Surrey, pp. 406–10.] N. and Q. Som. and Dorset, 1, pp. 246–47. 1890.

6351 Varah (William Edward). Barton. N. and Q., 164, p. 227. 1933.

93. PLACE-NAME STUDY

6352 Alexander (Henry). Place-names and dialect study. Trans. Yorks. Dialect Soc., 2, pt. 13, pp. 24–46. 1912.

6353 Bonner (Arthur). The study of place names, with illustrations from the south-east of England. S.E. Naturalist, 20, pp. 51–60. 1915.

6354 Ekwall (Eilert). Englische Ortsnamenforschung. Anglica [für A. Brandl] Bd. 1. Palaestra, 147, pp. 19–40. 1925.

6355 Gomme (*Sir* George Laurence), **Skeat** (Walter William), *etc.* Placenames of England. [Proposal for a dictionary of place-names.] N. and Q., 6th S. 1, pp. 433–34 : 2, pp. 50–51, 90–91, 192, 376–77, 455. 1880.

6356 Hruschka (Alois). Zur angelsächsischen Namenforschung. pp. 48 + 38. 2 Theile, 8° Prag, 1884–85.

6357 Marcus (Hans). Der gegenwärtige Stand der englischen Ortsnamenforschung. [A bibliography, here included.] Archiv Stud. neueren Spr., Bd. 169, pp. 18–29. 1936.

6358 Mawer (*Sir* Allen). English place-name study : its present condition and future possibilities. Proc. Brit. Acad., 10, pp. 31–44. 1921.

6359 —— Problems of place-name study. pp. xi, 140. 8° London, 1929.

6360 Skeat (Walter William). A plea for place-names. [To be collected.] N. and Q., 6th S. 10, pp. 109–10, 179. 1884.

6361 Zachrisson (Robert Eugen). Five years of English place-name study (1922–27). A critical survey. Engl. Studien, 62, pp. 64–105. 1927.

94. PLACE-NAME ELEMENTS

§ *a.* **Suffixes (-ing, Etc.)**

6362 Alexander (Henry). The genitive suffix in the first element of English place-names. Mod. Lang. Rev., 7, pp. 64–73. 1912.

6363 —— The particle *ing* in placenames. Essays and studies (English Assn.), 2, pp. 158–82. 1911.

6364 Alexander (John James). The element cote in place-names. Devon and Cornwall N. and Q., 21, pp. 105–07. 1940.

6365 Alexander (John James). The element cumb in place-names. [Occurs in over 800 place-names of Cornwall, Devon, Dorset and Somerset.] *Same jnl.*, 19, pp. 352–54. 1937.

6366 Anscombe (Alfred). -et in English place-names. [In A.–S. charters and Domesday.] N. and Q., 157, pp. 165–68, 291. 1929.

6367 —— P-names of places in Domesday ending with *-intune*. N. and Q., 153, pp. 59–62. 1927.

6368 —— Place-names in Domesday Book which end with *-intune*. Times Lit. Suppl., 1921, p. 484. 1921.

6369 Atkinson(John Christopher), *etc.* The patronymic -ing in north-English place-names. N. and Q., 4th S. 5, p. 559 : 6, pp. 61, 120–21, 303–04, 418–19, 509–10, 570–71. 1870.

6370 Boult (Joseph). On the syllable ' -ing ' in names of places in the British Isles. [*See also* **6384**.] Antiq. Mag., 1, pp. 295–98. 1882.

6371 Chope (Richard Pearse). The worthies and cots of the west of England. Devon N. and Q., 3, pp. 57–58. 1904.

6372 Cornelius (Heinrich). Die englische Ortsnamen auf *-wick, -wich*. Festschrift für L. Morsbach, pp. 352–416. 1913.

6373 Ekwall (Eilert). English place-names in *-ing*. *Skrifter utgivna av Kungl. Humanistiska Vetenskapssamfundet i Lund*, 6. pp. xix, 190. 8° Lund, 1923.

6374 Grundy (George Beardoe). The development of the meanings of certain Anglo-Saxon terms. [Original settlement of Saxon England : the termination *-ing* : *tun* : *ham* and *hamm* : *cot* : *weorth*, *worth*, *wyrth* : *wic* : *stede* : *leah* : *stocc*, *stoc* : *feld* : terms connected with agriculture.] Archaeol. J., 99 (1942), pp. 67–98. 1943.

6375 H. (D. R. S.), *etc.* The suffix *-shot* in place names. Word-lore, 1, pp. 116–17, 173–74. 1926.

6376 Hulburd (Percy). Final *den* in Kentish place-names. N. and Q., 12th S. 10, p. 116. 1922.

6377 Jolliffe (John Edward Austin). The Old English term ' snade '. [Suffix to place-names in S.E. England.] Antiquity, 9, pp. 220–22. 1935.

X

6378 Karlstroem (Sigurd). Old English compound place-names in *-ing*. *Diss., Uppsala.* Uppsala Univ. Årsskr., Filos., 1927, No. 2. Pp. xxiii, 194. 1927.

6379 Kemble (John Mitchel). On a peculiar use of the Anglo-Saxon patronymical termination, *ing*. Proc. Philol. Soc., 4, pp. 1–10. 1848.

6380 Kerslake (Thomas), *etc.* -hó= hoe. N. and Q., 4th S. 10, pp. 102–04, 171–72, 255, 298–99, 461, 507. 1872.

6381 March (Henry Colley). The place-names twistle, skip, and argh. Trans. Lancs. and Ches. Antiq. Soc., 8 (1890), pp. 72–96, + 3 plates (maps). 1891.

6382 Porter (William). The terminations ' hope ' and ' thorpe ', with some remarks on Mr. Cole's ' Scandinavian place names.' Antiq. Mag., 7, pp. 175–78. 1885.

6383 Pring (James Hurly). The place-name ' hampton ', with observations on Mr. J. R. Green's derivation of it. Antiq. Mag., 3, pp. 127–29. 1883.

6384 Round (John Horace). The terminal ' -ing ' in place-names. [Answering article by J. Boult, **6370**.] Antiq. Mag., 2, pp. 104–05. 1882.

6385 Schram (O. K.). Place-names in *-sett* in the east of England. Zeit. Ortsnamenforschung, 3, 1928.

6386 Skeat (Walter William), *etc.* Argh. [As termination place-names in Lancashire and Westmorland.= A.–S. *hearh* (heathen altar).] N. and Q., 9th S. 5, pp. 48, 97, 212, 346. 1900.

6387 Stevenson (William Henry), *etc.* The suffix -ny or -ney in place-names. N. and Q., 7th S. 4, pp. 56–57, 133–34, 349–50. 1887.

6388 Taylor (Isaac). The patronymic ing. N. and Q., 7th S. 10, pp. 362–63. 1890.

6389 Watkins (Alfred), *etc.* Leys. Word-lore, 2, pp. 65–66, 88–92, 140–41. 1927.

6390 Watts (Thomas). On the Anglo-Saxon termination *ing*. Proc. Philol. Soc., 4, pp. 83–86. 1849.

6391 Wheeler (G. H.). The method of formation of Old English place-names in '-haem', '-saetan', '-túningas'. Mod. Lang. Rev., 11, pp. 218–19. 1916.

6392 Zachrisson (Robert Eugen). English place-names in *-ing* of Scandinavian origin. *Språkvetenskapliga i Uppsala förhandlingar*, 1922–24. 8° Uppsala, 1924.

6393 —— The suffix *-ingja* in Germanic names. Archiv Stud. neueren Spr., Bd. 133, pp. 348–53. 1915.

6394 —— Studies on the *-ing* suffix in Old English place-names with some etymological notes. Studia Neophil., 9, pp. 66–129. 1937.

§ b. Other

6395 Alger (J. G.). Castra [*ceaster*] in English place-names. Palatine Note-bk., 4, pp. 7–11. 1884.

6396 Anscombe (Alfred). 'Cheese' in place-names. N. and Q., 156, pp. 419–20. 1929.

6397 Buckton (T. J.), *etc. Dun* as a local prefix. N. and Q., 4th S. 6, pp. 238–39, 556. 1870.

6398 Carbonell (Barbara M. H.), *etc. Thorn*, as a boundary name. Word-lore, 1, pp. 172–73, 216–17 : 2, pp. 100, 131. 1926–27.

6399 Earle (John), **Atkinson** (John Christopher), *etc.* Hell, as a place-name. N. and Q. Som. and Dorset, 3, pp. 125–26, 169–72. 1892–93.

6400 Earle (John). Kitum's well. [Place-names containing Saxon name Citta, Cyta, Cetta.] *Same jnl.*, 4, p. 194. 1895.

6401 Ekwall (Eilert). Ae. *botl, bold, boðl* in englischen Ortsnamen. Anglia, Beiblatt, 28, pp. 82–91. 1917.

6402 —— Studies on English place and personal names. [O.E. personal names in *-en* : Kentish names in *-ham* : *Church* in English place-names : various etymologies.] Bull. Soc. Roy. Lettres, Lund, 1930–1, pp. 1–110. 1931.

6403 —— Zu zwei keltischen Lehnwörtern im Altenglischen. [i. A.-S. *funta*, a spring : ii. A.-S. *torr*, a high rock.] Engl. Studien, 54, pp. 102–10. 1920.

6404 Evans (E. D. Priestley). The meaning of minster in place-names. Trans. Philolog. Soc., 1925–30, pp. 271–91. 1931.

6405 K. On the meaning of the word bury. Notes Beds. Archit. and Archaeol. Soc., 1, pp. 65–69. 1856.

6406 Llewellin (George T.), *etc.* Little Silver (Silver in place names). Devon, N. and Q., 2, pp. 2–4, 86–89. 1902.

6407 —— *etc.* The place-name Twitchen. *Same jnl.*, 5, pp. 258–62. 1909.

6408 Mawer (*Sir* Allen), *ed.* The chief elements used in English place-names. (Introduction to the survey of English place-names, pt. 2.) *English Place-name Society*, 1. *ii.* pp. 67. 8° Cambridge, 1924.

6409 Paterson (Donald Rose). The place-name *pill*. [On both sides of the Bristol Channel, and in Somerset and Lancs.] Arch. Camb., 85, pp. 426–27. 1930.

6410 Picton (*Sir* James Allanson), *etc.* Maiden in British place-names : Maiden Castle. N. and Q., 6th S. 2, pp. 68–70, 114, 195. 1880.

6411 Pogatscher (Alois). Die englische Æ/E-Grenze. [List of place-names containing original A.-S. æ and ē elements, arranged by counties.] Anglia, 23 (N.F. 11), pp. 302–09. 1901.

6412 Prideaux (W. F.). 'Tot' in place-names. [?Tōtian, to peep.] Home Counties Mag., 10, pp. 76–77. 1908.

6413 Sealy (H. N.). On the word pig as applied to a cross at Bridgwater and other objects. [Connects *pig* as a place-name element with A.-S. *piga* and Danish *pige*, a girl.] Proc. Somerset Arch. Soc., 9 (1859), pp. 5–7. 1860. *See also* vol. 17 (1871), p. 48. 1872.

6414 Sedgefield (Walter John). The place-name 'hale', 'haile', 'haugh', 'eale'. Mod. Lang. Rev., 9, pp. 240–41. 1914.

6415 Seyler (Clarence A.). The Old Welsh 'cruc' as a loan word in English : the Brydinga dic. Arch. Camb., 75 (6th S. 20), p. 280. 1920.

6416 Smith (Albert Hugh). Some place-names and the etymology of ' she '. [*See also* rejoinder by Martin B. Ruud (*She* once more) in 2, pp. 201–04. 1926.] Rev. Engl. Stud., 1, pp. 437–40. 1925.

6417 Taddy (John). On the use of the word bury. Notes Beds. Archit. and Archaeol. Soc., 1, pp. 119–26. 1858.

6418 Taylor (Isaac). Els- in place-names. N. and Q., 6th S. 12, p. 330. 1885.

6419 ——, *etc.* Pit in place-names. N. and Q., 7th S. 10, pp. 328–29. 1890.

6420 Walker (Bernard). Interchange and substitution of second elements in place names. [Derbyshire material only.] Engl. Studien, 51, pp. 25–36. 1917.

6421 Watkin (Hugh Robert). [The prefix Lide or Lyde in early nomenclature]. Devon and Cornwall N. and Q., 10, pp. 201–03. 1919.

6422 Zachrisson (Robert Eugen). English place-name compounds containing descriptive nouns in the genitive. Engl. Studien, 70, pp. 60–73. 1935.

6423 —— English place-names and river-names containing the primitive Germanic roots *vis, vask*. An essay on comparative place-name study. Uppsala Univ. Årsskr., 1926, Filos., 2, pp. 67. 1926.

6424 —— The French definite article in English place-names. [O.E., M.E., and N.E.] Anglia, 34 (N.F. 22), pp. 308–53. 1911.

95. FIELD NAMES, GENERAL

6425 Atkinson (John Christopher). Local nomenclature : field names. Reliquary, N. [2nd] S. 4, pp. 83–87. 1890.

6426 —— Notes on common-field names. Antiquary, 13, pp. 95–97, 150–52, 209–13, 255–60 : 14, pp. 72–76, 116–18, *also* 180 (note by H. W. Just). 1886.

6427 Mawer (*Sir* Allen). The study of field-names in relation to place-names. Hist. essays in honour of J. Tait, pp. 189–200. 1933.

6428 Middendorff (Heinrich). Altenglisches Flurnamenbuch. pp. iv, 156. 8° Halle, 1902. [Gross, 352.]

6429 Sawyer (Frederick Ernest). Field-name and toponymical collections. Antiquary, 10, pp. 6–8, *also* 85–86. 1884.

6430 Wainwright (Frederick Threlfall). Field-names. Antiquity, 17, pp. 57–66. 1943.

96. RIVER NAMES

6431 Alexander (John James). Devon river-names. Rept. and Trans. Devon. Assoc., 67, pp. 399–419. 1935.

6432 Anscombe (Alfred). The name of the river Trent. N. and Q., 12th S. 1, pp. 71–72. 1916.

6433 Cameron (A. N. F.). On the Celtic derivation of English river names. Trans. Gaelic Soc. Inverness, 11, pp. 166–71 ; 12, p. 429. 1885–86.

6434 Christy (Miller). Essex rivers and their names. Essex Nat., 21, pp. 275–302, + map. 1927.

6435 Connellan (Owen). On the rivers of Ireland, with the derivations of their names. Proc. R.I.A., 10, pp. 443–58. 1870.

6436 Ekwall (Eilert). Ablaut in Flussnamen. Anglia, Beiblatt, 36, pp. 276–87 : 37, pp. 54–56. 1925–26.

6437 —— English river-names. pp. xcii, 488. 8° Oxford, 1928.

6438 Eminson (Thomas Benjamin Franklin). The river Bain [Lindsey]. Lincs. N. and Q., 15, pp. 98–108. 1919.

6439 —— The river Dove. J. Derbs. Archaeol. Soc., 42, pp. 31–45. 1920.

6440 —— The river Humber. Lincs. N. and Q., 14, pp. 66–72. 1917.

6441 —— The river name Lindis. [But refuted by Sir A. C. E. Welby **6468**.] Lincs. N. and Q., 14, pp. 241–50. 1917.

6442 —— The river Till [West Lindsey]. Lincs. N. and Q., 14, pp. 174–83. 1917.

6443 —— The river Trent. J. Derbs. Archaeol. Soc., 39, pp. 154–73. 1917.

6444 —— The river Trent. Lincs. N. and Q., 14, pp. 117–28, 152–60. 1917.

6445 —— The river Witham. [British, not A.-S. : Domesday references.] Lincs. N. and Q., 14, pp. 200–10 : *see also* pp. 235–72. 1917.

6446 Evans (E. D. Priestley). The Severn and other Wye rivers. Trans. Philolog. Soc., 1925–30, pp. 260–70. 1931.

6447 F., *etc.* Derivation of Calder in Yorkshire. N. and Q., 6th S. 8, pp. 61–62, 114, 257. 1883.

6448 Flower (John Wickham). Surrey etymologies : rivers and streams, and towns on rivers, or streams. Surrey Archaeol. Collns., 5, pp. 15–20. 1871.

6449 Foerster (Max). Der Flussname Themse und seine Sippe. Studien zur Anglisierung keltischer Eigennamen und zur Lautchronologie des Altbritischen. pp. vii, 951. [Discusses many English and European place-names and other river-names besides Thames. *See also* **6458**.] Sitzungsb. bayer. Akad. Wiss., hist.-phil. Abt., 1941, Bd. 1. 1941.

6450 —— The river-name Tweed. Scot. Gaelic Stud., 3, pp. 1–9. 1931.

6451 Gordon (Eric Valentine) and **Smith** (Albert Hugh). The river names of Yorkshire. Trans. Yorks. Dialect Soc., 4, pt. 26, pp. 5–30. 1925.

6452 H. and **Weaver** (Frederic William). Somerset river-names (ancient). N. and Q. Som. and Dorset, 3, pp. 273–74 : 4, p. 327. 1893, 95.

6453 Heirmeier (A.). Die in Hogans Onomasticon Goedelicum vorkommenden keltischen Flussnamen. Sammlung und kartographische Fixierung mit einem typologischen Exkurs. Zeit. kelt. Philol., 23, pp. 55–120. 1943.

6454 —— IE *sreu̯/sru-*, to flow, to stream, in Celtic, especially Irish, river-names. J. Celtic Studies, 1, pp. 53–68. 1949.

6455 Hempl (George). The English river-names : Rea, Ree, Rhee, etc. [*ed*, water.] English miscellany presented to F. J. Furnivall, pp. 155–57. 1901.

6456 Jackson (Kenneth). Wallop. [As river-name : Welsh and A.-S.] Antiquity, 13, pp. 105–06. 1939.

6457 Kirkland (Walter). The river Trent. Notts. and Derbs. N. and Q., 1, pp. 187–88. 1893.

6458 Knoch (August). Der Flussname Themse. [Criticism of **6449**.] Archiv Stud. neueren Spr., Bd. 183, pp. 109–21. 1943.

6459 Marstrander (Carl Johan Sverstrup). Celtic river-names and river-goddesses. Norsk Tidsskr. for Sprogvidenskap, 7, pp. 344–46. 1934.

6460 Mawer (*Sir* Allen). The river-names of Northumberland and Durham. Archaeol. Æl., 4th S. 6, pp. 175–82. 1929.

6461 Mayo (Charles Herbert). Cernel bridge. [?Cern and river name.] N. and Q., Som. and Dorset, 8, pp. 24–25. 1903.

6462 Milne (George). The river-name Tweed. [*Tuidi* (Bede) : *Tweoda* (Hist. S. Cuthbert, c. 1050).] Scot. Gaelic Stud., 1, pp. 67–77. 1926.

6463 Pictet (Adolphe). De quelques noms celtiques de rivières. Rev. celt., 2, pp. 1–9. 1873.

6464 Quiggin (Edmund Crosby). Some Celtic river names. Trans. Philolog. Soc., 1911–16, pp. 99–100. 1920.

6465 Rose-Troup (Frances). The river-name Vine. [*Fyne*, moisture.] Devon and Cornwall N. and Q., 21, pp. 177–78. 1940.

6466 Walters (John). On the derivatives of the Welsh word *gwy*. [*Gwy*, a flow, in river names.] Proc. Philol. Soc., 1, p. 65. 1843.

6467 Watkin (Hugh Robert). The Lemon stream, Newton Bushel. [? from A.-S. *lemen*, loamy.] Devon and Cornwall N. and Q., 12, pp. 66–67. 1922.

6468 Welby (*Sir* Alfred Cholmeley Earle). River name Lindis. [Refuting **6441**.] Lincs. N. and Q., 15, pp. 26–27, 50–51. 1919.

6469 Wright (George R.). On the source and nomenclature of the river Thames. J. Brit. Archaeol. Assoc., 25, pp. 346–55. 1869.

6470 Zachrisson (Robert Eugen). Grendel in Beowulf and in local names. [Grindsworthy, Devon, ?from river-name, *grinde*, the gravel-brook.] Grammatical miscellany offered to O. Jespersen, pp. 39–44. 1930.

6471 Zachrisson (Robert Eugen). OE. wise, usan, wassan, waer-, ur-. Some etymological notes. Studia Neophil., 5, pp. 70–76. 1933.

6472 —— River-names in Suffolk and North Devonshire. *Same jnl.*, pp. 56–66. 1929.

97. PLACE-NAMES, EAST ANGLIA

(Norfolk, Suffolk, Essex, Cambs.)

6473 Charnock (Richard S.). On the etymology of Beccles. Proc. Suffolk Inst. Archaeol., 4, pp. 90–91. 1855.

6474 Coulton (John James). Names on the Nar [West Norfolk]. Norfolk Archaeology, 11, pp. 208–27. 1892.

6475 —— Names on the Wissey [West Norfolk]. *Same jnl.*, 12, pp. 13–24. 1895.

6476 Miller (Samuel Henry). Friday Bridge [3½ miles south of Wisbeach.] Fenland N. and Q., 3, pp. 151–53. 1896.

6477 —— Origin of the name Ely. *Same jnl.*, 2, pp. 316–18, 371. 1894.

6478 Munford (George). An attempt to ascertain the true derivation of the towns and villages and of rivers, and other natural features of the county of Norfolk. pp. xii, 239. 8° London, 1870. [Pp. 233–39, A.–S.]

6479 Picton (*Sir* James Allanson). On place-names in Norfolk. J. Brit. Archaeol. Assoc., 36, pp. 137–45. 1880.

6480 R. (E. G.). Scandinavian local names in East Anglia. [Wroo (Attleborough) : Filby.] East Anglian (N. and Q.), 2, p. 111. 1864.

6481 Reaney (Percy Hide). Essex place-name study. Trans. Essex Archaeol. Soc., N.S., 19, pp. 90–96. 1930.

6482 —— Essex place-names in ' -ing '. Mod. Lang. Rev., 19, pp. 466–69. 1924.

6483 —— The face of Essex. A study in place-names. Essex Rev., 58, pp. 10–21. 1949.

6484 —— The place-names of Cambridgeshire and the Isle of Ely. *English Place-name Society*, 19. pp. lxi, 396, + 3 maps. 8° Cambridge, 1943.

6485 Reaney (Percy Hide). The place-names of Essex. *Ph.D. thesis, London*. 1931. [Apply Univ. Library.]

6486 —— The place-names of Essex. *English Place-name Society*, 12. pp. lxii, 698, + 9 maps. 8° Cambridge, 1935.

6487 —— The place-names of Essex. (Summaries of theses. lxxxii). Bull. Inst. Hist. Res., 9, pp. 189–90. 1932.

6488 —— The place-names of Rochford hundred. Trans. Southend Antiq. and Hist. Soc., 2, pp. 103–12, + map. 1932.

6489 —— A survey of Essex place-names. Trans. Essex Archaeol. Soc., N.S. 16, pp. 251–57. 1923.

6490 Round (John Horace). Norse place-names in Essex. Trans. Essex Archaeol. Soc., N.S., 16, pp. 169–77. 1923.

6491 Rye (Walter). A list of Norfolk place-names. pp. 38. 4° Norwich, 1923.

6492 Schererz (C.). Studien zu den Ortsnamen von Cambridgeshire. [A.–S.] Zeit. Ortsnamenforschung, 3, pp. 13–26, 176–99. 1927–28.

6493 Schram (O. K.). The Celtic stratum in the place-name nomenclature of East Anglia. Aberystwyth Stud., 11, pp. 23–41. 1929.

6494 —— Fenland place-names. Chadwick Mem. Stud., pp. 427–41. 1950.

6495 —— Two Norfolk place-names (Testerton, Stibbard). [Frisian influence or settlements.] Rev. Engl. Stud., 5, pp. 73–76. 1929.

6496 Skeat (Walter William). The place-names of Cambridgeshire. 2nd edition. *Cambs. Antiq. Soc., 8° publicns.*, 36. pp. vi, 80. 8° Cambridge, 1913.

6497 —— The place-names of Suffolk. *Cambs. Antiq. Soc., 8° publns.*, 46. pp. x, 132. 8° Cambridge, 1913.

98. PLACE-NAMES, KENT

6498 Acum (Thomas Ethelbert Aldred). A study of the place-names of the pre-Conquest Kentish charters. *M.A. thesis, London*. pp. iii, 454. 1923. [Apply Univ. Library.]

6499 Gerould (Gordon Hall). Thunor in Kent. [7th c. SS. Ethelred and Ethelbert murdered by Thunur, who was swallowed by the earth at Thunerhleaw in Thanet.] Mod. Lang. Notes, 49, pp. 238–39. 1934.

6500 Horsley (John William). Place-names in Kent. pp. 84, + 7. 8° Maidstone, 1921.

6501 Shaw (W. Frank). Derivation of the name of Eastry. Arch. Camb., 13, pp. 557–55. 1880.

6502 Wallenberg (Johannes Knut). Kentish place-names. A topographical and etymological study of the place-name material in Kentish charters dated before the Conquest. Uppsala Univ. Årsskr., Filos, 1931, No. 2. Pp. xix, 378. 1931.

6503 —— The place-names of Kent. pp. xx, 626. 8° Uppsala, 1934.

99. PLACE-NAMES, MERCIA
§ a. North-West

(Cheshire, Shropshire, Hereford, Worcester, Warwick, Stafford)

6504 Andrews (William). The ancient British place names of Warwickshire. [A.–S. and Domesday included.] Proc. Warw. Archaeol. F.C., 46 (1901), pp. 3–10. 1903.

6505 Anscombe (Alfred), **Bowcock** (Elijah Wood), *etc.* Shropshire place-names. Shropshire N. and Q., 3rd S. 4, pp. 55–56, 58, 59, 60, 63, 76, 77. 1924.

6506 —— *Wiogora ceaster* : Worcester. N. and Q., 11th S. 1, pp. 123–24, 374. 1910.

6507 Baddeley (Welbore St. Clair). Herefordshire place-names. Trans. Bristol and Glos. Arch. Soc., 39, pp. 87–200. 1916.

6508 —— Place-names of Herefordshire. 8° Bristol, 1913.

6509 Bannister (Arthur Thomas). The place-names of Herefordshire, their origin and development. pp. xx, 231. 8° Cambridge, 1916.

6510 Bowcock (Elijah Wood). Shropshire place-names. With a prefatory note on Shropshire and a survey of English place-names, by Allen Mawer. pp. 271. 8° Shrewsbury, 1923.

6511 Collingwood (William Gershom). Norse place-names in Wirral. Saga-Book V.C., 2, pp. 143–47. 1899.

6512 Davis-Winstone (W. E.). Field names in the parish of Feckenham, [Worcs.]. B'ham. Arch. Soc., Trans., 46, pp. 36–48. 1920.

6513 Duignan (William Henry). Notes on Staffordshire place-names. pp. xix, 178. 8° London, 1902. [Gross, 352.]

6514 —— On some Midland place names. B'ham. and Midland Inst., Arch. Section, Trans., 20, pp. 45–59. 1894.

6515 —— On some Shropshire place-names. Trans. Shrop. Arch. Soc., 2nd S. 6, pp. 1–18 : 9, pp. 385–400 : 10, pp. 1–17. 1894–98.

6516 —— Warwickshire place-names. pp. 130. 8° Oxford, 1912. [Gross, 352.]

6517 —— Worcestershire place-names. pp. xi, 185. 8° London, 1905. [Gross, 352.]

6518 Earle (John). The ethnology of Cheshire, traced chiefly in the local names. [Pp. 105–09, ' lists of names occurring in Domesday Book under the several hundreds.'] Archaeol. J., 17, pp. 93–116. 1860.

6519 Ekwall (Eilert). The English place names Etchells, Nechells [Birmingham]. [O.E. *écan*, to increase. ?=addition.] Mélanges . . . offerts à J. Vising, pp. 104–06. 1925.

6520 Gover (John Eric Bruce), *etc.* The place-names of Warwickshire. *English Place-name Society*, 13. pp. li, 409, + 4 maps. 8° Cambridge, 1936.

6521 Irvine (William Fergusson). Place names in the hundred of Wirral. [Pp. 289–97, A.-S. : pp. 297–304, Norse.] Trans. Hist. Soc. Lancs. and Ches., 43/44 (1891–92), pp. 279–304. 1893.

6522 Jones (James P.). Tettenhall [Staffs.] place and field names. Midland Antiquary, 2, pp. 83–86. 1883.

6523 Mawer (*Sir* Allen), *etc.* The place-names of Worcestershire. *English Place-name Society*, 4. pp. xliv, 420, + map. 8° Cambridge, 1927.

6524 Phillimore (William P.). On the name Bridgnorth. Trans. Shropshire Arch. Soc., 1, pp. 129–33. 1878.

6525 Reade (Hubert). Welsh and English place-names in south Herefordshire. Trans. Woolhope N.F.C., 1921–23, pp. 18–29, + map. 1925.

6526 Thompson (H. V.). Scandinavian place-names in north Staffordshire. North Staffs. F.C., Trans., 51, pp. 77–83. 1917.

§ *b*. **North-East**

(Derbyshire, Notts., Leicester, Rutland, Northants.)

6527 [Anon.] Derivations of the names of Leicestershire villages. Midland Counties Hist. Coll., 1, pp. 82–85. 1855.

6528 B. (J. J.). Some Leicestershire place-names. Leic. and Rutl. N. and Q., 1, pp. 273–74. 1891.

6529 Barber (Henry). Etymologies of Derbyshire place-names. J. Derbs. Archaeol. Soc., 19, pp. 53–79. 1897.

6530 —— Place names of Northamptonshire which are included in the Fenland district. Fenland N. and Q., 3, pp. 312–15. 1897.

6531 Brushfield (Thomas Nadauld). Sharnford [Leic.], origin of name. Leic. and Rutl. N. and Q., 3, pp. 129–30. 1895.

6532 —— Tideswell and Tideslow. J. Derbs. Archaeol. Soc., 27, pp. 59–73. 1905.

6533 Carter (Thomas). Danish place-names of Leicestershire. Trans. Leic. Archaeol. Soc., 6, pp. 168–72, and map. 1888.

6534 Coleman (William L.). Some place and field names of the parish of Staveley. J. Derbs. Archaeol. Soc., 16, pp. 190–97. 1894.

6535 Cox (John Charles). Place and field names of Derbyshire which indicate the fauna. *Same jnl.*, 4, pp. 57–75. 1882.

6536 Cox (John Charles) Place and field names of Derbyshire which indicate vegetable productions. *Same jnl.*, 3, pp. 73–89. 1881.

6537 Davis (Frederick). The etymology of some Derbyshire place-names. *Same jnl.*, 2, pp. 33–71. 1880.

6538 Gover (John Eric Bruce), *etc.* The place-names of Northamptonshire. *English Place-name Society*, 10. pp. lii, 311, + 6 maps. 8° Cambridge, 1933.

6539 ——, *etc.* The place-names of Nottinghamshire. *English Place-name Society*, 17. pp. xlii, 348. + 5 maps. 8° Cambridge, 1940.

6540 Hipkins (Frederick Charles). The place-name Repton. Notts. and Derbs. N. and Q., 6, pp. 103–04. 1898.

6541 Hoskins (William George). The place-names of Leicestershire. [Appendix to his article on the Anglian and Scandinavian settlement of Leicestershire, **1862.**] Trans. Leic. Archaeol. Soc. 18, pp. 137–47. 1935.

6542 Kirke (Henry). On some ancient British and Anglo-Saxon names of places, etc., existing at the present day in the Peak of Derbyshire. Reliquary, 6, pp. 59–63. 1865.

6543 Kirkland (Walter). The place-name Derby. Notts. and Derbs. N. and Q., 1, pp. 105–06, 131–32. 1893.

6544 Morris (G. E.). The place-names and settlement of part of north Derbyshire. Proc. Leeds Phil. and Lit. Soc., 6, pp. 137–47, + map. 1946.

6545 Mutschmann (Heinrich). The place-names of Nottinghamshire : their origin and development. pp. xvi, 179. 8° Cambridge, 1913.

6546 Phillips (G.). Records of the past in Rutland place names. Rutland Mag., 1, pp. 245–58, + 1 map. 1904.

6547 R. (Y. S.). An enquiry into the origin and meaning of the names of Nottingham and Sneinton. [*See also* corrections by A. W. Whatmore, **6557.**] Notts. and Derbs. N. and Q., 2, pp. 84–88, 101–04. 1894.

6548 —— Sneinton [Nottingham] in Domesday Book. [*See also* corrections by A. W. Whatmore, **6557.**] *Same jnl.*, 4, pp. 97–99, 111–15. 1896.

6549 S. (C.). Ingleby, etc. [Notts.] *Same jnl.*, 4, pp. 180–81. 1896.

6550 Smith (Walter). Strines [Derbs.] and some other water-names. Word-lore, 3, pp. 114–18. 1928.

6551 Smithard (William). Place-names at or near Derby. [Normanton, etc.] J. Derbs. Archaeol. Soc., 34, pp. 139–44. 1912.

6552 Stenton (*Sir* Frank Merry). ' Godmundeslaech.' [=modern Gumley, Leicestershire.] E.H.R., 20, pp. 697–99. 1905.

6553 Walker (Bernard). The place-names of Derbyshire. [37, pp. 215–20, O.E. personal names ; pp. 220–21, Scandinavian personal names ; pp. 222–49, words of O.E. origin ; pp. 240–42, words of Scandinavian origin.] J. Derbs. Archaeol. Soc., 36, pp. 123–284 : 37, pp. 97–244. 1914–15.

6553a Ward (John) and **Kirkland** (Walter). The derivation of ' Derby '. Notts. and Derbs. N. and Q., 1, pp. 93–98. 1893.

6554 Watts (William). The place-names of Leicestershire. [Pp. 231–38, A.–S. names : pp. 238–41, Danish names.] Assoc. Archit. Socs'. Rpts., 31, pp. 225–42. 1911.

6555 Whatmore (A. W.). Derby : its derivation and pronunciation. Notts. and Derbs. N. and Q., 6, pp. 49–56. 1898.

6566 —— Ingleby, Stenson, Repton, and Snitterton. *Same jnl.*, 5, pp. 13–15, 29–32, 42. 1897.

6557 —— The origin and meaning of the names Nottingham and Sneinton. [Correcting articles of Y.S.R., 6547–48.] *Same jnl.*, 6, pp. 129–32, 145–49, 161–66. 1896.

6558 —— The place-name Repton. *Same jnl.*, 6, pp. 125–26. 1898.

6559 Williamson (F.). Notes on Walker's Place-names of Derbyshire [6553.] J. Derbs. Archaeol. Soc., N.S.2 (1927), pp. 143–98 ; 3 (1928–29), pp. 14–7. 1929–30.

§ *c*. Lincolnshire

6560 [Anon.] Lincolnshire names. [Alphabetical list of Lincs. places with A.–S., Danish, Domesday, etc., equivalents, and derivations.] Lincs. N. and Q., 6, pp. 20–28, 41–45, 67–71, 172–75, 203–06, 228–31 : 7, pp. 4–7, 50–53, 71–74, 106–08. 1901–04.

6561 Anscombe (Alfred). The ' Greeks ' of Lincolnshire. Engl. Studies, 3, pp. 74–78. 1921.

6562 —— A Lincolnshire place-name : Barnetby-le-wold. [Beornnôthesby : the dwelling of Beornnôth.] N. and Q., 158, pp. 24–25, 105, 140–41. 1930.

6563 Brown (Robert). The name Lincoln. Lincs. N. and Q., 9, pp. 50–52. 1907.

6564 —— The place-name Barrow [on-Humber]. Lincs. N. and Q., 7, pp. 61–62. 1904.

6565 Constable (J. Goulton). Place-name Alkborough. Lincs. N. and Q., 7, pp. 91–92. 1904.

6566 D. (M. M.). Threckingham. Fenland N. and Q., 4, p. 132. 1898.

6567 Eminson (Thomas Benjamin Franklin). Grantham, Cambridge, and the river Grant. Lincs. N. and Q., 15, pp. 72–82. 1919.

6568 —— The ingham names of West Lindsey. Lincs. N. and Q., 13, pp. 70–77. 1915.

6569 —— Kesteven. Lincs. N. and Q., 15, pp. 2–13. 1919.

6570 —— The place and river names of the West Riding of Lindsay. pp. 288, + map. 8° Lincoln, 1934.

6571 —— Scothorn and some other thorn names of Lindsey. Lincs. N. and Q., 12, pp. 182–88. 1913.

6572 —— Scotter and Scotton in Lindsey : a study in place-names. Antiquary, 48, pp. 417–21, 461–64. 1912.

6573 —— Torksey on Trent and Fosdike :—a study in place names. Lincs. N. and Q., 13, pp. 229–41. 1915.

6574 Johnston (K. J.). The Keltic element in the topographical nomenclature of the Isle of Axholme. Lincs. N. and Q., 1, pp. 172–73. 1889.

6575 Sills (George). Etymology of Gedney. Fenland N. and Q., 5, pp. 272–73, 314–15. 1913.

6576 Taylor (Isaac) and **Bradley** (Henry). The Danes in Lincolnshire. Academy, 25, pp. 206, 225. 1884.

6577 Venables (Edmund). Place names in the Isle of Axholme. Assoc. Archit. Socs', Rpts., 18, pp. 1–12. 1885.

§ *d.* **Gloucestershire, Oxon., Bucks.**

6578 Alexander (Henry). The place-names of Oxfordshire, their origins and development. pp. 251. 8° Oxford, 1912. [Gross, 352.]

6579 Anscombe (Alfred). The place-name Cheltenham. N. and Q., 156, p. 186. 1929.

6580 —— The place-name Oxford. N. and Q., 160, pp. 255–57. 1931.

6581 Baddeley (Welbore St. Clair), *etc.* Dumbleton [Glos.], place-name. N. and Q., 11th S. 4, pp. 136, 179. 1911.

6582 —— Place-names of Gloucestershire. pp. xxx, 185. 8° Gloucester, 1913.

6583 Bourke (Cecil Frederick Joseph). Notes on place-name endings in Buckinghamshire. Rec. Bucks., 8, pp. 327–41. 1903.

6584 Earle (John). On local names [in Gloucestershire]. Trans. Bristol and Glos. Arch. Soc., 8, pp. 50–61. 1884.

6585 —— Traces of history and ethnology in the local names in Gloucestershire. [Pp. 59–65, lists of names occurring in Domesday Book under the several hundreds.] Archaeol. J., 18, pp. 342–52 ; 19, pp. 50–67. 1861–62.

6586 Gelling (Margaret). The place-names of Oxfordshire. Based on material collected by Doris Mary Stenton. *English Place-name Society*, 23–24. 2 vol. 8° Cambridge, 1953–54. [Appendix (vol. 2) on charter boundaries.]

6587 Mawer (*Sir* Allen) and **Stenton** (*Sir* Frank Merry). The place-names of Buckinghamshire. *English Place-name Society*, 2. pp. xxxii, 274, + 2 maps. 8° Cambridge, 1925.

6588 Moberley (George H.). Local names near Cirencester. [1. Pure Saxon names : 2. Hybrid: 3. Purely Keltic names.] Trans. Bristol and Glos. Arch. Soc., 2, pp. 118–27. 1877.

6589 Parsons (Frederick Gymer). Some additional notes on the name of Risborough. [Notes on charter of 903.] Rec. Bucks., 13, pp. 470–72. 1940.

6590 Ritter (Otto). Zu einigen Ortsnamen aus Oxfordshire. [Abesditch-Avesditch, Bampton, Britwell, Bucknell, Calthorpe, Caversham, Charlbury, Cogges, Cokethorpe-Cockthorpe, Cold Norton, Cornbury, Emmington.] Engl. Studien, 56, pp. 292–300. 1922.

6591 Roach (Thomas). On the distribution of place-names [in Gloucestershire.] Glos. N. and Q., 2, pp. 145–49. 1884.

6592 Shore (Thomas William), *etc.* The origin and antiquity of the place-name Oxford. N. and Q., 9th S., 3, pp. 44–45, 309–10, 389–90 : 4, pp. 70–71, 130–31, 382–83, 479–81 : 5, pp. 69–71, 249–52, 517–20 : 6, pp. 108–11, 193–94, 312. 1899–1900.

6593 Taylor (Isaac), *etc.* Stroud as a place-name. N. and Q., 7th S. 6, pp. 309–10, 357, 449–50 ; 7, p. 77. 1888–89.

6594 Welch (F. B.). A miscellany of place-names. Proc. Cottesw. Nat. F.C., 37 (1939), pp. 21–25. 1940.

6595 —— Place names and trees in Gloucestershire. *Same jnl.*, 36, pp. 324–27. 1938.

6596 Winnington-Ingram (A. R.). On the origin of names of places with special reference to Gloucestershire, *etc.* Proc. Cottesw. Nat. F.C., 11, pp. 21–39. 1895.

§ *e.* **Beds., Hunts. and Herts.**

6597 Austin (Cedric R.). An introduction to Hertfordshire place-names. [i. Present-day methods of investigation : ii. Romans, Celts and Scandinavians : iii. Sounds and spellings : iv. Natural history, religion and social customs.] Hertfordshire Countryside, 6, pp. 138–39 : 7, pp. 18–19, 56–57, 90–91. 1952.

6598 Blair (Peter Hunter). The place-names of Hertfordshire. Trans. St. Albans Archit. Soc., N.S. 5 (1938), pp. 222–31. 1939.

6599 Faulke-Watling (C.), *etc.* Bedca: Bedford. N. and Q., 5th S. **3**, pp. 251–52, 311–12, 430–32 : 4, pp. 9–11, 56. 1875.

6600 Gover (John Eric Bruce), *etc.* The place-names of Hertfordshire. *English Place-name Society*, 15. pp. xliii, 342, + 5 maps. 8° Cambridge, 1938.

6601 Hall (Henry). Names of places in Hertfordshire. pp. 36. 8° Ware, 1902.

6602 Mawer (*Sir* Allen) and **Stenton** (*Sir* Frank Merry). The place-names of Bedfordshire and Huntingdonshire. *English Place-name Society*, 3. pp. xlii, 316, + 2 maps. 8° Cambridge, 1926.

6603 Mayhew (Anthony Lawson), *etc.* The etymology of Bedford. N. and **Q.**, 6th S. 1, pp. 173–74, 460–61 ; 2, pp. 249–50, 334, 474–75 : 3, pp. 318–19, 350–52 : 4, pp. 349–50. 1880–81.

6604 Skeat (Walter William). The place-names of Bedfordshire. *Camb. Antiq. Soc., 8° pubns.*, 42. pp. vii, 74. 8° Cambridge, 1906.

6605 —— The place-names of Hertfordshire. *East Herts. Archaeol. Soc.* pp. 75. 8° Hertford, 1904. *Same title.* [Old place-names, *etc.*] East Herts. Archaeol. Soc., Trans., 3. i (1905), pp. 107–09. 1906.

6606 —— Place-names of Hertfordshire. [Tring and Stevenage.] East Herts. Archaeol. Soc., Trans., 4, ii (1910), pp. 179–81. 1911.

6607 —— The place-names of Huntingdonshire. Proc. Camb. Antiq. Soc., 10, pp. 317–60. 1903.

6608 Taylor (Arthur). On the name of Godmanchester [Hunts.], as derived and explained by Camden. Proc. Soc. Antiq., 2, pp. 307–09. 1853.

§ *f.* **Middlesex and London Area**

(i.e. Southern suburbs here included)

6609 [Anon.] The name of Hornsey, [Middlesex]. Trans. Lond. and Middsx. Archaeol. Soc., N.S. 7, pp. 654–55. 1937.

6610 Bonner (Arthur). The name of Chelsea. *Same jnl.*, N.S. 2, pp. 356–66. 1913.

6611 —— A note on the name Battersea. *Same jnl.*, N.S. 2, pp. 434–37. 1913.

6612 De Montmorency (James Edward Geoffrey). Blackheath and Greenwich place names. Trans. Greenwich Antiq. Soc., 1, pp. 186–89. 1912.

6613 —— Weremansacre and the nucleus of Greenwich. *Same jnl.*, 3, pp. 97–102. 1927.

6614 Ekwall (Eilert). Notes on some Middlesex place-names. [Chelsea, etc.] Studia Neophil., 17, pp. 25–34. 1945.

6615 Gover (John Eric Bruce), *etc.* The place-names of Middlesex, apart from the city of London. *English Place-name Society*, 18. pp. xxxiv, 237, + 2 maps. 8° Cambridge, 1942.

6616 —— The place-names of Middlesex, including those parts of the county of London formerly contained within the boundaries of the old county. pp. xvi, 114. 8° London, **1922**.

6617 Heuser (Wilhelm). Alt-London mit besonderer Berücksichtigung des Dialeckts. pp. 64. 8° Osnabrück, 1914.

6618 Meiklejohn (M. J. C.). The place-names of Northfield and district. [General chat about place-names, including the north of London. Corrections, by W. F. Prideaux, 9, pp. 155–56. 1907.] Home Counties Mag., 8, pp. 102–10, 161–70. 1906.

6619 Skeat (Walter William). On the derivation and meaning of the name Lewisham. Lewisham Antiq. Soc., 12th Ann. Rept., pp. 3–4. 1897.

100. PLACE-NAMES, NORTHUMBRIA

§ *a.* **Yorkshire**

6620 Atkinson (John Christopher). On the Danish aspect of the local nomenclature of Cleveland. Abstract. [Place-names : personal names.] J. Anthrop. Inst., 3, pp. 115–20. 1874.

6621 —— Touching the meaning of ' castle ' in certain North Riding and other place-names. [A.-S. *castel.*] Reliquary, N [2nd] S. 7, pp. 132–36. 1893.

6622 Cole (Edward Maule). On Scandinavian place-names in the East Riding. Reliquary, 19 pp. 23–27, 88–92, 139–44. 1878–79.

6623 —— On the place-name Wetwang. Saga-Book V. C., 4, pp. 102–06. 1905.

6624 Goodall (Armitage). Place-names of south-west Yorkshire. Revised edition. pp. vi, 313. 8° Cambridge, 1914. [Gross, 352.]

6625 —— The Scandinavian element in Yorkshire place-names. Trans. Yorks. Dialect Soc., 3, pt. 17, pp. 28–54. 1915.

6626 Gordon (Eric Valentine). Scarborough and Flamborough. Acta Phil. Scand., 1, pp. 320–23. 1927.

6627 Gowland (Tom S.). Field names: their value and interest. [From the Yorkshire dales : descriptive of site or cultivation. Including O.E. and O. Norse.] Yorkshire Dalesman, 6, pp. 66–68, 73, 87–88, 93–94. 1944.

6628 Hardcastle (C. D.). Washburn place names. Yorkshire N. and Q., 2, pp. 57–61. 1890.

6629 Holderness (Thomas). Some place-names of the East Riding. pp. 32. 8° Driffield, 1881.

6630 Jackson (Kenneth). On the name Leeds. Antiquity, 20, pp. 209–10 : *corrections in* 21, p. 9 (1947). 1946.

6631 Liebermann (Felix). Streoneshealh. Archiv Stud. neueren Spr., Bd. 108, p. 368. 1902.

6632 Mawer (*Sir* Allen). Yorkshire history in the light of its place-names. Ann. Rept. Yorks. Philos. Soc., 1923, pp. 39–55. 1924.

6633 Moorman (Frederick William). The place-names of the West Riding. *Publications of the Thoresby Society*, 18. pp. lvi, 218. 8° Leeds, 1910.

6634 Morris (Marmaduke C. F.). East Riding field-names. Trans. East Riding Antiq. Soc., 1, pp. 59–65. 1893.

6635 Nicholson (John). Place-names of the East Riding.]Pp. 126–30, appendix 1, personal names from the Yorkshire section of Domesday Book]. Trans. E. Riding Antiq. Soc., 25, pp. 1–137. 1926.

6636 Rowe (Joseph Hambley). The place-names Menston and Manningham. [A.–S. personal name Mann.] Bradford Antiquary, 5 (N.S. 3), pp. 231–32. 1909.

6637 Skeat (Walter William). On the origin of Keighley. [A.–S. *Cyhhanleah.*] Bradford Antiquary, 5 (N.S. 3), pp. 326–28. 1910.

6638 Smith (Albert Hugh). Analogical development of -ing and the interpretation of Patrington. Leeds Studies in English, 5, pp. 71–73. 1936.

6639 —— East Riding place-names. Trans. E. Riding Antiq. Soc., 29, pp. 7–26. 1949.

6640 —— The place-names Jervaulx, Ure, and York. Anglia, 48 (N.F. 36), pp. 291–96. 1924.

6641 —— The place-names of north Yorkshire. Trans. Yorks. Dialect Soc., 4, pt. 27, pp. 7–19. 1926.

6642 —— Place names of the ancient parish of Halifax. Trans. Halifax Antiq. Soc., 1936, pp. 215–33. 1936.

6643 —— The place-names of the East Riding and York. *English Place-name Society*, 14. pp. lx, 351, + 7 maps. 8° Cambridge, 1937.

6644 —— The place-names of the North Riding. *English Place-name Society*, 5. pp. xlvi, 352, + map. 8° Cambridge, 1928.

6645 Stevenson (William Henry). Note on the place-name 'Filey'. Trans. E. Riding Antiq. Soc., 14, pp. 10–12. 1907.

6646 ——, *etc.* Streanaeshalch. [Sinus Fari. Etymology.] N. and Q., 7th S. 1, pp. 214, 255–56, 375, 413, 490–91 : 2, pp. 50–51, 111–12, 170–73. 1886.

6647 Turner (Joseph Horsfall). Yorkshire place-names, or toponomy as recorded in the Yorkshire Domesday Book, 1086. pp. xx, 301. 8° Bingley, [19—].

6648 Zachrisson (Robert Eugen). Six groups of Yorkshire place-names. Uppsala, 1926.

6649 —— Some Yorkshire place-names : Ilkley, Gilling, Ingetlingum. Upps. Univ. Årsskr., 1927, pp. 35–53. 1927.

6650 Zachrisson (Robert Eugen). Some Yorkshire place-names, York, Ure, Jervaulx. Mod. Lang. Rev., 21, pp. 361–67. 1926.

§ b. Other Counties

6651 Armstrong (Aileen M.), *etc.* The place-names of Cumberland. *English Place-name Society*, 20–22. pp. vi, lxxx, 565. 3 pts. 8° Cambridge, 1950–52.

6652 Carr (Ralph). Observations on composite names of places (chiefly in Northumberland) of Anglo-Saxon derivation. Trans. Tyneside Nat. F.C., 1, pp. 338–48. 1846.

6653 Carr-Ellison (Ralph). Names of the Farne Islands and of Lindisfarne. [*Fara*, a pilgrim.] Hist. Berwick. Nat. Club, 10, pp. 373–74. 1883.

**6654 —— On the significance of some names of places in north Northumberland. [Greves Ash, Hedgehope, Cunion Crag, Hedgeley, Yevering.] *Same jnl.*, 7, pp. 237–45. 1874.

6655 Chinnock (E. J.). The etymology of the word Ruthwell. [Argument for 'Red-pine wood'.] Trans. Dumfries. Antiq. Soc., 17 (1900–01), pp. 103–06. 1905.

6656 Collingwood (William Gershom). Mountain-names [of the Lake District]. Trans. Cumb. and Westm. Antiq. Soc., N.S. 18, pp. 93–104. 1918.

6657 Cummings (C. L.). The place-name of Sunderland. Antiq. Sunderland, 18 (1918–25), pp. 22–23. 1931.

6658 Ekwall (Eilert). The place-names of Lancashire. pp. xvi, 280. 8° Manchester, 1922.

6659 —— Scandinavians and Celts in the north-west of England. pp. xiv, 125. Lunds Univ. Årsskr., N.F., Avd. 1, 14, nr. 27. 1918.

6660 Embleton (Dennis). A catalogue of place-names in Teesdale. 8° Newcastle-upon-Tyne, 1887.

6661 F. Nomenclature near the border hills of Lancashire and Yorkshire. Antiq. Mag., 4, pp. 169–77. 1883.

6662 Flom (George Tobias). The origin of the place-name Keswick. J. Engl. and Germ. Phil., 18, pp. 221–25. 1919.

6663 Gregory (John V.). Place-names of the county of Durham. Archaeol. Æl., N.S. 10, pp. 173–85. 1885.

6664 —— Place-names of the county of Northumberland, with reference to the ancestry of the people. *Same jnl.*, N.S. 9, pp. 57–71. 1883.

6665 Hampson (Charles Phillips). Place-names of the Fylde. Trans. Lancs. and Ches. Antiq. Soc., 57 (1943–44), pp. 18–42, + 1 plate. 1946.

6666 Harrison (Henry). The place-names of the Liverpool district; or the history and meaning of the local and river names of south-west Lancashire and Wirral. pp. 104. 8° London, 1898. [Gross, 352.]

6667 Hedley (Anthony). An essay towards ascertaining the etymology of the names of places in the county of Northumberland. Archaeol. Æl. [1st S.] 1, pp. 242–62. 1822.

6668 Hood (Robert). On the derivation of the name Coldingham. ['*Cole* (cymric) narrow; *ing* (Danish) vale; *ham* (Saxon) vill.'] Hist. Berwick. Nat. Club, 5, p. 222. 1865.

6669 Jackson (Charles Edwyn). The place-names of Durham. pp. 115. 8° Durham, 1916.

6670 Johnston (James Brown). The origin of Durham and Haltwhistle. Anglia, Beiblatt, 41, pp. 91–94. 1930.

6671 Kay (J. Taylor). Lancashire and Cheshire place-names. [*See also* pp. 50–51.] Palatine Note Bk., 3, pp. 13–17, 63–67. 1883.

6672 Mawer (*Sir* Allen). Early Northumbrian history in the light of its place-names. Archaeol. Æl., 3rd S. 18, pp. 1–18. 1921.

6673 —— Notes on some place-names of Northumberland and county Durham. *Same jnl.*, 3rd S. 16, pp. 89–102. 1919.

6674 Mawer (*Sir* Allen). The place-names of Northumberland and Durham. pp. xxxviii, 271. 8° Cambridge, 1920.

6675 —— Scandinavian influence in the place-names of Northumberland and Durham. Saga-Book V.C., 8, pp. 172–210. 1914.

6676 Ritter (Otto). Ueber einige Ortsnamen aus Lancashire. [Accrington, Aldcliff, Alvedene, Arbury, Arkholme, Ashhurst, Audenshaw, Backbarrow, Barrowford, Bellfield, Birtle, Bleasdale, Blythe, Bowerham, Bradkirke, Bretherton, Bromiley.] Engl. Studien, 54, pp. 187–93. 1920.

6677 Sedgefield (Walter John). The place-names of Cumberland and Westmorland. *Pubns. Univ. Manchester*, 98. pp. xliv, 208. 8° Manchester, 1915.

6678 Sephton (John). A handbook of Lancashire place-names. pp. xi, 256. 8° Liverpool, 1913. [Gross, 352.]

6679 —— Notes on the south Lancashire place-names in Domesday Book. Otia Merseiana, 4, pp. 65–74. 1904.

6680 Wainwright (Frederick Threlfall). Field-names of Amounderness hundred: modern (c. 1840). [With O.E. and O.N. forms.] Trans. Hist. Soc. Lancs. and Ches., 97 (1945), pp. 181–222, + map. 1946.

6681 Warriner (Frank). Some south Cumberland place-names. Trans. Cumb. and Westm. Antiq. Soc., N.S. 26, pp. 72–102. 1926.

6682 Wyld (Henry Cecil Kennedy) and **Hirst** (Tom Oakes). The place-names of Lancashire: their origin and history. pp. xxiv, 400. 8° London, 1911.

101. PLACE-NAMES, SUSSEX

6683 Anscombe (Alfred). ' Halnaker ' or ' halfnaked '. Sussex N. and Q., 1, pp. 101–02. 1926.

6684 —— The name of Funtington. *Same jnl.*, 1, pp. 35–36. 1926.

6685 —— The name of Harpingden in Piddinghoe. *Same jnl.*, 1, pp. 203–05. 1927.

6686 —— The name of Portslade. *Same jnl.*, 1, pp. 70–72. 1926.

6687 Anscombe (Alfred). The Sussex place-names in Domesday Book which end in ' -intun '. Sussex Archaeol. Collns., 59, pp. 76–83. 1918.

6688 Brierley (G. H.). Earliest Sussex place names. Sussex County Mag., 17, pp. 201–03. 1943.

6689 Cooper (William Durrant). On the retention of British and Saxon [place-] names in Sussex. Sussex Archaeol. Collns., 7, pp. 1–21. 1854.

6690 Duckett (*Sir* George Floyd), *bart.* Hastings v. Senlac. Sussex Archaeol. Collns., 39, pp. 28–30. 1894.

6691 Holgate (Mary Scarlett). Old lands and ancient demesne. [Old Lands as a Sussex place-name, and its derivation.] Sussex N. and Q., 7, pp. 10–11 : *see also* : 9, pp. 141, 159. 1938, 1943.

6691a Jessup (Frank W.). The place-names of Sussex. [i. Introduction: ii. Gazeteer.] The Little Guides, Sussex, 9th. ed., pp. 282–98. 1938.

6692 Johnston (Philip Mainwaring). The derivation of Toddington. [Sussex and Middlesex.] Sussex Archaeol. Collns., 47, pp. 158–59. 1904.

6693 Keep (Herbert W.). Place-names —Framfield. Sussex N. and Q., 2, pp. 51–52. 1928.

6694 Mawer (*Sir* Allen) and **Stenton** (*Sir* Frank Merry). The place-names of Sussex. *English Place-name Society*, 6–7. pp. xlvi, vii, 613, + map. 2 vol. 8° Cambridge, 1929–30.

6695 Nicklin (Phyllis Amelia) and **Godfrey-Faussett** (E. G.). On the distribution of place names in Sussex. [Maps show (1) finds, Roman and Saxon, (2), -ingas, (3) -ington, -ingham, (4) -ton, (5) ham, hamm, ham(m), (6) -field, -fold, (7) woodland.] Sussex Archaeol. Collns., 76, pp. 212–21, + 3 folding plates (maps). 1935.

6696 Roberts (Richard G.). The place-names of Sussex. pp. xxxii, 210. 8° Cambridge, 1914.

6697 Salmon (E. F.) and **Mawer** (*Sir* Allen). Hove—origin of the name. [?Scandinavian origin: suggested and disproved.] Sussex N. and Q., 2, pp. 239–40 : 3, pp. 21–22. 1929–30.

6698 Zachrisson (Robert Eugen). Two Anglo-Keltic place-names, Sunt, Sompting in Sussex. Studia Neophil., 1, pp. 109–13. 1928.

102. PLACE-NAMES, WESSEX

§ *a*. **Surrey, Berkshire, Hampshire**

6699 Anscombe (Alfred). The name of Croydon. N. and Q., 152, pp. 401–2. 1927.

6700 —— *etc*. Penge as a place-name. [Surrey : since 1888 in Kent]. N. and Q., 12th S. 1, pp. 312–13, 433–34, 514–15. 1916.

6701 Bonner (Arthur). Surrey place-names. Surrey Archaeol. Collns., 36, pp. 85–101 : 37, pp. 117–43. 1935–27.

6702 Chancellor (E. C.). ' King- ' in place-names, and Roman roads. Proc. Dorset Archaeol. Soc., 64 (for 1942), pp. 25–33. 1943.

6703 Douse (T. Le Marchant). The derivation of ' Surrey '. Home Counties Mag,. 3, pp. 198–205. 1901.

6704 E. (F. A.). Etymology of Carisbrooke. Hampshire Antiquary, 1, pp. 15–16. 1891.

6705 Ekwall (Eilert). The place-name Lingfield. [Evidence from will of Ælfred, ealdorman of Surrey. Correcting K. Malone, **6718**.] Anglia, 63 (N.F. 51), pp. 392–97. 1939.

6706 Farnell (E. N.). Berkshire place names. Trans. Newbury F.C., 8, pp. 290–300. 1946.

6707 Flower (John Wickham). Surrey etymologies : the hundred of Wallington. Surrey Archaeol. Collns., 3, pp. 227–53. 1865.

6708 Godwin-Austen (Robert A. C.). Surrey etymologies : the hundred of Blackheath. Surrey Archaeol. Collns., 5, pp. 3–14. 1871.

6709 Gover (John Eric Bruce), *etc*. The place-names of Surrey. *English Place-name Society*, 11. pp. xlvi, 445, + 7 maps. 8° Cambridge, 1934.

6710 Grundy (George Beardoe). On place names in general, and the Hampshire place names in particular. Papers and Proc. Hants. F.C., 9, pp. 221–61. *See also* pp. 393–96. 1922.

6711 Hopwood (David). The place-names of the county of Surrey, including London in Surrey. pp. x, 101. Annals Univ. Stellenbosch, 4, section B, no. 2. 1926.

6712 Huntingford (George Wynn Brereton). Berkshire place-names. [i. River-names : ii. Hill-names : iii. Personal names : iv. Descriptive names. Addenda and corrigenda.] Berks. Archaeol. J., 38, pp. 109–27 ; 39, pp. 11–34, 198–99. 1934–35.

6713 —— The name Berkshire. *Same jnl.*, 37, pp. 34–37. 1933.

6714 Koekeritz (Helge). Några ortnamnstyper från ön Wight. Ortnamnssällskapets ... årsskr., 2, pp. 5–16. 1937.

6714a —— The place-names of the Isle of Wight. *Nomina Germanica*, 6. pp. cxi, 207, + 2 maps. 8° Uppsala, 1940.

6715 —— *Wihtgaraburh*. [Place-name in the Isle of Wight.] Mod. Lang. Notes, 58, pp. 181–91. 1943.

6716 Leveson-Gower (Granville). Surrey etymologies : Tandridge hundred. Surrey Archaeol. Collns., 6, pp. 78–108, 127–226. 1874.

6717 Liebermann (Felix). Southampton ältester Name. Archiv Stud. neueren Spr., Bd. 133, p. 133. 1915.

6718 Malone (Kemp). On the etymology of Lingfield (Surrey). (Lingfield again). [Proved far-fetched by E. Ekwall, **6705**.] Anglia, 60 (N.E. 48), pp. 366–68 : 63 (N.F. 51), pp. 65–66. 1936, 1939.

6719 Marble Arch, *pseud*. Local place names [in Hampshire]. Hants. N. and Q., 1, pp. 67–81. 1883.

6720 Sherwood (George F. Tudor). Berkshire—its derivation. [Celtic *Bear-ruc*, cognate with park.] Berks. N. and Q., 1, pp. 40–42. 1890.

6721 Shore (Thomas William). Traces of the language of the prehistoric and other ancient races of Hampshire contained in the place names of the county. Papers and Proc. Hants. F.C., 3, pp. 233–56. 1898.

6722 Skeat (Walter William). The place-names of Berkshire. pp. 118. 8° Oxford, 1911.

6723 Smith (Charles Roach). Derivation of Carisbrooke. Hampshire Antiquary, 1, p. 18. 1891.

6724 Stenton (*Sir* Frank Merry). The place-names of Berkshire. pp. viii, 56. 8° Reading, 1911.

6725 Stevenson (William Henry). Derivation of Nursling. Papers and Proc. Hants. F. C., 9, pp. 414–16. 1925.

6725a Stone (G.). The place-names of the Test valley. [O.E. and Domesday.] Papers and Proc. Hants. F.C., 18, pp. 154–56. 1953.

6726 Taylor (Isaac). The Meon valley: etymology of its place names. Hants. N. and Q., 3, pp. 3–4. 1887.

6727 Vincent (William Thomas). Local place names. Woolwich Antiq. Soc., Ann. Rpt., 2 (1896–97), pp. 30–42. 1897.

6728 Zachrisson (Robert Eugen). Descriptive words or personal names in Old English place-name compounds. A survey of some Surrey place-names. Studia Neophil., 7, pp. 30–39, 150–51. 1935.

§ *b*. **Wiltshire, Somerset, Dorset**
(For Celtic names in Somerset, see **103**).

6729 Arkell (William Joscelyn). Some topographical names in south Dorset. Proc. Dorset Archaeol. Soc., 62 (for 1940), pp. 39–49: 63 (for 1941), pp. 33–40. 1941–42.

6730 —— Some topographical names in Wiltshire. [Supplementary to Place-Name Society's volume.] Wilts. Archaeol. Mag., 49, pp. 221–24. 1940.

6731 Atkinson (John Christopher). Etymology of the place-name Somerset. N. and Q., Som. and Dorset, 1, pp. 153–54, 257–59. 1890.

6732 B. (C.). The name Somerset. [Saw mor sedd : hunt-sea-abode.] *Same jnl.*, 10, pp. 244–45. 1907.

6733 Bird (H.). On local names in the neighbourhood of Bath. Proc. Bath F.C., 4, pp. 305–23. 1881.

6734 Brentnall (Harold Cresswell). Wiltshire place-names. Antiquity, 15, pp. 33–44. 1941.

6735 Drew (Charles D.). Earnley; a lost place name recovered. [Now Bonville : A.–S. Earna Legh.] Proc. Dorset Archaeol. Soc., 71 (1949), pp. 85–87, + map. 1950.

6736 Earle (John). The place-name Somerset. N. and Q. Som. and Dorset, 1, pp. 174–75. 1890 .

6737 Ekblom (Einar). The place-names of Wiltshire, their origin and history. *Diss. Uppsala.* pp. xviii, 188. 8° Uppsala, 1917.

6738 Elworthy (F. T.) and **Dickinson** (Francis Henry). Selworthy place-names. N. and Q. Som. and Dorset, 1, pp. 203–05. 1890.

6739 Faegersten (Anton). The place-names of Dorset. [With bibliography. Review by Helge Kökeritz in Studia Neophilologica, 6, pp. 120–31. 1934.] Uppsala Univ. Årsskrift, 1933, Filos., 4. pp. xxiii, 336. 1933.

6740 Gover (John Eric Bruce), *etc.* The place-names of Wiltshire. *English Place-name Society*, 16. pp. xli, 547 + maps. 8° Cambridge, 1939.

6741 Gray (Louis H.). The origin of the name of Glastonbury. Speculum, 10, pp. 46–53. 1935.

6742 Greswell (William Henry Parr). Glaston, Glastonia, Glastonbury. [Derivation of Glastonbury as a place-name.] Proc. Somerset Arch. Soc., 57 (1911), pp. 114–19. 1912.

6743 —— The Quantocks and their place-names. *Same jnl.*, 46, pp. 125–48. 1900.

6744 Grundy (George Beardoe). The place-names of Wiltshire. Wilts. Archaeol. Mag., 41, pp. 335–53. 1921.

6745 Hancock (F.). Local place names in Selworthy parish. N. and Q., Som. and Dorset, 1, pp. 193–95. 1890.

6746 Hill (John Samuel). The place-names of Somerset. pp. vii, 373, + map. 8° Bristol, 1914. [Gross, 352.]

6747 Jones (William Henry Rich). The names of places in Wiltshire. [1. i–ii. On the Celtic element in Wiltshire local names. 2. On the Teutonic element in Wiltshire local names.] Wilts. Archaeol. Mag., 14, pp. 156–80, 253–79 : 15, pp. 71–98. 1874–75.

6748 —— On some place-names near Malmesbury, and their historic teachings. *Same jnl.*, 21, pp. 61–74. 1884.

6749 Longstaff (John Cleasbey). Notes on Wiltshire names. Vol. 1, place-names. pp. v, 166. 8° Bradford-on-Avon, 1911. [No more published.]

6750 Maskelyne (Nevil Story). The place-name Cricklade : a suggestion. Wilts. Archaeol. Mag., 30, pp. 95–99. 1899.

6751 Mawer (*Sir* Allen). Some notes from Wiltshire. [i. Canning marsh (*Caningan mærse*, A.-S., c. 1010) : ii. Fonthill and neighbourhood (land dispute, temp. Alfred) : iii. Lutegaresheale and Colungakrycge in the will of Æthelstan Ætheling : iv. Underditch hundred.] Studia Neophil., 14, pp. 89–96. 1942.

6752 Skeat (Walter William). Yetminster and Ockford. [Two Dorset Domesday names.] N. and Q., 8th S. 3, pp. 371–72, 409–10. 1893.

6753 Slover (Clark Harris). A note on the names of Glastonbury. [Correction of article by L. H. Gray, **6741**.] Speculum, 11, pp. 129–32. 1936.

6754 Stevenson (William Henry), *etc.* Errors in Anglo-Saxon names. [Sumorsaetan, Defnsaete, Dunsætas, *etc.*] Academy, 38, pp. 29, 44, 60, 74–75, 89, 105 : 31, p. 397. 1885–87.

6755 Tengstrand (Erik). Marginal notes to the place-names of Dorset. Studia Neophil., 6, pp. 90–103. 1934.

6756 Turner (A. G. C.). Notes on some Somerset place-names. Proc. Somerset Archaeol. Soc., 95 (1950), pp. 112–24. 1951.

6757 —— A selection of north Somerset place-names. *Same jnl.*, 96 (1951), pp. 152–59. 1952.

6758 Underdown (H. W.). Witham friary boundaries and place names [Somerset.] N. and Q. Som. and Dorset, 9, pp. 108–11, 189, 346–48 : 10, pp. 22–25, 59–64, 176–77, 206–08, 245–46, 292–96 : 11, pp. 204–05. 1905–09.

6759 Weaver (Frederic William). Notes on the names of parishes in the county of Somerset. N. and Q., 6th S. 7, pp. 462–63 : 8, pp. 23–24, 203–05, 342–43, 403–04, 461–62 : 9, pp. 43–44, 101–02, 161–62, 276, 318. 1883–84.

6760 Wildman (William Beauchamp). Yetminster, [Dorset]. N. and Q. Som. and Dorset, 10, pp. 11–12. 1906.

6761 Z. Kinwardstone. [?derived from earl Werstan or Wickstan, c. 800.] Wilts. N. and Q., 1, p. 139. 1893.

6762 Zachrisson (Robert Eugen). The meaning of the place-names of Dorset in the light of the terminal rule. Studia Neophil., 6, pp. 133–63. 1934.

§ c. Devon

6763 Alexander (John James). Devon names ending in ' tun '. (Résumé). Rept. and Trans. Devon. Assoc., 71, pp. 174–75. 1939.

6764 —— Devon names ending in ' worthy '. (Résumé). *Same jnl.*, 70, pp. 145–46. 1938.

6765 —— East and north Devon place-names. *Same jnl.*, 65, pp. 355–77. 1933.

6766 —— The place-names of Devon. Devonian Y.B., 21, pp. 65–70. 1930.

6767 —— The place-names of Torbay. Rept. and Trans. Devon. Assoc., 64, pp. 539–42. 1932.

6768 —— South Devon place-names. *Same jnl.*, 66, pp. 279–313, + map. 1934.

6769 —— Unredeemed Devon. [Place-names on the Tamar.] Devon and Cornwall N. and Q., 21, pp. 316–22. 1941.

6770 —— The western hundreds of Devon. [Place-name evidence.] Rept. and Trans. Devon. Assoc., 62, pp. 170–73. 1930.

6771 B. (J.). Hemyock. Devon and Cornwall N. and Q., 23, p. 47. 1947.

6772 Bate (Charles Spence). A contribution towards determining the etymology of Dartmoor names. [Including those containing Viking names.] Rept. and Trans. Devon. Assoc., 4, pp. 520–35. 1871.

6773 Blomé (Bertil). The place-names of north Devonshire. *Diss.* pp. xx, 189. 8° Uppsala, 1929.

6774 Brushfield (Thomas Nadauld) and **Reichel** (Oswald Joseph). Abbotskerswell, Kingskerswell. Devon N. and Q., 1, pp. 70–72. 1900.

6775 Chanter (John Frederick). Devonshire place-names. Part 1. The parishes. Rept. and Trans. Devon. Assoc., 50, pp. 503–32. 1918.

6776 Chope (Richard Pearse). Folk-etymology of Devonian place-names. Devonian Y.B., 25, pp. 48–53. 1934.

6777 Clarke (*Mrs.* Daisy Emily Martin). The phonological laws directly affecting Devon [place-names]. Rept. and Trans. Devon. Assoc., 62, pp. 168–70. 1930.

6778 Fortescue (Hugh Fortescue), *4th earl.* Some Devonshire farm names. *Same jnl.*, 62, pp. 311–40. 1930.

6779 Gover (John Eric Bruce), *etc.* The place-names of Devon. *English Place-name Society*, 8–9. pp. lx, xiv, 754, + 2 maps. 2 vol. 8° Cambridge, 1931–32.

6780 Hoskins (William George) and **Rose-Troop** (Frances). Burrow farm in Stoke Canon. Devon and Cornwall N. and Q., 20, pp. 27–28, 88. 1938.

6781 Hoskins (William George), *etc.* The meaning of Barton. [In Devon = *burh-tun* (demesne-farm). *Burh* = fortified house.] *Same jnl.*, 23, pp. 273–77, 326–28, 363, 398–99; 24, pp. 129–30. 1949–50.

6782 Karlstroem (Sigurd). Miscellaneous notes on the place-names of north Devonshire. Studia Neophil., 2, pp. 67–69. 1929.

6783 Llewellin (George T.) and **Rose-Troup** (Frances). Derivation of the name Heavitree. Devon and Cornwall N. and Q., 9, pp. 153–55, 180–81. 1916–17.

6784 Mawer (*Sir* Allen). Notes on the place-names of Devon. Trans. Phililog. Soc., 1931–2, pp. 68–72. 1933.

6785 Reichel (Oswald Joseph), *etc.* Clyst and week place-names. Devon and Cornwall N. and Q., 9, pp. 43–44, 92–93. 1916.

6786 —— and Watkin (Hugh Robert). Derivation of Haccombe. *Same jnl.*, 10, pp. 122–23. 1918.

6787 Reichel (Oswald Joseph). Etymology of Nympton and Chulmleigh. [Refuted by W. W. Skeat **6789**.] *Same jnl.*, 6, pp. 70–71, 128. 1910.

6788 Skeat (Walter William), *etc.* Etymology of Paignton [Devon]. N. and Q., 7th, S. 8, pp. 58, 117–18, 158–59, 252. 1889.

6789 —— Etymology of the place names Nympton and Chulmleigh. [Refuting **6787**.] Devon and Cornwall N. and Q., 6, pp. 43–46, 71–72, 132. 1910.

6790 T. (G.). The local termination -hay. [Exeter: A.-S. *haga*, haw, hedge.] Notes and gleanings ... Devon, 3, pp. 18–19. 1890.

6791 Watkin (Hugh Robert). Asprington place name. Devon and Cornwall N. and Q., 11, pp. 281–82. 1921.

6792 —— and Chope (Richard Pearse). Canna park. [Common field name in West Devon. From A.-S. *canne*, a cup: or from M.E. *canne*, a field in which canes grow.] *Same jnl.*, 12, pp. 71–72. 1922.

6793 Worth (Richard Hansford). A note on Dartmoor place-names. Rept. and Trans. Devon. Assoc., 58 (1926), pp. 359–72. 1927.

6794 Worth (Richard Nicholls) Notes on the historical connections of Devonshire place-names. *Same jnl.*, 10, pp. 276–308. 1878.

103. PLACE-NAMES, CELTIC GENERAL

6795 Crawford (Osbert Guy Stanhope). Celtic place-names in England. Archaeol. J., 77, pp. 137–47. 1920.

Y

6796 Hogan (Edmund Ignatius). Onomasticon Goedelicum locorum et tribuum Hiberniae et Scotiae. An index, with identifications, to the Gaelic names of places and tribes. pp. xvi, 696, + map. 4° London, Dublin, 1910. [Kenney, 1, p. 100.]

6797 Holder (Alfred). Altceltischer Sprachschatz. 2 vol. 8° Leipzig, 1896–1913. [Kenney, 1, p. 100. Early occurrences of Celtic place-names throughout Europe.]

6798 Loth (Joseph). Le brittonique en Somerset. Rev. celt., 20, pp. 340–42. 1899.

6799 Smith (Gilbert E.). Minehead. [And other Celtic place-names in Somerset.] N. and Q. Som. and Dorset, 7, pp. 258–59. 1901.

6800 Stevenson (William Henry), *etc.* Records of Celtic occupation in local names. N. and Q., 7th S. 4, pp. 1–3, 90–92, 134, 170–71, 249–52 : 5, pp. 9–12. 1887–88.

6801 Thomas (R. J.). Celtic place-names formed from animal-head names. Arch. Camb., 89, pp. 328–31. 1934.

6802 Turner (A. G. C.). Some Somerset place-names containing Celtic elements. Bull. Bd. Celtic Stud., 14, pp. 113–19. 1951.

6803 Varro, *pseud.* Derivation of Cymmer. [Junction of two streams.] Arch. Camb., 3, pp. 78–79. 1848.

6804 Watson (William John). Topographical varia. Celtic Rev. 5, pp. 148–54, 337–42 : 6, pp. 236–41 : 7, pp. 68–81, 361–71 : 8, pp. 235–45. 1908–13.

104. PLACE-NAMES, IRISH

6805 Butler (Elenor). Irish place names and geographical influences. Geog. Teacher, 12, pp. 191–98. 1923.

6806 Byrne (Matthew J.). Ancient names of Ireland. [Iberus, Hibernia, Scotia, Yrlande, *etc.*] Kerry Archaeol. Mag., 1, pp. 80–83. 1909.

6807 Dobbs (Margaret E.). Some ancient place-names [in Ulster]. [Pp. 111–18, those occurring in 5th c. campaigns of Conaill Gulban. Text edited

by Gustav Lehmacher *in* Zeit. celt. Philol., 14, pp. 212–69. 1923. **1020.**] J. Roy. Soc. Antiq. Ireland, 56 (6th S. 16), pp. 106–18. 1926.

6808 Duncan (James). Gaelic place names in Antrim. Ulster J. Archaeol., 2nd S. 12, pp. 131–34. 1906.

6809 Hickson (Mary Agnes). Danish names in Waterford and Cork. J. Waterford Archaeol. Soc., 3, pp. 44–46. 1897.

6810 —— Names of places and surnames in Kerry. J. Roy. Soc. Antiq. Ireland, 21 (5th S. 1. ii), pp. 685–96 : 22, pp. 137–44, 389–97 : 23, pp. 261–67 : 24, pp. 256–63. 1891–94.

6811 Joyce (Patrick Weston). Irish local names explained. New edition. pp. 107. 8° Dublin, 1884.

6812 —— On changes and corruptions in Irish topographical names. Proc. R.I.A., 9, pp. 225–52. 1865.

6813 —— On the occurrence of the number two in Irish proper names. Proc. R.I.A., 10, pp. 164–72. 1870.

6814 —— The origin and history of Irish names of places. 3 vol. 8° London, 1910–13.

6815 Little (George Aloysius). Pre-Norse Dublin. 1. The name. Dublin Hist. Rec., 8, pp. 1–16. 1946.

6816 MacNeill (Eoin). Sescenn Uarbeoil of the sagas and other ancient place-names to the south of Dublin. J. Roy. Soc. Antiq. Ireland, 65 (7th S. 5), pp. 9–22. 1935.

6817 Morris (Henry). 'Da' in Irish place names. County Louth Archaeol. J., 6, pp. 131–34. 1927.

6818 Murphy (Michael). Place names. The town, villages, and principal sites in county Cork. J. Ivernian Soc., 4, pp. 56–58 : 5–7, *passim.* 1911–15.

6819 O'Briain (Micheál). Hibernica. 6. On the names of Ireland. [Ériu, *etc.*] Zeit. celt. Philol., 14, pp. 326–34. 1923.

6820 O'Dowd (Peadar). Gaelic place-names in Omeath [Louth]. County Louth Archaeol. J., 3, pp. 232–36. 1914.

6821 O'Foley (Richard). Irish place-names. 8° Dublin, [193–].

6822 O'Oubhthaigh (Seosam). Gaelic place names in the glens of Antrim. [Irish, English and interpretation. Corrected, with notes, by John MacNeill.] Ulster J. Archaeol., 2nd S. 11, pp. 130–38, 180–89. 1905.

6823 O'Rahilly (Thomas Francis). Notes on Irish place-names. Hermathena, 23 (no. 48), pp. 196–220. 1933.

6824 Pictet (Adolphe). Inquiry into the origin of the name of Ireland. Ulster J. Archaeol., 5, pp. 52–60. 1857.

6825 Pokorny (Julius). *Da-* in irischen Ortsnamen. Zeit. celt. Philol., 14, pp. 270–71. 1923.

6826 —— Der Name Ériu. *Same jnl.*, 15, pp. 197–203. 1925.

6827 Power (Patrick). Place names of the Decies. J. Waterford Archaeol. Soc., 9–12, *passim*, + map. 1906–09. *Same title.* 2nd edition. pp. 489. 8° Cork, 1952.

6828 Price (Liam). Place-names of county Wicklow. The Irish form and meaning of parish, townland, and local names. pp. 72. 8° Wexford, 1935.

6829 —— The place-names of co. Wicklow. *Dublin Institute for advanced studies.* pp. 280. 4 pts. 8° Dublin, 1945–53.

6830 Stubbs (Francis William). Place names in the county of Louth. County Louth Archaeol. J., 2, pp. 29–39, 128–38, 285–98, 350–62. 1908–11.

6831 Todd (James Henthorn), *etc.* Etymology of Armagh. [Bede : *Dearmach.*] N. and Q., 1st S. 1, pp. 218–19, 264. 1850.

6832 Walsh (Paul). Place names in Vita Finniani. [i. Escair Branán : ii. Ros Findchuill : iii. Cell Rignaige.] Zeit. celt. Phil., 10, pp. 73–77. 1915.

6833 —— Some place-names in ancient Meath. Irish Eccles. Rec., 4th S. 32, pp. 601–10 : 5th S. 1, pp. 180–91 : 2, pp. 197–210. 1912–13.

105. PLACE-NAMES, MANX

6834 Collingwood (William Gershom). Some Manx names in Cumbria. With notes by Eiríkr Magnússon. Trans. Cumb. and Westm. Antiq. Soc., 13, pp. 403–14. 1895.

6835 Cumming (Joseph George). St. Patrick–Maune and Man. [?name of the Isle of Man.] N. and Q., 1st S. 8, p. 291. 1853.

6836 Gill (W. Walter). A Manx scrapbook. pp. xii, 532, + 7 plates. 8° London, Bristol, 1929. [Pp. 169–528, place-names and place-lore.]

6837 Gray (Louis H.). The name of the Isle of Man. Am. J. Philol., 50, p. 371. 1929.

6838 Harrison (S. N.) and **Tellet** (F. S.). Place names. [i. Maughold : ii. Lezayre.] Yn Lioar Manninagh, 1, pp. 75–78, 99–103. 1889.

6839 Jeffcott (John M.). Mann, its names and their origins. *Manx Society, vol.* 30. pp. 20. 8° Douglas, 1878.

6840 Kneen (John Joseph). Our Norse heritage. [Manx farms and place-names.] I.O.M., N.H. and Antiq. Soc., Proc., N.S. 3 (1930–32), pp. 482–95. 1934.

6841 —— The place-names Alkest and Cronk yn How. Arch. Camb., 85, pp. 307–08. 1930.

6842 —— Place names of the Isle of Man. *Manx Society.* 6 vol. 8° Douglas, 1925–29.

6843 —— The romance of place-names [in Man]. Arch. Camb., 85, pp. 103–14. 1930.

6844 Marstrander (Carl Johan Sverstrup). Remarks on the place-names of the Isle of Man. Norsk Tidsskr. for Sprogoldenskap, 7, pp. 287–334. 1934.

6845 Quine (John). Notes on Moore's surnames and place names in the Isle of Man [635]. Yn Lioar Manninagh, 3, pp. 444–51. 1899.

106. PLACE-NAMES, SCOTTISH

6846 Bentinck (Charles D.). Dornoch place-names. [A few of Pictish and Norse origin.] Trans. Gaelic Soc. Inverness, 31 (1922–24), pp. 98–115. 1927.

6847 Beveridge (Erskine). The Abers and Invers of Scotland. pp. xix, 128. 8° Edinburgh, 1923.

6848 Black (George William). The derivation of the word Glasgow. Trans. Glasgow Archaeol. Soc., 2, pp. 219–28. 1883.

6848a Borgstroem (Carl Hj.). The Norse place-names of Barra. Book of Barra, ed. John Lorne Campbell, pp. 287–95. 1936.

6849 Browne (Walter Raleigh). Distribution of place-names in the Scottish lowlands. Trans. Philol. Soc., 1880–81, pp. 322–34, + 2 folding charts. [1881].

6850 Cameron (   ), *Dr., of Brodick.* Arran place names. Trans. Gaelic Soc. Inverness, 15, pp. 122–39, + map. 1890.

6851 Carmichael (Alexander). The place-names of Iona. Scot. Geog. Mag., 2, pp. 461–74 : 3, pp. 80–87, 242–47. 1886–87.

6852 Christison (David). On the geographical distribution of certain place-names in Scotland. [23 headings : ben, pen, pin, fiold, barr, kame, ceom, ward, dale, hope, gill, lane, grain, beck, strand, lake, bal, pit, bie, ham, hirst, girth, thwaite.] Proc. Soc. Antiq. Scot., 27 (3rd S. 3), pp. 255–80. 1893.

6853 Coles (Frederick R.). Remarks on some of the place names of the Stewartry. Trans. Dumfries. Antiq. Soc., 12 (1895–96), pp. 56–66. 1897.

6854 Currie (R.). The place-names of Arran. 8° Glasgow, 1908.

6855 Diack (Francis C.). Aber and Inver in Scotland. Scot. Gaelic Stud., 1, pp. 83–98. 1926.

6856 —— Place-names of Pictland. Rev. celt., 38, pp. 109–32 : 39, pp. 125–74 : 41, pp. 107–48. 1920, 1922, 1924.

6857 Dobbs (Margaret E.). Cé : the Pictish name of a district in eastern Scotland [Aberdeenshire]. Scot. Gaelic Stud., 6, pp. 137–38. 1949.

6858 Edmondston (Thomas). Names of some places in Shetland with remarks on their origin and meaning. Trans. Philol. Soc., 1866 iii, pp. 149–66. 1866.

6859 Ellice (Edward Charles). Place-names in Glengarry [Inverness] and Glenquoich [Argyll], and their origin. 2nd and revised edition. pp. xii, 163. 8° London, 1931.

6860 Foerster (Max). Der Name *Edinburgh*. Anglia, 64 (N.F. 52), pp. 106–16. 1940.

6861 Forbes (Alexander Robert). Place-names of Skye, and adjacent islands : with lore, mythological, traditional and historical. pp. 495. 8° Paisley, 1923.

6862 Fraser (John). The name Alba. Scot. Gaelic Stud., 5, pp. 72–75. 1942.

6863 Galloway (Alexander). Enquiry into the origin and meaning of some names of places in Scotland, and particularly in Clydesdale. Trans. Glasgow Archaeol. Soc., 1, pp. 79–99. 1868.

6864 Gillies (Hugh Cameron). The place-names of Argyll. pp. xxvi, 273. 8° London, 1906.

6865 Gray (James). The Scandinavian place-names of Sutherland. (More *ditto*). [*See also* 3, pp. 69–70, 131.] Old-lore Misc. V.C., 2, pp. 213–26, + map : 3, pp. 14–21. 1909–10.

6866 Gunn (Adam). A review of Sutherland place-names. Old-Lore Misc., V.C., 3, pp. 182–87. 1910.

6867 Jakobsen (Jakob). The dialect and place-names of Shetland. Two popular lectures. pp. 125. 4° Lerwick, 1897.

6868 —— The place names of Shetland. pp. xiii, 273. 8° London, 1936.

6869 Johnson-Ferguson (*Sir* Edward Alexander James), *2nd bart.* Place-names. (—in Dumfriesshire and other notes). Trans. Dumfries. Antiq. Soc., 3rd S. 16 (1929–30), pp. 24–37 : 17 (1930–31), pp. 135–57 : 20 (1935–36), pp. 36–45. 1931–32, 1938.

6870 Johnston (Alfred Wintle). Orkney place-names. Old-lore Misc., 9, p. 9. 1921.

6871 —— Survey of Orkneyan place-names. Saga-Book V.C., 3, pp. 459–64 + table. 1904.

6872 Johnston (James Brown). The place-names of Berwickshire. *Roy. Scot. Geog. Soc., place-names of Scotland series*, 1. pp. 52. 8° Edinburgh, 1940.

6873 —— Place-names of Scotland. 3rd edition. pp. xvi, 335. 8° London, 1934.

6874 —— The place-names of Stirlingshire. Trans. Stirling Archaeol. Soc., 25 (1902–03), 1903.

6875 Liddall (William John Norbray). Kinross-shire place names. Trans. Gaelic Soc. Inverness, 14, pp. 153–58. 1889.

6876 —— The place-names of Fife and Kinross. pp. xii, 58. 8° Edinburgh, 1896. [1895].

6877 Livingstone (Colin). Lochaber place names. Trans. Gaelic Soc. Inverness, 13, pp. 257–69. 1888.

6878 MacBain (Alexander). The Norse element in the topography of the Highlands and Isles. *Same jnl.*, 19, pp. 217–45. 1895.

6879 —— Place names, highlands and islands of Scotland. pp. xxxii, 381. 8° Stirling, 1922.

6880 —— Place-names of Inverness-shire. Trans. Gaelic Soc. Inverness, 25 (1901–03), pp. 55–84. 1907.

6881 MacDonald (Angus). The place-names of West Lothian. pp. xl, 179. 8° Edinburgh, 1941.

6882 MacDonald (Archibald). Place-names of Kiltarlity and district. [Inverness-shire]. Trans. Gaelic Soc. Inverness, 28 (1912–14), pp. 441–51. 1918.

6883 MacDonald (James). Place-names in Strathbogie [Aberdeenshire] : with notes . . . map and plans. pp. xii, 300. 8° Aberdeen, 1891.

6884 —— Place names of west Aberdeenshire. pp. 376. 8° Aberdeen, 1899.

6885 MacEchern (Dugald). Place-names of Coll. [Argyllshire]. Trans. Gaelic Soc. Inverness, 29 (1914–19), pp. 314–35. 1922.

6886 Mackay (John). Sutherland place names. [i. General : ii. Parishes of Assynt : iii. Durness : iv. Farr, Tongue :

v. Kildonan, Reay : vi. Loth, Clyne : Golspie, Rogart : vii. Lairg, Creich : viii. Dornoch.] *Same jnl.*, 13, pp. 43–49 ; 15, pp. 107–22 ; 16, pp. 39–59 ; 17, pp. 101–25 ; 18, pp. 183–208, 325–40 ; 19, pp. 172–88 ; 20, pp. 103–25, 316–32. 1888–97.

6887 Mackenzie (Kenneth). Lewis place-names and relics of the Norse language in Lewis speech. *Same jnl.*, 26 (1904–07), pp. 368–87. 1910.

6888 MacKenzie (William Cook). Scottish place-names. pp. xi, 319. 8° London, 1931.

6889 —— Some oddities in Scottish place-names. [Including Norse derivations.] Scot. Geog. Mag., 54, pp. 143–48. 1938.

6890 —— The western isles : their history, traditions and place-names. pp. xv, 351, + 11 plates. 8° Paisley, 1932. [Pp. 1–14, Norse period : pp. 251–342, place-names.]

6891 McKie (J.). Galloway place names. Trans. Dumfries. Antiq. Soc., 4 (1885–86), pp. 134–41. 1887.

6892 MacKinlay (James Murray). Influence of the pre-reformation Church on Scottish place-names. pp. xx, 463. 8° Edinburgh, 1904. [Kils and saints, etc.]

6893 McLaughlan (Thomas). On the Kymric element in the Celtic topography of Scotland. Proc. Soc. Antiq. Scot., 6, pp. 315–24. 1868.

6894 Maclean (Hector). Brythonic and Gaelic place-names in Lanarkshire. Highland Monthly, 2, pp. 231–39. 1890.

6895 —— Notes on place names of Iona. Scot. Geog. Mag., 3, pp. 35–38. 1887.

6896 Maclean (Roderick). Notes on the parish of Kiltearn [Ross-shire]. [North side of Cromarty firth. Place-names.] Trans. Gaelic Soc. Inverness, 15, pp. 302–10. 1890.

6897 Martin (J. W.). The place names of the Cairn valley [Dumfries-shire.] Trans. Dumfries. Antiq. Soc., 16 (1899–1900), pp. 4–13. 1900.

6898 Marwick (Hugh). Celtic place-names in Orkney. Proc. Soc. Antiq. Scot., 57 (5th S. 9, 1922–23), pp. 251–65. 1923.

6899 —— Orkney farm-name studies. *Same jnl.*, 9 (1930–31), pp. 25–34. 1931.

6900 —— The place-names of North Ronaldsay. *Same jnl.*, 1 (1922–23), pp. 53–64. 1923.

6901 Matheson (Donald). The place-names of Elginshire. pp. 208. 8° Stirling, 1905.

6902 Maxwell (*Sir* Herbert Eustace), *7th bart.* Place-names of Galloway : their origin and meaning considered. pp. xlvi, 278. 8° Glasgow, 1930.

6903 —— Scottish land-names. Their origin and meaning. *Rhind Lectures in Archaeology*, 1893. pp. ix, 219. 8° Edinburgh, 1894.

6903a —— Studies in the topography of Galloway, with a list of nearly 4000 names of places, and remarks on their origin and meaning. pp. xv, 340. 8° Edinburgh, 1887.

6904 Meikle (James). Yarrow as a place-name. [Also Jarrow (Durham).] Scot. Geog. Mag., 59, pp. 100–02. 1944.

6905 Milne (John). Celtic place-names in Aberdeen. 1912.

6906 —— Gaelic place names of the Lothians. pp. viii, 51, 44, 30. 8° London, [19—?].

6907 Richardson (Ralph). Scottish place-names and Scottish saints. [Pp. 355–60, list of Scottish saints, with the place-names derived from them.] Scot. Geog. Mag., 21, pp. 352–60. 1905.

6908 Robertson (G. Philip). Stoney-kirk [Wigtownshire] : hints as to its history from place names. Trans. Dumfries. Antiq. Soc., N.S. 23, pp. 279–84. 1911.

6909 Russell ( ) *Miss, of Ashiesteel.* Some place-names in Scotland. Hist. Berwick. Nat. Club, 14, pp. 166–71 : 15, pp. 185–89. 1892–94.

6910 Shaw (James). Place names of Nithsdale. Trans. Dumfries. Antiq. Soc., 3 (1882–83), pp. 40–43. 1884.

6911 Stefánsson (Jón). Scandinavian place-names in Sutherland. Old-lore Misc. V.C., 3, pp. 234–36. 1910.

6912 Stratton (Thomas), *etc.* The Mearns or Kincardineshire. N. and Q., 6th S. 5, p. 275 : 6, pp. 42–43. 1882.

6913 Taylor (Alexander Burt). Identi-fication of saga place-names. Orkney Misc., 1, pp. 57–63. 1953.

6914 —— Some saga place-names. Proc. Orkney Antiq. Soc., 9 (1930–31), pp. 41–45. 1931.

6915 Thomas (F. W. L.). Did the Northmen extirpate the Celtic inhabitants of the Hebrides in the ninth century ? [Pp. 478–98, Scandinavian names of farms or townlands in Lewis, with Harris : pp. 498–502, Gaelic ditto : pp. 502–07, English ditto.] Proc. Soc. Antiq. Scot., 11, pp. 472–507. 1876.

6916 —— On Islay place-names, [Argyllshire]. [Scandinavian and Gaelic names of farms or townlands.] *Same jnl.*, 16 (N.S. 4), pp. 241–76. 1882.

6917 Watson (William John). The history of the Celtic place-names of Scotland. pp. xx, 558. 8° Edinburgh and London, 1926.

6918 —— The place-names of Breadal-bane [Perthshire]. Trans. Gaelic Soc. Inverness, 34 (1927–28), pp. 248–79. 1935.

6919 —— Place-names of Perthshire : the Lyon basin. *Same jnl.*, 35 (1929–30), pp. 277–96. 1939.

6920 —— Place names of Ross and Cromarty. pp. lxxxvi, 302. 8° Inverness, 1904.

6921 —— Place-names of Strathdearn. Trans. Gaelic Soc. Inverness, 30 (1919–22), pp. 101–21. 1924.

6922 —— The study of Highland place-names. [Including Pictish ele-ment.] Celtic Rev., 1, pp. 22–31. 1904.

6923 Whitelaw (J. W.). The origin of the name Dumfries. [Argument for ' Castle of the Frisians '. Of which no record : *See* next article in the volume.] Trans. Dumfries. Antiq. Soc., N.S. 24, pp. 229–31. 1912.

107. PLACE-NAMES, WELSH AND CORNISH

6924 Allen (W. Bird). Welsh place-names. [His explanation of Llan-.] Arch. Camb., 6th S. 15, pp. 430–31. 1915.

6925 Antiquary, An : *pseud.* Name of Radnor (Radenoure). Arch. Camb., 3rd S. 3, pp. 314–15, 393. 1857.

6926 Anwyl (*Sir* Edward). Notes on some Radnorshire place-names. Arch. Camb., 6th S. 11, pp. 161–69. 1911.

6927 Bushell (William Dene). Caldy island, Pemb., ' the isle of the fresh water springs '. Arch. Camb., 74 (6th S. 19), pp. 222–23. 1919.

6928 Charles (Bertie George). Non-Celtic place-names in Wales and Monmouthshire. *Ph.D. thesis, London.* 1935. [Apply Univ. Library.]

6929 —— Non-Celtic place-names in Wales. *London Mediaeval Studies : Monograph* 1. pp. xlviii, 326. 8° London, 1938. [Shows A.–S. and Norman penetration.]

6930 —— The substitution of Welsh sounds in place-names of English origin in the border counties of Wales. London Mediaeval Studies, 1, pp. 40–47. 1937.

6931 Cuillandre (J.). A propos des monographies du Rev. G. H. Doble sur les saints de Cornwall. [And their connection with place-names.] Rev. celt., 50, pp. 48–54. 1933.

6932 Dexter (Thomas Francis George). Cornish names. An attempt to explain over 1600 Cornish names. pp. 90. 8° London, 1926.

6933 Fisher (J.). Some place-names in the locality of St. Asaph. Arch. Camb., 6th S. 14, pp. 221–46. 1914.

6934 Glover (J. E.). Cornish place-names. Antiquity, 2, pp. 319–27. 1928.

6935 Gover (John Eric Bruce). The element *ros* in Cornish place-names. London Mediaeval Studies, 1, pp. 249–64. 1938.

6936 Jenner (Henry). Cornish place-names. [Suggestions for a survey.] J. Roy. Inst. Cornwall, 18, pp. 140–46. 1910.

6937 —— Some possible Arthurian place-names in west Penwith. *Same jnl.*, 19, pp. 46–89. 1912.

6938 Jones (M. H.). The ecclesiastical place-names of Carmarthenshire. Arch. Camb., 6th S. 15, pp. 321–32, 395–404. *See also note on* pp. 430–31. 1915.

6939 Jones (Thomas). The place-names of Cardiff. [Pp. 15–17, Early Welsh period, c. 450–1100.] S. Wales and Monmouth Rec. Soc. Publn., 2, pp. 1–206. 1950.

6940 Jones (Tom). A bibliography of monographs on the place-names of Wales. Bull. Bd. Celtic Studies, 5, pp. 249–64 : 6, pp. 171–78. 1931–33.

6941 Lloyd (*Sir* John Edward). Welsh place-names : a study of some common name-elements. With notes by the editor [Egerton Phillimore]. Y Cymmrodor, 11, pp. 15–60. 1892.

6942 Moffat (Alexander G.). Norse place-names in Gower (Glamorganshire). Saga-Book V.C., 2, pp. 95–117. 1898.

6943 Morgan (Thomas). Glamorgan place-names. 8° Newport, 1901.

6944 —— Handbook of the origin of place-names in Wales and Monmouthshire. pp. vii, 215. 8° Merthyr Tydfil, 1887.

6945 —— Place-names of Wales and Monmouthshire. 2nd and revised edition. pp. 262. 8° Newport, 1912.

6946 Norris (Edwin). On some names of places in Scilly. Arch. Camb., 8th S. 9, pp. 41–52. 1863.

6947 Owen (Robert). Place-names of Newtown and neighbourhood. ['Witnesses of the ebb and flow of Welsh and Saxon influence.'] Collns. hist. and archaeol. rel. to Montgom., 29, pp. 75–92. 1897.

6948 P. (W. R.), *etc.* Danes [or Norse] in Pembroke [and South Wales]. [?10th c. colony. With references. Place-name evidence.] N. and Q., 9th S. 10, pp. 132, 276–77. 1902.

6949 Paterson (Donald Rose). Scandinavian influence in the place-names and early personal names [pp. 74–89] of Glamorgan. Arch. Camb., 75 (6th S. 20), pp. 31–89. 1920.

6950 Paterson (Donald Rose). Womanby—a Cardiff place-name. [? Scandinavian origin.] Arch. Camb., 77 (7th S. 2), pp. 396–99. 1922.

6951 Picton (*Sir* James Allanson). Notes on the place-names in Pembrokeshire, illustrative of its history and ethnology. [Celtic and Scandinavian.] J. Brit. Archaeol. Assoc., 41, pp. 109–16. 1885.

6952 Williams (*Sir* Ifor). Some Welsh place-names in Denbighshire. J. Welsh bibliog. Soc., 5, pp. 249–61. 1941.

6953 Wood (James George). Radnor as a place-name. Trans. Woolhope N.F. Club, 1905–07, pp. 367–69. 1911.

108. GENERAL

§ a. Anglo-Saxon

6954 Allison (Thomas). Pioneers of English learning. pp. xix, 109. 8° Oxford, 1932. [Bede, etc.]

6955 Bugge (Alexander). Costumes, jewels, and furniture in Viking times. Saga-Book V.C., 7, pp. 141–76. 1912.

6956 Chambers (Raymond Wilson). The place of Anglo-Saxon civilization in European history. Chelmsford Diocesan Chronicle, Aug. 1933, pp. 121–24. 1933.

6957 Cook (Albert Stanburrough). Germans in England in the eighth century. [Wizo and Fredegis in Alcuin's school at York, etc.] Mod. Lang. Notes, 4, pp. 475–78. 1889.

6958 —— Old English literature and Jewish learning. [*See also* note by J. M. Hart, ' Judaism in early England ', 7, col. 53–56. 1892.] Mod. Lang. Notes, 6, col. 142–53. 1891.

6959 —— Possible begetter of the Old English Beowulf and Widsith. [Aldfrith, king of Northumbria.] Trans. Conn. Acad. Arts and Sci., 25, pp. 281–346. 1922.

6960 Dale (Edmund). National life and character in the mirror of early English literature. pp. xiv, 337. 8° Cambridge, 1907. [i. The Englishman of the conquest : ii. The advent and influence of Christianity : iii. The disconcerting factors : iv. The blending of the races : v. The resultant nation.]

6961 Draper (Warwick Herbert). King Alfred as man of letters. Antiquary, 36, pp. 102–05, 171–75, 230–35, 301–06. 1900.

6962 Eastwood (J. W.). York as an early British and English centre of life and learning. J. Brit. Archaeol. Assoc., 48, pp. 31–37. 1892.

6963 Field (Louise Frances), *Mrs. E. M. Field*. The child and his book. Some account of the history and progress of children's literature in England. 2nd edition. pp. vii, 358, + 4 plates. 8° London, [189–]. [Pp. 10–35, + 1 plate, ' before the Norman Conquest '.]

6964 Galbraith (Vivian Hunter). The literacy of the medieval English kings. [Including Aldfrith, Alfred, etc.] Proc. Brit. Acad., 21, pp. 201–38. 1935.

6965 Geyer (Bernhard). Die patristische und scholastische Philosophie. *Ueberweg* (F.) : *Grundriss der Geschichte der Philosophie, Teil* 2, 11. *Auflage*. pp. xviii, 826. 8° Berlin, 1928. [Bede, *passim* : Johannes Scotus Erigena, pp. 164–77, 693–94, and *passim*.]

6966 Girvan (Ritchie). Finnsburuh. [Including habits and culture depicted.] Proc. Brit. Acad., 26, pp. 327–60. 1940.

6967 Graham (Rose). The intellectual influence of English monasticism between the tenth and the twelfth centuries. Trans. R.H.S., N.S. 17, pp. 23–65. 1903.

6968 Grierson (Philip). Grimbald of St. Bertin's. [Scholar in England temp. Alfred.] E.H.R., 55, pp. 529–61. 1940.

6969 Harrison (Frederick). Medieval man and his notions. pp. viii, 276, + 24 plates. 8° London, 1947. [Popular. Pp. 30–46, meals, stars and chronology (Bede, etc.) : pp. 47–62, superstitions, etc. : pp. 63–78, A.–S. medicine (mostly Cockayne).]

6969 a Irwin (Raymond). In Saxon England. Studies in the history of libraries—vii. [Books, education, scholars.] Library Association Record, 57, pp. 290–96. 1955.

6970 James (Montague Rhodes). Learning and literature till the death of Bede. [Irish learning : Adamnan : Theodore, Hadrian : Benedict Biscop : Bede.] —— [from Alcuin] till pope Sylvester II. Camb. Med. Hist., 3, pp. 485–513, 514–38. 1922.

6971 James (Montague Rhodes). Two ancient English scholars ; St. Aldhelm and William of Malmesbury ... (The first lecture on the David Murray Foundation in the University of Glasgow ... 1931.) *Glasgow Univ. Publications*, 22. pp. 33. 8° Glasgow, 1931.

6972 Jones (Putnam Fennell). The Gregorian mission and English education. Speculum, 3, pp. 335–48. 1928.

6973 Knowles (Michael David). The cultural influence of English mediaeval monasticism. [' From 600 to 1066 the achievement of the monks was to preserve the legacy of the past. . . .'] C.H.J., 7, pp. 146–59. 1943.

6974 Laistner (Max Ludwig Wolfram). Thought and letters in western Europe, A.D. 500–900. pp. ix, 354. 8° New York, 1931. [Pp. 104–46, Irish and English scholars and missionaries to the death of Bede : The western European continent, c. 637–751, and the missionary labours of Boniface.]

6975 Leach (Arthur Francis). Our oldest school. [St. Peter's School, York.] Fortn. Rev., 58 (N.S. 52), pp. 638–50. 1892.

6976 Leitritz (Johannes). Altenglands Unterrichts- und Schulwesen. *Neusprachliche Abhandlungen*, 3. pp. 32. 8° Dresden, 1898.

6977 Lennard (Reginald). From Roman Britain to Anglo-Saxon England. [Influence of ancient world and its civilization on world of medieval Europe: early A.-S. tomb furniture and similar evidence : place-name evidence, etc.] Wirtschaft und Kultur : Festschrift . . . A. Dopsch, pp. 34–73. 1938.

6978 Lumby (Joseph Rawson). Greek learning in the Western Church during the seventh and eighth centuries, A.D. pp. 16. 8° Cambridge, 1878.

6979 Magoun (Francis Peabody) *jr.* King Alfred's letter on educational policy according to the Cambridge manuscripts. [Including A.-S. texts from MS. C.C.C. 12 and Camb. Univ. Library, MS. I.i 2–4.] Med. Stud., 11, pp. 113–22. 1949.

6980 Magoun (Francis Peabody) *jr.* Some notes on king Alfred's circular letter on educational policy addressed to his bishops. [With A.–S. text and English translation.] Med. Stud., 10, pp. 93–107. 1948.

6981 Manitius (Maximilian). Geschichte der lateinischen Literatur des Mittelalters. 1. Teil, Von Justinian bis zur Mitte des 10. Jahrhunderts. *Handbuch der klass. Altertumswiss.*, 9 *ii*. 1. pp. xiii, 766. 8° München, 1911. [Pp. 70–87, Bede : pp. 134–52, Aldhelm, Æthilwald, Bonifatius, Lul : pp. 181–87, Columbanus : pp. 236–42, Adamnan, Nennius : pp. 273–88, Alchvine : pp. 315–39, Sedulius, Johannes Scottus : etc.]

6982 Martin-Clarke (*Mrs.* Daisy Elizabeth). Culture in early Anglo-Saxon England. A study with illustrations. pp. xi, 100, + 19 plates. 8° Baltimore, 1947. [i. Age of Bede, *Beowulf* and the arts : ii. A.–S. sculpture : the Ruthwell Cross : iii. The epic *Beowulf* and its setting : iv. Technicalities, archaeological, literary and linguistic : v. A ship-burial (Sutton Hoo).]

6983 Ogilvy (Jack David Angus). Anglo-Saxon scholarship : 597–780. Univ. Colorado Stud., 22, pp. 327–40. 1935.

6984 —— Books known to Anglo-Latin writers from Aldhelm to Alcuin (670–804). *Medieval Academy of America, Studies and Documents*, 2. pp. xxii, 109. 8° Cambridge, Mass., 1936.

6985 Pierquin (Hubert). Les lettres, les sciences, les arts, la philosophie et la religion des Anglo-Saxons. pp. 118. 8° Paris, 1914.

6986 Raine (Angelo). History of St. Peter's School, York, A.D. 627 to the present day. pp. xii, 212, + 8 plates. 8° London, 1926. [Pp. 1–25, A.–S. : Alcuin, etc.]

6987 Ricci (Aldo). The Anglo-Saxon eleventh-century crisis. [Pessimism versus optimism : revenge versus love : emergence from ' Teutonic ' into ' European '.] Rev. Engl. Stud., 5, pp. 1–11. 1929.

6988 Roeder (Fritz). Neue Beiträge zur Erziehung der angelsächsischen adeligen Jugend. Festschrift für L. Morsbach, p. 625. 1913.

6989 —— Ueber die Erziehung der vornehmen angelsächsischen Jugend im fremden Häusern. pp. iv, 26. 8° Halle, 1910.

6990 Roesler (Margarete). Erziehung in England vor der normannischen Eroberung. [A supplement to Roeder (F.) **6989**. i. Weltliche Erziehung der Angelsachsen : ii. König Alfred : iii. Geistliche Erziehung, (1) Iona und Lindisfarne, (2) Malmesbury, (3) Wearmouth und Yarrow, (4) St. Augustine bei Canterbury, (5) Frauenklöster, (6) Kathedralschule zu York, (7) Die Klöster zur Zeit der Benediktinerreform.] Engl. Studien, 48, pp. 1–114. 1914.

6991 Roger (Maurice). L'enseignement des lettres classiques d'Ausone à Alcuin. Introduction à l'histoire des écoles carolingiennes. pp. xviii, 457. 8° Paris, 1905. [Gross, 1617a. ' On the Irish schools and the work of Aldhelm, Bede, Boniface, and Alcuin.']

6992 Slover (Clark Harris). Glastonbury abbey and the fusing of English literary culture. [' Contact with the cultural currents of Irish, Welsh, Anglo-Saxon, and Norman life.'] Speculum, 10, pp. 147–60. 1935.

6993 Stefánsson (Jón). Western influence on the earliest Viking settlers. Saga-Book V.C., 5, pp. 288–96. 1908.

6994 Wright (Thomas). An essay on the state of literature and learning under the Anglo-Saxons. pp. 112. 8° London, 1839.

6995 Wuelker (Richard). Grundriss zur Geschichte der angelsächsischen Litteratur. pp. xii, 532. 8° Leipzig, 1885. [Pp. 387–451, König Ælfred und sein Kreis : pp. 452–83, Die beiden Ælfric und Wulfstan : pp. 484–99, Geistliche Prosa : pp. 506–11, Mathematisch-naturwissenschaftliche Werke.]

6996 Wulf (Maurice de). History of mediaeval philosophy. Translated by Ernest C. Messenger. 3rd edition. Vol. 1. pp. xiv, 317. 8° London, 1935. [Bede, Alcuin, Lanfranc.]

§ b. Celtic

6997 [Anon.] Civilization and arts in ancient Ireland. Irish Eccles. Rec., 5, pp. 322–31, 349–60 ; 6, pp. 8–18. 1868.

6998 Arbois de Jubainville (Marie Henry d '). Les bardes. [Pp. 234–42, Les bardes d'Irlande.] Rev. archéol., N.S. 44, pp. 225–42. 1882.

6999 —— Les bardes en Irelande et dans le pays de Galles. Rev. hist., 8, pp. 1–9. 1878.

7000 Berardis (Vincenzo). Italy and Ireland in the Middle Ages. pp. 227. 8° Dublin, 1950. [Pp. 28–163 : St. Patrick, Irish classical culture (monastic schools), influence of Irish illuminative art in Italy, Columbanus and Bobbio, Irish saints and scholars in Italy, centres of expansion of Irish monasticism (Sedulius, etc.), Donough (son of Brian Boru) in Rome.]

7001 Cahill (E.). Irish in the early Middle Ages. [Monastic schools ; students ; curriculum, libraries, etc.] Irish Eccles. Rec., 5th S. 46, pp. 363–76. 1935.

7002 Corcoran (Timothy). Ireland and Pavia : 825–1925. Studies, 14, pp. 595–610. 1925.

7003 Cubbon (William). Early schools and scholarship in Mann. [Pp. 106–12, The Celtic period : the coming of the Norsemen : the scholarship of the monks : scholarship of the crosses, etc.] I.O.M., N.H. and Antiq. Soc., Proc., N.S. 3 (1925–26), pp. 106–29. 1927.

7004 Esposito (Mario). The knowledge of Greek in Ireland during the Middle Ages. Studies, 1, pp. 665–83. 1912.

7005 —— The Latin writers of mediaeval Ireland. [List of writers, 5th–12th c., and their works. *See also* **7007** and **7012**.] Hermathena, 14, pp. 519–29 : 15, pp. 353–64. 1907–09.

7006 —— Notes on Latin learning and literature in medieval Ireland. [5th c. —.] *Same jnl.*, 20, pp. 225–60 : 22, pp. 253–71 : 23, pp. 221–49 : 24, pp. 120–65 : 25 (no. 50), pp. 139–83. 1930–37.

7007 Esposito (Mario). Notes (Some further notes) on mediaeval Hiberno-Latin and Hiberno-French literature. [Supplementary to 7005.] *Same jnl.*, 16, pp. 58–72, 325–33. 1910–11.

7008 Flood (William Henry Grattan). The university of Lismore. [Founded by St. Carthage, early 7th c.] J. Waterford Archaeol. Soc., 5, pp. 3–20. 1899.

7009 Flower (Robin Ernest William). The Irish tradition. pp. 173. 8° Oxford, 1947.

7009a Fox (*Sir* Cyril). The personality of Britain : its influence on inhabitant and invader in prehistoric and early historic times. 4th edition, revised. *National Museum of Wales.* pp. 99, + maps. 4° Cardiff, 1943.

7010 Fryer (Alfred Cooper). Llantwit Major : a fifth century university. pp. x, 125, + 7 plates. 8° London, 1893. [St. Illtyd (teacher), St. Samson of Dol and Armorican missionaries (students).]

7011 Gougaud (Louis). Modern research, with special reference to early Irish ecclesiastical history. pp. 58. 8° Dublin, 1929. [Pp. 5–18, the Irish monasteries of the early Middle Ages, centres of production and store houses of original documents which constitute the materials for modern historical research.]

7012 —— and Esposito (Mario). Notes on the Latin writers of mediaeval Ireland. [5th–9th c. Supplementary to 7005 and 7007.] Irish Theol. Q., 4, pp. 57–65, 181–85. 1909.

7013 Graham (Hugh). The early Irish monastic schools. A study of Ireland's contribution to early medieval culture. pp. xvi, 206. 8° Dublin, 1923.

7014 —— Irish monks and the transmission of learning. Cath. Hist. Rev., 11 (N.S. 5), pp. 431–42. 1925.

7015 Gundersen (Borghild). Irish contributions to Norwegian Viking-culture. [Art, etc.] Irish Eccles. Rec., 5th S. 70, pp. 1063–67. 1948.

7016 Hanson (William George). The early monastic schools of Ireland : their missionaries, saints and scholars. Four lectures. pp. xi, 135. 8° Cambridge,

1927. [i. The schools : ii. St. Columban and his contemporaries : iii. Irish scholars of the 8th and 9th c. : iv. John Scotus Erigena.]

7017 Hayes (J. P.). The ancient school of Cork. [Loch Eirche, founded in 610 by St. Finn Barr, 1st bp. of Cork. With annals 610–1172.] J. Cork Hist. Soc., 2nd S. 1, pp. 369–77. 1895.

7018 Healy (John), *abp. of Tuam*. Ancient schools and scholars. From the time of St. Patrick to the Anglo-Norman invasion. 4th edition. pp. 652 + maps. 8° Dublin, 1902.

7019 —— Insula sanctorum et doctorum, or Ireland's ancient schools and scholars. pp. xviii, 638. 8° Dublin, 1890.
—— 4th edition. 8° Dublin, 1902. [Gross, 1614a. Kenney, 1, p. 288 : 'untrustworthy combination of romance and pseudo-criticism.']

7020 Henry (Françoise) and Ó Riordáin (Sean Pádraig). Irish culture in the seventh century. (Part 2 : a note on the archaeological evidence). Studies, 37, pp. 267–82. 1948.

7021 Hull (Eleanor). The Gael and the Gall : notes on the social condition of Ireland during the Norse period. Saga-Book V. C., 5, pp. 362–92. 1908.

7022 Hull (Vernam Edward). The wise sayings of Flann Fína (Aldfrith, king of Northumbria). [With text of 24 proverbs in Irish and in translation : edited from Yellow Book of Lecan, with variants from 4 other mss.] Speculum, 4, pp. 95–102. 1929.

7023 Jones (T. Gwynn). Bardism and romance, a study of the Welsh literary tradition. [i. Legal organisation of the literary classes : ii. Historical evidence : iii. Literary evidence.] Trans. Hon. Soc. Cymm., 1913–14, pp. 205–310. 1915.

7024 Lach-Szyrma (Wladyslaw Somerville). The ancient university of Britain. [i.e. that of St. Iltyd at Llaniltyd Fawr.] J. Brit. Archaeol. Assoc., 56 (N.S. 6), pp. 315–23. 1900.

7025 Lee (Timothy). Ancient Irish schools. Irish Eccles Rec., 3rd S. 6, pp. 249–57. 1885.

7026 Lindsay (Thomas Martin). Notes on education in Scotland in early days. 1.—To the wars of the Bruce succession. [Work of the Celtic monasteries, etc.] Trans. Glagow Archaeol. Soc., N.S. 1, pp. 13–31. 1890.

7027 Mackenzie (Donald A.). Phases of ancient Celtic civilization. [Picts, etc.] Trans. Gaelic Soc. Inverness, 33 (1925–27), pp. 225–45. 1932.

7028 MacNeill (Eoin). Beginnings of Latin culture in Ireland. Studies, 20, pp. 39–48, 449–60. 1931.

7029 Meyer (Kuno). Learning in Ireland in the fifth century and the transmission of letters. A lecture delivered before the School of Irish Learning . . . 1912. pp. 29. 8° Dublin, 1913.

7030 Moran (Patrick Francis) *cardinal, bp. of Ossory*. Irish civilization before the Anglo-Norman invasion. [Temp. Brian Borumha.] Irish Eccles. Rec., 3rd S. 1, pp. 57–77. 1880.

7031 Ryan (John). Irish learning in the seventh century. J. Roy. Soc. Antiq. Ireland, 80, pp. 164–71. 1950.

7032 Schlauch (Margaret). On Conall Corc and the relations of old Ireland with the Orient. J. Celtic Stud., 1, pp. 152–66. 1950.

7033 Stokes (George Thomas). On the knowledge of Greek in Ireland between A.D. 500 and 900. Proc. R.I.A., 3rd S. 2, pp. 187–202. 1893.

7034 Vendryes (Joseph). La connaissance du grec en Irlande du début du Moyen Âge. Rev. études grecques, 33, pp. 53–55. 1920.

7034a Waddell (Helen Jane). The wandering scholars. 7th edition [revised and enlarged]. pp. xxxi, 330. 8° London, 1932. —— *Pelican Books*. pp. 320. 8° Harmondsworth, 1954. [Chap. 2, Fortunatus to Sedulius of Liége : Chap. 3, 10th c.]

7035 Williams (Mary). Life in Wales in mediaeval times. [As depicted in the Mabinogion.] Trans. Hon. Soc. Cymm., 1914–15, pp. 136–94. 1916.

7036 Zimmer (Heinrich). The Irish element in mediaeval culture. Translated by J. L. Edmands. pp. vii, 139. 12° New York and London, 1891.

7037 —— Ueber die Bedeutung des irischen Elements für die mittelalterliche Cultur. Preuss. Jahrbücher, 59, pp. 27–59. 1887.

109. ANGLO-SAXON AND CELTIC SCHOLARS ON THE CONTINENT

§ *a*. **General and Miscellaneous**

7038 Born (Lester K.). The specula principis of the Carolingian renaissance. [Pp. 589–92, Alcuin : pp. 598–603, Sedulius Scotus.] Revue belge de Philol., 12, pp. 583–612. 1933.

7039 Boyer (Blanche B.). Insular contribution to medieval literary tradition on the continent. [Output of A.–S. and Irish scribes.] Class. Philol., 42, pp. 209–22. 1947.

7040 Clark (James Midgley). The abbey of St. Gall as a centre of literature and art. pp. vi, 322. 8° Cambridge, 1926. [Kenney, 1, pp. 206, 594. ' Gives special attention to Irish influences '. Its library, pp. 28 *et seq*.]

7041 Esposito (Mario). Dicuil, an Irish monk in the ninth century. [Kenney, 1, p. 545.] Dublin Rev., 137, pp. 327–37. 1905.

7042 —— Dungallus, ' praecipuus Scottorum '. J. Theol. Stud., 33, pp. 119–31. 1932.

7043 —— An Irish teacher at the Carolingian court : Dicuil. Studies, 3, pp. 651–76. 1914.

7043a Hauréau (Jean Barthélemy). Charlemagne et sa cour. (742–814). 5e édition. pp. 230. 12° Paris, 1880.

7044 Healy (John) *abp. of Tuam*. Ancient Irish scholars. Dicuil the geographer. [9th c.] Irish Eccles. Rec., 3rd S. 10, pp. 203–13. 1889.

7045 —— Dungal. [Irishman in France, 9th c.] *Same jnl.*, 3rd S. 3, pp. 296–309. 1882.

7046 Laistner (Max Ludwig Wolfram). The survival of Greek in western Europe in the Carolingian age. History, N.S. 9, pp. 177–87. 1924.

7047 Lehmann (Paul). The Benedictine Order and the transmission of the literature of ancient Rome in the Middle Ages. [Alcuin, etc.] Downside Rev.,71, pp. 407–21. 1953.

7048 Letronne (Jean Antoine). Recherches géographiques et critiques sur le livre De mensura orbis terrae, composé en Irlande au commencement du IXe siècle par Dicuil, suivies du texte restitué. 2 pt. 8° Paris, 1814.

7049 Martinus, *Hiberniensis. For* Martinus, of Laon [9th c.], *see* Kenney, 1, pp. 589–94.

7050 Meier (Gabriel). Geschichte der Schule von St. Gallen im Mittelalter. Jahrb. schweiz. Gesch., 10, pp. 35–128. 1885.

7051 Pfleger (Luzian). Beiträge zur Geschichte und Predigt und des religiösen Volksunterrichts im Elsass während des Mittelalters. Hist. Jh., 38, pp. 661–83. 1917.

7052 Schiaparelli (Luigi). Influenza straniere nella scrittura italiana dei secoli vii e ix. *Studi e testi*, 47. pp. 72, + 4 plates. 8° Roma, 1927.

7053 Strecker (Karl). Ein neuer Dungal? [? 4 persons of that name.] Zeit. roman. Phil., 41, pp. 566–73. 1921.

7054 Traube (Ludwig). Dungali. [i. Dungal reclusus in S. Denis : ii. Lehrer in Pavia : iii. Der Genosse des Sedulius : iv. Mönch von Bobbio.] Abh. bay. Akad. Wiss., Philos.-philol. Kl., 19, pp. 332–37. 1891.

7055 Turner (William). Irish teachers in the Carolingian revival of learning. [Kenney, 1, p. 530.] Cath. Univ. Bull., 13, pp. 382–99, 562–81. 1907.

7056 Zimmer (Heinrich). Über die Bedeutung des irischer Elemente für die mittelalterliche Kultur. Preuss. Jahrbücher, 59, pp. 27–59. 1887.

§ *b.* Alcuin

(735–804. See also F. W. Bateson : Cambridge Bibliography of English literature, vol. 1, pp. 106–07. 1940.)

7057 Alcuin. Un opusculo inedito di Alcuino. *Ottaviano* (*Carmelo*) : *Testi medioevali inediti* : *Alcuino, etc. pp.* 234. *Fontes Ambrosiani*, 3, *pp.* 1–18. 4° Firenze, 1933. [MS. S. 17. Sup. of the Ambrosian Library, Milan, known as Alcuini opusculum interrogationum.]

7058 —— The Rhetoric of Alcuin and Charlemagne. A translation, with an introduction, the Latin text, and notes, by Wilbur Samuel Howell. *Princeton Studies in English*, 23. pp. ix, 175. 8° Princeton, Oxford, 1941.

7059 Assmann (Bruno). Übersetzung von Alcuin's De virtutibus et vitiis liber. Ad Widonem comitem. [A.–S. and Latin texts.] Anglia, 11, pp. 371–91. 1889.

7060 Boas (Marcus). Alcuin and Cato. pp. 60. 8° Leiden, 1937. [With the text of the Praecepta vivendi per singulos versos quae monastica dicuntur, sometimes attributed to A., and a discussion of their relation to the Disticha of Dionysius Cato.]

7061 Browne (George Forrest) *bp. of Bristol.* Alcuin of York. pp. vii, 329. 8° London, 1908. [Gross, p. 319.]

7062 Buxton (Etheldreda Mary Wilmot). Alcuin. pp. 222. 8° London, 1922.

7063 Cabrol (Fernand). Les écrits liturgiques d'Alcuin. Rev. d'hist. ecclés., 19, pp. 507–21. 1923.

7064 Duckett (Eleanor Shipley). Alcuin, friend of Charlemagne : his life and his work. pp. xii, 337. 8° New York, 1951.

7065 Duemmler (Ernst). Alchuinstudien. [Kenney, 1, p. 534.] Sitzungsb. preuss. Akad. Wiss., 27, pp. 495–523. 1891.

7066 —— Zur Lebensgeschichte Alchvins. [Gross, 1624 : Kenney, 1, p. 534.] Neues Archiv, 18, pp. 51–70. 1893.

7067 Dupuy (Achille). Alcuin et l'école de Saint-Martin de Tours. 8° Tours, 1876.

7068 Flom (George Tobias) *ed.* Codex AM. 619 quarto ... containing ... Alcuin's De virtutibus et vitiis. *Univ. Illinois Studies in Language and Literature*, 14. *iv.* pp. 240. 8° Urbana, 1929. [Pp. 53–80, + 2 plates, Alcuin.]

7069 Frey (Joseph). De Alcuini arte grammatica commentatio. 1886.

7070 Ganshof (François Louis). La révision de le Bible par Alcuin. *Bibliothèque d'Humanisme et Renaissance, Travaux et documents*, 9. 8° Genève, 1947.

7071 Gaskoin (Charles Jacinth Bellairs). Alcuin, his life and his work. pp. 298. 8° London, 1904. [Gross, p. 319.]

7072 Hamelin (F.). Essai sur la vie et les ouvrages d'Alcuin. *Thèse, etc.* pp. 136. 8° Rennes, 1873.

7073 Jones (Thomas) [Bibliothecar. Chetham., *pseud.*]. A general literary index: index of authors : Alcuin. [Short bibliography of his Letters, with remarks.] N. and Q., 4th S. 3, pp. 230–31. 1869.

7074 Kleinclausz (Arthur). Alcuin. *Annales de l'Université de Lyon.* 3. *série, lettres*, 15. pp. 317. 8° Paris, 1948. [Pp. 18–28, La culture anglo-saxon au viiie siècle. L'école de York, etc.]

7075 Kowalski-Fahrun (Herta). Alkuin und der althochdeutsche Isidor. P.B.B., 47, pp. 312–24. 1923.

7076 Laforêt (Jean Baptiste). Alcuin, restaurateur des sciences en occident sous Charlemagne. *Diss.* pp. 254. 8° Louvain, 1851.

7077 —— Histoire d'Alcuin, moine anglo-saxon, natif d'York, restaurateur des sciences en Occident sous Charlemagne. 8° Namur, 1898. [Gross, 1625.]

7078 Liebermann (Felix). Ein Brief Alchwines an Offa von Mercien. Archiv Stud. neueren Spr., Bd. 146, pp. 115–16. 1923.

7079 Lietzmann (Hans). Handschriftliches zu Alkuins Ausgabe und Sacramentarium. Jahrbuch Liturgiewiss., 1925, pp. 68– . 1925.

7080 Long (Omera F.). The attitude of Alcuin towards Vergil. Studies in honor of B. L. Gildersleeve, pp. 377 *et seq.* 1902.

7081 Lorentz (Friedrich). Alcuins Leben. Ein Beitrag zur Staats-Kirchen- und Culturgeschichte des Karolinischen Zeit. pp. x, 278. 8° Halle, 1829. — Life of Alcuin ... translated ... by Jane M. Slee. pp. vi, 284. 8° London, 1837. [Gross, 1626.]

7082 Monnier (Francis). Alcuin, et son influence ... chez les Franks, avec des fragments d'un commentaire inédit d'Alcuin sur saint Matthieu. 8° Paris, 1853. — 2e édition. Alcuin et Charlemagne. pp. iv, 376. 8° Paris, 1863. [Gross, 1627.]

7083 Morin (Germain). L'homéliaire d'Alcuin rétrouvé. Rev. Bénédictine, 9, pp. 491–97. 1892.

7084 —— Un rédaction inédite de la préface au supplément du Comes d'Alcuin. *Same jnl.*, 29, pp. 341–48. 1912.

7085 Mullinger (James Bass). The schools of Charles the Great and the restoration of education in the ninth century. 8° London, 1877. [Gross, 1628. Ch. 1–2, Alcuin.]

7086 Papetti (M.). Intorno ai viaggi di Alcuino in Italia. Sophia, 3, pp. 216–18. 1936.

7087 Ramackers (Johannes). Eine unbekannte Handschrift der Alcuvīnbriefe. Neues Archiv, 50, pp. 425–28. 1935.

7087a Rand (Edward Kennard). A preliminary study of Alcuin's Bible. Cambridge, Mass., 1931.

7088 Sanford (Eva Matthews). Alcuin and the Classics. Class. J., 20, pp. 526–33. 1925.

7089 Schoenfelder ( ) *Oberlehrer in Zittau.* Alcuin. pp. 42. 4° Zittau, 1873.

7090 Seydl (Ernst). Alkuins Psychologie. [Analyse der Schrift De animae ratione, etc.] Jahrbuch Philos., 25, pp. 34–55. 1911.

7091 Sickel (Theodor). Alcuinstudien. [Kenney, 1, p. 534.] Sitzungsb. Akad. Wiss. Wien, 79, pp. 461–550. 1875.

7092 Strecker (Karl). Drei Rhythmen Alkuins. Neues Archiv, 43, pp. 386–93. 1922.

7093 Toyne (Stanley Mease). Alcuin and the school of York. *York minster historical tracts*, 6. pp. 16. 8° *n.p.*, [192–].

7094 Wells (Benjamin W.). Alcuin the teacher. Constructive Q., 7, pp. 531–52. 1919.

7095 Werner (Karl). Alcuin und sein Jahrhundert. Ein Beitrag zur christlich theologischen Literaturgeschichte. Neue Ausgabe. pp. xii, 415. 8° Wien, 1881. [Gross, 1629.]

7096 West (Andrew Fleming). Alcuin and the rise of the Christian schools. *The great educators*, 3. pp. 205. 8° New York, 1893 [1892]. [Gross, 1630. Pp. 197–98, bibliography.]

7097 Wilmart (André). Le lectionnaire d'Alcuin. Ephemerides Liturgicae, 51, pp. 136–97. 1937.

§ *c.* **Johannes Scotus Erigena**

(D. 886. For Johannes Scotus and the Irish colony of Laon and Rheims, *see* Kenney, 1, pp. 569–89. *See also* Bateson, Cambridge Bibliography of English Literature, vol. 1, pp. 109–10 : British Museum Catalogue, 28, col. 42–43 : Chevalier, p. 2491 : Geyer (**6965**), pp. 166, 693–94.)

7098 Albanese (Clodomiro). Il pensiero di Giovanni Eriugena. pp. 412. 8° Messina, 1929.

7099 Bett (Henry). Johannes Scotus Erigena. A study in mediaeval philosophy. pp. 204. 8° Cambridge, 1925.

7100 Bonafede (G.). Saggi sui pensiero de Scoto Eriugena. Atti Acad. Sci. Lett. e Arti di Palermo, ser. 4, 10 ii, Lettere, pp. 19–155. 1951.

7101 Cappuyns (Maïeul). Jean Scot Érigène, sa vie, son oeuvre, sa pensée. *Universitas Catholica Lovaniensis. Dissertationes*, ser. 2, 26. pp. xxiii, 410. 8° Louvain, Paris, 1933.

7102 Doerries (Hermann). Zur Geschichte der Mystik. Erigena und der Neuplatonismus. pp. 122. 8° Tübingen, 1925.

7103 Draeseke (Johannes). Johannes Scotus Erigena und dessen Gewährsmänner in seinem Werke De divisione naturae libri V. *Studien zur Geschichte der Theologie und der Kirche*, 9 *ii*. pp. 67. 8° Leipzig, 1902.

7104 Healy (John) *abp. of Tuam*. John Scotus Erigena. Irish Eccles. Rec., 3rd S. 1, pp. 3–18. 1880.

7105 Kletler (Paul). Johannes Eriugena. Eine Untersuchung über die Entstehung der mittelalterlichen Geistigkeit. Beiträge z. Kulturgesch. d. Mittelalters, 49, pp. 1–63. 1931.

7106 Labowsky (Lotte). A new version of Scotus Eriugena's commentary on Martianus Capella. Med. and Ren. Stud., 1, pp. 187–93. 1943.

7107 Pra (Mario dal). Scoto Eriugena. Secondo edizione. *Storia universale della filosofia*, 2. pp. 272. 8° Milano, 1951.

7108 Schneider (Arthur Carl August). Die Erkenntnislehre des Johannes Eriugena. *Schriften der Strassburger wissenschaftlichen Gesellschaft*, N.F. 3, 7. 2 Tl., 8° Berlin, 1921, 1923.

7109 Seul (W.). Die Gotteserkenntnis bei Joannes Scottus Eriugena unter Beruecksichtigung ihrer neoplatonischen und augustinischen Elemente. 8° Bonn, 1932.

7110 Techert (Marguerite). Le plotinisme dans la système de Jean Scot Erigène. Rev. néoscolastique de Philosophie, 29, pp. 28–68. 1927.

7111 Théry (P. G.). Scot Erigène, traducteur de Denys. Bull. du Cange, 4, pp. 185–278. 1931.

7112 Traube (Ludwig). Palaeographische Forschungen, Teil 5. Autographa des Johannes Scottus. Aus dem Nachlass herausgegeben von Edward Kennard Rand. pp. 12, + 12 plates. Abh. K. bay. Akad. Wiss., Philos.-Philol. Kl., 26 i. 1912.

§ *d.* **Sedulius Scotus**

(9th c. For Sedulius and his circle, *see* Kenney, 1, pp. 553–68.)

7113 Boyle (Patrick). Sedulius Scotus of Liège : an Irish scholar and poet of the ninth century. Irish Eccles. Rec., 5th S. 7, pp. 548–55. 1916.

7114 Green (Alice Stopford). Sedulius of Liège. J. Ivernian Soc., 6, pp. 231–34. 1914.

7115 Hellmann (Siegmund). Sedulius Scottus. . . . i. Liber de rectoribus Christianis. ii. Das Kollektaneum des Sedulius in dem Kodex Cusannus c. 14 nunc 37. iii. Sedulius und Pelagius. *Quellen und Untersuchungen zur lateinischen Philologie des Mittelalters*, i. 1. pp. xv, 203. 8° München, 1906.

7116 Pirenne (Henri). Sedulius de Liège. Mém. Acad. roy. Belg., Collection in 8°, 33, pp. 72, + facsimile. 1882.

7117 Traube (Ludwig). Sedulius Scottus. [i. Leben und Werke : ii. Von Sedulius und seinen irischen Genossen geschriebene Handschriften : iii. Kenntnis des Griechischen bei Iren zur Zeit Karl des Kahlen.] Abhand. philos.-philol. Cl., K. bayer. Akad. Wiss., 19, pp. 338–63. 1891.

§ *e*. **Virgilius, Bishop of Salzburg**

(Ferghil. Abbot of Aghaboe (Leix). Bishop of Salzburg from 755—or 767— till 784.)

7118 Healy (John) *abp. of Tuam*. St. Virgilius. Irish Eccles. Rec., 3rd S. 2, pp. 662–71. 1881.

7119 Krabbo (Hermann). Bischof Virgil von Salzburg und seine kosmologischen Ideen. [Kenney, 1, p. 523.] Mitth. Instit. österreich. Geschichtsforschung, 24, pp. 10–28. 1903.

7120 Laux (Johann Joseph) [George Metlake, *pseud*.]. St. Virgil the geometer. [Kenney, 1, p. 523.] Ecclesiastical Rev., 63, pp. 13–21. 1920.

7121 Loew (Heinz). Ein literarische Widersacher des Bonifatius : Virgil von Salzburg und die Kosmographie des Aethicus Ister. Akad. Wiss. Mainz, Abhandl. Geistes-u. Socialwiss. Kl., 2 (Nr. 11), pp. 899–988. 1951.

7122 Van der Linden (H.). Virgile de Salzbourg et les théories cosmographiques au viiie siècle. [Kenney, 1, p. 523.] Bull. Acad. roy. Belgique, Cl. lettres, 1914, pp. 163–87. 1914.

Z

110. LIBRARIES, SCRIPTORIA, MANUSCRIPTS

§ *a*. **Anglo-Saxon and Celtic in the British Isles**

7123 Bressie (Ramona). Libraries of the British Isles in the Anglo-Saxon period. The medieval library, by James Westfall Thompson, pp. 102–25. 1939.

7123a British Museum. A catalogue of the Harleian manuscripts. 4 vol. fol. [London], 1808–12.

7123b British Museum. A catalogue of the manuscripts in the Cottonian Library. pp. xvi, 618 + index. fol. [London], 1802.

7123c British Museum. Catalogue of western manuscripts in the old royal and king's collections, by Sir George F. Warner and Julius P. Gilson. 4 vol. fol. London, 1921.

7124 Clemoes (Peter). Liturgical influence on punctuation in late Old English and early Middle English manuscripts. Occas. Papers., Dept. A.-S., Camb., 1. pp. 22. 1952.

7125 Edmonds ( ) *Canon of Exeter*. The formation and fortunes of Exeter cathedral library. [Bishop Leofric's books, etc.] Rept. and Trans. Devon. Assoc., 31, pp. 25–50. 1899.

7126 Floyer (John K.). A thousand years of a cathedral library : being an account of the formation of the Worcester Cathedral library. Reliquary, 7, pp. 11–26. 1901.

7127 Gougaud (Louis). The remains of ancient Irish monastic libraries. Essays presented to Eoin MacNeill, pp. 319–34. 1940.

7128 —— Les scribes monastiques d'Irlande au travail. Rev. d'Hist. eccl., 27, pp. 293–306. 1931.

7129 Grierson (Philip). Les livres de l'abbé Seiwold de Bath. [11th c. 31 vols. : ?part of library of St. Peter at Bath, taken by Seiwold to continent when deprived by Norman conquest.] Rev. Bénédictine, 52, pp. 96–114. 1940.

7130 Harrsen (Meta). The countess Judith of Flanders and the library of Weingarten abbey. [Wife of Tostig, earl of Northumbria, and collector of mss. Plates are of mss. of Winchester School, etc.] Papers Bib. Soc. Amer., 24, pp. 1–12, + 8 plates. 1930.

7131 Haverfield (Francis John). The library of Æthelstan, the half-king. [From an empty page in MS. Cotton Domitian 1 (55b).] Academy, 26, p. 32. 1884.

7132 Hepple (Richard B.). Early Northumbrian libraries. [Lindisfarne, Hexham, Wearmouth and Jarrow, York.] Archaeol. Æl., 3rd S. 14, pp. 92–106, + 2 plates. 1917.

7133 —— The monastic school of Jarrow. History, N.S. 7, pp. 92–102. 1922.

7134 Hughes (Hubert David). A history of Durham cathedral library. pp. xlii, 134, + 24 plates, and plan. 8° Durham, 1925. [Pp. xxxvi–xlii, 12–14, 20–21, A.–S. mss., etc. : pp. 69–86, + 1 plate, St. Cuthbert's relics.]

7135 J. (C. D.). Anglo-Saxon mss. in Durham cathedral library. Ecclesiologist, 10, pp. 313–23. 1850.

7136 James (Montague Rhodes). The ancient libraries of Canterbury and Dover. The catalogues. . . . With an introduction and identifications of the extant remains. pp. xcv, 552. 8° Cambridge, 1903. [Gross, 787a.]

7137 —— Catalogue of manuscripts in the library of Corpus Christi college, Cambridge. 2 vol. 8° Cambridge, 1912.

7138 —— Catalogue of manuscripts in the library of Pembroke college, Cambridge. pp. xl, 314. 8° Cambridge, 1905.

7139 —— Lists of manuscripts formerly in Peterborough abbey library. With preface and identifications. Bibliog. Soc. Trans., Supp., 5. pp. 104. 8° Oxford, 1926. [Pp. 19–20, Æthelwold's (20) gifts, c. 984.]

7140 Ker (Neil Ripley). Aldred the scribe. [Writer of gloss to the Lindisfarne Gospels.] Essays and Studies (English Assocn.), 28, pp. 7–12. 1942.

7141 Kluge (Friedrich). AE. *gaerdas, bócstafas, bóc*. Z.f.d.A., 34, pp. 210–13. 1890.

7142 Laistner (Max Ludwig Wolfram). The library of the Venerable Bede. Bede, 12th centenary essays, ed. A. H. Thompson. pp. 237–66. 1935.

7143 O'Donovan (John). The lost and missing Irish manuscripts. Ulster J. Archaeol., 8, pp. 16–28. 1860.

7144 Phillips (David Rhys). The romantic history of the monastic libraries of Wales from the fifth to the sixteenth centuries (Celtic and mediaeval periods.) Library Assoc. Rec., 14, pp. 288–316. 1912.

7145 Quigley (E. J.). The Bible and Ireland. [Its introduction by St. Patrick, and work on it by Irish scribes.] Irish Eccles. Rec., 5th S. 35, pp. 449–73. 1930.

7146 Ross (Marvin Chauncey). An eleventh-century English book cover. [In Pierpont Morgan Library.] Art Bull., 22, pp. 83–85, + 2 plates. 1940.

7147 Sauvage (Eugène Paul Marie). Notes sur les manuscrits anglo-saxons et les manuscrits de Jumièges conservés à la bibliothèque de Rouen.

7148 Way (Albert). The gifts of Æthelwold, bishop of Winchester (A.D. 963–984), to the monastery of Peterborough. [Pp. 360–65, ' Notes on (20) books given by bishop Æthelwold to Peterborough.'] Archaeol. J., 20, pp. 355–66. 1863.

7149 Wright (Thomas). A leaden tablet, or book-cover, bearing an Anglo-Saxon inscription, in the possession of Lord Londesborough. [Opening of preface to first collection of Ælfric's Homilies. ? sample of A.–S. binding.] Proc. Soc. Antiq., 2, pp. 104–05. 1850.

7150 —— On bishop Leofric's library [Exeter]. J. Brit. Archaeol. Assoc., 18, pp. 220–24. 1862.

§ *b*. On the Continent
i. Bobbio

(Stocked originally by St. Columban *q.v.* 74 § *b*. Books brought together by Cassiodorus (6th c.). 29 books bequeathed to it by Dungal. For the Bobbio Missal, *see* 79 § *a*.)

7151 **Becker** (Gustavus). Catalogi bibliothecarum antiqui. pp. iv, 329. 8° Bonnae, 1885. [Kenney, 1, pp. 516, 599. Bobbio, no. xxxii, pp. 64–73 ; St. Gallen, no. xxii, pp. 43–53.]

7152 **Beer** (Rudolf). Bemerkungen über den ältesten Handschriften bestand des Klosters Bobbio. [Kenney, 1, p. 515.] Anzeiger K. Akad. Wiss. Wien, phil.-hist. Cl., 48, pp. 78–104. 1911.

7153 **Bobbio**, *monastery library*. Collezione paleografica Bobbiese. [In Univ. Library, Turin. 90 collotype plates.] Vol. 1, 2 pt. fol. Milano, 1907.

7154 **Cipolla** (Carlo) *count*. Attorno alle antiche biblioteche di Bobbio. [La biblioteca dell'abbazia di Bobbio al principio del sec. xviii, etc.] Riv. stor. benedettina, 3, pp. 561–80. 1908.

7155 —— —— and **Buzzi** (Guilio). Codice diplomatico del monasterio di San Colombano di Bobbio fino all' anno 1208. *Fonti per la storia d'Italia*, 52–54. 3 vol. 8° Roma, 1918. [Kenney, 1, p. 515. Corrections to vol. 1–2 *in* Buzzi (G.), Studi Bobbiesi, Roma, 1918.]

7156 **Collura** (Paolo). Studi palaeografici. La precarolina e la carolina a Bobbio. Fontes Ambrosiani, 22, pp. 1–98, 183–207. 1943.

7157 **Esposito** (Mario). The ancient Bobbio catalogue. [10th c. Discovered by Muratori on his visit in 1714.] J. Theol. Stud., 32, pp. 337–44. 1931.

7158 **Gebhardt** (Oscar von). Ein Bücherfund in Bobbio. [Kenney, 1, p. 85, note 360.] Cent. Bibliothekswesen, 5, pp. 343–64, 383–431, 538. 1888.

7159 **Gottlieb** (Theodor). Über Handschriften aus Bobbio. [Kenney, 1, p. 85, note 360.] *Same jnl.*, 4, pp. 442–463, 568 (Druckfehler). 1887.

7160 **Lejay** (Paul). Bobbio et la bibliothèque de Cassiodore. Bull. anc. lit. et archéol. Chrét., 3, pp. 265–69. 1913.

7161 **Lugnano** (Placido). Il codice diplomatico del monastero di S. Colombano di Bobbio. Riv. stor. benedettina, 11, pp. 173–84. 1916.

7162 **Mercati** (Giovanni) *cardinal*. M. Tulli Ciceronis, De re publica e codice rescripto Vaticano latino 5757. Prolegomena de fatis bibliothecae Monasterii S. Columbani Bobiensis e de codice ipso Vat. Lat. 5757. *Codices e Vaticanis selecti*, 23. 2 vol. fol. Romae, 1934. [From material collected by Cardinal Franz Ehrle.]

7163 **Muratori** (Lodovico Antonio). Antiquitates Italicae medii aevi. 6 vol. fol. Mediolani, 1738–42. [1, pp. 493–505 : Dissertatio 43, Bobbio Library catalogue (10th c.), attributed to Gerbert (Sylvester II) with list of c. 700 vols.]

7164 **Ottino** (Giuseppe). I codici Bobbiesi della Bibliotheca nationale di Torino indicati e descritti. pp. viii, 72. 8° Torino, 1890.

7165 **Peyron** (Amedeus). M. Tulli Ciceronis orationum . . . fragmenta inedita. . . . Idem praefatus est de bibliotheca Bobiensi, cuius inventarium anno 1861 confectum edidit atque illustravit. pp. xxxvii, 340, 228. 4° Stuttgardiae, 1824.

7166 —— M. Tulli Ciceronis orationum . . . fragmenta inedita. pp. lxxvi, 295. 8° Lipsiae, 1825. [Pp. iii–xxvii, De bibliotheca Bobiensi commentatio, also pp. 1–62. Kenney, 1, p. 85, note 36.]

7167 **Ratti** (Achille Ambrogio Damiano). [Pius XI, *Pope*]. Reliquie di antico codice bobbiese ritrovate. Miscellanea Ceriani (Bibl. Ambrosiana, Milano), pp. 789–810, + 4 plates. 1910.

7168 —— Le ultime vicende della biblioteca e dell' archivio di S. Columbano di Bobbio. pp. 43. 8° Milano, 1901. [Kenney, 1, p. 85, note 360.]

7169 **Sabbadini** (Remigio). Collezionc paleografica bobbiese, 1 : Codici bobbiesi della Biblioteca nazionale di Torino, con illustrazione di C. Cipolla. (Atlante di novanta tavole). 2 vol. fol. Milano, 1907. [= **7153**.]

7170 **Seebass** (Otto). Handschriften von Bobbio in den vatikanischen und ambrosianischen Bibliotheken. [Kenney, 1, p. 85, note 360.] Cent. Bibliothekswesen, 13, pp. 1–12, 57–79. 1896.

7171 Stokes (George Thomas). Ancient Celtic expositors. Columbanus and his library. Expositor, 3rd S. 9, pp. 460–72. 1889.

7172 Verrua (Pietro). Lo scrittorio di Bobbio. La Bibliofilia, 37, pp. 185–99. 1935.

ii. Swiss

(St. Gallen Library. Books of Irish bp. Marcus, uncle of Moengal, d. 871. Library transferred to Reichenau in 925 during an inroad of the Mongols : an equal number of books was returned. *See also* **7151.**)

7173 Bruckner (Albert) *ed*. Scriptoria medii aevi helvetica. 2 vol. fol. Genf, 1936–38. [With facsimiles.]

7174 Esposito (Mario). Hiberno-Latin manuscripts in the libraries of Switzerland. [i. Basel, Einsiedeln, Schaffhausen, St. Gallen, and Zürich (Kantonsbibliothek) : ii. Zürich (Stadtbibliothek) and Bern. Work of wandering Irish, 7th–10th c.] Proc. R.I.A., 28 c., pp. 62–95 : 30 c, pp. 1–14. 1910–12.

7175 Lehmann (Paul). Mittelalterliche Bibliothekskataloge Deutschlands und der Schweiz. München, 1918. [Kenney, 1, p. 594. Bd. 1, pp. 55–148, abbey of St. Gallen.]

7176 Loeffler (Karl). Die Sankt-Galler Schreibschule in der 2. Hälfte des viii. Jahrhunderts. Lindsay (W. M.) : Palaeographia Latina, 6, pp. 64, + 10 plates. (Univ. St. Andrews, pubn., 28.) 1929.

7177 Nigra (Costantino) *count*. Reliquie celtiche. 1. Il manoscritto irlandese di S. Gallo. pp. 55, + 3 plates. 4° Torino, 1872. [*No more published*. Second half of 9th c.]

7178 Scherrer (Gustav). St. Gallische Handschriften. In Auszügen herausgegeben von G.S. pp. 92. 8° St. Gallen, 1859.

7179 —— Verzeichniss der Handschriften der Stiftsbibliothek von St. Gallen. Halle, 1875. [Kenney, 1, p. 594.]

7180 Weidmann (Franz). Geschichte der Bibliothek von St. Gallen, seit ihrer Gründung um das Jahr 850 bis auf 1841. pp. iv, 493. 8° St. Gallen, 1841. [Kenney, 1, p. 207.]

iii. Other

7181 Bischoff (Bernhard). Südostdeutsche Schreibschulen und Bibliotheken in der Karolingerzeit. 1. pp. viii, 280. 8° Leipzig, 1940. [Hiberno-Latin, 9th–10th c.]

7182 Delisle (Léopold Victor). Mémoire sur l'école calligraphique de Tours au IXe siècle. pp. 32. [Kenney, 1, p. 654. Established by Alcuin, c. 800. Scribes English or Irish.] Mém. Acad. Inscr. et Belles Lettres, 32. 1885.

7183 Falk (Franz). Beiträge zur Rekonstruktion der alten Bibliotheca Fuldensis und Bibliotheca Laureshamensis. pp. 112. Zent. Bibliothekswesen, 26, Beiheft. 1902.

7184 Holder (Alfred) and **Preisandanz** (Karl). Die Reichenauer Handschriften. *Die Handschriften der grossherzoglich badischen Hof-und Landesbibliothek in Karlsruhe, Sekt.* 5–7. 3 vol. 8° Karlsruhe, 1906, 14, 18. [Kenney, 1, p. 86, note 363.]

7185 Lindsay (Wallace Martin). The (early) Lorsch scriptorium. [Pp. 30–33, MSS. of the Lorsch Library in A.-S. script.] Lindsay (W. M.) : Palaeographia Latina, 3, pp. 5–48, + 15 plates. (Univ. St. Andrews, pubn., 19). 1924.

7186 —— and **Lehmann** (Paul). The (early) Mayence scriptorium. Lindsay (W. M.) : Palaeographia Latina, 4, pp. 15–39, + 6 plates. (Univ. St. Andrews, pubn., 20). 1925.

7187 Leoffler (Karl). Die Fuldaer Klosterbibliothek. Zeit. Bücherfreunde, 1918–19, pp. 194–202. 1919.

7187a Rand (Edward Kennard). A survey of the manuscripts of Tours. *Mediaeval Academy of America*, 3. 2 vol. fol. Cambridge, Mass, 1929. [With plates (facsimiles). Period 2, the Irish at Tours : period 4, the reforms of Alcuin.]

111. INDIVIDUAL MANUSCRIPTS, ANGLO-SAXON

(See also Illuminations, **204**)

§ *a*. Codex Amiatinus

(Written at Jarrow or Monkwearmouth. Now in Laurentian Library, Florence.)

7188 Bible—*New Testament* : *Latin*. Codex Amiatinus. Novum Testamentum Latine interprete Hieronymo, ex celeberrimo Codice Amiatino . . . nunc primum edidit C. Tischendorf. . . . Accedit tabula lapidi incisa. 4° Lipsiae, 1854. [Reissue of edition of 1850.]

7189 Blum (Hans). Über den Codex Amiatinus und Cassiodors Bibliothek in Vivarium. Zent. Bibliothekswesen, 64, pp. 52–57. 1950.

7190 Boutflower (Douglas Samuel). More [10] leaves from an old Bible. [One of Ceolfrid's copies.] Antiq. Sunderland, 14, pp. 46–48. 1913.

7191 Chapman (John). The Codex Amiatinus and Cassiodorus. Rev. Bénédictine, 38, pp. 139–50. 1926.

7192 —— The Codex Amiatinus once more. *Same jnl.*, 40, pp. 130–33. 1928.

7193 Colgrave (Bertram). Two Jarrow bibles. [Ceolfrid's two copies.] Durham Univ. J., 30, pp. 208–09. 1937.

7194 Fowler (Joseph Thomas). The Codex Amiatinus at Jarrow or Wearmouth, cir. A.D. 700. *Same jnl.*, 7, pp. 153–55. 1887.

7195 Howorth (*Sir* Henry Hoyle). The Codex Amiatinus : its history and importance. Archaeol. J., 72, pp. 49–68. 1915.

7196 Low (John Low). The Codex Amiatinus : when and where written. pp. 13, iii. 8° Sunderland, 1903. *Reprinted from* Church Q. Rev., 25, pp. 435–48. 1888.

7197 —— St. Ceolfrid, abbot of Wearmouth and Jarrow, and the Amiatine Codex. [Summary of paper, and discussion.] Proc. Soc. Antiq. Newcastle, 2nd S. 3, pp. 51–52. 1887.

7198 Mercati (Angelo). Per la storia del codice Amiatino. Biblica, 3, pp. 324–28. 1922.

7199 Middlemiss (J. T.). A leaf from an old Bible. [From one of the two pandects of the same school as Codex Amiatinus. Given by William Greenwell, its finder, to British Museum.] Antiq. Sunderland, 12 (1911), pp. 13–18, + 1 plate. 1912.

7200 White (Henry Julian). The Codex Amiatinus and its birthplace. (Appendix, by W. Sanday, on the Italian origin of the Codex Amiatinus and the localizing of Italian MSS.). Studia Biblica et Ecclesiastica, 2, pp. 273–324. 1890.

7201 Whiting (Charles Edwin). A famous manuscript from the county of Durham. Durham Univ. J., 24, pp. 374–77. 1925.

7202 Wordsworth (John) *bp. of Salisbury*. The date and history of the great Latin Bible of Monte Amiata. Academy, 31, pp. 111–13. 1887.

§ *b*. Utrecht Psalter

(All aspects : ms. and its illuminations. Formerly MS. Cotton Claudius C. VII, but now in library of University of Utrecht. ?Written and illustrated at Reims c. 840 : deposited at St. Augustine's, Canterbury, and there copied, c. 1000 (B.M., MS., Harley 603). Second copy, 12th c. (Eadwine Psalter) at Trinity College, Cambridge.)

7203 [Anon.] The Urecht Psalter. [History and description of the ms. and its connection with the Athanasian Creed]. Church Q.R., 2, pp. 69–117. 1876.

7204 Benson (Gertrude R.). New light on the origin of the Utrecht Psalter. [Many references.] Art Bull., 13, pp. 13–79, + 29 plates. 1931.

7205 Bible—*Psalms*. Latin psalter in the University Library of Utrecht (formerly Cotton MS. Claudius C. VII) photographed and produced in facsimile [by the Palaeographical Society]. pp. 2, + 209 plates. large 4° London, 1874.

7206 Birch (Walter de Gray). The history, art, and palaeography of the . . . Utrecht Psalter. pp. v. xxiv, 318, + 3 plates. 8° London, 1876.

7207 Bond (*Sir* Edward Augustus) and 7 *others*. The Utrecht Psalter. Reports addressed to the trustees of the British Museum on the age of the manuscript, *etc.* pp. 14, + 3 facsimiles. fol. London, 1874. [? date : ? A.-S. artist of 9th c. copying 5th–6th c. drawings, added to 7th–8th c. text.]

7208 De Wald (Ernest Theodore) *ed.* The illustrations of the Utrecht Psalter. *Illustrated manuscripts of the Middle Ages*, 3. pp. 81, + 144 plates. fol. Oxford and Princeton, 1932. [With critical and descriptive text. A new facsimile to supplement that issued in London in 1875, and long out of print.]

7209 Durrieu (Paul). L'origine du manuscrit célèbre dit le Psautier d'Utrecht. *Mélanges* Julian Havet, pp. 639–57. 1895.

7210 Goldschmidt (Adolphe). Der Utrechtpsalter. Repertorium f. Kunstwissenschaft, 15, pp. 156–69. 1892.

7211 Hardy (*Sir* Thomas Duffus). The Athanasian creed in connexion with the Utrecht Psalter [= 1st report.] pp. 47, + 5 plates. fol. London, [1872]. [Dates ms. to 6th c.]

7212 —— Further report on the Utrecht Psalter, in answer to the eight reports [7207] made to the trustees of the British Museum and edited by the Dean of Westminster [A. P. Stanley]. fol. London, [1874]. [Suggestion that it was brought by queen Bertha to Reculver.]

7213 Lowe (Elias Avery). The uncial Gospel leaves attached to the Utrecht Psalter. Art Bull., 34, pp. 237–38, + 2 plates. 1952.

7214 Tietze-Cohrat (Erika). Der Utrecht-Psalter. *Kunst in Holland*, 3. pp. 17, + 10 plates. 8° Wien, 1921.

7215 Tikkanen (Johan Jakob). Abenländische Psalterillustration der Utrecht-Psalter. *Die Psalterillustration im Mittelalter, Bd.* 1, (*Heft* 3), *pp.* 153–320. 4° Leipzig, 1900. [77 figures in text.]

§ *c.* Other Anglo-Saxon MSS.

(*See also* Illuminations, **204**. For MSS. of Bede, *see* **66** §*b. v.*)

7216 Bateson (Mary). A Worcester Cathedral book of ecclesiastical collections, made c. 1000 A.D. [M.S. C.C.C.C. 265]. E.H.R., 10, pp. 712–31. 1895.

7216a Campbell (Alistair) *ed.* The Tollemache Orosius (British Museum Additional manuscript 47967). *Early English manuscripts in facsimile*, eds. B. *Colgrave, Kemp Malone, Knud Schibsbye*, 3. pp. 27, + 173 plates. 4° Copenhagen, 1952. [? early 10th c.]

7217 Craster (*Sir* Herbert Henry Edmund). The Laudian Acts. [Acts, codex E (Ms. Laud Greek 39; O.C. 1119). 7th c. Brought to England by Theodore in 668 and used by Bede, c. 731–5, for his Expositio Retractata of the Acts.] Bodl. Q.R., 2, pp. 288–90. 1919.

7218 Durham, *Monastery.* Liber vitae ecclesiae Dunelmensis. A collotype facsimile of the original manuscript, with introductory essays and notes. Vol. 1, facsimile and general introduction. *Surtees Society*, 136. pp. xxviii, + 138 plates. 8° Durham, 1923.

7219 Exeter Book. The Exeter Book of Old English poetry. With introductory chapters by R. W. Chambers, Max Förster and Robin Flower. pp. 94, + 260 plates. fol. London, 1933. [i. The Exeter Book and its donor Leofric, by R. W. Chambers : ii. The donations of Leofric to Exeter, by Max Förster : v. General description of the manuscript, by Max Förster : vii. The script of the Exeter Book, by Robin Flower.]

7220 Flom (George Tobias). On the Old English herbal of Apuleius, Vitellius C. III. [On the ms.] J. Eng. and Germ. Phil., 40, pp. 29–37, + 1 plate. 1941.

7221 Foerster (Max). Il codice Vercellese con omelie e poesie in lingua anglosassone, *etc. Codices e Vaticanis selecti photypice expressi, series minor*, 3. pp. 71, + 274 plates (facsimiles). 4° Roma, 1913. [Description and provenance of the ms.]

7222 Gasquet (Francis Aidan) *cardinal* and **Bishop** (Edmund). The Bosworth Psalter. . . . With an appendix on the birth-date of Saint Dunstan, by L. A. St. L. Toke. pp. 189. 4° London, 1908. [Account of B.M., Addit. MS. 37517.]

7223 Gilson (Julius Parnell). Description of the Saxon manuscript of the Four Gospels in the library of York Minster. 4° York, 1925.

7224 Hoops (Johannes). Die Foliierung der Beowulf-Handschrift, [Cotton Vitellius A XV.]. Engl. Studien, 63, pp. 1–11. 1928.

7225 Hoskier (Herman Charles) *ed.* The Golden-Latin Gospels in the library of J. Pierpont Morgan (formerly known as the Hamilton Gospels and sometimes as King Henry the VIIIth's Gospels), now edited . . . with notes . . . and . . . 4 facsimiles, by H. C. H. pp. cxvi, 363, + 4 plates. fol. New York, 1910. [Thought by Wattenbach to be ms. executed for St. Wilfrid : Hoskier agrees as to date (c. 700) and English provenance.]

7226 Kenyon (*Sir* Frederic George). Our Bible and the ancient manuscripts. 4th edition, revised. pp. xii, 266, + 32 plates. 8° London, 1939. [Pp. 175–76, + plate 25, Codex Amiatinus : pp. 184–88, + plates 26 and 27, Lindisfarne Gospels, etc. : pp. 194–99, English ms. Bibles.]

7227 Kuhn (Sherman M.). The *Vespasian Psalter* [MS. Cotton Vesp. A I] and the Old English charter hands. Speculum, 18, pp. 458–83, + 2 plates. 1943.

7228 Lega-Weekes (Ethel). Ancient liturgical ms. discovered in Exeter Cathedral Library. [? given by Leofric.] Devon and Cornwall N. and Q., 9, pp. 33–35, + 2 plates. 1916.

7229 Macalister (Robert Alexander Stewart). The colophon in the Lindisfarne Gospels. Essays presented to W. Ridgeway, pp. 299–305. 1913.

7230 Milner (John). Account of an ancient manuscript of St. John's Gospel. [Said to have been found in St. Cuthbert's tomb in 1104. 7th c. Now in Stonyhurst College library. *See* **7231**, p. 15. No. 2.] Archaeologia, 16, pp. 17–21, + 1 plate. 1812.

7231 Mynors (Roger Aubrey Baskerville). Durham cathedral manuscripts, to the end of the twelfth century. pp. x, 91, + 57 plates (10 in colour). fol. Oxford, 1939.

7232 Napier (Arthur Sampson). Bruchstück einer altenglischen Boetiushandschrift. [Ms. Bodl. Junius 86. Early 10th c. hand.] Z.f.d.A., 31, pp. 52–54. 1887.

7233 Peter (Thurstan). The Bodmin Gospels. [9th c. B.M. Addit. 9381.] J. Roy. Inst. Cornwall, 19, pp. 301–02, + 1 plate. 1913.

7234 Poole (Reginald Lane). A stage in the history of the Laudian MS. of Acts. [Bodl. Ms. Laud. Gr. 39. i.e. ' What happened to the manuscript after it left Bede's hands and before it was acquired by archbishop Laud.'] J. Theol. Studies, 29, pp. 399–400. 1928.

7235 Priebsch (Robert Charles). The Heliand manuscript, Cotton Caligula A. VII, in the British Museum. pp. 49, + 5 plates. 8° Oxford, 1925. [Mid 10th c. Assigns to Canterbury scriptorium.]

7236 Robinson (Stanford Frederick Hudson). On a fragment of an Anglo-Saxon benedictional preserved at Exeter Cathedral. Trans. St. Paul's Eccles. Soc., 5, pp. 221–28, + 1 plate. 1904.

7237 Rypins (Stanley I.). The *Beowulf* codex. [Cotton Vitellius A XV.] Mod. Phil., 17, pp. 173–79. 1919.

7238 Savage (Henry Edwin) *dean of Lichfield.* The story of St. Chad's Gospels. [i. The ms. itself : ii. The life history of the ms.] B'ham Archaeol. Soc., Trans., 41 (1915), pp. 5–21, + 6 plates. 1916.

7239 Sisam (Kenneth). MSS. Bodley 340 and 342 : Ælfric's *Catholic homilies.* [A study of the mss.] Rev. Engl. Stud., 7, pp. 7–22 : 8, pp. 51–68 : 9, pp. 1–12. 1931–33.

7240 Slater (D.). The Exeter Book (Codex Exoniensis). J. Brit. Archaeol. Assoc., 41, pp. 296–98, + 1 plate. 1885.

7241 Smyth (Charles). The Canterbury Gospels. [Corpus Christi, Camb., MS. 286. ? sent by Gregory to Augustine.] Friends of Canterbury Cathedral, Ann. Rept., 18, pp. 24–27, + 1 plate. 1945.

7242 Stettiner (Richard). Die illustrierten Prudentius-Handschriften. 695 Handschriftenseiten. Text, pp. 22, + 200 plates. 4° Berlin, 1905. [B.M., MS. Addit. 24199. Late 10th c.]

7243 Stoddard (F. H.). The Cædmon poems in MS. Junius XI. [A study of the ms. i. The binding and general character of the whole : ii. the gatherings or quires : iii. The signature marks : iv. The chapter or canto divisions, and illuminations : v. The penmanship.] Anglia, 10, pp. 157–67. 1887.

7244 Swarzenski (Hanns). The Anhalt Morgan Gospels. Art Bull., 31, pp. 77–83, + 6 plates. 1949.

7245 Turner (Cuthbert Hamilton) *ed.* Early Worcester MSS. Fragments of four books and a charter of the eighth century belonging to Worcester Cathedral. pp. lxxii, 31, + 32 plates. fol. Oxford, 1916. [Vulgate, etc. Charter is that of Uhtred, sub-king of the Hwiccas, 770, granting land at Aston on Salwarpe to the thane Æthelmund, with reversion to the Church of Worcester.]

7246 Warren (Frederick Edward). The Leofric Missal. Proc. Soc. Antiq., 2nd S. 9, pp. 17–25. 1881.

7247 Webb (Edward Doran). Notes on the Book of Cerne. Proc. Dorset Antiq. F.C., 21, pp. 158–61, + 2 plates. 1900.

7248 Westwood (John Obadiah). On an Anglo-Saxon ms. [10th c. Four Gospels, etc., belonging to Captain Carew. Abstract.] Proc. Oxford Archit. and Hist. Soc., N.S. 2, pp. 108–09. 1868.

7249 Williamson (Edward William) *bp. of Swansea.* The Gospels of St. Chad. Nat. Lib. Wales J., 4, pp. 46–49. 1945.

7250 Wrenn (Charles Leslie) *ed.* Beowulf. pp. 318. 8° London, 1953. [Pp. 9–14, the manuscript. Cotton Vitellius A XV.]

112. INDIVIDUAL MANUSCRIPTS CELTIC

(*See also* **Illumination, 204**)

§ *a.* **The Cathach of St. Columba**
(In library of Royal Irish Academy. Late 6th c. A Latin psalter. ? Copied by St. Columba in the cell of St. Finnian of Dromin. Also called 'Banner' of the O'Donnell, being borne to battle as a talisman of victory.)

7251 Chrétien (Douglas). The Battle Book of the O'Donnells. pp. 48. 8° Berkeley, 1935.

7252 Esposito (Mario). The Cathach of St. Columba. County Louth Archaeol. J., 4, pp. 80–83, + 1 plate. 1916.

7253 —— The so-called Psalter of St. Columba. [Kenney, 1, p. 629.] N. and Q., 11th S. 11, pp. 466–68 ; 12, pp. 253–54. 1915.

7254 Lawlor (Hugh Jackson). The Cathach of St. Columba. Proc. R.I.A., 33 c, pp. 241–443, + 5 plates. 1916.

7255 Lindsay (Wallace Martin). The Cathach of St. Columba. Appendix 2, Palaeographical notes. [i. The script of the Cathach : ii. The colophon of the Durrow Book.] Proc. R.I.A., 33 c, pp. 397–407, + 2 plates. 1916.

7256 Maclennan (Duncan M.). The Cathach of Colum-cille. Trans. Gaelic Soc. Inverness, 35 (1929–30), pp. 2–25. 1939.

§ *b.* **Other Celtic MSS.**

(*See also* **Illumination, 204**)

7257 Berger (Samuel). De quatre manuscrits des évangiles conservés à Dublin. Rev. celt., 6, pp. 348–57. 1885.

7258 Bernard (J. H.). On the Domnach Airgid ms. [?ms. belonged to St. Patrick.] Trans. R.I.A., 30, pp. 303–12, + 1 plate. 1893.

7259 Bieler (Ludwig). The Irish Book of hymns : a palaeographical study. [T.C.D., MS. E.4. 2 (11th c.), Franciscan Library, Merchants' Quay, Dublin, MS. A. 2. (end of 11th or early 12th c.] Scriptorium, 2, pp. 177–94. 1948.

7260 Cochrane (Robert). Notes on the ecclesiastical antiquities in the parish of Howth, county of Dublin : — iii. 'The Garland of Howth.' [7th c. ms. of the Gospels. 2 figures in text.] J. Roy. Soc. Antiq. Ireland, 23 (5th S. 33), pp. 404–07. 1893.

7261 David (Pierre). Un recueil de conférences monastiques irlandaises du VIIIe siècle. Note sur le manuscrit 43 de la Bibliothèque du Chapitre de Cracovie. [i. Description du manuscrit : ii. Les conférences monastiques du manuscrit 43 : iii. Caractére et origine du recueil.] Rev. Bénédictine, 49, p. 62–89, + 4 plates. 1937.

7262 Dold (P. Alban). Eine kostbare Handschriftenreliquie in irisch-angelsächsischen Schriftzügen des 8. Jahrhunderts mit dem monarchianischen Argumentum und den Kapiteleinteilungen zum Lukasevangelium (Hs. 702 der Universitätsbibliothek Freiburg im Breisgau). Zent. Bibliothekswesen, 52, pp. 125–35, + 2 plates. 1935.

7263 Dowden (John) *bp. of Edinburgh*. Notes on the MS. Liturg. f. 5 (' Queen Margaret's Gospel-book ') in the Bodleian library. [Early 11th c.] Proc. Soc. Antiq. Scot., 28 (3rd S. 4), pp. 244–53. 1894.

7264 Esposito (Mario). On the so-called Psalter of St. Caimin. [Mid 11th c.] Proc. R.I.A., 32 c, pp. 78–88, + 1 plate. 1913.

7265 Forbes (Alexander Penrose) *bp. of Brechin*. Account of a manuscript of the eleventh century by [the Scottish monk] Marianus of Ratisbon. Proc. Soc. Antiq. Scot., 6, pp. 33–40. 1868.

7266 Fraser (John). The Gaelic *notitiae* in the Book of Deer. [With text.] Scot. Gaelic Stud., 5, pp. 51–66. 1942.

7267 Gordon (James Frederick Skinner). Oldest Scottish MS. [Of Adamnan's Life of Columba : ? written by Dorbone of Iona in 715. Now in Public Library, Schaffhausen.] Scott. N. and Q., 2nd S. 3, p. 104. 1902.

7268 Graves (Charles) *bp. of Limerick*. On certain notes in the Ogham character on the margin of an ancient ms. of Priscian [at St. Gall]. [9th c.] Proc. R.I.A., 6 (1855), pp. 209–16. 1858.

7269 Halpin (James). Liturgical fragments of the early Irish Church. The Book of Dhimma. [T.D.C. Illuminated ms. of early 7th c.] Irish Eccles. Rec., 3rd S. 11, pp. 325–34. 1890.

7270 Hennessy (William Maunsell). On a manuscript written by St. Camin, of Inisceltra. [Fragment of psalm 119. 7th c. Now in Franciscan Convent, Dublin.] *Same jnl.*, 9, pp. 241–47. 1873.

7271 Kemp (R. S.). The Book of Deer. [? Pictish scribe.] Trans. Scot. Ecclesiol. Soc., 8, pp. 164–74. 1927.

7272 Leabhar Na h-Uidhri . . . now for the first time published . . . with an account of the manuscript. [A facsimile reproduction, made by Joseph O'Longan and collated by Brian O'Looney]. *Royal Irish Academy*. pp. xxv, 134, 8, + 2 plates. 4° Dublin, 1870.

7273 —— Lebor na Huidre. Book of the Dun Cow. Edited by Richard Irvine Best and Osborn Bergin. *Royal Irish Academy*. pp. xliv, 340, + 2 plates. 8° Dublin, 1929.

7274 MacBain (Alexander). The Book of Deer. [With extracts in Gaelic with translation, and index and vocabulary. 9th c.] Trans. Gaelic Soc. Inverness, 11, pp. 137–66. 1885.

7275 Mackay (Donald). New light on the [history of the] Book of Deer. Scot. Gaelic Stud., 5, p. 50. 1942.

7276 Nigra (Costantino) *count*. Un manuscrit irlandais de Vienne. [Imperial Library, Cod. 16. Latin texts of Probus, (8th c.) and of Eutychius (9th c.). Transcription of the Irish glosses.] Rev. celt., 1, pp. 58–59. 1870.

7277 Reeves (William) *bp. of Down*. The Antiphonary of Bangor. [Bobbio ms., now in Ambrosiana.] Ulster J. Archaeol., 1, pp. 168–79. 1853.

7278 —— On the Book of Armagh. Proc. R.I.A., 3rd S. 2, pp. 77–99. 1893.

7279 Todd (James Henthorn). Notice of an Irish ms. of the four Gospels, of the seventh century. [? given by Maelbrigid MacDornan, abp. of Armagh, to king Athelstan.] Proc. R.I.A., 1 (1837), pp. 40–41. 1841.

7280 —— On an ancient missal, and its silver box, described by Dr. O'Conor in his catalogue of the Stowe mss., and now the property of the earl of Ashburnham. [7th c. Gospel of St. John in box made between 1023 and 1064.] Proc. R.I.A., 6 (1856), pp. 393–98. 1858.

113. COLLECTIONS OF MANU-SCRIPT FACSIMILIES, ANGLO-SAXON AND CELTIC

(*See also* Illumination, 204)

7281 Cameron (John). Facsimiles of Anglo-Saxon manuscripts photozincographed by J. C., with translations by W. B. Sanders. 3 vol. elephant fol. Southampton, 1878–84. [Gross, 258.]

7282 Colgrave (Bertram), *etc.*, *ed.* Early English manuscripts in fascimile. 4° Copenhagen, 1951–. [*See also* under individual volumes **4213** and **7216a.**]

7283 Gilbert (*Sir* John Thomas). Account of facsimiles of national manuscripts of Ireland. . . . Edited . . . by J. T. Gilbert . . . and photozincographed . . . by Sir H. James. 2nd edition. pp. 95, ix, 8° London, 1879.

7284 —— ed. Facsimiles of National manuscripts of Ireland . . . photozincographed by Sir Henry James. Pt. 1. pp. xxiv, 89 + 45 coloured plates. Elephant fol. Dublin, 1874. [Domnach-Airgid ms., Cathach, Books of Durrow, Kells, Dimma, Mulling, Armagh, Gospels of Mac Regol, *etc.*]

7285 Gougaud (Louis). Répertoire des fac-similés des manuscrits irlandais. Rev. celt., 34, pp. 14–37 : 35, pp. 415–30: 38, pp. 1–14. 1913–14, 1920.

7286 Kenyon (*Sir* Frederic George) *ed.* Facsimiles of Biblical manuscripts in the British Museum. 25 plates, + letterpress. fol. London, 1900. [16 plates, A.–S. period.]

7287 Lowe (Elias Avery) *ed.* Codices Latini antiquiores : a palaeographical guide to Latin manuscripts prior to the ninth century. 2. Great Britain and Ireland. pp. xvii, 53, + 43 plates. fol. Oxford, 1935. [277 specimens. A.–S. and Irish. Distinguishing of Irish scripts from English.]

7288 New Palæographical Society. Facsimiles of ancient manuscripts. 2 vol. fol. London, 1903–12.—Second Series. 2 vol. fol. London, 1913–30. [A.–S. period, *passim.*]

7289 Palæographical Society. Facsimiles of ancient manuscripts. 259 plates. 3 vol. fol. London, 1873–83. —Second series. 209 plates. 2 vol. fol. London, 1884–94. [A.–S. period, *passim.*]

7290 Skeat (Walter William). Twelve facsimiles of Old English manuscripts, with transcriptions and introduction. pp. 36, + 12 plates. 4° Oxford, 1892.

114. SCRIPT

7291 Astle (Thomas). The origin and progress of writing, *etc.* pp. xxiv, 240, + 31 plates. fol. London, 1876. [Earliest work to deal with Irish script and illumination.]

7292 Bains (Doris). A supplement to Notae Latinae [**7307**] (Abbreviations in Latin mss. of 850 to 1050 A.D.). pp. xiv, 72. 8° Cambridge, 1936.

7293 Brandl (Alois). Chrousts Fund einer der ältesten ags. Aufzeichnungen. Archiv Stud. neueren Spr., Bd. 107, pp. 103–05, + 1 plate. 1901.

7294 Crawford (Samuel John). The Worcester marks and glosses of the Old English manuscripts in the Bodleian, together with the Worcester version of the Nicene creed. [The ' trembling hand.'] Anglia, 52 (N.F. 40), pp. 1–25, 1 plate. 1928.

7295 Fisher (John Hurt). The ancestry of the English alphabet. Archaeology, 4, pp. 232–42. 1951.

7296 Giles (John Allen). Anglo-Saxon typography. [With answers by ' Sob ', and George Stephens.] N. and Q., 1st S. 10, pp. 183–4, 248–50, 466–67. 1854.

7297 Humphreys (Henry Noel). The origin and progress of the art of writing. 2nd edition. pp. 178, + 28 plates. 8° London, 1855. [Pp. 130–37, + plate 15, A.–S. period.]

7298 Keller (Ferdinand). Bilder und Schriftzüge in den irischen Manuscripten der schweizerischen Bibliotheken. [Translated in Ulster J. Archaeol., 8, pp. 210–30 (1860) by W. Reeves.] Mitt. antiq. Gesell. in Zürich, 7, pp. 61–69. 1851.

7299 Keller (Wolfgang). Angelsächsische Palaeographie. Die Schrift der Angelsachsen mit besonderer Rücksicht auf die Denkmäler in der Volkssprache. 1. Theil, Einleitung. pp. vi, 56. 2. Theil, 13 Tafeln, nebst Transscriptionen. *Palaestra*, 43. 8° Berlin, 1906.

7300 —— Angelsächsische Schrift. Hoops : Reallexikon d. german. Altertumskunde, 1, pp. 98–103, + 3 plates. 1913.

7301 Ker (Neil Ripley). The date of the ' tremulous ' Worcester hand. [Evidence from MS. Bodley Hatton 114, f. 10 r.] Leeds Studies in English, 6, pp. 28–29. 1937.

7302 Lindsay (Wallace Martin). The Bobbio scriptorium : its early minuscule abbreviations. [Kenney, 1, p. 515.] Zent. Bibliothekswesen, 26, pp. 293–306. 1909.

7303 —— Breton scriptoria, their Latin abbreviation-symbols. [Orleans mss., 255 (302) and 193 (221).] *Same jnl.*, 29, pp. 264–72. 1912.

7304 —— Contractions in early Latin minuscule mss. pp. 54. 8° Oxford, 1908.

7305 —— Early Irish minuscule script. *St. Andrews Univ. Pubn.*, 6. pp. 74, + 12 plates. 8° Oxford, 1908.

7306 —— Early Welsh script. *St. Andrews University Pubn.*, 10. pp. 64, + 17 plates. 8° Oxford, 1912. [Kenney, 1, p. 657.]

7307 —— Notae Latinae. An account of abbreviations in Latin MSS. of the early minuscule period (c. 700–850). pp. xxiv, 500. 8° Cambridge, 1915. [For supplement, *see* **7292.**]

7308 Lowe (Elias Avery). Handwriting. Legacy of the Middle Ages, ed. C. G. Crump and E. F. Jacob, pp. 197–226, + 16 plates. 1927.

7309 —— The ' script of Luxeuil ', a title vindicated. Rev. bénédictine, 63, pp. 132–42, + 6 plates. 1953.

7310 Plummer (Charles). On the colophons and marginalia of Irish scribes. Proc. Brit. Acad., 12, pp. 11–44. 1926.

7311 Reeves (William) *bp. of Down.* Early Irish calligraphy. (*Including* : Illuminations and facsimilies from Irish manuscripts in the libraries of Switzerland, by Ferdinand Keller, *q.v.* **7298**). Ulster J. Archaeol., 8, pp. 210–30, 291–308, + 6 plates. 1860.

7312 Schiaparelli (Luigi). Note paleografiche : intorno all' origine e alcuni caratteri della scrittura e del sistema abbreviativo irlandese. Arch. stor. ital., 74, ii, pp. 3–126. 1916.

7313 Steffens (Franz). Die Abkürzungen in den lateinischen Handschriften des 8. und 9. Jahrhunderts in St. Gallen. [Pp. 488–99, note on the preceding article, by W. M. Lindsay.] Zent. Bibliothekswesen, 30, pp. 477–90. 1913.

7314 —— Über die Abkürzungsmethoden der Schreibschule von Bobbio. Mélanges Chatelain (Paris). 1910.

7315 Stewart (Zeph). Insular script without insular abbreviations : a problem in eighth-century palaeography. Speculum, 25, pp. 483–90. 1950.

7316 Thompson (*Sir* Edward Maunde). The history of English handwriting, A.D. 700–1400. [53 figures in text.] Trans. Bib. Soc., 5, pp. 109–142, 213–53. 1899.

7317 Wattenbach (Wilhelm). Das Schriftwesen im Mittelalter. 3. Auflage. pp. vi, 670. 8° Leipzig, 1896.

115. MUSIC

7318 [Anon.] Saint Dunstan's kyrie. Downside Rev., 5, pp. 45–51, + 2 plates. 1816.

7318a Bruce-Mitford (Rupert Leo Scott). The Sutton Hoo musical instrument. Archaeol. News Letter, 1. i, pp. 11–13. 1948.

7319 Buhle (Edward). Die musikalischen Instrumente in den Miniaturen des frühen Mittelalters. Ein Beitrag zur Geschichte der Musikinstrumente. 1. Die Blasinstrumente. pp. 119, + 14 plates. 8° Leipzig, 1903. [No more published.]

7320 Bunting (Edward). The ancient music of Ireland. pp. 100. 4° Dublin, 1840. [Pp. 45–56, A.-S. period.]

7321 C. (H. D.). The monster organ in Winchester cathedral of the 10th century. ['Description by the monk Wulston' (died 963) who 'dedicated his poem to bishop Elphege, by whose order the organ was built.' Translation of the passage.] Hants. N. and Q., 5, pp. 39–40. 1890.

7322 Chappell (William). On the use of the Greek language, written phonetically, in the early service books of the Church in England ; and on the earliest system of musical notation upon lines and spaces, one hitherto unnoticed, and seemingly peculiar to English use. [MS. Bodley 775 : of 10th c., from Winchester.] Archaeologia, 46, pp. 389–402, + 5 plates. 1881.

7323 Conran (Michael). The national music of Ireland, containing the history of the Irish bards, the national melodies, the harp, and other musical instruments of Erin. 2nd edition. pp. xii, 287. 8° London, 1850.

7324 Davey (Henry). History of English music. 2nd edition. pp. xix, 505. 8° London, 1921. [Pp. 3–15, A.–S. period, with list of mss.]

7325 Dolmetsch (Arnold). Ancient Welsh music. Trans. Hon. Soc. Cymm., 1933–35, pp. 115–25. 1936.

7326 Farmer (Henry George). A history of music in Scotland. pp. 557, + 14 plates. 8° London, 1947. [Pp. 16–31, + one plate, Celtic period.]

7327 Fleischmann (Aloys). References to chant in early Irish MSS. [? ecclesiastical chant brought to Ireland by St. Patrick himself.] Essays presented to . . . Torna, pp. 43–49. 1947.

7328 Flood (William Henry Grattan). A history of Irish music. pp. xiii, 353. 8° Dublin, 1905. [Pp. 9–45, Irish music from the 6th to the 9th c. : instruments, scales, etc.]

7329 —— Irish organ-builders from the eighth to the close of the eighteenth century. J. Roy. Soc. Antiq. Ireland, 40 (5h S. 20), pp. 229–34. 1910.

7330 French (W. H.). *Widsith* and the scop. [The wandering singer and his profession.] P.M.L.A., 60, pp. 623–30. 1945.

7330a Galpin (Francis William). Old English instruments of music, their history and character. *Antiquary's Books.* pp. xxv, 327, + 54 plates. 8° London, 1910. [A little of A.–S. period, including plates 1–3, 12 and 38.]

7331 Gougaud (Louis). Music in Celtic monasteries. [On the use of harps in church and the opposition to this practice.] Pax (Prinknash), 21, pp. 54–57. 1931.

7332 Handschin (J.). The two Winchester tropers. [10th c.] J. Theol. Stud., 37, pp. 34–49, 156–72. 1936.

7333 Jones (Edward). Musical and poetical relicks of the Welsh bards. . . . To the tunes are added variations of the harp. . . . Likewise a history of the bards, etc. pp. 78. (The Bardic museum of primitive British literary and other admirable varieties, forming the second volume, etc.). 4° London, 1784, 1802.

7334 Knowles (William James). Portion of a harp and other objects found in the crannoge of Carncoagh, co. Antrim. [?9th c.] J. Roy. Soc. Antiq. Ireland, 27 (6th S. 7), pp. 114–115. 1897.

7335 Ledwich (Edward). Inquiries concerning the ancient Irish harp. A letter . . . on the style of the ancient Irish music. In Walker (J. C.) : Historical memoirs of the Irish bards. [*q.v.* **7340**.] 4° London, 1786.

7336 Padelford (Frederick Morgan). Old English musical terms. *Bonner Beiträge zur Anglistik*, 4. pp. xii, 112. 8° Bonn, 1899. [Pp. 1–62, introduction on the various O.E. musical instruments.]

7337 Panum (Hortense). Harfe und Lyra im alten Nordeuropa. [Pp. 3–8, Die angelsächsische Harfe, die irische Harfe (with 13 figures in text) : pp. 13–14, Die Rundlyra bei den Angelsachsen (with 2 figures) : pp. 17–24, viereckige Saiteninstrumente, etc.] Sammelbände internat. Musik-Gesellschaft, 7, pp. 1–40. 1906.

7338 Pegge (Samuel). Observations on Dr. Percy's account of minstrels among the Saxons. Archaeologia, 2, pp. 100–06. 1772.

7339 Wackerbarth (Francis Diederich). Music and the Anglo-Saxons; being some account of the Anglo-Saxon orchestra, with remarks on the church music of the nineteenth century. 8° London, 1837. ['Its title is the best part of the book.'—Carl Engel.]

7340 Walker (Joseph Cooper). Historical memoirs of the Irish bards, . . . with . . . observations on the music of Ireland, also an historical . . . account of the musical instruments of the ancient Irish. pp. xii, 166, 124. 4° Dublin, 1786.

7341 Williams (Richard). The musical instruments of Cymru Fu. Cymru Fu, 2, pp. 5–8. 1889.

116. SCIENCE

(for Bede's Scientific works, *see* **66§b ii** : for Ælfric's, *see* **78**.)

§ *a*. **General and Miscellaneous**

7342 Anderson (George Kumler). The literature of the Anglo-Saxons. pp. 431. 8° London, 1949. [Pp. 384–402, Scientific writings in the Old English period.]

7343 Erhardt-Siebold (Erika von). Aldhelm in possession of the secrets of sericulture. Anglia, 60 (N.F. 48), pp. 384–89. 1936.

7344 Evans (Joan) and **Serjeantson** (Mary Sidney) *ed.* English mediaeval lapidaries. *Early English Text Society*, O.S. 190. pp. 205. 8° London, 1933. [Pp. 13–15, the Old English lapidary (11th c.) in MS. Cotton Tiberius A III : text (A.–S. and English) : pp. 131–32, notes.]

7345 Fleischhacker (Robert von). Ein altenglischer Lapidar. [Text from MS. B. M. Cotton Tib. A III, fol. 101 b and notes]. Z.f.d. A., 34, pp. 229–35. 1890.

7346 Foerster (Max). Die Weltzeitalter bei den Angelsachsen. Neusprachliche Studien. Festgabe K. Luick, pp. 183–203. 1925.

7347 Gregory (*Sir* Richard). British climate in historic times. [Part 1]. [Pp. 250–51, 8th–11th c.] Geog. Teacher, 12, pp. 248–58. 1924.

7348 Henel (Heinrich). Studien zum altenglischen Computus. *Beiträge zur englischen Philologie*, 26. pp. ix, 95. 8° Leipzig, 1934. [With special reference to Byrhtferth's Manuel].

7349 Hunt (Alfred). The Viking raft or pontoon bridge, made to rise and fall with the tide. Discovered in 1886 near Glamford-Brigg, north Lincs. Saga-Book V.C., 5, pp. 354–62. 1908.

7350 Jones (Charles Williams). Polemius Silvius, Bede, and the names of the months. Speculum, 9, pp. 50–56. 1934.

7351 Lerner (L. D.). Colour words in Anglo-Saxon. [No separate hue-words and brightness-words as now.] Mod. Lang. Rev., 46, pp. 246–49. 1951.

7352 Magnússon (Eiríkr). Notes on shipbuilding and nautical terms of old in the north. Saga-Book V.C., 4, pp. 182–237. 1905.

7353 Mead (William E.). Colour in Old English poetry. P.M.L.A., 14, pp. 169–206. 1899.

7354 Nilsson (Nils Martin Persson). Primitive time-reckoning. *Skrifter utgivna av Humanistiska Vetenskapssamfundet i Lund*, 1. pp. xiii, 384. 8° Lund, 1920. [P. 75, A.–S. seasons : pp. 293–97, A.–S. months and lunisolar year.]

7355 Quiggin (Edmund Crosby). A fragment of an old Welsh computus. [Calendar for 931–49, and 960–87 on the back. Text in Irish with English translation.] Zeit. celt. Phil., 8, pp. 407–10, + 1 plate. 1912.

7356 Schumacher (Karl Heinz). Die deutschen Monatsnamen. *Deutsches Werden*, 13. pp. 172. 8° Greifswald, 1937. [Pp. 31–45, A.–S.]

7357 Singer (Charles Joseph). The dark age of science. [Byrhtferth, etc.] Realist, 2, pp. 281–95. 1929.

7358 Skeat (Walter William). Anglo-Saxon names of the months. N. and Q., 7th S. 7, p. 301. 1889.

7359 Thomson (Ebenezer). On the archaic mode of expressing numbers in English, Saxon, Friesic, *etc.* pp. 16. 8° London, 1853.

7360 Willms (Johannes E.). Eine Untersuchung über den Gebrauch der Farbenbezeichnungen in den Poesie Altenglands. *Diss., Münster.* pp. 79. 8° Münster, 1902.

§ *b.* Byrhtferth

7361 Byrhtferth. Byrhtferth's Manual (A.D. 1011).. . . . Edited . . . from MS. Ashmole 328 . . . by S. J. Crawford. Vol. 1, text, translation, sources and appendices. *Early English Text Society, O.S.* 177. pp. 250, + 16 plates. 8° London, 1929.

7362 Classen (Karl Moritz). Über das Leben und die Schriften Byrhtferðs, eines angelsächsischen Gelehrten und Schriftstellers um das Jahr 1000. pp. 39. 4° Dresden, 1896.

7363 Forsey (George Frank). Byrhtferth's preface. [With text.] Speculum, 3, pp. 505–22 + 2 plates. 1928.

7364 Henel (Heinrich). Ein Bruchstück aus Byrhtferþs Handbuch. [Found in Camb. Univ. MS. Kk. 5. 32, f. 60 v. Text included.] Anglia, 61 (N.F. 49), pp. 122–25. 1937.

7365 —— Notes on Byrhtferth's *Manual.* J. Eng. and Germ. Phil., 41, pp. 427–43. 1942.

7366 Jones (Charles Williams). The Byrhtferth glosses. Medium Ævum, 7, pp. 79–97. 1938.

7367 Kluge (Friedrich). Angelsächsische Excerpte aus Byrhtferth's Handboc oder Enchiridion. [A.–S. text only.] Anglia, 8, pp. 298–337. 1885.

7368 Singer (Charles Joseph *and* Dorothea Waley). Byrhtferð's diagram. A restoration : Byrhtferð of Ramsey's diagram of the physical or physiological fours. [3 figures in text. MSS. Ashmole 328 and St. John's, Oxford, 17.] Bodl. Q. Rec., 2, pp. 47–51. 1917.

7369 —— An unrecognized Anglo-Saxon text. [i.e. MS. Ashmole 328.] Annals of medical history, 3, pp. 136–49. 1921.

§ *c.* Physiologus

7370 Cook (Albert Stanburrough) *ed.* The Old English Elene, Phoenix, and Physiologus. pp. 320. 8° New Haven, 1919.

7371 —— and **Pitman** (James Hall) *ed.* The Old English Physiologus. Text and translation. *Yale Studies in English,* 63. pp. 25. 8° New Haven, 1921.

7371a Cordasco (Francesco). The Old-English Physiologus : its problems. Mod. Lang. Quart., 10, pp. 351–55. 1949.

7372 Ebert (Adolf). Der angelsächsische Physiologus. Anglia, 6, pp. 241–47. 1883.

7373 Peebles (Rose Jeffries). The Anglo-Saxon *Physiologus.* Mod. Phil., 8, pp. 571–79. 1911.

7373a Sokoll ( ). Zum angelsächsischen Physiologus. Jahresb. d. K.u.K. Staats-Oberrealschule in Marburg, 27. 1897.

7374 Tupper (Frederick) *jr.* The Physiologus of the Exeter Book. J. Engl. and Germ. Philol., 11, pp. 89–91. 1912.

§ *d.* Animals, Birds, Fishes, Insects

7375 Bjoerkman (Erik). Zu den altenglischen Insektennamen. [i. *twinwyrm* : ii *stūt.*] Archiv Stud. neueren Spr., Bd. 117, pp. 364–66. 1906.

7376 Cook (Albert Stanburrough). The Old English whale. Mod. Lang. Notes, 9, col. 129–35. 1894.

7377 Cortelyou (John van Zandt). Die altenglischen Namen der Insekten, Spinnen-und Krustentiere. *Anglistische Forschungen,* 19. pp. vii, 124. 8° Heidelberg, 1906.

7378 Jordan (Richard). Die altenglischen Säugetiernamen, zusammengestellt und erläutert. *Anglistische Forschungen,* 12. pp. xii, 212. 8° Heidelberg, 1903.

7379 Koehler (Johann Jakob). Die altenglischen Fischnamen. *Anglistische Forschungen,* 21. pp. vii, 87. 8° Heidelberg, 1906.

7380 Schlutter (Otto Bernhard). Is there any evidence for OE. *weargincel* ' butcher-bird ' ? Neophilol., 8, pp. 206–08. 1923.

7381 —— Is there any real evidence for an alleged OE. *wyhtel* ' quail ' ? Neophilol., 8, pp. 303–04. 1923.

7382 Skeat (Walter William). Anglo-Saxon names for birds. [*Higora*, magpie or woodpecker : *hice-máse*, titmouse : and *géac*, cuckoo.] N. and Q., 9th S., p. 451. 1902.

7383 Swaen (A. E. H.). Some Old English birdnames. [*Huilpa*, *stint* (thrush), *wealhhafoe*, *nihtlecan* (quail), *frysca* (kite), *mūshafoc*.] Archiv Stud. neueren Spr., Bd. 118, pp. 387–89. 1907.

7384 Thomson (Alexander P. D.). A history of the ferret. [Pp. 473–75, A.-S. (*meard*, cognate with *marten*).] J. Hist. Med., 6, pp. 471–80. 1951.

7385 Whitman (Charles Huntington). The birds of Old English literature. J. Germ. Philol., 2, pp. 149–98. 1898.

7386 —— The Old English animal names : mollusks ; toads, frogs ; worms; reptiles. Anglia, 30 (N.F. 18), pp. 380–93. 1907.

7387 —— Old English mammal names. J. Engl. and Germ. Philol., 6, pp. 649–56. 1907.

§ *e*. **Plants**

7388 Earle (John). English plant names from the tenth to the fifteenth century. pp. cxii, 122. 16° Oxford, 1880.

7389 Ellacombe (Henry N.). Plant-names a thousand years ago. [List in Latin, with A.-S. and English. From Epinal Glossary.] Gardener's chronicle, Nov. 3, p. 502. 1888.

7390 Helbœck (Hans). Studies on prehistoric and Anglo-Saxon cultivated plants in England. Proc. Prehist. Soc., 6, pp. 176–78. 1940.

7391 Hoops (Johannes). Die forstliche Flora Altenglands. Verhandl. 46. Versammlung deut. Philologen, pp. 150–51. 1901.

7392 Hoops (Johannes). Pflanzen-aberglaube bei den Angelsachsen. Globus, 63, pp. 303 *et seq.*, 324 *et seq.* 1893.

7393 —— Über die altenglischen Pflanzennamen. *Diss., Freiburg i Br.* pp. 84. 8° Freiburg, 1889.

7394 Kaerre (Karl). The English plant-name grounsel. [A.-S. *gunde-* or *grunde-* plus *-swelge* or *-swylige*. Studier mod. Språkvetenskap, 9, pp. 67–78. 1924.

7395 Prior (Richard Chandler Alexander). On the popular names of British plants, being an explanation of the origin and meaning of the names of our indigeneous and most commonly cultivated species. 3rd edition. pp. xxviii, 294. 8° London, 1879. [Many A.-S. names given.]

7396 Reeves (W. P.). Felgerde. [= polipodium.] Mod. Lang. Notes, 23, pp. 186–87. 1908.

7397 Schlutter (Otto Bernhard). Is there an OE. plant-name *twínihte* ? [= twine-like, or byssus-like.] Neophilol., 12, pp. 117–19. 1927.

7398 —— Weiteres zu *disme* ' moschus '. [*See* Bd. 30, pp. 123–24.] Anglia, 32, p. 515. 1909.

7399 Skeat (Walter William). Anglo-Saxon plant names. N. and Q., 8th S. 9, pp. 163–64. 1896.

§ *f*. **Astronomy**

7400 Esposito (Mario). A ninth century astronomical treatise. [Irish. MS. Munic. Valenciennes, N.4.43. Compiled by Dicuil. Isidore, etc. and ff. 66a–118a Dicuil's Computus.] Mod. Philol., 18, pp. 177–88. 1920.

7401 —— An unpublished astronomical treatise by the Irish monk Dicuil. Proc. R.I.A., 26c, pp. 378–446. 1907.

7402 Harder (Hermann). Ein ags. Sternbildname. [*Raedgasram*. ? = Aries, rather than (Reuter's suggestion) = Hyades.] Archiv Stud. neueren Spr., Bd. 168, pp. 235–37. 1935.

7403 Henel (Heinrich). Planeten-glaube in Ælfrics Zeit. Anglia, 58 [N.F. 46), pp. 292–317. 1934.

7404 Macalister (Robert Alexander Stewart). Halley's and other comets in the Irish annals. [613, 676, 744, 916, 1011, 1018, etc.] J. Roy. Soc. Antiq. Ireland, 40 (5th S. 20), pp. 64–66. 1910.

7404a O'Connor (F. J.) Solar eclipses visible in Ireland between A.D. 400 and A.D. 1000. Proc. R.I.A., 55A, pp. 61–72. 1952.

7404b Schove (Derek Justin). The earliest British eclipse record (A.D. 400–600). [' 445 '=Dec. 23, 447 : 496 (A.U.) : 594 (A.U.).] J. Brit. Astron. Ass., 65, pp. 37–43. 1954.

7405 Schove (Derek Justin). Visions in north-west Europe (A.D. 400–600) and dated auroral displays. [A.D. 521–2, the aurora of Columba's birth : 594–600, the aurorae of Columba's death. With Chinese and other comparisons.] J.Brit. Archaeol. Ass., 3rd S. 13, pp. 34–49. 1950.

7406 Wright (Thomas). Popular treatises on science written during the Middle Ages, in Anglo-Saxon, Anglo-Norman and English. *Historical Society of Science*. pp. xvi, 140. 8° London, 1841. [Pp. 1–19, Anglo-Saxon manual of astronomy. A–S. and English translation. Abridgement of Bede's De natura rerum. Text printed from MS. Cotton Tib. B.V. c. 990.]

117. MEDICINE

§ *a*. Documents and Commentaries on them

7407 Apuleius, *Barbarus*. Herbarium Apuleii, Cotton MS. Vitellius C. III. Text and grammar, edited by A. J. G. Hilbelink. pp. 118. 8° Amsterdam, 1930.

7408 —— Das Herbarium Apuleii nach einer frühmittelenglischen Fassung, herausgegeben von Hugo Berberich. *Anglistische Forschungen*, 5. pp. iii, 140. 8° Heidelberg, 1902.

7409 Bradley (Henry). Some emendations in Old English texts. [iv. Leechdoms, ii, p. 52, l. 8–*pe fóporn* (=tenaculum) should probably read *pefoporn*, bramble-spine : v. Spider in Old English.] Mod. Lang Rev., 11, pp. 212–15. 1916.

7410 Cockayne (Oswald) *ed.* Leechdoms, wortcunning and starcraft of early England : being a collection of documents . . . illustrating the history of science [and medicine] . . . before the Norman Conquest. *Rolls series*. 3 vols. 8° London, 1864–66. [Gross, 1485. i. A–S. Herbal and Sextus Placitus : ii. Leech Books : iii. Lacnunga, περὶ διδά-ξεων, etc. A.–S. and translation.]

7411 Fazakerley (Mary Eleanor). Studies in the Old English Lacnunga. *B.A. thesis, Liverpool*. pp. viii, 80, + glossary. 4° 1945. [Typewritten. For text, apply University Library.]

7412 Fehr (Bernhard). Altenglische Ritualtexte für Krankenbesuch, heilige Ölung und Begräbnis. Texte u. Forschungen : Festgabe für F. Liebermann, pp. 20–67. 1921.

7413 Grattan (John Henry Grafton) and **Singer** (Charles Joseph). Anglo-Saxon magic and medicine, illustrated specially from the semi-pagan text Lacnunga. *Publications of the Wellcome Historical Medical Museum*, N.s.3. pp. xii, 234, + 6 plates. 8° London, 1952. [44 figures in text. Pt. 1, a general survey of magico-medical practice in A.–S. England : pt. 2, Lacnunga, a magico-medical commonplace book, edited with A.–S. text, translation, notes, glossary, etc.]

7414 Hilbelink (Aaltje Johanna Geertruida). Cotton MS. Vitellius C. III of the Herbarium Apuleii. *Academisch Proefschrift, Amsterdam*. pp. 118, + 2 plates. 8° Amsterdam, 1930. [A.–S. text.]

7415 James (R. R.). Ophthalmic leechdoms. [Material on eye diseases abstracted from Cockayne's Leechdoms.] Brit. J. Ophthalmology, 12, pp. 401–10. 1928.

7416 Myddfai. The physicians of Myddvai : Meddygon Myddfai, or the medical practice of . . . Rhiwallon and his sons of Myddvai in Caermarthenshire . . . translated by John M. Pughe . . . and edited by John Williams ab Ithel. *Society for the publication of ancient Welsh manuscripts*. pp. xxx, 470. 8° Llandovery, 1861. [Welsh and English.]

7417 Myddfai. Le plus ancien texte des Meddygon Myddveu. (Texte du Livre Rouge). [Edited with a glossary] par P. Diverrès. pp. cv, 300. 8° Paris, 1913. [Welsh and French.]

7418 Peri Didaxeon. Eine Sammlung von Rezepten in englischen Sprache aus dem 11./12. Jahrhundert. Nach einer Handschrift [Harl. 6258] des Britischen Museums, herausgegeben van Max Löweneck. *Erlanger Beiträge zur englischen Philologie*, 12. pp. viii, 57. 8° Erlangen, 1896. [Latin and A.-S.]

7419 Singer (Charles Joseph). A review of the medical literature of the Dark Ages, with a new text of about 1110. [Pp. 109–11, vernacular literature, esp. A.-S.] Proc. Roy. Soc. Med., Hist. Sectn., 10, pp. 107–60. 1917.

7420 Singer (Dorothea Waley). Survey of medical manuscripts in the British Isles dating from before the sixteenth century. [Pp. 103–04, list of 10 A.-S. medical mss.] *Same jnl.*, 22, pp. 96–107. 1919.

7421 Stokes (Whitley). A Celtic leech book. [Transcript of 4 pages of a 9th c. ms. in the University Library, Leiden. With glossary.] Zeit. celt. Philol., 1, pp. 17–25. 1897.

7422 Storms (Godfrid). An Anglo-Saxon prescription from the Lacnunga. [Lacnunga, 12 ; *to godre bansealfe*. Explains why the various ingredients possess *craft* to cure.] English Studies, 28, pp. 33–41. 1947.

7423 Sudhoff (Karl). Die gedruckten mittelalterlichen medizinischen Texte in germanischen Sprachen. [Pp. 297–30, nos. 70–80, A.-S.] Arch. Gesch. Med., 3, pp. 273–303. 1910.

§ b. Nomenclature

7424 Bonser (Wilfrid). Anglo-Saxon medical nomenclature. Engl. and Germanic Stud., 4, pp. 13–19. 1952.

7425 Bradshaw (Henry). On the oldest written remains of the Welsh language. [On ' 140 glosses or vernacular explanations ' in Welsh ' of hard words ' in an A.-S. ms. of Martianus Capella.] Camb. Antiq. Commns., 3 (1864–76), pp. 263–67. 1879.

A a

7426 Geldner (Johann). Untersuchung einiger altgenglischer Krankheitsnamen. 1. Folge. *Diss., Wurzburg.* pp. x, 50. 2. Folge. *Augsburg Programm.* pp. 48. 3. Folge. *Augsburg Programm.* pp. 48. 3 pt. 8° Braunschweig, 1906–08.

7427 Gillies (Hugh Cameron). Gaelic names of diseases and of diseased states. [Introduction, alphabetical list ; general words, the fevers, lung diseases, smallpox ; diarrhoea, skin diseases, the stomach and digestion, pregnancy and parturition, superstition, idiom of disease, philosophy of health.] Caledonian Med. J., N.S. 3, pp. 94–107, 183–94, 233–45. 1897–98.

7428 Lambert (Catherine). The Old English medical vocabulary. Proc. Roy. Soc. Med., 33, pp. 137–45. 1940.

7429 Osthoff (H.). Ags. *blǣc*, *blǣcðrustfel*. [*Blǣc*=pale and its compound *blǣcðrustfel* (glossed vitiligo) = lepra alba as opposed to lepra maculata nigra. ? vitiligo cognate with vitrum.] Engl. Studien, 32, pp. 181–85. 1903.

7430 Schlutter (Otto Bernhard). Anglo Saxonica. [*Disme* (muscus) : *hortu* (lapis) : *herse* m. — ahd. *hirsi* m. ? : *ǣwrænsian* ' geil werden ' : *arsgang* (latrina) : *ūf* (uvula) : *feporbyrste* ' vierberstig, *viergespalten* ' : *exe*, *ex* f. ' gehirn': *hælan* (castrare) : *lifrig* ' zum geliefern d. h. zum gerinnen geneigt ' : *gegymian* ' abkehlen ' : *gehnycned* ' gerunzelt ' : *burse*, *burs* f. ' bauchnetz, gekröse '.] Anglia, 30, pp. 123–34. 1907.

7431 —— Anglo-Saxonica. Altenglisches aus Leidener Handschriften : neuntes (zehntes) Jahrhundert. Anglia 33 (N. F. 21), pp. 239–51. 1910.

7432 —— Anglo-Saxonica. (= Weitere Nachträge zum Wörterbuche aus den Leechdoms). (Weitere keltische Spuren in altenglischen Glossaren). Anglia, 30, pp. 394–400 : 31, pp. 55–71, 135–40, 521–42 : 33, pp. 137–42. 1907–08, 1910.

7433 —— OE. *pillsǎpe* ' soap for removing hair '. Neophilol, 8, pp. 204–05. 1923.

7434 —— ' *Oððæt seo ex gesoht.*' [*Ex* = brain. Comparison of Lacnunga text with similar one in Leech-book.] Anglia, 32 (N.F. 20), pp. 257–58. 1909.

7435 Thoene (Franz). Die Namen der menschlichen Körperteile bei den Angelsachsen. *Diss., Kiel.* pp. xv, 132. 8° Kiel, 1912.

§ c. Epidemics
(Plague, pestilence, etc.)

7436 Bonser (Wilfrid). The date of Camlann—and of the pestilence of the same year. Antiquity, 24, pp. 142–43. 1950.

7437 —— Epidemics during the Anglo-Saxon period. With an appendix by Sir William MacArthur [*q.v.* **7442**.] J. Brit. Archaeol. Assoc., 3rd S. 9 (1944), pp. 48–71. [1946].

7438 Creighton (Charles). A history of epidemics in Britain from A.D. 664 to the extinction of plague. 2 vols., 8° Cambridge, 1891. [Vol. 1, pp. 1–16, A.–S. period.]

7439 Ireland. Census for the year 1851. Part 5. Tables of deaths, vol. 1, containing . . . tables of pestilences, *etc.* pp. iv, 560. fol. Dublin, 1856. [i. History of epidemic pestilences in Ireland : table of cosmical phenomena, epizootics, epiphitics, famines, and pestilences in Ireland : ii. Analysis of the table of cosmical phenomena : vii. Analysis of tables of pestilences and tables of deaths.]

7440 Lawlor (Hugh Jackson). Note on an Irish monastic office. [Recitation of an office against fire and against the ' Yellow Plague '. Notes on epidemic of 1091–96.] Hermathena, 10, pp. 212–25. 1899.

7441 MacArthur (*Sir* William Porter). Comments on Shrewbury's ' The Yellow Plague '. [**7447**.] J. Hist. Med., 5, pp. 214–15. 1950.

7442 —— Famine fevers in England and Ireland : the Yellow Pestilence, pestis flava, or *buidhe chonaill.* J. Brit. Archaeol. Assoc., 3rd S. 9 (1944), pp. 66–71. [1946].

7443 —— The identification of some pestilences recorded in the Irish annals. [i. *Blefed* (= bubonic plague) overlapped by *Buidhe Chonaill* (=relapsing fever) in 6th c. : ii. Bubonic plague in 7th c. : iii. Other outbreaks (*samtrusc, baccach,* etc. With an appendix (pp. 186–89) on ' leprosy '.] Irish Hist. Stud., 6, pp. 169–88. 1949.

7444 —— Old-time plague in Britain. [Pp. 404–05, A.–S., with much background.] J.R.A.M.C., 47, pp. 401–18. 1926.

7445 —— The pestilence called ' scamach '. [Deduces that ' the *scamach* was a widespread and virulent epidemic of influenza of which pneumonia was an outstanding feature.'] Irish Hist. Stud., 7, pp. 199–200. 1951.

7446 Piggott (Stuart). Pestilences in sixth century Britain. Antiquity, 24, pp. 143–45. 1950.

7447 Shrewsbury (John Findlay Drew). The Yellow Plague. [Argument that 6th and 7th c. visitations were both Yellow Plague : brought to England via Wales by ecclesiastics : identified as small pox.] J. Hist. Med., 4, pp. 5–48, + 1 plate. 1949.

§ d. General and Miscellaneous
(including diet and public health)

7448 Berdoe (Edward). The origin and growth of the healing art. pp. xii, 509. 8° London, 1893. [Pp. 273–86, A.–S. and Welsh medicine.]

7449 Blake (R. Marlay). Folk lore, with some account of the ancient Gaelic leeches and the state of the art of medicine in ancient Erin. County Louth Archaeol. J., 4, pp. 217–25. 1918.

7450 Bloch (Marc). Les rois thaumaturges. Étude sur le caractère surnaturel attribué à la puissance royale, particulièrement en France et en Angleterre. *Publ. Faculté des Lettres, Univ. Strasbourg,* 19. pp. 542, + 4 plates. 8° Strasbourg, 1914. [*Especially* Edward the Confessor, *passim.*]

7451 Bonser (Wilfrid). Medical lore and disease in Anglo-Saxon England. *Publications of the Wellcome Historical Medical Museum,* N.S. 9. pp. 470 (approx.). 8° London, 195–? (in the press). [Medical mss., epidemics, surgery, heathenism, relics, magical practices, food, herbals, leprosy, veterinary medicine, etc.]

7452 Bonser (Wilfrid). General medical practice in Anglo-Saxon England. Science, medicine and history : essays in honour of Charles Singer, 1, pp. 154–63. 1953.

7453 Butler (Hubert). The dumb and the stammerers in early Irish history. Antiquity, 23, pp. 20–31. 1949.

7454 —— Who were ' the stammerers ' ? [In early Ireland : dumbness and stammering.] J. Roy. Soc. Antiq. Ireland, 80, pp. 228–36. 1950.

7455 Creighton (Charles). Public health. Social England, ed. Traill and Mann, 1, pp. 253–56. 1891.

7456 Ellett (G. G.). [Anglo-] Saxon medicine. [General remarks.] B.M.J., 1908, 1, pp. 999–1000. 1908.

7457 Erhardt-Siebold (Erika von). The hellebore in Anglo-Saxon pharmacy. [=Mezereum.] Engl. Studien, 71, pp. 161–70. 1936.

7458 Fleetwood (John). History of medicine in Ireland. pp. xvi, 420, + 18 plates. 8° Dublin, 1951. [Pp. 10–14, ' The Brehon laws ', as far as they affect medicine and lunacy : pp. 15–23, ' medicine and Christianity ', but ?accuracy (including dating) as regards epidemics (Ed.)]

7459 Gayre (George Robert). Wassail ! in mazers of mead. An account of mead, metheglin, sack and other ancient liquors . . . with some comment upon the drinking customs of our forebears. pp. 176. 8° London, 1948. [Pp. 39–53, the ale and mead of our A.–S. and Norse ancestors : pp. 54–65, Celtic mead.]

7460 Gramm (Willi). Die Körperpflege der Angelsachsen. Eine kulturgeschichtlich-etymologische Untersuchung. *Anglistische Forschungen*, 86. pp. 137. 8° Heidelberg, 1938.

7461 Groen (Fredrik). Remarks on the earliest medical conditions in Norway and Iceland, with special reference to British influence. [Considers that dysentery and leprosy were imported from A.–S. England.] Science, medicine and history. Essays in honour of Charles Singer, 1, pp. 143–53. 1953.

7462 Grube (F. W.). Meat foods of the Anglo–Saxons. J. Engl. and Germ. Philol., 34, pp. 511–29. 1935.

7463 Hollingsworth (A. G.) *Rev.* Notes on the medical, surgical, and pharmaceutical archaeology of Suffolk. [Pp. 255–8, ' Dr. Cinfrid ' [!], etc.] Proc. Bury and W. Suffolk Archaeol. Inst., 1, pp. 253–67. 1852.

7464 James (R. R.). The medical history of William the Conqueror. Lancet, 232, p. 1151. 1937.

7465 Liebermann (Felix). Angelsächsische Arzneikunde im 12. Jahrhundert fortlebend. Archiv Stud. neueren Spr., Bd. 147, pp. 92–93. 1924.

7466 —— Speiseverbote der Angelsachsen. [Horseflesh.] *Same jnl.*, Bd. 147, p. 250. 1924.

7467 Loomis (Charles Grant). Hagiological healing. [Including various Celtic instances.] Bull. Hist. Med., 8, pp. 636–42. 1940.

7468 —— The miracle traditions of the Venerable Bede. [Derivation from Dialogues of Gregory the Great, etc. Bede's selection of narratives of healing and his omission of the unverified or more improbable elements.] Speculum, 21, pp. 404–18. 1946.

7469 Mac Arthur (*Sir* William Porter). Some notes on old-time leprosy in England and Ireland. [A small amount of A.–S. material, and much background.] J.R.A.M.C. ; 45, pp. 410–22. 1925.

7470 Moloney (Michael F.). Irish ethno-botany and the evolution of medicine in Ireland. pp. 96. 8° Dublin, 1919.

7471 Payne (Joseph Frank). English medicine in the Anglo-Saxon times. *Fitz-Patrick Lectures, Royal College of Physicians, for* 1903. pp. vii, 162, + 16 plates. 8° Oxford, 1904.

7472 Pearson (Karl). A myth about Edward the Confessor. [i.e. that he was an albino.] E.H.R., 25, pp. 517–20. 1910.

7473 Phillimore (Egerton). ' Homo planus ' and leprosy in Wales. [Some instances of leprosy in early Wales and Ireland.] Arch. Camb., 75 (6th S. 20), pp. 224–50. 1920.

7474 Rohde (Eleanour Sinclair). The Old English herbals, pp. xii, 243, + 18 plates. 8° London, 1922. [Pp. 1–41, + 4 plates, A.–S. herbals.]

7475 Singer (Charles Joseph). Early English magic and medicine. [Re-arranged and abbreviated in his From magic to science, pp. 133–67, + 7 plates (5 coloured). 1928.] Proc. Brit. Acad., [9], pp. 341–74. 1920.

7476 —— Magic and medicine in early England. [Synopsis of Fison Memorial lecture, Guy's Hospital Medical School.] Nature, 137, p. 1081. 1936.

7477 —— Sketches in the history of English medicine. 1. Dawn : Celtic and Anglo-Saxon medical and pharmaceutical practice from the 9th to the 13th centuries. Chemist and Druggist, 108, pp. 823–32. 1928.

7477a Smart (*Sir* William R. E.). Notes towards the history of the medical staff of the English army prior to the accession of the Tudors. Enlarged from a paper, *etc.* pp. 35. 8° London, 1873. *Also in* Brit. Med. J., 1873, 1, pp. 111–13 [A.–S.]. 1873.

7478 Strachan (Lionel Richard Mortimer). Hernia among the Anglo-Saxons. [Hēala.] N. and Q., 160, pp. 192–93. 1931.

7479 Thompson (Charles John Samuel). Chirurgie Anglo-Saxonne. Ier Congrès de l'histoire de l'art de guérir, 1920, Liber Memoralis, pp. 61–64, + 1 plate. 1921.

7480 Thorndike (Lynn). A history of magic and experimental science during the first thirteen centuries of our era. 4 vol. 8°New York, 1929–34. [Vol. I, ch. 4 (pp. 719–41), A.–S., Salernitan and other Latin medicine in mss. 9th–12th c.]

7481 Webb (George Herbert). Abnormal deposit of salivary calculus in the Anglo-Saxon. [A.–S. skull from east Yorks.] Brit. Dental J., 48, pp. 577–79. 1927.

118. MAGIC AND CHARMS

(including medical : *see also* Section **81** for loricas)

7482 Akerman (John Yonge). Notes on the ' *hwiting treow* ' of the Anglo-Saxons. [Argument that the dog-wood, rather than the linden, rowan, or way-faring-tree, was that used for augury (*tân*).] Archaeologia, 42, pp. 124–26. 1869.

7483 Arbois de Jubainville (Marie Henry d'). Des victimes immolées par les constructeurs pour assurer la solidité des édifices. Rev. celt., 26, p. 289. 1905.

7484 Assmann (Bruno). Prophezeiung aus dem I. Januar für das Jahr. [A.–S., text from MS. Cotton Vesp. D XIV., fol. 75 b.] Anglia, 11, p. 369. 1889.

7485 —— Eine Regel über den Donner. [A.–S. text. MS. Cotton Vesp. D. XIV, f.103b.] Anglia, 10, p. 185. 1888.

7486 Axon (William Edward Armitage). On a reference to the evil eye in the Anglo-Saxon poem of Beowulf. Trans. Roy. Soc. Lit., 2nd S. 21, pp. 117–19. 1900.

7487 Bonser (Wilfrid). A comparative study of magical practices among the Anglo-Saxons. *Ph. D. thesis, London.* pp. 218. fol. 1927. [Apply Univ. Library.]

7488 —— The dissimilarity of ancient Irish magic from that of the Anglo-Saxons. Folk-lore, 37, pp. 271–88. 1926.

7489 —— Magical practices against elves. [Elfshot in A.–S. medicine.] Folk-lore, 37, pp. 350–63. 1926.

7490 —— The Seven Sleepers of Ephesus in Anglo-Saxon and later recipes. Folk-lore, 56, pp. 254–56. 1945.

7491 —— The significance of colour in ancient and mediaeval magic, with some modern comparisons. [With many A.–S. examples.] Man, 25, pp. 194–98. 1925.

7492 Bradley (Henry). The song of the Nine magic herbs (Neunkräutersegen). Archiv Stud. neuren Spr., Bd. 113, pp. 144–45. 1904.

7493 Brandl (Alois). Vom kosmologischen Denken des heidnisch-christlichen Germanentums : Der früh-ags. Schicksalsspruch des Handschrift Tiberius B. 13 und seine Verwandtheit mit Boethius. pp. 12. Sitzungsb. preuss. Akad. Wiss., Hist.–philos. Kl., 1937, pp. 116–25. 1937.

7494 Brie (Maria). Der germanische, insbesondere der englische Zauberspruch. Mitth. d. schles. Ges. f. Volkskunde, 8, pp. 1–36. 1906.

7495 —— Über die angelsächsische Bezeichnung des Wortes Zauberer. Engl. Studien, 41, pp. 20–27. 1909.

7496 Dietrich (Franz Eduard Christoph). Drei altheidnische Segenformeln. Nebst einigen Jüngeren, auf Runendenkmälern und in Hss. aufgefunden. Z.f.d.A., 13, pp. 193–217. 1867.

7497 —— Fünf northumbrische Runenspruche. [i. Aus Cod. Cotton Otho C V, p. 41 : ii. Aus Whitakers Richmondshire II, 229 : iii. Aus Hickes Thesaurus, I, 135 : iv. Die Inschrift von Aylesbury : v. Die Runenverse des St. Galler Codex 878.] Z.f.d.A., 14, pp. 104–23. 1869.

7498 Foerster (Max). Die altenglischen Traumlunare. [With text from MS. Cotton Tib. A. III and from Cotton Cal. A. XV, and Bodl. Hatton, 115 (all end of 11th c.) Dream interpretation by the age of the moon.] Engl. Studien, 60, pp. 58–93. 1925.

7499 Foerster (Max). Die altenglischen Verzeichnisse von Glücks—und Unglückstagen. Studies in English philology . . . in honour of F. Klaeber, pp. 258–77. 1929.

7500 —— Beiträge zur mittelalterlichen Volkskunde. [Prognostications : contents of MS. Cotton Tib. A. III, etc.] Archiv Stud. neueren Spr., Bd. 120, pp. 43–52, 296–305 : 121, pp. 30–46 : 125, pp. 39–70 : 128, pp. 55–71. 1908–12.

7501 —— Die Kleinliteratur des Aberglaubens im Altenglischen. [Prognostications, blood-letting, dreams, etc.] *Same jnl.*, Bd. 110, pp. 346–58. 1903.

7502 Foerster (Max). Vom Forleben antiker Sammellunare im englischen und in anderen Volkssprachen. [Pp. 41–129, Die altenglische Version.] Anglia, 67–68 (N.F. 55–56), pp. 1–171. 1944.

7503 Gaidoz (Henri). L'origine de l'hymne de Colman. [Composed (as a protection against the Yellow Plague) 661.] Rev. celt., 4, pp. 94–103, 412. 1881–2.

7504 Grattan (John Henry Grafton). Three Anglo-Saxon charms from the Lacnunga. [i. For *fær-stice* : ii. Nineherbs charm : iii. For nightmare.] Mod. Lang Rev., 22, pp. 1–6. 1927.

7505 Graves (James). The discovery of an amber bead inscribed with an Ogham . . . used as an amulet for the cure of sore eyes. . . . J. Kilkenny Archaeol. Soc., [4] N.S. 1, pp. 149–50. 1856.

7506 Grendon (Felix). The Anglo-Saxon charms. J. American folk-lore, 22, pp. 105–227. 1909.

7507 Henel (Heinrich). Altenglischer Mönchsaberglaube. [i. Aderlass an den Hundstagen : ii. Ein altenglisches Aderlasslunar : iii. 24 kritische Aderlasstage: iv. 3 glückliche Nativitätstage : v. Die Pleiaden : vi. Die Bedeutung des Wortes Alleluia.] Engl. Studien, 69, pp. 329–39. 1935.

7508 Holthausen (Ferdinand). Altenglische Kleinigkeiten. 1. Fieberzauber. [MS. Vatican Regina 338, fol. 88 b. Names of Seven Sleepers as charm against *gedrif.*] Archiv Stud. neueren Spr., Bd. 99, p. 424. 1897.

7509 —— Die altenglischen Neunkräutersegen. [Text and notes.] Engl. Studien, 69, pp. 180–83. 1934.

7510 —— Zaubersegen. Anglia, Beibl., 31, pp. 30–32. 1920.

7511 —— Zum ae. Neunkräutersegen. Anglia, Beibl., 29, pp. 283–84. 1918.

7512 —— Zum ae. Zaubersprüchen und Segen. Anglia, Beibl., 31, pp. 116–20. 1920.

7513 —— Zum Zaubersprüchen. Anglia, Beibl., 36, p. 219. 1925.

7514 Horn (Wilhelm). Der altenglische Zauberspruch gegen den Hexenschuss. Probleme der engl. Sprache und Kultur. Festschrift J. Hoops, pp. 88–104. 1925.

7515 Horne (Ethelbert) *abbot of Downside*. Cowrie shells in Anglo-Saxon graves. [Evidence from Camerton.] Antiq. J., 13, p. 167. 1933.

7516 Huebener (Gustav). *Beowulf* and Germanic exorcism. Rev. Engl. Stud., 11, pp. 163–81. 1935.

7517 —— Beowulf's *seax*, the Saxons and an Indian exorcism. *Same jnl.*, 12, pp. 429–39. 1936.

7518 Hull (Eleanor). The ancient hymn-charms of Ireland. [Loricas, etc.] Folk-lore, 21, pp. 417–46. 1910.

7519 Hull (Eleanor). Old Irish tabus, or *geasa*. Folk-lore, 12, pp. 41–66. 1901.

7520 Lethbridge (Thomas Charles). The meaning of the cowrie : Fiji, Egypt, and Saxon England. [?against evil eye.] Man, 41, p. 48. 1941.

7521 Lindquist (Ivar). Galdrar. De gamla germanska trollsängernas stil undersökt i samband med en svensk runinskrift fran folkvandringstiden. Göteborgs Högskolas Årsskrift, 29, i. pp. viii, 193. 1923.

7522 MacBain (Alexander). Gaelic incantations. [St. Columba, passim.] Trans. Gaelic Soc. Inverness, 17, pp. 222–66. 1892.

7523 McBryde (J. M.) *jr.* Charms to recover stolen cattle. [*See also* for later examples, vol. 22, pp. 168–70. 1907.] Mod. Lang. Notes, 21, pp. 180–83, 254–55. 1906.

7524 Mackenzie (William). Gaelic incantations, charms, and blessings of the Hebrides. [St. Columba, passim.] Trans. Gaelic Soc. Inverness, 18, pp. 97–182. 1894.

7525 Magnússon (Eiríkr). Darraðarljóð. [11th c. Poem sung, according to Nialssaga, by ' weirds ' on Ap. 23, 1014, against Sigurd Silkbeard, king of Dublin, at battle of Clontarf.] Old-lore Misc., V.C., 3, pp. 78–94. 1910.

7526 Magoun (Francis Peabody) *jr.* OE charm A13 : *butan heardan bēaman.* [Grendon's notation A13. Fertiliser to make farm-land fertile to include all wood on the estate as an ingredient, except hard wood.] Mod. Lang. Notes, 58, pp. 33–34. 1943.

7527 —— Strophische Überreste in den altenglischen Zaubersprüchen. Engl. Studien, 72, pp. 1–6. 1937.

7528 —— Zu den ae. Zaubersprüchen. Archiv Stud. neueren Spr., Bd. 171, pp. 17–35. 1937.

7529 Meroney (Howard). Irish in the Old English charms. Speculum, 20, pp. 172–82. 1945.

7530 —— The Nine Herbs. [Lacnunga.] Mod. Lang. Notes, 59, pp. 157–60. 1944.

7531 Meyer (Kuno). Ein altirischer Heilsegen. [A spell to heal wounds inflicted by adders by covering them with blood.] Sitzungsb. preuss. Akad. Wiss., 1916, pp. 420–22. 1916.

7532 Mezger (Fritz). Der germanische Kult und die ae. Feminina auf -icge und -estre. [Feminine suffixes relating to magic and witchcraft.] Archiv Stud. neueren Spr., Bd. 168, pp. 177–84. 1935.

7533 Mincoff (Marko Konstantinov). Die Bodentungsentwicklung der ags. Ausdrücke für ' Kraft ' und ' Macht '. *Palaestra*, 188. pp. x, 156. 8° Leipzig, 1933.

7534 Napier (Arthur Sampson). Altenglische Miscellen. [A.–S. charms and prescriptions from Bodley MS. Auct. F.3.6, fol. 1 and 2 v. : from Worcester Cathedral MS. 4° 5 : from MS. fragments belonging to Lord Robartes (Viscount Clifden).] Archiv f. d. Stud. neueren Sprachen, Bd. 84, pp. 323–27. 1890.

7534a Ohrt (Ferdinand). Beiträge zur Segenforschung. [Pp. 5–7, ii. Der Woden-Auftritt im altenglischen ' Nigon wyrta galdar.'] Zeit. d. Vereins f. Volkskunde, 37, pp. 1–9. 1927.

7535 Pegge (Samuel). A dissertation of an ancient jewel of the Anglo-Saxons. [?a coin of Burgred of Mercia pierced for suspension. In Bodleian Library.] Archaeologia, 1, pp. 177–86. 1770.

7536 Plummer (Charles). Cáin Eimíne Báin. [Translation of an Irish tract which 'relates how Eïmíne Bán and 49 of his monks vicarously sacrificed themselves by voluntary death in order to save Bran úa Faeláin, king of Leinster, and 49 Leinster chiefs from the pestilence'.] Ériu, 4, pp. 38–46. 1908.

7537 Priebsch (Robert Charles). An Old English charm and the Wiener Hundesegen. Academy, 48 (May 23). 1896.

7538 Randolph (Mary Claire). Celtic smiths and satirists : partners in sorcery. E.H.L., 8, pp. 184–97. 1941.

7539 Reeves (William) *bp. of Down.* On the Hymnus Sancti Aidi. [8th c. charm for headache, and identification of Aedh as contemporary of Columba.] Proc. R.I.A., 7 (1858), pp. 91–96. 1862.

7540 Schroeder (Edward). Ueber das Spell. Z.f.d.A., 37, pp. 241–68. 1893.

7541 Shook (L. K.). Notes on the Old-English charms. Mod. Lang. Notes, 55, pp. 139–40. 1940.

7542 Skemp (Arthur Rowland). The Anglo-Saxon charms. [Reviewing **7506**.] Mod. Lang. Rev., 6, pp. 262–66. 1911.

7543 —— The Old English charms. Mod. Lang. Rev., 6, pp. 289–301. 1911.

7544 Storms (Godfrid). Anglo-Saxon magic. pp. ix, 336. 8° The Hague, 1948. [i. Comments : ii. Texts with translations. Other textual emendations are suggested by Karl Jost in his review *in* English Studies, 31, 1950, pp. 101–05.]

7545 Strobl (Joseph). Zur Spruchdichtung bei den Angelsachsen. Z. f.d. A., 31, pp. 54–64. 1887.

7546 Telting (A.). Angel-Saksische bezweringsformulieren. De Vrije Fries, 2, pp. 1–9. 1842.

7547 Townend (B. R.). The narrative charm with reference to toothache. Brit. Dent. J., 85, pp. 29–34, 86. 1948.

7548 Windisch (Ernst). Über das altirische Gedicht im Codex Boernerianus

und über die altirischen Zauberformeln. Ber. k. sächs. Gesell. Wiss., 1890, pp. 83–108. 1890.

7549 Wordsworth (Christopher). Two Yorkshire charms or amulets : exorcisms and adjurations. [Contains some A.-S. material : A.-S. Durham ritual, etc.] Yorks. Archaeol. J., 17, pp. 377–412 + 1 plate. 1903.

7550 Zimmer (Heinrich). Ein altirischer Zauberspruch aus der Vikingerzeit. [*Scyttisc gecost gealdor*, in Leech-Book, I. xlv. 5.] Zeit. f. vergl. Sprachforschung, 33, pp. 141–53. 1895.

7551 Zupitza (Julius). Kreuzandacht (Kreuzzauber). [Latin and A.-S. charms from pp. 611–15 (617) of MS. 391 in library of Corpus Christi College, Cambridge.] Archiv Stud. neueren Spr., Bd. 88, pp. 361–65. 1892.

7552 —— Ein Zauberspruch. [' Wenne, wenne, wenchichenne . . . ' in B.M. MS. Royal 4 A XIV, f. 106 b.] Z.f.d.A., 31, pp. 45–52. 1887.

119. FOLK-LORE

§ *a.* General, Anglo-Saxon

(A selection : articles from journals listed).

7553 Carter (George Edward Lovelace). Folk-lore of the saints. Devonian Y.B., 24, pp. 61–66. 1933.

7553a Chambers (Raymond Wilson). Six thirteenth century drawings illustrating the story of Offa and of Thryth (Drida). pp. 3, + 6 plates. 8° London, 1912. [Cotton Nero D I.]

7554 Cockayne (Oswald). Yule week. [MS. CCC. 41, p. 122 margin. A.-S. text.] The Shrine, pp. 29–35. 1864–67.

7555 Collingwood (William Gershom). King William the wanderer. Saga-Book V.C., 4, pp. 171–81. 1905.

7556 Cox (John Charles). On the flabellum. [Eucharistic fan. First plate shows ' Saxon figure, with flabellum, Enville, Staffs.'] Reliquary, N. [2nd] S., 1, pp. 65–68, + 2 plates. 1887.

7557 Emerson (Oliver Farrar). The legend of Joseph's bones in Old and Middle English. [Elene, lines 785 *et seq.* ?derived from Talmud.] Mod. Lang. Notes, 14, pp. 331–34. 1899.

7558 Fisher (August). Aberglaube unter den Angel-Sachsen. *Programme des Realgymnasiums zu Meiningen.* pp. 42. 4° Meiningen, 1891. [Reste des heidnischen Cultus : Böse Geister und Ungeheuer : Zauber : Weissagung : Schutz- und Heilmittel.]

7559 Fiske (Christabel Forsyth). Animals in early English ecclesiastical literature, 650–1500. [Service to man : as spiritual beings or devils disguised.] P.M.L.A., 28, pp. 368–87. 1913.

7560 Galbraith (Vivian Hunter). Edward the Confessor and the church of Clavering. [Ring-legend.] Trans. Essex Archaeol. Soc., N.S. 16, pp. 187–89 : 17, pp. 48–49. 1923, 26.

7561 Gough (Alfred Bradley). The Constance saga. *Palaestra*, 23. pp. 84. 8° Berlin, 1902. [On a legend contained in the Vita Offae primi and other mss., including the French Chronicle of Nicholas Trivet. Relation to history : the Northumbria saga of Ælla and Eadwine, Constantine II, king of Scots and Anlaf Cuaran of Northumbria, the lives of the two Offas, Cynethryth queen of Mercia in history, etc.]

7562 Heanley (R. M.). The Vikings : traces of their folklore in Marshland [i.e. the Fens.] Saga-Book V.C., 3 pp. 35–62. 1902.

7563 James (Montague Rhodes). Names of angels in Anglo-Saxon and other documents. J. Theol. Stud., 11, pp. 569–71. 1910.

7564 —— An ancient English list of the seventy disciples. [From 9th c. MS. Cotton Vesp. B. VI, with variants from 10th c. MS. C.C.C.C. 183.] *Same jnl.*, 11, pp. 459–62. 1910.

7565 Krappe (Alexander Haggerty). The Offa-Constance legend. [Theory that not of A.-S. but of Byzantine origin.] Anglia, 61 (N.F. 49), pp. 361–69. 1937.

7566 Liebrecht (Felix). Folk-lore. 1. Godiva. [Comparison of Godiva story with similar folk-lore themes.] Engl. Studien, 1, pp. 171–73. 1877.

7567 Murray (Margaret Alice). The divine king in England. pp. 279, + 12 plates. 8° London, 1954. [Pp. 44–55, Royal and substitute victims, Saxon period.]

7568 Napier (Arthur Sampson). Altenglische Kleinigkeiten. [Text of the Ages of the World, etc. *See also* 11, p. 174 for another text of it.] Anglia, 11, pp. 1–10. 1889.

7569 Sawyer (Frederick W.), **Skeat** (Walter William), *etc.* Totemism amongst the Anglo-Saxons. [-ing.] N. and Q., 6th S. 9, pp. 429, 494–95 : 10, pp. 73, 110–11, 225. 1884.

7570 Serjeantson (Mary Sidney). The vocabulary of folk-lore in Old and Middle English. Folk-lore, 47, pp. 42–73. 1936.

7571 Stefanović (Svetislav). Ein Beitrag zur angelsächsischen Offa-Sage. [Folk-lore basis of the saga.] Anglia, 35 (N.F. 23), pp. 483–525. 1912.

7572 —— Zur Offa-Thryðo-Episode im *Beowulf*. Engl. Studien, 69, pp. 15–31. 1934.

7573 Stredder (E.). The Yule of Saxon days. N. and Q., 8th S. 8, pp. 480–83 : 9, pp. 2–4, 102–04, 162–63, 262–63, 342–44. 1895–96.

7574 Tatlock (John Strong Perry). The dragons of Wessex and Wales. Speculum, 8, pp. 223–35. 1933.

7575 Thrupp (John). British superstitions as to hares, geese, and poultry. [Including some A.-S. and Welsh.] Trans. Ethnol. Soc., N.S. 5, pp. 162–67. 1867.

7576 Whistler (Charles Watts). Tradition and folklore of the Quantocks. Saga-Book V.C., 5, pp. 142–50. 1907.

7577 Wright (Thomas). On the legend of Weland the smith. Archaeologia, 32, pp. 315–24. 1847.

7578 —— On the legendary history of Wayland Smith. J. Brit. Archaeol. Assoc., 16, pp. 50–58. 1860.

7579 Zupitza (Julius). Die altenglische Bearbeitung der Erzählung von Apollonius von Tyrus. [With A.-S. text.] Archiv Stud. neueren Spr., Bd. 97, pp. 17–34. 1896.

§ b. General, Celtic

(A selection: articles from journals listed)

7580 Collingwood (William Gershom). A legend of Shetland from Fljótsdæla saga. Saga-Book V.C., 5, pp. 272–87. 1908.

7581 Cooke (Thomas Lalor). Description of the Barnaan Cuilawn, and some conjectures upon the original use thereof; together with an account of the superstitious purposes to which it was latterly applied. Also a description of the remains of an ancient mill, which were recently discovered near the ruins of Glankeen church, in the county of Tipperary. [?early 10th c.] Trans. R.I.A., 14 (Antiq.), pp. 31–45, + 1 plate. 1825.

7582 Crowe (John O'Beirne) *trs. and ed.* Siabur-Charpat con Culaind. [The demoniac chariot of Cu Chulaind]. From ' Lebor na h-Uidre ' (fol. 37, *et seq.*), a manuscript of the Royal Irish Academy. J. Roy. Hist. and Arch. Assoc. Ireland, [11], 4th S. 1 (1870–71), pp. 371–448. 1878.

7583 Dillon (Myles). The taboos of the kings of Ireland. [Irish from MS. Egerton 1782 : text and translation.] Proc. R.I.A., 54 c, pp. 1–36. 1951.

7584 Dobbs (Margaret E.). Manannan Mac Lir. [Synopsis of lecture]. J. Manx Mus., 1, pp. 106–08, 116–18. 1928.

7585 Dottin (Georges). Les deux chagrins du royaume du ciel. [' Dá brón flatha nime,' the legendary history of Elijah and Enoch.] Rev. celt., 21, pp. 349–87. 1900.

7586 Gaidoz (Henri). Comparative notes to the Mabinogion. I. Ransom by weight. Y Cymmrodor, 10, pp. 1–11. 1889.

7587 Gill (W. Walter). The Wonders of the Isle of Man. [From Irish version of Nennius : ? mid 11th c.] Folk-lore, 50, pp. 33–44. 1939.

7588 Gruffydd (W. J.). Mabon vab Modron. Y Cymmrodor, 42, pp. 129–47. 1930.

7589 Hamel (Anton Gerard van). Aspects of Celtic mythology. Proc. Brit. Acad., 20, pp. 207–48. 1934.

7590 Hutson (Arthur E.). Geoffrey of Monmouth : two notes. [i. Brychan and Geoffrey of Monmouth's Ebraucus : ii. Welsh heroes at Arthur's court.] Trans. Hon. Soc. Cymm., 1937, pp. 361–73. 1938.

7591 Jackson (Kenneth). The adventure of Laeghaire Mac Crimhthainn [Underworld story. ? of second half of 9th c. Irish text and English translation.] Speculum, 17, pp. 377–89. 1942.

7592 —— The motive of the threefold death in the story of Suibhne Geilt. Essays presented to E. MacNeill, pp. 535–50. 1940.

7593 —— The poems of Llywarch the Aged. Antiquity, 9, pp. 322–27. 1935.

7594 —— ' The wild man of the woods.' [Irish legend of Suibhne Geilt (' the madman ') Ulster king of 7th c., with analogous legends.] Yorks. Soc. Celtic Stud., Rpt. for 1934–35, pp. 13–14. 1935.

7595 Meyer (Kuno), *trs.* The wooing of Emer : an Irish hero-tale of the 11th century. [1st translation, from Lebor na-h-Uidre, compiled c. 1050.] Archaeol. Rev., 1, pp. 68–75, 150–55, 231–35, 298–307. 1888.

7596 O'Nolan (T. P.) *ed.* Mòr of Munster and the tragic fate of Cuann son of Cailchin. [Irish text and translation : historical references, glossary, names of persons and places, succession of Munster kings, 484–737]. Proc. R.I.A., 30 c, pp. 261–82. 1912.

7597 Rees (J. Rogers). The Norse element in Celtic myth. Arch. Camb., 5th S. 15, pp. 312–44. 1898.

7598 Seymour (St. John Drelincourt). The Book of Adam and Eve in Ireland. [Saltair na Rann. Epitome of story : apocryphal elements.] Proc. R.I.A., 36 c, pp. 121–33. 1922.

7599 —— The bringing forth of the soul in Irish literature. J. Theol. Stud., 22, pp. 16–20. 1921.

7600 Seymour (St. John Drelincourt.) Irish versions of the vision of St. Paul. *Same jnl.*, 24, pp. 54–59. 1923.

7601 —— The seven heavens in Irish literature. Zeit. celt. Philol., 14, pp. 18–30. 1923.

7602 Stokes (Whitley). A few parallels between the Old-Norse and the Irish literatures and traditions. Arkiv nord. Filol., 2, pp. 339–41. 1885.

7603 —— *ed.* Three legends from the Brussels manuscripts 5100–4. [i. Interview between Coirpre Crom, bp. in Clonmacnoise (d. 899) and soul of Maelsechlainn, overking 843–60 (*see* Four Masters, 899): ii. S. Ciarán of Clonmacnoise replaces head upon a wicked Coirpre Crom, who has been decapitated: iii. Story of S. Colmán mac Duach and Gúaire the Generous, king of Aidne (d. 622). Irish text and English translation.] Rev. celt., 26, pp. 360–77. 1905.

7604 Wentz (Walter Yeeling Evans). The fairy-faith in Celtic countries: its psychological origin and nature. *Thesis, Rennes.* pp. xxii, 314. 8° Rennes, 1909. [Pp. 201–41, Cult: Testimony of archaeology, paganism and of Christianity.]

7605 Westropp (Thomas Johnson). Notes and folklore from the Rennes copy of the Dindsenchas. [Wonders and monsters, magic, natural history, etc.] J. Roy. Soc. Antiq. Ireland, 29 (5th S. 9), pp. 21–27. 1899.

7606 Wilde (*Sir* William Robert Wills). On the ancient and modern races of oxen in Ireland. [Including cow-lore and mentions of cattle in Irish annals.] Proc. R.I.A., 7 (1858), pp. 64–75. 1862.

7607 Zimmer (Heinrich). Keltische Beiträge: 1. Germanen, germanische Lehnwörter und germanische Sagenelemente in der ältesten Überlieferung der irischen Heldensage. [For no. 2, *see* 6282.] Z.f.d.A., 32, pp. 196–334. 1888.

7608 —— Keltische Beiträge: 3. Weitere nordgermanische Einflusse in der ältesten Überlieferung der irischen Heldensage; Ursprung und Entwicke-lung der Finn-(Ossian-)sage; die Vikinger Irlands in Sage, Geschichte und Recht der Iren. Z.f.d.A., 35, pp. 1–172. 1891.

§ *c.* Arthuriana

(A selection: i.e. articles from journals listed, only)

7609 Bennett (R. E.). *Arthur and Gorlagon*, the Dutch *Lancelot*, and St. Kentigern. Speculum, 13, pp. 68–75. 1938.

7610 Davies (J. H.). A Welsh version of the birth of Arthur. [From Nat. Lib. Wales, Llanstephan MS. 201: 15th c., Welsh and translation.] Y Cymmrodor, 24, pp. 247–64 + 1 plate. 1913.

7611 Foulon (C.). Enchanted forests in Arthurian romance. Yorks. Celtic Stud., 5, pp. 3–18. 1952.

7612 Hamel (Anton Gerard van). Tristan's combat with the dragon. Rev. celt., 41, pp. 331–49. 1924.

7613 Hammer (Jacob). A commentary on the *Prophetia Merlini* (Geoffrey of Monmouth's *Historia Regum Britanniae*, Book VII). [With Latin text.] Speculum, 10, pp. 3–30; 15, pp. 409–31. 1935–40.

7614 Krappe (Alexander Haggerty). Arthur and Gorlagon. Speculum, 8, pp. 209–22. 1933.

7615 —— Arturus cosmocrator. ['Cornish tradition that king Arthur is still alive, though in the shape of a raven.'] Speculum, 20, pp. 405–14. 1945.

7616 —— The fighting snakes in the Historia Britonum of Nennius. [Temp. Vortigern.] Rev. celt., 43, pp. 124–31. 1926.

7617 —— Note sur un épisode de *l'Historia Britonum* de Nennius. [Chap. 41–42, human sacrifice by Vortigern on failure to build castle in Wales.] Rev. celt., 41, pp. 181–88. 1924.

7618 Llwyd (Angharad). Arthur and his knights—out of an old Welsh ms. in the possession of A. Llwyd. [Classification of 24 knights according to their gifts.] Arch. Camb., 1, pp. 48–49. 1846.

7619 Milne (Frank A.) *trs.* Arthur and Gorlagon. Translated by F. A. Milne, with notes by A. Nutt. Folk-lore, 15, pp. 40–67. 1904.

7620 Parry (John Jay). The triple death in the Vita Merlini [attributed to Geoffrey of Monmouth.] Speculum, 5, pp. 216–17. 1930.

7621 Rhŷs (*Sir* John). Notes on the hunting of Twrch Trwyth. Trans. Hon. Soc. Cymm, 1894–95, pp. 1–34, 146–48. 1896.

7622 Southward (Elaine C.). Arthur's dream. [Of a bear (*Arth*) withered by breath of a sea-dragon (*Mor-draig*): when on his way to Gaul, leaving Britain in care of Mordred.] Speculum, 18, pp. 249–51. 1943.

7623 —— The knight Yder and the *Beowulf* legend in Arthurian romance. Medium Ævum, 15, pp. 1–47. 1946.

7624 Tatlock (John Strong Perry). Geoffrey of Monmouth's *Vita Merlini.* Speculum, 18, pp. 265–87. 1943.

7625 Thompson (James Westfall). Ancient Celtic symptoms in Arthurian romance. Trans. Hon. Soc. Cymm., 1936, pp. 137–42. 1937.

7626 Veitsch (John). Merlin and the Merlinian poems. [? a real person.] J. Brit. Archaeol. Assoc., 45, pp. 123–30, 207–14. 1889.

7627 Yardley (E.), *etc.* Sleeping KingArthur. [Mugglewick (co. Durham), Eildon hills, Richmond castle, etc.] N. and Q., 9th S. 12, pp. 502–03 : 10th S. 1, pp. 77, 194. 1903–04.

§ *d.* Monsters (Grendel, Etc.)

7628 Chambers (Raymond Wilson). Beowulf and waterfall-trolls. Times Lit. Supp., 28, p. 383. 1929.

7629 —— Beowulf's fight with Grendel, and its Scandinavian parallels. [The story of Orm Storolfsson : Beowulf and the Sandhaugar episode : the saga of Samson the Fair.] English Studies, 11, pp. 81–100. 1929.

7630 Clarke (Esther Dinah). *Obthrust* in north Lincolnshire. Leeds studies in English, 4, pp. 78–79. 1935.

7631 Classen (Ernest). O.E. ' nicras ' (Beowulf, 422, 575, 845, 1427). Mod. Lang. Rev., 10, pp. 85–86. 1915.

7632 Crawford (Samuel John). Grendel's descent from Cain. *Same jnl.*, 24, p. 63. 1929.

7633 Donahue (Charles). Grendel and the *Clanna Cain.* J. Celtic Studies, 1, pp. 167–75. 1950.

7634 Gadde (Fredrik). Viktor Rydberg and some Beowulf questions. [Grendel and his mother, the Breca episode, the Herebeald-Hæthcyn episode, etc.] Studia Neophil., 15, pp. 71–90. 1942.

7635 Harder (Hermann). Zur Herkunft von ahd. thuris, ags. *þyrs*, aisl. *þurs.* Archiv Stud. neueren Spr., Bd. 175, p. 90. 1939.

7636 Krogmann (Willy). AE. *orc.* Anglia, 57 (N.F. 45), p. 110. 1933.

7637 —— AE. *orcnēas.* Anglia, 56 (N.F. 45), pp. 40–42. 1932.

7638 —— *Orc* und *orcnēas.* Anglia, 57 (N.F. 45), p. 396. 1933.

7639 Laborde (Edward Dalrymple). Grendel's glove and his immunity from weapons. Mod. Lang. Rev., 18, pp. 202–04. 1923.

7640 Paden (W. D.). Beowulf and the monster. Times Lit. Supp., 42, p. 247. 1943.

7641 Stedman (Douglas). Some points of resemblance betweeen Beowulf and the Grettla (or Grettis saga). [i.e. between ' (a) The Beowulf-Grendel and the Grettir-Glam story : (b) The Beowulf-Grendel's mother and the trollwife story in the Grettla."] Saga-Book V.C., 8, pp. 6–28. 1913.

7642 Tolkien (John Ronald Renel). Beowulf : the monsters and the critics. Proc. Brit. Acad., 22, pp. 245–95. 1936.

§ *e.* Visions and Eschatology

7643 Assmann (Bruno). Vorzeichen des Jüngsten Gerichts. [A.-S. text from MS. Cotton Vesp. D XIV, fol. 102a.] Anglia, 11, pp. 369–71. 1889.

7644 Boswell (Charles Stuart). An Irish precursor of Dante. A study of the vision of heaven and hell ascribed to the eighth-century Irish Saint Adamnan, with translation of the Irish text. *Grimm Library*, 18. pp. xiii, 262. 8° London, 1908. [Pp. 4–28, the seer (i.e. life of Adamnan); pp. 28–47, translation of the Fis Adamnáin; pp. 113–74, the legend in Ireland; pp. 174–206, the Fis Adamnáin.]

7645 Brown (Carleton Fairchild). Cynewulf and Alcuin. [Similarity and sources of two descriptions of purgatory.] P.M.L.A., 18, pp. 308–34. 1903.

7646 Judge (Cyril Bathurst). A note on the vision of a certain English prior. [As result of destruction he had seen during hard winter of 1046.] Speculum, 16, pp. 488–89. 1941.

7647 Konrath (M.). Eine altenglische Vision vom Jenseits. [Text in A.-S. and Latin from MS. Cotton Otho C.I. Statement by S. Boniface on vision of a monk of Wenlock.] Archiv Stud. neueren Spr., Bd. 139, pp. 30–46. 1919.

7648 Krogmann (Willy). Ags. *neorxenawang*. Anglia, 53 (N.F. 41), pp. 337–44 : 58 (N.F. 46), pp. 28–29. 1929, 1934.

7649 Langenfelt (Gösta). The OE. Paradise Lost. [*Neorxnawang*, etc.] Anglia, 55 (N.F. 33), pp. 250–65. 1931.

7650 MacNaught (John Campbell). Fis Adamnáin [the vision of Adamnan]. [Text in the Lebor na h-Uidhre (c. 1100) translated into modern Scottish Gaelic.] Trans. Gaelic Soc. Inverness, 34 (1927–28), pp. 153–69. 1935.

7651 Meyer (Kuno). Stories and songs from Irish mss. 1. The vision of Laisrén. [Abbot of Lethglenn in co. Carlow, d. 638. Irish text and English translation.] Otia Merseiana, 1, pp. 113–19. 1899.

7652 Napier (Arthur Sampson). An Old English vision of Leofric, earl of Mercia. [In MS. C.C.C.C. 367. Text in A.-S. and translation.] Trans. Philolog. Soc., 1907–10, pp. 180–88. 1910.

7653 Ritter (Otto). *Neorxnawang*. [*See also* 35 (1912), p. 428.] Anglia, 33 (N.F. 21), pp. 467–70 : 34, p. 528. 1910–11.

7654 Seymour (St. John Drelincourt). The eschatology of the early Irish Church. [With A.-S. comparisons. Hell, heaven, division of souls, fire of doom, purgatory.] Zeit. celt. Philol., 14, pp. 179–211. 1923.

7655 —— Irish visions of the other world : a contribution to the study of mediaeval visions. pp. 192. 8° London, 1930.

7656 —— The signs of doomsday in the Saltair na Rann. Proc. R.I.A., 36 c, pp. 154–63. 1923.

7657 —— The vision of Adamnan. Proc. R.I.A., 37 c, pp. 304–12. 1927.

7658 Silverstein (H. T.). The *Vision of Leofric* and Gregory's *Dialogues*. [Comparison of vision of narrow bridge over a river.] Rev. Engl. Stud., 9, pp. 186–88. 1933.

7659 Stokes (Whitley). Adamnan's second vision. [From Lebar Brecc, pp. 258b–259b. Irish text and English translation.] Rev. celt., 12, pp. 420–43. 1891.

7660 Vendryes (Joseph). Aislingthi Adhamnáin [vision of Adamnan] d'après le texte du manuscrit de Paris. [Irish text, with French translation.] Rev. celt., 30, pp. 349–83. 1909.

7661 Wright (Thomas). St. Patrick's purgatory ; an essay on the legends of purgatory, hell, and paradise, current during the Middle Ages. pp. xi, 192. 8° London, 1844. [Pp. 7–29, A.-S. and Celtic visions : pp. 186–90, A.-S. description of paradise in Exeter Book (A.-S. text and translation).]

§ f. Proverbs

(Supplementary to my Proverb Literature, Folk-lore Society Publication 89, 1930 : *q.v.* for A.-S., nos. 527–30, 543, 549, 603, 665 ; and for Irish, nos. 763–97, *passim*.)

7662 Anderson *afterwards* **Anderson-Arngart** (Olof Sigfrid). On some readings in the Proverbs of Alfred. Engl. Studies, 30, pp. 164–74. 1949.

7663 —— The proverbs of Alfred. 1. A study of the texts. *Skrifter utgivna av Kungl. Humanistiska Vetenskapssamfundet i Lund*, 32, i. pp. 162. 8° Lund, London, 1942.

7664 Gropp (Ernst). On the language of the proverbs of Alfred. *Diss., Halle.* pp. 61. 8° Berlin, 1879.

7665 Klaeber (Friedrich). An Old English proverb. ['*Donne se heretoga wacað ponne bið ealle se here swiðe gehindred.*'] J. Engl. and Germ. Philol, 5, p. 529. 1905.

7666 Kneuer (K.). Die Sprichwörter Hendyngs. *Diss.* 8° Weilheim, 1901.

7667 Schleich (G.). Zu den Sprichwörtern Hendings. Anglia, 5, pp. 5–8 : 51 (N.F. 39), pp. 220–77 ; 52 (N.F. 40), pp. 350–61. 1882, 1927–28.

7668 Singer (Samuel). Die Sprichwörter Hendings. Stud. Neophilol., 14, pp. 31–52. 1942.

7669 Skeat (Walter William). The proverbs of Alfred. Trans. Philol. Soc., 1895–98, pp. 399–418. 1898.

7670 South (Helen Pennock). The proverbs of Alfred, studied in the light of the newly discovered Maidstone manuscript. pp. vii, 168, + 1 plate. 8° New York, 1931.

§ g. Riddles

7671 Aldhelm, *St.* The riddles. Text and verse translation with notes by James Hall Pitman. *Yale Studies in English,* 67. pp. vii, 79. 8° New Haven, 1925.

7672 Bradley (Henry). Two riddles of the Exeter Book. [5 and 19. ? 5 'relates to some definite story of necromancy'.] Mod. Lang. Rev., 6, pp. 433–40. 1911.

7673 Brown (Carleton Fairchild). *Poculum mortis* in Old English. [Exeter Gnomic verses, lines 78–80.] Speculum, 15, pp. 389–99. 1940.

7674 Colgrave (Bertram). Some notes on riddle 21. [?=detailed description of the heavy type of plough.] Mod. Lang. Rev., 32, pp. 281–82. 1937.

7675 Dietrich (Franz Eduard Christoph). Die Rätsel des Exeterbuches. Z.f.d.A., 11, pp. 448–90 ; 12, pp. 232–52. 1864–65.

7676 Ebert (Adolf). Die Rätsel-Poesie der Angelsachsen. Bericht u.d. Verh. K. sächs. Gesell. Wiss., Phil.-hist. Cl., 19, pp. 30–56. 1867.

7677 Ehwald (Rudolf). De aenigmatibus Aldhelmi et acrostichis. Festschrift Albert von Bamberg, pp. 1–26. 1905.

7678 Eliason (Norman E.). Four Old English cryptographic riddles. [Exeter Book, 19, 36, 64 and 75.] Stud. Philol. (N.C.), 49, pp. 553–65. 1952.

7679 —— Riddle 68 of the Exeter Book. Malone (K.) : Philologica, pp. 18–19. 1949.

7680 Erhardt-Siebold (Erika von). Aldhelm's chrismal. [His 55th riddle : =portable reliquary in form of a house.] Speculum, 10, pp. 276–80 + plate. 1935.

7681 —— An archaeological find in a Latin riddle of the Anglo-Saxons. [Aldhelm's riddle 54—cocuma duplex—cooking pot.] Speculum, 7, pp. 252–55. 1932.

7682 —— History of the bell in a riddle's nutshell. [No. 7 of Tatwine's riddles—de tintinno. With remarks on Irish and other bells, etc.] Engl. Studien, 69, pp. 1–14. 1934.

7683 —— Die lateinischen Rätsel der Angelsachsen. *Anglistische Forschungen,* 61. pp. xvi, 276. 8° Heidelberg, 1925.

7684 —— Note on Anglo-Saxon riddle 74. Medium Ævum, 21, pp. 36–37. 1952.

7685 —— The Old-English hunt riddles. [36, water-fowl hunt : 19 and 64, falconry.] P.M.L.A., 63, pp. 1–6. 1948.

7686 —— The Old English loom riddles. Malone (K.) : Philologica, pp. 9–17, + 2 plates. 1449.

7687 —— Old English riddle no. 4 : handmill. [With diagram of A.-S. handmill in text.) (No. 39 : creature death. No. 57, O.E. Cā 'jackdaw'). P.M.L.A., 61, pp. 620–23, 910–15 : 62, pp. 1–8. 1946–47.

7688 —— Old English riddle 23, bow, O.E. *boga.* (Old English riddle 13). Mod. Lang. Notes, 65, pp. 93–96, 97–100. 1950.

7689 Exeter Book. The Exeter Book riddles (text after Grein). Seen through the press by T. Gregory Foster. pp. 39. 8° [London, 1905].

7690 Grein (Christian Wilhelm Michael). Zu den Rätseln des Exeterbuches. Germania, 10, pp. 307–09. 1865.

7691 Herzfeld (Georg). Die Rätsel des Exeterbuches und ihr Verfasser. *Acta Germanica*, 2 i. pp. 72. 8° Berlin, 1890.

7692 Hicketier (F.). Fünf Rätsel des Exeterbuches. Anglia, 10, pp. 564–600. 1888.

7693 Holthausen (Ferdinand). Nochmals die altenglischen Rätsel. Anglia, 38 (N.F. 26), pp. 77–82. 1914.

7694 —— Zu altenglischen Dichtungen. 1. Zu den Rätseln. Anglia, 44 (N.F. 32), pp. 346–52. 1920.

7695 —— Zu den ae. Rätseln. [*See also* Indogerm. Forsch., 4, pp. 386–88, 1894.] Anglia, 24 (N.F. 12), pp. 264–67 : 35 (N.F. 23), pp. 165–77. 1901, 1912. *Same title.* Anglia, Beiblatt, 30, pp. 50–55. 1919.

7696 Kennedy (Charles William). The earliest English poetry. pp. viii, 375. 8° London, 1943. [Pp. 131–46, riddles.]

7697 Kern (J. H.). Das Leidener Rätsel. (Noch einmal zum Leidener Rätsel). Anglia, 33 (N.F. 21), pp. 452–56 : 38 (N.F. 26), (N.F. 21), pp. 261–65. 1910, 1914.

7698 Lawrence (William Witherle). The first riddle of Cynewulf. [Answered by William Henry Schofield in the next article, ' Signy's lament '. (pp. 262–95).] P.M.L.A., 17, pp. 247–61. 1902.

7699 Mueller (Eduard). Die Rätsel des Exeterbuches. 8° Cöthen, 1861.

7700 Mueller (Lucien). Zu den Räthseln des h. Bonifacius. Rhein. Mus., N.F. 22, pp. 151–52. 1867.

7701 Nuck (R.). Zu Trautmann's Deutung des ersten und neunundachtzigsten Rätsels. Anglia, 10, pp. 390–94. 1888.

7702 O'Cavanagh (John Eugene). St. Aldhelm : the double acrostic. N. and Q., 3rd S. 11, pp. 249–50. 1867.

7703 Prehn (August). Komposition und Quellen der Rätsel des Exeterbuches. Dissertation. *Neuphilologische Studien, hrsg. von Gustav Körting (Heft 3)*, pp. 143–285. 8° Paderborn, 1883.

7704 Schlutter (Otto Bernhard). Zum Leidener Rätsel. Anglia, 33 (N.F. 21), pp. 457–66. 1910.

7705 Sonke (Emma). Zu dem 25. Rätsel des Exeterbuches. [Algora. ?= Woodpecker, but=a bird which mimics.] Engl. Studien, 37, pp. 313–18. 1907.

7706 Swaen (A. E. H.). Het Angelsaksische Raadsel 58. Neophilol., 13, pp. 293–96. 1928.

7707 —— The Anglo-Saxon horn riddles. Neophilol., 26, pp. 298–302. 1941.

7708 —— Riddle 9 (6, 8.). Facts and fancies. [No satisfactory solution yet found.] Studia Neophil., 14, pp. 67–70. 1942.

7709 —— Riddle XIII (XVI). [= Badger.] Neophilol., 26, pp. 228–31. 1941.

7710 Trautmann (Moritz). Alte und neue Antworten auf altenglische Rätsel. *Bonner Beiträge zur Anglistik*, 19 iii. Pp. 167–215. 8° Bonn, 1905.

7711 ——, *ed.* Die altenglischen Rätsel (Die Rätsel des Exeterbuchs). pp. xx, 203, + 16 plates [of the MS.]. 8° Heidelberg, 1915.

7712 —— Die Auflösungen der altenglischen Rätsel. Anglia, Beiblatt, 5, pp. 46–51. 1895.

7713 —— Die Quellen der altenglischen Rätsel. Anglia, 38 (N.F. 26), pp. 349–54. 1914.

7714 —— Das sogenannte erste Rätsel. Anglia, 36 (N.F. 24), pp. 133–38. 1912.

7715 —— Weiteres zu den altenglischen Rätseln und metrisches. Anglia, 43 (N.F. 31), pp. 245–60. 1919.

7716 —— Die Zahl der altengl. Rätsel. (Zu den Lösungen der Rätsel des Exeterbuches. Das Geschlecht in den altenglischen Rätseln). Anglia, Beiblatt, 25, pp. 272–99, 324–27. 1914.

7717 **Trautmann** (Moritz). Zeit, Heimat und Verfasser der altengl. Rätsel. Anglia, 38 (N.F. 26), pp. 365–73. 1914.

7718 —— Zu meiner Ausgabe der altenglischen Rätsel. Anglia, 42 (N.F. 30), pp. 125–41. 1918.

7719 —— Zum Streit um die altenglischen Rätsel. Anglia, 36 (N.F. 24), pp. 127–33. 1912.

7720 **Tupper** (Frederick), *jr.* Riddles of the Bede tradition : the ' Flores ' of pseudo-Bede. [With texts.] Mod. Phil., 2, pp. 561–72. 1905.

7721 —— *ed.* The riddles of the Exeter Book. Edited with introduction, notes and glossary. pp. cxi, 292. 8° Boston, 1910.

7722 **Walz** (John A.). Notes on the Anglo-Saxon riddles. Studies and Notes in Philol. and Lit., Harvard Univ., 5, pp. 261–68. 1936.

7723 **Whitbread** (L.). The Latin riddle [90] in the Exeter Book. N. and Q., 190, pp. 156–58 : 194, pp. 80–82. 1946, 1949.

7724 **Wood** (George A.). The Anglo-Saxon riddles. Aberystwyth Studies, 1, pp. 1–62 : 2, pp. 1–41. 1912–14.

7725 **Wyatt** (Alfred John). Old English riddles. pp. xxxviii, 193. 8° Boston, 1912.

7726 **Young** (Jean I.). Riddle 15 of the Exeter Book. [Argument for weasel.] Rev. Engl. Stud., 20, pp. 304–06. 1944.

120. GENERAL

7727 Aarberg (Nils). The Anglo-Saxons in England during the early centuries after the invasion. *Arbeten utgivna med understöd av v. Ekmans Universitetsfond, Uppsala,* 33. pp. ix, 219. 8° Uppsala, 1926. [319 figures in text of brooches and other jewellery. Archaeological investigations for estimating the chronology of the migration period.]

7728 Akerman (John Yonge). An archaeological index to remains of antiquity of the Celtic, Romano-British of Anglo-Saxon periods. pp. xii, 204, + 19 plates. 8° London, 1847.

7729 —— Remains of pagan Saxondom. pp. xxviii, 84, + 40 plates. 4° London, [1852]–55. [Gross, 393.]

7730 Anderson (Joseph). Scotland in pagan times: the Iron Age. *Rhind Lectures,* 1881. pp. xx, 314. 8° Edinburgh, 1883. [i. Viking burials: iv. Architecture of the brochs: v. The brochs and their contents.]

7731 Baron (John). On the study of Anglo-Saxon and its value to the archaeologist. Wilts. Archaeol. Mag., 17, pp. 36–46. 1878.

7732 Baye (Joseph de) *baron*. Études archéologiques: . . . industrie anglo-saxonne. pp. 133, + 17 plates. 4° Paris, 1889. The industrial arts of the Anglo-Saxons. . . . Translated by T. B. Harbottle. pp. xii, 135, + plates. 8° London, 1893. [Gross, 396.]

7733 Bloxam (Matthew Holbeche). The ancient British, Roman, and Anglo-Saxon antiquities of Warwickshire. B'ham and Midland Inst., Arch. Section, Trans., [6], pp. 25–38. 1875.

7734 British Museum. A guide to the Anglo-Saxon and foreign Teutonic antiquities. By Reginald Allender Smith. pp. xii, 179, + 17 plates. 8° (Oxford), 1923. [232 figures in text.]

7735 Burgess (Joseph Tom). Recent archaeological discoveries in Warwickshire (the pre-Domesday period). [Pp. 377–81 deal with ' the paucity of Saxon remains in Warwickshire.']. Archaeol. J., 33, pp. 368–81, + 4 plates. 1876.

7736 Crawford (Osbert Guy Stanhope). Air survey and archaeology. [Information re Saxon field system. Map on p. 355 of ' Saxon villages on Salisbury plain.'] Georg. J., 61, pp. 342–66, + 4 plates. 1923.

7737 Cunnington (*Mrs.* Maud Edith). An introduction to the archaeology of Wiltshire from the earliest times to the pagan Saxons. 4th edition. pp. xii, 172. 8° Devizes, 1949. [Pp. 34–43, A.-S. period: pp. 119–22, Wansdyke: pp. 141–44, Saxon jewellery from Roundway down: the Wilton bowl: the gold ring of Ethelwulf.]

7738 Davies (Oliver). A summary of the archaeology of Ulster. Part 2. [Pp. 43–56, + plates 5–8, early Christian period, break-up of Irish Christian culture.] Ulster J. Archaeol., 3rd S. 12, pp. 45–76. 1949.

7739 Dobson (Dina Portway). The archaeology of Somerset. *County Archaeologies.* pp. xv, 272, + map. 8° London, 1931. [Pp. 161–89, + 3 plates, A.-S. period.]

7740 Dodds (George). Figures found in Holderness. [Plate shows group of 4 wooden figures in boat found at Ross Carr, now in Museum of Hull Lit. and Phil. Soc. Disputes George Poulson's theory that they represent battle of Ella of Bernicia for York in 867, and says they have Eastern origin. *But see* **7753** (latest work).] Reliquary, 11, pp. 203–07, + 1 plate. 1871.

7741 Elgee (Frank *and* Harriet Wragg). The archaeology of Yorkshire. *County Archaeologies.* pp. xv, 272, + map. 8° London, 1933. [Pp. 177–201, Anglian Yorkshire; pp. 202–227, the Viking age.]

7742 Ellis *afterwards* **Davidson** (Hilda Roderick). The hill of the dragon: Anglo-Saxon burial mounds in literature and archaeology. [Mystery of cenotaphs, e.g. Sutton Hoo: possession of ancestor's barrow carries inheritance: king makes over land sitting on predecessor's tomb: barrows as boundaries: their treasures guarded by dragons.] Folk-lore, 61, pp. 169–85, + 2 plates. 1950.

7743 Evans (*Sir* John). An archaeological survey of Hertfordshire. [Introduction: topographical index of interments, coins, etc., with references to places of publication.] Archaeologia, 53, pp, 245–62, + folding map. 1892.

7744 Feddersen (Arthur). To Mosefund. [Pp. 383–85, Roos Carr boat models. *But see* **7753** (latest work).] Aarbøger nord. Oldk. og Hist., 1881, pp. 36–89. 1881.

7745 Ferguson (Richard Saul). An archaeological survey of Cumberland and Westmorland; and of Lancashire north-of-the-sands, by H. Swainson Cowper. [Introduction: topographical index of coins, brooches, etc., with references to places of publication.] Archaeologia, 53, pp. 485–538, and folding map. 1893.

7746 Gray (Harold St. George). Trial excavations at Cadbury castle, S. Somerset, 1913. (Ditto, 1922). [? 'head and front' of British resistance against S. and W. Saxons.] Proc. Somerset Arch. Soc., 59 (1913), pp. 1–24 + plan + 4 plates: 68 (1922), pp. 8–20 + map. 1914, 23.

7747 Hencken (Hugh O'Neill). The archaeology of Cornwall and Scilly. *County Archaeologies.* pp. xvii, 340, + 13 plates, + map. 8° London, 1932. [Pp. 203–89, A.D. 400–1066.]

7748 Hodgetts (James Frederick). Older England, illustrated by the Anglo-Saxon antiquities in the British Museum. pp. xv, 158: xvi, 226. 2 series, 8° London, 1884.

7749 Jessup (Ronald Frederick). The archaeology of Kent. *County Archaeologies.* pp. xiv, 272, + 13 plates, + map. 8° London, 1930. [Pp. 217–47, + plates 11–13 (jewellery), A.–S.]

B b

7750 Keiller (Alexander) and **Piggott** (Stuart). The chambered tomb in Beowulf. [?=description of an Irish or Scottish, not Scandinavian, megalithic tomb.] Antiquity, 13, pp. 360–61. 1939.

7751 Kendrick (*Sir* Thomas Downing) and **Hawkes** (Charles Francis Christopher). Archaeology in England and Wales, 1918–1931. pp. xix, 371, + 3 plates. 8° London, 1932. [Pp. 303–48, + plates 25–30, A.–S. period. Also figures 105–23 in text.]

7752 Leeds (Edward Thurlow). The archaeology of the Anglo-Saxon settlements. pp. 144, + 15 plates. 8° Oxford, 1913.

7753 Lindqvist (Sune). The boat models from Roos Carr. [Dated by earlier writters to c. 867 (Danish invasion of Holderness) but probably of Bronze Age. 5 figures (to support) in text.] Acta Archaeol., 13, pp. 235–42. 1942.

7754 London, *Guildhall Museum.* Catalogue of the collection of London antiquities. 2nd edition. pp. xii, 411, + 100 plates. 8° London, 1908. [Pp. 119–25, + plates 51–54, A.–S. period.]

7755 MacRitchie (David). Earthhouses and their inhabitants. [Maeshow, Orkney, etc.] Archaeol. Rev., 4, pp. 393–421. 1890.

7756 Manning (Percy) and **Leeds** (Edward Thurlow). An archaeological survey of Oxfordshire. [Introduction and topographical index, with references to publications.] Archaeologia, 71, pp. 227–65, + 2 folding maps. 1921.

7757 March (Henry Colley). The problem of lynchets. Proc. Dorset Antiq. F.C., 24, pp. 66–92. 1903.

7758 May (Akerman). The excavations at Wingham, Kent, in 1854. [Photograph of J. Y. Akerman excavating.] Antiq. J., 13, p. 172, + 1 plate. 1933.

7759 Megaw (Basil R. S.). The ancient village of Ronaldsway [Man]: a summary of recent investigations. [Inhabited from Roman occupation to Viking age, and possibly later. Plate shows small domestic objects.] J. Manx Mus., 4, pp. 181–82, + plate 181. 1940.

7760 Myres (John Nowell Linton). The present state of the archaeological evidence for the Anglo-Saxon conquest. History, N.S., 21, pp. 317–30. 1937.

7761 Noël-Hume (I.). Archaeology in Britain : observing the past. pp. 120. 8° London, 1953. [Pp. 85–93 (4 pp. of figures), A.–S.]

7762 Payne (George). An archaeological survey of Kent. [Introduction : topographical index of interments, coins, brooches, etc., with references to places of publication.] Archaeologia, 51, pp. 447–68, + folding map. 1888.

7763 Peake (Harold John Edward). The archaeology of Berkshire. *County Archaeologies.* pp. xi, 260, + 6 maps. 8° London, 1931. [Pp. 124–70, + 2 plates, A.–S. period.]

7764 Petrie (George). On the antiquities of Tara hill. Proc. R.I.A., 1 (1837), pp. 68–70, 75–76. 1841.

7765 Phillips (Charles William). The present state of archaeology in Lincolnshire, part 2. (An archaeological gazeteer of Lincolnshire.) [Pp. 137–151, A.–S. period, with map of pagan A.–S. Lincs., + plates 28–29.] Archaeol. J., 91 (1934), pp. 97–187, + 4 maps, + 9 plates. 1935.

7766 Roeder (Fritz). Neue Funde auf kontinental-sächsischen Friedhöfen der Völkerwanderungszeit. [With special reference to origins of subsequent settlement in England.] Anglia, 57 (N.F. 45), pp. 321–60, and 30 plates. 1933.

7767 Sheppard (Thomas). Notes on the ancient model of a boat, and warrior crew, found at Roos, in Holderness. (Additional note on the Roos Carr images). [Scandinavian origin ? *But see* 7753 (latest work).] Trans. East Riding Antiq. Soc., 9, pp. 62–74, + 2 plates : 10, pp. 76–79, + 1 plate. 1902–03.

7768 —— Viking and other relics at Crayke, Yorkshire. [Including pre-Norman cross, bronze ring, weapons, etc.] Yorks. Archaeol. J., 34, pp. 273–81, + 6 plates. 1939.

7769 Shetelig (Haakon) *ed.* Viking antiquities in Great Britain and Ireland. Part 1—6. *Scientific Research Fund of* 1919. 4° Oslo, 1940–54. [i. Introduction to the Viking history of western Europe, by H. Shetelig : ii. Viking antiquities in Scotland, by Sigurd Grieg : iii. Viking antiquities in Ireland, by Johs. Bøe : iv. Viking antiquities in England, by Anathon Bjørn and H. Shetelig : v. British antiquities of the Viking period found in Norway, by Jan Petersen : vi. Civilisation of the Viking settlers in relation to their old and new countries, by H. Shetelig.]

7770 Thropp (J.). A description of an ancient raft recently found by Messrs. Judge and Cole, in a field adjoining the brickyard, in their occupation . . . situate at Brigg in the county of Lincs. [Viking period.] Assoc. Archit. Socs.' Rpts., 19, pp. 95–97, + folding plate. 1887.

7771 Vulliamy (Colwyn Edward). [Anthony Rolls, *pseud.*] The archaeology of Middlesex and London. *County Archaeologies.* pp. xx, 308, + map. 8° London, 1930. [Pp. 220–68, + 2 plates, A.–S. period.]

7772 Whimster (Donald Cameron). The archaeology of Surrey. *County Archaeologies.* pp. xiv, 254, + 12 plates. 8° London, 1931. [Pp. 172–220, + plates 10–12, early Saxon period : Saxon and Viking.]

7773 Willis-Bund (John William). The true objects of Welsh archaeology. [Pp. 111–17 : iii. The Welsh Church.] Y Cymmrodor, 11, pp. 103–32. 1892.

7774 Wright (Thomas). On recent discoveries of Anglo-Saxon antiquities. [General survey.] J. Brit. Archaeol. Assoc., 2, pp. 50–59. 1847.

121. DYKES AND DITCHES

§ *a.* Cambridgeshire Dykes

7775 Babington (Charles Cardale). Ancient Cambridgeshire ; or, an attempt to trace Roman and other ancient roads that passed through the county of Cambridge. 2nd edition. *Cambs. Antiq. Soc.,* 8° *publicns,* 20. pp. viii, 116, + map. 8° Cambridge, 1883. [Pp. 95–110, dykes and ditches.]

7776 Beldam (Joseph). The Icenhilde road. [Pp. 35–41, the dykes which cross this British road : Devil's, Fleam, Bran, etc.] Archaeol J., 25, pp. 21–45. 1868.

7777 Fox (*Sir* Cyril), *etc.* Excavations in the Cambridgeshire dykes. [i. is pre-A.-S.]. ii. The Fleam dyke. [With plan and sections. Probably a 'work of entirely Anglo-Saxon date.'] iii. The Fleam dyke, Second report : excavations in 1922. [With plan and sections. ? of pagan A.-S. period.] iv. The Devil's Dyke : excavations in 1923 and 1924. [Probably A.-S. With plan, sections, and illustrations.] v. Bran or Heydon ditch. First report. vi. —. Second report. [Probably A.-S. With plans and sections.] Proc. Camb. Antiq. Soc., 24, pp. 28–53 : 25, pp. 21–36 : 26, pp. 90–129 : 27, pp. 16–35 : 30, pp. 78–93. 1923–26, 1929.

7778 Hughes (Thomas McKenny). The Cambridgeshire dykes. [Queries A.-S. origin.] J. Brit. Archaeol. Assoc., 69 (N.S. 19), pp. 135–60. 1913.

7779 Lethbridge (Thomas Charles). The Car dyke, the Cambridgeshire ditches, and the Anglo-Saxons. [With map.] Proc. Camb. Antiq. Soc., 35, pp. 90–96, + 1 plate. 1935.

7779a Lucas (Charles) *of Burwell.* The fenman's world [with a chapter by Sir Cyril Fox on excavations in the Cambridge dykes]. pp. xiii, 223. 8° Norwich, 1930.

7780 Palmer (William Mortlock) and **Lethbridge** (Thomas Charles). Further excavations at the Bran ditch. Proc. Camb. Antiq. Soc., 32, pp. 54–56, + 2 plates. 1932.

7781 Phillips (Charles William). Ancient earthworks. [Pp. 5–13, the dykes.] V.C.H., Cambs., 2, pp. 1–47, + 2 maps. 1948.

7782 Ridgeway (*Sir* William). Are the Cambridgeshire ditches referred to by Tacitus ? [Also their history in A.-S. times.] Archaeol. J., 50, pp. 62–72, + map. 1893.

7783 Stephenson (R.). The Devil's ditch. [Remarks on the dykes in general.] Trans. Cambs. and Hunts. Archaeol. Soc., 3, pp. 287–90. 1914.

7784 Tymms (Samuel). The Devil's dyke, Newmarket. Proc. Bury and W. Suffolk Archaeol. Inst., 1, pp. 167–76. 1851.

§ *b.* Offa's Dyke and Watt's Dyke

7785 B. (A.). Watt's dyke. [Plea for its preservation.] Arch. Camb., 4th S. 13, pp. 236–37. 1882.

7786 Bellows (John). Brief notes on Offa's dyke. Proc. Cottesw. Nat. F.C., 6, pp. 257–60. 1877.

7787 Cobbold (Edgar Sterling). Offa's dyke. [Topography and history.] Shropshire N. and Q., 1, pp. 66–68. 1885.

7788 Drinkwater (H.). Offa's dyke. Ann. Rpt. Chester Soc. Nat. Sci., Lit. and Art, 41. 1918.

7789 Earle (John). Offa's dyke, in the neighbourhood of Knighton. [Comments on pp. 397–98.] Arch. Camb., 3rd S. 3, pp. 196–210. 1857.

7790 Fox (*Sir* Cyril). The boundary line of Cymru. [With 2 plates and 4 maps of Offa's dyke.] Proc. Brit. Acad., 26, pp. 275–300. 1940.

7791 —— Dykes. [esp. Offa's, with maps, plates and profiles.] Antiquity, 3, pp. 135–54. 1929.

7792 —— Offa's dyke. Neath Antiq. Soc. Trans., 2nd S. 2, pp. 46–51. 1932.

7793 —— and Phillips (D. W.). Offa's dyke : a field survey. 1st (to 6th) report. [i. In northern Flintshire : ii. From Coed Talwrn (Treuddyn parish), Flintshire, to Plas Power park (Bersham parish), Denbighshire : iii. From Plas Power park to the river Vyrnwy on the boundary between Llanymynech (Shropshire) and Carreghofa (Montgomeryshire) parishes : iv. In Montgomeryshire: v. In the mountain zone : vi. In the Wye valley.] Arch. Camb., 81 (7th S. 6), pp. 133–79, + 6 plates : 82 (7th S. 7), pp. 232–68, + 11 plates : 83 (7th S. 8), pp. 33–110, + 15 plates : 84, pp. 1–60, + 3 plates : 85, pp. 1–73, + 2 plates, + map : 86, pp. 1–74, + 2 plates, + map. 1926–31.

7793a Fox (*Sir* Cyril). Offa's dyke. A field survey of the western frontier-works of Mercia in the seventh and eighth centuries. With a foreword by Sir Frank Stenton. *British Academy.* pp. xxvii, 317, + 46 plates. 4° London, 1955.

7794 Fox (*Sir* Cyril). Wat's dyke : a field survey. [Early 8th c. 39 figures in text.] Arch. Camb., 89, pp. 205–78, + 4 plates, + 2 maps. 1934.

7795 —— The western frontier of Mercia in the VIIIth century. [Offa's dyke, Wat's dyke, the short dykes.] Yorks. Celtic Stud., 1, pp. 3–10, + 2 plates, + 2 maps. 1938.

7796 Guest (Edwin). On the northern termination of Offa's dyke. Arch. Camb., 3rd S. 4, pp. 335–42. 1858.

7797 Hewlett (J. H.). Offa's dyke. pp. 32, + 4 plates, + photographic map. 8° London, 1924.

7798 Hogg (G.). Offa's dyke : a neglected monument. Country Life, 118, p. 197. 1945.

7799 Jones (Harry Longueville). Offa's dyke and Wat's dyke. Arch. Camb., 3rd S. 2, pp. 1–23, 151–54. 1856.

7800 Lines (H. H.). Saxon earthworks. [Watt's dyke and Offa's dyke and camps on their borders.] Collns. hist. and archaeol. ref. to Montgom., 24, pp. 237–41. 1890.

7801 Lloyd (John Maurice Edward). Wanten or Wanton dyke : with some remarks on upper and lower ' short dykes '. Arch. Cambs., 6th S. 1, pp. 279–98 : 2, pp. 159–60. 1901–02.

7802 Maclean (*Sir* John). The course of Offa's dyke in Gloucestershire. Trans. Bristol and Glos. Arch. Soc., 18, pp. 19–31. 1894.

7803 Mahler (Margaret). A history of Chirk castle and Chirkland, with a chapter on Offa's dyke. pp. xl, 231. 8° London, 1912. [Pp. 198–212, with 3 plates, Offa's dyke.]

7804 Milman (Henry Salusbury). The political geography of Wales. [Pp. 35–38, Offa's dyke and boundaries of Mercia.] Arch. Camb., 3rd S. 6, pp. 34–47. 1860.

7805 Moore (H. Cecil). Offa's dyke in Herefordshire : the Rowe ditch. Trans. Woolhope F. N. Club, 1895–97, pp. 251–56. 1898.

7806 —— Traces of Offa's dyke (Clewdd Offa) from Ross to Hereford. *Same jnl.*, 1902–04, pp. 29–31. 1905.

7807 Ormerod (George). Situation of Cingeston in Dyddenham, and the dyke therein. [Tidenham, Glos., at end of Offa's dyke.] Arch. Camb., 3rd S. 3, pp. 391–93. 1857.

7808 Owen (Elias). Offa's dyke. Collns. hist. and archaeol. rel. to Mongom., 29, pp. 93–111. 1897.

7809 Palmer (Alfred Neobard). Offa's and Wat's dykes. [Political aspect : boundaries, etc.] Y Cymmrodor, 12, pp. 65–86. 1897.

7810 Parkins (W. Trevor). Offa's dyke. Arch. Camb., 4th S. 6, pp. 275–81. 1875.

7811 Stenton (*Sir* Frank Merry). Offa's dyke : the course of the dyke in Herefordshire. [3 pages of maps in text.] Roy. Comn. Hist. Mon., Herefordshire, 3, pp. xxvii–xxxi. 1934.

7812 Watkins (Alfred) *etc.* Offa's dyke : the gap in the Weobley district, etc. [Various notes on a field meeting to explore the dyke.] Trans. Woolhope N. F. Club, 1902–4, pp. 241–55, + 1 plate. 1905.

7813 Williams (Jonathan). History of Radnorshire : section 7—Offa's dyke. Arch. Camb., 3rd S. 2, pp. 155–58. 1856.

7814 Wood (James George). Notes on the portions of Offa's dyke called the Stone row and Row ditch. Trans. Woolhope N.F. Club, 1900–2, pp. 148–51, + 2 plates. 1903.

7815 —— Offa's dike in Herefordshire. V.C.H., Hereford, 1, pp. 258–61. 1908.

§ *c*. Wansdyke

(Raised as last defence against invading Saxons.—Hamilton Thompson).

7816 Bothamley (C. H.). Ancient earthworks [in Somerset]. [Pp. 530–31, Wansdyke.] V.C.H., Somerset, 2, pp. 467–532, + map. 1911.

7817 Brentnall (Harold Cresswell). The age and purpose of Wansdyke. [?Built by Ceawlin in 557, or by Cenwahl in 650.] Wilts. Archaeol. Mag., 53, pp. 382–84. 1950.

7818 **Burne** (Alfred H.). Wansdyke west and south. *Same jnl.*, 55, pp. 126–34. 1953.

7819 **Cambrian Archæological Association.** Excursion 1, August 12, 1914. Wansdyke. Arch. Camb., 6th S. 14, pp. 116–20. 1914.

7820 **Crawford** (Osbert Guy Stanhope). The east end of Wansdyke. Wilts. Archaeol. Mag., 55, pp. 119–25, + 2 plates. 1953.

7821 **Major** (Albany Featherstonehaugh). The course of Wansdyke through Somerset. With an itinerary. Proc. Somerset Arch. Soc., 70 (1924), pp. 22–37. 1925.

7822 —— and **Burrow** (Edward J.). The mystery of Wansdyke. Being the record of research and investigation in the field. pp. viii, 200 + folding map. [112 drawings + 100 plans in text.] 4° Cheltenham, 1926.

7823 **Major** (Albany Featherstonehaugh). The problem of Wansdyke. [?Roman.] Antiq. J., 4, pp. 142–45. 1924.

7824 —— Wansdyke, its course through E. and S.E. Wiltshire. Wilts. Archaeol. Mag., 41, pp. 396–406. 1921.

7825 **Oman** (*Sir* Charles William Chadwick). Wansdyke. [?constructed in 6th c.]. Archaeol. J., 87 (1930), pp. 60–70. 1931.

7826 **Passmore** (A. D.). The age and origin of Wansdyke. [?first quarter of 5th c.]. Antiq. J., 4, pp. 26–29. 1924.

7827 **Scarth** (Harry Mengden). On ancient earthworks in the neighbourhood of Bath, on the south side of the river Avon. [Wansdyke, etc. 'Belgic origin, Roman adaptation, Saxon completion.'] J. Brit. Archaeol. Assoc., 13, pp. 98–113. 1857.

7828 —— On the course of the Wansdyke through Somerset, with a notice of the camps in it. Proc. Somerset Arch. Soc., 7 (1856–7), pp. 9–24. 1858.

7829 **Taylor** (Charles Samuel). The date of Wansdyke. [Evidence from A.–S. documents : probably constructed by Cuthred in 648–52.] Trans. Bristol and Glos. Arch. Soc., 27, pp. 131–55. 1904.

7830 **Willis** (F. M.). The Jutes and the Wansdyke. [Jutish settlements in Oxon., Glos., and Worcestershire. Attributes Wansdyke to them. Place-name evidence.] Antiquary, 29, pp. 255–56. 1894.

§ *d.* **Others in England**

7831 **Anderson** (Alan B.). Grimsdyke. N. and Q., 183, pp. 85–86, 148, 201. 1942.

7832 **Braun** (Hugh). Some earthworks of north-west Middlesex. [Pp. 379–88, Grims dyke.] Trans. Lond. and Middsx. Archaeol Soc., N.S. 7, pp. 365–92. 1937.

7833 **Clinch** (George). Ancient earthworks [in the county of Buckingham.] [10 figures in text. Pp. 34–35, Grimes dyke.] V.C.H., Bucks., 2, pp. 21–35, + map. 1908.

7834 **Cole** (Edward Maule). Danes' dike [Yorks. wolds]. [Earthwork utilized by invaders in turn, including A.–S. and Danes, whose name it bears.] Trans. East Riding Antiq. Soc., 1, pp. 39–58, + map. 1893.

7835 **Ekwall** (Eilert). Grim's ditch. Studia Germanica tillägnade E. A. Kock, pp. 41–44. 1934.

7836 **Esdaile** (George). Nico ditch. [Pre-9th c. Danish incursion.] Trans. Lancs. and Ches. Antiq. Soc., 10 (1892), pp. 218–20. 1893.

7837 **Godsal** (Philip Thomas). Woden's, Grim's, and Offa's dykes. pp. 23 + map. 8° London, 1913.

7838 **Hogg** (Alexander Hubert Arthur). Dyke near Bexley, Kent. [*Fæstendic* in grant of land dated 814. With map + cross-sections.] Antiquity, 8, pp. 218–22. 1934.

7839 —— Dyke on Hartford Bridge Flats. [Identified with the Festaen Dic of the Crondall boundary survey, 973–74. Full-page maps on pp. 71–72.] Papers and Proc. Hants. F. C., 13, pp. 70–74. 1935.

7840 Jones (William Henry). The ancient Wiltshire dykes. [i. Bokerly dyke : ii. Grimsdyke, to the south of Salisbury : iii. Grimsdyke, to the north of Salisbury : iv. The Old dyke : v. Wansdyke.] Wilts. Archaeol. Mag., 14, pp. 332–46. 1874.

7841 Little (E.). An exploration of Grim's ditch. Trans. Newbury District F.C., 8, pp. 124–28. 1939.

7842 Marshall (George). The defences of the city of Hereford. [Pp. 70–74, the Saxon ditches.] Trans. Woolhope N.F. Club, 1939–41, pp. 67–78, + 3 plates. 1942.

7843 Peake (Harold John Edward). Ancient earthworks [in Berkshire]. [Pp. 273–75, boundary ditches.] V.C.H., Berkshire, 1, pp. 251–84, + map. 1906.

7844 Piggott (C. M.). The Grim's ditch complex in Cranborne chase. [Argument for late bronze and early iron ages rather than to mark Saxon frontier. References to earlier articles, *pro* A.–S.] Antiquity, 18, pp. 65–71, + map. 1944.

7845 Stone (Horace J. W.). The Pinner Grims dyke. [7 maps in text. An earthwork ascribed to the pagan Saxon period.] Trans. Lond. and Middsx. Archaeol. Soc., N.S. 7. pp. 284–301. 1937.

7846 Thoyts (Emma Elizabeth). Entrenchments or dykes, British Roman or Saxon ? [E.g. that from Aldermaston park to Ireland farm, Ufton.] Berks. N. and Q., 1, pp. 49–50. 1890.

7847 Wheeler (*Sir* Robert Eric Mortimer). London and the Grim's ditches. Antiq. J., 14, pp. 254–63, + 2 plates, + map. 1934.

§ *e.* **Celtic**

7848 Brown (William). An account of Shenchy dyke, in the east of Fife. [And its possible connections with Danish invasions.] Archaeol. Scot., 2, pp. 192–98. 1822.

7849 Collingwood (William Gershom). The Deil's dyke [Galloway]. [Suggests that ' intended as the boundary of a post-Roman British region of which the religious centre was Whithorn '. 5th–6th c.] Trans. Dumfries. Antiq. Soc., 3rd S. 17 (1930–31), pp. 72–79. 1932.

7850 Craw (James Hewat). The Black Dykes of Berwickshire. [?date—possibly Danish period.] Hist. Berwick. Nat. Club, 26, pp. 359–75, + map. 1928.

7850a Irving (George Vere). Notes of an examination of ' the Devil's dyke in Dumfriesshire.' [?constructed c. 1000 A.D.] Proc. Soc. Antiq. Scot., 5, pp. 189–95. 1865.

7851 Jerman (H. Noel). A fieldsurvey of some dykes in central Wales. Antiq. J., 15, p. 67. 1935.

7852 —— A field-survey of some dykes in east central Wales. [7 figures in text.] Arch. Camb., 90, pp. 279–87. 1935.

7853 Kennedy (John W.). The Catrail. [? work of defence (before 600) : ? cattle road : ? boundary.] Trans. Hawick Archaeol. Soc., 1907, p. 52. 1907.

7854 Kennedy (W. N.). The Catrail. *Same jnl.*, 16. 1877.

7855 Reid (R. C.). The Galloway Deil's Dike from the Black Water of the Dee near Clatterinshaws Brig to the Deugh at Dalshangon. [?5th–6th c.] Trans. Dumfries. Antiq. Soc., 3rd S. 17 (1930–31), pp. 59–64. 1932.

7856 Russell ( ) *Miss, of Ashiesteel*. Notes on some historical and literary matter bearing on the works called the Catrail. [Considers it to be the boundary between Cumbria and Bernicia, *but see* 7858.] Hist. Berwick. Nat. Club, 10, pp. 89–105. 1882.

7857 Semple (William). A possible line of connection between the Galloway Deil's Dike and the Deil's Dike found in Nithsdale. Trans. Dumfries. Antiq. Soc., 3rd S. 17 (1930–31), pp. 64–72. 1932.

7858 Smail (James). The Catrail, or Picts-work-ditch in 1880. Hist. Berwick. Nat. Club, 9, pp. 105–21. 1880.

122. EARTHWORKS AND CASTLES, ANGLO-SAXON

§ a. Problem of *Burhs* and *Mottes* ; and General

7859 Addy (Sidney Oldall). A Norman motte theory. N. and Q., 11th S. 5, pp. 482–84. 1912.

7860 Allcroft (Arthur Hadrian). Earthwork of England, prehistoric, Roman, Saxon, Danish, Norman, mediaeval. pp. xix, 711. 8° London, 1908. [Pp. 379–99, Saxon and Danish earthworks : pp. 400–52, Norman castles.]

7861 Armitage (*Mrs.* Ella Sophia). Anglo-Saxon burhs and early Norman castles. Proc. Soc. Antiq. Scot., 34 (3rd S. 10, 1899–1900), pp. 260–88. 1900.

7862 —— The early Norman castles of England. [Argument for hillock and wooden stockade or tower rather than stone : pp. 452–55, table of 87 castles, giving type, probable date of stone keep, reference in Domesday, etc.]. E.H.R., 19, pp. 209–45, 417–55. 1904.

7863 —— The early Norman castles of the British Isles. pp. xvi, 408, + 45 plates. 8° London, 1912. [Gross, 422a. Pp. 11–47, A.–S. fortifications : pp. 48–62, Danish fortifications : pp. 63–79, origin of private castles : pp. 80–93, Motte–castles.]

7864 Ashdown (Charles Henry). British castles. pp. xx, 208. 8° London, 1911. [Pp. 38–47, A.–S. : pp. 48–63, Motte and bailey castle, c. 1066–c. 1100.]

7865 Baker (Harold). The origin and development of the English castle. B'ham Archaeol. Soc., Trans., 48, pp. 100–19. 1922.

7866 Braun (Hugh). Earthwork castles. [7 plates, paged in text.] J. Brit. Archaeol. Assoc., 3rd S. 1, pp. 128–56. 1937.

7867 Clark (George Thomas). Contribution towards a complete list of moated mounds or burhs. [*See also* **7883** for supplementary list.] Archaeol. J., 46, pp. 197–217. 1889.

7868 —— Earthworks of the post-Roman and English period. *Same jnl.*, 38, pp. 21–41. 1881.

7869 Clark (George Thomas). Of the castles of England at the Conquest and under the Conqueror. Arch. Camb., 4th S. 12, pp. 1–16. *Comment on* pp. 174–75. 1881.

7870 Earle (John) and **Bennett** (James Arthur). Camps and hundreds. [? early camps, e.g. Cadbury castle, centres ef the regular military organisation of the hundred.] N. and Q. Som. and Dorset, 1, pp. 12, 61. 1890.

7871 Evans (Herbert Arthur). Castles of England and Wales. pp. xvii, 368, + 34 plates. 8° London, 1912. [Pp. 34–230, 11th c. castles.]

7872 Garfitt (G. A.). The castle hill. [General discussion of the problem.] Trans. Hunter Archaeol. Soc., 1, pp. 187–92. 1918.

7873 Gould (Isaac Chalkley). Early defensive earthworks. [Pp. 29–36, A.–S. and Danish period.] J. Brit. Archaeol. Assoc., 57 (N.S. 7), pp. 15–38, + 1 plate + 5 plans. 1901.

7874 Honeyman (Herbert Lewis). The standard axial dimensions of English mound-and-bailey castles. Proc. Soc. Antiq. Newcastle, 4th S. 10, pp. 294–98. 1946.

7875 Hope (*Sir* William Henry St. John). English fortresses and castles of the tenth and eleventh centuries. Archaeol. J., 60, pp. 72–90. 1903.

7876 Morgan (W. Ll.). The classification of camps and earthworks. [Pp. 218–23, the Saxon invasion—the Danish invasion.] Arch. Camb., 75 (6th S. 20), pp. 201–23. 1920.

7877 Morris (John E.). Saxon burghs and Norman castles. Berks, Bucks and Oxon Archaeol. J., 31, pp. 81–110, + 2 plates. 1927.

7878 Neilson (George). The motes in Norman Scotland [and England]. [i. Early fortifications generally : ii. The motes : iii. English and other motes : iv. The motes in Scottish history : v. The Scottish motes feudal.] Scottish Rev., 32, pp. 209–38. 1898. [Gross, 409.]

7879 Painter (Sidney). English castles in the early Middle Ages : their number, location, and legal position. [William I→.] Speculum, 10, pp. 321–32. 1935.

7880 Pryce (T. Davies) and **Armitage** (*Mrs.* Ella Sophia), (rejoinder). The alleged Norman origin of ' castles ' in England. E.H.R., 20, pp. 703–18. 1905.

7881 Pryce (T. Davies). Earthworks of the moated mound type. [?A.–S. or Norman.] J. Brit. Archaeol. Assoc., 62 (N.S. 12), pp. 231–68, + 13 plates. 1906.

7882 Round (John Horace). The castles of the Conquest. Archaeologia, 58, pp. 313–40. 1902.

7883 Rutter (J. A.). Moated mounds. [Supplementary list to **7867**.] N. and Q., 9th S. 5, pp. 309–10, 399 : 6, *passim* (see index). 1900.

7884 —— Moated mounds. [?A.–S. or Norman.] Antiquary, 38, pp. 239–42, 271–76 : (correspondence, pp. 319–20, 351–53, by Ella S. Armitage.) 1902.

7885 Stenton (*Sir* Frank Merry). The development of the castle in England and Wales. *Historical Association, Leaflet*, 22. pp. 32, + 4 plates. 8° London, 1910 (revised, 1933).

7886 Thompson (Alexander Hamilton). Military architecture in England during the Middle Ages. pp. xxi, 384. 8° London, 1912. [Pp. 21–34, A.–S. and Danish.]

7887 Toy (Sidney). The castles of Great Britain. pp. xviii, 276, + 75 plates. 8° London, 1953. [Pp. 24–41, Romano-British and A.–S. fortresses, A.D. 400 to 1066.]

7888 Wall (James Charles). A Saxon *burh*. [8 figures in text.] J. Antiq. Assoc. Brit. Isles, 1, pp. 133–41, 1930.

7889 Watson (John). An account of some hitherto undescribed remains of antiquity. [Sundry fortifications which he ascribes to Saxons or Danes.] Archaeologia, 5, pp. 87–94, + plate. 1779.

§ *b*. East Anglia

7890 Clark (George Thomas). Castle Acre. Archaeol. J., 46, pp. 282–85. 1889.

7891 Clarke (William George). Thetford castle hill. [?early Norman.] Norfolk Archaeology, 16, pp. 39–45, + 2 plates. 1907.

7892 Cottrill (Frank). A trial excavation at Witham, Essex. [Site of *burh* constructed by Edward the Elder in 913 (A.–S. C.).] Antiq. J., 14, pp. 190–91. 1934.

7893 Downman (Edward A.). Great Canfield mount. [?A.–S. origin.] Trans. Essex Archaeol. Soc., N.S. 6, pp. 225–27, + plan. 1898.

7894 Francis (E. B.). Rayleigh castle : new facts in its history and recent exploration on its site. [Mentioned in Domesday : ?built by Conqueror. Mostly post A.–S. material.] *Same jnl.*, N.S. 12, pp. 147–85, + folding plan, + 7 plates. 1913.

7895 Gould (Isaac Chalkley). Ancient earthworks [in Essex]. [21 plans in text.] V.C.H., Essex, 1, pp. 275–314, + map. 1903.

7896 —— Bures mount. Trans. Essex Archaeol. Soc., N.S. 9, pp. 20–21. 1906.

7897 —— The burh at Maldon. *Same jnl.*, N.S. 10, pp. 79–81, + 1 plate. 1909.

7898 —— The castle of Ongar. [Plate ' shows the form of the existing works of the Anglo-Saxon period ' : p. 136, ' section of earthworks '.] *Same jnl.*, N.S. 7, pp. 136–41, + 1 plate. 1900.

7899 —— Great Easton mount. *Same jnl.*, N.S. 8, pp. 324–26. 1903.

7900 —— Rickling mount. *Same jnl.*, N.S. 9, pp. 377–79, + 1 plate. 1906.

7901 —— Traces of Saxons and Danes in the earthworks of Essex. [5 plans in text.] Archaeol. J., 64, pp. 227–42, + folding plan. 1907.

7902 Hartshorne (Albert). Castle Acre. [Roman, Saxon, Norman.] Archaeol. J., 47, pp. 1–8. 1890.

7903 Holmes (Thomas Vincent). Notes on ancient defensive earthworks in connection with those of Rayleigh ' castle ', Essex. [Discusses their dates. ?A.–S. Rayleigh mentioned in Domesday.] Essex Nat., 10, pp. 145–58. 1897.

7904 Hope (*Sir* William Henry St. John). On the Norman origin of Cambridge castle. [Mostly notes on burhs in general.] Proc. Camb. Antiq. Soc., 11, pp. 324–46, + 6 plans. 1906.

7905 Laver (Henry). Rayleigh mount: a British oppidum. [But Round says A.-S., not British : **7914.**] Trans. Essex Archaeol. Soc., N.S. 4, pp. 172–78 + folding plan, + 1 plate. 1893.

7906 —— Shoebury camp. [Its origin as narrated in A.-S. C. under date 893.] *Same jnl.*, N.S. 6, pp. 97–100, + plan. 1898.

7907 Laver (P. G.). Pandal Wood camp. [? of Viking period.] *Same jnl.*, N.S. 19, pp. 255–59. 1930.

7908 —— Sunecastre, or the camp at Asheldham. [? of Viking period.] *Same jnl.*, N.S. 19, pp. 180–85, + plan, + 2 plates. 1930.

7909 Manning (Charles Robertson). Eye castle. [?A.-S. earthworks, adapted to Norman use.] Proc. Suffolk Inst. Archael., 5, pp. 104–14, + plan. 1876.

7910 Morris (A. J.). The Saxon Shore fort at Burgh castle. [Pp. 116–19 + fig 7, Anglo-Saxon remains.] Proc. Suffolk Inst. Archaeol., 24, pp. 100–20, + 3 plates. 1947.

7911 Nichols (Francis Morgan). Colchester castle. [Earthworks, Saxon : a small amount of A.-S. and Domesday material.] Trans. Essex Archaeol. Soc., N.S. 3, pp. 1–35, + 3 plates. 1889.

7912 Round (John Horace). Pleshy. [? A.-S. mound.] *Same jnl.*, N.S. 5, pp. 83–86. 1895.

7913 —— Professor Freeman on his defence. [That Colchester keep was the work of Eudo de Rie.] Antiq. Mag., 7, pp. 264–67 : 8, pp. 69–75. 1885.

7914 —— Rayleigh mount. [Argument for A.-S. origin.] Trans. Essex Arch. Soc., N.S. 5, pp. 41–43. 1895.

7915 Spurrell (Flaxman Charles John). Danbury camp, Essex. [No date, but general likeness to Witham, built by Edward the Elder.] Essex Nat., 4, pp. 138–40. 1890.

7916 —— Haesten's camps at Shoebury and Benfleet, Essex. *Same jnl.*, 4, pp. 150–53. 1890.

7917 — Shoebury camp, Essex. [Constructed by Hæsten, 894.] Archaeol. J., 47, pp. 78–81, + plan. 1890.

7918 —— Withambury. [A.-S. C., 913. *Getimbred* by Edward the Elder.] Essex Nat., 1, pp. 19–22. 1887.

§ *c*. **Kent and Sussex**

7919 British Archaeological Association. Opening the Saxon barrows (Breach Down barrows and Bourne Park). [Near Canterbury.] Rept. of Proc., Brit. Archaeol. Assoc., 1 (Canterbury meeting, 1844), pp. 91–100, + 1 plate. 1845.

7920 Curwen (Eliot Cecil). The *burh* of Shermanbury. [Plan on p. 50.] Sussex N. and Q., 10, pp. 49–51. 1944.

7921 Holmes (Thomas Vincent). The deneholes of Kent. [?caverns made by the Danes or by people fleeing from them.] V.C.H., Kent, 1, pp. 446–54. 1908.

7922 Wheatley (Sydney Williams). Boley hill, Rochester, after the Roman period. [Motte dates from William I and not Danish ? Stone castle erected by Gundulf : 2 plans.] Arch. Cant., 41, pp. 127–41. 1929.

§ *d*. **Mercia**

7923 Andrews (Robert T.). Moats and moated sites in the parish of Reed [Herts.]. East Herts Archaeol. Soc., Trans., 2, iii (1904), pp. 265–72, + plan. 1905.

7924 Aylott (G.). Pirton castle. [Mound : ?A.-S.] *Same jnl.*, 4. i (1908–9), pp. 1–4, + folding plan. 1910.

7925 B. Saxon fortress at Bridgnorth. Shropshire N. and Q., 1, pp. 26–27. 1885.

7926 Blagg (Thomas Matthews). Bothamsall castle. [?an 11th c. motte.] Trans. Thoroton Soc., 35 (1931), pp. 1–3, + 1 plate. 1932.

7927 Braun (Hugh). Chiltern castles : the Conqueror's flank march round London in 1066. [1 map in text.] Trans. Lond. and Middsx. Archaeol. Soc., N.S. 7, pp. 602–09. 1937.

7928 —— London's first castle. [William I.] *Same jnl.*, N. S. 7, pp. 445–51. 1937.

7929 Burgess (Joseph Tom). The fortifications of Warwick. [Pp. 12–21, A.-S. period : fortifications by Æthelfleda, etc.] Proc. Warwickshire Nat. and Archaeol. F.C., [14] 1875, pp. 9–31. 1875.

7930 Campbell-Hyslop (C. W.) and **Cobbold** (Edgar Sterling) *eds.* Church Stretton. Vol. 3. Pre-Roman, Roman and Saxon archaeological remains. 8° Shrewsbury, 1903. [Pp. 75–91, reputed Saxon remains, by E.S.C. (Castle hill, All Stretton : Castle bank, Woolstaston : Castle hill, Lebotswood : Brockhurst castle).]

7931 Clark (George Thomas). The castle of Ewias Harold [Herefordshire]. Arch. Camb., 4th S. 8, pp. 116–24. 1877.

7932 —— The moated mound of Se[c]kington [Warwickshire : 4 miles N.E. of Tamworth.] Archaeol. J., 39, pp. 372–75, + plan. 1882.

7933 —— Richard's Castle [Herefordshire]. *Same jnl.*, 30, pp. 143–52. 1873.

7934 Cox (John Charles). Ancient earthworks [in Derbyshire.] [P. 376, Bakewell *burh*, etc.] V.C.H., Derbyshire, 1, pp. 357–96, + map. 1905.

7935 Downman (Edward A.). Forms and forming of mote castles in Herefordshire. [Argues that mote castles are works of Norman invaders rather than A.-S.] Trans. Woolhope N.F. Club, 1905–07, pp. 252–56. 1911.

7936 Downs (R. S.). Desborough castle [near Wycombe]. Rec. Bucks., 5, pp. 248–60. 1878.

7937 Goddard (A. R.). Ancient earthworks [in Bedfordshire]. [Including their use in A.-S. times. 28 plans in text.] V.C.H., Bedford, 1, pp. 267–308, + map. 1904.

7938 Gould (Isaac Chalkley) and **Downman** (Edward A.). Ancient earthworks [in Herefordshire]. [99 figures in text.] V.C.H., Hereford, 1, pp. 199–262, + map. 1908.

7939 Gould (Isaac Chalkley). The burh at Leicester. Antiquary, 36, pp. 372–74. 1900.

7940 —— Wymondley castle. [? temp. William I or Stephen.] East Herts Archaeol. Soc., Trans., 3. i (1905), pp. 10–11, + 2 plans. 1906.

7941 Ladds (Sidney Inskip). Ancient earthworks [in the county of Huntingdon]. [E.g. Huntingdon castle, built in 1068, pp. 288–90. 25 figures in text.] V.C.H., Huntingdon, 1, pp. 281–313, + map. 1926.

7942 Monkhouse (William). On Risinghoe castle, in Goldington, and Howbury, in Renhold [Beds.]. Assoc. Archit. Socs'. Rpts., 3, pp. 175–85. 1854.

7943 Phillips (William). The Saxon age of certain fortified posts in Shropshire. Shrop. N. and Q., N.S. 1, pp. 92–93. 1892.

7944 Round (John Horace). The origin of Belvoir castle [Leicestershire]. [?date of erection.] E.H.R., 22, pp. 508–10. 1907.

7945 Sutton (Edward). The ancient military walls and gates of Nottingham. 1 [i.e. in A.-S. period]. Notts. and Derbs. N. and Q., 4, pp. 49–52. 1896.

7946 Varley (W. J.). Excavations of the Castle Ditch, Eddisbury [Cheshire], 1935–1938. [21 plates interpaginated, + 18 figures in text. =Eadesbyrig of A.-S. C, MS. C. ; built by Aethelflaed.] Trans. Hist. Soc. Lancs. and Ches., 102 (1950), pp. 1–68. 1951.

7947 Wadmore (Beauchamp). The earthworks of Bedfordshire. pp. 270. 4° Bedford, 1920. [98 illustrations. Pp. 47–75, Saxon and Danish periods.]

7948 Whitehead (J. G. O.). Early Anglian defence works in the Arrow valley [Herefordshire]. [7th–8th c.] Trans. Woolhope N.F. Club, 1936–38, pp. 50–57, + 5 maps. 1940.

§ e. Northumbria

7949 Addy (Sidney Oldall). Some defensive earthworks in the neighbourhood of Sheffield. [?A.–S. Laughton-en-le-Morthen, Mexborough, Adwick-le-Street, Ratcliffe moat, Ecclesfield, Blueman's bower.] Trans. Hunter Archaeol. Soc., 1, pp. 357–64, + 4 plates and plans. 1918.

7950 Armitage (*Mrs.* Ella Sophia). Almondbury [near Huddersfield]. Bradford Antiquary, 3, pp. 396–403. 1900.

7951 —— The non-sepulchral earthworks of Yorkshire. [P. 15, ? used to shelter population from Danes.] *Same jnl.*, 4 (N.S. 2), pp. 1–21. 1901.

7952 —— On some Yorkshire earthworks. [?A.–S. or Norman.] Reliquary, 7, pp. 158–69. 1901.

7953 Armstrong (Albert Leslie). Sheffield castle : an account of discoveries made during excavations on the site from 1927 to 1929. [Pp. 22–24 + figure 14, ' the Saxon remains '.] Trans. Hunter Archaeol. Soc., 4, pp. 7–27, + plan, + 17 plates. 1937.

7954 Clark (George Thomas). Conisborough castle. [From time of Wulfric Spot, c. 1000 —.] Yorks. Archaeol. J., 8, pp. 125–57, + plan, + 4 plates. 1884.

7955 —— The defences of York. [Including A.–S. period.] Archaeol. J., 31, pp. 225–61, + plan. 1874. *Same title.* [Pp. 13–22, A.–S.] Yorks. Archaeol. J., 4, pp. 1–42 ; + folding plan. 1877.

7956 —— Observations on some moated mounds in Yorkshire. Yorks. Archaeol. J., 6, pp. 109–12. 1881.

7957 Collingwood (William Gershom). Aldingham [-in-Furness] mote. Antiquary, 45, pp. 252–58. 1909.

7958 Cooper (Thomas Parsons). York; the story of its walls, bars, and castles. pp. xx, 365. 8° London, 1904. [Pp. 22–46, A.–S. and Danish defences.]

7959 Cowper (Henry Swainson). The ancient settlements, cemeteries, and earthworks of Furness. [Pp. 422–26, ' post-Roman and Anglo-Saxon earthworks.'— Aldingham Moat hill and Pennington castle hill.] Archaeologia, 53, pp. 389–426, + map. 1893.

7960 Ferguson (Richard Saul). Two moated mounds, Liddell [at junction of Liddell and Esk] and Aldingham, [Lancs.]. [Ascribes to 8th to 11th c.] Trans. Cumb. and Westm. Antiq. Soc., 9, pp. 404–11, + 2 plans, + 1 plate. 1888.

7961 Gould (Isaac Chalkley). Some early defensive earthworks of the Sheffield district. [6 plans in text.] J. Brit. Archaeol. Assoc., 60 (N.S. 10), pp. 29–42. 1904.

7962 Hogg (Alexander Hubert Arthur). Earthwork at Old Yevering, Northumberland. [?=King Edwin's ' villa ' (7th c.)] Antiquity, 23, pp. 211–14. 1949.

7963 Kelly (Paul Vincent). Aldingham [Lancs.] motte and grange. [?A.–S. or early Norman.] Trans. Cumb. and Westm. Antiq. Soc., N.S. 24, pp. 271–77. 1924.

7964 Walker (John William). Sandall castle. [' True type of an English *burh*.'] Yorks. Archaeol. J., 13, pp. 154–88, + 3 plates, + 2 folding plans (one of earthworks). 1895.

§ f. Wessex

7965 Cornish (J. B.). Ancient earthworks and defensive enclosures [in Cornwall]. [Entrenchments are imprints of two centuries of border warfare between Cornish and A.–S. (735–936, when Athelstan made Tamar the boundary.) 7 plates, paginated as text.] V.C.H. Cornwall, 1, pp. 451–73, + map. 1906.

7966 Field (John Edward). The antiquities of Wallingford [Berks.]. [Pp. 20–23, the castle, completed by Robert d'Oilgi in 1071.] Q.J. Berks Archaeol. Soc., 3, pp. 18–23, *etc.* 1893.

7967 Finberg (Herbert Patrick Reginald). Lydford castle. [A.–S. *burh*, and early Norman motte.] Devon and Cornwall N. and Q., 23, pp. 386–87. 1949.

7968 Godwin-Austen (Robert A. C.). Hanstie or Anstie Bury [camp]. [? occupied by Saxons rather than by Danes.] Surrey Archaeol. Collns., 5, pp. 21–23, + map. 1871.

7969 Gould (Isaac Chalkley). The walls of Wallingford. [Castle dates from 1071?] J. Brit. Archaeol. Assoc., 62 (N.S. 12), pp. 119–24, + 2 plans. 1906.

7970 Hope-Taylor (Brian). The excavation of a motte at Abinger in Surrey. Archaeol. J., 107 (1950), pp. 15–43, + 9 plates. 1952.

7971 Irving (George Vere). On the earthworks at Old Sarum. [Inner citadel added by the Saxons.] J. Brit. Archaeol. Assoc., 15, pp. 291–302, + 1 plate. 1859.

7972 Lethaby (William Richard). The Conqueror's castles in Devonshire. Devon N. and Q., 3, pp. 179–81. 1905.

7973 Markland (James). Carisbrooke castle. [First plan (earthworks) shows ' work of 9th or 10th c. '] Papers and Proc. Hants. F.C., 2, pp. 257–70, + 3 plans. 1894.

7974 Montgomerie (D. H.). Old Sarum. [8 figures and plans in text.] Archaeol. J., 104 (1947), pp. 129–43. 1948.

7975 Myres (John Nowell Linton). Three unrecognised castle mounds at Hamstead Marshall [Berks.]. Trans. Newbury District F.C., 6, pp. 115–26, + map. 1932.

7976 Oliver (George). The castle of Exeter. [Pp. 128–31, A.–S. to William 1st]. Archaeol. J., 7, pp. 128–39 + 1 plate. 1850.

7977 Ramsden (Josslyn Vere). The hill fort and castle hill at Widworthy. [? Saxon *burh*. With plan.] Rept. and Trans. Devon. Ass., 79, pp. 193–96. 1947.

7978 Smart (T. W. Wake). Castle hill, Cranborne. [' Probably of Saxon age.'] Proc. Dorset Antiq. F.C., 11, pp. 148–58, + plan. 1890.

7979 Stone (Percy Goddard). A vanished castle : an attempt to reconstruct the castle of Southampton from observation, analogy and documentary evidence. [Pp. 241–43, 11th c., with plan c. 1070.] Papers and Proc. Hants. F.C., 12, pp. 241–70, + 4 plates. 1934.

7980 Underhill (F. M.). Notes on an earthwork in the parish of Tilehurst [Berks.]. Trans. Newbury F.C., 8, pp. 2–9. 1938.

123. EARTHWORKS AND FORTS, IRELAND

7981 Berry (R. G.). The royal residence of Rathmore of Moy-linne. With notes on other earthworks in Ulster. [*See also* note on pp. 111–12.] Ulster J. Arch., 2nd S. 5, pp. 9–19, 84–91. 1898–99.

7982 Kirker (Samuel Kerr). Cloughoughter castle, county Cavan. [? 11th c.] J. Roy. Soc. Antiq. Ireland, 20 (5th S. 1), pp. 294–97, + 1 plate. 1890.

7983 Knox (Hubert Thomas). The croghans and some Coanacht raths and motes. [Discusses the date question. See also **7990**.] *Same jnl.*, 41 (6th S. 1), pp. 93–116, 205–40, 301–42, + map. 1911.

7984 Lett (H. W.) and **Berry** (R. G.). The great wall of Ulidia ; commonly known as the Dane's Cast, or Gleann-na-muice-duibhe. A topographical description by H. W. Lett, with historical references and notes by R. G. Berry. Drawings, measurements and illustrations by W. J. Fennell. [Boundary of Ulidia till battle of Magh-Rath, 637.] Ulster J. Archaeol., 2nd S. 3, pp. 23–29, 65–82, + map. 1896–97.

7985 Morris (Henry). Motes [in county Louth] and their origin. County Louth Archaeol. J., 2, pp. 41–44. 1908.

7986 O'Connor (Michael). The excavation of three earthen ring-forts in the Liffey valley. [Rath na Frishtawn, Quinn's rath, and Tobin's rath. Adapted as habitation sites for poor families c. 800–900. Finds.] J. Roy. Soc. Antiq. Ireland, 74 (7th S. 14), pp. 53–60. 1944.

7987 O'Ríordáin (Seán Pádraig). The excavation of a large earthen ring-fort at Garranes, co. Cork. (Historical addendum by John Ryan). [Occupied c. 500 A.D.] Proc. R.I.A., 47c, pp. 77–150, + 12 plans and plates. 1942.

7988 —— and **Hartnett** (P. J.). The excavation of Ballycattern fort, co. Cork. [Occupied 600 A.D. →] Proc. R.I.A., 49 c, pp. 1–43, + 7 plates. 1943.

7989 O'Ríordáin (Seán P.). Lough Gur [co. Limerick] excavations: Carraig Aille and the 'Spectacles'. [Carraig Aille II fort, 8th late 10th c.] Proc. R.I.A., 52 c, pp. 39–111, + 17 plans and plates. 1949.

7990 Orpen (Goddard Henry). Croghans and Norman motes. [Reply to 7983.] J. Roy. Soc. Antiq. Ireland, 41 (6th S. 1), pp. 267–76. 1911.

7991 —— Motes and Norman castles in county Louth. *Same jnl.*, 38 (5th S. 18), pp. 241–69, + 1 plate. 1908.

7992 —— Motes and Norman castles in Ireland. *Same jnl.*, 37 (5th S. 17), pp. 123–52. 1907.

7993 —— The origin of Irish motes. County Louth Archaeol. J., 2, pp. 50–56. 1908.

7994 —— Rathgall, county Wicklow. J. Roy. Soc. Antiq. Ireland, 41 (6th S. 1), pp. 138–50, + 2 plates. 1911.

7995 Tempest (H. G.). The castles and motes of county Louth. [List of the 'motes which were the earliest Anglo-Norman fortifications before they had time to build in stone.'] County Louth Archaeol. J., 10, pp. 314–15. 1944.

7996 Westropp (Thomas Johnson). The ancient castles of the county of Limerick. Proc. R.I.A., 26 c, pp. 55–264, + 14 plates. 1906.

7997 —— The ancient forts of Ireland: being a contribution towards our knowledge of their types, affinities, and structural features. (Some further notes . . . especially as to the age of motes in Ireland). [Also age, use, distribution.] Trans. R.I.A., 31, pp. 579–730, + 8 plates. Proc. R.I.A., 24 c, pp. 267–76. 1902, 1904.

7998 Westropp (Thomas Johnson). The cahers of county Clare: their names, features, and bibliography. [Stone forts, ?8th–9th c.] Proc. R.I.A., 3rd S. 6, pp. 415–49. 1901.

7999 —— Irish motes and alleged Norman castles: note on some recent contributions to their study. J. Roy. Soc. Antiq. Ireland, 35 (5th S. 15), pp. 402–06. 1905.

8000 —— On Irish motes and early Norman castles. *Same jnl.*, 34 (5th S. 14), pp. 313–45. 1904.

8001 —— Types of the ring-forts and similar structures remaining in eastern Clare: the Newmarket group. (Ditto: Quin, Tulla and Bodyke). Proc. R.I.A., 27c, pp. 217–34, + 1 plate: pp. 371–400, + 1 plate. 1908–09.

124. EARTHWORKS AND FORTS, SCOTLAND

8002 Christison (David). Early fortifications in Scotland: motes, camps, and forts. *Rhind Lectures*, 1894. pp. xxvi, 407, + 3 maps. 8° Edinburgh, 1898. [137 figures in text.]

8003 —— Forts, camps, and motes of the upper ward of Lanarkshire. [30 figures in text. Undated and undatable: but in use during the period.] Proc. Soc. Antiq. Scot., 24 (N.S. 12), pp. 281–352, + 10 plates. 1890.

8004 —— The forts, 'camps', and other field-works of Perth, Forfar, and Kincardine. [From Roman to mediaeval times. 56 figures in text.] *Same jnl.*, 3rd S. 10 (1899–1900), pp. 43–120, + map. 1900.

8005 —— A general view of the forts, camps, and motes of Dumfriesshire, with a detailed description of those in upper Annandale, and an introduction to the study of Scottish motes. [27 figures in text.] *Same jnl.*, 25 (3rd S. 1), pp. 198–256, + map, + 1 plate. 1891.

8006 Coles (Frederick R.). The motes, forts, and doons of the stewartry of Kirkcudbright (—in the east and west divisions of *ditto*). [71 (66) figures in text.] *Same jnl.*, 25 (3rd S. 1), pp. 352–96: 26 (3rd S. 2), pp. 117–20: 27 (3rd S. 3), pp. 92–182. 1891–93.

8007 Curle (Alexander Ormiston). Report on the excavation, in September 1913, of a vitrified fort at Rockcliffe, Dalbeattie, known as the Mote of Mark, [Kirkcudbright]. [23 figures in text. Art is that of best epoch of Celtic design, early Christian period.] *Same jnl.*, 48 (4th S. 12, 1913–14). pp. 125–68. 1914.

8008 Fairhurst (Horace). The galeried dūn at Kildonan bay, Kintyre. [Period II shows ' that fort was occupied until after the 7th c., A.D. ' 13 figures in text.] *Same jnl.*, 73 (7th S. 1, 1938–39), pp. 185–228, + 7 plates. 1939.

8010 Mitchell (Arthur). Notice of buildings designed for defence on an island in a loch at Hogstetter, in Whalsay, Shetland. [Allied to brochs. 12 figures and plans in text.] *Same jnl.*, 15 (N.S. 3), pp. 303–15. 1881.

8011 Reid (R. C.). Dungarry fort. [Hypothesis that erected by Gaelic-speaking Scots, 8th c.] Trans. Dumfries. Antiq. Soc., 3rd S. 15, pp. 157–60. 1929.

8012 —— Dunragit. [Mote: link with kingdom of Rheged till 603.] *Same jnl.*, 3rd S. 29 (1950–51), pp. 155–64. 1952.

8013 Scott (Archibald Black). The earth-houses of Kildonan, Sutherland. [He dates to 300–750 A.D., from remains found : ?used owing to Viking raids.] Scottish Antiquary, 13, pp. 155–60. 1899.

8014 Stevenson (Robert B. K.). The nuclear fort of Dalmahoy, Midlothian, and other dark age capitals. Proc. Soc. Antiq. Scot., 83 (7th S. 11), pp. 186–98, + 1 plate. 1951.

125. BROCHS

§ *a*. **Their Problem and General**
(?Pictish, ?Scandinavian. In use, if not constructed, during the period)

8015 Anderson (Joseph). Notes on the structure, distribution, and contents of the brochs, with special reference to the question of their Celtic or Norwegian origin. [26 figures in text.] Proc. Soc. Antiq. Scot., 12, pp. 314–55. 1878.

8016 Cursiter (James Walls). The Scottish brochs, their age and destruction. A theory. 8° Kirkwall, 1898.

8017 Fergusson (James). On the Norwegian origin of Scottish brochs. Proc. Soc. Antiq. Scot., 12, pp. 630–69. 1878.

8018 —— A short essay on the age and uses of the brochs . . . of the Orkney islands and the north of Scotland. pp. 34. 8° London, 1877.

8019 Graham (Angus). A list of brochs and broch sites. [503 items.] Antiq. J., 23, pp. 19–25. 1943.

8020 —— Some observations on the brochs. [Numbers and distribution : architectural features : shape and dimensions : external defences.] Proc. Soc. Antiq. Scot., 81 (7th S. 9), pp. 48–99. 1949.

8021 Hudd (Alfred Edmund). Notes on some Scottish brochs. Proc. Clifton Antiq. Club, 2 (1888–93), pp. 239–43, + 1 plate. 1893.

8022 Laing (Samuel). On the age of the burgs or ' brochs ', and some other prehistoric remains of Orkney and Caithness. [' Of remote date,' but ' successive occupation '. Not built by the Scandinavians.] Proc. Soc. Antiq. Scot., 7, pp. 56–79. 1870.

8023 MacKenzie (Donald A.). The brochs of Scotland. J. Antiq. Assoc. Brit. Isles, 1, pp. 101–06, + 2 plates. 1930.

8024 Scott (*Sir* Lindsay). The problem of the brochs. [10 figures and maps in text. Broch culture in decline by 4th c., and brochs adapted to humbler occupation. By 10th c., used as burial howes (being already reduced to grassy mounds).] Proc. Prehist. Soc., N.S. 13, pp. 1–36. 1947.

§ *b*. **Orkney and Shetland**

8025 Acland (Charles Lawford). Notes on the broch of Copister in Yell Sound, Shetland. Proc. Soc. Antiq. Scot., 24 (N.S. 12), pp. 473–74. 1890.

8026 Bruce (John). Notice of the excavation of a broch at Jarlshof, Sumburgh, Shetland. [Plan and 14 figures in text. Disc of 9th c. found.] *Same jnl.*, 41 (4th S. 5, 1906–07), pp. 11–33. 1907.

8027 Cruden (Stewart). The brochs of Mousa and Clickhimin, Shetland. *Ancient monuments, Ministry of Works.* pp. 16, + 8 plates, + 2 plans. 8° Edinburgh, 1951. [' Problem of the brochs ', etc.]

8028 Cursiter (James). The Orkney brochs. Proc. Orkney Antiq. Soc., 1 (1922–23), pp. 49–52. 1923.

8029 Dryden (*Sir* Henry) *bart.* Notes on the brochs or ' Pictish towers ' of Mousa, Clickemin, etc., in Shetland, illustrative of part of the series of plans and sections deposited in the library of the Society [of Antiquaries of Scotland]. Archaeol. Scot., 5, pp. 199–212 + 6 plates. 1874.

8030 Fraser (John). Antiquities of Sandwick (Birsay, Firth, Evie) parish. Proc. Orkney Antiq. Soc., 2, pp. 23–29, + map : 3, pp. 21–30 : 5, pp. 51–56 : 7, pp. 41–46. 1924–25, 1927, 1929.

8031 Goudie (Gilbert). Notice of excavations in a broch and adjacent tumuli near Levenwick, in the parish of Dunrossness, Zetland [Shetland]. Proc. Soc. Antiq. Scot., 9, pp. 212–19. 1873.

8032 Graeme (A. Sutherland). An account of the excavation of the broch of Ayre, St. Mary's Holm, Orkney. [16 figures in text.] *Same jnl.*, 48 (4th S. 12, 1913–14), pp. 31–51. 1914.

8033 Johnman (W. A. P.). Shetland brochs and the Dwarfie stone. Trans. Hawick Archaeol. Soc., 1898, 1898.

8034 Paterson (John Wilson). The broch of Mousa [Shetland] : a survey by H.M. Office of Works. [8 figures and plans in text.] Proc. Soc. Antiq. Scot., 56 (5th S. 8), pp. 172–83. 1922.

8035 Petrie (George). Notice of the brochs or large round towers of Orkney. With plans, sections, and drawings, and tables of measurements of Orkney and Shetland brochs. [4 full page plans, etc. in text.] Archaeol. Scot., 5, pp. 71–94. 1874.

8036 Petrie (George). Primeval antiquities of Orkney. [Brochs, etc.] Proc. Orkney Antiq. Soc., 5, pp. 19–29, + 2 plates. 1927.

8037 Richardson (James Smith). The broch of Gurness, Aikerness, west mainland, Orkney. *Ancient Monuments : Ministry of Works.* pp. 7. 8° Edinburgh, 1948. [Pp. 4–5, plan.]

8038 Saxby (Jessie Margaret Edmonston) *Mrs. Henry Linckmyer Saxby.* Shetland traditional lore. pp. 208, + 8 plates. 8° Edinburgh, 1932. [Pp. 24–40, brochs.]

8039 Stout (Elizabeth). Some Shetland brochs and standing stones. [20 figures in text. ?date, but fortified against Vikings.] Proc. Soc. Antiq. Scot., 46 (4th S. 10, 1911–12), pp. 94–132. 1912.

8040 Traill (William). Results of excavations at the broch of Burrian, North Ronaldsay, Orkney, during the summers of 1870 and 1871. [21 figures in text : inscribed stones, implements, combs, etc., collected.] Archaeol. Scot., 5, pp. 341–64, + 2 plates. 1880.

8041 Watt (William G. T.). Notice of the broch known as Burwick or Borwick, in the township of Yescanabee and parish of Sandwick, Orkney. Proc. Soc. Antiq. Scot., 16 (N.S. 4), pp. 442–50. 1882.

§ *c.* Others

8042 Anderson (Joseph). Notice of the excavation of the brochs of Yarhouse, Brounaben, Bowermadden, Old Stirkoke, and Dunbeath, in Caithness, with remarks on the period of the brochs ; and an appendix containing a collected list of the brochs of Scotland, and early notices of many of them. [15 figures in text. Map northern Scotland.] Archaeol. Scot., 5, pp. 131–98, + map. 1874.

8043 Calder (Charles S. T.). Report on the excavation of a· broch at Skitten, in the Kilmster district of Caithness. With a report on the animal remains, by Margery I. Plant. Proc. Soc. Antiq. Scot., 82 (7th S. 10), pp. 124–45, + 7 plates. 1950.

8044 Childe (Vere Gordon). Unrecorded brochs in Scotland. [Islay, Struy, Mull.] Antiq. J., 15, pp. 204–05. 1935.

8045 Curle (Alexander Ormiston). Account of the excavation of a broch near Craigcaffie, Ince parish, Wigtownshire, known as the Teroy fort. Proc. Soc. Antiq. Scot., 46 (4th S. 10, 1911–12), pp. 183–88. 1912.

8046 —— An account of the ruins of the broch of Dun Telve, near Glenelg. [Invernessshire], excavated by H.M. Office of Works in 1914. [10 figures in text.] *Same jnl.*, 50 (5th S. 2, 1915–16), pp. 241–54. 1916.

8047 Curle (James). Notes on two brochs recently discovered at Bow, Midlothian, and Torwoodlee, Selkirkshire. [11 figures in text.] *Same jnl.*, 26 (3rd S. 2), pp. 68–84, + 1 plan. 1892.

8048 Duncan (Dalrymple). Notes on the broch of Tapock, Torwood, Stirlingshire. Trans. Glasgow Archaeol. Soc., N.S.1, pp. 398–404. 1890.

8049 Graham (Angus). Notes on some brochs and forts visited in 1949. Proc. Soc. Antiq. Scot., 83 (7th S. 11), pp. 12–24, + 4 plates. 1951.

8050 Hunter (D. M.). Note on excavations at the broch of Tappoch in the Tor wood, Stirlingshire. *Same jnl.*, 83 (7th S. 11), pp. 232–35. 1951.

8051 Joass (J. Maxwell). The brochs or 'Pictish towers' of Cinn-Trolla, Carn-Liath, and Craig-Carril, in Sutherland, with notes on other northern brochs. With a report upon the crania found in and about them. Archaeol. Scot., 5, pp. 95–130, + 6 plates. 1874.

8052 Judd (J. M.). Note of a broch at Dun Voradale, isle of Roasay, [Skye]. Proc. Soc. Antiq. Scot., 10, pp. 308–10. 1874.

8053 Leask (H.). Account of a Pictish burg or broach. Trans. Hawick Archaeol. Soc., 14. 1875.

8054 McConchie (   ) *bailie*. Teroy broch, [Wigtownshire]. Trans. Dumfries. Antiq. Soc., 3rd S. 17 (1930–31), pp. 181–83. 1932.

8055 Macdonald (James). Historical notice of ' the broch ', or Burghead, in Moray, with an account of its antiquities. Proc. Soc. Antiq. Scot., 4, pp. 321–69, + plan, + 4 plates. 1863.

8056 Mackay (James). Notice of the excavation of the broch at Ousdale, Caithness. *Same jnl.*, 26 (3rd S. 2), pp. 351–57. 1892.

8057 Mackenzie (Donald A.). A Berwickshire broch. [Eden's hall, on Cockburn law.] Trans. Hawick Archaeol. Soc., 1936, pp. 82–84, + 2 plates. 1936.

8058 Neilson (George). The monuments of Caithness. Scot. H. R., 9, pp. 241–52, + 5 plates. 1912.

8059 Nicol (John). Pictish tower at Kintradwell, parish of Loth [Sutherland.] Old-lore Misc. V.C., 3, pp. 230–33, + plan. 1910.

8060 —— Pictish tower at Salzcraggie, Helmsdale, [Sutherland]. *Same jnl.*, 3, pp. 107–10. 1910.

8061 Piggott (Stuart). Excavations in the broch and [Roman] hill-fort of Torwoodlee, Selkirkshire. Proc. Soc. Antiq. Scot., 85 (1950–51), pp. 92–117, + 3 plates, + plan. 1953.

8062 Polson (A.). Highland brochs. Trans. Gaelic Soc. Inverness, 19, pp. 115–21. 1895.

8063 Ross (Thomas). [The brochs of Tappock, Stirlingshire and Coldoch, Perthshire]. Proc. Soc. Antiq. Newcastle, 2nd S. 10, pp. 218–22. 1902.

8064 Thomas (F. W. L.). On the duns of the outer Hebrides. [Pp. 407–15, brochs.] Archaeol. Scot., 5, pp. 365–415, + 7 plates. 1890.

126. EARTHWORKS AND FORTS, WALES AND MAN

8065 Baring-Gould (Sabin). Early fortifications in Wales. Trans. Hon. Soc. Cymm., 1898–99, pp. 1–24. 1900.

8066 Bersu (Gerhard). A promontory fort on the shore of Ramsey bay, Isle of Man. [?early Viking age: 9th c. 8 figures in text.] Antiq. J., 29, pp. 62–79. 1949.

8067 Breese (Charles E.). The fort of Dinas Emrys [Carnarvonshire]. [?5th c.—period of Vortigern. 8 figures in text.] Arch. Camb., 85, pp. 342–54. 1930.

8068 Clark (George Thomas). Moated mounds. [In Wales and on Welsh border. ?A.–S. date.] Arch. Camb., 4th S. 6, pp. 63–69. 1875.

**8069 —— The moated mounds of the upper Severn. [5 plans of earthworks.] Collns. hist. and archaeol. rel. to Montgom., 10, pp. 329–48, and 1 plate. 1877. *Reprinted in* Arch. Camb., 4th. S. 11, pp. 200–12, + 2 plates. 1880.

8070 Gardner (Willoughby). Craig Gwrtheyrn hill fort, Llanfihangel ar Arth, Carmarthenshire. [Last refuge of Vortigern.] Arch. Camb., 87, pp. 144–50, + 1 plate. 1932.

8071 Glanusk (Joseph Russell Bailey) *1st baron*. Presidential address [to the Cambrian Archaeological Association, 1902]. [Pp. 71–72, Castles of the tenth century of Brecknockshire) : Norman castles.] Arch. Camb., 6th S. 3, pp. 68–73. 1903.

8072 Jones (Harry Longueville). On the study of Welsh antiquities–Glamorgan. [Pp. 189–93, Danish and post-Roman camps.] Arch. Camb., 3rd S. 15, pp. 187–93. 1869.

8073 Laws (Edward). Pembrokeshire earthworks. [Post-Roman defence v. Irish and Vikings.] Arch. Camb., 4th S. 11, pp. 241–48. 1880.

8074 Llewellin (William). The raths of Pembrokeshire. [Attributed to marauding Danes.] Arch. Camb., 3rd S. 10, pp. 1–13, + 2 plates. 1864.

8075 Richard (Arthur J.). A motte castle at Cwm Clais [Glamorgan]. Trans. Aberafon Hist. Soc., 6, pp. 54–56. 1934.

127. CEMETERIES AND 'FINDS' IN THEM, GENERAL AND MISCELLANEOUS

8076 Archaeological Institute. Catalogue of antiquities exhibited . . . during the annual meeting . . . at Bristol, July, 1851. [Pp. lxix–lxx, + 2nd plate
C C

(showing bronze Saxon brooch found near Warwick), A.–S.] Mems. Archaeol. Inst., [7] 1851, pp. lvii–xcv, + 3 plates. 1853.

8077 Bateman (Thomas). Ten years diggings in Celtic and Saxon grave hills, in the counties of Derby, Stafford and York, from 1848 to 1858 ; with notices of some former discoveries, hitherto unpublished, and remarks on the crania and pottery from the mounds. pp. vi, 309. 8° London, 1861.

8078 Crawford (Osbert Guy Stanhope). Barrows. [Pp. 432–4, A.–S.] Antiquity, 1, pp. 419–34. 1927.

8078a Douglas (James). Nenia Britannica, of a sepulchral history of Great Britain from the earliest period to its general conversion to Christianity. fol. London, 1793.

8079 Jewitt (Llewellynn). Grave-mounds and their contents . . . as exemplified in the burials of the Celtic, the Romano-British, and the Anglo-Saxon periods. pp. xxiv, 306. 8° London, 1870. [Pp. 202–97, with figures 325–489, A.–S.]

8080 Kemble (John Mitchell). Burial and cremation. [Reprinted in his Horae ferales, 1863, pp. 83–106, with additional note on 'Saxon graves discovered at Winster, Derbyshire']. Archaeol. J., 12, pp. 309–37. 1855.

8081 Kendrick (*Sir* Thomas Downing). Viking period antiquities in England. [800–1050, with map.] S.E. Naturalist, 38, pp. 42–49. 1933.

8082 Myres (John Nowell Linton). Cremation and inhumation in the Anglo-Saxon cemeteries. Antiquity, 16, pp. 330–41. 1942.

8083 Rolleston (George). On the modes of sepulture observable in late Romano-British and early Anglo-Saxon times in this country. pp. 9. [4th–6th c.] Trans. Internat. Congress of Preh. Archaeol., 3rd session (Norwich). [c. 1870?].

8084 Smith (Charles Roach). Anglo-Saxon and Frankish remains. [Various —near Derby ; Stowe Heath ; Searby, Lincs., etc.] Collectanea Antiqua, 2, pp. 203–48, + 10 plates. 1852.

8085 Smith (Charles Roach). Anglo-Saxon remains found in Kent and Lincolnshire. [Between Cuxton and Strood, Kent : Searby, Lincs.] *Same jnl.*, 5, pp. 129–40, + 3 plates. 1861.

8086 —— Anglo-Saxon remains found in Kent, Suffolk, and Leicestershire. [Strood, Otterham Creek, near Upchurch and Combe, Kent : Stowe Heath, Suffolk : Great Wigston, Leics.] *Same jnl.*, 2, pp. 155–70, + 9 plates. 1852.

8087 —— Anglo-Saxon remains recently discovered in Kent, Cambridgeshire, and in some other counties. [Faversham and Sarre, Kent : Chessell, I.o.W. : Barrington, Cambs. : Kempston, Beds.] *Same jnl.*, 6, pp. 136–72, + 13 plates. 1868.

8088 —— Researches and discoveries. [Little Wilbraham, Cambs. : Harnham hill, near Salisbury : Rochester, etc.] *Same jnl.*, 3, pp. 199–220, + 3 plates. [c. 1854].

8089 Wright (Thomas). On Anglo-Saxon antiquities, with a particular reference to the Faussett collection. [Weapons, fibulae, etc. With 40 figures in text.] Trans. Hist. Soc. Lancs. and Ches., 7, pp. 1–39, + map. 1855. *And in his* Essays on archaeological subjects, 1, pp. 107–71, + map. [51 figures in text.] 1861.

8090 Wylie (William Michael). Account of Teutonic remains, apparently Saxon, found near Dieppe. [9 figures, fibulae, etc., in text.] Archaeologia, 35, pp. 100–13. 1853.

8091 —— The burning and burial of the dead. [Pp. 470–78, A.–S.] *Same jnl.*, 37, pp. 454–78. 1857.

128. CEMETERIES, EAST ANGLIA

§ *a.* **Sutton Hoo**
(*See also* 15 § *b* (for history), and index.)

8092 [Anon.] A Saxon ship-burial in East Anglia. Discovery, N.S. 2, pp. 479–82. 1939.

8092a [Anon.] Sutton Hoo. Illustrated London News, Aug. 12 (p. 268), Aug. 19 (pp. 292–93), Aug. 26 (p. 346). 1939.

8092b [**Anon.**] The Sutton Hoo treasure : Anglo-Saxon finds presented to the nation. Museums J., 39, pp. 479–81, + 4 plates. 1940.

8092c Anderson (R. C.). The ribs of the Sutton Hoo ship. Mariner's Mirror, 36, p. 264. 1950.

8092d Birt (D. H. C.). The ancient history of the [Sutton Hoo] ship. Discovery, N.S. 2, pp. 461–67. 1939.

8093 British Museum. The Sutton Hoo ship burial. A provisional guide. [Prepared by R. L. S. Bruce-Mitford]. pp. 62. 8° London, (1947).

8094 Bruce-Mitford (Rupert Leo Scott). A new chapter in Anglo-Swedish relations. Anglo-Swedish Rev., 1950, pp. 69–72. 1950.

8094a Bruce-Mitford (Rupert Leo Scott). The problem of the Sutton Hoo cenotaph. ['No positive evidence whatsoever of a body'. Figure of 'the " body-area " . . . showing positions of the grave-goods with relation to a 6-foot hypothetical recumbent skeleton.'] Archaeol. News Letter, 2, pp. 166–69. 1950.

8094b —— Sutton Hoo—a rejoinder [to **8110**]. Antiquity, 26, pp. 76–82. 1952.

8094c —— Sutton Hoo and Sweden. Archaeol. News Letter, 1, ii, pp. 5–6. 1948.

8094d —— The Sutton Hoo ship-burial. [Substance of discourse at Royal Institution. General account, including description of reconstructed harp.] Nature, 165, pp. 339–41. 1950.

8094e —— The Sutton-Hoo ship burial. Proc. Roy. Institution, 24, pp. 440–49, + 2 plates. 1950.

8095 —— The Sutton Hoo ship-burial. Scientific American, 184, pp. 24–30. 1951.

8096 —— The Sutton Hoo ship burial : recent theories and some comments on general interpretation. Proc. Suffolk Inst. Arch., 25, pp. 1–78, + 15 plates. 1950.

8097 Crosley (A. S.) Survey of the 6th century Saxon burial ship. [11 figures.] Trans. Newcomen Soc., 22, pp. 109–16. 1943.

8097a Harcourt-Smith (*Sir* Cecil). The Sutton Hoo ship-burial. [8 figures.] Country Life, 87, pp. 377–79. 1940.

8098 Hill (*Sir* George). A note on the Sutton Hoo treasure trove inquest. Antiq. J., 30, pp. 67–68. 1950.

8099 Kendrick (*Sir* Thomas Downing). The discoveries at Sutton Hoo, Suffolk. [General notice.] Antiq. J., 20, p. 115. 1940.

8100 —— Una sepultura de rey anglosajon en un navio. Atlantis (Madrid), 16, pp. 190–92, + 1 plate. 1941.

8101 —— Kitzinger (Ernst) and **Allen** (Derek Fortrose). The Sutton Hoo finds. [i. The discovery : ii. The gold ornaments : iii. The silver : iv. The coins : v. Other finds : vi. Sutton Hoo and Saxon archaeology.] B.M.Q., 13, pp. 111–36, + plates 42–52. 1939.

8102 Lethbridge (Thomas Charles). Sutton Hoo. [6 figures in text.] Archaeology, 1, pp. 8–12. 1948.

8103 Lindqvist (Sune). Skeppsgraven å Sutton Hoo. Ett nytt Tolkningsförsök. Kungl. Human. Vetenskaps-Samfundet, Årsbok, 1951, pp. 78–102. 1951.

8104 Martin-Clarke (*Mrs.* Daisy Elizabeth). Significant objects at Sutton Hoo. [The standard, etc.] Chadwick Mem. Stud., pp. 107–19, + 1 plate. 1950.

8104a Moir (J. Reid). Treasure in East Anglia. Scientific American, 162, pp. 266–67. 1940.

8105 Phillips (Charles William). Ancestor of the British navy. [23 figures in text.] National Geographic Mag., 79, pp. 247–68. 1941.

8105a Phillips (Charles William). The [Anglo-Saxon] world from Sutton Hoo. Geog. Mag., 19, pp. 235–42. 1946.

8105b Phillips (Charles William). The excavation of the Sutton Hoo ship-burial. [Appendices : i. Inventory of the principal finds, by T. D. Kendrick : ii. Laboratory notes, by H. J. Plenderleith : iii. Report on timber, by H. Godwin : iv. Geological report.] Antiq. J., 20 , pp. 149–202, + 22 plates. 1940.

8106 —— The Sutton Hoo burial ship. Mariner's Mirror, 26, pp. 345–55, + 4 plates, 1940.

8107 —— The Sutton Hoo ship burial. [General survey.] Trans. Hunter Archaeol. Soc., 6, pp. 322–24. 1950.

8108 —— Kendrick (*Sir* Thomas Downing) *etc.* The Sutton Hoo ship-burial. [i. The excavation, by C. W. Phillips : ii. The gold ornaments, by T. D. Kendrick : iii. The large hanging-bowl, by T. D. Kendrick : iv. The archaeology of the jewellery, by T. D. Kendrick : v. The silver, by Ernest Kitzinger : vi. The coins, a summary, by O. G. S. Crawford : vii. The salvaging of the finds, by W. F. Grimes : viii. Who was He ? by H. Munro Chadwick.] Antiquity, 14, pp. 6–87, + 24 plates. 1940.

8109 Shetelig (Haakon). Skibsgraven ved Sutton Hoo i Suffolk. En angelsaksisk Kongegrave fra 600-årene. Viking, 4, pp. 167–72. 1940.

8110 Ward (Gordon). The silver spoons from Sutton Hoo. Antiquity, 26, pp. 9–13. 1952.

§ *b* **Others**

8111 Babington (Charles Cardale). On Anglo-Saxon remains found near Barrington, in Cambridgeshire. [Plate shows 2 fibulae.] Antiq. Commns. (Camb. Ant. Soc.), 2, pp. 7–10, + 1 plate. 1864.

8112 Bruce-Mitford (Rupert Leo Scott). The Snape boat-grave. [c. 635–50. Discovered 1862. Especially, pagan Saxon ring.] Proc. Suffolk Inst. Arch., 26 (1952), pp. 1–26, + 6 plates. 1953.

8113 Burrows (John William). Ten years of archaeological research in Southend-on-Sea and district. [Excavations at Shoebury, Prittlewell, etc. Figure in text of gold ornament, ?Jutish, from Prittlewell.] J. Brit. Archaeol. Assoc., N.S. 36 (1930), pp. 109–15. 1931.

8114 Carthew (George Alfred). Discovery of Anglo-Saxon remains in the parish of Castle Acre, Norfolk. Proc. Soc. Antiq., 4, p. 172. 1858.

8115 Davidson (Septimus). Discovery in . . . 1862 of antiquities on Snape common, Suffolk. [A.–S. urns : interment in boat : ?Danish.] *Same jnl.*, 2nd S. 2, pp. 177–82. 1863.

8116 Deck (Isaiah). Notice of remains of the Anglo-Saxon period, discovered at Little Wilbraham, Cambridgeshire. Archaeol. J., 8, pp. 172–78, + 1 plate. 1851.

8117 Draper (Warwick Herbert). Saxon remains at Leigh. [Skeleton and 7 coins (6 of Alfred, one of abp. Plegmund).] Essex Rev., 2, p. 187. 1893.

8118 Foster (Walter K.). Account of the excavations of an Anglo-Saxon cemetery at Barrington, Cambridgeshire. [Pp. 15–30, detailed account of graves. Plates mostly of fibulae.] Camb. Antiq. Commns., 5 (1880–84), pp. 5–32, + 12 coloured plates. 1886.

8119 Fowler (Gordon). Cratendune : a problem of the Dark Ages. [?to be identified with site of Ely Fields farm cemetery. The plates show finds from the cemetery—sword, brooches, and a string of amber beads.] Proc. Camb. Antiq. Soc., 41 (1943–47), pp. 70–73, + 3 plates. 1948.

8120 Fox (*Sir* Cyril). The archaeology of the Cambridge region. A topographical study of the bronze, early iron, Roman and Anglo-Saxon ages, *etc.*, pp. xxx, 360, 24, + 37 plates, + 5 maps. 8° Cambridge, 1923. — Reissue, with appendix 4. 8° Cambridge, 1948 [1949]. [Pp. 237–312, + plates 27–37, + map 5, A.–S. period.]

8121 Fox (*Sir* Cyril). Excavations at Foxton, Cambridgeshire, in 1922. [A.–S. burials overlying a La Tène settlement.] Proc. Camb. Antiq. Soc., 25, pp. 37–46. 1924.

8122 Hollingworth (Edith Joan), [*Mrs.* E. Savery], and **O'Reilly** (Maureen Margaret). Anglo-Saxon cemetery at Girton College, Cambridge ; a report based on the ms. notes of the excavations made by the late F. J. H. Jenkinson. pp. 38. 8° Cambridge, 1925.

8123 Housman (D.). Exploration of an Anglo-Saxon cemetery in the parish of Castleacre, Norfolk. Norfolk archaeology, 12, pp. 100–04. 1895.

8124 Hughes (Thomas McKenny). On some antiquities found near Hauxton, Cambridgeshire. [' Evidence of the overlap of . . . Saxon over Roman, and perhaps of Danish over Saxon.'] Proc. Camb. Antiq., Soc., 7 (1888–91), pp. 24–28, + 3 plates. 1893.

8125 —— [Report on] burying place of Saxon age [at Hunstanton, Norfolk]. Proc. Soc. Antiq., 2nd S. 18, pp. 318–21. 1901.

8126 Knocker (G. M.). Anglo-Saxon Thetford [Norfolk]. [Excavations.] Proc. Suffolk Inst. Arch., 25, pp. 109–10, + 1 plate. 1950.

8127 Layard (Nina Frances). Anglo-Saxon cemetery, Hadleigh road, Ipswich. Proc. Suffolk Inst. Archaeol., 13, pp. 1–19, + plan, + 5 plates. 1907.

8128 —— An Anglo-Saxon cemetery in Ipswich. Rept. Brit. Ass., 1906, pp. 694–95. 1907.

8129 —— An Anglo-Saxon cemetery in Ipswich. [The 3 plates show A.–S. bead necklaces.] Archaeologia, 60, pp. 325–52, + 3 coloured plates. 1907.

8130 —— and **Smith** (Reginald Allender). Discovery at Ipswich of an Anglo-Saxon cemetery of considerable extent. [Plates show 8 figures of brooches.] Proc. Soc. Antiq., 2nd S. 21, pp. 241–47, + 2 plates : p. 403. 1906–07.

8131 Layard (Nina Frances). Points of special interest in the Anglo-Saxon discoveries in Ipswich. [Plates show 'Anglian squareheaded brooch' and ' Jutish cloison brooch'.] Proc. Suffolk Inst. Archaeol., 16, pp. 278–80, + 2 coloured plates. 1918.

8132 Leeds (Edward Thurlow). Antiquities from Essex in the Ashmolean Museum, Oxford. [Pp. 253–54, + last plate, A.–S. period—pottery, etc.] Trans. Essex Archaeol. Soc., N.S., 19, pp. 247–54, + 4 plates. 1930.

8133 Lethbridge (Thomas Charles). Anglo-Saxon burials at Soham, Cambridgeshire. [With plan and illustrations.] Proc. Camb. Antiq. Soc., 33, pp. 152–63. 1933.

8134 —— The Anglo-Saxon cemetery, Burwell, Cambs. [With plans + illustrations.] *Same jnl.*, 27, pp. 72–79 : 28, pp. 116–23 : 29, pp. 84–94 : 30, pp. 97–109. 1926–29.

8135 —— and **O'Reilly** (Maureen Margaret). Archaeological notes. [Plate 5, A.–S. brooches, etc., Barton Road, Cambridge ; plate 6, A.–S. cinerary urn, Somersham, Hunts.] *Same jnl.*, 38, pp. 164–69, + 7 plates. 1938.

8136 Lethbridge (Thomas Charles). A cemetery at Lackford, Suffolk. Report of the excavation of a cemetery of the pagan Anglo-Saxon period in 1947. *Cambridge Antiquarian Society, Quarto Publications, N.S.*, 6. pp. 57. 4° Cambridge, 1951. [38 pages of figures.]

8137 —— A cemetery at Shudy camps, Cambridgeshire: report of the excavation of a cemetery of the Christian Anglo-Saxon period in 1933. *Cambridge Antiquarian Society. Quarto Publications, N.S.* 5. pp. 41, + 1 plate, + 2 plans. 4° Cambridge, 1936.

8138 —— East Angles, an account of recent fieldwork in Cambridgeshire and Suffolk. [Burwell, Mildenhall, Little Wilbraham, etc.] Ipek, 5, pp. 69–76, + 4 plates. 1930.

8139 —— and **Carter** (M. G.). Excavations in the Anglo-Saxon cemetery at Little Wilbraham. [With plan and illustrations.] Proc. Camb. Antiq. Soc., 29, pp. 95–104. 1928.

8140 Lethbridge (Thomas Charles). Excavations in the Bran ditch, Cambridgeshire. [Burials, including some A.–S. remains.] Antiq. J., 8, pp. 357–59. 1928.

8141 —— Further excavations at the War Ditches. [Fig. 1 shows bronze brooch of A.–S. (5th–6th c.) form. P. 127, bones of ancient (including A.–S. and Viking) sheep in the Cambridge region.] Proc. Camb. Antiq. Soc., 42 (1948), pp. 117–27, + 2 plates. 1949.

8142 —— Recent excavations in Anglo-Saxon cemeteries in Cambridgeshire and Suffolk. *Cambridge Antiquarian Society, Quarto Publications, N.S.* 3. pp. 90, + 6 plates, + 2 plans. 4° Cambridge, 1931.

8143 Lowerison (Bellerby). The sites of three Danish camps and an Anglian burying ground in East Anglia. [Camps at Holkham, Stiffkey and Creake. Burial ground in Hunstanton park. 2 plans in text.] Saga–Book V.C., 6, pp. 47–58. 1909.

8144 Maynard (Guy). Recent archaeological field work in Suffolk. [A.–S. sites : Ashbocking (Roman-Saxon huts), Butley (settlement sites and pottery), Fakenham (A.–S. burial), Ixworth Thorpe (A.–S. grave).] Proc. Suffolk Inst. Arch., 25, pp. 205–16. 1951.

8145 Middleton (John Henry). Discovery of a Saxon cemetery at Cambridge. [In cricket-field of St. John's college. Pagan.] Proc. Soc. Antiq., 2nd S. 12, pp. 132, 34. 1888.

8146 Neville (Richard Cornwallis) *4th baron Braybrooke*. Anglo-Saxon cemetery [on Linton heath, Cambridgeshire] excavated, January, 1853. Archaeol. J., 11, pp. 95–115, and 4 plates, p. 215. 1854.

8147 —— Saxon obsequies illustrated by ornaments and weapons : discovered by Hon. R. C. Neville in a cemetery near Little Wilbraham, Cambridgeshire. 40 coloured plates. fol. London, 1852.

8147a Palmer (William Mortlock) and **Fox** (*Sir* Cyril Fred). Shudy Camps, Castle Camps and Waltons Park, Ashdon. pp. 35. 8° Cambridge, [1924].

8148 Phillips (Charles William). An interesting effect of drought on barren land. [Revelation of a large A.-S. urn cemetery at Mill Heath, Cavenham, near Bury St. Edmunds.] Antiquity, 21, pp. 212–13. 1947.

8149 Pollitt (William). Anglo-Saxon remains (further Anglo-Saxon remains) in south-east Essex. [A.-S. cemetery, Southend : c. 500–650. 5 figures of pottery, etc.] Antiq. J., 10, pp. 386–88 : 11, pp. 61–62. 1930–31.

8150 —— The East Saxons of Prittle-well. Trans. Southend Antiq. Soc., 2, pp. 89–102, + plan, + 1 coloured plate (jewellery). 1932.

8151 —— The Roman and Saxon settlements. Southend-on-sea (excavated, 1923). (Appendix A, Report on three skulls, by Sir A. Keith : Appendix B, Archaeological evidences (pre-Norman) found in the Rochford hundred). [4 pp. of figures of A.-S., weapons, etc.]. Same jnl., 1, pp. 93–141, + 1 coloured plate. 1923.

8152 Prigg (Henry). The Anglo-Saxon graves, Warren Hill, Mildenhall. Proc. Suffolk Inst. Archaeol., 6, pp. 57–72. 1888.

8153 —— [Exhibition of A.-S. objects from West Stow heath, near Bury St. Edmunds]. J. Brit. Archaeol. Assoc., 47, pp. 94–95. 1891.

8154 Read (*Sir* Charles Hercules). Exploration of a Saxon grave at Broomfield, Essex. [6 figures in text.] Proc. Soc. Antiq., 2nd S. 15, pp. 250–55. 1894. *Reprinted in* Trans. Essex Arch. Soc., N.S. 5, pp. 237–420. 1895.

8155 Smith (Charles Roach). Saxon remains found near Ixworth, in Suffolk. [In the collection of Joseph Warren of Ixworth]. Collectanea Antiqua, 4, pp. 162–64, + 1 plate, 1857.

8156 Smith (Henry Ecroyd). An ancient cemetery at Saffron Walden. [Plates of A.-S. necklets and rings, etc.] Trans. Essex Archaeol. Soc., N.S. 2, pp. 311–34, + folding plan + 11 plates. 1884.

8157 Smith (Henry Ecroyd). Notes on an ancient cemetery at Saffron Walden. [Pottery 'A.-S. to A.-N. ', and ' rudely imitative of Roman patterns.'] *Same jnl.*, N.S. 2, pp. 284–87. 1884.

8158 Smith (Reginald Allender). Anglo-Saxon remains [in Essex]. V.C.H., Essex, 1, pp. 315–31, + map, + 1 coloured plate. 1903.

8159 —— Anglo-Saxon remains [in Norfolk]. V.C.H., Norfolk, 1, pp. 325–51, + 1 coloured plate, + map. 1901.

8160 —— Anglo-Saxon remains [in Suffolk]. V.C.H., Suffolk, 1, pp. 325–55, + 5 plates, + map. 1911.

8161 Tymms (Samuel). Anglo-Saxon relics from West Stow heath. Proc. Bury and W. Suffolk Archaeol. Inst., 1, pp. 315–28, + 8 plates. 1853.

8162 Walker (Frederick George)· Roman and Saxon remains from the Grange Road, Cambridge. Proc. Camb. Antiq. Soc., 16 (1911–12), pp. 122–27, + 2 plates. 1912.

8163 Wilkinson (Joseph). On the discovery of an Anglo-Saxon cemetery near Barrington, Cambridgeshire. Proc. London, Middlesex and Surrey Archaeol. Soc., 1, pp. 50–56, + 2 plates. 1862.

129. CEMETERIES, KENT

8164 Akerman (John Yonge). Notes on antiquarian researches in the summer and autumn of 1854. [A.-S. cemetery at Wingham : A.-S. grave at Stodmarsh, near Wingham.] Archaeologia, 36, pp. 175–86, + 1 coloured plate (Stodmarsh). 1855.

8165 Beck (R. T.). Unrecorded Saxon cemetery at Thurnham. [Plan in text.] Antiq. J., 20, pp. 380–82. 1940.

8166 Boulter (H. E.). Anglo-Saxon remains found at Ramsgate. [Incomplete skeleton, wattle knife, and glass. ? c. 670.] Arch. Cant., 45, pp. 283–84. 1933.

8167 Bowker (George). A Saxon cemetery at Wickhambreux. Arch. Cant., 17, pp. 6–9, + 3 coloured plates. 1887.

8168 Brent (Cecil). Notes on Anglo-Saxon discoveries at Stowting. J. Brit. Archaeol. Assoc., 39, pp. 84–86, + 1 plate. 1883.

8169 Brent (John). An account of researches in an Anglo-Saxon cemetery at Stowting, during the autumn of 1866. Archaeologia, 41, pp. 409–20, + 1 plate. 1867.

8170 —— Account of the [Kent Archaeological] Society's researches in the Saxon cemetery at Sarr. Arch. Cant., 5, pp. 305–22, + 3 plates : 6, pp. 157–85, + 1 plate : 7, pp. 307–21, + 8 plates. 1863, '66, '68.

8171 —— [Report on opening of an Anglo-Saxon grave in the King Field, Faversham]. [Figure of fibula on p. 381.] Proc. Soc. Antiq., 2nd S. 6, pp. 379–81. 1875.

8172 Conyngham (*Lord* Albert D.). Account of the opening of some Anglo-Saxon graves at Wingham. Archaeologia, 30, pp. 550–51. 1844.

8173 Cumberland (A.). Riseley Saxon cemetery, Horton Kirby. Interim report. Trans. Dartford Antiq. Soc., 7, pp. 17–18. 1937.

8174 —— Saxon cemetery, Riseley, Horton Kirby. Excavated 1937–1938. [Darenth valley.] *Same jnl.*, 8, pp. 14–30, + plan. 1938.

8175 Faussett (Bryan). Inventorium sepulchrale ; an account of some antiquities dug up at Gilton, Kingston, Sibertswold, Barfriston, Beakesbourne, Chartham and Crundale . . . from . . . 1757 to 1773. Edited by C. R. Smith. pp. lvi, 230, + 20 plates (7 coloured). 4° [privately printed], 1856.

8176 Godfrey-Faussett (Thomas Godfrey). The Saxon cemetery at Bifrons. Arch. Cant., 6, pp. 329–31 : 10, pp. 298–315, + 8 plates : 13, pp. 552–56. 1866, '76, '80.

8177 Hurd (Howard) and **Smith** (Reginald Allender). Discovery of an Anglo-Saxon burial ground at Broadstairs. [5 figures in text. Amber beads, etc.] Proc. Soc. Antiq., 2nd S. 23, pp. 272–82. 1910.

8178 Jenkins (Robert Charles). [Discovery of Saxon burial-place at Lyminge]. [Bones, weapons, fibulae, etc.] *Same jnl.*, 2nd S. 10, p. 206. 1885.

8179 Jessup (Ronald Frederick). An Anglo-Saxon cemetery at Westbere. Antiq. J., 26, pp. 11–21, + 4 plates. 1946.

8180 Naylor (George). [Exhibition of] antiquities discovered in October 1852 . . . on Star Hill, at Eastgate, [Rochester]. J. Brit. Archaeol. Assoc., 9, pp. 407–08, + 1 plate. 1854.

8181 Payne (George) *junr.* Anglo-Saxon remains from Sittingbourne. [Discovery of 2 graves, March 1882.] Proc. Soc. Antiq., 2nd S. 9, p. 162. 1882.

8182 —— Collectanea Cantiana. pp. xxiii, 218, + 25 plates, + 2 maps. 8° London, 1893. [Pp. 103–24, + 2 plates, + map, A.–S. cemeteries at Sittingbourne, Faversham, Milton and Rochester.]

8183 —— Discovery of Anglo-Saxon remains at Rochester. Antiquary, 26, pp. 166–67. 1892.

8184 —— Notes on Anglo-Saxon remains discovered in King's Field, Faversham. [Brooches, cups, etc.] Proc. Soc. Antiq., 2nd S. 15, pp. 122–24. 1894.

8185 —— Notes on Anglo-Saxon remains found at Dover. [5 figures on p. 180.] *Same jnl.*, 2nd S. 15, pp. 178–83. 1894.

8186 —— On the contents of nine Saxon graves . . . by the side of the road through Sittingbourne. *Same jnl.*, 2nd S, 8, pp. 506–08. 1881.

8187 —— Recent discoveries of Roman and Saxon remains near Sittingbourne. *Same jnl.*, 2nd S. 8, pp. 275–76. 1880.

8188 Smith (Charles Roach). Anglo-Saxon remains discovered at Ozingell [near Ramsgate]. Collectanea Antiqua, 3, pp. 1–18, + 6 plates. [c. 1854].

8189 —— A catalogue of Anglo-Saxon and other antiquities discovered at Faversham, and bequeathed by William Gibbs . . to the South Kensington Museum. pp. xxiv, 25. 8° London, 1871.

8190 Smith (Charles Roach). Discovery of Anglo-Saxon remains at Northfleet. J. Brit. Archaeol. Assoc., 3, pp. 235–40. 1848.

8191 —— The Faussett collection of Anglo-Saxon antiquities. [Tremworth down, Gilton, Kingston down, Sibertswold, etc.] Collectanea Antiqua, 3, pp. 179–92. [c. 1854].

8192 —— [Letter concerning Anglo-Saxon cemetery near Ramsgate]. J. Brit. Archaeol. Assoc., 1, pp. 242–43. 1846.

8193 —— On some Anglo-Saxon remains, discovered at Stowting. Archaeologia, 31, pp. 398–403. 1846.

8194 Smith (Reginald Allender). Anglo-Saxon remains [in Kent]. V.C.H., Kent, 1, pp. 339–87, + 5 plates, + map. 1908.

8195 —— Prehistoric and Anglo-Saxon remains discovered by Capt. L. Moysey at Howletts, near Bridge. Proc. Soc. Antiq., 2nd S. 30, pp. 102–13, + 3 plates. 1918.

8196 Spurrell (Flaxman Charles John). Dartford antiquities. Notes on the British, Roman and Saxon remains there found. Arch. Cant., 18, pp. 304–18, + map. 1889.

8197 Stebbing (William Pinckard Delane). A Jutish burial above Deal. Arch. Cant., 46, pp. 209–10. 1934.

8198 —— Jutish cemetery near Finglesham. [With introductory note by W. Whiting.] Arch. Cant., 41, pp. 115–25, + 1 plate. 1929.

8199 Vallance (William). Anglo-Saxon antiquities discovered at Sittingbourne, from 1825 to 1828. Collectanea Antiqua, 1, pp. 97–106, + 3 plates. 1848.

8200 Wright (Thomas). Articles found in an early Anglo-Saxon barrow on Barham Downs. Proc. Soc. Antiq., 2, pp. 58–60. 1850.

130. CEMETERIES, MERCIA

§ a. Bedfordshire Group

8201 Austin (William). A Saxon cemetery at Luton, Beds., with notes on the excavation by Thomas W. Bagshawe. Antiq. J., 8, pp. 177–92, + 13 plates. 1928.

8202 Austin (William). Saxon graves at Luton. Same jnl., 6, pp. 184–85, + 1 plate. 1926.

8203 Bagshawe (Thomas Wyatt). A Saxon burial at Luton. Same jnl., 11, pp. 282–84. 1931.

8204 Cooper (William Cooper). Remains . . . discovered in an Anglo-Saxon grave on the summit of Sheepwalk hill, in the parish of Toddington. Proc. Soc. Antiq., 2nd S. 10, pp. 36–38. 1884.

8205 Elger (Thomas Gwyn Empty). Discovery of Saxon remains at Bedford. [3 skeletons, 2 spearheads and a sword.] Same jnl., 2nd S. 16, p. 114. 1896.

8206 Fitch (S. Edward). Discovery of Saxon remains at Kempston. Assoc. Archit. Socs.' Repts., 7, pp. 269–99, + 6 coloured plates. 1864.

8207 Lawford (Edward). Anglo-Saxon remains at Leighton Buzzard. [Urns, etc.] Beds. N. and Q., 3, pp. 127–28. 1893.

8208 —— On Anglo-Saxon antiquities from Leighton Buzzard. Proc. Soc. Antiq., 2nd S. 9, p. 29. 1881.

8209 Littledale (Henry). [Exhibition of] relics . . . found in 1863 in an Anglo-Saxon cemetery at Kempston. Same jnl., 2nd S. 2, pp. 416–17, 420–21. 1864.

8210 Smith (Charles Roach). Anglo-Saxon remains discovered [at Kempston]. Collectanea Antiqua, 6, pp. 201–21, + 6 coloured plates. 1868.

8211 Smith (Reginald Allender). Anglo-Saxon remains [in Bedfordshire]. [12 figures in text.] V.C.H. Bedford, 1, pp. 175–190, + map, and 1 coloured plate (Kempston). 1904.

8212 —— Anglo-Saxon remains from Toddington, Bedfordshire, and King's Walden, Hertfordshire. Proc. Soc. Antiq., 2nd S. 25, pp. 183–89. 1913.

8213 Smith (Worthington George). Saxon remains from graves at Leagrave. Same jnl., 2nd S. 21, pp. 59–63, + 2 plates. 1906.

8214 Taddy (John). On the Roman and Saxon remains lately disinterred at Sandy. Assoc. Archit. Socs.' Rpts., 2, pp. 422–32. 1853.

8215 —— Roman and Saxon remains at Sandy. Notes Beds. Archit. and Archaeol. Soc., 1, pp. 33–35, + 1 plate. 1854.

§ b. Derbyshire Group

8216 Bateman (Thomas). Description of the contents of a Saxon barrow recently opened in Darbyshire. [At Benty Grange, near Monyash.] J. Brit. Archaeol. Assoc., 4, pp. 276–79. 1849.

8217 —— Discovery of Saxon graves at Winster. Same jnl., 13, pp. 226–28. 1857.

8218 Briggs (John Joseph). Notice of a discovery of ancient remains at King's Newton. [Plate shows 'Anglo-Saxon cinerary urns'.] Reliquary, 9, pp. 1–3, + 1 plate. 1868.

8219 Clarke (Camden) and **Fraser** (William), *etc.* Excavation of pagan burial mounds : Ingleby. (—2nd report). [Early Danish.] J. Derbs. Archaeol. Soc., 66, pp. 1–23 ; + 2 plates : 69, pp. 78–81. 1946, 1949.

8220 Cox (John Charles). Excavation at Repton. Same jnl., 35, pp. 245–46. 1913.

8221 Fraser (William). Anglian pagan cemetery at Ingleby, south Derbyshire. Antiq. J., 23, p. 159. 1943.

8222 —— Location of the alleged Anglian cemetery at Foremark. J. Derbs. Archaeol. Soc., N.S. 15, pp. 19–21. 1941.

8223 Heron (John). Report on the Stapenhill explorations. [i. The explorations ('finds' 1–44) : ii. Bearing on our knowledge of pagan English burials. Plates show pottery, weapons, fibulae, etc., + 3 plans.] Trans. Burton Archaeol. Soc., 1, pp. 156–93, + 11 plates. 1889.

8224 Jewitt (Llewellynn). On the discovery of an Anglo-Saxon cemetery at King's Newton. [Plates show A.–S. cinerary urns.] Reliquary, 9, pp. 6–8, + 2 plates. 1868.

8225 Lucas (John F.). Notice of the opening of a Celtic and Anglo-Saxon grave mound at Tissington. Reliquary, 5, pp. 165–69. 1865.

8226 Massey (William). Another account of the discovery at King's Newton. Reliquary, 9, pp. 3–5. 1868.

8227 Smith (Reginald Allender). Warrior's grave, Benty Grange. Proc. Soc. Antiq., 2nd S. 22, p. 68. 1908.

8228 Ward (John). Anglo-Saxon remains [in Derbyshire]. V.C.H., Derbyshire, 1, pp. 265–77, + map, + 1 coloured plate. 1905.

8229 —— A sketch of the archaeology of Derbyshire. [Pp. 18–20, 'Post-Roman or early Saxon interments : pre-Norman or late Saxon remains.'] J. Brit. Archaeol. Assoc., 56 (N.S. 6), pp. 1–25. 1900.

§ e. Gloucestershire Group

8230 Akerman (John Yonge). [Exhibition of] objects discovered in the Anglo-Saxon cemetery at Fairford. Proc. Soc. Antiq., 4, p. 258. 1859.

8231 Buckman (James). Notes on Saxon remains from Gloucestershire. [Fibulae, beads, etc., from Fairford and Stratton in Cirencester.] Same jnl., 4, pp. 38–40. 1857.

8232 Donovan (Helen E.) and **Dunning** (Gerald Clough). Iron age pottery and Saxon burials at Foxcote Manor, Andoversford. [Includes 'Saxon burials in the Cotswolds,' and 'distribution-map of Saxon spiral-headed pins'. Appendix : notes on the Foxcote skeletons, pp. 169–70.] Trans. Bristol and Glos. Arch. Soc., 58, opp. 157–7, + 1 plate. 1936.

8233 Smith (Charles Roach). Notes on Saxon sepulchral remains found at Fairford. [Plate shows fibulae, jewellery, etc.] Archaeologia, 34, pp. 77–82, + 1 plate. 1852.

8234 Wright (Thomas). Saxon remains found in Gloucestershire. [In field called Chavenage Sleight, between Avening and Chavenage, 1847.] J. Brit. Archaeol. Assoc., 4, pp. 50–54. 1849.

8235 Wylie (William Michael). Account of a further discovery of relics in the Anglo-Saxon cemetery at Fairford. Proc. Soc. Antiq., 3, pp. 105–06. 1854.

8236 —— Fairford graves. A record of researches. pp. 40, + 12 plates. 4° Oxford, 1852.

§ *d*. **Northamptonshire Group**

8237 Baker (Robert Sibley). Notes on archaeological discoveries at . . . Islip. [Bones, beads, fibulae, etc. Figure of bronze fibula with fylfot ornament.] Proc. Soc. Antiq., 2nd S. 9, pp. 89–91. 1882.

8238 —— On the discovery of Anglo-Saxon remains at Desborough. Archaeologia, 45, pp. 466–71, + 1 plate. 1880.

8239 —— Some Saxon antiquities found in the village of Desborough. [Gold necklace, bronze vessel, 2 glass bowls, etc.] Proc. Soc. Antiq., 2nd S. 6, p. 530. 1876.

8240 Bull (Frederick William). Recent discoveries of Roman and Anglo-Saxon remains at Kettering. [Plates show fibulae, pottery, etc.] Assoc. Archit. Socs.' Rpts., 27, pp. 382–87, + 4 plates. 1904.

8241 Dryden (*Sir* Henry) *bart*. An account of a discovery of early Saxon remains at Barrow Furlong, on the Hill Farm, in the parish of Marston St. Lawrence. Archaeologia, 33, pp. 326–34, + 3 plates. 1849.

8242 —— Excavation of an ancient burial ground at Marston St. Lawrence. [? pagan Saxon.] *Same jnl.*, 48, pp. 327–39, + 4 plates. 1885.

8243 George (T. J.). The Anglo-Saxon cemetery at Duston. J. Northants. Nat. Hist. Soc., 12, pp. 18, 280–81. 1903.

8244 —— The Anglo-Saxon cemetery at Kettering. [All 3 plates show cinerary urns.] *Same jnl.*, 12, pp. 121–27, + 3 plates. 1903.

8245 Gotch (John Alfred). Notes on some Anglo-Saxon antiquities found at Kettering. Proc. Soc. Antiq., 2nd S. 19, pp. 307–10. 1903.

8246 Hartshorne (Charles Henry). Saxon cemetery at Holdenby. [Plates show fibulae, beads, etc.] J. Northants. Nat. Hist. Soc., 11, pp. 3–7, + 2 plates. 1902.

8247 Hief (F. R. G.). Some Roman and Saxon antiquities found near Kettering. Proc. Camb. Antiq. Soc., 20 (1915–16), pp. 59–66, + 1 plate. 1917.

8248 Leeds (Edward Thurlow). Anglo-Saxon cemetery at Holdenby. J. Northants. Nat. Hist. Soc., 15, pp. 91–99, + plan, + 2 plates. 1909.

8249 —— Anglo-Saxon cemetery at Nassington. Antiq. J., 23, p. 58. 1943.

8250 —— and **Atkinson** (R. J. C.). An Anglo-Saxon cemetery at Nassington. *Same jnl.*, 24, pp. 100–28, + 9 plates, + folding plan. 1944.

8251 —— —— An Anglo-Saxon cemetery at Nassington. J. Northants. Nat. Hist. Soc. and F.C., 31, pp. 34–35, + 1 plate. 1946.

8252 Markham (Christopher A.). Anglo-Saxon cemetery at Kettering. [All 3 plates show cinerary urns.] J. Northants. Nat. Hist. Soc., 25, pp. 29–31, + plan + 3 plates. 1929.

8253 —— Anglo-Saxon cemetery at Kettering. Antiq. J., 10, pp. 254–55. 1930.

8254 Smith (Reginald Allender). Anglo-Saxon antiquities discovered at Islip. Proc. Soc. Antiq., 2nd S. 30, pp. 113–20, + 1 plate. 1918.

8255 —— Angle-Saxon remains [in Northamptonshire]. V.C.H., Northampton, 1, pp. 223–56, + 1 coloured plate, + map. 1902.

8256 Walker (Thomas James). Notes on two Anglo-Saxon burial-places at Peterborough [in Hunts.]. J. Brit. Archaeol. Assoc., 55 (N.S. 5), pp. 343–49, + 2 plates. 1899.

§ *e*. **Oxfordshire Group**

8257 Akerman (John Yonge). An account of researches in Anglo-Saxon cemeteries at Filkins, and at Broughton Poggs. Archaeologia, 37, pp. 140–46. 1857.

8258 Akerman (John Yonge). [Exhibition of a] collection of Anglo-Saxon relics from the cemetery at Brighthampton. Proc. Soc. Antiq., 4, pp. 231–32. 1858.

8259 —— Note on some further discoveries of Anglo-Saxon remains at Broughton Poggs. [Knives, fibulae, hair-pin.] *Same jnl.*, 4, pp. 73–74. 1857.

8260 —— Report of researches in a cemetery of the Anglo-Saxon period at Brighthampton. (2nd report, *etc.*, with postscript on crania by John Quekett). Archaeologia, 37, pp. 391–98 : 38, pp. 84,–97, + 2 plates. 1857–60.

8261 Kenward (J.). A first note on the Anglo-Saxon cemetery at Wheatley. Proc. B'ham Phil. Soc., 4, pp. 179–93. 1884.

8262 Leeds (Edward Thurlow). Anglo-Saxon cemetery at Wheatley. Proc. Soc. Antiq., 2nd S. 29, pp. 48–65, + 5 plates. 1916.

8263 —— An Anglo-Saxon cremation-burial of the seventh century in Asthall Barrow. [9 figures in text.] Antiq. J., 4, pp. 113–26. 1924.

8264 —— and **Riley** (Marjorie). Two early Saxon cemeteries at Cassington. [Illustrated.] Oxoniensia, 7, pp. 61–70. 1942.

8265 Leeds (Edward Thurlow). Two Saxon cemeteries in north Oxfordshire [North Leigh and Chadlington.] Oxoniensia, 5, pp. 21–30. 1940.

8266 Manning (Percy). Notes on the archaeology of Oxford and its neighbourhood. [P. 13, Interment at Brize Norton, ?A.–S. : pp. 15–16, A.–S. jewel from Dorchester : pp. 24–26, iron spearhead, etc., from St. Thomas's, Oxford : pp. 39–40, interment at Stanlake.] Berks, Bucks and Oxon Archaeol. J., 4, pp. 9–28, 39–47. 1898.

8267 Smith (Reginald Allender). [Saxon remains from] Ewelme. [Bronze bowl, etc.] Proc. Soc. Antiq., 2nd S. 22, pp. 71–73. 1908.

8268 Stone (Stephen). Account of certain (supposed) British and Saxon remains, recently discovered at Standlake [and Brighthampton]. *Same jnl.*, 4, pp. 92–100, 329. 1857, 1859.

8269 Stone (Stephen). British and Anglo-Saxon remains at Stanlake and Brighthampton. *Same jnl.*, 2nd S. 2, pp. 441–43. 1864.

8270 —— Discovery of Anglo-Saxon remains at Ducklington, near Witney. *Same jnl.*, 2nd S. 1, pp. 100–01. 1860.

8271 —— Recent explorations at Stanlake, Yelford, and Stanton Harcourt. *Same jnl.*, 4, pp. 213–19, 250–51. 1858.

§ ƒ. Rutland Group

8272 Cox (John Charles). Account of an Anglo-Saxon cemetery recently uncovered near Saxby, Leicestershire. [7th c. Middle Angle. Urns and pottery, fibulae, beads, etc.] Proc. Soc. Antiq., 2nd S. 13, pp. 331–36. 1891.

8273 Crowther-Beynon (Vernon Bryan). Anglo-Saxon remains found at North Luffenham, in the county of Rutland (ditto . . . found . . . previously to 1900). [Plates show weapons, fibulae, pottery, etc.] Assoc. Archit. Socs.' Rpts., 26, pp. 246–59, + 3 plates : 27, pp. 220–28, + 4 plates. 1901–03.

8274 —— [Finds at two Anglo-Saxon cemeteries in Rutland—Cottesmore and Market Overton]. [Plates show brooches.] Proc. Soc. Antiq., 2nd S. 22, pp. 50–53, + 2 plates. 1908.

8275 —— Notes on an Anglo-Saxon cemetery at Market Overton. With a supplementary note [on the gold bracteate and silver brooch] by E. T. Leeds. [Plate shows 6 brooches.] Archaeologia, 62, pp. 481–96, + 1 plate. 1911.

8276 —— Notes on finds of bronze age and Anglo-Saxon objects at Cottesmore in 1906. Rutland Mag., 3, pp. 215–19, + 1 plate. 1908.

8277 —— Notes on some Rutland antiquities. [iii. Anglo-Saxon, with illustrations of situla and fibulae.] Antiquary, 43, pp. 50–56. 1907.

8278 —— A Rutland Anglian cemetery. ['Chat'. ? What cemetery : probably North Luffenham. Description of some objects in the collection of a Mrs. Morris.] Rutland Mag., 1, pp. 87–92, 116–19, 152–57, + 5 plates. 1903–04.

8279 Haines (Reginald). Anglo-Saxon graveyard at North Luffenham. [2 full-page figures of a gilt bronze brooch in text.] Proc. Soc. Antiq., 2nd S. 19, pp. 195–98. 1903.

8280 Leeds (Edward Thurlow) and **Barber** (J. L.). An Anglian cemetery at Glaston. Antiq. J., 30, pp. 185–89, + 1 plate. 1950.

8281 Phillips (G.). Market Overton : the Roman and Anglo-Saxon finds. Rutland Mag., 4, pp. 161–67 ; 5, pp. 186–90, + 5 plates. 1910–12.

8282 Smith (Reginald Allender). Anglo-Saxon remains [in Rutland]. V.C.H., Rutland, 1, pp. 95–106, + 3 plates, + map. 1908.

8283 Thompson (James). Anglo-Saxon antiquities from Saxby [Leicester-shire]. [Pottery, ornaments, weapons.] Trans. Leic. Archit. Soc., 1, pp. 159–60. 1866.

8284 —— Roman and Anglo-Saxon antiquities. [From North Luffenham. Report of a paper.] Midland Counties Hist. Coll., 2, pp. 150–56, + 1 plate. 1856.

8285 —— Roman and Anglo-Saxon antiquities. [A.–S. ' weapons, and orna-ments of a female, found at North Luffenham '.] Trans. Leic. Archit. Soc., 1, pp. 77–80. 1866.

§ g. Warwickshire and Worcestershire Group

8286 Barnard (Etwell Augustine Bracher). Saxon finds at Blockley. Trans. Worcs. Archaeol. Soc., 3 (1925–26), pp. 128–32 + 1 plate. 1927.

8287 Bloxam (Matthew Holbeche). [Notice of the discovery of an Anglo-Saxon burial ground . . . at Marton, Warwickshire.] Proc. Soc. Antiq., 2nd S. 5, p. 303. 1872.

8288 —— On certain ancient British and Anglo-Saxon pagandom remains, mostly sepulchral, found in Warwick-shire, chiefly in the vicinity of Rugby. pp. 14. 8° *n.p.* [c. 1884].

8289 —— On some ancient British, Roman, Romano-British and early Saxon remains, mostly sepulchral, recently dis-covered in Warwickshire, and not hith-erto noticed. [A.–S., at Marton.] Assoc. Archit. Socs.' Rpts., 1, pp. 227–32. 1851.

8290 Burgess (Joseph Tom). Excava-tions at [Offchurch, between Leamington and] Longbridge in Warwickshire. J. Brit. Archaeol. Assoc., 32, pp. 106–11. 1876.

8291 —— Saxon remains at Offchurch. *Same jnl.*, 32, pp. 464–67, + 1 plate. 1876.

8292 Edwards (J. H.). [Note on the] Anglo-Saxon cemetery at Baginton, [Warw.]. Proc. Coventry N.H. Soc., 1, p. 72. 1933.

8293 —— The Anglo-Saxon pagan cemetery at Baginton. *Same jnl.*, 2, pp. 48–53, + 1 plate. 1948.

8294 Fetherston (John). [Exhibition of] four Anglo-Saxon ornaments found at Packwood, Aston Cantlow, Warwick-shire. [Fibulae and skeleton.] Proc. Soc. Antiq., 2nd S. 3, p. 424. 1867.

8295 Hertford (Francis Hugh George (Seymour)) *5th marquis of*. Anglo-Saxon relics found [with a female skeleton] in Ragley park, Warwickshire. [Fibulae, iron knife, part of a buckle.] *Same jnl.*, 2nd S. 5, pp. 453–54. 1873.

8296 Humphreys (John), **Ryland** (J. W.), **Barnard** (Etwell Augustine Bracher), **Wellstood** (Frederick Christian) and **Barnett** (Thomas George). An Anglo-Saxon cemetery at Bidford-on-Avon, Warwickshire. (Notes on the cranial and other skeletal characters, by James C. Brash). Archaeologia, 73, pp. 89–116, + 8 plates, + folding plan : 74, pp. 271–88, + 2 plates, + folding plan. 1923–25.

8297 Humphreys (John). Excava-tions of an Anglo-Saxon cemetery at Bidford-on-Avon, in 1922 and 1923. B'ham Arch. Soc., Trans., 49, pp. 16–25, + 6 plates : 50, pp. 32–36 + 1 plate. 1923–24.

8298 Ponting (William). [Notice of] the discovery of Anglo-Saxon remains . . . near Upton Snodsbury, Worcester-shire. Proc. Soc. Antiq., 2nd S. 3, p. 342. 1866.

8299 Ponting (William). On some Anglo-Saxon antiquities at Upton Snodsbury. [Weapons, beads, etc.] Reliquary, 13, pp. 206–08, + 1 plate. 1873.

8300 Smith (Reginald Allender). Anglo-Saxon remains [in Warwickshire]. V.C.H., Warwick, 1, pp. 251–68, + 1 coloured plate, + map. 1904.

8301 —— Anglo-Saxon remains [in Worcestershire]. V.C.H., Worcester, 1, pp. 223–33, + 1 coloured plate, + map. 1901.

8302 Spackman (F. T.). On some Anglo-Saxon antiquities from Bricklehampton, in the county of Worcester. [Amber bead, 6th c., one of glass paste, and a canine tooth : = part of a necklace.] Assoc. Archit. Socs.' Rpts., 30, pp. 597–604. 1910.

§ *h*. **Others**

8303 Bellairs (G. C.). Roman and Saxon pottery and fibulae found at Westcotes [near Leicester]. Trans. Leic. Archit. Soc., 6, p. 339, + 1 plate. 1888.

8304 Cocks (Alfred Heneage). Anglo-Saxon burials at Ellesborough [Bucks.]. [Pp. 429–30, ' description of the three Anglo-Saxon calvariae from Ellesborough, by Dr. William Wright.'] Rec. Bucks., 9, pp. 425–30, + 3 plates. 1909.

8305 Coote (C. M.). Saxon hut. [By Ouse, at Houghton, Hunts. Domestic fragments.] Trans. Cambs. and Hunts. Archaeol. Soc., 7, p. 71. 1950.

8306 Dunning (Gerald Clough). Anglo-Saxon discoveries at Harston. Trans. Leic. Arch. Soc., 28, pp. 48–54. 1952.

8307 Foster (Charles Wilmer). Excavation of an Anglian burial mound on Loveden hill [Lincs.] [Black pottery of 6th–7th c.] Assoc. Archit. Socs.' Rpts., 38, pp. 313–20, + 4 plates. 1927.

8308 Hawkes (Charles Francis Christopher). Anglian and Anglo-Danish Lincolnshire. The exhibition [Lincoln meeting of Royal Archaeological Institute, 1946]. [i. Pagan Anglian antiquities : ii. Hanging-bowls and escutcheons : iii. Later antiquities and coins.] Archaeol. J., 103 (1946), pp. 89–94, + 1 plate. 1947.

8309 Head (John Frederick). The excavation of the Cop round barrow, Bledlow. [' Saxon inhumations': ' Saxon cremations': 'A.–S. urns ' (2 figures on p. 337): 'A.–S. knife and spearhead and combs' (figures on p. 339): A.–S. period, pp. 336–39.] Rec. Bucks., 13, pp. 313–51, + 2 plates, + plan. 1938.

8310 Jewitt (Llewellynn). Notice of the discovery of an Anglo-Saxon interment at Barlaston, in Staffordshire. [Plates show bronze ring, helmet and enamelled pendant ornaments.] Reliquary, 11, pp. 65–66, + 2 plates. 1870.

8311 Kendrick (*Sir* Thomas Downing). An Anglo-Saxon cemetery at Ruskington, Lincolnshire. Antiq. J., 26, p. 69, + 1 plate. 1946.

8312 —— The art and archaeology of the early Anglo-Saxons. [Discusses Taplow finds.] S.E. Naturalist, 39, pp. 14–20. 1934.

8313 Lincoln and Nottingham Architectural Society. Discovery of the site of an Anglo-Saxon camp or settlement (?) near Woolsthorpe-by-Belvoir. Assoc. Archit. Socs.' Rpts., 18, pp. 132–34. 1886.

8314 Lincolnshire Architectural and Archaeological Society. Anglo-Saxon antiquities discovered at Caistor and Searby and elsewhere in Lincolnshire, now deposited in the Lincoln County Museum. [Plate shows bowl, rings, beads, etc.] *Same jnl.*, 31, pp. 375–77, + 1 plate. 1912.

8315 Lincoln County Museum. The Anglo-Saxon antiquities in the county Museum. [Bowls, fibulae, beads, etc.] Lincs. N. and Q., 12, pp. 67–70, + 1 plate. 1913.

8316 Lowndes (Charles). Discovery of Anglo-Saxon remains in Stone [Bucks.]. Rec. Bucks., 3, p. 164. 1870.

8317 —— On the discovery of Anglo-Saxon relics in Stone. Rec. Bucks., 5, pp. 23–25, + 2 plates. 1878.

8318 Myres (John Nowell Linton). Lincoln in the fifth century. [?early A.–S. cremation-cemetery: 2 urns.] Archaeol. J., 103 (1946), pp. 85–88. 1947.

8319 Newton (E. F.). Late Saxon sites and a mediaeval chapel at Weald, Hunts. [Pottery, etc.] Trans. Cambs. and Hunts. Archaeol. Soc., 6, pp. 167–75. 1943.

8320 North (Thomas). Anglo-Saxon cemetery at Melton Mowbray. Trans. Leic. Archit. Soc., 3, pp. 116–20. 1874.

8321 O'Sullivan (James). Some Anglo-Saxon antiquities, found at Wichnor, July 1899. Trans. Burton Archaeol. Soc., 4. ii, pp. 80–81. 1901.

8322 Ouvry (Frederic). Discovery of Saxon and other remains at or near Mentmore, Bucks. [Skeletons, 2 spearheads, knife, fibula, clasp.] Proc. Soc. Antiq., 3, pp. 72–73. 1854.

8323 —— Note on Saxon and other remains discovered at or near Mentmore. Archaeologia, 35, pp. 379–82. 1853. *Ditto.* Rec. Bucks., 1 (1855), pp. 108–12. 1858.

8324 Read (*Sir* Charles Hercules). [Exhibition of] a jewel, sword, shield-boss, and pottery from an Anglo-Saxon burial-place at Twickenham, Middlesex. Proc. Soc. Antiq., 2nd S. 24, pp. 327–29. 1912.

8325 Rutland (James). [Anglo-Saxon barrow at Taplow]. *Same jnl.*, 2nd S. 10, pp. 19–20. 1883.

8326 Sheppard (Thomas). Notes on a collection of Roman [and a few Anglo-Saxon] antiquities from South Ferriby, in north Lincolnshire. Trans. Hull Sc. F. N.C., 3, pp. 247–64 ; 4, pp. 55–69, + 13 plates. 1907–09.

8327 Shurlock (Manwaring). Urns, fragments of pottery, and bones from Shepperton, Middlesex. (Further excavations in an Anglo-Saxon cemetery at Shepperton). Proc. Soc. Antiq., 2nd S. 4, pp. 118–20, 191. 1868.

8328 Smith (Reginald Allender). Anglo-Saxon remains [in the county of Buckingham]. [5 figures in text.] V.C.H. Bucks, 1, pp. 195–205, + map, + 1 coloured plate (Taplow). 1905.

8329 —— Anglo-Saxon remains [in Hertfordshire]. V.C.H., Hertfordshire, 1, pp. 251–61, + map, + 1 plate. 1902.

8330 Smith (Reginald Allender). Anglo-Saxon remains [in the county of Huntingdon]. V.C.H., Huntingdon, 1, pp. 271–79, + 4 plates. 1926.

8331 —— Anglo-Saxon remains [in Leicestershire]. V.C.H., Leicester, 1, pp. 221–42, + 5 plates, + map. 1907.

8332 —— Anglo-Saxon remains [of London]. V.C.H., London, 1, pp. 147–70, + 3 plates, + map. 1909.

8333 —— Anglo-Saxon remains [in Nottinghamshire]. V.C.H., Nottingham, 1, pp. 193–205, + map. 1906.

8334 —— [Saxon remains from a grave at] Barlaston, Staffordshire. Proc. Soc. Antiq., 2nd S. 22, p. 67. 1908.

8335 Stevens (Joseph). On the remains found in an Anglo-Saxon tumulus at Taplow, Bucks. J. Brit. Archaeol. Assoc., 40, pp. 61–71, + 2 plates. 1884.

8336 Thomas (George William). On excavations in an Anglo-Saxon cemetery at Sleaford, in Lincolnshire. [Plates show fibulae, pottery, etc.] Archaeologia, 50, pp. 383–406, + 3 plates. 1887.

8337 Trolloppe (Edward). Saxon burial ground at Baston, Lincolnshire. Archaeol. J., 20, pp. 29–31, + 1 plate. 1863.

8338 Tucker (W. Trueman). Excavations at Rothley, Leicestershire : interesting Roman and Anglo-Saxon finds. Reliquary, 3, pp. 113–17. 1897.

131. CEMETERIES, NORTHUMBRIA

8339 Bouch (C. M. Lowther). A stone coffin at Kirkby Stephen church. [? pre-Norman. Skeleton 6 ft. high.] Trans. Cumb. and Westm. Antiq. Soc., N.S. 50, pp. 208–09, + 1 plate. 1951.

8340 Cole (Edward Maule). Duggleby howe. [A.–S. burial in British tumulus.] Trans. East Riding Antiq. Soc., 9, pp. 57–61. 1902.

8341 Combe (Taylor). Account of some Saxon antiquities found near Lancaster. [Pp. 201–02, list of coins of Canute found : plates show silver cup and torques.] Archaeologia, 18, pp. 199–202, + 2 plates. 1817.

8342 Congreve (Anthony L.). A Roman and Saxon site at Elmswell, east Yorks. 1935–1936. (Second interim report, 1937). [i. Pp. 15–19 : ii. pp. 22–25, the decorated Saxon pottery.] Hull Museum Publicns., 193, pp. 1–28, + 1 plate, + plan : 198, pp. 1–42, + 2 plates, + plan. 1937–38.

8343 Craw (James Hewat). Pillowstone from Lowick, [Northumberland]. [?7th or early 8th c.] Hist. Berwick. Nat. Club, 25, p. 228, + 1 plate. 1924.

8344 Garstang (John). Anglo-Saxon remains [in Lancashire]. V.C.H., Lancs., 1, pp. 257–68, + 8 plates, + map. 1906.

8345 Hall (J. G.). Ancient graveyard at Sancton. [Presumed A.–S.] Trans. East Riding Antiq. Soc., 5, pp. 115–20. 1897.

8346 Hildyard (E. J. W.). A Roman and Saxon site at Catterick. Yorks. Arch. J., 38, pp. 241–45, + 3 plates. 1953.

8347 Hornsby (William). An Anglian cemetery at Hob hill, near Saltburn. Yorks. Archaeol. J., 22, pp. 131–36. 1913.

8348 Jones (Bertram). Discoveries at Hartlepool. Antiq. J., 2, pp. 141–43. 1922.

8349 Keeney (George Stockdale). Anglo-Saxon burials at Galewood, within Ewart, near Milfield. Proc. Soc. Antiq. Newc., 4th S. 7, pp. 15–17. 1935.

8350 —— A pagan Anglian cemetery at Howick, Northumberland. Archaeol. Æl., 4th S. 16, pp. 120–28, + 1 plate. 1939.

8351 Lukis (William Collings). On some Anglo-Saxon graves on Howe hill, near Carthorpe, in the parish of Burneston, North Riding of Yorkshire. Yorks. Archaeol. J., 1, pp. 175–81 + 1 plate. 1870.

8352 Mortimer (John Robert). Forty years' researches in British and Saxon burial mounds of east Yorkshire. pp. 492. 4° London, 1905. [Pp. 94–95, 118, 182–83, 247–57, 264–69, 286–94, 344, 353, A.–S. material. Over 1000 illustrations.]

8353 Mortimer (John Robert). Notice of the opening of an Anglo-Saxon grave, at Grimthorpe, Yorkshire. [Weapons and ornaments.] Reliquary, 9, pp. 180–82, + 2 plates. 1869.

8354 Raine (James). Account of an early cemetery recently discovered at Selby. Ann. Rept. Yorks. Philos. Soc., 1876, pp. 19–26. 1877.

8355 Sheppard (Thomas). Anglo-Saxon cemeteries in east Yorkshire. [Reprinted from the Naturalist, Jan., April and June, 1938.] Hull Museum Publicns., 195, pp. 1–24, + 11 plates. 1938.

8356 —— An Anglo-Saxon cemetery at Hornsea. [=Hull Museum Publns., 97.] Trans. Hull Sc. F.N.C., 4, pp. 258–72, + 4 plates. 1913.

8357 —— An Anglo-Saxon grave [on the wolds] in east Yorkshire, and its contents. [Now in Hull Municipal Museum. With 6 figures. Hull Museum Pubns., 33, pp. 10–18.] Antiquary, 42, pp. 333–38, 440. 1906.

8358 —— Anglo-Saxon remains at Hornsea. [6th or 7th c. Figure shows 3 bronze brooches. Hull Museum Pubs., 95 (Quart. Record Addns., 45), pp. 14–16. 1913.

8359 —— Excavations at Eastburn, east Yorkshire. [Pp. 44–47, and plates 3–5, A.–S. remains. Hull Museum Publicn., 197.] Yorks. Archaeol. J., 34, pp. 35–47, + 5 plates. 1938.

8360 —— Excavations in an Anglo-Saxon cemetery near South Cave, Yorkshire. [Female skeleton, amber and glass beads, rings, fibulae, etc.] Rept. Brit. Ass., 1906, p. 685. 1907.

8361 —— Important archaeological discovery near Hull. (Saxon antiquities recently found near Hull). [North Newbold cemetery.] Hull Museum Pubns., 3, pp. 10–12 ; 11 (Quart. Rec. Addns., 2), pp. 1–8 ; 117. 1902.

8362 —— Notes on the more important archaeological discoveries in East Yorkshire. [Pp. 63–66, A.–S. period. = Hull Museum Publications, 46.] Trans. East Riding Antiq. Soc., 14, pp. 45–66. 1907.

8363 Sheppard (Thomas). Our German ancestors : being an account of the Anglo-Saxon remains found in east Yorkshire. [Hull Museum Publcns., 117. Driffield, Hornsea, Newbold, Sancton, etc.] Trans. Hull Sc. F. N. Club, 4, pp. 299–320. 1919.

8364 —— A recently discovered Anglo-Saxon cemetery in East Yorkshire [At Hornsea. With 13 figures.] Antiquary, 50, pp. 11–19. 1914.

8365 —— Saxon relics from Barton, Lincs., and from Elloughton, E. Yorks. [Reprinted from the Naturalist, 1939–40.] Hull Museum Publcns., 208, pp. 25. 1940.

8366 Smith (Reginald Allender). Anglo-Saxon remains [in Yorkshire]. V.C.H., York, 2, pp. 73–109, + 8 plates, + map. 1912.

8367 —— On the excavation by Canon Greenwell, in 1868, of an Anglo-Saxon cemetery at Uncleby, East Riding of Yorkshire. [7 figures in text.] Proc. Soc. Antiq., 2nd S., 24, pp. 146–58, + 1 plate, + map. 1912.

8368 Thurman (John). Description of an ancient tumular cemetery, probably of the Anglo-Saxon period, at Lamel hill, near York. Proc. Yorks. Philos. Soc., 1847–48, pp. 98–105. 1849.

8369 Waterman (Dudley M.). Anglian burial at Occaney, W. R. Yorks. Yorks. Archaeol. J., 37, pp. 440–41. 1951.

132. CEMETERIES, SUSSEX

8370 [Anon.] Anglo-Saxon burials. [Eastbourne.] Sussex N. and Q., 1, p. 112. 1926.

8371 Curwen (Eliot and Eliot Cecil). Anglo-Saxon burial, Portslade. *Same jnl.*, 1, pp. 186–87. 1927.

8372 Curwen (Eliot Cecil). Saxon interment near Portslade. *Same jnl.*, 3, pp. 214–15. 1931.

8373 Frere (Sheppard Sunderland). A survey of archaeology near Lancing. [Pp. 170–72, Saxon.] Sussex Archaeol. Collns., 81, pp. 141–72, + map. 1940.

8374 Frost (Marian). The Saxon cemetery at Highdown, and the romance of burial. Worthing Archaeol. Soc., Ann. Rept., 14, pp. 11–26. 1936.

8375 Griffith (A. F.) and **Salzmann** (Lewis Francis). An Anglo-Saxon cemetery at Alfriston. Sussex Archaeol. Collns., 56, pp. 16–53 : 57, pp. 197–208, + 30 plates, including folding plan. 1914–15.

8376 Griffith (A. F.). Notes on some Saxon interments at Ringmer. *Same jnl.*, 33, pp. 129–30. 1883.

8377 —— Some notes on Anglo-Saxon antiquities from High Down, near Worthing. *Same jnl.*, 66, pp. 219–24. 1925.

8378 Margary (Ivan D.). The Anglo-Saxon room [in the museum of the Sussex Archaeological Society]. [Figures of glass and buckles from A.-S. cemetery, Alfriston.] *Same jnl.*, 85, pp. 107–10. 1946.

8379 Read (*Sir* Charles Hercules). On excavations in a cemetery of South Saxons on High Down. (Further excavations, *etc.*) Archaeologia, 54, pp. 369–82, + 1 plate : 55, pp. 203–14, + 2 plates. 1895–96.

8380 Rice (Robert Garraway). Anglo-Saxon antiquities found at Portslade in July 1898. [3 skeletons, and iron objects.] Proc. Soc. Antiq., 2nd S. 18, pp. 28–29. 1900.

8381 Sawyer (John). Important archaeological discovery at Goring. Antiquary, 27, pp. 34–36. 1893.

8382 —— Important discovery of Anglo-Saxon remains at Kingston, Lewes. Sussex Archaeol. Collns., 38, pp. 177–83, + 1 plate. 1892.

8383 Smith (Reginald Allender). Anglo-Saxon remains [in Sussex]. V.C.H., Sussex, 1, pp. 333–49, + 2 plates, + map. 1905.

8384 Toms (Herbert S.). Saxon cremations near Saddlescombe. [With plan. Details of pottery.] Sussex Archaeol. Collns., 57, pp. 219–21. 1915.

8385 Whitley (H. Michell). [Discovery of] Saxon cemetery at Eastbourne. [No record of finds made.] Proc. Soc. Antiq., 2nd S. 15, p. 275. 1895.

8386 —— Notice of a cinerary urn found at the Mill Gap, Eastbourne. Trans. Eastbourne N.H. Soc., N.S. 1, pp. 5–7. 1885.

8387 —— Recent archaeological discoveries in the Eastbourne district. [Pp. 112–13, Saxon cemetery in the Mill Field, Eastbourne.] Sussex Archaeol. Collns., 37, pp. 111–15. 1890.

8388 Wilson (Arthur Ernest) and **Gerard** (Ethel). Worthing Museum Publications, No. 1. Guide to the Anglo-Saxon collection. pp. 16. 8° Worthing, 1947. [A.–S. cemetery on Highdown hill. 19 figures in text. Jewellery shows Roman influence and points to contact with Arthurian Britain. The glass shows link with Belgium and the Rhine valley.]

133. CEMETERIES, WESSEX
§ a. Berkshire Group

8389 [Anon.] Discovery of an Anglo-Saxon burial place near West Shefford. Q.J. Berks. Archaeol. Soc., 1, p. 81. 1890.

8390 Akerman (John Yonge). Report of excavations in an ancient cemetery at Frilford, near Abingdon. Proc. Soc. Antiq., 2nd S. 3, pp. 136–41. 1865.

8391 —— Report on researches in an Anglo-Saxon cemetery at Long Wittenham, 1859. (Report on further researches . . . in the summer of 1860). Archaeologia, 38, pp. 327–52, + 4 plates : 39, pp. 135–42, + 1 plate. 1860–63.

8392 —— Report on the results of his excavations in an Anglo-Saxon cemetery at Long Wittenham, near Abingdon. (Discovery . . . of sepulchral remains at *and* Further researches in . . . Long Wittenham.) Proc. Soc. Antiq., 2nd S. 1, pp. 20–21 : 2, pp. 37–38, 133–345. 1859, 1861–62.

D d

8393 Atkinson (R. J. C.). Archaeological notes . . . 1945. Blewbury. [A.S. burial on Blewburton hill. Figures of two bronze brooches.] Oxoniensia, 10, p. 93. 1945.

8394 Buxton (Leonard Halford Dudley). Excavations at Frilford. Antiq. J., 1, pp. 87–97. 1921.

8395 Clutterbuck (James C.). Discovery of a Saxon cemetery at Arne Hill near Lockinge. Proc. Soc. Antiq., 2nd S. 2, pp. 320–21. 1863.

8396 —— Discovery of a Saxon interment at Long Wittenham. Archaeol. J., 5, pp. 291–94, + 2 plates. 1848.

8397 Ditchfield (Peter Hampson). Discovery of a Saxon grave at Lockridge, near Wantage. Proc. Soc. Antiq., 2nd S. 14, p. 103. 1892.

8398 Leeds (Edward Thurlow) and **Harden** (Donald Benjamin). The Anglo-Saxon cemetery at Abingdon. *Ashmolean Museum*. pp. 63, + 19 plates. 8° Oxford, 1936.

8399 Leeds (Edward Thurlow). An Anglo-Saxon cemetery at Wallingford. [Also plates on pp. 39 and 40 of vol. 41, 1937.] Berks. Archaeol. J., 42, pp. 93–101, + plan, + 7 plates. 1938.

8400 Money (Walter). [Exhibition of] a sword, a fibula, some knives, and other relics found [in an Anglo-Saxon burial place] at East Shefford. Proc. Soc. Antiq., 2nd S. 13, pp. 107–08. 1890.

8401 Parker (James). On the Garford barrow, near Abingdon. Proc. Oxford Archit. and Hist. Soc., N.S. 3, pp. 6–13. 1872.

8402 Passmore (A. D.). Saxon interments at Coleshill. Antiq. J., 13, pp. 167–69. 1933.

8403 Peake (Harold John Edward) and **Hooton** (E. A.). Saxon graveyard at East Shefford, Berks. [i. The graves and their contents, by H. Peake : ii. Osteological report, by E. A. Hooton : iii. General conclusion, by H. Peake.] J.R.A.I., 45, pp. 92–130, + 7 plates, + table. 1915.

8404 Ravenscroft (William). The discovery of human remains in the Forbury, Reading. [Argument for this being ' original Saxon churchyard of Reading.'] Berks, Bucks and Oxon Archaeol. J., 13, pp. 5–16. 1907.

8405 —— The recent discovery of human remains at Reading. Antiquary, 43, pp. 91–98. 1907.

8406 Rolleston (George). Researches and excavations carried on in an ancient cemetery at Frilford, near Abingdon, Berks., in the years 1867–1868. [iii. Of the Anglo-Saxon interments in the way of cremation : iv. Of the Anglo-Saxon interments in the way of inhumation without orientation, but with insignia and in shallow graves, etc.] Archaeologia, 42, pp. 416–85, + 3 plates. 1869.

8407 —— Further researches in an Anglo-Saxon cemetery at Frilford, with remarks on the northern limit of Anglo-Saxon cremation in England. [Plate shows A.–S. urns from Sancton, Yorks.] Same jnl., 45, pp. 405–10, + 1 plate. 1880.

8408 Smith (Reginald Allender). Anglo-Saxon remains [in Berkshire]. [8 figures in text.] V.C.H., Berkshire, 1, pp. 229–49, + 3 plates, + map. 1906.

8409 Stevens (Joseph). The discoveries at Betterton. [Skeleton, ring, brooches, etc.] Q.J. Berks. Archaeol. Soc., 2, p. 118. 1892.

8410 —— The discovery of an ancient cemetery at Reading. [' Christian British cemetery, which was subsequently utilised by the Saxons at a time when the custom of placing pagan relics in the grave had not been wholly abandoned.'] Berks, Bucks and Oxon Archaeol. J., 1, pp. 100–05. 1896.

8411 —— The discovery of a Saxon burial-place near Reading. J. Brit. Archaeol. Assoc., 50, pp. 150–57, + 2 plates. 1894.

§ b. Hampshire Group

8412 [Anon.] Discovery of Anglo-Saxon remains in Hampshire. [Whitchurch.] Reliquary, 24, p. 230. 1884.

8413 Andrew (Walter Jonathan). Report on the first (–second) excavations at Oliver's Battery, [near Winchester] in 1930 (in 1931). [Pp. 7–8, ' the Saxon interment and bowl ' : pp. 166–67, ' the Anglo-Saxon interment.' c. 550.] Papers and Proc. Hants. F. C., 12, pp. 5–10, 163–68, + plate 1. 1932–33.

8414 Dale (William). Notes on the discovery of an Anglo-Saxon cemetery at Droxford. [6 figures of brooches, pendant and shield-handle, in text.] Proc. Soc. Antiq., 2nd S. 19, pp. 125–29. 1902.

8415 —— On the discovery of an Anglo-Saxon cemetery at Droxford. Papers and Proc. Hants. F.C., 5, pp. 173–77, + 1 plate. 1906.

8416 Hill (N. Gray). Excavations on Stockbridge down, 1935–36. [c. 50 skeletons in shallow graves, many decapitated and with wrists close together. Six silver coins of end of reign of Edward the Confessor found tucked in armpit of skeleton no. 19. Buckles, etc.] Same jnl., 13, pp. 247–59, + 8 plates, + 2 plans. 1937.

8417 Hillier (George). Excavations on Brightstone and Bowcombe downs, Isle of Wight. [Ascribed to transitional Roman—A.–S. period.] J. Brit. Archaeol. Assoc., 11, pp. 34–40, + 1 coloured plate. 1855.

8418 Kell (Edmund). Discoveries of early Saxon antiquities in the [Isle of Wight]. [Barrow on Arreton down.] Same jnl., 5, pp. 365–69. 1849.

8418a Muller (M. R. Maitland) and **Waterman** (Dudley M.). The Saxon town of Hamwih (Hamton) at Southampton, Hants. Report of excavations, 1946–1948. (Provisional reports . . . Easter, 1949 : summer, 1949 : Easter, 1950 : Summer, 1950 : for 6th year). Archaeol. News Letter, 2, pp. 13–14, 50, 142 : 3, pp. 36–37, 134–35 : 4, p. 62. 1949–51.

8419 Muller (M. R. Maitland). Southampton excavations : first (second) interim report, 1946 (1947). [Pp. 67–70, 125–29 + plate, the Saxon town of Hamwih.] Papers and Proc. Hants. F. C., 17, pp. 65–71, + plate : 125–29, + 1 plate. 1949–51.

8420 Pettigrew (Thomas Joseph). On the antiquities of the Isle of Wight, as illustrated by the British Archaeological Association. [Pp. 186–87, + first plate, A.–S. burials on Chessell downs.] J. Brit. Archaeol. Assoc., 11, pp. 177–193, + 2 plates. 1855.

8421 Smith (Charles Roach). Saxon remains found at Southampton. [8th–10th c. In possession of J. R. Keele.] Collectanea Antiqua, 4, pp. 58–62, + 1 plate. 1857.

8422 Smith (Reginald Allender). Anglo-Saxon remains [in Hampshire.] V.C.H., Hampshire, 1, pp. 373–98, + 1 coloured plate. 1900.

8423 —— [Saxon remains from] Basingstoke, Hants. [3 figures in text: iron spearheads and knife, bone draughtsmen : bronze bowl.] Proc. Soc. Antiq., 2nd S. 22, pp. 79–81. 1908.

8424 Stevens (Joseph). On newly discovered Roman and Saxon remains at Finkley, near Andover. J. Brit. Archaeol. Assoc., 28, pp. 327–36. 1872.

8425 Wilkins (E. P.), **Kell** (Edmund) and **Locke** (John). Account of the examination of the largest barrow in the Anglo-Saxon cemetery on Bowcombe down, Isle of Wight. *Same jnl.*, 16, pp. 253–61, + 1 plate. 1860.

§ *c*. **Somerset Group**
(With Devon and Cornwall)

8426 Dobson (Dina Portway). A Saxon burial at Evercreech. Proc. Spelaeological Soc., 4, p. 268. 1935.

8427 Gray (Harold St. George). Human remains found at Huish Episcopi. [Ring, ? 6th or 7th c., found on finger.] N. and Q. for Som. and Dorset, 23, pp. 141–42. 1940.

8428 Horne (Ethelbert) *abbot of Downside*. Camerton Saxon cemetery. Proc. Bath branch, Somerset Archaeol. Soc., 1928, pp. 206–07 : 1933, pp. 503–06. 1928, 1933.

8429 —— Saxon cemetery at Buckland Denham. Antiq. J., 6, pp. 77–8. 1926.

8430 Horne (Ethelbert) *abbot of Downside*. Saxon cemetery at Camerton, Somerset. Proc. Somerset Arch. Soc., 74 (1928), pp. 61–70 + folding plan : 75 (1929), pp. 107–08, + 1 plate : 76 (1930), pp. 101–02 : 77 (1931), p. 140 : 78 (1932), p. 129 : 79 (1933), pp. 39–63 + folding plan + 2 plates. 1929, 30, 31, 32, 33, 34.

8431 Smith (Reginald Allender). Anglo-Saxon remains [in Cornwall]. V.C.H., Cornwall, 1, pp. 375–78, + 2 plates. 1906.

8432 —— Anglo-Saxon remains [in Devon]. V.C.H., Devon, 1, pp. 373–74. 1906.

8433 Wingrave (Wyatt). An Anglo-Saxon burial on Hardown hill. Proc. Dorset Archaeol. Soc., 53 (for 1931), pp. 247–49, + 3 plates. 1932.

§ *d*. **Surrey Group**

8434 Bidder (Harold F.), **Smith** (Reginald Allender), *etc.* A burying ground of the early Anglo-Saxon period … at Mitcham. (Further excavations, *etc.*). Proc. Soc. Antiq., 2nd S. 21, pp. 3–10 : 32, pp. 201–02. 1905, 1920.

8435 —— Excavations in an Anglo-Saxon burial ground at Mitcham ; with notes on crania and bones found there by W. L. H. Duckworth. [12 figures in text.] Archaeologia, 60, pp. 49–68, + plan. 1906. *Reprinted in* Surrey Archaeol. Collns., 21, pp. 1–25, + plan. 1908.

8436 —— Mitcham : Saxon burial ground. [West Saxon : mid 6th c.] Surrey Archaeol. Collns., 34, pp. 109–10 : 37, p. 94. 1921, 1926.

8437 Brock (Edgar Philip Loftus). On an Anglo-Saxon interment at Beddington. J. Brit. Archeol. Assoc., 30, pp. 212–13. 1874.

8438 Burchell (J. P. T.) and **Frere** (Sheppard Sunderland). The occupation of Sandown Park, Esher, during the stone age, the early iron age, and the Anglo-Saxon period. [20 maps and diagrams in text.] Antiq. J., 27, pp. 24–46. 1947.

8439 Clinch (George). Discovery of Anglo-Saxon graves at Carshalton. Surrey Archaeol. Collns., 23, p. 213. 1910.

8440 Cotton (Arthur R.). Saxon discoveries at Fetcham. [Illustration of bronze bucket.] Antiq. J., 13, pp. 48–51. 1933.

8441 Dunning (Gerald Clough). A Saxon cemetery at Ewell. Antiq. J., 12, pp. 442–45 : 13, pp. 302–03 (with map and 2 figures of brooches in text). 1932–33.

8442 Escritt (L. B.) Report on the Saxon cemetery at the junction of Mitchley avenue and Riddlesdown road near Riddlesdown, Purley. (Report on human remains . . . by M. L. Tildesley). Proc. Croydon N.H. and Sci. Soc., 10, 10, pp. 199–201, + 1 plate. 1933.

8443 Finny (W. E. St. Lawrence). Kingston [on-Thames] : Saxon articles exhibited in the museum. [Notice re Bidder collection.] Surrey Archaeol. Collns. 35, p. 122. 1924.

8444 Flower (John Wickham). Notices of an Anglo-Saxon cemetery at Beddington. Same jnl., 6, pp. 122–24. 1874.

8445 —— Notices of an Anglo-Saxon cemetery at Farthing down, Coulsdon. Same jnl., 6, pp. 109–117 + 3 plates. 1874.

8446 Floyer (John K.). Two skeletons from Fetcham down. [Notice only.] Same jnl., 37, p. 93. 1926.

8447 Frere (Sheppard Sunderland). A Saxon burial on Farthing down, Coulsdon. Same jnl., 49, pp. 114–15. 1946.

8448 Gardner (Eric). Some prehistoric and Saxon antiquities found in the neighbourhood of Weybridge. [Pp. 133–35, Danish and Saxon weapons.] Same jnl., 25, pp. 129–35, + 4 plates. 1912.

8449 Griffith (Francis Llewellyn). On some Roman and Saxon remains found at Croydon in 1893–94. Proc. Soc. Antiq. Lond., 2nd S. 15, pp. 328–34. 1895. *Reprinted in* Surrey Archaeol. Collns., 13, pp. 18–25. 1897.

8449a Hope-Taylor (Brian). Excavations on Farthing down, Coulsdon, Surrey. [High proportion of children buried. ?victims of a mid-7th c. pestilence.] Archaeol. News Letter, 2, p. 170. 1950.

8450 Lambert (Henry). Find of skeletons at Banstead. [Pagan Saxon : with pottery.] Surrey Archaeol. Collns., 37, pp. 91–93. 1926.

8451 Lowther (Anthony William George). Excavations at Ewell in 1934. The Saxon cemetery and Stane Street. Same jnl., 43, pp. 16–35, + 2 plates, + folding map. 1935.

8452 —— The Saxon cemetery at Guildown, Guildford. Same jnl., 39, pp. 1–50, + 26 plates, + folding plan : 41, pp. 119–22, + 1 plate. 1931–33.

8453 Martin (Alan R.). The Saxon barrows in Greenwich park. Trans. Greenwich Antiq. Soc., 3, pp. 166–73, + plan, + 1 plate. 1929.

8454 Moodie (J. M.). Animal remains and Saxon burials found near Coulsdon. Surrey Archaeol. Collns., 26, pp. 139–40. 1913.

8455 Smith (Reginald Allender). Anglo-Saxon antiquities found at Mitcham. [Swords, brooches, etc.] Proc. Soc. Antiq., 2nd S. 28, pp. 230–33. 1916.

8456 —— Anglo-Saxon remains [in [in Surrey]. V.C.H., Surrey, 1, pp. 255–73, + 1 plate, + map. 1902.

8457 —— Recent and former discoveries at Hawkshill. [A.–S. cemetery in Mole valley of 5th or 6th century.] Surrey Archaeol. Collns., 20, pp. 119–28. 1907.

8458 —— Remarks on the antiquities discovered in the Mitcham cemetery. [9 figures in text.] Proc. Soc. Antiq., 2nd S. 21, pp. 4–10. 1906. *Reprinted in* Surrey Archaeol. Collns., 25, pp. 26–32. 1908.

8459 Willis (Cloudesley S.). Saxon burials at Ewell. Surrey Archaeol. Collns., 41, p. 122 : 42, p. 113. 1933–34.

§ e. Wiltshire Group

8460 Akerman (John Yonge). An account of excavations in an Anglo-Saxon burial ground at Harnham hill, near Salisbury. (Note on some further discoveries, etc.). Archaeologia, 35, pp. 259–78, + 3 plates, + maps : 475–79, + 1 plate. 1853.

8461 —— An account of the discovery of Anglo-Saxon remains at Kemble, in north Wilts ; with observations on a grant of land at Ewelme to the abbey of Malmesbury by king Æthelstan, in the year 931. *Same jnl.*, 37, pp. 113–21, + map. 1857.

8462 —— Report on researches . . . in an Anglo-Saxon cemetery at Harnham hill, Salisbury. Proc. Soc. Antiq., 3, pp. 30–32. 1853.

8463 Clay (Richard Challoner Cobbe). A pagan Saxon cemetery at Broadchalke. Wilts. Archaeol. Mag., 43, pp. 94–101, + plan, + 1 plates. 1925.

8464 —— A pagan Saxon burial at Ebbesbourne Wake. [Report on the bones by Sir Arthur Keith.] *Same jnl.*, 43, p. 101. 1925.

8465 Cunnington (*Mrs.* Maud Edith). Catalogue of antiquities in the museum of the Wiltshire Archaeological Society, at Devizes. Pt. 1, the Stourhead collection. Revised by E. H. Goddard. pp. iv, 96. 8° Devizes, 1896. [A.–S., passim.]

8466 —— and **Goddard** (E. H.). *Ditto.* Pt. 2. 2nd edition. pp. xiv, 294. 8° Devizes, 1934. [Pp. 239–56 (8 pp. of illustrations in text), Saxon period : Easton hill, Roundway down, Basset down, Broadchalke, Purton, *etc.*]

8467 Cunnington (*Mrs.* Maud Edith). Saxon burial at Netheravon. Wilts. Archaeol. Mag., 48, pp. 469–70. 1939.

8468 —— A Saxon burial of the pagan period at Woodbridge, North Newnton. [For report on human remains, pp. 266–67, *see* Cave (A.J.E.), **8751**.] *Same jnl.*, 47, p. 265. 1935.

8469 —— Saxon burials at Foxhill, Wanborough, 1941. *Same jnl.*, 49, pp. 542–43, + plate. 1942.

8470 Cunnington (*Mrs.* Maud Edith). and **Goddard** (E. H.). A Saxon cemetery at ' The Fox ', Purton. [Plate shows *seax*, spearhead and knife.] *Same jnl.*, 37, pp. 606–08, + 1 plate. 1912.

8471 Cunnington (*Mrs.* Maud Edith). Wiltshire in pagan Saxon times. [Dating: primary and secondary burials under barrows : cemeteries : isolated finds.] *Same jnl.*, 46, pp. 147–75. 1933.

8472 Cunnington (William). An account of the ancient British and Anglo-Saxon barrows on Roundway hill, in the parish of Bishop's Cannings. *Same jnl.*, 6, pp. 159–67. 1860.

8473 Goddard (E. H.). A list of prehistoric, Roman, and pagan Saxon antiquities in the county of Wilts. arranged under parishes. [With references, if described.] *Same jnl.*, 38, pp. 153–378. 1913.

8474 —— Notes on objects from a Saxon interment at Basset down. *Same jnl.*, 28, pp. 104–08, + 3 plates. 1895.

8475 Jackson (John Edward). Anglo-Saxon cemetery at Harnham, near Salisbury. *Same jnl.*, 1, pp. 196–208, + 1 plate. 1854.

8476 Leeds (Edward Thurlow) and **Shortt** (Hugh de Sausmarez). An Anglo-Saxon [pagan] cemetery at Petersfinger, near Salisbury, Wilts. With technical appendices by R. J. C. Atkinson, Mrs. G. M. Crowfoot and A. J. E. Cave. *Salisbury Museum.* pp. 64, + 11 plates. 4° Salisbury, 1953. [Appendices 1, construction of the swords, scabbards and shields : 2, The textile remains : 3, The human skeletal remains.]

8477 Meyrick (O.). A Saxon skeleton in a Roman well. [?6th c. Woman. Mildenhall parish.] Wilts. Archaeol. Mag., 53, pp. 220–22. 1949.

8478 Stevens (Frank). Saxon skeleton found at Perham down. *Same jnl.*, 49, p. 114. 1940.

8479 Stone (J. F. S.) and **Tildesley** (Miriam Louise). Saxon interments on Roche Court down, Winterslow, and a report on the human remains. *Same jnl.*, 45, pp. 568–99, + plan, + 4 plates. 1932.

134. CEMETERIES, VIKING

8480 [Anon.] Scandinavian relics found in Colonsay. [Viking grave at Kiloran bay. Bones, weapons, and styca of abp. Wigmund of York.] Highland Mag., 1, pp. 111–12. 1885.

8481 [Anon.] A Viking's tomb at Taplow [Bucks.] [Excavated by the Berkshire Archaeological Society.] Antiq. Mag., 5, pp. 14–21. 1884.

8482 Anderson (Joseph). Notes on the contents of two Viking graves in Islay, discovered by William Campbell of Ballinaby ; with notices of the burial customs of the Norse sea-kings, as recorded in the sagas and illustrated by their grave-mounds in Norway and in Scotland. [39 figures in text.] Proc. Soc. Antiq. Scot., 14 (N.S. 2), pp. 51–89. 1880.

8483 —— Notes on the relics of the Viking period of the Northmen in Scotland, illustrated by specimens in the museum. [35 figures in text. i. Stone urns : ii. Tortoise or bowl-shaped brooches : iii. Characteristic weapons of the Viking period : iv. Hoards of silver ornaments : v. Beaker of glass, found in a grave in Westray : vi. Scottish or Celtic brooches, etc., found in Viking graves in Scandinavia.] *Same jnl.*, 10, pp. 536–94. 1875.

8484 Auden (George Augustus). Abstract of a paper on antiquities dating from the Danish occupation of York. [6 figures and 2 plates in text : implements, etc.] Saga-Book V.C., 6, pp. 169–79. 1910.

8485 —— Some objects recently found in York referable to the Viking period. [Published in full **8488.**] Brit. Ass. Rept., 1907, p. 646. 1908.

8486 Balfour (John Alexander). Notes on a Viking-grave mound at Millhill, Lamlash, Arran. [8th or 9th c.] Proc. Soc. Antiq. Scot., 44 (4th S. 8, 1909–10), pp. 221–24. 1910.

8487 —— Notice of a Viking grave-mound, Kingscross, Arran. [? 9th c.] *Same jnl.*, 43 (4th S. 7, 1908–09), pp. 371–75. 1909.

8488 Benson (George) [and **Auden** (George Augustus)]. Notes on an excavation at the corner of Castlegate and Coppergate [York]. [' One of the most important finds belonging to the Viking period which has been made in Great Britain.'] Ann. Rpt. Yorks. Phil. Soc. 1906, pp. 72–76, + plan, + 2 plates. 1907.

8489 Charleston (Malcolm Mackenzie). Notes on some ancient burials in Orkney. [?date. Fig. 1 shows bronze bowl-shaped brooch of Viking type.] Proc. Soc. Antiq. Scot., 38 (4th S. 2, 1903–04), pp. 559–66. 1904.

8490 Coffey (George) and **Armstrong** (Edmund Clarence Richard). Scandinavian objects found at Island-bridge and Kilmainham [co. Dublin]. [Plate shows 5 sword-hilts. 24 figures in text.] Proc. R.I.A., 28 c, pp. 107–22, + 1 coloured plate. 1910.

8491 Coles (Frederick R.). The mound at Little Richorn, Dalbeattie, [Kirkendbright]. [?' a Norse grave-mound.' No description of contents.] Trans. Dumfries Antiq. Soc., 8 (1891–92), pp. 37–39. 1893.

8492 Cowen (John David). A catalogue of objects of the Viking period in the Tullie House museum, Carlisle. [i. The Ormside burial : ii. The Hesket burial : iii. Other weapons and tools : iv. Ornaments and jewellery : v. Sculptured stones.] Trans. Cumb. and Westm. Antiq. Soc., N.S. 34, pp. 166–87, + 4 plates. 1934.

8493 —— Viking burials in Cumbria. *Same jnl.*, N.S. 48, pp. 73–76. 1949.

8494 Croker (Thomas Crofton). Antiquities discovered in Orkney, the Hebrides, and Ireland, compared. [Larne, Antrim, 1840 : Pier-o-wall, Orkney : of period of Danish invasions.] J. Brit. Archaeol. Assoc., 2, pp. 328–33. 1847.

8495 Curle (James). On recent Scandinavian grave-finds from the island of Oronsay, and from Reay, Caithness, with notes on the development and chronology of the oval brooch of the Viking time. [22 figures, mostly of brooches, in text.] Proc. Soc. Antiq. Scot., 48 (4th S. 12, 1913–14), pp. 292–315. 1914.

8496 Edwards (Arthur J. H.). Excavation of a number of graves in a mound at Ackergill, Caithness. With a report on the skeletal remains from the graves by Thomas H. Bryce. [Viking period. 10 figures in text.] *Same jnl.*, 60 (5th S. 12, 1925–26), pp. 160–82. 1927.

8497 —— Excavation of graves at Ackergill, and of an earth-house at Freswick Links, Caithness, and a description of the discovery of a Viking grave at Reay, Caithness. With a preliminary note on the skeletal remains from the various graves, by Thomas H. Bryce. [12 figures in text.] *Same jnl.*, 61 (6th S. 1, 1926–27), pp. 196–209. 1927.

8498 —— A Viking cist-grave at Ballinaby, Islay. With a note on the skeletel remains by Thomas H. Bryce. [c. 950–1000.] *Same jnl.*, 68 (6th S. 8, 1933–34), pp. 74–78. 1934.

8499 Grieve (Symington). Note upon Carn nan Bharraich, or cairn of the men of Barra, a burial mound of the Viking time on the island of Oronsay, Argyllshire, with an outline of the political history of the Western Isles during the latter half of the ninth century. *Same jnl.*, 48 (4th S. 12, 1913–14), pp. 272–91. 1914.

8500 Kaye (Walter Jenkinson). A Viking grave near Harrogate. Durham Univ. J., 35, pp. 381–84. 1928.

8501 Kendrick (*Sir* Thomas Downing). Viking period antiquities in England. Trans. S.E. Union of Sci. Socs., 1933, pp. 42–49. 1933.

8502 Kermode (Philip Moore Callow). Ship-burial in the Isle of Man. Antiq. J., 10, pp. 126–33, + 1 plate. 1930.

8503 Lethbridge (Thomas Charles). A burial of the Viking age in Skye. Archaeol. J., 77, pp. 135–36. 1920.

8504 McCrie (George M.). Notice of the discovery of an urn of steatite in one of five tumuli excavated at Corquoy, in the island of Rousay, Orkney. [? Viking.] Proc. Soc. Antiq. Scot., 15 (N.S. 3), pp. 71–73. 1881.

8505 McNeill (Malcolm). Notice of excavations in a burial mound of the Viking time in Oronsay. *Same jnl.*, 25 (3rd S. 1), pp. 432–35. 1891.

8506 McNeill (Malcolm). Notice of the discovery of a Viking interment, in the island of Colonsay. *Same jnl.*, 26 (3rd S. 2), pp. 61–62. 1892.

8507 Marwick (Hugh). Notes on Viking burials in Orkney. Proc. Orkney Antiq. Soc., 10 (1931–32), pp. 27–29. 1932.

8508 Megaw (Basil R. S.). An ancient cemetery at Balladoyne, St. John's, [Isle of Man]. New discoveries near Tynwald hill. [Viking weapons, etc.] J. Manx Mus., 4, pp. 11–14, + 2 plates. 1938.

8509 Milligan (Seaton Forrest). Danish finds [at Bangor, co. Down] in Ireland. J. Roy. Soc. Antiq. Ireland, 36 (5th S. 16), pp. 205–06. 1906.

8510 Paget ( ) *Lady*. Notes on sepulchral crosses and slabs in Shetland. [In Viking churchyards at Norwick and Sandwick. No carving.] J. Brit. Archaeol. Assoc., 50, pp. 306–07, + 2 plates. 1894.

8511 Shetelig (Haakon). Ship-burial at Kiloran bay, Colonsay, Scotland. [?early 10th c.] Saga-Book V.C., 5, pp. 172–74. 1907.

8512 —— The Viking graves in Great Britain and Ireland. [i. The Viking graves and the geography of Viking settlements : ii. Burial customs and grave goods. 28 figures in text.] Acta Archaeol., 16, pp. 1–55. 1945.

8513 Sheppard (Thomas). Viking and other relics at Crayke, Yorkshire. [Hull Museum Publicn., 203.] Yorks. Archaeol. J., 34, pp. 273–81, + 6 plates. 1939.

8514 Smith (John Alexander). Note of the discovery of sepulchral urns in Fair Isle, with letter from John Bruce of Sumburgh, Shetland. [Steatite vessels of heathen Viking period, 8th–11th c.] Proc. Soc. Antiq. Scot., 11, pp. 530–34. 1876.

8515 Smith (Reginald Allender). Notes on some objects of the Viking period recently discovered at York. [4 figures in text of sword-chapes, axehead, and portion of a bone casket : described by G. A. Auden in Man, 1907.] Proc. Soc. Antiq., 2nd S. 22, pp. 5–9. 1907.

8516 Whistler (Charles Watts). Battle burial, probably of Danes. [Combwich, on the Parrett.] Saga-Book V.C., 4, pp. 22–23. 1905.

8517 —— The battle burials at Cannington Park [Somerset]. [Viking period.] *Same jnl.*, 5, pp. 237–42. 1908.

8518 Williams (John). Antiquities recently discovered by [Commander Edge] in the island of Barra, Hebrides. [?interment of a 9th or 10th c. Danish chieftain.] Proc. Soc. Antiq., 2nd S. 2, pp. 229–31. 1863.

135. CEMETERIES, CELTIC

8519 [Anon.] The grave of Sawyl Benisel, king of the Britons. [?7th c.] Arch. Camb., N.S. 2, pp. 159–62. 1851.

8520 Armstrong (Edmund Clarence Richard). Some Irish antiquities of unknown use. [9th–10th c. Killua and Navan.] Antiq. J., 2, pp. 6–12, + 1 plate. 1922.

8521 Beaumont (William). An account of an ancient sepulchre discovered in the county of Kildare, Ireland, in the year 1788. [?Irish, not later than 7th c. ?Danish.] Trans. R.I.A., 2 (Antiq.), pp. 51–55, + 1 plate. 1788.

8522 Bruce (J. Ronald) and **Cubbon** (William). Cronk yn How. An early Christian and Viking site, at Lezayre, Isle of Man. [Mound erected in 7th or 8th c. for reception of a Keeill.] Arch. Camb., 85, pp. 267–308, + 3 maps, etc. 1930. *Also* I.O.M. N.H. and Antiq. Soc., Proc., N.S. 3 (1928–30), pp. 282–97, + 6 plates. 1931.

8523 Calder (Charles S. T.) and **Feachem** (R. W.). Cemetery, Dunbar, East Lothian. [?Early Christian.] Proc. Soc. Antiq. Scot., 85 (1950–51), p. 179. 1953.

8524 Casson (Stanley). American archaeological research of the year. [Describes a penannular bronze brooch of 7th c. and the Ballinderry gaming board found in Ireland.] Discovery, 15, pp. 286–88. 1934.

8525 Cubbon (William). Early Christian graves at Ballaqueeney. [Parish of Rushen, Isle of Man]. J. Manx Mus., 3, p. 12. 1935.

8526 Duignan (Michael). Early monastic site, Kiltiernan East Townland, co. Galway. J. Roy. Soc. Antiq. Ireland, 81, pp. 73–75. 1951.

8527 Edmond (J. P.). The burial-place of Malcolm I. [Died 953.] Antiq. Mag., 7, pp. 121–25. 1885.

8528 Ffoulkes (W. Wynne). Tumulus, Gorsedd Wen, and the reasons for supposing it to be the tomb of Gwen, one of Llywarch Hen's sons. [Denbighshire, 6th c.] Arch. Camb., N.S. 2, pp. 9–19. 1851.

8529 Fox (Aileen Mary) *Lady Fox*. Early Christian period [in Wales]. Settlement sites and other remains. Cambrian Archaeol. Assoc. Centenary vol., pp. 105–22, + 2 plates. 1946.

8530 Frazer (William). The Aylesbury-road [co. Dublin] sepulchral mound. Description of certain human remains, articles of bronze, and other objects obtained there. [10th–11th c.] Proc. R.I.A., 2nd S. 2 (Antiq.), pp. 116–18. 1883.

8531 —— Description of a great sepulchral mound at Aylesbury road, near Donnybrook, in the county of Dublin, containing human and animal remains, as well as some objects of antiquarian interest, referable to the tenth or eleventh centuries. Proc. R.I.A., 2nd S. 2 (Antiq.), pp. 29–55. 1880.

8532 Hencken (Hugh). Lagore crannog : an Irish royal residence of the 7th to 10th centuries A.D. With sections by Liam Price and Laura E. Start. [Brooches, pins, implements, etc.] Proc. R.I.A., 53 c, pp. 1–247, + 19 plates. 1950.

8533 Henry (Françoise). Habitation sites on Inishkea North, co. Mayo. [Early 8th c.] J. Roy. Soc. Antiq. Ireland, 81, pp. 75–76. 1951.

8534 Kermode (Philip Moore Callow) and **Kneen** (John Joseph). Knoc y Doonee [tumulus]. [?burial place of 'Athacan the Smith', c. 950.] I.O.M. N.H. and Antiq. Soc., Proc., N.S. 3 (1927–28), pp. 241–49, + 3 plates. 1930.

8535 Kermode (Philip Moore Callow). Ship burial in the Isle of Man. [?9th c., Celto-Scandinavian, heathen.] Antiquity, 2, pp. 91–3. 1928.

8536 McCulloch (W. T.). Notice of coffins (formed of stone slabs) found on the farm of Milton, Haddingtonshire. [Similar to A.–S. cemeteries of 6th–10th c.] Proc. Soc. Antiq. Scot., 3, pp. 503–06. 1862.

8537 Manx Museum. Excavations at Cronk Conoly, Lezayre. [7th–8th c. graves, etc.] J. Manx Mus., 1, pp. 131–32. 1928.

8538 Monro (Robert). Notice of an ancient kitchen-midden near Largo bay, Fife, excavated by W. Baird, Esq., of Elie. (Notes on the bones [of animals]). [Post-Roman : ?7th or 8th c.] Proc. Soc. Antiq. Scot., 35 (3rd S. 11, 1900–01), pp. 281–300. 1901.

8539 Power (Patrick). The *cill* or *cillín* : a study in early Irish ecclesiology. [Grave-yards : place-names in *kill* or *kil.*] Irish Eccles. Rec., 5th S. 73, pp. 218–25. 1950.

8540 Robertson (James S.). Find of a Pictish urn at Inverurie [Aberdeenshire]. [?burial of king Oadh, 878.] Scot. N. and Q., 2nd S. 4, pp. 102–03. 1903.

8541 Stuart (   ) *professor, of Aberdeen.* Account of the discovery of an ancient tomb at Fetteresso, in Kincardineshire, in January, 1822. [?that of Malcolm I.]. Archaeol. Scot., 2, pp. 462–65. 1822.

8542 Stuart (John). Account of the recent examination of a cairn called ' Cairngreg ', on the estate of Linlathen [Forfarshire]. [Pagan interment : pre-6th c.?] Proc. Soc. Antiq. Scot., 6, pp. 98–103. 1868.

8543 —— Notices of two ancient graves recently opened in the vicinity of Dunrobin castle, Sutherlandshire. [? Scandinavian cist.] *Same jnl.*, 1, pp. 297–99. 1852.

8544 Taylor (George). Early Christian graves at Hoprig, [Cockburnspath, Berwickshire.]. Hist. Berwick. Nat. Club, 25, pp. 440–42, + 1 plate. 1925.

8545 Wakeman (William Frederick). Irish antiquities of the Saxon period. [Dunshaughlin, Lagore, etc.] Collectanea Antiqua, 3, pp. 37–44, 43 plates. [c. 1854].

8546 Williams (John) *ab Ithel.* British interments. [Inhumation *v.* cremation, etc.] Arch. Camb., N.S. 3, pp. 81–92. 1852.

136. BOWLS AND OTHER VESSELS

(Pottery, Metal and Glass)

8547 [Anon.] Post-Roman pottery from Worth and Deal [Kent]. [Teutonic, but pre-Jutish.] Antiq. J., 17, pp. 312–13, + 1 plate. 1937.

8548 Addy (John). Discovery of a Roman villa at Beddington, Surrey . . . together with cinerary urns of the Anglo-Saxon period from a cemetery on the same site. [Also penny of Athelstan : Eadmund, moneyer.] Proc. Soc. Antiq., 2nd S. 5, pp. 149–55. 1871.

8549 Allen (John Romilly). Metal bowls of the late-Celtic and Anglo-Saxon periods. [7 figures in text.] Archaeologia, 56, pp, 39–56. 1898.

8550 Andrew (Walter Jonathan). The Winchester Anglo-Saxon bowl. [4 figures in text.] Antiq. J., 11, pp. 1–13, 160. 1931.

8551 —— The Winchester Anglo-Saxon bowl, and bowl-burial. [Gilded, with base silver escutcheons and enamel disks. Excavated at Oliver's Battery. Pagan, probably c. 550.] Papers and Proc. Hants. F.C., 12, pp. 11–19, + plate. 1932.

8552 Armstrong (Edmund Clarence Richard). Stone chalices, so called. [Probably lamps, used by the early Irish Church.] Proc. R.I..A, 26c, pp. 318–26 + 1 plate. 1907.

8553 Auden (George Augustus) *photographer.* The Great Ormside bowl. [Anglian : ? c. 670.] Reliquary, N. [3rd] S. 13, pp. 200–04. 1907.

8554 Baker (Robert Sibley) and **Franks** (*Sir* Augustus Wollaston). 'Find' of bronze vessels in the parish of Irchester, Northamptonshire. [?A.–S. rather than Roman.] Proc. Soc. Antiq., 2nd S. 6, pp. 475–76. 1876.

8555 Barker (Horace R.). Anglo-Saxon urns found near Lackford. Proc. Suffolk Inst. Archaeol., 16, pp. 181–82, + 1 plate. 1917.

8556 Baynes (Edward Neil). Notes on two small urns and a glass beaker and bowl of Saxon date, found at Buttsole, Eastry, Kent. [4 figures in text.] Proc. Soc. Antiq., 2nd S. 22, pp. 363–67. 1909.

8557 Beloe (Edward Milligen). [Exhibition of] a quern of late Roman or Saxon date, still retaining its iron handle. [Figure in text.] *Same jnl.*, 2nd S. 14, p. 183. 1892.

8558 Bromehead (Cyril Edward Nowill). On an Anglian glass vessel in the Yorkshire Museum. Ann. Rept. Yorks. Philos. Soc., 1927, pp. 7–10. 1928.

8559 Bruce-Mitford (Rupert Leo Scott). The Castle Eden vase. [Glass. 6th c.] B.M.Q., 15, p. 73, + plate 34 (a). 1952.

8560 —— and Jope (Edward Martyn). Eleventh and twelfth century pottery from the Oxford region. [Illustrated.] Oxoniensia, 5, pp. 42–49. 1940.

8561 Burchell (J. P. T.) and **Brailsford** (J. W.). Pottery from Northfleet, Kent. [? Invasion period, mid 5th c. 2 figures in text.] Antiq. J., 28, pp. 186–89. 1948.

8562 Carr (Ralph). Note on a bronze patella, having an Anglo-Saxon inscription on the handle, found at Friar's Carse, Dumfriesshire. [Ansiepharr : = head-cook.] Proc. Soc. Antiq. Scot., 9, pp. 567–68. 1873.

8563 Clarke (Roy Rainbird). Romano-Saxon pottery in East Anglia. Archaeol. J., 106 (1949), pp. 69–71. 1951.

8564 Cowen (John David). The Capheaton [Nrhb.] bowl. [A.–S. 'hanging bowl'.] Archaeol. Æl., 4th S. 8, pp. 328–38, + 2 plates. 1931.

8565 Curwen (Eliot and Eliot Cecil). A Saxon hut-site at Thakeham, Sussex. [Pottery, etc.] Antiq. J., 14, pp. 425–26. 1934.

8566 Dalton (Ormonde Maddock). On a silver bowl and cover of the ninth or tenth century. [B.M., Franks collection. N.W. Europe, ?A.–S. Vine-motive, with comparisons.] Archaeologia, 61, pp. 357–60, + 1 plate. 1909.

8567 Davies (Ellis W.). An early bronze hanging-bowl, found at Cerrig-y-Druidion [Denbigh]. [Ancestor of A.–S. hanging-bowls ; with remarks on the latter.] Arch. Camb., 81 (7th S. 6), pp. 335–39, + 1 plate. 1926.

8567a Dunning (Gerald Clough). Dating medieval pottery. [Late Saxon period.] Archaeol. News Letter, 1. x, pp. 1–3. 1949.

8568 —— A note on the late Saxon pot containing the [Chester] hoard [of 1950]. [*See also* **9137**.] Antiq. J., 33, pp. 31–32. 1953.

8569 Dyke (*Sir* Percyvall Hart) *bt.* [Exhibition of] a bronze bowl with its ornaments and some other objects, found at Lullingstone, Kent. Proc. Soc. Antiq., 2nd S. 1, pp. 187–88. 1860.

8570 Fox (*Sir* Cyril). A settlement of the early iron age at Abington Pigotts, Cambs., and its subsequent history ; as evidenced by objects preserved in the Pigott collection. [Pp. 227–31, the settlement in the Anglo-Saxon and mediaeval periods. Pottery.] Proc. Prehist. Soc. E. Anglia, 4, pp. 211–33. 1924.

8571 Franks (*Sir* Augustus Wollaston). [Exhibition of] a bronze bowl, probably of Anglo-Saxon workmanship. [Found in the Thames.] Proc. Soc. Antiq., 2nd S. 3, p. 45. 1865.

8572 Garrood (Jesse Robert). Late Saxon and early mediaeval pottery in Huntingdonshire. [One full page of diagrams in text.] Trans. Cambs. and Hunts. Archaeol. Soc., 6, pp. 107–10, + 1 plate. 1941.

8573 Green (Charles). An Anglian cinerary urn from Hibaldstow, Kirton-in-Lindsey [Lincs.]. Trans. East Riding Antiq. Soc., 27, pp. 174–77. 1932.

8573a Harden (Donald Benjamin). Glass vessels in Anglo-Saxon Britain. [Imported, and therefore predominantly S.E. distribution. Distribution map, 12 figures of types.] Archaeol. News Letter, 3, pp. 21–27. 1950.

8574 —— Saxon glass from Sussex. [List of A.–S. glasses from Sussex cemeteries (High Down and Alfriston). 10 figures in text.] Sussex County Mag., 25, pp. 260–68. 1951.

8575 Henry (Françoise). Hanging bowls. [Discusses their use, technique, and enamelled decoration, deriving the type from Ireland, and describes surviving examples.] J. Roy. Soc. Antiq. Ireland, 66 (7th S. 6), pp. 209–46, + 20 plates : 67, pp. 130–31, + 1 plate. 1936–37.

8576 Hope-Taylor (Brian). Saxon pot from Thursley. Surrey Archaeol. Collns., 51, pp. 152–53, + 1 plate. 1950.

8577 Jope (Edward Martyn). Medieval and Saxon finds from Felmersham, Bedfordshire. [Pottery, etc.] Antiq. J., 31, pp. 45–50. 1951.

8578 —— Mediaeval pottery in Berkshire. [Including late Saxon.] Berks. Archaeol. J., 50, pp. 49–76. 1947.

8579 Kendrick (*Sir* Thomas Downing). Escutcheon of a pagan Saxon hanging-bowl from Willoughton, Lincs. Antiq. J., 25, p. 149, + 1 plate. 1945.

8580 —— A late Saxon hanging-bowl. [Found in the Witham near Lincoln.] Antiq. J., 21, pp. 161–62, + 2 plates. 1941.

8581 —— A new escutcheon from a hanging-bowl. [From Benniworth, Lincs. ?c. 600.] Antiq. J., 16, pp. 98–99. 1936.

8582 —— The Scunthorpe [Lincs., hanging] bowl. Antiq. J., 41, pp. 236–38, + 2 plates. 1941.

8583 Kilbride-Jones (Howard Edward). A bronze hanging-bowl from Castle Tioram, Moidart [Inverness-shire] and a suggested absolute chronology for British hanging-bowls. [Group i, Romano-British : group ii, Celtic : group iii, Kentish. 13 figures in text.] Proc. Soc. Antiq. Scot., 71 (6th S. 11, 1936–37), pp. 206–47. 1937.

8584 Leeds (Edward Thurlow). An enamelled bowl from Baginton, Warwickshire. [Plates show brooches as well as the bowl.] Antiq. J., 15, pp. 109–12, + 3 plates. 1935.

8585 Lethbridge (Thomas Charles) and **Tebbutt** (C. F.). Ancient lime-kilns at Great Paxton, Hunts., their relation to the Anglo-Saxon church at Great Paxton, and a tentative scheme for dating pottery of the late Saxon period. [Illustrated.] Proc. Camb. Antiq. Soc., 35, pp. 97–105, + 1 plate. 1935.

8585a —— and **Dunning** (Gerald Clough). Anglo-Saxon glazed pottery. [Letters.] Archaeol. News Letter, 2, pp. 26, 42. 1949.

8586 Lethbridge (Thomas Charles). Bronze bowl of the Dark Ages from Hildersham, Cambridgeshire. [Hanging bowl, c. 650.] Proc. Camb. Antiq. Soc., 45 (1951), pp. 44–47, + 4 plates. 1952.

8587 —— Byzantine influence in late Saxon England. [Comparison between late Saxon and Byzantine glazed works.] *Same jnl.*, 43 (1949), pp. 2–6, + 2 plates. 1950.

8588 Lowther (Anthony William George). Saxon pottery from Walton-on-Thames, Wotton, and Farnham, Surrey. [3 figures on p. 324.] Antiq. J., 19, pp. 323–25. 1939.

8589 Myres (John Nowell Linton). The Anglo-Saxon pottery from Elkington, [Lincs.]. Archaeol J., 108, pp. 60–64. 1952.

8590 —— The Anglo-Saxon pottery of Lincolnshire. [12 figures and map in text. 26 sites.] Archaeol. J., 108, pp. 65–99, + 1 plate. 1952.

8591 —— The Anglo-Saxon pottery of Norfolk. Norfolk Archaeology, 27, pp. 185–249, + 12 plates. 1941.

8592 —— Anglo-Saxon urns from North Elmham, Norfolk : some corrected attributions. [Trollope collection.] Antiq. J., 27, pp. 47–50, + 1 plate. 1947.

8593 —— The Saxon pottery from Theale [Berks.]. Trans. Newbury District F.C., 8, pp. 60–62. 1938.

8594 Myres (John Nowell Linton). Some Anglo-Saxon potters. Antiquity, 11, pp. 389–99, + 4 plates. 1937.

8595 ——Some English parallels to the Anglo-Saxon pottery of Holland and Belgium in the migration period. ['These objects form a valuable body of evidence for the course and character of the Anglo-Saxon invasion of Britain.' 6 full pages of figures in text.] Antiquité classique, 17, pp. 453–72. 1948.

8595a —— South Elkington [Lincs.], Anglican cemetery. [Notes on the pottery.] Archaeol. News Letter, 2, p. 189. 1950.

8596 —— Three styles of decoration on Anglo-Saxon pottery. Antiq. J., 17, pp. 424–37, + 4 plates. 1937.

8597 —— Wingham villa and Romano-Saxon pottery in Kent. [With 4 figures.] Antiquity, 18, pp. 52–55. 1944.

8598 Oswald (Adrian). Saxon pottery from Sutton Bonington, Notts. Antiq. J, 27, pp. 85–86. 1947.

8599 Pickering (A. J.). A hanging-bowl from [Stoke Golding,] Leicestershire. Antiq. J., 12, pp. 174–75. 1932.

8600 Power (Patrick). On four (or five) ' stone chalices ' from early church sites in the Decies. J. Waterford Archaeol. Soc., 9, pp. 143–49, + 1 plate. 1906.

8601 Read (*Sir* Charles Hercules). A bronze vessel and a glass tumbler of the Saxon period from Wheathampstead, Herts. Proc. Soc. Antiq., 2nd S. 18, pp. 110–14. 1900.

8602 Rudkin (*Mrs.* E. H.). A hanging-bowl from [Willoughton,] Lincolnshire. Antiq. J., 12, pp. 452–53. 1932.

8603 St. Croix (William de). On a vessel found near Glynde. [? early A.-S.] Sussex Archaeol. Collns., 23, pp. 82–84, + 1 plate. 1871.

8604 Sheppard (Thomas). Anglo-Saxon remains at Newark. [Two cinerary urns.] Antiquary, 40, pp. 150–51. 1904.

8605 Sheppard (Thomas). Some Anglo-Saxon vases in the Hull Museum. [From Sancton Anglian cemetery. = Hull Museum Publications, 66–67.] Trans. E. Riding Antiq. Soc., 16, pp. 50–70, + 14 plates. 1909.

8606 Smith (Arthur). Saxon cup with glass insertion. [Found near Stamford : now in Lincoln Museum.] Lincs. N. and Q., 11, p. 101, + plate. 1911.

8607 Smith (Charles Roach). Inscribed funereal urn in the museum of Joseph Mayer, Esq. [From Fausett collection. ?from North Elmham, Norfolk.] Collectanea Antiqua, 5, pp. 115–21, + 1 plate. 1861.

8608 —— Remarkable Saxon urn, discovered at Kempston, Beds. *Same jnl.*, 4, pp. 159–61. 1857.

8609 Smith (Reginald Allender). Enamelled mount of a hanging bowl of Saxon date, found at Mildenhall, Suffolk. [5 figures in text.] Proc. Soc. Antiq., 2nd S. 22, pp. 75–77. 1908.

8610 —— From a Saxon weaver's hut. [Tools and pottery from Bourton-on-the-Water, Glos.] B.M.Q., 7, pp. 138–39, + plate 42. 1933.

8611 —— Glass of Anglo-Saxon date. [From A.-S. cemetery at Newport Pagnell, Bucks.] B.M.Q., 11, p. 168, + plate 49. 1937.

8612 —— The Winchester bowl. [Bronze hanging bowl, dug up in Aug. 1930, at Oliver's Battery, 1¾ miles, S.W. of Winchester.] B.M.Q., 5, pp., 104–06, + plate 50. 1931.

8613 Stevens (Courtenay Edward). The hanging bowl in Irish literature, [c. 600 A.D.]. Antiquity, 8, pp. 93–94. 1934.

8614 Stevens (Frank). The Wilton hanging bowl. [?5th c.] Wilts. Archaeol. Mag., 46, pp. 441–44, + plate. 1934.

8615 Webster (Graham). An Anglo-Saxon urnfield at South Elkington, Louth, Lincolnshire. [18 figures (of pottery) in text.] Archaeol. J., 108, pp. 25–59, + plan. 1952.

8616 Whiting (W.). On some Jutish pottery found in Kent. Arch. Cant., 39, pp. 35–36 + plate. 1927.

8617 Wilson (Arthur Ernest). Late Saxon and early medieval pottery from selected sites in Chichester. (Description ... by G. C. Dunning and A. E. Wilson). Sussex Archaeol. Collns., 91, pp. 140–50, + 13 plates. 1953.

8618 Winbolt (Samuel Edward). The Surrey-Sussex glass industry. Sussex County Mag., 5, pp. 286–91. 1931.

8619 Woodward (Bolingbroke Bernard). An Anglo-Saxon urn [from Evesham, Norfolk, near Bungay]. Proc. Soc. Antiq., 2nd S. 1, p. 29. 1859.

8620 Wright (Thomas). Fragments of Roman and Saxon pottery, recently found in the neighbourhood of Folkestone. *Same jnl.*, 2, pp. 175–76. 1851.

137. IMPLEMENTS AND UTENSILS, DOMESTIC

8621 [Anon.] Irish bucket from Sweden. [Early 10th c., evidently looted by Vikings.] Antiq. J., 5, pp. 167–68. 1925.

8622 [Anon.] Three late Saxon and mediaeval sharpening-stones from Longworth, Sunningwell and Wallingford. Berks. Archaeol. J., 51, pp. 68–70. 1949.

8623 Anderson (Joseph). Notes on the evidence of spinning and weaving in the brochs or Pictish towers supplied by the stone whorls and the long-handled ' broch combs ' found in them. [12 figures in text.] Proc. Soc. Antiq. Scot., 9, pp. 548–61. 1873.

8624 Auden (George Augustus). Recent finds in York. [Axe-head, horse's bit, etc., of Danish period.] Saga-Book V.C., 5, pp. 53–55. 1907.

8625 Becker (C. J.). An Irish bronze cauldron found in Jutland. [5 figures in text.] Acta Archaeologica, 20, pp. 265–70. 1949.

8626 Buckman (James). On Saxon situlae, or buckets. Proc. Dorset Antiq. F.C., 4, pp. 98–101, + 1 plate. 1882.

8627 —— Saxon situla found at Fairford, Gloucestershire. [Bucket ' intended to hold food and not drink '.] Archaeol. J., 25, pp. 137–38, + 1 plate. 1868.

8628 Buick (George Raphael). Bronze bridle-bit found recently near Portglenone, co. Antrim. [With comparisons. 6 figures in text.] Ulster J. Archaeol., 2nd S. 9, pp. 145–51. 1903.

8629 Charlton (Edward). Implements of the Saxon period, found near Lanchester [co. Durham]. Archaeol. Æl., N.S. 5, pp. 159–61. 1861.

8630 Coughtrey (Millen). Notes on materials found in a kitchen midden at Hillswick, Shetland, with special reference to long-handled combs. Proc. Soc. Antiq. Scot., 9, pp. 118–51, + 6 plates. 1873.

8631 Cox (John Charles). A Saxon or Danish comb found in Fish Street, Northampton. Proc. Soc. Antiq., 2nd S. 17, pp. 165, 167 (for figure). 1898.

8632 Davis (*Sir* Edmund). Loom-weights from Chilham castle, [Kent]. Antiq. J., 16, pp. 467–68. 1936.

8633 Dickins (Bruce). Old Norse ' trog '. [=trencher, from Shetland glossaries.] Proc. Orkney Antiq. Soc., 10 (1931–32), p. 31. 1932.

8634 Elger (Thomas Gwyn Empty). Anglo-Saxon combs found at Bedford. Proc. Soc. Antiq., 2nd S. 12, pp. 115–16. 1888.

8635 Fox (*Sir* Cyril). A jug of the Anglo-Saxon period. Antiq. J., 4, pp. 371–73. 1924.

8636 Grove (L. R. A.). An Anglo-Saxon loom-weight from York castle. Yorks. Archaeol. J., 34, pp. 112–13. 1939.

8637 Head (John Frederick). An Anglo-Saxon strap-end from Bledlow, Bucks. Antiq. J., 22, p. 221. 1942.

8638 Hencken (Hugh O'Neill). Ballinderry crannog no. 1 [co. Westmeath]. [Site occupied from close of Viking age to 17th c. Discusses wooden gaming-board of Celto-Norse workmanship made in Man in 10th c. (plate 25), and bronze lamp with decoration of six-petalled rosettes, Irish, c. 1000.] Proc. R.I.A., 43c, pp. 103–239, + 13 plates. 1936.

8639 Kendrick (*Sir* Thomas Downing). An Anglo-Saxon cruet. [Franks collection, B.M.] Antiq. J., 18, pp. 377–81, + 4 plates. 1938.

8640 —— Bone pins found with the Cuerdale treasure. [10th c.] Antiq. J., 21, pp. 162–63. 1941.

8641 —— Gourd bottles from Sutton Hoo. Antiq. J., 21, pp. 73–74. 1941.

8642 —— Portion of a basalt hone from North Wales. Antiq. J., 21, p. 73, + 1 plate. 1941.

8643 Leeds (Edward Thurlow). A Saxon village near Sutton Courtenay, Berkshire. (—second report, third report). [Saxon houses, pottery, rings, implements, etc., of later part of 5th c.] Archaeologia, 73, pp. 147–92, + 8 plates : 76, pp. 59–80, + 4 plates : 92, pp. 79–93, + 3 plates. 1923, 1927, 1947.

8644 Lethbridge (Thomas Charles). An Anglo-Saxon hut on the Car dyke, at Waterbeach [Cambs.]. [The building and its contents. Pagan period.] Antiq. J., 7, pp. 141–46. 1927.

8645 Lower (Mark Antony). On an ancient leaden coffer found at Willingdon. [c. 10th c. ?use.] Sussex Archaeol. Collns., 1, p. 160. 1848.

8646 McCall (Hardy Bertram). Anglian comb from Whitby. [8th c.] Yorks. Archaeol. J., 29, p. 350, + 1 plate. 1929.

8647 Megaw (Basil R. S.). The balance-beam from Ronaldsway, Isle of Man. Antiq. J., 20, pp. 382–85. 1940.

8648 Munro (Robert). Notes on ancient bone skates. [Fig. 2, skate and runner, found at Arches, and Stixwold ferry, Lincoln. Pre-12th c.] Proc. Soc. Antiq. Scot., 28 (3rd S. 4), pp. 185–97. 1894.

8649 Murray (R. W.). An inquiry regarding the date of some old English horse-shoes. [Pp. 20–24, 32 (plate), Saxon period.] J. Brit. Archaeol. Assoc., 3rd S. 1, pp. 14–33. 1937.

8650 Oswald (Adrian). A bronze Viking drinking-horn mount from Fetter Lane, London. Antiq. J., 28, p. 179, + 1 plate. 1948.

8651 Power (Patrick). A decorated quern-stone, and its symbolism. [Cf. Stowe missal.] Proc. R.I.A., 45c, pp. 25–30, + 1 plate. 1939.

8652 Price (Frederick George Hilton). A Viking horse-bit . . . found [at the back of St. Ann and St. Zachary's church] in London. [Figures in text.] Proc. Soc. Antiq., 2nd S. 21, pp. 401–02. 1907.

8653 Radford (Courtenay Arthur Ralegh). Small bronzes from St. Augustine's abbey, Canterbury. [Pins, etc.] Antiq. J., 20, pp. 506–08. 1940.

8654 Scarth (Harry Mengden). Notes on a pair of Celtic spoons found near Weston, Bath, in 1866. [? late 5th c. 4 figures in text.] Proc. Bath F.C., 2, pp. 112–16. 1870.

8655 Skinner (F. G.) and **Bruce-Mitford** (Rupert Leo Scott). A Celtic balance-beam of the Christian period. [From Ronaldsway, I.O.M.] Antiq. J., 20, pp. 87–102, + 1 plate. 1940.

8656 Sutcliffe (Frank M.). Bronze comb from Whitby. Antiq. J., 9, pp. 158–59. 1929.

8657 Traill (William). Collections from the broch or Pictish tower of Burrian, North Ronaldsay, Orkney. Proc. Soc. Antiq. Scot., 10, pp. 5–23. 1874.

8658 Ward (Gordon). The iron age horsehoe and its derivatives. [Pp. 17–19, Saxon, of 'Winchester type'.] Antiq. J., 21, pp. 9–27. 1941.

8659 White (G. M.). A settlement of the South Saxons. [At Medmerry farm, Selsey, Sussex. Pottery, querns, loom-weights, etc.] Antiq. J., 14, pp. 393–400, + 1 plate. 1934.

8660 Wood-Martin (William Gregory). Bronze serpentine latchets, and other cumbrous dress fasteners. [20 figures in text.] Ulster J. Archaeol., 2nd S. 9, pp. 160–66 ; 10, pp. 12–20 ; 11, pp. 33–39. 1903–05.

138. TRAPS

8661 Allingham (Hugh). Wooden objects found in peat bogs, supposed to have been otter traps. J. Roy. Soc. Antiq. Ireland, 26 (5th S. 6.), pp. 379–82. 1896.

8662 **Buick** (George Raphael). Notice of an ancient wooden trap, probably used for catching otters. [Found at Clontrace, co. Antrim.] *Same jnl.*, 21 (5th S. 1. ii), pp. 536–41, + 1 plate. 1891.

8663 **Graham-Smith** (G. S.). On the method employed in using the so-called 'otter or beaver traps'. [6 figures in text.] Proc. Soc. Antiq. Scot., 57 (5th S. 9, 1922–23), pp. 48–54. 1923.

8664 **Kinahan** (George Henry). Ancient otter traps. J. Roy. Soc. Antiq. Ireland, 27 (5th S. 7), pp. 184–85. 1897.

8665 **Munro** (Robert) and **Gillespie** (Patric). Further notes [to a book] on ancient wooden traps—the so-called otter and beaver traps. (Note on the sculptured figure of a stag on a cross-shaft at Clonmacnois, Ireland, in relation to the ancient wooden objects known as otter or beaver traps). [4 figures in text : sculpture at Clonmacnois, 8th–9th c.] Proc. Soc. Antiq. Scot., 53 (5th S. 5, 1918–19), pp. 162–67. 1919.

8666 —— Notice of some curiously constructed wooden objects found in peat bogs in various parts of Europe, supposed to have been otter and beaver traps. *Same jnl.*, 25 (3rd S. 1), pp. 73–89. 1891.

8667 —— Some further notes on otter and beaver-traps. J. Roy. Soc. Antiq. Ireland, 28 (5th S. 8), pp. 245–49. 1898.

8668 **Reid** (R. W.). Ancient wooden trap from the moss of Auquharney, Aberdeenshire. [Figures in text.] Proc. Soc. Antiq. Scot., 56 (5th S. 8), pp. 282–87. 1922.

8669 **Wheeler** (*Sir* Robert Eric Mortimer). An ancient trap from [Caio in] Carmarthenshire. [4 figures in text. List of 38 known examples.] Arch. Camb., 79 (7th S. 4), pp. 198–202. 1924.

139. WEAPONS AND ARMOUR

§ *a*. Anglo-Saxon, Etc.

8670 [Anon.] A Saxon spear head, Eastbourne. Sussex N. and Q., 2, p. 193, + 1 plate. 1929.

8671 **Akerman** (John Yonge). On some of the weapons of the Celtic and Teutonic races. Archaeologia, 34, pp. 171–89. 1852.

8672 —— Part of an Anglo-Saxon sword . . . found in June 1831 . . . at Reading. [Whole page figure in text.] Proc. Soc. Antiq., 2nd S. 3, pp. 461–63. 1867.

8673 —— Weapons of the Celtic and Teutonic races. *Same jnl.*, 2, pp. 168–70. 1851.

8674 **Austin** (Roland). Saxon headpiece, Leckhampton. Trans. Bristol and Glos. Arch. Soc., 59, pp. 324–26. 1937.

8675 **Beck** (James). An Anglo-Saxon sword-knife, or *scramura-seax* [from] Little Bealings, Suffolk. Proc. Soc. Antiq., 2nd S. 10, pp. 17–18. 1883.

8676 **Carpenter** (L. W.). Saxon spearhead from Cheam. Surrey Archaeol. Collns., 51, pp. 151–52. 1950.

8677 **Clutterbuck** (James C.). Anglo-Saxon spear-head of iron . . . found in the parish of Dorchester (Oxon.). Proc. Soc. Antiq., 2nd S. 2, p. 209. 1863.

8678 **Cowen** (John David). Two spearheads of the middle Saxon period from Ferrybridge. Yorks. Archaeol. J., 33, pp. 196–98, + 1 plate. 1938.

8679 **Cuming** (Henry Syer). On some Anglo-Saxon arms found in the Thames. J. Brit. Archaeol. Assoc., 13, pp. 302–06, + 1 plate. 1857.

8680 **Cutts** (Edward Lewes). Scenes and characters of the Middle Ages. pp. xiii, 546. 8° London, 1872. [Pp. 311–25, A.-S. arms and armour.]

8681 **Ely** (Talfourd). The shield as a weapon of offence. [Pp. 304–06, on A.-S. shields.] Proc. Soc. Antiq., 2nd S. 14, pp. 297–307. 1893.

8682 **Evans** (*Sir* John). Note on an Anglo-Saxon knife, found [at Sittingbourne] in Kent, bearing an inscription. [?9th c. Bearing names of owner and maker.] Archaeologia, 44, pp. 331–34, + 1 plate. 1873.

8683 Fox *afterwards* **Pitt-Rivers** (Augustus Henry Lane). An iron sword . . . from the bed of the Thames near Battersea. Proc. Soc. Antiq., 2nd S. 4, p. 143, + 1 plate. 1868.

8684 Hallam (W. H.). Saxon remains in Berkshire. [Spear-head and knife from Stockholm farm between Woolstone and Uffington.] Berks. Archaeol. J., 37, p. 78. 1933.

8685 Hawkes (Charles Francis Christopher). A Saxon spear-head and scramasax from the disputed long barrow at Preston Candover, Hants. Antiq. J., 20, pp. 279–80. 1940.

8686 Henniker (John Major (Henniker-Major)) *5th baron*. [Exhibition of] an Anglo-Saxon knife or ' scramasax ' found at Hoxne, in Suffolk. Proc. Soc. Antiq., 2nd S. 8, p. 80. 1879.

8687 Herben (Stephen J.) *jr.* A note on the helm in Beowulf. [A.-S. *freā-wrāsen.*] Mod. Lang. Notes, 52, pp. 34–36. 1937.

8688 Hewitt (John). Mediaeval arms and armour. [Plates show A.–S. warriors from MSS. Cotton Tib. C. VI and Cotton Claudius B. IV, also A.–S. weapons and armour.] Reliquary, 10, pp. 13–15, 113–15, 161–63, + 5 plates. 1869–70.

8689 Higgs (Frederick). A Saxon spear. [Dug up in 1926 at Cobham, Surrey.] Surrey Archaeol. Collns., 37, p. 93. 1926.

8690 Keller (May Lansfield). The Anglo-Saxon weapon names treated archaeologically and etymologically. *Anglistische Forschungen*, 15. pp. vii, 275. 8° Heidelberg, 1906.

8691 Leeds (Edward Thurlow). The Wallingford sword. [Now in Ashmolean. ?2nd half of 9th c.] Antiquary, 46, pp. 348–49. 1910.

8692 Maryon (Herbert). The Sutton Hoo helmet. Antiquity, 21, pp. 137–44, + 4 plates. 1947.

8693 —— The Sutton Hoo shield. [Plan of burial chambers on p. 22.] Antiquity, 20, pp. 21–30, + 8 plates. 1946.

8694 Maryon (Herbert). A sword of the Nydam type from Ely Fields farm, near Ely. [On iron swords and their construction.] Proc. Camb. Antiq. Soc., 41, pp. 73–76, + plates, 18, 21, 22. 1948.

8695 O'Neil (B. H. St. J.). Excavations at Titterstone Clee hill camp, Shropshire, 1932. [Early Iron Age : but p. 32 and figure 2, Saxon spear-head.] Antiq. J., 14, pp. 13–32, + 5 plates, + 3 plans. 1934.

8696 Page (Samuel). Antiquarian discovery at Aslockton, Notts. [5th–6th c. sword. *See also* pp. 121–22.] Notts. and Derbs. N. and Q., 1, pp. 107–08. 1923.

8697 Payne (George). Anglo-Saxon antiquities found . . . near Grove Ferry, in the parish of Wickham, Kent, including a sword pommel and two iron umbos of shields. Proc. Soc. Antiq., 2nd S. 15, p. 178. 1894.

8698 Rice (Robert Garraway). Find of Anglo-Saxon antiquities at Lewes, [Sussex]. [Iron axe and sword blade.] *Same jnl.*, 2nd S. 18, p. 29. 1900.

8699 Romans (Thomas). An early spear-head from Pittington, [co. Durham]. [?A.–S.] Trans. Archit. Soc. Durham, 9, pp. 139–42. 1941.

8700 Sheppard (Thomas). Early German relics in Lincs. [Plate shows A.–S. sword and spears found at Horncastle.] Lincs. N. and Q., 15, pp. 97–98, + 1 plate. 1919.

8701 Smith (H. P.). The 6th century helmet unearthed at Hamworthy in the summer of 1923. Proc. Dorset Archaeol. Soc., 54 (for 1932), pp. 1–4, + 2 plates (one in colour). 1933.

8702 Smith (John Alexander). Notes of small ornamented stone balls found in different parts of Scotland, etc., with remarks on their supposed age and use. (Additional notes . . .). [? of 9th–10th c. ? used as mace-heads.] Proc. Soc. Antiq. Scot., 11, pp. 29–62. + 2 plates : pp. 313–19. 1876.

8703 Smith (Reginald Allender). Anglo-Saxon sword with stamps. [c. 700 A.D. From the Thames at Syon reach.] B.M.Q., 4, p. 109, + plate 61. 1929.

8704 Spain (George R. B.). Anglo-Saxon spear head. [Found at Burradon in Coquetdale, Nhd. : now in Blackgate museum, Newcastle.] Proc. Soc. Antiq. Newcastle, 4th S. 1, pp. 78–79. 1923.

8705 Vulliamy (Colwyn Edward). Discovery of a Saxon sword in Wales. Man, 31, pp. 86–87. 1931.

8706 Walker (Warren S.). The brūn-ecg sword. [Beowulf, lines 1546, 2577–78, etc. Table of temperatures, and colours, required when sword must be 'drawn'.] Mod. Lang. Notes, 67, pp. 516–20. 1952.

8707 Watson (Christopher Knight). [Exhibition of] three Anglo-Saxon weapons [from] Little Hampton [Glos., near Evesham]. Proc. Soc. Antiq., 2nd S. 2, pp. 163–64. 1862.

8708 Williams (John) *ab Ithel*. On the gold corselet found near Mold, Flintshire. Arch. Camb., 3, pp. 98–104. 1848.

8709 Wilson (Daniel). An iron dagger and knife found on the farm of East Langton, Mid-Lothian. Proc. Soc. Antiq. Scot., 1, pp. 73–74. 1852.

8710 Wright (Thomas). Three early Saxon weapons, found with a skeleton . . . near [Lowesby Hall, Leicestershire]. [Sword, spear-head and iron arrow-head.] Proc. Soc. Antiq., 2, p. 255. 1852.

8711 Young (Hugh W.). Stone ball with projecting knobs . . . found at Lumphanan, Aberdeenshire. [3 figures in text. Similar to mace-heads in the Bayeux tapestry.] *Same jnl.*, 2nd S. 16, pp. 407–09. 1897.

§ *b*. Viking

8712 [Anon.] An account of some ancient arms and utensils found in Lincolnshire, chiefly in the bed of the river Witham, between Kirksted and Lincoln, when it was scoured out in 1787 and 1788. [Danish, etc.] Lincs. N. and Q., 3, pp. 196–201, 232–36 : 4, pp. 20–21, 61–62, 124–27, 184–85, 238–41. 1893–96.

8713 Acland (John E.). Sword of the Viking period. [From bed of the Frome at Wareham.] Antiq. J., 8, pp. 361–62, + 1 plate. 1928.

E e

8714 Bolton (William Thomas (Orde Powlett)) *4th baron*. A sword of the Viking period . . . found in Wensley churchyard, [Yorks.]. [Figures in text.] Proc. Soc. Antiq., 2nd S. 28, pp. 229–30. 1916.

8715 Brett (*Hon*. Maurice). Viking axe from the Thames. [Kew]. Antiq. J., 7, p. 320. 1927.

8716 Chatwin (Philip Boughton). Viking axe found at Studley, [Warw.]. Trans. B'ham. Arch. Soc., 68 (1949–50), p. 126, + 1 plate, 1952.

8717 Collingwood (William Gershom). The Workington sword. Saga-Book V.C., 3, pp. 302–03. 1904.

8718 Collins (A. E. P.). Some Viking-period weapons from the Thames. Berks. Archaeol. J., 51, pp. 17–19. 1949.

8719 Cowen (John David). A rare iron axe-head. [?Viking, 11th c. Found at Bawtry, Notts.] Arch. Æl., 4th S. 26, pp. 146–49, + 1 plate. 1948.

8720 —— A spear-head from Festiniog, North Wales. [Probably Viking, c. 10th c.] Arch. Æl., 4th s. 26, pp. 144–46, + 1 plate. 1948.

8721 —— A Viking sword from Eaglesfield, near Cockermouth, [Cumb.]. Arch. Æl., 4th S. 26, pp. 55–61, + 1 plate. 1948.

8722 Curle (Alexander Ormiston). Notices of the discovery of a hoard of rapier-shaped blades of bronze at Drumcoltran, in the stewartry of Kirkcudbright, and of a Viking sword at Torbeckhill, near Ecclefechan. Proc. Soc. Antiq. Scot., 48 (4th S. 12, 1913–14), pp. 333–35. 1914.

8723 Day (Robert). Flint spear-head of Danish origin, found at Scarriff [co. Clare]. J. Roy. Soc. Antiq. Ireland, 25 (5th S. 5), p. 176, + full page illustn. 1895.

8724 Evans (*Sir* John). Notes on a Danish sword-hilt found near Wallingford [Berks.]. Archaeologia, 50, pp. 534–36, + 1 plate. 1887.

8725 Gaythorpe (Harper). Notes on the Rampside sword. [Low Furness.] Year-Book Viking Club, 1, pp. 57–61. 1909.

8726 Grove (L. R. A.). Five Viking-period swords. [5 figures in text.] Antiq. J., 18, pp. 251–57. 1938.

8727 Lenihan (M.). Weapon of war, probably Danish . . . recently found in Scattery island, [co. Clare]. J. Roy. Hist. and Arch. Assoc. Ireland, [13] 4th S. 3 (1874–75), p. 182. 1876.

8728 McCall (Hardy Bertram). Viking axe-head found near Harrogate. Yorks. Archaeol. J., 29, pp. 133–34. 1929.

8729 MacDermott (Máire) and **May** (A. McL.). A sword-handle of the Viking period from the Bann. J. Roy. Soc. Antiq. Ireland, 82, pp. 151–52, + 1 plate. 1952.

8730 Macintosh ( ) Rev. [Exhibition of] bronze hilt and fragments of the blade of a double-edged sword of the Viking period . . . dug up in the island of Eriskay [Inverness]. [Figure in text.] Proc. Soc. Antiq. Scot., 40 (4th S. 4, 1905–06), pp. 215–16. 1906.

8731 Macpherson (Norman). Notes on antiquities from the island of Eigg, [Inverness]. [Plate shows richly ornamented sword-hilt of the Viking time.] Same jnl., 12, pp. 577–97, + 1 plate. 1878.

8732 Maryon (Herbert). A sword of the Viking period from the river Witham. Antiq. J., 30, pp. 175–79, + 2 plates. 1950.

8733 Megaw (Basil R. S.). Weapons of the Viking age found in Man. [Mostly of 10th c. : none earlier than 800.] J. Manx Mus., 3, pp. 234–36, + 1 plate. 1937.

8734 Nordman (Carl Axel). Vapnen i Nordens forntid. *Nordisk Kultur, XII* : B-Vapen, utgiven av Bengt Thordeman, pp. 1–66. 8° Stockholm, 1944. [Pp. 46–66, Vikingatiden.]

8735 Oakeshott (R. E.). An ' Ingelri ' sword in the British Museum. Antiq. J., 31, pp. 69–71, + 1 plate. 1951.

8736 Price (Frederick George Hilton). Notes on a Viking sword from the Thames at Wandsworth. Proc. Soc. Antiq., 2nd S. 21, pp. 147–50, + 1 plate : pp. 402–03. 1906–07.

8737 Raphael (Oscar). An inlaid knife from Southwark. Antiq. J., 14, p. 61. 1934.

8738 Read (Sir Charles Hercules). On an iron sword of Scandinavian type found in London, now in the British Museum, and a bronze stirrup of the same period found near Romsey, in Hampshire, in the possession of Philip B. Davis Cook, Esq. Archaeologia, 50, pp. 530–33. 1887.

8739 —— A Viking sword found in the Lea near Edmonton. Proc. Soc. Antiq., 2nd S. 27, pp. 215–16, + 1 plate. 1915.

8740 —— A Viking sword found in the Thames. [2 figures in text.] Same jnl., 2nd S. 16, pp. 390–92. 1897.

8741 Seaby (W. A.). Late Dark Age finds from the Cherwell and Ray, 1876–86. [Mostly weapons, and in use (871–1013) in Viking raids on Wessex.] Oxoniensia, 15 (1950), pp. 29–43. 1952.

8742 Smith (Reginald Allender). A bronze-gilt sword-pommel of the Viking period, found probably in East Anglia. Proc. Soc. Antiq., 2nd S. 23, pp. 302–07. 1910.

8743 Vassall (Harry Greame). Discovery of a Viking-axe at Repton, [Derbs.]. J. Derbs. Archaeol. Soc., N.S. 1, pp. 118–19. 1925.

8744 Waddington (Quinton). Viking sheath of leather. [For sword-knife, c. 1000.] Antiq. J., 7, p. 526–27, + 1 plate. 1927.

140. PHYSICAL ANTHROPOLOGY (CRANIA, ETC.)

§ a. Anglo-Saxon and Jutish

8745 Bentham (James). Extract of a letter . . . concerning certain discoveries in Ely minster. [' Concerning the removal of some bones,' in 1769 ; with particulars of them = 7 A.-S. bishops.] Archaeologia, 2, pp. 364–66. 1772.

8746 Bevan (James Oliver). [Exhibition of] three skulls, two femora and a knife . . . found . . . in a field in the parish of Alfriston, Sussex. Proc. Soc. Antiq., 2nd S. 16, pp. 91–92. 1896.

8747 Brash (James Cooper), **Layard** (Doris) and **Young** (Matthew). The Anglo-Saxon skulls from Bidford-on-Avon, Warwickshire and Burwell, Cambridgeshire, with a comparison of their principal characters and those of the Anglo-Saxon skulls in London museums. Biometrika, 27, pp. 273–408, + 7 plates, + 2 folding tables. 1935.

8748 Brash (James Cooper). Notes on the cranial and other skeletal characters [at the Anglo-Saxon cemetery at Bidford-on-Avon, Warwickshire, excavated by John Humphreys, etc., q.v. **8296**.] Archaeologia, 73, pp. 106–10. 1923.

8749 Cave (Alexander James Edward). Dark age burial on Barham downs [Kent]. ['Middle-aged male of Saxon stock.'] Arch. Cant., 57 (1944), pp. 71–72. 1945.

8750 —— Report on a human skull from the Freedown, Ringwould, Kent. [At latest, of pagan Saxon period.] Arch. Cant., 58 (1945), pp. 83–85, + 1 plate. 1946.

8751 —— Report on human remains from Woodbridge, North Newnton. [Pagan Saxon. Submitted by Mrs. M. E. Cunnington, q.v., **8468**]. Wilts. Archaeol. Mag., 47, pp. 266–67. 1935.

8752 Curwen (Eliot and Eliot Cecil). Human remains at the [Devil's] Dyke. Sussex N. and Q., 4, pp. 7–8. 1932.

8753 Davies (D. Alexander). Report on Jutish skeleton [Deal, Kent]. Arch. Cant., 46, p. 210. 1934.

8754 Davis (Joseph Barnard) and **Thurnam** (John). Crania Britannica: Delineations and descriptions of the skulls of the early inhabitants of the British Isles. 2 vol. 4° and fol., London, [1856–] 1865. [Gross, 1244. Text and plates.]

8755 Davis (Joseph Barnard). Notes on the Anglo-Saxon skulls from Long Wittenham [Berks.]. Archaeologia, 38, pp. 349–50. 1860.

8756 Duckworth (Wynfrid Laurence Henry). A brief report on human bones [Roman and Saxon, from Grange Road, Cambridge] sent to the Anatomy School, Cambridge, in the months of May and August, 1911, by F. G. Walker. Proc. Camb. Antiq. Soc., 16 (1911–12), pp. 128–32. 1912.

8757 Duckworth (Wynfried Laurence Henry). Note on a collection of crania and bones from Mitcham, [Surrey]. Archaeologia, 60, pp. 60–68. 1906. *Reprinted in* Surrey Archaeol. Collns., 21, pp. 15–25. 1908.

8758 —— Notes on human remains from Mr. Lethbridge's excavations of the Bran ditch in 1927. [Comparison with those from A.–S. cemetery at Burwell.] Proc. Camb. Antiq. Soc., 30, pp. 94–96. 1929.

8759 —— Notes on skeletons of two children discovered at Foxton, Cambs., on 7 May, 1922, in the course of excavations conducted by Dr. C. Fox for the Cambridge Antiquarian Society. [A.–S. period.] *Same jnl.*, 25, pp. 47–49. 1924.

8760 —— Report on human bones from the Anglo-Saxon cemetery at Burwell excavated by Mr. Lethbridge in 1925–26. *Same jnl.*, 28, pp. 124–25. 1927.

8761 —— Report on some human remains from Hyning in Westmorland. [?Saxon.] *Same jnl.*, 16 (1911–12), pp. 133–44. 1912.

8762 Hall (T. G.). On human remains in the crypt of St. Leonard's church, Hythe. [Large proportion of Celtic type: the greater part of the remainder of A.–S. type. Chiefly of men in prime of life. ? slain in battle. *N.b.* disproved by F. G. Parsons, q.v. **8778**.] Arch. Cant., 18, pp. 333–36. 1889.

8763 Harrison (James Park). Note on photographs of inhabitants of Britain of Jutish type. J.R.A.I., 13, pp. 86–87. 1883.

8764 Hodge (E. Humfrey V.). The human remains of the Anglo-Saxon period found in Rutland, with some remarks on comparative osteology. [Mostly 'chat'. Description of 4 skeletons. ? what cemetery.] Rutland Mag., 2, pp. 44–52. 1905.

8765 Hooton (E. A.). Osteological report on the Saxon cemetery at East Shefford, Berks. [=ii. of article by Peake (H. J. E.) and Hooton (E. A.), q.v. **8403**.] J.R.A.I., 45, pp. 99–105. 1915.

8766 Horton-Smith (R. J.). The cranial characteristics of the South Saxons compared with those of some of the other races of south Britain. [i.e. with the West Saxons, Jutes, and East Anglians.] J.R.A.I, 26, pp. 82–102. 1896.

8767 Keith (*Sir* Arthur). Copy of a report on three skulls from ancient cemetery at Southend-on-Sea. Trans. Southend Antiq. Soc., 1, pp. 131–32. 1923.

8768 —— A pagan Saxon cemetery at Broadchalke [Wilts.]. Detailed description of the burials : report on bones. Wilts. Archaeol. Mag., 43, pp. 95–100. 1925.

8769 Knox (Robert). Some observations on a collection of human crania and other human bones at present preserved in the crypt of a church at Hythe in Kent. (Some additional observations, etc.). [? A.–S. and Danes slain in 842. *But see* **8778**.] Trans. Ethnol. Soc., N.S. 1, pp. 238–45 : 2, pp. 136–40. 1861–63.

8770 Kraag (C. M.). Report on a skeleton discovered at Hoe Court in the grounds of Lancing College, March, 1936. [6th c.] Sussex N. and Q., 6, pp. 91–93. 1936.

8771 Layard (Doris) and **Young** (Matthew). The Burwell skulls, including a comparison with those of certain other Anglo-Saxon series. [7th c. Christian.] Biometrika, 27, pp. 388–408, + 3 plates, + folding table. 1935.

8772 Lower (Mark Antony). Report on the antiquities lately found at Lewes. [Tomb of William and Gundrada de Warenne ; with description of the bodies.] J. Brit. Archaeol. Assoc., 1, pp. 346–57. 1846.

8773 Morant (Geoffrey McKay). A first study of the craniology of England and Scotland from neolithic to early historic times, with special reference to the Anglo-Saxon skulls in London museums. [6 whole-page figures + 18 tables in text.] Biometrika, 18, pp. 56–98, + 2 folding tables. 1926.

8774 Mortimer (John Robert). The stature and cephalic index of the prehistoric [and other] men whose remains are preserved in the Mortimer Museum, Driffield. [(c). 'Anglo-Saxon remains obtained from five cemeteries.'] Man, 9, pp. 35–36. 1909.

8775 —— The stature of early man in east Yorkshire. [Pp. 28–31, 'Pagan Saxons'.] Trans. East Riding Antiq. Soc., 17, pp. 23–31. 1910.

8776 Muenter (A. Heinrich). A study of the length of the long bones of the arms and legs in man, with special reference to Anglo-Saxon skeletons. Biometrika, 28, pp. 258–94, + 3 folding tables. 1936.

8777 Parsons (Frederick Gymer). Anglo-Saxon skull contours. *Royal Anthropological Institute* : *Occasional papers, no.* 9. pp. iv, + 66 plates. 8° London, 1923. [A portfolio of 66 drawings to scale, with measurements of the skulls of the most important collections and museums of Great Britain.]

8778 —— An explanation of the Hythe bones. [Probably townsfolk of 13th–15th centuries : disproves theory of relics of a battle in early A.–S. times.] Arch. Cant., 30, pp. 203–13. 1914.

8779 —— On some Saxon bones from Folkestone. J.R.A.I., 41, pp. 101–29, + 2 plates. 1911.

8780 —— A Saxon cemetery at Luton, Beds. (Details of graves and contents, with description of skeletal remains by Prof. Parsons). Antiq. J., 8, pp. 186–92. 1928.

8781 —— Speenhamland [Berks.] skeleton. Trans. Newbury District F.C., 6, pp. 33–34. 1930.

8782 Rolleston (George). Frilford [Berks.] crania. Proc. Soc. Antiq., 2nd S. 3, pp. 139–41. 1865.

8783 Sansbury (Arthur R.) and **Parsons** (Frederick Gymer). Kintbury skeleton no. 1 (no. 2). [Berks.] Trans. Newbury District F.C., 6, pp. 30–33. 1930.

8784 **Stoessiger** (Brenda N.) and **Morant** (Geoffrey McKay). A study of the crania in the vaulted ambulatory of Saint Leonard's church, Hythe. [Negative A.–S. evidence.] Biometrika, 24, pp. 135–202, + 7 plates, + 2 tables. 1932.

8785 **Thurnam** (John). Notes on skulls from Long Wittenham, [Berks.] Archaeologia, 38, pp. 348–49. 1860.

8786 **Tildesley** (Miriam Louise). The human remains from Roche Court down [Winterslow, Wilts.]. [*See also under* Stone (J.F.S.), **8479.**] Wilts. Archaeol. Mag., 45, pp. 583–99. 1932.

8787 **Wright** (William). Description of the three Anglo-Saxon calvariae from Ellesborough. Rec. Bucks., 9, pp. 429–30, + 2 plates. 1909.

§ b. Viking

8788 **Bryce** (Thomas H.). On the bones from graves at Ackergill, Caithness, and an underground building at Rennibister, Orkney. [Viking period.] Proc. Soc. Antiq. Scot., 61 (6th S. 1, 1926–27), pp. 301–17. 1927.

8789 —— Preliminary note on the skeletal remains [from graves at Ackergill and a Viking grave at Reay, Caithness]. [Appendix to account of excavation, by A. J. H. Edwards, **8497**. *See also* pp. 301–17 for fuller account.] *Same jnl.,* 61 (6th S. 1, 1926–27), pp. 207–09. 1927.

8790 —— Report on the bones from the graves [in a mound at Ackergill, Caithness]. [Viking period. Appendix to account of the excavation by A. J. H. Edwards, **8497.**] *Same jnl.,* 60 (5th S. 12, 1925–26), pp. 180–82. 1927.

8791 —— Report on the bones [in a Viking cist-grave at Ballinaby, Islay, Argyllshire]. [c. 950–1000. Report on excavation by A. J. H. Edwards, *q.v.* **8498.**] *Same jnl.,* 68 (6th S. 8, 1933–34), pp. 77–78. 1934.

8792 **Little** (K. L.). A study of a series of human skulls from Castle Hill, Scarborough. [Including alien community of pre-Conquest and Scandinavian origin : base for Vikings till 11th c.] Biometrika, 33, pp. 25–35, + 1 table. 1943.

8793 **Thurnam** (John). Observations on Danish tumuli, and on the importance of collecting crania found in them. [e.g. in Yorkshire.] Archaeol. J., 7, pp. 34–35. 1850.

8794 **Ward** (John). Antiquarian discovery at Aslockton, Notts. [?5th–6th c. burial. ?Danish. *See also* pp. 107–08.] Notts. and Derbs. N. and Q., 1, pp. 121–23. 1893.

§ c. Celtic

8795 **Bruce** (J. Ronald). Note on human remains found at the Smelt, Fort St. Mary [Isle of Man]. [Early Christian : 750–1000 A.D.] I.O.M. N.H. and Antiq. Soc., Proc. N.S. 3 (1925–26), pp. 100–01. 1927.

8796 **Dawkins** (*Sir* William Boyd). On some human bones found at Buttington, Montgomeryshire. [And their connection with battle of 894.] Collns. hist. and archaeol. rel. to Montgom., 6, pp. 141–45. 1873.

8797 **Foot** (Arthur Wynne). An account of a visit to the cave of Dunmore, co. Kilkenny, with some remarks on human remains found therein. [Catalogue of 113 bones removed from Dunmore to museum of the Association. ?remains of persons slaughtered by the Danes in 928.] J. Roy. Hist. and Arch. Assoc. Ireland, [11], 4th S. 1 (1870–71), pp. 65–94. 1878.

8798 **Grattan** (John). Notes on the human remains discovered within the round towers of Ulster, with some additional contributions towards a Crania Hibernica. Ulster J. Archaeol., 6, pp. 27–39, 221–46, + 5 plates, + 3 tables. 1858.

8799 **Howells** (W. W.). The early Christian Irish : the skeletons at Gallen priory, [Ferbane, Offaly]. [Pp. 104–06, historical note on the priory, by Michael Duignan. 36 tables in text.] Proc. R.I.A. 46c, pp. 103–219, + 8 plates. 1941.

8800 **Hughes** (Henry Harold). Discovery of [?pre-Norman] burials at Bangor [Wales]. Arch. Camb., 93, pp. 262–64. 1938.

8801 Macalister (Robert Alexander Stewart) and **Holtby** (J. R. D.). On some interments at Mooretown, co. Meath. [Probably pre- or early Christian.] Proc. R.I.A., 34c, pp. 68–71, + 1 plate. 1917.

8802 Martin (Cecil Percy). Prehistoric man in Ireland. pp. xi, 184, + 11 plates, + 10 tables. 8° London, 1935. [Pp. 133–50, + plates 9–10, + tables 14–16, The people of the early Christian era, the Norsemen.]

8803 Morris (Henry). The Belladooan skeleton [co. Mayo]. [' Early Irish Christian era '.] J. Roy. Soc. Antiq. Ireland, 62 (7th S. 2), pp. 191–200. 1932.

141. ETHNOLOGY

*(See also **Place-Names**, passim)*

8804 Atkinson (John Christopher). On the Danish element in the population of Cleveland, Yorkshire. J. Ethnol. Soc., N.S. 2, pp. 351–66. 1870.

8805 Beddoe (John). A contribution to the anthropology of Wiltshire. [Including A.–S. and Domesday evidence.] Wilts. Archaeol. Mag., 34, pp. 15–41. 1906.

8806 —— On the ancient and modern ethnography of Scotland. Proc. Soc. Antiq. Scot., 1, pp. 243–57. 1852.

8807 —— The races of Great Britain. pp. viii, 271. 8° Bristol, 1885. [Gross, 1243. Chap. ix, Norman Conquest.]

8808 Bjoerkman (Erik). Über den Namen der Jüten. Engl. Studien, 39, pp. 356–61. 1908.

8809 Bugge (Alexander). The Norse settlements in the British Islands. [Mostly from place-name evidence.] Trans. R.H.S., 4th S., 4, pp. 173–210. 1921.

8810 Buxton (Leonard Halford Dudley). The sea raiders : a contribution to the ethnology of Britons and Saxons in the Oxford district. Custom is king : essays presented to R. R. Marett, pp. 201–13. 1936.

8810a Copley (Gordon J.). The tribal complexity of Middle Anglia. [Boundary between Angles and Saxons. Map shows grave-fields and tribal place-names of the Cambridge region.] Archaeol. News Letter, 4, pp. 152–56. 1952.

8810b Copley (Gordon J.). The tribal complexity of the early Kentish kingdom. [Jutes and Saxons. Map of Kent in 5th–6th c.] Archaeol. News Letter, 5, pp. 24–28. 1954.

8811 Craigie (*Sir* William Alexander). The Gaels in Iceland. Proc. Soc. Antiq. Scot., 31 (3rd S. 7), pp. 247–64. 1897.

8812 Crawfurd (John). On the so-called Celtic languages in reference to the question of race. Arch. Camb., 3rd S. 10, pp. 181–212. 1864.

8813 Davies (John). The Celtic element of the English people. [i. Historical : ii. Philological element.] Arch. Camb., 4th S. 10, pp. 195–221, 252–67 : 11, pp. 10–24, 97–105. *Also* 9, pp. 77–78, 152–53, 234–35, for discussion. 1879–80.

8814 —— On the races of Lancashire, as indicated by the local names and the dialect of the county. Trans. Philol. Soc., 1855, pp. 210–84. [1855].

8815 Ekwall (Eilert). The proportion of Scandinavian settlers in the Danelaw. Saga-Book V.C., 12 (1936–37), pp. 19–34. 1937.

8816 Ellis (George). Irish ethnology socially and politically considered ; embracing a general outline of the Celtic and Saxon races. pp. vii, 156. 8° Dublin, 1852.

8817 Ewen (Cecil Henry L'Estrange). Are the British Anglo-Saxons or Celts ? The onomatologist to the aid of the anthropologist. pp. 14. 8° London. 1938.

8818 Ferguson (James). The Celtic element in Lowland Scotland. Celtic Rev., 1, pp. 246–60, 321–32. 1905.

8819 —— The Scottish peoples : their origin, constituents, and continuity. Trans. Gaelic Soc. Inverness, 28 (1912–14), pp. 466–96. 1918.

8820 Fiske (Christabel Forsyth). Old English modification of Teutonic racial conceptions. Studies . . . in celebration of J. M. Hart, pp. 255–94. 1910.

8821 Frazer (William). A contribution to Irish anthropology. J. Roy. Soc. Antiq. Ireland, 20 (5th S. 1), pp. 391–404. 1891.

8822 Gray (Arthur). On the late survival of a Celtic population in East Anglia. [i.e. in A.–S. times.] Proc. Camb. Antiq. Soc., 15 (1910–11), pp. 42–52. 1911.

8823 Headlam (*Sir* Cuthbert) *bart.* The three northern counties of England. pp. xiii, 343. 4° Gateshead upon Tyne, 1939. [Pp. 1–14, racial settlement in the north of England.]

8824 Hodgetts (James Frederick). On the Scandinavian elements in the English race. Antiquary, 13, pp. 137–43, 205–09, 245–47 : 14, pp. 137–47 : *also* 13, pp. 279 (note by A. Hall). 1886.

8825 Howorth (*Sir* Henry Hoyle). Some unconventional views on primitive man in western Europe from the earliest times to the seventh century A.D. [Pp. 63–78, A.–S., Picts, etc.] Arch. Camb., 6th S. 10, pp. 1–78. 1910.

8826 Jabet (George). The ethnology of Warwickshire, traced in the names of places. [3.—Of the Saxons (Angles) in Warwickshire.] B'ham and Midland Inst., Arch. Section, Trans., [4], pp. 1–26. 1873.

8827 Johnston (Alfred Wintle). Orkney and Shetland folk, 872–1350. ['Attempt to describe the mixed races.'] Old-lore Misc., 7, pp. 84–96, 131–43, 183–92 : 8, pp. 17–21. 1914–15.

8828 Jones (W. Basil). On certain terms of Celtic ethnology, and on a recent theory [of Thomas Wright] of the origin of the Welsh. Arch. Camb., 3rd S. 4, pp. 125–51. 1858.

8829 —— On the origin of the Welsh. [Reply to Thomas Wright, **8855**]. Arch. Camb., 3rd S. 5, pp. 27–44, 224–31: 6, pp. 319–22. 1859–60.

8830 La Borderie (Louis Arthur Le Moyne de). Origin of the Welsh. Arch. Camb., 3rd S. 5, pp. 293–97. 1859.

8831 Latham (Robert Gordon). The ethnology of the British Isles. 8° London, 1852. [Gross, 1250. Influence of Celtic, Roman, German and Danish elements.]

8832 Laws (Edward). The ethnology of Pembrokeshire. J. Brit. Archaeol. Assoc., 41, pp. 22–27. 1885.

8833 Lewin (Thomas). Primitive races and early inhabitants of Great Britain. [i. Celts : ii. Cwmri : iii. Belgae : iv. Saxons.] Proc. Soc. Antiq., 2nd S. 3, pp. 474–78. 1867.

8834 Mackenzie (William Cook). The origin of the Gael. Trans. Gaelic Soc. Inverness, 28 (1912–14), pp. 67–100. 1918.

8835 Mackintosh (D.). Results of ethnological observations made during the last ten years in England and Wales. [Distinction between Jutes, Frisians, and Saxons.] Trans. Ethnol. Soc., N.S. 1, pp. 211–21. 1861.

8836 MacRitchie (David). The Finnmen of Britain. [Shetland. *See also* **8839**.] Archaeol. Rev., 4, pp. 1–26, 107–29. 1889.

8837 Malone (Kemp). The meaning of Bede's *Iutae*. Anglia, Beibl., 51, pp. 262–64. 1940.

8838 Morris (Henry). Picts, Scots and Gaels : some views of Scottish writers. County Louth Archaeol. J., 6, pp. 190–93. 1928.

8839 Nutt (Alfred). The Finn-men of Britain. [Criticism of D. MacRitchie's article, *q.v.*, **8836**, and his views on the identity of Finn MacCumhail and his warriors with an historical race akin to the present Finns]. Archaeol. Rev., 4, p. 232. 1889.

8840 Palmer (J. Foster). The Saxon invasion and its influence on character and race. Trans. R.H.S., N.S. 2, pp. 173–96. 1885.

8841 Parsons (Frederick Gymer). The earlier inhabitants of London. pp. 240. 8° London, 1927. [Pp. 171–231, the Picts, Scots and Saxons : Saxon London : London and the Danes.]

8842 Petrie (*Sir* William Matthew Flinders). British and Saxon fusion. Man, 37, pp. 97–98. 1937.

8843 Picton (J.). The ethnology of Wiltshire as illustrated in the place-names. J. Brit. Archaeol. Assoc., 37, pp. 229–38. 1881. *Also in* Wilts. Archaeol. Mag., 20, pp. 16–26. 1882.

8844 Picton (*Sir* James Allanson). A few notes on the ethnology and development of the bishopric and county palatine of Durham. [Scrappy: nothing new.] J. Brit. Archaeol. Assoc., 43, pp. 133–36. 1887.

8845 Rhys (*Sir* John). The early ethnology of the British Isles. [Gross, 1254. Rhind Lectures.] Scottish Rev., 15, pp. 233–52; 16, pp. 30–47, 240–56; 17, pp. 60–82, 332–49; 18, pp. 120–43. 1890–91.

8846 —— Peoples of ancient Scotland. *Same jnl.*, 17, pp. 60–84. 1891.

8847 Robinson (T.). The ancient population of Lincolnshire. Lincs. N. and Q., 2, pp. 103–05. 1891.

8848 Schuette (Gudmund). The Geats of Beowulf. [Equates with Jutes of Jutland.] J. Engl. and Germ. Philol., 11, pp. 574–602. 1912.

8849 Scott (Archibald Black). The historical sequence of the Celtic people in Scotland. Trans. Gaelic Soc. Inverness, 34 (1927–28), pp. 314–37. 1935.

8850 Scouler (John). On the early population of Scotland. Trans. Glasgow Archaeol. Soc., 1, pp. 124–34. 1868.

8851 Turner (Sharon). On the Asiatic origin of the Anglo-Saxons. Trans. Roy. Soc. Lit., 2, pp. 252–62. 1834.

8852 Wallis (E. W.). The pre-Conquest English. Word-lore, 3, pp. 97–99. 1928.

8853 Wardale (Edith). ' Béowulf ': the nationality of Ecgðeow. Mod. Lang. Rev., 24, p. 322. 1929.

8854 Williams (Robert). On the origin of the Welsh. Arch. Camb., 3rd. S. 6, pp. 196–210; 7, pp. 82–83. 1860–61.

8855 Wright (Thomas). On the origin of the Welsh. [Reply to W. B. Jones, **8828**.] Arch. Camb., 3rd S. 4, pp. 289–305 : *also* 5, pp. 145–47. 1858–59.

8856 Yeatman (John Pym). The Shemetic origin of the nations of Western Europe, *etc.* pp. xx, 292. 8° London, 1879. [Pp. 197–207, the Anglo-Saxons.]

142. GENERAL TEXT BOOKS

8857 Brooke (George Cyril). English coins from the seventh century to the present day. pp. xii, 277, + 64 plates. [Pp. 1–86, 249–55, + plates 1–18, 65–66, A.–S. *Plus*: pp. 249–68, + plates 65–72, supplement.]

8858 Engel (Arthur) and **Serrure** (Raymund). Traité de numismatique du moyen âge. 3 vol. 8° Paris, 1891–1905. [Gross, 373. Includes coinage of British Isles to end of 13th c.]

8859 Hawkins (Edward). The silver coins of England. pp. 308, + 47 plates. 4° London, 1841. [Pp. 16–78, A.–S.]

8860 Lindsay (John). A view of the coinage of the heptarchy, to which is added a list of unpublished mints and moneyers of the chief or sole monarchs, from Egbert to Harold II, *etc.* 4° Cork, 1842. [Gross, 390.]

8861 Oman (*Sir* Charles William Chadwick). The coinage of England. pp. xii-395, + 44 plates. 8° Oxford, 1931. [Pp. 1–90, + plates 1–13, A.–S.]

8861a Seaby (Peter John). The story of the English coinage. pp. xii, 110. 8° London, 1952. [Pp. 15–25, A.–S. coins.]

8862 Thwaites (Edward). Notes upon the Anglo-Saxon coins. *In* Wotton (William): Short view of George Hickes's . . . Treasury, translated by M. Shelton. 2nd edition. pp. 156–82. 4° London, 1737.

143. CATALOGUES OF, AND NOTES ON, COLLECTIONS

8863 Allan (John). Barnett collection of pre-Conquest coins. B.M.Q., 10, pp. 124–27, + plates 35–36. 1936.

8864 British Museum. A catalogue of English coins in the British Museum. Anglo-Saxon series, by H. A. Grueber and C. F. Keary. 2 vol. 8° London, 1887–93. [Gross, 389. With map + 62 plates.]

8865 British Museum. A catalogue of English coins in the British Museum. The Norman kings, by G. C. Brooke. 2 vol. 8° London, 1916.

8866 British Museum. Handbook of the coins of Great Britain and Ireland in the British Museum. By H. A. Grueber. pp. lxiii, 272, + 64 plates. 8° London, 1899. [Pp. 1–35, + plates 1–6, 56, A.–S. period.]

8867 Hildebrand (Bror Emil). Monnaies Anglo-Saxonnes du Cabinet royal de Stockholm, toutes trouvées en Suède. Anglosachsiska Mynt, etc. 4° Stockholm, 1846. [Swedish and French.] Anglo-Saxon coins in the Royal Swedish Cabinet of medals. New augmented edition. pp. viii, 502, + 14 plates. 8° Stockholm, 1881. [Gross, 388.]

8868 Holm (Sigurd). Studien äfver Uppsala Universitets anglosaxiska mynt-samling. Uppsala Univ. Årsskr., Filos., 1917, No. 1. Pp. vii, 34, 75. 1917.

8869 Lindsay (John). Notices of remarkable Greek, Roman and Anglo-Saxon and other mediaeval coins in the cabinet of the author. [Illustrated.] 4° Cork, 1860.

8870 Sotheby, Wilkinson and **Hodge.** The Montague collection of coins. Catalogue of the British and Anglo-Saxon series. 8° London, 1895.

144. ' FINDS '

§ *a.* Cuerdale Hoard

(Near Preston, Lancs. Viking treasure: the bulk of Danish kings of Northumbria, plus A.–S. coins of 860–925, including coins of St. Edmund, and foreign.)

8871 [Anon.] Report to the Chancellor and council of the Duchy of Lancaster on the subject of the treasure recently found at Cuerdale. Trans. R. Soc. Lit., 2nd S. 1, pp. 209–25. 1843.

8872 Andrew (Walter Jonathan). Buried treasure: some traditions, records, and facts. [Pp. 11–13, the Cuerdale hoard: the Beaworth hoard.]. J. Brit. Archaeol. Assoc., 59 (N. S. 9), pp. 8–32. 1903. *Also in* Brit. Num. J., 1, pp. 9–59, + 4 plates, 1905. [Pp. 12–26, + plates 1–2, Cuerdale hoard: pp. 26–29, + plate 3, Beaworth hoard: pp. 51–57, description of plates.]

8873 Bergsöe (S.). Critical remarks on the uncertain coins of the Cuerdale find. [Cunnetti and miscellaneous.] Num. Chron., N.S. 20, pp. 192–204. 1880.

8874 Haigh (David Henry). On the coins of the Cuerdale find, with the names 'Siefredus', 'Cunnetti', and 'Ebraice'. Num. Chron., 5, pp. 105–117. 1842.

8875 Hawkins (Edward). An account of coins and treasure found in Cuerdale. [*See also*: Proceedings of the Numismatic Society. Jan. 1842, pp. 49–56.] Num. Chron., 5, pp. 1–48, 53–104, + 10 plates. 1842.

8876 Hugo (Thomas). On the field of Cuerdale. [Penny of Alfred, silver armlet, etc.] J. Brit. Archaeol. Assoc., 8, pp. 330–35, + 1 plate. 1853.

8877 Kenyon (Joseph). Discovery of ancient coins and other treasure near Preston. Num. Chron., 3, pp. 62–65. 1841.

8878 Longpérier (Adrien de). Note on some coins of the Cuerdale find. Num. Chron., 5, pp. 117–20. 1842.

§ *b.* **Others (Miscellaneous)**

8879 Allan (John). A find of sceattas at Southampton. Num. Chron., 6th S. 6, p. 73. 1946.

8880 Allen (Derek Fortrose). The Sutton Hoo finds. [4. The coins. All from Merovingian mints.] B.M.Q., 13, pp. 126–28. 1939.

8881 —— Treasure trove, 1933–9. [Pp. 269–74: Rotherham, Yorks., 1939. Buried c. 1069. Harold II—William I.] Brit. Numism. J., 23 (1938–41), pp. 269–86. 1941.

8882 Bliss (Thomas). Anglo-Saxon coins found at Croydon. [Cenwulf of Mercia, Ceolnoth of Kent (i.e. abp. of Canterbury) and Ecgbeorht of Wessex, 796–839.] Num. Chron., 4th S. 7, pp. 339–42. 1907.

8883 Blunt (Christopher E.). The date of the Croy hoard. [Mains of Croy, Inverness-shire. 2 coins (one of Cenwulf of Mercia, the other of Æthelwulf of Wessex) now reattributed.] Proc. Soc. Antiq. Scot., 84 (1949–50), p. 217. 1952.

8884 Brooke (George Cyril). Beeston Tor [Staffs.] find of Anglo-Saxon coins. [49. 9th c. A.–S. pennies, with 3 gold rings and a silver brooch. Burgred of Mercia (20): abp. Ceolnoth (1): Æthelwulf of Wessex (1): Æthelred of Wessex (7): Alfred (20).] Num. Chron., 5th S. 4, pp. 322–25. 1924.

8885 Carlyon-Britton (Philip William Poole). On some coins of the tenth century, found in the Isle of Man, with special reference to a penny of Anlaf struck at Derby. Brit. Num. J., 5, pp. 85–96, + 2 plates. 1909.

8886 Carruthers (James). Discovery of Saxon coins [at Derry Kearhan, co. Antrim,] in Ireland. Num. Chron., 6, pp. 112–14, 213–16. 1843–44.

8887 Christmas (Henry). Discovery of Anglo-Saxon coins at White Horse, near Croydon. [Æthelweard (1) and Edmund (6) of East Anglia: Æthelred I (10) and Alfred (12): Burgred of Mercia (51): etc. 850–73.] Num. Chron., N.S. 2, pp. 302–04. 1862.

8888 Churchill (William S.). The Harkirke find. [Included sundry A.–S. coins.] Trans. Lancs. and Ches. Antiq. Soc., 5 (1887), pp. 219–35, + 1 plate. 1888.

8889 Crawford (Osbert Guy Stanhope). The Sutton Hoo ship-burial. 6. The coins: a summary. Antiquity, 14, pp. 64–68. 1940.

8890 Edleston (J.) *possessor*. Find of Anglo-Saxon coins at Gainford, Durham. [4 pennies of Alfred and Burgred.] Num. Chron., N.S. 4, p. 225. 1864.

8891 Evans (*Sir* John). Discovery of Anglo-Saxon coins at White Horse, near Croydon. [Burgred of Mercia (51): Æthelweard (1) and Edmund (6) of East Anglia : Æthelred I (10) and Alfred (12).] Num. Chron., N.S. 6, pp. 232–40. 1866.

8892 —— On a hoard of early Anglo-Saxon coins found in Ireland. [Delgany, co. Wicklow. Kent (Eadbearht—Baldred), Mercia (Offa—Beornvulf), Egbert, archiepiscopal coins.] Num. Chron., 3rd S. 2, pp. 61–86, + plate 4. 1882.

8893 —— On some Anglo-Saxon sceattas found in Friesland. [Probably mid 6th c., and ' struck by Frisian tribes, either in Britain or Friesland, rather than by the Angles '.] Num. Chron., N.S. 4, pp. 22–27. 1864.

8894 Grierson (Philip). The Canterbury (St. Martin's) hoard of Frankish and Anglo-Saxon coin-ornaments. Br. Num. J., 27, pp. 39–51, + 1 plate. 1953.

8895 —— The dating of the Sutton Hoo coins. Antiquity, 26, pp. 83–86. 1952.

8896 Grueber (Herbert Appold). A find of Anglo-Saxon coins. [B.M., Franks collection. 241 coins of Mercia, Kent, Canterbury, East Anglia and Wessex.] Num. Chron., 3rd S. 14, pp. 29–76, + 2 plates. 1894.

8897 Hawkins (Edward). On some Saxon coins discovered near Gravesend, in 1838. [Mercia and East Anglia, 830–98 : 429 of Burgred.] Num. Chron., 3, pp. 14–34. 1841.

8898 Heywood (Nathan). Saxon coins found on the site of Waterloo bridge, London. [Burgred of Mercia and Æthelred I. of Wessex.] Num. Chron., 3rd S. 4, pp. 349–50. 1884.

8899 Le Gentilhomme (P.). La circulation des monnaies d'or mérovingiennes en Angleterre. [Finds at Sutton Hoo, Crondall, Hants., etc.] Br. Num. J., 23 (1938–41), pp. 395–98. 1941.

8900 Lindsay (John). Anglo-Saxon coins found in May [1843] at Lough Lyn, near Mullingar, co. Westmeath. Num. Chron., 6, pp. 216–17. 1844.

8901 Lindsay (John). Anglo-Saxon coins lately found in the county of Tipperary. Num. Chron., 6, p. 217. 1844.

8902 Lockett (Richard Cyril). Hoard of nine Anglo-Saxon pennies found in Dorsetshire. [i–iii, Cenwulf of Mercia : iv–vii, Egbert of Wessex : viii. Wulfred, abp. Cant., 805–33 : ix. ? sede vacante.] Num. Chron., 4th S. 15, pp. 336–44, + plate 17. 1915.

8903 Mattingley (Harold). A Bermondsey coin-hoard, 5th century. [Late Roman coins and copies of them : used in post-Roman times before there was a mint in this island.] Antiquity, 20, pp. 158–59. 1946.

8904 Milne (J. Grafton). A note on the Harkirke find. [*See* article by W. S. Churchill, **8888.**] Num. Chron., 5th S. 15, p. 292. 1935.

8905 Nordman (Carl Axel). Anglo-Saxon coins found in Finland. pp. 92, ii. 4° Helsingfors, 1921.

8906 Peacock (John). Saxon coins found at Chester. [Edward the Elder (7), St. Peter (9), St. Edmund (1).] Num. Chron., N.S. 2, pp. 305–06. 1862.

8907 Puttock (James). Saxon coins found near Dorking [Surrey] in 1817. [Miscellaneous.] Num. Chron., 7, pp. 199–200. 1845.

8908 Rashleigh (Jonathan). An account of [114] Anglo-Saxon coins and gold and silver ornaments found at Trewhiddle, near St. Austell, Cornwall, A.D. 1774. [Mercia : Offa (1), Coenvulf (2), Beornvulf (1), Berhtulf (10), Burgred (45), Ciolvulf (1) : Eanred of Northumbria (1) : Cealnoth, abp. of Canterbury (6) : Egbert (3), Ethelvulf (10), Ethelred I (2), Alfred (2), etc.] Num. Chron., N.S. 8, pp. 137–57. 1868.

8909 Rashleigh (Philip). Account of antiquities discovered [at Trewhiddle] in Cornwall, 1774. Archaeologia, 9, pp. 187–88, + 1 plate. 1789.

8910 Rogers (John Jope). Saxon silver ornaments and coins found at Trewhiddle, *etc.* J. Roy. Inst. Cornwall, 2, pp. 292–305. 1867.

8911 Sutherland (Carol Humphrey Vivian). Anglo-Saxon gold coinage in the light of the Crondall hoard [1828]. *Ashmolean Museum.* pp. 106, + 5 plates. 4° London, 1948. [Pp. 74–99, Catalogue of A.–S. gold coins.]

145. COINS, GENERAL AND MISCELLANEOUS

8912 Andrew (Walter Jonathan). The early Anglo-Danish coinage. [i. The Guthred-Cnut theory : ii. Who was Cnut, king of the Northumbrians?] Brit. Num. J., 20 (1929–30), pp. 314–15 : 21 (1931–3), pp. 188–89. 1932–35.

8913 —— Evolution of portraiture on the silver penny. [Pp. 361–74, A.–S. period.] Brit. Num. J., 5, pp. 361–80, + 1 plate. 1909.

8914 —— Numismatic sidelights on the battle of Brunan-burh, A.D. 937. [Plates, Brough-in-the Peak.] Brit. Num. J., 20 (1929–30), pp. 1–25, + 2 plates. 1932.

8915 Belaiew (Nikolai Timothyee-vich). On the ' dragon ' series of the Anglo-Saxon sceattas. [13 figures.] J. Brit. Archaeol. Assoc., 3rd S. 1, pp. 35–51. 1937.

8916 —— On the ' Wodan-monster ' or the ' dragon ' series of the Anglo-Saxon sceattas. [Discusses Scandinavian and Scythian affinities.] Seminarium Kondakovianum : receuil d'études, archéologie, etc., 7, pp. 169–84. 1935.

8917 Carlton-Britton (Philip William Poole). British numismatics. [Pp. 2–4, A.–S. period.] Brit. Num. J., 1, pp. 1–8. 1905.

8918 —— Cornish numismatics. [Plate shows ' coins of Æthelred II, Harold I, William I,' etc. Mint at Launceston.] Brit. Num. J., 3, pp. 107–16, + 1 plate. 1906. *Also in* J. Roy. Inst. Cornwall, 17, pp. 52–62, + 1 plate. 1907.

8919 Dirks (Jacob). Les Anglo-Saxons et leur petits deniers dit sceattas. Essai historique et numismatique. [Gross 385.] Rev. num. belge, 5e S. 2, pp. 81–128, 269–320, 387–409, 521–41. 1870.

8920 Evans (*Sir* Arthur). Notes on early Anglo-Saxon gold coins. Num. Chron., 6th S. 2, pp. 19–41, + plate 1. 1942.

8921 Haigh (Daniel Henry). [H.L.Y., *pseud.* (last letters of name)]. Sceattas. Num. Chron., 2, pp. 152–60. 1840.

8922 —— Miscellaneous notes on the Old English coinage. [A.–S. gold coins, etc.] Num. Chron., N.S. 9, pp. 171–96, + 1 plate. 1869.

8923 Head (Barclay Vincent). Anglo-Saxon coins with runic legends. Num. Chron., N.S. 8, pp. 75–90, + plate 4. 1868.

8924 Hill (Philip V.). The animal, 'Anglo-Merovingian', and miscellaneous series of Anglo-Saxon sceattas. Br. Num. J., 27, pp. 1–38, + 5 plates. 1953.

8925 —— The coinage of Britain in the Dark Ages. [Till c. 600—' probable burial dates '.—Roman coins.] Br. Num. J., 26 (3rd S. 6, 1949), pp. 1–27, + 1 plate. 1950.

8926 —— Saxon sceattas and their problems. Br. Num. J., 26 (3rd S. 6), pp. 129–54, + 4 plates. 1951.

8927 —— The ' standard ' and ' London ' series of Anglo-Saxon sceattas. Br. Num. J., 26 (1949–51), pp. 251–79, + 4 plates. 1952.

8928 Holmboe (C. A.). Le mancus des Anglo-Saxons. [?=manica (bracelet) ?= *baug* (ring) in old Norwegian laws for payment for crimes.] Num. Chron., 20, pp. 149–50. 1857.

8929 Holmes (Urban T.) *jr.* Old French *mangon*, Anglo-Saxon *mancus*, late Latin *mancussus, mancosus, mancessus*, etc. [=ring, then money bracelet, then a sum of indefinite value greater than the solidus or dînâr.] P.M.L.A., 53, pp. 34–37. 1938.

8930 Keary (Charles Francis). Coinage of the British islands. Part 1. [Pp. 256–57, ' coinage of the Saxons '.] Antiquary, 7, pp. 255–6. 1883.

8931 —— The coinages of western Europe : from the fall of the western empire to the accession of Charlemagne. —iv. The growth of a silver currency in Europe and the earliest coinage of England. Num. Chron., N.S. 19, pp. 23–61, + 1 plate. 1879.

8932 L. (C. W.). Sceattas. Num. Chron., 1, pp. 66–67. 1839.

8933 Lawrence (L. A.). Forgery in relation to numismatics. [Pp. 401–09 and the first 7 plates, forgeries of A.-S. coins.] Br. Num. J., 2, pp. 397–409 : 3, pp. 281–90, + 11 plates. 1905–06.

8934 Lefroy (J. H.). Further notice of gold coins discovered in 1828, by the late C. E. Lefroy, and described in the Numismatic Chronicle, vol. 6. [Considered by D. H. Haigh to be South Saxon.] Num. Chron., N.S. 10, pp. 164–76. 1870.

8935 Longpérier (Adrien de). Gold triens with 'Dorovernis'. [?earliest A.-S.] Num. J., 2, pp. 232–34. 1838.

8936 Oman (*Sir* Charles William Chadwick). Notes on certain Anglo-Saxon coin-types. [Peace commemoration?] Num. Chron., 5th S. 9, pp. 169–79, + plate 7. 1929.

8937 Parsons (H. Alexander). Art and the coins of England. [Pp. 294–98, + plates 1–2, A.-S. period.] Br. Num. J., 3, pp. 291–310, + 4 plates. 1906.

8938 Radford (A. J. V.). The coins and tokens of Devon. Rept. and Trans. Devon. Assoc., 39, pp. 349–59. 1907.

8939 S. (R.). An attempt to locate some coins of unappropriated mints, in Ruding from Domesday, and the New Topographical Dictionary. Num. J., 2, pp. 45–51. 1837.

8940 Salis (J. F. W. de). On some looped coins found with Anglo-Saxon ornaments [near Reculver] in Kent. [6th–7th c. Coins of south of Gaul bearing name and effigy of Heraclius.] Num. Chron., N.S. 1, pp. 58–59. 1861.

8941 Salisbury (F. S.). The Richborough coins and the end of the Roman occupation. ['The money of the latter half of the fourth century, and its bearing . . . on the origin of the A.-S. coinage.'] Antiq. J., 7, pp. 268–81, + 1 plate. 1927.

8942 Schive (C. J.). Some account of the weight of English and Northern coins in the tenth and eleventh centuries, and an attempt at comparison between these weights and the weight system for coins which apparently belong to the same period. Translated from the Danish by [Sir] John Evans. Num. Chron., N.S. 11, pp. 42–66. 1871.

8943 Schwabe (H. O.). Germanic coin-names. Mod. Phil., 13, pp. 583–608 : 14, pp. 42–56. 611–90. 1916–17.

8944 Stirling (James) *of Leadhills*. An account of the money, coins, and weights, used in England, during the reigns of the Saxon princes. Archaeol. Scot., 1, pp. 216–33. 1792.

8945 Sutherland (Carol Humphrey Vivian). Anglo-Saxon sceattas in England : their origin, chronology, and distribution. Num. Chron., 6th S. 2, pp. 42–70, + plate 2. 1942.

8946 —— The Canterbury *minissimi* again. [Answering query : no coins used in this island from c. 450 to c. 600.] Num. Chron., 6th S. 9, pp. 242–44. 1949.

8947 Thomsen (C. J.). Remarks on the ancient British and Anglo-Saxon coinage. Num. Chron., 3, pp. 116–22. 1841.

8948 —— Uncertain coins of the Anglo-Saxon period. Num. Chron., 16, pp. 104–07, + 1 plate. 1854.

146. NOTES ON INDIVIDUAL COINS

8949 Akerman (John Yonge). On a gold coin found near Canterbury. [? struck by A.-S. bishop or archbishop. Runic ⋈ on reverse.] Num. Chron., N.S. 5, pp. 166–67. 1865.

8950 —— Rude coins discovered in England. [Including a sceatta imitated from Roman coins.] Num. Chron., 4, pp. 30–34, + 1 plate. 1841.

8951 Anscombe (Alfred). The golden *solidus* of Hama ['rex Britanniae']. [c. 465 A.D.] Br. Num. J., 16 (1921–2), pp. 292–94. 1924.

8952 Blunt (Christopher E.). Four Italian coins imitating Anglo-Saxon types. Br. Num. J., 25 (3rd S. 5), pp. 282–85. 1949.

8953 —— On a coin of the 'temple' type bearing the name of Aethelred, king of England. [Polish coin.] Num. Chron., 6th S. 3, pp. 101–02. 1943.

8954 Blunt (Christopher C.) Three Anglo–Saxon notes [i. A coin of Heaberht, king of Kent: Lord Grantley's attribution vindicated: ii. A Burgred-type coin with, apparently, the name of king Aethilbearht of Wessex: iii. A die-identity between a coin of Alfred and one of Aethelstan II of East Anglia.] Br. Num. J., 27, pp. 52–57, + 1 plate. 1953.

8955 Brooke (George Cyril). An English gold coin of the seventh century. B.M.Q., 3, p. 100, + plate 52 (c.). 1929.

8956 Christmas (Henry). Unpublished English and Anglo-Gallic coins. [i. Cenwulf: ii–iii. Eric of Northumbria: iv. Penny of St. Edmund: v. Penny of Edgar, struck at St. Edmundsbury: vi. Harold II.] Num. Chron., N.S. 1, pp. 17–31. 1861.

9857 Dale (William). [A coin of] the sceat series [from the Roman site of Clausentum, Hants.] [?5th c. Showing Romulus and Remus suckled by the wolf.] Proc. Soc. Antiq., 2nd S. 22, pp. 376–77. 1909.

8958 Dolley (R. H.). English coins. [Silver penny of Wulfred, abp. of Canterbury, and unique silver penny with obverse of Beorhtwulf of Mercia (839–53) and reverse of Æthelwulf of Wessex (838–59).] B.M.Q., 18, pp .54–55, + plate 15. 1953.

8959 Grantley (John Richard Brinsley Norton) 5*th baron*. On some unique Anglo-Saxon coins. [Ecgberht of Kent: Beorhtwulf of Mercia and Æthelwulf of Wessex: Egbert of Wessex.] Num. Chron., 3rd S. 20, pp. 148–61. 1900.

8960 Hoare (Edward). Another uncertain Anglo-Saxon, or Anglo-Danish coin. Num. Chron., 16, pp. 146–49. 1854.

8961 Smith (Joseph Huband). On certain antiquities . . . found near a cavern at Cushendall, in the county of Antrim. [Including coin of Beorhtwulf, king of Mercia, 839, and of Ceolnoth, abp. of Canterbury, 839.] Proc. R.I.A., 4, pp. 395–96. 1850.

147. EAST ANGLIA AND KENT
(including Archbishops of Canterbury)

8962 Bergne (John B.). Another type of Baldred. Num. Chron. 15, pp. 102–03. 1853.

8963 —— Unpublished coins of Cuthred, Baldred, and William the Conqueror. Num. Chron., 14, pp. 145–50. 1852.

8964 Brooke (George Cyril). Anglo-Saxon acquisitions of the British Museum. ii. Kent; archbishops of Canterbury; East Anglia. Num. Chron., 5th S. 3, pp. 243–59, + plate 11. 1923.

8965 Carlyon-Britton (Philip William Poole). A penny of St. Æthelberht, king of East Anglia. [With a biography of Æthelberht.] Br. Num. J., 5, pp. 73–84, + 1 plate. 1909.

8966 —— A penny of St. Æthelberht, king of East Anglia. Proc. Soc. Antiq., 2nd S. 22, pp. 432–42, + 1 plate. 1909.

8967 Christmas (Henry). Numismatic scraps. No. 4. A coin of Plegmund. [*Obv.* + Plegmvnd. Archiep.: R. + Sigehelm. Mōn.] Num. Chron., 8, pp. 126–27. 1845.

8968 D. (F.). Coins of Ethelstan [of East Anglia.] Num. Chron., 5, pp. 124–27. 1842.

8969 Evans (*Sir* John). Coins of archbishops Jaenberht and Æthilheard. Num. Chron., N.S. 5, pp. 351–60, + plate 14. 1865.

8970 Grantley (John Richard Brinsley Norton) 5*th baron*. Penny of Baldred. [King of Kent, 807–25.] Num. Chron., 4th S. 6, pp. 90–91. 1906.

8971 Haigh (Daniel Henry). An essay on the numismatic history of the ancient kingdom of the East Angles. 4° Leeds, 1845.

8972 —— On the arrangement of the coins of the archbishops of Canterbury. Num. Chron., 2, pp. 209–15, + 1 plate. 1840.

8973 —— On the coins of East Anglia. Num. Chron., 2, pp. 47–51. 1840.

8974 Haigh (Daniel Henry). On the gold triens inscribed ' Dorovernis civitas '. [Argument that it is a specimen of the earliest Saxon coinage, minted at Canterbury.] Num. Chron., 4, pp. 120–21. 1841.

8975 —— Remarks upon the numismatic history of East Anglia during the vii. and viii. centuries. (Further remarks on *ditto*, during the ninth century.) Num. Chron., 4, pp. 34–41, 195–200. 1841.

8976 Hill (Philip V.). An unpublished sceatta in Norwich museum. [Dragon type : mid 8th c.] Num. Chron., 6th S. 10, pp. 150–51. 1950.

8977 Howorth (*Sir* Henry Hoyle). The coins of Ecgbeorht [as king of Kent] and his son Athelstan. [9th c.] Num. Chron., 4th S. 8, pp. 222–65, + plates 16–18. 1908.

8978 Kenyon (Joseph). Unpublished penny of Ethelstan I of East Anglia. Num. Chron., 7, pp. 38–39. 1844.

8979 Lindsay (John). Presumed skeatta of archbishop Theodore. Num. Chron., 5, pp. 158–59, + 1 plate. 1842.

8980 Mack (R. P.). A new type for archbishop Wulfred. [Abp. of Canterbury, 805–32.] Br. Num. J., 26, pp. 343–44. 1952.

8981 Madden (Frederic William). On an unpublished variety of the coins of Ethelstan, king of East Anglia. Num. Chron., N.S., 1, pp. 85–86. 1861.

8982 Potts (Robert Ullock). The gold medalet of Leudard the bishop—the oldest English gold coin. [Temp. Ethelbert of Kent. Bp. sent with queen Bertha from Paris.] Archaeol. Cant., 57 (1944), pp. 72–74. 1945.

8983 Pownall (Assheton). Account of an Anglo-Saxon coin found at Bulwick [Northants.]. [Obverse, Ethelstani: reverse, Torhthelm. Athelstan I, king of Kent and East Anglia.] Assoc. Archit. Socs.' Rpts., 7, pp. 252–56. 1864.

8984 —— New types of the first Ethelstan. Num. Chron., N.S. 4, pp. 190–92. 1864.

8985 Pownall (Assheton). On a unique penny of Athelstan I. [Obverse, Ethelstani : reverse, Torhthelm.] Trans. Leices. Archit. Soc., 2, pp. 274–75. 1870.

8986 Shaw (Samuel). New coin of Beorchtric. Num. Chron., 17, pp. 59–61. 1854.

148. MERCIA

8987 Allan (John). Offa's imitation of an Arab dinar. Num. Chron., 4th S. 14, pp. 77–89. 1914.

8988 Bergne (John B.). [Coin of Offa]. J. Brit. Archaeol. Assoc., 21, pp. 353–54. 1865.

8989 Boileau (*Sir* John P.) *bart.* Notice of a Saxon silver coin found at Burgh castle, [Suffolk]. [Ceolwulf I of Mercia, 819–21 : Ferbald, moneyer.] Norfolk archaeology, 6, pp. 38–41. 1864.

8990 Brooke (George Cyril). Anglo-Saxon acquisitions of the British Museum. i. Thrymsa and sceatta series, Mercia. Num. Chron., 5th S. 2, pp. 214–44 + plate 10. 1922.

8991 Carlyon-Britton (Philip William Poole). The gold mancus of Offa. Br. Num. J., 5, pp. 55–72, + 2 plates, + map. 1909.

8992 —— A penny of Æthelred, subregulus of Mercia, son-in-law of Ælfred the Great. Br. Num. J., 8, pp. 55–59. 1912.

8993 D. (F.). Arrangement of Mercian pennies, bearing the inscription, ' Ceolwulf ', or ' Ciolwulf rex '. Num. Chron., 4, pp. 23–27. 1841.

8994 Evans (*Sir* John). Note upon two unpublished Saxon pennies. [Offa and Ceolwulf.] Num. Chron., N.S. 6, pp. 307–10. 1866.

8995 Faulkner (Charles). [Exhibition of a penny of Offa from Deddington Castle, Oxon., and of a penny of Ethelred (' Rex Ang '.) from Brackley, Northants.] J. Brit. Archaeol. Assoc., 22, p. 245. 1866.

8996 Grantley (John Richard Brinsley Norton) *5th baron*. Notes on a penny of Offa with new type of reverse. Num. Chron., 3rd S. 16, pp. 270–71. 1896.

8997 Haigh (Daniel Henry). Coin of Offa with scs Petrvs [on its reverse]. Num. Chron., N.S. 4, pp. 223–24. 1864.

8998 Hamper (William). On a penny of Offa. Archaeologia, 23, pp. 403–05. 1831.

8999 Hawkins (Edward). Remarks on the coins of the kings of Mercia. *Same jnl.*, 23, pp. 395–98, + 1 plate. 1831.

9000 Heywood (Nathan). The kingdom and coins of Burgred, [852–74]. Trans. Lancs. and Ches. Antiq. Soc., 2 (1884), pp. 46–53. 1885.

9001 —— The kingdom and coins of Burgred. Br. Num. J., 3, pp. 59–66, + 1 plate. 1906.

9002 Keary (Charles Francis). Art on the coins of Offa. Num. Chron., N.S. 15, pp. 206–15, + plate 5. 1875.

9003 Kell (Edmund). Ancient site of Southampton. [Particulars of ' 11 sceattæ and 14 A.–S. pennies' (Mercian).] J. Brit. Archaeol. Assoc., 20, pp. 68–73. 1864.

9004 Kenyon (Joseph). Mercian penny of Heribert. Num. Chron., 6, pp. 163–68. 1843.

9005 Latchmore (Frank). Saxon coins found near Hitchin. [Burgred and Æthelred I.] Num. Chron., 3rd S. 17, p. 248. 1897.

9006 Lockett (Richard Cyril). The coinage of Offa. Num. Chron., 4th S. 20, pp. 57–89, + plates 4–12. 1920.

9007 Longpérier (Adrien de). The gold mancus [of Offa]. Num. Chron. 5, pp. 122–24. 1842.

9008 —— Remarkable gold coin of Offa. [Arabic dinar, of 157=774.] Num. Chron., 4, pp. 232–34. 1841.

9009 [?]Longstaffe (William Hylton Dyer). Coins of Aelfred and Burgred found at Gainford [co. Durham.] Archaeol. Æl., N.S. 6, pp. 233–34. 1865.

9010 Lucas (John Clay). Anglo-Saxon coins found in Sussex. [Of Offa and of Cenwulf.] Sussex Archaeol. Collns., 21, pp. 219–20. 1869.

9011 Ouvry (Frederic). Coin of Offa [discovered at Mentmore, Bucks.]. [Figure in text.] Proc. Soc. Antiq., 3, p. 222. 1856.

9012 Pownall (Assheton). The coins of Offa. Trans. Leic. Archit. Soc., 4, pp. 326–27. 1878.

9013 —— Offa, king of Mercia. Num. Chron., N.S. 15, pp. 196–205, + plate 5. 1875.

9014 Shetelig (Haakon). A coin of Offa found in a Viking-age burial at Voss, Norway. Br. Numism. J., 5, pp. 51–54. 1909.

9015 Smith (Charles Roach). Coins found in Kent. [Offa; Berhtulf; Æthilheard, abp. Canterbury; Cenwulf, etc., from collection of W. H. Rolfe.] Collectanea Antiqua, 1, pp. 63–64, + 2 plates. 1848.

9016 —— Penny of Ceolwulf, from [Toddington], Bedfordshire. Num. Chron., N.S. 5, p. 168. 1865.

149. NORTHUMBRIA (INCLUDING ARCHBISHOPS OF YORK)

9017 [Anon.] Penny of Regnald. [10th c. ? coins of Irish origin.] Num. Chron., 1, p. 119. 1839.

9018 Adamson (John). An account (Further account, etc.) of the discovery at Hexham, Northumberland, of a brass vessel containing a number of the Anglo-Saxon coins called stycas. [Eanred, Æthelred II, Redulf (=Rædwulf), abps. Eanbald, Wigmund, etc. Early 9th c.] Archaeologia, 25, pp. 279–310, + 25 plates: 26, pp. 346–48, + 7 plates. 1834–36.

9019 Allan (John). A collection of Northumbrian stycas in the possession of Sir Carnaby Haggerston. [9th c. Eanred (36), Æthelred II (34), Rædwulf (1): abps. of York—Eanbald II (1), Wigmund (19).] Hist. Berwick. Nat. Club, 29, pp. 289–91, + 1 plate. 1937.

9020 Allen (Derek Fortrose). Northumbrian pennies of the tenth century. Br. Num. J., 22 (1934–7), pp. 175–86. + 1 plate. 1938.

9021 Andrew (Walter Jonathan). Coins commemorating the rebuilding of York minster, A.D. 921–25. Br. Num. J., 20 (1929–30), pp. 31–32. 1932.

9022 Auden (George Augustus). A leaden cross bearing a styca impression and other antiquities found in York. Br. Num. J., 4, pp. 235–37, + 1 plate. 1908.

9023 B—. Saxon skeatta of Wildfrid, [abp. of York]. [Eotberchtul, moneyer. *See also* **9037, 9062.**] Num. J., 1, pp. 18–25, 204 [not Wilfrid's]. 1836–37.

9024 Benson (George). Coins: especially those relating to York. [Pp. 12–17, 33–52, 65–68, 73–79, 100, 102–3, plates 5, 6, 8, the Anglian kingdom of Northumbria, the Viking kingdom of York, the Anglo-Danish mint. William I, the York archiepiscopal mint.] Ann. Rept. Yorks. Phil. Soc., 1913, pp. 1–104, + 8 plates. 1914.

9025 Brooke (George Cyril). Anglo-Saxon acquisitions of the British Museum. iii. Northumbria. Num. Chron., 5th S. 4, pp. 86–95. 1924.

9026 Caine (Caesar). The archiepiscopal coins of York. pp. 74. 8° York, 1908.

9027 Cowper (Henry Swainson). Bone cave at Grange[-over-Sands]. [Discovery of 7 Northumbrian stycas of Eanred, Æthelred II, and abp. Wigmund.] Proc. Soc. Antiq., 2nd S. 14, pp. 227–30. 1892.

9028 Creeke (Anthony Buck). On silver coins of Eanred and Ethelred II, of Northumbria. Num. Chron., N.S. 20, pp. 62–65. 1880.

9029 —— On the coinage of Northumbria. Trans. Lancs. and Ches. Antiq. Soc., 2 (1884), pp. 28–32. 1885.

9030 —— The regal sceatta and styca series of Northumbria. Br. Num. J., 1, pp. 65–96, + 2 plates. 1905.
F f

9031 Creeke (Anthony Buck). The sceatta and styca coinage of the early archbishops of York. Br. Num. J., 2, pp. 7–20, + 1 plate. 1906.

9032 —— Unpublished stycas of Ælfwald I and Æthelred I. Num. Chron., 4th S. 2, pp. 310–11. 1902.

9033 Cuff (James Dodsley). On Anglo-Saxon coins [stycas] discovered at York in the year 1842. [531 of Eanred, 919 of Æthelred II, 63 of Redulf (=Rædwulf) 61 of Osberht, 1 of Eanbald, 237 of Wigmund, 23 of Wulfhere, 423 illegible.] Num. Chron., 9, pp. 121–27, + 1 plate 1846.

9034 D. (F.) and **Hawkins** (Edward). On the Northumbrian skeattas. Num. Chron., 3, pp. 184–57. 1841.

9035 Ellis (*Sir* Henry). Styca of Huth. Num. J., 2, pp. 99–100. 1837.

9036 Evans (*Sir* John). On a small hoard of Saxon sceattas found near Cambridge. [Northumbrian.] Num. Chron., 3rd S. 14, pp. 18–28, + plate 2. 1894.

9037 Fairless (Joseph) and **Cuff** (James Dodsley). On the skeatta attributed to Wildfrid, archbishop of York, in article 3[**9023**]. [Both attribute to Aldfrith.] Num. J., 1, pp. 187–89. 1837.

9038 Fairless (Joseph). Stycas found at York. [Eanred, Edilred (=Æthelred II).] Num. Chron., 7, pp. 34–36. 1844.

9039 Featherstonhaugh (Walker). The stycas of Northumbria. Proc. Soc. Antiq. Newcastle, 2nd S. 5, pp. 206–13. 1892.

9040 Fennell (William). An account of a hoard of Northumbrian stycas discovered in Yorkshire. [In field near Ulleskelf, 1846.] J. Brit. Archaeol. Assoc., 4, pp. 127–32. 1849.

9041 Grantley (John Richard Brinsley Norton), *5th baron*. On a unique styca of Alchred of Northumbria and archbishop Ecgberht. Num. Chron., 3rd S. 13, pp. 266–72. 1893.

9042 —— On the North-humbrian coinage of A.D. 758–808. Num. Chron., 3rd S. 17, pp. 134–44, + plate 7. 1897.

9043 Grantley (John Richard Brinsley Norton). St. Cuthbert's pennies. Br. Num. J., 8, pp. 49–53. 1912.

9044 —— A unique styca of Ethelred I, king of Northumbria. Num. Chron., 3rd S. 12, pp. 87–88. 1892.

9045 Haigh (Daniel Henry). The coins of the Danish kings of Northumberland. Archaeol. Æl., N.S. 7, pp. 21–77, + 7 plates. 1876.

9046 —— On the pennies of Regnald of Northumbria. Num. Chron., 2, pp. 7–11. 1840.

9047 Hawkins (Edward). Remarks on the coins of Northumbria. Num. Chron., 1, pp. 1–4. 1839.

9048 —— Remarks upon the skeattae and styca attributed to Huth of Northumbria. Num. Chron., 1, pp. 5–12. 1839.

9049 Heywood (Nathan). Coinage of Elfwald II, A.D. 806–807. Num. Chron., 3rd S. 7, pp. 220–21. 1887.

9050 —— A find of Anglo-Saxon stycas at Lancaster. Br. Num. J., 11 (1915), pp. 1–2. 1916.

9051 —— Find of stycas. Num. Chron., 3rd S. 8, pp. 95–96. 1888.

9052 —— Notes on Northumbrian stycas inscribed 'hoavð re✠'. Num. Chron., 3rd S. 10, p. 335. 1890.

9053 —— A parcel of stycas from the York find, 1842. Br. Num. J., 7, pp. 331–34. 1911.

9054 —— The stycas of North Humbria. Trans. Lancs. and Ches. Antiq. Soc., 15 (1897), pp. 81–99. 1898.

9055 Hodgson (John). An account of a Saxon coin of Ecgfrith, king of Northumberland. [sic.] Archaeol. Æl. [1st S.] 1, pp. 124–25, + plate 6, fig. H. 1822.

9056 Keary (Charles Francis). On the coins of Ethelred, king of Northumbria. [Attributes to Æthelred II coins attributed by Rashleigh [9075] to Æthelred I.] Num. Chron., N.S. 14, pp. 94–99. 1874.

9057 L. (C. W.). Skeatta of Aldfrith, king of Northumbria. Num. J., 1, pp. 78–79. 1836.

9058 Liebermann (Felix). Der angebliche Hammer Thors auf Yorker Münzen 10. Jhs. Arch. Stud. neueren Spr., Bd. 142 (N.S. 42), pp. 127–28. 1921.

9059 Lindsay (John). Coins of Huath, king of Northumberland. Num. J., 2, pp. 234–36. 1838.

9060 —— On some Anglo-Saxon stycas. [Legend ✠ Edredmre, retrograde.] Num. Chron., 6, pp. 38–41. 1843.

9061 —— On the appropriation of certain coins to Northumbria and East Anglia. Num. Chron., 2, pp. 132–38. 1840.

9062 —— On the skeatta ascribed to Wildfrid in article 3 [9023]. [Assigns to Egfrid, king of Mercia.] Num. J., 1, pp. 86–88. 1836.

9063 —— On the styca, supposed of Huth, or Huath of Northumbria. Num. Chron., 1, pp. 141–45. 1839.

9064 Montagu (H.). Silver stycas of Northumbria and York. Num. Chron., 3rd S. 3, pp. 26–31. 1883.

9065 Nelson (Philip). Notes on Danish and Anglo-Saxon coins : were Cunnetti coins struck at York ? [Silver coins of Guthred-Cnut struck at York.] Num. Chron., 6th S. 5, pp. 137–42. 1945.

9066 — A rare York coin of Guthred-Cnut, [king of York]. Num. Chron., 6th S. 8, pp. 236–37. 1948.

9067 —— Some rare Norman coins of York. [William I—Stephen.] Num. Chron., 6th S. 7, pp. 72–73. 1947.

9068 —— Some unpublished coins of Northumbria. [Cnut, Siefred, Regnald, 877–921.] Num. Chron., 6th S. 4, pp. 120–22. 1944.

9069 —— Three unpublished coins of Siefred of Northumbria [894–98]. Num. Chron., 6th S. 3, pp. 106–07. 1943.

9070 —— An unpublished archiepiscopal coin of York. [?New coin-type of Siefred, ob. 898.] Num. Chron., 6th S. 7, pp. 71–72. 1947.

9071 Nelson (Philip). An unpublished penny of Anlaf [II], Sihtricson. [York, 941–43.] Num. Chron., 6th S. 8, p. 97. 1948.

9072 —— An unpublished York penny of Guthred-Cnut. Num. Chron., 6th S. 10, p. 318. 1950.

9073 Parsons (H. Alexander). The coins of Æthelred I. of Northumbria. Br. Num. J., 10, pp. 1–8. 1914.

9074 —— The coins of archbishop Eanbald II of York. Br. Num. J., 12 (1916), pp. 1–14. 1918.

9075 Rashleigh (Jonathan). Remarks on the coins of the Anglo-Saxon and Danish kings of Northumberland. Num. Chron., N.S. 9, pp. 54–107, + 2 plates. 1869.

9076 Selby (John S. Donaldson). On the foundations of ancient buildings, and coins of the Saxon kingdom of Northumbria, recently discovered at Holy Island. [Styca of Æthelred II, king of Northumbria (840–48) and styca of Wigmund, abp. of York (851–54).] Hist. Berwick. Nat. Club, 2, pp. 159–63. 1845.

9077 Smith (Charles Roach). On a hoard of stycas discovered at York, and sent by Mr. William Hargrove to the recent congress at Gloucester. J. Brit. Archaeol. Assoc., 2, pp. 230–33. 1847.

9078 —— On some Anglo-Saxon stycas discovered at York. [365 stycas, Eanred to Osbercht, 808–40.] Num. Chron., 7, pp. 99–104, + 1 plate. 1844.

9079 Smith (John Alexander). Notice of an Anglo-Saxon styca of Osbercht, king of Northumbria. [Found near Jedburgh.] Proc. Soc. Antiq. Scot., 3, pp. 300–03. 1862.

9080 Webster (W.). Attribution of a new Saxon type to a king of Northumbria. Num. Chron., 16, pp. 183–84. 1854.

150.   WESSEX, PRE-ALFRED

9081 [Anon.] Coin of Ethelwulf. [From London Wall.] Num. J., 2, p. 109. 1837.

9082 Allan (John). A find of [9th c.] Saxon and Carolinian coins in S. Wales. [Penny of Egbert of Wessex.] Num. Chron., 6th S. 8, p. 236. 1948.

9083 Brooke (George Cyril). Anglo-Saxon acquisitions of the British Museum. iv. Wessex. Num. Chron., 5th S. 4, pp. 239–53. 1924.

9084 Carlyon-Britton (Philip William Poole). A penny of Beorchtric, king of Wessex. Num. Chron., 5th S. 10, pp. 39–43. 1930.

9085 Combe (Taylor). An account of some Anglo-Saxon pennies found at Dorking, in Surrey. [Mostly Ethelwulf and Ethelbert.] Archaeologia, 19, pp. 109–19, + 2 plates. 1821.

9086 Howorth (*Sir* Henry Hoyle). Ecgberht, king of the West Saxons and the Kent men, and his coins. Num. Chron., 3rd S. 20, pp. 66–87. 1900.

9087 —— Some early gold coins struck in Britain. [? at Winchester. ?by earliest bishops, before beginning of the regal series of Wessex.] Num. Chron., 3rd S. 13, pp. 259–66. 1893.

9088 Lawrence (L. A.). Coinage of Æthelbald [of Wessex]. Num. Chron., 3rd S. 13, pp. 40–45, + plate 4. 1893.

9089 Montagu (H.). Coinage of Æthelbald of Wessex. Num. Chron., 3rd S. 7, pp. 132–38. 1887.

9090 Whitbourn (Richard). On two unpublished coins of Egbert. Num Chron., N.S. 3, pp. 46–47. 1863.

151.   ALFRED

9091 Anscombe (Alfred). The inscription on the Oxford pennies of the *Ohsnaforda* type. Br. Num. J., 3, pp. 67–100. 1906.

9092 Blunt (Christopher E.). A new type for Alfred [from Southampton]. Brit. Num J., 26 (3rd S. 6), pp. 213–15. 1951.

9093 Evans (*Sir* John). The cross and pall on the coins of Ælfred the Great. Num. Chron., 4th S. 2, pp. 202–07. 1902.

9094 Grueber (Herbert Appold). A find of coins of Alfred the Great at Stamford [Lincs.]. Num. Chron., 4th S. 3, pp. 347–55. 1903.

9095 Haigh (Daniel Henry). Coins of Ælfred the Great. Num. Chron., N.S. 10, pp. 19–39, + 7 plates. 1870.

9096 Hills (William). Coin of Alfred. [Found at Chichester, 1871.] Sussex Archaeol. Collns., 24, p. 298. 1872.

9097 Kenyon (Joseph). Worcester penny of Alfred. Num. Chron., 7, pp. 39–40. 1844.

9098 Lawrence (L. A.). A remarkable penny of king Alfred. Brit. Num. J., 3, pp. 101–06. 1906.

9099 Marsh (William E.). Note on pennies of Alfred and Great with the obverse legend divided into three or four parts. Num. Chron., 4th S. 19, pp. 253–54. 1919.

9100 Schnittger (Bror). Ett Alfred den stores mynt funnet i svensk jord. Fornvännen, 2, pp. 191–92. 1917.

152. EDWARD THE ELDER TO EDGAR

9101 [Anon.] Saxon coins found at Bangor, Caernarvonshire. [Edgar (2). *See also* pp. 403–04, to account for their presence at Bangor.] Arch. Camb., 1, p. 276. 1846.

9102 Andrew (Walter Jonathan). An unpublished coin of Athelstan. Br. Num. J., 21 (1931–3), pp. 194–96. 1935.

9103 Anscombe (Alfred). ' Fastolfi moneta ', ' Fastolfes môt ', and the like, on coins of Eadgar rex Anglorum. Br. Num. J., 20 (1929–30), pp. 33–48. 1932.

9104 Bateman (Thomas). List of a portion of the Anglo-Saxon pennies found in June 1855 . . . at Scotby, near Carlisle. [Edward the Elder and Athelstan.] J. Brit. Archaeol. Assoc., 11, pp. 350–51. 1855.

9105 Blunt (Christopher E.). A gold penny of Edward the Elder. Br. Num. J., 25 (3rd S. 5), pp. 277–81. 1949.

9106 Brooke (George Cyril). Anglo-Saxon acquisitions of the British Museum. v. Alfred to Eadwig. Num. Chron., 5th S. 5, pp. 343–65. 1925.

9107 —— An Anglo-Saxon find, *temp.* Edward the Elder—Aethelstan. Num. Chron., 5th S. 11, pp. 133–35. 1931.

9108 Christmas (Henry). Unedited Saxon and English coins. [Penny of Eadgar struck at St. Edmundsbury.] Num. Chron., 7, pp. 135–42. 1844.

9109 D. (F.). Penny of Æthelstan. Num. Chron., 5, pp. 127–29. 1842.

9110 Dolley (R. H.). Two coins [pennies] of Edgar recently discovered at York. Num. Chron., 6th S. 12, pp. 118. 1952.

9111 Evans (*Sir* John). Anglo-Saxon coins found in Meath. [Edward the Elder, Athelstan, Edmund I and Edred : and 3 Northumbrian coins (Eric, Anlaf II and ? Anlaf III).] Num. Chron., 3rd S. 5, pp. 128–44. 1885.

9112 —— On a hoard of [48] Anglo-Saxon coins found in Ireland. [Edward the Elder—Edgar, and 6 of Anlaf of Northumbria.] Num. Chron., N.S. 3, pp. 48–54. 1863.

9113 Grueber (Herbert Appold). An Anglo-Saxon brooch. [Copy of reverse type of penny of Edward the Elder, c. 920. Found at Winchester.] Num. Chron., 4th S. 8, pp. 83–84. 1908.

9114 —— The Douglas find of Anglo-Saxon coins and ornaments. [95 coins : Athelstan—Edgar, and one of Anlaf of Northumbria.] Num. Chron., 4th S. 13, pp. 322–48. 1913.

9115 Hughes (Thomas). On some Anglo-Saxon coins discovered in the foundations of St. John's church, Chester. [Edward the Elder.] J. Archit., Archaeol., and Hist. Soc. Chester, 2 (1855–62), pp. 289–308, + 5 plates. 1864.

9116 Keary (Charles Francis). A hoard of Anglo-Saxon coins found in Rome and described by Sig. de Rossi. [Alfred—Edmund.] Num. Chron., 3rd S. 4, pp. 225–55. 1884.

9117 Lindsay (John). Penny of Edward the Elder. Num. Chron., 3, p. 195. 1841.

9118 Lumb (George Denison). Edward the Elder—pennies with façade of a building. Br. Num. J., 20 (1929–30), pp. 27–29. 1932.

9119 Malcomson (Robert) and **Smith** (Aquilla). Five silver coins, part of a recent railway 'find' in the north of Ireland. [Edgar.] J. Kilkenny Archaeol. Soc., [8] N.S. 5, pp. 51–52. 1864.

9120 Montagu (H.). Halfpenny of Eadred. Num. Chron., 3rd S. 4, p. 350. 1884.

9121 Nelson (Philip). Some unpublished Anglo-Saxon coins. [Edward the Elder to Eadwig.] Num. Chron., 6th S. 7, pp. 68–71. 1947.

9122 —— A unique penny of Edward the Elder. Num. Chron., 6th S. 4, p. 122. 1944.

9123 —— An unpublished York penny of Edred. Num. Chron., 6th S. 8, p. 96. 1948.

9124 Newstead (Robert). A find of coins of Eadred, Eadwig, and Eadgar at Chester. Br. Num. J., 24 (1941–2), pp. 47–49. 1943.

9125 Peacock (John). Find of Saxon coins at Chester. [Eadred, Eadwig and Eadgar.] Num. Chron., N.S. 6, p. 322. 1866.

9126 Porter (J. L.). Find of coins in Ireland. [At Burt, Donegal. Silver pennies of Edgar.] Num. Chron., N.S. 4, pp. 156–57. 1864.

9127 Quine (John). The Douglas treasure trove [June, 1894]. [Alias Woodbourne treasure-trove. Coins, temp. Athelstan, Edwy and Edgar : and (?) Danish jewellery, also of 10th c.] Yu Lioar Manninagh, 2, pp. 242–45. 1901.

9128 Reade (George H.) and **Smith** (Aquilla). [Report on seven Saxon pennies (Athelstan to Edgar)] discovered in June 1864, on the property of Travers Wright, Esq., Killincoole Castle, County Louth. J. Kilkenny Archaeol. Soc., N.S. 5, pp. 373–76. 1867.

9129 Richardson (Adam B.). Notice of a hoard of broken silver ornaments and Anglo-Saxon and Oriental coins found in Skye. [Edward the Elder (31), Athelstan (56), abp. Plegmund (1), Sihtric of Northumbria (1).] Proc. Soc. Antiq. Scot., 26 (3rd S. 2), pp. 225–40. 1892.

9130 Rotheram (Edward Crofton). Find of tenth century coins in co. Meath. [Eadred, Eadwig, Edmund, Anlaf.] J. Roy. Soc. Antiq. Ireland, 30 (5th S. 10), pp. 253–54. 1900.

9131 S. Penny of Edred. Num. Chron., 4, p. 184. 1841.

9132 Scott (W. H.). Report on a large hoard of Anglo-Saxon pennies, in silver, found in the island of Islay [in 1850]. [Largely Athelstan-Edgar.] Proc. Soc. Antiq. Scot., 1, pp. 74–81. 1852.

9133 Skippon (*Sir* Philip). An account of some Saxon coins found [at Honedon, near Clare] in Suffolk. (Remarks upon the foregoing observations, by W.W.). [21. Athelstan, Edmund, Edred.] Phil. Trans. Roy. Soc., 16, pp. 356–61, 361–66. 1687.

9134 Smith (Aquilla). On Anglo-Saxon coins found in Ireland. [8 pennies of Edward the Elder, one of St. Edmund, and a Cufic coin.] Num. Chron., N.S. 3, pp. 255–57. 1863.

9135 —— Saxon coins found in Ireland. [Edward the Elder and Athelstan.] Num. Chron., 3rd S. 2, pp. 103–07, 298 : 3, pp. 282–87. 1882–83.

9136 Walker (John). A hoard of Anglo-Saxon coins from Tetney, Lincolnshire. [Silver pennies of Eadred, Eadwig and Eadgar (with 6 exceptions).] Num. Chron., 6th S. 5, pp. 81–95, + 1 plate. 1945.

9137 Webster (Graham). A Saxon treasure hoard found at Chester, 1950. [522 coins, Alfred to Eadgar. Pp. 29–31, A note on the coins, by R. H. Dolley : pp. 31–32, A note on the late Saxon pot containing the hoard, by G. C. Dunning, 8568.] Antiq. J., 33, pp. 22–32, + 1 plate. 1953.

9138 Wright (Travers) and **Smith** (Aquilla). Saxon coins discovered in June 1864 [at] Killincoole castle, county of Louth. [Pennies of Athelstan (1), Eadred (3), Eadwig (2), Edgar (1).] J. Kilkenny Archaeol. Soc., [8] N.S. 5, pp. 373–76. 1865.

153. EDWARD THE MARTYR AND ÆTHELRED II

9139 Baldwin (A. H.). A hoard of Æthelred II coins, 1940. Br. Num. J., 24 (1941–2), pp. 49–50. 1943.

9140 Brooke (George Cyril). Mr. Parsons' arrangement of the coin-types of Æthelred II. [*See also* **9153** and **9154**.] Num. Chron., 4th S. 10, pp. 370–80. 1910.

9141 Carlyon-Britton (Philip William Poole). The chronological sequence of the types of Eadweard the Martyr and Æthelræd II. Br. Num. J., 16 (1921–2), pp. 5–31. 1924.

9142 Dickinson (W. Binley). Find of Anglo-Saxon coins in the Isle of Man. [All of Æthelred II, of crux type.] Num. Chron., 16, pp. 99–104. 1854.

9143 —— Saxon coins found in the Isle of Man. [Further specimens (of Pax type) of Æthelred II.] Num. Chron., 17, p. 130. 1854.

9144 Evans (*Sir* John). Discovery of Anglo-Saxon coins at Ipswich. [c. 500 pennies of Æthelred II. *See also* **9155**.] Num. Chron., N.S. 4, pp. 28–33, 225. 1864.

9145 Francis (R. S.). Account of Saxon coins found at Ipswich. J. Brit. Archaeol. Assoc., 21, pp. 190–91. 1865.

9146 —— Saxon coins found at Ipswich. [c. 500 coins. Æthelred II. With names of moneyers.] East Anglian (N. and Q.), 2, p. 8. 1864.

9147 Gordon (H. D.). Find of Saxon coins at Harting, June, 1892. [5 silver pennies of Æthelred II.] Sussex Archaeol. Collns., 39, p. 225. 1894.

9148 Grueber (Herbert Appold). A rare penny of Æthelred II. Num. Chron., 3rd S. 19, pp. 344–49. 1899.

9149 Grueber (Herbert Appold). Recent hoards of coins. [Pp. 161–63, Isleworth find (Æthelred II).] Num. Chron., 3rd S. 6, pp. 161–67. 1886.

9150 Hill (George Francis). A find of coins of Eadgar, Eadweard II, and Æthelred II at Chester. Num. Chron., 4th S. 20, pp. 141–65. 1920.

9151 Holmboe (C. F.). On coins of Ethelred II. Num. Chron., 17, pp. 95–97. 1854.

9152 Mateu y Llopis (F.) and **Dolley** (R. H.). A small find of Anglo-Saxon pennies from Roncesvalles. [6, temp. Æthelred II.] Br. Num. J., 27 (1952), pp. 89–91. 1953.

9153 Parsons (H. Alexander). The coin-types of Æthelred II. [*See also* **9140** and **9154**.] Num. Chron., 4th S. 10, pp. 251–90, + plates 6 and 7. 1910.

9154 —— Mr. G. C. Brooke on ' the coin-types of Æthelred II.' A reply. [*See also* **9140** and **9153**.] Num. Chron., 4th S. 10, pp. 381–87. 1910.

9155 Pollexfen (John Hutton). Anglo-Saxon coins found at Ipswich. [Æthelred II. Additions to those described by Sir John Evans, **9144**.] Num. Chron., N.S. 8, pp. 179–80. 1868.

9156 Stephenson (Mill). A series of finds at Ewell. [P. 137 : silver penny of Æthelred II.] Surrey Archaeol. Collns., 26, pp. 135–39. 1913.

9157 Wells (William Charles). A hoard of coins of Æthelræd II found in Ireland. Br. Num. J., 17 (1923–4), pp. 51–59, + 1 plate. 1927.

154. DANISH KINGS

9158 Cursiter (James Walls). Coins found at Caldale, [Orkney]. [300. Cnut.] Old-lore Misc., V.C., 2, p. 192 : 3, pp. 11–12. 1909–10.

9159 Fonahn (A.). Notes on a hoard of medieval coins found at Stein, Ringerike, Norway. [Including A.–S., 4 of Æthelred II and 15 of Cnut.] Num. Chron., 5th S. 6, pp. 279–86. 1926.

9160 Gibbs (E. M.) and **Gunston** (Thomas). [Exhibition of a penny of Canute found in Cornwall : exhibition of 2 gold A.–S. coins found at Whaddon chase, Bucks.] J. Brit. Archaeol. Assoc., 11, pp. 261–62. 1855.

9161 Gough (Richard). A catalogue of the coins of Canute, etc. pp. 23. 4° London, 1777.

9162 Henfrey (Henry William). Penny of Canute the Great : a rectification. [To Thomsen : *in* O.S. 3, p. 121 : **8947**.] Num. Chron., N.S. 19, p. 220. 1879.

9163 Herbst (C. F.) and **Henfrey** (Henry William). Some further notes upon [**9162**]. Num. Chron., N.S. 20, pp. 226–33. 1880.

9164 Herbst (C. F.). Note upon [**9162**.] Num. Chron., 3rd S. 1, pp. 65–66. 1881.

9165 Parsons (H. Alexander). The Anglian coins of Cnut the Great. Br. Num. J., 19 (1927–8), pp. 25–67. 1930.

9166 —— The Anglo-Saxon coins of Harthacnut. Br. Num. J., 11 (1915), pp. 21–55. 1916.

9167 —— The coins of Harold I. [With 17 figures in text.] Br. Num. J., 15 (1919–20), pp. 1–48. 1921.

9168 —— Some coins of Sigtuna [near Stockholm] inscribed with the names of Æthelred, Cnut, and Harthacnut. Br. Num. J., 11 (1915), pp. 3–19. 1916.

9169 Smith (Aquilla). Did Suein as sole monarch coin money in England? Num. Chron., 3rd S. 3, pp. 63–64. 1883.

9170 Symonds (Henry). Anglo-Saxon coins found at Wedmore in 1853. [Majority of Cnut.] Proc. Somerset Arch. Soc., 69 (1923), pp. 30–37. 1924.

9171 Webster (W.). Remarks on the blundered legends found upon the Anglo-Saxon coins. [? executed by Danes during reigns of Æthelred II, Canute, and Edward the Confessor.] Num. Chron., 17, pp. 89–93. 1854.

155. EDWARD THE CONFESSOR AND HAROLD II

9172 [Anon.] Gold coin of Edward the Confessor. Num. J., 2, pp. 54, 106–07. 1837.

9173 Allen (Derek Fortrose). Edward the Confessor's gold penny. Br. Num. J., 25 (3rd S. 5), pp. 259–76, + 1 plate. 1949.

9174 Bergne (John B.). [On] six silver coins of Edward the Confessor and Harold II . . . found in a field in Washington parish [Sussex]. J. Brit. Archaeol. Assoc., 23, pp. 201–03. 1867.

9175 Burton (Frank E.). Coins of Edward the Confessor (1042–1046) and Harold II (1066). Trans. Thornton Soc., 39 (1935), pp. 37–42, + 2 plates. 1936.

9176 Carlyon-Britton (Phillip William Poole). Eadward the Confessor and his coins. Num. Chron., 4th S. 5, pp. 179–205, + plates 7–8. 1905.

9177 Combe (Boyce Harvey). Discovery at Seddlescomb of Saxon pennies of Edward the Confessor. Sussex Archaeol. Collns., 27, pp. 227–28. 1877.

9178 Evans (*Sir* John). On a hoard of Saxon pennies found in the city of London in 1872.—Appendix. [Appendix to article by Ernest Willett **9216**. Æthelred II—William I, but mostly Edward the Confessor.] Num. Chron., 3rd S. 5, pp. 254–73. 1885.

9179 Gill (Henry Septimus). Hoard of Edward the Confessor's pennies found at Sedlescombe, near Battle. Num. Chron., N.S., 19, pp. 154–56. 1879.

9180 Griffith (Guyon). Account of coins, etc., found in digging up the foundations of some old houses near the church of St. Mary Hill, London, 1774. [Coins of Edward the Confessor, Harold II and William I. P. 363, 'list of moneyers and towns' for these three reigns.] Archaeologia, 4, pp. 356–63, + 1 plate. 1786.

9181 Head (Barclay Vincent). An account of the hoard of Anglo-Saxon coins found at Chancton farm, Sussex. [c. 1720 coins. 58 of Harold II ; the rest, pennies of Edward the Confessor.] Num. Chron., N.S. 7, pp. 63–126, + plates 5 + 6. 1867.

9182 Hoare (Edward). Coin of Edward the Confessor, with probable surname. Num. Chron., 14, pp. 176–77. 1882.

9183 Lindsay (John). Unpublished pennies of Edward the Confessor. Num. Chron., 1, pp. 146–47. 1839.

9184 Lucas (John Clay). The hoard of Anglo-Saxon coins found at Chancton farm, Sussex. [1720 sent to B.M. 58 pennies of Harold II, rest of Edward the Confessor.] Sussex Archaeol. Collns., 20, pp. 212–21, + 1 plate. 1868.

9185 Margary (Ivan D.). The Penfold bequest ; coins and tokens. The Anglo-Saxon coins : addenda. [Edward the Confessor pennies. See also **9198.**] Sussex N. and Q., 10, p. 186. 1945.

9186 Parsons (H. Alexander). The first authorized issue of Edward the Confessor. Br. Num. J., 20 (1929–30), pp. 95–104. 1932.

9187 R. (E. S. G.). An English gold penny. [Of Edward the Confessor.] B.M.Q., 17, pp. 10–11, + 1 plate. 1952.

9188 Raper (W. A.) and **Willett** (Ernest H.). On the silver pennies of Edward the Confessor found at Sedlescomb. Sussex Archaeol. Collns., 33, pp. 1–38, + 1 plate. 1883.

9189 Smith (Samuel) *junr.* A rare variety of the penny of Edward the Confessor. Num. Chron., 3rd S. 5, pp. 145–47. 1885.

9190 Wakefield (Charles). Description of the coins of Edward the Confessor in the collection of the Yorkshire Philosophical Society. Ann. Rept. Yorks. Philos. Soc., 1910, pp. 1–12, + 1 plate. 1911.

156. GENERAL AND MISCELLANEOUS, 9th–11th c.

9191 [Anon.] Discovery of Anglo-Saxon coins [of 10th and 11th centuries at Egersund] in Norway. Num. Chron., 1, p. 207. 1839.

9191a [Anon.] Iona : discovery of a silver coin hoard. [Over 300. Athelstan-Æthelred II : more than half, Edgar.] Archaeol. News Letter, 3, p. 86. 1950.

9192 [Anon.]. Saxon coins found in the island of Gothland. [c. 600, from Eadgar to Edward the Confessor.] Num. Chron., 8, pp. 170–71. 1845.

9193 Ade (Charles). Account of the discovery of Anglo-Saxon coins at Milton Street, near Alfriston. [From Canute to Edward the Confessor.] Sussex Archaeol. Collns., 1, pp. 38–42. 1848.

9194 Andrews (James Petit). [Exhibition to the Society of Antiquaries of] forty-seven coins of Anglo-Saxon kings . . . found July 1762, under a skull in the churchyard of Kintbury, Berks. . . . [also] about forty other Saxon coins. . . [Athelstan to Harold II.] Archaeologia, 8, pp. 430–31. 1787.

9195 Boyd (William C.). Some unpublished varieties of Saxon coins, [Eanred, Æthelred II (stycae) : Burgred. Ælfred, Eadred, Eadgar, Æthelred II, Cnut, Harthacnut, Edward the Confessor, Harold II (pennies).] Num. Chron., 3rd S. 20, pp. 265–69. 1900.

9196 Brøegger (Anton Wilhelm). Anglo-Saxon silver coins from the XIth century in a silver-hoard from Ryfylke, Norway. Saga-Book V.C. 7, pp. 232–46. 1912.

9197 Brooke (George Cyril). Quando moneta vertebatur : the change of coin-types in the eleventh century ; its bearing on mules and overstrikes. Br. Num. J., 20 (1929–30), pp. 105–16. 1932.

9198 Caldecott (J. B.). The Penfold bequest : coins and tokens. [Pp. 100–04 : 1. Anglo-Saxon pennies of Æthelred II—William I. See also **9185.**] Sussex Archaeol. Collns., 83, pp. 100–14. 1943.

9199 Caraher (Patrick) *finder.* Recent finds in county Louth : Saxon coins at Smarmore, Ardee. [10th c.] County Louth Archaeol. J., 6, p. 254. 1928.

9200 Creeke (Anthony Buck). Unpublished varieties of Anglo-Saxon and English coins. [Pennies of Ergbeorght, Anlaf, Eadred, Eadgar, Canute, Harold I.] Num. Chron., N.S. 16, pp. 150–52. 1876.

9201 Evans (*Sir* John). On gold coins struck in late Saxon times. Num. Chron., N.S. 19, pp. 62–65. 1879.

9202 Hawkins (Edward). Account of some Saxon pennies, and other articles [e.g. forks], found at Sevington, north Wilts. [9th c. coins] Archaeologia, 27, pp. 301–05, + 2 plates. 1838.

9203 Lindsay (John). Unpublished penny of Aethelstan, and half-penny of Edward the Confessor. Num. Chron., 2, pp. 35–37. 1840.

9204 Parsons (H. Alexander). Assays and imitations, foreign and native, of the late Saxon period, A.D. 975–1066. Br. Num. J., 17 (1923–4), pp. 61–97. 1927.

9205 —— Remarks on hoards of late Anglo-Saxon coins. Br. Num. J., 16 (1921–2), pp. 33–57, + 2 plates. 1924.

9206 —— Symbols and double names on late Saxon coins. [59 figures in text.] Br. Num. J., 13 (1917), pp. 1–74. 1919.

9207 Person (Erik). Anglo-Saxon coins in the find of Torlarp, Sweden. [*Temp.* Æthelred II, Cnut and Edward the Confessor.] Num. Chron., 5th S. 15, pp. 42–45. 1935.

9208 Petersen (Jan). Anglo-Saxon finds in Norway : coins of the Danegeld. J. Brit. Archaeol. Assoc., N.S. 29, pp. 264–66. 1923.

9209 Rasmusson (N. L.). Nordens tidigaste import av engelska mynt. [Probably in 10th c.] Fornvännen, 29, pp. 366–72. 1934.

9210 Smith (Henry Ecroyd). A record of the archaeological products of the sea-shore of Cheshire in 1867. [Pp. 169–71, Saxon and Danish. Coins of Canute and Edward the Confessor, beads, etc.] Reliquary, 19, pp. 167–76. 1869.

9211 Stevenson (Robert B. K.). A hoard of Anglo-Saxon coins found at Iona abbey. [c. 350 coins from Athelstan to Æthelred II, also York (Viking).] Proc. Soc. Antiq. Scot., 85 (1950–51), pp. 170–75. 1953.

9212 —— The Iona hoard of Anglo-Saxon coins. Num. Chron., 6th S. 11, pp. 68–90, + chart (of 7th–11th c. coin finds in Scotland). 1951.

9213 Symonds (Henry). Anglo-Saxon coins in Taunton museum. [Pennies of Edgar (1), and of Edward the Confessor

(3).] Proc. Somerset Arch. Soc., 73 (1927), pp. 125–26. 1928.

9214 Vaux (W. Sandys Wright). An account of a find of coins in the parish of Goldborough, Yorkshire. [One of Alfred, one of Edward the Elder : the rest Oriental from 889–932.] Num. Chron., N.S. 1, pp. 65–71, + 1 plate. 1861.

9215 —— [Two Anglo-Saxon] coins discovered in Orkney. [St. Peter's penny, 10th c., and Athelstan, 925.] Proc. Soc. Antiq. Scot., 3, p. 250. 1862.

9216 Willett (Ernest H.). On a hoard of Saxon pennies found in the city of London in 1872. [Æthelred II (4), Cnut (19), Edward the Confessor (2,798), Harold II (1), William I (5).] Num. Chron., N.S. 16, pp. 328–94, + 3 plates. 1876.

157. WILLIAM I

(including find at Beaworth, near Winchester of 8000–9000 William I pennies)

9217 [Anon.] Coins of the Conqueror discovered at York. [Mostly struck at York : list of moneyers and mints given.] Num. Chron., 8, pp. 123–25. 1845.

9218 B. (J.). Pennies of William the Conqueror. Num. Chron., 1, pp. 119–22. 1839.

9219 Bergne (John B.). [Exhibition of] three pennies of William the Conqueror and William Rufus. [From Beaworth hoard.] J. Brit. Archaeol. Assoc., 21, pp. 227–28. 1865.

9220 Brooke (George Cyril). Notes on the reign of William I. [i. The Berkeley mint : ii. Comparison of dies : iii. Alterations of dies.] Num. Chron., 4th S. 11, pp. 268–90, + plates. 14–17. 1911.

9221 Carlyon-Britton (Philip William Poole). A numismatic history of the reigns of William I and II (1066–1100). Br. Num. J., 2, pp. 87–184 : 3, pp. 117–72 : 4, pp. 47–78 : 5, pp. 97–122 : 6, pp. 147–76 : 7, pp. 1–25 : 8, pp. 61–81 : 9, pp. 129–43 : 10, pp. 33–41 : + 30 plates [in all]. 1905–14.

9222 Carlyon-Britton (Philip William Poole). On the coins of William I and II and the sequence of the types. Num. Chron., 4th S. 2, pp. 208–23. 1902.

9223 Carlyon-Britton (Raymond C.). A hoard of coins of William the Conqueror found in a trench in the war area. Br. Num. J., 12 (1916), pp. 15–32, + 4 plates. 1918.

9224 Crowther (G. F.). Pennies of William I and William II. ['Pax' pennies.] Num. Chron., 3rd S. 11, pp. 25–33. 1891.

9225 (?) **Dale** (William). Beauworth. [Pax pennies of William I.] Papers and Proc. Hants. F. C., 7 i, pp. 52–58. 1914.

9226 Hawkins (Edward). Description of a large collection of coins of William the Conqueror, discovered at Beaworth, in Hampshire, with an attempt at a chronological arrangement of the coins of William I and II. Archaeologia, 26, pp. 1–25, + 1 plate. 1836.

9227 J. (J.). Unpublished penny of William I. [?as to Ælner on Snvd.] Num. Chron., 5, p. 159. 1842.

9228 Keary (Charles Francis). Discovery of coins of William I and William II at Tamworth [Staffs.]. Num. Chron., N.S. 17, pp. 340–41. 1877.

9229 L. (C. W.). Pennies of William the Conqueror. [From Malmesbury.] Num. J., 2, p. 106. 1837.

9230 Lawrence (L. A.). On some coins of William I and II. Num. Chron., 3rd S. 17, pp. 226–34, + plate 10. 1897.

9231 Montagu (H.). Note on an unpublished penny of William I and on the word pax. Num. Chron., 3rd S. 4, pp. 59–65. 1884.

9232 Nelson (Philip). Three rare Norman coins of York. [Two of William I.] Num. Chron., 6th S. 8, p. 237. 1948.

9233 —— Two unpublished Norman coins of London mint [in writer's collection.]. [William I, type VI, moneyer Edred: and William II, type II.] Num. Chron., 6th S. 9, p. 258. 1949.

9234 Ogden (William Sharp). Concerning the evolution of some reverse types of the Anglo-Norman coinage. [William I, etc. 5 pp. of illustrations in text.] Br. Num. J., 2, pp. 57–85, + 1 plate. 1906.

9235 Packe (Alfred E.). The coinage of the Norman kings. [Plate 11, coins of William I and II.] Num. Chron., 3rd S. 13, pp. 129–45, + 2 plates. 1893.

9236 Parsons (H. Alexander). The prototype of the first coinage of William the Conqueror. Br. Num. J., 15 (1919–20), pp. 49–56. 1921.

9237 S. (R.). On the coins of William the Conqueror. Num. Chron., 2, pp. 42–47. 1840.

9238 Spicer (F.). The coinage of William I and William II. Chapter 1, William I. Num. Chron., 4th S. 4, pp. 144–79, + plate 10. 1904.

158. CELTIC COINS

9239 [Anon.] Coins found in the Isle of Man. [Now in B.M. Imitations of money of Æthelred and Edward the Confessor, etc.] Num. Chron., 11, p. 180, + 2 plates. 1849.

9240 Allen (Derek Fortrose). The Irish bracteates: two little-known hoards in the National Museum of Ireland. Num. Chron., 6th S. 2, pp. 71–85. 1942.

9241 Cane (Robert) and **Windele** (John). On the ring-money of ancient Ireland. Trans. Kilkenny Archaeol. Soc., 1, pp. 322–33, + 3 plates. 1851.

9242 Carlyon-Britton (Philip William Poole). The Saxon, Norman and Plantagenet coinage of Wales. [Coinage of Howel Dda, 913–948: coinage of William I . . . at Rhuddlan: coinage at St. David's in the time of William I.] Br. Num. J., 2, pp. 31–56, + 1 plate. 1906. *Also in* Trans. Hon. Soc. Cymm., 1905–06, pp. 1–30, + 1 plate. 1907.

9243 Carruthers (James). On the coins discovered in the cairn on Scraba mountain [co. Down]. [9th c.] Ulster J. Archaeol., 3, pp. 320–21, + 1 plate. 1855.

9244 Hoare (Edward). [An] unknown variety of the ancient Celto-Irish penannular gold ring-money. J. Kilkenny Archaeol. Soc., [4] N.S. 1, pp. 391–92. 1857.

9245 Jennings (J. R. B.). On some ancient coins found [at Knockmaon] in West Waterford. [Hiberno-Danish : Edgar, Edred, etc.] J. Waterford Archaeol. Soc., 15, pp. 163–67, + 1 plate. 1912.

9246 Lindsay (John). On the bracteate and other early coins of Ireland. Trans. Brit. Archaeol. Assoc., 3rd Congress (Gloucester) 1846, pp. 181–88, + 2 plates. 1848.

9247 MacAdam (Robert). Opening of a cairn on Scraba mountain (county of Down), and discovery of Danish coins. [9th c.] Ulster J. Archaeol., 3, pp. 315–320. 1855.

9248 Nolan (Patrick). Studies in Irish monetary history. [Esp. 19, pp. 172–76, 'Irish coins of the Danes and Anglo-Saxons.'] Irish Eccles. Rec., 5th S. 17, pp. 610–19 : 18, pp. 41–54, 170–81 : 19, pp. 172–76, 274–83. 1921–22.

9249 O'Sullivan (William). The earliest Irish coinage. J. Roy. Soc. Antiq. Ireland, 79, pp. 190–235, + 4 plates. 1949.

9250 Parsons (H. Alexander). The chronology of the Hiberno-Danish coinage. Br. Num. J., 17 (1923–4), pp. 99–124, + 3 plates. 1927.

9251 —— An Irish eleventh-century coin of the southern O'Neil. Br. Num. J., 16 (1921–2), pp. 59–71. 1924.

9252 Roth (Bernard). The coins of the Danish kings of Ireland. Hiberno-Danish series. Br. Num. J., 6, pp. 55–146 + 10 plates. 1910.

9253 Simon (James). An essay towards an historical account of Irish coins, *etc.* pp. xv, 184. 4° Dublin, 1749. [Pp. 1–10, A.–S. period.]

9254 Smith (Aquilla). The human hand on Hiberno-Danish coins. Num. Chron., 3rd S. 3, pp. 32–39, + plate 3. 1883.

9255 —— When was money first coined in Ireland ? Num. Chron., 3rd S. 2, pp. 308–18. 1882.

159. MINTS AND MONEYERS

9256 [Anon.] Penny of Harthacnute, of the Dover mint. Num. Chron., 7, p. 202. 1845.

9257 [Anon.] Saxon coin minted at Malmesbury. [Penny of Edward the Confessor.] J. Brit. Archaeol. Assoc., N.S. 23, p. 189. 1917.

9258 Akerman (John Yonge). On the mint of Winchester. Trans. Brit. Archaeol. Ass., 2nd Congress (Winchester 1845), pp. 285–88. 1846.

9259 Allan (William). The Cricklade mint. [Æthelred II, Canute, Edward the Confessor, William I and II.] Wilts. Archaeol. Mag., 19, pp. 283–98, + 1 plate. 1881.

9260 Andrew (Walter Jonathan). Stockbridge, an Anglo-Saxon mint. Br. Num. J., 20 (1929–30), pp. 49–61, + 1 plate. 1932.

9261 —— The title *monetarius*. Br. Num. J., 20 (1929–30), pp. 302–04. 1932.

9262 Anscombe (Alfred). The names of Old-English mint-towns : their original form and meaning and their epigraphical corruption. [1. The names of Old-English mint-towns which occur in Bede. i. Introduction : ii. The phonology of Latin loan-words in Old English : iii. The case-endings preserved in Old-English place-names : iv. Words entering into combination in the place-names of Bede : v. Particles in combination : vi. The place-names. 2. The names of Old-English mint-towns which occur in the Saxon chronicles. A–L (L–Z).] Br. Num. J., 8, pp. 9–48 : 9, pp. 89–118 : 10, pp. 9–31. 1912–14.

9263 —— Odilo, a Northumbrian moneyer of the ninth century, and his issues. [i. Northumbrian coins which bear the name of Odilo : ii. The name and nationality of Odilo : iii. King Eardulf's connection with Charles the Great.] Br. Num. J., 14 (1918), pp. 1–12. 1920.

9264 Bateman (Thomas). Coins of Anglo-Saxon and Norman kings, minted at Derby. [*See also* note by Richard Sainthill, on pp. 126–27.] Reliquary, 1, pp. 1–4, + 1 plate. 1860.

9265 Bayley (Arthur R.) *etc.* Local mints. [Totnes, Oxford, etc.] N. and Q., 183, pp. 52, 85, 144–45, 171–73, 204, 358, 387–88. 1942.

9266 Benson (George). Coins : especially those relating to York. (List of coins in the Royal York mint). Ann. Rept. Yorks. Philos. Soc., 1913, pp. 1–104, + 8 plates. 1914.

9267 —— Coins in the York Museum. Trans. Yorks. Num. Soc., 1, pp. 107–10, + 2 plates. 1913.

9268 Bramble (James R.). Coins of the Bristol mint, in the collection of Col. Bramble. [Including penny of Harold I, and two pennies of William I.] Proc. Clifton Antiq. Club, 3 (1893–96), pp. 128–31. 1897.

9269 Brooke (George Cyril). Huntingdon borough : history of early mint. V.C.H., Huntingdon, 2, pp. 121–22, + 1 plate. 1932.

9270 —— A Leicester penny of William I. Num. Chron., 5th S. 3, p. 157. 1923.

9271 —— The medieval moneyers. [Pp. 59–61, A.–S. period.] Br. Num. J., 21 (1931–3), pp. 59–66. 1935.

9272 Burton (Frank E.). The coins of king Athelstan (of king Canute : of William the Conqueror) of the Nottingham mint. Trans. Thoroton Soc., 31 (1927), pp. 105–07, + 1 plate : 37 (1933), pp. 41–44, + 2 plates : 42 (1938), pp. 15–18, + 2 plates. 1928, 1934, 1939.

9273 Carlyon-Britton (Philip William Poole). Bedwin and Marlborough and the moneyer Cilda. [Edward the Confessor and William I.] Num. Chron., 4th S. 2, pp. 20–25. 1902.

9274 —— The Berkeley mint. [Pp. 17–20, coins of Edward the Confessor and William I.] Br. Num. J., 4, pp. 17–31. 1908.

9275 —— The 'Gothabyrig' mint. Br. Num. J., 4, pp. 33–45. 1908.

9276 —— The Oxford mint in the reign of Alfred. Br. Num. J., 2, pp. 21–30, + 1 plate. 1906.

9277 Carlyon-Britton (Philip William Poole). 'Uncertain' Anglo-Saxon mints and some new attributions. Br. Num. J., 6, pp. 13–47. 1910.

9278 —— The Winchcombe mint. Br. Num. J., 6, pp. 49–54, + 1 plate. 1910.

9279 Carson (R. A. G.). The mint of Thetford. [Eagdar to Henry II.] Num. Chron., 6th S. 9, pp. 189–236, + 4 plates. 1949.

9280 Conyngham (*Lord* Albert D.). On the coinage of Chester. J. Brit. Archaeol. Assoc., 5, pp. 233–35. 1849.

9281 Cox (James Stevens). The Ilchester mint and Ilchester trade tokens. *Ilchester Historical Monographs*, 3. pp. 37–68. 8° Ilchester, 1948. [Æthelred II–Henry III.]

9282 —— Somerset mints. [11 A.–S. mints.] N. and Q. Som. and Dorset, 25, p. 127. 1948.

9283 Crowther (G. F.). Cnut's York coins. [With list of his York moneyers.] Yorkshire N. and Q., 2, pp. 241–44. 1890.

9284 —— Coins struck in Yorkshire. [York mint.] *Same jnl.*, 1, pp. 226–28. 1888.

9285 —— On a pax penny attributed to Witney. [But probably from Wilton mint. Moneyer Sefmroi. Harold II.] Num. Chron., 3rd S. 11, pp. 161–63. 1891.

9286 Dale (William). Famous Winchester moneyers. [Æthelred II—William II.] Papers and Proc. Hants. F.C., 7 i, pp. xxi–xxii. 1914.

9287 Davies (Robert). Historical notices of the royal and archiepiscopal mints and coinages at York. pp. 79. 8° York, 1854.

9288 Doxey (John S.). Anglo-Saxon and Norman coins minted at Derby. [Athelstan—William I.] Proc. Manch. Num. Soc., 1, pp. 163–66. 1869.

9289 —— Notices of Anglo-Saxon coins minted at Derby. (Additional notes on Anglo-Saxon coins struck at Derby : by Llewellynn Jewitt). [Athelstan—William I.] Reliquary, 15, pp. 129–32. 1875.

9290 Evans (*Sir* John). Additional note on Bardney as a mint. [?Bardney or Barnstaple, for *bear*, *bard*, etc.] Num. Chron., 3rd S. 18, pp. 275–77. 1898.

9291 —— The mint of Gothabyrig. [?=Idbury, Oxon.] Num. Chron., 3rd S. 15, pp. 45–50. 1895.

9292 —— A new Saxon mint, Weardbyrig. Num. Chron., 3rd S. 13, pp. 220–27. 1893.

9293 Fitch (E. W.). Saxon mints at Maldon and Colchester. [Silver coins of Edward the Confessor discovered at Sedlescombe, Sussex, in 1876.] Essex Rev., 2, pp. 123–24. 1893.

9294 Fletcher (W. G. D.). Saxon and Norman coins minted at Shrewsbury. Trans. Shrop. Arch. Soc., 3rd S., 1, p. 150. 1901.

9295 Francis (Grant R.). Some notes on a coin of Anlaf from the Derby mint. [Northumbria, 10th c.] Br. Num. J., 16 (1921–2), pp. 1–4. 1924.

9296 Gardner (Willoughby). The mint of Chester. [Synopsis]. Br. Num. J., 16 (1921–2), pp. 300–01. 1924.

9297 Gill (Henry Septimus). On silver regal money coined in Devonshire mints. (Devonshire coins and moneyers). Rept. and Trans. Devon. Assoc., 10, pp. 589–610. 1878.

9298 Haigh (Daniel Henry). Yorkshire mints under the Danish kings. Yorks. Archaeol. J., 4, pp. 73–83, + 1 plate. 1877.

9299 Harding ( ) *Lt.-Col.* On the coinage of Exeter. J. Brit. Archaeol. Assoc., 18, pp. 97–111. 1862.

9300 Hawkes (Arthur John). A Saxon moneyer's hoard at Chester. Trans. Lancs. and Ches. Antiq. Soc., 61 (1949), pp. 190–92. 1951.

9301 Hawkins (Edward). The ancient mint of Lincoln. Mems. Archaeol. Inst., [4] (1848), pp. 49–57. 1850.

9302 —— Dorsetshire numismatics : the ancient mints, with notices of some medals connected with the county. [A.–S. mints at Dorchester, Bridport, Shaftesbury and Wareham.] Archaeol. J., 23, pp. 122–30. 1866.

9303 Hawkins (Edward). Notices of the mint and exchange at Winchester. [Pp. 41–43, list of moneyers from Æthelstan to Henry III.] Proc. Archaeol. Inst., [1] (1845), pp. 33–43. 1846.

9304 —— Notices on the mints of Wiltshire. Mems. Archaeol. Inst. [5] (1849), pp. 234–40. 1851.

9305 Henfrey (Henry William). The ancient coins of Norwich. J. Brit. Archaeol. Assoc., 36, pp. 291–315, 418–31, + 2 plates. 1880.

9306 —— The Bristol mint and its productions. [Æthelred II—William I.] *Same jnl.*, 31, pp. 339–68, + 1 plate. 1875.

9307 Kenyon (R. Lloyd). History of the Shrewsbury mint, with an account of the coins struck there. [Pp. 251–59 + plates 1–2, A.–S. period.] Trans. Shrop. Arch. Soc., 2nd S. 10, pp. 251–72, + 6 plates. 1898.

9308 Kershaw (Samuel Wayland). Canterbury's ancient coinage. J. Brit. Archaeol. Assoc., 58 (N.S. 8), pp. 161–66. 1902.

9309 King (Horace Herbert). The Steyning mint. Br. Num. J., 24 (1941–2), pp. 1–7, + 1 plate. 1943.

9310 Lawrence (L. A.). The Anglo-Saxon moneyer Torhtulf and characteristics of die-sinking. Br. Num. J., 2, pp. 411–16. 1905.

9311 —— On the mint of Barnstaple. [?Bardney or Barnstaple for *bear*, *bard*, etc. *See also* **9290, 9322.**] Num. Chron., 3rd S. 17, pp. 302–08. 1897.

9312 —— The two mints at York. [Pp. 366–67, A.–S. mints.] Num. Chron., 5th S. 5, pp. 366–79. 1925.

9313 Longstaffe (William Hylton Dyer). The earliest coins of Durham. Archaeol. Æl., N.S. 6, pp. 234–38. 1865.

9314 McCall (Hardy Bertram). York penny of Eadward the Elder. Yorks. Archaeol. J., 30, pp. 309–10. 1931.

9315 Manning (Charles Robertson). On Saxon coins struck at Norwich, with the moneyer's name of Manning. Norfolk Archaeology, 13, pp. 93–99 + 1 plate. 1898.

9316 Manton (J. O.). An Aethelstan penny (925–941). [Derby mintage.] J. Derbs. Archaeol. Soc., 50 (N.S. 3, 1928–29), pp. 101–02. 1930.

9317 —— An outline of the coinage of Britain, with special references to Derby mintages, to A.D. 1066. *Same jnl.*, 44, pp. 23–43. 1922.

9318 Mayo (Charles Herbert). Warne's collection of Dorset coins. [Sold by auction 25. v. 1889. Includes 25 lots of coins from Athelstan to William I from mints of Shaftesbury, Wareham, Dorchester and Bridport.] N. and Q. Som. and Dorset, 1, pp. 225–26. 1890.

9319 Milne (J. Grafton). An Anglo-Saxon moneyer. [Aegelwine of Cricklade and Oxford.] Oxoniensia, 10, pp. 90–101. 1945.

9320 Montagu (H.). The Anglo-Saxon mints of Chester and Leicester. Num. Chron., 3rd S. 11, pp. 12–24. 1891.

9321 —— The mint of Castle Rising, in Norfolk. Num. Chron., 3rd S. 9, pp. 335–43. 1889.

9322 Napier (Arthur Sampson). On Barnstaple as a minting-place. [?Bardney or Barnstaple for *bear, bard*, etc.] Num. Chron., 3rd S. 18, pp. 274–75. 1898.

9323 Nelson (Philip). An Athelstan penny of Derby. [Sigar of Derby, moneyer.] Num. Chron., 6th S. 10, pp. 151–52. 1950.

9324 —— The Cunnetti mint. [Cnut. Northumbrian mint.] Num. Chron., 6th S. 8, p. 96. 1948.

9325 —— The St. Peter coins of York. [From archiepiscopal mint subsequent to 910.] Num. Chron., 6th S. 9, p. 116. 1949.

9326 Noble (Rose). The Shrewsbury mint. [Temp. William I.] Shrop. N. and Q., 3rd S. 1, p. 26. 1911.

9327 North (Jeffery J.). The mints of Sussex. [Chichester, Hastings, Lewes, Pevensey, Rye, Steyning: with names of A.-S. moneyers.] Sussex County Mag., 14, pp. 255–56. 1940.

9328 P. (C. D.). The Cricklade mint. [Moneyer Aegelwine of Cricklade and Oxford, temp. Cnut.] Wilts. Archaeol. Mag., 52, pp. 393–94. 1949.

9329 Parsons (H. Alexander). The coins of Eadmund's moneyers Faraman and Ingelgar, A.D. 939–46. Br. Num. J., 23 (1928–41), pp. 1–5. 1941.

9330 —— The Dunwich mint. Br. Num. J., 9, pp. 119–28. 1913.

9331 Passmore (A. D.). A Saxon mint at Chippenham ? Wilts. Archaeol. Mag., 46, p. 100. 1932.

9332 Perry (Marten). Stamford mint. Fenland N. and Q., 6, pp. 369–72. 1906.

9333 Pickersgill (T.). English regal coins struck at York. Trans. Yorks. Num. Soc., 2, pp. 169–77. 1925.

9334 —— Regal coins struck at York. *Same jnl.*, 1, pp. 18–21, + 1 plate. 1909.

9335 Pownall (Assheton). Coins of the Stamford mint. [Athelstan-Stephen.] Num. Chron., N.S. 20, pp. 66–73. 1880.

9336 —— Treasure trove, in connection with Anglo-Saxon coins struck at Leicester. [Coins of the Chancton find: 6 minted at Leicester.] Assoc. Archit. Socs.' Rpts., 12, pp. 140–44, + 1 plate. 1873. *Also in* Trans. Leic. Archit. and Archaeol. Soc., 4, pp. 194–99, + 1 plate. 1878.

9337 Robertson (J. Drummond). The mint of Gloucester. (and supplement). [Contains (pp. 17–20) general remarks on A.-S. coins and moneyers and (pp. 31–55) illustrations and descriptions of individual A.-S. coins.] Trans. Bristol and Glos. Arch. Soc., 10, pp. 17–66: 13, pp. 205–11. 1886, 89.

9338 Sharp (Samuel). Early moneys of this country, and the Anglo-Saxon mint of Stamford. Assoc. Archit. Socs.' Rpts., 10, pp. 71–85. 1869.

9339 —— The Stamford mint. [Pp. 335–57, list of coins, Eadgar to Henry II, pp. 358–68, list of moneyers.] Num. Chron., N.S. 9, pp. 327–68: N.S. 19, p. 153: 20, pp. 205–25, + 1 plate. 1869, 1879–80.

9340 Shepherd (E. J.). On the mint-marks of certain Saxon coins which are presumed to have been struck at York. Mems. Archaeol. Inst., [2] (1846), pp. 1–8. 1848.

9341 Shortt (Hugh de Sausmarez). Bibliography of Wiltshire coins in early mediaeval hoards. Wilts. Archaeol. Mag., 53, pp. 413–18, + 2 tables of moneyers and types. 1950.

9342 —— The mints of Wiltshire. [Edgar—William I.] Num. Chron., 6th S. 8, pp. 169–87, + 3 plates. 1948.

9343 —— The mints of Wiltshire from Eadgar to Henry III. Archaeol. J., 104 (1947), pp. 112–28, + 3 plates. 1948.

9344 Smith (Samuel) *junr.* Is it certain that the Anglo-Saxon coins were always struck at the towns named on them ? Num. Chron., 3rd S. 8, pp. 138–44. 1888.

9345 Stainer (Charles Lewis). Oxford silver pennies from A.D. 925–A.D. 1272. *Oxford Historical Society*, 46. pp. xlv, 94, + 15 plates. 8° Oxford, 1904.

9346 Stapleton (A.). The Nottingham mint. Notts. and Derbs. N. and Q., 2, pp. 17–20, 38–42, 49–50. 1894.

9347 Symonds (Henry). Bridport as an Anglo-Saxon mint. Num. Chron., 5th S. 2, pp. 144–45. 1922.

9348 —— Coins struck in Dorset during the Saxon, Norman and Stuart periods. [At Shaftesbury, Wareham and Dorchester. Athelstan—.] Proc. Dorset Antiq., F.C., 28, pp. 159–67, + 1 plate. 1907.

9349 —— The evidence for an Anglo-Saxon mint at Bridport. *Same jnl.*, 43, pp. 37–40. 1923.

9350 T. Royal mint at Bedford. [Edwy to Stephen.] Notes Beds. Archit. and Archaeol. Soc., 1, pp. 189–92. 1863.

9351 Turner (Joseph Horsfall). Canute's York coins. Yorkshire N. and Q., 2, pp. 187–89. 1890.

9352 Turner (Thomas M.). Pennies of the Colchester mint. Br. Num. J., 24 (1941–2), pp. 8–21, + 1 plate. 1943.

9353 W. (G.). Coins of the Chester mint. [Athelstan.] Cheshire Historian, 3, pp. 49–50. 1953.

9354 Wainwright (Thomas). Barnstaple, a mint town in Anglo-Saxon and early Norman times. Devon N. and Q., 2, pp. 60–61. 1902.

9355 Wedlake (A. L.). The Watchet mint. [Æthelred II—Stephen.] Proc. Somerset Arch. Soc., 94 (1948–9), pp. 111–17, + 1 plate. 1950.

9356 Wells (William Charles). The Northampton and Southampton mints. Br. Num. J., 17 (1923–4), pp. 1–49, + 2 plates : 19 (1927–8), pp. 69–91, + 2 plates : 20 (1929–30), pp. 63–93, + 2 plates : 21 (1931–3), pp. 1–57, + 2 plates. 1927–35.

9357 —— The Stamford and Peterborough mints. [30 figures in text.] Br. Num. J., 22 (1934–7), pp. 35–77 : 23 (1938–41), pp. 7–28 : 24 (1942–3), pp. 69–109 : + 6 plates. 1938–44.

9358 Whitbourn (Richard). The mints of Surrey. Surrey Archaeol. Collns., 3, pp. 37–38. 1865.

9359 Willett (Ernest H.). On the resident character of the office of monetarius in Saxon times. Num. Chron., 3rd S. 1, pp. 32–36. 1881.

9360 Williams (W. I.). The foundation-dates of the churches of St. Werburgh and St. Peter in Chester. [Evidence from coins from Chester mint.] J. Chester and N. Wales Archit. Soc., N.S. 37, pp. 299–302. 1949.

9361 Windeatt (Edward). Anglo-Saxon coins from Totnes mint. Devon N. and Q., 2, p. 86, + 1 plate. 1902.

160. SEALS

9362 Birch (Walter de Gray). On the great seals of William the Conqueror (with addendum). Trans. Roy. Soc. Lit., 2nd S. 10, pp. 149–84, + 2 plates. 1874.

9363 —— On the three great seals of king Edward the Confessor. *Same jnl.*, 2nd S. 10, pp. 613–48, + 3 plates. 1874

9364 British Museum. Catalogue of British seal-dies. By Alec Bain Tonnochy. pp. lxxii, 212, + 32 plates. 4° London, 1952. [Pp. 1–3 + plate 1, A.-S. (Ethilwald, c. 850: Godwin, 'minister' and Godgytha nun, 10th–11th c. Ælfric, 10th–11th c.] 1952.

9365 —— Catalogue of seals . . . by W. de G. Birch. Vol. 1. pp. viii, 863. 8° London, 1887. [Pp. 1–5, A.-S. sovereigns.]

9366 Douce (Francis). Some remarks on the original seal belonging to the abbey of Wilton. [And on the early history of the abbey.] Archaeologia, 18, pp. 40–54. 1817.

9367 Ellis (*Sir* Henry). Account of the discovery of the matrix of an Anglo-Saxon seal. [' Sigillum Ælfrici,' ? alderman of Mercia, 983–1007. Figure in text.] *Same jnl.*, 24, pp. 359–61. 1832.

9368 —— Observations on the history and use of seals in England. [Pp. 14–20, A.-S. period.] *Same jnl.*, 18, pp. 12–20. 1817.

9369 —— Seal of Coenulf, king of Mercia [796–819]. [2 figures in text.] *Same jnl.*, 32, pp. 449–50. 1847.

9370 —— Seal of king William the Conqueror. [Exhibition of a cast of the seal to the Society of Antiquaries.] *Same jnl.*, 25, pp. 616–17, + 1 plate. 1834.

9371 Franks (*Sir* Augustus Wollaston). An Anglo-Saxon seal of Godwin, from Wallingford, Berks. Proc. Soc. Antiq., 2nd S. 8, pp. 468–70, + 1 plate. 1881.

9372 Gurney (Hudson). Observations on the seal of Ethilwald, bishop of Dunwich, lately discovered at Eye, in Suffolk. [Mid 9th c.] Archaeologia, 20, pp. 479–83. 1824.

9373 Harmer (Florence Elizabeth). The English contribution to the epistolary usages of early Scandinavian kings. Saga-Bk. Viking Soc., 13, pp. 115–55, + 4 plates. 1950.

9374 Kingsford (Hugh Sadler). The epigraphy of medieval English seals. [Including those of William I's reign.] Archaeologia, 79, pp. 149–78. 1929.

9375 Liebermann (Felix). Zur Geschichte des Siegels in England. [Including remarks on its first use in A.-S. times.] Arch. Stud. neueren Spr., Bd. 142 (N.S. 42), pp. 254–55. 1921.

9376 Piggot (John) *jun.* Seal of Ethilwald, bishop of Dunwich, A.D. 850. N. and Q., 3rd S. 12, p. 167. 1867.

9377 Poole (Reginald Lane). Seals on Anglo-Saxon charters. N. and Q., 12th S. 2, pp. 169–70. 1916.

161. RUNES, GENERAL

9378 Arntz (Helmut). Handbuch der Runenkunde. pp. xvii, 329. 8° Halle, 1935. [xi. Ogom und Runen.]

9379 —— Runen und Runennamen. [A. Die Handschriften Brüssel Nr. 9565–66 und St. Gallen Nr. 270.] Anglia, 67–68 (N.F. 55–56), pp. 172–250. 1944.

9380 Baesecke (Georg). Die Herkunft der Runen. Germ.-roman. Monatsschr., 22, pp. 413–17. 1934.

9381 Bennett (J. A. W.). The beginnings of runic studies in England. Saga-Book V. Soc., 13, pp. 269–83. 1951.

9382 Blomfield (Joan). Runes and the Gothic alphabet. Saga–Book V.C., 12, pp. 177–94, 209–31. 1941–42.

9383 Brade-Birks (S. Graham). Teach yourself archaeology. pp. 220. 8° London, 1953. [Pp. 174–82, runes and Ogham : a summary.]

9384 Brodeur (Arthur G.). The riddle of the runes. [Germanic runic alphabet and its problems.] Univ. Cal., Pubns. in English, 3, pp. 1–15. 1932.

9385 Cahen (Maurice). Origine et développement de l'écriture runique. [Pp. 37–41, runes in England.] Mém. Soc. Ling. de Paris, 23, pp. 1–46. 1923.

9386 Cook (Albert Stanburrough). Runic monuments known as obelisks. [Considered analogous by 16th–17th c. antiquaries.] Arch. Stud. neueren Spr., Bd. 132, pp. 394–97. 1914.

9387 Friesen (Otto von). Runenschrift. Hoops : Reallexikon d. german. Altertumskunde, 4, pp. 5–51, + 7 plates. 1918.

9388 Grienberger (Theodor von). Beiträge zur Runenlehre. [i. Die nordischen Namenreihen.] Arkiv nord. Filol., 14, pp. 101–36. 1898.

G g

9389 Hempl (George). The runic words, Hickes 135. [Use of runic u for runic w.] Engl. Studien, 32, pp. 317–18. 1903.

9390 King (Richard John). Runes and rune-stones. [Popular account.] Fraser's Mag., 93 (N.S. 13), pp. 747–57. 1876.

9391 Marstrander (Carl Johan Sverstrup). Om runene og runenavnenes oprindelse. Norsk Tidsskrift for Sprogvidenskap, 1, pp. 85–179. Resumé in French, pp. 180–88. 1928.

9392 Neckel (Gustav). Zur Einführung in die Runenforschung. Germ.-rom. Monatsschrift, 1, pp. 7–19, 81–95. 1909.

9393 Palmer (J. Linton). Notes on runes. Proc. Lit. and Phil. Soc. L'pool, 37, pp. 143–59, + 4 plates. 1883.

9394 Paues (Anna Carolina). Runes and manuscripts. Camb. Hist. English Lit., 1, pp. 7–18. 1907.

9395 Pedersen (Holger). L'origine des runes. Mém. Soc. roy. Antiq. Nord, 1920–25, pp. 88–136. [1925.]

9396 —— Runernes oprindelse. Aarbøger for nordisk Oldkyndighed, 3 raekke, 13, pp. 37–82. 1923.

9397 Sievers (Eduard). Runen und Runeninschriften. Pauls Grundriss d. german. Philol., 2. Aufl., Bd. 1, Abschnitt 4. i, pp. 248–62, + 1 plate. 1901.

9398 Taylor (Isaac). Greeks and Goths. A study of the runes. pp. vii, 139. 8° London, 1879. [Pp. 108–39, Oghams.]

9399 Wimmer (Ludvig Frands Adalbert). Runeskriftens Oprindelse og Udvikling i Norden. pp. 270, + 3 plates. 8° København, 1874. —Die Runenschrift. . . . Vom Verfasser umgearbeitete und vermehrte Ausgabe . . . aus dem Dänischen übersetzt von F. Holthausen. pp. xxiv, 394, + 3 plates. 8° Berlin, 1887.

162. RUNES, ANGLO-SAXON, GENERAL

9400 Dickins (Bruce). A system of transliteration for Old English runic inscriptions. Leeds Studies in English, 1, pp. 15–21. 1932.

9401 Grienberger (Theodor von). Die angelsächsischen Runenreihen und die s. g. Hrabanischen Alphabete. Arkiv nord. Filol., 15, pp. 1–40. 1899.

9402 —— Neue Beiträge zur Runenlehre. [32, pp. 295–302, Zu den angelsächsischen und deutschen Inschriften : 39, pp. 95–100, Zu den ags. Inschriften.] Z. f. d. P., 32, pp. 289–304 : 39, pp. 50–100. 1900, 1907.

9403 —— Runensachen. [Pp. 279–80, Zu den ags. Münzinschriften.] Z. f. d. P., 50 , pp. 274–83. 1926.

9404 Hempl (George). Hickes's additions to the Runic Poem. Mod. Phil., 1, pp. 135–41, + 2 plates. 1904.

9405 —— The Old-English runes for *a* and *o*. Mod. Lang. Notes, 11, col. 348–52. 1896.

9406 —— Old-English runic *ōenipu lufu.* Proc. Am. Phil. Ass., 27, pp. lxiv–vi. 1896.

9407 Holthausen (Ferdinand). Altenglische Kleinigkeiten. 2. Altenglische Runennamen. [In MS. Vatican, Regina 338, fol. 90.] Archiv Stud. neueren Spr., Bd. 99, p. 425. 1897.

9408 Huebner (Emil) *ed.* Inscriptiones Britanniae Christianae. *Corpus Inscriptionum Latinarum,* 7. pp. xxiv, 101, + 2 maps. 4° Berolini, 1876. [Gross, 1484. Mostly A.–S. Many illustrations.]

9409 Keller (Wolfgang). Zur Chronologie der AE. Runen. [From continental period to 7th c.] Anglia, 62 (N.F. 50), pp. 24–32. 1938.

9410 Kemble (John Mitchell). On Anglo-Saxon runes. Archaeologia, 28, pp. 327–72, + 6 plates. 1840.

9411 Logeman (Henri). The name of the Anglo-Saxon rune *P.* Academy, 39, p. 284. 1891.

163. INSCRIPTIONS ON ANGLO-SAXON RINGS

9412 Dickins (Bruce). Runic rings and Old English charms. [Criticism of **9418.**] Archiv Stud. neueren Spr., Bd. 167, p. 252. 1935.

9413 Douce (Francis). Dissertation on the runic jasper ring belonging to George Cumberland. [*See also* under Hamper (W.). **9416.**] Archaeologia, 21, pp. 119–37. 1827.

9414 Ferguson (Robert). Copper ring . . . having an inscription in Anglo-Saxon runes. [Rendered by Haigh : '*Ar hriuf el hriurithon glus tacon tel.*'] Proc. Soc. Antiq., 2nd S. 4, p. 439. 1870.

9415 Franks (*Sir* Augustus Wollaston). On a ring with a runic inscription. [*See also* vol. 21, p. 117.] Archaeologia, 44, pp. 481–82. 1873.

9416 Hamper (William). Explanation of a runic inscription upon a jasper ring [belonging to George Cumberland]. [Dano-Saxon amulet ' against pestilence'. Interprets inscription as '*Æræra of moldan ; ara ure wolan, hwiles ðe pytte nold.*' (Raise us from the dust, save us from pestilence).] *Same jnl.,* 21, pp. 117–18. 1827.

9417 —— Observations on a gold ring, with a runic inscription, in the possession of . . . the earl of Aberdeen. [Found on Greymoor hill, Kingmoor, near Carlisle, in 1817. Now in British Museum. Hamper translates : ' Febriculosus vel leprosus : laetus in morbo.'] *Same jnl.,* 21, pp. 25–30. 1827.

9418 Harder (Hermann). Eine angelsächsische Runeninschrift. [On ring, from Greymoor hill.] Archiv Stud. neueren Spr., Bd. 160, pp. 87–89. 1931.

9419 Harder (Hermann). Eine angelsächsische Ring-Inschrift. [In British Museum. Guide to A.–S. antiquities (1923), p. 116.] *Same jnl.,* Bd. 161, pp. 37–39. 1932.

9420 Harder (Hermann). Die Inschriften angelsächsischen Runenringer. [New readings of examples from Stephens, taken from his Handbook. Not merely ' abracadabra'.] *Same jnl.,* Bd. 169, pp. 224–28. 1936.

9421 McCaul (John). Description of a fibula found in Sealand, with an inscription in Anglo-Saxon runes, translated from the Society's Annals. [Ðorir o. (Thorir owns).] Mém. Soc. roy. Antiq. Nord, 1836–39, pp. 163–64, + plate 7 (fig. 10). [1839?].

9422 Magnuson (Finn). De annulo aureo runicis characteribus signato, nuper in Anglia invento, et pluribus ejusdem generis, brevis dissertatio. Archaeol. Æl., [1st S.] 1, pp. 136–41. 1822.

9423 Newton (William Waring Hay). Inscribed runic ring. [Found in 1849 in the Abbey park, St. Andrews, Fife.] Proc. Soc. Antiq. Scot., 1, pp. 22–25. 1852.

164. ANGLO-SAXON INDIVIDUAL INSCRIPTIONS

(for Franks casket, *see* 195 § *b*)

§ *a*. General and Miscellaneous

9424 Buck (Carl Darling). An ABC inscribed in Old English runes. [?a piece of an urn decorated by an A.-S. pilgrim visiting Rome. Purchased in Rome by C. H. Moore.] Mod. Phil., 17, pp. 219–24. 1919.

9425 Cook (Albert Stanburrough). The date of the Old English inscription on the Brussels cross. Mod. Lang. Rev., 10, pp. 157–61. 1915.

9426 Cuming (Henry Syer). On a runic epigraph found in the Thames. J. Brit. Archaeol. Assoc., 24, pp. 178–82, + 1 plate. 1868.

9427 D'Ardenne (S. T. R. O.). The Old English inscription on the Brussels cross. English Studies, 21, pp. 145–64, + 4 plates : 271–72. 1939.

9428 Gibson (A. Craig). Runic inscriptions : Anglo-Saxon and Scandinavian. Trans. Hist. Soc. Lancs. and Ches., 11, pp. 111–32, + 2 plates. 1859.

9429 Grienberger (Theodor von). Zwei altenglische Runeninscriften. [Remarks on **9431**.] Z. f. d. P., 43, pp. 377–78. 1911.

9430 Harder (Hermann). Die Runen der ags. Schwertinschrift im Britischen Museum. [Ækosoeri.] Archiv. Stud. neueren Spr., Bd. 161, pp. 86–87. 1932.

9431 Holthausen (Ferdinand). Zwei altenglische Runeninschriften. [i. Die Beinlamelle des Brit. Museums : ii. Die Inschrift des Braunschweiger Reliquiars. For comments by T. von Grienberger, *see* **9429**.] Z. f. d. P., 42, pp. 331–33. 1910.

9432 Logeman (Henri). L'inscription anglo-saxonne du reliquaire de la Vrai Croix au trésor de l'église des SS. Michel et Gudule à Bruxelles. pp. 31, + 2 plates. Mém. Acad. roy. Belgique (8°), 45, viii. 1891.

9433 Nesbitt (Alexander). Observations on Professor Stephens' reading of the runic inscription on the casket preserved in the museum at Brunswick. [*q.v.* **9438–39**.] J. Kilkenny Archaeol. Soc., [8] N.S. 5, pp. 14–16, 376–79. 1864–65.

9434 Selmer (Carl). The runic inscription of Codex Latinus Monacensis 13067 [in the Staatsbibliothek at Munich]. [A.-S. character of 9th–11th c. Transcribes phrase Jhesus Nazarenus Rex Iudaeorum.] P.M.L.A., 53, pp. 645–55, + 1 plate. 1938.

9435 Sperber (Hans). Eine altnordische Runeninschrift in einer englischen Handschrift. [Cotton Caligula A XIV.] P.B.B., 37, pp. 150–56. 1912.

9436 Stephens (George). Handbook of Old-Northern runic monuments of Scandinavia and England. pp. xxiv, + 281. 4° London, 1884.

9437 —— The Old northern runic monuments of Scandinavia and England. 4 vol. fol. London, Köbenhavn, 1866–1901.

9438 —— On an ancient runic casket now preserved in the ducal museum, Brunswick. [?Northumbrian. ?7–9th c. *See also* **9433**.] J. Kilkenny Archaeol. Soc., [7] N.S. 4, pp. 267–76, + 4 plates : N.S. 5, pp. 134–37. 1863–64.

9439 —— On the Brunswick coffer [and its A.-S. runes]. [Reply to Alexander Nesbitt, **9433**.] *Same jnl.*, N.S. 5, pp. 134–37. 1867.

9440 Wright (Thomas). On a leaden tablet or book cover, with an Anglo-Saxon inscription. [The opening of Ælfric's preface to his first collection of A.-S. homilies.] Archaeologia, 34, pp. 438–40, + 1 plate. 1852.

§ *b*. **Mercia**

9441 [Anon.] Saxon inscription at St. Mary-le-Wigford, Lincoln. [' *Eadwig me let wircean . . .*'.] J. Brit. Archaeol. Asscn., 33, pp. 132–33. 1876.

9442 Allen (John Romilly). Early inscribed cross-slab at Llanveynoe, Herefordshire. Arch. Camb., 6th S. 2, p. 239. 1902.

9443 Browne (George Forrest) *bp. of Bristol.* On a sculptured stone with a runic inscription in Cheshire. [Upton, Wirral.] Archaeol. J., 46, pp. 395–99, + 1 plate. 1889.

9444 —— On a sculptured stone with a runic inscription [at Overchurch] in Cheshire. [' The people raised a memorial. Pray for Æthelmund '.] J. Chester Archaeol. and Hist. Soc., N.S.3, pp. 178–84, + 2 plates. 1890.

9445 Dallow (Wilfrid). Notes on the Overchurch runic stone. *Same jnl.*, N.S. 3, pp. 185–91. 1890.

9446 Dietrich (Franz Eduard Christoph). Die Runeninschriften der Goldbracteaten entziffert und nach ihrer geschichtlichen Bedeutung gewürdigt. [P. 25, § 15 b. Warwickshire, England.] Z. f. d. A., 13, pp. 1–105. 1867.

9447 Grienberger (Theodor von). The Thames Fitting. [Inscription found at Westminster bridge in 1866.] Z. f. d. P., 45, pp. 47–55. 1913.

9448 Knowles (James S.). Letter accompanying the cast of an inscribed monumental stone, found in St. Paul's churchyard, London.

[Ina : let : legia : st.
in : thiasi : aug : tuki.

Interpreted as Old Norse of 10th or early 11th c.] Proc. R.I.A., 5, pp. 351–54. 1853.

9449 Radford (Courtenay Arthur Ralegh). A lost inscription of pre-Danish age from Caistor [Lincs.]

[S/CRUCISPOL/QUODECBEREC/INHONOR/
. . T . . . D]

Archaeol. J., 103 (1946), pp. 95–99. 1947.

9450 Rafn (Charles Christian). Remarks on a Danish runic stone from the eleventh century found in the central part of London. [From St. Paul's churchyard.] Mém. Soc. roy. Antiq. Nord, 1845–49, pp. 286–318, + 1 plate. 1849. *Also separately*, pp. 70, + 3 plates. 8° Copenhagen, 1854.

9451 Wordsworth (J.). Anglo-Saxon dedicatory inscription on the tower of St. Mary-le-Wigford church in Lincoln, *etc.* Assoc. Archit. Socs.' Rprts., 15, pp. 16–17, + 1 plate. 1879.

§ *c*. **Northumbria**
i. **Bewcastle and Ruthwell Crosses**

(*See also* 188 § *b*. for their sculpture)

9452 Black (George F.). The Ruthwell cross. Trans. Dumfries. Antiq. Soc., 4 (1885–86), pp. 123–33. 1887.

9453 Brown (Gerard Baldwin). The Bewcastle and Ruthwell crosses. (Letter). Burl. Mag., 21, p. 113. 1912.

9454 Charlton (Edward). On the runic inscription on the cross at Bewcastle. Midland counties Hist. Coll., 2, pp. 40–42. 1856.

9455 Cook (Albert Stanburrough). Cædmon and the Ruthwell cross. [? date.] Mod. Lang. Notes, 5, col. 153—55. 1890.

9456 —— Notes on the Ruthwell cross. [Discovery and inscription.] P.M.L.A., 17, pp. 367–90. 1902.

9457 Dietrich (Franz Eduard Christoph). De cruce Ruthwellensi et de auctore [Cynewulf] versuum in illa inscriptorum qui ad passionem Domini pertinent. *Diss. Marburg.* pp. 15. 4° Marburg, 1865.

9457a The **Dream of the Rood.** Edited by Bruce Dickins and Alan S. C. Ross. *Methuen's Old English Library.* pp. xii, 50, + plate. 8° London, 1934. [Pp. 1–13, the Ruthwell cross: pp. 13–16, the Brussels cross.]

9458 Forbes (M. D.) and **Dickins** (Bruce). The inscriptions of the Ruthwell and Bewcastle crosses and the Bridekirk font. [1 plate included in pagination.] Burl. Mag., 25, pp. 24–29. 1914.

9459 —— and —— The Ruthwell and Bewcastle crosses. [? dates—from inscriptions.] Mod. Lang. Rev., 10, pp. 28–36. 1915.

9459a Hewison (James King). The romance of Bewcastle cross. The mystery of Alcfrith and the myths of Maughan, *etc.* pp. 52, + 10 plates. 4° Glasgow, 1923. [A criticism of the seventh report (1920) of the Royal Commission on the Ancient . . . monuments . . . of Scotland, and of John Maughan's reading of the runes on the cross and his conclusions, **9462.**]

9460 Kemble (John Mitchell). Additional observations on the runic obelisk at Ruthwell; the poem of the Dream of the Holy Rood; and a runic copper dish found at Chertsey [pp. 40–46, on which *see* **9522**]. Archaeologia, 30, pp. 31–46. 1844.

9461 Magnusen (Finn). Om obelisken i Ruthwell og om de Angel-saxiske runer. [*Also* in English, *in* Report addressed by Roy. Soc. northern Antiquaries to its British members, 1836, pp. 81–188.] Annaler nordisk Oldkynd., 1836, pp. 243–337. 1836.

9462 Maughan (John). A memoir on the Roman station and runic cross at Bewcastle . . . and the runic inscription in Carlisle cathedral. pp. 44. 8° London, 1857.

9463 Muir (P. McAdam). The Ruthwell cross. [And its connection with Caedmon.] Trans. Scottish Ecclesiol. Soc., 1, pp. 135–40. 1905.

9464 Nanson (William). Bewcastle. [Especially the runes on the cross.] Trans. Cumb. and Westm. Antiq. Soc., 3, pp. 215–31. 1878.

9465 Nicolson (William). A letter concerning a runic inscription at Beaucastle. Phil. Trans. Roy. Soc., 15, pp. 1287–91. 1685.

9466 Reeves (William Peters). The date of the Bewcastle cross [and its inscription]. [7th c.] Mod. Lang. Notes, 35, pp. 155–60. 1920.

9467 Repp (Thorlief Gudmundson). Letter . . . regarding the runic inscription on the monument at Ruthwell. [In Latin.] Archaeol. Scot., 4, pp. 327–36. 1857.

9468 Ross (Alan Strode Campbell). The linguistic evidence for the date of the Ruthwell cross. Mod. Lang. Rev., 28, pp. 145–55. 1933.

9469 Smith (George). [Bewcastle cross.] (The explanation of the runic obelisk). Gent. Mag., 12, pp. 132, 318–19, 368–69, 529. 1742.

9470 Stephens (George). The Ruthwell cross, *etc.*, pp. 46, + 2 plates. fol. London, 1866. [Reprinted from vol. 1 of **9437.**]

ii. Other

9471 Addison (F.). The Saxon inscription at Beckermont, [Cumberland]. [Two contradictory readings.] Archaeol. Æl., N.S. 6, pp. 60–62. 1865.

9472 Brooke (John Charles). An illustration of a Saxon inscription on the church of Kirkdale in Rydale in the North Riding of the county of York. Archaeologia, 5, pp. 188–205, and plate, and ' tabula genealogica . . . Ormi filii Gamellonis, domini de Kirdale '. 1779.

9473 —— An illustration of a Saxon inscription remaining in the church of Aldbrough, in Holdernesse, in the East Riding of the county of York. *Same jnl.*, 6, pp. 39–53, and plate, and ' stemma Ulphi comitis . . . d'ni de Aldburgh.' 1782.

9474 Browne (George Forrest) *bp. of Bristol.* On inscriptions at Jarrow and Monkwearmouth. Archaeol. Æl., N.S.11, pp. 27–32. 1886.

9475 Browne (Geoage Forrest) *bp. of Bristol.* On various inscriptions and supposed inscriptions. [i. The font at Wilne, Derbs. : ii. The Jarrow inscription, *In hoc singular[i an]no vita redditur mundo* : iii. The Jarrow inscription, . . . *berchti* : . . . *edveri* : . . . *c crucem* : iv. The Monkswearmouth inscription, *Hic in sepulchro requiescit corpore Hereberecht Prb* : v. The cross at Hawkswell, Yorks.] Camb. Antiq. Commns., 6 (1884–88), pp. 1–16, + 2 plates. 1891.

9476 Chadwick (Hector Munro). Early inscriptions in the north of England. Trans. Yorks. Dialect Soc., 1, pt. 3, pp. 79–85, + 1 plate. 1900.

9477 Charlton (Edward). On an inscription in runic letters in Carlisle cathedral. [' Tolfilen wrote these runes upon this stone.'] Archaeol. Æl., N.S. 3, pp. 65–68. 1859.

9478 Charlton (William L.). Runic inscription on Hazel-Gill crags, near Bewcastle. ['Asker, the bold, at Hazel-Gill to his house carl.' c. 950–1000.] *Same jnl.*, N.S. 17, pp. 53–56. 1895.

9479 Cox (John Charles). On a portion of an early dial bearing runes, recently found. [At Skelton, in Cleveland.] Reliquary, N. [2nd] S. 6, pp. 65–67. 1892.

9480 Dickins (Bruce) and **Ross** (Alan Strode Campbell). The Alnmouth cross. [Concerns the inscription.] J. Engl. and Germ. Phil., 39, pp. 169–78. 1940.

9481 Ellison (Ralph Carr). The Anglo-Saxon monumental stone found at Falstone [Nhd.] in 1813. Archaeol. Æl., N.S. 7, pp. 272–73. 1876.

9482 Foerster (Max). Zwei altenglische Steininschriften. [Above south door of Kirkdale church, Yorks., and in Breamore church, Hants.] Engl. Studien, 36, pp. 446–49. 1906.

9483 Fowler (Joseph Thomas). Runic dial found at Skelton [in Cleveland.] Yorks. Archaeol. J., 13, pp. 189–90. 1895.

9484 —— Runic inscription at Kirkheaton. *Same jnl.*, 12, pp. 136–38. 1893.

9485 Gage (John). Sepulchral stones found at Hartlepool in 1833. [With ' runic inscription '.] Archaeologia, 26, pp. 479–82, + 1 plate. 1836.

9486 Haigh (Daniel Henry). The dedication stone of the church of St. Mary in Castlegate [York]. [11th c., in A.–S. and Latin mixed.] Communications Yorks. Philos. Soc., 1870, pp. 27–32, + 2 plates. 1870.

9487 —— Note on an inscribed stone at Wensley. [' Orate pro Eatbereht et Aruini,' A.D. 740.] Yorks. Archaeol J., 6, pp. 45–46. 1881.

9488 —— Notes on the monumental stones discovered at Hartlepool in the years 1833, 1838, 1843. [17 figures in text.] J. Brit. Archaeol. Assoc., 1, pp. 185–96. 1845.

9489 —— On an inscribed stone found at Yarm. [?' For Hereberht priest Alla erected this cross . . .' *but see* Stephens (G.): **9506**, for alternative names, etc.] Yorks. Archaeol. J., 6, pp. 47–52, + 1 plate. 1881.

9490 —— The runic monuments of Northumbria. Rept. of Proc. Geol. Soc. W. Riding of Yorks, 5, pp. 178–217, + 2 plates. 1870.

9491 —— Yorkshire runic monuments. [Pp. 255–78, + middle plate, Franks casket.] Yorks. Archaeol. J., 2, pp. 252–88, + 3 plates. 1873.

9492 Hamper (William). An account of a runic inscription on an ancient cross, discovered at Lancaster, in the year 1807. [' Gebyt for oczelbrit fruh-burug '. With figure.] Archaeol. Æl., [1st S.] 2, pp. 111–12. 1832.

9493 Hemingway ( ) *Dr.* Portion of a Saxon inscription. [At Dewsbury, Yorks.] Archaeologia, 34, p. 437, + 1 plate. 1852.

9494 Hempl (George). The Collingham [Yorks.] runic inscription. Mod. Lang. Notes, 12, col. 123–24. 1897.

9495 Howard (Henry). Observations on [runic inscription on] Bridekirk font and on the runic column at Bewcastle, in Cumberland. [4 plates of Bridekirk, and one (runes) of Bewcastle.] Archaeologia, 14, pp. 113–18, + 5 plates. [read] 1801.

9496 Just (John). On the reading of the Lancaster rune inscription. [2 figures in text.] Hist. Soc. Lancs. and Ches., Proc., 1, pp. 121–28. 1849.

9497 Kaye (Walter Jenkinson) *junr.* Notes on an inscription in Scandinavian runes found near Harrogate. ['Suna'. 11th or 12th c.] Proc. Soc. Antiq., 2nd S. 19, p. 55. 1902.

9498 Kemble (John Mitchell). Further notes on the runic cross at Lancaster. [Further to **9410**.] Archaeologia, 29, pp. 76–79, + 2 plates. 1842.

9499 Levison (Wilhelm). The inscription on the Jarrow cross. Archaeol. Æl., 4th S. 21, pp. 121–26, + 1 plate. 1943.

9500 Lyttelton (Charles) *bp. of Carlisle.* Description of an ancient font at Bridekirk, in Cumberland. [With runic inscription, which he translates : 'Here Ekard was converted, and to this man's example were the Danes brought.'] Archaeologia, 2, pp. 131–32. 1772.

9501 Maughan (John). A runic inscription on Hessilgil crags : Murchie's cairn [Cumberland]. [?reads : askr hritah aft Gil himthiga=Askr wrote this in memory of the son of his companion Hessil. Also ? pagan Saxon burial.] Trans. Cumb. and Westm. Antiq. Soc., 1, pp. 318–21, + 1 plate. 1874.

9502 Nicolson (William). A letter concerning a runic inscription on the font at Bridekirk, [Cumberland]. Phil. Trans. Roy. Soc., 15, pp. 1291–95. 1685.

9503 Olsen (Magnus). Notes on the Urswick [Lancs.] inscription. [Furness. 2 figures in text.] Norsk Tidsskr. for Sprogvidenskap, 4, pp. 282–86. 1930.

9504 Ross (Alan Strode Campbell). Notes on the runic stones at Holy Island. Engl. Studien, 70, pp. 36–39. 1935.

9505 Stephens (George). The Beckermont [Cumberland] inscription. [Cannot decipher.] Archael. Æl., N.S. 6, pp. 191–92, + 1 plate. 1865.

9506 —— Further remarks on an inscribed stone found at Yarm. [*See also* **9489**.] Yorks. Archaeol. J., 7, pp. 112–18, + 2 plates. 1882.

9507 Stephens (George). Pre-Conquest stone from Holy Island. Proc. Soc. Antiq. Newcastle, 2nd S. 5, pp. 189–90, + 1 plate. 1892.

9508 —— Runic inscription found at Brough, Westmorland. Date about A.D. 550–600. Trans. Cumb. and Westm. Antiq. Soc., 5, pp. 291–310, + 1 plate. 1881.

9509 Viëtor (Wilhelm). Beiträge zur Textkritik der northumbrischen Runensteine. *Diss. Marburg.* pp. 16. [Later embodied in **9511**.] 8° Marburg, 1894.

9510 —— The Collingham [Yorks.] runic inscription. Mod. Lang. Notes, 12, col. 120–22. 1897.

9511 —— Die northumbrischen Runensteine. Beiträge zur Textkritik, *etc.* pp. viii, 50, + 7 plates, + map. 4° Marburg, 1895. [Gross, 412a, note.]

9512 Waller (Thomas). Two Saxon inscriptions. [On dials at Kirkdale and Edstone, Yorks.] Old Yorkshire, ed. William Smith, vol. 1, pp. 33–35. 1881.

9513 Whitbread (L.). The Thornhill cross inscription [West Riding]. N. and Q., 193, p. 156. 1948.

9514 Wood (James). Some account of a Saxon inscription, on a stone found near Falstone, in the county of Northumberland. Archaeol. Æl., [1st S.] 1, pp. 103–04, + folding plate. 1822.

9515 Y. (X.). Runic gravestones found at Hartlepool. [2 figures in text.] Gent. Mag., 103 II, pp. 218–20. 1833.

§ *d.* Wessex and Kent

9516 Haigh (Daniel Henry). Notes in illustration of the runic monuments of Kent. Arch. Cant., 8, pp. 164–270 + 23 plates. 1872.

9517 Hempl (George). The runic inscription on the Isle of Wight sword. [c. 800.] P.M.L.A., 18, pp. 95–98. 1903.

9518 Macalister (Robert Alexander Stewart). The ancient inscriptions of the south of England. [Cornwall, Devon, Somerset, Dorset. 11 figures in text.] Arch. Camb., 84, pp. 179–96. 1929.

9519 McClure (Edmund). The Wareham inscriptions. [Breton refugees to England, temp. Athelstan.] E.H.R., 22, pp. 728–30. 1907.

9520 Milles (Jeremiah). Observations on an inscription in the church of Sunninghill, Berks. [Which he reads : ' Undecimo kalendarum Martii obiit Livingus presbiter': A.–S. proper name.] Archaeologia, 2, pp. 129–30. 1772.

9521 Potts (Robert Ullock). An eleventh century burial cross at St. Augustine's, Canterbury. [Inscribed ' on the eleventh of March 1063 departed out of this life Wulfmaeg sister of Wulfric the abbot.'] Antiq. J., 4, pp. 422–25. 1924.

9522 Ralston (William Ralston Sheddon). Remarks on an inscription on a copper disk found at Chertsey [Surrey]. [*See* article by J. M. Kemble, **9460.**] Archaeologia, 44, pp. 63–64. 1873.

9523 Westwood (John Obadiah). An Anglo-Saxon sepulchral slab at Stratfield Mortimer, Berks. [' + viii kl' octb fuit positvs Ægelþardus filvs Kyppingvs in isto loco beatvs sit omo qui orat pro anima eivs Toki me scripsit.'] Proc. Soc. Antiq., 2nd S. 11, pp. 224–26. 1886.

9524 —— On an Anglo- or Dano-Saxon memorial preserved in Stratfield Mortimer church, Berks. Proc. Oxford Archit. and Hist. Soc., N.S. 5, pp. 293–95. 1890.

165. OGHAMS, CELTIC, GENERAL

(Script originated in Ireland. Dating very difficult. No evidence for any existing before 5th c. Most belong to 6th c., a small proportion belong to 7th c. —MacNeill.)

9525 Abercromby (*Hon.* John). The Ogham alphabet. (The Oghams). [Answered by Isaac Taylor on p. 311.] Academy, 18, pp. 294, 346. 1880.

9526 Arntz (Helmut). Das Ogom. P.B.B., 59, pp. 321–413. 1935.

9527 —— Ogom und Runen. Nachr. Giessener Hochschulges., 10, pp. 27–40. 1934.

9528 Brash (Richard Rolt). The Ogam inscribed monuments of the Gaedhil in the British Islands ; with a dissertation of the Ogam character. . . . Edited by G. M. Atkinson. Pp. xvi, 45, + map, + 50 plates. 4° London, 1879.

9529 —— The Oghm inscribed monuments of the Gaedhil in the British Islands. [Notice of posthumous work.] J. Roy. Hist. and Arch. Assoc. Ireland, [15], 4th S. 5 (1879–82), pp. 450–52. 1882.

9530 Browne (George Forrest), *bp. of Bristol*. The origin of the Ogam alphabet, properly called the Bethluisnion. Proc. Soc. Antiq., 2nd S. 28, pp. 258–60. 1916.

9531 Burton (*Sir* Richard Francis). The Ogham runes and El-Mushajjar, a study. Trans. Roy. Soc. Lit., 2nd S. 12, pp. 1–46, + 5 plates. 1882.

9532 Derolez (R.). Ogam, ' Egyptian ', 'African' and ' Gothic ' alphabets. Some remarks in connection with Codex Bernensis 207. Scriptorium 5, pp. 1–19. 1951.

9533 —— Richtingen in de runenkunde, met enkele beschonwingen over het probleem, ogam-runen. Rev. belge Philol., 30, pp. 5–49. 1952.

9534 Diack (Francis C.). The origin of the Ogam alphabet. Scot. Gaelic Stud., 3, pp. 86–91, + 1 plate. 1931.

9535 Ferguson (*Sir* Samuel). Ogham inscriptions in Ireland, Wales, and Scotland. pp. xi, 164. 8° Edinburgh, 1887.

9536 —— On the difficulties attendant on the transcription of Ogham legends and the means of removing them. Proc. R.I.A., 2nd S. 1 (Antiq.), pp. 30–64. 1879.

9537 Graves (Charles) *bp. of Limerick*. Note on Ogams. J. Roy. Hist. and Arch. Assoc. Ireland, [16], 4th S. 6 (1883–84), pp. 439–40. 1884.

9538 —— The Ogam alphabet. Hermathena, 2, pp. 443–72. 1879.

9539 —— On Ogham inscriptions. Hermathena, 6, pp. 241–68. 1888.

9540 —— and **Windele** (John). On the age of Ogham writing. Trans. Kilkenny Archaeol. Soc., 1, pp. 305–21. 1851.

9541 Graves (Charles) *bp. of Limerick.* On the Ogam Beithluisnin, with a note on Scythian letters. Hermathena, 3, pp. 208–52. 1880.

9542 —— On the Ogham character. Proc. R.I.A., 4, pp. 173–80, 356–68. 1850.

9543 Graville (C. R.). On Oghams. Scottish Antiquary, 15, pp. 132–40, 211–13. 1901.

9544 Haigh (Daniel Henry). Cryptic inscriptions on the cross at Hackness, in Yorkshire. [And on Oghams.] J. Kilkenny Archaeol. Soc., [5] N.S. 2, pp. 170–94, + 1 plate. 1858.

9545 Keller (Wolfgang). Die Entstehung des Ogom. P.B.B., 62, pp. 121–32. 1938.

9546 Macalister (Robert Alexander Stewart). Celtic inscriptions. [Synopsis of a lecture.] J. Manx Mus., 2, pp. 22–23. 1931.

9547 —— Corpus inscriptionum insularum celticarum. *Irish Manuscripts Commission.* 3 vol. 8° Dublin, 1945–49. [Vol. 1, pp. 1–305, Ogham and analogous inscriptions of Ireland : pp. 306–434, do. of Wales : pp. 435–78, do. of England (Cornwall, etc.) : pp. 479–83, do. of Man : pp. 484–501, do. of Scotland.]

9548 —— The cryptic element alleged to exist in Ogham inscriptions. J. Roy. Soc. Antiq. Ireland, 29 (5th S. 9), pp. 52–55. 1899.

9549 —— Do Ogham inscriptions contain Latin words ? *Same jnl.*, 26 (5th S. 6), pp. 175–77. 1896.

9550 —— The ecclesiology of Ogham inscriptions. Trans. St. Paul's Eccles. Soc., 4, pp. 53–64. 1896.

9551 —— The Ogham word for ' daughter '. J. Roy. Soc. Antiq. Ireland, 31 (5th S. 11), pp. 439–40. 1901.

9552 —— The origin of the Forfeada. [5 symbols at end of Ogham alphabet.] *Same jnl.*, 30 (5th S. 10), pp. 255–56. 1900.

9553 MacNeill (Eoin). Archaisms in the Ogham inscriptions. Proc. R.I.A., 39 c, pp. 33–53. 1931.

9554 O'Daly (John). Ogham inscriptions. Evidence of their antiquity. Ulster J. Archaeol., 3, pp. 9–13. 1855.

9555 Pettigrew (Thomas Joseph). On Ogham inscriptions. J. Brit. Archaeol. Assoc., 17, pp, 293–310, + 1 plate. 1861.

8556 Plummer (Charles). On the meaning of Ogam stones. [?sepulchral : ? boundary stones.] Rev. celt., 40, pp. 387–90. 1923.

9557 Rhys (*Sir* John). The oldest Ogam. [From Silchester, Berks.] Arch. Camb., 5th S. 10, pp. 355–57. 1893.

9558 Richardson (L. J. D.). The word Ogham. Hermathena, no 62, pp. 96–105. 1943.

9559 Southesk (James Carnegie), *9th earl of.* The Ogam sign X. Academy, 45, pp. 229–30. 1894.

9560 Thurneysen (Rudolf). Du language secret dit *Ogham.* Rev. celt., 7, pp. 369–74. 1886.

9561 —— Zum Ogom. P.B.B., 61, pp. 188–208. 1937.

166. INSCRIPTIONS, CORNWALL
(including a few in Devon)

9562 Alexander (John James). The ancient inscribed stones [of Devon]. [10 Pre-coming of the Saxons : probably ranging from 450–700 A.D.] Rept. and Trans. Devon. Assoc., 69, pp. 153–54. 1937.

9563 Barham (C.). The ancient inscribed stones at Tregoney and Cubert. J. Roy. Inst. Cornwall, 2, pp. 47–58, + 1 plate. 1866. *Reprinted in* Arch. Camb., 3rd S. 12, pp. 417–29, + 1 plate. 1866.

9564 Hencken (Hugh O'Neill). Inscribed stones at St. Kew and Lanteglos by Fowey. [Chi–Rho, etc. ?5th–8th c.] Arch. Camb., 90, pp. 156–59. 1935.

9565 Iago (William). Discovery of an Ogham inscription [at Lewannick, near Launceston]. [' Ingenvi ma.'] Proc. Soc. Antiq., 2nd S. 14, pp. 214–15. 1892.

9566 —— The inscribed stone at Bleu-Bridge, Gulval. [Romano-British, ?6th or 7th c.] J. Roy. Inst. Cornwall, 8, p. 366 + 1 plate. 1885.

9567 Iago (William). Inscribed stones of Cornwall. [South-hill, Callington: St. Hilary 'Noti-Noti' stone: Bleu-Bridge, Gulval.] *Same jnl.*, 12, pp. 109–14, + 1plate. 1894.

9568 —— The Lanhadron inscribed stone. [Latin.] *Same jnl.*, 6, pp. 397–401, + 1 plate. 1881.

9569 —— Lanteglos-by-Camelford church and inscribed stone. Arch. Camb., 5th S. 13, pp. 146–48. 1896.

9570 —— Mawgan cross, the inscribed stone of the Meneage. J. Roy. Inst. Cornwall, 8, pp. 276–84, + 1 plate. 1884.

9571 —— Notes on some inscribed stones in Cornwall. [i. The Phillack stone deciphered: ii. Menscryfa, Madron. 6th–9th c.] *Same jnl.*, 4, pp. 59–71. 1872.

9572 —— Notes on three Ogham-inscribed stones in Cornwall. *Same jnl.*, 12, pp. 172–74. 1896.

9573 —— South Hill church and inscribed stone with chi-rho monogram. Arch. Camb., 5th S. 13, pp. 254–57. 1896.

9574 —— Trevena village and inscribed cross. Arch. Camb., 5th S. 13, pp. 153–55. 1896.

9575 —— Worthyvale, early Christian inscribed stone. Arch. Camb., 5th S. 13, pp. 149–50. 1896.

9576 Jenner (Henry). The Men scrifa. [Dates inscription to c. 600.] J. Roy. Inst. Cornwall, 21, pp. 56–62. 1922.

9577 Jones (Harry Longueville). Early British inscribed stones: The Fardel stone [near Ivybridge], Devonshire. [Fanoni/Maqvirini: Sasramni and Oghams.] Arch. Camb., 3rd S. 8, pp. 134–42. 1862.

9578 —— Early inscribed stones of Cornwall. [The Vitalis stone, St. Clement's: the Quenatavus stone, Gulval: the Conetocius stone, St. Cubert's. 6th–9th c.] Arch. Camb., 3rd S. 9, pp. 286–90, + 1 plate. 1863.

9579 Langdon (Arthur Gregory) and **Allen** (John Romilly). Catalogue of the early Christian inscribed monuments in Cornwall. Arch. Camb., 5th S. 12, pp. 50–60, + 7 plates. 1895.

9580 Langdon (Arthur Gregory). The chi-rho monogram upon early Christian monuments in Cornwall. Arch. Camb., 5th S. 10, pp. 97–108, + 2 plates. 1893.

9581 —— Lewannick church and Ogam inscribed stones. Arch. Camb., 5th S. 13, pp. 245–51. 1896.

9582 —— An Ogam stone at Lewannick. J. Brit. Archaeol. Assoc., 48, pp. 336–39. 1892. *Same title.* Arch. Camb., 5th S. 9, pp. 251–52, + plate. 1892. *Reprinted in* J. Roy. Inst. Cornwall, 11, pp. iv, 285–88. 1893.

9583 —— A second Ogam inscribed stone found at Lewannick. Proc. Soc. Antiq., 2nd S. 15, pp. 279–82. 1895. *Also in* J. Roy. Inst. Cornwall, 12, pp. 169–71, + 1 plate. 1896.

9584 —— [Two inscribed stones at] Tavistock [Devon]. Arch. Camb., 5th S. 13, pp. 234–37. 1896.

9585 Radford (Courtenay Arthur Ralegh). Report on the excavations at Castle Dore [near Fowey]. [Old site re-occupied 5th–8th c. Pp. 117–19, the Cunomorus stone, with 6th c. inscribed stone to Drustaus (son of Cunomorus = king Mark).] J. Roy. Inst. Cornwall, N.S. 1 (Appendix), pp. 1–119, + 13 plates, + plan. 1951.

9586 Rhys (Sir John). Inscribed stone at Lustleigh in Devon. Arch. Camb., 4th S. 11, pp. 161–63. 1880.

9587 —— The Lustleigh stone. [Figure in text.] Arch. Camb., 4th S. 13, p. 50. 1882.

9588 Wills (Samuel J.). Inscribed stone at Southhill. Arch. Camb., 5th S. 8, pp. 324–26. 1891.

167. INSCRIPTIONS, IRELAND
§ a. General

9589 [Anon.] Christian inscriptions in the Irish language. Arch. Camb., 4th S. 1, pp. 101–16, + 2 plates. 1870.

9590 Atkinson (George Mouncey). Some account of ancient Irish treatises on Ogham writing [in the Book of Ballymote] illustrated by tracings from the original mss. J. Roy. Hist. and Arch. Assoc. Ireland, [13] 4th S. 3 (1874–75), pp. 202–36, + 4 folding plates. 1874.

9591 Auraicept. Auraicept na n'Éces. The scholars' primer. Being the texts of the Ogham tract from the Book of Ballymote and the Yellow Book of Lecan, and the text of the Trefhocul from the Book of Leinster. Edited from eight manuscripts, with introduction, translation of the Ballymote text, notes, and indices, by George Calder. pp. lvi, 374. 8° Edinburgh, 1917.

9592 Brash (Richard Rolt). Ogham readings : no. 1 [only]. J. Hist. and Archaeol. Assoc. Ireland, [10] 3rd S. 1, pp. 168–86, + 1 plate, 438–39. 1868–69.

9593 Cochrane (Robert). Ogam inscriptions discovered in Ireland in the year 1898. J. Roy. Soc. Antiq. Ireland, 28 (5th S. 8), pp. 399–408. 1898.

9594 Ferguson (*Sir* Samuel). Fasciculus of prints from photographs of casts of Ogham inscriptions. Trans. R.I.A., 27, pp. 47–56, + 5 plates. 1881.

9595 —— Inscribed cromlechs in Ireland. J. Roy. Hist. and Arch. Assoc. Ireland, [12], 4th S. 2 (1872–73), pp. 523–31, + 3 plates. 1874.

9596 Gaidoz (Henri). Notice sur les inscriptions latines de l'Irlande. [Kenney 1, p. 103.] Mélanges publiés par la section historique et philologique de l'École des hautes études, pp. 121–35. 1878.

9597 Macalister (Robert Alexander Stewart). The secret languages of Ireland . . . partly based upon collections and manuscripts of the late John Sampson. pp. x, 284. 8° Cambridge, 1937. [Pp. 1–36, Ogham.]

9598 —— Studies in Irish epigraphy, a collection of revised readings of the ancient inscriptions of Ireland. 3 parts. 8° London, 1897–1902, 1907. [Kenney, 1, p. 103. Best collection of Ogam inscriptions.]

9599 MacNeill (John). Notes on the distribution, history, grammar, and import of the Irish Ogham inscriptions. Proc. R.I.A., 27 c, pp. 329–70. 1909.

9600 Nash (D. W.). On the Irish Ogham inscriptions. Ulster J. Archaeol., 2, pp. 60–66. 1854.

9601 Petrie (George). Christian inscriptions in the Irish language from the earliest known to the end of the twelfth century. Collected by G. Petrie, edited by Margaret Stokes. *Royal Hist. and Archaeol. Association of Ireland.* 128 plates. 2 vol. 4° Dublin, 1872–78. [Gross, 1486.]

9602 Rhys (*Sir* John). The Ogam-inscribed stones in the collection of the Royal Irish Academy, in the Dublin Museum. pp. 43. 8° Dublin, 1902.

9603 —— On Irish Ogam inscriptions. Proc. R.I.A., 2nd S. 1 (Antiq.), pp. 298–302. 1879.

9604 Vallancey (Charles). Ogham inscriptions. *Collectanea de rebus Hibernicis, vol. vi, pp. 157–236, + 5 plates.* 8° Dublin, 1804.

9605 Windele (John). Ancient Irish Ogham inscriptions. [3 comments, signed Psi, C. MacSweeney, and R. Hitchcock, on pp. 101–05.] Ulster J. Archaeol., 1, pp. 43–52, + 1 plate. 1853.

§ b. Co. Antrim, Connor

9606 Buick (George Raphael). The recent discovery of Ogams [at Connor]. J. Roy. Soc. Antiq. Ireland, 28 (5th S. 8), pp. 392–95. 1898.

9607 —— Report on the Ogams recently discovered near Connor. Proc. R.I.A., 3rd S. 6, pp. 265–71. 1901.

9608 —— A further notice of the Connor Ogams, and on a cross at Connor. J. Roy. Soc. Antiq. Ireland, 32 (5th S. 12), pp. 239–45. 1902.

9609 Carmody (W. P.). Ogam stones in the parish of Connor. (Further notes about the Connor Ogams). Ulster J. Archaeol., 2nd S. 5, pp. 47–50 : 9, pp. 66–68. 1898, 1903.

9610 Cochrane (Robert). The Connor Ogams. A new reading of the inscriptions. Ulster J. Archaeol., 2nd S. 5, pp. 105–08. 1899.

§ c. Co. Cork

i. Monataggart

9611 Brash (Richard Rolt). On an Ogham-inscribed pillar-stone at Monataggart. (Further remarks on the Monataggart Ogham inscription, No. 1). Proc. R.I.A., 2nd S. 1 (Antiq.), pp. 172–75, 213–14. 1879.

9612 Ferguson (*Sir* Samuel). On an Ogham-inscribed stone (No. 1) at Monataggart. (On further inscriptions discovered, etc. : Additional note . . . with a communication from Dr. Graves). Proc. R.I.A., 2nd S. 1 (Antiquities), pp. 207–10, 292–94, 295–97. 1879.

9613 Graves (Charles) *bp. of Limerick.* Remarks on the Ogham inscription (No. 1). Proc. R.I.A., 2nd S. 1 (Antiquities), pp. 211–12. 1879.

9614 Quarry (J.). On stones bearing Ogham inscriptions at Monataggart. Proc. R.I.A., 2nd S. 1 (Antiq.), pp. 289–91. 1879.

9615 Rhys (*Sir* John), **Haigh** (Daniel Henry) and **Stokes** (Whitley). Three additional notes on Ogham inscriptions at Montaggart. Proc. R.I.A., 2nd S. 1 (Antiq.), pp. 351–53. 1879.

ii. Others

9616 Atkinson (George Mouncey). Cill-caet-iairn and Ogham stones at Lisgenan and Glenawillen. J. Roy. Hist. and Arch. Assoc. Ireland, [16], 4th S. 6 (1883–84), pp. 307–10. 1884.

9617 Barry (Edmund). Discovery of an Ogham inscription at Rathcanning. J. Cork Hist. Soc., 2nd S. 3, pp. 41–44. 1897.

9618 —— Ogham inscription [at Rathcanning]. J. Roy. Soc. Antiq. Ireland, 27 (5th S. 7), pp. 79–80. 1897.

9619 —— On an Ogham monument at Rathcobane. Proc. R.I.A., 2nd S. 2 (Antiq.), pp. 485–89. 1888.

9620 —— On fifteen Ogham inscriptions recently discovered at Ballyknock in the barony of Kinnatalloon. J. Roy. Soc. Antiq. Ireland, 21 (5th S. 1, ii), pp. 514–35. 1891.

9621 Brash (Richard Rolt). On an Ogham-inscribed pillar-stone, at Ballycrovane. Proc. R.I.A., 2nd S. 1 (Antiq.), pp. 196–200. 1879.

9622 —— On an Ogham-inscribed pillar-stone, at Kilcullen. Proc. R.I.A., 2nd S. 1 (Antiq.), pp. 304–06. 1879.

9623 —— and **Ferguson** (*Sir* Samuel). On an Ogham-inscribed stone from Mount Music. Proc. R.I.A., 2nd S. 1 (Antiq.), pp. 190–95. 1879.

9624 Brash (Richard Rolt). On two Ogham inscribed stones from the county of Cork. [From Leades and Gurranes.] J. Hist. and Archaeol. Assoc. Ireland, [10] 3rd S. 1, pp. 254–64. 1869.

9625 Buckley (James). On an Ogham stone recently discovered at Greenhill. J. Cork Hist. Soc., 2nd S. 13, pp., 116–18, + 1 plate. 1907.

9626 Caulfield (Richard). Note on a supposed Ogham inscription, from Rus-Glass. J. Ethnol. Soc., N.S. 2, pp. 400–01 + 1 plate. 1870.

9627 Cochrane (Robert). Ancient monuments in the county of Cork. XI. Ogam inscribed stones . . . Alphabetical list. J. Cork Hist. Soc., 2nd S. 18, pp. 175–78. 1912.

9628 Coleman (James). The Knockshanawee Ogham stones. *Same jnl.*, 2nd S. 20, pp. 39–42. 1914.

9629 FitzGerald (Edward). [An Ogham stone 5 miles S.W. of Youghal.] J. Kilkenny Archaeol. Soc., [5] N.S. 2, pp. 286–87. 1859.

9630 Graves (Charles) *bp. of Limerick.* On the identification of the proper names appearing on two monuments bearing Ogam inscriptions. [At Aghabulloge, near Macroom, co. Cork, and at Cynffic, near Margam, Glamorganshire.] Proc. R.I.A., 2nd S. 2 (Antiq.), pp. 283–89. 1885.

9631 Hayman (Samuel). On an Ogham stone found built into the wall of a house close to St. John's priory, Youghal. J. Roy. Hist. and Arch. Assoc. Ireland, [15], 4th S. 5 (1879–82), pp. 38–40. 1882.

9632 Henebry (Richard). An Ogham inscribed stone in University College, Cork. [From Gurranes.] J. Ivernian Soc., 3, pp. 73–81, + 1 plate. 1911.

9633 Lee (Philip G.). Notes on the Ogham chamber at Knock-shan-a-wee. J. Cork Hist. Soc., 2nd S. 17, pp. 59–62. + 3 plates. 1911.

9634 Lionárd (Padraig). A reconsideration of the dating of the slab of St. Berichter at Tullylease. [Not to Berichter, d. 839, but to son (of same name) of Saxon prince who left England after Synod of Whitby, 664.] *Same jnl.,* 58, pp. 12–13. 1953.

9635 Macalister (Robert Alexander Stewart). Eight newly-discovered Ogham inscriptions in county Cork. J. Roy. Soc. Antiq. Ireland, 36 (5th S. 16), pp. 259–61. 1906.

9636 —— The Glounagloch Ogham. *Same jnl.,* 41 (6th S. 1), p. 68. 1911.

9637 —— Notes on certain Irish inscriptions. [14, mostly in co. Cork.] Proc. R. I. A., 33 c, pp. 81–92 + 1 plate. 1916.

9638 —— Ogham graffiti. [At Barrymore castle and Greenhill.] J. Roy. Soc. Antiq. Ireland, 62 (7th S. 2), p. 223. 1932.

9639 —— The Ogham inscriptions preserved in the Queen's College, Cork. J. Cork Hist. Soc., 2nd S. 13, pp. 36–42. 1907.

9640 —— On some county Cork Ogham stones in English museums. J. Roy. Soc. Antiq. Ireland, 36 (5th S. 16), pp. 166–78. 1906.

9641 O'Crowley (James). Newly-discovered Ogham stones, county Cork. *Same jnl.,* 36 (5th S. 16), p. 204. 1906.

9642 Power (Patrick). The latest Ogham discovery. [Watergrasshill.] J. Ivernian Soc., 6, pp. 201–05, + 1 plate. 1914.

9643 Rhys (*Sir* John). Another Greenhill Ogam. J. Roy. Soc. Antiq. Ireland, 38 (5th S. 18), pp. 201–04, + 1 plate. 1908.

9644 Stokes (Whitley). The Ogam inscriptions at Ballyknock. Arch. Camb., 5th S. 9, pp. 163–64. 1892.

9645 Waters (Eaton W.). Ballyknock Ogham stones. J. Cork Hist. Soc., 2nd S. 27, pp. 89–90. 1921.

9646 Windele (John). Ogham inscriptions. [In Cork Museum (from Gleunn-na-g-cloch, Burnfort, Barachaurin) and at Ballyboodan.] Trans. Kilkenny Archaeol. Soc., 1, pp. 142–45, + 1 plate. 1850.

§ d. Co. Galway

9647 Colles (J. A. Purefoy). Note on a supposed Ogham stone at Ross Hill. [Habam.] J. Roy. Hist. and Arch. Assoc. Ireland, [11], 4th S. 1 (1870–71), p. 268. 1878.

9648 Joyce (Patrick Weston). On the headstone of Lugna, or Lugnaed, St. Patrick's nephew, in the island of Inchagoill, in Lough Corrib. ['To commemorate Lugnaed, the son of Liemania.'] J. Roy. Soc. Antiq. Ireland, 36 (5th S. 16), pp. 1–10. 1906.

9649 Macalister (Robert Alexander Stewart). The Inchagoill inscription. *Same jnl.,* 36 (5th S. 16), pp. 297–302. 1906.

9650 —— The inscriptions of Iniscaltra, Lough Derg. [15 figures in text.] *Same jnl.,* 36 (5th S. 16), pp. 303–10. 1906.

9651 Trench (W. F.). The stone of Luguaedon on Inchagoill. J. Galway Archaeol. Soc., 3, pp. 146–47. 1904.

§ e. Co. Kerry

i. Dunloe Ogham Cave

9652 Allen (John Romilly). Dunloe Ogam cave. J. Roy. Soc. Antiq. Ireland, 22 (5th S. 2), pp. 166–70. 1892.

9653 Atkinson (George Mouncey). Notice of the Ogham cave at Dunloe. J. Kilkenny Archaeol. Soc., [8] N.S. 5, pp. 523–24, + 2 plates. 1866.

9654 Brash (Richard Rolt). On an Ogham inscribed stone at Dunloe. Arch. Camb., 4th S. 2, pp. 324–27. 1871.

9655 Graves (Charles) *bp. of Limerick.* Note on the Ogam cave at Dunloe. J. Roy. Hist. and Arch. Assoc. Ireland, [17], 4th S. 7, pp. 605–07. 1885.

9656 —— On the proper names occurring in the Ogam inscriptions found in the cave of Dunloe. J. Roy. Soc. Antiq. Ireland, 21 (5th S. 1. ii), pp. 665–72. 1891.

9657 Rhys (*Sir* John). Dunloe Ogam cave [and a description of the inscribed stones, with Sir John Rhys' readings.] Arch. Camb., 5th S. 9, pp. 50–54, + 1 plate. 1892.

ii. Others

9658 [Anon.] Ballintaggart killeen and Ogam inscribed stones. Arch. Camb., 5th S. 91, pp. 132–39. 1892.

9659 [Anon.] Oratory of Temple Managhan and Ogam-inscribed pillar. Arch. Camb., 5th S. 9, pp. 151–52. 1892.

9660 Allen (John Romilly). Notes on the antiquities in co. Kerry visited by the . . . Society . . . Aug. 1891. [Aghadoe cathedral (Ogam) : Dunloe Ogam cave : Ballintaggart killeen and Ogam-inscribed stones : Emlagh West Ogam-inscribed stone : Ogam-inscribed pillar at Kilmalkedar : oratory of Gallerus and inscribed stone : oratory of Temple Managhan and Ogam-inscribed pillar.] J. Roy. Soc. Antiq. Ireland, 22 (5th S. 2), pp. 158–70, 255–84. 1892.

9661 Brash (Richard Rolt). The Camp, or Glenfais, Ogam-inscribed stone. J. Roy. Hist. and Arch. Assoc. Ireland, [13], 4th S. 3 (1874–75), pp. 320–22. 1876.

9662 —— On an Ogham inscribed monument in Glen Fais. [Plate is ' map of Ireland showing the districts in which Ogham inscriptions have been found '.] Proc. R.I.A., 10, pp. 384–95, + plate 28. 1870.

9663 —— On an Ogham-inscribed stone, at Kilbonane. Proc. R.I.A., 2nd S. 1 (Antiq.), pp. 27–29, + 1 plate. 1879.

9664 —— On two Ogham inscribed stones from Tinnahally. Proc. R.I.A., 2nd S. 1 (Antiq.), pp. 186–89. 1879.

9665 Delap (M. J.). Ogham stone, Drung Hill. Kerry Archaeol. Mag., 2, pp. 159–62. 1913.

9666 Graves (Charles) *bp. of Limerick.* On an Ogam inscription [from the killeen of Aglish.] Trans. R.I.A., 27, pp. 31–40, + 1 plate. 1879.

9667 —— On an Ogam inscription lately discovered near Gortatlea. [NIOTTACOBRANORA . . ./DUMELI MAQI GLASICONAS.] J. Roy. Soc. Antiq. Ireland, 25 (5th S. 5), pp. 1–4. 1895.

9668 —— On an Ogam inscription supposed to bear an Anglo-Saxon name. [At Ballintaggart, near Dingle.] Trans. R.I.A., 30, pp. 97–108. 1892.

9669 —— On an Ogam monument recently found [at Ballinvoher]. Proc. R.I.A., 3rd S. 3, pp. 374–79. 1894.

9670 —— On the Ogam monument at Kilcolman. Trans. R.I.A., 29, pp. 33–42. 1887.

9671 —— On [two] Ogham monuments. [Both found in co. Kerry, and presented to the museum of the Royal Irish Academy.] Proc. R.I.A., 5, pp. 401–03. 1853.

9672 —— Remains of an Ogam monument [found in 1877 near Killorglin, and presented to the Royal Irish Academy], with some introductory remarks by Sir Samuel Ferguson. Proc. R.I.A., 2nd S. 2 (Antiq.), pp. 279–82. 1885.

9673 —— Remarks upon an Ogham inscription at Cahirciveen. [Christian.] Proc. R.I.A., 2nd S. 1 (Antiq.), pp. 157–59. 1879.

9674 Lynch (Patrick J.). Discovery of an Ogham stone [at Gurrane]. J. Roy. Soc. Antiq. Ireland, 24 (5th S. 4), pp. 291–92. 1894.

9675 —— Ogam stone at Lackareigh. *Same jnl.,* 38 (5th S. 18), pp. 278–80. 1908.

9676 —— Ogham stone in Cloghanecarhan, with a note by R. A. S. Macalister. *Same jnl.,* 39 (5th S. 19), pp. 164–69, + 1 plate. 1909.

9677 Macalister (Robert Alexander Stewart). A new Ogham inscription. [At Rathduff, near Anascaul, ' LLON-OCC MAQQ.'] J. Roy. Soc. Antiq. Ireland, 72 (7th S. 12), p. 76. 1942.

9678 —— The Ogham inscription at Maumanorig. Proc. R.I.A., 44c, pp. 241–47, + 1 plate. 1938.

9679 —— The Ogham inscriptions at Kilfontain and Ballymorereigh (St. Manchan's) in the Dingle peninsula. J. Roy. Soc. Antiq. Ireland, 67 (7th S. 7), pp. 221–28, + 1 plate. 1937.

9680 —— The Ogham monument at Kilbonane. *Same jnl.*, 33 (5th S. 13), pp. 175–78. 1903.

9681 —— Recent epigraphic discoveries in co Kerry. [Ogham, etc.]. Proc. R.I.A., 45 c., pp. 13–23, + 1 plate. 1939.

9682 Rhys (*Sir* John). Emlagh West Ogam-inscribed stone. Arch. Camb., 5th S. 9, p. 139. 1892.

9683 —— Ogam-inscribed pillar [and stones] at Kilmalkedar. Arch. Camb., 5th S. 9, pp. 143–47, + 1 plate. 1892.

9684 —— Query as to Killarney Oghams. J. Roy. Hist and Arch. Assoc. Ireland, [16] 4th S. 6 (1883–84), pp. 314–15. 1884.

9685 Rice (Richard Justice). Kerry Ogham finds, 1896. J. Roy. Soc. Antiq. Ireland, 28 (5th S. 8), pp. 69, 176. 1898.

§*f*. Co. Kildare
i. Killeen Cormac, near Colbinstown

9686 Brash (Richard Rolt). On the Ogam inscribed stones at Killeen Cormac. J. Roy. Hist. Arch. Assoc. Ireland, [13] 4th S. 3 (1874–75), pp. 165–82, + 1 plate. 1876.

9687 Fitzgerald (*Lord* Walter). Killeen Cormac. [8 figures and 2 plans in text.] J. co. Kildare Archaeol. Soc., 3, pp. 149–163. 1900.

9688 FitzGerald (William). Killeen Cormac inscribed stones. J. Roy. Soc. Antiq. Ireland, 25 (5th S. 5), pp. 380–82. 1895.

9689 —— On the lost Ogham ' Deccedda ' stone, once at Killeen Cormac. J. co. Kildare Archaeol. Soc., 2, pp. 206–08. 1896.

9690 Macalister (Robert Alexander Stewart). The ' Druuides ' inscription at Killeen Cormac. Proc. R.I.A., 32 c., pp. 227–38, + 1 plate. 1914.

9691 —— The Killeen Cormac stones. J. Roy. Soc. Antiq. Ireland, 26 (5th S. 6), pp. 81–83. 1896.

9692 —— and **Praeger** (R. Lloyd). Report on excavations recently conducted in Killeen Cormac. [Pp. 255–59, + plate 28, pillar-stones with Ogham inscriptions.] Proc. R.I.A., 38 c., pp. 247–61, + 5 plates. 1929.

9693 Marstrander (Carl Johan Sverstrup). The *Druuides* inscription at Killeen Cormac. [Ogham and Roman characters.] Norsk Tidsskr. for Sprogvidenskap, 13, pp. 353–56. 1945.

9694 O'Hanluain (Enri). The Druuides stone of Killeen Cormaic. (Short history of Ogham decipherment). J. co. Kildare Archaeol. Soc., 12, pp. 66–73. 1937.

9695 —— The Killeen Cormaic Ogham stone. *Same jnl.*, 12, pp. 201–13. 1941.

9696 —— On the occurrence of Roman capital letters at Killeen Cormaic. *Same jnl.*, 12, pp. 1–11. 1935.

9697 Rethwisch (Ernst). Die Inschrift von Killeen Cormac und der Ursprung der Sprache. pp. 38. 8° Norden, 1886.

9698 Shearman (John Francis). Bilingual Ogham inscription at Kileen Cormac. J. Roy. Hist. and Arch. Assoc. Ireland, [12], 4th S. 2 (1872–73), pp. 544–60. 1874.

9699 —— Inscribed stones of Killeen Cormac. An essay to identify that church with the Cell Fine of Palladius. Irish Eccles. Rec., 4, pp. 421–32. 1868.

9700 —— The Killeen Cormac stone again. Rev. celt., 3, pp. 453–57, + 1 plate. 1878.

9701 —— On some inscribed stones at Killeen Cormac. Proc. R.I.A., 9, pp. 253–62. 1865.

ii. Maynooth

9702 FitzGerald (*Lord* Walter). Discovery of an Ogham stone near Maynooth. J. Roy. Soc. Antiq. Ireland, 32 (5th S. 12), pp. 267–68. 1902.

9703 —— Notes on an Ogham inscribed stone recently discovered in the Donaghmore churchyard, near Maynooth, with a reading of its inscription by J. Rhys. [5 figures in text.] J. co. Kildare Archaeol. Soc., 4, pp. 155–60. 1903.

9704 O'Hanluain (Enri). The Maynooth Ogham stone [co. Kildare].—A new reading, and a new decipherment of the British Oghams. *Same jnl.*, 12, pp. 170–87. 1939.

9705 Rhys (*Sir* John). Notes on the Ogam-inscribed stones of Donaghmore, co. Kildare, and Inisvickillane, co. Kerry. J. Roy. Soc. Antiq. Ireland, 33 (5th S. 13), pp. 75–87. 1903.

§ g. Co. Kilkenny

9706 Barry (Edmund). On Oghamstones seen in Kilkenny county. [The Gowran stone, the Dunbell stones, the Clara stone, Tullaherin, Ballyboodan: Lamogue, Legan, Hook point, Kilbeg stone, Topped mountain, Ballyspallan brooch.] J. Roy. Soc. Antiq. Ireland, 25 (5th S. 5), pp. 348–68: 26, pp. 122–35. 1895–96.

9707 Brash (Richard Rolt). County of Kilkenny inscribed pillar-stones: Gowran. J. Roy. Hist. and Arch. Assoc. Ireland, [12], 4th S. 2 (1872–73), pp. 437–44. 1874.

9708 —— The Dunbel Ogham inscriptions. *Same jnl.*, [12], 4th S. 2 (1872–73), pp. 238–46. 1874.

9709 Ferguson (*Sir* Samuel). The Ogham monuments of Kilkenny. With some introductory observations by John G. A. Prim. *Same jnl.* [12], 4th S. 2 (1872–73), pp. 222–38. 1874.

9710 Hewson (Edward F.). On Ogams, including three recently discovered in the county Kilkenny, and one in the county Waterford. [At Legan castle and at Lamogue (co. Kilkenny)

and at Garraun (co. Waterford).] J. Roy. Soc. Antiq. Ireland, 26 (5th S. 6), pp. 22–28. 1896.

9711 Langrische (Richard). Ballyboodan Ogham-stone. *Same jnl.*, 26 (5th S. 6), pp. 177–78. 1896.

9712 Macalister (Robert Alexander Stewart). A county Kilkenny Ogham stone. [At Brittas, near Inistioge.] *Same inl.*, 70 (7th S. 10), pp. 92–93. 1940.

9713 —— Notes on some Kilkenny Oghams. *Same jnl.*, 27 (5th S. 7), pp. 221–31. 1897.

9714 Prim (Christopher Humphrey). The Ogham monument existing in the burial-ground of Tullaherin, barony of Gouran. Proc. and Trans. Kilkenny Archael. Soc., 3, pp. 86–87. 1854.

9715 Prim (John G. A.). On the discovery of Ogham monuments and other antiquities in the raths of Dunbel. *Same jnl.*, 3, pp. 397–408, + 2 plates (inscriptions). 1855.

§ h. Co. Louth

9716 Garstin (John Ribton). Some inscriptions in Irish in the county of Louth. [*See also* note, by Henry S. Crawford, on p. 226.] County Louth Archaeol. J., 5, pp. 3–12. 1921.

9717 Lefroy (J. H.). On a bronze object bearing a runic inscription found at Greenmount, Castle-Bellingham. [DOMNAL SELSHOFOTh A SO-ERTh ThETA] J. Roy. Hist. and Arch. Assoc. Ireland, [11], 4th S. 1, (1870–71), pp. 471–502. 878.

9718 Macalister (Robert Alexander Stewart). Ancient inscribed tombstones at Drogheda and Dunleer. County Louth Archaeol. J., 4, pp. 104–05. 1916.

9719 —— The Ogham inscription at Barnafeadog. *Same jnl.*, 3, pp. 385–86. 1915.

9720 Morris (Henry). Kilnasaggart stone [near Dundalk]. [?8th c. Inscription runs: 'This place, Ternóc, son of Ciaran the Little, bequeathed it under the protection of the apostle Peter.'] *Same jnl.*, l i, pp. 47–49, + 1 plate. 1904.

9721 Quinn (James). Kilnasagart [inscribed stone]. *Same jnl.*, 2, pp. 186–90. 1909.

9722 Reeves (William) *bp. of Down*. Kilnasaggart. Ulster J. Archaeol., 1, pp. 221–25, + 1 plate. 1853.

§ *i*. Co. Mayo

9723 Ferguson (*Sir* Samuel). On a recently-discovered Ogham inscription at Breastagh. Proc. R.I.A., 2nd S. 1 (Antiq.), pp. 201–06. 1879.

9724 Knox (Hubert Thomas). Note in reference to the Breastagh Ogham-stone. J. Roy. Soc. Antiq. Irealnd, 28 (5th S. 8), pp. 272–73, + 1 plate. 1898.

9725 Rhys (*Sir* John). The Kil-mannin Ogam. *Same jnl.*, 37 (5th S. 17), pp. 61–68. 1907.

9726 —— Report on the Island Ogam at Brackeaghboy, near Ballyhaunis. Proc. R.I.A., 3rd S. 6, pp. 279–82. 1901.

9727 —— The Tullaghane Ogam-stone. J. Roy. Soc. Antiq. Ireland, 31 (5th S. 11), pp. 176–78. 1901.

§ *j*. Co. Waterford

9728 Barry (Edmond). Three Ogham stones [at Garranmillion and Rath-gormuck] near Kilmacthomas. J. Waterford Archaeol. Soc., 2, pp. 228–33. 1896.

9729 Blackett (W. R.). The discovery of a new Ogham inscription [at Temple-anvach]. J. Kilkenny Archaeol. Soc., [6] N.S. 3, pp. 7–9. 1860.

9730 Brash (Richard Rolt). An account of the Ogham chamber at Drumloghan. Proc. R.I.A., 10, pp. 103–19, + 7 plates. 1870.

9731 —— On an Ogham inscribed stone, at Kiltera. Proc. R.I.A., 2nd S. 1 (Antiq.), pp. 4–7, + 1 plate. 1879.

9732 —— On the Seskinan Ogham inscriptions. J. Hist. and Archaeol. Assoc. Ireland, [10] 3rd S. 1, pp. 118–30, + 1 plate. 1868.

9733 Fitzgerald (Edward). Jottings in archaeology. [Pp. 43–47, Ardmore Oghams.] J. Kilkenny Archaeol. Soc., [4] N.S. 1, pp. 40–49. 1856.

H h

9734 Graves (Charles) *bp. of Limerick*. Observations on Mr. Brash's paper ' on the Ogham chamber of Drumlohan.' [9730.] Proc. R.I.A., 10, pp. 119–21. 1870.

9735 Henebry (Richard). The Ard-more Ogam. J. Ivernian Soc., 7, pp. 123–41. 1915.

9736 Macalister (Robert Alexander Stewart). The excavation of Kiltera. [Pp. 10–14, Oghams.] Proc. R.I.A., 43 c., pp. 1–16, + 3 plates. 1935.

9737 —— The Ogham inscription from Fox's Castle. J. Roy. Soc. Antiq. Ireland, 65 (7th S. 5), pp. 149–50, + 1 plate. 1935.

9738 Power (Patrick). Another Og-ham discovery [at Seemochuda.] J. Waterford Archaeol. Soc., 5, pp. 146–50, + 1 plate. 1899.

9739 —— Another Ogham discovery in co. Waterford. [At Kiltire, near Villierstown.] *Same jnl.*, 12, pp. 77–80, + 1 plate. 1909.

9740 —— On an early Christian inscription from [Shankill]. [*Aedui*, + two crosses.] *Same jnl.*, 13, pp. 103–06, + 1 plate. 1910.

9741 —— On an Ogham inscribed pillar stone recently discovered [near Dunhill. CUMNI MAQI MUCOI FAGUFI]. *Same jnl.*, 2, pp. 170–75, + 1 plate. 1896.

9742 Redmond (Gabriel). Remarks on an Ogham stone lying in Salterbridge demesne. J. Roy. Hist. and Arch. Assoc. Ireland, [17], 4th S. 7, pp. 418–19. 1885.

9743 Rhys (*Sir* John). The Ardmore Ogam stones. J. Roy. Soc. Antiq. Ireland, 33 (5th S. 13), pp. 381–86 : *also* pp. 373–74. 1903.

9744 —— The Drumloghan Ogams. *Same jnl.*, 29 (5th S. 9). pp. 390–403. 1899.

9745 Williams (William). Ocham readings ; with an account of an Ocham monument recently discovered in the ruins of the church of Kilrush, near Dungarvan. J. Kilkenny Archaeol. Soc., [4] N.S. 1, pp. 324–40, + 5 plates. 1857.

9746 Williams (William). On an Ogham chamber at Drumloghan. J. Hist. and Archaeol. Assoc. Ireland, [10], 3rd S. 1, pp. 35–39, + 1 plate. 1868.

§ *k.* **Co. Wicklow**

9747 Cochrane (Robert). Castletimon Ogam stone. J. Roy. Soc. Antiq. Ireland, 40 (5th S. 20), pp. 61–63. 1910.

9748 Crawford (Henry Saxton). Note on an inscription at Glendalough. [Cairbre, son of Cathal, d. 1013.] *Same jnl.,* 42 (6th S. 2), pp. 60–61. 1912.

9749 Graves (James). On a sepulchral slab found at the Reefert, Glendalough, bearing an Irish inscription, and also one in Greek letters. J. Roy. Hist. and Arch. Assoc. Ireland, [16] 4th S. 6 (1883–84), pp. 42–48. 1884.

9750 Macalister (Robert Alexander Stewart). On an Ogham inscription recently discovered [at Knickeen, or Cnuicin]. Proc. R.I.A., 33 c., pp. 230–32, + 1 plate. 1916.

9751 Tuomey (J. C.). Description of a cromleac and Ogham monument near Castletimon church. Proc. and Trans. Kilkenny Archaeol. Soc., 3, pp. 187–94. 1854.

§ *l.* **Other Counties**
(and in several counties)

9752 Armstrong (Edmund Clarence Richard). An inscribed cross-slab from Gallen priory, Ferbane, King's County. [10th c. Sexton, p. 155.] J. Royal Soc. Antiq. Ireland, 38 (5th S. 18), pp. 173–74. 1908.

9753 Callwell (Joseph). A sculptured slab, found in an old wall near Brookborough [co. Fermanagh]. [10th or 11th c. 'A prayer for Dunchad, the presbyter, here.'] Proc. R. I.A., 6 (1857), p. 512. 1858.

9754 Cochrane (Robert). Notes on the newly-discovered Ogam-stones [at Painestown and St. Cairan] in county Meath. With readings by [Sir John] Rhys. [*See also* (St. Cairan) **9783.**] J. Roy. Soc. Antiq. Ireland, 28 (5th S. 8), pp. 53–60. 1898.

9755 —— Ogam inscriptions discovered in Ireland in the year 1898. [The Island Ogam, or Bracklaghboy stone, co. Mayo (with 4 figures): the Ballyandreen stone, co. Kerry: the Aultagh Ogams, co. Cork: Bally-havenooragh Ogam, co Kerry: Knochalafalla, or Comeragh Ogam, co. Waterford.] *Same jnl.,* 28 (5th S. 8), pp. 399–408. 1898.

9756 Cooke (Thomas Lalor). On an ancient monumental slab at Athlone, [co. Westmeath]. [? 9th c. to Torpaith.] Trans. Kilkenny Archaeol. Soc., 1, pp. 409–12. 1851.

9757 Crawford (Henry Saxton). Description of an Ogam stone at Mountrussell, county Limerick: with a reading of the inscription by Sir John Rhys, and note by R. A. S. Macalister. J. Roy. Soc. Antiq. Ireland, 38 (5th S. 18), pp. 52–60. 1908.

9758 —— On an Ogham stone [at Ballingarry] in county Limerick. (Notes by Sir John Rhys and R. A. S. Macalister). *Same jnl.,* 36 (5th S. 16), pp. 47–50, + 1 plate. 1906.

9759 Elcock (Charles). Notes on an Ogam stone [at Lower Dungimmin, Kilbride parish] in the county Cavan. [Now illegible.] J. Roy. Hist. and Arch. Assoc. Ireland, [18] 4th S. 8, pp. 503–04. 1887.

9760 Ferguson (*Sir* Samuel). On an Ogham inscription at Mullagh, co. Cavan. Proc. R.I.A., 2nd S. 1 (Antiq.), p. 303. 1879.

9761 —— On the Ogham-inscribed stone on Callan mountain, co. Clare. Proc. R. I. A., 2nd S. 1 (Antiq.), pp. 160–71. 1879.

9762 Gógan (Liam S.). Observations on the inscription and decoration of the Dún Laoghaire stones [co. Dublin]. J. Roy. Soc. Antiq. Ireland, 62 (7th S. 2), pp. 214–19. 1932.

9763 Graves (James). On stone and bone antiquities, some with oghamic inscriptions, found at a crannog in Ballinderry Lough, parish of Cumreragh, county Westmeath. J. Roy. Hist. and Arch. Assoc. Ireland, [16] 4th S. 6 (1883–84), pp. 196–202. 1884.

9764 Henry (Françoise). L'inscription de Bealin, [Westmeath]. [c. 800.] Rev. archéol., 5 S. 32, pp. 110–15, + 2 plates. 1930.

9765 Lindsay (A. W.). The Dunalis [co. Derry] souterrain and Ogham stone. Proc. Belfast N. H. and Phil. Soc., 1934–5, pp. 61–70. 1936.

9766 Macalister (Robert Alexander Stewart). The inscriptions on the slab at Fahan Mura, co. Donegal. [Greek words. Interlacing ornament.] J. Roy. Soc. Antiq. Ireland, 59 (6th S. 19), pp. 89–98, + 4 plates. 1929.

9767 —— A newly discovered Ogham and some other antiquities in county Carlow. [At Crosslow, near Tullow.] *Same jnl.*, 40 (5th S. 20), pp. 349–51. 1910.

9768 —— Notes on some Ogham inscriptions, including two recently discovered. [Baltinglass, co. Wicklow: Connor, co. Antrim: Aghaleague and Breastach, co. Mayo: The Cotts, co. Wexford: Windele collection.] Proc. R.I.A., 34 c., pp. 400–04. 1919.

9769 —— Notes on the inscriptions at Kilpeacani, [co. Limerick]. J. Roy. Soc. Antiq. Ireland, 39 (5th S. 19), pp. 67–69. 1909.

9770 —— The Ogham inscription of Hook Point, co. Wexford. *Same jnl.*, 60 (6th S. 20), pp. 52–55. 1930.

9771 —— Ogham stone at The Cotts, co. Wexford. *Same jnl.*, 51 (6th S. 11), p. 77 + 1 plate. 1921.

9772 —— The Ogham stones near Clonmel and Carrick-on-Suir, [co. Tipperary]. *Same jnl.*, 39 (5th S. 19), pp. 294–96. 1909.

9773 —— On a (further notes on the) runic inscription at (in) Killaloe cathedral, [co. Clare]. ['Thorgrim raised this stone.' ? 11th c.] Proc. R.I.A., 33 c., pp. 493–98: 38 c, pp. 236–39, + 1 plate. 1917, 1929.

9774 —— On some recently discovered Ogham inscriptions. [i. Kilkeshagh, co. Kerry: ii. Drummin, co. Roscommon: iii–viii. Knockshanawee, co. Cork.] Proc. R.I.A., 32 c., pp. 138–46, + 2 plates. 1914.

9775 MacNeill (John). Ogham inscription at Cloonmorris, county Leitrim. J. Roy. Soc. Antiq. Ireland, 39 (5th S. 19), pp. 132–36. 1909.

9776 Marstrander (Carl Johan Sverstrupp). Killaloe korset og de Norske kolonier i Irland. [Co. Clare. With English summary. 6 figures in text.] Norsk Tidsskr. for Sprogvidenskap, 4, pp. 378–400. 1930.

9777 Milligan (Seaton Forrest). Ogham inscription, co. Tyrone. Proc. Belfast N. H. and Phil. Soc., 1887–88, p. 64. 1889.

9778 O'Connell (Philip) and **Meehan** (Joseph B.). Cavan Ogham stones. [i. Mullagh Ogham: ii. Dungimmin Ogham. 2 figures in text.] Breifny Antiq. Soc. J., 1, pp. 154–63. 1921.

9779 O'Toole (Edward) and **Macalister** (Robert Alexander Stewart). Ogham stone at Tuckamine, near Rathvilly, co. Carlow. J. Roy. Soc. Antiq. Ireland, 68 (7th S. 8), pp. 304–05. 1938.

9780 Patterson (William Hugh). Ancient sculptured stones at Maghera, county of Down. [Church founded by St. Donard; d. 506.] J. Roy. Hist. and Arch. Assoc Ireland, [16], 4th S. 6 (1883–84), pp. 20–22. 1884.

9781 Power (Patrick). A new Ogham from [Priesttown], Tipperary. J. Waterford Archaeol. Soc., 6, pp. 97–100, + 1 plate. 1900.

9782 Reeves (William), *bp. of Down*. [An] Ogham stone, now preserved at the Public Library, Armagh. J. Roy. Hist. and Arch. Assoc. Ireland, [16] 4th S. 6 (1883–84), pp. 367–70. 1884.

9783 Rhys (*Sir* John). The Cairon [co. Meath] Ogam stone (a correction) [to an appendix to R. Cochrane: **9754.**] J. Roy. Soc. Antiq. Ireland, 29 (5th S. 9), pp. 426–27. 1899.

9784 —— Newly discovered Ogams in Mayo and Antrim, with readings of some hitherto undescribed in Cork and Waterford. [Bracklaghboy (Mayo), Connor (Antrim), Aultagh (Cork), Knockalafalla (Waterford).] *Same jnl.*, 28 (5th S. 8), pp. 396–98. 1898.

9785 Rhys (*Sir* John). Notes on an Ogam hunt in the north of Ireland. *Same jnl.*, 25 (5th S. 5), pp. 101–05. 1895.

9786 —— Notes on Ogam inscriptions. [i. The Oldmills Piper stone, Donard, co. Wicklow: ii. The Carncomb Ogam, Connor, co. Antrim.] *Same jnl.*, 33 (5th S. 13), pp. 113–118. 1903.

9787 Rhys (*Sir* John). The Ogaminscribed stones of the Royal Irish Academy, and of Trinity College, Dublin. *Same jnl.*, 32 (5th S. 12), pp. 1–41. 1902.

9788 —— The Rathcroghan Ogams [co. Roscommon]. *Same jnl.*, 28 (5th S. 8), p. 409. 1898.

9789 —— Some Ogam-stones in Connaught. [Rathcroghan, co. Roscommon: Doughmaksone, co. Mayo: Breastagh, co. Mayo.] *Same jnl.*, 28 (5th S. 8), pp. 230–36. 1898.

9790 Ronan (Myles V.). The Dún Laoghaire inscribed and ornamented stones [co. Dublin]. *Same jnl.*, 62 (7th S. 2), pp. 212–14. 1932.

9791 Wakeman (William Frederick). Kilcoo [co. Leitrim]. [3 inscribed stones.] J. Roy. Hist. and Arch. Assoc. Ireland, [15], 4th S. 5 (1879–82), pp. 24–34. 1882.

9792 —— Note on an Ogam pillarstone in Aughascribbagh, co. Tyrone: with some notice of the Doonfeany stone, near Ballycastle, co. Mayo. *Same jnl.*, [15] 4th S. 5 (1879–82). pp. 750–56. 1882.

9793 —— On an Ogham, from the carn on Topped mountain, co. Fermanagh. *Same jnl.*, [13[, 4th S. 3 (1874–75), pp. 529–42, + 1 plate. 1876.

9794 —— Two hitherto undescribed inscriptions, in Irish, on stone slabs at Clonmacnoise, [King's County]. J. Roy. Soc. Antiq. Ireland, 20 (5th S. 1), pp. 273–75. 1890.

9795 Westropp (Thomas Johnson). The 'Knockfierna' Ogham stone, county Limerick. J. Roy. Soc. Antiq. Ireland, 37 (5th S. 17), pp. 242, 244–45. 1907.

168. INSCRIPTIONS, ISLE OF MAN

9796 Bradley (Henry). The runic crosses in the Isle of Man. Academy, 30, pp. 126–27. 1886.

9797 Brate (Erik). Runinkrifterna på Ön Man. Fornvännen, 2, pp. 20–34, 77–95. 1907.

9798 Cambrian Archaeological Association. Report of the 83rd annual meeting held at Douglas. [Descriptions of places visited: information largely on inscribed crosses, by P.M.C. Kermode, etc.] Arch. Camb. 84, pp. 348–71. 1929.

9799 Craigie (*Sir* William Alexander). Gaelic words and names in the Icelandic sagas. [Gaelic names on Manx runic crosses.] Zeit. celt. Phil., 1, pp. 439–54. 1897.

9800 Cumming (Joseph George). On the inscribed stones in the Isle of Man. Proc. R.I.A., 6 (1854), pp. 73–77. 1858.

9801 —— The runic and other monumental remains of the Isle of Man. pp. vii, 44, + 14 plates. 4° London, [1857].

9802 —— The runic inscriptions of the Isle of Man. Arch. Camb., 3rd S. 12, pp. 251–60, + 1 plate. 1866.

9803 —— The runic monumental remains in the Isle of Man. J. Archit. and Hist. Soc. of Chester, 1 (1849–55), pp. 445–49, + 2 plates. 1857.

9804 Haviland (Alfred). The Manx Oghams and the Manx alphabet. 1 page. 4° Douglas, 1887.

9805 Kermode (Philip Moore Callow). Brief note on the runic stones of the Isle of Man. Blandinger til oplysning om danske sprog i ældre og nyere tid udg. af Univ.-Jubilaets danske Samfund ved samfundets sekretær, pt. 4, pp. 281–86. 1886.

9806 —— Catalogue of the Manks crosses with the runic inscriptions and various readings compared. Second edition. pp. viii, 60. 8° [Ramsay, 1892].

9807 —— Early inscribed stone found at Santon. Arch. Camb., 5th S. 12, pp. 205–06. 1895.

9808 Kermode (Philip Moore Callow). Inscription in Anglian runes, from Kirk Maughold. Reliquary, N. [3rd] S. 13, pp. 265–67. 1907.

9809 —— Manx crosses, or the inscribed sculptured monuments of the Isle of Man from about the end of the fifth to the beginning of the thirteenth century. pp. xxii, 221, + 66 plates. 4° London, 1907.

9810 —— Note on the Ogam and Latin inscriptions from the Isle of Man, and a recently found bilingual in Celtic and Latin. [13 figures in text.] Proc. Soc. Antiq. Scot., 45 (4th S. 9, 1910–11), pp. 437–50. 1911.

9811 —— A Welsh inscription in the Isle of Man. [9th c. ' Crux Guriat.' *See also* pp. 52–55, note on Guriat, by Sir John Rhys.] Zeit. celt. Phil., 1, pp. 48–51, + 1 plate. 1897.

9812 Kinnerbrook (William). Etchings of the runic monuments in the Isle of Man, with remarks. pp. 14, + 26 plates. 8° London, 1841.

9813 Kneale (William). The discovery of Ogams in the Isle of Mann. Manx Note Bk., 3, pp. 163–66 + 1 plate. 1887.

9814 MacArthur (William). Runic inscriptions on crosses in the Isle of Man. N. and Q., 11th S. 6, p. 26. 1912.

9815 Marstrander (Carl Johan Sverstrup). Jurbykorset. [With English summary. 3 figures in text.] Norsk Tidsskr. for Sprogvidenskap, 4, pp. 370–77. 1930.

9816 —— Om sproget i manske runeinnskrifter. [Pp. 255–56, English summary.] *Same jnl.*, 8, pp. 243–56. 1937.

9817 Munch (Peter Andreas). Runeindskrifter fra Øen Man og Sydevøerne, meddelte. Annaler Nordisk Oldkyndighed, 10, pp. 273–87. 1850.

9818 —— Runic inscriptions in Sodor and Man. [i. Runic inscriptions in the Ile [sic] of Man : ii. A hitherto unknown runic inscription from Sodor.] Mém. Soc. roy. Antiq. Nord, 1845–49, pp. 192–208. [1849.]

9819 Olsen (Magnus). Om sproget i de manske runeinskrifter. Vid. Selsk. Forhandlingar, Christiania, 1909, No. 1, pp. 26. 1909.

9820 Rhys (*Sir* John) and **Browne** (George Forrest) *bp. of Bristol*. Manx Ogams. [Arbory, Ballaqueeney, Kirk Michael.] Arch. Camb., 5th S. 8, pp. 38–41. 1891.

9821 —— Why I visited the Manx Mona. [Concerning Ogam insciptions.] Manx Note Bk., 3, pp. 61–66. 1887.

9822 Savage (Ernest B.). Ogam inscriptions at Ballaqueeney, Rushen. [5th or 6th c.] *Same jnl.*, 2, pp. 145–48. 1886.

9823 Shetelig (Haakon). Stil og tidsbestemmelær i de nordiske korsene paa Øen Man. Opuscula archaeol. O. Montelio dedicata, pp. 391–403. 1913.

9824 Taylor (Isaac). The Manx runes. [Comments by Sir W. Boyd Dawkins and Henry Bradley on pp. 164–68. Further comments by Isaac Taylor on pp. 34–37, 78–90 of vol. 3, 1887.] Manx Note Book, 2, pp. 97–113, + 2 plates. 1886.

9825 —— *etc.* Runic inscriptions in the Isle of Man. Academy, 31, pp. 113, 131, 150, 167, 184, 202, 221, 275, 290. 1887.

9826 Vigfusson (Gudbrand) and **Savage** (Ernest B.). The Manx runic inscriptions re-read. [Pp. 78–90, is correspondence (between Isaac Taylor, P. M. C. Kermode, and G. V.) on this article, reprinted from the Academy.] Manx Note Bk., 3, pp. 5–22, 78–90. 1887.

169. INSCRIPTIONS, SCOTLAND

§ a. General

9827 Allen (John Romilly). Classification and geographical distribution of early Christian inscribed monuments in Scotland. J. Brit. Archaeol. Assoc., 45, pp. 299–305. 1889.

9828 Macalister (Robert Alexander Stewart). The inscriptions and language of the Picts. Essays presented to E. MacNeill, pp. 184–226, + 2 plates. 1940.

9829 Nicholson (Edward Williams Byron) *etc.* The North-Pictish inscriptions. Academy, 44–45, *passim* (6 articles). 1894.

9830 Rhys (*Sir* John). The inscriptions and language of the northern Picts. (——: addenda and corrigenda). Proc. Soc. Antiq. Scot., 26 (3rd S. 2), pp. 263–351 : 27 (3rd S. 3), pp. 411–12. 1892–93.

9831 —— A revised account of the inscriptions of the northern Picts. *Same jnl.*, 32 (3rd S. 8), pp. 324–98. 1898.

9832 Skene (William Forbes). Ancient Gaelic inscriptions in Scotland. *Same jnl.*, 1, pp. 81–83. 1852.

9833 Southesk (James Carnegie), *9th earl of.* The Ogham inscriptions of Scotland. [Newton stone, and others.] *Same jnl.*, 18 (N.S.6), pp. 180–206. 1884.

9834 Westwood (John Obadiah). On runic and other cryptic classes of inscriptions. [Abstract. Cat-stone, near Edinburgh, etc.] Proc. Oxford Archit. and Hist. Soc., N.S. 2, pp. 52–53. 1867.

§ b. Kirkmadrine, Wigtonshire

9835 Collingwood (Robin George). The Kirkmadrine inscriptions. Trans. Dumfries Antiq. Soc., 3rd S. 21 (1936–38), pp. 275–89, + 3 plates. 1939.

9836 Collingwood (William Gershom). Note on the Kirkmadrine stone. *Same jnl.*, 3rd S. 5, Pp. 141–43. 1918.

9837 Dowden (John), *bp. of Edinburgh.* Observations and conjectures on the Kirkmadrine epigraphs. (Appendix by Joseph Anderson.) Proc. Soc Antiq. Scot., 32 (3rd S. 8), pp. 247–74. 1898.

9838 Macalister (Robert Alexander Stewart). The ancient inscriptions of Kirkmadrine and Whithorn. *Same jnl.*, 70 (6th S. 10, 1935–36), pp. 315–25. 1936.

9839 Mitchell (Arthur). Inscribed stones at Kirkmadrine, in the parish of Stoneykirk. *Same jnl.*, 9, pp. 568–86, + 2 plates. 1873.

9840 Robertson (G. Philip). The lost stone at Kirkmadrine. Trans. Dumfries. Antiq. Soc., 3rd S. 5, pp. 136–41, + 1 plate. 1918.

9841 —— The stones of Kirkmadrine. *Same jnl.*, N.S. 21 (1908–09), pp. 130–34. 1910.

9842 Starke (James Gibson Hamilton). The Kirkmadrine crosses. [7th c.] *Same jnl.*, 6 (1887–88), pp. 53–56, + 4 plates. 1890.

§ c. Maes-Howe, Orkney

9843 Barclay (T.). Explanation of the inscriptions found in the chambers of the Maes-howe. Coll. Archaeol., 2, pp. 9–17, + 2 plates. 1871.

9844 Carr (Ralph). Note on no. vii of Mr. Petrie's copy of the Maeshow runes. Proc. Soc. Antiq. Scot., 8, pp. 139–42. 1871.

9845 —— Observations on some of the runic inscriptions at Meshowe, *Same jnl.*, 6, pp. 70–83. 1868.

9846 Farrer (James). Notice of runic inscriptions discovered during recent excavations in the Orkneys. (Readings of the inscriptions by Professors Stephens, March, Rafn.) pp. 40, + 13 plates. 4° Edinburgh, 1862. [Maes Howe, *etc.*]

9847 Mitchell (John M.). Meshowe : illustrations of the runic literature of Scotland. Translations in Danish and English of the inscriptions in Meshowe, etc. pp. 70, + 8 plates. 8° Edinburgh, 1863.

9848 Olsen (Magnus). Tre orknøske runeindskrifter (Maeshowe XXII, XVIII og XVI). Vid. Selsk. Forhandlingar, Christiania, 1930, no. 10. pp. 30. 1930.

9849 Pettigrew (Thomas Joseph). On the tumulus of Maes-howe in the Orkneys. [Comparative statement of the translation of the several inscriptions found in the great chamber by Barclay, Stephens, Munch, and Rafn.] Coll. Archaeol., 2, pp. 1–8, + 2 plates. 1871.

9850 Stephens (George) and **Farrer** (James). The runic inscriptions at Maeshowe. Gent. Mag., N.S. 13, pp. 286–91, 343. 1862.

9851 Stuart (John). Notice of excavations in the chambered mound of Maeshowe, in Orkney, and of the runic inscriptions on the walls of its central chamber. Proc. Soc. Antiq. Scot., 5, pp. 247–79, + 3 plates. 1865.

§ d. Newton Stone, Garioch, Aberdeenshire

9852 Bannerman (William). The Newton stone. A critical examination and translation of its main inscription. [' Draw near to the soul of Molung from whom came knowledge of the faith. He was of the island of Lorn.' d. 592.] Proc. Soc. Antiq. Scot., 42 (4th S. 6, 1907–08), pp. 56–63. 1908.

9853 Brash (Richard Rolt). Remarks on the Ogham inscription of the Newton pillar-stone. *Same jnl.*, 10, pp. 134–41. 1874.

9854 Carr (Ralph). On the inscriptions upon the stone at Newton Insch, Aberdeenshire, and on the inscription on a sculptured stone at St. Vigeans, Forfarshire. *Same jnl.*, 7, pp. 11–23, + 4 plates. 1870.

9855 Craigie (*Sir* William Alexander). The Picts and the Newton stone. [?8th c. In answer to various queries and unscientific answers in former parts. i. Ethnology of the Picts : ii. History of the Picts : iii. Language.] Scottish N. and Q., 5, pp. 101–02 : *See also* plate in no. for Mch., 1891, vol. 4. 1891.

9856 Diack (Francis C.). The Newton stone. Trans. Buchan Club, 13, pp. 179–87, + 2 plates. 1928.

9857 —— The Newton stone and other Pictish inscriptions. pp. 66, + 1 plate. 8° Paisley, 1922.

9858 Ellison (Ralph Carr). On the inscription at Newton-Insch. Proc. Soc. Antiq. Scot., 14 (N.S. 2), pp. 292–94. 1880.

9859 Graves (Charles), *bp. of Limerick*. An attempt to decipher and explain the inscriptions on the Newton stone. *Same jnl.*, 20 (N.S. 8), pp. 298–313. 1886.

9860 Moore (George), *etc.* The Newton stone. [Concludes that erected to memory of a Hebrew Buddhist missionary to Scotland !] N. and Q., 3rd S. 5, pp. 110–11, 245–46, 428. 1864.

9861 Skene (William Forbes). Notes on the Ogham inscription on the Newton stone. Proc. Soc. Antiq. Scot., 5, pp. 289–98, + 1 plate. 1865.

9862 Southesk (James Carnegie), *9th earl of*. The Newton stone. *Same jnl.*, 17 (N.S. 5), pp. 21–45. 1883.

9863 Thomson (Alexander). Notice of the various attempts which have been made to read and interpret the inscription on the Newton stone. *Same jnl.*, 5, pp. 224–34, + 2 plates. 1865.

§ e. St. Vigeans, Forfarshire

9864 Bannerman (William). The inscription on the Drosten stone at St. Vigeans. [' Drosten, thou wrought'st repentance.'] Proc. Soc. Antiq. Scot., 44 (4th S. 8, 1909–10), pp. 343–52. 1910.

9865 Carr (Ralph). The inscription on the sculptured stone at St. Vigeans. *Same jnl.*, 7, pp. 19–23, + 2 plates. 1870.

9866 Macrae (Donald). The Drostan stone (St. Vigeans). [?8th c.] *Same jnl.*, 43 (4th S. 7, 1908–09), pp. 330–34. 1909.

9867 Ramsay (John) and **Petrie** (George). On some ancient inscriptions in Scotland. [On cross of St. Vigeans.] Proc. R.I.A., 3, pp. 445–54. 1847.

§ f. Others

9868 [Anon.] Account of a stone with a runic inscription, presented to the Society [of Antiquities of Scotland] by the late Sir Alexander Seton of Preston, and of other inscriptions of the same kind in the Isle of Man. Archaeol. Scot., 2, pp. 490–501, + 1 plate. 1822.

9869 Anderson (Joseph). Notices of some recently discovered inscribed and sculptured stones. [i. Rune-inscribed cross at Thurso : ii. Stone, with symbols and Ogham inscription, at Keiss, Caithness : iii. Sculptured slab at Murroes, Forfarshire : iv. Incised symbol stone at Pabbay, Barra Island, Outer Hebrides : v. Portion of cross-shaft, sculptured in relief, from the island of Canna, etc.] Proc. Soc. Antiq. Scot., 31 (3rd S. 7), pp. 293–308. 1897.

9870 Bannerman (William). On the Ogham inscriptions of the Lunnasting [Shetland] and Golspie [Sutherland] stones. [Duichad, of Manan-land, son of Fife : Alldall Deyad, son of Nur.] *Same jnl.*, 42 (4th S. 6, 1907–08), pp. 342–52. 1908.

9871 Borland (Robert). The Liberalis stone [Whitehope, Yarrow]. [Considers was erected by Nudus (Nud Hael, ' the liberal '), king of the Strathclyde Britons, to commemorate his 2 sons, killed there in 6th c. battle.] Hist. Berwick Nat. Club, 19, pp. 169–72. 1904.

9872 Boyd (Halbert J.). The standing stones of Yarrow, [Selkirkshire]. [Plate shows ' Liberalis ' stone.] *Same jnl.*, 32, pp. 87–92, + 1 plate. 1951.

9873 Brate (Erik). Runic inscriptions in the cell of St. Molaise. Balfour (J. A.): The book of Arran, 1, pp. 261–67. 1910.

9874 Browne (George Forrest), *bp. of Bristol.* On some antiquities in the neighbourhood of Dunecht house, Aberdeenshire. pp. xiv, 170, + 63 plates. 4° Cambridge, 1921. [Including Ogam inscriptions, the Newton stone. Pictish sculptured stones.]

9875 Calder (Charles S. T.). Notice of two standing stones (one with Pictish symbols [goose]) on the lands of Parterhead farm, near Gleneagles, Perthshire. Proc. Soc. Antiq. Scot., 81 (7th S. 9), pp. 1–7, + 2 plates. 1949.

9876 Cunningham (James). An essay upon the inscriptions of Macduff's crosse in Fyfe. 4° Edinburgh, n.d. [Reprinted in Tracts illustrative of the . . . antiquities of Scotland. Edinburgh, 1836. Now lost.]

9877 Diack (Francis C.). The Dumnoqeni inscription at Yarrow (Selkirk) and the lociti inscription at Whithorn (Wigtown). Scot. Gaelic Stud., 2, pp. 221–32. 1927.

9878 —— A pre-Dalriadic [Ogham] inscription of Argyll : the Gigha stone. *Same jnl.*, 1, pp. 3–16. 1926.

9879 Goudie (Gilbert). Notice of a fragment of an Ogham-inscribed slab from [Cunningsburgh,] Shetland. Proc. Soc. Antiq. Scot., 17 (N.S. 5), pp. 306–11. 1883.

9880 Goudie (Gilbert). On rune-inscribed relics of the Norsemen in Shetland. *Same jnl.*, 13 (N.S. 1), pp. 136–64. 1879.

9881 —— On two monumental stones with Ogham inscriptions recently discovered in Shetland. [9th c. Christian.] *Same jnl.*, 12, pp. 20–32. 1878.

9882 Graves (Charles), *bp. of Limerick.* On the Ogham inscriptions appearing on a sculptured monument found at Bressay, in Shetland. [i. Crux : Natdodds : dattr : ann.: ii. Benres : meccudroi : ann.] Proc. R.I.A., 6 (1855), pp. 248–49. 1858.

9883 Macalister (Robert Alexander Stewart). The Greenloaning stone, [Perthshire]. Trans. Stirling Archaeol. Soc., 60, pp. 114–15. 1938.

9884 Macdonald (*Sir* George). On two inscribed stones of the early Christian period from the border district. [i. The Liddesdale stone : ii. The Manor Water stone, Peebles.] Proc. Soc. Antiq. Scot., 70 (6th S. 10, 1935–36), pp. 33–39. 1936.

9885 Marwick (Hugh). A rune-inscribed stone from Birsay, Orkney. *Same jnl.*, 56 (5th S. 8), pp. 67–71. 1922.

9886 Michie (J. G.). The Aboyne Ogham stone, Aberdeenshire. Scottish N. and Q., 7, p. 49, + 1 plate : *see also* p. 66. 1893.

9887 Munch (Peter Andreas). Om de ved steinsnes paa Orknøerne nys apdagede runeindskrifter. Illustreret Nyhedsblad, 10, pp. 201–02, 206–08 : 11, pp. 14–15. 1861–66.

9888 Petrie (George). Discovery of runic inscriptions in Orkney. Gent. Mag., 211, pp. 179–81. 1861.

9889 Rhys (*Sir* John). The Gigha Ogam, [Argyllshire]. J. Roy. Soc. Antiq. Ireland, 29 (5th S. 9), pp. 346–49: 31 (5th S. 11), pp. 18–23. 1899, 1901.

9890 Roger (James C.). Notes on two additional runic ristings in St. Molio's cave, Holy Isle, Lamlash bay, island of Arran. Proc. Soc. Antiq. Scot., 19 (N.S. 7), pp. 378–80. 1885.

9891 Russell ( ) *Miss, of Ashiesteel.* The Yarrow inscription. [' Liberalis ' stone, erected to the two sons of Nudd Hael, 6th c.] Hist. Berwick. Nat. Club, 10, pp. 105–08, + 1 plate. 1882.

9892 Simpson (William Douglas). The Maiden stone, [Aberdeenshire]. [Early Christian monument, with Pictish symbolism.] Trans. Buchan Club, 13, pp. 188–190. 1928.

9893 Skene (William Forbes). Notice of an Ogham inscription in the church-yard of Aboyne, Aberdeenshire. Proc. Soc. Antiq. Scot., 10, pp. 602–03. 1875.

9894 Southesk (James Carnegie), *9th earl of.* An Ogam inscription at Abernethy, [Perthshire], 1895. *Same jnl.,* 29 (3rd S. 5), pp. 244–51. 1895.

9895 —— The Oghams of the Brodie [Moray] and Aquhollie [Kincardine] stones, with notes on the inscriptions of the Golspie and Newton stones, and a list of the [14] Oghams in Scotland. *Same jnl.,* 20 (N.S. 8), pp. 14–40. 1886.

9896 Stephens (George). Note of a fragment of a rune-inscribed stone from Aith's Voe, Cunningsburgh, Shetland. *Same jnl.,* 10, pp. 425–30. 1875.

9897 Stevenson (Robert B. K.). A new Pictish symbol-stone in the Low-lands. [Borthwick Mains, near Hawick.] *Same jnl.,* 84 (1949–50), pp. 206–08, + 2 plates. 1952.

9898 Wilson (Daniel). Holy Island, and the runic inscriptions of St. Molio's cave, county of Bute. *Same jnl.,* 17 (N.S. 5), pp. 45–56. 1883.

9899 ——, *etc.* Runic inscription at St. Molio['s cave, Holy Isle, Bute]. N. and Q., 3rd S. 11, pp. 334–35, 499–500: 12, pp. 36–37. 1867.

170. INSCRIPTIONS, WALES
§ *a.* General

9900 Brash (Richard Rolt). Inscribed stones of Wales. Arch. Camb., 4th S. 4, pp. 285–87, 335–36. 1873.

9901 —— The Ogham inscribed stones of Wales. Arch. Camb., 3rd S. 15, pp. 148–67, + 2 plates. 1869.

9902 Ferguson (*Sir* Samuel). On the completion of the biliteral key to the values of the letters in the south British [= Welsh and Devonian] Ogham alphabet. (On the collateral evidences corroborating the biliteral key, *etc.*). Proc. R.I.A., 2nd S. 1 (Antiq.), pp. 176–80, 181–85. 1879.

9903 Jackson (Kenneth). Notes on the Ogam inscriptions of southern Britain. [54: of which, 16 Pembroke, 7 Carmarthen, 7 Breconshire, etc.] Chadwick Mem. Stud., pp. 197–213. 1950.

9904 Macalister (Robert Alexander Stewart). The ancient inscriptions of Wales. [11 figures in text.] Arch. Camb., 83 (7th S. 8), pp. 285–315. 1928.

9905 —— Notes on some early Welsh inscriptions. Arch. Camb., 77 (7th S.2), pp. 198–219. 1922.

9906 Nash-Williams (Victor Erle). Some dated monuments of the ' Dark Ages' in Wales. Arch. Camb., 93, pp. 31–56, + 10 plates. 1938.

9907 Owen (Edward). Lewis Morris's notes on some inscribed stones in Wales. Arch. Camb., 5th S. 13, pp. 129–44. 1896.

9908 Rhys (*Sir* John). The early inscribed stones of Wales. pp. 12. 8° Carnarvon, 1873. Carnarvon and Denbigh Herald, Nov. 29 and Dec. 6. 1873.

9909 —— Notes on some early inscribed stones in South Wales. Arch. Camb., 5th S. 10, pp. 285–91. 1893.

9910 —— Notes on some of the early inscribed stones of Wales, Devon and Cornwall. Arch. Camb., 6th S. 18, pp. 181–94. 1918.

9911 —— On some of our British inscriptions. Arch. Camb., 4th S. 4, pp. 74–77, 197–200, 386–88: 5, pp. 17–21, + 1 plate, 330–35. 1873–74.

9912 —— On some of our early inscribed stones. Arch. Camb., 4th S. 8, pp. 135–44, 239–40, + 1 plate. 1877.

9913 —— On some of our inscribed stones. Arch. Camb., 4th S. 6, pp. 359–71. 1875.

9914 Stephens (Thomas). An essay on the Bardic alphabet called ' Coelbren y Beirdd '. Arch. Camb., 4th S. 3, pp. 181–210. 1872.

9915 Westwood (John Obadiah). Early crosses and Christian inscriptions in Wales. Proc. Oxford Archit. and Hist. Soc., N. S. 1, pp. 30–37. 1861.

9916 —— Notes of several inscribed stones recently found in various parts of Wales. (Further notices . . .). Arch. Camb., 3rd S. 1, pp. 4–10, 153–56, 213 : 2, pp. 49–52, 139–46, 249–52, 319–21 : 3, pp. 55–61 : 4, pp. 161–65, 405–08 : 5, pp. 53–57, 287–92 : 6, pp. 47–57, 128–36, 223–28 : 11, pp. 59–66 : 13, pp. 342–44 : 4th S. 2, pp. 256–66, 339–42 : 6, pp. 283–84 : 7, pp. 195–97 : + 15 plates. 1855–76.

9917 —— Further notices of the early inscribed stones of South Wales. Arch. Camb., 4th S. 13, pp. 40–42. 1882.

9918 —— Further notes on ancient inscribed and sculptured stones. [Crossed stone near Goodwic, Pembroke : sculptured stones at Llanddew church, near Brewn, Brecknockshire.] Arch. Camb., 5th S. 2, pp. 146–50, + 2 plates. 1885.

9919 —— Observations on some of the early inscribed and carved stones in Wales. Arch. Camb., N.S. 2, pp. 144–49, 226–28, + 3 plates. 1851.

9920 —— On the early inscribed and sculptured stones of Wales, with introductory remarks. Arch. Camb., 4th S. 7, pp. 34–41, + 2 plates. 1876.

9921 Williams (*Sir* Ifor) and **Nash-Williams** (Victor Erle). Some Welsh pre-Norman stones. Arch. Camb., 92, pp. 1–10, + 4 plates. 1937.

9922 Williams (*Sir* Ifor). When did British become Welsh? Anglesey Antiq. Soc., Trans., 1939, pp. 27–39. 1939.

§ *b*. **Brecknockshire**

9923 Allen (W. Bird). The Llywel stone. Arch. Camb., 6th S. 17, pp. 159–63. 1917.

9924 Brash (Richard Rolt). Notes on the Ogham inscribed stone at Crickhowel. Arch. Camb., 4th S. 2, pp. 158–62, + 1 plate. 1871.

9925 Browne (George Forrest), *bp. of Bristol*. The Llywel stone. Arch. Camb., 6th S. 17, pp. 1–14, + 1 plate. 1917.

9926 Graves (James). Inscription at Trallong, in Roman and Ogham characters. J. Kilkenny Archaeol. Soc., [7] N.S. 4, pp. 206–09, + 1 plate. 1862.

9927 Robinson (George E.). Ogham inscribed stone at Pentre-Poeth, near Trecastle. [To B.M. since this article was written.] Arch. Camb., 4th S. 9, pp. 221–24, + 1 plate. 1878.

9928 Westwood (John Obadiah). Inscribed font at Patrishow. ['Menhir me fecit i(n) tē(m)pore Gēnillin': 1060.] Arch. Camb., 3rd S. 2, pp. 286–90. 1856.

9929 —— Notice of an early inscribed stone at Llangors, Talgarth. Arch. Camb., 4th S. 5, pp. 232–34. 1874.

9930 —— On an inscribed stone at Llangorse church. [Not later than mid 11th c.] Arch. Camb., 5th S. 7, pp. 224–35, + 1 plate. 1890.

9931 —— The Turpillian inscription, near Crickhowel ; Welsh Oghams, Bardic alphabet and destruction of ancient monuments. Arch. Camb., 2, pp. 25–29, 183. 1847.

9932 Williams (*Sir* Ifor). Names on the Llanddetty stone. [?9th c.] Arch. Camb., 90, pp. 87–94. 1935.

§ *c*. **Glamorgan**

9933 Allen (John Romilly). Iolo Mirganwg's [Edward Williams'] readings of the inscriptions on the crosses at Llantwit Major. Arch. Camb., 5th S. 10, pp. 326–31, + 3 plates. 1893.

9934 Ferguson (*Sir* Samuel). On the Kenfig inscription. Proc. R.I.A., 2nd S. 2 (Antiq.), pp. 347–54. 1886.

9935 Fox (Aileen Mary), *Lady Fox*. The siting of some inscribed stones of the Dark Ages in Glamorgan and Breconshire. Arch. Camb., 94, pp. 30–41, + 2 plates, + map. 1939.

9936 Jones (Harry Longueville). Roman altar bearing Oghams at Loughor. Arch. Camb., 3rd S. 15, pp. 258–62. 1869.

9937 Macalister (Robert Alexander Stewart). Early inscribed and carved stones at Llantwit Major. [8th c., etc. Figure in text.] Arch. Cam., 83 (7th S. 8), pp. 405–08. 1928.

9938 —— The second inscription on the Conbelin cross at Margam, [Glamorgan]. [Interlacing ornament.] Arch. Camb., 93, pp. 248–49. 1938.

9939 Nash-Williams (Victor Erle). Four early Christian stones from South Wales. [Ogmore stone and its inscriptions, etc. 7 figures in text.] Arch. Camb., 85, pp. 394–402. 1930.

9940 Rhys (*Sir* John). Some Glamorgan inscriptions. Arch. Camb., 5th S. 16, pp. 132–68, + 4 plates. 1899.

9941 Richard (Arthur J.). The Punpeius Carantorius stone, [near Eglwys Nunyd farm]: (Ogham stones—a revision). [Ogham and Latin inscriptions.] Trans. Aberafan Hist. Soc., 1, [pp. 44–46]; 2, pp. 30–31. 1928–29.

9942 Richards (Arthur). Ecclesiastical monuments at Port Talbot. [8th c. cross inscribed with name Geluguin.] Arch. Camb., 80 (7th S. 5), pp. 424–28. 1925.

9943 Robinson (George E.). The [Punpeius] Carantorius stone. (Eglwys Nunnydd). Cardiff Nat. Soc., Rpt. and Trans., 13 (1881), pp. 54–57. 1882.

9944 Stephens (Thomas). On an inscribed stone at Capel Brithdir. [*See also* **10016**.] Arch. Camb., 3rd S. 8, pp. 130–34. 1862.

9945 Thomas (Thomas Henry). Inscribed stones : some account of the pre-Norman inscribed and decorated monumental stones of Glamorganshire, being explanatory notes upon the series of photographs made by T. Mansel Franklen. Cardiff Nat. Soc., Rpt. and Trans., 25, pp. 34–46, + 4 plates. 1893.

9946 Wakeman (Thomas). On the age of some of the inscribed stones. [Crosses of Howel ap Rhys and of Samson, Llantwirt.] Arch. Camb., 4, pp. 18–21. 1849.

9947 Westwood (John Obadiah). Ogham characters [on a stone between Kenfegge and Margam]. [*See also*

(correspondence), p. 290, + pp. 413–16.] Arch. Camb., 1, pp. 182–83. 1846.

9948 Williams (C.). The inscribed stone at Capel Brithdir. Arch. Camb., 5th S. 11, pp. 330–32. 1894.

9949 Williams (*Sir* Ifor). The Ogmore castle inscription. [2 figures in text.] Arch. Camb., 87, pp. 232–38. 1932.

§ *d.* **Merioneth**

9950 Anwyl (*Sir* Edward). The Llandecwyn inscribed stone. [?8th–9th c.] Arch. Camb., 6th S. 6, pp. 121–24. 1906.

9951 Breese (Charles E.). Inscribed stone at Llanfihangel y Traethau. [' + Hic est sepulchrum Wleder matris Odelev qvi primum edificavit hanc ecclesiam in tempore Wini regis.'] Arch. Camb., 6th S. 16, pp. 235–38. 1916.

9952 —— Llandecwyn inscribed stone. [?8th–9th c.] Arch. Camb., 6th S. 5, pp. 237–41, + 1 plate. 1905.

9953 L. (H. W.). The Llan Elltyd stone. [Late Hiberno-Saxon characters.] Arch. Camb., 4th S. 9, p. 76. 1878.

9954 Rhys (*Sir* John). The St. Cadfan [Towyn], and other stones. Arch. Camb., 4th S. 5, pp. 243–48. 1874.

9955 Stephens (Thomas). St. Cadvan, Arthur, Caerfill. [Inscription on St. Cadvan s stone, Towyn.] Arch. Camb., N.S. 2, pp. 58–69. 1851.

9956 Thomas (David Richard). The Porivs stone. [Near Dolgelly.] Arch. Camb., 5th S. 2, pp. 143–45, + 1 plate. 1885.

9957 Wakeman [Thomas]. The stone of St. Cadvan, [Towyn.] [6th c.] Arch. Camb., N.S. 1, pp. 205–12. 1850.

9958 Westwood (John Obadiah) and **Williams** (John) *ab Ithel*. Observations on the stone of St. Cadfan, at Towyn, and on some other inscribed and carved stones in Wales. Arch. Camb., N.S. 1, pp. 90–100, + 1 plate. 1850.

9959 Williams (*Sir* Ifor). The Towyn inscribed stone. [8th c.] Arch. Camb., 100, pp. 161–72, + 1 plate. 1949.

§ e. Pembrokeshire and Carmarthenshire

9960 [Anon.] [An early Christian inscription on stone at Conwil Gaio, Carmarthenshire]. Arch. Camb., 5th S. 10, p. 94. 1893.

9961 [Anon.] The Llanwinio Ogam stone, [Carmarthenshire]. Arch. Camb., 5th S. 10, pp. 139–40, + 1 plate. 1893.

9962 [Anon.] Parcau and Gwarmacwydd, Llandyssilio, and Traws Mawr [Carmarthenshire and Pembrokeshire]. [Inscribed stones.] Arch. Camb., 6th S. 7, pp. 242–48, + 2 plates. 1907.

9963 [Anon.] ['Paulinus' and 'Talori' inscribed stones at Dolau Cothy, Carmarthenshire]. [2 figures in text.] Arch. Camb., 5th S. 10, pp. 91–93. 1893.

9964 Allen (John Romilly). Catalogue of the early Christian monuments in Pembrokeshire. [With table of references.] Arch. Camb., 5th S. 13, pp. 290–306. 1896.

9965 —— and **Westwood** (John Obadiah). Discovery of two Ogham stones at Castell Villia, and four crosses at St. Edren's, Pembrokeshire. Arch. Camb., 5th S. 1, pp. 46–50, + 2 plates. 1884.

9966 Allen (John Romilly). Early Christian inscribed stones at St. David's and St. Edren's, Pembrokeshire. Arch. Camb., 5th S. 10, pp. 281–82. 1893.

9967 —— The inscriptions at Carew, Pembrokeshire, and Fethard and Baginbun, co. Wexford. Arch. Camb., 5th S. 12, pp. 236–37, + 1 plate. 1895.

9968 —— On an inscribed Ogham stone at Little Trefgarne, [Pembrokeshire]. Arch. Camb., 4th S. 7, pp. 54–55, + 1 plate. 1876.

9969 —— Recent discoveries of inscribed stones in Carmarthenshire and Pembrokeshire. Arch. Camb., 5th S. 6, pp. 304–10, + 6 plates. 1889.

9970 Anwyl (*Sir* Edward). Inscribed stone at Eglwys Cymmyn, Carmarthenshire. [Oghams.] Arch. Camb., 6th S. 7, pp. 231–32. 1907.

9971 Birch (Walter de Gray). Notes on the inscription of the Carew cross, Pembrokeshire. J. Brit. Archaeol. Assoc., 41, pp. 405–11. 1885.

9972 Brash (Richard Rolt). The Bridell stone, [Pembrokeshire]. Arch. Camb., 4th S. 4, pp. 103–04. 1873.

9973 —— The inscribed stones at Clydai, Pembrokeshire. Arch. Camb., 4th S. 5, pp. 277–84, + 3 plates : 6, pp. 284–86. 1874–75.

9974 —— On an Ogham inscribed pillar at Bridell, Pembrokeshire. Arch. Camb., 4th S. 3, pp. 249–57, + 1 plate. 1872.

9975 Bushell (William Dene). Sir John Rhŷs and the Caldey Ogam. Arch. Camb., 6th S. 16, pp. 95–97. 1916.

9976 Davies (D. H.). Removal of Gellydywyll inscribed stone to Cenarth churchyard, [Carmarthenshire]. [Figure in text.] Arch. Camb., 5th S. 11, pp. 80–82. 1894.

9977 Ferguson (*Sir* Samuel). The Bridell stone [Pembrokeshire]. Arch. Camb., 4th S. 3, pp. 355–56. 1872.

9978 Fisher (J.). Discovery of an inscribed stone at Llansadyrnin [Carmarthenshire]. [6th c. ?[Arch. Camb., 75 (6th S. 20), pp. 190–92. 1920.

9979 Francis (George Grant). Stone with inscriptions in Latin letters and Ogham characters, discovered in 1846 at Llanwinio, in Carmarthenshire. [Figure in text.] Proc. Soc. Antiq., 2nd S. 3, pp. 446–47. 1867.

9980 Laws (Edward). Discovery of the tombstone of Vortipore, prince of Demetia at Llanfallteg, Carmarthanshire. Arch. Camb., 5th S. 12, pp. 303–07. 1895.

9981 Llanllawg, *pseud.* The Ogham stones of Pembrokeshire. Arch. Camb., 4th S. 3, pp. 356–57. 1872.

9982 Nash-Williams (Victor Erle). Early Christian stones. [Six. In Carmarthen Museum. Latin and Ogam inscriptions. 5th–6th c.] Arch. Camb., 100, pp. 127–28. 1948.

9983 —— Five new Pembrokeshire monuments. Arch. Camb., 92, pp. 325–30, + 4 plates. 1937.

9984 Radford (Courtenay Arthur Ralegh). The inscription on the Carew cross, [Pembrokeshire]. [11th c.] Arch. Camb., 100, pp. 253–55. 1949.

9985 Rhys (*Sir* John). The Capel Mair stone [Carmarthenshire]. Arch. Camb., 6th S. 7, pp. 293–310, + 1 plate. 1907.

9986 —— The inscribed stones at Clydai, Pembrokeshire. [Corrections of R. R. Brash's article, **9973**.] Arch. Camb., 4th S. 6, pp. 186–87. 1875.

9987 —— The Llandrudian stones, Pembrokeshire. Arch. Camb., 5th S. 15, pp. 54–63. 1898.

9988 —— Notes on inscribed stones at Egrement and Llandilo, [Carmarthenshire]. [5 plates in previous article.] Arch. Camb., 5th S. 6, pp. 311–13. 1889.

9989 —— Notes on inscribed stones in Pembrokeshire. [Llangwaran, Steynton, Brawdy, etc.] Arch. Camb., 5th S. 14, pp. 324–31, + 2 plates. 1897.

9990 —— Notes on the inscriptions on the tombstone of Voteporis, prince of Demetia, [at Llanfallteg, Carmarthenshire]. [Ogams, etc] Arch. Camb., 5th S. 12, pp. 307–13. 1895.

9991 —— Ogam stones in Pembrokeshire. Arch. Camb., 6th S. 10, pp. 327–30. 1910.

9992 —— The Steynton inscribed stone, Pembrokeshire. Arch. Camb., 4th S. 12, pp. 217–19. 1881.

9993 —— Three ancient inscriptions. [Nevern and Trehowel, Pembrokeshire.] Arch. Camb., 6th S. 13, pp. 376–90. 1913.

9994 Robinson (George E.). On the Gelli-Dywell [Carmarthenshire] and Wareham [Dorset] inscribed stones. Arch. Camb., 4th S. 7, pp. 141–45, + 2 plates. 1876.

9995 Schaaffs (G.). Die lateinischen Bemerkungen auf den Ogamsteinen Camp 1 und Calday island. Zeit. celt. Philol., 14, pp. 164–72. 1923.

9996 Southesk (James Carnegie), *9th earl of*. The inscriptions at Carew [Pembrokeshire], Fethard, and Baginbun, [co. Wexford]. Arch. Camb., 5th S. 12, pp. 325–29. 1895.

9997 Treherne (G. G. T.), **Rhys** (*Sir* John) and **Allen** (John Romilly). Notice of the discovery of an Ogam stone at Eglwys Cymun church, Carmarthenshire. Arch. Camb., 5th S. 6, pp. 95–96, 176–77, 224–32, + 2 plates. 1889.

9998 Westwood (John Obadiah). Description of the Vitalianus stone [at Cwm Glöyne, Pembrokeshire.] Arch. Camb., 5th S. 1, pp. 50–52, + 1 plate. 1884.

9999 —— Early inscribed stones in Wales.—Notice of an inscribed stone on Caldy island, Pembrokeshire. [7th–9th c.] Arch. Camb., 3rd S. 1, pp. 258–61, + 1 plate. 1855.

10000 —— Inscribed stone [of the two sons of bishop Abraham, 1076–78] at St. David's. Arch. Camb., 5th S. 9, pp. 78–80, + 3 plates. 1892.

10001 —— Notice of early inscribed stones found in the church of Llanwnda, Pembrokeshire. Arch. Camb., 4th S. 13, pp. 104–07, + 2 plates. 1882.

10002 —— On some inscribed stones in Pembrokeshire. [Steynton Ogham stone : Caldy island : Upton chapel font : St. Florence : Rhoscrowther.] Arch. Camb., 4th S. 11, pp. 292–99, + 1 plate. 1880.

10003 —— On the Gurmarc stone, St. David's, with observations on the introduction of the alpha and omega on ancient monuments. Arch. Camb., 5th S. 3, pp. 43–52, + 1 plate. 1886.

10004 Wilkinson (*Sir* John Gardner). The Menvendanus stone [near Llanboidy, Caermarthenshire]. Arch. Camb., 4th S. 2, pp. 140–57, + 2 plates. 1871.

§ *f*. Other Counties

(and in several counties)

10005 [Anon.] Inscribed stone with Oghams at Llanarth, Cardiganshire. Arch. Camb., 3rd S. 9, pp. 262–64. 1863.

10006 Allen (John Romilly). The discovery of an early Christian inscribed stone at Treflys, Carnarvonshire. Arch. Camb., 6th S. 5, pp. 70–72. 1905.

10007 Allen (John Romilly). Early inscribed stones visited during the Llanrwst meeting. Arch. Camb., 5th S. 5, pp. 176–78, + 2 plates. 1888.

10008 —— Eliseg's pillar. [Near Llangollen, Denbigh.] Arch. Camb., 5th S. 11, pp. 220–23. 1894.

10009 —— Llanwnws church and inscribed stone [Cardiganshire]. Arch. Camb., 5th S. 14, pp. 156–58. 1897.

10010 Boston (George Ives (Irby)), *4th baron.* Early inscribed stone, Anglesey. [St. Macutus, in Penrhos Llugwy churchyard.] Arch. Camb., 3rd S. 10, pp. 105–06. 1864.

10011 Brash (Richard Rolt). On an inscribed stone at Penrhos Llugwy, Anglesey. Arch. Camb., 4th S. 2, pp. 266–70. 1871.

10012 —— The Priscian Ogham glosses. Arch. Camb., 4th S. 4, pp. 105–06. 1873.

10013 Davies (Ellis W.). Llystyn Gwyn inscribed stone [Carnarvonshire]. [Latin & Ogham.] Arch. Camb., 90, pp. 307–09. 1935.

10014 Fox (*Sir* Cyril), **Williams** (*Sir* Ifor), *etc.* The Domnic inscribed slab, Llangwyryfon, Cardiganshire. Topographical survey by Sir Cyril Fox; epigraphy by Ifor Williams, R. A. S. Macalister and V. E. Nash-Williams. [Probably late 5th c.] Arch. Camb., 97, pp. 205–12, + 2 plates. 1943.

10015 James (T. D.). Llanerfyl: inscribed stone [Montgomeryshire]. [? 5th–6th c.] Arch. Camb., 6th S. 15, pp. 440–42. 1915.

10016 Jones (Harry Longueville). Early inscribed stones of Wales. [i. Erect stone with Oghams at Bridell, Pembrokeshire: ii. Llanfechan, Cardiganshire: iii. Stackpole-Elidyr, or Cheriton, Pembrokeshire: iv. Spittal, Pembrokeshire, Penbryn, Cardiganshire: v. Trallong, Brecknockshire: vi. Capel Brithdir, Glamorganshire—TEGERNA/ CUS FILI / US MARTI / HIC IACIT. Remarks on **9944**.] Arch. Camb., 3rd S. 6, pp. 314–17: 7, pp. 42–45, 137– 39, 302–08: 8, pp. 52–56, 220–23. 1860–62.

10017 Llanfwrog, *Pool Park*, Denbighshire. Latin-Ogam inscribed stone. [5th–7th c. = (The monument of) prince Sumilin. Figure in text.] Arch. Camb., 76 (7th S. 1), pp. 376–77. 1921.

10018 Macalister (Robert Alexander Stewart). Two Welsh inscriptions. [Capel Mair, Carmarthenshire, Llandanwg, Merioneth. Roman and Ogham letters.] Arch. Camb., 91, pp. 152–54. 1936.

10019 Nash-Williams (Victor Erle). Inscribed stone at Llanwnnws, Cardiganshire. [9th c.] Arch. Camb., 93, pp. 253–55. 1938.

10020 Owen (Aneurin). Welsh incised stone [at Wareham] in Dorsetshire. Arch. Camb., 4th S. 3, pp. 65–67. 1872.

10021 Radford (Courtenay Arthur Ralegh) and **Williams** (*Sir* Ifor). The early medieval period [in Anglesey], (c. 400–c. 1100). The early inscriptions. Personal names in the early inscriptions. Roy. Commission Hist. Mon., Anglesey, pp. civ–cvii. 1937.

10022 Rhys (*Sir* John). Epigraphic notes. [The Llanmadoc inscription (Gower): the Loughor altar: the Caswilia stones (Pembroke): the Carew cross inscription (Pembroke), with plate and note by J. R. Allen: the Garreg Lwyd, near Cefn Gwifed, Montgomeryshire.] Arch. Camb., 5th S. 12, pp. 180–90. 1895.

10023 —— Epigraphic notes. [Pembrokeshire—Caldey island, Cas-wilia, Carn Hedryn: Carmarthenshire—Castell Dwyran: Cardiganshire—Henfynyw, Llanddewi Aber Arth, Llanarth, Llanllyr: Brecknockshire—Devynnock: Glamorganshire—Pen y Mynydd, Ystrad Fellte.] Arch. Camb., 5th S. 13, pp. 98–128, + 5 plates. 1896.

10024 —— Epigraphic notes. [Pembrokeshire—Clydney, Rickardston hall: Merionethshire—Llech Idris, Trawsfynydd, Llanelltyd, Towyn: Tyddyn Holland, Little Druse, near Llandudno.] Arch. Camb., 5th S. 14, pp. 125–46. 1897.

10025 Rhys (*Sir* John). Epigraphic notes. [Carmarthenshire—Llansaint, Llandawke : Pembrokeshire—Nevern : Carnarvonshire—Treflys, Llystyn Gwyn.] Arch. Camb., 6th S. 7, pp. 66–102. 1907.

10026 —— The Gesail Gyfarch stone. [Near Tremadoc, Carnarvonshire.] Arch. Camb., 4th S. 13, pp. 161–65, + 1 plate. 1882.

10027 —— An inscription at Penmachno, [Carnarvonshire]. [6th or 7th c.] Arch. Camb., 74 (6th S. 19), pp. 201–05. 1919.

10028 —— The Pentre Poeth inscribed stone. [Now in B.M.] Arch. Camb., 6th S. 1, pp. 240–44. 1901.

10029 Roberts (Thomas). Inscribed stone, Penmachno, [Carnarvonshire]. Arch. Camb., 6th S. 15, pp. 442–43. 1915.

10030 Sayce (Archibald Henry). The inscription on the pillar of Eliseg, near Llangollen. Arch. Camb., 6th S. 9, pp. 43–48. 1909.

10031 Westwood (John Obadiah). The sepulchral stone of Emlyn, [near Ruthin]. [Note by William Owen, p. 214.] Arch. Camb., 3rd S. 1, pp. 115–17, + 1 plate. 1855.

10032 Williams (*Sir* Ifor). The Trescawen stone (Llangwyllog). [2 figures in text.] Roy. Commission on Hist. Mon., Anglesey, pp. cix–cxiii. 1937.

10033 —— and **Nash-Williams** (Victor Erle). Two early Christian stones from Tregaron, Cardiganshire. [7th or 8th c.] Arch. Camb., 91, pp. 15–19. 1936.

10034 Williams (John) *ab Ithel.* The pillar of Eliseg. [Near Valle Crucis abbey. Prince of Powys, d. 773.] Arch. Camb., N.S. 2, pp. 295–302. 1851.

10035 Willis-Bund (John William) and **Westwood** (John Obadiah). Cardiganshire inscribed stones. [Pontfaen stone, near Lampeter : Idnert-stone and another, at Llanddewibrefi.] Arch. Camb., 5th S. 8, pp. 233–35, 318–20, 328 : 9, pp. 170–71. 1891–92.

XII. ART

171. GENERAL

§ a. Anglo-Saxon and Viking

10036 Åberg (Nils). The occident and the orient in the art of the seventh century: the British Isles. pp. 135. Kungl. Vitterhets Hist. och Antik. Akad. Handlingar, 56 i. 1943.

10037 Brock (Edgar Philip Loftus). Saxon art and architecture. [Especially on interlaced work.] Antiquary, 3, pp. 103–09. 1881.

10037a Brown (Gerard Baldwin). The arts and crafts of our Teutonic forefathers. Being the substance of the Rhind Lectures for 1909. pp. xviii, 250, + 22 maps. 8° Edinburgh, 1910. [130 figures in text.]

10038 Brown (Gerard Baldwin). The arts in early England. 6 vol. (in 7), 8° London, 1903–37. [Gross, 425.] ——New and revised edition. vol. 1–2. *No more published.* 8° London, 1926, '25. [i. Life of Saxon England and its relation to the arts: 2. Ecclesiastical architecture: 3–4. Saxon art and industry in the pagan period: 5. The Ruthwell and Bewcastle crosses, the Gospels of Lindisfarne and other Christian monuments of Northumbria: 6. i. Completion of the study of the monuments of the great period of the art of Anglian Northumbria: 6. ii. A.-S. sculpture. The last vol. seen through the press by E. H. L. Sexton.]

10039 —— Was the Anglo-Saxon an artist ? Archaeol. J., 73, pp. 171–94, + 4 plates. 1916.

10040 Clemen (Paul). i. Die irische und angelsächsische Metallurgie. ii. Die irische und angelsächsische Steinplastik. [10 figures (brooches, etc.) in text.] Jahrbücher des Vereins von Alterthumsfreunden im Rheinlandes, 92, pp. 60–96. 1892.

10041 Collingwood (William Gershom). An inventory of the ancient monuments of Cumberland. [Churches, crosses, earthworks, etc.] Trans. Cumb. and Westm. Antiq. Soc., N.S. 23, pp. 206–76. 1923.

10042 —— An inventory of the ancient monuments of Westmorland and Lancashire-north-of-the-sands. [Mostly negative evidence as regards A.-S. period.] *Same jnl.*, N.S. 26, pp. 1–62. 1926.

10043 Dobson (Dina Portway). Anglo-Saxon buildings and sculpture in Gloucestershire. Trans. Bristol and Glos. Arch. Soc., 55, pp. 261–76, + 4 plates. 1933.

10044 Dunning (Gerald Clough). Medieval finds in London. [Fig. 1, Part of a leather scabbard decorated with interlacing. c. 10th–11th c.] Antiq. J., 12, p. 177. 1932.

10045 Goldschmidt (Adolph). English influence on medieval art of the continent. [29 figures in text. Ornament, especially illuminations.] Porter (A. K.): Medieval studies, 2, pp. 709–28. 1939.

10046 Holmqvist (Wilhelm). Viking art in the eleventh century. [42 figures in text.] Acta Archaeol., 22, pp. 1–56. 1951.

10047 Hughes (Reginald). Art and architecture. [Including coins.] Social England, ed. Traill and Mann, 1, pp. 278–93. 1891.

10047a Jenny (Wilhelm Albert von). Die Kunst der Germanen im frühen Mittelalter. pp. 86, + 152 plates. 8° Berlin, 1940. [Pp. 35–40, + plates 74, 75, 77, A.-S.]

10048 Jonas (Alfred Charles). Heraldry before the Conquest. N. and Q., 9th S. 9, pp. 124–25, 290–91 : 10, p. 110 : 10th S. 1, p. 76. 1902, 1904.

10049 Kendrick (*Sir* Thomas Downing). Anglo-Saxon art to A.D. 900. pp. xvi, 227, + 104 plates. 8° London, 1938.

10050 —— The art and archaeology of the early Anglo-Saxons. S. E. Naturalist, 39, pp. 14–20. 1934.

10051 —— Early Christian art in the British Isles. [Discusses Book of Durrow and Lindisfarne Gospels, Clapham's theory of development of Anglo-Celtic style, and vine-scroll ornament on Northumbrian crosses.] S. E. Naturalist, 40, pp. 14–20. 1935.

10052 —— Late Saxon and Viking art. pp. xv, 152 + 96 plates. 8° London, 1949.

10053 —— The Viking taste in pre-Conquest England. Antiquity, 15, pp. 125–41 + 4 plates. 1941.

10054 Leeds (Edward Thurlow). Early Anglo-Saxon art and archaeology. *Rhind Lectures*, 1935. pp. xii, 130, + 33 plates. 8° Oxford, 1936.

10055 March (Henry Colley). Scando-Gothic art in Wessex. Proc. Dorset Antiq. F.C., 34, pp. 1–16, + 3 plates. 1913.

10056 Mildenberger (Kenneth). Unity of Cynewulf's *Christ* in the light of iconography. [5 figures of St. Cuthbert's coffin.] Speculum, 23, pp. 426–32, + 5 plates. 1948.

10057 Mitchell (H. P.). Flotsam of later Anglo-Saxon art. [*See also* note on this article by Rose Graham, 43, p. 49. 1923.] Burl. Mag., 42, pp. 63–72, 162–69, 303–05 : 43, pp. 104–17, + 8 plates. 1923.

10058 Pfeilstuecker (Suse). Spätantikes und germanisches Kunstgut in der frühangelsächsischen Kunst. Nach lateinischen und altenglischen Schriftquellen. *Diss., Bonn,* 1936. pp. 244, + plates. 8° Berlin, 1936.

10059 Phythian (John Ernest). The story of art in the British Isles. pp. 246. 8° London, 1901. [Pp. 27–42, Celtic Christian art : pp. 42–53, Art in Saxon England.]

10060 Picton (Harold). Early German art and its origins. pp. xii, 148, + 102 plates. 8° London, 1939. [A little A.-S. and Celtic background.]

10061 Pite (Beresford). The study of Anglo-Saxon art. J.R.I.B.A., 3rd S. 24, pp. 33–38. 1917.

10062 Radford (Courtenay Arthur Ralegh). Roma e l'arte dei Celti e degli Anglosassoni dal v all'viii secolo D.C. *Istituto di studi Romani, Quaderni dell'Impero, Roma e le provincie,* 3. pp. 15, + 1 plate. 8° Roma, 1938.

10063 Rice (David Talbot). The Byzantine element in late Saxon art. *W. H. Charlton memorial lecture,* 1946. pp. 20, + 1 plate. 8° London, 1947.

10064 —— English art, 871–1100. *Oxford History of English art,* ed. T. S. R. Boase, 2. pp. xxii, 280, + 97 plates. 8° Oxford, 1952. [Architecture, sculpture, ivories, mss., minor arts.]

10065 Saunders (O. Elfrida). A history of English art in the Middle Ages. pp. xxii, 272, + 77 plates. 8° Oxford, 1932. [Pp. 1–38, + plates 1–12, A.-S. art.]

10066 Saxl (Fritz) and **Wittkower** (Rudolf). British art and the Mediterranean. pp. 56. fol. London, 1948. [Plates and commentary : nos. 12–18, A.-S. art and the south : 19–23, the ' Carolingian Renaissance' in Britain : 31, A.-S. herbals.]

10067 Shetelig (Haakon). Specimens of the Urnes style in English art of the late eleventh century. Antiq. J., 15, pp. 22–25. 1935.

10068 Smith (Reginald Allender). Examples of Anglian art. [26 figures in text.] Archaeologia, 74, pp. 233–54. 1925.

10069 Strzygowski (Josef). Origin of Christian church art. New facts and principles of research. pp. xvii, 267, + 47 plates. 4° Oxford, 1923. [Pp. 230–52 : Hiberno-Saxon art in the time of Bede.]

I i

§ b. Celtic

10070 Allen (John Romilly). Celtic art in pagan and Christian times. Second edition, revised. *Antiquary's Books.* pp. xxii, 315. 8° London, 1912.

10071 —— Celtic art in Wales and Ireland compared. Arch. Camb., 5th S. 10, pp. 17–24. 1893.

10072 —— The early Christian monuments of Scotland ; and an introduction, being the Rhind Lectures for 1892, by Joseph Anderson. pp. cxxii, 522. 4° Edinburgh, 1903. [567 figures, on plates and in letterpress.]

10073 —— A monumental history of the early British Church [to 1066]. pp. xvi, 255, + 16 plates. 8° London, 1889. [Gross, 394.]

10074 Bain (George). Celtic art. The mathematical basis of the construction of the art of the Pictish school. [7 pp. of figures in text.] Trans. Gaelic Soc. Inverness, 37 (1934–36), pp. 136–54. 1946.

10075 —— The methods of construction of the Pictish school of Celtic art. [2 maps, + 2 pp. of illustrations of ' one continuous line, symbolical of eternity '.] Trans. Glasgow Archaeol. Soc., N.S. 9, pp. 83–91. 1938.

10076 Beaufort (L. C.). An essay upon the state of architecture and antiquities, previous to the landing of the Anglo-Normans in Ireland. Trans. R.I.A., 15 (Antiq.), pp. 101–242, + 15 plates. 1828.

10077 Brash (Richard Rolt). The precious metals and ancient mining in Ireland. [Pre- and early Christian metallurgic arts.] J. Roy. Hist. and Arch. Assoc. Ireland, [11] 4th S. 1 (1870–71), pp. 509–34. 1878.

10078 Curle (Cecil L.) and **Henry** (Françoise). Early Christian art in Scotland. [Outline 5th–11th c. with contemporary English and Irish affinities. 13 figures in text.] Gaz. beaux arts, 6th S. 24, pp. 257–72. 1943.

10079 Dublin, *National Museum of Science and Art.* Royal Irish Academy collection. Guide to the Celtic antiquities of the Christian period preserved in the National Museum. By George Coffey. 2nd edition. pp. ix, 111, + 19 plates. 8° Dublin, 1910. [Kenney, 1, p. 103. 114 figures in text. Brooches, shrines, croziers, bells, etc.]

10080 —— Guide to the collection of Irish antiquities. Part 4.—The Christian period, by Thomas J. Westropp. 3rd edition. pp. 27, + 6 plates. 8° Dublin, 1911. [Shrines, bells, croziers, brooches, etc.]

10081 Frazer (William). On ' Patrick's crosses '—stone, bronze and gold. [i. Stone and bronze (Corp Naomh, etc.) : ii. Gold—a further contribution to the history of gold ornaments found in Ireland.] J. Roy. Soc. Antiq. Ireland, 29 (5th S. 9), pp. 35–43. 1899.

10082 Galbraith (James John). Celtic art. Trans. Gaelic Soc. Inverness, 29 (1914–19), pp. 182–94. 1922.

10083 Gerke (Friedrich). Die Anfänge der frühchristlichen Kunst in Irland. [4 figures in text.] Kunst u. Kirche, 16, pp. 104–08. 1939.

10084 Gógan (Liam S.). The Ardagh chalice. pp. 94. 8° Dublin, 1932. [18 plates and figures. Notes on other chalices : its A.-S. pendant, 7th c., from Kent : inscription, etc.]

10085 Gougaud (Louis). L'art celtique chrétien. [Kenney, 1, p. 98. 13 figures in text. Architecture, work in wood and metals, mss. and miniatures, motifs of ornament.] Rev. de l'art chrét., 61, pp. 89–108. 1911.

10086 —— The earliest Irish representations of the crucifixion. [Illuminated mss., sculptured stone crosses, etc. List of carvings.] J. Roy. Soc. Antiq. Ireland, 50 (6th S. 10), pp. 128–39, + 5 plates. 1920.

10087 —— Liturgies et arts celtiques. [ii. L'art celtique chrétien.] Rev. celt., 32, pp. 250–53. 1911.

10088 Henry (Françoise). Un domaine nouveau de l'histoire de l'art : l'art irlandais du VIIIe siècle et ses origines. [15 figures in text.] Gaz. des Beaux-Arts, 79 (pér. 6, 17), pp. 131–44. 1937.

10089 —— Irish art in the early Christian period. 2nd edition. pp. xix, 220, + 80 plates. 8° London, 1947. [55 figures in text. Especially 10th c. Lindisfarne Gospels and other illuminated mss.]

10090 —— Les origines de l'iconographie irlandaise. Rev. archéol., 5 S. 32, pp. 89–109. 1930.

10091 Jacobsthal (Paul). Early Celtic art. 2 vol. (text and plates). 4° Oxford, 1944.

10092 Lamb (Helen A.). The art of the Celtic Church. Soc. Friends Dunblane Cath. Bk., 2, pp. 7–24. 1937.

10093 Lamont (Augusta). The history of Celtic art. Proc. Scot. Anthrop. Soc., 3, pp. 29–55, + 4 plates. 1939.

10094 Lawlor (Henry Cairnes). Ulster, its archaeology and antiquities. pp. xiv, 224. 8° Belfast, 1928.

10095 Lee (Philip G.). Notable Celtic monuments illustrated. [Pp. 71–77, Early Christian period, round towers, high crosses, illumination, metal work.] J. Ivernian Soc., 2, pp. 65–78, + 6 plates. 1910.

10096 —— Notable Celtic monuments. [Round towers, high crosses, illumination, etc.] J. Antiq. Assoc. Brit. Isles, 1, pp. 3–24. 1930.

10097 Macalister (Robert Alexander Stewart). The archaeology of Ireland. 2nd edition, revised. pp. xx, 386, + 16 plates. 8° London, 1949.

10098 MacKenna (James Edward). Irish art. pp. 59. 8° Dublin, 1910.

10099 Mahr (Adolf) and **Raftery** (Joseph), *ed.* Christian art in ancient Ireland. 2 vol. fol. Dublin, 1932–41.

10100 Mahr (Adolf). Irish early Christian handicraft. [Summary, dealing in particular with the development of penannular brooches and shrines.] N. Munster Antiq. J., 1, pp. 57–66, + 18 plates. 1937.

10101 March (Henry Collery). Early Christian intrecci : their origin and meaning. [' An inquiry into the origin of mediaeval Irish art.'] Trans. Lancs. and Ches. Antiq. Soc., 19 (1901), pp. 242–44. 1902.

10102 Moore (Courtenay). The connection of early Irish and Italian Christian art. J. Cork Hist. Soc., 2nd S. 15, pp. 181–83. 1909.

10103 O'Neill (Henry). The fine arts and civilization of ancient Ireland. 4° London, 1863 [1862].

10104 Radford (Courtenay Arthur Ralegh). The early Christian monuments of Scotland. Antiquity, 16, pp. 1–18. 1942.

10105 Rivoira (Giovanni Teresio). Antiquities of S. Andrews. [Church and tower of St. Regulus : early carvings in the cathedral museum : archaeological discussions arguing for an earlier date for the Ruthwell and Bewcastle crosses. Plates show cross-shaft in cathedral museum (not earlier than 8th c.) with comparisons. *See also* p. 113.] Burl. Mag., 21, pp. 15–25, + 3 plates. 1912.

10106 Roe (Helen M.). The ' David cycle ' in early Irish art. [12 figures in text. 50 instances in illumination, sculpture, metalwork or ivory.] J. Roy. Soc. Antiq. Ireland, 79, pp. 39–59. 1949.

10107 Simpson (William Douglas). The early stones. *The stones of Scotland, edited by George Scott-Moncrieff.* pp. 6–24, + 10 plates. 8° London, 1938. [Brochs, early churches, crosses, etc.]

10108 Stokes ( ), *Miss.* Observations on two ancient Irish works of art known as the Breac Moedog, or shrine of St. Moedoc of Ferns, and the Soiscel Molaise, or Gospel of St. Molaise of Devenish. Archaeologia, 43, pp. 131–50, + 8 plates. 1871.

10109 Stokes (M.). Irish art in Bavaria. J. Roy. Hist. and Arch. Assoc. Ireland [11], 4th S. 1 (1870–71), pp. 352–59. 1878.

10110 Stokes (Margaret MacNair). Early Christian art in Ireland. *National Museum of Ireland.* 2 pts. 8° Dublin, 1932. [Gross, 413. 157 figures in text.]

10111 Thomas (Thomas Henry). Celtic art, with a suggestion of a scheme for the better preservation and freer study of the monuments of the early Christian Church in Wales. Y Cymmrodor, 12, pp. 87–111. 1897.

10112 Turchi (Nicola). L'arte irlandese. *L'isola di smeraldo.* 8° Torino, 1914.

10113 Waring (John Burley). Stone monuments, tumuli and ornament of remote ages ; with remarks on the early architecture of Ireland and Scotland. pp. x, 96, + 108 plates. fol. London, 1870. [Plates 70–79, Irish (round towers, etc.) : 88–94, Celtic ornament : 106–08, A.–S. fibulae, etc.]

10114 Warren (Frederick Edward). The influence of Celtic art in England. Church Q. Rev., 75, pp. 1–20. 1912.

10115 Yorke (P. A.). Early Christian art in Ireland. [Illuminations, and works in metal.] Irish Eccles. Rec., 3rd S. 9, pp. 233–43, 340–49. 1888.

172. ARCHITECTURE, DOMESTIC

10116 [Anon.] Saxon pit dwelling at Bourton-on-the-Water. Glos. Countryside, 1, p. 45. 1932.

10117 Addy (Sidney Oldall). The *stapol* in Beowulf : hall and chamber. [Flight of steps.] N. and Q., 152, pp. 363–65. 1927.

10118 Butterworth (George). A Saxon house at Deerhurst, near Tewkesbury. Arch. Camb., 5th S. 2, pp. 234–35. 1885. *Same title.* Walford's Antiquarian, 9, pp. 46–48, 96. 1886.

10119 Childe (Vere Gordon). Another late Viking house at Freswick, Caithness. Proc. Soc. Antiq. Scot., 77 (7th S. 5, 1942–43), pp. 5–17, + 4 plates. 1943.

10120 Curle (Alexander Ormiston). An account of the excavation of a dwelling of the Viking period at ' Jarlshof', Sumburgh, Shetland. [58 figures in text.] *Same jnl.,* 69 (6th S. 9, 1934–35), pp. 265–321, + folding plate. 1935.

10121 Curle (Alexander Ormiston). An account of the excavation of further buildings of the Viking period (Viking house no. ii), at ' Jarlshof '. [18 figures in text.] *Same jnl.,* 70 (6th S. 10, 1935–36), pp. 251–70, + folding plan. 1936.

10122 —— The excavations at Jarlshof, *etc.* Antiq. J., 15, pp. 26–29. 1935.

10123 —— A Viking settlement at Freswick, Caithness. Report on excavations carried out in 1937 and 1938. (Report on the animal remains, by Margery I. Platt). Proc. Soc. Antiq. Scot., 73 (7th S. 1, 1938–39), pp. 71–110, + 14 plates. 1939.

10124 Dunning (Gerald Clough). Bronze age settlements and a Saxon hut near Bourton-on-the-Water, Gloucestershire. [Roof construction, pottery, etc.] Antiq. J., 12, pp. 279–93, + 4 plates. 1932.

10125 Files (George Taylor). The Anglo-Saxon house, its construction, decoration, and furniture. Together with an introduction in English miniature drawing of the 10th and 11th centuries. *Diss.* p. 65. 8° Leipsic, 1893. [Gross, 429.]

10126 Gloucestrensis, *pseud.* Discovery of a Saxon house at Deerhurst. Glos. N. and Q., 3, pp. 221–22. 1887.

10127 Henry (Françoise). Habitations irlandaises du haut moyen âge. [c. 7th c. 9 figures in text. Result of excavations in 1938 in the island of Inishkea, co. Mayo.] Rev. archéol., 6e S. 28, pp. 157–76. 1947.

10128 —— Remains of the early Christian period on Inishkea North, co. Mayo. [Excavation of houses in a settlement dating 6th–10th c.] J. Roy. Soc. Antiq. Ireland, 75, pp. 127–55, + 12 plates + 2 folding plans. 1945.

10129 Henry (Françoise). A wooden hut on Inishkea North. [Late 7th c.] *Same jnl.,* 82, pp. 163–78, + 6 plates. 1952.

10130 Jacobs (Harry). Die Namen der profanen Wohn-und Wirtschaftsgebäude und Gebäudeteile im Altenglischen. *Diss.,* Kiel. pp. 108. 8° Kiel, 1911.

10131 Leask (Harold G.). St. Mochta's house, Louth. [?9th c.] County Louth Archaeol. J., 9, pp. 32–35, + 1 plate. 1937.

10132 Lethaby (William Richard). The palace of Westminster in the eleventh and twelfth centuries. [Pp. 131–32, ' the Saxon, or old, palace.'] Archaeologia, 60, pp. 131–48, + plan. 1906.

10133 Lethbridge (Thomas Charles) and **Tebbutt** (C. F.). Huts of the Anglo-Saxon period. 1. Huts of the pagan period at Waterbeach and West Row. 2. Late Saxon huts at St. Neots, [Hunts.]. [With tables and illustrations.] Proc. Camb. Antiq. Soc., 33, pp. 133–151, + 3 plates. 1933.

10134 Lowry-Corry (*Lady* Dorothy). St. Molaise's house at Devenish, lough Erne, and its sculptured stones. J. Roy. Soc. Antiq. Ireland, 66 (7th S. 6), pp. 270–84, + 4 plates. 1936.

10135 O'Kelly (Michael J.). St. Gobnet's house, Ballyvourney, co. Cork. [6th c. or later.] J. Cork Hist. Soc., 2nd S. 57, pp. 18–40, + 3 plans, + 4 plates. 1952.

10136 Scarth (Harry Mengden). Excavations at Mudgley, Wedmore, the site of a manor-house of king Alfred. [Pottery from early Saxon to Norman times found.] Proc. Soc. Antiq., 2nd S. 8, pp. 169–72. 1879.

173. ARCHITECTURE, ECCLESIASTICAL, GENERAL

10137 [Anon.] English architecture before the Conquest. [Appendix : Architectural details in A.–S. mss., c. 1000.] Archaeologia Oxon., 3, pp. 114–38, + 4 plates. 1893.

10138 A. (A.). Bishop Gundulf and his architecture. N. and Q., 4th S. 4, pp. 321–22. 1863.

10139 —— Stone and wooden altars in [A.–S.] England. N. and Q., 3rd S. 5, p. 499. 1864.

10140 Barnes (W. Miles). On the form and probable history of Saxon church architecture. Proc. Dorset Antiq. F.C., 23, pp. 87–122, + 5 plates. 1902.

10141 Bilson (John). The eleventh century east-ends of St. Augustine's, Canterbury, and St. Mary's, York. Archaeol. J., 63, pp. 106–16, + 2 plans. 1906.

10142 —— Wharram-le-Street church, Yorkshire, and St. Rule's church, St. Andrews. [' Both towers represent the pre-Norman building tradition of the old Northumbria.'] Archaeologia, 73, pp. 55–72, + 4 plates. 1923.

10143 Brown (Gerard Baldwin). List of churches in England that exhibit traces of Saxon building. Builder, 84, pp. 453–55. 1903.

10144 —— Notes on pre-Conquest architecture in England. [i. The surviving evidence : ii. Monkwearmouth church : iii. The basilican plan : iv. Cruciform plans and towers : v. The tradition of Rome : vi. Celtic influence : vii. Timber construction and its traces in stonework : viii. Roman or Romanesque ? Summary. 46 figures in text.] Builder, 69, pp. 215–17, 250–52, 288–90, 326–28, 370–72, 410–12, 454–55, 474–76. 1895.

10145 —— Some characteristics of pre-Conquest architecture. J.R.I.B.A., 3rd S. 2, pp. 485–505. 1895.

10146 Clapham (*Sir* Alfred William). English romanesque architecture before the Conquest. pp. xx, 168, + 65 plates. 8° Oxford, 1930. [51 figures in text.]

10147 —— Romanesque architecture in England. *British Council.* pp. 47, + 5 plates. 8° London, 1950. [Pp. 7–23, + 7 plates, A.–S.]

10148 —— The Saxon gap. Archit. Rev., 108, pp. 281–84. 1950.

10149 Crossley (Frederick Herbert). Timber buildings in England from early times to the end of the seventeenth century. pp. 168, + plates with 202 figures. 8° London, 1951. [Pp. 7–13, 79–83, A.–S. period : pp. 88–93, forts and castles.]

10150 Duesbury (Henry). On the architecture of pre-Norman England. J. Brit. Archaeol. Assoc., 10, pp. 142–59. 1855.

10151 Ferrey (Benjamin). Remarks upon the works of the early mediaeval architects, Gundulph . . . and others. Papers read at R.I.B.A., 1863–64 [1st S., 14], pp. 130–46. 1864.

10152 Fletcher (Eric George Molyneux) and **Jackson** (Edward Dudley Colquhoun). ' Long and short ' quoins and pilaster strips in Saxon churches. (Further notes on ' long and short ' quoins in Saxon churches). J. Brit. Archaeol. Assoc., 3rd S., 9 (1944), pp. 12–29, + 8 plates : 3rd S. 12, pp. 1–18, + 10 plates. [1946]–49.

10153 Harrison (James Park). Note on the use of lead as a covering for Saxon churches. Archaeologia Oxon., pp. 211–14, + 1 plate. 1895.

10154 Hartshorne (Charles Henry). On some anomalies observable in the earlier styles of English architecture. [e.g. A.–S. long and short work.] Archaeol. J., 3, pp. 285–97. 1846.

10155 Innocent (Charles Frederick). Romano-British precedents for some English romanesque details. J.R.I.B.A., 3rd S. 15, pp. 649–50. 1908.

10156 Jackson (Edward Dudley Colquhoun) and **Fletcher** (Eric George Molyneux). Constructional characteristics in Anglo-Saxon churches. J. Brit. Archaeol. Ass., 3rd S. 14, pp. 11–26, + 2 plates. 1951.

10157 Lovegrove (E. W.). Influence. [International influences in mediaeval architecture, with special reference to A.–S.] Trans. Bristol and Glos. Archaeol. Soc., 56, pp. 45–64. 1934.

10158 Micklethwaite (John Thomas). On the growth of English parish churches. [A.–S. period, pp. 364–71.] Archaeol. J., 37, pp. 364–77. 1880.

**10159 —— ** Something about Saxon church building. (Some further notes on Saxon churches). [With 41 figures, mostly plans.] Archaeol. J., 53, pp. 293–351 : 55, pp. 340–49. 1896–98.

10160 Moule (H. J.). Notes about Saxon churches. Proc. Dorset Antiq. F. C., 19, pp. 51–54, + 1 plate. 1898.

10161 Parker (John Henry). Anglo-Saxon architecture. [A.–S. diaper work discovered by scraping off plaster during Victorian ' restoration ' at Kirton-in-Lindsay, Wallingford and Bampton.] Antiquary, 5, pp. 37–38. 1882.

**10162 —— ** Architecture in the eleventh century. Archaeol. J., 30, pp. 117–26, + 2 plates. 1873.

**10163 —— ** The buildings of bishop Gundulph. Reprinted from Gentleman's Magazine. pp. 16. 8° London, 1863. [11 figures in text.]

10164 Peers (*Sir* Charles Reed). On Saxon churches of the St. Pancras type. [7 plans in text.] Archaeol. J., 58, pp. 402–34. 1901.

10165 Picton (*Sir* James Allanson). Anglo-Saxon architecture. Timber or stone ? [Probably wood : *timbrian*= to build]. N. and Q., 4th S. 11, pp. 209–10. 1873.

10166 Rickman (Thomas). Further observations on the ecclesiastical architecture of France and England. [' Such buildings as are known to be prior to 1,000.'] Archaelogia, 26, pp. 26–46, and 2 plates. 1836.

10167 Rivoira (Giovanni Teresio). Lombardic architecture, its origin, development and derivatives. Translated by G. McN. Rushforth. Re-edited, with additional notes. 2 vol. 4° Oxford, 1933. [Vol. 2, pp. 130–210 (with figures 534–640), ecclesiastical architecture in England from Constantine to the Norman Conquest.]

10168 Roberts (Harold Vernon Molesworth). Anglo-Saxon churches : an index of illustrations. pp. 20. MS. in library of the Royal Institute of British Architects. (To which apply). fol. 1951.

10169 Salzman (Louis Francis). Building in England down to 1540. A documentary history. pp. xvi, 629, + 21 plates. 8° Oxford, 1952. [Pp. 356–62, passages from A.–S. writers to show the nature of the material for the study of the documentary history of building.]

10170 Savage (Henry Edwin). Saxon architecture. [Notes on Micklethwaite's paper **10158**.] Proc. Soc. Antiq. Newcastle, 2nd S. 8, pp. 21–29. 1897.

10171 Sorby (Henry Clifton). On Saxon church architecture. Proc. Oxford Archit. and Hist. Soc., N.S. 5, pp. 305–09. 1890.

10172 Waller (John Green). Notes on Anglo-Saxon masonry. J. Brit. Archaeol. Ass., 1, pp. 117–20. 1846.

10173 Warre (Frank). On the distinction between Anglo-Saxon and Norman architecture. Proc. Somerset Arch. Soc., [2] 1851, pp. 1–13, + plate. 1852.

10174 Wilkinson (*Sir* John Gardner). Long and short work. Assoc. Archit. Socs.' Rpts., 7, pp. 41–52, + 2 plates. 1863.

10175 Wright (Thomas). Anglo-Saxon architecture, illustrated from illuminated manuscripts. [19 figures in text. Reprinted in his Essays on archaeological subjects, 1, pp. 186–201. 1861.] Archaeol. J., 1, pp. 24–35. 1844.

10176 —— Medieval architecture illustrated from illuminated manuscripts — builders at work. [First figure shows building of Babel from MS. Cotton Claudius B. IV, f. 19, 10th–11th c.] J. Brit. Archaeol. Ass., 1, pp. 22–25. 1846.

10177 Young (J. P. W.). Greek influence in the early British Church. [Especially in architecture.] Trans. Scot. Ecclesiol. Soc., 8, pp. 110–20, + 2 plates. 1926.

174. ARCHITECTURE, ECCLESIASTICAL, EAST ANGLIA

10178. Brock (Edgar Philip Loftus). The round towers of Norfolk and Suffolk. [Ascribes earliest to A.-S. period.] J. Brit. Archaeol. Assoc., 37, pp. 32–37. 1881.

10179 Burkitt (A. H.). Notes on a wooden church, and the remains of the shrine of St. Edmund the Martyr, at Greenstead, Essex. *Same jnl.*, 5, pp. 1–6, + 1 plate. 1849.

10180 Butterick (T.) ['B.T.R.C.'] Remains of a pre-Conquest church at North Elmham in Norfolk. [Plan and 2 figures in text.] Builder, 84, pp. 267–70. 1903.

10181 Clapham (*Sir* Alfred William) and **Godfrey** (Walter Hindes). The Saxon cathedral of [North] Elmham, [Norfolk]. Antiq. J., 6, pp. 402–09, + 2 plates. 1926.

10182 —— and —— The Saxon cathedral of Elmham. [Plan on p. 58.] Norfolk Archaeology, 23, pp. 56–67, + 2 plates. 1929.

10183 Gunn (John). Notices of remains of ecclesiastical architecture in Norfolk, supposed to be of the Saxon period. [Witton, etc.] Archaeol. J., 6, pp. 359–63 + 1 plate. 1849.

10184 —— Saxon remains in the cloisters of Norwich cathedral. Norfolk Archaeology, 8, pp. 1–9 + 2 plates. 1879.

10185 Harley (Laurence S.). The pre-Conquest churches of Essex and the method of laying-out their groundplans. Essex Nat., 28, pp. 275–77. 1951.

10186 Harrison (James Park). The date of Waltham church [Essex]. [?part of Harold's church still in existence.] Antiquary, 34, pp. 63–64, 149–50. 1898.

10187 Johnston (Philip Mainwaring). Holy Trinity church, [Colchester]. [A.-S. west doorway ; with figure in text.] J. Brit. Archaeol. Assoc., N.S. 25, pp. 137–39. 1919.

10188 Kent (Ernest A.). On the Saxon windows in Hales Church, Norfolk. *Same jnl.*, N.S. 33, pp. 187–88, + 1 plate. 1927.

10188a Laing (G. E.). Saxon tower of Trinity church, Colchester. *Same jnl.*, 3, pp. 19–22, + 1 plate. 1848.

10189 Laver (Henry). The chapel of St. Elene at Wicken Bonhunt, [Essex]. Trans. Essex Archaeol. Soc., N.S. 9, pp. 404–07, + 2 plates. 1906.

10190 —— Copford church [Essex]. [Dated to c. 1080.] *Same jnl.*, N.S. 11, pp. 295–309, + 4 plates. 1911.

10191 —— Greenstead church. *Same jnl.*, N.S. 10, pp. 97–103, + 4 plates. 1909.

10192 —— St. Peter ad Murum, [Ythancaester]. [Criticising article by J. C. Wall, *q.v.* **10201.**] Reliquary, N. [3rd] S. 15, pp. 39–50. 1909.

10193 Lynam (Charles). The chancel arch of White Notley church. Trans. Essex Archaeol. Soc., N.S. 9, pp. 228–30, + 2 plates. 1906.

10194 Micklethwaite (John Thomas)· The old minster at South Elmham classified and described. Proc. Suffolk Inst. Archaeol., 16, pp. 29–35. 1916.

10195 Morley (Claude). Circular towers. [Theoretical reasons : i. Saxon lord's bell-tower : ii. Danish national influence : iii. Exigencies of local geological strata.] *Same jnl.*, 18, pp. 144–55. 1923.

10196 —— On traces of Saxon architecture yet remaining in the county of Suffolk. [i. Historical : ii. Domesday Book : iii. The argument : iv. Church constituents : v. Saxon features in Suffolk churches.] *Same jnl.*, 18, pp. 1–28. 1922.

10197 Raven (John James). The ' old minster ', South Elmham. *Same jnl.*, 10, pp. 1–6. 1898.

10198 Salvin (A.). Anglo-Saxon discovery. [Castle-Rising, Norfolk.] Ecclesiologist, 1, pp. 167–68. 1842.

10199 Spurgeon (Joseph W.). Church at Greenstead, [Essex]. [?Chestnut.] N. and Q., 7th S., 10, pp. 297, 330, 371–72, 397–98, 476–77 : 10th S. 8, pp. 26, 154, 196, 275–76, 416–17. 1890, 1907.

10200 Suckling (Alfred). Supposed Anglo-Saxon remains near Bungay, Suffolk. [South Elmham.] Ecclesiologist, 1, pp. 165–67. 1842.

10201 Wall (James Charles). St. Peter ad Murum, [Ythancaester, Essex]. [*See also* **10192.**] Reliquary, N. [3rd] S. 14, pp. 257–63. 1908.

10202 Warburton (Joseph Robert). North Elmham : the Saxon cathedral. [Plan in text.] J. Brit. Archaeol. Assoc., N.S. 40, pp. 53–54. 1935.

10203 Woodward (Bolingbroke Bernard). The old minster, South Elmham. Proc. Suffolk Inst. Archaeol., 4, pp. 1–7, + 2 plans. 1864.

175. ARCHITECTURE, ECCLESIASTICAL, KENT

10204 Brock (Edgar Philip Loftus). The Saxon church at Whitfield, near Dover. Arch. Cant., 21, pp. 301–07. 1895.

10205 Denne (Samuel). Observations on Canterbury cathedral. Archaeologia, 10, pp. 37–49. 1792.

10206 Doré (Alice). St. Martin's church, Canterbury. Antiquary, 39, pp. 207–08. 1903.

10207 Elliston - Erwood (Frank Charles). The pre-Conquest church at Lydd. Archaeol. J., 78, pp. 216–26, + plan, + plate. 1921.

10208 —— The Saxon church of St. Margaret, Darenth. Invicta Mag., 3, pp. 183–87. 1913.

10209 Harrison (James Park). Saxon remains in Minster church, Isle of Sheppy. Archaeol. J., 41, pp. 54–57, + 1 plate. 1884.

10210 Hope (*Sir* William Henry St. John). The architectural history of the cathedral church and monastery of St. Andrew at Rochester. 1. The cathedral church : 2. The monastery. [First plan shows A.–S. church.] Arch. Cant., 23, pp. 194–328, + 3 plans, and 1 plate : 24, pp. 1–85 + 2 plans, and 2 plates. 1898.

10211 —— Excavations at St. Austin's abbey, Canterbury. 1. The chapel of St. Pancras. [Plan shows Saxon church.] Arch. Cant., 25, pp. 222–37, + 6 plates and coloured plan. 1902.

10212 —— The foundations of St. Augustine's abbey, Canterbury—important discoveries. J. Brit. Archaeol. Assoc., 71 (N.S. 21), pp. 86–88. 1917.

10213 —— Gundulf's tower at Rochester, and the first Norman cathedral church there. Archaeologia, 49, pp. 323–34, + 2 plans. 1886.

10214 —— Notes on the architectural history of Rochester cathedral church. [Pp. 217–19, A.–S. church.] Trans. St. Paul's Eccles. Soc., 1, pp. 217–30, + 2 plans. 1885.

10215 —— The plan and arrangement of the first cathedral church of Canterbury. [4 plans in text.] Proc. Soc. Antiq., 2nd S. 30, pp. 136–58, + 2 folding plans. 1918.

10216 Hope (*Sir* William Henry St. John). Recent discoveries at St. Austin's abbey, Canterbury. [Work of abbot Wulfric, between 1056 and 1059, etc.] Arch. Cant., 31, pp. 294–96, + 2 plates ; 32, pp. 1–26, + 8 plates, + coloured plan. 1915–17.

10217 —— Recent discoveries in the abbey church of St. Austin at Canterbury. [Abbot Wulfric's building, etc.] Archaeologia, 66, pp. 377–400, + coloured folding plan. 1915.

10218 —— Recent discoveries in the abbey church of St. Augustine at Canterbury. [In full in Archaeologia, **10217.** With discussion by G. F. Browne, etc.] Proc. Soc. Antiq., 2nd S. 27, pp. 250–53. 1915.

10219 Irvine (James Thomas). Dover castle church. J. Brit. Archaeol. Assoc., 41, pp. 284–88, + plan, + 1 plate. 1885.

10220 —— On the remains of the Saxon or early Norman work in the church of Stone juxta Faversham. *Same jnl.*, 31, pp. 249–58, + 3 plates. 1875.

10221 Jenkins (Robert Charles). Observations on the remains of the basilica of Lyminge. Arch. Cant., 18, pp. 46–54. 1889.

10222 —— On the connection between the monasteries of Kent in the Saxon period ; in illustration of the ruined church within the precincts of Dover castle. Arch. Cant., 3, pp. 19–34. 1860.

10223 Jessup (Ronald Frederick). Reculver. [With ground plan of A.–S. church.] Antiquity, 10, pp. 179–94, + 7 plates. 1936.

10224 Livett (Grevile Mairis). Foundations of the Saxon cathedral at Rochester. Arch. Cant., 18, pp. 261–78, + coloured plan, + 1 plate. 1889.

10225 —— Lydd church. [Pp. 72–87, the Saxon basilica.] Arch. Cant., 42, pp. 61–92, + 2 plans, and 4 plates. 1930.

10226 —— Mediaeval Rochester. [Pp. 17–38 ; pt. 1, concerning the Saxon city or the ' castellum which is called Hrofescester,' and the Norman ' castellum ' or castle.] Arch. Cant., 21, pp. 17–72, + plan, + 6 plates. 1895.

10227 Livett (Grevile Mairis). Whitefield *alias* Beuesfield. [i. A Saxon three compartment church: ii. Other examples of the type . . . : v. Saxon remains . . . : viii. The Saxon apse . . .] Arch. Cant., 40, pp. 141–58, + 2 plates. 1928.

10228 Peers (*Sir* Charles Reed). Reculver : its Saxon church and cross. Archaeologia, 77, pp. 241–56, + 3 plates. 1928.

10229 —— and **Clapham** (*Sir* Alfred William). St. Augustine's abbey church, Canterbury, before the Norman Conquest. Archaeologia, 77, pp. 201–18, + 7 plates, + coloured folding plan. 1928.

10229a Potts (Robert Ullock). The abbey of St. Augustine, Canterbury. *Notes on famous churches and abbeys*, 29. 16° London, [1927].

10230 —— The latest excavations at St. Augustine's abbey, [Canterbury]. [Resumé of its architectural history, with plan.] Arch. Cant., 35, pp. 117–26. 1921.

10231 —— A note on the plan of St. Augustine's abbey church, [Canterbury]. Arch. Cant., 40, pp. 65–66, + large coloured plan. 1928.

10232 Puckle (John). The ancient fabric of the church of St. Mary the Virgin, Dover. Arch. Cant., 20, pp. 119–27 + 4 plates. 1893.

10233 Routledge (Charles Francis). St. Martin's church, Canterbury. Arch. Cant., 14, pp. 108–12, + 2 plates: 22, pp. 1–28, + 5 plates, + plan. 1882, 1897. *Same title.* J. Brit. Archaeol. Assoc., 40, pp. 47–51. 1884.

10234 Scott (George Gilbert). The church on the castle hill, Dover. Arch. Cant., 5, pp. 1–18, + 4 plates, + plan. 1863.

10235 Smith (Charles Roach) and **Jenkins** (Robert Charles). Lyminge. [Architectural discoveries of R. C. Jenkins : also a history of it in A.–S. times.] Collectanea Antiqua, 5, pp. 185–200, + 1 plate. 1861.

10236 Walcott (Mackenzie Edward Charles). Vestiges of St. Augustine's abbey without the walls of Canterbury. J. Brit. Archaeol. Assoc., 35, pp. 26–58, + plan. 1879.

176. ARCHITECTURE, ECCLESI-ASTICAL, MERCIA

§. *a.* Deerhurst, Glos.

10237 Bazeley (William). Deerhurst church and Saxon chapel. [Plan in text.] J. Brit. Archaeol. Assoc., 69 (N.S. 19), pp. 62–70. 1913.

10238 Bell (Charles L.) Deerhurst. [?Was abbot Baldwin of Bury its designer.] Antiquary, 6, p. 85. 1882.

10239 Buckler (John Chessell). Notes on Saxon architecture, with a description of Deerhurst priory, Gloucestershire. Trans. Bristol and Glos. Arch. Soc., 11, pp. 6–83, + 2 plans, + 5 plates. 1887.

10240 Butterworth (George). The ancient apse of Deerhurst church. Trans. Bristol and Glos. Arch. Soc., 14, pp. 48–49. 1890.

10241 —— Deerhurst, a parish in the vale of Gloucester. 2nd and revised edition. pp. xii, 252, + 10 plates. 8° Tewkesbury, 1890. [Including plans of the Saxon church and chapel, etc.]

10242 —— Discovery of a Saxon chapel at Deerhurst. Glos. N. and Q., 3, pp. 303–07, 519–20. 1887.

10243 —— The history of Deerhurst church. Ecclesiologist, 23, pp. 89–101, + 2 plates. 1862.

10244 —— Newly discovered Saxon chapel, Deerhurst. J. Brit. Archaeol. Assoc., 41, pp. 414–18, + 1 plate. 1885.

10245 —— Notes on the priory and church of Deerhurst. Trans. Bristol and Glos. Arch. Soc., 1, pp. 96–104. 1876. *Same title.* pp. iv, 30, + 1 plate. 8° Tewkesbury, 1878.

10246 —— The Saxon chapel at Deerhurst. Trans. Bristol and Glos. Arch. Soc., 11, pp. 105–16, 280, + 1 plan, + 1 plate. 1887.

10247 Gilbert (E. C.). Deerhurst priory church. *Same jnl.*, 61, pp. 294–307. 1939.

10248 Haigh (Daniel Henry). Deerhurst church. J. Brit. Archaeol. Ass., 1, pp. 9–19. 1846.

10249 Hudd (Alfred Edmund). The Saxon chapel recently discovered at Deerhurst. Proc. Clifton Antiq. Club, 1 (1884–88), pp. 27–32, + 1 plate. 1888.

10250 Knowles (W. H.). Deerhurst priory church, including the result of the excavations conducted during 1926. [With 22 plans and figures.] Trans. Bristol and Glos. Arch. Soc., 49, pp. 221–58, + 1 plate. 1927.

Same title. [With 19 plans and figures in text.] Archaeologia, 77, pp. 141–64, + 1 plate. 1928.

10251 Massé (Henri Jean Louis Joseph). The abbey church of Tewkesbury, with some account of the parish church of Deerhurst. *Bell's Cathedral series.* pp. xii, 131. 8° London, 1901. [Pp. 104–26, + plan, Deerhurst and its Saxon chapel. 9 figures in text.]

10252 Middleton (John Henry). [Newly discovered Saxon church at Deerhurst]. Proc. Soc. Antiq., 2nd S. 11, pp. 15–19, 155. 1885.

10253 —— On a Saxon chapel at Deerhurst. Archaeologia, 50, pp. 66–71, + 1 plate. 1887.

10254 Moore (H. Cecil). Deerhurst—its Saxon church and Saxon chapel. Trans. Woolhope N.F. Club, 1893–94, pp. 25–28. 1896.

10255 Pope (Thomas S.). On some architectural remains at Deerhurst priory church. Proc. Clifton Antiq. Club, 1 (1884–88), pp. 18–21, + 1 plate. 1888.

§ *b.* Lincolnshire Group

10256 [Anon.] Saxon churches [in Lincs.]. Ecclesiologist, 3, pp. 138–39, + 1 plate. 1844.

10257 Atkinson (George). On Saxon architecture, and the early churches in the neighbourhood of Grimsby. Assoc. Archit. Socs.' Rpts., 5, pp. 23–33, + 2 plates. 1859.

10258 Bilson (John). The plan of the first cathedral church at Lincoln. Archaeologia, 62, pp. 543–64, + 3 folding plans. 1911.

10259 Brock (Edgar Philip Loftus). The churches of the city of Lincoln. [Plate shows 'Saxon architecture at Stow and St. Peter's-at-Gowts.'] J. Brit. Archaeol. Assoc., 46, pp. 17–28, + 1 plate. 1890.

10260 Clapham (*Sir* Alfred William). Barton-on-Humber, St. Peter. [With 2 plans in text.] Archaeol. J., 103 (1946), pp. 179–81. 1947.

10261 —— Lincolnshire priories, abbeys and parish churches. [Pp. 168–70, Stow (with plan) : pp. 179–81, Barton-on-Humber, St. Peter (with plan).] Archaeol. J., 103 (1946), pp. 168–88, + 4 plates. 1947.

10262 Fowler (C. Hodgson). Glentworth church. Assoc. Archit. Socs.' Repts., 14, pp. 57–60, + 2 plates. 1877.

10263 Fowler (Joseph Thomas). Discovery of a primitive nave at Winterton. [Lower part of tower also found to be pre-Norman after removal of plaster.] Proc. Soc. Antiq., 2nd S. 20, pp. 20–24. 1904.

10264 Livett (Grevile Mairis). Notes on Barholme church. Assoc. Archit. Socs.' Repts., 32, pp. 341–50, + plan. 1914.

10265 Saxl (Fritz). Lincoln cathedral : the eleventh-century design for the west front. (Notes on the reconstruction, by W. Frankl [p. 118.]). Archaeol. J., 103 (1946), pp. 105–18, + 6 plates. 1947.

10266 Thompson (Alexander Hamilton). The churches of St. Mary-le-Wigford, St. Benedict, and St. Peter-at-Gowts, Lincoln. [P. 164, plans of St. Mary and St. Peter.] Archaeol. J., 103 (1946), pp. 162–66. 1947.

10267 —— Pre-Conquest church-towers in north Lincolnshire. Assoc. Archit. Socs.' Repts., 29, pp. 43–70, + 3 plates. 1907.

10268 Varah (William Edward). The notable churches of Barton on Humber. pp. 48, + 8 plates. 8° Barton on Humber, [19—?].

§ *c.* London

10269 Borenius (Tancred). Anglo-Saxon London. [As revealed by bombing. Editorial]. Burl. Mag., 79, p. 139. 1941.

10270 Clayton (P. B.). Saxon discoveries at All Hallows [Barking] church. [Illustration of Saxon wall on p. 254, and of 'part of shaft of a sculptured Saxon cross' on p. 255.] Builder, 161, pp. 254–55. 1941.

10271 —— Saxon discoveries in London. [All-Hallows, Barking. 3 figures in text.] Naft Mag., xx No. 2, pp. 1–3. 1944.

10272 Kendrick (*Sir* Thomas Downing). Recent discoveries at All-Hallows, Barking. [As a result of enemy action ' a portion of a Saxon church on the site was uncovered, and also some fragments of what must have been an imposing Saxon cross.' 'Fragments of masonry are the most important remains of Saxon building yet found in the City of London.'] Antiq. J., 23, pp. 14–18, + 3 plates. 1943.

10273 Lethaby (William Richard). Note on the existing remnants of the Confessor's church [at Westminster]. [Appendix to **10274**.] Archaeologia, 62, pp. 97–100. 1910.

10274 Robinson (Joseph Armitage). The church of Edward the Confessor at Westminster. (Note on the existing remnants of the Confessor's church, by W. R. Lethaby). *Same jnl.*, 62, pp. 81–100, + 3 plans. 1910.

10275 Tanner (Lawrence Edward) and **Clapham** (*Sir* Alfred William). Recent discoveries in the nave of Westminster abbey. [Plan shows 11th c. church and monastic buildings.] *Same jnl.*, 83, pp. 227–36, + 1 plate, + folding coloured plan. 1933.

§ *d.* Northamptonshire Group

10276 Argles (Marsham). On the tower of Barnack church. J. Brit. Archaeol. Assoc., 22, pp. 346–49. 1866.

10277 Barrett (Lionel). The church of All Saints, Earls Barton. Proc. Clapton Archit. Club, 12, pp. 48–49. 1901.

10278 Boyle (John Roberts). Notes of a visit to the Saxon churches of Northamptonshire. Proc. Soc. Antiq. Newcastle, 2nd S. 2, pp. 116–23. 1885.

10279 Brereton (R. P.). Notes on some unrecorded Saxon work in and near Northamptonshire. [Nassington, Wansford, etc.] Assoc. Archit. Socs.' Rpts., 27, pp. 397–400. 1904.

10280 Carpenter (R. Herbert). St. Andrew's church, Brigstock. *Same jnl.*, 13, pp. 237–48, + 4 plates. 1876.

10281 Dryden (*Sir* Henry E. L.) *bart.* On the chancel of Brixworth church. *Same jnl.*, 20, pp. 343–52, + 2 plates. 1890.

10282 Irvine (James Thomas). Account of the discovery of part of the Saxon abbey church of Peterborough. J. Brit. Archaeol. Assoc., 50, pp. 45–54, + plan, + 1 plate. 1894.

10283 —— Account of the pre-Norman remains discovered at Peterborough cathedral in 1884. Assoc. Archit. Socs.' Rpts., 17, pp. 277–83, + 3 plates. 1884.

10284 —— Fragment of Saxon stonework with painting on it, discovered at Peterborough cathedral. J. Brit. Archaeol. Assoc., 47, pp. 184–85. 1891.

10285 Poole (George Ayliffe). On the Saxon church of All Saints, Brixworth. Assoc. Archit. Socs.' Rpts., 1, pp. 122–33, + plan, + 4 plates. 1851.

10286 Roberts (Edward). On Brixworth church. J. Brit. Archaeol. Assoc., 19, pp. 285–305, + 2 plates. 1863.

10286a Segger (Arthur Thomas). Earl's Barton church. *Notes on famous churches and abbeys*, 39. 12° London, [1929].

10287 Syers (Henry Sam). Barnack church. *Same jnl.*, 55 (N.S. 5), pp. 13–28, and 4 plates. 1899.

10288 —— The building of Barnack church. Assoc. Archit. Socs.' Rpts., 23, pp. 143–51. 1895.

10289 Thoyts (E.). Brixworth basilican church. Trans. Aberdeen Ecclesiol. Soc., 3 (1894), pp. 90–92. 1896.

10290 Traylen (Henry T.). Ravensthorpe church. Ancient [pre-Norman] font restored to use. Northants. N. and Q., N.S. 6, pp. 95–96. 1928.

10291 Watkins (Charles Frederic). The basilica ; . . . and a description and history of the basilican church of Brixworth. pp. 64, + 4 plates. 8° London, 1867.

10292 Wildridge (T. Tindall). Earls Barton church. Byegone Northamptonshire, ed. William Andrews, pp. 89–96. 1891.

§ *e*. Repton, Derbs.

10293 Ashpitel (Arthur). Repton church and priory. J. Brit. Archaeol. Assoc., 7, pp. 263–83, + 5 plates. 1852.

10294 Cox (John Charles). A note on discoveries at Repton priory and church. [Plate showing ' stump of Saxon pier '.] J. Derbs. Archaeol. Soc., 34, pp. 75–78, + 2 plates. 1912.

10295 —— A note on the restoration of Repton church. *Same jnl.*, 8, pp. 231–36. 1886.

10296 Fletcher (A. W.). The south transept of Repton church. *Same jnl.*, 71, pp. 82–83, + 1 plate. 1951.

10297 Hipkins (Frederick Charles). A note on the most recent discoveries in Repton church crypt. *Same jnl.*, 23, pp. 105–07. + plan. 1901.

10298 Irvine (James Thomas). On the crypt beneath the chancel of Repton church. *Same jnl.*, 5, pp. 165–72, + 2 plates. 1883.

10299 —— Plans of discoveries lately made in the nave of Repton church. J. Brit. Archaeol. Assoc., 50, pp. 248–50, + 2 plans. 1894.

§ *f*. Others

10300 Brereton (R. P.). Some unrecorded Saxon churches. [Nassington, Northants. : Wansford, Northants. : Thornage, Norfolk : Woodstone, Hunts., etc. With 12 figures in text.] Reliquary, 11, pp. 111–26. 1905.

10301 British Archaeological Association. Saxon architecture at Worcester. Rept. of Proc., Brit. Archaeol. Assoc., 5 (meeting at Worcester, 1848), pp. 403–17. 1851.

10302 Cavalier (H. O.). St. Stephen's church, St. Albans : repairs to the mediaeval roof and discovery of an early [A.–S.] window. Trans. St. Albans Archaeol. Soc., 1934, pp. 188–95. 1934.

10303 Chafy (William Kyle Westwood). A short history of Rous Lench, [Worcs.]. pp. xv, 197. 8° Evesham, 1901. [Pp. 118–22, + 5 plates, A.–S. architecture and sculpture, including pair of peacocks.]

10304 Cobbett (Louis) and **Fox** (*Sir* Cyril). The Saxon church of Great Paxton, Huntingdonshire. [With 9 illustrations, + 3 plans.] Proc. Camb. Antiq. Soc., 25, pp. 50–77. 1924.

10305 Currey (Percy H.) and **Cox** (John Charles). The Saxon window in Mugginton church. J. Derbs. Archaeol. Soc., 25, pp. 225–28. 1903.

10306 Fane (William Dashwood). The date of the parish church of Melbourne, Derbyshire. ['May not Melbourne church be, in the main, the church mentioned in the Domesday record ? "] *Same jnl.*, 17, pp. 82–94. 1895.

10307 Fraser (William). The Derbyshire Trent and its early churches. *Same jnl.*, 71, pp. 87–105. 1951.

10308 Freeman (Edward Augustus). On Anglo-Saxon remains in Iver church, Bucks. Archaeol. J., 7, pp. 147–56, + 1 plate. 1850.

10309 Harrison (James Park). An account of the discovery of the remains of three apses at Oxford cathedral. pp. 23, + 2 plates. 8° London, 1891.

10311 —— On a pre-Norman clerestory window and some additional early work recently discovered in Oxford cathedral. Archaeol. J., 49, pp. 155–60, + 1 plate. 1892. *Same title.* Archaelogia Oxon., 1, pp. 23–31. 1892. *Same title.* pp. 11. 8° London, 1892. *Same title.* J. Brit. Archaeol. Assoc., 48, pp. 141–43. 1892.

10312 —— The pre-Norman date of the design and some of the stone-work of Oxford cathedral. pp. 23, + 3 plates. 8° London, 1891.

10313 Haswell (George W.). The abbey church of Saint Werburgh, Chester, in pre-Norman times. J. Chester and N. Wales Archaeol. and Hist. Soc., N.S. 22, pp. 142–65, and plan, + 3 plates. 1918.

10314 Hill (A. du Boulay). Plumtree church [Notts.]. [Discovery of inner, Saxon, wall of tower.] Trans. Thoroton Soc., 9 (1905), pp. 79–82, + 2 plates. 1906.

10315 —— St. Peter's church, East Bridgford, Notts. [Pp. 99–101, + 2 plates, ' the Saxon church '.] *Same jnl.*, 7 (1903), pp. 99–118, + plan, + 5 plates. 1904.

10316 Hills (Gordon M.). Stanton Lacy church, Shropshire, and Saxon architecture in England. J. Brit. Archaeol. Assoc., 24, pp. 360–82, + map of England, + plans. 1868.

10317 Hopkins (W. J.). Wyre Piddle church, Worcestershire. Assoc. Archit. Socs.' Rpts., 19, pp. 424–35, + 1 plate. 1888.

10318 Knowles (W. H.). The development of architecture in Gloucestershire to the close of the twelfth century. [With 30 figures, 7 of A.–S. period—mostly of Deerhurst.] Trans. Bristol and Glos. Arch. Soc., 50, pp. 57–96. 1928.

10319 Mayer (Joseph). On Shotwick church [Wirral] and its Saxon foundation. [Fourth plate is of ' Saxon porch.'] Hist. Soc. Lancs. and Ches., Proc., 6, pp. 77–83, + 5 plates. 1854.

10320 Medland (Henry). St. Oswald's priory, Gloucester. [With 4 plates of remains of A.–S. cross.] Trans. Bristol and Glos. Arch. Soc., 13, pp. 118–29. 1889.

10321 Petit (J. L.). Stanton Lacy church, near Ludlow, Shropshire. [Pilaster strips, etc.] Archaeol J., 3, pp. 297–98. 1846.

10322 Pollard (H. P.). Reed church. East Herts Archaeol. Soc., Trans., 2. iii (1904), pp. 261–64, + 1 plate. 1905.

10323 Scott (George Gilbert). On the supposed Saxon work at Iver and at Wing. Rec. Bucks., 1 (1854), pp. 36–38. 1858.

10324 Sheppard (Lewis). The Saxon wall and the monastic ruins under the south-west corner of Worcester cathedral. Assoc. Archit. Socs.' Rpts., 30, pp. 589–96, + plan, + 1 plate. 1910.

10325 Smith (Henry Ecroyd). Reliques of the Anglo-Saxon churches of St. Bridget and St. Hildeburga, West Kirkby, Cheshire; with some of their sepulchral monuments. pp. iv, 34, + 7 plates. 8° Liverpool, 1870.

10326 Wilkins (William). A description of the church of Melbourne, in Derbyshire, with an attempt to explain from it the real situation of the porticus in the ancient churches. Archaeologia, 13, pp. 290–308, + plan, + 2 plates. 1798.

10327 Wilson (James Maurice) and **Sheppard** (Lewis). Some notes on the building stones used in Worcester cathedral, and on the quarries from which they were brought. [Pp. 259–61, ' the Saxon period '.] Assoc. Archit. Socs.' Rpts., 31, pp. 259–70. 1911.

177. ARCHITECTURE, ECCLESIASTICAL, NORTHUMBRIA

§ *a*. **Escombe, Jarrow and Monkwearmouth**

10328 Architectural and Archaeological Society of Durham and Northumberland. St. Peter's, Monkwearmouth. Trans. Archit. Soc. Durham and Nhd., 1 (1862–68), pp. 141–44, Appendix, pp. 1–8, + 5 plates. 1870.

10329 Boyle (John Roberts). On the monastery and church of St. Paul, Jarrow. Archaeol. Æl., N.S. 10, pp. 195–216, + plan, + 7 plates. 1885.

10330 —— On the windows in the south wall of the chancel of St. Paul's church, Jarrow. *Same jnl.*, N.S. 10, pp. 217–19, + 1 plate. 1885.

10331 Gilbert (Edward). Anglian remains at St. Peter's, Monkwearmouth. *Same jnl.*, 4th S. 25, pp. 140–78, + 1 plate. 1947.

10332 Greenwell (William). Features of Anglo-Saxon architecture recently brought to light in Monkwearmouth church. Proc. Soc. Antiq., 2nd S. 3, pp. 450–51. 1867.

10333 Hall (John). The dates of the monastic remains at St. Peter's church, Monkwearmouth. Antiq. Sunderland, 18 (1918–25), pp. 36–62, + 4 plates. 1931.

10334 Hodges (Charles Clement). Escomb church, Durham. [With illustrations and plan.] Illust. Archaeologist, 1, pp. 225–36. 1894.

10335 Hodgson (J. F.). The churches of Escomb, Jarrow and Monkwearmouth. [Last plate is of part of cross-shaft from Jarrow.] Trans. Archit. Soc. Durham and Nhd., 6 (1906–11), pp. 109–87, + 32 plates. 1912.

10336 Hooppell (R. E.). On a perfect Saxon church at Escombe in the county of Durham. J. Brit. Archaeol. Assoc., 35, pp. 380–84, + 1 plate. 1879.

10337 Johnson (R. J.). S. Peter's, Monkwearmouth. Ecclesiologist, 27 (N. S. 24), pp. 361–64, + 2 plates. 1866.

10338 Longstaffe (William Hylton Dyer). Escombe church. Archaeol. Æl., N.S. 8, pp. 281–86. 1880.

10339 Lord (T. E.). Escombe. [Plan and 4 figures in text.] Proc. Soc. Antiq. Newcastle, 2nd S. 7, pp. 53–63. 1895.

10340 Lynam (Charles). Escomb church, Bishop Auckland. J. Brit. Archaeol. Assoc., 43, pp. 44–46, + 2 plates. 1887.

10341 Ml. (J.). Excavations at Monkwearmouth. N. and Q., 3rd S. 10, p. 348 : 11, p. 61. 1866–67.

10341a Patterson (James). A handbook to the church of St. Peter, Monkwearmouth. 3rd edition. 1920.

10342 —— Some Saxon remains at Monkwearmouth church. Antiq. Sunderland, 2 (1901), pp. 73–82, + 2 plates. 1903.

10343 Peers (*Sir* Charles Reed). Monkwearmouth and Jarrow. Bede : 12th centenary essays, ed. A. H. Thompson, pp. 102–10. 1935.

10344 Romans (Thomas). Escomb church. Trans. Cumb. and Westm. Antiq. Soc., N.S. 36, pp. 221–22, + plate. 1936.

10345 —— Monkwearmouth. *Same jnl.*, N.S. 36, pp. 216–18, + plate. 1936.

10345a Rose (James Dudfield). Jarrow church and monastery. 3rd edition. pp. 56. 8° Jarrow, 1932.

10346 Savage (Henry Edwin). Jarrow church and monastery. [6 figures of sculpture in text.] Archaeol. Æl., N.S. 22, pp. 30–60, + 5 plates. 1900.

10347 Smithwhite (J. H.). Biscop's twin churches. Antiq. Sunderland, 20 (1932–43), pp. 31–36. 1951.

10348 Whiting (Charles Edwin). Jarrow. Trans. Cumb. and Westm. Antiq. Soc., N.S. 36, pp. 214–16. 1936.

§ b. Hexham and Ripon

10349 Farquhar (James Vaux Cornell). The Saxon cathedral and priory church of S. Andrew, Hexham. pp. 34, + plan. 8° Hexham, 1935.

10350 Hodges (Charles Clement). Ecclesia Hagustaldensis. The abbey of St. Andrew, Hexham. pp. 62, + 60 plates. large fol. *n.p.*, 1888. [Pp. 14–21, + plates 39–40, St. Wilfrid's church.]

10351 Longstaffe (William Hylton Dyer). Hexham church. [Pp. 150–54, Saxon Hexham.] Archaeol. Æl., N.S. 5, pp. 150–58. 1861.

10352 Micklethwaite (John Thomas). On the crypts at Hexham and Ripon. [670 and 674.] Archaeol. J., 39, pp. 347–54, + 2 plates. 1882.

10353 Peers (*Sir* Charles Reed). Recent discoveries in the minsters of Ripon and York. Antiq. J., 11, pp. 113–22, + 2 plates, + 2 plans. 1931.

10354 Turner (T. H.). Observations on the crypt of Hexham church, Northumberland. Arch. J., 2, pp. 239–42. 1846.

10355 Walbran (John Richard). Observations on the Saxon crypt under the cathedral church of Ripon, commonly called St. Wilfrid's needle. Mems. Archaeol. Inst., [2] (1846), pp. 1–11. 1848.

10356 —— On a crypt in Ripon cathedral, commonly called St. Wilfrid's needle ; with observations on the early history of the church of Ripon. Trans. Brit. Archaeol. Assoc., 2nd congress, Winchester, 1845, pp. 339–54. 1846.

10357 Wilson (F. R.). Hexham abbey church. Ecclesiologist, 23, pp. 309–17, + plan. 1862.

§ c. Others

10358 [Anon.] Anglo-Saxon church. [St. Mary Bishophill junior, York.] Ecclesiologist, 1, pp. 190–92. 1842.

10359 Aird (R. Anderson). Recent discoveries at Seaham church, [co. Durham.] [Saxon window.] Antiq. Sunderland, 15, pp. 7–81, + 4 plates. 1914.

10360 —— Seaham. [? A.–S. church. Plan + 2 full page illustrations in text.] Proc. Soc. Antiq. Newcastle, 3rd S. 6 (1913), pp. 59–71. 1915.

10361 Boddington (Edgar). Pre-Conquest discoveries at Greatham church [co. Durham]. [Including A.–S. balusters and sculpture.] Archaeol. Æl., 3rd S. 9, pp. 11–24. 1913.

10362 Boutflower (Douglas Samuel). Types of Saxon churches in the county of Durham. Antiq. Sunderland, 17 (1916–17), pp. 9–21. 1925.

10363 Clift (J. G. Neilson). An early instance of billet-moulding. [At Beverley, between 1050 and 1060?] J. Brit. Archaeol. Assoc., 63 (N.S. 13), pp. 29–31. 1907.

10364 Cudworth (W.). Leathley church, Yorkshire. [? A.–S., ? early Norman.] Reliquary, 11, pp. 204–08. 1905.

10365 Dunn (J. W.). On the vestiges of Saxon work revealed during the restoration of Warkworth church [Nhb.]. Archaeol. Æl., N.S. 5, pp. 100–02, + 1 plate. 1861.

10366 Gilbert (Edward). Anglo-Saxon work at Billingham [co. Durham]. Proc. Soc. Antiq. Newcastle, 4th S. 11, pp. 195–204, + 1 plate. 1948.

10367 —— New views on Warden, Bywell and Heddon-on-the Wall churches. [Warden-on-Tyne, Anglo-Danish belfry window : Bywell-on-Tyne, Anglo-Danish tower : Bywell St. Peter, A.–S. nave wall, etc. : Heddon, A.–S. nave.] Arch. Æl., 4th S. 24, pp. 157–76, + 4 plates. 1946.

10368 Hodges (Charles Clement). The church of St. Bartholomew, Whittingham, Northumberland. Archaeol. Æl., 4th S., 5, pp. 81–86, + plan + 3 plates. 1928.

10369 —— The pre-Conquest churches of Northumbria. [With many illustrations in text, including drawings of crosses.] Reliquary, N. [2nd] S. 7, pp. 1–18, 65–85, 140–56 : 8, pp. 1–12, 65–83, 193–205, + 7 plates. 1893–94.

10370 Honeyman (Herbert Lewis). Some early masonry in north Northumberland. [Details of 15 churches with pre-conquest work : with plans.] Archaeol. Æl., 4th S., 12, pp. 158–86, + 2 plates. 1935.

10371 Hooppell (R. E.). On the ruins of an early church at North Gosforth, near Newcastle-on-Tyne. [?Saxon or very early Norman.] J. Brit. Archaeol. Assoc., 38, pp. 117–21, + 1 plate. 1882.

10372 Hope (*Sir* William Henry St. John). Notes on recent excavations in the cloister of Durham abbey. [Plan= ' Suggested plan of Aldhun's church and Walcher's monastic buildings.'] Proc. Soc. Antiq., 2nd S. 22, pp. 416–24, + plan. 1909.

10373 Hudleston (Ferdinand). The recent find in Dacre churchyard [Cumberland]. [Argument for sewer to Bede's monastery ' which being built near the river Dacore has taken its name from the same.'] Trans. Cumb. and Westm. Antiq. Soc., N.S. 32, pp. 75–77, + plate, + plan. 1932.

10374 Longstaffe (William Hylton Dyer). Norton [co. Durham]. Archaeol. Æl., N.S. 15, pp. 1–13, + 2 plates. 1892.

10375 Lynam (Charles). Laughton-en-le-Morthen church, Yorkshire. J. Brit. Archaeol. Assoc., 60 (N.S. 10), pp. 195–98, + 1 plate. 1904.

10375a Newell (Charles S.). The story of Kirk Hammerton parish church. pp. 31, + 8 plates. 8° Leeds, 1938.

10376 Pegge (Samuel). Observations on the present Aldbrough church at Holderness, proving that it was not a Saxon building, as Mr. Somerset contends. Archaeologia, 7, pp. 86–89. 1785.

10376a Powell (W. F.). St. Gregory's minster, Kirkdale. 1909.

10377 Rigby (T.). Laughton-en-le-Morthen church, Yorkshire. [Plate shows Saxon doorway.] J. Brit. Archaeol. Assoc., 60 (N.S. 10), pp. 189–94, + 2 plates. 1904.

10378 Robson (John). Notes on a visit to Heysham, [Lancs.]. Hist. Soc. Lancs. and Ches., Proc., 3, pp. 27–29, + 1 plate. 1850.

10379 Rowe (George). On the churches of Lastingham and Kirkdale, in Yorkshire, with some remarks on ancient Saxon sundials. Assoc. Archit. Socs.' Rpts., 12, pp. 202–10, + 5 plates, + 1 plan. 1874.

10380 —— On the Saxon church of All Saints, Kirby Hill, Boroughbridge, [Yorks.]. *Same jnl.*, 10, pp. 239–43, + 4 plates. 1870.

10380a Thompson (Alexander Hamilton), *etc.* The church of St. John the Baptist, Kirk Hammerton, York. 1911.

10380b Tudor (Charles L. R.). A brief account of Kirkdale church, with plans, *etc.* fol. London, 1876.

10381 Wall (James Charles). Pure Norman. [On Lastingham crypt, ?1078–88.] Reliquary, 12, pp. 145–51. 1906.

178. ARCHITECTURE, ECCLESIASTICAL, SUSSEX

10382 André (James Lewis). Sompting church. Sussex Archaeol. Collns., 41, pp. 7–24, + 2 plates, + plan. 1898.

10383 Beckett (J. H.). Saxon masonry in Sussex. North Staffs. F.C., Trans., 64, pp. 33–40, + 5 plates. 1930.

10384 Brakspear (*Sir* Harold). Battle abbey. [Figure shows ' plan of the original east end,' and ?spot where Harold fell.] Antiq. J., 11, pp. 166–68. 1931.

10385 Bridge (Arthur). Worth church. pp. 56. 8° London, 1911.

10386 Dale (Joseph). Notice of the south doorway of the church at Bolney. Sussex Archaeol. Collns., 10, pp. 59–62. 1858.

10387 Elrington (H.). The ancient church of Bosham. Reliquary, 4, pp. 82–90. 1898.

10388 Fox (G. J. B.). Worth, Sussex. Proc. Croydon N.H. and Sci. Soc., 10, pp. 37–42, + 1 plate. 1926.

10389 Gardner (Samuel). Architectural notes : . . . Sompting church. Proc. Clapton Archit. Club, 14, pp. 19–20. 1903.

10390 Godfrey (Walter Hindes). Guide to the church of St. Andrew, Bishopstone. *Sussex Arch. Soc., Sussex churches*, 9. pp. 12. [Plan + 4 figures in text.] 8° Lewes, 1948.

10391 —— Guide to the church of St. Mary, Sompting. *Same series*, 16. pp. 20. 8° Lewes, 1951. [Plan + 7 figures in text.]

10392 —— Guide to the church of St. Nicholas, Worth. *Same series*, 18. pp. 16. 8° Lewes, 1952. [Plan + 6 figures in text.]

10393 —— The parish church of St. Andrew, Bishopstone. [Plan, + 6 figures in text.] Sussex Archaeol. Coll., 87, pp. 164–83. 1948.

10394 —— Sussex church plans, 92. Parish church of Holy Trinity, Bosham. Sussex N. and Q., 13, pp. 109–10. 1951.

10395 Hills (Gordon M.). The church of West Hampnett, Sussex, chiefly in reference to its Roman remains. [Saxon chancel-arch and side-walls.] J. Brit. Archaeol. Assoc., 24, pp. 209–18, + plans, and 1 plate. 1868.

10396 Jessep (Henry Lethbridge). Anglo-Saxon church architecture in Sussex. pp. 62, + 12 plates, + map. 8° Winchester, [1914].

10397 Johnston (Philip Mainwaring). Chithurst church. [Largely c. 1080. With plan.] Sussex Archaeol. Collns., 55, pp. 97–107, + 3 plates. 1912.

10398 —— The church of Lyminster and the chapel of Warningcamp, with some notice of the dependent manors. [Nave and chancel, c. 1040.] *Same jnl.*, 46, pp. 195–230, + 4 plates, + plan : (*note also in* 47, pp. 158–59). 1903–04.

ᴋ k

10399 Johnston (Philip Mainwaring). Clayton church. [Saxon church, altered in 13th c., ? A.–S frescoes.] J. Brit. Archaeol. Assoc., N.S. 23, pp. 154–57 : *see also* N.S. 24, pp. 275–77. 1917–18.

10400 —— Ford and its church. (Addenda and corrigenda). [Pp. 116–19, A.–S. features.] Sussex Archaeol. Collns., 43, pp. 105–57, + 2 plates, + plan : 44, pp. 206–08. 1900–01.

10401 —— Hardham church, and its early paintings. [11th c.] Archaeol. J., 58, pp. 62–92, + 5 plates. 1901.

10402 —— Saxon doorway, St. John-sub-Castro, Lewis. [Measured drawing.] J. Brit. Archaeol. Assoc., N.S. 23, pp. 161–62. 1917.

10403 —— A supposed pre-Conquest font at Waldron. [No carving.] Sussex Archaeol. Collns., 49, pp. 126–27, + 1 plate. 1906.

10404 Leeney (O. M.). The church of Bishopstone. Antiquary, 47, pp. 369–74. 1911.

10405 Poole (Herbert). The Domesday Book churches of Sussex. [18 figures in text.] Sussex Archaeol. Coll., 87, pp. 29–76. 1948.

10406 Roberts (Harold Vernon Molesworth). A Saxon doorway. [St. John-sub-Castro, Lewes.] Builder, 137, p. 298. 1929.

10407 Stebbing (William Pinckard Delane). The church of Worth. pp. 29, + 5 plates. 8° Broad Campden, *Essex House Press*, 1908.

10408 Walford (Weston Styleman). On the church of Worth. Sussex Archaeol. Collns., 8, pp. 235–49, + 2 plates. 1856.

10409 Wallis (W. Cyril). Some Saxon churches in Sussex. [6 figures in text.] Sussex County Mag., 5, pp. 345–51. 1931.

179. ARCHITECTURE, ECCLESI-ASTICAL, WESSEX

§ a. Bradford-on-Avon, Wilts.

10410 Addy (Sidney Oldall), *etc.* The so-called Saxon church of Bradford-on-Avon. [Not A.–S.] N. and Q., 152, pp. 237–39, 322. 1927.

10411 Astley (Hugh John Dukinfield). The Saxon church at Bradford-on-Avon. J. Brit. Archaeol. Assoc., 61 (N.S. 11), pp. 211–30, + 3 plates. 1905.

10412 —— The Saxon church at Bradford-on-Avon. Wilts. Archaeol. Mag., 34, pp. 374–87, + 2 plates. 1906.

10413 Batten (Edmund Chisholm). Saxon church of St. Lawrence, Bradford-on-Avon. Archaeol. J., 45, pp. 1–6. 1888.

10414 Beddoe (John). On the date of the ecclesiola at Bradford-on-Avon. Wilts. Archaeol. Mag., 36, pp. 359–63. 1910.

10415 Brentnall (Harold Cresswell). The ground-plan of the Saxon church, Bradford-on-Avon. [Plan on p. 499.] *Same jnl.*, 50, pp. 498–500. 1944.

10416 Burder (Alfred William Newsam). Notes on the parish church and Saxon church, Bradford-on-Avon. [Pp. 322–23, Saxon church—notes on repairs to chancel and drainage in 1908.] *Same jnl.*, 36, pp. 318–23. 1910.

10416a —— A short account of the Saxon church of St. Laurence, Bradford-on-Avon, Wilts. 8° Bradford-on-Avon, [1912?].

10417 Collisson (S. O.). The Saxon church [of Bradford-on-Avon]. Proc. Dorset Antiq. F.C., 26, pp. l–lii. 1905.

10418 Davis (C. E.). [The Saxon church of Bradford-on-Avon : remarks at visit.] J. Brit. Archaeol. Assoc., 31, pp. 326–28. 1875.

10419 Ingledew (Walter A.). A consecration cross at the Saxon church of St. Lawrence, Bradford-on-Avon. Proc. Soc. Antiq. Newc., 4th S. 6, pp. 175–77. 1933.

10420 Jones (William Henry Rich). An account of the Saxon church of St. Laurence, Bradford-on-Avon. pp. 17. + 5 plates. 4° Devizes, [?1873].

10421 —— The Saxon church of St. Laurence, Bradford-on-Avon. [Brief statement and appeal.] Wilts. Archaeol. Mag., 13, pp. 274–75, + 2 plates. 1872.

10422 MacGibbon (A. L.). The church of S. Laurence at Bradford-on-Avon. Trans. Scot. Ecclesiol. Soc., 2, pp. 288–95. 1908.

10423 Radford (Courtenay Arthur Ralegh). The church of St. Lawrence, Bradford-on-Avon. Proc. Somerset Archaeol. Soc., 95 (1950), pp. 31–32. 1951.

10424 Williams (Philip). On the Anglo-Saxon church at Bradford-on-Avon. Trans. Exeter Diocesan Archit. Soc., N.S. 5, pp. 157–67, + 1 plate. 1892.

§ *b*. Others

10425 [Anon.] Saxon doorway at Somerford-Keynes, Wilts. Illust. Archaeologist, 1, pp. 46–49. 1894.

10426 [Anon.] Saxon window, Boarhunt church. Papers and Proc. Hants. F.C., 2, pp. 255–56. 1894.

10427 Baron (John). The church of Maningford Bruce, Wilts. [10th c.] Proc. Soc. Antiq., 2nd S. 9, pp. 26–28. 1881.

10428 Cave (Walter). Notes on the Saxon crypt, Sidbury church, Devonshire. Archaeol. J., 56, pp. 74–76. 1899.

10429 —— Sidbury church. [A.-S. crypt.] Rept. and Trans. Devon. Assoc., 35, pp. 353–59. 1903.

10430 Cooper (A. J. Campbell). Evidences of Saxon work at Boxford church, Berks. Trans. Newbury District F.C., 8, pp. 105–08, + 1 plate. 1939.

10431 Cresy (Edward). Winchester cathedral. Trans. Brit. Archaeol. Ass. (2nd congress, Winchester, 1845), pp. 355–400, + 5 plates. 1846.

10432 Fanshawe (G. C.). Godalming: the Saxon windows in the church. Surrey Archaeol. Collns., 33, pp. 116–17. 1920.

10433 Finny (W. E. St. Lawrence). The Saxon church at Kingston [-on-Thames]. *Same jnl.*, 37, pp. 211–19, + 1 plate. 1927.

10434 Freeman (George H.). The site of the Saxon church at Kingston [-on-Thames]. *Same jnl.*, 35, pp. 98–104, + 1 plate. 1924.

10435 Green (Arthur Robert *and* Phyllis Mary). Saxon architecture and sculpture in Hampshire. pp. viii, 67, + 20 plates. 8° Winchester, 1951.

10436 Green (Arthur Robert). Saxon churches of Hampshire. [Record of excursion.] Papers and Proc. Hants. F.C., 13, pp. 232–33. 1936.

10437 Hardy (William Masters). A study on the work of preservation of the church of St. Nicholas, Studland, Dorset, from its original foundation by the Saxons to the date of its completion by the Normans. Proc. Dorset Antiq. F.C., 12, pp. 164–79, + plan, + 3 plates. 1891.

10437a Harrison (James Park). Notes on St. Leonard's church, Wallingford, [Berks.]. [?A.–S. piers, with diaper pattern, to chancel arch.] J. Brit. Archaeol. Assoc., 47, pp., 135–38, + 1 plate. 1891.

10438 Hill (A. du Boulay). A Saxon church at Breamore, Hants. Archaeol. J., 55, pp. 84–87, + 3 plates. 1898.

10439 Irvine (James Thomas). Description of the Saxon church of Boarhunt, in Hampshire. J. Brit. Archaeol. Assoc., 33, pp. 367–80, + 2 plates. 1877.

10440 Jessep (Henry Lethbridge). Notes on pre-Conquest church architecture in Hampshire and Surrey. pp. 32. [Illustrated.] 8° Winchester, 1913.

10441 Johnston (Philip Mainwaring). The discovery of a pre-Conquest window, with early painting on the internal splays, in Witley church, Surrey. Proc. Soc. Antiq., 2nd S. 29, pp. 189–203. 1917.

10442 —— Pre-Conquest churches in Surrey. A note upon the antiquity of West Horsley church and other churches. Surrey Archaeol. Collns., 36, pp. 117–19. 1925.

10443 —— Stoke d'Abernon church : some recent discoveries. [With plan of pre-Conquest church.] *Same jnl.*, 26, pp. 121–33, + 3 plates. 1913.

10444 —— Studland church, and some remarks on Norman corbel-tables. [Plan, + 17 figures in text.] J. Brit. Archaeol. Assoc., N.S. 24, pp. 33–68, + 2 plates. 1918.

10445 Johnston (Philip Mainwaring). Witley and Thursley churches : recent discoveries. Surrey Archaeol. Collns., 39, pp. 104–11, + 2 plates. 1931.

10445a Kaines-Thomas (E. G.). Saxon and Norman architecture in the Newbury district. Trans. Newbury F.C., 9, pp. 44–51, + 4 plates. 1951.

10446 Minns (G. W.). On a Saxon sepulchral monument at Whitchurch. Papers and Proc. Hants. F.C., 4 (1898–1903), pp. 171–74, + 1 plate. 1905.

10447 Nisbett (Norman C. H.). Notes on some examples of Saxon architecture in Hampshire. *Same jnl.*, 2, pp. 309–16, + 1 plate. 1894.

10448 Parker (James). Glastonbury : the abbey ruins. [Pp. 51–60 : description of the church before the fire, 1184 : tombs of Edmund I, Edgar, Edmund Ironside, Dunstan, etc.] Proc. Somerset Arch. Soc., 26 (1880), pp. 25–106, + 2 pl ns, + 2 plates. 1881.

10449 Parker (John Henry). The church of St. Mary, Guildford. [11th c.] Archaeol. J., 29, pp. 170–80, + 4 plates. 1872.

10450 Peers (*Sir* Charles Reed), **Clapham** (*Sir* Alfred William) and **Horne** (Ethelbert) *abbot of Downside.* Interim report on the excavations at Glastonbury abbey. [The A.–S. church (Ine to Dunstan) : with plan.] Antiq. J., 10, pp. 24–29. 1930.

10451 Ponting (C. E.). All Saints', Somerford Keynes. [Plate is ' Elevation of Saxon doorway '.] Wilts. Archaeol. Mag., 27, pp. 27–29, + 1 plate. 1894.

10452 —— A description of the Saxon work in the church of S. James, Abury. *Same jnl.*, 21, pp. 188–93, + 2 plates. 1884.

10453 Prideaux (E. K.). Illustrated notes on the church of St. Candida and Holy Cross at Whitechurch Canonicorum, Dorset. [Part 1, the Saxon and Norman churches.] Archaeol. J., 64, pp. 119–50, + 15 plates. 1907.

10454 Radford (Courtenay Arthur Ralegh). Excavations at Glastonbury abbey, 1952. [The Saxon church.] Antiquity, 27, p. 41. 1953.

10455 Robinson (Joseph Armitage) *dean of Wells.* The historical evidence as to the Saxon church at Glastonbury. Proc. Somerset Arch. Soc., 73 (1927), pp. 40–89. 1928.

10456 Saunders (G. W.) and **Allen** (F. J.). Milborne Port church. [Pilaster strip work : the one example in Somerset.] N. and Q. for Som. and Dorset, 18, p. 169, + 1 plate : 211–12. 1925–26.

10457 Sayer-Milward (W. C.). Notes on St. Leonard's church, Wallingford, [Berks.] [Queries Parker's article **10161,** as to A.–S. piers of chancel arch.] J. Brit. Archaeol. Assoc., 47, pp. 132–34. 1891.

10458 Swayne (Henry I. F.). [Saxon arch, and its carving, Britford church, near Salisbury]. *Same jnl.,* 32, p. 497, + 1 plate. 1876.

10459 Talbot (C. H.). Downton and Britford churches. [Plate shows Saxon arch, Britford.] Wilts. Archaeol. Mag., 17, pp. 238–53, + 1 plate. 1878.

10460 —— The Saxon arches of Britford church, near Salisbury, Wilts. J. Brit. Archaeol. Assoc., 33, pp. 345–48. 1877.

10461 Yarborough (J. Cooke). An account of some recent discoveries in Romsey abbey. Papers and Proc. Hants. F.C., 4 (1898–1903), pp. 227–33, + plan. 1905.

180. ARCHITECTURE, IRELAND
§ *a.* General

10462 Bagnall-Oakeley (Mary Ellen). Early Christian settlements in Ireland. [Architectural development. Enclosing walls for protection and seclusion show provenance from the East. Round towers later for protection.] Proc. Clifton Antiq. Club, 3 (1893–96), pp. 22–24. 1897.

10463 Beckley (F. J.). Notes in Irish architecture. [Primitive Christian edifices, round towers, etc.] Trans. St. Paul's Eccles. Soc., 3, pp. 142–54. 1895.

10464 Brash (Richard Rolt). The ecclesiastical architecture of Ireland to the close of the twelfth century. pp. xii, 174, + 52 plates. 4° Dublin, 1875. [Gross, 424.]

10465 Champneys (Arthur Charles). Irish ecclesiastical architecture, with some notice of similar or related work in England, Scotland and elsewhere. pp. xxxiii, 258, + 114 plates. fol. London, 1910. [Kenney, 1, p. 103. Early churches, round towers, early ornament and carving, high crosses, etc.]

10466 Cochrane (Robert). Notes on the 'Ancient monuments protection (Ireland) Act, 1892,' and the previous legislation connected therewith. [Pp. 415–19, schedule of monuments (churches, forts, etc.)] J. Roy. Soc. Antiq. Ireland, 22 (5th S. 2), pp. 411–29. 1892.

10467 Davies (Oliver). The earliest Irish church architecture. [5th c.] Proc. Belfast N. H. and Phil. Soc., 2nd S. 3, pp. 99–101, + 3 plates. 1948.

10468 —— Early Irish stone building. [Rejoinder to **10472.**] County Louth Archaeol. J., 12 (1949), pp. 11–12. 1950.

10469 Du Noyer (George Victor). Notes on some peculiarities in ancient and mediaeval Irish ecclesiastical architecture. [Including oratories, 5th c., etc.] J. Kilkenny Archaeol. Soc., N.S. 5, pp. 27–40, + 4 plates. 1867.

10470 Dunraven (Edwin Richard Wyndham) *3rd earl of.* Notes on Irish architecture, edited by Margaret Stokes. 2 vol. fol. London, 1875–77. [125 plates (photographs) : plates 66–89, round towers.]

10471 Ferguson (*Sir* Samuel). On sepulchral cellae. [12 figures in text.] Trans. R.I.A., 27, pp. 57–66. 1882.

10472 Henry (Françoise). Early Irish monasteries, boat-shaped oratories, and beehive huts. [6th–7th c.] County Louth Arch. J., 11, pp. 296–304, + 2 plates. 1949.

10473 Keane (Marcus). The towers and temples of ancient Ireland : their origin and history discussed. 4° Dublin, 1867.

10474 Leask (Harold G.). The characteristic features of Irish architecture from early times to the twelfth century. [13 figures in text.] N. Munster Antiq. J., 1, pp. 10–21. 1936.

10475 Lynch (Patrick J.). Early Christian architecture of Ireland. J. Limerick F.C., 2, pp. 18–33, 82–104, + 8 plates. 1901–02.

10476 M. (J. J.). Remarks on the early architecture of Ireland. [Round towers, etc.] Ulster J. Archaeol., 6, pp. 247–49. 1858.

10477 O'Connell (Jerome). The Roman basilica and Irish churches. Irish Eccles. Rec., 4th. S. 5, pp. 136–49. 1899.

10478 Phipps (C. B.). The problem of dating ancient Irish buildings. Hermathena, no. 54, pp. 54–92, + 1 plate. 1939.

10479 Ronan (Myles V.). Patrician churches : their form and material. Irish Eccles. Rec., 5th S. 41, pp. 356–69. 1933.

10480 Stokes (Margaret Mac Nair). Early Christian architecture in Ireland. 4° London, 1878. [Gross, 439. Forts, church towers, etc. 52 plates.]

10481 Trusted (Charles J.). Some remarks on early Christian remains in Ireland. Proc. Clifton Antiq. Club, 2 (1888–93), pp. 47–56, + 3 plates. 1893.

§ b. Individual

10482 Bigger (Francis Joseph). Cruach MacDara, off the coast of Connamara : with a notice of its church, crosses and antiquities. [Oratory, 6th or 7th c.] J. Roy. Soc. Antiq. Ireland, 26 (5th S. 6), pp. 101–12, + 1 plate. 1896.

10483 Currey (Francis Edmund). St. Bridget's church, Britway parish, co. Cork. *Same jnl.*, 24 (5th S. 4), pp. 129–31. 1894.

10484 Davies (Oliver). Killeavy churches. [Founded by St. Moninna at beginning of 6th c. Originally 2 churches, 33 feet apart. Eastern church ? Norman.] County Louth Archaeol. J., 9, pp. 77–86. 1938.

10485 Drew (Thomas). The Danish Christchurches of Dublin and Waterford. [Waterford, founded by Reginald, son of Sigtryg, c. 1050 : Dublin, 1038.] J. Waterford Archaeol. Soc., 1, pp. 194–97, + coloured plan [Waterford].

10486 Fitzgerald (Edward). On St. Declan's oratory at Ardmore, county of Waterford, and the old Irish inscription built into its east wall. Proc. and Trans. Kilkenny Archaeol. Soc., 3, pp. 223–31, + 1 plate (inscription) : 282–84. 1855.

10487 Graves (James). The Damhliag of Achadhabhall [Aghowle, co. Wicklow]. J. Roy. Hist. and Arch. Assoc. Ireland, [16], 4th S. 6 (1883–84), pp. 72–85, + 1 plate. 1884.

10488 Hill (Arthur). Ancient Irish architecture : Kilmalkedar, co. Kerry. pp. 6, + 12 plates. 4° n.p., 1870.

10489 Hills (Gordon M.). Innisclothran [in Lough Ree], and other island churches in Ireland. Ecclesiologist, 21, pp. 331–40, + 2 plates. 1860.

10490 Kinahan (George Henry). Cyclopean churches in the vicinity of Loughs Corrib, Mask and Carra. [Co. Galway.] J. Hist. and Archaeol. Assoc. Ireland, [10] 3rd S. 1, pp. 76–80, 131–38, + 4 plates. 1868.

10491 Leask (Harold G.). Killoughternane church, co. Carlow. [?8th c.] J. Roy. Soc. Antiq. Ireland, 73 (7th S. 13), pp. 98–100. 1943.

10492 —— and Macalister (Robert Alexander Stewart). Liathmore-Mochoemóg (Leigh), county Tipperary. [i. The partial excavation of a site at Liathmore or Leigh, county Tipperary : ii. The churches at Liathmore, by H. G. Leask.] Proc. R.I.A., 51 c, pp. 1–14. 1946.

10493 Lynch (Patrick J.). Liathmore-Mochoemog. [Architecture of 2 churches, co. Tipperary.] J. North Munster Archaeol. Soc., 3, pp. 73–84, + 3 plates. 1914.

10494 Macalister (Robert Alexander Stewart). The antiquities of Ardoiléan, county Galway. [Monastery founded by St. Féichin of Fore, c. 630–40. Chapel, clocháns, crosses, etc.] J. Roy. Soc. Antiq. Ireland, 26 (5th S. 6), pp. 196–210. 1896.

10495 —— Ballywiheen church, Ballyneanig, co. Kerry. [850–1000 A.D.] *Same jnl.*, 28 (5th S. 8), pp. 15–20. 1898.

10496 Malone (Michael). The ancient church of Donaghmore [near Limerick]. J. Roy. Hist. and Arch. Assoc. Ireland, [12] 4th S. 2 (1872–73), pp. 77–81, + 1 plate. 1874.

10497 O'Reilly (Joseph P.). Notes on the architectural details and orientations of the old churches of Kill-of-the-Grange, Killiney, and St. Nessan, Ireland's Eye [co. Dublin]. Proc. R.I.A., 24 c, pp. 107–16, + 1 plate. 1905.

10498 —— Notes on the orientations and certain architectural details of the old churches of Dalkey town and Dalkey island. Proc. R.I.A., 24c, pp. 195–236, + 5 plates. 1903.

10499 Power (Patrick). The ancient ruined churches of co. Waterford. [1, pp. 247–50, + plate, Kilbunny (pre-Norman) : 3, pp. 3–5, Clonea.] J. Waterford Archaeol. Soc., 1, p. 247–53 : 3, pp. 3–12. 1895–97.

10500 Rolleston (Thomas William). The church of St. Patrick on Caher island, county Mayo. J. Roy. Soc. Antiq. Ireland, 30 (5th S. 10), pp. 357–63. 1900.

10501 Wakeman (William Frederick). Ante-Norman churches in the county of Dublin. *Same jnl.*, 22 (5th S. 2), pp. 101–06, + 3 1892.

10502 —— The antiquities of Devenish, [co. Fermanagh]. [Establishment of St. Molaisse in Loch Erne. Round tower, etc. 20 figures in text.] J. Roy. Hist. and Arch. Assoc. Ireland, [13] 4th S. 3 (1874–75), pp. 59–94, + 1 plate. 1876.

10503 —— On the ecclesiastical antiquities of Cluain-Eois, now Clones, county of Monaghan. [Round tower, cross, etc.] *Same jnl.*, [13] 4th S. 3 (1874–75), pp. 327–40. 1876.

10504 —— Primitive churches in county Dublin. J. Roy. Soc. Antiq. Ireland, 21 (5th S. 1. ii), pp. 697–702, + 2 plates. 1891.

10505 Westropp (Thomas Johnson). A description of the ancient buildings and crosses at Clonmacnois, King's County. (*See also*, pp. 329–40. Sexton, pp. 101–14). *Same jnl.*, 37 (5th S. 17), pp. 277–306. 1907.

181. ARCHITECTURE, SCOTLAND

10506 Bryce (Thomas H.) and **Knight** (George Alexander Frank). Report on a survey of the antiquities on Eileach an Naoimh, [Argyllshire]. [' Underground cell, graveyards and tomb on the hill ' belong to ' the earliest phase of the Celtic church.'] Trans. Glasgow Archaeol. Soc., N.S. 8, pp. 62–102, + 14 plates, + plan. 1930.

10507 Gibbon (Robert W.) and **Kelly** (Francis). Three Orkney churches. [ii. (with plate) : S. Magnus, Egilsey, 11th c.] Trans. Aberdeen Ecclesiol. Soc., 3 (1896), pp. 367–72, + 4 plates. 1898.

10508 MacGibbon (David) and **Ross** (Thomas). The ecclesiastical architecture of Scotland from the earliest Christian times to the seventeenth century. 3 vol. 8° Edinburgh, 1896–97. [Vol. 1, pp. 64–108, the Celtic monastic and ecclesiastical structures ; pp. 109–73, churches in Orkney and Shetland ; pp. 174–80, transition from Celtic to Norman architecture. Figures 27–158.]

10509 Maxwell (*Sir* John Stirling). Shrines and homes of Scotland. pp. xx, 264, + 119 plates. 8° London, 1937. [Pp. 10–18, + plates 2, 7–9, primitive churches, c. 800–1124.]

10510 Radford (Courtenay Arthur Ralegh). The excavations at Chapel Finnian, Mochrum [Wigtownshire]. [? 10th–11th c.] Trans. Dumfriesshire Antiq. Soc., 3rd S. 28 (1949–50), pp. 28–40, + 1 plate. 1951.

10511 —— Excavations at Whithorn [Wigtownshire]. [?Chapel, c. 450.] Antiquity, 23, pp. 217–18. 1923.

10512 —— Excavations at Whithorn, first season, 1949. [Early history of Whithorn : excavations and the early church.] Trans. Dumfriesshire Antiq. Soc., 3rd S. 27 (1948–49), pp. 85–126, + 4 plates, + plan. 1950.

10513 Roussel (Aage). Norse building customs in the Scottish isles. pp. 113. 8° Copenhagen and London, 1934.

10514 Thoms (Alexander). St. Regulus tower, St. Andrews—Where did the stones with which it was built come from? Proc. Soc. Antiq. Scot., 47 (4th S. 11, 1912–13), pp. 426–28. 1913.

10515 **Waddell** (J. Jeffrey). The chapel or oratory of St. Columba at Iona. Trans. Glasgow Archaeol. Soc., N.S. 10, pp. 55–59. 1941.

182. ARCHITECTURE, WALES, CORNWALL AND ISLE OF MAN

10516 **Badger** (A. B.) and **Green** (Francis). The chapel traditionally attributed to St. Patrick, Whitesand bay, Pembrokeshire. [6th–10th c.] Arch. Camb., 80 (7th S. 5), pp. 87–120. 1925.

10517 **Collins** (Morley B.). St. Piran's oratory, Perranporth. J. Roy. Inst. Cornwall, 18, pp. 390–97, + 1 plate. 1911.

10518 **Halliday** (George Eley). Llantwit Major church, Glamorgan. [Excavation of pre-Norman church : plan, plate 1.] Arch. Camb., 6th S. 5, pp. 242–50, + 4 plans, + 5 plates. 1905.

10519 **Haslam** (William). Perranzabuloe ; with an account of the past and present state of the oratory of St. Piran in the Sands, and remarks on its antiquity. 8° London, 1844. [Built 6th or 7th c.]

10520 **Kermode** (Philip Moore Callow). An early church. [Excavations at Cronk Keeillane, near Peel, Isle of Man. ?6th c.]. J. Manx Mus., 1, p. 21. 1925.

10521 —— Introduction to the study of the church buildings in the Isle of Man earlier than the eleventh century. [Read, Dec. 18, 1907.] I.O.M., N.H. and Antiq. Soc., Proc., N.S., 1, pp. 421–26. 1913.

10522 **Radford** (Courtenay Arthur Ralegh). The excavations at Tintagel. [Pottery indicates that buildings belong to Celtic monastery deserted before Norman Conquest.] Antiq. J., 14, pp. 64–65. 1934.

10523 **Tyrrell-Green** (E.). The church architecture of Wales. [Pp. 57–70, the architecture of the early Celtic Church.] Trans. Hon. Soc. Cymm., 1916–17, pp. 52–118, + 2 plates. 1918.

10524 ——The ecclesiology of Anglesea. [Pp. 47–63 : churches of the native Celtic plan.] Y Cymmrodor, 40, pp. 43–117. 1929.

183. ARCHITECTURE, CELTIC ROUND TOWERS
§ a. General

10525 **Bagnall-Oakeley** (Mary Ellen). Notes on round towers. [Scotland, Ireland (and elsewhere). Correspond with the 3 chief invasions by the Northmen in dates.] Proc. Clifton Antiq. Club, 2 (1888–93), pp. 142–51, + 2 plates. 1893.

10526 **Barnwell** (Edward Lowry). On the analogy between our Irish round towers and the French fanaux de cemetière. J. Kilkenny Archaeol. Soc., [7] N.S. 4, pp. 317–19. 1863.

10527 **Brash** (Richard Rolt). Notes on the round tower controversy. Ulster J. Archaeol., 7, pp. 155–65. 1859.

10528 —— The round tower controversy—the belfry theory examined. *Same jnl.*, 8, pp. 280–91. 1860.

10529 **Davis** (Thomas). The round towers of Ireland. Davis (T.) : Prose writings (Camelot series), pp. 90–103. 1889.

10530 **De Montmorency-Morris** (Hervey). A historical and critical inquiry into the origin and primitive use of the Irish pillar-tower. pp. 75, + 2 plates. 4° London, 1821.

10531 **Du Noyer** (George Victor). On the analogy between the Irish round towers and fanaux de cemetière. J. Kilkenny Archaeol. Soc., [8] N.S. 5, pp. 131–33. 1864.

10532 **Eassie** (W.). Round towers. [?communication between stories.] N. and Q., 3rd S. 9, pp. 260–61. 1866.

10533 **F.** (E.) *of Youghal*. The round towers of Ireland, and a national style of church architecture. Ulster J. Archaeol., 2, pp. 67–68. 1854.

10534 **Gaidoz** (Henri). A propos des tours rondes d'Irlande. Rev. celt., 6, pp. 493–95. 1885.

10535 **Greg** (Robert Hyde). Observations on the round towers of Ireland. Mems. Manch. Lit. and Phil. Soc., 2nd S. 4, pp. 332–62. [c. 1825.]

10536 Ledwich (Edward). A dissertation on the round towers in Ireland. *In* Vallancey (Charles): Collectanea de rebus Hibernicis, vol. 2 (no. 6), pp. 117–43. 8° Dublin, 1781.

10537 O'Brien (Henry). The round towers of Ireland or the mysteries of freemasonry . . . unveiled. Prize essay of the Royal Irish Academy, enlarged. New edition, with introduction, synopsis, index, *etc.* pp. xcv, 551. 8° London, 1898.

10538 Petrie (George). The ecclesiastical architecture of Ireland anterior to the Anglo-Norman invasion, comprising an essay on the origin and uses of the round towers of Ireland. [Republished in book form (as 2nd edition) in 1845. Gross, 434.] Trans. R.I.A., 20, pp. i–xix, 1–521. 1845.

10539 Power (Patrick). The round towers. J. Ivernian Soc., 6, pp. 83–90, 155–63. 1914.

10540 Salmon (John). The round towers of Ireland : their origin and uses. pp. 68. 8° Belfast, 1886.

10541 Smiddy (Richard). An essay on the druids, the ancient churches and the round towers of Ireland. pp. ix, 242. 8° Dublin, 1871.

10542 Vallancey (Charles). Some remarks on the round towers of Ireland. *Collectanea de rebus Hibernicis, vol.* 3 (no. 10), *pp.* 191–96 : *vol.* 6, *pp.* 121–56. 8° Dublin, 1782, 1804.

10543 Westropp (Hodder Michael). [On the Irish round towers and their analogy with the French fanaux or lanternes de morts]. J. Kilkenny Archaeol. Soc., [7] N.S. 4, pp. 190–95 : N.S. 5, pp. 18–20. 1862–64.

10544 —— The rounded towers of Ireland and the French fanaux de cimetière. Ulster J. Archaeol, 8, pp. 171–76. 1860.

10545 Westropp (Thomas Johnson). A list of the round towers of Ireland, with notes on those which have been demolished, and on four in the county of Mayo. Proc. R.I.A., 3rd S. 5, pp. 294–311. 1899.

10546 Wise (Thomas Alexander). The pillar-towers of Scotland. [Abernethy and Brechin, contemporaneous with those of Ireland.] Ulster J. Archaeol., 5, pp. 210–15. 1857.

10547 Zehender (W. von). Die runden Thürme in Irland. Rostock, 1885.

§ *b.* Individual

10548 Brash (Richard Rolt). Notices, historical and architectural, of the round tower of Brechin, [Angus]. Proc. Soc. Antiq. Scot., 4, pp. 188–210, + 1 plate. 1863.

10549 —— The round tower and church of Dysert, county of Limerick. J. Hist. and Archaeol. Assoc. Ireland, [10] 3rd S. 1, pp. 54–61, + 1 plate. 1868.

10550 —— The round tower of Abernethy, [Perthshire]. Proc. Soc. Antiq. Scot., 3, pp. 303–19, + 1 plate. 1862.

10551 Buckley (James). The round tower of Kinneigh, co. Cork. J. Cork Hist. Soc., 2nd S. 11, pp. 135–38, + 1 plate. 1905.

10552 Caulfield (Richard), **Harkness** (William) and **Haines** (J.). Examination and measurements of the round tower of Kineigh, barony of West Carbery, co. Cork. J. Roy. Hist. and Arch. Assoc. Ireland, [15] 4th S. 5 (1879–82), pp. 16–24. 1882.

10553 Clark (Jane). Kilree church and round tower, county Kilkenny. J. Roy. Soc. Antiq. Ireland, 33 (5th S. 13), pp. 213–16. 1903.

10554 Cochrane (Robert). Ancient monuments in the county of Cork. x. Round towers. J. Cork Hist. Soc., 2nd S. 18, pp. 132–33. 1912.

10555 —— Notes on the round tower, etc., of Kilmacduagh [co. Galway]. J. Roy. Soc. Antiq. Ireland, 34 (5th S. 14), pp. 234–38. 1904.

10556 Coleman (James). The round towers of Cloyne and Kinneigh, co. Cork. J. Cork Hist. Soc., 3, pp. 177–82, 201–06. 1894.

10557 —— The round towers of the co. Kerry. Kerry Archaeol. Mag., 1, pp. 95–102, + 1 plate. 1909.

10558 Crawford (Henry Saxton). Oran round tower, co. Roscommon. J. Roy. Soc. Antiq. Ireland, 43 (6th S. 3), pp. 170–72. 1913.

10559 —— The round tower and castle of Timahoe [Queen's County]. *Same jnl.*, 54 (6th S. 14), pp. 31–45, + 4 plates. 1924.

10560 —— The round tower of Aghagower [co. Mayo]. *Same jnl.*, 35 (5th S. 15), pp. 416–18. 1905.

10561 —— The round tower of Kinneigh, co. Cork. [?built c. 1014.] *Same jnl.*, 57 (6th S. 17), pp. 67–68, + 2 plates. 1927.

10562 FitzGerald (*Lord* Walter). The round tower of Castledermot, [co. Kildare]. J. Roy. Soc. Antiq. Ireland, 22 (5th S. 2), pp. 66–69, + 4 plates. 1892.

10563 —— The round towers of the co. Kildare, their origin and use. [Castledermot, Old Kilcullen, Oughterard, Kildare, Taghadoe.] J. co. Kildare Archaeol. Soc., 1, pp. 71–94, + 5 plates. 1892.

10564 Getty (Edmund). Notices of the round towers of Ulster. [i. Introduction, theories ; ii. Drumbo, co. Down ; iii. Trummery, co. Antrim ; iv. Clones tower, co. Monaghan ; v. Downpatrick, co. Down ; Ram's Island, co. Antrim ; Nendrum, co. Down ; vi. Armoy tower, co. Antrim ; Devenish tower, co. Fermanagh ; vii. Drumlane tower, co. Cavan ; Iniskean tower, co. Monaghan ; Tory island, co. Donegal.] Ulster J. Archaeol., 3, pp. 14–32, 110–16, 292–300 ; 4, pp. 62–71, 128–39, 173–91 ; 5, pp. 110–22. 1855–57.

10565 Hitchcock (Richard). Notes on the round towers of the county of Kerry. Trans. Kilkenny Archaeol. Soc., 2 (1853), pp. 242–54, + plate. 1855.

10566 Jervise (A.). Remarks on the round tower of Brechin, [Angus]. [?built c. 1020 (Petrie).] Proc. Soc. Antiq. Scot., 3, pp. 28–35, + 1 plate. 1862.

10567 Kelly (Richard J.). Notes on the round tower of Kilbannon . . . co. Galway. J. Roy. Soc. Antiq. Ireland, 31 (5th S. 11), pp. 379–84. 1901.

10568 Kirker (Samuel Kerr). Armoy round tower, co. Antrim. *Same jnl.*, 29 (5th S. 9), pp. 121–25. 1899.

10569 Wakeman (William Frederick). Roscam round tower, near Galway. [3 figures in text.] *Same jnl.*, 25 (5th S. 5), pp. 284–86. 1895.

10570 Windele (John). The round tower of Ardmore [co. Waterford], and its siege in 1642. J. Kilkenny Archaeol. Soc., [4], N.S. 1, pp. 196–202. 1856.

184. SCULPTURE, GENERAL (Anglo-Saxon, Celtic and Viking)

10571 [Anon.] Ancient crosses. Ecclesiologist, 8, pp. 220–39. 1848.

10572 [Anon.] Recent discoveries of early Christian monuments. Illust. Archaeologist, 1, pp. 117–20. 1894.

10573 Allen (John Romilly) and **Browne** (George Forrest), *bp. of Bristol*. List of stones with interlaced ornament in England. [By county. With references.] J. Brit. Archaeol. Assoc., 41, pp. 351–58. 1885.

10574 Allen (John Romilly). Notes on interlaced crosses. *Same jnl.*, 34, pp. 352–59, + 2 plates. 1878.

10575 —— On recent discoveries of pre-Norman sculptured stones. [Rockland, Norfolk ; Colsterworth, Lincs. ; Bexhill, Sussex.] *Same jnl.*, 41, pp. 267–77, + 2 plates. 1885.

10576 —— On some points of resemblance between the art of the early sculptured stones of Scotland and of Ireland. [7 figures in text.] Proc. Soc. Antiq. Scot., 31 (3rd S. 7), pp. 309–32. 1897.

10577 —— On the antiquity of fonts in Great Britain. [Pp. 169–71, 172–73, fonts with Celtic and Saxon forms of ornament : fonts made from Roman and Saxon materials.] J. Brit. Archaeol. Assoc., 44, pp. 164–73, + 2 plates. 1888.

10578 Allen (W. Bird). Some early crosses. [Relics of Saxon sun worship.] Arch. Camb., 76 (7th S. 1), pp. 306–07. 1921.

10579 Black (William George). Hogbacked monuments. Scots lore, 1, pp. 106–08. 1895.

10580 Brown (Stephen J.). The high crosses of Great Britain and Ireland, with special reference to a collection of books. [Sculptured and otherwise. Bibliography, with comments.] Irish Eccles. Rec., 5th S. 78, pp. 285–88 : 79, pp. 271–75 : 80, pp. 225–29. 1952–53.

10581 Browne (George Forrest), *bp. of Bristol*. Disney lectures, 1888. The sculptured stones of pre-Norman type in the British Isles. 26 large 4° plates (with 8° syllabuses). 4° Cambridge, 1888. [In library of the Society of Antiquaries.]

10582 —— On basket-work figures of men represented on sculptured stones. Archaeologia, 50, pp. 287–94, + 1 plate. 1887.

10583 —— On sculptured 'memorials of the dead' of pre-Norman type,—(1) coped stones, (2) flat stones, (3) standing stones, (4) pillars, (5) crosses. Assoc. Archit. Socs.' Rpts., 18, pp. 122–29. 1886.

10584 —— On the early lapidary art and the inscriptions of the English, the Irish, and the Caledonians. [Report of a lecture.] J. Brit. Archaeol. Assoc., N.S. 23, pp. 141–42. 1917.

10585 Casson (Stanley). Byzantinism. [Claiming Langford and Romsey roods, Chichester reliefs and Bradford-on-Avon angels to be A.-S. work : disputed by Sir Eric Maclagan, p. 325 : S. Casson's reply, pp. 325–26.] Burl. Mag., 59, pp. 208–13, 1 plate. 1931.

10586 —— Byzantium and Anglo-Saxon sculpture. [Argument for earlier date of Romsey rood, Chichester reliefs, etc., owing to Byzantine connexions.] Burl. Mag., 61, pp. 265–74 : 62, pp. 26–36, 5 plates. 1932–33.

10587 —— Late Anglo-Saxon sculpture. Am. Mag. of Art, 28, pp. 327–35. 1935.

10588 Chambers (John David). On ancient crosses. Ecclesiologist, 9, pp. 85–101. 1849.

10589 Clapham (*Sir* Alfred William). Some disputed examples of pre-Conquest sculpture. [i. Reculver cross-shaft : ii.

Romsey rood : iii. Langford (Oxon.) draped rood : iv. Barnack Majesty : v. Daglingworth (Glos.) figures]. Antiquity, 25, pp. 191–95, + 6 plates. 1951.

10590 Clapham (*Sir* Alfred William). Three carved stones in the collection of the Society [of Antiquaries]. [Danish influence, early 11th c.] Antiq. J., 11, pp. 133–35, + 2 plates. 1931.

10591 Collingwood (William Gershom). The dispersion of the wheel-cross. [Sketch-map on p. 325.] Yorks. Archaeol. J., 28, pp. 322–31. 1926.

10592 —— On some ancient sculptures of the devil bound. [8 figures in text.] Trans. Cumb. and Westm. Antiq. Soc., N.S. 3, pp. 380–89. 1903.

10593 —— A pedigree of Anglian crosses. Antiquity, 6, pp. 35–54 : illustrated. 1932.

10594 —— Some illustrations of the archaeology of the Viking age in England. [31 figures of sculpture in text.] Saga-Book V.C., 5, pp. 108–41. 1907.

10595 Cottrill (Frank). A study of Anglo-Saxon stone sculpture in central and southern England. *M.A. Thesis, London.* 1931. [Apply Univ. Library.]

10596 Dobson (Dina Portway). Primitive figures on churches. [Sheela-na-gigs at Fiddington, Somerset and Abson, Glos. : at Oaksey, Wilts. and Ampney St. Peter, Glos.] Man, 30, pp. 10–11 : 31, pp. 3–4. 1930–31.

10597 Ellis *afterwards* **Davidson** (Hilda Roderick). Gods and heroes in stone. Chadwick Mem. Stud., pp. 121–39. 1950.

10598 —— Sigurd in the art of the Viking age. [Manx, Halton (Lancs.) : early 11th c., etc.] Antiquity, 16, pp. 216–36. 1942.

10599 —— The story of Sigurd in Viking art. J. Manx Mus., 5, pp. 87–90. + 2 plates. 1942.

10600 French (Gilbert). On the ancient sculptured stones of Scotland, Ireland, and the Isle of Man. J. Brit. Archaeol. Assoc., 15, pp. 63–80, + 8 plates. 1859.

10601 Gardner (Arthur). English medieval sculpture. pp. viii, 352. 8° Cambridge, 1951. [683 figures in text. (2nd edition of Handbook of English medieval sculpture, 1935.) Pp. 21–51, and figures 23–80, A.–S. i. Anglian crosses : ii. Mercian School : iii. Wessex sculpture.]

10602 —— Saxon crosses. Proc. Harrow Archit. Club, 1935, pp. 11–14. 1935.

10603 Hencken (Hugh O'Neill). A gaming board of the Viking age. [Found at Ballinderry, co. Westmeath, and now in Nat. Mus. of Ireland. Made in Isle of Man, 3rd quarter of 10th c.] Acta Archaeol., 4, pp. 85–104, + 1 plate. 1933.

10604 Innocent (Charles Frederick). Romano-British precedents for some English romanesque details. J.R.I.B.A., 3rd S. 15, pp. 649–50. 1908.

10605 Kendrick (*Sir* Thomas Downing). Instances of Saxon survival in post-Conquest sculpture. Proc. Camb. Antiq. Soc., 39, pp. 78–84, + 5 plates. 1940.

10606 March (Henry Colley). The pagan-Christian overlap in the north. [i. The Sigurd overlap : ii. The wise-bird overlap : iii. Mr. Lees on the Heysham hog-back : iv. The doomsday overlap : v. The renunciation overlap. Plates of Halton cross, Lancaster, Heysham hog-back, etc.] Trans. Lancs. and Ches. Antiq. Soc., 9 (1891), pp. 49–89, + 12 plates. 1892.

10607 —— Rending the wolf's jaw. [Fig. 1, on Gosforth cross.] *Same jnl.*, 11 (1893), pp. 113–17, + 8 plates. 1894.

10608 Murray (Margaret Alice). Female fertility figures. [Sheela-na-gigs.] J.R.A.I., 64, pp. 93–100, + 5 plates. 1934.

10609 Ó Riordáin (Seán Pádraig). The genesis of the Celtic cross. Essays presented to . . . Torna, pp. 108–14, + 5 plates. 1947.

10610 Richard (Arthur J.). The early Christian monuments of the British Isles. Trans. Aberafan Hist. Soc., 4, pp. 41–45. 1932.

10611 Robinson (John L.). Celtic remains in England. [i.e. sculptured crosses in England with Celtic designs.] J. Roy. Soc. Antiq. Ireland, 20 (5th S. 1), pp. 31–35, + 4 plates. 1890.

10612 Roosval (Johnny). Swedish and English fonts. [2 plates, included in pagination : 17 figures in text.] Burl. Mag, 32, pp. 85–94. 1918.

10613 Seaver (Esther Isabel). Some examples of Viking figure representation in Scandinavia and the British Isles. [29 figures in text.] Porter (A. K.) : Medieval Studies, 2, pp. 589–610. 1939.

10614 Shetelig (Haakon). Queen Asa's sculptors. Wood carvings found in the Oseberg-ship, Norway. [21 figures (photos) in text. Viking ' background '.] Saga-Book V.C., 10, pp. 12–56. 1928.

10615 Underwood (Eric Gordon). A short history of English sculpture. pp. xiv, 192, + 48 plates. 8° London, 1933. [Pp. 11–21, + plates 2–4, A.–S.]

10616 Walker (J. Russell). Notes on a peculiar class of recumbent monuments. [Hogbacks. 12 whole-pages of figures in text. 9th–12th c.] Proc. Soc. Antiq. Scot., 19 (N.S. 7), pp. 406–24. 1885.

10617 Wall (James Charles). Hogback stones. [Map, + 11 figures in text.] J. Antiq. Assoc. Brit. Isles, 1, pp. 41–52. 1930.

185. SCULPTURE, EAST ANGLIA

10618 Allen (John Romilly). Early Christian art [in Norfolk]. V.C.H., Norfolk, 2, pp. 555–63, + 6 plates. 1906.

10619 Bale (J. E.). On the Norman font in the church of All Saints, Toftrees, Norfolk. [Anglo-Celtic design]. Archaeol. J., 47, pp. 160–63, + 1 plate. 1890.

10620 Benton (Gerald Montague). Early sepulchral monuments in Stapleford church, Cambs. [11th c.] Antiquary, 46, pp. 229–30. 1910.

10621 Brown (George Forrest) *bp. of Bristol*. On a supposed Saxon altar-slab at St. Benet's, Cambridge. [The cutting of five crosses on altar-slabs.] Antiquary, 21, pp. 2–4, *also* pp. 75–78 (discussion). 1890.

10622 Burrell (H. J. E.). Pre-Conquest tomb-slab from Balsham, Cambs. Antiq. J., 11, pp. 423–24. 1931.

10623 Cobb (F. W.). A cross in a strange place. [Part of Saxon cross found in the foundations of ' The Close ', Saffron Walden, Essex.] Architects' J., 81, p. 18. 1935.

10624 Cobbett (Louis). Saxon carving found at Ely. Antiq. J., 14, pp. 62–63. 1934.

10625 Cogswell (Thomas Smith). On some ancient stone fragments found in Cringleford church [near Norwich]. Norfolk Archaeology, 14, pp. 99–102, + 2 plates. 1901.

10626 Collingwood (William Gershom). The Whissonsett cross, [Norfolk]. [6 figures in text.] *Same jnl.*, 15, pp. 316–23, + 2 plates. 1904.

10627 Fox (*Sir* Cyril). Anglo-Saxon monumental sculpture in the Cambridge district. Proc. Camb. Antiq. Soc., 23, pp. 15–45, + 8 plates. 1922.

10628 —— Saxon grave-slab at Balsham, Cambridgeshire. *Same jnl.*, 32, p. 51 + plate. 1932.

10629 Hill (H. Copinger). Great Ashfield cross. Proc. Suffolk Inst. Archaeol., 20, pp. 280–86, + 1 plate. 1930.

10630 —— Kedington cross. [c. 900]. *Same jnl.*, 20, pp. 287–89, + 1 plate. 1930.

10631 Morley (Claude). Suffolk ' Dane stones '. [Halesworth and Hunston.] *Same jnl.*, 17, pp. 93–96, + 2 plates. 1920.

10632 Sperling (C. F. D.). Discovery of a portion of a pre-Norman stone coffin-lid at Great Maplestead. Trans. Essex Archaeol. Soc., N.S. 16, pp. 139–40. 1923.

10633 Turnbull (W. H.). St. Peter and Paul, Kedington : a notable church in East Anglia. [West Suffolk. Pp. 296–98, and figure on p. 299, Saxon cross on east-end gable.] J. Brit. Archaeol. Assoc., N.S. 36 (1930), pp. 291–317. 1931.

186. SCULPTURE, KENT AND SUSSEX

10634 Birch (Walter de Gray). The ancient sculptures in the south aisle of the choir of Chichester cathedral. J. Brit. Archaeol. Assoc., 42, pp. 255–62, + 1 plate. 1886.

10635 Curwen (Eliot Cecil). The Steyning grave slab. [11th c. carving ?] Sussex N. and Q., 8, pp. 169–70, + 1 plate. 1941.

10636 Dowker (George). On the cross and platform at Richborough. [Platform Roman : cross probably A.–S.] Arch. Cant., 24, pp. 201–19, + 2 plans. 1900.

10637 Johnston (Philip Mainwaring). A pre-Conquest coffin-slab from Arundel castle. Sussex Archaeol. Collns., 47, pp. 148–50. 1904.

10638 —— A pre-Conquest grave-slab at Bexhill. *Same jnl.*, 48, pp. 153–55, + 1 plate. 1905.

10638a Martin-Clarke (*Mrs.* Daisy Elizabeth). The Reculver cross. [Letter on fragments now in Canterbury cathedral crypt.] Archaeol. News Letter, 2, p. 123. 1950.

10639 Potts (Robert Ullock). A Saxon burial cross found in St. Austin's abbey [Canterbury]. Arch. Cant., 37, pp. 211–13 + plate. 1925.

187. SCULPTURE, MERCIA
§ a. Cheshire

10640 Allen (John Romilly). The early Christian monuments of Lancashire and Cheshire. Trans. Hist Soc. Lancs. and Ches., 45 (1893), pp. 1–32a, + 18 plates. 1894. *Same title.* [63 figures in text.] J. Archit. and Hist. Soc. of Chester, N.S. 5, pp. 133–74, + 6 plates. 1895.

10641 Browne (George Forrest) *bp. of Bristol.* Brief precis of the description of the early sculptured stones of Cheshire. Archaeol. J., 44, pp. 146–56. 1887.

10642 —— The Sandbach crosses. [11 pages of figures in text.] Arch. Camb., 6th S. 10, pp. 283–304 : *also* pp. 184–85, + 2 plates. 1910.

10643 Cox (E. W.). Fragment of a Saxon cross found at West Kirby. J. Archit. and Hist. Soc. of Chester, N.S. 5, p. 108. 1895.

10644 Croston (James). Anglo-Saxon cross discovered in Prestbury church. Palatine Note-bk., 4, pp. 1–7, + 1 plate. 1884.

10645 —— On an Anglo-Saxon cross, at Prestbury. Reliquary, 25, pp. 1–9, + 1 plate. 1884.

10646 Ditchfield (Peter Hampson). The Sandbach crosses. J. Brit. Archaeol. Assoc., N.S. 32, pp. 72–75. 1926.

10647 Earwaker (John Parsons). The history of . . . Sandbach, *etc.* pp. xiv, 316, + 7 plates. 4° *n.p.*, 1890. [Pp. 11–15, + 3 plates (the crosses).]

10648 Egerton (Ethel). The Saxon crosses, Sandbach. 8° Sandbach, 1930.

10649 Harper (W. J.). The ancient crosses at Sandbach. 8° Tunstall, c. 1890. *Same title.* [9 figures in text.] Cheshire N. and Q., N. [3rd] S. 6, pp. 16–26. 1901.

10650 Heywood (Nathan). The crosses at Sandbach. [For a plate showing detail of their ornament, *see* J. Chester and N. Wales Archit. Soc., 32, opp., p. 75, 1938]. Trans. Lancs. and Ches. Antiq. Soc., 29 (1911), pp. 44–52, + 1 plate. 1912.

10651 Hume (Abraham). The Hilbre cross. [1 figure in text.] Trans. Hist. Soc. Lancs. and Ches., 15 (N.S. 3), pp. 232–33. 1863.

10652 Kendrick (*Sir* Thomas Downing). Two Saxon sculptures from Cheshire. [2 grave-stones, of red sandstone, probably from Chester, c. 950.] B.M.Q., 14, pp. 35–36, + plates 11–12. 1940.

10653 Moorhouse (Frederick). [On three pre-Norman circular pillar crosses, now in Macclesfield park]. Trans. Lancs. and Ches. Antiq. Soc., 32 (1914), pp. 264–68, + 1 plate. 1915.

10654 P. (H.). Sandbach crosses : their history and description. Cheshire N. and Q., 7 (N.S. 2), pp. 100–02. 1887.

10655 Phelps (Joseph James). Pre-Norman cross at Cheadle. Trans. Lancs. and Ches. Antiq. Soc., 37 (1919), pp. 95–109, + 1 plate. 1921.

10656 Smith (Henry Ecroyd). Archaeology in the Mersey district, . . . in 1874 : Anglo-Saxon and mediaeval sculptures at Neston. Trans. Hist. Soc. Lancs. and Ches., 3rd S. 3 [=27], pp. 88–94. 1875.

10657 Tait (A. C. F.). The Sandbach crosses. [c. 850. 8 figures in text.] *Same jnl.*, 98 (1946), pp. 1–20, + 1 plate. 1948.

10658 Taylor (Henry). [Crosses at St. John's church and at Grosvenor museum, Chester.] Arch. Camb., 5th S. 8, pp. 113–15, 119–20, + 2 plates. 1891.

10659 Yates (O. V.). Sandbach crosses. Cheshire N. and Q., N. [3rd] S. 3, pp. 133–35. 1898.

§ *b.* Derbyshire

10660 Allen (John Romilly). Early Christian art [in Derbyshire]. [1 plate paginated in text.] V. C. H., Derbyshire, 1, pp. 279–92. 1905.

10661 —— Notes on two pre-Norman cross shafts found at Norbury in 1902. J. Derbs. Archaeol. Soc., 25, pp. 97–102, + 3 plates. 1903.

10662 Andrew (W. J.). The Shall cross : a pre-Norman cross, now at Fernilee hall. *Same jnl.*, 27, pp. 201–14, + 1 plate. 1905.

10663 Bateman (Thomas). Notes on Saxon remains, from Bakewell church. J. Brit. Archaeol. Assoc., 2, pp. 303–05. 1847.

10664 Brown (C. E.) *photographer.* Restored cross-shaft at Bradbourne. J. Derbs. Archaeol. Soc., 67, p. 120, + 1 plate. 1947.

10665 Brown (George Forrest) *bp. of Bristol*. Bradbourne cross. Archaeol. J., 45, pp. 7–11, + 1 plate. 1888.

10666 —— The font at Wilne, near Draycott. Assoc. Archit. Socs.' Rpts., 21, pp. 7–10, + 1 plate. 1891.

10667 —— On the pre-Norman sculptured stones of Derbyshire. J. Derbs. Archaeol. Soc., 8, pp. 164–84, + 4 plates. 1886.

10668 Collingwood (William Gershom). The Brailsford cross. [Illustrated.] *Same jnl.*, 45, pp. 1–13. 1923.

10669 Hanbury (W. H.). A pre-Norman carved stone at Darley. *Same jnl.*, 71, pp. 84–86, + 2 plates. 1951.

10670 Haslam (Victor A.) *photographer*. Two pre-Norman cross-shafts found at Norbury. Reliquary, 9, pp, 128–30. 1903.

10671 Lynam (Charles). Some pre-Norman crosses in Derbyshire. J. Brit. Archaeol. Assoc., 56 (N.S. 6), pp. 305–14, + 3 plates. 1900.

10672 Routh (Theodore E.). A corpus of the pre-Conquest carved stones of Derbyshire, with introduction [pp. 1–3] by W. G. Clark-Maxwell. Archaeol. J., 94 (1937), pp. 1–42, + 21 plates. 1938. *Same title.* J. Derbs. Archaeol. Soc., N.S. 11 (1937), pp. 1–46, + 22 plates. 1938.

10673 Smith (G. Le Blanc). Notes on pre-Norman crosses in Derbyshire. [Hope ; Blackwell ; St. Alkmund's, Derby, now in the Derby Museum. With 11 figures in text.] Reliquary, 11, pp. 95–110. 1905.

10674 —— Notes on some Derbyshire fonts. 1.—The Saxon font at Wilne. Antiquary, 39, pp. 81–83. 1903.

10675 —— Three pre-Norman crosses in Derbyshire. [Bakewell, Eyam and Bradbourne. With 9 figures in text.] Reliquary, 10, pp. 194–204. 1904.

10676 Steventon (William). Blackwell, and its sculptured cross. J. Derbs. Archaeol. Soc., 39, pp. 75–80. 1917.

10677 Tudor (Thomas L.). Ancient cross-head discovered at Rowsley. *Same jnl.*, N.S. 6 (1932), pp. 98–99, + 1 plate : N.S. 7 (1933), pp. 7–11, + frontispiece. 1933–34.

10678 —— Pre-Norman cross-shaft in Two Dales, Darley Dale. *Same jnl.*, N.S. 10 (1936), pp. 105–12, + 2 plates. 1937.

10679 Walker (John Holland). The Stapleford cross shaft. [He dates to reign of Canute. Discursive.] Trans. Thoroton Soc., 49 (1945), pp. 1–11, + 6 plates [4 being of Bewcastle cross]. 1946.

10680 Walton (W. H.). The Burbage cross-shaft. J. Derbs. Archaeol. Soc., N.S. 6 (1932), pp. 99–100, + 1 plate. 1933.

10681 Ward (John). Pre-Norman tombstone of Bakewell. [Its removal to the Weston Park Museum at Sheffield.] Notts. and Derbs., N. and Q., 2, pp. 59–60, 88–89. 1894.

§ *c*. Gloucestershire

10682 [Anon.] Carved stone in South Cerney church. [Late pre-Conquest Christ in majesty, etc.] Antiq. J., 15, pp. 203–04, + plate. 1935.

10683 Allen (John Romilly). Pre-Norman cross-shaft recently found at Newent. Reliquary, N. [3rd] S. 13, pp. 197–200. 1907.

10684 Baddeley (Welbore St. Clair). The Lypiatt cross. Trans. Bristol and Glos. Arch. Soc., 51, pp. 103–07, + 2 plates. 1929.

10685 Clifford (*Mrs.* Brookes). An Anglian cross in Gloucestershire. [Lypiatt.] Antiq. J., 13, pp. 301–02, + 1 plate. 1933.

10686 Conder (Edward). Discovery of a very early sculptured stone tablet [at] St. Mary's church, Newent. [2 photos in text.] Proc. Soc., Antiq., 2nd S. 24, pp. 323–26. 1912.

10687 —— A pre-Norman cross shaft found at Newent. *Same jnl.*, 2nd S. 21, pp. 478–79, + 2 plates. 1907.

10688 Dobson (Dina Portway). A Saxon stone from Berkeley castle. Antiq. J., 16, pp. 100–01. 1936.

10689 Hudd (Alfred Edmund). On the Saxon baptismal font in Deerhurst priory church, with notes upon other early fonts. Trans. Bristol and Glos. Arch. Soc., 11, pp. 84–104, + plate. 1887.

10690 Smith (Reginald Allender). Four sculptures of the Viking period from Bibury. [13 figures in text.] Proc. Soc. Antiq., 2nd S. 26, pp. 60–72. 1914.

§ *d*. **Leicestershire**

10691 Clapham (*Sir* Alfred William). The carved stones at Breedon on the Hill, and their position in the history of English art. Archaeologia, 77, pp. 219–40, + 11 plates, 1928. *Same title.* Trans. Leic. Archaeol. Soc., 15, pp. 309–32, + 21 plates. 1928.

10692 Irvine (James Thomas). On an early Celtic sepulchral slab [at Hickling church, near Melton Mowbray]. [?A.S.] J. Brit. Archaeol. Assoc., 46, pp. 71–72. 1890.

10693 Rix (Michael M.). The treasures of Breedon church. [5 photographs of A.–S. sculpture in text.] Derbs. countryside, 18, pp. 78–80. 1950.

10694 Routh (Theodore E.). The church of Breedon-on-the-hill. Trans. Thoroton Soc., 32 (1928), pp. 1–16, + 6 plates. 1929.

10695 —— The Rothley cross-shaft and the Sproxton cross. Trans. Leic. Archaeol. Soc., 20, pp. 65–76, + 6 plates. 1938.

§ *e*. **Lincolnshire**

10696 Allen (John Romilly). Early Norman sculpture at Lincoln and Southwell [Notts.]. [Dates to c. 1075.] J. Brit. Archaeol. Assoc., 48, pp. 292–99. 1892.

10697 Davies (D. S.). Ancient stone crosses in Kesteven. [Including 14 of A.S. period.] Lincs. N. and Q., 12, pp. 129–50, + 2 plates. 1913.

10698 Davies (D. S.). Ancient stone crosses in Lindsey and Holland. *Same jnl.*, 13, pp. 129–57, 161–180, 212–23, 225–29, + 6 plates. 1915.

10699 —— Conisholme stone. [? 10th c. cross-head.] *Same jnl.*, 9, pp. 1–2, + 1 plate. 1926.

10700 —— Pre-Conquest carved stones in Lincolnshire. With an introduction by A. W. Clapham. [P. 6, map showing A.–S. sites : 4 figures in text.] Archaeol. J., 83, pp. 1–20, + 8 plates. 1926.

10701 —— Saxon stones and stone crosses in Lincolnshire. Ann. Rpt. Rutland Archaeol. Soc., 12 (1914), pp. 50–63. 1915.

10702 —— Stone crosses (Additional stone crosses). [Crowle, *etc.*] Lincs. N. and Q., 13, pp. 180–81 : 14, pp. 21–31, 55–64. 1915–17.

10703 Dodds (George). Observations on the [shaft of a runic cross used as the] lintel of a doorway at Crowle church. [Plate 1, the lintel, plate 2, runes, ?early 11th c.] Reliquary, 10, pp. 1–8, + 2 plates. 1869.

10704 Fowler (Joseph Thomas). Discovery of a shaft of a stone cross, with a runic inscription at Crowle church [St. Oswald's]. [3 figures in text.] Proc. Soc. Antiq., 2nd S. 4, pp. 187–190, 378–79. 1868–69.

10705 —— Early sculptured stones [in Lincolnshire]. [List of eleven.] Lincs. N. and Q., 5, pp. 3–4. 1898.

10706 —— Notes on an ancient doorhead [at South Ferriby.] [?1020–1150]. Proc. Soc. Antiq., 2nd S. 8, pp 26–28, + 1 plate, 1879.

10707 Hunt (Alfred). Celtic cross at Digby. [Late 7th c.] Lincs. N. and Q., 20, p. 81, + 1 plate. 1929.

10708 Penny (James A.). Sepulchral stones at Miningsby, etc. [Interlaced sculpture.] *Same jnl.*, 4, pp. 225–28, + 1 plate. 1896.

10709 Sympson (Edward Mansel). Pre-Norman stone at St. Michael's church, Cammeringham. *Same jnl.*, 12, p. 225, + plate. 1913.

10710 Tempest (E. B.). Pre-Conquest stones. [Plate shows : ' carved stone found at Coleby Hall, 1879.'] *Same jnl.*, 5, pp. 113–14, + 1 plate. 1898.

10711 Trollope (Edward). The Norman sculpture of Lincoln cathedral. [' Gough, Wild and even Cockerell, deemed them to be Saxon,'—but later : compared with ' Saxon ' sculpture of Chichester—which also probably later.] Archaeol. J., 25, pp. 1–20, + 6 plates. 1868. *Same title.* Assoc. Archit. Socs.' Rpts., 8, pp. 279–93, + 4 plates. 1866.

§ f. Northamptonshire

10712 Allen (John Romilly). Early Christian art and inscriptions [in Northamptonshire]. V.C.H., Northampton, 2, pp. 187–99, + 4 plates. 1906.

10713 —— Early Christian sculpture in Northamptonshire. Assoc. Archit. Socs'. Repts., 19, pp. 398–423, + 4 plates. 1888.

10714 Clapham (*Sir* Alfred William). A figure of Christ in majesty at Barnack. Antiq. J., 13, p. 468, + 1 plate. 1933.

10715 Crawley (M.). Early crosses. [Stow-Nine-Churches.] Northants. N. and Q., 2, p. 223. 1888.

10716 Irvine (James Thomas). [On] various fragments of Saxon work found in the immediate neighbourhood of Peterborough. J. Brit. Archaeol. Assoc., 45, pp. 179–80, + 2 plates. 1889.

10717 K. The stone crosses of Northamptonshire. [Criticism of paper by C. A. Markham, **10719.**] Northants. N. and Q., 6, pp. 233–36. 1896.

10718 Markham (Christopher A.). Anglo-Saxon cross, Sudborough. *Same jnl.*, N.S. 1, pp. 23–24, + 1 plate. 1905.

10719 —— The stone crosses of the county of Northampton. [Including a few A.-S. : Barnack, Nassington, St. Peter's, Northampton, etc.] Assoc. Archit. Socs'. Rpts., 23, pp. 157–93, + 3 [not A.-S.] plates. 1895.

10720 Tom (E. N.). St. Peter's church, Northampton. [1st and 3rd plates give drawings of A.-S. sculpture.] Northants. N. and Q., 4, pp. 1–8, + 3 plates. 1892.

§ g. Staffordshire

10721 Auden (George Augustus). Pre-Conquest cross at Rolleston. Reliquary, N. [3rd] S. 14, pp. 47–49. 1908.

10722 Baylay (Atwell Mervyn Yates). Rolleston. [Plate 3 is ' fragments of Celtic cross '] Trans. Thoroton Soc., 17 (1913), pp. 49–53, + 4 plates. 1914.

10723 Browne (George Forrest) *bp. of Bristol*. An account of three ancient cross shafts, and the font, St. Bertram's, Ilam. pp. 32. 8° London, 1888.

10724 —— Notes on pre-Norman carved stone recently found at Leek. North Staffs. F.C., Trans., 32, p. 125. 1898.

10725 Jeavons (Sidney A.). Anglo-Saxon cross-shafts in Staffordshire. Trans. B'ham Archaeol. Soc., 66 (1945–46), pp. 110–22, + 7 plates. 1950.

10726 Keyser (Charles Edward). Notes on a sculptured tympanum at Kingswinford church, and other early representations in England of St. Michael the archangel. [?pre-Norman or early Norman.] Archaeol. J., 62, pp. 137–46, + 1 plate. 1905.

10727 Levien (Edward), **Hills** (Gordon M.), *etc.* [Wolverhampton pillar]. [?Saxon or Norman.] J. Brit. Archaeol. Assoc., 29, pp. 105–07, + 1 plate. 1873.

10728 Lynam (Charles). The ancient churchyard-crosses of Staffordshire. *Same jnl.*, 33, pp. 432–40, + 3 plates. 1877.

10729 —— Part of a pre-Norman sculptured cross-shaft found at Leek. [2 figures in text.] Proc. Soc. Antiq., 2nd S. 16, pp. 289–94. 1897.

10730 —— Pre-Norman carved stone, lately found at Leek. North Staffs. F.C., Trans., 31, pp. 155–58, + 2 plates [photos]. 1897.

10731 Pape (T.). The round-shafted (The rectangular-shafted) pre-Norman crosses of north Staffordshire. Trans. N. Staffs. F.C., 80, pp. 25–49, + 5 plates : 81, pp. 20–51, + 6 plates. 1946–47.

10732 Smith (G. Le Blanc). Some Norman and pre-Norman remains in the Dove-dale district. [Alstonefield, Ilam, etc. With 12 figures in text, 10 of crosses, 2 of fonts.] Reliquary, 10, pp. 232–47. 1904.

10733 —— Some pre-Norman crosses in Staffordshire. [Checkley, Leek, etc. With 10 figures in text.] Reliquary, 12, pp. 229–46. 1906.

10734 Steele (H. J.). A photographic survey of the pre-Conquest crosses of Staffordshire : with an account of the Wolverhampton pillar. Trans. N. Staffs. F.C., 82, pp. 116–25, + 4 plates. 1948.

§ *h*. **Other Counties**

10735 Allen (John Romilly). Early Christian art [in Worcestershire]. V.C.H. Worcs., 2, pp. 183–95, + 4 plates. 1906.

10736 Bailey (George). Tympanum at Elstow [Beds.]. [Late 10th c. or early 11th c. With figure.] Antiquary, 23, pp. 69–70. 1891.

10737 Bede (Cuthbert) *pseud*, [= Edward Bradley]. Early crosses. [Stretton, Rutland.] Northants. N. and Q., 2, p. 189. *See also* p. 148. 1888.

10738 Brown (Gerard Baldwin). The Lechmere stone. [In house of Sir E. Lechmere, near Hanley Castle, Worcs.] Antiq. J., 11, pp. 226–28, + 1 plate. 1931.

10739 Browne (George Forrest) *bp. of Bristol.* ' Scandinavian ' or ' Danish ' sculptured stones found in London ; and their bearing on the supposed ' Scandinavian ' or ' Danish ' origin of other English sculptured stones. Archaeol. J., 42, pp. 251–59, + 2 plates. 1885.

10740 Chafy (William Kyle Westwood). A carved stone of the Saxon period lately found built into the wall of Rous Lench church, Worcestershire. [2 figures (photos) on p. 260]. Proc. Soc. Antiq., 2nd S. 17, pp. 259–61. 1898.

10741 Cottrill (Frank). A pre-Norman cross-shaft at Rugby [Warw.]. Antiq. J., 15, p. 475, + 2 plates. 1935.

10742 Crowther-Beynon (Vernon Bryan). Saxon cross shaft, Normanton, Rutland. Reliquary, N. [3rd] S. 15, p. 137. 1909.

10743 Dale (Thomas Lawrence). Langford church [Oxon.]. [Plates show A.-S. crucifix : c. 900.] Oxfordshire Archaeol. Soc. Rpt., 80 (1934), p. 62, + 2 plates. 1934.

10744 Guest (Edith M.). A sculptured stone in Burford church. [Sole survival from its Saxon church?] Antiq. J., 10, pp. 159–60. 1930.

10745 Hill (A. du Boulay). East Bridgford church [Notts.]. [Pp. 51–52, Saxon church, pp. 54–55, Saxon cross, with 2 figures.] Trans. Thoroton Soc., 19 (1915), pp. 47–55, + 4 plates. 1916.

10746 —— Pre-Norman churches and sepulchral monuments of Nottinghamshire. [5 figures in text.] Archaeol. J., 73, pp. 195–206, + 4 plates. 1916.

10747 Kendrick (*Sir* Thomas Downing) and **Radford** (Courtenay Arthur Ralegh). Recent discoveries at All Hallows, Barking. [Early 11th c. cross : also blocked Saxon archway.] Antiq. J., 23, pp. 14–18, + 3 plates. 1943.

10748 Knowles (James T.) *junr.* Sculptured stone found . . . on the south side of St. Paul's Churchyard, bearing, beside a rude sculptured figure, a runic inscription. [' Ina let to lay this stone.' 2 figures in text.] Proc. Soc. Antiq., 2, pp. 284–85. 1853.

10749 Martin (R. R.). The Sheela-na-gig at Oxford. Man, 29, pp. 134–35. 1929.

10750 Mason (W. H.). Discovery of a Saxon grave-cover [at Coates, Notts.]. Trans. Thoroton Soc., 8 (1904), pp. 63–65, + 1 plate. 1905.

10751 Peers (*Sir* Charles Reed). Notes on a [Saxon] bronze casting, probably part of the cover of a censer, found at Pershore in the eighteenth century. [5 figures in text.] Proc. Soc. Antiq., 2nd S. 21, pp. 52–59. 1906.

10752 Rice (David Talbot). The Gloucester Christ. [Late Saxon.] Trans. Bristol and Glos. Arch. Soc., 71 (1952), pp. 98–100, + 1 plate. 1953.

10753 Smith (Worthington George). Two incised stones [from Stanbridge and Milton Bryan, Beds.]. Proc. Soc. Antiq., 2nd S. 20, pp. 354–56. 1905.

10754 Standish (John). Shelford [Notts.]. [Plate opposite p. 42 shows 3 figures of pre-Norman cross.] Trans. Thoroton Soc., 7, pp. 38–62, + 4 plates, + plan. 1904.

10755 Stevenson (W.). Discovery of a Saxon inscribed and ornamented cross-shaft at Rolleston, Notts. Reliquary, 3, pp. 181–82. 1897.

10756 Watkins (Alfred). Tenth century crucifixion and emblem stones at Llanveyno, [Herefordshire]. [With remains of Hiberno-Saxon inscription.] Trans. Woolhope N.F.C., 1927–29, pp. 204–06, + 1 plate. 1931.

10757 Weir (W.). Fragments of a pillar piscina, found in the church of North Stoke, Oxon. ['Possibly of Saxon workmanship.' Figure in text.] Proc. Soc. Antiq., 2nd S. 19, pp. 224–26. 1903.

188. SCULPTURE, NORTHUMBRIA

§ a. General

10758 Collingwood (William Gershom). Northumbrian crosses of the pre-Norman age. pp. 196. 4° London, 1921. [227 figures in text.]

10759 —— On a group of Northumbrian crosses. [With page of 22 figures.] Antiquary, 49, pp. 167–72. 1913.

10760 Howorth (Sir Henry Hoyle). The great crosses of the seventh century in northern England. Archaeol. J., 71, pp. 45–64. 1914.

10761 Kendrick (Sir Thomas Downing). Late Saxon sculpture in northern England. J. Brit. Archaeol. Assoc., 3rd S. 6, pp. 1–19, + 8 plates. 1941.

10762 Stephens (George). Prof. S. Bugge's studies in northern mythology. [Pp. 348–400, The Ruthwell cross : art-motives in England : Caedmon's devil : pp. 7–45, Gosforth cross.] Mém. Soc. roy. Antiq. Nord, 1878–83, pp. 289–414 : 1884–89, pp. 1–56. 1883–89.

10763 Stone (J. M.). The runic crosses of Northumbria. Stone (J. M.); Studies from court and cloister : essays : pp. 207–222, + 1 plate. 1905.

§ b. Bewcastle and Ruthwell Crosses

(*See also* **164**, § c i. for inscriptions)

10764 [Anon.] The Ruthwell cross. [Description.] Reliquary, N [2nd] S. 2, pp. 85–88. 1888.

10765 Barbour (James). Regarding the origin of the Ruthwell cross. [Geological origin.] Trans. Dumfries. Antiq. Soc., 16 (1899–1900), pp. 28–31. 1900.

10766 Brandl (Alois). Zur Zeitbestimmung des Kreuzes von Ruthwell. Arch. Stud. neueren Spr., Bd. 136, pp. 150–51. 1917.

10767 Brown (Gerard Baldwin) and **Lethaby** (William Richard). The Bewcastle and Ruthwell crosses. Burl. Mag., 23, pp. 43–49. 1913.

10768 Brown (Gerard Baldwin) *etc*. Report on the Ruthwell cross. With some references to that at Bewcastle in Cumberland. [Sculpture and inscription.] Roy. Commission on hist. mon., Dumfries, pp. 219–86, + 11 plates. 1920.

10769 Browne (George Forrest) *bp. of Bristol*. The ancient cross shafts at Bewcastle and Ruthwell. Enlarged from the Rede lecture . . . 1916. pp. x, 92, + 3 plates. 4° Cambridge, 1916.

10770 —— The ivory chair of archbishop Maximianus at Ravenna. ['Examples of ornamentation from which the vine-scrolls might have been directly copied for the shafts of Anglian crosses at Rothwell and Bewcastle.' With discussion by Sir Martin Conway, W. R. Lethaby, etc.] Proc. Soc. Antiq., 2nd S. 28, pp. 260–61, 203–05. 1916.

10771 Calverley (William Slater). Bewcastle cross. Trans. Cumb. and Westm. Antiq. Soc., 12, pp. 243–46, + 2 plates. 1892.

10772 Collingwood (Robin George). The Bewcastle cross. [With 6 figures in text.] *Same jnl.*, N.S. 35, pp. 1–29, + 4 plates. 1935.

10773 Collingwood (William Gershom). Bewcastle. Proc. Soc. Antiq. Newcastle, 3rd S. 1 (1904), pp. 219–34, + 1 plate : 3rd S. 6 (1914), pp. 214–18, + 2 plates. 1905. 1915.

10774 —— Ruthwell and Bewcastle crosses. Yorks. Archaeol. J., 22, pp. 294–95. 1913.

10775 —— The Ruthwell cross and its relation to other monuments of the early Christian age. [Diagrams of many crosses.] Trans. Dumfries. Antiq. Soc., 3rd S. 5, pp. 34–52, + 32 plates. 1918.

10776 —— The story of Bewcastle cross. [3 figures in text.] Northern Counties Mag., 1, pp. 32–42. 1901.

10777 Conway (*Sir* William Martin). The Bewcastle and Ruthwell crosses. Burl. Mag., 21, pp. 193–94, + 1 plate. 1912.

10778 Cook (Albert Stanburrough). The Bewcastle cross. pp. 10. 8° New Haven, Conn., 1913.

10779 —— The date of the Ruthwell and Bewcastle crosses. [Also published separately.] Trans. Conn. Acad. Arts and Sci., 17, pp. 213–361. 1912.

10780 —— The date of the Ruthwell cross. Academy, 37, pp. 153–54. 1890.

10781 —— Some accounts of the Bewcastle cross between the years 1607 and 1861 reprinted and annotated. *Yale Studies in English*, 50. pp. iv, 148. 8° New Haven, 1914. [Reprints all early publications.]

10782 Dinwiddie (J. L.). The Ruthwell cross and its story. pp. xiv, 153. [7 figures in text.] 8° Dumfries, 1927.

10782a —— The Ruthwell cross and the story it has to tell. [Its history, etc.] Trans. Dumfries. Antiq. Soc., N.S. 22 (1909–10), pp. 109–21. 1911.

10783 Duncan (Henry). An account of the remarkable monument in the shape of a cross, inscribed with Roman and runic letters, preserved in the garden of Ruthwell manse, Dumfriesshire. Archaeol. Scot., 4, pp. 313–26, + 3 plates. 1857.

10784 Ferguson (Richard Saul). Report on injury to the Bewcastle obelisk. Trans. Cumb. and Westm. Antiq. Soc., 12, pp. 51–56. 1892.

10785 Gough (Richard). Description of a cross at Rothwell in Annandale. Vet. Mon., 2, pp. 3 + plates 54 and 55. 1789.

10786 Haigh (Daniel Henry). The Saxon cross at Bewcastle. Archaeol. Æl., N.S. 1, pp. 149–95, + 1 plate (inscriptions). 1857.

10787 Hewison (James King). Notes on the runic roods of Ruthwell and Bewcastle. Proc. Soc. Antiq. Scot., 47 (4th S. 11, 1912–13), pp. 348–59. 1913.

10787a —— The runic roods of Ruthwell and Bewcastle. With a short history of the cross and crucifix in Scotland. pp. xii, 178, + 30 plates. 8° Glasgow, 1914.

10788 —— The runic roods of Ruthwell and Bewcastle. . . . A reply to . . . G. B. Brown, *etc.* pp. 16. 8° Dumfries, 1921. [With reference to vol. 5 of The arts in early England.]

10789 Lea (Harry). A 1,200 years' old cross. [Bewcastle. 5 photographs in text.] Country Life, 96, pp. 638–39. 1944.

10790 Lethaby (William Richard). Is Ruthwell cross an Anglo-Celtic work ? [14 figures in text.] Archaeol. J., 70, pp. 145–61, + 1 plate. 1913.

10791 —— The Ruthwell cross. Archit. Rev., 32, pp. 59–63. 1912. *Same title.* Burl. Mag., 21, pp. 145–146. 1912.

10792 MacFarlan (James). The Ruthwell cross. 2nd edition. pp. 28. 8° Dumfries, 1896.

10793 McKerrow (M. H.). The Ruthwell cross. [Summary of history and literature.] Trans. Hawick Archaeol. Soc., 1936, pp. 65–66. 1936.

10794 Rydberg (Viktor). Skalden Kadmon och Ruthwellkorset. Göteborgs Handelstidning, Sept. 1874 : *reprinted in* Rydberg (V.) : Skrifter, 14, pp. 516–23. 1899.

10795 Saxl (Fritz). The Ruthwell cross. J. Warburg and Courtauld Insts., 6, pp. 1–19, + 8 plates. 1943.

10796 Schapiro (Meyer). The religious meaning of the Ruthwell cross. Art Bull., 26, pp. 232–45, + 4 plates. 1944.

10797 Seton (George). Statement relative to the Ruthwell cross. [Plan to shelter from the weather.] Proc. Soc. Antiq. Scot., 21 (N.S. 9), pp. 194–97. 1887.

§ *c*. **Cumberland and Westmorland**

i. **Gosforth**

10798 Calverley (William Slater). The find of a coped tombstone at Gosforth. Proc. Soc. Antiq., 2nd S. 16, pp. 297–98, + 2 plates. 1897.

10799 —— Finds made in 1897 at Gosforth, Cumberland, namely a coped tombstone and a portion of the head of a pre-Norman cross. *Same jnl.*, 2nd S. 17, pp. 80–82. 1898.

10800 —— The sculptured cross at Gosforth, west Cumberland. Archaeol. J., 40, pp. 143–58, + 5 plates. 1883.

10801 —— The sculptured cross at Gosforth. Drawings, measurements, and some details by C. A. Parker. [7 figures in text.] Trans. Cumb. and Westm. Antiq. Soc., 6, pp. 373–404, + 1 plate. 1883.

10802 —— Shrine-shaped or coped tombstones at Gosforth. *Same jnl.*, 15, pp. 239–46, + 6 plates. 1898.

10803 Collingwood (William Gershom). The Gosforth cross. [2 figures in text.] Northern Counties Mag., 2, pp. 312–21. 1901.

10804 Parker (Charles Arundel). Ancient cross at Gosforth. Antiquary, 14, pp. 204–05 ; *also* p. 279 (note by John Honeyman). 1886.

10805 —— The ancient crosses at Gosforth. pp. 86, + 6 plates. 8° London, 1896.

10806 Parker (Charles Arundel)· Notes on Gosforth church and churchyard, and on sculptured monuments there. Trans. Cumb. and Westm. Antiq· Soc., 6, pp. 405–12, + 1 plate. 1883.

10807 —— and **Collingwood** (William Gershom). A reconsideration of Gosforth cross. [With 3 full page illustrations in text.] *Same jnl.*, N.S. 17, pp. 99–113, and 6 plates. 1917.

ii. **Other**

10808 Bower (R.). Notes on discoveries at Crosscanonby church, near Maryport [Cumb.]. Trans. Cumb. and Westm. Antiq. Soc., 5, pp. 149–52, + 4 plates. 1881.

10809 Calverley (William Slater). Coped or hogbacked tombstone at St. Michael's church, Bongate, or Old Appleby [Westm.]. *Same jnl.*, 9, pp. 118–20, + 1 plate. 1887.

10810 —— Cross fragment at St· Michael's church, Workington [Cumb.]· *Same inl.*, 9, pp. 458–60, + 1 plate. 1888.

10811 —— Crosses at Walberthwaite church and at High Aketon farm in the parish of Bromfield [Cumb.]. *Same jnl.*, 12, pp. 458–62, + 4 plates. 1893.

10812 —— Early sculptured cross shaft at Dearham church, Cumberland. [2 figures in text.] *Same jnl.*, 7, pp. 289–94. 1884.

10813 —— Fragments of pre-Norman crosses at Workington and Bromfield, and the standing cross at Rocliffe [Cumb.]. *Same jnl.*, 12, pp. 171–76, + 4 plates. 1892.

10814 —— Illustrations of Teutonic mythology from early Christian monuments at Brigham and Dearham [Cumb.]. *Same jnl.*, 6, pp. 211–15, + 2 plates. 1882.

10815 —— Notes on sculptured stones at Dearham church [Cumb.]. *Same jnl.*, 5, pp. 153–56, + 3 plates. 1881.

10816 —— Notes on some coped pre-Norman tombstones at Aspatria [Cumb.], Lowther [Westm.], Cross Canonby [Cumb.], and Plumbland [Cumb.]. *Same jnl.*, 9, pp. 461–71, + 4 plates. 1888.

10817 Calverley (William Slater). Notes on the early sculptured crosses, shrines and monuments in the present diocese of Carlisle, edited by W. G. Collingwood. *Cumberland and Westmorland Ant. Soc., Extra series*, 11. pp. xix, 319, + plates. 8° Kendal, 1899. [Gross, 397. 185 figures and plates.]

10818 —— Notice of the discovery of a sculptured stone at Dearham, in Cumberland. [2 figures in text.] Reliquary, 25, pp. 81–84. 1884.

10819 —— Pre-Norman cross fragments at Aspatria, Workington, Distington, Bridekirk, Gilcrux, Plumbland and Isell [Cumb.]. Trans. Cumb. and Westm. Antiq. Soc., 11, pp. 230–37, + 10 plates. 1890.

10820 —— Pre-Norman cross-shaft at Heversham [Westm.]. *Same jnl.*, 13, pp. 118–24, + 1 plate. 1894.

10821 —— A quadrangular stone from Isel, Cumberland. Proc. Soc. Antiq., 2nd S. 10, pp. 330–31, + 1 plate. 1885.

10822 —— Red sandstone cross shaft at Cross-Canonby [Cumb.]. [2 figures in text.] Trans. Cumb. and Westm. Antiq. Soc., 9, pp. 472–74. 1888.

10823 —— Sculptured stone at Isell church, bearing the 'swastika', 'triskele' and other symbols. *Same jnl.*, 9, pp. 29–31, + 1 plate. 1887.

10824 —— The swastika and triskele, with other symbols sculptured on stone at Isel church. Reliquary, N.[2nd] S., pp. 165–67, + 1 plate. 1887. *Same title.* Manx Note Bk., 3, pp. 131–33, + plate. 1887.

10825 Collingwood (William Gershom). An Anglian cross at Tullie House [Carlisle]. [One figure in text.] Trans. Cumb. and Westm. Antiq. Soc., N.S. 16, pp. 279–81. 1916.

10826 —— An Anglian cross-fragment at Kendal [Westm.]. Reliquary, 9, pp. 204–05. 1903. *Same title.* Trans. Cumb. and Westm. Antiq. Soc., N.S. 4, pp. 330–33, + plate. 1904.

10827 Collingwood (William Gershom). Anglian cross-shafts at Dacre [Cumb.] and Kirkby Stephen [Westm.]. Trans. Cumb. and Westm. Antiq. Soc., N.S. 12, pp. 157–63, + 2 plates. 1912.

10828 —— A cross-shaft of the Viking age at Kirkby Stephen. *Same jnl.*, N.S. 12, pp. 29–32, + 1 plate. 1912.

10829 —— Fragments of an early cross at the abbey, Carlisle. [2 figures in text.] *Same jnl.*, N.S. 1, pp. 292–94. 1901.

10830 —— The Giant's Grave, Penrith [Cumb.]. [With 13 figures in text.] *Same jnl.*, N.S. 23, pp. 115–28. 1923.

10831 —— The Giant's Thumb [Penrith]. *Same jnl.*, N.S. 20, pp. 53–65, + 1 plate. 1920.

10832 —— Great Clifton cross-shaft [Cumberland]: Glassonby shaft. [1 figure in text, 10–11 c.] Saga–Book V.C., 2, pp. 257–60. 1901.

10833 —— The Lowther hogbacks [Westm.]. Trans. Cumb. and Westm. Antiq. Soc., N.S. 7, pp. 152–64, + 3 plates. 1907.

10834 —— Note on the early cross-fragments at Addingham church [Cumberland]. [8th c.] *Same jnl.*, N.S. 13, pp. 164–66, + 1 plate. 1913.

10835 —— Notes on early crosses at Carlisle, Bewcastle and Beckermet, [Cumb.]. [One figure (Carlisle) in text. Plate shows inscribed panel on cross-shaft, Beckermet.] *Same jnl.*, N.S. 15, pp. 125–31, + 1 plate. 1915.

10836 —— Pre-conquest cross-fragment from Glassonby, [Cumb.]. [3 figures in text]. *Same jnl.*, N.S. 1, pp. 289–91. 1901.

10837 —— Pre-Norman cross-head at Harrington, Cumberland. Antiq. J., 5, pp. 76–77. 1925.

10838 —— Pre-Norman cross-shaft at Great Clifton, near Workington, and two minor pre-Norman fragments [at Glassonby and at the abbey, Carlisle]. Proc. Soc. Antiq., 2nd S., 18, pp. 323–24. 1901.

10839 Collingwood (William Gershom). Remains of the pre-Norman period [in Cumberland]. [27 figures in text. Anglian and Cumbrian cross-heads, round shafted crosses, hogbacks, minor Scandinavian crosses, chain-pattern, later zoomorphic sculptures, the dragonesque series, inscriptions, metal-work, earthworks, motes.] V.C.H., Cumberland, 1, pp. 253–93, + map, + 19 plates. 1901.

10840 —— Rockcliff cross and the Knowes of Arthuret [Cumb.]. Trans. Cumb. and Westm. Antiq. Soc., N.S. 26, pp. 378–89. 1926.

10841 —— Some crosses at Hornby and Melling in Lonsdale, [Westm.]. [With 5 figures in text.] Reliquary, 10, pp. 35–42. 1904.

10842 —— The Waberthwaite crosses, [Cumb.]. [With 2 pages of illustrations in text.] Trans. Cumb. and Westm. Antiq. Soc., N.S. 25, pp. 80–85. 1925.

10843 Curwen (John F.). Heversham church, [Westm.]. [P. 29, figures of cross as reconstructed by W. G. Collingwood.] Same jnl., N.S. 25, pp. 28–79. 1925.

10844 Fair (Mary C.). The West Cumberland group of pre-Norman crosses. [21 crosses: no illustrations.] Same jnl., N.S. 50, pp. 91–98. 1951.

10845 Hodgson (J. F.). Kirkby Stephen church, [Westm.]. [Pp. 9–11, and plates 1–2, parts of Saxon crosses.] Trans. Archit. Soc. of Durham and Nhd., 2 (1869–79), pp. 1–124, + 8 plates. 1883.

10846 —— Kirkby Stephen church. [Pp. 186–88, + plates 1–2, A.–S. sculptured stones.] Trans. Cumb. and Westm. Antiq. Soc., 4, pp. 178–249, + 8 plates. 1880.

10847 Hogg (Robert). Cross-head from Stanwix, Carlisle. [c. 900. With figures.] Same jnl., N.S., 47, pp. 239–41. 1948.

10848 —— Some recent accessions to the Carlisle Museum. 4. An Anglian cross-head from Walton, Cumberland. Same jnl., N.S. 50, pp. 177–78, + 1 plate. 1951.

10849 Jewitt (Llewellynn). Occurrence of the fylfot cross on a sculptured stone at Dearham, co. Cumberland. [6 figures in text.] Reliquary, 25, pp. 84–85. 1884.

10850 Knowles (E. H.) *canon*. Fragments at St. Bees, [Cumb.]. [Pp. 27–28, + first plate : A.–S. sculpture.] Trans. Cumb. and Westm. Antiq. Soc., 2, pp. 27–30, + 5 plates. 1875.

10851 —— A miscellany of notes on fragments [of A.–S. crosses, etc.] in and near St. Bees. Same jnl., 3, pp. 95–98, + 6 plates. 1877.

10852 —— Notes on fragments at St. John's, Beckermet : Whitbeck : Corney, [Cumb.]. [Pp. 143–45, + plates 1–8, pre-Norman period.]. Same jnl., 4, pp. 139–48, + 13 plates. 1879.

10853 Lidbetter (Robert M.). A pre-Norman shaft, recently found at Great Clifton church, [Cumberland]. Same jnl., N.S. 2, pp. 108–12, + 1 plate. 1902.

10854 Lyttelton (Charles), *bp. of Carlisle*. An account of a remarkable monument in Penrith church yard, Cumberland. [The Giant's Grave.] Archaeologia, 2, pp. 48–53, + 1 plate. 1772.

10855 Marsh (W. J.). Crosscanonby church [Cumb.] (Note on the pre-Norman remains at Crosscanonby, by W. G. Collingwood). [Plates show sculptured cross-shaft, slab and hogback.] Trans. Cumb. and Westm. Antiq. Soc., N.S. 13, pp. 255–60, + 3 plates. 1913.

10856 Mason (J. R.) and **Valentine** (Herbert). Find of pre-Norman stones at St. Michael's church, Workington, [Cumb.]. Same jnl., N.S. 28, pp. 59–62, + 3 plates. 1928.

10857 Mathews ( ) *canon*. The Dacre stone [Cumb.]. (Note by W. S. Calverley). Same jnl., 11, pp. 226–29, + 2 plates. 1890.

10858 Richardson (Henry). On an ancient sculptured stone at Dacre, Cumberland. [Found in 1874.] Reliquary, 16, pp. 33–34, + 1 plate. 1875.

10859 Stephens (George). The bound man devil at Kirkby Stephen, [Westm.]. Trans. Cumb. and Westm. Antiq Soc., 7, pp. 300–09, + frontispiece. 1884.

10860 —— and **Calverley** (William Slater). Sculptured runic grave-block at Dearham, W. Cumberland, date about A.D. 850–950. [2 figures in text.] *Same jnl.*, 6, pp. 358–66. 1883.

10861 Valentine (Herbert). Harrington cross-head, [Cumb.]. *Same jnl.*, N.S. 25, pp. 369–71, + 1 plate. 1925.

§ *d.* **Durham**

10862 [Anon.] Cross shaft, St. Oswald's, Durham. Trans. Archit. Soc. of Durham and Nhd., 3 (1880–89), p. 32, + 1 plate. 1890.

10863 Brock (Edgar Philip Loftus). Notes on some sculptured stones in various churches visited during the Darlington congress [of the British Archaeological Association], 1886. J. Brit. Archaeol. Assoc., 44, pp. 174–79, 408–09, + 2 plates. 1888.

10864 Brown (Gerard Baldwin). The Hartlepool tombstones, and the relations between Celtic and Teutonic art in the early Christian period. [14 figures in text.] Proc. Soc. Antiq. Scot., 53 (5th S. 5, 1918–19), pp. 195–228, + 1 plate. 1919.

10865 —— Saxon and Norman sculpture in Durham. Antiquity, 5, pp. 438–40 + 6 plates. 1931.

10866 Bull (Thomas). Crosses at Escombe church. Proc. Soc. Antiq. Newc., 4th S. 4, pp. 292–94, + 1 plate. 1930.

10867 Clapham (*Sir* Alfred William). Two carved stones at Monkwearmouth. [Before 890.] Arch. Æl., 4th S. 28, pp. 1–6, + 1 plate. 1950.

10868 Durham, *Cathedral library.* A catalogue of the sculptured and inscribed stones in the library. The Roman series, by F. J. Haverfield : the Anglian series, by William Greenwell. pp. 162. 8° Durham, 1899. [13 plates interpaginated. Pp. 51–162, A.-S.]

10869 Greenwell (William). An account of the heads of four memorial crosses found in the foundations of the chapter house, Durham [in 1891]. [1000–83.] Trans. Archit. Soc. of Durham and Nhd., 4 (1890–95), pp. 123–33, + 5 plates. 1896.

10870 —— An account of the memorial crosses found at St. Oswald's, Durham. [? 9th and 10th or early 11th c.] *Same jnl.*, 4 (1890–95), pp. 281–85, + 2 plates. 1896.

10871 Hodges (Charles Clement). Anglo-Saxon remains [in the county of Durham]. [Grave at Darlington and cemetery at Hartlepool, otherwise meagre except for sculpture.] V.C.H., Durham, 1, pp. 211–40, + 11 plates, + map. 1905.

10872 Hodgson (J. F.). The church of Auckland St. Andrew (or North Auckland), commonly called South Church. [Pp. 28–39, 'Anglo-Saxon relics,' with plates 2–5 of cross-shaft, etc.] Archaeol. Æl., N.S. 20, pp. 27–206, + 12 plates. 1899.

10873 Knowles (W. H.). Sockburn church. [With descriptions of ' 22 A.–S. crosses and grave-covers '. 12 figures in text]. Trans. Archit. Soc. of Durham and Nhd., 5 (1896–1905), pp. 99–120, + 3 plates. 1907.

10874 Kurth (Betty). Ecclesia and an angel on the Andrew Aukland cross. J. Warburg and Courtauld Insts., 6, pp. 213–14, + 1 plate. 1943.

10875 Rose (James Dudfield). Notes on the cross-slab at St. Paul's church, Jarrow. [7th c.] Antiq. Sunderland, 12 (1911), pp. 37–40, + 3 plates. 1912.

10876 Smith (I. W.). Carved stone slab found during some alterations at Dinsdale church near Darlington. J. Brit. Archaeol. Assoc., 32, pp. 495–96. 1876.

10877 Stephens (George). On the shaft of an Anglic inscribed cross discovered in the church at Chester-le-Street. ? date about A.D. 700–800. [2 figures : interlacing work.] Archaeol. Æl., N.S. 10, pp. 88–92. 1885.

10878 Wilkinson (J. J.). The Monk-wearmouth amphisbaena. [Dragon: on tomb stone of Herebericht.] Antiq. Sunderland, 19 (1929–32), pp. 1–12, + 1 plate. 1939.

10879 Wooler (Edward). Anglian crosses in Aycliffe churchyard. Proc. Soc. Antiq. Newcastle, 3rd S. 3 (1907), pp. 65–66, + 2 plates. 1909.

§ e. Lancashire

10880 Allen (John Romilly). Description of Winwick cross. J. Brit. Archaeol. Assoc., 37, pp. 91–93, + 1 plate. 1881.

10881 —— Pre-Norman crosses at Halton and Heysham. *Same jnl.*, 42, pp. 328–44, + 1 plate. 1886.

10882 Bailey-Kempling (W.). The architectural antiquities of Heysham. [Chapel, church and hogs-back. No illustrations.] Antiquary, 39, pp. 357–58. 1903.

10883 Browne (George Forrest) *bp. of Bristol*. Pre-Norman sculptured stones in Lancashire. Trans. Lancs. and Ches. Antiq. Soc., 5 (1887), pp. 1–18, + 6 plates. 1888.

10884 Collingwood (William Gershom). Pre-Norman cross fragments at Lancaster. Reliquary, 8, pp. 272–74. 1902.

10885 —— A pre-Norman cross-shaft from Urswick church. Trans. Cumb. and Westm. Antiq. Soc., N.S. 10, pp. 307–11, + 1 plate. 1910.

10886 —— A rune-inscribed Anglian cross-shaft at Urswick church. *Same jnl.*, N.S. 11, pp. 462–68, + 2 plates. 1911.

10887 —— Some pre-Norman finds at Lancaster. [With 9 figures of cross-shaft sculpture.] Reliquary, 9, pp. 257–66. 1903.

10888 —— [The Urswick cross.] [1 figure in text.] Year-Book Viking Club, 2, pp. 37–38. 1910.

10889 Collingwood (William Gershom). Viking-age cross at Lancaster. [Figured on p. 303.] Saga–Book V.C., 3, p. 304. 1904.

10889a Ditchfield (Peter Hampson). The crosses of Lancashire. Memorials of old Lancashire, ed. Henry Fishwick and P. H. Ditchfield, 2, pp. 112–22, + 6 plates. 1909.

10890 Grafton (E. M.). Some notes on Heysham church and parish. [One plate shows 'portion of shaft of runic cross', another the hogback.] Trans. Hist. Soc. Lancs. and Ches., 55–56 (1903–04), pp. 150–62, + 5 plates. 1905.

10891 Green (Charles). Some stone monuments. [P. 417, map of 'Danish settlement near Manchester', the westernmost of the Danelaw, in which a group of crosses located.] Trans. Lancs. and Ches. Antiq. Soc., 56 (1941–2), pp. 114–20. 1944.

10892 Lees (Thomas). An attempt to interpret the meaning of the carvings on certain stones in the churchyard of Heysham. [i. The hog-backed stone: ii. The ancient cross shaft. No illustrations.] *Same jnl.*, 9 (1891), pp. 38–48. 1892.

10893 May (Thomas) *photographer*. Pre-Norman cross-head at Winwick. Reliquary, 12, pp. 134–35. 1906.

10894 Nicholson (J. Holme). The sculptured stones at Heysham. [No illustrations.] Trans. Lancs. and Ches. Antiq. Soc., 9 (1891), pp. 30–38. 1892.

10895 Phelps (Joseph James). An ancient sculptured stone in Manchester cathedral. *Same jnl.*, 23 (1905). pp. 172–98, + 7 plates. 1906.

10896 Roberts (William John). Description of the ancient font at Kirkby, in the parish of Walton-on-the-Hill. Hist. Soc. Lancs. and Ches., Proc., 6, pp. 85–88, + 2 plates. 1854.

10897 Taylor (Henry). The ancient crosses of Lancashire. [Pp. 42–43, pre-Norman crosses. No illustrations.] Trans. Lancs. and Ches. Antiq. Soc., 16 (1898), pp. 39–61. 1899.

10898 Taylor (Henry). The ancient crosses of Lancashire. [1.] The hundred of Blackburn. [Pp. 14–20, + first plate, the pre-Norman crosses in Whalley churchyard.] [2.] The hundred of West Derby. [Pp. 219–25, + 2nd and 3rd plates, Winwick churchyard cross.] [3.] The hundred of Lonsdale. [Pp. 45–62, + 5 plates, pre-Norman cross, Lancaster : pp. 78–108, + 6 plates, Halton, Heysham, Hornby, etc.] [4.] The hundred of Salford. *Same jnl.*, 18 (1900), pp. 1–60, + map, + 5 plates ; 19 (1901), pp. 136–238, + 2 maps, + 4 plates ; 21 (1903), pp. 1–110, + 2 maps, + 13 plates ; 22 (1904), pp. 73–153, + 7 maps, + 6 plates. 1901–02, 1904–05.

10899 Wallis (John E. W.). [A.-S. crosses in Whalley churchyard]. *Same jnl.*, 39 (1921), pp. 190–91, + 1 plate. 1923.

10900 Wickham (W. A.). The Anglian cross-head at Aughton and other recent discoveries there. [Pp. 171–78, + first and last plates of the cross.] Trans. Hist. Soc. Lancs. and Ches., 66 (1914), pp. 151–80, + 6 plates. 1915.

§ f. Northumberland

10901 Berwickshire Naturalists' Club. Rothbury, [excursion]. [4 plates (photographs) of A.-S. cross : now in Black Gate museum, Newcastle-upon-Tyne.] Hist. Berwick. Nat Club, 27, p. 47, + 4 plates. 1929.

10902 Boyle (John Roberts). Fragment of a Saxon cross from Tynemouth. Proc. Soc. Antiq. Newcastle, 2nd S. 2, pp. 23–24, + 1 plate. 1885.

10903 Carr (Sidney S.). Pre-Conquest cross shaft at Tynemouth. *Same jnl.*, 2nd S. 7, pp. 163–64, + 1 plate. 1895.

10904 Charlton (Edward). On an ancient Saxon cross from the church of Rothbury. Archaeol. Æl., [1st S.], 4, pp. 60–62, + 1 plate. 1855.

10905 Collingwood (William Gershom). Early carved stones at Hexham. [With 19 figures.] Archaeol. Æl., 4th S., 1, pp. 65–92. 1925.

10906 Dickson (William). Rothbury and its Saxon cross. [2 figures in text.] Hist. Berwick. Nat. Club, 4, pp. 66–75. 1858.

10907 Featherstonhaugh (Walker). Saxon sculpture at St. Andrews, Bywell. Archaeol. Æl., N.S. 3, pp. 33–35, + 1 plate. 1859.

10908 Gibson (J. Pattison). Small Anglian cross, 13 in. + 9½ in., found on 18 January, 1911, at Hexham. Proc. Soc. Antiq. Newcastle, 3rd S. 5, pp. 1–2, + 1 plate. 1913.

10909 Hall (G. Rome). Notes on a pre-Conquest memorial stone from Birtley, and fragments of crosses from Falstone, North Tynedale [etc.]. [Second plate shows ' bi-literal runic and romanesque inscription from Falstone.'] Arch. Æl., N.S. 13, pp. 252–77, + 2 plates. 1889.

10910 Hastings (Frank) and **Romans** (Thomas). Two fragments of pre-Norman cross-shafts from Ovingham church. Arch. Æl., 4th S. 24, pp. 177–82, + 3 plates. 1946.

10911 Hodges (Charles Clement)· The ancient cross of Rothbury. Arch· Æl., 4th S., 1, pp. 159–68, + 3 plates. 1925.

10912 —— Anglo-Saxon memorial cross. [Portion of head of cross at Hexham, in possession of H. F. Lockhart.] Proc. Soc. Antiq. Newcastle, 3rd S. 10, pp. 292–95. 1922.

10913 —— The memorial stone, supposed to be that of Tidfirth, the last bishop of Hexham. [9th c.] Antiq. Sunderland, 7 (1906), pp. 13–16, + 2 plates. 1908.

10914 —— A note on the piece of the shaft of a Saxon cross at Alnwick castle. Proc. Soc. Antiq. Newcastle, 4th S. 2, pp. 91–92, + 1 plate. 1925.

10915 —— Simondburn church. [Contains 6 pre-Conquest carved stones, of which one plate and 2 figures are given.] Arch. Æl., 4th S., 1, pp. 179–88, + 4 plates. 1925.

10916 Knowles (W. H.). Church of St. John the Baptist, Edlingham. [Pp. 37–39, pre-Conquest period, with figure of part of sculptured cross-shaft.] Trans. Archit. Soc. Durham and Nhd., 5 (1896–1905), pp. 37–48, + 4 plates. 1907.

10917 Laidlaw (Walter). Sculptured and inscribed stones in Jedburgh and vicinity. [Figures 5–10 show interlaced work, etc.] Proc. Soc. Antiq. Scot., 39 (4th S. 3, 1904–05), pp. 21–54. 1905.

10918 Longstaffe (William Hylton Dyer). Winston. [Saxon cross-head.] Archaeol. Æl., N.S. 6, pp. 24–26, 62, + 1 plate. 1865.

10919 Peers (*Sir* Charles Reed). The inscribed and sculptured stones of Lindisfarne. Archaeologia, 74, pp. 255–70, + 8 plates. 1925.

10920 —— A Saxon pillow-stone, recently discovered at Lindisfarne. [3 figures in text.] Proc. Soc. Antiq., 2nd S. 27, pp. 132–37. 1915.

10921 Phillips (Maberly). Pre-Conquest cross at Nunnykirk. [2 figures in text.] Proc. Soc. Antiq. Newcastle, 2nd S. 8, pp. 84–86. 1897. *Reprinted in* Reliquary, 4, pp. 53–57. 1898.

10922 —— A pre-Conquest cross shaft at Nunnykirk. Archaeol. Æl., N.S. 19, pp. 192–96, + 1 plate. 1898.

10923 Smith (John Alexander). Notes respecting a fragment of an ancient sculptured stone or Anglo-Saxon cross, found at Gattonside, near Melrose, and a portion of the old [?9th c.] cross of Jedburgh. Proc. Soc. Antiq. Scot., 10, pp. 448–57. 1875.

10924 Tate (George). Saxon sculptured stones at Norham [Nhd.]. Hist. Berwick. Nat. Club, 4, p. 218, + 2 plates. 1860.

§ g. Yorkshire

10925 Allen (John Romilly). The crosses at Ilkley. (— pt. 2, List of mss. containing Celtic ornament : Celtic metalwork : — pt. 3, conclusion). J. Brit. Archaeol. Assoc., 40, pp. 158–72, + 2 plates : pp. 409–417 ; 41, pp. 332–58. 1884–85.

10926 Allen (John Romilly). The early sculptured stones of the West Riding of Yorkshire. (Descriptive catalogue of ditto). [No illustrations in first article : 29 figures in text of 2nd.] *Same jnl.*, 46, pp. 288–310 : 47, pp. 225–46, + 2 plates. 1890–91.

10927 —— Pre-Norman cross-shaft at Nunburnholme. Reliquary, 7, pp. 98–106. 1901.

10928 Auden (George Augustus). Cresset stone in York museum. [11th c. Figure in text.] Antiq. J., 6, p. 84. 1926.

10929 —— Danish monuments in Yorkshire. [Synopsis of lecture to Yorks. Philos. Soc.] Yorks. N. and Q., 3, p. 21. 1906.

10930 —— Two early sculptured stones in Birstall church. Yorks. Archaeol. J., 20, pp. 20–23, + 2 plates. 1909.

10931 Batty (John). Ancient carved stones in Holy Trinity parish church, Rothwell, near Leeds. *Same jnl.*, 7, pp. 464–66. 1882.

10932 Brigg (John J.). Pre-Norman crosses at Kildwick-in-Craven. Reliquary, N. [3rd] S. 14, pp. 165–71. 1908.

10933 Browne (George Forrest) *bp. of Bristol*. The ancient sculptured shaft in the parish church at Leeds. J. Brit. Archaeol. Assoc., 41, pp. 131–43, + 2 plates. 1885.

10934 Clapham (*Sir* Alfred William). The York Virgin and its date. [Holds it to be pre-Norman.] Archaeol. J., 105 (1948), pp. 6–13, + 2 plates. 1950.

10935 Collingwood (William Gershom). Anglian and Danish sculpture [1] in the North Riding, [2] at York, [3] in the East Riding, with addenda to the North Riding, [4] in the West Riding, with addenda to the North and East Ridings and York, and a general review of the early Christian monuments of Yorkshire. Yorks. Archaeol. J., 19, pp. 266–413 (map + 44 plates in pagination : 20, pp. 149–213, + 22 plates : 21, pp. 254–302, with many illustrations : 23, pp. 129–299, + 1 plate, + map, with 77 illustrations, many full-paged, in text. 1907, 1909, 1911, 1915.

10936 Collingwood (William Gershom.) Anglo-Saxon sculptured stone [in Yorkshire]. V.C.H., York, 2, pp. 109–31, + 7 plates. 1912.

10937 —— Crosses lately found at Hovingham and Hawnby. Yorks. Archaeol. J., 29, pp. 111–12. 1929.

10938 —— A cross-fragment at Sutton-on-Derwent. *Same jnl.*, 29, pp. 238–40, + 1 plate. 1929.

10939 —— The early crosses of Leeds. Pubs. Thoresby Soc., 22 (1912–14), pp. 267–338, + 10 plates. 1915.

10940 —— Fragment of early grave-monument at Kirkheaton. Yorks. Archaeol. J., 24, pp. 213–15. 1917.

10941 —— New find of pre-Norman stones at Bedale. *Same jnl.*, 20, pp. 259–60. 1909.

10942 Douce (Francis). Illustration of the reliefs on the font at Thorpe Salvin. ['Probably Saxon.'] Archaeologia, 12, pp. 209–10. 1796.

10943 Fowler (James). Two fragments of an [A.–S.] cross . . . at Crofton. [P. 34, figures.] Proc. Soc. Antiq., 2nd S. 4, pp. 33–35. 1867.

10944 Fryer (Alfred Cooper). The Bingley font. [With 4 figures. *See also* p. 64 of this vol.] Antiquary, 39, pp. 19–22. 1903.

10945 Gilchrist (Anne G.). A late Anglian cross-head and an Anglo-Saxon crucifix at Bentham. Trans. Cumb. and Westm. Antiq. Soc., N.S. 33, pp. 278–82, + 2 plates. 1933.

10946 Grove (L. R. A.). A pre-Norman cross fragment in York castle museum. [1 figure in text.] Yorks. Archaeol. J., 35, pp. 2–4. 1940.

10946a Haigh (Daniel Henry). A paper on the fragments of crosses discovered at Leeds, in 1838. pp. 32, + 3 plates. 8° Leeds, 18—?

10947 Hodges (Charles Clement). North Frodingham cross. *Same jnl.*, 20, pp. 258–59, + 1 plate. 1909.

10948 Holden (Richard). Description of the reliefs on the font at Thorpe Salvin. Archaeologia, 12, pp. 207–08, + plate. 1796.

10949 Holmes (Richard). Discovery of a fragment of a Saxon cross in the tower of Kippax church. Yorks. Archaeol. J., 8, pp. 377–80. 1884.

10950 Howarth (E.). Pre-Norman cross-shaft at Sheffield. Reliquary, N. [3rd] S. 13, pp. 204–08. 1907.

10951 Innocent (Charles Frederick). The early history of the Sheffield district as told by the Christian monuments. [Synopsis of lecture. Absence of crosses in area S.E. of the Don.] Trans. Hunter Archaeol. Soc., 1, pp. 247–48. 1918.

10952 Irvine (James Thomas). Sculptured slab in Rothwell church, Leeds. J. Brit. Archaeol. Assoc., 50, p. 328, + 1 plate. 1894.

10953 Kenworthy (Joseph). Some ancient stones at Ecclesfield. [8th or 9th c.] Yorks. N. and Q., 2, pp. 207–09. 1905.

10954 Kirk (George Edward). A short history of the parish church of St. Oswald, Collingham. pp. 35, + 13 plates. 8° Leeds, 1937. [Pp. 8–10, + plates 7–9, A.–S., crosses. ?9th c.]

10955 Longhurst (Margaret Helen). The Easby cross. Archaeologia, 80, pp. 43–47, + 5 plates. 1931.

10956 McCall (Hardy Bertram). Pre-Norman cross-head at Lowthorpe. Yorks. Archaeol. J., 31, p. 4. 1934.

10957 —— Pre-Norman stone at Masham. *Same jnl.*, 31, p. 94. 1934.

10958 MacMichael (James Holden). West Riding (East Riding, North Riding) crosses. [*See also* : 3, pp. 49–50, 133–34 (list, by Arthur W. Millar.) Yorks. N. and Q., 2, pp. 359–74. 1906.

10959 Meigh (Alfred) *photographer*. Pre-Norman cross at Thrybergh, [near Rotherham]. Reliquary, N. [3rd] S. 15, pp. 132–33. 1909.

10960 Milner (George). Remarks on the sculptured font in Kirkburn church, near Driffield, with additional observations by J. G. Waller and William Bell. [Considered to be A.–S.] J. Brit. Archaeol. Assoc., 7, pp. 38–52. 1852.

10961 Parez (C. H.). Remains of pre-Norman crosses found at Gargrave. Yorks. Archaeol. J., 12, pp. 87–91, + 1 plate. 1893.

10962 Pettigrew (Thomas Joseph). The monumental crosses at Ilkley and Collingham. J. Brit. Archaeol. Assoc., 20, pp. 308–14, + 1 plate. 1864.

10963 Pritchett (J. P.). St. Peter's church, Croft. [Pp. 242–43, + plate, A.-S. sculpture built into aumbrey.] *Same jnl.*, 44, pp. 241–50, + plan, + 1 plate. 1888.

10964 Raine (James). Note on the sculptured stone, with spectacle ornament, recently discovered at Bilton. [With figure. Interlaced ornament.] Proc. Soc. Antiq. Scot., 9, p. 177. 1873.

10965 Rowe (George). Remarks on some monumental stones found at Brompton, Northallerton. Assoc. Archit. Socs.' Rpts., 14, pp. 61–65, + 3 plates. 1877.

10966 Sheppard (Thomas). Easby cross. [2 figures in text.] Hull Museum Publicns., 181, pp. 3. 1932.

10967 —— Fragments of an early cross from Patrington. [Late pre-Conquest.] Reliquary, N. [3rd] S. 15, pp. 207–08. 1909.

10968 Skene (William Forbes). Notice of a remarkable sculptured cross at Bilton. Proc. Soc. Antiq. Scot., 8, pp. 417–18. 1871.

10969 Speight (H.). The Bingley rune stone. [Corrections of **10944**.] Antiquary, 39, p. 64. 1903.

10970 Stephens (George). On a runic stone at Thornhill. [? c. 700–800.] Yorks. Archaeol. J., 8, pp. 49–58, + 3 plates. 1884.

10971 Turner (Joseph Horsfall). Walton cross [Hartshead church]. [Quotation from vol. 8 of ' Smith's Old Yorkshire,' to describe the plate.] Reliquary, 24, p. 178, + plate. 1884.

10972 Victoria and Albert Museum. Early mediaeval art in the north. pp. vi, + 28 plates. 8° London, 1949. [Plates 10–15, fragment of a cross from Easby church, near Richmond.]

10973 Wall (James Charles). Lastingham relics. [With 27 figures in text.] Reliquary, 12, pp. 152–61. 1906.

10974 Waterton (Edmund). Part of an Anglo-Saxon cross [from Wakefield]. [Found in use as a doorstep.] Proc. Soc. Antiq., 2nd S. 2, pp. 124–25. 1862.

10975 Young (C.). Discovery of Saxon monumental stones at Kirklevington church. Yorks. Archaeol. J., 7, pp. 458–59. 1882.

189. SCULPTURE, WESSEX

§ *a*. **Surrey, Berkshire and Hampshire**

10976 Allen (John Romilly). Early Christian art and inscriptions [in Hampshire]. V.C.H., Hampshire, 2, pp. 233–49, + 7 plates. 1903.

10977 Bunt (Cyril George Edward). An important relic of south Saxon art. [Preaching stone found at Reigate, carved with device of interlaced ovals.] Builder, 149, p. 863. 1935.

10978 Clark (C. R.). Saxon stoup at Shefford Woodlands [Berks.]. Trans. Newbury District F.C., 6, p. 227. 1933.

10979 Collingwood (William Gershom). A cross-base at Winchester. Papers and Proc. Hants. F.C., 9, pp. 219–20, + 2 plates. 1922.

10980 Harris (John). Saxon font in South Hayling church, Hayling Island, Hants. J. Brit. Archaeol. Assoc., 42, pp. 65–67, + 1 plate. 1886.

10981 Johnston (Philip Mainwaring). The parish church of All Saints, Kingston-upon-Thames. [First plate shows ' eighth century Saxon carving on a stone ' in the church.] *Same jnl.*, N.S. 32, pp. 229–47, + 3 plates. 1926.

10982 Lamborn (Edmund Arnold Greening). A note on a fragment of an Anglo-Saxon wheel cross found at Abingdon. Berks. Archaeol. J., 39, pp. 58–59, + 2 plates. 1935.

10983 —— The Wantage crosses. *Same jnl.*, 41, pp. 122–24. 1937.

10984 Piggott (Stuart). A Saxon cross shaft-fragment from Wantage. [With carved interlace, c. 950.] Trans. Newbury District F.C., 7, pp. 149–50. 1936.

10985 Seaby (Allen W.). Some Berkshire interlacings. [With 16 figures.] Antiquity, 18, pp. 98–94. 1944.

§ *b*. **Wiltshire and Somerset**

10986 Allen (John Romilly). Notes on the ornamentation of the early Christian monuments of Wiltshire. [19 figures in text.] Wilts. Archaeol. Mag., 27, pp. 50–65, + 9 plates. 1894.

10987 Appleby (E. J.). Notes on ancient stone crosses of Somerset. [Pp. 194–95, + plate, the Saxon period (4 crosses).] Proc. Bath F.C., 10, pp. 192–203, + 5 plates. 1903.

10988 Bagnall-Oakeley (Mary Ellen). Ancient sculptures in the south porch of Malmesbury abbey church. Trans. Bristol and Glos. Arch. Soc., 16, pp. 16–19, + 4 plates. 1892.

10989 Barron (John). A sculptured stone discovered in St. Peter's church, Codford, Wilts. [?c. 1000 A.D. With figure in A.–S. costume.] Proc. Soc. Antiq., 2nd S. 7, pp. 429–30. 1878.

10990 Brentnall (Harold Cresswell). More carved stones from Teffont Magna. Wilts. Archaeol. Mag., 51, pp. 350–51, + 1 plate. 1946.

10991 Brock (Edgar Philip Loftus). [Anglo-Saxon arch at Britwell church, Wilts.]. J. Brit. Archaeol. Assoc., 33, pp. 218–19. 1877.

10992 Browne (George Forrest) *bp. of Bristol*. The Aldhelm crosses in Somerset and Wilts. Proc. Clifton Antiq. Club, 6 (1906–08), pp. 121–27, + 2 plates. 1908.

10993 —— Early sculptured stone at West Camel church, Somersetshire. Proc. Somerset Arch. Soc., 36 (1891), pp. 70–81, + 1 plate. 1891.

10994 —— Pre-Norman sculptured stones of Wiltshire. *In* Dryden (Alice) *ed.* Memorials of old Wiltshire. pp. x, 267. 8° London, 1906.

10995 Browne (George Forrest) *bp. of Bristol*. Sculptured stone found on site of chapel ' by the cloister ' in burial ground of Wells cathedral church. Proc. Somerset Arch. Soc., 40 (1894), p. 275. 1894.

10996 Brownlow (William Robert Bernard) *bp. of Clifton*. The Saxon cross found in Bath, 1898. Proc. Clifton Antiq. Club, 4 (1897–99), pp. 252–56, + 1 plate. 1900.

10997 Buck (A. G. Randle). Some Wiltshire fonts. [Pp. 461–64, A.–S.: pp. 464–67, early Norman, 1066–1100.] Wilts. Archaeol. Mag., 53, pp. 458–70, + 4 plates. 1950.

10998 Clapham (*Sir* Alfred William) and **Charlton** (John). Note on pre-Conquest cross-shaft from Broad Chalke, Wiltshire. Antiq. J., 19, pp. 83–84, + 1 plate. 1939.

10999 Cottrill (Frank). Some pre-Conquest stone carvings in Wessex. [Illustrations show Colerne, Wilts.; Tenbury, Worcs.; Ramsbury, Shaftesbury, Glastonbury, West Camel.] Antiq. J., 15, pp. 144–51, + 4 plates. 1935.

11000 Dickinson (Francis Henry). Sculptured stone . . . West Camel church, Somersetshire. Proc. Soc. Antiq., 2nd S. 3, p. 493. 1867.

11001 Dobson (Dina Portway). Saxon sculptures at Chew Stoke, Somerset. Antiq. J., 18, p. 178. 1938.

11002 Goddard (E. H.). Notes on pre-Norman sculptured stones in Wilts. [Figure on p. 47, of part of cross (?), Wantage, Berks.] Wilts. Archaeol. Mag., 27, pp. 43–49. 1894.

11003 —— On fragments of a Saxon cross shaft, found at Minety, and Saxon silver ornament from Cricklade. *Same jnl.*, 30, pp. 230–32, + 1 plate. 1899. *Same title* [with 4 figures]. Reliquary, 5, pp. 129–31. 1899.

11004 Horne (Ethelbert) *abbot of Downside*. Fragment of a Glastonbury Saxon cross. N. and Q. for Som. and Dorset, 20, 1 p., + 1 plate. 1930.

11005 Irvine (James Thomas). Notes on [Bradford-on-Avon] church. [Plate shows carving.] J. Brit. Archaeol. Assoc., 33, pp. 215–16, + 1 plate. 1877.

11006 Kendrick (*Sir* Thomas Downing). Fragment of a cross-head from Bath. Antiq. J., 21, pp. 75–76, + 1 plate. 1941.

11007 Murray (Margaret Alice) and **Passmore** (A. D.). The sheela-na-gig at Oaksey [north Wilts.]. [2 figures in text.] Man, 23, pp. 140–41. 1923.

11008 Newall (R. S.). Two recently-discovered fragments of pre-Norman cross shafts in S. Wilts. [Hanging Langford and Teffont Magna.] Wilts. Archaeol. Mag., 48, pp. 183–84, + 2 plates [photos.]. 1938.

11009 Scarth (Henry Mengden). Remarks on some ancient sculptured stones . . . particularly those recorded to have stood in the cemetery at Glastonbury. [Including Bewcastle and Rothwell crosses.] Proc. Somerset Arch. Soc., 10 (1860), pp. 113–30, + 1 plate. 1861.

11010 Webb (Edward Doran). Notes on some recent discoveries at Ramsbury. [10th c. cross.] Trans. Salisbury F.C., 1, pp. 90–91, + 1 plate. 1894.

§ *c.* **Dorset and Devon**

11011 Allen (John Romilly). The font at Dolton, Devonshire. [' Constructed from the remains of certainly one, and perhaps two, highly ornamented pre-Norman cross-shafts.' With 12 figures.] Reliquary, 8, pp. 243–56. 1902.

11012 Barnes (W. Miles). A brief historical and descriptive sketch of the churches in the rural deanery of Dorchester (Dorchester portion). [Pp. 46–47, + plate 2 : Toller Fratrum and its Saxon font.] Proc. Dorset Antiq. F.C., 12, pp. 36–70, + 3 plates. 1891.

11013 Browne (George Forrest) *bp. of Bristol.* Fragment of Anglo-Saxon carving. [Gillingham vicarage, Dorset.] N. and Q. Som. and Dorset, 15, pp. 233–34, + 1 plate. 1917.

11014 Carter (George Edward Lovelace). The Sticklepath [Devon] stone. [Interpretation of the incised symbols. Probably to be dated 1065. Figure in text.] N. and Q., 169, pp. 219–20. 1935.

11015 Clarke (Kate M.). The baptismal fonts of Devon. Part I. [Pp. 315–17, the 2 A.-S. fonts, Dolton and Luppitt.] Rept. and Trans. Devon. Assoc., 45, pp. 314–29. 1913.

11016 —— The Dolton font. Devon N. and Q., 5, pp. 25–28. 1908.

11017 —— The Luppitt font. [10–11th c.] Devon and Cornwall N. and Q., 7, pp. 201–05, + 2 plates. 1913.

11018 Dicker (Charles William Hamilton). Important find [of Saxon cross] at Whitcombe church. [?10th c.] Proc. Dorset Antiq. F.C., 33, pp. xvi–xvii + 1 plate [photo]. 1912.

11019 Ditchfield (Peter Hampson). The priory of St. Nicholas [Exeter]. [Figure on p. 9 shows part of Saxon cross.] J. Brit. Archaeol. Assoc., N.S. 33, pp. 7–10. 1927.

11020 Dobson (Dina Portway). Carved angel from [Winterbourne Steepleton], Dorset. [10th c.] Antiq. J., 13, pp. 315–16. 1913.

11021 Fowler (Joseph). Saxon cross at Yetminster [Dorset]. N. and Q. for Som. and Dorset, 23, pp. 307, 309, + 1 plate. 1942.

11022 Gray (M.). Symbolic art as illustrated by the Romanesque [A.-S.] font at St. Marychurch. Trans. Exeter Diocesan Archit. Soc., 12 (3rd S. 2), pp. 160–66, + 1 plate. 1906.

11023 Joce (T. J.). Coplestone, [Devon]. Devon and Cornwall N. and Q., 20, pp. 208–10. 1938.

11024 Jones (Winslow). Font in Dolton church, north Devon. Rept. and Trans. Devon. Assoc., 23, pp. 197–202, + 4 plates. 1891.

11025 King (Richard John). Coplestone cross ; and a charter of Eadgar, A.D. 974. [Text in Latin, and translation: plates of the cross.] *Same jnl.*, 8, pp. 351–59, + 2 plates. 1876.

11026 March (Henry Colley). Portions of a cross-shaft recently discovered at Whitcombe church, Dorset. [Figure (photo) in text.] Proc. Soc. Antiq., 2nd S. 25, pp. 177–79. 1913.

11027 Phillips (Edwin Noel Masson). The ancient stone crosses of Devon. [69, pp. 293–94 : 6 examples left (detailed in list) for references to which see index on pp. 334–40 of vol. 70.] Rept. and Trans. Devon. Assoc., 69, pp. 289–342 : 70, pp. 299–340, + 27 plates. 1937–38.

11028 —— Anglo-Saxon crosses in Devon. Devon and Cornw. N. and Q., 19, pp. 224–25. 1937.

11029 Pope (William). The old ' Copelan-Stan ' at Copplestone. [Saxon or earlier.] *Same jnl.*, 18, pp. 112–14, + 1 plate. 1934.

11030 Reed (Harbottle). Saxon cross in the church of St. Andrew, Colyton, Devon. [c. 800. Recently found in walling of tower.] Rept. and Trans. Devon. Assoc., 67, pp. 285–89, + 3 plates. 1935.

11031 Rowley (F. R.). An early Christian cross-shaft in the Royal Albert Memorial Museum, Exeter. Devon and Cornwall N. and Q., 7, pp. 65–69, + 1 plate. 1912.

11032 Watkin (Hugh Robert). Ancient sepulchral slab with cross found at Harberton [Devon]. [Queries A.-S.] *Same jnl.*, 11, pp. 113–16, + 1 plate. 1920.

11033 Way (R. E.). The ancient cross at Coplestone, near Crediton, Devon. J. Brit. Archaeol. Assoc., 34, pp. 122–23, 242, + 1 plate. 1878.

11034 Westwood (John Obadiah). Notice of an early sculptured stone in the church of Winterborne Steepleton. [?end of 10th or early 11th c.] Proc. Dorset Antiq. F.C., 5, pp. 81–87. 1883.

11035 White (R. H.). Toller Fratrum church. [Saxon font. Illustrated in 12, p. 46.] Proc. Dorset Archaeol. Soc., 53 (for 1931), pp. lxxvi–viii. 1932.

190. SCULPTURE, CORNWALL

11036 Andrew (C. K. Croft). Ancient monuments near Liskeard. 9. King Doniert's stone, St. Cleer. [?9th c. Interlacing ornament.] Devon and Cornwall N. and Q., 19, pp. 112–15, + 2 plates. 1936.

11037 —— The Doniert stone, St. Cleer. J. Roy. Inst. Cornwall, 24, pp. 112–39. 1933.

11038 Blight (John Thomas). Ancient crosses and other antiquities in the east (in the West: 2nd edition) of Cornwall. pp. vi, ff. 133 ; pp. vii, ff. 73. 2 vol. 4° London, 1858.

11039 Dexter (Thomas Francis George *und* Henry). Cornish crosses, Christian and pagan. pp. xxxi, 301. 4° London, 1938. [190 figures in text.]

11040 Ellis (G. E.). Cornish crosses. [Supplementary to Langdon's work, *q.v.*, **11045–53.**] Devon and Cornwall N. and Q., 24, pp. 105–11, 137–42, 201–03, 217–20, + 7 plates. 1950–51.

11041 Hare (N.). The St. Neot stone. J. Roy. Inst. Cornwall, 8, pp. 19–21. 1883.

11042 —— The Quethiock cross. *Same jnl.*, 7, pp. 139–40, + 1 plate. 1882.

11043 Iago (William). Cardinham : its inscribed stones and other antiquities. [Pp. 363–64, + 1 plate, A.-S. inscribed stone.] *Same jnl.*, 5, pp. 358–65, + 2 plates. 1877.

11044 —— Waterpit Down inscribed and ornamented cross-shaft. Arch. Camb., 5th S. 13, pp. 150–52. 1896.

11045 Langdon (Arthur Gregory). Celtic ornament on the crosses of Cornwall. [Pp. 337–47, analysis of the patterns.] J. Brit. Archaeol. Assoc., 45, pp. 318–47, + 3 plates. 1889.

11046 —— Coped stones in Cornwall. *Same jnl.*, 49, pp. 274–84, + 2 plates. 1893.

11047 —— Early Christian monuments [in Cornwall]. [43 inscribed stones, 352 crosses, 4 coped stones, 5 early recumbent cross slabs. 18 plates paginated as text.] V.C.H., Cornwall, 1, pp. 407–49. 1906.

11048 Langdon (Arthur Gregory) and **Allen** (John Romilly). The early Christian monuments of Cornwall. J. Brit. Archaeol. Assoc., 44, pp. 301–25, + 1 plate. 1888.

11049 Langdon (Arthur Gregory). The inscribed and ornamented cross-shaft at Biscovey, St. Blazey. Arch. Camb., 5th S. 11, pp. 308–15. 1894.

11050 —— Old Cornish crosses. . . . With an article on their ornament by J. R. Allen. pp. xxviii, 439. 8° Truro, 1896.

11051 —— The ornament on the early crosses of Cornwall. [i. Celtic : ii. incised : iii. miscellaneous : iv. subjects.] J. Roy. Inst. Cornwall, 10, pp. 33–96, + 8 plates. 1890.

11052 —— The Padstow crosses. J. Brit. Archaeol. Assoc., 47, pp. 301–07, + 2 plates. 1891.

11053 —— and **Opie** (Otho B.). Two early sculptured stones in St. Stephen's church, Launceston. [?A.–S., ? early Norman.] Devon and Cornwall N. and Q., 6, pp. 81–83, + 1 plate : 105–06. 1910.

11054 Stephens (William J.). St. Allen crosses. J. Roy. Inst. Cornwall, 19, pp. 397–99, + 3 plates. 1914.

191. SCULPTURE, IRELAND

§ a. General

11055 Allen (John Romilly). Early Christian symbolism in Great Britain and Ireland before the thirteenth century. *Rhind Lectures for* 1885. pp. xix, 408. 8° London, 1887. [Pp. 130–235, High crosses of Ireland. 154 figures in text.]

11056 Bigger (Francis Joseph). The *dextera Dei* sculptured on the high crosses of Ireland. Proc. R.I.A., 3rd S. 6, pp. 79–84. 1900.

11057 Brash (Richard Rolt). The sculptured crosses of Ireland, and what we learn from them. J. Roy. Hist. and Arch. Assoc. Ireland, [12] 4th S. 2 (1872–73), pp. 98–112. 1874.

11058 Chart (David Alfred) *ed.* A preliminary survey of the ancient monuments of Northern Ireland, conducted by the Ancient Monuments Advisory Council for Northern Ireland. pp. xxiv, 284, + 74 plates. 4° Belfast, 1940.

11059 Crawford (Henry Saxton). A descriptive list of the early Irish crosses. J. Roy Soc. Antiq. Ireland, 37 (5th S. 17), pp. 187–239, + 4 plates : 38, pp. 181–82. 1907–08.

11060 —— A descriptive list of early cross-slabs and pillars [in Ireland]. (Supplementary lists . . .). [By counties.] *Same jnl.*, 42 (6th S. 2), pp. 217–44, + map, + 2 plates : 43, pp. 151–69, + 2 plates, 261–65, 326–34 : 46, pp. 163–67 : 48, pp. 174–79. 1912–13, 1916, 1918.

11061 Davies (D. Griffith). Early sculptured stones in Ireland. [8 figures in text.] Arch. Camb., 5th S. 14, pp. 255–60. 1897.

11062 F.R.S.A.I. Figures known as hags of the castle, sheelas or sheela na gigs [in Ireland]. (Carved female figures found in early churches, castles, etc. Supplemental list). J. Roy. Soc. Antiq. Ireland, 24 (5th S. 4), pp. 77–81, 392–94. 1894.

11063 Graves (Charles) *bp. of Limerick.* On the croix gamée, or swastika [on early Christian monuments in Ireland]. Trans. R.I.A., 27, pp. 41–46. 1879.

11064 Guest (Edith M.). Irish sheela-na-gigs in 1935. [List with references.] J. Roy. Soc. Antiq. Ireland, 66 (7th S. 6), pp. 107–29, + 8 plates. 1936.

11065 Healy (John) *abp. of Tuam.* The baptism of Our Lord, as represented at Kells and Monasterboice. *Same jnl.*, 23 (5th S. 3), pp. 1–6, + 2 plates. 1893.

11066 Henry (Françoise). Early Christian slabs and pillar stones in the west of Ireland. [6th–7th c.] *Same jnl.*, 67 (7th S. 7), pp. 265–79, + 11 plates. 1937.

11067 —— La sculpture irlandaise pendant les douze premiers siècles de l'ère chrétienne. 2 vol. (text and plates), 4° Paris, 1933. [171 plates.]

11068 Lawlor (Henry Cairnes). Grotesque carvings improperly called sheelana-gigs. Irish Naturalists' J., 1, pp. 182–85, + 1 plate. 1927.

11069 Ledwich (Edward). Antiquities of Ireland. 2nd edition. pp. 526. 4° Dublin, 1804.

11070 Mason (T. H.). The devil as depicted on Irish high crosses. J. Roy. Soc. Antiq. Ireland, 72 (7th S. 12), pp. 131–35, + 2 plates. 1942.

11071 O'Neill (Henry). The most interesting of the ancient crosses of ancient Ireland. Drawn to scale and lithographed. fol. London, [1853]–57.

11072 Porter (Arthur Kingsley). The crosses and culture of Ireland. pp. xxiv, 143, + plates with 276 figures. 4° New Haven, 1931. [i. St. Patrick : ii. Columbcille : iii. The great missionaries (Columbanus, etc.) : iv. Fall of the Celtic Church : v. The Vikings in Ireland. Plates are all of sculpture.]

11073 —— An Egyptian legend in Ireland. [SS. Anthony and Paul breaking the bread. Parallels with Coptic art in subjects on Irish crosses.] Marburger Jahrb. Kunstwiss., 5, pp. 1–14. 1930.

11074 —— Notes on Irish crosses. Konsthistoriska Studier . . . Festschrift J. Roosval (Stockholm), pp. 84–94. 1929.

11075 Roe (Helen M.). An interpretation of certain symbolic sculptures of early Christian Ireland. [Grotesque figures with animal attributes derive from pagan times and come to bear symbolic significance of demons.] J. Roy. Soc. Antiq. Ireland, 75, pp. 1–23, + 3 plates. 1945.

11076 Sexton (Eric Hyde Lord). A descriptive and bibliographical list of Irish figure sculptures of the early Christian period, with a critical assessment of their significance. pp. xxvii, 300, + 55 plates. 8° Portland, Maine, 1946. [Alphabetical : showing where illustrated. The standard work, with which the references in this section are correlated.]

M m

11077 Smith (Joseph Huband). Ancient stone crosses of Ireland. Ulster J. Archaeol., 1, pp. 53–57. 1853.

11078 Ullrich (H.). Irische Hochkreuze als Zeugen nordische Frömmigheit. [4 figures in text.] Kunst u. Kirche, 16, pp. 112–16. 1939.

11079 Wakeman (William Frederick). On the earlier forms of inscribed Christian crosses found in Ireland. J. Roy. Soc. Antiq. Ireland, 20 (5th S. 1), pp. 350–58, + 3 plates. 1891.

§ *b*. **Clonmacnoise, King's County**

(North cross, 7 feet high : South cross, 12 feet high : West cross, 13 feet high, carved all over with figure subjects in panels : East cross, 5 feet high, removed from Banagher. For details, see Sexton [11076], pp. 101–14, 65–66).

11080 Crawford (Henry Saxton). Note on the high cross of Clonmacnoise. J. Roy. Soc. Antiq. Ireland, 40 (5th S. 20), p. 356. 1910.

11081 —— Notes on several of the Clonmacnois slabs. *Same jnl.*, 41 (6th S. 1), pp. 51–57. 1911.

11082 —— A sepulchral slab lately found at Clonmacnois. [?c. 900.] *Same jnl.*, 40 (5th S. 20), pp. 235–37. 1910.

11083 Gillespie (Patrick). Note on the sculptured figure of a stag on a cross-shaft at Clonmacnois, in relation to the ancient wooden objects known as otter or beaver traps. [Whole page figure : 8th–9th c.] Proc. Soc. Antiq. Scot., 53 (5th S. 5, 1918–19), pp. 165–67. 1919.

11084 Graves (James). A list of the ancient Irish monumental stones at present existing at Clonmacnoise. [6 figures in text.] Proc. and Trans. Kilkenny Archaeol. Soc., 3, pp. 293–303. 1855.

11085 Guest (Edith M.). A sheelana-gig at Clonmacnoise. [On a 10th c. cross.] J. Roy. Soc. Antiq. Ireland, 69 (7th S. 9), p. 48, + 1 plate. 1939.

11086 Ireland. 75th Annual Report from the Commissioners of Public Works. [Sexton, pp. 105–14.] Dublin, 1907. [Pp. 8–17, 59–73, West Cross, Clonmacnoise.]

11087 Macalister (Robert Alexander Stewart). The memorial slabs of Clonmacnois : with an appendix on the materials for a history of the monastery. *Extra vol. of the Roy. Soc. Antiq. Ireland for* 1907–08. pp. xxxii, 159, + 40 plates. 8° Dublin, 1909. [Kenney, 1, p. 103.]

§ *c.* **Monasterboice, co. Louth**

(West cross, 21½ feet high, 50 sculptured panels : South (abbot Muiredach's) cross (d. 922), 17 feet 8 inches high, 22 panels : North cross, 16 feet high. For details, see Sexton [**11076**], pp. 221–45.)

11088 Hunt (John). The cross of Muiredach, Monasterboice. J. Roy. Soc. Antiq. Ireland, 81, pp. 44–47, + 1 plate. 1951.

11089 Lucas (A. T.). The west cross, Monasterboice : a note and a suggestion. J. County Louth Archaeol. Soc., 12, pp. 123–25, + 1 plate. 1951.

11090 Macalister (Robert Alexander Stewart). The ancient inscriptions of Kells [co. Meath]. [Identifies Muiredach as the sculptor of the Kells and Monasterboice crosses, and confutes previous evidence of date.] J. Roy. Soc. Antiq. Ireland, 64 (7th S. 4), pp. 16–21, + 2 plates. 1934.

11091 ——The cross of Muiredach. County Louth Archaeol. J., 3, pp. 209–12, + 2 plates. 1914.

11092 —— Guide to Monasterboice. pp. 24. 8° Dundalk, 1944. [4 plates of crosses in text. History of the monastery, crosses, etc.]

11093 —— Monasterboice, co. Louth. pp. 79, + 19 plates. 8° Dundalk, 1946.

11094 —— Muiredach, abbot of Monasterboice, 890–923 A.D., his life and surroundings. pp. xii, 85, + 7 plates. fol. Dublin, 1914. [Mostly devoted to his cross there, 10th c.]

11095 —— The panel representing the *Traditio evangelii* on the cross of Muiredach. J. Roy. Soc. Antiq. Ireland, 62 (7th S. 2), pp. 15–18, + 2 plates. 1932.

11096 Morris (Henry). The Muiredach cross. A new interpretation of three of its panels. [Suggests that they represent the conversion of the Norsemen.] *Same jnl.*, 64 (7th S. 4), pp. 203–12, + 2 plates. 1934.

11097 Pentland (George Henry). The great cross at Monasterboice. [Taking of a cast. *See also* 29, pp. 68–71, 1899.] *Same jnl.*, 28 (5th S. 8), pp. 264–66, + 1 plate. 1898.

11098 Stephens (Francis E.). The tall cross at Monasterboice. *Same jnl.*, 43 (6th S. 3), p. 267. 1913.

11099 Stokes (Margaret MacNair). Early Christian art in Ireland. Bas-relief on [South] cross at Monasterboice. Reliquary, N. [3rd] S. 5, pp. 110–15. 1899.

§ *d.* **White Island, Lower Lough Erne, co. Fermanagh**

(Seven carved figures in a recess inside the northern wall of the ruined church. ?7th c. For details, see Sexton [**11076**], pp. 296–300.)

11100 Du Noyer (George Victor). Remarks on ancient Irish effigies sculptured on the walls of the ancient church on White Island, parish of Magheraculmoney. J. Kilkenny Archaeol. Soc., 6 (2nd S. 3), pp. 62–69, + 3 plates. 1860.

11101 Ettlinger (*Mrs.* Ellen). The stone sculptures on White Island. [? Represent St. Patrick, king Loiguire and king Enna.] Man, 53, pp. 33–34, + 1 plate. 1953

11102 Guest (Edith M.). Some notes on the dating of sheela-na-gigs. [That at White Island, 7th–8th c., but most, probably, much later.] J. Roy. Soc. Antiq. Ireland, 67 (7th S. 7), pp. 176–80. 1937.

11103 Lowry-Corry (*Lady* Dorothy). Report on the preservation of the ruin of White Island church. [Pp. 16–17, + plate, sheela-na-gig, 8th–9th c.] Proc. Belfast N.H. and Phil. Soc., 1927–28, pp. 13–18, + 1 plate. 1929.

11104 McKenna (James Edward) and **Lowry-Corry** (*Lady* Dorothy). White Island: its ancient church and unique sculptures. J. Roy. Soc. Antiq. Ireland, 60 (6th S. 19), pp. 23–37, + 4 plates. 1930.

11105 O'Driscoll (Desmond) and **Macalister** (Robert Alexander Stewart). The White Island sculptures. J. Roy. Soc. Antiq. Ireland, 72 (7th S. 12), pp. 116–19. 1942.

11106 Wakeman (William Frederick). The church on White Island. J. Roy. Hist. and Arch. Assoc. Ireland, 15, pp. 276–92. 1882.

11107 —— White Island. *Same jnl.*, 15, pp. 66–69. 1879.

§ e. Others

11108 Armstrong (Edmund Clarence Richard). An account of some early Christian monuments discovered at (A cross-slab and fragment from) Gallen priory, [King's County]. [Sexton, pp. 153–55.] J. Roy. Soc. Antiq. Ireland, 38 (5th S. 18), pp. 61–66, 390–93. 1908.

11109 Bigger (Francis Joseph). The ancient cross of Drumgolan in the co. Down. [Figure in text. Interlacing.] Ulster J. Archaeol., 2nd S. 14, pp. 56–58. 1908.

11110 —— and **Fennell** (William J.). Ardboe [or Arboe], co. Tyrone: its cross and churches. *Same jnl.*, 2nd S. 4, pp. 1–7, + 1 plate. 1897.

11111 —— and —— The high cross of Downpatrick. [1 figure in text. Sexton, p. 121.] *Same jnl.*, 2nd S. 3, pp. 272–74. 1897.

11112 Bremer (Walther Erich Emanuel Friedrich). Note on the Holywood stone [co. Wicklow]. [Not Danish period as assigned by G. H. Orpen, **11155**, but ? Bronze Age.] J. Roy. Soc. Antiq. Ireland, 56 (6th S. 6), pp. 51–54, + 1 plate. 1926.

11113 Buick (George Raphael). The high cross of Connor, co. Antrim. [1 figure in text. Sexton, p. 116.] Ulster J. Archaeol., 2nd S. 9, pp. 41–42. 1903.

11114 Cochrane (Robert). Ancient monuments in the county of Cork. 18. Ancient crosses. J. Cork Hist. Soc., 2nd S. 18, pp. 131–32. 1912.

11115 Coleman (James). Irish crosses in the county Cork. [Almost total absence of.] *Same jnl.*, 2nd S. 14, pp. 38–39. 1908.

11116 Crawford (Henry Saxton) and **Moore** (Courtenay), *etc.* Ancient carved stone near Bantry [co. Cork]. *Same jnl.*, 2nd S. 20, pp. 51–52, 204–05. 1914.

11117 Crawford (Henry Saxton). Bealin cross, Twyford, county Westmeath. [P. 321, whole page figure. Sexton, pp. 68–69.] J. Roy. Soc. Antiq. Ireland, 37 (5th S. 17), pp. 320–22. 1907.

11118 —— The churches and monuments of Inis bó finne, county Westmeath. *Same jnl.*, 47 (6th S. 7), pp. 139–52, + 2 plates. 1917.

11119 —— The crosses and slabs of Inishowen, [co. Donegal.] *Same jnl.*, 45 (6th S. 5), pp. 183–92, + 1 plate. 1915.

11120 —— The crosses of Kilkieran [co. Kilkenny] and Ahenny [co. Tipperary]. [Sexton, pp. 194–95.] *Same jnl.*, 39 (5th S. 19), pp. 256–60, + 1 plate. 1909.

11121 —— Description of a carved stone at Tybroughney, co. Kilkenny. [Sexton, pp. 288–89.] *Same jnl.*, 38 (5th S. 18), pp. 270–77. 1908.

11122 —— The early cross-slabs and pillar stones at Church Island, near Waterville, co. Kerry. [10th–11th c.] *Same jnl.*, 56 (6th S. 16), pp. 43–47. 1926.

11123 —— The early crosses of East and West Meath. *Same jnl.*, 56 (6th S. 16), pp. 1–10, 71–81 : 57, pp. 1–6, + 14 plates. 1926–27.

11124 —— The early slabs at Lemanaghan, King's County. *Same jnl.*, 41 (6th S. 1), pp. 151–56. 1911.

11125 —— Notes on the crosses and carved doorways at Lorrha, in north Tipperary. [Crosses, ? 10th c. But 8th c. (F. Henry). Sexton, pp. 214–15.] *Same jnl.*, 39 (5th S. 19), pp. 126–31. 1909.

11126 Crawford (Henry Saxton). The sepulchral slab and round tower at Meelick, co. Mayo. [?10th–11th c. Figure of slab in text.] *Same jnl.*, 52 (6th S. 12), pp. 179–81. 1922.

11127 —— Some early monuments in the glen of Aherlow [co. Tipperary]. With notes on the inscriptions at Kilpeacan [co. Limerick], by R. A. S. Macalister. [?date.] *Same jnl.*, 39 (5th S. 19), pp. 59–69, + 1 plate. 1909.

11128 Crozier (Isabel) and **Lowry-Corry** (*Lady* Dorothy). Some Christian cross-slabs in co. Donegal and co. Antrim. [6th–7th c.] *Same jnl.*, 68 (7th S. 8), pp. 219–25, + 2 plates. 1938.

11129 Davies (Oliver). Clogher [co. Tyrone] crosses and other carved stones. [9th or 10th c. Figure in text.] Ulster J. Archaeol., 3rd S. 1, pp. 227–30. 1938.

11130 —— and **Paterson** (T. G. F.). The head of St. Patrick at Armagh. [From Armagh cathedral. After 9th c.] *Same jnl.*, 3rd S. 3, p. 68, + 1 plate. 1940.

11131 Doherty (William). Some ancient crosses . . . of Inishowen, co. Donegal. Proc. R.I.A., 3rd S. 2, pp. 100–16. 1893.

11132 FitzGerald (W.). The Dysart O'Dea high cross, parish of Dysart (Tola) [co. Clare]. [Sexton, pp. 143–46.] J. Ass. Preservation Memorials of the Dead in Ireland, 9, p. 21. 1913.

11133 FitzGerald (*Lord* Walter). On a holed cross at Moone [co. Kildare]. [Combination of pagan and Christian forms. Sexton, pp. 253–54.] J. Roy. Soc. Antiq. Ireland, 29 (5th S. 9), pp. 385–89. 1899.

11134 Galpin (Francis William). Ullard [co. Kilkenny] : its church and its cross. [Cross, 9th c. : 2 illustrations of it. *See also* Sexton, pp. 293–95.] Antiquary, 49, pp. 11–14. 1913.

11135 Given (Maxwell). The high cross of Saint Comgall at Camus-juxta-Bann [co. Derry]. [2 figures in text.] Ulster J. Archaeol., 2nd S. 11, pp. 145–52. 1905.

11136 Henry (Françoise). The decorated stones at Ballyvourney, co. Cork. J. Cork Hist. Soc., 57, pp. 41–42, + 2 plates. 1952.

11137 —— Figure in Lismore cathedral [co. Waterford]. [7th–8th c. ? Sexton, p. 212.] J. Roy. Soc. Antiq. Ireland, 67 (7th S. 7), pp. 306–07, + 1 plate. 1937.

11138 —— New monuments from Inishkea north, co. Mayo. *Same jnl.*, 81, pp. 65–69, + 2 plates. 1951.

11139 —— Three engraved slabs in the neighbourhood of Waterville (Kerry) and the cross on Skellig Michael. *Same jnl.*, 78, pp. 175–77, + 1 plate. 1948.

11140 Hitchcock (Francis Ryan Montgomery). The Kinnitty stone [King's County]. [9th c. *See also* Sexton, pp. 210–11.] *Same jnl.*, 47 (6th S. 7), p. 185, + 1 plate. 1917.

11141 Hunt (John). An unrecorded sheela-na-gig from [Caherelly], co. Limerick. *Same jnl.*, 77, pp. 158–59. 1947.

11142 Kendrick (*Sir* Thomas Downing). Gallen priory [King's County] excavations, 1934–5. [Lists and plates of sculptured slabs.] *Same inl.*, 69 (7th S. 9), pp. 1–20, + 6 plates. 1939.

11143 Lawlor (Henry Cairnes). Some primitive crosses in counties Antrim and Down. [Broughanlea cross, near Ballycastle : ?5th–7th c., erected to commemorate St. Fiachrius : figure.] Irish Naturalists' J., 6, pp. 294–97. 1937.

11144 Leask (Harold G.). Carved stones discovered at Kilteel, co. Kildare. J. Roy. Soc. Antiq. Ireland, 65 (7th S. 5), pp. 1–8, + 3 plates. 1935.

11145 Lett (H. W.). St. MacErc's cross, Donaghmore, co. Down. Ann. Rep. and Proc. Belfast Nat. F.C., N.S. 3, pp. 390–94, + 1 plate. 1892.

11146 Lowry-Corry (*Lady* Dorothy). The market cross at Lisnaskea [co. Fermanagh]. [9th or 10th c., with carving of Adam and Eve and the tree of knowledge. Sexton, p. 213.] J. Roy. Soc. Antiq. Ireland, 65 (7th S. 5), pp. 153–56, + 1 plate. 1935.

11147 Lowry-Corry (*Lady* Dorothy). The sculptured crosses of Galloon [co. Fermanagh]. [Probably late 9th or early 10th c. Sexton, pp. 156–59]. *Same jnl.*, 64 (7th S. 4), pp. 165–76, + 4 plates. 1934.

11148 —— The sculptured stones at Killadeas [co. Fermanagh]. [A cross-shaft, a stone with a Greek cross, probably 8th c., and a stone with human figure carvings, possibly 7th or 8th c. Sexton, p. 196.] *Same jnl.*, 65 (7th S. 5), pp. 23–33, and 3 plates. 1935.

11149 Macalister (Robert Alexander Stewart). Notes on the sculptured slabs at Gallen priory [King's County]. *Same jnl.*, 38 (5th S. 18), pp. 323–27. 1908.

11150 —— Some cross-slabs in the neighbourhood of Athlone [co. Westmeath]. *Same jnl.*, 42 (6th S. 2), pp. 27–31, + 1 plate. 1912.

11151 MacDermott (Máire). Terminal mounting of a drinking horn from Lismore, co. Waterford. [8th–9th c.] *Same jnl.*, 80, p. 262, + 1 plate. 1950.

11152 Macnamara (George U.). The ancient stone crosses of Ui-Fearmaic, county Clare. *Same jnl.*, 29 (5th S. 9), pp. 244–55 : 30, pp. 22–33. 1899–1900.

11153 —— The cross of Dysert O'Dea, [co. Clare]. *Same jnl.*, 30, pp. 377–78. 1900.

11154 O'Reilly (Patrick J.). The early Christian leacs and free-standing crosses of the Dublin half-barony of Rathdown. *Same jnl.*, 31 (5th S. 11), pp. 134–61, 246–58, 385–403. 1901.

11155 Orpen (Goddard Henry). The Hollywood stone [co. Wicklow] and the labyrinth of Knossos. [? of Danish period. But *see* **11112**. Answered by G. H. O., vol. 59 (6th S. 19), pp. 176–79, 1929.] *Same jnl.*, 53 (6th S. 13), pp. 177–89, + 2 plates. 1923.

11156 Paterson (T. G. F.). Brigid's crosses in co. Armagh. Ulster J. Arch., 3rd S. 8, pp. 43–48. 1945.

11157 Porter (Arthur Kingsley). A relief of Labhraidh Loingseach at Armagh. [Sexton, pp. 61–64.] J. Roy. Soc. Antiq. Ireland, 61 (7th S. 1), pp. 142–56, + 1 plate. 1931.

11158 Power (Patrick). The Celtic crosses of Kilkieran [co. Kilkenny], Kilklispeen [now called Ahenny, co. Tipperary] and Killamory [co. Kilkenny]. [Sexton, pp. 194–95, 48–52, 198–201.] J. Waterford Archaeol. Soc., Suppl. to 9, pp. 1–20. 1906.

11159 —— Curious inscribed stone at Tybroghney [co. Kilkenny, near Carrick-on-Suir]. [Sexton, pp. 288–89.] *Same jnl.*, 3, pp. 47–48, + 1 plate. 1897.

11160 Price (Liam). Glencolumbkille, county Donegal, and its early Christian cross-slabs. J. Roy. Soc. Antiq. Ireland, 71 (7th S. 11), pp. 71–88, + 4 plates. 1941.

11161 Purser (Olive). Fragment of a Celtic cross found at Drumcullin, King's County. [Sexton, p. 127.] *Same inl.*, 48 (6th S. 8), pp. 74–77, + 1 plate. 1918.

11162 Reade (George H.). The pillar-stone of Kilnasaggart, [co. Louth]. J. Kilkenny Archaeol. Soc., [4] N.S. 1, pp. 315–18, + 2 plates. 1857.

11163 Reeves (William) *bp. of Down*. Tynan and its crosses. (Clonarb and its crosses). [co. Armagh. 11 figures in text.] J. Roy. Hist. and Arch. Assoc. Ireland, [16] 4th S. 6 (1883–84), pp. 412–30, + 1 plate. 1884.

11164 Ronan (Myles V.). Cross-in-circle stones of St. Patrick's cathedral, [Dublin]. J. Roy. Soc. Antiq. Ireland, 71 (7th S. 11), pp. 1–8, + 1 plate. 1941.

11165 Scott (George Digby). The stones of Bray [co. Wicklow] and the stories they can tell of ancient times in the barony of Rathdown. pp. 247. 8° Dublin, 1913.

11166 Stokes (Margaret MacNair). Celtic crosses at Castledermot, [co. Kildare]. [Sexton, pp. 91–96.] J. co. Kildare Archaeol. Soc., 1, pp. 281–85, + 1 plate. 1895.

11167 —— The high crosses of Castledermot and Durrow, with an introduction on the high crosses of Ireland. *Royal Irish Academy*. pp. xiv, 12. fol. Dublin, 1898. [Kenney, 1, p. 103. 12 illustrations. Reviewed in Church Q. Rev., 48, pp. 121–43. 1899.]

11168 Stokes (Margaret MacNair). The holed-stone cross at Moone. [3 figures in text. Sexton, pp. 253–54.] J. co. Kildare Archaeol. Soc., 3, pp. 33–38. 1899.

11169 —— Notes on the high crosses of Moone, Drumcliff, Termonfechin, and Killamery. [co. Kildare, Sligo, Louth, Kilkenny. Sexton, pp. 246–52, 124–26, 277–79, 198–201.] Trans. R.I.A., 31, pp. 541–78, + 24 plates. 1901.

11170 —— Old Kilcullen [co. Kildare]. [Cross-shaft in churchyard : 3 figures.] J. co. Kildare Archaeol. Soc., 2, pp. 431–46. 1899.

11171 Vigors (Philip D.). The antiquities of Ullard, co. Kilkenny. [Pp. 255–57 with figure, cross. Sexton, pp. 293–95.] J. Roy. Soc. Antiq. Ireland, 23 (5th S. 3), pp. 251–60. 1893.

11172 Wallace (J. N. A.). Carved stone pillar at Bantry, co. Cork. [*See also* Sexton, p. 67.] N. Munster Antiq. J., 2, pp. 153–55. 1941.

11173 Wheeler (Henry). Cross slabs at Inishkeel, co. Donegal. [Sexton, p. 172.] J. Roy. Soc. Antiq. Ireland, 64 (7th S. 4), p. 262, + 2 plates. 1934.

11174 Williams (Sterling de Courcy). The old graveyards in Durrow [King's County] parish. [9 figures of crosses, etc., in text. Sexton, pp. 135–44.] *Same inl.*, 27 (5th S. 7), pp. 128–49. 1897.

11175 Windle (*Sir* Bertram Coghill Alan). Note on an early cross found at Reask, co. Kerry. [Not later than 7th c.] J. Ivernian Soc., 3, p. 249, + 1 plate. 1911.

192. SCULPTURE, ISLE OF MAN
§ *a*. General

11176 Allen (John Romilly). The early Christian monuments of the Isle of Man. J. Brit. Archaeol. Assoc., 43, pp. 240–66, + 1 plate. 1887.

11177 Barnwell (Edward Lowry). Notes on the stone monuments of the Isle of Man. Archaeol. Camb., 12, pp. 46–60. 1866.

11178 Cumming (Joseph George). On the ornamentation of the runic monuments in the Isle of Man. Arch. Camb., 3rd S. 12, pp. 156–67, + 2 plates. 1866.

11179 Jewitt (Llewellynn). Passing notes on some of the sculptured stone crosses and other remains of past ages in the Isle of Man. [18 figures in text.] Reliquary, 25, pp. 97–112, + 2 plates. 1884.

11180 Kermode (Philip Moore Callow). Manx crosses as illustrations of Celtic and Scandinavian art. Report Brit. Assoc., 66, pp. 934–35. 1896.

11181 —— The monumental crosses of Mann : with suggestions as to means to be adopted for their better preservation. Trans. I.O.M., N.H. and Antiq. Soc., 1 (1879–84), pp. 148–57. 1888.

11182 —— Saga illustrations of early Manks monuments. [3 figures in text.] Saga-Book V.C., 1, pp. 350–69, + 6 plates. 1897.

11183 —— Traces of Norse mythology in the Isle of Man. pp. 30, + 10 plates. 8° London, 1904. [The plates are all cross-sculpture.]

11184 Kermode (R. D.). The Vikings in Man. Haakon Shetelig's view of the Scandinavian-Manx crosses. J. Manx Mus., 3, pp. 23–25, 45–49, + 1 plate. 1935.

11185 Knox (Archibald). Ancient crosses in the Isle of Man. [16 figures in text.] Builder, 65, pp. 243–46. 1893.

11186 Liverpool, *Public Museums*. Handbook and guide to the replicas and casts of Manx crosses on exhibition. pp. 23, + 4 plates. 8° Liverpool, 1930.

11187 MacArthur (William). Norse myths illustrated on Manx crosses. N. and Q., 11th S. 5, p. 506. 1912.

11188 Mayhew (Samuel Martin). Notes on the Isle of Man. [Pp. 51–53, runic monuments.] J. Brit. Archaeol. Assoc., 37, pp. 47–55. 1881.

11189 Oswald (H. R.). Notes of references to the series of delineations of the runic and other ancient crosses found in the Isle of Man. Archaeol. Scot., 2, pp. 502–08, + 3 plates. 1822.

11190 Shetelig (Haakon). Manx crosses—relating to Great Britain and Norway. [14 figures in text.] Saga–Book V.C., 9, pp. 253–74. 1925.

11191 Windele (John). On the runic crosses of the Isle of Man. Proc. and Trans. Kilkenny Archaeol. Soc., 3, pp. 151–60. 1854.

11192 Wood (G. W.). The earliest drawings of the runic crosses of the Isle of Man. I.O.M. N.H. and Antiq., Soc., Proc., N.S. 2 (1917–23), pp. 302–03. 1924.

§ *b*. Individual

11193 [Anon.] Unique carved slab found at Ronaldsway. [Probably an altar slab of 8th c.] J. Manx Mus., 3, p. 43, + 1 plate. 1935.

11194 Banks (*Mrs*. Mary Macleod). Gerth at Kirk Michael : a new interpretation. J. Manx Mus., 3, pp. 207–08, + 1 plate. 1937.

11195 Black (George F.). Notice of a sculptured stone [at Kirk Andreas] with representation of Sigurd Fafni's bane. [?late 11th c. With ' other examples '. 6 figures in text.] Proc. Soc. Antiq. Scot., 21 (N.S. 9), pp. 325–38. 1887.

11196 —— Notice of two sculptured stones at Kirk Andreas, one bearing an inscription in bind-runes ; with notices of other bind-rune inscriptions. [9 figures in text.] *Same jnl.*, 23, (N.S. 11), pp. 332–43. 1889.

11197 Bowdin ( ). Monument at Kirk Michael. Gent. Mag., 68, p. 749, + 1 plate. 1798.

11198 Cumming (Joseph George). On a newly recovered runic monument at Kirk Braddan. Archaeol. J., 14, pp. 263–66, + 1 plate. 1857.

11199 —— On some more recently discovered Scandinavian crosses in the Isle of Man. Arch. Camb., 3rd S. 12, pp. 460–65, + 4 plates. 1866.

11200 Dodds (George). Observations on the symbolism of an incised stone in Kirk-Braddon churchyard. [? early 10th c.] Reliquary, 14, pp. 137–42, + 2 plates. 1874.

11201 Dodds (George). On an ancient stone found in the ruins of the old chapel in the Calf of Man. [?early 8th c.] Reliquary, 14, pp. 81–84, + 1 plate. 1872.

11202 Ellis *afterwards* **Davidson** (Hilda Roderick) and **Megaw** (Basil R. S.). Gaut the sculptor. [Name found in inscription at Kirk Michael cut in Norse runes by him. c. 1000.] J. Manx Mus., 5, pp. 136–39. 1944.

11203 Ffrench (James F. M.). On an inscribed [?=carved] monumental stone from the Isle of Man. [Andreas.] J. Roy. Hist. and Arch. Assoc. Ireland, [18] 4th S. 8, pp. 438–40. 1887.

11204 Hencken (Hugh O'Neill). A Manx gaming board of the Viking age. [10th c. Plates show ornament with comparisons from crosses.] J. Manx Mus., 2, pp. 164–65, + 4 plates. 1934.

11205 Jewitt (Llewellynn). A few words on the fylfot, and its occurrence on a sculptured stone at Onchan. [33 figures in text.] Manx Note Bk., 1, pp. 4–16. 1885.

11206 Kermode (Philip Moore Callow). The antiquities of the parish of Bride. [Crosses, keeils (chapels), etc.] Yn Lioar Manninagh, 1, pp. 182–89. 1890.

11207 —— Cross-slabs in the Isle of Man brought to light since December 1915. Proc. Soc. Antiq. Scot., 55 (5th S. 7, 1920–21), pp. 256–60. 1921.

11208 —— Cross-slabs recently discovered in the Isle of Man. [18 figures in text.] *Same jnl.*, 46 (4th S. 10, 1911–12), pp. 53–76. 1912.

11209 —— Descriptive particulars of places visited [by the Royal Society of Antiquaries of Ireland : Isle of Man, 1910]. [The sculptured and inscribed stones of the Isle of Man : the cross-slabs at Kirk Conchan : Kirk Braddan crosses : the Peel cross-slabs : the cross-slabs of Kirk Michael : the crosses of Maughold.] J. Roy. Soc. Antiq. Ireland, 40 (5th S. 20), pp. 393–427, + 5 plates. 1910.

11210 Kermode (Philip Moore Callow). First appearance of a Viking ship on a Manx monument. [Figure in text.] Mannin, no. 3, pp. 178–80. 1914.

11211 —— Further discoveries of cross-slabs in the Isle of Man. [9 figures in text.] Proc. Soc. Antiq. Scot., 50 (5th S. 2, 1915–16), pp. 50–62. 1916.

11212 —— The Hedin cross, Maughold. [2 figures in text.] Saga-Book V.C., 9, pp. 333–42. 1925.

11213 —— Horleif's cross, Kirk Braddon. [4 drawings.] J. Manx Mus., 3, plate 71. 1936.

11214 —— Inscribed cross-slab from keeill at Ballavarkish, Bride. [7th or early 8th c.] I.O.M. N.H. and Antiq. Soc., Proc., N.S. 1, pp. 593–95. 1914.

11215 —— More cross-slabs from the Isle of Man. Proc. Soc. Antiq. Scot., 63 (6th S. 3, 1928–29), pp. 354–60. 1929.

11216 —— A rune-inscribed slab from Kirk Maughold ; and the first figure of a Viking ship on a Manx monument. I.O.M. N.H. and Antiq. Soc., Proc., N.S. 2 (1913–15), pp. 107–13. 1923.

11217 —— Sculptured and inscribed stones recently found at Kirk Maughold. [P. 631, 7th c. Anglian runes, similar to Bewcastle cross and Frank's casket.] Yn Lioar Manninagh, 3, pp. 629–33. 1902.

11218 —— A sculptured stone recently discovered in Ramsey, and the story of Sigurd the Volsung, as illustrated on monuments in the Isle of Man. [4 figures in text.] *Same jnl.*, 4, pp. 60–68. 1910.

11219 —— Some early Christian monuments recently discovered at Kirk Maughold. [With 16 figures.] Reliquary, 8, pp. 182–93. 1902.

11220 Kermode (R. D.). The Vikings in Man. [Analysis of the style and ornament of Gaut's and later crosses.] J. Manx Mus., 3, pp. 45–49. 1935.

11221 Megaw (Basil R. S.). An ancient carving from Kirk Maughold. [Capital : c. 1000.] J. Manx Mus., 3, pp. 209–10, + 1 glate. 1937.

11222 Megaw (Basil R. S.). Seven crosses and an unusual carved slab found since 1932. J. Manx Mus., 4, pp. 163–64, + 2 plates. 1939.

11223 Quine (John). Anglian crosses in Maughold. I.O.M. N.H. and Antiq. Soc., Proc., N.S. 1 (1913–15), pp. 129–31. 1923.

11224 Styrap (H. G. Jukes de). St. Maughold. [Sculptured stone, including figure of a bishop, over west door. ?bp. Roolver, c. 1050.] Arch. Camb., 4th S. 9, p. 77. 1878.

11225 Way (Albert). Sketches of some remarkable sculptured crosses [at Kirk Braddan, Kirk Andreas and Kirk Michael]. [With 3 figures.] Archaeol. J., 2, pp. 74–76. 1846.

193. SCULPTURE, SCOTLAND

§ a. General

11226 [Anon.] The sculptured and cross stones of Scotland. Ecclesiologist, 23, pp. 129–31. 1862.

11227 Allen (John Romilly). Preliminary list of sculptured stones older than 1100, with symbols and Celtic ornament in Scotland. Proc. Soc. Antiq. Scot., 24 (N.S. 12), pp. 510–25. 1890.

11228 —— Report on the sculptured stones (on the photographs of the sculptured stones) older than A.D. 1100, with symbols and Celtic ornament, in the district of Scotland north of the river Dee. (*Ditto* south of the river Dee). *Same jnl.*, 25 (3rd S. 1), pp. 422–31 : 26 (3rd S. 2), pp. 251–59 : photographs, 28 (3rd s. 4), pp. 150–77 : 31 (3rd S. 7), pp. 147–52. 1891–92 ; 1894, 1897.

11229 Anderson (Joseph). Notices of some undescribed sculptured stones and fragments in different parts of Scotland. [13 figures in text.] *Same jnl.*, 23 (N.S. 11), pp. 344–55. 1889.

11230 Crawford (Osbert Guy Stanhope). The vine-scroll in Scotland. Antiquity, 11, pp. 469–73, + 4 plates. 1937.

11231 Curle (Cecil L.). The chronology of the early Christian monuments of Scotland. [Map, + 15 figures in text.] Proc. Soc. Antiq. Scot., 74 (7th S. 2), pp. 60–116, + 40 plates. 1940.

11232 Galbraith (James John). Some problems of the sculptured monuments. (—2. Chronology.) Trans. Gaelic Soc. Inverness, 33 (1925–27), pp. 245–52 : 36 (1931–33), pp. 218–39. 1932–41.

11233 Graham (Robert C.). The early Christian monuments of Scotland. Scot. H. R., 1 pp. 58–61, + 2 plates. 1904.

11234 Hannah (Ian Campbell). Story of Scotland in stone. pp. xv, 332. 8° Edinburgh, 1934. [Pp. 13–49, figures 1–26, A.–S. period.]

11235 Hibbert-Ware (S.). On the sculptured stones of Scotland. Archaeol. Scot., 4, pp. 415–18. 1857.

11236 Lowson (George). The early sculptured monuments of Scotland. Trans. Stirling N.H. and Archaeol. Soc., 18 (1895–96). 1896.

11237 Mackenzie (Donald A.). Ancient sculptured stones of Scotland. J. Antiq. Assoc. Brit. Isles, 1, pp. 156–63, + 2 plates. 1931.

11238 MacLagan (C.) *Miss.* Sculptured stones in the east and west of Scotland. Trans. Stirling N.H. and Archaeol. Soc., 12 (1889–90). 1890.

11239 MacLagan (Christian). A catalogue raisonné of the British Museum collection of rubbings from ancient sculptured stones. A chapter of Scotland's history. pp. 99. Small 4° Edinburgh, 1898.

11240 Simpson (William Douglas). Pictish symbolism and the sculptured stones of Scotland. A study of the early Christian monuments. Falkirk Archaeol. Soc., Proc., 2, pp. 67–70, + 1 plate. 1938.

11241 Stuart (John). Sculptured stones of Scotland. *Spalding Club.* 2 vol. fol. Aberdeen, 1856–67. [With 269 plates.]

§ *b.* **Argyllshire**

11242 Allen (John Romilly). The early Christian monuments of Iona ; with some suggestions for their better preservation. [12 figures in text.] Proc. Soc. Antiq. Scot., 35 (3rd S. 11, 1900–01), pp. 79–93. 1901.

11243 Anderson (Joseph). The great cross of Kildalton [Islay]. [2 figures in text. Reprinted from Proc. Soc. Antiq. Scot., N.S. 5, 1883.] J. Roy. Soc. Antiq. Ireland, 29 (5th S. 9), pp. 157–60. 1899.

11244 Collingwood (William Gershom). Viking-age cross at Iona. [2 figures in text.] Saga-Book V.C., 3, pp. 304–06. 1904.

11245 Crawford (W. C.). Notes on the grave slabs and cross at Keills, Knapdale. [Figures show zoomorphic and interlaced patterns.] Proc. Soc. Antiq. Scot., 54 (5th S. 6, 1919–20), pp. 248–52. 1920.

11246 Drummond (James). Archaeologia Scotica. Sculptured monuments in Iona and the West Highlands. *Soc. Antiq. Scotland.* pp. 19, + 100 plates, + their letterpress. fol. Edinburgh, 1881. [Kenney, 1, p. 422. A.–S. and later.]

11247 Graham (Robert C.). The carved stones of Islay. pp. xvi, 119, + 32 plates, + map. 4° Glasgow, 1895.

11248 Macalister (Robert Alexander Stewart). An inventory of the ancient monuments remaining in the island of Iona. Proc. Soc. Antiq. Scot., 48 (4th S. 12, 1913–14), pp. 421–30. 1914.

11249 MacLagan (C.) *Miss.* Iona and its sculptured stones. Trans. Stirling Archaeol. Soc., 8 (1885–86). 1887.

11250 —— Scultured stones and crosses of Islay. *Same jnl.*, 5 (1882–83). 1883.

§ *c.* **Dumfriesshire**

11251 Charleson (C. Forbes). Fragments from old Kirkconnel. [3 plates show cross-fragments.] Trans. Dumfries. Antiq. Soc., 3rd S. 15, pp. 119–37, + 3 plates. 1929.

11252 Charleson (C. Forbes). Notes on the site of a pre-Norman chapel of S. Conal in upper Nithsdale. [Fragments of 4 crosses. 6 figures in text.] Trans. Scot. Ecclesiol. Soc., 9, pp. 158–71. 1930.

11253 Clapham (*Sir* Alfred William). The cross-shaft at Nith Bridge. [9th c. Anglian tradition. No illustration.] Trans. Dumfries. Antiq. Soc., 3rd S. 22 (1938–40), pp. 183–84. 1942.

11254 Collingwood (William Gershom). The early Church in Dumfriesshire and its monuments. [i. St. Kentigern : ii. Monuments. Plates show crosses.] *Same jnl.*, 3rd S. 12 (1924–25), pp. 46–62, + 5 plates. 1926.

11255 Gibson-Craig (James T.). Saxon cross, found in the ruins of Hoddam church. Proc. Soc. Antiq. Scot., 1, pp. 11–12. 1852.

11256 Hewat (Kirkwood). Notice of a peculiar stone cross, found on the farm of Cairn, parish of New Cumnock, upper Nithsdale. [2 figures in text, showing interlacing.] *Same jnl.*, 34 (3rd S. 10, 1899–1900), pp. 300–03. 1900.

11257 Mann (Ludovic MacLellan). The archaic sculpturings of Dumfries and Galloway ; being chiefly interpretations of the local cup and ring markings, and of the designs of the early Christian monuments. Trans. Dumfries. Antiq. Soc., 3rd S. 3, pp. 121–66, + 6 plates. 1915.

11258 Radford (Courtenay Arthur Ralegh). An early cross at Ruthwell. [7th–9th c.] *Same jnl.*, 3rd S. 28 (1949–50), pp. 158–60. 1951.

§ d. Orkney and Shetland

11259 Charlton (Edward). On the Ogham inscription from the island of Bressay, Shetland, 1853. [Monsters, interlacing work, etc.] Archaeol. Æl., [1st S.] 4, pp. 150–56, + 1 plate. 1855.

11260 Cursiter (James Walls). Notice of a wood-carver's tool-box, with Celtic ornamentation, recently discovered in a peat-moss in the parish of Birsay, Orkney. [8th–9th c. 2 figures in text.] Proc. Soc. Antiq. Scot., 20 (N.S. 8), pp. 47–50. 1886.

11261 Dietrichson (Lorentz Henrik Segelcke). Monumenta Orcadica. Normændene paa Orknøerne, *etc.* pp. xvi, 200, + 86 plates. 4° Kristiania, 1906. [Pp. 43–57, + 2 plates, De Kristnede Kelters mindesmærker, c. 600–872.] —[English summary]. Monumenta Orcadica : the Norsemen in the Orkneys and the monuments they have left. With a survey of the Celtic (pre-Norwegian) ... monuments on the islands. With 152 illustrations. pp. xiv, 77. 4° Kristiania, 1906. [Pp. 7–8, brochs : pp. 8–11, c. 600–872 : pp. 13–44, Norwegian monuments under Celtic influence (872–c. 1200.]

11262 Goudie (Gilbert). Notice of a sculptured slab from the island of Burra, Shetland. Proc. Soc. Antiq. Scot., 15 (N.S. 3), pp. 199–209. 1881.

11263 Hamilton (Zachary Macaulay) *donor*. Sculptured stone with Ogham inscriptions, found at Bressay, Shetland, in the Museum of the Antiquaries of Scotland. *Same jnl.*, 5, pp. 239–40, + 2 plates. 1865.

11264 Jewitt (Llewellynn). Sculptured stone, with Ogham inscription, on the island of Bressay, in Shetland. Reliquary, 25, p. 232, + 2 plates. 1885.

11265 Mackenzie (W. Mackay). The dragonesque figure in Maeshowe, Orkney. [12th c., but remarks on A.–S., Viking, etc., zoomorphic ornament. 15 figures in text.] Proc. Soc. Antiq. Scot., 7 (6th S. 11, 1936–37), pp. 157–73. 1937.

11266 Marwick (Hugh). Ancient monuments in Orkney. *H.M.S.O.* pp. 40, + 12 plates, + map. 8° Edinburgh, 1952.

11267 Moar (Peter) and **Stewart** (John). Newly discovered sculptured stones from Papil, Shetland. Proc. Soc. Antiq. Scot., 78 (7th S. 6, 1943–44), pp. 91–99, + 2 plates. 1944.

11268 Tait (Edwyn Seymour Reid). Fragment of a cross-slab from the churchyard of Whiteness, Shetland. [With figure.] *Same jnl.*, 71 (6th S. 11, 1936–37), pp. 369–70. 1937.

§ e. Perthshire

11269 Aglen (Anthony Stocker). The sculptured stones at Meigle. pp. 18. 8° Dundee, 19-. [? 7th, ?11th c.]

11270 Allen (John Romilly). Notice of sculptured stones at Kilbride [Perthshire], Kilmartin [Argyllshire] and Dunblane [Perthshire]. Proc. Soc. Antiq. Scot., 15 (N.S. 3), pp. 254–61. 1881.

11271 —— On the discovery of a sculptured stone at St. Madoes, with some notes on interlaced ornament. [223 figures in text.] Same jnl., 17 (N.S. 5), pp. 211–71. 1883.

11272 Anderson (Arthur). Notice of the discovery of a sculptured stone at Logierait. [Serpent-symbol and interlacing.] Same jnl., 12, pp. 561–64, + 1 plate. 1878.

11273 Calder (Charles S. T.). Note on a Pictish cross-slab from Gellyburn. Same inl., 85 (1950–51), pp. 175–77, + 1 plate. 1953.

11274 Galloway (William). Notice of several sculptured stones at Meigle, still undescribed. Same jnl., 12, pp. 425–34, + 3 plates. 1878.

11275 Hutcheson (Alexander). Notice of a sculptured stone recently discovered at Murtly, and now presented to the museum by Sir Douglas Stewart, bart., of Grantully. [With figure in text : cf. animal figures at Meigle.] Same jnl., 20 (N.S. 8), pp. 252–56. 1886.

11276 Laing (Alexander). Notice of a fragment of an ancient stone cross found at Carpow, in the parish of Abernethy. [8th c. Interlacing.] Same jnl., 12, pp. 462–65, + 1 plate. 1878.

§ c. St. Andrews, Fife

11277 Allen (John Romilly). A missing fragment of the pre-Norman altar tomb at St. Andrews, N.B. [Part also in York museum.] Reliquary, 12, pp. 270–73. 1906.

11278 Fleming (D. Hay). Further discovery of three Celtic cross-slabs at St. Andrews... [Interlacing.] Proc. Soc. Antiq. Scot., 52 (5th S. 4, 1917–18), pp. 126–30. 1918.

11279 Fleming (D. Hay). Note on a Celtic cross-slab and two fragments recently found at St. Andrews. [4 figures in text.] Same jnl., 47 (4th S. 11, 1912–13), pp. 463–68. 1913.

11280 —— Notice of a sculptured cross-shaft and sculptured slabs recovered from the base of St. Andrews cathedral by direction of Mr. Oldrieve of H.M. Office of Works, with notes of other sculptured slabs at St. Andrews. [23 figures in text.] Same jnl., 43 (4th S. 7, 1908–09), pp. 385–414. 1909.

11281 —— Two sculptured stones, a coped coffin-cover [etc.] found in St. Andrews. [Interlacing.] Same jnl., 58 (5th S. 10, 1923–24), pp. 330–32. 1924.

11282 Hutcheson (Alexander). Notice of the recent discovery of fragments of ancient sculptured crosses at the cathedral church, St. Andrews. Same jnl., 26 (3rd S. 2), pp. 215–20. 1892.

11283 MacLagan (C.) *Miss.* The recently discovered sculptured stones at St. Andrews. Trans. Stirling Archaeol. Soc., 17 (1894–95), 1895.

1284 Mowbray (Cecil). Eastern influence on carvings at St. Andrews and Nigg [Ross], Scotland. [With parallels with 7th–8th c. Irish and Manx crosses and Northumbrian art.] Antiquity, 10, pp. 428–40, + 9 plates. 1936.

§ g. Wigtownshire
(Galloway)

11285 Anderson (Robert S. G.) Crosses and rock sculptures recently discovered in Wigtownshire. [Late 11th c., etc.] Proc. Soc. Antiq. Scot., 61 (6th S. 1, 1926–27), pp. 115–22. 1927.

11286 —— Crosses from the Rhinns of Galloway. [6 figures in text.] Same jnl., 71 (6th S. 11, 1936–37), pp. 388–97. 1937.

11287 —— Sculptured stones of Old Luce church. [10th–11th c. 4 figures in text.] Same jnl., 70 (6th S. 10, 1935–36). pp. 139–45. 1936.

11288 —— Two Celtic crosses from the Machars. Same jnl., 57 (5th S. 9, 1922–23), pp. 17–19. 1923.

11289 Collingwood (William Gershom). The early crosses of Galloway. [i. Relics of the primitive Church (Kirkmadrine, etc.): ii. Anglian remains in Galloway (Northumbrian crosses, Anglo-Cumbrian stones): iii. Whithorn school: iv. Later Galloway crosses.] Trans. Dumfries. Antiq. Soc., 3rd S. 10 (1922–23), pp. 205–31, + 15 plates. 1925.

11290 —— and **Reid** (R. C.). Whithorn priory. *H.M.S.O.*, pp. 27. 8° London, 1928. [9 pages of plates of sculptured crosses interpaginated.]

11291 Glenluce, *Local authority.* [Exhibition of] sculptured stone from Glenluce. [5½ feet high. Interlacing.] Proc. Soc. Antiq. Scot., 15 (N.S. 3), pp. 8–9. 1881.

11292 Maxwell (*Sir* Herbert Eustace) *7th bart.* The crosses of Kirkmadrine: discovery of the missing third cross. [6 figures in text.] *Same jnl.,* 51 (5th S. 3, 1916–17), pp. 199–207. 1917.

11293 —— Notice of the further excavation of St. Ninian's cave, parish of Glasserton. [Discovery of cross with 'intricate interlaced design of Celtic character', + 5 runic letters. ?6th c.] *Same jnl.,* 21 (N.S. 9), pp. 137–41. 1887. *Same title.* Archaeol. and Hist. Collns. Ayrshire and Galloway, 6. 1889.

11294 —— Shaft of a Celtic cross from Longcastle. [2 figures showing interlaced work.] Proc. Soc. Antiq. Scot., 55 (5th S. 7, 1920–21), pp. 276–77. 1921.

11295 Radford (Courtenay Arthur Ralegh). The Pictish symbols at Trusty's Hill, Kirkcudbrightshire. [Early 8th c.] Antiquity, 27, pp. 237–39, + 1 plate. 1953.

11296 —— Two unrecorded crosses found near Stranraer. [Liddesdale cross, c. 820: Glaik cross, c. 1100.] Trans. Dumfriesshire Antiq. Soc., 3rd S. 27 (1948–49), pp. 193–96, + 2 plates. 1950.

§ *h.* Others

11297 [Anon.] The Fordoun [Kincardine] sculptured stone. [?Commemorates Kenneth III.] Scottish N. and Q., 7, pp. 81–82, + 1 plate. 1893.

11298 [**Anon.**] Harvey and his theory of the circulation of the blood as represented on a sculptured stone at Montrose [museum.] [From Inchbrayock, Forfar.] Scot. N. and Q., 3rd S. 6, pp. 205–08, + 1 plate. 1928.

11299 Allen (John Romilly). The early Christian monuments of the Glasgow district. Trans. Glasgow Archaeol. Soc., N.S. 4, pp. 394–405, + 7 plates. 1913.

11300 Anderson (Joseph). Description of a collection of objects found in excavations at St Blane's church, Bute. [36 figures in text, including some of sculptured stones, showing interlacing.] Proc. Soc. Antiq. Scot., 34 (3rd S. 10, 1899–1900), pp. 307–25. 1900.

11301 —— Notices of a sculptured stone with ogham inscription, from Latheron [Caithness], presented to the National Museum [of Scotland] by Sir Francis Tress Barry, bart., . . . and of two sculptured stones, recently discovered by Rev. D. Macrae at Edderton, Ross-shire. [Interlaced pattern, also bird and fish.] *Same jnl.,* 38 (4th S. 2, 1903–04), pp. 534–41. 1904.

11302 Anderson (Robert S. G.). Three crosses in the south-west of Scotland. [iii. Fardenreoch, Colmonell, Ayrshire. Late 10th c. One figure in text.] *Same jnl.,* 60 (5th S. 12, 1925–26), pp. 266–68. 1927.

11303 Beaton (Donald). The early Christian monuments of Caithness. Oldlore Misc., 6, pp. 75–85, 119–129, 195–201, + 11 plates. 1913.

11304 Calder (Charles S. T.). Three fragments of a sculptured cross of Anglian type now preserved in Abercorn church, West Lothian. [3 figures in text.] Proc. Soc. Antiq. Scot., 72 (6th S. 12, 1937–38), pp. 217–23. 1938.

11305 Callander (J. Graham). Crossshaft from Morham, East Lothian. [4 figures in text.] *Same jnl.,* 67 (6th S. 7, 1932–33), pp. 241–43. 1933.

11306 Clark (Ivo M.). Farnell sculptured stone [Aberdeenshire]. [2 figures in text.] Scot. N. and Q., 3rd S. 3, pp. 62–63. 1925.

11307 Cooke (T. Etherington). Notice of a cross-shaft at Arthurlee, Renfrewshire. [Interlacing.] Proc. Soc. Antiq. Scot., 9, pp. 451–52, + 1 plate. 1873.

11308 Davidson (James Milne). A Pictish symbol stone from Golspie, Sutherland. *Same jnl.*, 77 (7th S. 5, 1942–43), pp. 26–30, + 1 plate. 1943.

11309 Duke (William). Notice of a recumbent hog-backed monument, and portions of sculptured slabs with symbols recently discovered at St. Vigeans church, Forfarshire. [4 figures in text.] *Same jnl.*, 22 (N.S. 10), pp. 143–46. 1888.

11310 —— Notice of the fabric of St. Vigeans church, Forfarshire ; with notice and photographs of early sculptured stones recently discovered there. [Interlacing.] *Same jnl.*, 9, pp. 481–98, + 4 plates. 1873.

11311 Eeles (Francis Carolus). Notice of a Celtic cross-slab recently discovered at Kinneff, Kincardineshire. *Same jnl.*, 33 (3rd S. 9), pp. 163–67. 1899.

11312 —— Undescribed sculptured stones and crosses at Old Luce [Wigtown], Farnell [Angus], Edzell [Angus], Lochlee [Angus], and Kirkmichael (Banffshire), *etc.* [13 figures in text.] *Same jnl.*, 44 (4th S. 8, 1909–10), pp. 354–72. 1910.

11313 Fraser (J. E.). Small fragment of a sculptured stone, with a fretwork pattern, found on the shore of Loch Ness, near Dores. *Same jnl.*, 35 (3rd S. 11, 1900–01), pp. 106–07. 1901.

11314 Galbraith (James John). The chi-rho crosses on Raasay [Skye] : their importance and chronological relationships. [c. 560–590.] *Same jnl.*, 67 (6th S. 7, 1932–33), pp. 318–20. 1933.

11315 Galloway (William). Early Christian remains in Ayrshire. Archaeol. and Hist. Collns. Ayr and Wigton, 3, pp. 99–109, + 3 plates. 1882.

11316 —— Notice of a sculptured stone in the churchyard at Tullibole, Kinross-shire. [Interlacing.] Proc. Soc. Antiq. Scot., 13 (N.S. 1), pp. 316–20, + 1 plate. 1879.

11317 Hewison (James King). Notice of a Celtic cross-shaft in Rothesay churchyard. [?11th c. 2 figures in text.] *Same jnl.*, 25 (3rd S. 1), pp. 410–16. 1891.

11318 Lacaille (Armand D.). The Capelrig cross, Mearns, Renfrewshire ; St. Blane's chapel, Lochearnhead, Perthshire ; and a sculptured slab at Kilmaronock, Dumbartonshire. *Same jnl.*, 61 (6th S. 1, 1926–27), pp. 122–42. 1927.

11319 —— Ecclesiastical remains in the neighbourhood of Luss [Dumbartonshire], with notes on some unrecorded crosses and hog-backed stones. [9 figures in text.] *Same jnl.*, 62 (6th S. 2, 1927–28), pp. 85–106. 1928.

11320 Laing (Henry). A note respecting the sculptured cross at St. Vigeans, near Arbroath. *Same jnl.*, 1, pp. 294–96. 1852.

11321 Maclagan (C.) *Miss.* Notice of the discovery of two sculptured stones, with symbols, at Rhynie, Aberdeenshire. [Circles and horse's head.] *Same jnl.*, 14 (N.S. 2), pp. 11–13. 1880.

11322 —— Sculptured stones in the Western Isles of Scotland. Trans. Stirling F.C., 4 (1881–82), 1882.

11323 Miller (Hugh). Note on fragments of two sculptured stones of Celtic workmanship found in the churchyard of Tarbat, Easter Ross. [4 figures in text.] Proc. Soc. Antiq. Scot., 23 (N.S. 11), pp. 435–44. 1889.

11324 Milne (George). Sculptured cross at St. Vigeans. [Late 9th c.] Scottish N. and Q., 4, p. 83, + 1 plate. 1890.

11325 Mitchell (George Bennet). Glamis [Angus] church—its history and reconstruction. [3 crosses, 9th c. Plate shows Manse stone.] Trans. Scot. Ecclesiol. Soc., 11, pp. 106–13, + 2 plates. 1935.

11326 Morris (James A.). Notice of an undescribed slab with Celtic ornament ... at Girvan, Ayrshire. [Pp. 175–77, + 3 figures.] Proc. Soc. Antiq. Scot., 47 (4th S. 11, 1912–13), pp. 174–96. 1913.

11327 Morrison (Hew). Notices of the discovery of a stone coffin and fragment of a Celtic cross at Lethnott, Forfarshire, . . . [?9th c. Interlacing.] *Same jnl.*, 19 (N.S. 7), pp. 315–20. 1885.

11328 Napier (Alexander). Pre-Norman cross-shaft at Cambusnethan, Lanarkshire. [Strathclyde group.] Reliquary, 5, pp. 49–50. 1899.

11329 National Museum of Scotland. Fragment of cross-shaft from Cambusnethan, Lanarkshire. [4 figures in text.] Proc. Soc. Antiq. Scot., 72 (6th S. 12, 1937–38), pp. 12–13. 1938.

11330 Neish (James). Note of a donation of four sculptured stones from Monifieth, Forfarshire. [7th–9th, c.] *Same jnl.*, 9, pp. 71–77, + 3 plates. 1873.

11331 Petley (Charles Carter). A short account of some carved stones in Ross-shire, accompanied with a series of outline engravings. [Interlacing.] Archaeol. Scot., 4, pp. 345–52, + 8 plates. 1857.

11332 Ritchie (James). Description of a simple inscribed cross observed in the churchyard of Tarbat [Ross] and now destroyed. [Early Christian.] Proc. Soc. Antiq. Scot., 49 (5th S. 1, 1914–15), pp. 304–06. 1915.

11333 Ross (Thomas). Notice of undescribed hog-backed monuments at Abercorn [West Lothian] and Kirknewton [Midlothian]. [5 figures in text.] *Same jnl.*, 38 (4th S. 2, 1903–04), pp. 422–27. 1904.

11334 Simpson (William Douglas). The Augustinian priory and parish church of Monymusk, Aberdeenshire. [Pp. 36–40, 9th c. sculptured stone, with figure, and the ' Brechbannoch ' or reliquary of St. Columba : with 2 figures.] *Same jnl.*, 59 (5th S. 11, 1924–25), pp. 34–71. 1925.

11335 Stephens (George). Notice of a sculptured stone, bearing on one side an inscription in runes, from Kilbar, island of Barra, [Inverness]. [Norse, *c.* 11th c. 2 figures in text]. *Same jnl.*, 15 (N.S. 3), pp. 33–36. 1881.

11336 Story (R. Herbert). Note of a sculptured stone recently discovered at Rosneath, [Dumbarton]. [' Ornament much defaced, but seems to consist entirely of interlaced work and fret.' No illustration.] *Same jnl.*, 16 (N.S. 4), pp. 72–73. 1882.

11337 Waddell (J. Jeffrey). The cross of S. Kentigern at Hamilton, [Lanarkshire], and its environment. Trans. Scot. Ecclesiol. Soc., 5, pp. 247–56, + 2 plates. 1918.

11338 —— Cross-slabs recently discovered at Fowlis Wester, [Perth] and Millport, [Bute]. [2 figures in text. Interlaced ornament.] Proc. Soc. Antiq. Scot., 66 (6th S. 6, 1931–32), pp. 409–12. 1932.

11339 Wilson (Daniel). Some illustrations of early Celtic Christian art. [Kilbride cross, Argyllshire, and others. 5 figures in text.] *Same jnl.*, 20 (N.S. 8), pp. 222–39. 1886.

194. SCULPTURE, WALES

§ *a.* General

11340 Allen (John Romilly). Early Christian art in Wales. Arch. Camb., 5th S. 16, pp. 1–69, + 13 plates. 1899.

11341 —— The early Christian monuments of North Wales. [1. Early Celtic period, c. 450–600 : ii. Hiberno-Saxon period, 600–1066.] J. Chester Archaeol. and Hist. Soc., N.S. 4, pp. 34–51, + 3 plates. 1892.

11342 Hemp (Wilfrid J.). Some unrecorded ' sheela-na-gigs ' in Wales and the border. Arch. Camb., 93, pp. 136–39, + 3 plates. 1938.

11343 Jones (Harry Longueville). The crosses of Wales. [6th–7th c.] Arch. Camb., 3rd S. 7, pp. 205–13. 1861.

11344 Macalister (Robert Alexander Stewart). Early Christian period [in Wales]. Inscribed and sculptured stones. [Plate shows sculptured crosses at Nevern (Pemb.) and (Llanynis (Breck.).] Cambrian Archaeol. Assoc. Centenary vol., pp. 123–28, + 1 plate. 1946.

11345 Macalister (Robert Alexander Stewart). The sculptured stones of Wales. [2 plates interpaginated.] Porter (A. K.) : Medieval studies, 2, pp. 577–87. 1939.

11346 Nash-Williams (Victor Erle). The early Christian monuments of Wales. pp. xxiii, 258, + 71 plates. 4° Cardiff, 1950. [Both sculpture and inscriptions. 261 figures in text.]

11347 —— An inventory of the early Christian stone monuments of Wales, with a bibliography of the principal notices. [i. Anglesey to Flintshire : ii. Glamorganshire to Radnorshire. c. 400–1100.] Bull. Board Celt. Stud., 8, pp. 62–84, 161–88. 1935–36.

11348 —— Some early Welsh crosses and cross-slabs. Arch. Camb., 94, pp. 1–20, + 11 plates. 1939.

11349 —— Some Welsh early Christian monuments. Antiq. J., 19, pp. 147–56, + 3 plates. 1939.

11350 Westwood (John Obadiah). Lapidarium Walliae : the early inscribed and sculptured stones of Wales. *Cambrian Archaeological Association.* pp. viii, 246, + 101 plates. 4° Oxford, 1876–79. [Gross, 417. Including Ogham inscriptions.]

§ *b* Anglesey

11351 Allen (John Romilly). Crosses at Penmon. Arch. Camb., 5th S. 12, pp. 153–54. 1895.

11352 Allen (W. Bird). Notes on the Penmon cross. (Note on Penmon cross no. 1). Arch. Camb., 75 (6th S. 20), pp. 193–95, 291–92. 1920.

11353 Hughes (Henry Harold). The ancient churches of Anglesey. [11th c. → 18 figures in text, mostly of sculpture (fonts and crosses).] Arch. Camb., 85, pp. 237–66. 1930.

11354 —— Cross in the refectory at Penmon. Arch. Camb., 5th S. 13, pp. 62–63, + 2 plates. 1896.

11355 —— Early Christian decorative art in Anglesey. [81 figures in text.] Arch. Camb., 74 (6th S. 19), pp. 477–98 : 75 (6th S. 20), pp. 1–30 : 76 (7th S. 1), pp. 84–114 : 77 (7th S. 2), pp. 61–79 : 78, pp. 53–69 : 79, pp. 39–58. 1919–24.

11356 Hughes (Henry Harold). An early crucifix-head at Llanfachreth. [Figure in text.] Arch. Camb., 87, pp. 397–99. 1932.

11357 Macalister (Robert Alexander Stewart). Penmon [crosses]. [Figure in text.] Arch. Camb., 85, pp. 444–45. 1930.

11358 Radford (Courtenay Arthur Ralegh). The early mediaeval period [in Anglesey]. [Stones, crosses and sculpture. Illustrated.] Roy. Commission on hist. mon., Anglesey, pp. cxi–cxiii. 1937.

§ *c.* Carmarthenshire

11359 [Anon.] Inscribed wheel cross, Llanarthney. Arch. Camb., 5th S. 10, pp. 137–38. 1893.

11360 [Anon.] Llandeilo-Fawr. [2 cross-heads. 3 figures in text.] Arch. Camb., 5th S. 10, pp. 129–32. 1893.

11361 Allen (John Romilly). The cross of Eiudon, Golden Grove. Arch. Camb., 5th S. 10, pp. 48–55, + 2 plates. 1893.

11362 Hughes (Henry Harold). Cae'r Castell cross, Llanarthney church. [Figure in text. ?early 11th c.] Arch. Camb., 80 (7th S. 5), pp. 463–64. 1925.

11363 —— The cross at Eiudon. [? 10th c.]. Arch Camb., 80 (7th S. 5), p. 465. 1925.

11364 —— Cross-slab from Hen Gapel, Aberafon. [Now in museum of Carmarthenshire Antiquarian Society. 2 figures in text.] Arch. Camb., 81 (7th S. 6), pp. 193–97. 1926.

11365 —— [Two crosses in Llandilo churchyard]. [4 figures in text. 10th–11th c.] Arch. Camb., 80 (7th S. 5), pp. 492–96. 1925.

11366 Price (Lewis). Cross-heads at Llandeilo Fawr. Arch. Camb., 5th S. 11, pp. 79–80. 1894.

11367 Westwood (John Obadiah). The inscribed stones of Wales.—The Llech Eiudon. [Plate shows 4 sides—interlacing work.] Arch. Camb., 4th S. 2, pp. 339–42, + 1 plate. 1871.

11368 —— The Llandeilo cross. [2 figures in text.] Arch. Camb., 3rd S. 5, pp. 136–38. 1859.

§ d. Flintshire

Maen Ackwyfan

11369 Davies (Ellis W.). Letters relating to Maen Achwyfan. Arch. Camb., 77 (7th S. 2), pp. 155–58. 1922.

11370 —— Notes on the origin of Maen Achwyfan, Whitford, near Holywell. J. Brit. Archaeol. Assoc., N.S. 32, pp. 70–71. 1926.

11371 Hughes (Henry Harold). The carving on Maen Achwyfan. [5 figures in text.] Arch. Camb., 81 (7th S. 6), pp. 36–47. 1926. *Same title.* [6 figures in text, also on p. 41.] J. Brit. Archaeol. Assoc., N.S., pp. 59–69. 1926.

11372 —— Maen Achwyfan. [Figures in text.] Arch. Camb., 76 (7th S. 1), pp. 408–10. 1921.

11373 Westwood (John Obadiah). The Maen Achwynfan. Arch. Camb., 3rd S. 11, pp. 364–68, + 1 plate. 1865.

11374 [Anon.] Maen y Chwyfan. Arch. Camb., 5th S. 8, pp. 74–76, + 1 plate. 1891.

§ e. Glamorgan

i. Llantwit Major

11375 Allen (John Romilly). The cylindrical pillar at Llantwit Major. Arch. Camb., 5th S. 6, pp. 317–26, + 3 plates. 1889.

11376 —— The inscribed and sculptured stones at Llantwit Major. Arch. Camb., 5th S. 6, pp. 118–26, + 5 plates. 1889.

11377 Halliday (George Eley). Fragments of pre-Norman crosses found at Llantwit Major. Arch. Camb., 6th S. 1, p. 148. 1901.

11378 —— Llantwit Major church. [Pp. 148–55, the pre-Norman stones, with 5 figures.] Arch. Camb., 5th S. 17, pp. 129–56. 1900.

11379 —— The removal of the cross of Iltyd at Llantwit Major [into the church]. Arch. Camb., 6th S. 3, pp. 56–64. 1903.

11380 Rodger (John W.). The ecclesiastical buildings of Llantwit Major. [6 pre-Norman stones.] Cardiff Nat. Soc., Rpt. and Trans., 39 (1906), pp. 18–48, + 7 plates, + plan. 1907.

11381 Thomas (Thomas Henry)· Sculptured stones, Llantwit Major. Arch· Camb., 6th S. 13, pp. 90–94. 1913.

ii Other

11382 Allen (John Romilly). The cross of Irbic at Llandough. Arch. Camb., 6th S. 4, pp. 247–52, + 4 plates. 1904.

11383 —— The early Christian monuments of Glamorganshire. J. Brit. Archaeol. Assoc., 49, pp. 15–22, + 1 plate. 1893.

11384 —— Pre-Norman cross-base at Llangefelach. Arch. Camb., 6th S. 3, pp. 181–88, + 2 plates. 1903.

11385 —— Pre-Norman sculptured stone . . . at Llanrhidian, Gower. Arch. Camb., 5th S. 5, pp. 173–76, + 1 plate. 1888.

11386 Gardner (Iltyd). The Celtic 'cross' at Llandough, near Cardiff. Arch. Camb., 11th S. 13, pp. 149–51, + 1 plate. 1913.

11387 Halliday (George Eley). Pre-Norman cross, Llangan, near Cowbridge. [Figure in text.] Arch. Camb., 6th S. 9, pp. 373. 1909.

11388 Hemp (Wilfrid J.). Wheel cross discovered at Port Talbot. [10th or 11th c.]. Arch. Camb. 76 (7th S. 1), p. 296, + 1 plate. 1921.

11389 Jones (Harry Longueville). Monumental stones, Caerleon. [?late 12th c. Interlacing.] Arch. Camb., 3rd S. 2, p. 311, + 1 plate. 1856.

11390 Macalister (Robert Alexander Stewart). The 'Conbelin' cross, Margam. [9th c. Figure in text.] Arch. Camb., 83 (7th S. 8), pp. 392–93. 1928.

11391 —— [Two sculptured stones at Merthyr Mawr]. [2 figures in text. 'Margam type'.] Arch. Camb., 83 (7th S. 8), pp. 366–69. 1928.

11392 Radford (Courtenay Arthur Ralegh). Margam museum, Glamorgan. *Ancient monuments*: *Ministry of Works*. pp. 32, + 4 plates. 8° London, 1949. [Pumpeius stone, mid 6th c. (plate); Boduoc stone, 6th c.; pillar of St. Thomas, 8th c.; crosses of Einion, c. 870 (plate), Grutne, c. 900, Cynfelyn, 9th–10th c. (plate), from Eglwys Nunydd, 11th c., of Ieci, 11th c., Ilquici, 11th c., etc.]

11393 Robinson (George E.). Sculptured stone near Brigend. [?early 11th c.] Arch. Camb., 4th S. 8, pp. 62–64, + 1 plate. 1877.

11394 Thomas (Thomas Henry). Cross-slab at Llantrisant church. [' Probably pre-Norman.'] Arch. Camb., 5th S. 10, p. 348. 1893.

11395 Ward (John). Casts of ancient crosses at Margam. [In Cardiff Museum.] Arch. Camb., 5th S. 11, pp. 250–53, + 1 plate. 1894.

§ f. Pembrokeshire

11396 Allen (John Romilly). Head of cross at St. David's. [2 figures in text.] Arch. Camb., 6th S. 5, pp. 89–90. 1905.

11397 Costello (Dudley). Cross in Nevern churchyard. Gent. Mag., 104 (N.S. 2), pp. 369–70, + 1 plate. 1834.

11398 Grimes (W. F.). A leaden tablet of Scandinavian origin from south Pembrokeshire. [Figure of dragon 10th–11th c. (Viking).] Arch. Camb., 85, pp. 416–17. 1930.

11399 Hughes (Henry Harold). St. Brynach's cross, Nevern. [c. 10th c. Figure in text.] Arch. Camb., 77 (7th S. 2), pp. 501–03. 1922.

11400 Lynam (Charles). The cross at Carew. [Drawing on p. 410.] J. Brit. Archaeol. Assoc., 41, pp. 129–30. 1885.

11401 Macalister (Robert Alexander Stewart). A slab in St. David's cathedral. [Seraph and interlacing: figure in text.] Arch. Camb., 86, pp. 353–54. 1931.

11402 Westwood (John Obadiah). The great cross in Nevern churchyard. Arch. Camb., 3rd S. 6, pp. 47–51, + 1 plate. 1860.

N n

11403 Westwood (John Obadiah). The small cross at Penally. Arch. Camb., 3rd S. 10, pp. 328–29, + 1 plate. 1864.

§ g. Other Counties

11404 [Anon.] Llanbadarn Fawr church [Cardiganshire]. [Plate of cross.] Arch. Camb., 5th S. 14, pp. 152–53, + 1 plate. 1897.

11405 Hartland (Ernest). Notes on a Radnorshire cross [at Llowes]. [?early 11th c.] Arch. Camb., 4th S. 4, pp. 321–26, + 1 plate. 1873.

11406 Hughes (Henry Harold). Llanrhaiadr. [Montgomeryshire. Notice of 2 pre-Conquest sculptured stones.] Arch. Camb., 78 (7th S. 3), pp. 402–03, + 1 plate. 1923.

11407 —— Meifod. [Montgomeryshire. Notice of pre-conquest sculptured stone. Figure in text.] Arch. Camb. 78 (7th S. 3), pp. 450–52. 1923.

11408 —— Pre-Norman cross and cross-base in Diserth church [Radnor]. [4 figures in text.] Arch. Camb., 80 (7th S. 5), pp. 149–56. 1925.

11409 —— Pre-Norman stone at Rhuddlan, [Denbighshire]. [4 figures in text.] Arch. Camb., 91, pp. 140–42. 1936.

11410 Lloyd (Howel William). The Llowes cross [Radnorshire]. Arch. Camb., 4th S. 5, pp. 83–85. 1874.

11411 Macalister (Robert Alexander Stewart). The sculptured stones of Cardiganshire. Trans. Cards. Antiq. Soc., 5, pp. 7–20, + 1 plate. 1927.

11412 Nash-Williams (Victor Erle). A cross-slab from Llanfeigan, Brecknockshire. [Figure in text.] Arch. Camb., 91, pp. 134, 137. 1936.

11413 Radford (Courtenay Arthur Ralegh). The pillar of Eliseg, Llantysilio-yn-ial, Denbighshire. H.M.S.O. pp. 7. 8° London, 1953.

11414 Thomas (David Richard). Notes on the sculptured stone and church at Llandrinio, Montgomeryshire. Arch. Camb., 5th S. 10, pp. 25–28, + 2 plates. 1893.

11415 Thomas (David Richard). Sculptured tombstone in Meifod church. Arch. Camb., 4th S. 11, pp. 182–85, + 1 plate. 1880. *Reprinted in* Collns. hist. and archaeol. rel. to Montgom., 14, pp. 33–35, + 1 plate. 1881.

11416 Thomas (Thomas Henry). Monuments of the pre-Norman period recently discovered in Breconshire. [i. Gurdan stone : ii. Erwhelme shaft : iii. Llanlleonfil stone.] Cardiff Nat. Soc., Rpt. and Trans., 39 (1906), pp. 103–07. 1907.

11417 Thomas (Thomas Henry). Pen-y-Mynnid stone, Brecknockshire. Arch. Camb., 5th S. 11, pp. 329–30. 1894.

11418 Westwood (John Obadiah). Notice of the early sepulchral stone at Llandevaelog, Brecon. Arch. Camb., 3rd S. 4, pp. 306–09. 1858.

195. IVORY (AND BONE) CARVINGS

§ *a*. General

11419 British Museum. Catalogue of the ivory carvings of the Christian era ... by O. M. Dalton. pp. iii, 194, + 125 plates. 4° London, 1909. [Pp. 27–32, plates 17–18, Franks casket : pp. 32–40, plates 19–21, A.-S. : etc.]

11420 Cust (Anna Maria Elizabeth). The ivory workers of the Middle Ages. pp. xix, 169. 8° London, 1902. [Pp. pp. 99–106, A.-S.]

11421 Goldschmidt (Adolf). Die Elfenbeinskulpturen aus der Zeit der karolinischen und sächsischen Kaiser, 8.–11. Jahrhundert. (-aus der romanischen Zeit, 11–13. Jahrhundert). 4 Bde., large fol. Berlin, 1914–26. [A.-S. background.]

11422 Longhurst (Margaret Helen). English ivories. pp. xvii, 123, + 57 plates. 4° London, 1926. [Pp. 1–36, 17 plates, A.-S.]

§ *b*. Franks Casket

(In British Museum. Northumbrian, c. 700. Both aspects, sculpture and inscription.)

11423 Boer (Richard Constant). Über die rechte Seite des angelsächsischen Runenkästchens. Arkiv nord. Filol., 27 (N.F. 23), pp. 215–59, + 1 plate. 1911.

11424 Bugge (Sophus). The Norse lay of Wayland (' Volundarkuiða '), and its relation to English tradition. [Plate shows Franks casket, lid and front, full size.] Saga-Book V.C., 2, pp. 271–312, + plate. 1901.

11425 Clark (Eleanor Grace). The right side of the Franks casket. P.M.L.A., 45, pp. 339–53, + 1 plate. 1930.

11426 Craigie (*Sir* William Alexander). [Discussion on three books on Franks casket : by Wadstein, Napier and Viëtor.] Arkiv nord. Filol., 19, pp. 364–67. 1903.

11427 Dalton (Ormonde Maddock). The animal-headed figure on the Franks casket. Man, 8, pp. 177–78, + 1 plate. 1908.

11428 Gering (Hugo). Zum Clermonter Runenkästchen (Franks' casket). Z.f.d.P., 33, pp. 140–41, 287. 1901.

11429 Grienberger (Theodor von). Schriften über das ags. Runenkästchen. Z.f.d.P., 33, pp. 409–21. 1901.

11430 —— Zu den Inschriften des Clermonter Runenkästchens. Anglia, 27 (N.F. 15), pp. 436–49. 1904.

11431 Hempl (George). The variant runes on the Franks casket. Trans. Am. Philol. Ass., 32, pp. 186–95. 1901.

11432 Hofmann (Konrad). Ueber die Clermonter Runen. Sitzb. k. bayer. Akad., Philos.-philol. Kl., 1871, pp. 665–76 : 1872, pp. 461–62. 1871–72.

11433 Holthausen (Ferdinand). Zum Clermonter Runenkästchen. Anglia, Beibl., 16, pp. 229–31 ; 17, p. 176. 1905–06.

11434 Jenny (Wilhelm Albert von). Angelsächsischer Runenschrein, genannt Franks' Schrein. Deutsche Kunst, 3, p. 97. 1937.

11435 Napier (Arthur Sampson). Contributions to Old English literature : 2. The Franks casket. English miscellany presented to F. J. Furnivall, pp. 362–81. 1901.

11436 Napier (Arthur Sampson). The Franks casket. *In Furnivall celebration volume*. pp. 22, + 6 plates. 4° Oxford, 1900.

11437 Souers (Philip Webster). The top of the Franks casket. (The Franks casket: left side. The magi on the Franks casket). [Description, interpretation, runes, linguistic notes.] Harvard Stud. and Notes in Phil. and Lit., 17, pp. 163–79, + plate: 18, pp. 199–209, + plate: 19, pp. 249–54, + plate. 1935, 1937.

11438 —— The Wayland scene on the Franks casket. Speculum, 18, pp. 104–111, + 1 plate. 1943.

11439 Viëtor (Wilhelm). The Anglo-Saxon runic casket (the Franks casket.) pp. 12, + 5 plates. 2 parts, 8° Marburg, 1901. [In German and in English.]

11440 Wadstein (Elis). The Clermont runic casket. [Interpretation of missing side (in Florence) and discussion of rest of the carving.] Skrifter K. Hum. Vet.-Samf. Upsala, 6. vii. Pp. 55, + 5 plates. 1900.

11441 —— Zum Clermonter Runenkästchen. Z.f.d.P., 34, p. 127. 1902.

11442 Walker (Francis G.). Fresh light on the Franks casket. Wash. Univ. Stud., 2 ii, pp. 165–76. 1915.

§ *c*. **Other**

11443 Allen (John Romilly). A carved bone of the Viking age. [With 7 figures in text.] Reliquary, 10, pp. 270–75. 1904.

11444 Anderson (Joseph). Notice of a casket of cetacean bone, carved with interlaced patterns in panels, exhibited by Miss Drysdale, Kilrie House, Kirkcaldy. [?7th c. 5 figures in text.] Proc. Soc. Antiq. Scot., 20 (N.S. 8), pp. 390–96. 1886.

11445 Carrington (Samuel) *finder*. Bone draughtsmen of the Saxon period, found [in a grave-mound near Cold Eaton] in Derbyshire. Reliquary, 26, p. 276, + 1 plate. 1886.

11446 Cottrill (Frank). Bone trial-piece found in Southwark. [?10th c.] Antiq. J., 15, pp. 69–71. 1935.

11447 Dalton (Ormonde Maddock). Early chessmen of whale's bone excavated in Dorset. [?10th c. A.–S. or Viking.] Archaeologia, 77, pp. 77–86, + 2 plates. 1928.

11448 —— Medieval objects in the Borradaile collection. [Pp. 8–12, carved ivory horn, 10th–11th c.?]. Proc. Soc. Antiq., 2nd S. 26, pp. 8–21, + 2 plates. 1913.

11449 —— Note on an Anglo-Saxon ivory carving. [Found near St. Cross, and now in the Winchester museum. Figure in text.] *Same jnl.*, 2nd S. 32, pp. 45–47. 1919.

11450 Davies (Robert). The horn of Ulphus. [All aspects. *See also* 52 § *a*.] Archaeol. J., 26, pp. 1–11, + 1 plate. 1869.

11451 Fox (*Sir* Cyril). Two Anglo-Saxon bone carvings [from Leicester]. [9th c.] Antiq. J., 13, pp. 303–05, + 1 plate. 1933.

11452 Franks (*Sir* Augustus Wollaston). Carved bone disk, London. [Figure in text. Interlacing with snakes, etc.] Proc. Soc. Antiq., 2nd S. 3, pp. 224–25. 1866.

11453 Kendrick (*Sir* Thomas Downing). The horn of Ulph. [As a work of art.] Antiquity, 11, pp. 278–82, + 5 plates. 1937.

11454 —— Note on an ivory implement from Bramham, Yorks. [Probably Anglo-Danish work of c. 1000, with incised ornament of a crude type.] Yorks. Archaeol. J., 32, pp. 339–40. 1935.

11455 Perkins (J. B. Ward). An eleventh-century bone stylus from York. Antiq. J., 29, pp. 207–09, + 1 plate. 1949.

11456 Read (*Sir* Charles Hercules). An English ivory of the eleventh century. [Head of crozier in B.M.] Burl. Mag., 3, pp. 99–100, + 1 plate. 1903.

11457 —— On a morse ivory tau cross head of English work of the eleventh century. Archaeologia, 58, pp. 408–12, + 1 plate. 1903.

196. JEWELLERY, ANGLO-SAXON

§ *a.* **General and Miscellaneous**

11458 Addis (John) *etc.* Œstel. [For notes *see* **11537.**] N. and Q., 4th S. 10, pp. 436–37 : 6th S. 3, pp. 14–15 : 4, p. 75. 1872, 1881.

11459 Allen (John Romilly). Anglo-Saxon pins found at Lincoln. [? first half of 9th S.] Reliquary, 10, pp. 52–53, + 1 plate. 1904.

11460 —— The thurible of Godric. [?10th c. With 4 figures in text.] Reliquary, 12, pp. 50–52. 1906.

11461 Armistead (C. J.). Anglo-Saxon remains . . . discovered . . . in the modern cemetery at Soham, Cambridge-shire. [6 fibulae, beads and ' key-shaped ornament of unknown use ', figured.] Proc. Soc. Antiq., 2nd S. 5, pp. 496–97. 1873.

11462 Bartlett (J. Pemberton). [Exhibition of] objects of the Anglo-Saxon period obtained from tumuli . . . on Breach Down, in Kent. [Beads, amber, rings and hairpin.] *Same jnl.*, 3, pp. 137–38. 1855.

11463 Bateman (Thomas). Anglo-Saxon antiquities in the possession of T. Bateman, Esq. [Plate shows fibula-shaped ornament, Northants., and a bridle-bit.] Reliquary, 1, pp. 189–90, + coloured plate. 1861.

11464 Baye (Joseph de) *baron.* Les bijoux francs et la fibule anglo-saxonne de Marilles (Brabant). pp. 11, + 1 plate. 8° Caen, 1889. [Offprinted from Bull. monumental, 1889.]

11465 Beck (Horace Courthope). Note on three beads from Camerton cemetery. Antiq. J., 13, pp. 169–70. 1933.

11466 Benton (Gerald Montagu). A Saxon brooch from Brislingcote, near Burton-on-Trent [Staffs.] Proc. Camb. Antiq. Soc., 17 (1912–13), pp. 137–38, + 1 plate. 1914.

11467 Brent (John). Circular enamelled ornaments found . . . at Greenwich. [A.-S. plaques. Figure in text.] Proc. Soc. Antiq., 2nd S. 2, pp. 201–03. 1863.

11468 Brewis (Parker). A cruciform brooch from Benwell, Newcastle upon Tyne. Archaeol. Æl., 4th S. 13, pp. 117–21, + 2 plates. 1936.

11469 British Museum. Anglo-Saxon antiquities from Kent. [Exhibition of pendants, brooches, etc., from Darent valley and Howletts.] B.M.Q., 12, pp. 70–71, + plate 23. 1938.

11470 —— Anglo-Saxon jewels from [Milton Regis, near Sittingbourne,] Kent. Antiq. J., 6, pp. 446–47. 1926.

11471 Brown (Gerard Baldwin). Notes on a necklace of glass beads found in a cist in Dalmeny park, South Queens-ferry. [?belonging to Anglo-Saxon raiders in northern Britain, from resemblance to those found in A.-S. graves.] Proc. Soc. Antiq. Scot., 49 (6th S. 1, 1914–15), pp. 332–38. 1915.

11472 Bruce-Mitford (Rupert Leo Scott). Anglo-Saxon brooch and pot from Brixworth, Northants. Antiq. J., 19, pp. 325–26, + 1 plate. 1939.

11473 —— An Anglo-Saxon gold pendant from High Wycombe, Bucks. [c. 600.] B.M.Q., 15, p. 72, + plate 33 (c.) 1952.

11474 —— The Fuller brooch. [The five senses. Late Saxon : nielloed-silver.] B.M.Q., 17, pp. 75–76, + plate xxx, 1952.

11475 —— A late Saxon disk-brooch and sword pommel. B.M.Q., 15, pp. 74–75, + plate 33 (a, d.). 1952.

11476 —— A late-Saxon silver disk-brooch from the Isle of Ely. B.M.Q., 17, pp. 15–16, + plate V. 1952.

11477 —— A Saxon jewelled circular brooch from Long Bennington, Lincs. Antiq. J., 31, pp. 67–68, + 1 plate. 1951.

11478 Buckman (James). Notes on a [Saxon?] pendant from Dorchester. Proc. Dorset Antiq. F.C., 2, pp. 109–11, + 1 coloured plate. 1878.

11479 —— On a bracelet (armilla) of supposed Saxon workmanship. *Same jnl.*, 1, pp. 38–39, + 1 plate. 1877.

11480 Bulleid (Arthur). Saxon gold pendant from [Burnett,] Somerset. Antiq. J., 2, p. 383. 1922.

11481 Burgess (Joseph Tom). [Exhibition of 14] fibulae from Warwickshire. [Mostly found at Longbridge.] Proc. Soc. Antiq., 2nd S. 7, pp. 78–79. 1876.

11482 Byles (   ) of *Boxmoor*. Antiquities found at Barrington, near Cambridge. [A.–S. knife, beads and brooch. Figure of brooch.] Proc. Soc. Antiq., 2nd S. 5, pp. 13–14. 1870.

11483 —— A Saxon fibula recently found at Orwell, Cambridgeshire. *Same jnl.*, 2nd S. 5, p. 380. 1872.

11484 Chatwin (Philip Boughton). Anglo-Saxon finds at [Emscote near] Warwick. [Mostly brooches.] Antiq. J., 5, pp. 268–72, + 2 plates. 1925.

11485 Clark (Mary Kitson). Bracelet and toilet set from Burton Fields gravel pit. Proc. Leeds Phil. and Lit. Soc., 5, pp. 339–43. 1942.

11486 —— Late Saxon pin-heads from Roos, east Yorkshire, and South Ferriby, Lincolnshire, now in the collections at Hull. *Same jnl.*, 5, pp. 333–38, + 1 plate. 1942.

11487 Collingwood (William Gershom). Silver fibula found in Westmorland. [10th c.] Saga-Book V.C., 5, p. 230. 1908.

11488 Crowther-Beynon (Vernon Bryan). On recent finds, chiefly of the Anglo-Saxon period, at Market Overton, Rutland. [Gold bracteate, gold bead, silver torc, clasps, brooches, etc.] Proc. Soc. Antiq., 2nd S. 23, pp. 412–14. 1911.

11489 —— Some Anglo-Saxon personal ornaments, with special reference to Rutland finds. Ann. Rpt. Rutland Archaeol. Soc., 14 (1916), pp. 48–57. 1917.

11490 Cumberland (A.). Riseley Saxon cemetery. [Gold ornaments: second plate shows silver-gilt brooches from Jutish cemetery at Howletts, near Canterbury.] Arch. Cant., 53, p. 142, + 2 plates. 1941.

11491 Cuming (Henry Syer). Ancient ornaments. [Pp. 272–4, A.–S. and Danish fibulae.] J. Brit. Archaeol. Assoc., 16, pp. 269–74, + 2 plates. 1860.

11492 Cuming (Henry Syer). On ancient fibulae. *Same jnl.*, 18, pp. 224–26, + 1 plate. 1862.

11493 —— On semicircular-topped fibulae. *Same jnl.*, 17, pp. 232–34. 1861.

11494 Cunnington (*Mrs.* Maud Edith). Three brooches from Wiltshire. ['Applied' Saxon type. ?5th c.] Antiq. J., 11, pp. 160–61. 1931.

11495 Dalton (Ormonde Maddock). On some early brooches of cloisonnée in the British Museum, with a note on the Alfred jewel. [? Castellani, Towneley and Dowgate Hill brooches, of continental origin, though hitherto accounted as A.–S.] Proc. Soc. Antiq., 2nd S. 20, pp. 64–77, + 1 plate. 1904.

11496 —— Sarmatian ornaments from Kerch in the British Museum, compared with Anglo-Saxon and Merovingian ornaments in the same collection. Antiq. J., 4, pp. 259–62, + 2 plates. 1924.

11497 Evans (*Sir* Arthur) and **Smith** (Reginald Allender). [Discussion on E. T. Leeds'] paper on the distribution of the Anglo-Saxon saucer brooch in relation to the battle of Bedford in 571 A.D. [**11524**]. Proc. Soc. Antiq., 2nd S. 24, pp. 78–80. 1912.

11498 Evans (Joan). English jewellery from the fifth century A.D. to 1800. pp. xxxi, 168, + 34 plates. 4° London, 1921. [Pp. 1–25, + plates 1–9, A.–S., and Celtic jewellery].

11499 Evans (*Sir* John). An Anglo-Saxon brooch found [at Tuxford] in Nottinghamshire. [Figure in text.] Proc. Soc. Antiq., 2nd S. 21, pp. 34–37. 1905.

11500 Evison (V. I.). The white material in Kentish disc brooches. Antiq. J., 31, pp. 197–200, + 1 plate. 1951.

11501 Fairholt (Frederick William). Remarks on ancient fibulae, recently exhibited to the British Archaeological Association. [Various finds.] J. Brit. Archaeol. Assoc., 2, pp. 309–15. 1847.

11502 Franks (*Sir* Augustus Wollaston). A gold ornament found at [Little] Hampton in Gloucestershire. Proc. Soc. Antiq., 2nd S. 3, p. 27. 1864.

11503 Garrett (Robert Max). Precious stones in Old English literature. *Münchener Beiträge zur romanischen und englischen Philologie*, 47. pp. xiv, 91. 8° München, 1909.

11504 Goldney (Francis Bennett). [Exhibition of] a number of antiquities of the bronze, Roman and Saxon periods, found near Canterbury. [4 fibulae, one with garnets.] Proc. Soc. Antiq., 2nd S. 18, pp. 279–80. 1901.

11505 Green (Charles). An Anglo-Saxon necklace from Yorkshire. [45 beads. 3 of amber. Now in Royal Museum, Peel Park, Salford.] Trans. East Riding Antiq. Soc., 27, pp. 164–67. 1932.

11506 Haseloff (Günther). An Anglo-Saxon openwork mount from Whitby abbey. Antiq. J., 30, pp. 170–74, + 2 plates. 1950.

11507 Hawkins (Edward). An account of coins and treasure found in Cuerdale [near Preston, Lancs.]. [Ornaments worn c. time of Alfred.] Archaeol. J., 4, pp. 111–30, 189–99. 1847.

11508 Heaton (Harriet A.). The brooches of many nations. Edited by John Potter Briscoe. pp. xv, 50, + 32 plates [drawings]. 4° Nottingham, 1904. [Pp. 36–50, Celtic, Scottish and A.–S. fibulae.]

11509 Hertford (Francis Hugh George Seymour) 8*th marquess.* On an Anglo-Saxon brooch found in Ragley Park, Warwickshire. [Notice of exhibit.] Archaeologia, 44, pp. 482–83, + 1 plate. 1873.

11510 Jessup (Ronald Frederick). Anglo-Saxon jewellery. pp. 148, + 44 plates (4 coloured). 8° London, 1950.

11511 —— Saxon England. *Young Britain—Highlights of history*, 2. pp. 31. 8° n.p., n.d. [Photographs of brooches, etc.]

11512 Jewitt (Llewellynn). Notice of a [Saxon] brooch of penannular form, found in Derbyshire. [With comparisons with Tara brooch, etc.] Reliquary, 4, pp. 65–74, + 4 plates. 1863.

11513 Kendrick (*Sir* Thomas Downing). Polychrome jewellery in Kent. Antiquity, 7, pp. 429–52, + 5 plates. 1933.

11514 —— St. Cuthbert's pectoral cross, and the Wilton and Ixworth crosses. Antiq. J., 17, pp. 283–93, + 6 plates. 1937.

11515 —— Saxon art at Sutton Hoo. Burl. Mag., 77, pp. 174–83, + 3 plates. 1940.

11516 —— The Sutton Hoo finds. [2. The gold ornaments.] B.M.Q., 13, pp. 115–17, + plates 42–44. 1939.

11517 —— and **Kitzinger** (Ernest). The Sutton Hoo ship-burial. 2. The gold ornaments. 3. The large hanging-bowl. 4. The archaeology of the jewellery. 5. The silver. Antiquity, 14, pp. 28–63. 1940.

11518 Kilbride-Jones (Howard Edward). The evolution of penannular brooches with zoomorphic terminals in Great Britain and Ireland. [30 figures in text and chronological table. Fig. 1 shows distribution in the British Isles, and shows their relation to Roman roads in south Britain]. Proc. R.I.A., 43C, pp. 379–455. 1937.

11519 Kitzinger (Ernst). The Sutton Hoo finds. [3. The silver. Bowls, cups, spoons, etc.] B.M.Q., 13, pp. 118–26, + plates 45–49. 1939.

11520 Leeds (Edward Thurlow). The brooch from West Stow, Suffolk. [Bought for Ashmolean Museum. ?Frankish type, c. 500.] Antiq. J., 29, p. 91. 1949.

11521 —— A corpus of early Anglo-Saxon square-headed brooches. pp. xv, 138, + 47 plates. 8° Oxford, 1949.

11522 —— Denmark and early England. [Gold bracteates.] Antiq. J., 26, pp. 22–37, + 3 plates. 1946.

11523 —— The distribution of the Angles and Saxons archaeologically considered. [19 maps, and 21 collections of figures of brooches, etc., in text. Appendix 1, catalogue of small-long brooches: appendix 2, associated groups of brooches.] Archaeologia, 91, pp. 1–106. 1945.

11524 Leeds (Edward Thurlow). The distribution of the Anglo-Saxon saucer brooch in relation to the battle of Bedford, A.D. 571. [22 figures in text. *See also* **11497**.] *Same jnl.*, 53, pp. 159–202, + 4 plates. 1912.

11525 —— A late British brooch from Glaston, Rutland. [?c. 500. 3 figures in text.] Antiq. J., 28, pp. 169–73, + 1 plate. 1948.

11526 —— Notes on examples of late Anglo-Saxon metal work. Annals of Archaeol. (L'pool), 4, pp. 1–10. 1912.

11527 —— Supplementary note [to **8275**] on the gold bracteate and silver brooch from Market Overton [Rutland]. Archaeologia, 62, pp. 491–96. 1911.

11528 —— Two cruciform brooches from Islip, Northants. Antiq. J., 41, pp. 234–36, + 2 plates. 1941.

11529 —— Two types of brooches from the island of Gotland, Sweden. [Brooches in the Ashmolean from the 'collection of Anglo-Saxon, Scandinavian and Teutonic objects which was formed by the late Sir John Evans.'] Archaeol. J., 67, pp. 235–58, + 3 plates. 1910.

11530 Le Strange (Hamon). Saxon brooch found at Hunstanton, [Norfolk]. [Figure, whole size, in text.] Proc. Soc. Antiq., 2nd S. 19, pp. 172–74. 1902.

11531 Lethbridge (Thomas Charles). Jewelled Saxon pendant from the Isle of Ely. Proc. Camb. Antiq. Soc., 46 (1952), pp. 1–3, + plate. 1953.

11532 Littledale (Henry). [Exhibition of] an Anglo-Saxon brooch, found in the cemetery at Kempston, Beds. Proc. Soc. Antiq., 2nd S. 3, pp. 97–98. 1865.

11533 Low (Charles William). A few notes on an iron Anglo-Saxon brooch supposed to have been found at Hoxne, Suffolk. Proc. Suffolk Inst. Archaeol., 14, pp. 1–5, + 2 plates. 1910.

11534 Manning (Charles Robertson). Notice of a gold pendant ornament, found at Palgrave, Suffolk. *Same jnl.*, 2, pp. 88–89. 1859.

11535 Melton Mowbray. The temporary museum. [Notice of exhibition, 1865. Two plates of a 'Saxon fibula, found at Saxby, co. Leicester.'] Trans. Leic. Archit. Soc., 3, p. 39, + 2 plates. 1874.

11536 Mickelthwaite (John Thomas). Notes on the cross said to have been taken out of the coffin of king Edward the Confessor in 1685. Proc. Soc. Antiq., 2nd S. 9, pp. 227–30. 1883.

11537 Milles (Jeremiah). Observations on the aestel. [=tablet, worth 50 mancuses, attached to each copy of Alfred's translation of the Cura Pastoralis. Probably was framed in gold to this value.] Archaeologia, 2, pp. 75–79. 1772.

11538 Mitchell (H. P.). English or German ?—a pre-Conquest gold cross. [10th–11th c. German : figure of Christ, A.-S.] Burl. Mag., 47, pp. 324, 29–30, + 2 plates. 1925.

11539 O'Neil (B. H. St. J.). An enamelled penannular brooch from the Scilly Isles. Antiq. J., 33, pp. 210–11. 1953.

11540 Oswald (Adrian). An Anglo-Saxon brooch from Notts. Antiq. J., 18, p. 411. 1938.

11541 Passmore (A. D.) *owner.* Saxon button brooch from Silchester. [Figure in text.] Papers and Proc. Hants. F. C., 12, p. 212. 1933.

11542 —— A Saxon saucer brooch from Mildenhall. Wilts. Archaeol. Mag., 46, p. 393, + plate. 1933.

11543 Payne (George). Anglo-Saxon antiquities . . . recently found in graves near Faversham, [Kent]. [Brooches, rings, vases, etc.] Proc. Soc. Antiq., 2nd S. 14, pp. 311–14. 1893.

11544 —— Anglo-Saxon objects, from the collection of Henry Durden, . . . from graves on Wye and Crundale downs, Kent, where they were discovered in 1858, and later. [Brooches, etc.] *Same jnl.*, 2nd S. 14, pp. 314–15. 1893.

11545 Payne (George). Anglo-Saxon ornaments found near Teynham, Kent. [Fibula, pendants, etc.] *Same jnl.*, 2nd S. 15, p. 184. 1894.

11546 Pegge (Samuel). Observations on two jewels in the possession of Sir Charles Mordaunt, bart. [?A.–S., ? early 11th c. Dug up at Compton Verney, Warw., 1774.] Archaeologia, 3, pp. 371–75. 1786.

11547 Pollitt (William). Anglo-Saxon saucer brooches in south-west Essex. [From Southend cemetery.] Antiq. J., 11, pp. 284–85, + 1 plate. 1931.

11548 Pownall (Assheton). Anglo-Saxon antiquities discovered at Glen Parva in Leicestershire. [Beads, fibulae, etc.] Proc. Soc. Antiq., 2nd S. 3, pp. 344–46. 1866.

11549 Robinson (*Sir* Charles). An Anglo-Saxon brooch. [In his possession. Silver brooch, 10th c., engraved and inlaid with niello. Northumbrian]. Antiquary, 46, p. 268 (illustration on p. 269). 1910.

11550 Robson (Isabel Suart). England's oldest handicrafts.—Working in precious metals. [Including A.–S. period, and Alfred jewel.] Antiquary, 35, pp. 200–04. 1899.

11551 Rogers (John Jope). [Exhibition of] some Anglo-Saxon antiquities of silver, discovered many years since at Trewhiddle, near St. Austell, Cornwall. [Jewellery, miscellaneous coins, etc. Deposit c. 878.] Proc. Soc. Antiq., 2nd S. 8, pp. 313–14. 1880.

11552 Ross (Alexander). Notice of the discovery of portions of two penannular brooches of silver with beads of glass and amber, and of a silver coin of Coenwulf, king of Mercia (A.D. 795–818), at Mains of Croy, Inverness-shire. [7 figures in text.] *Same jnl.*, 20 (N.S. 8), pp. 91–96. 1886.

11553 Smith (A. E.) *photographer.* Ornamental metal disc found at Ixworth, Suffolk. [Anglian.] Reliquary, N. [3rd] S. 13, pp. 133–34. 1907.

11554 Smith (Charles Roach). An account of some antiquities found in the neighbourhood of Sandwich, Kent. [Fibulae, etc.] Archaeologia, 30, pp. 132–36, + 1 plate. 1844.

11555 —— Fibulae discovered in the Crimea. [At Kertch. He classifies as A.–S.] Collectanea Antiqua, 5, pp. 140–45, + 1 plate. 1861.

11556 —— On an ancient enamelled ouche in gold. [?A.–S., fibula.] Archaeologia, 29, pp. 70–75, + 1 coloured plate. 1842.

11557 —— On Anglo-Saxon remains discovered recently in various places in Kent. [With 5 plates (4 in colour)]. Arch. Cant., 3, pp. 35–46. 1860.

11558 —— On Anglo-Saxon remains recently discovered at Faversham, at Wye, and at Westwell, in Kent. [With 3 plates (2 in colour) of A.–S. fibulae.] Arch. Cant., 1, pp. 42–49. 1858.

11559 —— and **Fairholt** (Frederick William). On fibulae in the museum of the Hon. R. C. Neville. J. Brit. Archaeol. Assoc., 5, pp. 113–18, + 1 coloured plate. 1849.

11560 Smith (Charles Roach). On the so-called Anglo-Saxon antiquities discovered near Kertch, in the Crimea. [Plate shows 3 fibulae.] Trans. Hist. Soc. Lancs. and Ches., 10, pp. 59–60, + 1 plate. 1858.

11561 Smith (Harold Clifford). Jewellery. pp. xlvii, 410, + 54 plates. 4° London, 1908. [Pp. 56–79, + plates 11–14, A.–S. and Celtic.]

11562 Smith (Reginald Allender). Anglo-Saxon antiquities (Fenton collection). [*See also* V.H.S., Suffolk 1, pp. 336–37, 342, 346.] B.M.Q., 2, pp. 90–91, + plate 59. 1928.

11563 —— Anglo-Saxon ornaments from Holme Pierrepont [Notts.]. [Plate shows 5 fibulae. Found 1842. *See* V.H.C., Notts., 1, p. 195.] B.M.Q., 6, pp. 16–17, + plate 11. 1932.

11564 —— Art in the Dark Ages. [Including A.–S. brooches, etc.] Burl. Mag., 57, pp. 3–10, 2 plates. 1930.

11565 Smith (Reginald Allender). The Beeston Tor hoard [Staffs.]. [5 figures of brooches, etc., in text.] Antiq. J., 5, pp. 135–40. 1925.

11566 —— The evolution and distribution of some Anglo-Saxon brooches. [23 figures in text.] Archaeol. J., 65, pp. 65–88. 1908.

11567 —— A fragment of gold filigree from Selsey. [Late A.–S. Figure in text.] Proc. Soc. Antiq., 2nd S. 26, pp. 133–34. 1914.

11568 —— A gold ornament from Selsey beach. [Late A.–S. filigree.] B.M.Q., 7, p. 126, + plate 39. 1933.

11569 —— Note on a coin-brooch [of the later Saxon period] found at Canterbury. [Silver.] Proc. Soc. Antiq., 2nd S. 19, pp. 210–12, + 1 plate. 1903.

11570 —— Notes on a bronze-gilt brooch found at Canterbury. ['Scandinavian edition of a Keltic original'. Figure on p. 299.] *Same jnl.*, 2nd S. 19, pp. 298–305. 1903.

11571 —— On some Anglo-Saxon silver ornaments found at Trewhiddle, Cornwall, in 1774. *Same jnl.*, 2nd S. 20, pp. 47–55, + 1 plate. 1904.

11572 —— [On the brooches from the] Anglo-Saxon cemetery at Ipswich. *Same jnl.*, 2nd S. 21, pp. 242–47, + 2 plates. 1906.

11573 —— A pewter brooch of late Saxon date found at Castleacre, Norfolk. *Same jnl.*, 2nd S. 22, p. 66, + 1 plate (opp. p. 63). 1908.

11574 —— The Pitney brooch. [c. 950. *See* V.C.H., Somerset, 1, p. 380.] B.M.Q., 6, pp. 39–40, + plate 19 (b). 1931.

11575 —— Roman and Anglo-Saxon jewellery. B.M.Q., 10, pp. 161–62, + plate 61. 1936.

11576 —— [Saxon remains from] Dover, Kent. [Enamelled discs with hooks from hanging bowls : 5 figures in text.] Proc. Soc. Antiq., 2nd S. 22, pp. 76–78. 1908.

11577 —— [Saxon remains from] Faversham, Kent. [3 figures in text : enamelled disk and escutcheons.] *Same jnl.*, 2nd S. 22, pp. 69, 78–9. 1908.

11578 Sutherland (Carol Humphrey Vivian). Numismatic parallels to Kentish polychrome brooches. Archaeol. J., 94 (1937), pp. 116–27, + 2 plates. 1938.

11579 Taylour (Charles) *Gent.*, [*pseud. of Henry Keepe*]. A true . . . narrative of the . . . finding the crucifix and gold chain of . . . Edward the king and Confessor, which was found after 620 years interment, *etc.* pp. 34. 4° London, 1688.

11580 Thurnam (John). On an Anglo-Saxon fibula in the museum of the Society [of Antiquaries]. Archaeologia, 41, pp. 479–81, + 1 plate. 1867.

11581 Tymms (Samuel). Fibulae and buckles from a cemetery on Stow Heath, in Suffolk. [3 figures in text.] Proc. Soc. Antiq., 3, pp. 165–67. 1855.

11582 Victoria and Albert Museum. Enamelled bowl-escutcheons [from Hitchin]. [c. 550–650.] Antiq. J., 5, pp. 168–69. 1925.

11583 Walford (Edward Gibbs). [Exhibition of four] fibulae, apparently of Saxon manufacture, discovered . . . at Badby, in Northamptonshire. [Figure in text.] J. Brit. Archaeol. Assoc., 1, pp. 60–61. 1846.

11584 Warren (Joseph). [Exhibition of A.–S. and Danish fibulae, found at Stow Heath and Icklingham, Suffolk]. *Same jnl.*, 21, pp. 82–84, + 1 plate. (figs. 5 and 6). 1865.

11585 —— Saxon remains found near Ixworth, [Suffolk]. [Gold ornaments, and 2 slabs showing interlacing, in churchyard.] Proc. Suffolk Inst. Archaeol., 3, pp. 296–98, + 2 plates. 1862.

11586 Way (Albert). Ancient armillae of gold recently found in Buckinghamshire and north Britain : with notices of ornaments of gold discovered in the British islands. Archaeol. J., 6, pp. 48–61 + 4 plates. 1849.

11587 —— Notice of a Saxon brooch, found [at Myton] in Warwickshire. [Gilt-bronze fibula.] Archaeol. J., 9, pp. 179–80, + 1 plate. 1852.

11588 Whincopp (William). Ornaments found in Suffolk. [2 ear-rings : ?A.–S.] Archaeologia, 32, p. 395. 1847.

11589 Wilson (Arthur Ernest). Saxon jewellery from Sussex. [9 figures in text. Brooches from Highdown and Alfriston.] Sussex County Mag., 25, pp. 21–25. 1951.

11590 Worsaae (Jens Jacob Asmussen). A few remarks upon the antiquities of silver found at Cuerdale [near Preston, Lancs.]. Archaeol. J., 4, pp. 200–03. 1847.

11591 Wright (Thomas). Account of Anglo-Saxon jewellery, etc., found at Seamer in the East Riding of Yorkshire. J. Brit. Archaeol. Assoc., 21, pp. 329–32, + 1 plate. 1865.

11592 Wylie (William Michael). [Exhibition of] two fibulae, of dish-forms, . . . found in the Anglo-Saxon cemetery at Fairford [Glos.]. [Figures in text.] Proc. Soc. Antiq., 2, p. 132, 137. 1851.

§ *b*. **Alfred Jewel**

11593 [Anon.] The Alfred jewel. Antiquary, 37, pp. 212–16. 1901.

11594 [Anon.] Alfred the Great's jewel. Berks, Bucks and Oxon Archaeol. J., 5, pp. 59–61. 1899.

11595 Browne (George Forrest) *bp. of Bristol*. Presidential address [on the Alfred jewel]. Proc. Somerset Arch. Soc., 47 (1901), pp. 9–23. 1902.

11596 Earle (John). The Alfred jewel. pp. xxii, 196. [Coloured frontispiece.] 8ᶜ London, 1901.

11597 Jewitt (Llewellynn). A note on king Alfred's jewel. Reliquary, 20, pp. 65–66, + 1 plate. 1879.

11598 Kirk (Joan R.). The Alfred and Minster Lovel jewels. *Ashmolean Museum*. pp. 12. 8° Oxford, 1948.

11599 Macray (J.). King Alfred's jewel. N. and Q., 3rd S. 2, p. 493. 1862.

11600 Pegge (Samuel). Observations on the mistakes of Mr. Lisle and Mr. Hearne, in respect to king Alfred's present to the cathedrals. The late use of the stylus, or metalline pen. Mr. Wise's conjecture concerning the famous jewel of king Alfred, further pursued, shewing it might possibly be part of the stylus sent by that king, with Gregory's Pastoral, to the monastery of Athelney. Archaeologia, 2, pp. 68–74. 1772.

11601 Smith (Herbert Luther). Alfred's jewel. [?Head of a sceptre.] N. and Q., 2nd S. 6, pp. 46–47, 78, 312–13, 357–58. 1858.

11602 Smith (Reginald Allender). Anglo-Saxon remains [in Somerset]. [Mostly on the Alfred jewel and other jewellery.] V.C.H., Somerset, 1, pp. 373–81, + 2 plates, + map. 1906.

§ *c*. **Bronze Ornaments and other Bronze Objects**

11603 Böe (Johs.). An Anglo-Saxon bronze mount from [Bjoerke], Norway. Antiq. J., 12, pp. 440–42, + 2 plates. 1932.

11604 Cowen (John David). A 9th–10th century bronze mounting from York. Saga-Book V.C., 11 (1928–36), pp. 125–28. 1935.

11605 Crawford (Osbert Guy Stanhope). West-Saxon graves in Berks. [Exhibition of 6 bronzes.] Antiq. J., 12, p. 445, + 1 plate. 1932.

11606 George (Thomas). A series of bronze ornaments from Anglo-Saxon burials at Duston, [Northants.]. [2, full-size, figures of brooches in text.] Proc. Soc. Antiq., 2nd S. 19, pp. 310–14. 1903.

11607 Head (John Frederick). An Anglo-Saxon strap-end from Bledlow, Bucks. [Bronze : end of 9th c.] Antiq. J., 22, p. 221. 1942.

11608 Lewes Museum. A rare bronze [from Broyle, near Chichester] in Sussex. [5th c., A.–S.] Antiq. J., 4, pp. 49–50. 1924.

11609 Sheppard (Thomas). Anglo-Saxon bronze pendant. [Found in a gravel pit at Roos in Holderness, and now in Hull Museum.] Trans. East Riding Antiq. Soc., 20, p. 52. 1914.

11610 —— A fifth-century bronze buckle from Lincolnshire. [Now in Hull Museum. With 5 figures.] Antiquary, 50, pp. 207–08. 1914.

11611 Shortt (Hugh de Sausmarez). A Saxon bronze girdle-end from East Harnham, Wilts. [3 figures in p. 349.] Wilts. Archaeol. Mag., 52, pp. 345–49. 1949.

11612 Smith (Reginald Allender). A bronze penannular brooch of about the fifth century, found at Stratford-on-Avon. [Between Roman period and foundation of the A.–S. kingdoms.] Proc. Soc. Antiq., 2nd S. 27, pp. 95–98, + 1 plate. 1915.

11613 Stevenson (Alexander S.). Pre-Conquest fibula of bronze found at Whitehill Point in Northumberland. Proc. Soc. Antiq. Newcastle, 2nd S. 5, p. 236, + 1 plate. 1892.

11614 Westell (William Percival). Bronze objects found in Hertfordshire. [A.–S. book-clasp(?) From Letchworth. ?9th c.] Antiq. J., 15, pp. 349–51. 1935.

§ *d.* **Rings**

11615 Akerman (John Yonge). Silver ring found near Bifrons [Kent]. [? second half of 10th c.] Archaeologia, 32, p. 423. 1847.

11616 Anscombe (Alfred). The ring of Eolla, bishop of Selsey, circa A.D. 720. [In the Ashmolean.] Sussex N. and Q., 1, pp. 136–39, + 1 plate. 1927.

11617 British Museum. An Anglo-Saxon finger-ring [from Ebbesbourne, near Salisbury]. Antiq. J., 6, pp. 186–87. 1926.

11618 —— Franks bequest. Catalogue of the finger rings, *etc.* By O. M. Dalton. pp. lvii, 366, + 30 plates. 4° London, 1912. [Pp. 29–36, + plate 2, A.–S. and Viking.]

11619 Bull (Frederick William). Discoveries near Tickford abbey, Bucks. [Skeletons and ring of silver wire of c. 6th c.] Antiq. J., 5, p. 289. 1925.

11620 Evans (B. E.). The story of a ring. [That of abbot Hedda of Peterborough, slain by the Norsemen, 870. Found 1860, and now in the B.M.] J. Northants. Nat. Hist. Soc., 24, pp. 150–52. 1928.

11621 Fowler (Joseph Thomas). An account of the Anglo-Saxon ring discovered near Driffield, Yorks., now in possession of Geo. Welby, Barrowby, Grantham. [With inscription ' ✠ Ecce Agnvs Dei.'] Rept. of Proc. Geol. Soc. W. Riding of Yorks., 5, pp. 157–62, + 1 plate. 1870.

11622 Franks (*Sir* Augustus Wollaston). [Remarks at exhibition of] the gold ring of Æthelswith, queen of Mercia. [Wife of Burhred. Died 888. Figures on p. 306.] Proc. Soc. Antiq., 2nd S. 6, pp. 305–07. 1875.

11623 Nelson (Philip). An Anglo-Saxon finger-ring. [Late A.–S. period: silver gilt : from Grantley collection.] Antiq., J., 24, p. 154. 1944.

11624 —— An Anglo-Saxon gold finger-ring. [From York.] Antiq. J., 19, pp. 182–84, + 2 plates. 1939.

11625 Oman (Charles Chichele). Anglo-Saxon finger-rings. [7 figures in text.] Apollo, 14, pp. 104–08. 1931.

11626 Pegge (Samuel). Illustration of a gold enamelled ring, supposed to have been the property of Alhstan, bishop of Sherburne ; with some account of the state and condition of the Saxon jewelry in the more early ages. Archaeologia, 4, pp. 47–68. 1786.

11627 Pollexfen (John Hutton). [Exhibition of] a small gold ring found at West Bergholt in Essex. [Figure in text.] Proc. Soc. Antiq., 2nd S. 2, p. 247. 1863.

11628 Sheppard (Thomas). Saxon gold ring found at Driffield, East Yorks. [Hull Museum Publn. 134. 16 figures in text.] Trans. East Riding Antiq. Soc., 24, pp. 43–50. 1923.

11629 Smith (Harold Clifford). [Exhibition of] a gold ring, the property of Mrs. Richardson. [Dug up c. 1867 at Meaux abbey, near Beverley. 9th or early 10th c. Figure in text.] Proc. Soc. Antiq., 2nd S. 32, pp. 112–13. 1920.

11630 Smith (Reginald Allender). Anglo-Saxon gold ring found at Oxford. [10th c.] *Same jnl.*, 2nd S. 29, p. 123. 1917.

11631 Stephens (George). Notice of the runic ring recently found in Cramond churchyard, [Midlothian]. [? 10th c. Figure in text. No reading given.] Proc. Soc. Antiq. Scot., 9, pp. 458–59. 1873.

11632 Waterman (Dudley M.). A gold ring found at Malton [Yorks.] in 1774. Antiq. J., 31, p. 192, + 1 plate. 1951.

11633 Whitbourn (Richard). [Exhibition of] an Anglo-Saxon ring of gold ... found at Witley in Surrey. Proc. Soc. Antiq., 2nd S. 2, p. 88. 1862.

197. JEWELLERY, JUTISH

11634 Hooley (*Mrs.* R. W.) and **Crawford** (Osbert Guy Stanhope). Jutish buckle-plate. [From Meon valley. Now in Winchester Museum.] Antiq. J., 17, pp. 199–200, 441–42. 1937.

11635 Kendrick (*Sir* Thomas Downing). A Jutish fragment from [Dover Museum,] Kent. [Embossed silver-gilt mount of late 6th c. 2 figures.] Antiq. J., 17, pp. 76–77. 1937.

11636 —— and **Hawkes** (Charles Francis Christopher). Jutish jewellery from Preshaw, Hants. [Meon-Wara, c. 600.] Antiq. J., 17, pp. 322–24. 1937.

11637 Kendrick (*Sir* Thomas Downing). The Kingston brooch. [Early 6th c. From Jutish grave at Kingston, Kent. Figure in text. ' Most splendid jewel ever found in the soil of England.'] Antiq. J., 19, pp. 195–96. 1939.

11638 Smith (Reginald Allender). Jutish finds in Kent. [From Howletts gravel-pit, near Bekesbourne, 3 miles east of Canterbury.] B.M.Q., 10, pp. 131–32, + plate 38. 1936.

11639 —— Jutish ornaments from Kent. [From Howletts gravel-pit.]. B.M.Q., 11, pp. 51–52, + plate 15. 1937.

198. JEWELLERY, VIKING

11640 Allen (John Romilly). The Orton Scar brooch. Reliquary, 9, pp. 203–04. 1903.

11641 Anderson (Joseph). Notice of bronze brooches and personal ornaments from a ship burial of the Viking time in Oronsay, and other bronze ornaments from Colonsay. . . . With a description, from notes by the late William Galloway, of a ship-burial of the Viking time at Kiloran bay, Colonsay. [9 figures in text.] Proc. Soc. Antiq. Scot., 41 (4th S. 5, 1906–07), pp. 437–50. 1907.

11642 Armstrong (Edmund Clarence Richard). Catalogue of the silver and ecclesiological antiquities of the Royal Irish Academy, by the late Sir William Wilde. [Largely Viking period.] Proc. R.I.A., 32c, pp. 287–312, + 3 plates. 1915.

11643 Baynes (Edward Neil). Five armlets of the Viking period. Antiq. J., 8, pp. 359–60. 1928.

11644 Böe (Johs.). A hoard from west Norway. [Brooches, etc., of Irish-Scandinavian craftsmanship.] Antiq. J., 14, pp. 159–62, + 1 plate. 1934.

11645 Cochrane (Robert). [Exhibition of] two Viking brooches and a bowl . . . found . . . at Ballyholme, . . . co. Down . . . 1903. J. Roy. Soc. Antiq. Ireland, 36 (5th S. 16), pp. 450–54. 1906.

11646 —— Ornamental pin of the Viking period found at Clontarf, co. Dublin. Reliquary, 12, pp. 131–32. 1906.

11647 —— and **Smith** (Reginald Allender). Two Viking brooches and a bowl found . . . at Ballyholme . . . county Down. [2 figures in text.] Proc. Soc. Antiq., 2nd S. 21, pp. 72–79. 1906.

11648 Coffey (George). A pair of brooches and chains of the Viking period recently found in Ireland. J. Roy. Soc. Antiq. Ireland, 32 (5th S. 12), pp. 71–73. 1902.

11649 Corrie (John M.). Viking brooch of silver from Skaill Bay, Orkney. [With figure.] Proc. Soc. Antiq. Scot., 66 (6th S. 6, 1931–32), pp. 84–85. 1932.

11650 Curle (James). A find of Viking relics in the Hebrides. Burl. Mag., 29, pp. 241–42, + 1 plate. 1916.

11651 Goudie (Gilbert). A gold armlet of the Viking time discovered [in the isle of Oxna] in Shetland. Proc. Soc. Antiq. Scot., 47 (4th S. 11, 1912–13), pp. 444–50. 1913.

11652 Greenwell (William). Scandinavian brooches found at Santon, in Norfolk. Proc. Suffolk Inst. Archaeol., 4, pp. 208–17, + 1 plate. 1870.

11653 Grove (L. R. A.). A Viking bone trial-piece from York castle. Antiq. J., 20, pp. 285–87. 1940.

11654 Henderson (James). [Donation of] a pair of ' tortoise ' or bowl-shaped brooches of brass or bronze, of the Viking period found . . . near Wick, [Caithness]. [9th–11th c. Figure in text.] Proc. Soc. Antiq. Scot., 11, pp. 152–53. 1876.

11655 Jarvis (Edwin). Account of the discovery of ornaments and remains, supposed to be of Danish origin, in the parish of Caenby, Lincolnshire. Archaeol. J., 7, pp. 36–44 + 2 plates. 1850.

11656 Kendrick (*Sir* Thomas Downing). The Claughton hall [Lancs.] brooches. [10th c. Found in Viking grave, 1822.] Saga-Book V.C., 11 (1928–36), pp. 117–24. 1935.

11657 —— A gaming-board of the Viking period found in Ireland. ['From its ornament, probably made in the Isle of Man by a Celto-Norse craftsman of the third quarter of the 10th century.'] *Same jnl.*, 11 (1928–33), pp. 82–83. 1934.

11658 Kermode (Philip Moore Callow). The Woodbourne [Douglas] treasure-trove, 1894. [Silver coins of Athelstan to Edgar : also gold and silver armlets, ring, silver pin, etc.] I.o.M., N.H. and Antiq. Soc., Proc., N.S. 1, pp. 437–40. 1913.

11659 Kirk (John Lamplugh). Trefoil brooch from Yorkshire. [c. 900. Found near Pickering.] Antiq. J., 7, pp. 526, 528 (figure). 1927.

11660 Leeds (Edward Thurlow). A bronze Viking pin from Castor, Northants. [Figure in text.] Antiq. J., 30, p. 75. 1950.

11661 MacLeod (D. J.). An account of a find of ornaments of the Viking time from Valtos, Uig, in the island of Lewis, [Ross]. With a detailed description of the objects by W. J. Gibson, and a note upon the find by James Curle. Proc. Soc. Antiq. Scot., 50 (5th S. 2, 1915–16), pp. 181–89. 1915.

11662 Megan (Basil R. S.). The Douglas treasure trove. A hoard of the Viking age. [Woodbourne estate. Coins, rings, bracelets, brooches, etc. ?deposited 960–80]. J. Manx Mus., 4, pp. 27–80, + 3 plates. 1938.

11663 Milligan (Seaton Forrest). Pin found at Clontarf, Dublin. [Early 9th c. Scandinavian work, ornamented and inlaid with a white metal.] J. Roy. Soc. Antiq. Ireland, 36 (5th S. 16), pp. 87, 218–19 (figures). 1906.

11664 Patterson (William Hugh). [Exhibition of] a bronze and gilt disc of a fibula, probably of the Viking type [found at Budore, co. Antrim.]. J. Roy. Hist. and Arch. Assoc. Ireland, [17], 4th S. 7, pp. 125–26. 1885.

11665 Quine (John). The Douglas treasure trove. [Woodbourne estate. 1894.] Yn Lioar Manninagh, 2, pp. 242–45. 1901.

11666 Scott-O'Connell (D. H.). Viking period silver ornaments from Rathmoley, county Tipperary. J. Cork Hist. Soc., 2nd S. 43, pp. 125–26, + 1 plate. 1948.

11667 Shetelig (Haakon). Vikingeminner i Vest-Europa. *Inst. for Sammenlignende Kultur forskning, serie A*, 16. pp. xii, 270. 8° Oslo, 1933.

11668 Sjøvold (Thorleif). A bronze ornament of western European origin, found [at Hillesøy] in northern Norway. [Brooch of Viking period : 'originates from England '.] Antiquity, 25, pp. 127–30, + 1 plate. 1951.

11669 Smith (Reginald Allender). A bronze panel of the Viking period from Winchester cathedral. [5 figures in text.] Proc. Soc. Antiq., 2nd S. 23, pp. 397–402. 1911.

11670 Smith (Reginald Allender). Remarks on the pin and [penannular] brooches exhibited [from Fluskew Pike, Newbiggin Moor, Cumberland and from Killucan, co. Westmeath], and on other examples of the 'thistle' type. [' Link connecting the "thistle" ornament on penannular brooches of Viking times with the late-Keltic period.' 7 figures in text.] Proc. Soc. Antiq., 2nd S. 21, pp. 63–91, + 1 plate. 1906.

11671 Society of Antiquaries of Scotland, *Museum*. Pair of oval bowl shaped brooches and a trefoil-shaped brooch found at Clibberswick, Unst, Shetland. [Scandinavian types. 2 figures in text.] Proc. Soc. Antiq. Scot., 17 (N.S. 5), p. 17. 1883.

11672 Walker (Thomas James). Notice of a large cruciform fibula or brooch of bronze, overlaid with gold, found in Peterborough in 1878. [Whole page figure. Scandinavian design.] Proc. Soc. Antiq. Scot., 22 (N.S. 10), pp. 263–65. 1888. *Reprinted in* Northants. N. and Q., 4, pp. 105–06, + plate. 1892.

11673 Waterman (Dudley M.). Viking antiquities from Sawdon, N.R. Yorks. [Pin, etc. 2 figures in text.] Antiq. J., 28, pp. 180–83. 1948.

11674 Wilde (*Sir* William Robert Wills). On the Scandinavian antiquities lately discovered at Islandbridge, near Dublin. [10 figures in text]. Proc. R.I.A., 10, pp. 13–22. 1870.

199. JEWELLERY, CELTIC

11675 [Anon.] The Dalriada brooch. Ulster J. Archaeol., 4, pp. 1–3, + 1 coloured plate. 1856.

11676 [Anon.] The Roscommon brooch. [10th c.] J. Roy. Soc. Antiq. Ireland, 58 (6th S. 18), p. 166, + 1 plate. 1928.

11677 Allen (John Romilly). The Celtic brooch, and how it was worn. Illust. Archaeol., 1, pp. 162–75. 1893.

11678 Anderson (Joseph). Notes on the ornamentation of the silver brooches found at Skaill, Orkney, and now in the museum. [Mixed Celtic and Scandinavian. 23 figures in text.] Proc. Soc. Antiq. Scot., 15 (N.S. 3), pp. 286–98. 1881.

11679 —— Notice of a fragment of a silver penannular brooch, ornamented with gold filigree work and amber settings, found at Achavrole, Dunbeath, Caithness, in 1860 ; and of two silver brooches, the property of Andrew Heiton, said to have been found in the neighbourhood of Perth. *Same jnl.*, 14 (N.S. 2), pp. 445–52. 1880. *See also* 40 (4th S. 4, 1905–06), pp. 347–50 (figured on p. 349). 1906.

11680 Armstrong (Edmund Clarence Richard). Four brooches preserved in the library of Trinity College, Dublin. [Two from La Tène period : one c. 600 A.D. and one early 10th c. 3 figures in text]. Proc. R.I.A., 32 c, pp. 243–48. 1915.

11681 —— An Irish bronze casting formerly preserved ay Killua castle, co. Westmeath. [8th c. Figures.] Antiq. J., 1, pp. 122–24. 1921.

11682 —— Irish bronze pins of the Christian period. Archaeologia, 72, 71–86, + 3 plates. 1922.

11683 Atkinson (George Mouncey). Glass beads and jet ornaments. J. Roy. Hist. and Arch. Assoc. Ireland, [16], 4th S. 6 (1883–84), pp. 69–71. 1884.

11684 Barker (W. R.). An ancient bronze collar from Wraxall, Somerset, recently presented to the Bristol museum. [' Late-Celtic ' ornament.] Proc. Clifton Antiq. Club, 3 (1893–96), pp. 89–94, + 1 plate. 1897.

11685 —— Part of a late Celtic bronze collar found at Llandyssil, Cardiganshire, [' Late Celtic ' ornament.] *Same jnl.*, 3 (1893–96), pp. 210–13. 1897.

11686 Bellingham (*Sir* Henry) *bart.* Annual address [to the County Louth Archaeological Society, on the Ardagh chalice.] County Louth Archaeol. J., 1. iii, pp. 5–14, + 2 plates. 1906.

11687 Cochrane (Robert). The Clonmacnoise brooch. J. Roy. Soc. Antiq. Ireland, 20 (5th S. 1), pp. 318–19, + 1 plate. 1890.

11688 Cursiter (James Walls). Notes on a hoard of silver ornaments and coins, discovered in the island of Burray, Orkney. [Armlets and 3 coins—pennies of Edward the Elder, Edgar and Ethelred II.] Proc. Soc. Antiq. Scot., 23 (N.S. 11), pp. 318–22. 1889.

11689 Day (Robert). Ornaments in glass from Egypt to illustrate those found in Ireland. J. Roy. Hist. and Arch. Assoc. Ireland, [18], 4th S. 8, pp. 112–14, + 1 coloured plate. 1887.

11690 Dunglas (Charles Alexander) *lord, afterwards 12th earl of Home*. Notice of the discovery of a massive silver chain of plain double rings or links at Hordwell, Berwickshire. With notes of similar silver chains found in Scotland, by John Alexander Smith. [With ' the peculiar C-like curves of the late Celtic period of art.'] Proc. Soc. Antiq. Scot., 15 (N.S. 3), pp. 64–70. 1881.

11691 Dunraven (Edwin Richard Wyndham) *3rd earl of*. On an ancient chalice and brooches lately found at Ardagh, in the county of Limerick. [10th c.] Trans. R.I.A., 24 (Antiq.), pp. 433–55, + 3 plates. 1873.

11692 —— On an ancient cup and brooches, found near Ardagh. (Abstract). [10th c.] Proc. R.I.A., 10, pp. 458–59. 1870.

11693 Edwards (Arthur J. H.). Three penannular armlets and two finger-rings of silver. Proc. Soc. Antiq. Scot., 73 (7th S. 1, 1938–39), p. 327, + 1 plate. 1939.

11694 Fairholt (Frederick William). Remarks on Irish fibulae. Trans. Brit. Archaeol. Ass., 3rd Congress (Gloucester, 1846), pp. 86–93, + 1 plate. 1848.

11695 Fraser (Thomas). Notice of a find of silver ornaments, etc., at Croy, Inverness-shire, now presented to the museum, with notes, descriptive of the objects, by Joseph Anderson. [Including silver penny of Coenwulf.] Proc. Soc. Antiq. Scot., 11, pp. 588–92. 1876.

11696 Fraser (William). On gold linulae, with descriptions of those contained in the Royal Irish Academy's museum, and other collections ; and on the source of the gold employed to make Irish gold ornaments. (On Irish gold ornaments. Whence came the gold and when ? Article no. 2). [1st c. to about 620 A.D. ?products of remolten Roman and Byzantine gold.] J. Roy. Soc. Antiq. Ireland, 27 (5th S. 7), pp. 53–66, 359–70. 1897.

11697 Graves (James) and **Clibborn** (Edward). [The Kilkenny brooch]. J. Kilkenny Archaeol. Soc., [5] N.S. 2, pp. 242–50, + 2 plates. 1859.

11698 Hassé (Leonard). Statistics of ornamented glass beads in Irish collections. J. Roy. Soc. Antiq. Ireland, 20 (5th S. 1), pp. 359–66. 1891.

11699 Hoare (Edward). Ancient Celto-Irish, silver penannular brooch, dug up . . . about three miles south-east of Galway. [?Scandinavian workmanship : ? date.] Proc. and Trans. Kilkenny Archaeol. Soc., 3, pp. 10–11, + 1 plate. 1854.

11700 Horne (Ethelbert), *abbot of Downside*. Celtic discs of enamel. [From Saxon cemetery at Camerton, near Bath.] Antiq. J., 10, pp. 53–54. 1930.

11701 Kermode (Philip Moore Callow). Bronze pin from the Isle of Man. Antiq. J., 11, pp. 163–64. 1931.

11702 Knowles (William James). Ancient Irish beads and amulets. [Stone, jet, amber, lead, glass, etc. ? dates.] J. Roy. Hist. and Arch. Assoc. Ireland, [15], 4th S. 5 (1879–82), pp. 522–37, + 2 coloured plates. *See also* pp. 392–96. 1882.

11703 Lethbridge (Thomas Charles) and **David** (H. E.). A brooch of the ' dark ages ' from Kenfig, [Glamorgan]. [Probably 6th c.] Arch. Camb., 83 (7th S. 8), pp. 200–02. 1928.

11704 Mac an Bháird (E. R.). The Belcoo brooch [co. Fermanagh]. [7th c. Penannular bronze brooch.] J. Roy. Soc. Antiq. Ireland, 59 (6th S. 19), pp. 69–71. 1929.

11705 MacLeod (Norman). Tortoise-shaped brooch of bronze [and bronze pin] from the island of Tiree, [Argyllshire]. [c. 8th c.] Proc. Soc. Antiq. Scot., 9, pp. 532–33. 1873.

11706 Mahr (Adolf). Ancient Irish handicraft. *Thomond Archaeological Society.* pp. 24, + 24 plates. 4° Limerick, 1939.

11707 —— The Blackrock brooch. [Penannular : ? late 6th c.] County Louth Archaeol. J., 7, pp. 530–31, + 1 plate. 1932.

11708 —— Irish early Christian handicraft. N. Munster Antiq. J., 1, pp. 57–66, + 12 plates. 1937.

11709 Maxwell (*Sir* Herbert Eustace), *7th bart.* Notes on a hoard of personal ornaments, implements, and Anglo-Saxon and Northumbrian coins from Talnotrie, Kinkcudbrightshire. Proc. Soc. Antiq. Scot., 47 (4th S. 11, 1912–13), pp. 12–16. 1913.

11710 Miller (Hugh) and **MacLeod** (Donald). Notice of the discovery of a hoard of silver penannular armlets and coins at Tarbat, Ross-shire. [13 coins (one of Edgar) and 2 penannular armlets.] *Same jnl.,* 23 (N.S. 11), pp. 314–17. 1889.

11711 Morris (Henry). The Tara brooch. [700–1000, A.D.] County Louth Archaeol. J., 1. i, pp. 21–22, + 1 plate. Another plate opp. p. 84 in 1. iii. 1904.

11712 Nesbitt (Alexander). Observations relative to the probable origin of beads of glass found in Ireland. [Remarks on paper by W. J. Knowles, **11702.**] J. Roy. Hist. and Arch. Assoc. Ireland, [15], 4th S. 5 (1879–82), pp. 592–96. 1882.

11713 Nordman (Carl Axel). Irish metal-work in Finland. [?8th c., looted by Vikings. Bronze fragment, from Ristimäki cemetery near Åbo.] Antiq. J., 5, pp. 169–70. 1925.

11714 Olden (Thomas). The paten of Gourdon, illustrated from the Book of Armagh. [5th–6th c. ?] Proc R.I.A., 3rd S. 3, pp. 784–89. 1896.

11715 Ó Ríordáin (Seán Pádraig). Recent acquisitions from county Donegal in the National Museum. With addendum : chemical examination of ancient Irish bronze and silver objects, by Kenneth C. Bailey. [Pp. 174–83, early Christian objects. (Silver bracelets and brooches—some Viking type, probably 10th c.)] Proc. R.I.A., 42c, pp. 145–91, + 8 plates. 1935.

11716 O'Toole (Edward). Two early penannular brooches from Bough, Rathvilly, co. Carlow. [6th–7th c. Bronze, with traces of red enamel.] J. Roy. Soc. Antiq. Ireland, 64 (7th S. 4), pp. 263–64, + 1 plate. 1934.

11717 Paterson (T. G. F.) and **Davies** (Oliver). The Craig collection in Armagh museum. [Including two early Christian penannular brooches (Illustrated).] Ulster J. Archaeol., 3rd S. 3, pp. 70–72. 1940.

11718 Patterson (William Hugh). Notice of a silver brooch found at the crannog in the bog of Aghaloughan, near Randalstown, county of Antrim. [Figure in text. Not later than 10th c.] J. Roy. Hist. and Arch. Assoc. Ireland, [12], 4th S. 2 (1872–73), p. 74. 1874.

11719 Petrie (George). On an ancient brooch found near Drogheda [co. Louth]. [?11th c.] Proc. R.I.A., 5, pp. 36–40. 1853.

11720 Read (*Sir* Charles Hercules) and **Smith** (Reginald Allender). The Breadalbane brooch. [c. 770–80.] Proc. Soc. Antiq., 2nd S. 32, pp. 63–66, + 1 plate. 1920.

11721 Smith (J. Richardson). An ancient brooch, found in the cave of Bhreacain on the Jura shore of the gulf of Corryvreckan [and] another found in the island of Mull. Proc. and Trans. Kilkenny Archaeol. Soc., 3, pp. 339–40, + 1 plate. 1855.

11722 Smith (John Alexander). Notice of a massive bronze armlet, the property of the earl of Strathmore. [' Late Celtic ' style.] Proc. Soc. Antiq. Scot., 17 (N.S. 5), pp. 90–92. 1883.

11723 Smith (Reginald Allender). A bronze-gilt boss from Steeple Bumpstead church, Essex. [5 figures in text. Irish, presumably plundered from an Irish monastery in an 8th c. Viking raid.] Proc. Soc. Antiq., 2nd S. 28, pp. 87–95. 1916.

11724 —— Irish brooches of five centuries. [14 figures in text. Pp. 247–50, ' chronological list of the principal penannular brooches and allied forms dating about 500–1000 A.D.'] Archaeologia, 65, pp. 223–50, + 4 plates. 1914.

11725 Society of Antiquaries of Scotland. [Exhibition of] two silver brooches and one of bronze, found in Sutherlandshire. Proc. Soc. Antiq. Scot., 8, pp. 305–10, + 1 plate. 1871.

11726 Stephens (George). The Hunterston brooch. [Silver, gold filigree, set with amber. ?8th or 9th c. 2 inscriptions in Scandinavian (?Manx) runes.] Archaeol. and Hist. Collns. Ayr and Wigton, 1, pp. 76–79, + 2 coloured plates. 1878.

11727 —— Note on the Hunterston brooch, Ayrshire, with a reading of the runic inscription on it. [?8th or 9th c.] Proc. Soc. Antiq. Scot., 7, pp. 462–64, + 2 coloured plates. 1870.

11728 Stewart (John Lorne). [Exhibition of] penannular brooch of bronze, with settings of glass, and bronze pin, with ornamental head, found in the island of Coll, [Argyll.]. [Late Christian period, 9th–12th c.] Same jnl., 15 (N.S. 3), pp. 79–81. 1881.

11729 Stokes (Margaret MacNair). Inquiry as to the probable date of the Tara brooch and chalice found near Ardagh. [Chart is ' chronological table of those examples of Irish architecture, sculpture, metal-work, and manuscripts, the dates of which can be approximately fixed.'] Proc. R.I.A., 2nd S. 2 (Antiq.), pp. 451–55, + chart. 1888.

11730 Wakeman (William Frederick). Two ancient pins [from counties Roscommon and Fermanagh]. J. Roy. Hist. and Arch. Assoc. Ireland, [13], 4th S. 3 (1874–75), pp. 153–60. + 1 plate. 1876.

o o

11731 Waterhouse and Co. Antique Irish brooches. 8° Dublin, 1872.

11732 Way (Albert). Notices of a remarkable discovery of silver ornaments in a tumulus at Largo, in Fifeshire. [Some ornament comparable to Irish-Saxon School of 7–8th century.] Archaeol. J., 6, pp. 248–59, + 3 plates. 1849.

11733 Weston *afterwards* **Hunter-Weston** (Gould Read). [Exhibition of] Hunterston brooch [with] remarks. [' Finest fibula ever found in Scotland, and the only one known to exist in that country bearing runes.'] Proc. Soc. Antiq., 2nd S. 7, pp. 47–49. 1876.

11734 Westropp (Hodder Michael). [Bronze] fibula found at Ridgemount, near Frankfort, King's County. J. Hist. and Archaeol. Assoc. Ireland, [10] 3rd S. 1, pp. 279–81, + 1 plate. 1869.

11735 Wheeler (H. A.). The Tara brooch : where was it found ? [Now in National Museum, Dublin. P. 156, whole page fig.] County Louth Archaeol. J., 12 (1950), pp. 155–58. 1951.

11736 Windele (John). Ancient Irish gold. [Finds of, etc.] Ulster J. Archaeol., 8, pp. 28–50, + 1 plate. 1860.

11737 —— Ancient Irish gold and its origin, with notes on early Irish navigation and commerce. *Same jnl.*, 8, pp. 197–222. 1860.

200. BELLS

(All aspects—artistic, historical, etc. Earlier type, backwards to 5th c. : later type, 10th c.)

11738 [Anon.] The bell of St. Ceneu, or St. Keyna, daughter of Brychan. [5th c. Given by T. Kerslake to library of Univ. Coll., Cardiff.] Cymru Fu, 1, p. 365. 1889.

11739 Abgrall (Jean Marie). Quatre vieilles cloches et deux pierres sonnantes. [Bells of SS. Paul Aurelian, Goulven, Ronan and Mériadec.] Bull. Soc. archéol. du Finistère, 22, pp. 17–32, + 1 plate. 1895.

11740 Anderson (Joseph). Notice of a Celtic bell of bronze, from Little Dunkeld. Proc. Soc. Antiq. Scot., 23 (N.S. 11), pp. 118–21. 1889.

11741 —— Notice of a bronze bell of Celtic type at Forteviot, Perthshire. [?10th c.] *Same jnl.*, 26 (3rd S. 2), pp. 434–39. 1892.

11742 —— Notice of ancient Celtic bells at Glenlyon [Perth], Fortingall [Perth], and Inch, [Inverness]. [Also, p. 107, 'healing stones of St. Fillan', against insanity and rheumatism.] *Same jnl.*, 14 (N.S. 2), pp. 102–08. 1880.

11743 Anker (Joseph). Saxon bell found at Peterborough. [?Saxon.] Northants. N. and Q., 2, p. 104. 1888.

11744 Barnwell (Edward Lowry). On some ancient Welsh bells. Arch. Camb., 4th S. 2, pp. 271–75. 1871.

11745 Bell (John). On an ancient bell, said to have belonged to St. Murus. [7th c. Used as a drinking cup, especially by women during pregnancy.] Proc. R.I.A., 5, pp. 206–07. 1853.

11746 Coleman (James). Irish bells in Brittany. J. Roy. Soc. Antiq. Ireland, 28 (5th S. 8), pp. 167–70. 1898.

11747 Cooke (Thomas Lalor). On ancient Irish bells. Trans. Kilkenny Archaeol. Soc., 2 (1852), pp. 47–63. 1853.

11748 Doherty (William). St. Boedan's bell. Proc. R.I.A., 3rd S. 2, pp. 114–16. 1893.

11749 Dottin (Georges). Le celtique clocca. Rev. études anciennes, 22, pp. 39–40. 1920.

11750 Eeles (Francis Carolus). The Guthrie bell and its shrine. [4 figures in text. ?5th c. From Guthrie castle, Forfar, and now in National Museum.] Proc. Soc. Antiq. Scot., 60 (5th S. 12, 1925–26), pp. 409–20. 1927.

11751 Fisher (John). The Welsh Celtic bells. [Figures of 8 bells.] Arch. Camb., 81 (7th S. 6), pp. 324–34. 1926.

11752 Forbes (Alexander Penrose) *bp. of Brechin.* Notice of the ancient bell of St. Fillan. Proc. Soc. Antiq. Scot., 8, pp. 265–76. 1871.

11753 Franks (*Sir* Augustus Wollaston). Four ancient Irish bells from [the archbishop of Armagh's] collection. [i. The Clog Mogue or Bell of St. Mogue : ii. The Clog-na-fullah, or Bell of Blood : iii. The Barry Garioh : iv. A Monaghan bell.] Proc. Soc. Antiq., 2nd S. 3, pp. 149–51, + 1 plate. 1865.

11754 Jones (Morris Charles). Celtic bell from Llangystenyn. [Cast-bronze bell, now in Powys-land museum : early Christian.] Arch. Camb., 5th S. 9, pp. 252–55. 1892.

11755 McClelland (John) *jr.* The bell of Saint Mura. [7th c.] Ulster J. Archaeol., 1, pp. 274–75, + 2 plates. 1853.

11756 McGovern (J. B.). The bell of St. Mogue. Breifny Antiq. Soc. J., 2, pp. 20–24. 1923.

11757 McInroy (William). The bell of St. Fillan of Struan in Athole. [2 figures in text. Of type in use in earliest ages of the Celtic Church.] Proc. Soc. Antiq. Scot., 13 (N.S. 1), pp. 345–46. 1879.

11758 Meehan (Joseph B.). The bell of Fenagh. [Clogh-na-Righ, given to St. Caillin by St. Patrick.] Breifny Antiq. Soc. J., 2, pp. 99–106. 1923.

11759 Milligan (Seaton Forrest). Ancient ecclesiastical bells in Ulster. J. Roy. Soc. Antiq. Ireland, 33 (5th S. 13), pp. 46–57. 1903.

11760 Morris (Ernest). Ancient bells of Celtic saints. [9 figures in text.] Apollo, 28, pp. 282–87. 1938.

11761 Morris (Henry). Some Ulster ecclesiastical bells. [i. Badoney (N. Tyrone) bell : ii. Drumragh or Mac-Enhill bell : iii. Ballymagroarty bell : iv. St. Buadan's bell.] J. Roy. Soc. Antiq. Ireland, 61 (7th S. 1), pp. 61–64, + 2 plates. 1931.

11762 Petrie (George). On an ancient Irish bell. [Inscribed ' Pray for Cumuscach, son of Ailill.' Died 904.] Proc. R.I.A., 1 (1840), p. 477. 1841.

11763 —— On ancient Irish consecrated bells. Proc. R.I.A., 1 (1838), pp. 174–75. 1841.

11764 Quick (Richard). Notes on an ancient Celtic bell. [?6th c. Found at Bosbury, 1888. Probably used by Christian missionaries in England.] J. Brit. Archaeol. Assoc., 52 (N.S. 2), pp. 34–36, + 1 plate. 1896.

11765 Reeves (William) *bp. of Down.* Five chrome-lithographic drawings, representing an Irish ecclesiastical bell, which is supposed to have belonged to St. Patrick, and the several sides of a jewelled shrine in which it is preserved; accompanied by a description. 2nd edition. pp. 6, + 5 plates. fol. Belfast, 1850.

11766 —— On some ecclesiastical bells in the collection of the Lord Primate. Proc. R.I.A., 8, pp. 441–45. 1864.

11767 —— On the bell of St. Patrick, called the Clog an Edachta. Trans. R.I.A., 27, pp. 1–30. 1877.

11768 Smith (John Alexander). Notice of an ancient Celtic ecclesiastical bell, now preserved in the museum, Kelso. [From Ednam, Roxburghshire.] Proc. Soc. Antiq. Scot., 16 (N.S. 4), pp. 277–84. 1882. *Also in* Hist. Berwick. Nat. Club, 10, pp. 184–91. 1882.

11769 Smythe (William Barlow). On the bell from Lough Lene in the [Royal Irish] Academy's museum. [?belonged to St. Fechin of Fore, 7th c.] Proc. R.I.A., 2nd S. 2 (Antiq.), pp. 164–66, + 1 plate. 1883.

11770 Westwood (John Obadiah). Ecclesiastical hand-bells. Arch. Camb., N.S. 3, pp. 212–13. 1852.

11771 —— On the ancient portable hand-bells of the British and Irish churches. Arch. Camb. 3, pp. 230–39, 301–09; 4, pp. 13–18, 167–76. 1848–49.

11772 Wilson (Daniel). Notes on the Buidhean or bell of Strowan, and other primitive ecclesiastical bells of Scotland. Proc. Soc. Antiq. Scot., 1, pp. 18–22. 1852.

201. CROZIERS, ETC.

11773 Anderson (Joseph). Notice of the Quigrich or crosier, and [4] other relics of St. Fillan, in possession of

their hereditary keepers, or Dewars, in Glendochart, in 1549–50. Proc. Soc. Antiq. Scot., 23 (N.S. 11), pp. 110–18. 1889.

11774 Frazer (William). On an Irish crozier, with early metal crook, probably the missing ' crozier of St. Ciaran ', of Clonmacnoise. Proc. R.I.A., 3rd S. 1, pp. 206–14. 1891.

11775 Garstin (John Ribton). On the identification of a bronze shoe-shaped object as part of the head of an ancient Irish crozier. [' Between 8th and 12th c.' (Heads of croziers used to contain relics).] Proc. R.I.A., 2nd S. 1 (Antiquities), pp. 261–64. 1879.

11776 Gibb (Robert) *illustr.* The Quigrich, or crozier of St. Fillan. [Notice of acquisition by the National Museum of the Antiquities of Scotland, with 2 full-size coloured drawings.] Archaeol. Scot., 5, pp. 339–40, + 2 plates. 1880.

11777 Kendrick (*Sir* Thomas Downing). Flambard's crozier. [Resemblances to Viking work in design and craftsmanship.] Antiq. J., 18, pp. 236–42, + 3 plates. 1938.

11778 Olden (Thomas). On the culebath. [=a liturgical fan, e.g. that belonging to Columba.] Proc. R.I.A., 2nd S. 2 (Antiq.), pp. 355–58. 1886.

11779 Stuart (John). Historical notices of St. Fillan's crozier, and of the devotion of king Robert Bruce to St. Fillan. Proc. Soc. Antiq. Scot., 12, pp. 134–82, + 2 plates. 1878.

11780 Thomson (William). An account of the ancient crosier of St. Fillan's. Archaeol. Scot., 3, pp. 289–91. 1831.

11781 Way (Albert). The Quigrich, or crosier of St. Fillan: with a notice of its present existence in Canada. [With appendices: Documents relating to the relics of St. Fillan: Note on the bells of St. Fillan and St. Medan.] Archaeol. J., 16, pp. 41–52, + plate. 1859.

11782 Westropp (Thomas Johnson). The croziers of Rath and Dysert. [Figures of both in text.] J. Roy. Soc. Antiq. Ireland, 24 (5th S. 4), pp. 337–40. 1894.

11783 Wilson (Daniel). Notice of the Quigrich, or crozier of St. Fillan. Proc. Soc. Antiq. Scot., 3, pp. 233–34, and 1 plate. 1862.

11784 —— Notices of the Quigrich or crozier of St. Fillan and of its hereditary keepers. *Same jnl.*, 12, pp. 122–31. 1878.

11785 —— The Quigrich, or crozier of St. Fillan. pp. 14, + 1 plate. 8° Toronto, 1859.

202. RELIQUARIES AND SHRINES

11786 [Anon.] An Anglo-Saxon reliquary in France. [Northumbrian, c. 660–725. Now at Mortain.] Antiq. J., 11, pp. 161–62. 1931.

11787 [Anon.] The shrine of Dachonna and Peel islet, A.D. 797. [Refers to **11804.**] J. Manx Mus., 3, pp. 26–27, + 1 plate. 1935.

11788 Anderson (Joseph). The architecturally shaped shrines and other reliquaries of the early Celtic Church in Scotland and Ireland. [14 figures in text.] Proc. Soc. Antiq. Scot., 44 (4th S. 8, 1909–10), pp. 259–81. 1910.

11789 —— Notice of an ancient Celtic reliquary exhibited to the Society by Sir Archibald Grant, bart., of Monymusk. [Interlacing ' knot-work ' pattern.] *Same jnl.*, 14 (N.S. 2), pp. 431–35. 1880.

11790 Armstrong (Edmund Clarence Richard). The Cathach of St. Columba. Appendix 1.– The shrine of the Cathach. [Between 1062 and 1098.] Proc. R.I.A., 33 c, pp. 390–96, + 3 plates. 1916.

11791 —— An imperfect Irish shrine recently purchased by the Royal Irish Academy. [Killua shrine : ?8th c.] Antiq. J., 1, pp. 48–61, + 1 plate. 1921.

11792 —— Lord Emly's shrine ; two ridge-poles of shrines, and two bronze castings. [8th c.] Antiq. J., 2, pp. 135–37, + 2 plates. 1922.

11793 Beard (Charles R.). The Monymusk reliquary. [8th c. P. 183 is plate.] Connoisseur, 92, pp. 182–83. 1933.

11794 Bigger (Francis Joseph). Notice of an ancient Celtic shrine. [5th–6th c. Dredged from Lower Loch Erne.] Ann. Rep. and Proc. Belfast Nat. F.C., N.S. 3, pp. 394–95. 1892.

11795 Conway (*Sir* William Martin). Portable reliquaries of the early medieval period. [Pp. 234–37, Celtic group.] Proc. Soc. Antiq., 2nd S. 31, pp. 218–40. 1919.

11796 Crawford (Henry Saxton). A descriptive list of Irish shrines and reliquaries. [i. Tomb-shaped reliquaries : ii. Cross-shaped : iii. Hand-shaped : iv. Miscellaneous reliquaries : v. Cumdachs, or book-shaped : vi. Bell shrines : vii. Croziers : viii. Miscellaneous shrines.] J. Roy. Soc. Antiq. Ireland, 53 (6th S. 13), pp. 74–93, 151–76, + 14 plates. 1923.

11797 Duignan (Michael). The Moylough (co. Sligo), and other Irish belt-reliquaries. [7th–8th c.] J. Galway Hist. Soc., 24, pp. 83–94, + 3 plates. 1951.

11798 Duns (John). Notice of an ancient Celtic reliquary ornamented with interlaced work. [Found in the Shannon with bronze implements.] Proc. Soc. Antiq. Scot., 14 (N.S. 2), pp. 286–91. 1880.

11799 Eeles (Francis Carolus). The Monymusk reliquary or Brecbennoh of St. Columba. *Same jnl.*, 68 (6th S. 8, 1933–34), pp. 433–38, + 1 coloured plate. 1934.

11800 Gougaud (Louis). Fragments of two shrines, probably Irish, found at Angers. Irish Eccles. Rec., 5th S. 2, pp. 606–13, + 1 plate. 1913.

11801 Graves (James). The church and shrine [1166] of St. Manchán, [abbot of Mendroichet, Leix]. pp. 20, + 8 plates. 8° Dublin, 1875. [At Lemanaghan, King's County (Offaly). Died 664, of the Yellow Plague.]

11802 Gwynn (Lucius). The reliquary of Adomnán. [Died, at Iona, 702. Its history.] Irish Eccles. Rec., 5th S. 4, pp. 457–62. 1914. *Same title.* Archivium Hibernicum, 4, pp. 199–214. 1915.

11803 Kendrick (*Sir* Thomas Downing) and **Senior** (Elizabeth). St. Manchan's shrine. Archaeologia, 86, pp. 105–18, + 6 plates. 1936.

11804 Kermode (Philip Moore Callow). Peel island and the shrine of St. Mochonna. [Manx work of 8th c. Now in Copenhagen Museum. Carried off by Norsemen in 797.] I.O.M., N.H. and Antiq. Soc., Proc., N.S. 1, pp. 585–91. 1914.

11805 MacKenna (James Edward). Two Clogher [co. Tyrone] relics. . . . The Domnach Airgid. [5 figures in text.] Ulster J. Archaeol., 2nd S. 7, pp. 118–25. 1901.

11806 Menzies (William Gladstone). Art in the saleroom : Monymusk reliquary, Celtic, late 8th century. Apollo, 18, pp. 65–66. 1933.

11807 Morris (Henry). The shrine of St. Patrick's bell. [Late 11th c.] County Louth Archaeol. J., 1, iv, p. 28, + 1 plate. 1907.

11808 Murphy (Denis). On a shrine lately found in Lough Erne, now belonging to Thomas Plunkett, Enniskillen. Proc. R.I.A., 3rd S. 2, pp. 290–94. 1893.

11809 —— On the ornamentation of the Lough Erne shrine. [9 figures in text.] J. Roy. Soc. Antiq. Ireland, 22 (5th S. 2), pp. 349–55. 1892.

11810 Petersen (Th.). A Celtic reliquary found in a Norwegian burial mound. 8° Trondhjem, 1907. [7th c. Discovered at Melhus in 1906. Viking plunder. Trumpet patterns.]

11811 Petrie (George). An account of an ancient Irish reliquary, called the Domnach-Airgid. Trans. R.I.A., 18 (Antiq.), pp. 14–24, + 5 plates. 1839.

11812 Stevenson (Robert B. K.). The Shannon shrine. J. Roy. Soc. Antiq. Ireland, 77, pp. 156–57, + 1 plate. 1947.

11813 Wall (James Charles). Shrines of British saints. *Antiquary's Books.* pp. xii, 252, + 27 plates. 8° London, 1905.

11814 Westropp (Thomas Johnson). The Clog an oir or bell shrine of [St. Senan of] Scattery. J. Roy. Soc. Antiq. Ireland, 30 (5th S. 10), pp. 237–44. 1900.

11815 Wilde (W. R.). Description of an ancient Irish shrine, called the ' Mias Tighearnain '. [St. Tighearnain, end of 5th c.] Trans. R.I.A., 21 (Antiq.), pp. 16–19, + 1 plate. 1848.

203. TEXTILES

(For the Bayeux tapestry, *see* 18 § *d*.)

11816 Brown (Gerard Baldwin) and **Christie** (A. Grace I.) *Mrs. Archibald H. Christie.* S. Cuthbert's stole and maniple at Durham. [4 plates, included in pagination, and 10 figures in text.] Burl. Mag., 23, pp. 3–17, 67–72. 1913.

11816a Calberg (Marguerite). Tissus et broderies attribués aux saintes Harlinde et Relinde. [Founders of monastery of Aldeneyck, 8th c., and consecrated by SS. Willibrord and Boniface. ' Unique spécimen de broderie de style anglo-saxon.' 21 figures in text.] Bull. Soc. roy. d'Archéol. Bruxelles, Oct. 1951, pp. 1–26, + plate. 1951.

11817 Christie (A. Grace I.) *Mrs. Archibald H. Christie.* English mediaeval embroidery : a brief survey . . . from the beginning of the tenth century until the end of the fourteenth, together with a descriptive catalogue of the surviving examples. pp. xviii, 206, + 160 plates. fol. Oxford, 1938. [Plates 1–3, St. Cuthbert's relics.]

11818 Crowfoot (*Mrs.* Grace Mary). Anglo-Saxon tablet weaving. Antiq. J., 32, pp. 189–91, + 2 plates. 1952.

11819 —— The tablet-woven braids from the vestments of St. Cuthbert at Durham. Antiq. J., 19, pp. 57–80, + 6 plates. 1939.

11820 —— Textiles from a Viking grave at Kildonan, on the isle of Eigg. Proc. Soc. Antiq. Scot., 83 (7th S. 11), pp. 24–28, + 1 plate. 1951.

11821 —— Textiles of the Saxon period in the Museum of Archaeology and Ethnology, [Cambridge]. [i. Mildenhall, ii. St. John's cricket field, iii. Barrington cemetery.] Proc. Camb. Antiq. Soc., 44 (1950), pp. 26–32, + 2 plates. 1951.

11822 Doran (Joseph M.). St. Cuthbert's stole and maniple. [Letter.] Burl. Mag., 23, p. 115. 1913.

11823 Duclos (   ). De mantelinc van Ste. Brigida in de kathedrale te Brugge. Rond den Heerd, 3, pp. 67–69. 1868.

11824 McClintock (Henry Foster). The 'mantle of St. Brigid' at Bruges. [Said to have been given to St. Donatien by Gunhild, sister of Harold II, d. 1087 : now in St. Sauveur. Description of the material and of the technique of the weaving.] J. Roy. Soc. Antiq. Ireland, 66 (7th S. 6), pp. 32–40, + 2 plates. 1936.

11825 —— The mantle of Saint Brigid at Bruges. [' Genuine piece of Irish cloth at least as old as 1050.'] J. County Louth Archaeol. Soc., 12, pp. 119–22, + 1 plate. 1951.

11826 Smith (Reginald Allender). St. Cuthbert's stole. [Early 10th c.] B.M.Q. 11, pp. 4–5, + plate 3. 1937.

11827 Street (G. E.). On mediaeval embroidery. [Pp. 51–52, on St. Cuthbert's stole and maniple.] Trans. Archit. Soc. Durham, 1 (1862–68), pp. 47–72. 1870.

204. ILLUMINATION

§ a. General

11828 Beissel (Stephan). Geschichte der Evangelienbücher in den ersten Hälfte des Mittelalters. *Ergänzungshefte zu den Stimmen aus Maria-Laach*, 92–93. pp. vii, 365, + 91 plates. 8° Freiburg im Breisgau, 1906. [Kenney, 1, p. 98. Pp. 102–38, with figures 26–38, Angelsächsische und irische Evangelienbücher.]

11829 Birch (Walter de Gray) and **Jenner** (Henry). Early drawings and illuminations . . . with a dictionary of subjects in the British Museum. pp. lxiii, 310, + 12 plates. 8° London, 1879.

11830 Boeckler (Albert). Abendländische Miniaturen bis zum Ausgang der romanischen Zeit. pp. viii, 133, + 106 plates. 4° Berlin, 1930. [Pp. 5, 19–20, + plate 12, Codex Amiatinus : pp. 15–19, + plates 8–11, Irische Handschriften, Hiberno-sächsische Handschriften : pp. 40–41, + plate 29, St. Gallen : etc.]

11831 Boeckler (Albert). Deutsche Buchmalerei vorgotischer Zeit. pp. 80. 4° Königstein im Taunus, 1952. [66 plates, many in colour, in pagination. Includes 12 from Fulda, St. Gallen, Reichenau, etc.]

11832 Boinet (Amédée). La miniature carolingienne : ses origines, son développement. pp. 12, 160 plates. large 4° Paris, 1913. [Plates 61–65, Utrecht Psalter.]

11833 British Museum. Schools of illumination. Reproductions from manuscripts in the British Museum. Part I, Hiberno-Saxon and early English schools, A.D. 700–1100. pp. 11, + 16 plates. fol. London, 1914.

11834 Bruun (Johan Adolf). An enquiry into the art of the illuminated manuscripts of the Middle Ages. Pt. 1, Celtic illuminated manuscripts. pp. xiv, 86, + 10 plates. 4° Edinburgh [also Stockholm], 1897. [Kenney, 1, p. 98.]

11835 Burlington Fine Arts Club. Exhibition of illuminated manuscripts. pp. xxviii, 135, + 162 plates. fol. London, 1908. [Plates 10, 11, 15–18, 21. 27, A.-S.]

11836 Cook (Albert Stanburrough). Bishop Cuthwini of Leicester (680–691), amateur of illustrated manuscripts. Speculum, 2, pp. 253–57. 1927.

11836a Dodwell (C. R.). The Canterbury School of Illumination, 1066–1200. pp. xv, 139, + 72 plates. 4° Cambridge, 1954. [Pp. 21–32, The continuity of A.-S. illumination.]

11837 Ebersolt (Jean). Miniatures irlandaises à sujets iconographiques. Rev. archéol., 5. Sér., 13, pp. 1–6. 1921.

11838 Fahey (J. A.). Early Irish Christian art. Illumination. Irish Eccles. Rec., 3rd S. 10, pp. 891–901. 1889.

11839 Goldschmidt (Adolph). Der angelsächsische Stil in der mittelalterlichen Malerei. Texte u. Forschungen. Festgabe für F. Liebermann, pp. 271–76. 1921.

11840 —— Die deutsche Buchmalerei. 2 Bde., 4° Firenze, München, 1928. [200 plates. i. Die karolinische Buchmalerei : ii. Die ottonische Buchmalerei. A.-S. background.]

11841 Herbert (John Alexander). Illuminated manuscripts. *Connoisseur's Library*. pp. xiii, 356, + 51 plates. 4° London, 1911. [Kenney, 1, p. 98. Pp. 66-8, + plates 7-8, Celtic : pp. 106-21, outline drawings of the 9th-11th c., especially in England : pp. 122-42, + plates 12-15, English illumination to A.D. 1200.]

11842 Hermann (Hermann Julius). Die frühmittelalterlichen Handschriften des Abenlandes. *Die illuminierten Handschriften . . . der Nationalbibliothek in Wien*, N.F.1. pp. xii, 239, + 36 plates. 4° Leipzig, 1923. [Pp. 50-56, + plates 11-20, Südenglische Handschrift. 1224 [Salisb. 32]. Evangeliarium, sogen. Cutbercht-Evangeliar. Lateinisch, Folio, viii. Jahrhundert.]

11843 Hieber (Hermann). Die Miniaturen des frühen Mittelalters. pp. 147, 2 plates. 4° München, 1912. [80 figures in text.]

11844 Homburger (Otto). Die Anfänge de Malschule von Winchester im 10. Jahrhundert. *Studien über christliche Denkmäler, hrsg. von J. Ficker. N.F. der archäol. Studien*, 13. pp. 76, + 12 plates. 8° Leipzig, 1912.

11845 Hovey (Walter Read). Sources of the Irish illuminative art. Art Studies, 6, pp. 105-20, + 7 plates. 1928.

11846 Humphreys (Henry Noel). The illuminated books of the Middle Ages . . . from the IVth to the XVIIth centuries. Illustrated by a series of examples the size of the originals . . . printed in colours. pp. 15, + 39 plates. Elephant fol. London, 1849. [Plates 1-8, A.-S.]

11846a Italy, *Ministero della Publica Istruzione*. Mostra storica nazionale della miniatura, Palazzo di Venezia, Roma. Catalogo. pp. xxxvii, 528, + 5 coloured + 104 black plates. Sm. 4° Firenze, 1953. [Pp. xix-xxxvii, bibliography : nos. 31, + plate xi (Codex Amiatinus)—34 (Biblia sacra, detta di Alcuino, 9th c.), etc., A.-S. period.]

11847 Kantorowicz (Ernst Hartwig). The quinity of Winchester. [Group of 5 persons framed by studded circular

aureole. 1012-20 ms. of officia of New Minster, Winchester School.] Art Bull., 29, pp. 73-85, + 4 plates. 1947.

11848 Kobell (Luise von). Kunstvolle Miniaturen und Initialen aus Handschriften des 4. bis 16. Jahrhunderts. 2. Auflage. pp. x, 116, + 60 plates. fol. München, 1892. [Pp. 6-9, Der Einfluss der irischen Mönche auf die Schrift-und Buchmalerei im frühen Mittelalter.]

11848a Koehler (Wilhelm Reinhold Walter). Die karolinischen Miniaturen. *Denkmäler deutscher Kunst*. 4° Berlin, 1930— [Bd. 1 School of Tours. Plates in folio.]

11849 Koemstedt (Rudolf). Zur Beurteilung der frümittelalterlichen Buchmalerei. [Pp. 32-43, Irish and A.-S. mss., in particular the Book of Kells and the Lindisfarne Gospels.] Westdeutsches Jahrbuch für Kunstgeschichte, 9, pp. 31-58. 1936.

11850 Laurie (Arthur Pillans). On the palette of illuminators from the seventh to the end of the fifteenth century. [Abstract of paper, with discussion]. Proc. Soc. Antiq., 2nd S. 25, pp. 10-13. 1912.

11851 —— The pigments and mediums of the old masters. pp. xiv, 192. 8° London, 1914. [' Minute study of pigments employed by insular illuminators, Irish and Anglo-Saxon, based chiefly on the Book of Lindisfarne.' Red—red lead : yellow—orpiment (a sulphite of arsenic) : blue—from lapis lazuli : green—malachite : purple—from Irish shell-fish (murex), c.f. Bede, E.H., I. 1 : no gold used.]

11852 —— The pigments used in painting the Rosslyn missal in the Advocates' Library, and the Celtic psalter D. p. 11, 8, in the library of the University of Edinburgh. [Though the mss. are later, the article discusses also pigments used in early Celtic mss.] Proc. Soc. Antiq. Scot., 57 (5th S. 9, 1922-23), pp. 41-45. 1923.

11853 Lawlor (Hugh Jackson). Lecture on Irish illuminated manuscripts. County Louth Archaeol. J., 4, pp. 17-25. 1916.

11854 Leitschuh (Franz Friedrich). Geschichte der karolinischen Malerei : ihr Bilderkreis und seine Quellen. pp. xii, 471. 8° Berlin, 1894. [Kenney, 1, p. 98. 59 figures.]

11855 Lemoine (J. G.). Les origines de la miniature irlandaise. L'art vivant, 5, pp. 274–79. 1929.

11856 Leprieur (Paul). La peinture en occident du Ve au Xe siècle en dehors de l'Italie. La miniature : les écoles britanniques. Michel (A.) : Histoire de l'art, tome 1, partie 1, pp. 314–21. 1905.

11857 Masai (F.). Essai sur les origines de la miniature dite irlandaise. *Publications de Scriptorium*, 1. pp. 146, + 64 plates. 4° Bruxelles, 1947.

11858 Micheli (Geneviève Louise). L'enluminure du haut moyen âge et les influences irlandaises. pp. xiii, 231, + 280 figures (in plates). 4° Bruxelles, 1939.

11859 Middleton (John Henry). Illuminated manuscripts in classical and mediaeval times, their art and technique. pp. xxiv, 270. 4° Cambridge, 1892. [56 figures in text. Pp. 80–97, Celtic school : pp. 98–105, A.–S. school.]

11860 Millar (Eric George). English illuminated manuscripts from the Xth to the XIIIth century. pp. xii, 146, + 100 plates. fol. Paris, 1926.

11861 Moé (Émile A. van). Illuminated initials in mediaeval manuscripts. Translated by Joan Evans. pp. 120. [Reproductions]. 4° London, [1950].

11862 Muentz (Eugène). La miniature irlandaise et anglo-saxonne au IXe siècle. *Études iconographiques et archéologiques sur la moyen âge*. Paris, 1887. [Kenney, 1, p. 98.]

11863 Oakeshott (Walter Fraser). The sequence of English medieval art, illustrated chiefly from illuminated mss., 650–1450. pp. xi, 55, + 56 plates (16 being in colour). 4° London, 1950. [Pp. 8–16, + plates 2–4, A.–S. period : pp. 22–26, the conditions in which illuminated books were produced (clerics).]

11864 Pfister (Kurt). Irische Buchmalerei ; Nordeuropa und Christentum in der Kunst des frühen Mittelalters.

pp. 24, + 40 plates (4 in colour). 4° Potsdam, 1927. [Plates 1–19, Book of Kells.]

11865 Pfister (Kurt). Die mittelalterliche Buchmalerei des Abenlandes. pp. 40, + 4 plates. 4° München, [1922].

11866 Quaile (Edward). Illuminated manuscripts : their origin, history, and characteristics. pp. xi, 149, + 26 plates. 4° Liverpool, 1897. [Pp. 32–49, A.–S.]

11867 Quaritch (Bernard) *owner*. Examples of the art of book-illumination during the Middle Ages, reproduced in facsimile. Pt. 1. 8 plates. 4° London, 1889. [Plates 1 and 2, from purple ms. called Henry VIII's Golden Gospels, c. 750.]

11868 Réau (Louis). Historie de la peinture au moyen-âge. La miniature. pp. 256, + 96 plates. 4° Melun, 1946. [Pp. 67–74, + plates 16–19, 25, A.–S. and Celtic.]

11869 Saunders (O. Elfrida). English illumination. pp. xx, 132, + 129 plates. 2 vol. 4° Firenze, Paris, [1928]. [Vol. 1, pp. 1–44, + plates 1–33, Celtic and A.–S.]

11870 Schapiro (Meyer). The image of the disappearing Christ. The ascension in English art around the year 1000. [9 figures in text.] Gaz. beaux arts, 6e sér. 23, pp. 135–52. 1943.

11871 Schardt (Alois Jakob). Das Initial : Phantasie und Buchstabenmalerei des frühen Mittelalters. *Kunstbücher des Volkes*, 25. pp. 180, + 4 coloured plates. 4° Berlin, 1938. [106 plates interpaginated. Book of Kells, etc.]

11872 Shaw (Henry). A handbook of the art of illumination as practised during the Middle Ages. With a description of the metals, pigments, and processes employed, *etc.* pp. viii, 66, + 16 plates. 4° London, 1866. [Plates 2–4, A.–S.]

11873 —— Illuminated manuscripts . . . from the sixth to the seventeenth centuries . . . with descriptions by Sir Frederic Madden. pp. 18, + 40 coloured plates. 4° London, 1833. [Plates 2 and 3, A.–S. ii. 8th c. Latin and Saxon Gospels (MS. Cotton Nero, D. IV) : iii. 10th c. Psalter (MS. Cotton Tib. C. VI.]

11874 Springer (Anton). Der Bilder-schmuck in den Sacramentarien des frühen Mittelalters. Abhandl. k. sächs. Gesellschaft der Wiss., 25 (hist.-phil. Cl. 11), pp. 337–78. 1890.

11875 —— Die Genesisbilder in der Kunst des frühen Mittelalters, mit besonderer Rücksicht auf den Ashburn-ham-Pentateuch, [which is, however, north Italian work (O. von Gebhardt) of 7th c.; or Spanish, 8th c. (Otto Schmitt, Reallexikon, 1939, p. 482).] *Same jnl.*, 21, (phil.-hist. Cl. 9), pp. 665–733, + 2 plates. 1884.

11876 —— Die Psalter-Illustrationen im frühen Mittelalter, mit besonderer Rücksicht auf den Utrechtpsalter. Ein Beitrag zur Geschichte der Miniatur-malerei. *Same jnl.*, 19 (phil.-hist. Kl. 8), pp. 187–296, + 10 plates. 1880.

11877 Stanford (R.). Celtic illumin-ative art. Dublin, 1908.

11878 Stoessel (Waldemar). Nor-dische Stilelemente in der karolinischen Buchmalerei. *Diss., Halle.* pp. 87. 8° Borna-Leipzig, 1935. [25 figures in text. Pp. 38–48, Tierornamentik und irischer Stil.]

11879 Swarzenski (Hanns) *introdn.* Early mediaeval illumination. pp. 23 and 21 colour plates. fol. London, 1951. [Reichenau: also 8th c. Northumbrian from Bibl. Nat., Paris, MS. Lat. 9389.]

11880 Thompson (*Sir* Edward Maunde). English art in illuminated manuscripts. J. Soc. Arts, 46, pp. 461–70. 1898.

11881 —— English illuminated manu-scripts. pp. 67, + 21 plates. 4° London, 1895. [Plates 1–8, A.–S.]

11882 —— English illuminated manu-scripts, A.D. 700–1066. Bibliographica, 1, pp. 129–53, + 8 plates. 1895.

11883 —— Notes on the illuminated manuscripts in the exhibition of English medieval paintings [June 1896]. [Pp. 214–16, on A.–S. mss.] Proc. Soc. Antiq., 2nd S. 16, pp. 213–32. 1896.

11884 Thomson (Richard). A lecture on … illuminated manuscripts from the viii. to the xviii. century. … To which is added a second lecture on the materials and practice of illuminators, *etc.* pp. vi, 138. 8° London, 1857. [A little A.–S. material.]

11885 Tikkanen (Johan Jakob). Studien über die Farbengebung in der mittelalterlichen Buchmalerei. … Heraus-gegeben von Tancred Borenius. *Soc. Sc. Fennica. Commentationes humanarum litterarum, v. i.* pp. vii, 452. 4° Helsing-fors, 1933. [Pp. 216–27, Die irische Buchmalerei : pp. 247–64, Die früangel-sächsische Buchmalerei.]

11886 Todd (James Henthorn). [Ex-hibition of] twelve … facsimiles from pages of Irish illuminated manuscripts … with some illustrative remarks. Proc. Soc. Antiq., 2nd S. 3, pp. 271–75. 1866.

11887 Unger (F. W.). La miniature irlandaise, son origine et son développe-ment. Rev. celt., 1, pp. 9–26. 1870.

11888 Warner (*Sir* George Frederic). Illuminated manuscripts in the British Museum. Miniatures, borders, and initials, reproduced in gold and colours. With descriptive text. Series 1–4, 60 plates. 4° London, 1899–1903. [7 plates, A.–S.]

11889 Weisbach (Werner). Manier-ismus in mittelalterlicher Kunst. pp. 40, + 33 plates. fol. Basel, 1942. [Plates 12–17, Winchester School.]

11890 Westwood (John Obadiah). Facsimiles of the miniatures and orna-ments of Anglo-Saxon and Irish manu-scripts. pp. xv, 155 + 53 coloured plates. fol. London, 1868. [Gross, 266.]

11891 —— On the distinctive char-acter of the various styles or ornamenta-tion employed by the early British, Anglo-Saxon and Irish artists. Archaeol. J., 10, pp. 275–301, + 3 plates. 1853.

11892 —— On the peculiarities ex-hibited by the miniatures and ornamenta-tion of ancient Irish illuminated mss. Archaeol. J., 7, pp. 17–25. 1850.

11893 Wormald (Francis). Decorated initials in English mss. from A.D. 900 to 1100. Archaeologia, 91, pp. 107–35, + 9 plates. 1945.

11894 —— English drawings of the tenth and eleventh centuries. pp. 83, + 21 plates. 8° London, 1952. [Introduction, catalogue and illustrations.]

11895 —— The survival of Anglo-Saxon illumination after the Norman Conquest. Proc. Brit. Acad., 30, pp. 127–45, + 9 plates. 1944.

11896 Worringer (Wilhelm). Über den Einfluss der angelsächsischen Buchmalerei auf die frühmittelalterliche Monumentalplastik des Kontinents. Schriften Königsberger Gelehrten Gesellschaft, 8, pp. 1–16, + 12 plates. 1931.

11897 Wyatt (*Sir* Matthew Digby). The art of illuminating: what it was, what it should be, and how it may be practised. pp. 104, + 85 plates. fol. London, 1860. [Plates 1–27, A.–S. period, many being A.–S.]

11898 Zimmermann (Benedikt Ernst Heinrich). Die Fuldaer Buchmalerei in karolinischer und ottonischer Zeit. Kunstgesch. Jahrb. (Wien), 4, pp. 1–104, + 12 plates. 1910. [Also separately, *Diss.*, *Halle-Wittenberg*. pp. 104. 36 figures. 4° Halle a. S., 1911.]

11899 —— Vorkarolingische Miniaturen. pp. xii, 330, + 341 plates. Text and plates. fol. (45 × 34 cm.) Berlin, 1916. [Includes many reproductions of Irish mss.]

§ *b*. St. Gallen

11900 Duft (Johannes) and **Meyer** (Peter). Die irischen Miniaturen der Stiftsbibliothek von St. Gallen. Faksimile-Aufgabe. 19 coloured and 24 other plates. 4° Olten, 1953.

11900a —— The Irish miniatures in the abbey library of St. Gall. pp. 150, + 43 plates (mostly coloured). 4° Berne and Lausanne, 1954.

11901 Ebersolt (Jean). Manuscrits à miniatures de Saint-Gall. Rev. archéol., 5e série, 9, pp. 225–43. 1919.

11902 Hogan (J. F.). Art and literature at St. Gall. [Illuminations of Irish provenance.] Irish Eccles. Rec., 3rd S. 15, pp. 289–301. 1894.

11903 Keller (Ferdinand). Illuminations and facsimilies from Irish manuscripts in the libraries of Switzerland. Ulster J. Archaeol., 8, pp. 212–30, 291–308, + 6 plates. 1860.

11904 Landsberger (Franz). Der St. Galler Folchart-Psalter. Eine Initialenstudie. *Diss.*, *Breslau*. pp. 28. large 4° St. Gallen, 1912. [9th c.]

11905 Merton (Adolf). Die Buchmalerei des IX. Jahrhunderts in St. Gallen, unter besonderer Berücksichtigung der Initial-Ornamentik. *Diss.*, *Halle*. pp. viii, 101, + 4 plates. 8° Halle a. S., 1911. [Einleitung: Die Stellung des Klosters St. Gallen in der karolinischen Kultur; Die St. Galler Schreibschule in der kunsthistorischen Forschung.]

11906 —— Die Buchmalerei in St. Gallen von neunter bis zum elften Jahrhundert. pp. 107, iii, + 100 plates. 4° Leipzig, 1912.

11907 Micheli (Geneviève Louise). Recherches sur les manuscrits irlandais décorés de saint Gall et de Reichenau. [Examination of the mss. themselves, local copies of Irish models and continental interpretations of Irish and A.–S. style. 11 figures in text.] Rev. archéol., série 6, 7, pp. 189–223; 8, pp. 54–79. 1936.

11908 Rahn (Johann Rudolf). Das Psalterium aureum von Sanct Gallen. Ein Beitrag zur Geschichte der karolinischen Miniaturmalerei. *Hist. Verein des Kantons St. Gallen*, pp. 67, + 17 coloured plates. fol. St. Gallen, 1878.

§ *c*. Book of Kells

(all aspects)

11910 Crawford (Henry Saxton). Notes on the 'doubtful' portrait and the cross-bearing pages in the Book of Kells. J. Roy. Soc. Antiq. Ireland, 49 (6th S. 9), pp. 153–54, + 3 plates. 1919.

11911 Duignan (Michael). Three pages from Irish Gospel-books, Codex Sangallensis LI, p. 267, Codex Cenannensis, 187v and 202v. [Book of Kells.] J. Cork Hist. Soc., 2nd S. 57, pp. 11–17, + 2 plates. 1952.

11912 Field (A. M.) *jr.* The canon tables of the Book of Kells. Porter (A. K.): Medieval studies, 2, pp. 611–41, + 24 plates. 1939.

11913 Gunn (John). Letters in ancient Ireland. The Book of Kells. Irish Eccles. Rec., 3rd S. 9, pp. 130–40. 1888.

11914 Hartley (W. N.). On the colouring matters employed in the illuminations of the Book of Kells. 8° Dublin, [188–?].

11915 Kells, *Book of.* The Book of Kells, described by Sir Edward Sullivan, *etc.* 5th edition. *Studio Publications.* pp. 111, + 24 coloured plates. 4° London, 1952.

11916 —— The Book of Kells in three volumes. 3 vol. fol. Bernae Helvetiorum, 1950. [i. Reproduction of folios 1–182 : ii. Reproduction of folios 183–339 (end): iii. Introductory. Many plates are in colour.]

11917 —— Celtic ornaments from the Book of Kells, by T. K. Abbott. pp. xii, + 5 plates. 4° Dublin, 1895.

11918 —— Reproductions from the Book of Kells. Explanatory text by T. K. Abbott. pp. 50, + 53 plates. 4° Dublin, 1896.

11919 Nyhan (Daniel). The Book of Kells. [Brief account of it.] J. Cork Hist. Soc., 2nd S. 34, pp. 111–13, + 1 plate. 1929.

11920 Picton (Harold). Kells portraits and eastern ornament. Burl. Mag., 73, pp. 121–22, and 1 plate. 1938.

11921 Rosenau (Helen). The prototype of the Virgin and Child in the Book of Kells. [Egyptian, etc.] Burl. Mag., 83, pp. 228–31, 2 plates. 1943.

11922 Stephens (Francis E.). An interlinear design in the Book of Kells. J. Roy. Soc. Antiq. Ireland, 76, pp. 213–14, + 2 plates. 1946.

11923 Westwood (John Obadiah). The Book of Kells. A lecture . . . before . . . the Oxford Architectural and Historical Society. pp. 18, + 2 plates. 4° Dublin, 1887.

§ *d.* **Other Individual Manuscripts**

11924 Æthelwold, *St. bp. of Winchester.* The Benedictional of St. Æthelwold, bp. of Winchester, an illuminated Anglo-Saxon ms. of the tenth century, in the library of . . . the duke of Devonshire, with a prefatory dissertation, and a description of the Benedictional of archbishop Robert [of Jumièges], an illuminated Anglo-Saxon ms. of the same century in the public library at Rouen. By John Gage. *Soc. Antiquaries.* pp. 136, + 34 plates. fol. London, 1832.

11925 —— The Benedictional of Saint Æthelwold, bishop of Winchester, 963–984. Reproduced in facsimile from the manuscript . . . and edited, with text and introduction, by Sir George Frederic Warner and Henry Austin Wilson. *Roxburghe Club.* pp. ix, 56, iv, + 239 plates. fol. London, 1910.

11926 Braeude (M. A.). The wanderings of two ancient manuscripts. [In Pierpont Morgan library : from Holkham hall. MSS. 708 and 709 (Winchester School.)] History To-day, 2, pp. 323–31. 1952.

11927 Burkitt (Francis Crawford). Kells, Durrow and Lindisfarne. [Comparison of Irish art and Lindisfarne Gospels.] Antiquity, 9, pp. 33–37. 1935.

11928 Caedmon. The Caedmon manuscript of Anglo-Saxon biblical poetry, Junius XI in the Bodleian Library. With introduction by Sir Israel Gollancz. *British Museum.* pp. cxxvii, + 232 plates. fol. London, 1927. [Ascribed to Canterbury Scriptorium.]

11929 Doran (Joseph M.). The enamelling and metallesque origin of the ornament in the Book of Durrow. [8th c.: 8 figures in text.] Burl. Mag., 13, pp. 138–45. 1908.

11930 Ellis (*Sir* Henry). Account of Caedmon's metrical paraphrase of scripture history, an illuminated manuscript of the tenth century. [MS. Bodl. Junius XI.] Archaeologia, 24, pp. 329–40, + 53 plates. 1832. *Also separately.* pp. 14, + 53 plates. 4° London, 1833.

11931 Gage (John). A description of a benedictional, or pontifical, called 'Benedictionarius Roberti Archiepiscopi', an illuminated manuscript of the tenth century, in the Public Library at Rouen, communicated as an accompaniment to St. Æthelwold's Benedictional. [Robert of Jumièges, abp. of Rouen.] Archaeologia, 24, pp. 118–36, + 2 plates. 1832.

11932 —— A dissertation on St. Æthelwold's benedictional, an illuminated ms. of the 10th century, in the library of the duke of Devonshire. *Same jnl.*, 24, pp. 1–117, + 32 plates. 1832.

11933 Harrison (James Park). On a Saxon picture in an early ms. at Cambridge. [Frontispiece to Bede's Life of Cuthbert, MS. C.C.C.C. 183. 10th c.] J. Brit. Archaeol. Assoc., 49, pp. 268–73, + 1 plate. 1893.

11934 Hemphill (Samuel). The Gospels of Mac Regol of Birr : a study in Celtic illumination. [Bodley, MS. Auct. D. II. 19. MacRegol (or, better, Mac Réguil), abbot of Birr, co. Offaly, d. 821 (=822) A.U.] Proc. R.I.A., 29c, pp. 1–10, + 5 plates. 1911.

11935 Margaret, *St.*, *queen of Scotland.* The Gospel-Book of St. Margaret. Being a facsimile reproduction, *etc.* Edited by William Forbes-Leith. pp. 14, ff. 68. 4° Edinburgh, 1896. [MS. Bodl. Latin Liturg. F.5. Mid 11th c.]

11936 Millar (Eric George) *ed.* The Lindisfarne Gospels ; three plates in colour and 36 in monochrome from Cotton MS. Nero D. IV, in the British Museum, with pages from two related manuscripts, with introduction. pp. 52. fol. Oxford, 1924.

11937 Niver (Charles). The psalter in the British Museum, Harley 2904. [4 figures in text. Probably from Ramsey

abbey scriptorium, between 974 and 986.] Porter (A. K.) : Medieval studies, 2, pp. 667–87. 1939.

11938 Nordenfalk (Carl). Eastern style elements in the Book of Lindisfarne. [15 figures in text.] Acta Archaeol., 13, pp. 157–69. 1942.

11939 Robinson (Stanford Frederick Hudson). Celtic illuminative art in the Gospel Books of Durrow, Lindisfarne, and Kells. pp. xxx, + 31 plates, and their letterpress. 4° Dublin, 1908.

11940 Thomas (Thomas Henry). Notes upon the Psalter of Ricemarch. [11th c., at T.C.D.] Cardiff Nat Soc., Rpt. and Trans., 33 (1900–01), pp. 47–52, + 6 plates. 1902.

11941 Todd (James Henthorn). Descriptive remarks on illuminations in certain ancient Irish manuscripts. pp. 16, + 14 coloured plates. Elephant fol. London, 1869. [Book of Kells, Garland of Howth (2), Psalter of Ricemarch.]

11942 —— Remarks on illuminations in some Irish illuminated manuscripts. [In colour : Book of Kells, Garland of Howth, Psalter of Ricemarch.] Vetusta Monumenta, 6, pp. 16, + plates 43–46. 1885.

11943 Tolhurst (J. B. L.). An examination of two Anglo-Saxon manuscripts of the Winchester School : the Missal of Robert of Jumièges, and the Benedictional of St. Æthelwold. Archaeologia, 83, pp. 27–44. 1933.

11944 Wattenbach (Wilhelm). Un Evangéliare à miniatures d'origine irlandaise, dans la Bibliothèque princière d'Œttingen-Wallerstein. [2 figures in text.] Rev. celt., 1, pp. 27–31. 1870.

11945 Wormald (Francis). The miniatures in the Gospels of St. Augustine, [Canterbury], Corpus Christi College, [Cambridge], MS. 286. pp. ix, 17, + 19 plates (2 in colour). [6th c. MS.] 4° Cambridge, 1954.

11946 —— Two Anglo-Saxon miniatures compared. [Cotton Tib. A III f. 26 and Durham Cath. Biii, 32, f. 566. Both mid 11th c.] B.M.Q., 9, pp. 113–15, + plate 35. 1935.

205. ORNAMENT AND DESIGN, GENERAL

(See also Art Section passim and the index, and 184 especially.)

11947 Allen (John Romilly). List of mss. containing Celtic ornament : Celtic metal work. [=Pt. 2 of **10925**]. J. Brit. Archaeol. Assoc., 40, pp. 409–17. 1884.

11948 —— Notes on Celtic ornament —the key and spiral patterns. [Early Christian period. 94 figures in text.] Proc. Soc. Antiq. Scot., 19 (N.S. 7), pp. 253–308, + 1 plate. 1885.

11949 Astley (Hugh John Dukinfield). Scandinavian motifs in Anglo-Saxon and Norman ornamentation. [17 figures in text.] Saga-Book V.C., 4, pp. 132–70. 1905.

11950 Brønsted (Johannes). Early English ornament : the sources, development and relation to foreign styles of pre-Norman ornamental art in England. Translated . . . by A. F. Major. pp. 352. 8° London, Copenhagen, 1924. [217 figures in text.]

11951 Carr (Ralph). The symbolism of the sculptured stones of eastern Scotland—an ecclesiastical system of monograms and decorative characters. Meanings of the several symbols. pp. 38, + plates. 8° Edinburgh, 1867.

11952 Cinthio (Erik). Anglo-Saxon and Irish style-influences in Skåne during the 8th century. [10 figures of ornament in text.] Årsberättelse K. Human. Vetenskapssamfundet i Lund. (Bull. Soc. Roy. Lettres, Lund), 1946–47, pp. 113–35. 1947.

11953 Crawford (Henry Saxton). Handbook of carved ornament from Irish monuments of the Christian period. Royal Society of Antiquaries of Ireland. pp. viii, 79, + 51 plates. 4° Dublin, 1926. [Kenney 1, p. 774.]

11954 Dauncey (Kenneth Douglas Masson). The intrusive elements in Anglo-Saxon zoomorphic style. J. Brit. Archaeol. Assoc., 3rd S. 6, pp. 103–26, + 5 plates. 1941.

11955 Dawkins (Sir William Boyd). The ornamentation of the early Irish manuscripts and of the runic crosses. Manx Note Bk., 3, pp. 120–24. 1887.

11956 Delmar (E.). Observations on the origin of the arms of Edward the Confessor. [' Composed upon a Coptic pattern—as were his coins, showing 4 birds and a cross.] Burl. Mag., 95, pp. 359–62, + plate. 1953.

11957 Forssander (J. E.). Irland-Oseberg. [54 figures, in text, of ornament from Irish mss., A.–S. sculpture, etc.] Årsberättelse, etc. (Bull. Soc. Roy. Lettres, Lund), 1942–43, pp. 294–404. 1943.

11958 Gabrielsson (Ruben). Kompositionsformer i senkeltisk orneringsstil. Diss., Stockholm. pp. 192. 8° Lund, 1945. [27 plates interpaginated. Pp. 182–92, English summary : Composition forms in late Celtic ornamentation style, seen against the background of the general development of European art. 7th–11th c.]

11959 Gerke (Freiedrich). Ornament und Figur in der angelsächsischen Kunst. [4 figures in text.] Kunst u. Kirche, 16, pp. 108–12. 1939.

11960 Gray (Nicolete). Jacob's ladder: a Bible picture book from Anglo-Saxon and 12th century English mss. pp. 118, 48 plates included in pagination. 8° London, (1949).

11961 Harrison (James Park). Anglo-Norman ornament compared with designs in Anglo-Saxon mss. Archaeol. J., 47, pp. 143–53, + 3 plates. 1890.

11962 Herringham (Christiana J.). The snake pattern in Ireland, the Mediterranean and China. [Irish ms. illumination and metal-work of 400–1100 and comparisons : 48 figures in text.] Burl. Mag., 13, pp. 132–37. 1908.

11963 Kendrick (Sir Thomas Downing). The development of barbaric ornament in Britain. [7 plates, paged in text.] J. Brit. Archaeol. Assoc., 3rd S. 1, pp. 79–92. 1937.

11964 Kendrick (*Sir* Thomas Downing). Some types of ornamentation on late Saxon and Viking weapons in England. [5 figures in text.] Eurasia Septentrionalis Antiqua, 9, pp. 392–98. 1934.

11965 —— Style in early Anglo-Saxon ornament. Ipek, 9, pp. 66–76, + 7 plates. 1934.

11966 Kitzinger (Ernest). Anglo-Saxon vine-scroll ornament. Antiquity, 10, pp. 61–71, + 7 plates. 1936.

11967 Leeds (Edward Thurlow). Celtic ornament in the British Isles, down to A.D. 700. pp. xix, 170, + 22 plates. 8° Oxford, 1933.

11968 Matheson (Colin). Hippocampus as a *motif* in Celtic art. [Figure of brooch from Lamberton moor, Berwickshire, compared with Hippocampus antiquorum.] Arch. Camb., 86, pp. 179–81. 1931.

11969 Nordenfalk (Carl). Before the Book of Durrow. [Ornamentation, sculpture and mss. 26 figures in text.] Acta Archaeologica, 18, pp. 141–74. 1947.

11970 Peers (*Sir* Charles Reed). English ornament in the seventh and eighth centuries. Proc. Brit. Acad., 12, pp. 45–54. 1926.

11971 Ringbom (Lars-Ivar). Entstehung und Entwicklung der Spiralornament. [33 figures in text.] Acta Archaeol., 4, pp. 151–200. 1933.

11972 Salin (Bernhard). Die altgermanische Thierornamentik. Typologische Studie über germanische Metallgegenstände aus dem iv. bis ix. Jahrhundert, nebst einer Studie über irische Ornamentik. Übersetzt von J. Mestorf. Neue Auflage. pp. xvi, 388. 4° Stockholm, 1935. [Kenney, 1, p. 98. Pp. 322–49 and figures 699–740, Die angelsächsische und die irländische Thierornamentik.]

11973 Shetelig (Haakon). The Norse style of ornamentation in the Viking settlements. [Brooches, sculpture, shrines, etc. 36 figures in text.] Acta Archaeologica, 19, pp. 69–113. 1948.

11974 —— The origin of the Scandinavian style of ornament during the migration period. [Background : ' the peculiar decorative style of the Migration period is common to Anglo-Saxon England and to Scandinavia '.] Archaeologia, 76, pp. 107–20, + 8 plates. 1927.

11975 Trench (Thomas Cooke). Notes on Irish ribbon work in ornamentation. J. co. Kildare Archaeol. Soc., 1, pp. 240–44, + 3 plates. 1894.